STRATEGIC MANAGEMENT

A Choice Approach

John R. Montanari
Arizona State University

Cyril P. Morgan
Washington State University

Jeffrey S. Bracker
George Mason University

The Dryden Press
Chicago Fort Worth San Francisco Philadelphia
Montreal Toronto London Sydney Tokyo

Acquisitions Editor: Robert Gemin
Developmental Editor: Penny Gaffney
Project Editor: Cathy Crow
Design Manager: Alan Wendt
Production Manager: Bob Lange
Permissions Editor: Cindy Lombardo

Director of Editing, Design, and Production: Jane Perkins
Text and Cover Designer: C.J. Petlick, Hunter Graphics
Copy Editor: Jean Berry
Indexer: Leoni McVey
Compositor: Impressions, Inc.
Text Type: 10/12 Times Roman

Library of Congress Cataloging-in-Publication Data

Montanari, John R.
Strategic management : a choice approach / John R. Montanari, Cyril P. Morgan, Jeffrey S. Bracker.
p. cm.
Includes bibliographical references.
ISBN 0-03-008857-7
1. Strategic planning. I. Morgan, Cyril P., 1936– II. Bracker, Jeffrey S. III. Title.
HD30.28.M6451990
658.4′012—dc20 89-27596
CIP

Printed in the United States of America
12-040-98765432

Address orders:
The Dryden Press
Orlando, FL 32887

Address editorial correspondence:
The Dryden Press
908 N. Elm Street
Hinsdale, IL 60521

The Dryden Press
Holt, Rinehart and Winston
Saunders College Publishing

In memory of Sally Lemak,
who was so proud to be working
on our manuscript. We wish she
could have seen the final product.

The Dryden Press Series in Management

Bartlett
Cases in Strategic Management for Business

Bedeian
Management, *Second Edition*

Bedeian
Organizations: Theory and Analysis, Text and Cases, *Second Edition*

Boone and Kurtz
Contemporary Business, *Sixth Edition*

Bowman and Branchaw
Business Communication: From Process to Product

Bowman and Branchaw
Business Report Writing, *Second Edition*

Cullinan
Business English for Industry and the Professions

Czinkota, Rivoli, and Ronkainen
International Business

Daft
Management

Efendioglu and Montanari
The Advantage Ski Company: A Strategic Simulation

Gaither
Production and Operations Management: A Problem-Solving and Decision-Making Approach
Fourth Edition

Forgionne
Quantitative Management

Gatewood and Feild
Human Resource Selection, *Second Edition*

Greenhaus
Career Management

Higgins
Strategy: Formulation, Implementation, and Control

Higgins and Vincze
Strategic Management: Text and Cases
Fourth Edition

Hills
Compensation Decision Making

Hodgetts
Modern Human Relations at Work, *Fourth Edition*

Holley and Jennings
The Labor Relations Process, *Third Edition*

Holley and Jennings
Personnel/Human Resource Management: Contributions and Activities, *Second Edition*

Huseman, Lahiff, and Penrose
Business Communication: Strategies and Skills
Third Edition

Jauch, Coltrin, and Bedeian
The Managerial Experience: Cases, Exercises, and Readings, *Fifth Edition*

Kemper
Experiencing Strategic Management

Kuehl and Lambing
Small Business: Planning and Management
Second Edition

Kuratko and Hodgetts
Entrepreneurship: A Contemporary Approach

Lee
Introduction to Management Science
Second Edition

Luthans and Hodgetts
Business

Montanari, Morgan, and Bracker
Strategic Management: A Choice Approach

Northcraft and Neale
Organizational Behavior: A Management Challenge

Tombari
Business and Society: Strategies for the Environment and Public Policy

Varner
Contemporary Business Report Writing

Vecchio
Organizational Behavior

Weekly and Aggarwal
International Business: Operating in the Global Economy

Wolters and Holley
Labor Relations: An Experiential and Case Approach

Zikmund
Business Research Methods, *Second Edition*

Preface

When we conceived the idea for *Strategic Management: A Choice Approach*, we conducted a survey to determine what potential users would like to see in a strategic management text. The survey results indicated that a need exists for a text that can translate leading edge theory and research into an understandable discussion of strategic management. Respondents suggested an applications focus with particular emphasis on strategic management in the global societies of the future. We believe that this textbook answers these needs.

Features of the Book

Four features of the text reflect our personal philosophies toward education in strategic management and, we believe, contribute to meeting the needs of future strategic managers.

1. *A choice perspective.* We agree with many other strategic management writers that the primary function of a strategic manager is to make choices or decide among alternatives. The correct solution is seldom obvious to senior executives of an organization, whether the organization is private, public, or not for profit. Often information is incomplete, the problem poorly defined, and the results uncertain, which creates an ambiguous decision-making situation. Under these conditions, the manager must conduct the appropriate analyses, evaluate the alternatives, and choose the best direction for his or her organization. This book focuses on the content and process of the choices that managers make in the strategic management of their organizations. It thus provides a realistic look at the complexity of managing strategically and suggests tools to help tomorrow's managers make better choices.

2. *An applications orientation.* We have attempted to make the text portion of the book as comprehensive as possible while presenting the information in a manner that is easily understood and usable. By combining descriptions of what managers do with advice given by scholars about what managers should do, we provide a description of how to perform the strategic management process.

3. *An in-depth discussion of strategy implementation.* This feature mirrors recent trends in the strategic management field. We have developed three chapters on strategy implementation. They focus on implementation issues such as functional strategies, organization structure, culture, leadership, and human resource management. In addition, we have included a chapter on strategic control. This aspect of the strategic management process is discussed in detail and distinguished from operational control. In the opinion of reviewers, it is a particularly strong feature of the text.

4. *New and updated cases.* The 32 cases provided in the book are a mix of new and contemporary cases, updated classics such as The Lincoln Electric Company case, and industry notes on dynamic industries such as airlines and financial services. Many of the previously published cases now include Case Updates with recent financial data. The cases were selected to complement the material in the text and include small, entrepreneurial, and high-tech firms.

Several other features contribute to achieving our goals for the book:

- A minimum of three Strategic Applications examples in every chapter, generally including one international and one social responsibility example
- Extensive coverage of international issues in a chapter on strategic management in the international arena
- In-depth discussions of social issues and ethics in a chapter devoted to social issues in management
- A special chapter on strategic management in entrepreneurial and not-for-profit organizations
- An innovative chapter on future directions in strategic management
- Numerous examples, tables, and figures to illustrate complex concepts
- Short end-of-chapter cases related to the chapter content
- Thoughtful discussion questions at the end of each chapter, some of which require outside or library research
- Case analysis and financial analysis appendixes. Both were written specifically for this book. The case analysis format described in Appendix A, which follows the content and flow of the text, shows how to analyze a case. Financial analyses (Appendix B) are presented in a manner that highlights the practical uses of the results obtained from such analyses.

Supplements

A comprehensive teaching package has been assembled to support the textbook.

- An extensive *Instructor's Manual* prepared by the authors includes a chapter outline, a chapter summary, answers to the discussion questions, teaching notes for the end-of-chapter Cases for Discussion, and complete casenotes for the 32 cases included in the book. The casenotes are presented in a consistent format to make case analysis more convenient. The *Instructor's Manual* also contains transparency masters of important figures and tables from the text.
- The *Test Bank* provides true/false, multiple choice, and essay questions for each text chapter and case. The text page number where the correct answer can be found

is also given. A *computerized* version of the test bank is available for IBM-PC and compatible microcomputers. The *Test Bank* was written by Marshall Schminke of Creighton University.

- A *Videotape* is available to supplement several of the cases in the text, featuring Delta Airlines, America West, the NASA Space Shuttle Challenger, and others.
- A *Computer Disk* of templates provides financial data from selected cases and guides the student through several important strategic analyses.

A computer simulation entitled *The Advantage Ski Company: A Strategic Simulation* is available for the IBM PC and compatibles. The software and accompanying manual allow students to strategically manage their own firm in a competitive arena consisting of other companies (teams) in the class. The simulation is written by Alev M. Efendioglu and John R. Montanari.

Acknowledgments

Many competent professionals and policy-making groups have contributed to the material contained in this book. To the pioneers who first conceived of strategic planning and strategic management as a discipline worthy of study and research, we owe a special debt of gratitude. To the AACSB, who recognized strategy as an important component of a business education, we applaud their foresight. To the Academy of Management and the Strategic Management Society, which provide forums to present and discuss strategic issues, many of them having become the foundations for the field of strategic management, we express our thanks. Finally, to the universities that have encouraged our pursuit of strategy knowledge and experience, we are extremely grateful.

Special gratitude must be expressed to the people who were responsible for the creation, assimilation, and preparation of the content of this book. For the many strategic management scholars who conducted the research and developed the theories from which the essence of this text is drawn, no expression of gratitude is sufficient. Cy feels a particular intellectual debt to William Newman, Louis Allen, James D. Thompson, and Lyle Ball. Each has unknowingly provided inspiration and stimulation at important points in his career. Colleagues such as Richard Reed, Art Bedeian, Larry Jauch, Jack Pearce II, Greg Moorhead, and Bob Kreitner, renowned authors in their own right, provided encouragement at critical points in the development of our project. We must also recognize the strategy practitioners who contributed many of the insights contained in this book through their writings in business periodicals and examples documented in the popular business press. Strategic managers and friends like Bill Stalnaker, David Renke, Ken Kucera, and Gerry Hauer allowed us to work with them over the years to refine some of our ideas about how strategy is actually developed and implemented.

More directly involved in the creation of *Strategic Management: A Choice Approach* were those who contributed illustrations, figures, and quotations for inclusion in the book. We wish to acknowledge and thank the colleagues who contributed many of the cases for this text. They are Sexton Adams, *University of North Texas*; Larry D. Alexander, *Virginia Polytechnic Institute and State University*; Alan Bauerschmidt, *University of South Carolina*; Roger C. Blackwell, *The Ohio State University*; Chris Cairns, *Pacific Telesis*; Michael Cavanaugh, *University of Massachusetts–Amherst*; James W. Clinton, *University of Northern Colorado*; David B. Croll, *University of Virginia*; Xavier Gilbert, *IMEDE*; Adelaide Griffin, *Texas Women's University*; John M. Gwin, *University of Virginia*; Jean M. Hanebury, *Salisbury State University*; David B. Jemison, *Stanford University*; Per V. Jensen, *University of Virginia*; Wesley J. Johnston, *The Ohio State University*; Raymond M. Kinnunen, *Northeastern University*; Donald F. Kuratko, *Ball State University*; Patricia P. McDougall, *Georgia State University*; Stewart C. Malone, *University of Virginia*; Robert Marx, *University of Massachusetts–Amherst*; Bernard A. Morin, *University of Virginia*; George A. Overstreet, Jr., *University of Virginia*; Dan S. Prickett, *University of Dayton*; James Brian Quinn, *Dartmouth College*; Leslie W. Rue, *Georgia State University*; Joseph A. Schenk, *University of Dayton*; John A. Seeger, *Bentley College*; Arthur Sharplin, *McNeese State University*; Steven A. Sinclair, *Virginia Polytechnic Institute and State University*; Stanley J. Stough, *University of Dayton*; Charles Stubbart, *University of Massachusetts–Amherst*; W. Wayne Talarzyk, *The Ohio State University*; Arthur A. Thompson, *University of Alabama*; Virginia Traub, *University of Massachusetts–Amherst*; Fred C. Walters, *Virginia Polytechnic Institute and State University*; William D. Wilsted, *University of Colorado–Boulder*; and Julian W. Vincze, *Rollins College.*

We also wish to thank Maria Muto for her excellent assistance with the cases selected for use in the text, and Marshall Schminke of Creighton University for creating the *Test Bank* that accompanies the text.

Other colleagues contributed immeasurably to the style and quality of the finished product. Their excellent critiques, comments, and suggestions resulted in rewrites of the original text and case material and many modifications to the case list. These reviewers were:

R. Duane Ireland, *Baylor University*; Howard D. Feldman, *University of Colorado*; Thomas W. Sharkey, *University of Toledo*; Ellen Foster Curtis, *University of Lowell*; Peter Smith Ring, *University of Minnesota*; Gordon E. Von Stroh, *University of Denver*; Kenneth W. Olm, *University of Texas at Austin*; Peter Goulet, *University of Northern Iowa*; James B. Thurman, *The George Washington University*; Marilyn L. Taylor, *University of Kansas*; Bruce T. Lamont, *University of North Carolina–Chapel Hill*; Sharon G. Johnson, *Baylor University*; Michael W. Pitts, *Virginia Commonwealth University*; Daniel A. Sauers, *Louisiana Tech University*; Gaber Abou El Enein, *Mankato State University*; William T. Flannery, *University of Texas at San Antonio*; James E. Post, *Boston University*; Charles M. Byles, *Oklahoma State University*; and Joseph G. P. Paolillo, *University of Mississippi.*

The organization and development of the vast amounts of material necessary to complete this project was no small task. We would like to acknowledge the help, patience, and professionalism of the staff at The Dryden Press. To Bill Schoof, Butch Gemin, Becky Ryan, Penny Gaffney, Cathy Crow, and others with whom we have worked, we express our gratitude for their guidance, encouragement, and commitment to our project.

We would also like to thank the many people who contributed to the preparation of the manuscript. A thank-you is owed to the many students who contributed their ideas, experiences, and stimulation. Of special note are research assistants Paul Walker, Greg Dunn, and Alan Belton and our secretary, Caryl Jones, who were extremely helpful in the preparation of drafts of the manuscript. Also, we would like to express special gratitude to Sally Lemak for devoting many months to the preparation of the first two drafts. She was tireless in her efforts to meet deadlines and caught many omissions of the authors. She was a cheerful and enthusiastic assistant and a good friend who made the authors' work much more enjoyable.

Finally, thank you to our families, who encouraged and motivated us through the preparation of the manuscript. Ellen was a constant source of encouragement for Dick at times when the work on the project seemed most difficult. Sharon, Pat, Sean, and Matt, having suffered through several books, know when to stay out of the way and when to get Cy to go fishing, as well as when he needs "strokes." Peggie and Rachel were there when Jeff needed them most. To all of our families we owe more than gratitude. They shared our joys and frustrations and continued to provide selfless support throughout the entire project.

John R. Montanari
Cyril P. Morgan
Jeffrey S. Bracker

November 1989

About the Authors

John R. (Dick) Montanari received his Doctorate in Business Administration from the University of Colorado in Management and Administrative Policy. He has served on the faculties of the University of Houston and Arizona State University since receiving his degree in 1976. He is currently Professor of Management at Arizona State University. He has published several articles on management and business strategy in journals such as the *Academy of Management Review, Strategic Management Journal, Human Relations, Journal of Management,* and *Journal of Management Studies.* He is on the Editorial Review Board of the *Journal of Management* and is an active member of the Academy of Management. His awards include several grants for research in the area of strategic management. Dr. Montanari was selected as a Distinguished Visiting Professor by the United States Air Force Academy. He has been actively involved in consulting and training for a number of firms in the private and public sectors. His consulting and training experiences include strategic management, long-range planning, and leadership. He has helped a number of public and private organizations develop strategic plans and strategic management systems.

Cyril P. Morgan is a Professor and Chairman of the Department of Management and Systems at Washington State University. His research interests include organization structure as well as its interface with business policy and organizational behavior, collaborative group processes, risk taking, and R&D project management. He has taught courses in business strategy and policy, organizational theory, organizational behavior, and introduction to management. His work has been published in such journals as *Administrative Science Quarterly, Journal of Experimental Psychology, Management Science, Academy of Management Journal, Journal of Management Studies, Human Relations*, and *Management Informational Review.* He is also the author of case studies and articles for practitioners. He is the coauthor of *Organizational Theory* (three editions) and *Administering Real Property.* Dr. Morgan has engaged in extensive consulting and training with public and private organizations. He received his Ph.D. from Case Institute of Technology, his M.B.A. from Xavier University, and his B.S. from Miami University. He has also received three teaching awards from M.B.A. and doctoral students.

Jeffrey S. Bracker (Ph.D., Georgia State University) is an Associate Professor of Strategic Management at George Mason University. He was one of the founders and former chief executive officer of Biosurge Inc., a New York–based medical products firm. He has more than 75 articles, proceedings, and scholarly presentations to his credit. Some of his work appears in the *Academy of Management Review, Strategic Management Journal*, and *Journal of Applied Psychology*, and *Planning Review.*

Contents

Alphabetical Listing of Cases

A Note to the Student

The material in this book presents you with a unique opportunity to practice as a strategic manager. More specifically, it is aimed at allowing you to integrate all that you have already learned in business courses as you focus on top management decision making and policy making. You are given the opportunity to put yourself in the position of the top level executive in an organization and to experience the choices and decisions that strategic managers make, without the associated risks. Through case analysis you can assume the role of a staff expert or consultant in strategic management.

From this book and the materials that complement it, especially the *Advantage Ski Company* simulation, you can expect to gain an understanding of the type and magnitude of issues that strategic managers face in setting the long-term direction of their organizations. You will discover the principles of strategic planning and management that have been successfully practiced by managers of a variety of organizations. In addition, you will be exposed to "leading edge" strategic management knowledge being developed by management scholars and practitioners. You will learn analysis methods and tools that you can combine with the techniques learned in other courses to become a more effective strategic manager. Finally, you will acquire analysis and decision-making skills by using the methods and tools in actual case situations.

The book was written to be both informative and useful. We hope that you will take the information about current thinking on strategic management presented here, and use it as you apply the methods, techniques, and tools that you take from this course to "real world" strategic situations.

Chapter 1

The Choice Perspective of Strategic Management

We've come to praise strategic planning, not to bury it.
—Daniel Gray, President and CEO of Gray-Judson, Inc.[1]

Learning Objectives

- To discover the difference between strategic management and strategic planning.
- To learn how strategic management thought developed and why it is important today.
- To understand the levels of strategy development and the stages of the strategic management process.
- To be introduced to the choice model of strategic management.
- To appreciate the flow and direction of the strategic management process.
- To learn the situational, organizational, group, and personal factors that influence managers' strategic choices.
- To understand how to recognize effective organizations.

The Strategic Management Perspective

When Lee Iacocca came to Chrysler Corporation, the company was on the verge of closing its doors. The K-car was on the drawing boards, but Chrysler's management could not generate financing to bring it to market. Sweeping changes under Iacocca's administration have since turned the company around dramatically.

Why do some firms succeed while others fail? Why do similar firms in the same industry pursue different courses of action? The answers to these questions lie in the strategic direction that top-level decision makers such as Iacocca set for the organization.

The strategic direction is based on answers to questions such as "What business should we be in?" and "Which approach to that business should we take?" These answers determine the other individuals and organizations with which the firm must transact its business. Asking and answering such questions is the basis of the **strategic**

management of the organization—that is, the choices of the analyses, plans, decisions, and actions that determine the strategic direction of the organization and lead to accomplishment of its strategic goals and objectives in a dynamic environment. Whether a firm is large or small, is not-for-profit or profit-making, or is privately held or a publicly traded corporation, successful strategic managers engage in similar activities. The senior executives who make the top-level, long-term decisions of strategic management are referred to as **strategic managers**. These managers spend most of their time analyzing, planning, and deciding on issues that give the firm a competitive advantage in an increasingly turbulent business environment. To accomplish this, managers must perform in different capacities in the organization.

Mintzberg refers to these as the roles that top managers occupy in the organization.[2] According to Mintzberg, the primary roles involve making decisions, handling information, and managing people. Strategic managers handle external and internal information by matching external environmental opportunities with internal organizational capabilities. Once the managers believe they have a match, they make strategic choices as to how to use the firm's capabilities to take advantage of the opportunity. Last, they organize, motivate, and direct people to utilize their capabilities to contribute to the success of the organization. Performing all of these roles well is the key to being an effective strategic manager.

At the very top levels of the organization, management is more complex than it is at lower levels. Strategic managers make novel choices that involve the success and survival of the organization. Because strategic problems are unique, managers draw upon their judgment and experience to commit vast amounts of the organization's resources to projects that may or may not be appropriate for tomorrow's marketplace. The amount of resources and degree of uncertainty involved make the strategic manager a key figure in the firm's success. The central challenge of tomorrow's strategic manager is to match the opportunities in the environment to the firm's capabilities and then manage those capabilities toward accomplishment of organizational goals.

Strategic managers are the captains of their organization. They set the long-term course of the firm and ensure that resources are available to steer the organization along that course. Therefore, it is not surprising that the average chief executive officer (CEO) of a major corporation receives total compensation of over $1.1 million.[3] These managers are highly valued because they deal with strategic issues that are critical to the firm's survival. Iacocca, for example, was a creative and charismatic CEO who was able to convince suppliers, unions, bankers, and the government to fund Chrysler until he could turn it around. He was the right strategic manager for the environment that Chrysler faced and the right person to manage Chrysler's turnaround.

Why Learn about Strategic Management

Learning about strategic management is more important today than it has been at any time in the past. The growth of a world economy, rapid technological advances, and the shortage of critical resources (for example, crude oil and water) are just a few of the factors that make today's business conditions more dynamic and complex than those of even a decade ago. Effective strategic management is typically associated with improved organizational performance. Those who learn to view the organization from a strategic perspective will benefit personally and professionally.

Changing Business Conditions

In the early 1960s, the big three U.S. automobile manufacturers were in the driver's seat in the huge U.S. auto market. These companies were increasing the size of cars to improve their profit margins, and demand was strong. Foreign automobile manufacturers had only five to seven percent of the market, and brand loyalty for GM, Ford, and Chrysler was high. But during the next two decades, the United States experienced two fuel crises, which created a demand for smaller, fuel-efficient foreign cars. Impressed by the high quality of these autos, many U.S. consumers switched loyalties to the foreign manufacturers. Today foreign autos enjoy a 30 to 35 percent share of the market.

This cycle of rapid and dramatic change is not limited to the automobile industry. Many other industries as diverse as semiconductors and home appliances are experiencing turbulent change. Not only has the environment in which managers conduct business changed, but so have the nature of organizations and the view that managers hold in setting the strategic direction for their firms.

Before the mid-1950s, most organizations were thought of as **closed systems**. That is, strategic managers assumed that knowledge would expand at a steady rate that would allow ample time to plan for obsolescence. They also assumed that resources were abundant and available, both in terms of the materials and knowledge needed to provide a good or service and in terms of the customers for that good or service. Thus, the success and survival of the organization depended upon the efficiency of its internal operations. Planning concentrated on internal processes associated with operations. Managers did not need to look outside the organization, because the environment would favor the firm with the most efficient operations.

Strategic managers of some organizations, such as General Electric and Du Pont, recognized early that there was a need for a more external or open view of the firm. However, several events that occurred after 1960 convinced other strategic managers to change the way they viewed their organizations.

One such event was the energy crisis of 1973, which dramatically illustrated to managers the degree to which U.S. business had become internationally dependent. Another event was the widespread acceptance of the computer in scientific and business applications. The processing speed of computers dramatically shortened the time required to analyze data, greatly increasing the rate at which new knowledge is created and transferred. The effect of the resulting knowledge explosion has been more rapid technological development, which causes more rapid obsolescence of existing products and services. Today's strategic managers must expend more energy looking outside of the firm for new competing technologies and market entrants.

These events and many others highlighted the importance of the firm's external environment, forcing strategic managers to view the organization as an **open system**. This perspective entails viewing the organization as being open to changes in the environment and in a state of continuous interaction with it. Managers depend upon the environment for opportunities, resources, and customers. They are also the key individuals responsible for adapting the firm to its dynamic environment. Today's successful managers have adopted a more open perspective in order to strategically manage both the organization and its interactions with the environment.

Improved Organizational Performance

Mounting evidence indicates that firms using formal strategic planning and management outperform firms without it.[4] In one review of prior research, 12 of 20 studies conclude that strategic planning improved organizational performance. According to many studies, as strategic plans become more sophisticated, performance improves. Other research reports that the mere practice of strategic planning results in improved performance. Based on these studies and the experience of practicing managers, strategic planning is generally acknowledged as a way to improve organizational performance.

Personal and Professional Benefits

On a more personal note, if you, as a possible future strategic manager, learn to view the firm from a strategic perspective, you will be better prepared to understand your organizational surroundings. In addition, this book will give you a better understanding of the decisions that top managers make in the firms in which you are employed. The insights that you gain will help you prepare to chart your course up the career ladder through the organization. In many cases, advancement in a firm depends on being in the right place at the right time. Understanding which factors affect top management improves your chances of being where you need to be when you need to be there.

The Evolution of Strategic Management

Strategic planning and management have interested senior executives for the past two decades. **Strategic planning** is the analysis of environmental conditions and organizational capabilities, and the formulation of plans to match the firm's capabilities with those conditions. Most managers consider strategic planning absolutely necessary to allow their organization to cope with a more dynamic environment. Others believe that the planning process has been overformalized to the point of little use.[5] As one senior executive put it: "What we had [our plan] was a kind of strategic rain dance—war cries, smoke signals, sacrificial offerings."[6] However, a recent survey of senior-level executives reported that most companies remain firmly committed to strategic planning.

Why this confusion about strategic planning? As the business environment became more turbulent,[7] managers discovered that strategic *planning*, with its emphasis on environmental assessment, analysis of internal capabilities, and plan formulation, was insufficient. They realized that the strategic planning process did not specify how plans should be translated into action. A gap existed between the strategic direction set by senior executives and the results obtained by the firm.

As Alex R. Oliver, Vice President at Booz, Allen and Hamilton, Inc., suggests, one of the most common strategic planning mistakes is inadequate involvement of line management in strategic planning.[8] In addition, discussions with 216 strategic managers indicated that the greatest source of frustration and disappointment in their strategic planning systems was difficulties in implementation.[9] As one executive stated, "We actually used to tell ourselves our planning system was OK, even though we admitted it fell apart at implementation. That was our way of telling ourselves that the trouble was not at the top."

These problems with the implementation of the strategic plan led to the evolution of **strategic management**. Strategic management includes not only the elements of strategic planning, environmental analysis, and strategy formulation, but also strategy implementation and control. This current view of strategically managing the enterprise extends the responsibilities of strategic managers beyond planning to the design of implementation and control systems. Therefore, strategic management is not merely a new name for strategic planning. It is a comprehensive process for strategically managing the organization, a process that evolved in response to the demands of changing business conditions.

The Strategic Management Process

In a survey of CEOs, 91 percent stated that their firms engaged in some type of formal long-range planning.[10] However, planning does not always result in effective organizational performance. If plans are to succeed, they must be developed and implemented with equal care. Once implementation begins, managers must evaluate actual performance to verify progress toward accomplishing the plans and trigger corrective action when needed. Depending on the organization, this process can operate at any of four levels.

Levels of Strategy Development

In most larger firms, strategies are developed at various levels within the firm. It makes sense that department heads will develop strategies that are different from those developed by top-level managers. Managers at each level have a different perspective of the organization, and managers at higher levels are responsible for choices that have a greater impact on the organization. The choices at all levels are important, but some have consequences that are farther reaching for the firm than do others.

A useful way to view these levels of strategy development is to use the four levels first specified by Schendel and Hofer,[11] drawing from the work of Ansoff.[12] They are the functional, business, corporate, and enterprise levels. Figure 1.1 illustrates each of these levels and the areas of the firm's environment addressed by managers at each level.

Figure 1.1 Levels of Strategy Development

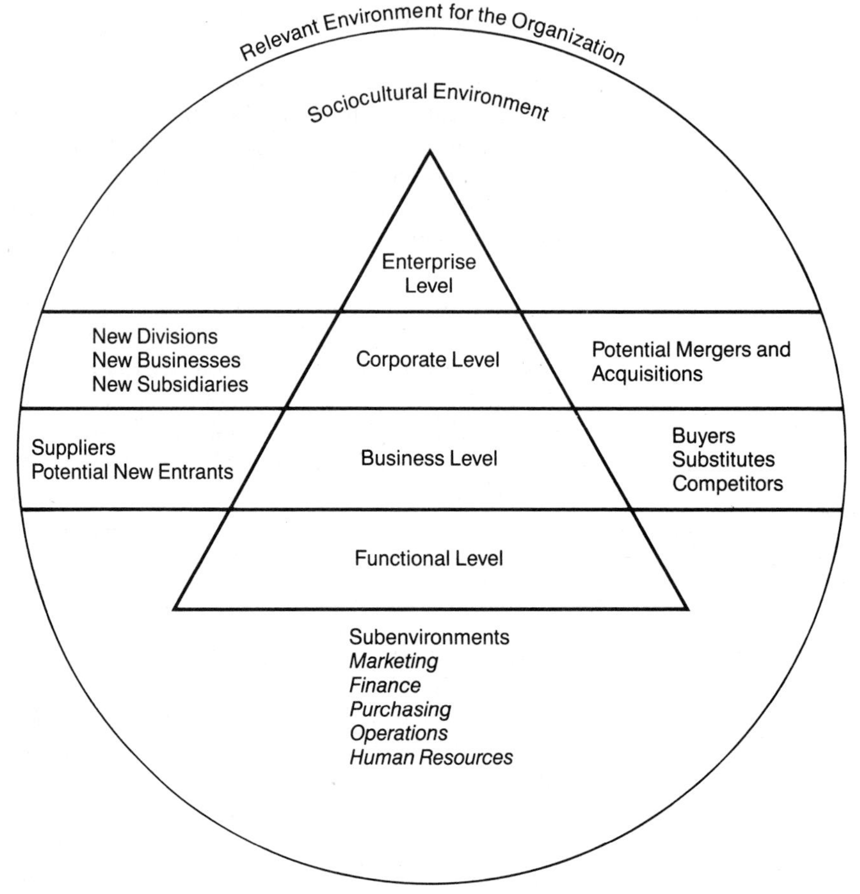

The levels at which strategies must be developed depend on the type of organization. Smaller, single-purpose businesses in a large community may not need to be as concerned with strategies for the enterprise and corporate levels, whereas large, visible, multibusiness firms may need to devote management attention to all levels.

According to Schendel and Hofer, the strategic management process can be applied to each level at which strategies are developed. In other words, regardless of level, strategies must be effectively managed to assure that they move the organization toward its goals.

Enterprise Level The highest level of strategy development, the enterprise level, involves strategies that encompass the organization's interactions with its publics. In a broad sense, the publics include the firm's sociocultural environment, which consists of the general publics that provide the culture, populations, communities, and economic system in which the firm conducts its business. The organization not only is influenced by the sociocultural environment in which it conducts business, but also influences that environment through its products and the choices that it makes. Society can accept the firm's choices or act through special interest groups or legislators to object to the firm's actions. The organization therefore must be prepared to analyze its sociocultural environment and develop enterprise-level strategies appropriate to this environment.

The society in which the firm is located gives it both legal and practical permission to operate. This permission from society is referred to as a **charter**. The **legal charter** is the granting of the licenses, registrations, and permissions that the organization needs in order to conduct business. The **practical charter** is society's willingness to purchase the firm's products or services at a price that allows the firm to make a profit. In many situations, these charters are influenced as much by the way the organization interacts with its relevant publics as by the products or services it provides.

The enterprise level of strategy development also includes strategies for social responsibility and ethics. The awarding of the legal and practical charters depends in part upon the public's belief that the company conducts its business responsibly and ethically. **Social responsibility**, discussed in Chapter 11, is the posture a firm takes in its attitudes, policies, and actions with respect to the duties, obligations, and expectations for which society believes the business should be held accountable in the conduct of its affairs or pursuit of its purpose. Fundamentally, it is the expectations that society holds for the manner in which the firm conducts its business. **Ethics** is a set of moral principles or values that forms the basis for accepted professional standards of conduct.

Society demands ethical and responsible behavior as preconditions for giving an organization a charter to operate. At the enterprise level, managers must therefore develop strategies for this behavior. Failure to do so may result in scenarios such as the alleged one in the Strategic Application "The Saga of Paul Bilzerian."

Corporate Level Firms engaged in multiple businesses or single-business firms pursuing growth through diversification into other businesses need to develop corporate-level strategies. The corporate level of strategy development requires the manager to analyze the environment for opportunities to acquire, develop, or divest businesses that will strengthen the organization's portfolio and to develop strategies to capitalize on those opportunities. The central issue is how best to manage the firm's portfolio of businesses to achieve the organization's strategic goals and to protect it from unexpected changes in the environment. This is one of the most important strategic choices for the top executives of a multibusiness firm.

Managing the firm's business portfolio involves integrating businesses with different market and operating characteristics. For example, many businesses are affected differently by general economic cycles, so that some are strong during periods of economic decline, whereas others closely follow the economic cycle. Another reason for corporate-level strategies is to manage the product life cycles of the various businesses.

STRATEGIC APPLICATIONS: SOCIAL RESPONSIBILITY

The Saga of Paul Bilzerian

Paul Bilzerian was an expression of the American dream. A high school dropout, Vietnam veteran, and self-made multimillionaire, he was the CEO of Singer Corporation by the age of 37. However, mounting evidence suggests that he may have "ridden roughshod over the securities laws" of the United States on his way to the top. Mr. Bilzerian was investigated by the SEC for alleged violations of securities law. According to *The Wall Street Journal*, the charges

> are outlined in documents obtained by *The Wall Street Journal*—including many filed by the SEC in federal court in New York—and interviews with many of Mr. Bilzerian's colleagues and people involved in his takeover raids. The details disclosed an even broader pattern of questionable conduct than anything that has heretofore emerged. For all his derring-do the details of his tactics amount to a catalog of possible securities crimes: insider trading, "parking" of stock in accounts to conceal its true ownership, false public disclosure documents filed with the SEC, aiding and abetting the keeping of false books and records, conspiracy to violate the securities laws, and tax fraud.
>
> While some of these are sometimes dismissed as technical violations, in the hands of Mr. Bilzerian these practices became weapons to force large corporations into unwanted takeovers or liquidations that gained him hundreds of millions of dollars.

The message here is that Mr. Bilzerian may have violated the legal and moral charter granted by society by engaging in unethical business practices.

Source: *The Wall Street Journal*, May 19, 1988.

Business Level Most discussions of strategic planning and management focus on the business level of strategy development. This level involves the choices relating to the strategies the firm will use to compete in a single business area. At this level, strategic managers are responsible for analyzing the environment for opportunities and threats in the firm's chosen business. They must then match the organization's internal capabilities to these opportunities and threats, and develop the strategies that will direct organizational members toward accomplishment of the organization's goals. Next, they must design structures, processes, and systems to guide all of the functional areas of the firm toward implementation of those strategies. If the organization consists of many businesses, then each business develops strategies for its product-markets. For example, the Strategic Application "Audi Aims for the U.S. Market" describes strategy development at the international business level at the Audi Car Company.

Functional Level Functional units of the firm handle business functions such as marketing, production, and finance. Each functional unit must develop strategies that contribute to the success of the overall business strategy.

Variations in functional strategies reflect that each functional unit of the organization interacts with unique segments of the environment. Purchasing deals with suppliers. Personnel recruits and trains employees. Marketing is responsible for distribution and sales. Operations must maintain the systems to produce the product or service.

STRATEGIC APPLICATIONS: INTERNATIONAL

Audi Aims for the U.S. Market

Audi, a subsidiary of Volkswagen, designated 1989 as its comeback year. In 1985 Audi sold 74,100 cars in the United States. However, a weaker dollar and allegations of mechanical defects caused U.S. sales to drop to just 22,900 autos in 1988. The new CEO of Audi projected an increase to 30,000 units for 1989. The U.S. National Highway Traffic Safety Administration was joined by similar agencies in Canada and Japan in a March 1989 ruling that cleared several auto manufacturers, including Audi, of the alleged mechanical problem. This, and a rejuvenated business-level strategy, are the bases for Audi's optimism.

Audi's turnaround strategy combined cost cutting to boost profits with aggressive advertising touting Audi's 12 first- or second-place finishes in 13 Sports Car Club of America Trans-Am races to assure the U.S. consumer of the cars' safety and reliability. In addition, Audi launched two new models in an attempt to capture a larger share of the declining U.S. market for European luxury cars. One model is an ultra luxury sedan with a V8 engine that gives it the highest power-to-size ratio in its field of competitors. The other model is a sporty coupe version of its four-wheel-drive Quattro. These new models combine power, handling, and luxury to appeal to the more affluent car buyer.

As a subsidiary of Volkswagen, Audi is engaged in the single business of providing autos for domestic and export sales to the middle class car enthusiast. Their business-level strategy focuses on recapturing a lost share of the U.S. auto market. This strategy must be consistent with Volkswagen's corporate-level strategy while specifying how Audi plans to compete successfully in the international luxury car market.

Source: Jim Treece and J. Templeman, "Can Audi Start Winning Races in the Showroom, Too?" *Business Week*, May 29, 1989, 47.

The manager of the functional unit not only monitors the actions of organizations outside the firm but also integrates the unit's activities with those of other units in the firm. For example, the personnel department must be aware of the local labor market and also coordinate with the other departments within the firm to ensure that the right employees are hired for each department.

Phases of Strategic Management

Regardless of the level at which the manager develops strategy, the same basic process is used to manage the strategy. This process consists of three phases: strategy formulation, strategy implementation, and strategic control and evaluation.

Strategy Formulation In the first phase of strategic management, the manager assesses current business conditions, analyzes internal capabilities, and develops plans. Like strategic planning, strategic management considers the environment a source of opportunities and threats for the organization. A strategically well-managed firm scans the environment for opportunities and threats as an initial stage in the planning process. In addition, it continually monitors the environment for changes that will present new opportunities or interfere with the achievement of the organization's goals.

At the same time, managers analyze the organization's internal capabilities. These include the managerial, technical, informational, organizational, and financial resources necessary for the business to continue to serve existing customers and clients plus what is needed to pursue new opportunities or respond to new threats. The capabilities analysis provides information upon which the manager can base a decision whether to adapt to environmental changes by using internal capabilities or by acquiring needed capabilities from outside the organization.

Combining the environmental assessment and the analysis of internal capabilities allows the manager to progress to formulating a strategy. Here, the manager chooses the firm's principal business relationships and develops a mission and strategy to take advantage of opportunities. This phase also includes strategic goals and objectives to guide the activities of members of the organization.

Strategy Implementation The action phase of strategic management is strategy implementation. This is the phase at which lower level managers must convert the strategic plans received from the strategic managers into the functional plans and strategies that guide the activities of organization members in a way that should lead the firm to achieve its strategic goals. Senior executives design organization structures and develop annual objectives to guide this process. These objectives are converted into functional-level plans, including objectives and strategies, that specify each unit's contribution to meeting the organization's overall strategic goals.

Good implementation requires that each department fulfill its purpose in the best way possible to contribute to the firm's strategic goals. It is hard to recommend specific implementation principles for department managers, because what they need to do varies with the organization and the strategic plan. In addition, these managers are seldom rewarded for their contributions to the strategic plan, because of the difficulty in tying one unit's efforts to overall organization performance. The combination of few guidelines and little recognition makes the implementation phase extremely challenging for functional-level managers.

Strategic Control and Evaluation A plan must be developed in the present to prepare for the future. But conditions inside and outside the firm change rapidly, making some aspects of the plan obsolete. Therefore, businesses need processes for evaluating these changes to determine their source (inside or outside) and importance. In addition, systems and techniques must be in place to trigger action to adjust to the changes and return the firm to the planned course, or to modify the plan to reflect the real world that the firm now faces. By using these processes and systems, the business completes the final phase of strategic management: control and evaluation.

A Choice Model of the Strategic Management Process

Most issues that senior managers address are either strategic or operational. **Strategic issues** concern the future decisions and actions that set the long-term direction of the firm.[13] Examples of strategic issues are: Which business(es) should the firm be engaged in over the next three, five, or ten years? Which major market segments, consumer or commercial, should the firm concentrate on over the next decade?

Operational issues are shorter-term decisions made in order to keep the firm competitive. These issues typically concern the functional areas of the firm rather than the entire organization. Examples of major operational issues are: Which manufacturing processes should be used? How can we best market our product or service? Which inventory costing method is most appropriate for our firm? Although operational issues have a narrower scope and focus on shorter time periods, they are as important as strategic issues. Both categories of issues influence the overall success of the organization.

Strategic issues are the focus of the strategic management process. The outputs of this process are the choices that managers make to direct the firm toward the pursuit of its mission. Unlike the daily operating choices of the lower level managers, these choices are strategic in nature.

Strategic choices usually depend on the prior experience of senior executives. They involve unique problems with major long-term consequences for the organization. Very little precedent exists to guide the manager, and an incorrect choice can seriously impair the success and survival of the firm. Therefore, these choices reflect the manager's best judgments among alternatives generated from previous analyses. The specific alternative that the executive chooses reflects environmental conditions, situational and organizational factors, and the individual and collective personalities of senior executives involved in the strategic management of the firm.

To make these choices successfully, managers should follow a logical process of analyzing information, formulating strategies, implementing the strategies, and evaluating and controlling them. Figure 1.2 illustrates the way many executives perform these tasks. Notice that strategic management is a series of choices. These choices determine the success and survival of the organization. Besides the strategic choices, Figure 1.2 indicates some of the important functional-level choices that are necessary to effectively implement top management's strategies.

This model of the strategic management process applies to all of the levels of strategy development—enterprise, corporate, business, and functional. This chapter concentrates on the business level of strategy development. In discussing the actual strategies that a manager may choose, Chapter 4 will distinguish corporate and business-level strategies. Functional-level strategies will be discussed in Chapters 5, 6 and 7 on implementation. Chapter 11 will address enterprise-level strategies under social issues in strategic management.

Environmental Assessment Why have foreign automobile manufacturers captured one-third of the U.S. car market? Why did so many savings and loan associations go under in the late 1980s while other financial institutions thrived? The answers to such questions are complex, but the single most important reason for the success or failure of an organization is its ability to assess current business conditions, accurately predict future trends, and use this information to make good strategic choices.

Strategic management therefore begins with acquiring an understanding of the business environment in which the organization operates. The firm's environment consists of other organizations, government agencies, special interest groups, and individuals with which the firm must transact business. From this arena, the firm draws its life's blood in the form of capital, raw materials, labor, and operating revenue

Figure 1.2 Choice Model of the Strategic Management Process

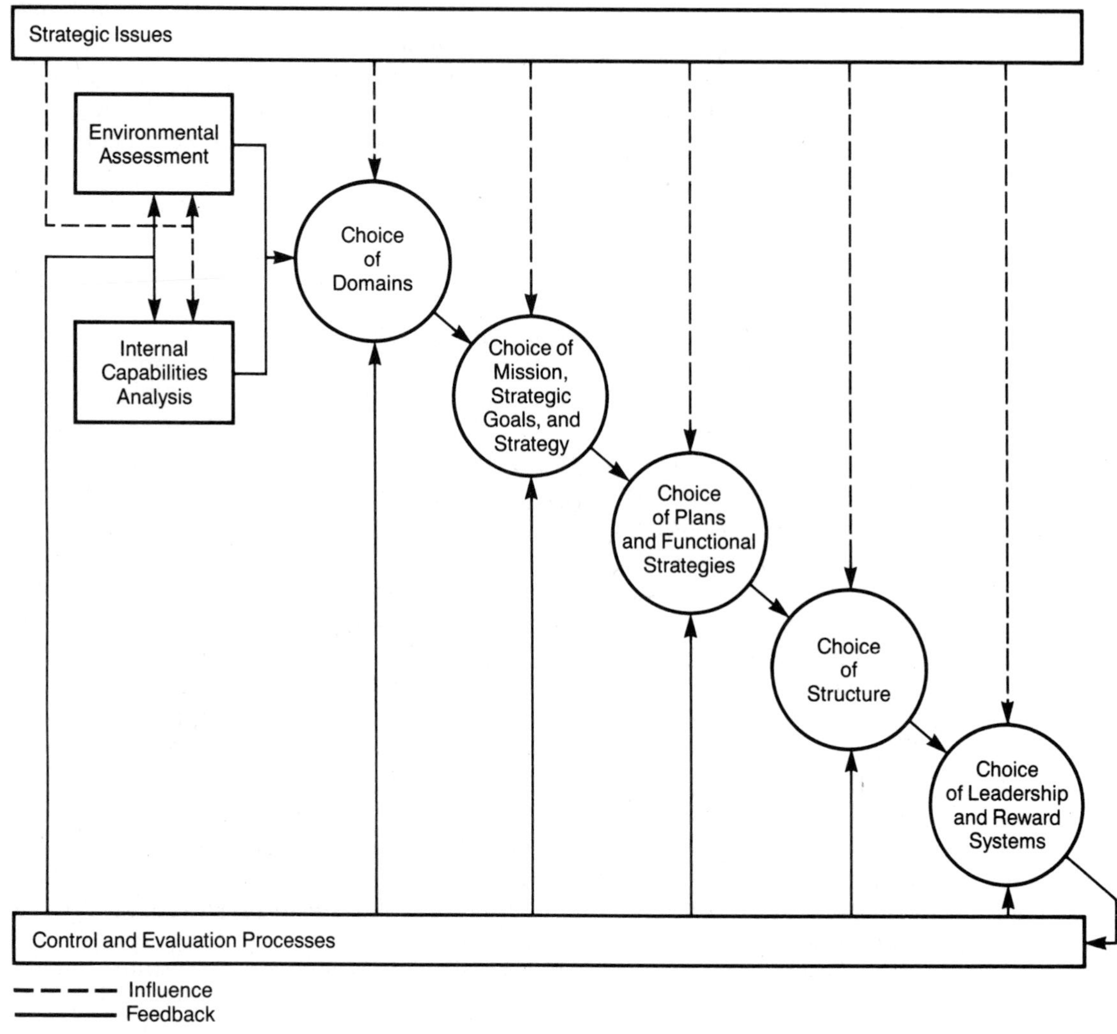

(whether from sales or appropriations). This information does not come cheap. Indeed, deciding how much to spend for the acquisition of environmental data is one of top management's most important strategic choices. Chapter 2 will discuss specific elements in the firm's environment and provide insight into aspects of the environment that require special scrutiny.

Determination of Internal Strategic Capabilities Strategic management must also look inward to the organization and determine the capabilities of its technical and human

systems. This analysis reveals the demands that current operations place upon the firm's resources, material and human. It also provides information about the slack that the firm has available to absorb new demands that may emerge from the environment. A thorough analysis of internal strategic capabilities allows the manager to match current capabilities to environmental conditions and to assess the feasibility of possible strategies. If additional resources are necessary, then the acquisition of those resources can be incorporated into the strategic plan.

This stage of the strategic management process is extremely important. The strengths and weaknesses of the firm's managerial, technical, financial, and human resource capabilities determine to a large extent which environmental opportunities the firm can pursue in the short run. For example, Sony used its strength of an innovative culture to shift its dependence from the highly competitive consumer electronics market to new opportunities in commercial telecommunications, office automation, and health care. With its relatively high commitment to research and development, Sony was able to use existing capabilities to enter these markets.[14]

Choice of Domain Not all of the components of the environment are relevant for every firm. Depending on the organization's size, industry, customers, and products, more or less of the environment will be important to the organization's success and survival. To use a term chosen by Dill,[15] the part of the total environment that is relevant to the organization for goal setting and goal attainment is the task environment. Most business task environments are limited geographically to a single nation, region, city, or town.

Not all of the components of a firm's environment transact with the firm. For example, suppliers of inputs and buyers of the firm's products may be potentially relevant and, therefore, part of the firm's task environment. However, managers typically choose to buy from a few reliable suppliers and sell to only a segment of the total market.

Therefore, once strategic managers are familiar with the environment and with the firm's capabilities, they must choose the portion of the task environment in which they wish to conduct business. The portion of the task environment that the manager chooses is called the **domain**. It is defined as all of the organizations, agencies, groups, and individuals in the task environment with which the manager chooses to transact business.[16] For example, the decision to make Dillards' a national rather than regional retailer was the specific choice of William T. Dillard.[17] He chose this expanded domain with its increased complexity on the basis of his assumptions about the environment and his personal aspirations for the organization.

The choice of a domain is extremely important. The correct choice will give the firm a competitive advantage, while an incorrect choice will force the firm to operate in an unfriendly environment, as Quadram Corporation unfortunately learned. Explosive growth and financial success caused J. Leland Strage, CEO of this small high-tech firm, to rapidly make a series of acquisitions. An 80 percent drop in earnings in one year convinced him that the company's domain had expanded faster than his ability to manage it. He later decided to restrict expansion to more familiar businesses.[18]

Choice of Mission, Strategic Goals, and Strategy Within the selected domain, the manager must choose which environmental opportunities to pursue. This choice results in a clear statement of the firm's primary business or **mission**. A mission states the firm's primary purpose or business, indicating to its employees and publics the firm's products, markets, method of conducting business, and approach to dealing with constituents. The mission specifies whether the firm intends to be proactive or reactive and whether it will emphasize R&D, finance, operations, or marketing. Finally, the mission gives the firm's employees and publics a clear picture of where it is positioned in its competitive arena and who are its primary stakeholders.[19] The Strategic Application "Mission Statement" provides examples of mission statements for several types of firms.

Strategic management is designed to enable the firm to accomplish its mission over an extended period. To plan how the firm can do this, managers set **strategic goals**, sometimes called long-term objectives. These goals state the general targets that the firm intends to achieve in strategic areas such as market share, profitability, productivity, growth, and return. To serve their purpose, strategic goals must be consistent with the mission of the firm. For example, to fulfill a mission of being a proactive, high-growth firm, managers might set a strategic goal of 15 percent annual growth rate in an industry in which growth of seven to eight percent is average. These are strategic-level goals that reflect the combined performance of all of the organizational units (strategic business units, divisions, or departments).

STRATEGIC APPLICATIONS

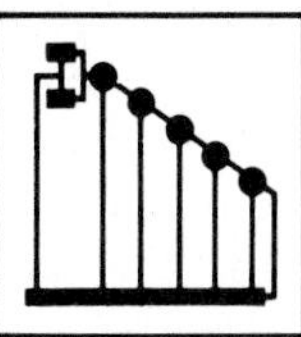

Mission Statements

Entrepreneurial Organization: The Anchor Companies We are an integrated financial services organization with the mission of profitably selling and servicing a broad mix of investment-oriented life insurance, annuities, and securities to meet the needs of the nationwide marketplace served by independent financial services professionals.

Established Organization: Public Service Company of New Mexico Recognizing the advantages of our placement, we are pursuing a growth-oriented corporate strategy. In New Mexico we are promoting economic development through direct investment and other inducements to industry. Simultaneously, we are seeking wider regional and national markets for our energy products. We are broadening our base and spreading shareholder risk through a variety of nonutility investments.

Public Organization: Texas Department of Human Services The mission of this department is to promote the individual's worth and dignity by providing services to families and children, elderly, and disabled individuals to encourage their self-sufficiency and prevent long-term dependence on public assistance. These services will be provided humanely, efficiently, within available resources, and consistent with legislative provisions.

Source: The Anchor Companies, 1987; 1988 annual report, Public Service Company of New Mexico; *Strategic Plan for the Texas Department of Human Services 1986–1991*, internal document, September 1985.

The specifics of how the firm will exploit the opportunities that top management has chosen from among those available are laid out in the **strategy**. This functions as the organization's compass to point to the general methods that the organization will use to achieve its strategic goals. The strategy guides and directs the activities of organization members toward accomplishment of the mission.

Strategies fall into three general types: generic strategies, master strategies, and ancillary strategies. Table 1.1 shows these types along with brief definitions of strategy categories under each type. Many of the master strategies in these categories are most appropriate for the business level of strategy development. Others apply more directly to the corporate level. Chapter 4 will describe specific strategies in each category and at which level they are appropriate.

Strategies describe broad ranges of actions available to the organization to accomplish its strategic goals. For example, a cost-leadership generic strategy helps the firm be a more effective competitor within its industry by incurring the lowest costs to provide its product or service. Internal-growth master strategies promote the firm's growth through developing new products or services in-house, whereas external-growth master strategies use acquisition or merger as the method for growth. In some cases, a firm may need to shrink to control costs and improve management control before launching into a growth mode. This would require rejuvenation master strategies. At other times, it is financially more appropriate to concentrate on maintaining the current level of business performance than to attempt to grow. This frequently happens in times of economic decline and results in the adoption of a stabilization master strategy. On occasion, it may be best to harvest or divest all or part of the business, which calls for a termination master strategy. Last, a manager may choose to focus on establishing cooperative ventures with other organizations as a means to improve organization performance. These strategies are referred to as ancillary strategies. The factors that determine the choice of a strategy are discussed later in this chapter.

Table 1.1 Types of Strategies

Strategy Type	Definition	Examples of Strategies
Generic	Generic approaches to outperform industry competitors.	Cost Leadership Differentiation Niche (Focus)
Master	Strategic actions that a single business or SBU takes to achieve its strategic goals.	Vertical Integration Concentration Product Diversification Concentric Diversification Conglomerate Diversification Rejuvenation through Retrenchment Stabilization through Maintenance Termination through Divestment
Ancillary	Strategies that work in conjunction with other strategies and facilitate achievement of strategic goals.	Rationalization through Consolidation Cooperation through Joint Venture

Choice of Plans, Objectives, and Functional Strategies Strategies and strategic goals are implemented through plans that include objectives and functional-level strategies. Objectives provide specific targets that indicate expected levels and time frames and serve as guides to organization action. Functional-level strategies are the means or activities that the organization will use to achieve its objectives. Managers are responsible for selecting the best strategy for each objective.

To merely develop a new strategy is not enough. Organizational performance depends on effectively implementing strategies through plans and functional-level strategies. For example, after Black & Decker, the medium-sized power tool manufacturer, experienced a $158 million loss in 1985 due primarily to foreign competition, the board hired a new CEO, Noland D. Archibald, with a background in consumer marketing. Archibald immediately devised a retrenchment–turnaround strategy designed to position the company to face foreign competition head-on and diversify its product mix. He purchased GE's small-appliance division and devised an implementation plan that included closing seven plants, eliminating 2,000 jobs, and reorganizing operations around product-markets.[20]

A formulated strategy is lifeless until members of the organization implement it. All of an organization's activities either help or hinder the successful implementation of the strategy.

Choice of Organization Structure Implementation plans usually include changes to the structure, processes, and systems of the organization. Choosing the appropriate organization structure involves selecting the structural design that leads to accomplishment of strategic goals. General Electric appeared to pursue a master strategy of external growth when it acquired Kidder, Peabody & Company, one of the larger Wall Street brokerage houses. To implement this growth strategy and integrate Kidder, Peabody into its organization, GE had to modify its structure by creating a new division for financial services.[21] Not only acquisition but most changes in strategy are accompanied by alterations in the firm's structure. Motorola Inc. has an implementation procedure that automatically elevates a unit from division to group status when it reaches a certain level of sales. Staff functions are then added to the group's organization chart, and group managers receive more decision authority.

The organization structure is originally designed during the initial stages of strategy implementation. Senior executives handle this formal organization design, which is represented by the organization chart. So that it will help managers and employees implement the strategy, the organization design must be consistent with the mission and strategy stated in the strategic plan. However, organizations also have an informal structure that is based on past working relations and friendships among employees, developed over a period of time. This informal structure can either help or hinder the successful accomplishment of the firm's goals and objectives.

While senior management must design an appropriate overall organization structure, unit managers must modify the department's structure. All levels of management need to closely monitor the informal structure to determine whether changes are necessary. For example, Gillette formally committed $7 million to the introduction of its electric shaver produced by its West German subsidiary. However, Gillette's

top management remained apathetic about the project. As one executive put it, "Those electric razors are getting better, but they're still not as good as a blade."[22] The informal structure did not truly support the product development strategy, and as a result the product was not successful.

Choices of Leadership, Culture, and Human Resource Processes and Reward Systems To implement new or changing mission, strategic goals, and strategy, the organization needs new processes and systems for leading and rewarding employees. A **process** is a series of actions or operations directed toward a particular result. A process or several processes focused on a particular aspect or activity of the organization form a **system**. Leadership processes play an important role in the implementation of plans and strategies. The system of rewards with which the organization acknowledges the contributions of its members also encourages employees to perform the actions necessary to achieve strategic goals and objectives.

The implementation of strategic and functional plans depends on the choices of the most effective leadership processes and reward systems. For example, Intel Inc., a large semiconductor manufacturer, has a master strategy of internal growth through innovation. To implement this strategy, the company decided to make leadership more participative and to reward creative thinking. In contrast, Texas Air has chosen external growth through acquisition and low-cost leadership. Texas Air reward systems place less emphasis on people, and reward using traditional means such as money and movement up the hierarchy. In both cases, the implementation processes and systems must be consistent with the mission and strategy.

The culture operating at all levels of the organization can be a key to the efficient and effective implementation of a strategy. Organization culture is the structures, behaviors, processes, rites, rituals, myths, symbols, and traditions that distinguish the organization from other organizations. In many respects, culture is the link between plans and action. Well-developed plans clearly specify what actions are necessary. However, unless the organization has a culture that supports taking the specified actions, the plan cannot be successfully implemented. Managers should be sensitive to the organization's culture and to how employees operate within that culture, so that they can design a process that maximizes each employee's contribution to achieving functional objectives and strategic goals.

Senior management also must choose the most appropriate reward system for the organization's mission and strategy. The reward system gives managers a powerful tool to use in influencing the actions of organization members toward accomplishment of strategic goals and functional objectives. The expectation of receiving a desired reward usually motivates employees to higher performance. Managers can modify organizational rewards to reflect what employees value. Managers can use the promise of rewards as an incentive and the awarding of rewards as a reinforcement.

A company that designed a reward system to direct and reward action toward the firm's goals and objectives is Mesa Petroleum. When T. Boone Pickens, the celebrated corporate raider, was chairman of Mesa Petroleum, the strategy was external growth through acquisition. A unit of the company was devoted to searching for potential acquisitions. In this unit, the speed with which information was obtained and decisions were made was critical for taking advantage of the very narrow windows of opportunity that appeared for corporate takeovers. The unit's performance appraisal system was designed to reward analysts for their thorough and timely research and willingness to make risky decisions. In that regard, the system was designed to facilitate movement in the strategic directions set forth for the organization.

Choice of Processes and Techniques for Control and Evaluation Throughout each phase of the strategic management process, management must control and evaluate the activities of the organization. Control processes and techniques provide the means to monitor the firm's progress toward its goals and objectives. Evaluation criteria are the triggers that tell when the limits of the objectives have been reached.

Senior management designs and activates the control processes, techniques, and evaluation criteria used to keep the organization's progress on track. A variety of control techniques are available, including statistical testing, employee surveys, and financial reports. These techniques use several different evaluation criteria such as cost, stress levels, profitability, and satisfaction levels. The manager must design the most effective process and appropriate techniques with relevant criteria to ensure that the firm is on track toward meeting its strategic goals and objectives.

Control mechanisms should include recommendations for corrective action. A report that simply observes that an objective was missed is of little use to a manager. By the time the manager receives the report, it may be too late to take any timely corrective action. Therefore, the control mechanism itself should initiate intermediate corrective action until the manager can analyze the condition in more detail.

One clear example is Pan American World Airways. Pan Am's management was aware that its Panamac reservation system was obsolete and costing sales. Yet the control mechanisms that alerted management to the problem failed to indicate a way to respond. Because other matters were more pressing for the airline, nothing was done. Finally, the problem became a crisis, and Pan Am was forced to negotiate the use of the reservation system owned by American Airlines.[23] Pan Am could have avoided this threat if the company's control mechanism had been designed to initiate action to develop a new reservation system as soon as Pan Am learned the old system was hurting sales.

Choices of control processes, techniques, and evaluation criteria are, perhaps, some of the most important choices that managers must make as part of the strategic management process. Top-level executives specify overall strategic goals and approve budgets that serve as standards by which to judge the firm's performance. Unit managers then must design control processes and techniques that monitor the day-to-day activities of their unit and that prompt corrective action when the managers detect a deviation from objectives. This arrangement allows unit managers to identify and quickly correct small internal deviations, freeing senior management to focus on attempting to adapt to external factors such as changes in the actions of competitors or general business conditions.

Feedforward and Feedback Any dynamic process such as strategic management must include a feedback loop to the preceding stages. Control mechanisms compare actual performance to desired levels specified in strategic goals and objectives. If an unacceptable gap exists between desired and actual performance, corrective action must be taken. Short-term corrective action should be specified as part of the control mechanism. However, long-term remedies require the manager to review the preceding stages of the process to determine the source of the gap and take more permanent corrective action. The feedback indicated in Figure 1.2 directs the manager back to preceding stages. If strategic plans are carefully developed, the gap is more likely caused by an implementation or control issue than by a faulty strategic plan.

Recent writings in strategic management suggest that control and evaluation include more than merely reacting to gaps between the desired and actual levels of performance.[24–27] After all, even if the organization has quick-reacting control mechanisms, the gap already exists and part of the damage is done. These strategic management experts argue that management should continually look forward to try to anticipate future gaps rather than waiting until they happen. This idea, referred to as **feedforward** control, is the active anticipation of strategic and operational gaps, and the timely and effective closing of those gaps. By using a combination of feedforward and feedback control, managers at all levels can provide better direction toward the accomplishment of the organization's strategic goals and objectives.

Flow and Direction of the Strategic Management Process

One frequent misconception regarding the process of strategic management is that it always flows from the top-level decision makers down to lower level managers. Although the determining of the strategic direction for the firm is the responsibility of top management, much information about the internal and external environment comes from department managers, sales staff, and other employees. Once the strategic direction is decided, it is communicated downward, where it starts a series of cycles for objective setting, strategy formulation, implementation, and monitoring, as shown in Figure 1.3. Note that the levels in Figure 1.3 refer to level of responsibility rather than level of strategy development.

The first two cycles involve formulating enterprise-, corporate-, and business-level strategic goals, and forwarding them upward or downward for review and approval. Next, divisions and departments develop budgets based on the approved objectives and again forward them to higher level management for review and approval. In the fourth cycle, department managers report their performance to top management, where performance is compared to objectives to determine if strategy adjustments are necessary. This process is consistent with the ideas of many experts, who say that strategy development is highly interactive among top management and operational units (divisions or departments). It also suggests a sequence that will result in more effective strategic management for the organization.

The cycles in Figure 1.3 correspond to the stages in the choice model (Figure 1.2). The development of a mission, enterprise-level strategy, or charter is assumed to be based on an environmental assessment and analysis of internal capabilities. This mission or charter is a formal statement of the domain that the firm's management has selected. Division objectives and strategies are the choices of strategic goals

Figure 1.3 Strategy Development Cycles

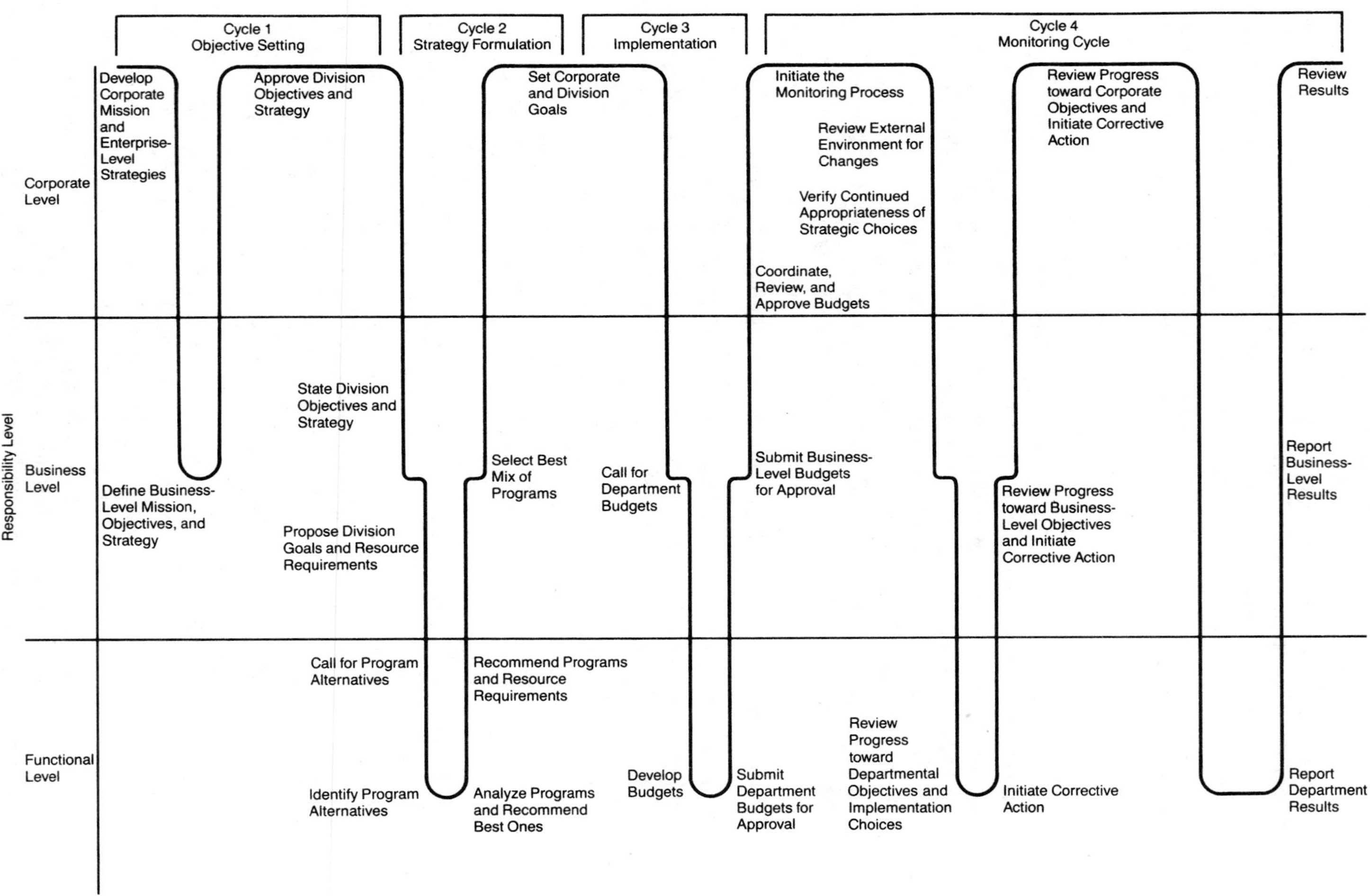

Source: Modified and reprinted by permission of *Harvard Business Review*. An exhibit from "Strategic Planning in Diversified Companies" by Richard F. Vancil and Peter Lorange, January–February 1975, pp. 84–85.

and master strategies. The third cycle involves the flow of plans, objectives, and functional-level strategies required to effectively implement the firm's strategic goals. The last cycle describes the possible flow of review activities undertaken in the control and evaluation stage of the strategic management process.

Influences on Managers' Choices

Because the essence of strategic management is making choices, it is important to understand what influences these choices. Many firms that are in the same industry and are apparently facing identical environmental conditions elect to pursue different strategies. One explanation for these differences is that factors within the organization and unique to the manager may influence the manager's choice of one strategy over others.

The influences on the choices that managers make in the course of strategically managing their organizations fall into five basic categories: environmental, situational, organizational, group, and personal. Environmental factors, discussed in Chapter 2, are the forces in the firm's business arena that cause the manager to select a course of action. These factors are the focus of most discussions of strategy formulation and provide the opportunities and threats that act on the organization. Situational, organizational, group, and individual factors also exert substantial influence on managerial choices but have received much less attention from management writers.

Situational Factors Situational factors include organization size, shape, and technology. Size usually refers to the level of the firm's sales, value of assets, or number of employees. Managers of larger organizations have the option to choose strategies that require large amounts of extra resources typically unavailable in smaller, leaner organizations. However, smaller firms are usually less constrained by rigid bureaucratic structures or inflexible cultures and can be more responsive to opportunities by pursuing rapid-growth strategies than their larger counterparts. Thus, size can expand or limit the number of strategies available to the organization.

Organization shape is the configuration of the firm's structure at the corporate, business, and functional levels. This is typically represented by the organization chart. The shape of the organization limits the choices of the strategic manager.[28] If the organization has a history of a tall, rigid structure, the strategic manager will likely choose a strategy that fits within that structure. The manager who is accustomed to operating in a very flexible, organic structure is less limited in selecting strategies because he or she knows that the organizational configuration can adjust to the design requirements of the new strategy. Chapter 6 discusses organization shapes in more detail.

The level of sophistication of the organization's technology influences the strategic manager's choices in two ways. First, the type of technology directly limits the number of alternatives available to the manager. Traditional smokestack industries—for example, steel producers or auto makers—require large capital investments. Strategic managers are frequently reluctant to abandon such a large asset base to pursue a completely different strategy. This limits strategic options to those that fit within the constraints of the current industry. Second, the type of technology inevitably influences the manager's point of reference. That is, a manager trained in a particular industry, with its associated traditions and accepted practices, would probably continue to evaluate choices based on this initial point of reference. The Strategic Application "Sun National Bank" provides a case in point.

Organizational Factors: Culture and Politics Organizational factors that influence managers' choices include the organization's culture and politics. Remember from page 17 that an organization's culture is the structures, behaviors, processes, rites, rituals, myths, symbols, and traditions that distinguish the organization from other organizations. Interest in organization culture grew with the publication of Peters and Waterman's book *In Search of Excellence.*[29]

Peters and Waterman studied several successful firms and determined that they had certain aspects of culture in common. Some readers assumed that all organizations that have or acquire these characteristics will be successful. However, just three years after publication of their book, a report in *Business Week* indicated that 13 of the 25 firms listed as excellent by Peters and Waterman were no longer excellent according to their same criteria.[30] This suggests that no one culture is best.

On one hand, the manager's experience in the firm's existing culture will bias him or her toward choosing a strategy that is compatible with the firm's current culture. On the other hand, it is most important that the culture match the demands of existing business conditions. Furthermore, changing an entire organization's culture is slow and difficult. These opposing forces push the manager to choose the best strategy that

STRATEGIC APPLICATIONS

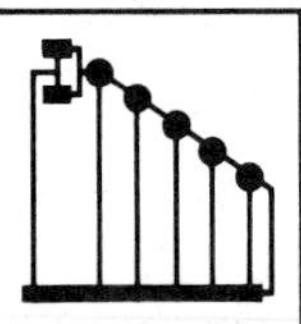

Sun National Bank

Sun National Bank (SNB) is the largest bank in Arizona and the 39th largest bank in the United States. SNB has been profitable since it was founded and has gained a reputation as a solid and fiscally conservative institution. Like other traditional financial institutions, SNB felt that its primary purpose was to serve as an intermediary between the saver and the borrower.

With the deregulation of the financial services industry, competition from savings and loans, credit unions, and out-of-state banks has threatened SNB's market position. One executive stated, "We are still profitable because of our older accounts, but we are losing the new account battle." To cope with increased competition, the strategic managers of SNB launched a program to become more marketing oriented.

However, the conservative philosophy of SNB's management resulted in extreme resistance to the shift in the bank's orientation. An executive said, "If I had wanted to be a salesman, I would have worked in a department store rather than a bank." In spite of SNB's stated commitment to a marketing orientation, managers continued to evaluate decisions on the basis of the old, regulated banking criteria. As a consequence, the switch to a marketing orientation had yet to be completed after five years.

is acceptable to the firm's current culture, even though this may not be the best strategy for prevailing business conditions.

Organizational politics are especially likely to affect strategy development if strategic choices are made by a group of top-level senior executives rather than a single CEO. In many organizations, such a group is called the executive committee, strategic planning committee, or planning committee. Its purpose is to draw from the collective experience and knowledge of several senior executives to arrive at a consensus regarding the strategic direction of the firm. When strategy development involves the high stakes of corporate leadership, organizational politics are highly likely to become important.

Robert E. Jones[31] warns of several political games that are played in organizations. These games diminish the advantages of using a group for strategy development because little exchange of ideas takes place. Furthermore, these games can be harmful if they result in political infighting among the members of the senior executive group.

Group Factors Strategic managers seldom act in isolation. More often, their choices and actions result from input and discussions with trusted individuals or their peer group. Members of this group may come from various levels of the organization and have varying degrees of influence on the choices of the manager. James D. Thompson refers to this group as the dominant coalition of organization decision makers.[32] They are the "relevant others" who apply direct and indirect pressure on the executive to conform to the choices that are acceptable to the entire group.

The manager may reject feasible strategies because he or she knows that they are inconsistent with the wishes of the management group. In some instances, the manager's choice may not be his or her preferred strategy but a consensus of the members of the executive group. Other choices may merely be influenced by information from members of the group. Regardless of the degree of influence, the opinions and suggestions of the executive's peer group affect the executive's choices.

Personal Factors Strategic managers are not robots, but thinking and feeling human beings. When senior executives make choices, they typically use a combination of intuition and analysis based on aspects of their personalities. In addition, their diagnosis of a strategic situation is frequently biased by their preferred choices.[33] It is important to understand the personality factors that contribute to intuition and, therefore, influence strategic choices. Three of the most important personality factors that influence managers' choices are their functional perspective, individual characteristics, and previous professional experience. Definitions and examples of these factors are provided in Table 1.2.

Performance and Organization Effectiveness

The central theme of this book is that strategic managers make complex choices that influence the success and survival of the firm. Effective strategic management results in improved short- and long-term performance. To relate the strategic manager's

Table 1.2 Personality Factors Influencing Choices

Factor	Definition	Examples
Functional perspective	The functional background of the managers, such as accounting, engineering, or production/operations	Functional area of the firm in which the manager received his or her formal education (e.g., engineering, accounting) Functional area of the firm in which the manager received his or her on-the-job training
Individual characteristics	The personality attributes that managers bring to strategic choice situations	Values: Managers tend to choose the strategies that promote what they personally value (e.g., creativity). Geographical perspective: Managers think in either global or local terms.[a] Demographics: Sex and ethnic background may influence values and biases.[b] Judgment biases: Managers can display biases in their judgment when making choices based on partial data.[c] Problem simplification: Because managers have varying abilities to mentally process complex strategic data, they use simplification processes.[d] Use of power and authority: All managers have authority but vary in their power to implement strategic choices.[e] Degree of assertiveness: Managers vary in the degree to which they are assertive or aggressive.[f] Decision-making profile: Managers differ in how they gather and evaluate information for decision making.[g] Cognitive beliefs: Managers have varying beliefs about which factors cause which outcomes.[h] Motivational orientation: Managers are motivated by different factors.[i]
Professional experience	The experiences of the manager during his or her professional career that have influenced the way he or she evaluates strategic choices and makes decisions.	Initial professional exposure: The first professional job or activity performed by a manager in an organizational setting. This is the period when the new professional is most impressionable and results in lasting opinions of what constitutes good management practice.[j] Role models: Superiors or peers of the manager whom he or she admired for their management accomplishments. Attempts to emulate the role model result in lasting management preferences and opinions.

[a]Frank Feather, "Geo-Strategic Thinking . . . and Its Courageous Application to Planning," *Managerial Planning* 33 (November–December 1984): 4–8, 60.

[b]Andre Von der Merwe, "Strategic Leadership and the Chief Executive," *Long Range Planning* 18 (February 1985): 100–111.

[c]James H. Barnes, Jr., "Cognitive Biases and Their Impact on Strategic Planning," *Strategic Management Journal* 5 (April–June 1984): 129–137.

[d]Charles R. Schwenk, "Cognitive Simplification Processes in Strategic Decision Making," *Strategic Management Journal* 5 (April–June 1984): 111–128.

[e]David C. Calabria, "CEO's and the Paradox of Power," *Business Horizons* 25 (January–February 1982): 29–31.

[f]James A. Walters, "Managerial Assertiveness," *Business Horizons* 25 (September–October 1982): 24–29.

[g]John W. Slocum, Jr., and D. Hellriegel, "A Look at How Managers' Minds Work," *Business Horizons* 26 (July–August 1983): 58–68.

[h]Jeffrey D. Ford and W. H. Hegarty, "Decision Makers' Beliefs about the Causes and Effects of Structure: An Exploratory Study," *Academy of Management Journal* 27 (June 1984): 271–291.

[i]H. R. Bobbit, Jr., and J. D. Ford, "Decision-Maker Choice as a Determinant of Organizational Structure," *Academy of Management Review* 5 (January 1980): 13–23.

[j]John R. Montanari, "Managerial Discretion: An Expanded Model of Organization Choice," *Academy of Management Review* 3 (April 1978): 231–241.

choices and actions to the firm's performance, managers need to understand the complex nature of organizational performance and effectiveness. Furthermore, managers need to understand how to measure effectiveness in a way that will provide accurate feedback on how effectively they are strategically managing their firm.

Effectiveness is a measure of the long-term viability of the organization. This definition, which pertains to organizations in all sectors of the economy, is too broad to be used by individual organizations to determine their long-term performance. Therefore, managers have developed more direct ways to measure effectiveness. Table 1.3 provides a list of 15 effectiveness measures, their time perspectives, and the organizational setting in which they would be most appropriate. When selecting the most appropriate measure, managers should consider the time perspective and the type of measure that are appropriate.

Three broad time periods are usually considered: short range (one to three years), intermediate (two to five years), and long range (three to 15 years). Some measures are more suited to assess performance over the long term. For example, the organization's ability to adapt to a rapidly changing environment is critical to the long-term success of the enterprise, but this criterion is impossible to assess in the short run.

The effectiveness measure may be financial, operational, or behavioral. Financial measures assess the financial performance of the organization or unit. Operational

Table 1.3 Effectiveness Measures

Criteria	Time Perspective[a]	Type[b]
Adaptability	I	Beh
Productivity	SR	Ops
Satisfaction	SR	Beh
Profitability	SR-I-LR	Fin
Resource Acquisition	SR-I	Ops
Absence of Strain	SR-I	Beh
Control over Environment	I-LR	Fin-Ops
Development	I-LR	Beh
Efficiency	SR-LR	Ops
Employee Reaction	SR-I	Ops
Growth	LR	Fin
Integration	I-LR	Ops-Beh
Open Communication	SR-I	Beh
Survival	LR	Fin-Ops
Financial Operations (e.g., return on investment, gross profit margin, inventory turnover, cash flow)	SR-I-LR	Fin

[a]SR = Short-Range (1–3 years), I = Intermediate (2–5 years), LR = Long-Range (3–15 years)
[b]Fin = Financial Effectiveness Criteria, Ops = Operational Effectiveness Criteria, Beh = Behaviorial Effectiveness Criteria

measures assess the effectiveness of work flow and work support. Behavioral effectiveness measures determine individual performance. The type of measure used depends on which aspect of performance the manager wishes to evaluate.

Managers can select effectiveness measures using this straightforward method:

1. Determine the type and time perspective that is most appropriate to determine the organization's and/or unit's performance.

2. Review the list of criteria available (see Table 1.3), and select the most appropriate criteria.

In today's dynamic business environment, firms must be effective to survive. Thus strategic managers must be able to assess the effectiveness of their organization over the correct time period, using the proper measure. Strategic managers cannot hope to correctly determine the effectiveness of a selected strategy unless they use an accurate measure of the performance attributed to that strategy. Therefore, the selection of the appropriate measure of effectiveness is an important managerial choice in the strategic management process.

Summary

Unlike strategic planning, strategic management recognizes the need for extensive strategy implementation and control to effectively manage organizations under dynamic business conditions. The strategic management perspective, like strategic planning, is based on the open-systems view of the organization. It has evolved in response to the changing needs of the organization in a more uncertain environment.

Strategy development takes place on four levels. First, enterprise-level strategies focus on the firm's transactions with its sociocultural environment. Corporate-level strategies are concerned with the mix of the firm's various businesses to create a portfolio to achieve corporate strategic goals. Business-level strategies integrate the efforts of several components of a single business to take advantage of the opportunities present in the business environment. Finally, functional-level strategies assure that each functional unit manages its environment in a manner that will contribute to the accomplishment of strategic goals and objectives. The strategies that are appropriate for each level vary depending on the type of organization.

The strategic management process involves a series of choices. First, the manager assesses current business conditions to determine opportunities and threats and analyzes the firm's internal strategic capabilities. Then senior managers determine the gaps between opportunities and capabilities and select the domain that offers the most opportunities with the fewest threats. Then these managers choose the firm's mission, strategic goals, and strategy. At this stage, the managers are in a position to develop a mission and specific strategic goals. These goals guide the choice of a strategy to specify how the firm intends to accomplish its goals and objectives.

The strategic management process continues with the choices necessary to implement the strategies developed. Managers choose plans and functional-level strategies necessary to transform the strategic plan into action. Depending on the nature of the strategic and implementation plans, a new or modified organization structure may be necessary. Leadership and culture processes and reward systems also must contribute to the successful implementation of plans. Last, control processes, techniques, and evaluation criteria must be set in place to anticipate and track the progress of actual organization performance toward the goals and objectives. If the actual results fail to meet the levels specified in the strategic goals and objectives, feedback from this last stage triggers corrective action at preceding stages. If changes in conditions could hinder the accomplishment of strategic goals and objectives, feedforward triggers the required changes in plans, implementation strategies, or evaluation criteria.

The fundamental goal of the strategic management process is improved performance. The choice model presented in this chapter shows the type and location of critical choices that the manager must make to assure effective organizational performance.

The remaining chapters of this book will discuss the various stages of the choice model in detail and will describe the decision support tools managers can use for assistance in making these important strategic choices.

Questions

1. In recent years, deregulation in the airline industry in the United States has led to intense competition. Discuss how strategic managers in this industry would benefit from assuming a choice perspective and practicing strategic management.

2. Obtain an annual report for a large, publicly held Fortune 500 firm, and read the part that precedes the financial statements. Attempt to determine which levels of strategy development are addressed in this annual report.

3. Why is it important for managers of a multinational firm to practice strategic management rather than to use only strategic planning? Discuss this question in terms of the phases of strategic management and how they might differ for domestic and multinational firms.

4. One of the unique features of the choice model of strategic management is the explicit recognition of the choices that top-level executives must make. Why is it important to acknowledge that strategic management is a series of choices rather than merely a sequence of action steps?

5. Assume that you are a senior executive and a member of the strategic management team for Coors Brewers Inc. The CEO has asked you to recommend a method to assess the total effectiveness of the organization. Discuss which effectiveness criteria you would recommend and why you selected those particular criteria.

Notes

1. Daniel Gray, "Uses and Misuses of Strategic Planning," *Harvard Business Review* 64 (January–February 1986): 89–97.

2. H. Mintzberg, *The Nature of Managerial Work* (New York: Harper and Row, 1973): 92–93.

3. John A. Byrne, Ronald Grover, and Todd Vogel, "Is the Boss Getting Paid Too Much," *Business Week*, May 1, 1989, 46–93.

4. John A. Pearce II, D. K. Robbins, and R. B. Robinson, Jr., "The Impact of Grand Strategy and Planning Formality on Financial Performance," *Strategic Management Journal* 8 (March–April 1987): 125–134.

5. "Business Fads: What's In—and Out," *Business Week*, January 20, 1986, 52–61.

6. Gray, "Uses and Mususes of Strategic Planning," 88–89.

7. F. E. Emery and E. I. Trist, "The Causal Texture of Organizational Environments," *Human Relations* 18 (Feb. 1965): 21–32.

8. Alex R. Oliver and J. R. Garber, "Implementing Strategic Planning: Ten Sure-Fire Ways to Do It Wrong," *Business Horizons* (March–April 1983): 49–51.

9. Christopher Oyeen, "Long Range Planning in Large Corporations: A Cross-National Survey," *Managerial Planning* 33 (November–December 1984) 18–23.

10. Ibid.

11. D. E. Schendel and C. Hofer, eds., *Strategic Management: A New View of Business Policy and Planning* (Boston: Little Brown and Co., 1979): 11–13.

12. H. Igor Ansoff, *Corporate Strategy: An Analytic Approach to Business Policy* (New York: McGraw-Hill, 1965), 37–38.

13. Jane E. Dutton and R. B. Duncan, "The Influence of the Strategic Planning Process on Strategic Change," *Strategic Management Journal* 8 (March–April 1978): 103–116.

14. "Sony's Challenge," *Business Week*, June 1, 1987, 64–69.

15. W. R. Dill, "Environment as an Influence on Managerial Autonomy," *Administrative Science Quarterly* 2 (March, 1958): 409–442.

16. James D. Thompson, *Organization in Action* (New York: McGraw-Hill, 1967), 25–27.

17. Jim Hurlock, "Why William Dillard Loves a Lost Cause," *Business Week*, May 5, 1986, 100.

18. Pete Engardio, "How Last Year's No. 11 Tumbled Off the List," *Business Week*, May 26, 1986, 102.

19. R. Edward Freeman, *Strategic Management: A Stockholders Approach* (Boston: Pitman, 1984).

20. Christopher S. Eklund, "How Black & Decker Got Back in the Black," *Business Week*, July 13, 1987, 86–90.

21. Anthony Blanko, "Generous Electric: We Bring Good Things to Kidder Peabody," *Business Week*, May 12, 1986, 27–28.

22. Alex Beam, "Gillette: Not Quite So Sharp," *Business Week*, May 12, 1986, 92 and 94.

23. Chuck Hawkins, "Does Pan Am Have a Ticket Out of the Industry Slide?" *Business Week*, May 5, 1986, 32.

24. Georg Schreyogg and H. Steinmann, "Strategic Control: A New Perspective," *Academy of Management Review* 12 (January 1987): 91–103.

25. J. Camillus and R. Velizath, "Organization Control: A Conceptual Typology." Paper presented at the Academy of Management annual meeting, Boston, August 1984.

26. J. K. Gardner, "A Systems Approach to Bank Prudential Management and Supervision: The Utilization of Feedforward Control," *Journal of Management Studies* 22 (January 1985): 1–24.

27. P. Lorange, "Strategic Control: Some Issues in Making It Operationally More Useful," in *Competitive Strategic Management*, ed. R. B. Lamb (Englewood Cliffs, N.J.: Prentice-Hall, 1984), 247–271.

28. D. J. Hall and M. A. Saias, "Strategy Follows Structure!" *Strategic Management Journal* 1, (April/June 1980): 149–163.

29. Thomas J. Peters and R. H. Waterman, *In Search of Excellence: Lessons from America's Best-Run Companies* (New York: Harper & Row, 1982), x.

30. "Who's Excellent," *Business Week*, November 5, 1984, 76–79.

31. Robert E. Jones, "Internal Politics and the Strategic Business Plan," *Journal of Small Business Management* 23 (January 1985): 31–37.

32. Thompson, *Organization in Action*, 125–127.

33. Daniel J. Isenberg, "How Senior Managers Think," *Harvard Business Review*, 62 (November–December 1984): 81–90.

Case for Discussion

Strategic Management in a Changing Business Environment

U.S. exports are rising and unemployment is low. Why is there still talk in the country and Congress about protectionist legislation as the 1980s end? After all, the Reagan Administration had a reputation as being a "free trade" administration. Yet, in a 2½-year period near the end of the second term, it initiated or threatened twice as many actions against U.S. foreign trading partners as it did in its entire first term. Why the push for protection against foreign competition under circumstances that would historically signal the opposite?

According to some experts, we are starting a period of "economic nationalism" that is prompted by a general feeling among the American population that we are losing control of our economic and financial destiny. Recent polls indicate that a majority of U.S. citizens consider our trade imbalance a "serious national-security problem." It threatens to change our definition of national security to include economic imperialism.

What does this mean for today's strategic managers? For the manager of the domestic corporation serving only domestic markets, it may mean that the American society and federal government have become important allies in dealing with foreign competitors. However, for firms that market, produce, or import from locations off U.S. shores, the news may be a severe threat to their survival. Many U.S. manufacturing organizations are learning to cope with foreign competition by taking advantage of world sources of parts, labor, and materials. These firms may find that their recently developed capabilities to allow them to compete in today's global markets may be liabilities in a protectionist era.

Already, "piecemeal protectionism" is appearing in several industries such as pasta, aircraft, meat, computer chips, leather, construction, and even financial services. The great pasta war saw the U.S. impose a 40 percent duty on certain European pasta. The EC retaliated with duties on U.S. walnuts and lemons. The U.S. followed by delaying a promised concession on semifinished steel, only to see the EC respond with duties on U.S. fertilizer, paper, and beef products. For organizations in these industries, this international tit for tat could spell an end to their competitive future.

One major battleground may be in the commercial aircraft industry. Boeing is in a bitter competitive battle with Airbus Industrie, a consortium of Britain, France, West Germany, and Spain. The United States has threatened to ban Airbus sales in

Source: "Protectionist Attitudes Grow Stronger in Spite of Healthy Economy," *The Wall Street Journal*, May 16, 1988.

the United States and/or deny landing rights to certain airlines from those countries. Such action could affect everyone from the U.S. traveling public to major U.S. airlines like United that already have some Airbus planes.

The protectionist movement is still low-key, but for how long? As the environment becomes more competitive, managers must learn to strategically manage in an international arena.

Discussion Questions

1. Why is environmental assessment critical under newly emerging environmental conditions?

2. Do you think that a protectionist strategy on the part of the United States is appropriate? Why or why not?

3. What effect do the attitudes of the present administration have on the choices currently governing U.S. trade policy?

4. If you were the CEO of an import–export trading company, how would you likely view the trends described here?

5. As the CEO in Question 4, what choices could you make to adapt to these conditions?

Part One

Strategy Formulation

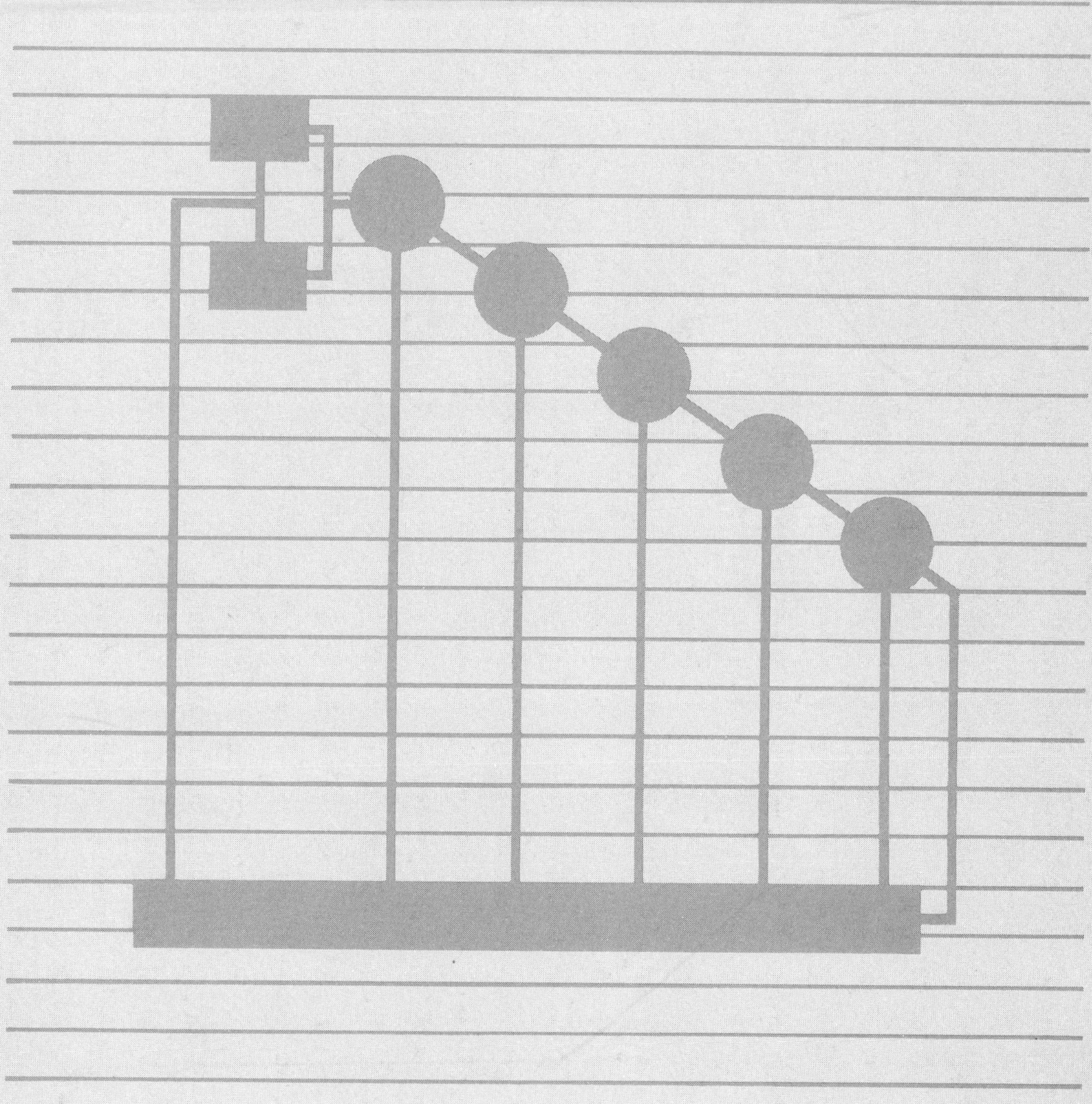

Chapter 2

External Environmental Assessment and Choice

Universe to each must be
All that is, including me.
Environment in turn must be
All that is, excepting me.

—Richard Buckminster Fuller, Synergetics 2 (1979), Sec. 100.12, Universal Requirements

Learning Objectives

- To gain a working knowledge of environmental assessment.
- To learn to distinguish environmental sectors and stakeholders.
- To understand the difference between remote, general, competitive, and task environments.
- To learn how to systematically scan the organization's environment.
- To become aware of where and how to obtain relevant environmental information.
- To learn several methods for assessing the organization's environment.
- To understand how to interpret the results of an environmental assessment.

THE price of oil may rise by 50 percent. Congress passes a law reducing the federal budget. An inexpensive, biodegradable alternative to plastic is invented. The growth in the young adult population is slowing. Economists expect a major recession during the next decade.

These statements represent current or possible changes in the environment that may have dramatic consequences for organizational performance. If you are the strategic manager for a chemical company, an increase in the price of oil means an increase in the cost of your primary raw material. Legislation to cut the federal budget could reduce demand for a defense contractor's products. The invention of an alternative to plastic may hurt the sales of those who make plastic while providing exciting opportunities to the inventor. Slower growth in the population of young adults limits the labor force available for entry-level jobs and may lead to higher wages for those jobs. And if a major recession occurs, sales at most organizations will decline, and funding will become more difficult or expensive.

To be prepared to confront changes such as these, organizations must continually assess the environment. This chapter stresses the importance of environmental assessment to the effective strategic management of the organization. In addition, it provides the information necessary to conduct a thorough environmental assessment.

Importance of the Environmental Choice

The environment is the source of opportunities and threats for the firm and, therefore, is vital to its growth and survival. One of the most important tasks of a strategic manager, therefore, is to assess the organization's environment. In a recent survey of strategic managers in 40 of the top 100 U.S. industrial firms, 64 percent said that environmental assessment was a formal component of their planning process. Of those managers responding to the survey, 47 percent had departments devoted to environmental assessment.[1]

One reason why strategic managers devote so much time and energy to assessing the environment is the complexity of the business conditions facing most modern organizations. Organizations compete with one another for capital, materials, labor, and customers. New technologies and new entrants into the market can erode the firm's competitive advantage and market share. To complicate the problem, these components can change from day to day.

The complexity of the environment that most modern organizations face creates many challenges for the strategic manager. Managers must choose which components in the total environment are important to the success of the firm, how to collect accurate information on important components, and which components offer the greatest opportunities and fewest threats. Further complicating these choices is the increasing rate of change of many of these components.

A recent example of change in the environment concerns the tobacco industry. This industry had accepted the federal government's passive actions to discourage smoking for health reasons and concentrated its efforts on developing a less harmful product. However, the federal regulatory environmental threat became more important when the Surgeon General announced that tobacco is as addictive as hard drugs. The regulatory component of the environment suddenly emerged as a critical factor in the survival of the industry.[2]

Environmental assessment is one of the most important functions of the strategic manager. Therefore, the manager should try to have the most timely and accurate environmental information possible.

Understanding Environments

Strategic managers operate in two different environments, actual and observed.[3] The **actual environment** contains all components of the total environment that are important to the organization, whether or not the manager recognizes them. The **observed environment** is a subset of the actual environment and consists of all components of the total environment that the manager recognizes as relevant and considers important enough to act on.[4]

Managers make choices based on the environmental components that they observe, while organizational success is determined by the conditions in the actual environment. Therefore, the observed environment must accurately reflect the actual environment if the manager is to make effective choices. The Strategic Application "The Automobile Industry" shows how U.S. automakers have tried to match the observed environment to the actual environment. Differences in their observations are one cause of differences in their chosen competitive strategies.

Conditions in the environment affect the organization whether or not the strategic manager observes them. Failure to observe important activities in the actual environment can be catastrophic. For example, the U.S. consumer electronics industry failed to recognize the extent of the Japanese commitment to establish videocassette recorder (VCR) technology as the industry standard. U.S. firms such as RCA continued to develop and market laser disk technology, which provided superior picture quality but did not permit home recording, as does VCR technology. RCA and others failed to recognize the American consumer's desire to be able to record programs as well as watch prerecorded videos. When RCA realized its failure to recognize the consumer's taste and the Japanese threat, it was too late. Businesses producing machines utilizing laser video disk technology had to abandon their efforts in favor of the VCR technology.

Thus, while managers would like to understand the actual environment, they must react to, plan for, and choose strategies appropriate for the observed environ-

STRATEGIC APPLICATIONS

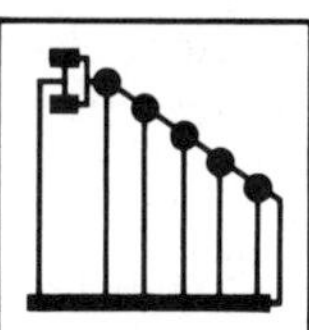

The Automobile Industry

The U.S. automobile industry's response to foreign competition provides an interesting example of how different firms in the same actual environment observe that environment differently. General Motors has viewed the competition as an opportunity to expand small-car sales, and therefore embarked on a joint venture with Toyota. Ford has considered foreign competitors threats and aggressively tried to challenge them by stressing quality and foreign styling. Chrysler has viewed foreign competitors as just more entrants into its competitive environment and reacted as it would to any other form of competition. The company competes on the basis of price by taking advantage of favorable wage rates and offering an extended warranty.

To date, all three of these perspectives of the competitive environment appear to have resulted in adequate strategies. GM's joint venture product with Toyota, the Geo, is holding its own but has not run away with the small-car market as GM had hoped that it would. Chrysler's extended warranty (the longest in the automobile industry) and lower prices have allowed the company to maintain a profit over several successive quarters. The Ford Motor Company strategy appears to be superior, because Ford surpassed GM in annual profits in the late 1980s—for the first time in decades.

ment. The rest of the chapter focuses on the observed environment and describes ways that managers can assess it to make sure that the observed environment more accurately represents the actual environment of the firm.

Environmental Sectors, Elements, and Stakeholders

The first step in analyzing the environment is to separate it into its parts. Environments can be broken into sectors, elements, and stakeholders. Sectors are subsets of the total environment that can be uniquely described by similar characteristics, known as elements, and can be distinguished from other environmental subsets. As Figure 2.1 shows, some of the more important sectors of the business environment are the input, human resources, financial resources, market, technology, economic conditions, government, sociocultural, and competitive sectors.

Elements describe those factors in the sector that are relevant or potentially relevant to the success and survival of the organization. For example, the competitive sector consists of elements that relate to the firm's industry in its environment. These elements could be industry size, concentration ratio, stage of maturity, or other substitute products. The elements of the technology sector might include production techniques, level of automation in the industry, and the extent to which new materials are used.

An element may or may not include stakeholders. **Stakeholders** are identifiable groups or individuals in the organization's environment who interact with the organization to an extent that can affect the achievement of the organization's goals or threaten its survival.[5] The stakeholders in a sector are the people who function within an element. In the market sector, for example, stakeholders could be the firm's customers or clients. In contrast, the average level of advertising in the industry is an element of the market sector but not a stakeholder. Because a sector is defined by its elements and stakeholders, whenever the term *element* or *stakeholder* is used, we are referring to elements or stakeholders within a sector. Figure 2.1 includes many of the elements and stakeholders that are important to most organizations.

The environmental assessment should include as many relevant sectors, elements, and stakeholders as possible. This helps ensure that the observed environment closely resembles the organization's actual environment.

Types of Environment

Another way to look at the firm's environment is to separate it into four types: remote, general, competitive, and task.[6] Figure 2.2 shows the relationship of these four environmental types to one another and to the organization. Elements and stakeholders in these environments can have varying degrees of impact on the firm's performance. The importance of an element or stakeholder determines the environmental type in which it is located. The least important and least controllable elements are classified in the remote environment, while the most important elements are part of the task environment.

Figure 2.1 Environmental Sectors, Elements, and Stakeholders

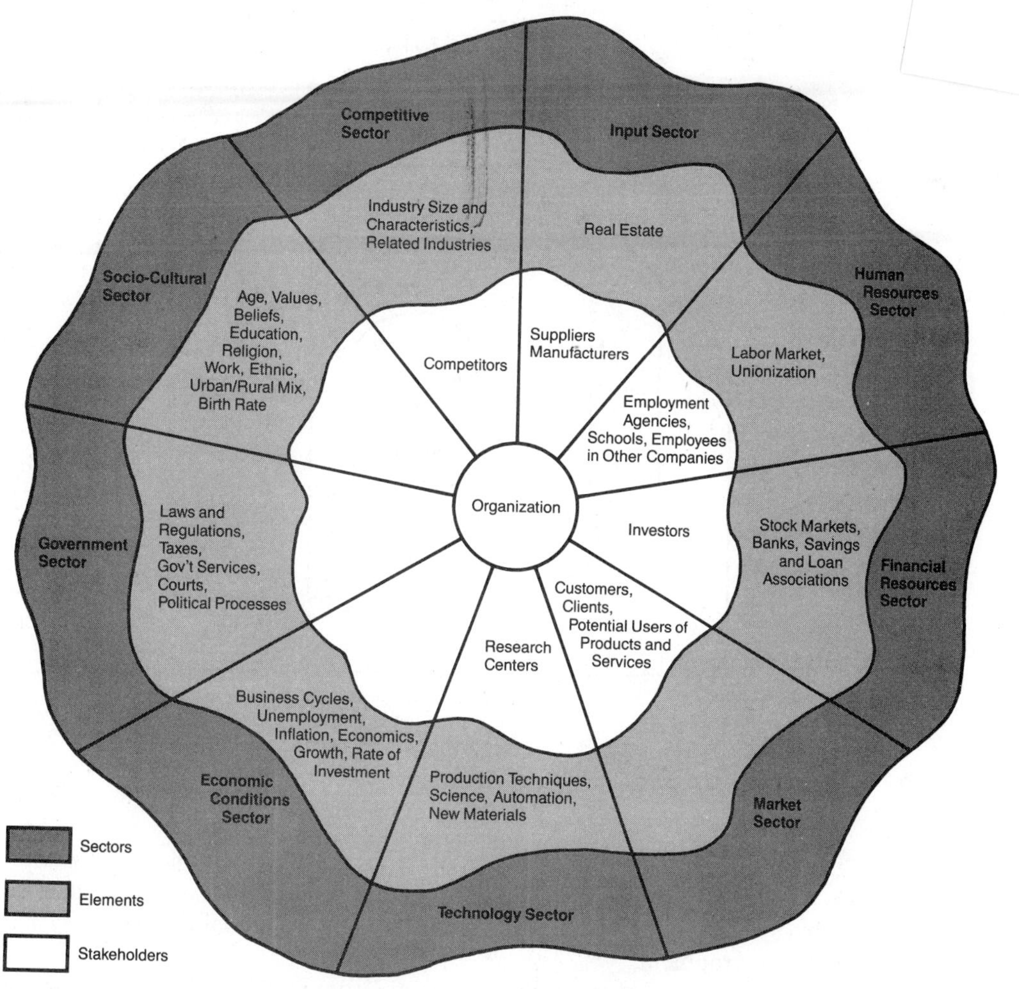

Source: Adapted by permission from page 46 of *Organization Theory and Design*, 3/e by Richard L. Daft; copyright © 1989 by West Publishing Company. All rights reserved.

This classification scheme is useful because classifying the element or stakeholder tells the manager how much relative attention to give it. Elements and stakeholders of the task environment demand the most attention, while competitive, general, and remote environmental components receive relatively less attention.

Remote Environment The remote environment is composed of all the elements in the total environment that have little chance of affecting the success and survival of the organization.[7] For United Airlines in the 1980s, an example might have been

Figure 2.2 Types of Environments

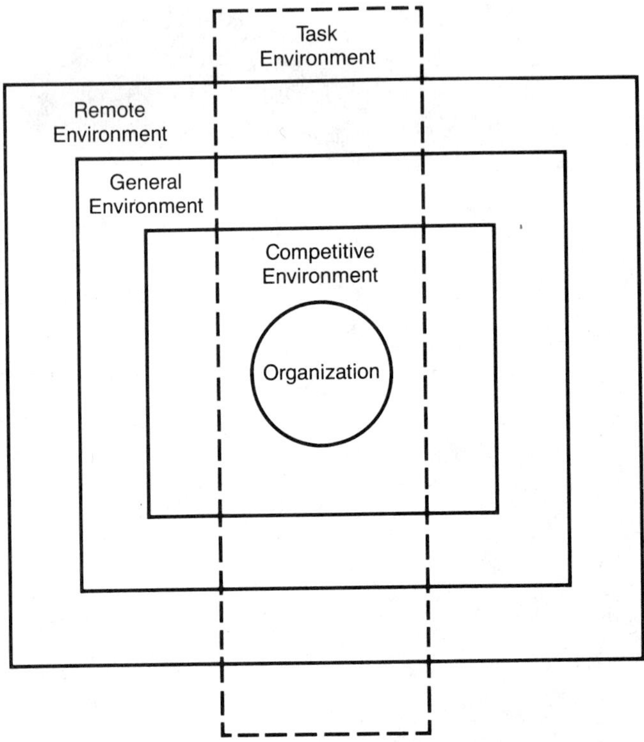

Texas International, the predecessor of Texas Air Corporation. The possibility that this relatively small, low-cost airline would threaten United probably seemed unlikely. United's strategic managers considered Texas International a minor player in their remote environment.

Because the elements in the remote environment have little effect on the firm, managers do not devote much time and attention to them. Over time, however, elements can move from the remote to a more important type environment, as Texas International did between 1975 and the late 1980s. Texas Air Corporation, under the direction of Frank Lorenzo, became the largest airline company in the world and a major competitor of United Airlines. Because an element can move into a more important environmental type, managers must periodically monitor elements in the remote environment to guard against environmental jolts that can surprise strategic managers and threaten the firm's existence.[8]

General Environment Other elements in the organization's environment can affect the firm but are too large or powerful to be influenced by the firm. These elements are located in the general environment. The general environment typically includes elements in the political, general economic, social, and legal sectors of the total environment. With a few notable exceptions such as GM, Exxon, or General Electric, a single firm rarely can influence national politics, economic conditions, social norms, or legislation of its host country. For most small to medium-sized organizations, the general environment is limited to a state or local community.

Regardless of geographic area, sectors in the general environment have a profound effect on the operations of the firm. A federal law to reduce the deficit, for example, may have a dramatic impact on governmental agencies that provide services to the poor or on businesses that sell to the government, yet these agencies and businesses acting alone have little power to influence that political–legal sector. Likewise, government actions to drive down the value of the U.S. dollar on foreign exchange markets may help some U.S. businesses by discouraging imports but increase the cost to U.S. manufacturers that use imported raw materials.

Events that occur in the general environment affect the firm but limit the choices available to the manager. Nevertheless, the manager must try to adapt to the changed environment. For example, if government actions drive down the value of the dollar, the managers of a U.S. manufacturing firm will need to reevaluate sources of raw materials. Materials that the company has been importing may have become relatively less expensive from a domestic supplier.

The general environment is only a periodic source of opportunities and threats for the organization and involves events beyond the control of the manager. Therefore, the strategic manager should monitor the general environment periodically but not devote a great deal of time and attention to the elements in this part of the environment. Recognizing that some elements are in the general environment allows the manager to develop procedures to monitor them but spend most of his or her planning time on elements more directly under his or her control and probably more important to the success of the firm.

Competitive Environment A type of environment that is of more immediate importance is the competitive environment. The competitive environment consists of the forces driving industry competition. According to Michael Porter, author of several books on competitive strategy, these forces include the threat of new entrants, threat of substitutes, bargaining power of buyers, bargaining power of suppliers, and rivalry among current competitors. Notice that these forces go beyond the business's direct competitors in the same line of business. Porter explains:

> Customers, suppliers, substitutes, and potential entrants are all "competitors" to firms in the industry and may be more or less prominent depending on the particular circumstances. Competition in this broader sense might be termed extended rivalry.
>
> All five competitive forces jointly determine the intensity of industry competition and profitability, and the strongest force or forces are governing and become crucial from the point of view of strategy formulation.[9]

Porter's view of these competitive forces is illustrated in Figure 2.3.

The forces originate from five stakeholder groups in the firm's competitive environment. According to Porter, the most important stakeholders are customers (buy-

Figure 2.3 Elements of the Competitive Environment

Competitive Force:
Threat of New Entrants

Potential New Entrants

Industry Competitors

Suppliers

Buyers

Competitive Force:
Threat from Bargaining Power of Suppliers

Competitive Force:
Threat from Competitors

Competitive Force:
Threat from Bargaining Power of Buyers

Substitutes

Competitive Force:
Threat of Substitution

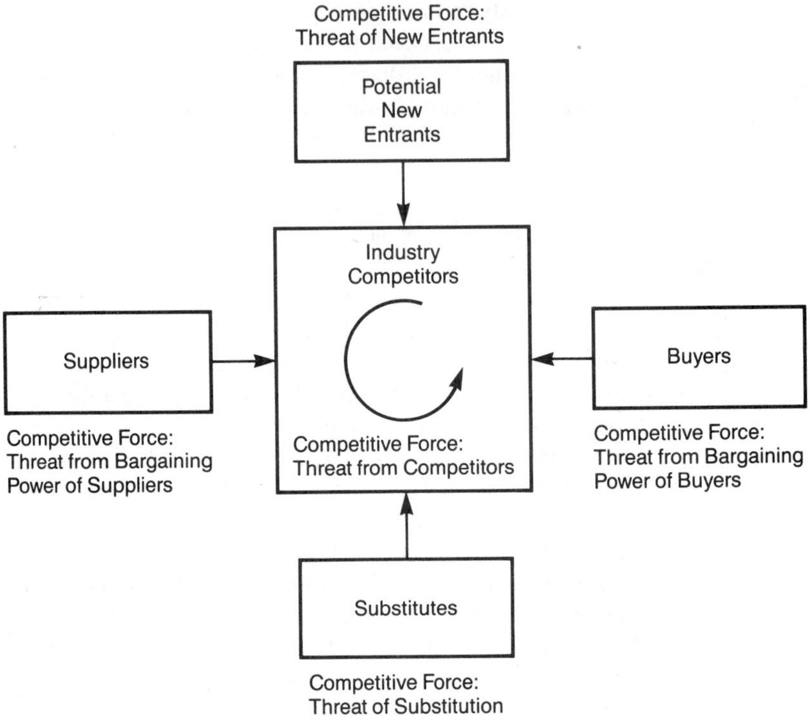

Source: Reprinted with permission of The Free Press, a Division of Macmillan, Inc. from *Competitive Strategy: Techniques for Analyzing Industries and Competitors* by Michael E. Porter, p. 4. Copyright © 1980 by The Free Press.

ers), suppliers, firms that are potential entrants into the market, firms with substitute products or services, and competitors within the industry. Because these stakeholders are extremely important, the manager should devote substantial planning attention to frequently monitoring their activity. In this way, he or she can develop strategies to protect the organization from threats that they impose on the firm and to point out opportunities that they provide.

Task Environment The task environment is the portion of the total environment that is relevant to the organization for strategy development and implementation at a given time.[10] As shown in Figure 2.2, it includes most of the competitive environment, some of the general environment, and, periodically, some elements and stakeholders from the remote environment. Other elements and stakeholders in the firm's remote, general, and competitive environments are not seen as important at this particular time. Therefore, the task environment is the portion of the observed environment that currently concerns the strategic manager. It is where managers should devote most of their time and attention to develop strategies for coping with threats and taking advantage of opportunities.

Developing a general understanding of elements and stakeholders is the first step toward determining which environmental components are most important for the success and survival of the organization. Strategic managers must be able to locate relevant elements and stakeholders and classify them into the appropriate type of environment: remote, general, or competitive. This classification allows the manager to locate the task environment and develop strategies to exploit opportunities or avoid threats that are important to the firm.

Environmental Assessment

Environmental assessment is conducted in three stages: scanning, environmental analysis, and interpretation.[11] **Scanning** refers to gathering and synthesizing information from environmental sectors (elements and stakeholders) about opportunities or threats that are relevant to the organization. **Environmental analysis** is processing that information to locate important elements and stakeholders that are critical for the firm's success and survival. The **interpretation** stage involves applying judgment to the results of the analysis to forecast future environmental conditions and formulate strategies.

The Phillip Morris Company went through these stages in the introduction of Miller Lite beer. Phillip Morris had an extensive scanning system in place from its vast experience in the consumer tobacco industry. An analysis of environmental information indicated that the beverage industry was a good diversification target. The existing consumer data suggested that little demand existed for "diet" beer, but an analysis of consumer trends indicated a growing concern for health-related issues and weight control. The company correctly interpreted these trend data to indicate rapid growth for the light beer segment of the beverage market.

Environmental Scanning

How can the manager acquire the information necessary to recognize opportunities and cope with threats that may affect the organization's long-term success and survival? The answer is through the environmental scanning process.

Scanning Levels Scanning can range from a broad, informal review of industry periodicals to focused, formal market surveys involving the collection of primary data. Figure 2.4 presents a model of the scanning process. The circles on the left of the model represent four basic scanning levels: exploratory search, source search, secondary search, and primary search.[12]

Exploratory Search The first scanning level, the **exploratory search**, involves the information gathering that managers do in the normal course of their jobs. This includes reading the standard business periodicals (such as *Business Week*, *Fortune*, *Barron's*,

Figure 2.4 The Environmental Scanning Process

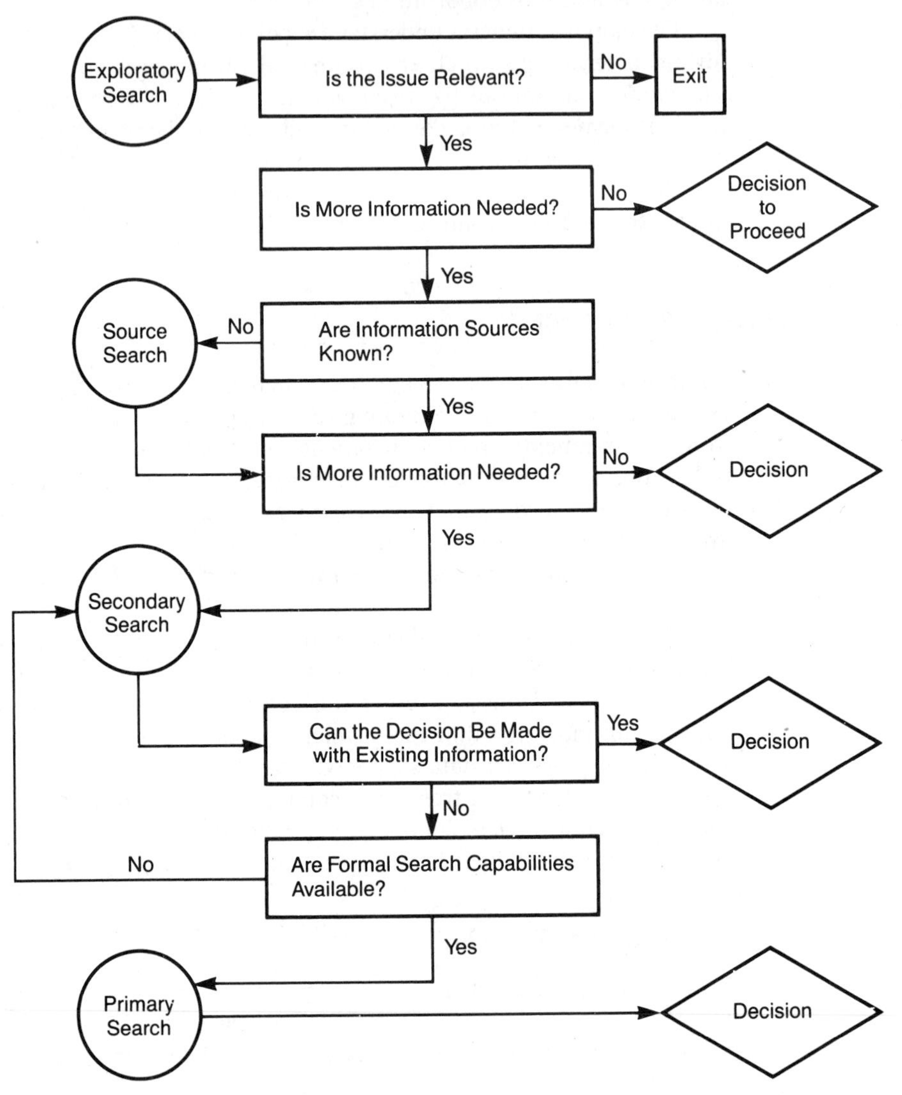

Source: F. Aguilar, *Scanning the Business Environment* (New York: Trustees of Columbia University, 1967).

Inc., Forbes, and *The Wall Street Journal*) and trade periodicals for their industry. In addition, this search includes information gathered from conversations with executives and officials of other organizations. The president of a small manufacturer of computer components reports that he scans over 50 trade magazines each week. This is a very informal search of potentially useful material to keep abreast of the trends in the industry. He searches for issues that pose possible opportunities for the firm or threats to its success.

The strategic manager then asks whether he or she needs more information in order to make a decision. If not, the manager makes the decision. However, if more information is needed, the manager moves to the next level of search. IBM's managers did this when they realized that they needed more information before entering the PC market. They believed that a market opportunity existed but felt that they could lose their reputation as the foremost computer company in the world if the new product failed. IBM management therefore used more sophisticated scanning methods to gather more accurate information.

Source Search If the strategic manager determines that more information is needed, he or she needs to know the relevant sources of additional information that are available. If the manager already knows what these sources are, he or she can proceed to the next search level. If a list of relevant sources is not available, then the manager should conduct a source search to create this list. The **source search** is a review of all potentially relevant sources of secondary information to compile a final list of information sources for later use.

Because the source search focuses on where to find relevant information, managers only rarely find the information necessary to make a decision at this stage. However, if a strategic manager is fortunate enough to discover the necessary information, he or she can make the decision and initiate the necessary action.

Secondary Search The secondary search uses the results of the source search to survey all relevant historical information that relates to the issue about which the manager must make a decision. It is an important level of the scanning process because it is relatively inexpensive yet provides high-quality historical information. Firms with limited resources may be unable to afford to search beyond this level.

A major weakness of the secondary search is that the manager has no control over the quality of the information. That is, the data are only as current and accurate as the procedures used by the source publications in which they are published. If the manager needs to be sure that the information is accurate and current, the data must be gathered through a primary search.

Primary Search The highest level of scanning sophistication is the primary search. At this level, the firm designs a search procedure and systematically collects original information about the environmental issue. A typical procedure is a market-research survey. This level of scanning gives the firm current and accurate information about a specific environmental issue. Current information helps the manager make better projections about trends and possible actions by competitors. For example, a Denver, Colorado, bank established a five-person staff, including a lawyer and an accountant, to monitor 18 federal and state agencies that affected the bank. The staff sent the bank's strategic managers regular reports highlighting trends and potential threats. This group was credited with recognizing the need for separate personal credit cards for spouses and gained several months' advantage over competitors.

The ability to conduct a primary search requires the knowledge and experience to gather original information about an issue. Primary-search capabilities exist in a firm if it has the financial resources to hire primary-search specialists or if these specialists are employed in the firm. For example, if a firm has the capability to conduct market research, then the manager initiates such a primary search. The absence of this capability forces the manager to accept a less sophisticated search procedure, the secondary search. Figure 2.4 indicates this condition with an arrow that returns to the secondary search even when the decision requires more information.

Since a primary search is the most current and accurate level of scanning, why doesn't the manager initiate scanning at this level? The answer lies in the cost of the scanning effort. Costs increase greatly as the firm moves from the exploratory to the primary level. After all, the exploratory level is merely the scanning that any good strategic manager would do as part of his or her daily activities. In contrast, the costs associated with developing an internal market-research capability or hiring consultants to conduct market research could run to millions of dollars. The prudent strategic manager uses the most cost-effective search.[13]

Sources of Environmental Information Strategic managers do not have unlimited time to scan the environment at even the exploratory level. The president of the electronics firm mentioned earlier spends from two to three hours a day scanning business and trade publications. Nor do even large firms have unlimited resources to spend on scanning. Therefore, it is important that environmental analysts know where to find the most accurate and timely information.

There are two basic sources of environmental information, internal and external. Internal sources are individuals within the organization who have frequent contact with the environment. External sources consist of publications, consultants, and other miscellaneous sources outside the organization (for example, commercial data banks). Chapter Appendix 2.1 identifies a variety of external sources used by businesses.

Internal Sources of Information Specific sources of internal information are functional areas of the organization, internal reports, and management experience. Table 2.1 describes where these internal sources might be located in the organization, as well as the aspects of the environment about which they provide information. Functional managers within the organization are excellent internal sources of expertise on probable future events in the environment.[14] Marketing managers should have their hand on the pulse of the firm's product-markets. Operations managers should be aware of the latest developments in process technology. The purchasing manager should be familiar with the status of input suppliers. Finally, the R&D manager is responsible for knowing the most recent advances in product development and new technology.

Internal reports are continually being generated by units within the organization. Market research reports, supplier pricing reports, and employee productivity reports are common in many firms. These reports provide valuable information about a segment of the environment. For example, automotive manufacturers frequently use productivity reports from their various plants to assess the work habits of the labor

Table 2.1 Internal Sources of Environmental Information

Source	Organizational Location	Environmental Sector, Element, or Stakeholder
Functional Area	Marketing	Competitive, market, and economic conditions
	Operations	Technology, input, and government
	Personnel	Human resources, government, and sociocultural
	Purchasing	Input, technology, and government
	Research and Development (R&D)	Technology and competitive
	Strategic Analysis Staff	Financial resources, economic conditions, sociocultural, government, and market
Internal Reports	Sales—Sales Reports	Market
	Marketing—Competitor Reports	Competitors
	R&D—Competitor Product Analysis	Competitors
	Purchasing—Supplier Pricing Report	Suppliers
	Personnel—Labor Pool & Equal Employment Opportunity Reports	Human resources and minority groups
	Production—Production, Productivity, Quality Control, and Safety Reports	Competitors, human sources, competitor technologies, regulators
Management Experience	Chief Executive Officer and Senior Executives	Financial, sociocultural, economic conditions, market, government, and competitive
	Functional Unit Managers	Managers of functional areas have knowledge and experience relating to their function's portion of the environment
	Strategic Staff	All sectors, elements, and stakeholders

Source: Adapted from J. A. Pearce II, B L. Chapman, and F. R. David, "Environment Scanning for Small and Growing Firms," *Journal of Small Business Management* 20 (July 1982): 27–34. Adapted with permission.

element in different parts of the country. In some instances, they have shifted production from one plant to another based on this information.

Senior executives typically have vast experience and expertise in the functioning of their firms. They have probably learned to effectively read and analyze their environments while performing as functional managers. This experience in environmental assessment provides the firm with an internal source of scanning information. One of the reasons for Pennzoil's success is the ability of its CEO, Hugh Liedtke, to quickly read the environment for opportunities and act on them. For example, his decision to buy a 25 percent stake in a Texaco project to lease an off-shore oil-drilling site increased Pennzoil's daily oil production by almost 33 percent in 1987.[15]

Many examples illustrate the importance of internal information. In one case, the purchasing manager of a military research and development laboratory realized that certain materials for an experiment were available from several sources. This eliminated the laboratory's dependence on a single supplier and resulted in a

43 percent reduction in the cost of these materials and a 25 percent reduction in the cost of the project.

External Sources of Information Publications are the least expensive source of external information. Most businesses make some use of general business and government publications. Over 80 publications provide general business information, and countless trade and industry publications devote special issues to business conditions within a particular industry segment. For example, a recent issue of *Financial Planning*, the trade magazine for professional financial planners, contained a survey of retail financial services businesses.[16] It would be impossible to list all of the specialized publications, but the manager should be aware that specific industry data are usually available in trade periodicals. Also, many major libraries are U.S. Federally Designated Government Depositories with large holdings of government documents that provide a wealth of environmental information broken out by industry or market.

Another excellent source of external information is consultants who have studied the industry in detail. Consulting available to the firm may be commercial consultants, government-sponsored consulting, and nonprofit consulting services. Many organizations use paid, commercial consultants who have experience in their industry or have expertise in a specific environmental issue. For example, most firms hire Equal Employment Opportunity (EEO) consultants to help them keep track of the latest developments and trends in EEO regulations. In addition, the Small Business Administration offers low-cost consulting to new businesses. Many cities have chambers of commerce or industrial development offices to assist new or relocating firms.

Other nonprofit organizations that provide environmental information are universities and foundations. Most major colleges of business have research bureaus or centers that can help the manager scan the local or regional environment.

Miscellaneous sources of external information are varied and tend to be unique to a particular industry. Commercial data bases are computerized sources of information on a broad range of topics that are increasing in popularity with the widespread use of microcomputers. It is possible to access over 1,000 commercial data bases covering a broad range of environmental issues. For example, the legal data bases called LEXIS and WESTLAW make it possible to identify and retrieve information about cases pertaining to a subject of concern to a company.

Other sources of information about the competition range from actually purchasing a competitor's product and inspecting it, to hiring employees who previously worked for competitors. For example, Ford Motor Company inspected over 50 mid-size cars and bought a Honda Accord and Toyota Corolla to tear them down to find engineering ideas for the development of the Taurus and Sable automobiles.[17]

One very common source of competitor information is industry trade shows. These shows typically include product displays for all major competitors as well as brochures showing market data and specifications for competing products. The practice of a medium-sized manufacturer of computer components is to send three people to trade shows. Two individuals staff the company's display to respond to the questions of potential customers, while the third person walks to each competitor's display to gather technical and market information by posing as a potential customer.

Environmental Analyses

Once accurate and current information is gathered, it must be analyzed to determine its impact on the success and survival of the organization. The systematic application of procedures and techniques to external information to determine how and why current and projected environmental changes affect or will affect the strategic management of the organization is referred to as **environmental analysis.**[18] In a recent survey, presidents of Fortune 500 firms listed the following payoffs of formal environmental analysis:[19]

1. Increased general awareness by management of environmental changes
2. Better strategic planning and decision making
3. Greater effectiveness in government matters
4. Better industry and market analysis
5. Sound decisions concerning diversification and resource allocation
6. Better results in foreign business
7. Better energy planning

Environmental analysis begins with selection of the procedure that is most appropriate for the situation. This chapter introduces four analysis methods that can be used for a broad range of situations and industries. Three of these are currently used by managers: opportunities and threats (O&T) analysis, industry analysis, and financial analysis. The final approach—strategic importance analysis (SIA)—was developed by the authors and holds promise as a useful analysis technique.

Opportunities and Threats Analysis Today organizations frequently use opportunities and threats (O&T) analysis. It is usually combined with the analysis of internal strengths and weaknesses, which will be discussed in the next chapter, under the label of SWOT analysis—analysis of *s*trengths, *w*eaknesses, *o*pportunities, and *t*hreats.[20] The O&T analysis involves rating each element and stakeholder in the firm's task environment on the basis of its potential to provide the firm with opportunities to meet its strategic objectives or threats to its success or survival.

Opportunities can be either financial or nonfinancial. Anchor National Life Insurance Company perceived an environmental opportunity where other insurance companies saw only a threat. When interest rates "inverted" (meaning that short-term interest rates became higher than long-term rates), most standard insurance-type investments became unattractive. Anchor managers used this opportunity to introduce a new product, Q Plan, that would take advantage of the temporary interest rate inversion. As a result of seizing this environmental opportunity, Anchor became the fastest growing insurance company in the United States during that period. Like this one, most opportunities involve the chance to increase market penetration, develop new markets, or generate growth of a new product.

Threats are environmental issues that can potentially damage the firm. They can come from any element or stakeholder such as adverse government regulation or competitive pressures. For example, one unforeseen threat to major U.S. banks was the decline in the price of crude oil on the world markets. The drop in price lowered revenues to oil-producing nations, which severely hampered their ability to repay loans to U.S. banks. Banks with a large percentage of their loans to foreign countries were forced to restructure the loans or accept default by these countries.

One very new threat that most organizations face is the product of modern computer technology in the hands of unethical computer professionals. The social implications of these "computer viruses" are staggering, as the Strategic Application "A 'Virus' Epidemic Strikes Computers" suggests. As environmental threats such as these "viruses" become more common and more difficult to recognize, managers will need to be more astute at environmental assessment.

STRATEGIC APPLICATIONS: SOCIAL RESPONSIBILITY

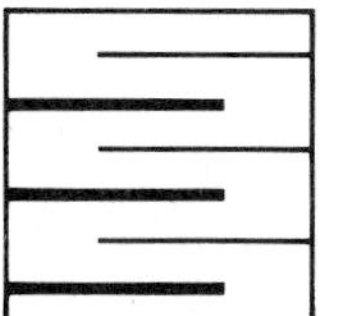

A "Virus" Epidemic Strikes Computers

A new environmental threat is facing the computer industry that promises to have dramatic effects on society. This threat is not biological nor chemical but promises to be as devastating to advanced cultures as either of these forms of warfare. An epidemic of computer viruses is spreading to personal computers around the world without the knowledge of manufacturers or users. One virus, labeled the "Pakistani Virus" has already attacked over 250,000 machines. People who depend on computers to perform their jobs and provide products and services to society are frightened of the potential disruption and danger that could result from this technical plague.

Computer viruses, like their biological counterpart, are information malfunctions. They contain instructions for their own replication and actually take over the host PC operating system. Not only can they wreak havoc with the information in a host machine, but they can secretly attach to clean disks that are used in the host and, thereby, be carried to uninfected computers. More frightening, they can also be carried over data transmission lines to other computers. They can interrupt computer operations with harmless messages such as "Merry Christmas" or "Universal Peace" like a virus developed by a 23 year old programmer from Tucson. Or, they can be used to create a "computer time bomb" that is linked to a PC's internal clock and programmed to destroy all data files on a specified day and time, as with one virus in several machines at Hebrew University.

To this point, real social harm has been avoided. However, a virus called SCORES has appeared in computers at EDS, Boeing, Arco, and even NASA and the IRS. Managers of all major firms using PCs must be aware of this potential threat. Organizations such as banks with electronic funds-transfer systems, stock exchanges, and U.S. military defense systems are all vulnerable to sabotage from computer viruses.

With the growing dependence on desktop computers for data analysis, word processing, electronic mail, record keeping, scheduling, and a host of other vital operating functions within the firm, it is critical that managers be aware of this threat. What started as a prank on the part of youthful programming geniuses could turn into a major disruption of the way business is conducted in today's environment. As Thomas Lunger says, "We're harvesting our first crop of a computer literate generation. The social responsibility hasn't caught up with them." What is needed to deal with this threat may be no less than an international code of ethics on computer abuse. Until that code is developed and accepted, computer viruses remain a threat to be dealt with by the manager.

"Invasion of the Data Snatchers," *Business Week*, Sept. 26, 1988, 62–67.

Elements or stakeholders can be either opportunities or threats. Therefore, O&T analysis will be most effective if it follows a systematic procedure for recognizing and analyzing environmental opportunities and threats. Figure 2.5 is a sample of a form for conducting an O&T analysis. After scanning the environment, the manager enters on the form each element and stakeholder in an environmental sector and writes in the issue that relates to it. The manager then rates each element or stakeholder in terms of its potential as an opportunity or threat. The rating may show that an element poses a critical, immediate threat to the survival of the firm that must be dealt with quickly or a lesser threat that can be monitored for possible damage to the organization. Likewise, some opportunities must be seized immediately, whereas others can be investigated more slowly and thoroughly.

An element or stakeholder can be the source of more than one opportunity or

Figure 2.5 Form for Opportunities and Threats Analysis

Environmental Sector, Element, or Stakeholder	Critical and Immediate Threat	Important Potential Threat	Possible Threat	Neutral	Possible Opportunity	Good Long-Range Potential Opportunity	Short-Term Definite Opportunity
Element: ______ Description of Issue: ______ ______ ______	1	2	3	4	5	6	7
Element: ______ Description of Issue: ______ ______ ______	1	2	3	4	5	6	7
⋮	⋮	⋮	⋮	⋮	⋮	⋮	⋮
Stakeholder: ______ Description of Issue: ______ ______ ______	1	2	3	4	5	6	7

threat to the firm. In that case, the manager can enter the element or stakeholder on the form twice but record a different issue. For example, in the input sector of the federal government's environment several suppliers produce military aircraft. These multiple stakeholders give the Pentagon the opportunity to use a fixed-price contracting policy that awards the contract to the lowest bidder. However, if the most efficient aircraft manufacturer is always the same and is always awarded the contract, then the other manufacturers would be forced out of business. Reliance on a single remaining supplier would be a threat in the event of war. Therefore the same stakeholders could be both short-term opportunities and long-term threats for the Pentagon.

Each manager involved in environmental assessment should complete the O&T analysis form for all relevant environmental issues. A number of techniques are available for combining the managers' ratings. Organizations frequently use brainstorming, the Delphi technique, the nominal group technique, and the modified nominal group technique:

- **Brainstorming** occurs when a group of strategic managers meet to openly discuss the issues. Communication flows in all directions, and all members are considered to be of equal status and authority. Consensus determines the relevant issues and managers forecast the future direction of those issues.
- **Delphi** is a procedure whereby managers who are not assembled in a group are polled by questionnaire regarding relevant environmental issues. Each manager lists his or her view of the issues and forecasts the future direction of those issues. These independent observations and forecasts are compiled and fed back to all managers independently. This process is repeated until all managers agree on the relevant issues and forecasts.
- **Nominal Group Technique (NGT)** is a procedure whereby strategic managers are assembled and asked to write down their views of the relevant issues and forecast the future direction of those issues. Each issue and its forecast is listed so that all managers present can view it. Participants in the process can ask questions of clarification but cannot debate an issue or forecast. The group is then directed to rank the issues with their forecasts. The issues ranked highest are the group's recommendations for further consideration.
- **Modified NGT** involves a group of strategic managers meeting to write down their views of the relevant issues and their forecasts, as with the NGT process. Again, each issue and forecast is listed for all participants to see. Next the meeting is changed to a brainstorming format, in which open discussions of listed issues and forecasts can take place. The group reaches consensus on the relevant issues and forecasts.

Regardless of the procedure used, the managers jointly analyze the issues in terms of the rating of those issues on the form in Figure 2.5 and assign top priority to the critical and immediate threats and the short-term definite opportunities. The remaining issues are ranked according to their ratings. Short-term, immediate threats must be dealt with to ward off damage to the organization. The short-term, definite opportunities should be evaluated in terms of the firm's capabilities and resources. Analysis of internal strategic capabilities will be described in Chapter 3.

Industry Analysis The industry analysis framework developed by Michael Porter concentrates exclusively on the competitive task environment of the firm.[21] This environmental sector consists of suppliers, potential new entrants, buyers, substitutes, and competitors that are most important to the success and survival of the organization. According to Porter, these five stakeholder groups are the competitive forces that affect the organization. Therefore, the environmental assessment focuses on these stakeholders in order to determine the competitive posture of each relative to the firm. Figure 2.6 illustrates Porter's basic approach. To use this analysis technique effectively, the strategic manager must determine which stakeholder is most critical and the primary competitive issues operating within that stakeholder group.

Suppliers According to Porter, when suppliers have relatively greater power than do purchasing firms, the competitive forces in the environment are operating against the organization. The effective manager will analyze the supplier environment to determine the direction of the competitive forces (favorable or unfavorable for the organization) and design strategies to exploit favorable forces and cope with unfavorable forces. For example, because Chrysler was the only buyer for many of its suppliers, it was able to force them to lower their prices and extend credit.

Figure 2.6 Bases for an Industry Analysis

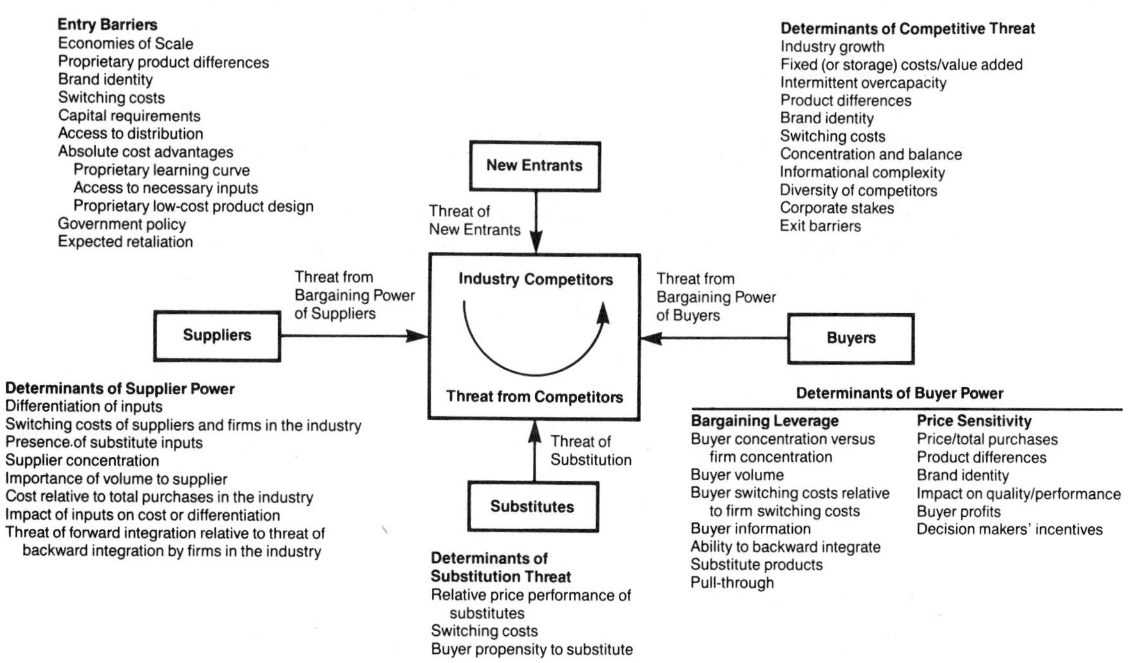

Source: Reprinted with permission of The Free Press, a Division of Macmillan, Inc. from *Competitive Advantage: Creating and Sustaining Superior Performance* by Michael E. Porter, p. 6. Copyright © 1985 by Michael E. Porter.

The manager conducts the supplier analysis by answering the following questions:

Do we have many suppliers of our most important material to select from?

Are there many substitutes for our most important input material?

Are we a major customer for the supplier of our most important input material?

Is it true that no single supplier is critical to our business?

Can we easily switch suppliers for most of our input materials?

Are our suppliers relatively small compared to our firm?

If the manager must answer no to any of these questions, suppliers can pose threats to the firm.

Potential New Entrants Firms that are thinking of entering the same industry are potential threats. To evaluate the likelihood of potential new entrants, managers look for forces in the industry that make it attractive or unattractive for a potential competitor to enter. To identify these forces, managers can ask the following questions:

Is the cost to enter this business great?

Are our products highly differentiated?

Does it take a great deal of capital to get into this business?

Would it be expensive for our customers to switch to another supplier?

Is it difficult to gain access to channels of distribution?

Is it very difficult to get government approval to operate a business like ours?

Again, if after thorough review, the manager must answer no to any of these questions, environmental forces may encourage new firms to enter the industry.

Buyers Buyers or customers may also have power over the organization by virtue of their control over the firm's output. If buyers refuse to purchase the firm's products, it will go out of business. Therefore, the manager must determine the direction of the competitive forces for this stakeholder group. If the firm has the only product of its kind and customers need it, forces are in favor of the firm. When Xerox was the only manufacturer of dry photocopiers, it could name its price and sit back and wait for orders.

The following questions measure the buyer-related competitive forces in the industry:

Do we have many customers who purchase in small volume?

Is it true that none of our products accounts for a large part of the customer's purchasing dollar?

Do most firms in our business offer a unique, highly differentiated product?

Is it difficult for our customers to switch to another supplier?

Is there substantial profit in the products that our customers offer?

Is it true that none of our customers is large enough to own us?

Does our product contribute little to the *quality* of our customer's product?

Do our customers know little about our business and how profitable it is?

A "no" answer to any of these questions should alert the manager to a possible threat from the customer sector of the environment.

Substitutes Occasionally substitute products or services become available that threaten the firm's major business. For example, firms in the copper business were seriously threatened with the advent of plastics for automobiles and fiber optics for telephone lines. The manager should be aware of possible substitutes and be prepared to cope with these threats.

The following questions will help the manager recognize threats from substitute products or services:

Is it true that no other products serve the same purpose as ours?

Can we say that no other type of product can do what ours does for the same cost?

Are firms that produce a product that performs the same function as ours very profitable in their other markets?

Substitute products or services can pose subtle threats to the firm. Therefore, the manager must be prepared to take fast action if the answer to any of these questions is no.

Competitors The most obvious stakeholders in the firm's environment that can threaten its success and survival are its competitors. The power of competitors within the industry determines the organization's profit, market share, and future growth. The manager can gain insight into the strength of the firm's competitors by answering the following questions:

Are there many competitors in this business?

Are all competitors in this business about equal in size and market power?

Are markets for our products growing rapidly?

Is this a low-overhead business?

Is it hard for our customers to switch to other suppliers?

Is it easy to add small quantities of capacity to our operations process?

Can it be said that no two firms are alike in this business?

Can most firms in this business easily switch to another business?

Are only a few firms in this business here to stay?

Competitors that are highly dependent on the industry for survival make fierce rivals. Therefore, the manager must be keenly aware of any "no" answers to these questions.

The output of the industry analysis is a thorough assessment of the competitive environment of the organization. In addition, the analysis isolates specific issues that are critical to the firm's success. Chapter Appendix 2.2 includes a form and procedure that managers can use to conduct an industry analysis. Understanding the opportunities and threats present in the organization's competitive task environment is one of the most important aspects of the firm's environmental assessment.

Strategic Groups Many industries contain strategic groups—subsets of firms that are strategically similar. For example, there are over 300 firms that assemble personal computers. However, only a relatively few of them are backed by large, vertically integrated organizations like Apple, IBM, Zenith and Tandy. These large diversified parent companies provide capabilities to their P.C. subsidiaries that make them a strategic group within the microcomputer industry.

According to Michael Porter, firms within these groups follow the same or similar strategies for specialization, brand identification, push versus pull marketing strategy (selling to the ultimate consumer versus distributors), channel selection, product quality, technological leadership, vertical integration, cost position, service, price policy, leverage, relationship with parent company, and relationship to home and host governments. A manager who determines that the firm is a member of a strategic group within the industry should be aware that the primary competition will probably come from other members of the group.

To conduct a thorough industry analysis when the firm is a member of a strategic group, the manager should analyze the competitive environment both outside and within the strategic group. Looking outside the group, the manager is concerned with the height of the barriers that protect the strategic group from invasion by outside firms and constrain the firm from moving to another group.[22] Also of concern is the bargaining power of the group in dealing with customers and suppliers, as well as the group's vulnerability to substitute products and competition from other groups.

Within the strategic group, the manager should be aware of the degree of competition and cost of entry into the group. The relative size and influence of the firm in the strategic group establishes its power to influence other group competitors. Management's ability to implement chosen strategies helps determine its relative position in the group.

Industry analysis forms can be modified to add an analysis of the firm's position in its strategic group. This combined analysis of industry competitive forces and strategic group characteristics helps clarify the firm's position in its competitive environment. As U.S. firms move from a national to an international business arena and as competition increases, a systematic method for looking at a complex competitive environment becomes more important.

Financial Analyses Businesses have traditionally used financial analyses to establish internal controls for the firm, analyze potential prospects for acquisition or merger, or track the firm's performance by comparing it to the industry average or historical performance. Financial analyses can also be used to assess the positions of competitors and substitutes in terms of their financial strengths and other internal capabilities. An added advantage of this type of environmental analysis is that, for many firms, the information is readily available in annual reports or industry periodicals.

The financial analysis appendix (Appendix B) explains various financial analyses in detail. This discussion is primarily concerned about information regarding competitors' capabilities that can be obtained from analyses of their financial condition. For example, a competitor's liquidity provides information about its ability to finance major expansion programs or promotional efforts to gain market share. The requirement to pay interest on a heavy debt load will limit what a competitor can do to expand its markets. The activity ratios can tell the astute strategic manager the level of competence of a competitor's management team. The profitability ratios can convey the pricing strategy of the competitor and its ability to control expenses. Finally, analysis of a competitor's cash flow can provide information about its ability to generate revenues to cover obligations.

The information obtained from a review of competitors' financial performance can tell the strategic manager a great deal about their current strategies and capabilities. More important, it can be used to generate pro forma projections of competitors' financial health. This can help the manager anticipate the future actions and reactions that competitors might take.

Strategic Importance Analysis Based on previous management writings and procedures in use by practicing managers, strategic importance analysis (SIA) considers the vulnerability of the firm to the actions of its elements and stakeholders. Vulnerability is defined as the level of uncertainty concerning the elements' or stakeholders' actions and the degree to which the organization is dependent on its elements and stakeholders. For example, if a critical input resource is available from only one supplier, who often changes prices without notice, the firm is very vulnerable to the actions of that supplier. SIA enables the strategic management team to rank elements and stakeholders based on this definition of vulnerability, so that managers can focus on developing strategies for those elements and stakeholders that present the most immediate opportunity or threat.

Level of Uncertainty Environmental uncertainty is defined in terms of the number and rate of change of elements and stakeholders. It applies to all sector elements and stakeholders in the firm's task environment. When the task environment consists of many elements and stakeholders that change rapidly, it is described as uncertain. The level of uncertainty in the task environment dictates the difficulty of environmental analysis and strategy formulation. Therefore, determining the level of uncertainty is an important step in conducting a thorough environmental analysis.

As Figure 2.7 shows, environmental uncertainty is defined by two dimensions, number of elements or stakeholders, and rate of change. The number of elements or stakeholders determines the breadth or scope of the environmental analysis. For example, a $37 billion company like General Electric conducts business in several countries and offers many varied product lines. It acquires raw materials, operates facilities, and sells products to many diverse groups of customers who live under different social, political, and economic systems. The many elements and stakeholders in GE's customer, supplier, sociopolitical, and government sectors call for such a broad system of environmental analysis that it could consume vast organizational resources, human and financial. In contrast, a local restaurateur with only one location faces an environment with relatively few customers and employees.

Figure 2.7 Level of Uncertainty in the Environment

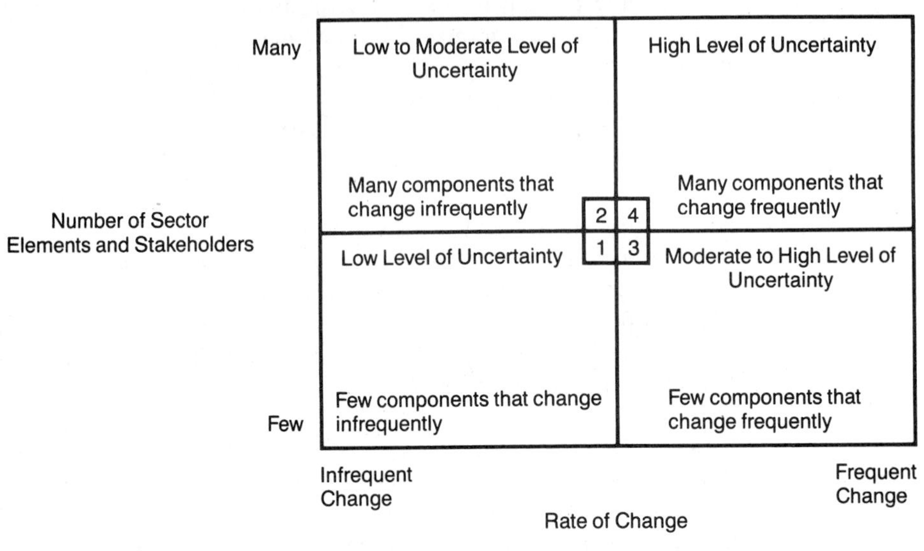

The rate of change refers to how frequently elements and stakeholders change in a way that affects their relationships with the organization. If stakeholder groups change frequently, a high rate of change exists. For example, recent actions in the health care industry illustrate rapid change in the customer stakeholders. Before 1983, the customer movement to control health care costs was limited to a loose collection of individuals who had experienced large medical bills. By the following year, several firms faced with growing expenses for employee health insurance formed an alliance to cut the cost of providing health care. They were quickly joined by federal and state legislators and citizen groups with the same aim. In addition, the expectations of these stakeholders had changed from the highest quality health care available at any price to adequate health care at a reduced price. This rapid shift caught many health care executives by surprise, and many failed to develop effective strategies to cope with the changes. Eventually a number of CEOs of major health care systems were removed from their positions.

The numbers in each cell of Figure 2.7 indicate the relative environmental uncertainty for that cell. Cell 1 is the least uncertain because there are few elements and stakeholders to contend with, and they are not changing very rapidly. Cell 2 is more uncertain due to the large number of elements and stakeholders. However, because they are not changing rapidly, the firm has time to adjust to the various demands of the stakeholders in each element. Low diversity and a high rate of change characterize cell 3. Here the number of components are relatively few, but they are changing rapidly. This condition requires that the firm monitor stakeholders in the cell closely to plan for unexpected changes in their demands. Cell 4 is the most uncertain for the organization because there are many elements and stakeholders to monitor, and they are continually changing. The higher the level of uncertainty of the environmental element and stakeholder, the higher its priority should be for the strategic manager.

Degree of Dependence Dependence is a stakeholder's control over a resource that is important to the success and survival of the organization. A government contractor that does 90 percent of its business with the federal government is very dependent on the government as the major source of its revenues. The degree of dependence is determined by two key dimensions, availability and importance.

Availability is the number of alternative sources for a resource supplied by a stakeholder. Customers, suppliers, capital markets, labor markets, any element or stakeholder can control a critical resource (see Figure 2.1). If the company can find many alternative sources of the resource, availability is high. When availability is low, the firm is vulnerable to the few sources of a critical resource. For example, a company that sells through catalogs is dependent on the Postal Service, because few alternatives are available for widespread, inexpensive distribution of catalogs. In contrast, companies that do much business over the phone have benefited from the availability of more long-distance telephone services since the deregulation of the telephone industry. These companies are less vulnerable because they are less dependent on AT&T.

The second dimension of dependence is **importance** and it refers to how critical the resource supplied by a particular stakeholder is to the success and survival of the firm. A firm is more dependent on a stakeholder that controls an important resource than it is on one that provides a resource that is insignificant to the firm's operations. For example, firms in the commercial real estate business recently discovered that they were dependent on the tax element in the government sector. Favorable tax laws encouraged many investors to buy commercial property even if they had little hope of complete occupancy in the short run. When later tax legislation removed the tax benefit, a shock went through the commercial real estate industry.

Together, the two dimensions of dependence form four cells, as shown in Figure 2.8. The conditions of high availability and low importance in cell 1 mean that the firm is not dependent on environmental stakeholders because they supply resources that are of little importance to the firm and for which there are many sources. In cell 2, importance is high, but so is availability. Even though stakeholders control a critical resource, the readily available alternative sources make the firm less dependent. In cell 3, the stakeholder has almost complete control of a moderately unimportant resource. Dependence is greater in this situation because the firm has no other source and is vulnerable to the actions of the stakeholder. Cell 4 is the most vulnerable position for the organization. The stakeholder in this cell has exclusive control over an important resource without which the firm cannot succeed or survive. Organizations must devote constant attention to stakeholders in this cell and closely monitor their activities, or risk the stakeholder withholding a critical resource.

The SIA Procedure The first step in SIA is to determine the level of uncertainty and degree of dependence for each element or stakeholder that is the firm's task environment. To conduct this analysis, the manager can use a form such as the one in Figure

Figure 2.8 Degree of Dependence in the Environment

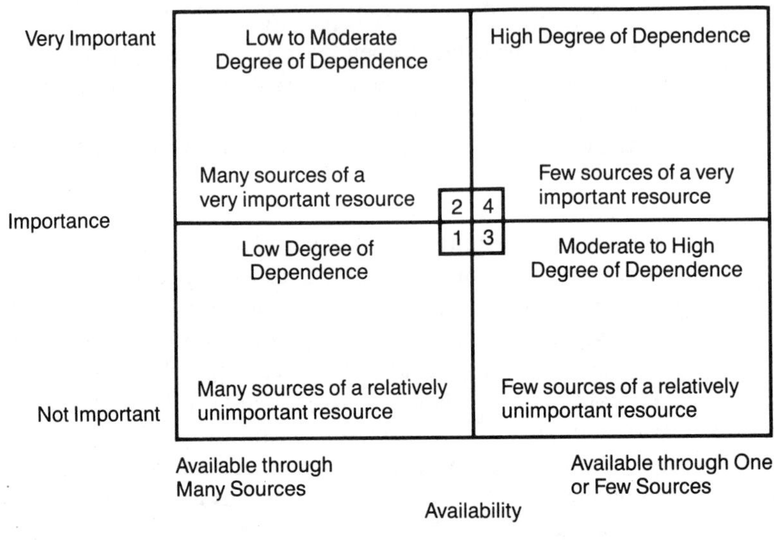

Figure 2.9 Uncertainty-Dependence Profile

Element or Stakeholder					
1. How many parts are there to this component?	One 1	Few 2	Several 3	Many 4	Very Many 5
2. How often do the parts of this component change?	Very Often 5	Often 4	Not Very Often 3	Hardly Ever 2	Very Infrequently 1
3. Are there substitutes for what this component provides to our firm?	Very Many 1	Many 2	Some 3	Few 4	None 5
4. How important is this component to the success of our business?	Very Important 5	Somewhat Important 4	Neutral 3	Little Importance 2	Not Important 1

Total Score for this Element or Stakeholder ______________

2.9. After answering the four questions in Figure 2.9 for each element and stakeholder, the manager sums the scores for each. The elements and stakeholders are ranked according to their scores, with the highest score ranked first.

After ranking the elements and stakeholders, managers meet to list all critical issues under each high-ranking element or stakeholder. For example, a supplier may be the most important stakeholder because it controls a critical input resource. The issue related to this stakeholder may be the possibility of a reduced supply of this critical resource. This was the case for many electric utilities when OPEC restricted the supply of oil in 1973.

Finally, the managers determine which issues most require management attention. These are the issues with an SIA Index closest to −100 or 100, according to the following equation:

$$\text{SIA Index} = (C_w \times P_c)\, W_{ud}$$
$$(\text{Range} = -100 \text{ to } +100)$$

Where: C_w = consequences weight for the issue. The weight ranges from +5 to −5, with +5 indicating high positive consequences for the firm, and −5 high negative consequences.

P_c = probability that the consequences will occur.

W_{ud} = uncertainty–dependence score for the element or stakeholder that relates to the issue.

C_w and P_c values are obtained from the estimates of senior executives based on their training and experience. One or more of the techniques described on page 50 can be used to combine executive estimates. The environmental issues with the most extreme SIA Index scores are the issues to which the organization is most vulnerable. The strategic manager should single out these issues for immediate attention because they are possible opportunities or threats.

The Strategic Application "Two Luxury Goods Giants Wed" describes how three

STRATEGIC APPLICATIONS: INTERNATIONAL

Two Luxury Goods Giants Wed

Moët-Vuitton, seller of champagne and luggage, calls itself the world's biggest luxury conglomerate. Guinness PLC, best known for its liquor operations under its United Distillers Group, is also a large luxury goods firm. These two giants decided to merge after looking at the growing uncertainty and dependence in the international market for luxury goods.

The real winner in this merger strategy was Bernard Arnault, who used astute environmental assessment to forecast the possibility of such a merger and purchased large quantities of Moët-Vuitton stock. Mr. Arnault is the Senior Executive for Financiere Agach S.A., which controls the Christian Dior high-fashion house and the successful new Christian Lacroux house. The result of this three-way marriage is the creation of the world's largest luxury goods conglomerate.

Using principles of strategic importance analysis, the two major firms chose to reduce dependence on competitors through merger. Their management, however, did not expect an outsider to use environmental assessment to benefit from their merger. This strategic application is an example of a stakeholder in Moët's and Guinness's general environment quickly moving into their task environment.

Source: "Moët-Vuitton Dispute Resolved in Accord with Guinness, French Outside Investor," *Wall Street Journal*, July 10, 1988, 15.

firms used the principles of strategic importance analysis to gain a competitive advantage in their international markets through merger.

The four analysis methods discussed in this section can be used independently or together. Each method provides the manager with information about a different aspect of the firm's task environment. The manager should remember that (1) the greater the opportunity or threat is, (2) the more unfavorable the competitive forces are, (3) the more capable a competitor is of using aggressive strategies, and (4) the more dependent the firm is, the more strategic management attention he or she must devote to that element or stakeholder. All of these analysis methods are therefore designed to enable managers to select the most important environmental elements and stakeholders.

Interpretation of Environmental Information

Interpretation is using previously analyzed environmental information that has been determined to be relevant for the firm, to project future business conditions and set future directions for the organization. That is, strategic managers use environmental information in two ways: to forecast future events and to formulate strategy to prepare the firm for those events. Forecasting is predicting, projecting, or estimating some future event, series of events, or condition that is outside the direct control of the organization. It is not planning, because planning involves actions, events, or conditions over which the organization has some control. Managers *plan* to take certain action because they have *forecast* that certain environmental events will occur. If the events fail to happen as predicted, the plans must be altered.

The most popular forecasting techniques currently in use by managers are those listed in Figure 2.10. These techniques vary in their sophistication and the conditions under which they are most appropriate. Figure 2.11 provides a series of criteria that

Figure 2.10 Forecasting Techniques

Judgment Techniques

Naive Extrapolation
Sales Force Composite
Jury of Executive Opinion
Scenario
Delphi
Historical Analogy

Counting Techniques

Market Testing
Consumer Market Survey
Industrial Market Survey
Purchasing Survey

Time Series Techniques

Moving Averages
Exponential Smoothing
Adaptive Filtering
Time-Series Extrapolation
Time-Series Decomposition
Box-Jenkins

Association/Causal Techniques

Correlation
Regression
Leading Indicators
Econometric Models
Input–Output Models

Figure 2.11 Forecasting Criteria and Questions

Criteria	Question
Time Requirements	
Span	How far into the future is the forecast period?
Urgency	How quickly is the forecast needed?
Frequency	Are forecast updates needed frequently?
Resource Requirements	
Computer	Are computers necessary, and to what extent?
Financial	How expensive is this technique to use?
Input Requirements	
Mathematical sophistication	How mathematically sophisticated must we be to use this technique?
Completeness	How complete must the historical input data be?
Fluctuations	Does the technique need to handle wide fluctuations in input data?
Internal change	Must the technique handle changes in internal decision criteria?
External change	Must the technique handle shifts among variable relationships?
Output Relationships	
Detail	Are detailed forecasts required?
Accuracy	Is a high level of accuracy required?
Turning points	Should the technique reflect turning points quickly?
Probabilities	Are probability estimates required as part of the forecast?

Source: David M. Georgoff and Robert G. Murdick, "Manager's Guide to Forecasting," *Harvard Business Review* 64 (January–February 1986): 110–120.

the manager should use when selecting a forecasting technique, along with questions for each criterion. The results of the forecasts establish the future environmental conditions for which the firm must plan.

A plan is only as good as the forecast on which it is based, and a forecast is meaningless without a plan. Strategy formulation consists of using forecasts of future environmental events to set a direction for the firm that will take advantage of those events. Utility companies failed to forecast the increased cost of nuclear safety and decreased energy usage when they contracted to increase power generation capacity through nuclear reactors. As a result, nuclear power generation is no longer cost effective nor needed by consumers. Many nuclear power generation projects have either been reduced in size or abandoned altogether. Better environmental analyses and forecasting may have saved utilities billions of dollars in construction costs and their loss of goodwill with the consuming public.

Summary

This chapter described how managers conduct environmental assessments through scanning, analysis, and interpretation. In addition, the chapter included discussions of four analysis methods.

The environment consists of a number of sectors, which contain elements and stakeholders. Depending on the organization's control over the elements and stakeholders, they may be part of the remote, general, competitive, or task environment. The task environment consists of elements and stakeholders from the remote, general, and competitive environments that are relevant to the organization for its success and survival. Therefore, the task environment is that portion of the total environment on which the strategic manager must focus.

After learning which elements and stakeholders are relevant for the firm's success and survival, the senior executive can initiate a scan to gather information about the issues within each of them. The levels of scanning are exploratory search, source search, secondary search, and primary search. The extent of the scanning effort depends on the amount of information required to make a decision, the costs and potential benefits of the information, and the capabilities of the firm.

Of the four environmental analyses presented, the most commonly used is the opportunities and threats (O&T) analysis, which rates elements and stakeholders on their potential as opportunities or threats to the firm. Another technique, industry analysis, involves a detailed analysis of direct competitors, suppliers, buyers, potential new entrants to the industry, and possible substitutes. Financial analysis helps determine the financial capabilities and strategic intentions of competitors in the firm's task environment. A relatively new approach to environmental analysis is the strategic importance analysis, which allows the strategic manager to prioritize the relevant elements and stakeholders according to the firm's vulnerability to them, measured in terms of uncertainty and dependence.

Managers conduct environmental assessments in order to forecast future conditions and formulate strategies. Several forecasting techniques and the criteria for selecting them were given. The knowledge gained from the environmental analysis enables the manager to formulate a strategic direction that will allow the firm to successfully exploit opportunities and cope with threats. As this strategy must be within the firm's capabilities, Chapter 3 discusses the analysis of internal strategic capabilities and how it helps the manager choose the portion of the task environment in which the firm will conduct business.

Questions

1. Select a major firm in the electronics industry and, using the sectors, elements, and stakeholders in Figure 2.1, list ten elements or stakeholders that are in the firm's task environment. In which type of environment (remote, general, or competitive) is each element or stakeholder, and why?

2. Many major U.S. businesses hire market research firms to gather information about their markets. According to the discussion of environmental scanning, under what conditions is this approach cost effective?

3. You have been hired by a consortium of wealthy business tycoons to help them determine the feasibility of starting a national professional soccer league in the United States. The first thing that you must do is conduct an industry analysis as part of your assessment. How would you go about conducting this analysis? How would you conduct the analysis for competitors and suppliers?

4. Assume that you are in charge of assessing the environment for a large multinational organization. Because the stakes are high, you have decided to conduct an opportunities and threats analysis, industry analysis, financial analysis, and strategic importance analysis. Discuss the additional insight you would expect the SIA to give you over the first three analyses.

Notes

1. J. Diffenbach, "Corporate Environmental Analysis in Large U. S. Corporations," *Long Range Planning*, vol. 16, no. 3, 1983, 107–116.

2. Amy Dunkin, M. Oneal, and K. Kelly, "Beyond Marlboro Country," *Business Week* (August 8, 1988): 54–58.

3. A great deal has been written about the difference between the actual and perceived environments (e.g. Paul R. Lawrence and J. W. Lorsch, *Organization and Environment* (Homewood, IL.: Richard D. Irwin, 1967); R. B. Duncan, "Characteristics of organizational environments and perceived environmental uncertainty," *Administrative Science Quarterly*, vol. 17, no. 3, 1972, 313–327.

4. Richard L. Daft, *Organization Theory and Design* (St. Paul, Minn.: West Publishing Company, 1986).

5. R. Edward Freeman and D. L. Reed, "Stockholders and stakeholders: A new perspective on corporate governance," *California Management Review*, vol. 25, no. 3, 1983, 88–106.

6. Dill (W. R. Dill, "Environment as an influence on managerial autonomy," *Administrative Science Quarterly*, vol. 2, no. 4, 1958, 409–442) refers to the task environment as the relevant portion of the general environment. Emery and Trist (F. E. Emery and E. L. Trist, "The causal texture of organizational environments," *Human Relations*, vol. 18, no. 1, 1965, 21–32) considered four types of environments: placid-randomized, placid-clustered, disturbed-reactive and turbulent-field. In 1984, McCann and Selsky (Joseph E. McCann and J. Selsky, "Hyperturbulence and the emergence of Type 5 environments," *Academy of Management Review*, vol. 8, no. 3, 1983, 460–470) extended the Emery and Trist typology to include hyperturbulent environments. Lawrence and Lorsch and others (e.g. James D. Thompson, *Organizations in Action* (New York: McGraw-Hill, 1967); Duncan, 1972, op cit; Ray Jurkovich. "A core typology of organization environments," *Administrative Science Quarterly,* vol. 19, 1974, 380–394) describe the environment in terms of level of uncertainty. Emerson (Emerson, "Power-dependence relations," *American Sociological Review* 27 (1974):31–41) and later, Pfeffer and Salancik (Jeffery Pfeffer and G. R. Salancik, *The External Control of Organizations* (New York: Harper & Row, 1978) argue that the level of interdependence among environmental elements and stakeholders best describes the type of environment that a firm faces. More recently, authors have used variations of these schemes to describe a firm's environment. Examples are Dess and Beard (Gregory Dess and D. W. Beard, "Dimensions of organizational task environments," *Administrative Science Quarterly*, vol. 29, no. 1, 1984, 52–73)—level of munificence, dynamism and complexity; Fischer (David W. Fischer, "Strategies toward political pressures: A typology of firm responses," *Academy of Management Review*, vol. 7, no. 3, 1983, 403–412)—product and impact environments; Astley and Frombrun (Graham W. Astley and C. J. Frombrun, "Collective strategy: The social ecology of organizational environments," *Academy of Management Review*, vol. 8, no. 4, 1983, 576–587)—interorganizational, general and task environments; Bourgeois (L. J. Bourgeois III, "Strategy and environment: A conceptual integration," *Academy of Management Review*, vol. 5, no. 1, 1980, 25–40)—general and task environments; Astley and Ven de Ven (Graham W. Astley and A. Van de Ven, "Central perspectives and debates in organization theory," *Administrative Science Quarterly,* vol. 28, no. 2, 1983, 245–273)—micro-macro and deterministic-voluntaristic, and Pearce and Robinson (John A. Pearce and R. B. Robinson, Jr.,

Strategic Management: Strategy Formulation and Implementation (3rd). Homewood, IL: Richard D. Irwin, 1988)—remote and operating.

7. Another way to look at this is to think in terms of the probability that an action by that element or stakeholder will influence the success or survival of the firm. If the probability is less than .05 (approximately 2 standard deviations) that action taken by the element or stakeholder will have consequences for the firm, then it should be classified in the remote environmental type.

8. Alan D. Meyer, "Adapting to environmental jolts," *Administrative Science Quarterly*, vol. 27, no. 4, 1982, 515–537.

9. Michael E. Porter, *Competitive Strategy* (New York: The Free Press, 1980), 6.

10. Dill, 1958.

11. Fahey and Narayanan describe four stages to environmental analysis: scanning, monitoring, assessment, and forecasting (Liam Fahey and V. K. Narayanan, *Macroenvironmental Analysis for Strategic Managers*. St. Paul, Minn.: West Publishing Company, 1986). Their interpretations are similar to ours except for terms used in some cases. Their use of scanning is identical to that used here. The distinction between scanning and monitoring as they use them is subtle, and these were combined under scanning here. Fahey and Narayanan use assessment and forecasting in a manner similar to our use of analysis and interpretation.

12. The description presented here is based primarily on the pioneering work of Aguilar (F. Aguilar, *Scanning the Business Environment*. New York: MacMillan, 1967). However, his basic framework has been modified substantially to incorporate a number of subsequent contributions of other authors (e.g. Donald C. Hambrick, "Environmental scanning and organization strategy," *Strategic Management Journal*, vol. 3, no. 2, 1982, 159–174; Stoffels, "Environmental scanning for future success," *Managerial Planning*, vol. 31, no. 3, 1982, 4–12; R. Whaley, "Data bank on the future business environments," *Long Range Planning*, vol. 18, no. 4, 1984, 83–90; Allen H. Mesch, "Developing an effective environmental assessment function," *Managerial Planning*, vol. 32, no. 5, 1984, 17–22; Mark W. Dersmith and M. A. Covaleski, "Strategy, external communication and environmental context," *Strategic Management Journal*, vol. 4, no. 2, 1983, 137–151; B. Nanus, "QUEST—Quick environmental scanning technique," *Long Range Planning*, vol 15, no. 2, 1982, 39–45; Liam Fahey , W. R. King, and V. K. Narayanan, "Environmental scanning and forecasting in strategic planning—The state of the art," *Long Range Planning*, vol. 14, no. 1, 1981, 32–39; S. C. Jain, "Environmental scanning in U. S. Corporations," *Long Range Planning*, vol. 17, no. 2, 1984, 117–128; Joseph E. McCann, "Analyzing industrial trends—A collaborative approach," *Long Range Planning*, vol. 18, no. 5, 1985, 116–123; James Belohlav and L. Sussman, "Environmental scanning and dialectical inquiry," *Managerial Planning*, vol. 32, no. 2, 1983, 46–49; C. B. Arrington and R. N. Sawaya, "Issues management in an uncertain environment," *Long Range Planning*, vol. 17, no. 6, 1984, 17–24).

13. This is only one of several descriptions of the scanning process. Aguilar's (1968) original version and a more recent version by Nanus (1982) in which he describes the QUEST technique are two examples. The process discussed above follows Aguilar's. The QUEST environmental scanning technique was developed to "provide a broad and comprehensive first approximation to environmental trends and events that are critical to strategic decisions." It contains four stages: preparation, divergent planning session, scenario development, and strategic options identification. Fahey & King (Liam Fahey and W. R. King, "Environmental scanning for corporate planning," *Business Horizons*, vol. 20, no. 4, 1977, 61–75; Fahey and King, 1981) propose three types of scanning; irregular, periodic, and continuous. They argue that firms move toward the continuous scanning mode. However, Stubbert (C. Stubbart, "Why we need a revolution in strategic planning," *Long Range Planning*, vol. 18, no. 6, 1985, 68–76) found that four of the twelve firms in their survey regressed toward the irregular mode.

14. Nanus (1982).

15. James R. Norman, Terri Thompson, Cynthia Green, and Jo Ellen Davis, "The Scrappy Mr. Penzoil," *Business Week*, Jan. 27; 1986: 88–95.

16. Robert Veres, "Surveying the Market." *Financial Planning*, 14, Nov. 1985, 88–99.

17. Russell Mitchell, "How Ford Hit the Bull's-Eye with Taurus," *Business Week*, June 30, 1986, 69–70.

18. Adapted from the definition of Assessment in Fahey and Narayanan, p. 42.

19. Diffenbach, "Corporate Environmental Analyses." *Macroenvironmental Analysis for Strategic Management* (New York: West Publishing Co.).

20. Some authors have used similar labels such as TOWS Analysis—Threats, Opportunities, Weaknesses and Strengths and WOTS-UP Analysis—Weaknesses, Opportunities, Threats and Strengths.

21. Porter, *Competitive Strategy*.

22. Kathryn Harrigan, *Strategic Flexibility* (Lexington, Mass.: Lexington Books, 1985).

Case for Discussion

Motorola and Congress on Defense Contract Fraud

During the period from 1979 to 1984, more than 50 employees of the Government Electronics Group of Motorola Inc., a major U.S. government contractor, improperly moved more than $2.5 million in labor and materials from troubled contracts to other defense contracts. One project involved a communications satellite, and another involved a surface-to-air missile for the Navy. These charges were filed by the U.S. Department of Justice after an extensive investigation of Motorola and other defense contractors.

Congress is up in arms over the pervasive fraud being committed by defense contractors. Congresswoman Pat Schroeder of Colorado complained that employees and corporate officers found guilty of fraud were going unpunished and should be sent to prison. John Dingell, Congressman from Michigan, agrees. Two other members of Congress indicated that they might initiate their own probes of defense contractors if Justice did not get tougher on contract abuse. Most observers agree that Congress is leaning toward tighter controls and stiffer penalties.

As far as Motorola is concerned, senior executives refused to admit guilt. However, they did settle out of court and agree to pay the government $16.7 million in restitution and penalties. This agreement is on the heels of a $17 million penalty paid by TRW Inc. for defense fraud just one year earlier. In addition, Motorola dismissed or froze the salaries of 20 managers implicated in the investigation. The toll from the settlement in dollars and personal hardship, not to mention damage to the reputation of the firm, is tremendous.

What is the reaction of many defense contractor employees and managers? Many have trouble understanding the fuss. In interviews some say, "It is common practice in the industry," or, "When the technology is this sophisticated, you need to shift costs to be competitive," or, "If the government procurement people would stop changing specifications, the problem would go away." Senior managers realize that they are on the horns of an ethical dilemma but don't know exactly what to do.

Discussion Questions

1. Which stakeholders in Motorola's environment are mentioned in this case?

2. Using an industry analysis approach, analyze Motorola's social responsibility environment.

3. In which type of environment (remote, general, competitive, task) would Motorola probably classify Congress and the Justice Department before the investigation? After the investigation? Support your classification.

4. What level of scanning (exploratory, source, secondary, primary) did Motorola apparently use when looking at Congress?

5. If Motorola management were to conduct an SIA, how would it likely rate the stakeholders listed in your answer to Question 1 in terms of uncertainty and dependence? Justify your answer.

Appendix 2.1

Sources of Business Information

Numerous business-information sources are available in most libraries. The following selections are meant only to give the reader an idea of what is available and a place to start. For information pertaining to a specific area of interest, the bibliographies and special guides in most libraries will provide complete lists of pertinent publications.

Government Publications

Indexes

American Statistics Index Issued monthly. A comprehensive, descriptive guide and index to statistics published by all government agencies, Congressional committees, and statistics-producing programs. Washington: Congressional Information Service, 600 Montgomery Bldg., 20014, 1973.

Index to U.S. Government Periodicals Issued quarterly. An index from 1980 to present of government periodicals.

Monthly Catalog of United States Publications (GPO) Issued Monthly. A comprehensive listing of the publications issued by all branches of the federal government during each month.

Selected Basic Sources

County and City Data Book (U.S. Department of Commerce, Bureau of the Census) Issued annually. Statistical information for counties, cities, Standard Metropolitan Statistical Areas, unincorporated places, and urbanized areas.

County Business Patterns (U.S. Department of Commerce, Bureau of the Census) Issued annually. County, state, and U.S. summary statistics on employment categorized under approximately 15 industry headings.

Economic Indicators Issued monthly. Charted and tabulated current information on economic conditions of prices, wages, production, business activity, purchasing power, credit, money, and federal finance.

Federal Reserve Bulletin (Board of Governors of the Federal Reserve System) Issued monthly. Numerous financial statistics on banking, deposits, loans and investments, money market rates, securities prices, industrial production, and so forth relating to government, business, real estate, and the consumer.

Monthly Bulletin of Statistics (New York: United Nations) Issued monthly. The current supplement to the United Nations Statistical Yearbook.

Monthly Labor Review (U.S. Department of Labor, Bureau of Labor Statistics) Issued monthly. Current statistics, trends, and information on labor, including employment, wages, weekly working hours, collective agreements, and industrial accidents.

Statistical Abstract of the United States (U.S. Department of Commerce, Bureau of the Census) Issued annually. Summary statistics on the social, political, and economic organization of the United States.

Statistical Reporter (U.S. Office of the President, Office of Management and Budget, Statistical Policy Division) Issued annually. Selected information on federal statistical programs and lists of statistical sources.

Statistical Yearbook (New York: United Nations) Issued annually. International statistics covering a variety of areas, including population, agriculture, mining, manufacturing, finance, trade, and education.

Survey of Current Business (U.S. Department of Commerce, Bureau of Economic Analysis) Issued monthly. The official source for reporting the gross national product, national income, and international balance of payments. Numerous different statistical series are brought up to date in each issue under various headings including General Business Indicators, Domestic Trade, Labor Force, Employment and Earnings, Finance, and Foreign Trade of the United States.

Census Data

Bureau of the Census Catalog of Publications (U.S. Department of Commerce, Bureau of the Census) Issued quarterly. An index to Census Bureau data, publications, and unpublished materials.

Census of Housing (U.S. Department of Commerce, Bureau of the Census) Issued every ten years, it includes five volumes:

I States and Small Areas
II Metropolitan Housing
III City Blocks
IV Components of Inventory Change
V Residential Financing

Census of Manufacturers (U.S. Department of Commerce, Bureau of the Census) Issued every five years. Geographical and industrial data on manufacturers.

Census of Population (U.S. Department of Commerce, Bureau of the Census) Issued every ten years. The 1980 edition includes series A through D:

A Number of Inhabitants
B General Population Characteristics
C General Social and Economic Characteristics
D Detailed Characteristics

Census of Retail Business, Census of Service Business, Census of Transportation, Census of Wholesaling, Census of Construction (U.S. Department of Commerce, Bureau of the Census) Issued every five years. Most of these contain total sales, number of firms, various information about incorporated versus unincorporated status, and size of payroll, and are arranged by standard industrial classification (SIC) codes and also by geographical area.

Business Guides and Services

Directory of American Firms Operating in Foreign Countries Juvenal L. Angel, ed. (New York: Simon & Schuster, 1975) Three volumes. Over 4,300 firms and their foreign subsidiaries by country where they operate. The companion to this is the *Directory of Foreign Firms Operating in the United States.*

Directory of Corporate Affiliations (Skokie, Ill.: National Register Publishing Company) Published annually. A directory that lists over 3,000 parent companies with their 16,000 divisions, subsidiaries, and affiliates.

Middle Market Directory (New York: Dun & Bradstreet) Published annually. A directory that lists over 31,000 U.S. companies with an indicated worth of $500,000 to $999,999. The format is similar to Dun & Bradstreet's Million Dollar Directory.

Million Dollar Directory (New York: Dun & Bradstreet) Published annually. A directory that lists approximately 39,000 U.S. companies with an indicated worth of $1 million or over. Gives officers, products (if manufacturers), standard industrial classification (SIC), approximate sales, and number of employees.

Moody's Annuals (New York: Moody's Investors Service) Published annually with semiweekly or weekly supplements.

Moody's Bank and Finance Manual
Moody's Industrial Manual
Moody's Municipal and Government Manual
Moody's OTC Industrial Manual
Moody's Public Utilities Manual
Moody's Transportation Manual

Reference Book of Corporate Managements (New York: Dun & Bradstreet) Published annually. Lists over 30,000 officers and directors of some 2,400 companies whose combined revenues equal 80 percent of the gross national product and that employ approximately 20 million people.

Regional and State Manufacturers Directories State directories of manufacturing companies. Several examples are:

California Manufacturers Register
Directory of New England Manufacturers
Industrial Directory of Massachusetts Manufacturers

Standard & Poor's Corporation Services (New York: Standard & Poor's) Included among these services are "Industry Surveys," an annual survey that includes three or four current surveys of each industry and a monthly trends and projections section; "The Outlook," a weekly stock market letter; "Stock Guide," a monthly summary of investment data; and "Trade and Securities," a monthly listing of statistics on business and finance.

Standard & Poor's Register of Corporations, Directors and Executives (New York: Standard & Poor's) Issued annually, Volume 1 is an alphabetic listing of more than 36,000 U.S. and Canadian corporations with titles of their important executives, names of directors and principals, and annual sales. Volume 2 is an alphabetic listing of executives and directors. Volume 3 is an index of corporations arranged under several headings, including standard industrial classification (SIC), geographic area, and new companies.

Standard Directory of Advertisers (Skokie, Ill.: National Register Publishing Company) Published annually. A listing of more than 17,000 companies and their agencies doing national and regional advertising, grouped by line of business and by state and city.

Standard Rate & Data Service Publications (Skokie, Ill.: Standard Rate & Data Services) Examples of these publications include "Direct Mail List Rates and Data," a semiannual listing of more than 22,000 mailing lists available; "Network Rates and Data," a list of national radio and television networks with basic marketing information that is published every other month; and "Newspaper Rates and Data," a monthly compilation of over 1,600 U.S. newspapers and newspaper groups.

Indexes

Accountant's Index (New York: American Institute of Certified Public Accountants) A comprehensive list, indexed by author, subject, and title, of books, government documents, pamphlets, and periodicals that concern accounting, auditing, data processing, financial management and investments, financial reporting, management, and taxation.

Business Periodicals Index (New York: H. W. Wilson) A cumulative subject index covering numerous periodicals in the field of business.

F & S Index of Corporations and Industries (Cleveland, Ohio: Predicasts, Inc.) Published weekly. A current index to company, industry, and product information from more than 750 business-oriented newspapers, financial publications, special reports, and trade magazines.

F & S Index International (Cleveland, Ohio: Predicasts, Inc.) Published monthly. An index that covers articles on foreign companies and industries that have appeared in some 1,000 foreign and domestic periodicals and other documents.

Index to Legal Periodicals Issued monthly. Subject and author index to legal periodicals in the English language. Table of cases and book review index at end. New York, H. W. Wilson Co. in cooperation with American Association of Law Libraries. Frequency varies.

The New York Times Index (New York: The New York Times Company) A detailed index to articles and news items giving date of issue, page, and column number for each indexed item.

Public Affairs Information Service Bulletin (New York: Public Affairs Information Service) A selective list by subject of government documents, pamphlets, periodical articles, and recent books relating to economics and public affairs.

Reader's Guide to Periodical Literature (New York: H. W. Wilson) An index by subject and author of the contents of general magazines in the United States.

Social Science Citation Index (Philadelphia, Pa.: Institute for Scientific Information) Issued every four months. Subject, author, and citation indexes of research literature in the social sciences field. Index to articles cited in other publications.

Social Sciences Index (New York: H. W. Wilson) Issued quarterly. Author–subject index to more than 260 scholarly journals in broad areas of the social sciences.

The Wall Street Journal Index (Princeton, N.J.: Dow Jones) An index of all articles that have appeared in the paper, grouped in two parts: corporate news and general news.

Periodicals and Periodical Directories

Hundreds of business periodicals are of interest to the business manager and student. The following are a selected few: *Accounting Review, Advertising Age, Business Week, Dun's, Forbes, Fortune, Harvard Business Review, Industrial Marketing, Journal of Advertising Research, Journal of Business, Journal of Finance, Journal of Marketing, Journal of Marketing Research, Journal of Retailing, Management Accounting, Management Science, Modern Packaging, Nation's Business, Personnel, Personnel Management, Sales Management, The Wall Street Journal.*

Ayer Directory of Publications (Philadelphia, Pa.: Ayer Press, 1975) A comprehensive directory of newspapers, magazines, and trade publications of the United States, Canada, Bermuda, Republic of Panama, Republic of the Philippines, and the Bahamas.

Business Publications Rates and Data (Skokie, Ill.: Standard Rate & Data Services) Issued monthly. This directory lists over 3,000 U.S. business, trade, and technical publications.

Ulrich's International Periodicals Directory (New York: Bowker) Issued every two years. An index by subject to over 55,000 current periodicals published throughout the world.

Bibliographies and Special Guides

Bibliography of Publications of University Bureaus of Business and Economic Research (Boulder, Colo.: Business Research Division, University of Colorado) Published annually. A bibliography of publications by bureaus of business and economic research and by members of the American Association of Collegiate Schools of Business.

Business Information Sources Lorna M. Daniells (Berkeley: University of California Press, 2nd Ed., 1985). Basic annotated guide not only to the most important reference sources such as indexes, directories, financial manuals, and statistical publications, but also to selected books, periodicals, and reference works pertaining to each management function.

Business Reference Sources: An Annotated Guide for Harvard Business School Students Lorna M. Daniells (Boston: Baker Library, Harvard Business School, 1979) Best student guide to a business school library.

Directory of Business and Financial Services Riva Belleaut-Schiller and Norma Cote, eds. (New York: Special Libraries Association, 2nd Ed., 1984) Directory describing business, economic, and financial services that are published regularly.

Encyclopedia of Business Information Sources (Detroit: Gale Research Company, 7th Ed., 1988) A list of subjects of interest to managers, which includes bibliographies, directories, handbooks, organizations, periodicals, sourcebooks, and other sources of information on each topic.

How to Use the Business Library with Sources of Business Information (Cincinnati, Ohio: South-Western Publishing Company, 5th Ed., 1984) A guide to learning the use of a business library.

Industrial Products Directory Published annually, four volumes. Information on 40,000 companies. Alphabetic listing of all companies, trade name directory, product categories directory, and directory of industrial literature (product catalogs and technical literature).

The Journal of Economic Literature (Nashville, Tenn.: American Economic Association) Issued quarterly. An annotated guide to new books and current periodical articles in economics, finance, management and labor, and trade and industry.

Management Information Guides (Detroit: Gale Research Company) Numerous bibliographic references to business information sources. Each volume includes books, dictionaries, encyclopedias, filmstrips, government and institutional reports, periodical articles, and recordings on the featured subject. Guides are available from this series in almost every field. Selected volumes include:

- Accounting Information Sources
- American Economic and Business History Information Sources
- Commercial Law Information Sources
- Communication in Organizations: An Annotated Bibliography and Sourcebook
- Computers and Data Processing Information Sources
- Ethics in Business Conduct: Selected References from the Record—Problems, Attempted Solutions, Ethics in Business Education
- Investment Information Sources
- Public and Business Planning in the United States

Sources of Business Information (Berkeley: University of California Press, 1964) A guide to reference materials in various business fields.

Statistics Sources (Detroit: Gale Research Company, 8th Ed., 1984) Publication designed to locate current statistical data. Includes a subject guide to data on many topics, including business, finance, and industry for the United States and some foreign countries. Issued in parts.

Where to Find Business Information: A Worldwide Guide for Everyone Who Needs the Answers to Business Questions (New York: David M. Brownstone, 2nd Ed., 1982) Book in three parts: Source Finder (subject section); Publishers' Index; Sources of Business Information (describes each item listed in first two parts).

Trade Associations

Encyclopedia of Associations (Detroit: Gale Research Company, updated irregularly) Volume 1: National Organizations of the United States; Volume 2: National Organizations of the United States; Volume 3: New Associations and Projects.

National Trade and Professional Associations of the United States and Labor Unions (Washington, D.C.: Columbia Books) Issued annually. Directory listing over 4,700 organizations, trade and professional associations, and labor unions with national memberships.

Yearbook of International Organizations (Brussels: Union of International Associations) A computer-produced directory that covers politics, professions, trade unions, economics, finance, and industry, among other topics. Includes information on international organizations that are members.

Other Basic Sources

Commercial Atlas and Marketing Guide (New York: Rand McNally) Published annually. A guide that includes statistics and maps that provide data on population estimates, principal cities, business centers and trading areas, county business, sales and manufacturing units, zip code marketing information, and transportation data for the United States.

The Conference Board Record (New York: The Conference Board) Published monthly. A report to management on business statistical tabulations.

National Economic Projection Series (Washington, D.C.: National Planning Association) Published annually. This report provides forecasts of the gross national product and its principal components, including historical and projected five-, ten-, and fifteen-year forecasts for capital investment, consumption and savings, government revenues and expenditures, output and productivity, and population and employment.

Sources of Information on Foreign Companies

Directory of European Business Information Sources Irene Kingston and William A. Benjamin, eds. A comprehensive guide to business information in Europe. In three parts: (1) basic information sources and services; (2) subject information sources and services; (3) country information sources and services (with cross-references to parts 1 and 2). Subject/title index. (Cambridge, Mass.: Bullenger, 1979).

Bottin International: International Business Register (Paris: Société Didot-Bottin) Published annually. An international directory listing manufacturers, distributors, importers, and exporters.

Europe's 5,000 Largest Companies (New York: Bowker) Published annually. A listing of the 5,000 largest European industrials and trading companies ranked by sales and number of employees.

European Companies: A Guide to Sources of Information G. P. Henderson, ed. (Bechenham, England: CBD Research, 1972) A guide to information on companies in Western and Eastern Europe. Includes official records, financial and commercial services, directories, newspapers, and journals.

Jane's Major Companies of Europe (New York: F. Watts) Published annually. This sourcebook gives financial data on 1,000 Western European companies arranged by industry.

Principal International Businesses (New York: Dun & Bradstreet) Published annually. This sourcebook provides addresses, sales, and number of employees for more than 44,000 international companies.

Who Owns Whom? Continental Edition (London: O. W. Roskill) Published annually. A directory to parent and subsidiary companies in industry and commerce.

Kelly's Manufacturers and Merchants Directory Including Industrial Services (Kingston-upon-Thames, England) Published annually. Volume 1: Great Britain, Northern Ireland, Republic of Ireland; Volume 2: Europe, Africa, the Americas, Asia, Oceania.

Information Sources on Small Business

Barometer of Small Business (San Diego, Calif.: Accounting Corporation of America) Published semiannually. Operating statistics for about 50 small retail and service businesses compiled from the books of ACA clients. The statistics are analyzed and summarized by industry type, size category, and geographic region.

Small Business Information Sources Joseph C. Schabacker. (Tempe, Ariz.: Publication Services, 1976) An annotated bibliography that lists publications with their tables of contents. Included are books on small-business practice, pamphlets, periodicals, Small Business Administration (SBA) research summaries, and SBA free publications.

Small Business Survival Guide Joseph R. Mancuso. (Englewood Cliffs, N.J.: Prentice-Hall, 1980) A comprehensive guide listing sources of information of interest to the small-business owner. The book includes chapters on advertising and public relations, bankruptcy, books, business associations, business plans, sources of help, and data processing.

Appendix 2.2

Industry Analysis

A procedure for using Porter's industry analysis approach is presented in Figure 2.2A. This procedure specifies a series of statements or items to which the manager either agrees or disagrees. The items correspond directly to the issues developed by Porter and are broken down by his five competitive stakeholder groups. A score is calculated for each stakeholder group using the following equation:

$$\text{Stakeholder Score} = (X/n)I$$

where: X = summed score for all items within that stakeholder that were answered by the manager;

n = number of items answered within that stakeholder; and

I = importance score for the stakeholder as measured by the manager's response to the last item.

The stakeholder score indicates to the manager how critical each stakeholder is to the firm's competitive success. After determining the most critical stakeholders, the manager locates the items within those stakeholders with high scores (4 or 5) to isolate the issues that must be dealt with immediately. When a group of individuals is involved in environmental assessment, the procedures discussed in this chapter can once again be used.

Figure 2.2A Sample Industry Analysis Format

Competitive Forces	Strongly Agree				Strongly Disagree
I. Potential Entrants					
1. The cost to enter this business is great.	1	2	3	4	5
2. Our products are highly differentiated.	1	2	3	4	5
3. It takes a great deal of capital to get into this business.	1	2	3	4	5
4. It would be very expensive for our customers to switch to another supplier.	1	2	3	4	5
5. It is difficult to gain access to channels of distribution.	1	2	3	4	5
6. It is very difficult to get government approval to operate a business like ours.	1	2	3	4	5
7. The chances of a new firm entering this business and threatening our firm are not very great.	1	2	3	4	5

Score = (summed score from all items answered ÷ number of items answered) × (score from item 7)

Figure 2.2A *(continued)*

	Strongly Disagree				Strongly Agree
II. Industry Competitors					
1. There are many competitors in this business.	1	2	3	4	5
2. All competitors in this business are about equal.	1	2	3	4	5
3. The markets for our products are growing slowly.	1	2	3	4	5
4. There is a great deal of costly overhead in this business.	1	2	3	4	5
5. It is easy for our customers to switch to other suppliers.	1	2	3	4	5
6. It is very difficult to add small quantities of capacity to our operations process.	1	2	3	4	5
7. No two firms are alike in this business.	1	2	3	4	5
8. Most firms in this business must succeed or they will go out of business.	1	2	3	4	5
9. The majority of firms in this business are here to stay.	1	2	3	4	5
10. What my competitors do really doesn't make much difference to my firm.	1	2	3	4	5

Score = (summed score from all items answered ÷ number of items answered) × (5 − score from item 10)

	Strongly Disagree				Strongly Agree
III. Substitutes					
1. There are many other products that have the same purpose as ours.	1	2	3	4	5
2. Other types of products can do about what ours does but at a lower cost.	1	2	3	4	5
3. Firms that produce a product that performs the same function as ours are very profitable in their other markets.	1	2	3	4	5
4. I am very concerned about other types of products that can do exactly what ours does.	1	2	3	4	5

Score = (summed scores from all items answered ÷ number of items answered) × (score from item 4)

	Strongly Disagree				Strongly Agree
IV. Buyers					
1. We have relatively few customers who purchase a large part of our sales volume.	1	2	3	4	5
2. Our product accounts for a large part of the customer's purchasing dollar.	1	2	3	4	5
3. Most firms in our business offer a standard, commodity-like product.	1	2	3	4	5
4. It is easy for our customers to switch to another supplier.	1	2	3	4	5
5. There is very little profit in the products that our customers offer.	1	2	3	4	5
6. Some of our customers are large enough to own us.	1	2	3	4	5
7. Our product contributes little to the *quality* of our customer's product.	1	2	3	4	5
8. Our customers know all about our business and how profitable it is.	1	2	3	4	5
9. If I were totally honest, I would say that our customers have very little influence over suppliers in our business.	1	2	3	4	5

Score = (summed scores from all items answered ÷ number of items answered) × (5 − score from item 9)

Figure 2.2A *(continued)*

	Strongly Agree				Strongly Disagree
V. Suppliers					
1. We have many suppliers of our most important material to select from.	1	2	3	4	5
2. There are many substitutes for our most important input material.	1	2	3	4	5
3. We are a major customer for the supplier of our most important input material.	1	2	3	4	5
4. No single supplier is critical to our business.	1	2	3	4	5
5. We can easily switch suppliers for most of our input materials.	1	2	3	4	5
6. None of our suppliers are very large when compared to our firm.	1	2	3	4	5
7. Suppliers are a critical part of our business.	1	2	3	4	5

Score = (summed score from all items answered ÷ number of items answered) × (5 − score from item 7)

Chapter 3

Analysis of Internal Strategic Capabilities

Non omnia possumus omnes. [We are not all capable of everything.]

—Virgil, 70–19 B.C.

Learning Objectives

- To learn the type, level, and location of an organization's capabilities.
- To learn how to construct a profile of strategic capabilities.
- To learn to analyze strategic capabilities.
- To understand the various types of analyses that can be used to conduct an internal strategic capabilities study.
- To learn how to use the results of strategic analyses to choose a domain in which the organization can successfully conduct business.

WHEN Robert C. Stempel became president of General Motors, the company was in a state of decline. GM's U.S. market share tumbled from 44 percent in 1982 to less than 37 percent in 1987. In addition, shrinking profit margins caused profits to fall. Although Stempel is sure that GM knows the U.S. automobile marketplace, he is concerned that GM is losing its capability to remain competitive with other automobile producers. For example, GM makes about 70 percent of its parts in-house as compared to 50 percent for Ford and 30 percent for Chrysler. However, GM's internal capability to produce high-quality parts at a competitive cost has been hampered by obsolete production facilities that produce parts for more than it would cost to buy them from outside vendors. This internal weakness jeopardizes GM's ability to succeed in a very competitive environment.[1]

As Stempel has realized, a thorough environmental assessment is useless if the firm lacks the capability to act on the results of that assessment. Therefore, in the strategic management process, the environmental analysis is followed by an analysis of the organization's internal strategic capabilities to determine its ability to successfully conduct business in selected product markets.[2] This chapter describes how the manager analyzes the firm's current internal capabilities at two levels, business and corporate.

Business-Level Strategic Capabilities

The business level of strategy development relates to how a firm will compete in a single business area. The organizational unit at this level is often called the **strategic business unit (SBU)**. All organizations have business-level capabilities that act as sources of strength or weakness. Each functional department of the firm has its own unique strategic capability, as do the management and staff who coordinate the efforts of these functional units. Understanding these business-level capabilities is vital for positioning the firm to take advantage of environmental opportunities. For example, TRW built on its strength as a supplier of seat belts to capture contracts with Ford and Chrysler to supply air bags or air bag components. Eaton Corporation had tried earlier to get into the air bag business but, with no strength in this area, lost $20 million.[3]

Types of Business-Level Capabilities

Strategic capabilities at the business level are internal to the organization and spring from its managerial, technical, informational, and organizational competencies. These capabilities are classified as strengths or weaknesses based on how they relate to the firm's strategic goals, functional objectives, and daily plans. Capabilities that facilitate accomplishment of goals, objectives, and plans are strengths. Weaknesses are capabilities that detract from goal, objective, and plan accomplishment. Figure 3.1 illustrates how the types of capabilities relate to the goals of the firm.

Managerial Capabilities At the senior executive level of the SBU, managerial capabilities are the experience, skill, and talent that strategic managers use to direct the organization through dynamic environmental conditions. Top-level decision makers

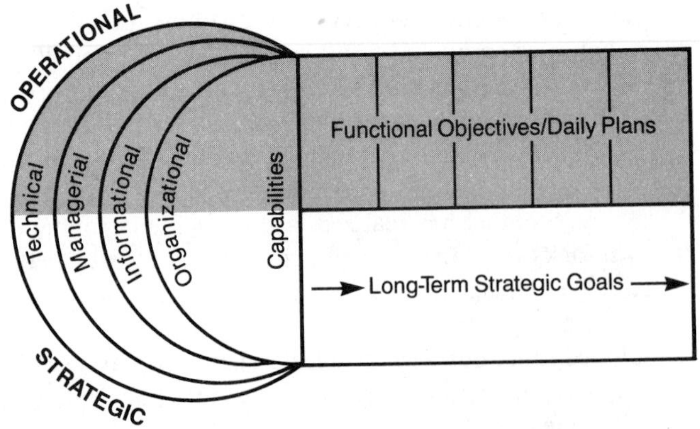

Figure 3.1 Types of Organizational Capabilities and Organization Goals

must diagnose strategic problems and select and implement the appropriate solutions. Some managers have a track record of making good strategic choices in varying environmental conditions. For example, Lee Iacocca has built a reputation as an effective strategic decision maker by orchestrating the turnaround of Chrysler Corporation.

At the middle management level, managerial capabilities focus on the day-to-day operations of the enterprise. Operational managerial capabilities help implement the organization's strategies in the short term. Highly qualified managers of functional units (for example, marketing and production) translate the strategic plans sent from the senior executives into the short-term objectives necessary to implement the firm's strategy during the next business cycle.

Some experts predict that many organizations are jeopardizing today's operational managers and tomorrow's strategic managers for short-term productivity gains. The overall social implications of this practice could be dramatic, as the Strategic Application "Where Have All the Middle Managers Gone" suggests. However, the short-term social costs in terms of layoffs and increased human stress may be less than the long-term social costs—deterioration of our capability to develop managers who are prepared to assume the strategic management of tomorrow's major organizations.

An organization with both strategic and operational managerial capabilities is Triangle Industries, Inc. The two strategic minds behind this new industrial giant are Nelson Pelty and Peter May. Their combined strategic capabilities resulted in some shrewd acquisitions in several highly profitable basic industries. Pelty and May acquire only firms that are run by talented managers with strong operational capabilities and a track record of effectively managing their companies. In one year, this combination of managerial capabilities moved Triangle from a firm that did not qualify as one of the top 1,000 U.S. firms to one of the top 250.[4]

Technical Capabilities Technical capabilities strengthen or weaken the firm's ability to compete in its task environment. Technical capabilities lie in the areas of new-product technology, process technology, operations support technology, and human resource management. All capabilities apply their particular technologies to the efficient operation of the company.

New-product technology is most familiar. It can produce a new state-of-the-art product that is a strength for the firm and a source of a product-based competitive advantage. By the same token, an obsolete product or one that is poorly designed can put the firm at a competitive disadvantage. Schering-Plough, a large pharmaceutical manufacturer, depended on a single product. When that product lost patent protection, generic equivalents caused sales to drop. Because the company was not developing any new products, its new-product technology capability was a serious weakness. A new CEO, Robert P. Luciano, increased research and development to record levels, making new-product technology a strength for Schering-Plough so that the company once again became a viable competitor.[5]

A firm can also gain a competitive advantage through its **process technology**—the processes used to produce a product or service. Process technology can be a strength by giving a cost or quality advantage. Obsolete or inadequate process tech-

STRATEGIC APPLICATIONS: SOCIAL RESPONSIBILITY

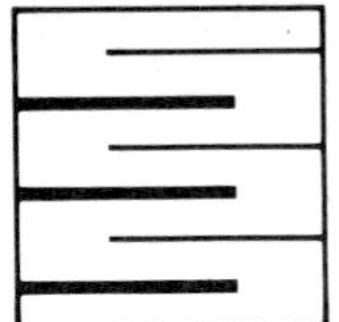

Where Have All the Middle Managers Gone?

U.S. businesses are becoming more productive—or are they? Increases in productivity have usually come from increased output resulting from more efficient use of the factors of production—land, labor, capital and energy. By far, the largest productivity gains have come from the substitution of capital for labor. Machines and processes to increase the output per unit of labor have helped make the United States the industrial giant of the free world. However, recent productivity gains may merely reflect the elimination of layers of middle managers as firms rush to downsize. We are only now beginning to learn the social costs of this massive reduction in middle management.

Some estimates are that more than one million U.S. managers and staff persons have lost their jobs in the past 10 years. The list of firms using middle management layoffs as the vehicle for downsizing is impressive: Mobil Oil—17 percent reduction; Dupont—15 percent laid off; GE—35 percent of middle managers gone. These reductions have resulted in a restless and dissatisfied middle management work force. Managers who have been laid off feel insecure, hurt, and betrayed. Many say that they can never again trust corporate management in any firm. Of the managers who have kept their jobs, many report being overworked, highly stressed, and vulnerable to losing their own jobs. As Peter Drucker says, middle managers "feel like slaves on an auction block."

In recent interviews with several middle managers who, to date, have held onto their jobs, *Business Week* reports some of the following comments:

> "Some days it's difficult to get up and go to work. . . . The majority of people I know who are sitting here, toughing it out, are doing it for their families."
>
> "The current morale is, without exaggeration, the worst I've ever seen."
>
> "I'm not disappointed at not moving higher up. When you enter the bonus rolls, the corporation owns you. . . . This way I can leave the office at night confident that my principles remain intact."
>
> "The other day, one of my [subordinate] managers . . . walked up to me . . . and said, 'Hi! Remember me? I work for you. . . .' That makes me feel bad as a manager."
>
> "The problem for them [new managers] is that they no longer have mentors. The layer of management that was eliminated mentored many of them."

Today's strategic manager must be prepared to face the social consequences, both external and internal, to the firm for this thinning of middle management ranks. The social question is, have U.S. corporations gone too far? The practical questions are more direct. Will the increased stress imposed on remaining middle managers drive qualified future strategic managers from the firm? Will current operations go undermanaged? Where is the training ground for tomorrow's strategic managers?

Source: Byrne, John A., W. Zellner and S. Ticer, "Caught in the Middle," *Business Week*, Sept. 12, 1988, 80–88.

nology can drive up costs and lower profits. The introduction of robotics is one process technology that revolutionized the operations of many businesses. One example is the automotive industry, where robots weld, assemble, and paint automobiles. Robotics has even moved into agriculture for picking and sorting produce. Some managers believe that robots are the most significant improvement in process technology since the assembly line. They can give the small firm the same automated capabilities as the large firm and remove some of the cost advantage of economies of scale. Without this process technology, an organization could face serious weaknesses. However, neither robots nor any process technology is a complete ticket to the firm's future success. Executives must be capable of managing these technologies.

Operations support technologies are the techniques, procedures, and systems that directly support the product and process technologies used to produce the good or service. One operations support area in which new technologies have significantly improved some firms' ability to compete is information transmission. New techniques and systems can transmit accurate information across the country in only a few milliseconds (thousandths of a second). Federal Express uses a computerized information transmission system that can immediately trace the location of any package in its network. This capability is an operations support strength that Federal Express promotes in its advertising.

Other operations support technologies include order-processing techniques, logistics systems, and transportation capabilities. Toyota of Japan has its own fleet of ships to transport automobiles to foreign markets. This capability reduces shipping costs and allows Toyota to be certain that transportation is available when it is needed.

Unlike the capabilities of Toyota and Federal Express, some operational support technologies can be a weakness for the firm. Anchor National Life Insurance Company purchased a data-processing system that was obsolete shortly after it was installed. The limitations of the system hindered Anchor's ability to develop new products. Ultimately the company's management was forced to go outside the firm for data-processing support.

Human resource management (HRM) involves the operations support procedures and practices that recruit, select, and reward the human component of the organization, the employees. Every person who contributes either directly or indirectly to the firm's output must have the support of the human resource management function. If HRM procedures and practices improve employees' dedication and competence, then they are sources of competitive strength for the firm. The absence of adequate HRM capabilities can cause organization members to become unproductive and dissatisfied.

Informational Capabilities All sources of information that help the firm compete effectively in its product-markets are known as informational capabilities. Some capabilities relate to external information about the firm's environment—its competitors and its markets. An organization that is good at gathering information about market trends and competitor activity has an advantage over other firms in the industry. Additional informational capabilities pertain to the management information system that the organization uses to communicate within and among work units. An efficient and effective internal information system, whether automated or manual, can reduce mistakes and help make the organization more responsive to its environment.[6]

As an example, the Goodyear Corporation has an extensive international communications network with over 40 dedicated circuits devoted to the transmission of corporate information of various types. International market data are sent to manufacturing facilities worldwide to quickly adjust production to demand in each country. Information on the most recent technological advances of international competitors is forwarded instantly to corporate headquarters. This allows Goodyear to quickly formulate a response to the new competitive threat. Test data from testing facilities around the world are sent to the main laboratory for analysis. Through these and many other uses, the Goodyear communication network is a source of competitive strength as it helps strategic managers stay informed about developments in the company's vast international business arena.

Organizational Capabilities An SBU's organizational capabilities can affect external exchanges that the firm has with its task environment or internal relationships among organizational units or individuals. An external exchange capability may be the firm's reputation as an industry leader in new-product technology or its influence as the industry price leader. The firm may be well known for high-quality products, which gives it a competitive advantage. Toyota and IBM enjoy such a reputation in automobiles and mainframe computers, respectively.

Another exchange capability relates to the strength of the firm's position within the industry in terms of customer goodwill. Customers favor some products even though they do not possess any technological advantage. For example, Volvo automobiles are renowned for their reliability and long life, even though industry studies show that other autos last just as long as Volvos.

External capabilities can provide the firm with a competitive advantage through enhancing its strength in the marketplace. The firm's image, prestige, and flexibility within the industry often allow it to recruit top managers and employees[7] or obtain more favorable terms from its suppliers. The reputation of one SBU may spread to become an external capability for another SBU. For example, Boeing Airframe's reputation as a reliable defense contractor, which stems from its successful development of the B-52 bomber, has carried over to its commercial aircraft sales.

Like external exchange strengths, internal relationship capabilities can be a source of organizational strength. The organization's internal structural design may help it to be extremely responsive to its customers, thereby strengthening its competitive position. Its culture may encourage productivity and commitment, resulting in low turnover and lower costs of production.

Exchange and relationship organizational capabilities can also be weaknesses. A high level of goodwill with customers can allow a company to charge a premium for its products. However, customer ill will can mean that the firm cannot sell its products even at below cost. The same can be said for internal organizational capabilities. A structural design and culture that frustrates customers and employees will result in the firm becoming noncompetitive.

The organization's managerial, technical, informational, and organizational capabilities help determine the strengths that the firm can use to take advantage of opportunities. Weak or absent capabilities increase the likelihood that the firm will fail to exploit opportunities or will be threatened by environmental conditions that it does not have the capabilities to recognize or avoid.

Location of Business-Level Strategic Capabilities

To determine which capabilities provide a strategic advantage, the manager must know where to look for the firm's capabilities. Primary capabilities are located in five areas that have the greatest effect on the competitive strengths of the firm:

1. Marketing
2. Research and development
3. Production and operations
4. Finance and accounting
5. General management

These five areas have the potential for all four types of capabilities: technical, managerial, informational, and organizational. Figure 3.2 shows these capabilities located in an organization's finance and accounting unit.

Marketing Capabilities associated with the marketing function are price, promotion, and distribution of the product as well as characteristics of the product itself. Table 3.1 lists several marketing capabilities with competitive consequences for the firm. These capabilities include, among others, the breadth of the product mix and the extent of product protection. A business with a broad product mix is usually protected from the threat of the decline of a single primary product. Patent protection for a

Figure 3.2 Organizational Capabilities in One Functional Unit of an Organization

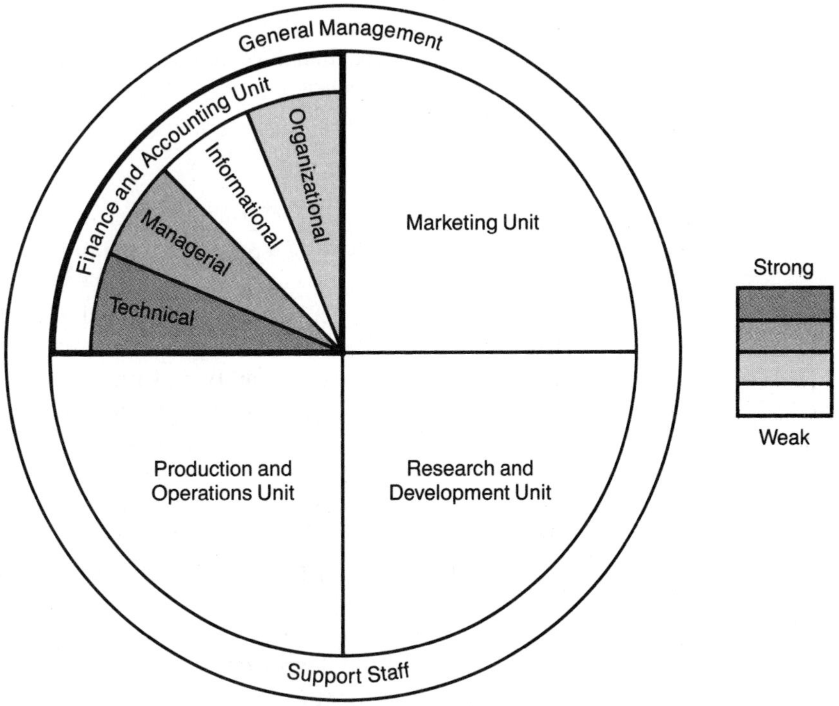

Table 3.1 Marketing Capabilities

Capability	Strength	Weakness
1. Product mix	Broad	Narrow
2. Concentration of sales to few products or customers	No	Yes
3. Market share	High	Low
4. Market research	Strong	Weak
5. Product service		
a. Function	Good	Poor
b. Reputation	Good	Poor
6. Product development		
a. Function	Leads market	Follows
b. Reputation	Good	Poor
7. Patent protection for product or process	Yes	No
8. Life cycle of products	Balanced	Unbalanced
9. Distribution systems	Strong	Weak
10. Sales organization		
a. Size	Appropriate	Too large or small
b. Experience	Qualified	Unqualified
c. Reputation	Good	Poor
d. Ability	High	Low
11. Customer goodwill and brand loyalty	High	Low
12. Promotion	Successful	Unsuccessful
13. Pricing	Competitive	Too high or low
14. Product stability over economic cycles	Good	Poor
15. Degree of differentiation of products	High	Low

very popular product ensures the differentiation of the product and protects its competitive advantage.

Marketing capabilities can be either strengths or weaknesses. For example, having a strong market research capability within the firm will give the organization an edge over competitors, whereas a weak capability will limit the organization's ability to act on market opportunities. To measure whether each of the marketing capabilities in Table 3.1 is a strength or a weakness, the manager ranks it on the continuum in the right hand column. If the assessment of the capability is toward the left side of the continuum, the capability is most likely a strength. If the manager's assessment is more toward the right, then the capability is probably a weakness.

Two marketing capabilities of particular importance are product stability over economic cycles and the degree of product differentiation. If the business has products that do not follow the standard ups and downs of the economic cycle, then it can be confident of continuous revenue flows from those products. Likewise, if its products are highly differentiated from competitors' products, the firm can generate a higher margin on the product, which can fund the development of new products.

Research and Development The firm's research and development (R&D) capabilities can directly and indirectly affect the organization's competitive position. Strategic managers need to monitor their R&D function to determine the success ratio of innovations produced to innovations profitably brought to market. A high ratio qualifies the R&D capability as a strength that the business can use to obtain a competitive advantage. Table 3.2 lists several R&D capabilities and a scale for measuring whether they are strengths or weaknesses. The firm's senior management can use these capabilities as a guide to evaluate the organization's position in terms of R&D.

An R&D function may be creative but produce few products that contribute to the organization's product mix and profitability. This type of R&D unit can be a financial drain on the firm, provide it little competitive advantage, and even jeopardize its survival. This is particularly a problem when competitors have high success ratios. The Strategic Application "The Polaroid Company" describes how Polaroid, under the direction of Edwin H. Land, was envied across the industry for its R&D capabilities. However, this strength became a weakness when new-product development, rather than the production and sale of products, became the goal.

R&D capabilities can indirectly strengthen the firm's competitive position by building a reputation in new-product development that can attract customers. Hewlett-Packard, for example, has a reputation for innovation in scientific calculators. Most engineers and scientists look first to HP for the latest in scientific calculating instruments. This reputation became a weakness when HP attempted to enter the market for home personal computers. Consumers perceived HP's product as too

Table 3.2 R&D Capabilities

Capability	Strength	Weakness
1. Basic and applied product research competencies		
a. Department operations	Efficient	Inefficient
b. Department reputation	Good	Poor
2. Process research competencies		
a. Timely introduction of new processes	Yes	No
b. Cost-effective	Yes	No
3. Effective use of resources	High return on investment	Low return on investment
4. Physical facilities		
a. Development laboratories	Good	Poor
b. Testing laboratories	Good	Poor
5. Organization of R&D unit	Facilitates innovation	Hinders innovation
6. Communication and coordination between R&D and operations and marketing	Good	Poor
7. Quality of technological forecasting	Good	Poor
8. Success ratio of new product innovations to products brought to market	High	Low

STRATEGIC APPLICATIONS

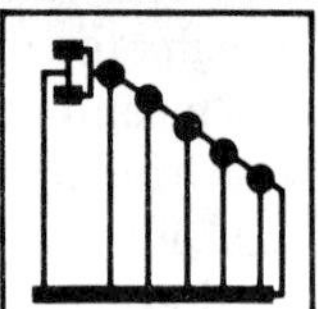

The Polaroid Company

Under the leadership of its founder, Edwin Land, the Polaroid Company was driven by its research development efforts. The company's philosophy, modeled after Land's, was based on "building a better mousetrap." Polaroid led the market from its beginnings when Land invented instant photography. The company enjoyed patent protection for its instant photography process and would develop new generations of its products to make the old products obsolete. To promote this R&D and new-product orientation within Polaroid, the company gave its R&D group a great deal of latitude.

The fortunes of the company and its founder turned for the worse when the Polarvision instant movie camera and projection system were introduced with much fanfare in the mid-1970s. Land's R&D unit believed that customers would jump at the chance to make home movies and immediately play them back for viewing. Market research said otherwise, but Land's confidence in R&D convinced him that the market research was inaccurate. As it turned out, customers were not prepared to pay the price of the Polaroid camera and projector merely to see silent moving images of their family. After a great deal of expense, the product was removed from the market, and Polaroid took a $68.5 million write-off in 1979. Polaroid learned that its R&D capability was a strength only if the company used it to develop products that could be economically produced and sold and that consumers were willing to purchase.

technical for the nonscientific user. On the other hand, the smaller scientific market readily accepted HP personal computers.

Production and Operations The organization's production and operations function is where the product is produced or the service provided. Here, all direct and support capabilities come together to create the firm's output. In this area capabilities can most directly affect the organization's competitiveness. That is, production and operations is the primary function in which cost savings and operations quality can translate directly into increased profits. Table 3.3 presents the ten primary capabilities of the production unit.

One important capability is the firm's purchasing function. The purchasing department's success in obtaining high-quality input at the best price and delivery schedule translates dollar-for-dollar into profit for the firm.[8] Therefore, this capability is a strength that provides a direct competitive advantage to help fund other projects that will contribute to the organization's long-term success.

The operations function is also where the firm can benefit from economies of scale and new process technologies. These capabilities affect the cost and quality of the product or service. SGS, a new entrant into the semiconductor manufacturing industry, recently completed a "clean" manufacturing facility that allows only one particle of dirt per million cubic feet of air to enter the room. This clean environment is one of the first such facilities in the United States and gives SGS a quality advantage over competitors. Also, the facility is designed for production runs of hundreds of thousands of units, so that the company can benefit from economies of scale. This

Table 3.3 Production and Operations Capabilities

Capabilities	Strength	Weakness
1. Lower cost of operations	Yes	No
2. Purchasing		
a. Function	Qualified	Not Qualified
b. Costs	Low	High
c. Relations with suppliers	Good	Poor
3. Capacity (plant and equipment)		
a. Sufficient to meet demand	Yes	No
b. Modern and efficient	Yes	No
c. Maintains high quality standards	Yes	No
4. Location of facilities		
a. For transportation	Centrally located	Remote
b. For experienced employees	Good	Poor
c. For facilities costs	Low cost/sq. ft.	High cost/sq. ft.
5. Inventory		
a. Scheduling	Efficient	Not Efficient
b. Storing	Low costs	High costs
c. Using	Responsive	Not Responsive
6. Maintenance		
a. Adequately staffed	Yes	No
b. Modern	Yes	No
7. Use of economies of scale	Yes	No
8. Use of modern technologies (e.g., robotics)	Extensive	Little
9. Effective use of subcontracting	Frequently	Seldom
10. Extent of value added	Much	Minimal

is the only way that SGS could competitively price its products in a very price-sensitive market. Without both capabilities, SGS would have little hope of a triumphant entry into the industry.

Finance and Accounting Some organizations have an easier time attracting financing than others. The ability to develop relationships with sources of debt and equity financing can be an organization's primary strategic strength. All products or services eventually reach the maturity and decline stages of their life cycles. To guarantee its long-term survival, a firm must recognize and exploit new opportunities. The inability to secure financing to take advantage of these opportunities can be a serious weakness.

In addition, the finance function is responsible for monitoring the organization's vulnerability to an unfriendly takeover. In recent years, corporate takeovers have increased in frequency. A new type of celebrity has emerged, the corporate raider. T. Boone Pickens, Jr., former CEO of Mesa Petroleum and celebrated corporate raider, has perhaps been the most famous of the raiders.[9] Because of this new environmental threat, many top-level managers have reevaluated their organizations' financial capabilities to look for any weakness that would increase the firm's takeover potential.

Another financial capability is the financial controls that the firm has in place to guide it toward accomplishment of strategic goals. These control systems are the key methods used to determine progress toward achieving objectives. Effective financial controls not only monitor the movement toward an objective but also signal when acceptable limits have been exceeded and trigger short-term corrective action.

General Management In addition to the functional units of marketing, R&D, production and operations, and finance, staff units within the organization can provide strategic strengths. These units, such as human resources, legal, community relations, and strategic analysis, support the functional units by providing information or maintaining coordination and control. In insurance companies, for example, the legal department monitors the legislation that affects the financial services industry and works with marketing to develop new products that take advantage of the most recent laws. Such a capability can provide a competitive strength.

Many other aspects of the general management function can help or impair the firm in its efforts to compete effectively in its task environment. One such capability is the strategic management of the organization as measured by the track record of current managers in strategically directing the firm and their visibility in the business environment. Highly visible managers can make it easier for the organization to attract financing or customers. They can also attract unwanted attention from stakeholders such as government regulators. Carl Icahn, CEO of TWA Inc., is a famous, visible corporate raider. His activities have brought much unwanted attention to TWA.

One of the capabilities that provides the most direct benefit to the firm is the contacts of the strategic manager. Many prior high-ranking military commanders and federal government officials are hired as executives for firms engaged in defense contracting. The influential contacts of these individuals provide the firm with strengths that may not be available to competitors.

Corporate-Level Strategic Capabilities

Diversified organizations are engaged in more than one business. Depending on their degree of diversification and strategic goals, they will build a portfolio of more or less related businesses. Corporate-level capabilities consist of the capabilities of the combination of SBUs that make up this portfolio of businesses.

If the enterprise is diversified with several SBUs operating as profit centers under a single headquarters or corporate umbrella, then internal strategic capabilities can operate at the corporate level as well as the SBU level. Senior managers of multiple-SBU organizations must understand how the company's different businesses provide capabilities that are the sources of competitive strengths. Single-SBU managers must analyze the business's internal strengths to determine where they can gain a competitive advantage in their single-business area.

Corporate-level strategic capabilities fall into three categories: general, portfolio-related, and financial. General capabilities include the strengths that senior management provides to the firm and the characteristics of the firm's businesses. Portfolio-related capabilities are the time, life cycle, and risk advantages that diversification into multiple businesses brings to the firm. Finally, financial capabilities give the organization the strength to adapt to opportunities and threats in its environment.

General Capabilities

Managers, including members of the board of directors, provide strategic capabilities to the organization. Chapter 2 discussed management as a source of external information for the organization. This ability to scan and interpret the firm's environment is a function of the managers' experience and knowledge. As long as the business situation remains similar to the situation in which the managers gained their knowledge and experience, managers can contribute an important strength to the success of the organization. If conditions change but managers do not, a mismatch is created that becomes a weakness.

This type of mismatch apparently occurred for Valley National Bank. According to Donald Crowley of Keefe, Bruyette and Woods Inc., a San Francisco-based brokerage firm, "Like many organizations with a long and august history of growth and success, Valley National Bank in many respects has developed a deep bureaucracy that is resistant to change, even when directed from the top." The bank found itself facing increased competition. This combination of a changing competitive situation and managers who were resistant to change resulted in the removal of three senior executives.[10]

The board of directors of a corporation can also be a source of general managerial capabilities. Because of the increasing frequency of shareholder lawsuits charging directors with failure to oversee the operations of the firm, increased surveillance of boards by the Securities and Exchange Commission, and Congress's passage of the 1977 Foreign Corrupt Practices Act, boards of directors have become more involved in the strategic management of the corporation. This more active role for directors can be a strength if they are selected for the specific capabilities they bring to the firm. Outside directors may be senior executives in firms that provide important resources to the corporation. For example, bankers, government or former government officials, and university presidents and deans are frequently selected for boards of local corporations. The relationships that these directors have with the corporation can be important strengths if the resources they control ever become scarce. A banker on the board can be helpful if the corporation needs a new loan. Relationships developed through board membership can be important strengths for the corporation.

General capabilities also include the characteristics of the businesses in the firm's portfolio. Based on his classification of organizations according to type of business and degree of diversification, Rumelt discovered that organizations that were diversified into related businesses had the highest financial performance.[11] This is consistent with the idea of synergy, which suggests that similar businesses can share common resources resulting in the whole being greater than the sum of the parts ($2 + 2 = 5$). Related businesses can often benefit from shared staff functions, shared marketing and distribution, or shared production facilities. If the businesses in the firm's portfolio are synergistically related, the organization usually has an advantage over firms with unrelated businesses that must duplicate all functions for each business.

Portfolio-Related Capabilities

Some capabilities at the corporate level involve relationships among the businesses in the organization's portfolio. A carefully constructed portfolio is a strategic strength because it helps the firm maintain a long-term competitive advantage by ensuring that new businesses grow and mature as older businesses decline.

Life Cycles Knowing when products, businesses, and industries reach the various stages of their lives is a major part of planning at the corporate level. To take full advantage of portfolio-related capabilities, the manager must understand the product, firm, and industry life cycles for each business in the portfolio.

Product Life Cycle The product life cycle depicts the birth, growth, and decline of a single product in the firm's portfolio of products. The first graph in Figure 3.3 shows the standard representation of a product life cycle. The initial stage is the embryonic or introductory stage. This is the stage at which the firm first conceives and develops the product or service. Then, during the growth stage, the product or service experiences rapid growth in volume and usually market share. It is here that competitors are attracted to the market and price competition begins. During the maturity stage, volume starts to level off as the market becomes saturated and less efficient competitors are driven out. Finally, a product enters the decline stage; demand begins to decline as new or substitute products gain consumer favor. Organizations are continually trying to revitalize products or services that have reached the decline stage in an attempt to push them back into the growth mode.

Firm Life Cycle Firms typically have a five-stage life cycle, as shown in the middle graph of Figure 3.3. The initial stage, the entrepreneurial stage, begins when an entrepreneur starts a new venture to introduce a product or service to an existing market or to develop a new market for an existing product. This stage requires that one or a few entrepreneurs nurture an idea through its initial development.

If the new firm successfully negotiates the development stage, then it will enter the growth stage. Growth is characterized by increased demand for the product or service, which usually stimulates growth in personnel. Most important, the firm reaches a point at which the skills required to manage an established firm are no longer the entrepreneurial skills that were necessary to start it.

The maturity stage is as far as the firm can go on its initial product or service. Once demand for the firm's first product starts to level off and competition becomes more intense, the firm must develop new products or new markets to return to a growth condition. If the firm fails to develop a new product or market, it will be overtaken by the competition and end as one of the 95 percent of new businesses that fail during the first three years of operation.

Industry Life Cycle Like products and firms, industries experience birth, growth, and decline. As shown in Figure 3.3, they typically start as fledgling offshoots of other industries. Such an offshoot is created by the invention of a revolutionary new product. An example is the semiconductor industry, which started as an offshoot of the elec-

Figure 3.3 Life Cycles

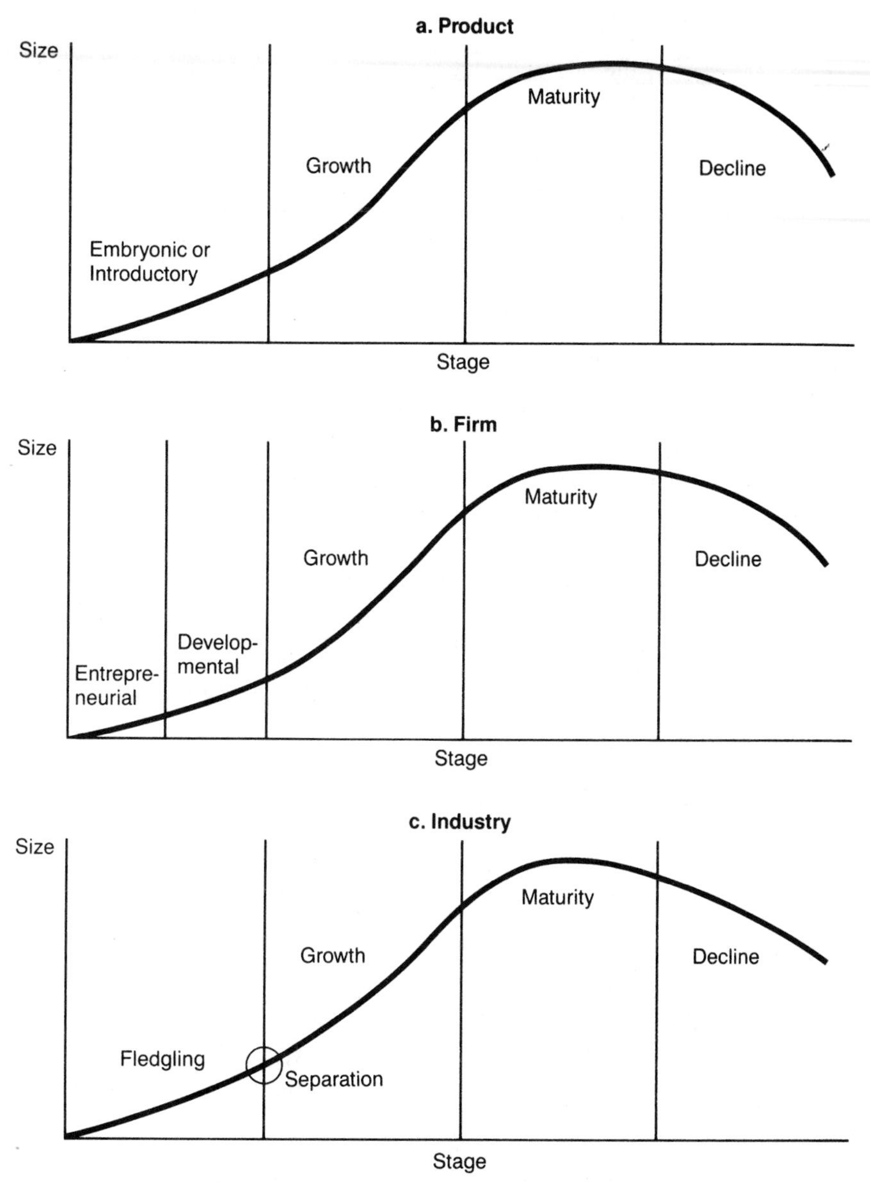

tronics industry. If the new product replaces an obsolete product, it will be absorbed into the original industry. However, if the new product is sufficiently different from existing products and if some level of demand remains for the parent industry's current products, then a new industry will emerge. If demand is strong enough, firms in the new industry will spin off from the parent industry. The spinoff is followed by total separation from the original industry. The new industry is recognized by both insiders and outsiders as a distinct group of firms focused on a unique new line of products or services.

If the new industry survives the separation, it will enter a period of growth in which industry sales and capacity increase as new firms are attracted to the industry by the promise of high profits and growth. Industries grow as long as the demand for the product or service continues. When increased capacity enables supply to catch up with demand, profits decline and the industry may enter the maturity and even the decline phase. Again, the semiconductor industry provides an excellent example. Profit margins during the late 1970s and early 1980s were averaging over 25 percent. These profits were obtained in a period of 50 percent growth for early entrants into the industry. By 1982 several additional major U.S. manufacturers had entered the market. This created excess manufacturing capacity, which led to an industry slump over the next several years.

Until this point, the new industry has been a one-product industry. The maturing of the single product requires that the industry develop new products to maintain its growth. If new products are not developed, the industry will mature and decline along with its product.

Portfolio Analysis Knowledge of life cycles helps the manager understand how a portfolio of diversified businesses can be a corporate-level strength for the firm. Firms that have a strategic goal of long-term profitability will build a diversified and balanced portfolio, one that consists of businesses that are in various stages of their life cycles.

Businesses in the developmental and growth stages of their life cycles currently use more resources than they generate but are sources of future revenues. This strength ensures the firm's future viability. A portfolio of businesses primarily in the developmental and growth stages of their life cycles is appropriate for a strategic goal of high growth. This portfolio also can result in industry dominance for businesses when the market matures.

Businesses in the mature and early decline stages strengthen the firm's position by providing revenues for current operations and development of newer products and businesses. A portfolio of successful, mature businesses is therefore associated with a strategic goal of high short-term profits. Organizations in this position frequently have large cash reserves that can help during economic downturns.

A portfolio that reflects the strategic goals of the organization is a source of competitive strengths. An inappropriate portfolio for the firm's strategic goals or improper goals for prevailing business conditions will be weaknesses for the firm. Managers must be able to analyze the organization's current portfolio of businesses to determine their fit with its existing strategic goals.

The analysis of corporate-level capabilities can also determine the long-term competitiveness of the multiple-SBU organization's portfolio of businesses. Each business should reduce long-term risk by contributing to the effectiveness and survival of the organization. However, since SBUs are at different stages of their life cycles, not all will contribute equally to reducing long-term risk. Therefore, an organization's portfolio should combine businesses that reduce long-term risk because they may become major contributors to profitability and businesses that ensure short-term survival because they are currently profitable.

The firm's portfolio should provide competitive strength and reflect the firm's strategic goals. To make sure that the portfolio is consistent with strategic goals, the manager must analyze the firm's current business portfolio. Three approaches that are frequently used to determine the firm's corporate-level, portfolio-related strategic capabilities are the Boston Consulting Group (BCG) growth-share matrix, the General Electric (GE) planning grid, and Hofer's product/market-evolution matrix.

BCG Growth-Share Matrix One of the first uses of a portfolio approach to corporate-level analysis was developed by the Boston Consulting Group (BCG). The BCG growth-share matrix suggests that the two most important factors to consider in evaluating the strength of an SBU within a portfolio are its relative market share and the growth rate of the market it serves. These two market-related dimensions are combined to form the four-cell matrix shown in Figure 3.4.

The **market growth rate**, plotted on the vertical axis, is usually measured as the market's growth in dollar or unit volume over a specified period of time. Businesses

Figure 3.4 BCG Growth-Share Matrix

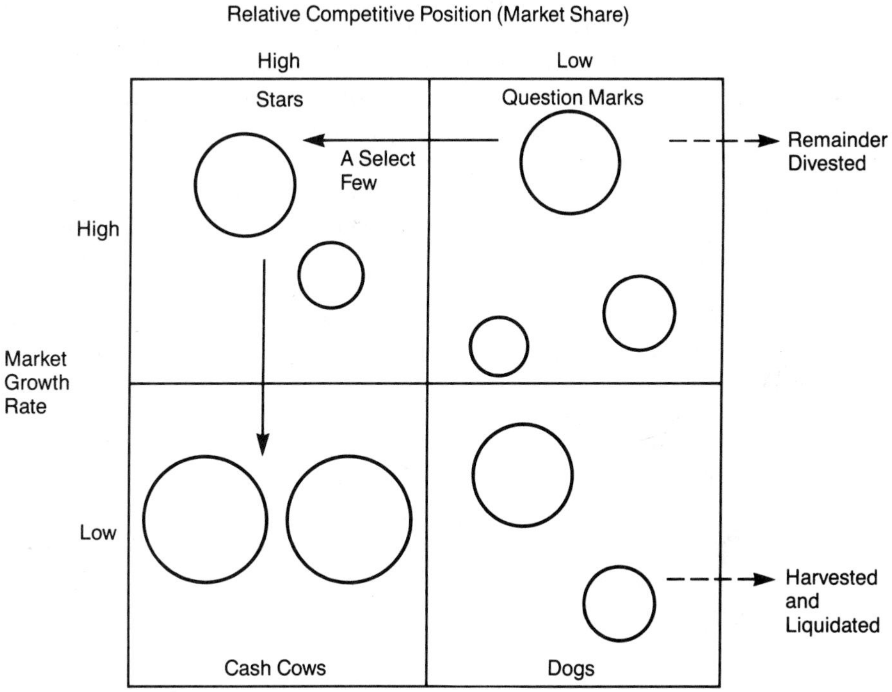

Source: Adapted with permission from *Long Range Planning*, February 1977, Barry Hedley, "Strategy and the Business Portfolio," p. 10. Copyright 1977 Pergamon Press PLC.

experiencing market growth greater than 10 percent are in a high-growth market, whereas less than 10 percent is considered low market growth. This standard is somewhat arbitrary and may be changed for different industries.

The second dimension, the **relative competitive position**, is plotted on the horizontal axis. The axis is divided into high and low, with the midpoint typically set at either 1.0 or 1.5. The SBU's relative market share is calculated by dividing its market share by the market share of the next largest competitor. If the firm is not the industry leader, then the market share of the dominant firm in the industry is used as the denominator. If the firm is the market share leader in the industry, the market share for the second largest firm in the industry is used.

This type of matrix analysis frequently incorporates additional information. For example, in Figure 3.4 each circle is a separate SBU, perhaps operating in a different industry. The size of the circle represents the percentage of total corporate revenue generated by the SBU. Thus, the two SBUs in the lower left-hand cell of Figure 3.4 generate the largest percentage of the organization's revenues.

The BCG matrix recommends a different strategy for businesses in each cell. Businesses in the upper right cell are labeled question marks, because they are in high-growth areas but have relatively small market shares. This could lead managers to choose one of two different strategies. The industry could be in the fledgling stage of its life cycle and about to experience rapid growth. If this is the case, the firm's strategic management team may choose to invest in the SBU to try to capture the dominant position in the industry. Or the team could choose to forgo the opportunity and divest of the SBU at a time when it can be sold at a premium. Regardless of the strategy chosen, the intention is to move SBUs out of the question mark cell either by investing in them to move them into a high-market-share cell or by divesting and removing them from the firm's portfolio.[12]

Firms in the upper left cell are classified as stars. These SBUs have relatively large market shares in growth industries. Businesses that are in the star category are vital to the future profitability of the enterprise. The strategy associated with this cell is one of continued investment to maintain or expand the current large market share. Stars are resource users that require the infusion of capital to meet the demand of the growing market.

The lower left cell is labeled cash cows. SBUs in this cell are in industries in which the market growth rate has slowed to below 10 percent. These are typically businesses in mature markets with little growth. However, they have a large, profitable share of that market. The organization can reduce its investment for expansion and benefit from the revenues generated from being dominant in the industry. The strategies appropriate in this condition are market penetration and cost reduction in order to maintain or increase market share and profitability. Revenues produced by the firm's cash cows are used to fund star and future star (question mark) SBUs to develop them into the next generation of cash cows.

SBUs in the low-growth and low-market-share cell are referred to as dogs. Some of the organization's businesses may be in this category for a number of reasons. The SBU could have started as a question mark that was insufficiently funded and therefore never achieved star status. It could have been a cash cow that has declined to the point of losing market dominance to a competitor. Or it could have been a part of another firm that was recently acquired by the organization. The strategy typically recommended for businesses in this cell is divestment. Recently, some strategic management researchers have shown that it is possible to operate these businesses profitably.[13] The SBU must be extremely well managed and cost effective and have enough surplus working capital to outlast weaker competitors. In this situation, even though the market is shrinking, the SBU is gaining market share. However, this set of conditions is rare, which suggests that divestment is generally most suitable for dog SBUs.

General Electric Planning Grid Another matrix approach, the GE planning grid, has three distinct advantages over the BCG growth-share matrix: It uses multiple factors for the two dimensions or axes. It uses nine rather than four cells. And, it avoids negative labels. Figure 3.5 illustrates the important characteristics of the GE approach. The horizontal dimension is labeled industry or product-market attractiveness, and

Figure 3.5 GE Planning Grid

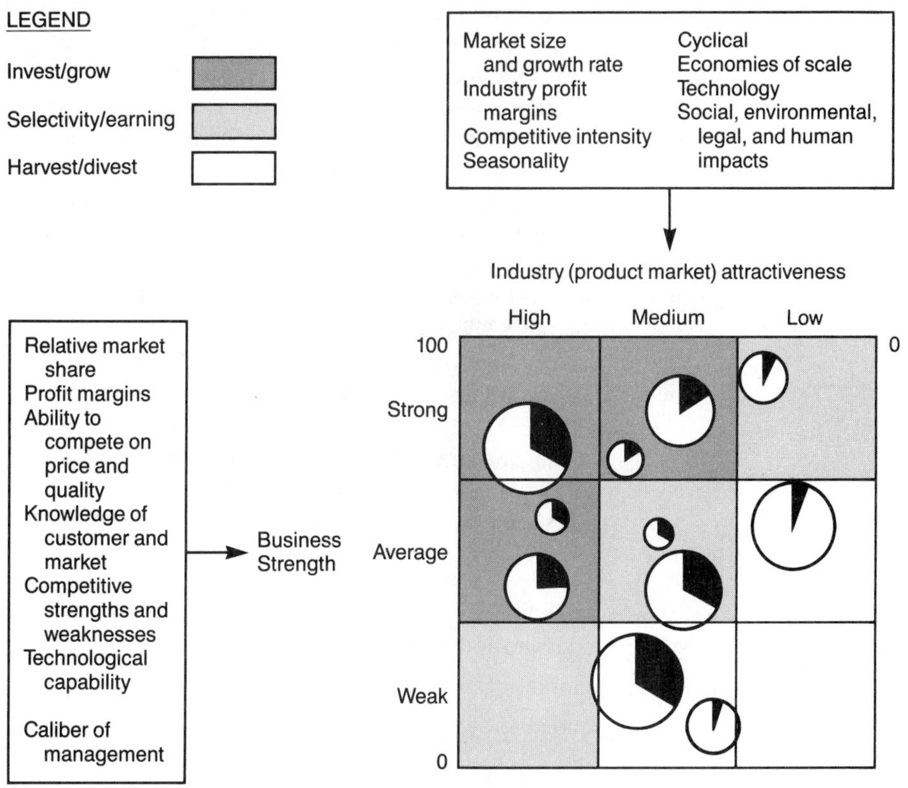

LEGEND
Invest/grow
Selectivity/earning
Harvest/divest

Market size and growth rate
Industry profit margins
Competitive intensity
Seasonality
Cyclical
Economies of scale
Technology
Social, environmental, legal, and human impacts

Industry (product market) attractiveness
High Medium Low
100 0

Relative market share
Profit margins
Ability to compete on price and quality
Knowledge of customer and market
Competitive strengths and weaknesses
Technological capability
Caliber of management

Business Strength

Strong
Average
Weak
0

the vertical dimension indicates the relevant strengths of the SBU. These dimensions are each broken into three levels, which yield nine cells.

The **industry attractiveness** dimension includes market growth, as does the BCG matrix. However, it also incorporates other competitive factors such as the average industry profit margin, number and size of competitors, seasonal and cyclical demand trends, barriers to entry (such as economies of scale present in the industry and protected technological advantages), and other factors that characterize the industry. Each SBU is rated high, medium, or low in terms of the attractiveness of its industry or product-market and placed in the appropriate cell in the grid.

A similar procedure is used to locate the SBUs on the **business strength** dimension. This dimension includes the BCG factor of relative market share, as well as several other potential strengths of the SBU: the SBU's history of profit margins; the demonstrated ability to compete on the basis of price and quality; the SBU's knowledge of the customer and market; a list of the SBU's competitive strengths and weaknesses; the SBU's use of modern and reliable technology; and the proven capabilities of the SBU's management. Again, each SBU is located on this axis as weak, average, or strong in terms of business strengths. This combination of the SBU's location on the two axes will indicate its position on the grid.

Once the SBU is located on the GE grid, the manager can determine the balance of the organization's portfolio and the most appropriate strategy for its various businesses. The strategies are invest/grow, selectivity/earning, and harvest/divest. The invest/grow strategy directs the firm to expend resources on these businesses to build a high market share and dominant position in the industry. Selectivity/earning as a strategy suggests that the manager should selectively designate businesses with high industry attractiveness but weak business strengths for funding to build upon their strengths. Likewise, businesses in the low-attractiveness but high-business-strength cell should be selectively evaluated for retention as an earnings generator or for divestment. Harvest/divest is a strategy that the firm uses when it wishes to dispose of businesses that are low in industry attractiveness and business strength. These strategies are applied to SBUs that are located in the lower right cells of the grid as shown on Figure 3.5. Although the GE grid contains nine cells, three cells are combined for the purpose of specifying a strategy.

As with the BCG matrix, the size of the circles in Figure 3.5 represents the relative percentage of total corporate revenue contributed by the SBU. In addition, the circles have wedges drawn inside to illustrate the market share of the SBU within its industry. Thus, the figure showing the GE Grid can provide four important items of information to the executive:

1. An indication of each SBU's competitive position
2. Relative contribution to total corporate revenue
3. Relative market share
4. Recommended strategy for each SBU

Many strategic managers have expressed a preference for the GE grid over the BCG matrix.[14] Nevertheless, it displays several limitations. The GE grid is subject to the strategic manager's interpretation of the appropriate industry segment or product market, as is the BCG matrix. Although it increases the number of cells to nine, it reduces the grid to three categories for the purpose of specifying strategies. Also, it can be used only to classify SBUs and does not guide the manager in the selection of businesses to introduce into the portfolio. Finally, the GE grid adds only one strategy to the two indicated in the BCG matrix, which may restrict the applicability of this approach in today's complex environment.

Life Cycles and Corporate-Level Capabilities Two other perspectives of corporate-level capabilities that have gained recent attention directly incorporate the life cycle concept into the discussion of corporate-level capabilities. The product/market-evolution matrix method, developed by Charles Hofer, looks at the **competitive position** of each business in the firm's portfolio and compares it to the stages of **product/market evolution**. The combination of these two axes yields the 15-cell matrix shown in Figure 3.6.[15] The circles represent the relative size of each industry in which SBUs

Figure 3.6 Hofer Product Market-Evolution Matrix

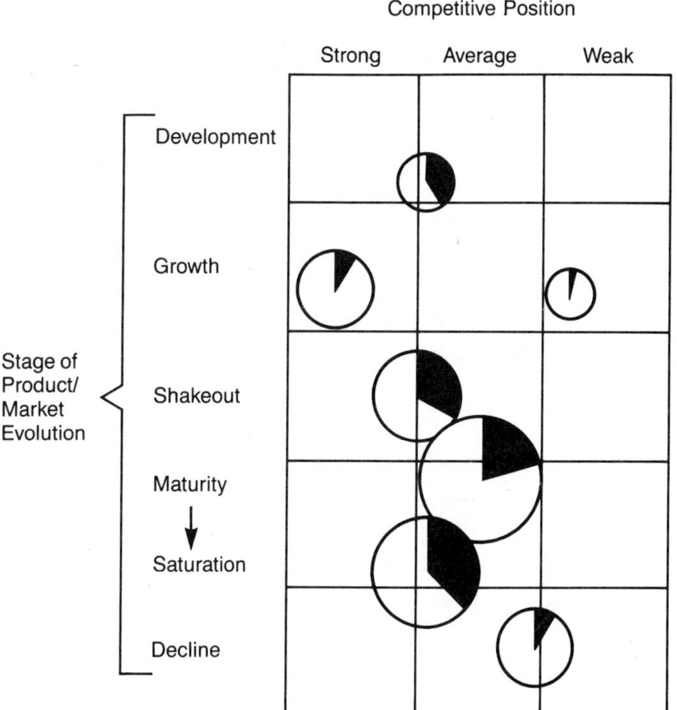

Source: C. W. Hofer, "Conceptual Constructs for Formulating Corporate and Business Strategies" (Dover, Massachusetts: Lord Publishing Company, BP-0041, p. 3). Copyright © 1977 by C. W. Hofer. Used by permission.

are located. As with the GE Grid, the wedge within each circle illustrates the market share that the SBU holds for its market within its industry.

A fourth portfolio approach to analyzing corporate-level capabilities incorporates the product-market life cycle into the BCG growth-share matrix directly by expanding it from four to eight cells as shown in Figure 3.7.[16] Infants are product-markets that are in the early stages of development. In this case, relative market share has no meaning, and so no distinction is made in the matrix. Infants are always resource users and contribute nothing to the firm's cash flow. The middle four cells are identical to the BCG matrix and appear in the growth and maturity stages of the life cycle.

The product-life-cycle-portfolio matrix differs substantially from the previously described approaches in its bottom two cells. It includes SBUs in a negative-growth market that are in the decline stage of their life cycle. High-market-share "war horses" can continue to generate profits for the firm with little in the way of additional investment. These SBUs should not be divested until they can no longer justify their cost of capital. Dodos, unlike dogs that can generate a positive cash flow under certain favorable conditions, should be immediately divested.

This approach suffers from many of the same limitations as the BCG matrix because of its close similarity. However, it has the advantage of directly including all of the stages of the product-market life cycle.

Financial Capabilities

For an organization to build and maintain a portfolio, it must have enough financial resources to acquire or develop new businesses. Therefore, the firm's financial capabilities determine, to a great extent, its ability to pursue corporate-level strategies. If the firm is financially strong, it can manage its portfolio in a way that provides a competitive advantage. For example, Ford Motor Company has $10 million in cash reserves from several years of industry-leading profitability. With financial strength, Ford can acquire major firms in other industries. This results in a competitive advantage from the potential for immediate industry dominance through acquisition. A firm with fewer financial capabilities might be forced to acquire a weaker competitor in other industries.

Analysis Methods

When choosing to enter any competitive arena, top management must be aware of the capabilities at its disposal. Three methods for identifying these capabilities as a basis for strategic decisions are the strategic capabilities profile, strategic capabilities analysis, and SWOT analysis.

Strategic Capabilities Profile

Armed with an understanding of the type and location of the firm's capabilities, the manager is prepared to develop a **strategic capabilities profile**. This gives the manager

Figure 3.7 Product-Life-Cycle-Portfolio Matrix

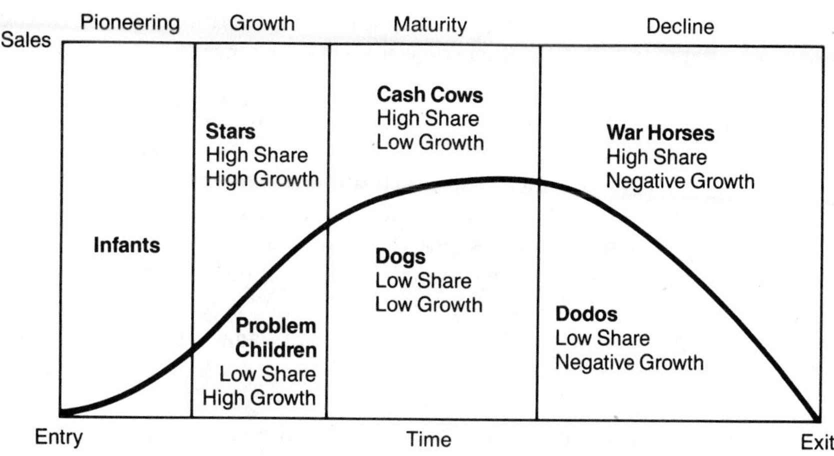

a. Combined life-cycle-product-portfolio concepts

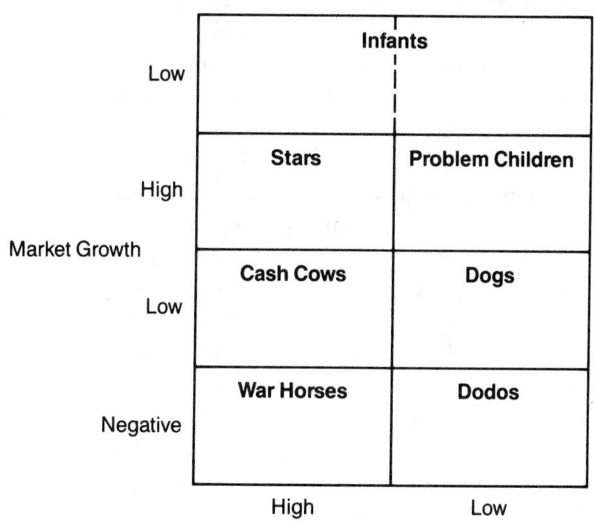

b. Product-life-cycle-portfolio matrix

Source: Reprinted with permission from *Long Range Planning*, Journal No. 358, Vol. 15, No. 6, 1982, Hiram C. Backsdale and Clyde E. Harris, Jr., "Portfolio Analysis and the Product Life Cycle," pp. 74–83. Copyright 1982 Pergamon Press PLC.

a description of the strengths and weaknesses of the firm in terms of its relative position in the industry and its internal capabilities. The strategic capabilities profile consists of techniques that have been used extensively in strategic management in the past,[17] as well as some novel approaches that have recently been introduced.

Analysis of External Exchange Capabilities The relative position that the firm occupies in its industry is known as **exchange capability**. Some firms, because of the nature of the industry or their dominant position within the industry, enjoy protection from competitive pressures. This protection operates as a strength for these firms. Other organizations lack this protection and are vulnerable to outside competitive forces. The manager should conduct an analysis of exchange capabilities to determine the extent to which they are present. Three techniques for analyzing exchange capabilities are the competitive industry analysis, the PIMS analysis, and the strategic advantage analysis.

Competitive Industry Analysis The competitive industry analysis looks at competitive factors in the firm's chosen markets and identifies those that give an advantage over competitors. Like the industry analysis in Chapter 2, this analysis can be separated into five forces that may limit the organization's ability to compete: forces from potential entrants, buyers, substitutes, suppliers, and competitors.[18] Figure 3.8 shows how five categories of competitive factors shield the firm from the five competitive forces. For example, competitors' efforts will be limited by high overhead costs, a slowly growing market, or easily differentiated products. Likewise, substitutes will be hard to locate if the technology of the industry is difficult to copy or protected by patents. Many potential entrants will be dissuaded by high entry costs and high customer-switching costs. Having many reliable suppliers to choose from will protect the firm from competition for a limited number of suppliers.

Protection from competitive pressures through industry-related exchange advantages may last only until new process technologies are available to overcome these shielding forces. Several years ago, high customer-switching costs protected manufacturers of large mainframe computers from competition. Many large organizations such as Honeywell and Sperry investigated the new mainframe computer market but quickly learned that IBM so dominated the market that the costs for most users to switch their computer systems were prohibitive. However, the introduction of the personal computer and standardization of operating system software reduced the importance of this external capability for most IBM competitors. Because such exchange advantages may shift, the strategic manager should review the firm's external capabilities at the beginning of each planning cycle.

PIMS Analysis In the 1960s, General Electric in conjunction with the Strategic Planning Institute embarked on a project to determine the characteristics of many of the most profitable firms in the United States. The project has become known as the Profit Impact of Marketing Strategies (PIMS) program.[19] This project produced a list of factors—such as market share, investment intensity, and product quality—proposed to be the most important in predicting the performance of an organization. The

Figure 3.8 Competitive Industry Capabilities

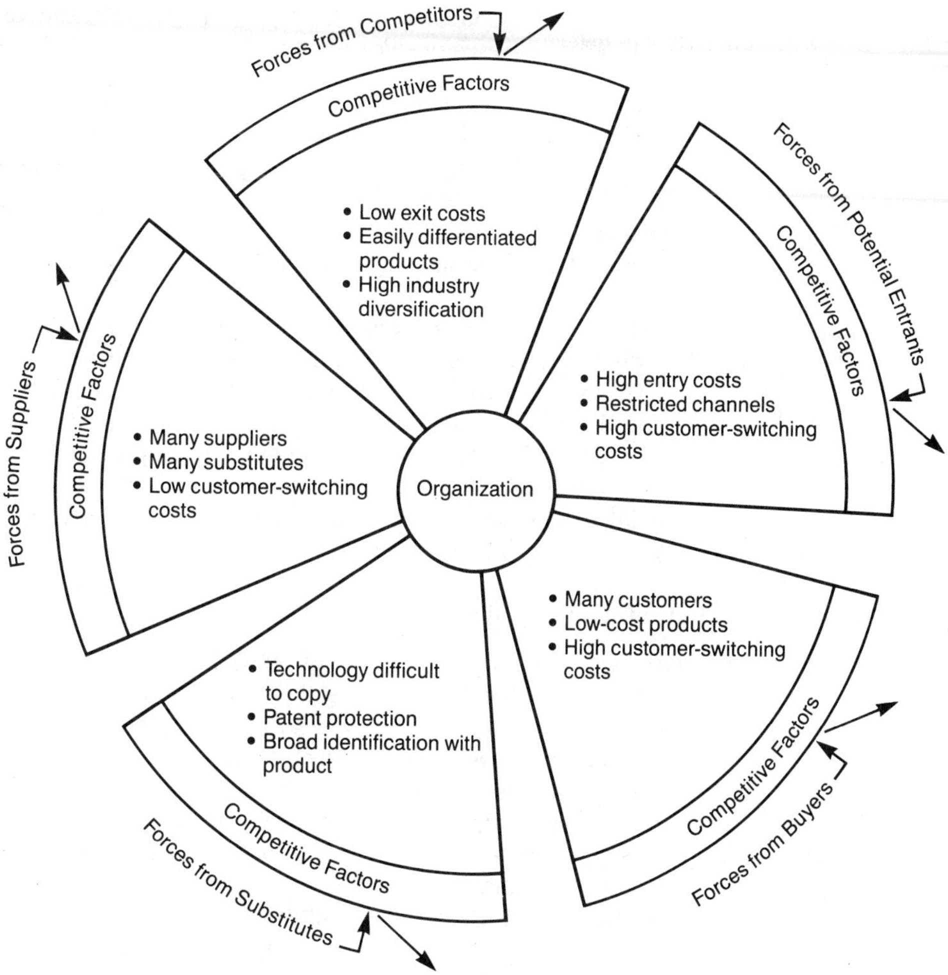

Forces from Competitors
Competitive Factors
• Low exit costs
• Easily differentiated products
• High industry diversification

Forces from Potential Entrants
Competitive Factors
• High entry costs
• Restricted channels
• High customer-switching costs

Forces from Buyers
Competitive Factors
• Many customers
• Low-cost products
• High customer-switching costs

Forces from Substitutes
Competitive Factors
• Technology difficult to copy
• Patent protection
• Broad identification with product

Forces from Suppliers
Competitive Factors
• Many suppliers
• Many substitutes
• Low customer-switching costs

Organization

Source: Adapted with permission of The Free Press, a Division of Macmillan, Inc. from *Competitive Strategy: Techniques for Analyzing Industries and Competitors* by Michael E. Porter, p. 49. Copyright © 1980 by The Free Press.

relative importance of each factor varies from industry to industry and determines the formula for success in each industry.

The PIMS data base provides a convenient method for determining relative performance within an industry. This procedure begins with obtaining the relative weightings for performance factors for the organization's industry. The firm then compares its performance on highly weighted factors to the averages for its industry. Factors for which the firm falls below the average represent capabilities that are weaknesses for the organization. Factors on which the organization is above average represent strengths. In addition, the PIMS data base can provide information on the position of competitors on the relevant factors for the industry. With this information, the manager can determine the organization's strengths or weaknesses relative to specific competitors.

An example of such a comparison is General Motors, which enjoys the strength of having the highest market share in the U.S. auto market. However, GM's share of the market declined in the late 1980s. A comparison of market shares across foreign and domestic auto manufacturers reveals that GM lost competitive ground. The wise strategic manager will use such information from the PIMS analysis to capitalize on the firm's strengths and protect it from attacks on its weaknesses.

Strategic Advantage Analysis Strategic advantage analysis involves gathering information about the relevant strengths and weaknesses of the major competitors in the industry. The firm then compares its capabilities to those of its competitors. Strengths that exceed those of any major competitor are potential advantages. Weaknesses greater than those of major competitors pose a serious problem for the organization. The capabilities that are reviewed and compared include external and internal capabilities. Figure 3.9 is an example of a strategic advantage analysis for a marketing department.

Analysis of Internal Capabilities

Corporate-Level Analysis The analysis of corporate-level internal capabilities focuses on the portfolio of SBUs that make up the multiple-SBU organization. As discussed earlier in this chapter, these businesses will probably be at different stages of their respective life cycles and have different competitive characteristics. Therefore, a corporate-level analysis informs the firm about how its current portfolio of businesses is positioned to take advantage of corporate-level environmental opportunities. The more consistent the organization's portfolio is with its strategic goals, the more capable is the firm of remaining effective over the long term. Three of the most frequently used corporate-level analyses are those discussed earlier in this chapter: the BCG growth-share matrix, the GE planning grid, and Hofer's product/market-evolution matrix.

Regardless of which technique is used, a similar procedure is followed to analyze the strength of the corporation's portfolio. The following five steps apply to all of the corporate-level approaches:

1. Identify the relevant factors determining industry attractiveness (see Figure 3.5) and calculate the degree of industry attractiveness for each SBU.

2. Identify the relevant factors determining business strength (see Figure 3.5), and calculate the overall business strength for each SBU.

3. Determine the stage of the life cycle at which each SBU's products are currently operating (see Figure 3.6).

4. Locate each SBU on the matrix for the analysis approach selected (BCG, GE, or Product/market-evolution).

Figure 3.9 Strategic Advantage Analysis—Marketing

Factor	Weakness: Much Less than	Weakness: Equal to or Less than	Strength: Equal to or More than	Strength: Much Greater than
As compared to the competition, our . . .				
External				
Market share is			X	
Distribution channels are		X		
Buyer switching costs are				X
Product differentiation is				X
Internal				
Market research unit is			X	
Product mix is		X		
Completeness of product line is	X			
Protection from patents is		X		
Customer goodwill is				X
Quality reputation is				X
Service system is			X	

5. Determine the consistency of the portfolio with the firm's strategic goals, and formulate the appropriate strategy for the corporation and each SBU.

Portfolio analyses can provide the strategic manager with valuable tools to determine the organization's corporate-level capabilities. First, the manager can determine the degree of balance in the firm's portfolio of businesses. Some of the typical bases used to balance a corporation's portfolio are economic cycle, life cycle, cash posture, and relatedness/synergy.

While a balanced portfolio is not the only strategic goal that a firm may have, it is a relatively common goal because it offers many benefits to the organization. These benefits are a function of the basis for the portfolio balance. A portfolio that includes businesses with cycles counter to the general economic cycles gives the firm a source of revenue in periods of general economic decline. A mix of businesses at various stages of their life cycle helps ensure that new successful businesses will contribute to company profits in the future when currently successful businesses mature and decline. A portfolio might balance cash users and cash generators. Last, managers may wish to build a portfolio that is balanced in terms of relatedness. Some businesses would be closely related to take advantage of synergy, whereas others would be unrelated to diversify more completely. In these ways, a balanced portfolio will assure the firm of benefits over the long term.

Another benefit of portfolio analyses is that they provide the manager with information regarding appropriate strategies for various SBUs. Most important, they alert the manager to SBUs that should be considered for divestiture. In addition, these corporate-level analyses help the firm's strategic managers consider master strategies for individual SBUs.

These benefits suggest that strategic management conduct corporate-level internal strategic capabilities analyses frequently and regularly. This will furnish valuable information on the effectiveness of the organization's SBU mix. However, the ultimate success and survival of the multiple-SBU firm depends on the effective strategic management of the individual SBUs or businesses, just as the success of the single-business firm depends on its effective strategic management. Therefore, the internal capabilities of each SBU must also be reviewed to determine whether they match the demands of environmental opportunities.

Business-Level Analysis An analysis that focuses on the strengths and weaknesses of a single business or SBU is a business-level analysis. The starting point for this analysis is identification of the type and location of the business's capabilities. Six steps are required:

1. Develop a list of the organization's major capabilities.[20]
2. Evaluate each capability on the list, and label it a definite weakness, potential weakness, potential strength, or definite strength.
3. Compile the ratings for the relevant internal capabilities to obtain a profile of the firm's internal business-level capabilities.
4. Gather similar lists and ratings from other senior executives in the firm.
5. Compile the analyses of all the firm's managers to obtain the results of the business-level analysis.
6. Incorporate the business-level information into the external and corporate-level capabilities analyses to develop a complete profile of external and internal capabilities.

Constructing the Strategic Capabilities Profile The sixth step above combines the results of the external exchange and internal capabilities analyses to accurately indicate the capabilities of the organization as viewed by its senior management. Results of the strategic capabilities profile specify the organizational capabilities that are available for two fundamental purposes: to meet the current demands operating on the organization and to supply resources for exploiting new environmental opportunities.

Strategic Capabilities Analysis

The strategic capabilities analysis, a relatively new capabilities analysis developed by these authors, combines the results of the strategic capabilities profile with an analysis of current organizational demands and the requirements of new markets. The method of this analysis is illustrated in Figure 3.10.

Figure 3.10 Strategic Capabilities Analysis

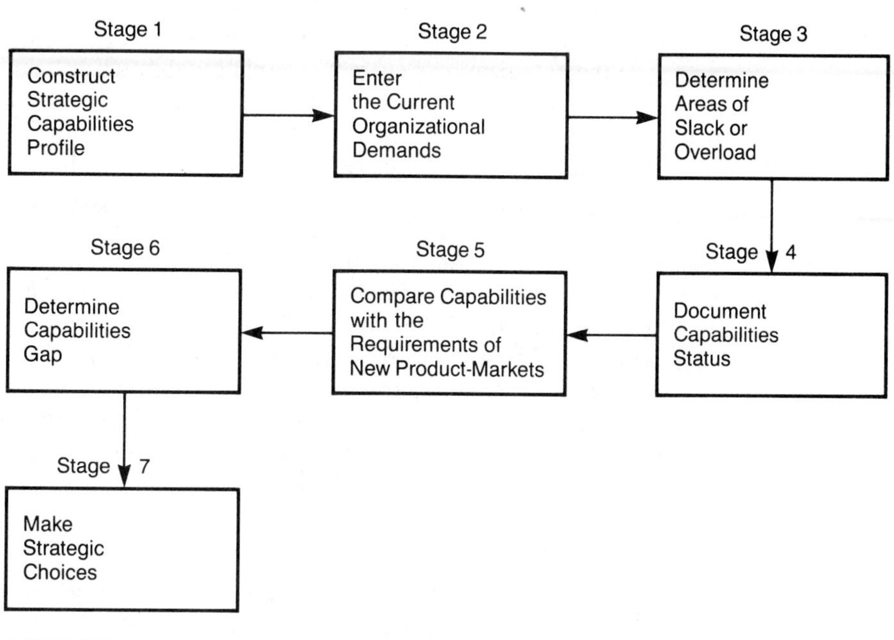

The analysis starts with construction of the strategic capabilities profile, as just described (Stage 1). Next, the manager determines the firm's current organizational requirements for its current business operations (Stage 2). Every firm that is currently in business has obligations to its existing stakeholders (customers, suppliers, and employees). Knowledge of these requirements allows the strategic executive to compare current capabilities with current operational demands.

Based on this information, the manager determines the degree of slack or overload in the organization (Stage 3). Slack occurs when the current capabilities as reflected in the strategic capabilities profile exceed the current demands of the firm's existing operations and stakeholders. An overload happens when the current requirements are greater than current capabilities. Osborn Computers created an overload condition when it announced a new generation of computers and prompted a barrage of new orders from its dealers. The firm did not have the capability to meet this demand, much less to take on another product or market under these conditions.

The manager should document the status of each relevant capability, slack, or overload (Stage 4). Knowledge of the slack/overload condition of the firm's relevant capabilities permits the manager to compare these capabilities with requirements for new products or markets (Stage 5). The manager compares the requirements of the new product or market opportunity with the firm's current capabilities, highlighting areas in which a capabilities gap exists (Stage 6). Based on this comparison, the manager determines where gaps exist and whether the organization can fill them by using slack resources. This information becomes the foundation for the manager's strategic choices (Stage 7).

This strategic capabilities analysis provides the manager with a systematic method to analyze the organization's current internal capabilities in light of the demands of existing operations. Furthermore, it allows the manager to include the requirements of the new opportunities into the analysis. The results of this procedure help the manager choose the most effective means to acquire capabilities necessary to take advantage of opportunities presented by the environmental analysis.

Such an analysis could have helped Anchor National Life Insurance Company avoid a strategic error. Anchor's marketing department took advantage of an environmental opportunity by developing a new product with high market potential. However, the firm lacked the data-processing capabilities to administer the product along with its existing data processing workload. If slack had existed between the requirements of its existing products and its capabilities, Anchor could have cross-trained employees and shifted equipment to handle processing of the new product. The absence of slack caused the firm to go to an outside vendor to acquire the data-processing capabilities needed for the new product.

SWOT Analysis

Another capabilities analysis technique is the SWOT analysis mentioned in Chapter 2.[21] SWOT identifies the strengths, weaknesses, opportunities, and threats associated with the firm's anticipated strategic actions. (This technique is also known as TOWS or WOTS-UP analysis, rearranging the list of factors identified.)

SWOT analysis uses a logical, systematic procedure to combine the results of the opportunities and threats analysis with a strengths and weaknesses analysis that forms the basis for the strategic capabilities profile. First, the opportunities and threats in the firm's markets are analyzed. These opportunities and threats are compared with the firm's capabilities (strengths and weaknesses). Strategies are designed to exploit the opportunities that carry the fewest threats and are within the organization's capabilities.

Comparison of Methods

Both the SWOT analysis and strategic capabilities analysis provide information about the current level of strategic capabilities when compared to opportunities presented by the task environment. These analyses give the strategic manager information on the capabilities available to pursue environment opportunities. Information obtained from either analysis helps the manager determine which of the following actions are most advantageous for the organization:

- Pursue the opportunity using existing organizational capabilities.
- Reject the opportunity because the organization has inadequate capabilities.

The choice of which action to take influences the organization's strategy.

In an organization using the SWOT analysis, the pursuit of an environmental opportunity may be limited by the availability of organizational capabilities. If this occurs, managers may reject highly profitable markets because the firm lacks the necessary capabilities.

However, strategic choices that result from the strategic capabilities analysis are based on the recognition of an environmental opportunity uncovered in the environmental assessment described in Chapter 2. If the opportunity is attractive enough, only the following choices are reasonable:

- Pursue the opportunity, using existing organizational slack.
- If an overload condition exists, acquire resources to pursue the opportunity.
- Decrease the requirements associated with the new opportunity but continue to pursue it.

These choices focus on the alternative ways to pursue the opportunity and do not consider abandoning the new market. This method helps assure the long-term success of the organization because the pursuit of opportunities steers strategic choices at this stage of the process. The lack of capabilities does not constrain the manager's choices.

The SWOT and strategic capabilities analyses can also be used to analyze and adapt to environmental threats. Using the SWOT approach, the firm would cope with the environmental threat by using existing organizational capabilities. Where capabilities fall short, the firm would be vulnerable to the consequences of the threat. Approaching the same threat based on a strategic capabilities analysis would require the firm to obtain the resources necessary to confront the threat or avoid it by changing its task environment. The Strategic Application "Japan's Social Responsibility Abroad" describes how some Japanese companies selected the former option by using financial resources to overcome a potential threat in lucrative U.S. markets.

Domain Choice

The environmental assessment highlights the elements or stakeholders that offer the most favorable opportunities to the organization. The internal strategic capabilities analysis identifies the organizational resources available to pursue the recognized opportunities. The strategic manager should combine these analyses in a SWOT and/or strategic capabilities analysis to determine what is feasible for the organization. This is an important choice, for it determines the firm's specific business arena for the next planning cycle. The name given to this portion of the task environment with its associated elements and stakeholders is the firm's domain—all of the organizations, agencies, groups, or individuals in the task environment with which the manager chooses to transact business.

According to this definition, when a manager chooses opportunities to pursue, he or she also determines the elements and stakeholders in the firm's task environment. If the manager chooses to conduct business in residential construction in Dallas, then Dallas customers, suppliers, local laws, labor, financing, and regional economy all become part of the firm's task environment. However, the construction company manager is not required to conduct business with all of these elements in the firm's

STRATEGIC APPLICATIONS: INTERNATIONAL

Japan's Social Responsibility Abroad

Because Japanese imports have been blamed for the loss of many American jobs, Japanese firms were faced with growing American opposition to their products and growing support for protectionist legislation. In the past, the Japanese dealt with this opposition by improving the quality and appeal of their products. However, their dependence on the U.S. market and huge Japanese investments in the United States dramatically increased the consequences of the threat of protectionist legislation.

Japanese managers decided to meet this threat head-on by going directly to the U.S. public. In the words of Robert S. Ingersoll, former ambassador to Japan, "They're trying to point out that they are of value to the American citizens, to counteract the negative impact their imports have had on American jobs."

Japanese firms are using their substantial organizational financial slack to build a positive reputation with Americans through socially responsible activities. Japanese companies donated an estimated $140 million to public television, museums, universities, and think tanks in the United States in 1988, up from $85 million in 1987. Good corporate citizenship is a hot topic in Tokyo; over 100 Japanese leaders attended a Foreign Affairs Ministry symposium on how to be socially responsible abroad. These business leaders realize that socially responsible activities improve their image and protect their investments in the United States. They also appreciate the importance of responding to threats as well as opportunities.

Source: Mason, Todd and J. Hoerr, "Japan Digs Deep to Win the Hearts and Minds of America," *Business Week*, July 1, 1988, 73–75.

task environment. The strategic manager initially has a choice of the elements and stakeholders with which he or she will conduct business. Typically, the manager will depend on referrals from other contractors or previous business acquaintances to select only a few suppliers, banks, and so on, with which to conduct business. Through this process the manager selects the elements and stakeholders that compose the firm's domain from all possible elements and stakeholders in the task environment.

Selection of a firm's domain should follow a systematic procedure that produces the greatest opportunities while limiting the threats to the organization's survival. Table 3.4 specifies the steps for such a procedure.

The first step in the selection process is to review the results of the environmental assessment. If the firm is newly formed and not committed to an industry or current markets, the assessment can produce a broad list of opportunities. However, in most cases the firm's task environments are partially defined by the existing markets in which the firm operates. Next, the manager identifies the greatest opportunities and determines which task environments are associated with the new opportunities. This information can usually be taken directly from the opportunities and threats (O&T) analysis conducted in the environmental assessment.

Also available from the O&T analysis is information about the threats that accompany each opportunity. These threats are evaluated for each of the opportunities selected in Step 2. Especially important is to identify any terminal threats associated with a particular task environment. **Terminal threats** are those that have a high prob-

Table 3.4 Domain Selection

Step	Procedure
1	Review the results of the environmental assessment.
2	Select the greatest opportunities and determine their task environments.
3	Evaluate the threats that exist in each task environment selected in Step 2.
	a. Check for any terminal threats.
	b. Describe the remaining threats.
4	Analyze internal strategic capabilities, and compare the capabilities of the organization with the demands of the opportunity.
5	Select the task environments with no terminal threats and the fewest nonterminal threats that fall within the capabilities of the organization.
6	Consider all environmental and organizational constraints that are operating on each task environment.
	a. Accept the constraints.
	b. Eliminate the constraints.
7	Select the task environments that offer the greatest opportunities and fewest nonterminal threats and that fall within the firm's capabilities in Step 4.
8	List all of the organizations and agencies with which the firm should or must establish relationships (e.g., suppliers, distributors, customers).
9	Evaluate all of the organizations and agencies in Step 8 to determine which of these should be selected for inclusion in the firm's domain.

ability of occurrence and can cause the firm to fail. If a task environment associated with an opportunity contains a terminal threat, this task environment should be eliminated from further consideration. The strategic manager then describes any remaining nonterminal threats that are a part of the opportunities that have not been eliminated.

Next the manager analyzes internal strategic capabilities to identify the firm's capabilities. The manager compares these capabilities with the demands of the new opportunity.

In Step 5, the strategic manager makes an initial selection of all task environments that have minimal threats and fall within the organization's capabilities. Before the manager can make a final selection, he or she must consider the constraints on the selection process. These constraints limit the feasibility of some opportunities for a particular organization. For example, if the manager insists on maintaining total ownership of the business, this constraint may limit the opportunities available to the firm to obtain funding. Basically, the manager has two ways to deal with these constraints. The manager either can accept the constraints as legitimate and incorporate them into the selection process, or can eliminate their influence from the process.

In light of the accepted constraints, the manager narrows the selection of the task environments to those that will form the basis for the firm's operations and relationships. Once the manager selects the task environments associated with the best opportunities, all elements and stakeholders within these task environments become part of the firm's newly expanded task environment. This expanded task environment includes all relevant elements and stakeholders from both the old and the new businesses of the firm.

To identify these elements and stakeholders, the manager lists the organizations and agencies with which the firm should or must establish relationships. This step involves an evaluation of the organizations that may be part of the firm's domain. Here, the manager selects those organizations that are critical to the success of the firm or that provide the firm with a competitive advantage. Some regulatory agencies *must* be part of the firm's task environment. For example, the Securities and Exchange Commission must be in the firm's domain if the firm is in the securities industry. The Environmental Protection Agency must be part of the domain of a firm in the mining industry. The Internal Revenue Service is a necessary stakeholder in the domain of a firm headquartered in the United States.

The firm may *select* other organizations to be part of the domain because they improve organizational performance. For example, a supplier that has a reputation for high-quality materials would be a good selection for the firm's domain. Or a useful addition to the domain might be a distributor with a reputation for hiring aggressive sales personnel. Many suppliers or distributors from which to select may exist in the task environment, but only certain ones can give the firm a competitive advantage. The last step in the selection process is therefore actually to select the organizations and agencies that will compose the firm's domain.

In reality, most organizations do not follow this ideal process for domain selection. Except for new entrepreneurial organizations, most firms have served specific markets for a number of years and have established relationships with suppliers and regulators. Furthermore, over the years an organization has developed a culture, which is difficult to change in the short term. Therefore, for most established organizations, the selection of a domain is constrained by factors beyond the manager's control.

Nor should all of these steps be followed in practice. Many organizations currently operate in secure and profitable task environments, and their CEOs do not wish to modify them in any way. For these organizations, managers need only follow the steps that identify and weight threats and constraints. Even the manager of a stable and secure firm wants to protect the organization from events that could threaten its survival.

Summary

Internal strategic capabilities are located at two levels of strategy development: corporate and business. At the business level, strategic capabilities consist of the human, material, and informational resources of the firm that enable it to pursue the opportunities in its environment. The types of capabilities that exist in the firm can be managerial, technical, information, or organizational. Major locations for capabilities are the marketing, R&D, production/operations, finance, and management functions of the firm. Knowing the type and location of organizational capabilities allows the manager to determine the firm's ability to take advantage of environmental opportunities.

At the corporate level, strategic capabilities relate to how well the firm balances its portfolio of businesses or SBUs. The portfolio should consider the product, firm, and industry life cycles. Three popular approaches to portfolio analysis are the BCG growth-share matrix, the GE planning grid, and the product/market-evolution matrix.

This chapter described three methods of analyzing capabilities: the strategic capabilities profile, the strategic capabilities analysis, and the SWOT analysis. The strategic capabilities profile identifies external exchange capabilities and internal capabilities. To analyze external capabilities, the industry competitive analysis compares the competitive position of the organization to industry competitive forces. The profit impact of marketing strategies (PIMS) approach compares the firm's position on several important performance criteria to the values of a large number of other firms on those same criteria. The strategic advantage analysis develops a list of the competitive factors for which the organization enjoys a competitive advantage. Analysis of internal capabilities takes place at both the corporate and the business levels.

The strategic capabilities analysis combines the results of the strategic capabilities profile with the opportunities and threats analysis conducted as part of the environmental assessment discussed in Chapter 2. This method treats organizational opportunities as the force that drives managers' choices about the acquisition of additional capabilities.

The SWOT analysis encompasses a systematic review of the firm's strengths and weaknesses coupled with environmental opportunities and threats. Unlike strategic capabilities analysis, it constrains managers' choices to areas in which threats are limited, rather than providing a way of overcoming threats to pursue an exceptional opportunity.

Finally, the results of the environmental assessment and internal capabilities analysis are used to select the domain in which the firm should conduct business. Accurate and reliable information allows the strategic manager to evaluate alternative task environments and compare their demands with the firm's capabilities. Selection of the firm's domain is based on this comparison. The resulting strategic direction exploits opportunities within the limits of the firm's capabilities.

Questions

1. At the library, look up information on AT&T after its breakup. Locate its businesses in the BCG growth-share matrix. Discuss your rationale for placing each business in a specific cell. (Hint: Start at the library's reference section to determine the industries under which AT&T is classified.)

2. Select a firm in your local community and conduct a marketing capabilities analysis using the format illustrated in Table 3.1. Explain why you rated the firm as you did on each of the 15 items that are relevant for that organization.

3. Using the college or university that you are currently attending, determine the location of greatest strength and greatest weakness. Discuss your reasons for selecting these two capabilities. (Hint: The location of the capability will probably be in an academic or administrative unit within the college or university.)

4. Compare and contrast the three external capabilities analyses described in this chapter: competitive industry analysis, PIMS analysis, and strategic advantage analysis. Which one would be most effective to use for a small to medium-sized firm in a regional market with a single product? Why?

5. You have been hired as a consultant to United Airlines Inc. (UAL). UAL's managers have asked you to help them conduct a strategic capabilities analysis for their next planning cycle. You know that UAL wants to continue to recapture a larger share of its commercial airline business, but the managers have also decided to pursue an opportunity in overnight delivery of freight to compete with UPS and Federal Express. Given this limited information, describe the process that you would recommend to UAL for conducting the analysis.

6. Discuss how K mart, McDonald's, and Radio Shack may have followed the steps in Table 3.4 to choose their domain.

Notes

1. James B. Treece, "It Is Time for a Tune-Up at GM," *Business Week*, September 7, 1987, 22–23.
2. D. E. Hussey provides a discussion of planning techniques in "Strategic Management: Lessons for Success and Failure," *Long Range Planning* 17 (February 1984): 43–53.
3. Stephen Phillips and Seth Payne, "TRW's Air Bag Business Looks Ready to Balloon," *Business Week*, November 2, 1987, 74–78.
4. Christopher Farrell, "The New Aces of Low Tech," *Business Week*, September 15, 1986, 132–137.
5. Christopher Power, "Schering May Have a Cure for Anemic Profits," *Business Week*, September 15, 1986, 118+.
6. Harvey J. Brightman and S. E. Harris, "Is Your Information System Mature Enough for Computerized Planning?" *Long Range Planning* 18 (October 1985): 68–73.
7. David A. Aaker and B. Mascarenhas, "The Need for Strategic Flexibility," *The Journal of Business Strategy* 5 (Fall 1984): 74–82.
8. Harold E. Fearon, William A. Ruch, and C. David Wieters, *Fundamentals of Production/Operations Management*, 4th ed. (St. Paul, Minnesota: West Publishing Company, 1989), 120.
9. Judith H. Dobryzinski and Jo Ellen Davis, "Business Celebrities," *Business Week*, June 23, 1986, 100–107.
10. Barbara Rose, "Valley Bank Shifts Expected," *The Arizona Republic*, May 18, 1988, C1–2.
11. R. Rumelt, *Strategy, Structure and Economic Performance.* (Boston: Harvard Business School, 1974).
12. Robert E. Linneman and M. J. Thomas. "A Common Sense Approach to Portfolio Planning," *Long Range Planning* 15 (February 1982): 77–92.
13. Carolyn Y. Woo and A. C. Cooper. "Strategies of Effective Low Share Businesses," *Strategic Management Journal* 2 (July–September 1981): 301–318.
14. Anil K. Gupta and V. Govindarajan. "Build, Hold, Harvest: Converting Strategic Intentions into Reality," *Journal of Business Strategy* 4 (Winter 1984): 34–47.
15. Charles Hofer, *Conceptual Constructs for Formulating Corporate and Business Strategies,* 9-378-754 (Boston: Intercollegiate Case Clearing House, 1977), 3.
16. Hiram C. Barksdale and C. E. Harris, Jr. "Portfolio Analysis and the Product Life Cycle," *Long Range Planning* 15 (December 1982): 74–83.
17. Hussey, 1984.
18. Michael E. Porter, *Competitive Strategy* (New York: The Free Press, 1980).

19. The PIMS approach has been criticized on methodological grounds and modified in several articles. Two of these articles are: Arthur R. Burgess, "The Modeling of Business Profitability: A New Approach," *Strategic Management Journal* 3 (January–March 1982): 53–66; Carolyn Y. Woo, "Evaluation of the Strategies and Performance of Low RDI Market Share Leaders," *Strategic Management Journal* 4 (April–June 1983): 123–135.

20. Leidecker and Bruno refer to these as critical success factors and describe an alternative method of identification in Joel K. Leidecker and A. V. Bruno, "Identifying and Using Critical Success Factors," *Long Range Planning* 17 (February 1984): 23–32.

21. Heinz Weihrich provides an excellent description of how to use a TOWS (SWOT) matrix for capabilities analysis in "The TOWS Matrix—A Tool for Situational Analysis," *Long Range Planning* 15 (April 1982): 54–56.

Case for Discussion

American Airlines' Tough CEO

The reputation, visibility, contacts, and experience of senior management can be important strategic capabilities for the organization. Robert Crandall has been the successful CEO of American Airlines for over a decade. During the difficult years following deregulation, American has compiled an impressive profit record. American was the industry leader of major U.S. airlines with a five-year average of 13 percent return on equity. Its 1987 operating revenues were 20 percent higher than they were in 1986, while passenger traffic industrywide was up 11 percent. However, Crandall has had problems penetrating European and Asian markets.

American lost an opportunity for a lucrative contract with British Airways, Swissair, KLM, and Alitalia to use their Sabre computer reservation system. The Europeans chose instead to go with United Airlines' Apollo system. In addition, no European airlines will include American foreign flights on their reservation computers. British Airways will not let travel agents using its computerized ticketing system even sell an American Airlines ticket. Crandall is suing in Britain's High Court over the British Airways policy.

Industry analysts are confused by the reaction of the Europeans toward the most successful U.S. airline. American seems to have all of the technical, financial, and operational capabilities to compete in the European market. Crandall is a tough, successful CEO. According to one article, "No one would describe Robert Crandall as easy to deal with. He has made few allies in the airline business." European airline executives, especially, seem to have difficulty with his aggressive style. Whatever the reason, American's expansion into Europe appears to be in for turbulent flying conditions.

Discussion Questions

1. What are American Airlines' capabilities mentioned in the case? Are they strengths or weaknesses?

Source: "Calmness Itself," *Forbes*, March 21, 1988, 39–40.

2. How does your analysis change when you compare the domestic and European markets?

3. Using the information in the case, conduct a SWOT analysis for American.

4. Using a strategic capabilities analysis, how should American acquire additional capabilities to take advantage of the European opportunity?

5. At what stage in the process of domain selection did American Airlines' managers encounter difficulty when they chose to expand their domain to Europe? Explain.

Chapter 4

Strategy Formulation: Choice of Mission, Strategic Goals, and a Strategy

In the construction of a country, it is not the practical workers but the idealists and planners that are difficult to find.

—Chung-shan Ch'iian-shu, 1936[1]

Learning Objectives

- To understand the nature of strategy formulation.
- To learn the components of a mission statement and how it is generated.
- To learn how to develop strategic goals.
- To gain an understanding of the major strategies that an organization can adopt.
- To examine how competitive, environmental, and internal factors affect the selection of the organization's strategy.
- To obtain a working knowledge of the Strategy Selection Technique (SST).

ONCE the manager has assessed the environment, analyzed the firm's capabilities, and selected the domain in which to conduct business, he or she is ready to formulate a mission, strategic goals, and a strategy that directs the organization's activities toward taking advantage of opportunities and warding off threats. The strategic choices resulting from the environmental assessment and analysis of strategic capabilities have positioned the firm in a task environment and domain. Equally important are the choices that determine the firm's ability to successfully compete within its chosen domain. These choices are the essence of strategy formulation, which includes choices of a mission, strategic goals, and a strategy.

Modern managers use many different strategies to guide their organizations. Choosing the correct strategy to take advantage of environmental opportunities and gain a competitive edge is the primary responsibility of the firm's strategic managers.

Nature of Strategy Formulation

The word strategy is derived from the Greek word *strategos*, meaning general, and was used to describe the military plans developed by the ancient Greek generals. Until the Industrial Revolution, the use of the term was limited to military strategies developed to coordinate the movement and efforts of large numbers of soldiers on the battlefield. The challenge of running large organizations spawned by the Industrial Revolution prompted some managers to apply military planning techniques to private enterprise. Since that time, managers have used **strategy** to describe the plans and actions necessary to coordinate the activities of organization members toward the accomplishment of organizational goals and objectives.

This chapter discusses strategy formulation in terms of the strategic management process. Strategy formulation is the stage of the process in which the information obtained from the environmental assessment and internal capabilities analysis is used to develop a strategy for accomplishing the firm's mission and strategic goals. Not all experts agree on how strategy formulation is conducted in organizations. In general, there are two different perspectives of how strategy is formulated, synoptic and incremental. The model discussed in this book draws from both views.

Synoptic Perspective

A synoptic perspective is a formal approach that applies the rational problem-solving technique. Rational problem solving follows five steps: identifying the problem, analyzing the problem, generating alternative solutions, evaluating these alternatives, and recommending courses of action to solve the problem. When a manager applies the synoptic perspective to strategic management, he or she assumes that the problem is how best to meet the demands of the organization's constituents, for example, owners and employees. Problem analysis consists of the environmental assessment and internal-capabilities analysis described in Chapters 2 and 3. Alternative generation—the topic of this chapter—identifies several strategies that may be used to meet constituents' demands. Managers evaluate these strategies in light of environmental and organizational information and choose the most appropriate strategy to ensure the organization's success.

Critics of the synoptic perspective argue that actual business conditions seldom evolve as expected, and the elaborate synoptic plan quickly becomes obsolete. They claim that once conditions change, operational managers throw away the plan and pursue short-term strategies.

One company that encountered the limitations of the synoptic perspective is IBM. Long an industry giant and blue-chip corporation, IBM generated $46 billion in revenues in 1984 and developed detailed plans based on forecasts of $200 billion in revenue by 1995. By the end of 1985, however, conditions dramatically changed. Revenues rose only 9 percent that year, earnings flattened, and return on equity dropped. In the words of one former IBM scientist, "We simply read the market wrong." Immediately the company replaced long-term growth objectives with short-term cost cutting, new-product introduction, management streamlining, and more aggressive marketing objectives. Diversification took the place of a strategy for long-term internal growth. Thus, the new competitive conditions facing IBM meant that the company had to modify its "ponderous planning process."[2]

Incremental Perspective

While the synoptic perspective sets forth an idealized approach to strategy formulation, the incremental perspective focuses on how managers actually formulate strategy. According to Lindbloom,[3] Quinn,[4] and others,[5] many managers do not plan a series of decisions and actions that they follow to completion. Rather, these managers establish an initial plan, implement it, and wait to see the response. The next activity they plan is based on the response to the first, and so on until the strategy formulation and implementation cycle is complete. Based on this perspective, all strategy formulation is essentially short range, and the sum of the series of incremental plans, activities, and reactions appears rational and systematic only after the fact.

Managers are forced to use the less rational incremental approach because most modern firms face dynamic environmental conditions. Table 4.1 sets forth the key differences between the strategic assumptions of the synoptic perspective and the environmental realities that cause the manager to use the incremental approach, as summarized by Charles Stubbart.[6]

According to Quinn, support for the use of the incremental approach comes from examples of the strategy changes that occurred at General Mills and other companies.[7] In 1969, General Mills began a planned acquisition program into food-related and nonfood growth markets. During the initial stages of implementing this plan, managers at General Mills discovered that acquisition targets in food-related areas were greatly overpriced. In response to this discovery, they substantially altered their original acquisition strategy and purchased firms in primarily nonfood markets. When nonfood acquisitions faltered, this incremental change was followed by another incremental change, to refocus on the more expensive food-related businesses.

Table 4.1 Synoptic Formal Assumptions and Environmental Realities

Synoptic Formal Assumptions	Environmental Realities
The strategic manager adapts and coaligns his organization to its environment.	• The environment cannot be understood or predicted. • Change proceeds much faster and more radically than the organization can change its form.
Top management decides on a mission/strategy.	• Diverse strategies intensify turbulence. The larger system is suboptimized.
Good strategies can control organizational outcomes.	• Control over future outcomes is impossible. • Myths of control are frustrated by realities of change.

Source: Reprinted with permission from *Long Range Planning*, Vol. 18, December 1985, Charles Stubbart, "Why We Need a Revolution in Strategic Planning," pp. 68–76. Copyright 1985 Pergamon Press PLC.

Critics argue that because the incremental perspective emphasizes the short term, organizations with long planning cycles—such as public utilities or manufacturers of capital goods—cannot use it successfully. Furthermore, this perspective implies that managers are reactive or passive and that they adapt to changes in the firm's environment by initiating only incremental adjustments. On the other hand, the synoptic perspective allows strategic managers to develop a long-term strategy to influence the environment in a direction that is more favorable for the organization.

In the choice model, we incorporate both perspectives. The rational synoptic approach is represented by the logical series of stages shown in the model. (See Figure 1.2.) Each stage should be completed in sequence. However, the incremental approach is used to describe how the choice model is applied to "real world" organizations. By using strategic control, described in Chapter 8, the rational synoptic process is constantly monitored and incrementally adjusted to reflect changes in the firm's business conditions.

Choice of Mission

Whether managers take a synoptic or incremental perspective, their initial step in formulating a strategy should be to formally state the purpose of the organization. This statement, called the mission statement, flows directly from previous analyses and provides a clear picture of the firm's position in its competitive arena. The mission statement should clearly and concisely state the firm's unique purpose or business in words that indicate to employees and publics the firm's products, markets, methods of conducting business, and approach to dealing with constituents. The mission statement specifies the firm's chosen product-markets and the competitive philosophy that it will employ in those product-markets, as well as the capabilities that it will emphasize to gain a competitive advantage.

The firm's mission can be developed by answering the following four questions:

1. What is the firm's business?
2. What is the firm's intended strategic posture?
3. What is the firm's main functional orientation?
4. What is the firm's orientation toward its primary constituents?

Stating the firm's **business** communicates information about the competitive elements in the task environment: suppliers, customers, and competitors. **Strategic posture** is the organization's proactive or reactive competitive philosophy. A proactive posture is aggressive and characterizes a firm that is first to enter the market with an innovation and exercise market or industry dominance by capturing a large share of the market. Reactive organizations are passive and let other firms incur the expense and risk associated with the introduction of new products. Neither posture is considered superior, and firms can be successful with either one if it is effectively implemented.

An example of a mission statement for a company with a reactive posture appears in the Strategic Application "Anchor National Life Insurance Company Mission Statement." This mission statement, for a medium-sized insurance company in the southwestern United States, indicates that the firm is in the financial services business. It offers a full line of proprietary and nonproprietary financial planning products. The emphasis on Anchor's distribution network and quality support, rather than innovative products, demonstrates the company's reactive posture.

Functional orientation identifies a functional capability that provides a strong competitive advantage for the firm. For example, a firm that has a strong marketing capability will emphasize marketing in its mission statement. The firm's functional orientation informs external constituents about its basis for competing in the industry. Also, it notifies employees which functional unit is emphasized within the firm. For Anchor, the emphasis on low cost, high quality, and timely service indicates that it is an operations-oriented organization.

The final component of the mission is the organization's orientation toward its **primary constituents**. If the organization is particularly vulnerable to social issues (e.g., pollution or safety), then its mission statement will include words about its commitment to a clean and safe working environment. Practically all firms depend upon the support of their employees and therefore include a sentence in their mission statement about concern for employee welfare. These items send a clear message that the organization is aware of the importance of its critical constituents. Anchor's mission statement lists several such commitments under "management philosophy."

STRATEGIC APPLICATIONS

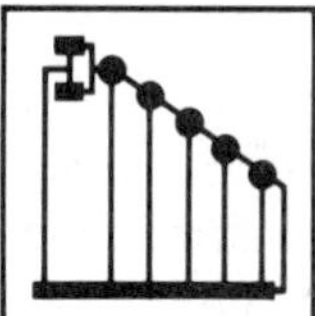

Anchor National Life Insurance Company Mission Statement

The Anchor Companies constitute a financial services organization with the mission of profitably selling and servicing a *full line* of financial planning products, proprietary and nonproprietary. These consist of both traditional and equity oriented life insurance and annuity products that are aggressively sold to a national market. Anchor will obtain its competitive advantage through its unique distribution network of financial planners and its proven commitment to high-quality broker/dealer support.

Management Philosophy

Anchor is an equal opportunity employer that is committed to providing each employee with an opportunity to maximize his or her potential.

Anchor expects honesty and integrity from its employees and rewards them commensurate with their contributions to the success of Anchor. We are demanding but fair.

The management of the Anchor Companies recognizes community involvement as an important corporate responsibility and a viable business objective.

Anchor is a low-cost provider of life insurance and annuity products to its customers.

Quality and timeliness of customer service are equal to or superior to 80 to 90 percent of our competitors.

Source: Anchor National Life Insurance Company, 1987.

Development of Strategic Goals

Once management chooses the firm's mission, senior executives are in a position to develop strategic goals. These are the long-term goals that the organization intends to achieve by effectively formulating and implementing strategies. These goals specify the outcome or performance areas that the firm wishes to emphasize over the long term, typically three to five years.

Performance Areas for Strategic Goals

The performance areas in which a manager may choose to establish strategic goals depend, to a great extent, on the demands of the firm's primary stakeholders and constituents. In addition, these goals must be consistent with the firm's mission statement. For example, if the mission includes a commitment to social responsibility, the manager should develop a socially responsive strategic goal to chart the firm's performance in pursuit of that aspect of the mission. Strategic goals are typically developed for one or more of the following areas:

Employee relations and development
International competitive position
Market position
Productivity
Profitability
Return growth
Service leadership
Social responsibility
Technology leadership

Most firms find it important to maintain cooperative relations with their staff employees, managers, and direct line personnel. For the unionized firm, good employee relations are essential to prevent work slowdowns or stoppages resulting from grievances or strikes. Employee cooperation is also important for the nonunion organization, not only because it frequently improves employee morale and productivity, but also because it prevents expensive turnover and absenteeism while simplifying recruitment of new employees.

Most employees also have needs for advancement and personal growth that they hope to fulfill through the organization. If their workplace fails to provide for these needs, employees typically seek their fulfillment outside the firm by quitting or reducing their commitment. Senior managers provide for employee personal growth through employee development programs that prepare employees for advancement. For example, Ford Motor Company has a strategic goal of minimizing employee layoffs that it has negotiated as part of its current labor contract with the United Auto Workers. One means to make this goal achievable is to cross-train employees for different jobs that are still available within the company.

Many companies have started to include international competitive position as a strategic goal. Such goals are usually stated in terms of international expansion or market penetration. Expansion could involve producing or selling in other countries. In the words of a senior vice president of Caterpillar Inc., "The way to gain worldwide market share is to get worldwide competitive, not hide behind quotas."[8]

Many larger organizations establish strategic goals for their relative position in their markets. Some firms strive to be industry leaders in market share or sales volume. Others have goals to capture a certain percentage of the market for all of their products. Qume Corporation, a revitalized printer company, has a strategic goal of $300 million in sales.[9]

A strategic goal of many U.S. manufacturing firms during the 1980s and 1990s is increased productivity. The results show that U.S. firms, on the average, are achieving higher productivity gains than Japan or western Europe. This renewed emphasis on productivity is rapidly moving into service industries. Organizations such as banks and scientific laboratories are concerned about increased productivity. Los Alamos National Laboratory doubled the productivity of its purchasing department in three years.

A major strategic goal of most businesses is profitability. To ensure an attractive return to investors and continued internal capital for operations and expansion, senior management establishes a strategic goal of a certain profit level or rate of profit increase. Ford Motor Company was more profitable than General Motors in 1988, and Ford's managers continue to have ambitious profitability goals for the future.

Related to profitability and productivity are the firm's return on investment (ROI) and return on equity (ROE). These two profitability ratios—explained in more detail in Appendix B—give the firm's stakeholders an indication of how effectively management is using the firm's assets and equity. Strategic goals for return are usually stated in terms of a projected percentage increase in ROI or ROE. For example, in the Strategic Application, Anchor National Life Insurance Company stated the following strategic goals for the mission:

> Anchor will obtain a minimum of 12 percent return on equity and 10 percent annual sales growth through the sale of proprietary products and commission income generated from the sale of nonproprietary equity and insurance products.

Some organizations gain an advantage by being better at servicing their products than competitors are. Firms such as IBM and Lincoln Electric have reputations for superior service, which increase the attractiveness of their products to customers. Strategic goals to become the industry leader in customer service or to keep service time at a certain level make it clear to employees that service is a primary focus of the company.

As the U.S. public expects more socially responsible actions from private-sector firms, managers increasingly must establish strategic goals for social responsibility. These goals provide a standard for the manager to use to measure the firm's progress in this area. For example, the director of a major federal agency determined that the agency could be more socially responsible in awarding contracts to minority vendors. The agency's senior management created a strategic goal to increase the amount of contracts awarded to minority vendors by $10 million in one year. The goal was exceeded by $3 million because employees saw the strategic goal as a target the agency should achieve.

Being in the forefront of technological development can allow the firm to capture a large market share before competition catches up. Also, technology leadership may give the firm an opportunity to skim higher profits from the market because of its temporary monopoly position with the new technology. For example, Hewlett-Packard enjoyed very large profit margins for laser printers when the company was the only supplier of that technology. Competing manufacturers of laser printers have since decreased the price of this technology and HP's profit margins. Thus, a strategic goal of technological leadership is an initial if temporary step in gaining a competitive advantage.

Characteristics of Strategic Goals

Well-developed strategic goals are linked to effective strategy formulation. To serve as guides for the strategic activities of senior management and facilitate implementation of the firm's strategy, strategic goals should be:

- Clear
- Acceptable
- Flexible
- Achievable
- Action-oriented

Strategic goals must be clearly stated and understood by all organizational members. If the same goal means different things to different members of the firm, implementation activities will be confused and inefficient. In addition, goals should be measurable so that all employees know when they have achieved the goals. Strategic goals have meaning only when organizational members can mark their progress toward meeting those goals.

Strategic goals cannot be achieved by top management alone. The firm's success depends on the efforts of all employees to pull together toward goal accomplishment. Commitment to the organization's goals can be guaranteed only if the goals are acceptable to the employees responsible for accomplishing them. For IBM employees, quality service is a source of pride and provides a focus for their efforts. It has the additional benefit of increasing customer acceptance of IBM's products.

Strategic goals must be flexible because they depend on the organization's using its internal capabilities to pursue opportunities in its task environment. When external conditions or internal capabilities change, the firm must accommodate these changing conditions. General Motors needed flexibility when it discovered in midstream that its program for modernizing its plants was not producing the cost savings or quality improvements projected. GM's managers changed the strategic goals for productivity to focus more on the individual worker's productivity.

Strategic goals that are impossible to achieve only frustrate employees. Goals should stretch the organization to perform well and operate effectively. However, employees interpret too much stretch as unattainable and may respond by developing their own informal goals. As one executive stated, "Our sales goals are extreme 'stretch' goals. I would be happy if [our salespeople] achieved half that level." As you would expect, only half *was* achieved.

To motivate employees to action, strategic goals should be stated in active terms. Action-oriented goals use verbs: *increase* productivity, return, or market position; *establish* or *maintain* technological leadership in an industry; *develop* a social responsibility thrust for the firm; or *expand* service quality to generate a competitive advantage. It is easy to see how these terms move the organization to action in pursuit of its mission.

Strategic goals, if effectively developed, are targets for organization members to strive for; they motivate employees to action. They clearly and concisely state the long-term results that management intends to achieve. These results are based on using the firm's internal capabilities to take advantage of environmental opportunities. Strategic goals are destinations on a map of organizational success. Managers also must determine the most effective route to that destination—the firm's strategies.

Selection of the Appropriate Strategy

Strategies specify how management will achieve strategic goals in the long-range management of the firm. The remaining sections of this chapter describe a process for formulating strategies by using information from the environmental assessment and capabilities analysis. External and/or internal events can alter the appropriateness of these strategies. Therefore, the process allows for modification based on the feedback from the strategic control stage of the strategic management process, which will be discussed in Chapter 8.

Levels of Strategy Development

Chapter 1 identified four levels of strategy development: enterprise level, corporate level, business level, and functional level. Specific types of strategies are associated with each of these levels. Enterprise-level strategies ensure that the firm acts properly as a corporate citizen. We will discuss enterprise-level strategies in detail in Chapter 11. Corporate-level strategies focus on the firm's portfolio of businesses. Strategies at the corporate level determine which businesses the firm should be in and how these businesses should be developed. Business-level strategies are designed to improve the firm's competitive advantage in its product-markets. Last, functional-level strategies support and implement strategies from the other three levels.[10] We will discuss corporate- and business-level strategies in the remainder of this chapter. Strategies at the functional level will be discussed in Chapter 5.

Strategies may be formulated at any of the four levels. If the organization is highly visible in its task environment and includes social responsibility in its mission, it

Table 4.2 Types of Strategies

Type	Category	Strategy	Definition
Generic	Generic: Approaches to outperform competitors in the industry	Cost leadership	Using economies of scale, scope, and technology to reduce cost and increase profit or sales
		Differentiation	Developing ways to make product or service appear unique
		Focus (Niche)	Focusing product development and marketing efforts to a particular market segment in which the firm has a cost or differentiation advantage
Master	Internal growth: Growth at a steady rate each year through internal innovation and development	Vertical integration	Steadily growing through development of sources of input or channels of distribution
		Market penetration (concentration)	Inventing or developing ways to capture larger shares of the market for existing products
		Market development	Developing new markets for existing products
		Product diversification	Inventing or developing new products for new markets
	External growth: Growth through acquisition and merger	Vertical integration	Growing through greater ownership of sources of input or channels of distribution
		Horizontal integration	Acquisition or merger with competitors
		Horizontal diversification	Acquisition of new product lines for existing customers
		Concentric diversification	Acquiring new but related product lines for new customers
		Conglomerate diversification	Acquiring new and unrelated product lines for new customers
	Rejuvenation: Reducing the scope of business to emphasize areas of strength in either products or markets	Retrenchment	Reducing costs and assets as a response to declining profitability

should have strategic goals and a strategy for social responsibility. Multiple SBU organizations or firms anticipating diversification should formulate corporate-level strategies. All SBUs and single-business firms need business-level strategies to direct their efforts toward accomplishment of strategic goals. Likewise, all SBUs and single-business firms must have functional-level strategies to implement their strategy. As discussed previously, strategies can be more or less formal, but senior management must have an understanding of the firm's direction and how it will proceed in that direction.

At the corporate or business level, a firm can pursue three types of strategies. These are generic strategies (approaches to outperforming industry or strategic group

Table 4.2 *(continued)*

Type	Category	Strategy	Definition
		Turnaround	Transition strategy moving from retrenchment to growth after a period of retrenchment
	Stabilization: Maintenance of the firm's current competitive position in order to cope with a short-term environmental condition	Maintenance	Protecting the firm's current competitive position during periods of economic downturn until the next growth period
		Defense	Financially and organizationally restructuring the firm to protect it from an unfriendly takeover
	Termination: Relinquishing control of the organization by selling assets or ceasing operations	Divestment (harvesting)	Selling a subsidiary, division, product line, or other part of the organization in order to fund remaining parts
		Liquidation	Selling all of the company's assets for their tangibile worth and ceasing operations
Ancillary	Rationalization: Eliminating inefficient or unproductive parts of the organization and combining operations	Consolidation	Closing a facility and ceasing operations at that location because of obsolescence or inactivity (e.g., declining sales)
	Cooperation: Obtaining access to needed resources (financial, human, materials) or customers by engaging in formal agreements	Joint venture	Two or more organizations committing financial resources to the same project
		Agency agreement	One organization agreeing to act as the agent for another
		Credit agreement	One organization assisting another in obtaining a line of credit
		Management agreement	One organization agreeing to manage a facility owned by another

competitors)[11]; master strategies (primary strategic actions that a business will use to gain a competitive advantage; and ancillary strategies (strategic moves that amplify the effectiveness of the master strategy). All of these strategies are the result of choices by the firm's strategic management and influence the direction that the organization will take. If strategies are chosen to take advantage of environmental opportunities and build on organizational strengths, the organization will most likely succeed. Several strategies, along with their type and category, are shown in Table 4.2.

Generic Strategies

Porter defines generic strategies as approaches that managers choose to direct the firm in outperforming its competitors in an industry and strategic group.[12] These strategies help the organization cope with the five competitive forces described in Chapters 2 and 3. Porter proposes three generic strategies: cost leadership, differentiation, and focus. The manager may select any of the three generic strategies. Once a strategy has been chosen, all organizational actions must be committed to the effective implementation of the strategy.

Cost Leadership Cost leadership consists of using economies of scale, scope, and technology to reduce the costs of producing a good or providing a service. High-tech firms like Intel Inc. must design a new integrated circuit product and its production process for production runs of several hundred thousand units. This allows Intel to get the unit cost down to a level that will make the company a low-cost supplier in a cost-competitive industry.

Differentiation A strategy of differentiation is based on developing ways to make the product or service appear unique. Luxury automobile manufacturers such as the makers of Mercedes Benz, BMW, and Volvo cars use this strategy. Mercedes automobiles are differentiated on the basis of quality and prestige, BMW on handling and performance at high speeds, and Volvo on dependability. The BMW 735i series of automobiles was developed to compete head-on with Mercedes. However, even though the 735i is a major entrant into the luxury segment of the auto market, it is differentiated from its Mercedes competition on the basis of handling and performance. The Strategic Application "A Flyer from BMW of North America" is an example of how BMW of North America attempts to differentiate its products in the United States through promotional material targeted to an upper socioeconomic bracket.

Focus A niche, or focus, generic strategy is similar in some respects to differentiation. While differentiation attempts to segment the market on the basis of a characteristic of the product or service, the niche strategy focuses on a particular market segment in which the firm has a competitive advantage. Therefore, the niche strategy segments the market on the basis of a characteristic of the market. Examples would be geographical, age, or sex niches. Hewlett-Packard, for example, markets its calculators to the scientific segment of the calculator market.

Focus generic strategies can be based on either cost leadership or differentiation within a market niche. Once a subset of a market is chosen, the firm can differentiate its product or be cost leader within that niche. Remember, generic strategies are approaches for achieving success against industry competitors. Therefore, a firm can choose the entire industry as its task environment or focus on a niche within the industry. In either case, managers can choose to be cost leaders or to differentiate depending on conditions in the firm's competitive environment. The three generic strategies are discussed in more detail in Chapter Appendix 4.1.

Master Strategies

The idea of a master strategy to guide the organization in accomplishing its strategic goals and pursuing its mission is well accepted by strategic management experts. Writers such as Pearce and Robinson, Jauch and Glueck, Certo and Peter, and Thompson and Strickland refer to master strategies as grand strategies or general strategies.[13]

STRATEGIC APPLICATIONS: INTERNATIONAL

A Flyer from BMW of North America Inc.

A Cordial Invitation
From Your Local BMW Dealers.

The product of an eight-year, billion-dollar quest, the 735i is not merely superior to the conventional luxury car, it is a boldly innovative, brilliantly successful new conception of the luxury car.

We're now pleased to announce that a new BMW 735i just became more attainable than ever.

Through the resources of BMW Credit Corporation, your local BMW dealers are able to offer favorable financing on this luxury performance sedan for a limited time.

So please visit your nearby BMW dealer soon for a test drive. We can assure you, you will not be disappointed.

In the 735i, BMW engineers have seized the opportunity to rethink every aspect of the luxury automobile—comfort, aesthetics, quality, reliability and safety.

They have combined the results with even higher levels of BMW's extraordinary performance. And they have created today's most thorough definition of what makes an expensive car worth the money.

As the editors of *AutoWeek* have observed, "There is a completeness, a cohesiveness to the new Seven that is its most remarkable attribute. It is a true performance sedan that gives up nothing in comfort. It is a luxury sedan that will embarrass most sports cars."

For thrilling corroboration, visit your participating BMW dealer today, and ask about our special financing arrangements. Or if you would prefer, just call one of the participating dealers to arrange for a test drive at your convenience at your home or office. And as a memento of your test drive, you'll receive an elegant gift from Tiffany. See the enclosed card for details.

Sincerely,

Source: 1988 brochure from BMW

All master strategies indicate the primary strategic actions that the senior managers will use to effectively compete in the firm's task environment. We have chosen to use **master strategy** here because, like a ship's master, the master strategy guides the organization through uncharted business conditions and coordinates the activities of members to keep the firm on course.

Most master strategies can be used at both the corporate and business levels of strategy development. Single-business firms can spawn new businesses by creating a new-product division and watching it grow into a major player in the industry. Or they can choose to diversify and acquire existing companies. Corporations typically add to their business portfolios through acquisition or merger but could choose to use internal resources to develop a new "question mark" business.

Whether a manager chooses an internal or an external master strategy depends on the firm's capabilities and the manager's judgment of which strategy will provide a competitive advantage. A financial strength coupled with a shortage of experienced managers will usually prompt a manager to choose diversification through acquisition or merger to obtain competent management with the acquired company. Managerial and operational strength combined with a shortage of acquisition capital usually calls for the internal development of new products or businesses.

As explained in detail in Chapter Appendix 4.1, five categories of master strategies give rise to the 15 possible strategies defined in Table 4.2.

Internal Growth Master strategies for internal growth promote firm growth through internal innovation and development. New products or services are internally developed by the firm. If new markets materialize, the firm benefits from the product during the growth stage of its life cycle. Sales, profits, and asset creation usually increase slowly and gain speed as the product moves up the growth curve. Figure 4.1 illustrates a possible growth curve for a firm that pursues internal growth strategies.

Internal strategies for growth may take several forms: vertical integration, market penetration, market development, and product diversification. Vertical integration is a strategy of growth through internal development of sources of input or channels of distribution. This could include manufacturing 70 percent of the input assemblies for an automobile as General Motors does or owning and operating several thousand retail outlets as does Exxon Corporation.

Market penetration (sometimes called concentration) refers to developing ways to capture larger shares of markets for the firm's existing products. Two of the many ways that firms attempt to use penetration are major advertising campaigns and price promotions. Phillip Morris has developed aggressive tactics to pursue its penetration strategy in response to former Surgeon General C. Everett Koop's announcements about the health hazards of smoking. In spite of proven risks from smoking, Phillip Morris has launched a massive campaign including pamphlets, state newsletters, and a full-color magazine to promote smoking. The Strategic Application "Phillip Morris Companies" discusses the aggressive tone of the Phillip Morris pamphlet designed to stem the reduction in smoking and attract a larger share of the smoker's market.

In contrast, a master strategy of market development consists of developing new markets for existing products. There are several examples of market development strategies in consumer goods. Honda attempted to develop a new market for its

Figure 4.1 Internal Growth Strategy Curve

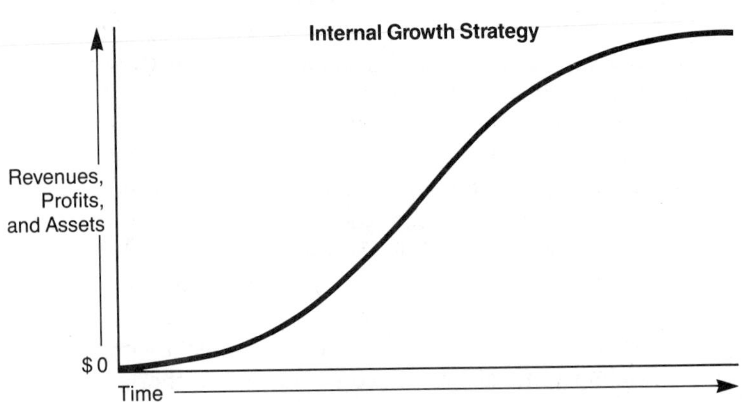

STRATEGIC APPLICATIONS: SOCIAL RESPONSIBILITY

Phillip Morris Companies

Phillip Morris has launched an aggressive advertising campaign in response to the Surgeon General's antismoking announcements. Reacting to the Surgeon General's pronouncement regarding the hazards of smoking, Phillip Morris has developed a proactive strategy to promote its smoking products. In an attempt to rally smokers behind Phillip Morris and its products, the company has initiated a program aimed at "smokers' rights." This program depicts smokers as citizens who are unfairly overtaxed and denied their freedom of choice. As one ad reads, "It's up to smokers to remind Congress that discrimination against smokers is unfair and un-American."

The strategy is designed to maintain Phillip Morris's market share by solidifying customers' commitment to smoking and increase penetration by attracting new customers to Phillip Morris products. The social responsibility issues involved in this situation are very complex. They can be summarized in the following question: Is it socially responsible to use a campaign based on patriotism to promote the use of a product proclaimed to be a health hazard by the senior health official of the United States?

recreational all-terrain vehicle (ATV) by promoting it as a small farm and construction work vehicle. Perhaps the best known example is Arm & Hammer baking soda. Markets were developed for this baking supplement as a refrigerator deodorizer and carpet cleaner.

The product diversification master strategy is taken from the work of Igor Ansoff and involves the internal development of new products for new markets.[14] When IBM decided to enter the retail computer market with a personal computer, it was radically departing from its major product—mainframe computers—and its sophisticated commercial users.

Internal growth master strategies provide the firm with a great deal of control over the sources of its growth and can be relatively inexpensive to pursue. However, some risks are associated with internal growth. First, it typically takes longer to develop new products or services internally, and the organization may miss the growth portion of the product's life cycle. Also, risks are great that the firm will develop an expensive new product only to find that its market fails to materialize. Last, these strategies leave the organization extremely vulnerable to innovations. If new ideas do not appear at the appropriate time, the firm may fail to obtain any competitive advantage. When deciding whether to adopt an internal growth strategy, managers must weigh the benefits of greater control against the risks of failure.

External Growth: Merger and Acquisition Growth master strategies at the corporate level and, under some circumstances, at the SBU level may involve merger or acquisition. Sometimes the firm lacks the time, management expertise, and operations knowledge to take advantage of environmental opportunities for growth by engaging in internal innovation and development. In this case, it may use its financial capabilities to acquire existing organizations that have already taken advantage of the opportunity. The acquisition of or merger with another organization produces a rapid or incremental growth in revenue, profits, assets, or all of these at the completion of the transaction. Figure 4.2 illustrates the changes in the firm's growth curve as a result of an acquisition or merger.

Many of the master strategies discussed here cause long-term growth in revenues, profits, or assets. However, growth through acquisition or merger takes place in discrete jumps, whereas internal growth is slower and continuous.

Master strategies for external growth include vertical integration, horizontal integration, horizontal diversification, concentric diversification, and conglomerate diversification. External vertical integration involves acquiring other organizations that are sources of input or provide channels of distribution. For example, rather than expand its own manufacturing capabilities, IBM purchased a large percentage of Intel to supply needed integrated circuits for its computers.

Merger and/or acquisition are also mechanisms for a master strategy of horizontal integration. With this strategy, the firm acquires or merges with existing competitors to capture a larger share of the market. As with the internal strategy of market penetration, increased market share is the desired result. When National Semiconductor purchased Fairchild Semiconductor from Schlumberger Ltd., it became the sixth largest chipmaker in the world.[15]

Horizontal diversification consists of acquiring new product lines for existing customers. Cullinet Software Inc. was the number-one independent software producer until IBM entered the marketplace. After losing market share to IBM, Cullinet decided to employ a horizontal diversification strategy to reduce its dependence on data-base software (which accounted for 86 percent of total revenues in 1984). Cullinet acquired five smaller companies that produce applications software. By 1987, 45 percent of its sales came from applications software sold to the same customers that purchased its data-base software.[16]

Figure 4.2 External Growth Strategy Curve

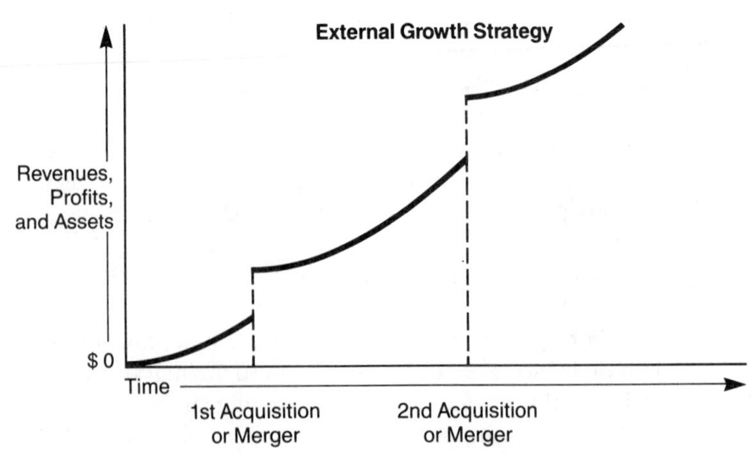

A firm pursues a master strategy of concentric diversification by acquiring new but related product lines for new customers. Southwest Bell Corporation acquired Metromedia Inc.'s cellular telephone business to expand its regular telephone service to a new region of the United States through a related (in this case, cellular) telephone product.[17]

Conglomerate diversification is a strategy involving an unrelated new product that targets new customers. It parallels the product diversification internal strategy but uses acquisition or merger rather than internal development. This strategy is being vigorously pursued by American Brands Inc., a long-time tobacco company. Besides cigarettes, American Brands' stable of products now contains such dissimilar products as Swingline staplers, Jim Beam bourbon, Titleist golf balls, Franklin life insurance, Master locks, and Pinkerton's security services.[18]

External growth master strategies have many benefits relative to internal growth strategies. They permit the acquiring organization to purchase a proven competitor with a track record of success. The firm also usually obtains an experienced management team with the acquisition. The growth in sales, market share, or operating assets (plant and equipment) is rapid and allows the acquiring firm to quickly enter a desirable market and seize an opportunity.

However, external strategies also incorporate several risks. The cost of acquisition may exceed the benefits accrued to the acquiring firm. The organization cultures of the two firms may not be compatible, causing an exodus of the management personnel who made the acquisition attractive. The financial and managerial demands of the new acquisition may drain vitality from the previously healthy acquiring organization. The manager must weigh these and other costs and benefits before electing to pursue growth through acquisition or merger.

Rejuvenation In the life of many organizations, growth eventually stagnates and costs rise. These occurrences could result from the simultaneous maturing of all the products or businesses in the firm's portfolio. Or the strategic managers of the organization might have failed to recognize that competitors were gaining market share at the firm's expense. Regardless of the reason for this condition, the firm must respond with a rejuvenation strategy.

This category of strategies consists of reducing the scope of the business by cutting costs and emphasizing areas of strength in products or markets. Scope reductions are frequently called downsizing and consist of trimming the firm's product or service offerings to concentrate on more profitable markets. The reduction can include decreasing the number of employees or facilities or increasing the number of operations performed in-house (as opposed to purchased services).

An organization cannot continue to downsize indefinitely, as Figure 4.3 shows. Eventually competition will overtake the firm's position in the market and use new technologies or economies due to increased market share to secure industry dominance. Downsizing should be considered a temporary condition that leads to renewed growth. This cycle of downsizing and revitalization gives these strategies the label "rejuvenation."

Master strategies in the rejuvenation category are retrenchment and turnaround. When a firm's managers believe the firm has been overwhelmed by too rapid expan-

Figure 4.3 Rejuvenation Strategy Curve Compared to Internal and External Growth Strategy

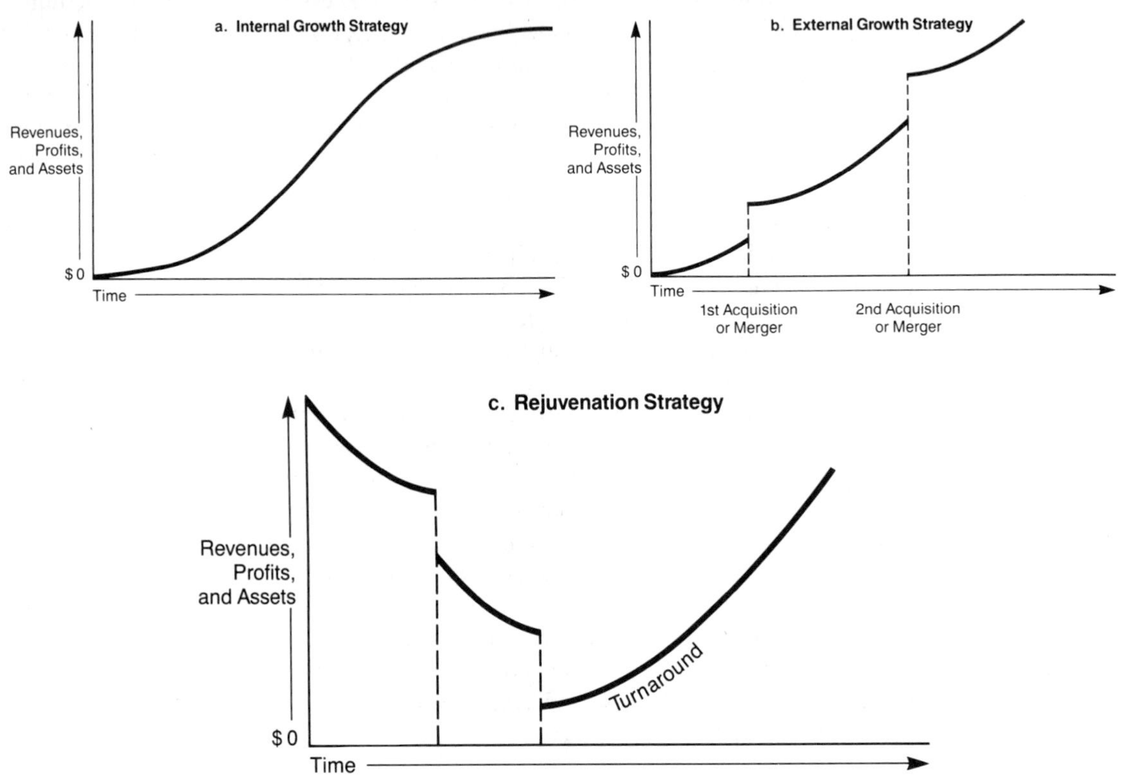

sion or unprofitable acquisitions, they often decide that they need to regain control of the company's core business. To regain this control, they use a retrenchment strategy to reduce costs and assets to a downsized core business (or businesses) that is better handled by the firm's existing managerial capabilities. This allows senior executives to concentrate on a smaller, more manageable asset base.

The conventional retrenchment strategy consists of three steps: focus on monthly profits, streamline operations, and cut out the fat.[19] A more comprehensive approach to retrenchment proposed by Donald Heany suggests a redefinition of the current business. He discusses the direction to a successful retrenchment as retreat and charge. Retreat consists of a systematic streamlining of the firm's operations, while charge involves the initial actions toward redefinition of the firm's operational thrust. This approach can be the first step in a turnaround strategy. If the strategic manager redefines the current concept of the business, then it is easier to turn the firm toward growth.

A retrenchment master strategy positions the organization for turnaround, which moves the firm from a retrenchment posture to selective growth. Selective growth involves conservative moves toward market expansion, taking care not to stretch the firm's weakened financial position beyond reasonable limits. The Strategic Application "The Chrysler Corporation" shows how Lee Iacocca used a strategy of retrenchment and turnaround to pull Chrysler from the brink of disaster.

As with all master strategies, the rejuvenation strategies must be managed carefully. The unwise executive may be tempted to dwell in a retrenchment condition for too long, because it allows the firm to once again be profitable—albeit marginally profitable. However, cost cutting and downsizing are effective only for a limited time. Soon obsolescence of equipment and low employee morale take their toll on the organization. Careful and steady growth are necessary to generate real profits, motivate employees, and keep competitors at bay.

Stabilization During periods of economic instability, an organization may benefit from a stabilization strategy. Stabilization refers to maintaining the firm's current competitive position or defending the firm from a hostile takeover. The strategies that fall under this category are temporary for most organizations and should be changed to growth strategies once the crisis has ended. They are used as strategies to protect the firm from short-term threats and not as long-term master strategies for success and growth.

STRATEGIC APPLICATIONS

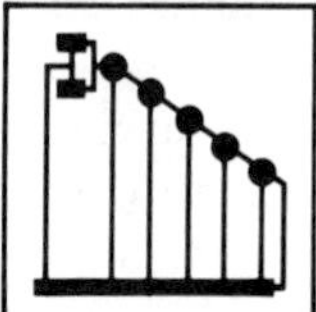

The Chrysler Corporation

Under Lee Iacocca, the Chrysler Corporation has navigated a successful retrenchment-turnaround in an industry that is currently undergoing retrenchment itself.[1] In 1979, Chrysler was on the brink of failure. The quality of its products and productivity were down. Energy and pollution legislation were threatening to drive the cost of manufacturing an automobile beyond the reach of the mass market. Foreign competition was becoming a viable force in the U.S. auto market. These environmental forces and Chrysler's internal inefficiencies combined to produce a $1.7 billion loss in 1980.

Enter Iacocca and his retrenchment strategy. The firm drastically reduced salary expenses. Fixed costs were reduced by approximately $2 billion annually. Chrysler streamlined operations by building all of its cars on the K-car chassis, which saved $1 billion in inventory alone. The company embarked on a program to increase quality while it restructured its balance sheet to reduce interest expense.

Having successfully cut costs and emphasized its operation strength through quality improvements, Chrysler embarked on a five-year $6.6 billion turnaround strategy that stressed product development to ensure future growth.[2] Gradually, Iacocca expanded Chrysler's product line to include upscale products and purchased large shares of foreign auto manufacturers to fill out Chrysler's U.S. product lines. Through retrenchment and turnaround strategies Chrysler has, once again, emerged as a major player in the U.S. automobile industry.

[1] Eugene Finken, "Company Turnaround," *Journal of Business Strategy* 5 (Spring, 1985): 14–24.

[2] Lee Iacocca, "The Rescue and Resuscitation of Chrysler," *Journal of Business Strategy* 4 (Summer, 1983): 67–73.

Some organizations by their nature or the choices of management continue to use a stabilization strategy for a longer term. Owners of small mom-and-pop businesses that provide an adequate income for the family unit may prefer to maintain a comfortable size by continuing their current local market position. Public utilities and some not-for-profit organizations may wish not to grow if their constituents are adequately served by the firm's present size. For these organizations, master strategies for maintenance of existing market share and size are consistent with the strategic goals of the owners, sponsors, and managers.

A maintenance strategy protects the firm's current competitive position during downturns in the economic cycle. This strategy suspends all activities channeled toward internal or external growth until market conditions are favorable enough to support growth strategies. Many organizations that produce durable goods, such as office equipment or commercial vehicles, attempt to maintain their revenue flow during economic recessions by emphasizing the service, repair parts, and service contracts portion of their businesses. They rarely view these peripheral markets as sources of growth, and when economic conditions rebound, they immediately return to emphasizing their major products.

A defensive strategy has recently become more important to protect businesses from unfriendly takeover. This strategy usually involves actions to make the firm appear less attractive as a takeover target. Some of these actions include acquiring another firm to drain the company's cash reserves and to become larger and more expensive to acquire. Or a firm may seek a friendly merger to discourage a potential buyer. When T. Boone Pickens, Jr., the famous corporate raider, targeted asset-rich Newmont Mining Corporation for an attempted takeover, Newmont's management tried to strike an alternate deal with Consolidated Gold Fields PLC, a British company that controlled 26 percent of Newmont's stock. Because of Newmont's defensive actions, Pickens had to battle to acquire the organization.[20]

Stabilization master strategies provide valuable mechanisms for surviving undesirable conditions in the firm's competitive environment. Whether these conditions are produced by temporarily declining markets or hostile takeover attempts, they require a rapid but well-thought-out strategy shift to maintain the firm's competitive position. Strategic managers should be prepared to institute these strategies when they are needed and to move on to other strategies when the crisis passes.

Termination Termination master strategies relinquish control of the firm by selling all or part of its assets. The primary termination strategies used today are divestiture and liquidation. These strategies differ in terms of the degree of termination of the firm's activities. Divestment is only a partial termination of the enterprise, while liquidation is complete termination. Ceasing operations is a traumatic event for the management and employees of the organization and should not be taken lightly as a master strategy. However, it is sometimes in the best interest of the firm's owners (individuals or stockholders) to discontinue operations.

A divestment master strategy, sometimes called harvesting, consists of selling a subsidiary, division, product line, or other part of the organization in order to generate funds for the remaining parts. Unlike retrenchment, divestment is not prompted by an overextension of management capabilities but is a choice by senior managers to divest part of the organization for the purpose of channeling funds to more profitable businesses, selling a subsidiary when the price is high, or becoming less visible to the public. The top management team of UAL Corporation divested its successful Hertz Rental subsidiary to channel more resources into its United Airlines division.[21] Union Carbide sold several profitable subsidiaries to decrease its public visibility after the Bhopal, India, accident in which a Union Carbide plant released toxic gases. The divested unit is not always highly profitable, but more funds can be charged for the sale of a successful subsidiary than for a loser.

The final and most dramatic termination strategy is liquidation, which involves selling all of the company's assets. This action signals that the organization has been unable to remain a viable competitor in its product-markets. Liquidation is usually an attempt to pay as many of the firm's creditors as possible and minimize the disruptions to the local economy. When W. T. Grant decided to close its doors and cease operations as one of the country's larger rural department store chains, its management formulated a liquidation strategy that would clear out its inventories, be fair to its loyal employees, and sell as many of its locations as possible.

Termination strategies can be difficult for the firm's senior managers but may be in the best interest of the stockholders and employees. If the firm becomes a stronger competitor through a divestment, those remaining with the organization will have benefited. In the case of liquidation, it may eliminate the need for investors and employees to continue to contribute money and time to an organization that is ill equipped to compete.

Combination Strategies Seldom does a firm adopt only one of the "pure" master strategies discussed here. More often managers combine master strategies to meet the organization's strategic goals. For example, a firm can use an external growth strategy at the corporate level while employing an internal growth strategy for some of its SBUs. Likewise, a corporate-level master strategy of external growth could include divestment to remove the "dogs" from the firm's portfolio of businesses. Retrenchment strategies typically involve some harvesting. In any case, managers should use the single or a combination of master strategies most appropriate for their business circumstances.

IBM used a combination of master strategies to engineer its recovery from the earnings slump it experienced in the mid-1980s. Harvesting and streamlining of management were used as part of IBM's retrenchment. At the same time, innovation and market development were used to initiate a turnaround. Next, IBM instituted a product diversification master strategy as part of its long-term strategy for internal growth.[22] This stream of master strategies ultimately took the company in the direction of growth.

Ancillary Strategies

Many organizations use ancillary strategies to help amplify the effectiveness of their chosen master strategy. These strategies involve choices at the top levels of management but alone do not set the firm's direction. They are chosen to increase the firm's operations efficiency or to provide access to otherwise restricted resources. Because they involve major commitments and actions by the firm's management, we will discuss them here.

The basic ancillary strategies are consolidation and a variety of approaches to cooperation. A firm that adopts a **consolidation** strategy closes a facility or ceases operations at one or more locations because of obsolescence or inactivity. These choices are made at the highest organizational levels and help improve the positive impact of other strategies such as market penetration through cost leadership. For example, to stem a decline in market share and profits, General Motors closed several of its older and less productive manufacturing plants across the United States. This move was designed to cut production costs and improve quality, which GM hopes will differentiate its products.

Many organizations are faced with situations in which they depend on other firms to carry out their master strategy. For example, Chrysler Corporation needed to purchase 300,000 engines from Volkswagen for its subcompact cars until its own engine plant could meet demand. A push in subcompact cars was one aspect of Chrysler's turnaround strategy. When managers need the support of other organizations in their task environment, cooperative strategies may be appropriate. Ancillary strategies that promote cooperation among organizations include joint ventures, agency agreements, credit agreements, and management agreements.

Joint venturing is the most common cooperative ancillary strategy. In a joint venture, two or more organizations commit financial resources to the same project. This strategic relationship is designed to benefit all parties involved. Joint ventures are frequently used in multinational situations in which government restrictions or cultural prohibitions prevent foreign firms from entering a domestic market. One of the most recent examples of a joint venture is the cooperative agreement between Toyota and General Motors to develop the Chevrolet Geo. This project combined the small-car manufacturing capabilities of Toyota with the physical facility and marketing capabilities of GM to produce a new entry into the U.S. market for compact autos.

When a joint venture is not feasible, organizations can use several forms of **cooperative agreements**. Under one common cooperative agreement, an organization agrees to act as an agent for another. Long-standing examples of this arrangement are the famous Dutch trading companies. These companies neither manufacture nor assemble the goods that they trade, but act as distribution agents for other firms.

Under a credit agreement, one organization assists another in obtaining a line of credit. Some large real estate brokerages will guarantee a short-term loan from a financial institution for an organization that is a trusted client. This is typically used for clients that have entered into the early stages of a major real estate development project and have employed the brokerage firm.

A management agreement is frequently used when absent owners of a physical facility or piece of equipment lack the expertise or interest to manage it themselves. Organizations may own deep-water oil-drilling rigs, commercial office complexes, or nuclear power plants that they wish to have managed. Another firm may not wish to invest the capital to acquire these expensive assets but has managerial and operational capabilities to manage them. The cooperative agreement links these two firms for their mutual benefit. Management agreements are appearing more frequently in an attempt to separate the liability of the managing firm from that of the owning firm.

Cooperative ancillary strategies are useful to provide the organization with capabilities that it could not obtain on its own. However, any form of cooperative agreement reduces each organization's control over its operations. Strategic managers usually choose these strategies carefully and devote much time and attention to the selection of a cooperative partner.

Determinants of the Appropriate Master Strategy

Three categories of factors help determine which strategy is best for the firm: competitive factors, other environmental factors, and organizational factors. The strategy of an effective organization is appropriate for competitive and environmental conditions and uses organizational strengths.

Competitive Factors A strategy must be appropriate for the conditions in the firm's competitive arena. Ian MacMillan argues that the most effective strategy is one that involves acting ahead of competitors. He refers to such a strategy as a preemptive strategy and defines it as "a major move by a focal business ahead of moves by its adversaries, which allows it to secure an advantageous position from which it is difficult to dislodge because of the advantages it has captured by being the first mover." According to MacMillan, the astute strategic manager uses the results of the environmental assessment to recognize preemptive opportunities and chooses a strategy that best takes advantage of one or more of them.[23] For example, if competitors are fighting for cost leadership, the manager might choose a differentiation strategy to avoid cutthroat pricing.

A related consideration is the firm's ability to capture enough early market share to take advantage of the experience curve to gain an initial price advantage. Several studies of the experience curve suggest that operations costs decline by 10 to 30 percent with each doubling of the cumulative output.[24] The result is a substantial savings for firms that can maintain a high market share. Thus, the cost leadership strategy of entering the market at a low price to quickly gain share can increase profits over the long term only if competitive conditions allow the firm to quickly capture the lion's share of the market. If the firm cannot generate sufficient demand to take advantage of the experience curve effects, cost leadership is not an effective strategy to select.

Other Environmental Factors Several external factors besides competitors affect the selection of a strategy. Some of these factors are current business and competitive conditions, regulations that govern the industry, technological developments, and social issues. No one knows exactly how all of these factors interact to point to a specific strategy. However, some previous writings help the manager select a strategy under a given set of external conditions. For example, George Yip reports that the firm that chooses to pursue an opportunity in an industry with high entry barriers should adopt an acquisition strategy. If the opportunity is in an industry that is highly compatible with the firm's current businesses, then product diversification is the better strategy.[25]

Three additional external factors that influence the selection of a strategy are the nature of the industry, entry barriers, and exit barriers. The nature of the industry refers to its life cycle position, technology, and regulation. Research conducted by William Hall suggests that firms in mature industries such as steel, beer, home appliances, and tobacco are most successful if they adopt a cost leadership or differentiation strategy.[26] Firms in developing industries with new technologies are seldom regulated and can use market-related strategies such as penetration or development to promote continuous growth.[27] In a similar vein, Woo and Cooper suggest that the choice of a strategy is at least partially affected by the firm's location on the BCG matrix. They report that firms in the low-share, low-growth quadrant of the matrix are more successful if they use a focus (niche) strategy that emphasizes quality or cost.[28]

Firms in industries with large entry and exit barriers must concentrate on strategies that enhance their ability to compete within the industry. This is because, to a great extent, they are captive within their industries. Organizations in industries without these barriers can consider strategies that include acquisition and divestment as options.[29]

Finally, some experts suggest that the nature of the environment itself affects the choice of a strategy.[30] For example, Mascarenhas proposes that the stability of the environment is important to consider when choosing a strategy. He states that firms in stable environments should use a market penetration strategy, while firms in unstable environments need more flexible strategies.[31]

Organizational Factors As with external factors, experts are not sure of the exact relationship among various internal organizational factors and the appropriateness of a strategy. However, recent work gives us some insight into the effect of organizational factors on the choice of a strategy. Internal factors that have been related to strategies are organization structure, culture, background and experience of the CEO, and the chosen strategy itself.

One of the first organizational factors to be related to strategy was organization structure. In 1962, Chandler conducted a historical analysis and concluded that the structure of the firm must be consistent with and facilitate the implementation of the firm's strategy.[32] Several studies supported Chandler's observations until Berg, Hall and Sais, and others presented arguments that the relationship may not be that clear. Rather, in some firms, strategy may follow the structure that is operating in the organization.[33] The current speculation is that large, mature firms with rigid structures will select strategies that fit their existing structure. Managers prefer this to experiencing the trauma associated with a massive structural change.

Another internal organization factor that can influence strategy formulation is the organization's culture. As mentioned in Chapter 1, Peters and Waterman's book *In Search of Excellence* helped turn management attention to organization culture—the structures, behaviors, processes, rites, rituals, myths, symbols, and traditions that distinguish one organization from another. Peters and Waterman reported that certain organization cultures were closely related to excellent performance. However, later research indicates that there is no one best culture to fit all situations; instead, it is most important that the culture match the demands of the chosen strategy and existing business conditions.[34]

Culture appears to have both short- and long-term effects on strategy formulation. Consistent with Peters and Waterman,[35] most strategic managers believe that an organization's existing culture cannot be changed in the short term. Therefore, the current culture constrains the firm's choices of which strategies are most feasible. Culture influences the way that the manager sees the world and the role of the firm in that world. Alternative strategies will be considered feasible only if they are consistent with the manager's perspective of business conditions. For example, Valley National Bank had a traditional banking culture that espoused personal contact with the customer. Influenced by this, the bank's managers developed a strategy to respond to the competitive pressures of deregulation, instituting a personal selling program in all branches. Some of the strategic managers were later surprised by the success of telemarketing in other Arizona banks because they had not even considered it a feasible alternative approach.

However, the organization's culture can itself be a strategic choice for the manager in the long term. The organization's top executives can institute a program to change the culture and align it with the future strategy of the firm. The manager first selects the future strategy for the firm and determines which type of culture would be supportive of that strategy. Next, the strategic manager should implement a long-term program of cultural socialization to adapt the culture to the firm's long-term strategy.[36] In this way, culture becomes a vehicle to carry the organization to high performance rather than an obstacle to be overcome.

Jae Song writes that the background and experience of the CEO is an important factor in the choice of a firm's strategy. Song's work supports the preferences of the manager as a major consideration in the strategy selection process. Therefore, if the strategic manager has a strong preference for growth through acquisition as opposed to internal innovation and development, then the firm will probably adopt an external growth strategy.[37]

Work by Richard Rumelt mentioned in Chapter 3 indicates that some strategies, by their very nature, are more profitable than others. Rumelt looked at several organizations that ranged from single-business firms to conglomerates with unrelated businesses. He found that firms with vertical integration and conglomerate diversification strategies were less profitable. This indicates that the strategic manager should carefully analyze his or her business conditions before selecting one of these two strategies.[38]

Strategy Selection Techniques

To choose the appropriate strategy, the manager may use the strategy selection technique based on the model presented in this book. This technique consists of using the following list of questions to determine if the proposed strategy takes into account all of the preceding stages of the strategic management process:

1. Is the strategy consistent with the results of the environmental assessment?
   a. Does it consider all of the relevant elements and stakeholders within the task environment?
   b. Does it minimize uncertainties and dependencies so that the firm is not vulnerable as a result of this strategy?
   c. Is the strategy appropriate for the firm's selected domain?
2. Does the strategy use the strengths of the organization?
   a. Does it provide for the existing demands of the firm's current constituents?
   b. Is the strategy the most effective way to meet the demands of the new opportunity?
   c. Does the strategy use existing slack in areas where the firm has strengths to meet the demands of the new opportunity?
3. Is the strategy consistent with the firm's stated mission, and does it accomplish strategic goals?
   a. Does the strategy reflect the organization's strategic posture?
   b. Does the strategy build on the firm's functional orientation (e.g., market-oriented strategy with a marketing functional orientation)?
   c. Does the strategy provide the best method available to meet the firm's strategic goals?

Another approach to strategy evaluation is based on the list of questions in Chapter Appendix 4.2. This list, based on the work of Tilles,[39] was developed by Steiner, Miner, and Gray to evaluate master strategies.[40] Regardless of which list the manager uses, he or she should attempt to answer these questions to evaluate the appropriateness of the chosen strategy in light of the firm's current business conditions and its current capabilities.

Summary

This chapter has described the strategy formulation stage of the strategic management process, the stage at which the information from the environmental assessment and the capabilities analysis is used to develop a strategy for achieving strategic goals. Strategy formulation may follow a synoptic or an incremental approach.

Strategy formulation begins with the creation of a statement setting forth the purpose of the organization. The mission statement should specify the firm's business, strategic posture, functional orientation, and orientation toward its primary constituencies.

Senior managers use this mission as the basis for developing strategic goals, which may cover a variety of performance areas: employee relations and development, international competitive position, market position, productivity, profitability, return growth, service leadership, social responsibility, and technology leadership.

To specify how the organization will achieve these strategic goals, managers develop strategies. These strategies may be formulated at any of the four levels of strategy development. Several strategies were defined and classified into three general categories:

Generic strategies

Master strategies

Ancillary strategies

The manager may choose from a variety of strategies at both corporate and business levels. Generic strategies are cost leadership, differentiation, and focus. Master strategies include internal growth, external growth, rejuvenation, stabilization, or termination of the business. Ancillary strategies increase the organization's operations efficiency and provide access to otherwise restricted resources. They include both consolidation and cooperation strategies. The selection of one or a combination of these strategies depends on three categories of factors: competitive, environmental, and organizational. In weighing these factors to choose a strategy, the manager asks whether a given strategy is consistent with the results of the environmental assessment, uses the organization's strengths, and is consistent with the firm's mission and strategic goals.

Depending on the competitive and environmental conditions that the company faces and its internal capabilities, the manager selects the strategy that will best utilize its strengths to achieve organizational goals.

Questions

1. What is the difference between the rational synoptic and logical incremental views of strategy formulation? Which perspective is considered by some to be impractical for most major organizations? Why is this perspective impractical? Why do strategic management experts continue to recommend it?

2. At the library, obtain copies of annual reports of three major firms in the United States. Read the material that precedes the presentation of the financial statements. What is the mission of each firm? (Be sure to look for answers to the questions that relate to a mission statement.)

3. Select a major firm such as Motorola or Ford Motor Company and trace its history over the past 20 years through business periodicals and annual reports. What major types of strategies were used (e.g., internal growth, external growth)? Why do you think the company used that strategy?

4. Look at a medium-sized firm in your region and determine the strategy under which it is currently operating. Next, apply the strategy selection technique described at the end of this chapter to evaluate the appropriateness of this strategy for current business conditions.

5. In groups or teams for a simulation exercise or case analyses, use the process described in the first four chapters of this book to develop a strategy for your team. During the planning process, look at your environment, capabilities, and mission.

Notes

1. From William T. DeBary, ed., *Sources of Chinese Tradition*, Vol. II.

2. Marilyn A. Harris, Gordon Bock, Anne R. Field and Geoff Lewis, "How IBM Is Fighting Back," *Business Week*, November 17, 1986, 152–157.

3. C. E. Lindbloom, "The Science of 'Muddling Through,' " *Public Administration Review* 19 (Spring 1959): 79–88.

4. J. B. Quinn, *Strategies for Change: Logical Incrementalism* (Homewood, Ill.: Irwin, 1980), 14–15.

5. For example, B. L. T. Hedberg, P. C. Nystrom, and W. H. Starbuck, "Camping on Seesaws: Prescriptions for a Self-Designing Organization," *Administrative Science Quarterly* 26 (March 1976): 41–65.

6. Charles Stubbart, "Why We Need a Revolution in Strategic Planning," *Long Range Planning* 18 (December 1985): 68–76.

7. Quinn, *Strategies for Change*, 13–152.

8. Kathleen Deveny, Corie Brown, William J. Hampton, James B. Treece, "Going for the Lion's Share," *Business Week*, July 18, 1988, 70–72.

9. Mario Shao, "David Lee Is Back at Square One—and He's Thrilled," *Business Week*, July 25, 1988, 62–63.

10. Dan E. Schendel and C. W. Hofer, *Strategic Management: A New View of Business Policy and Planning* (Boston: Little, Brown, 1979), 13.

11. Michael E. Porter, *Competitive Strategy* (New York: The Free Press, 1980), 35.

12. Porter, *Competitive Strategy*, 35.

13. See John A. Pearce II and R. B. Robinson, Jr., *Strategic Management: Strategy Formulation and Implementation*, 3d ed. (Homewood, Ill.: Irwin, 1988); Lawrence R. Jauch and W. E. Glueck, *Business Policy and Strategic Management*, 5th ed. (New York: McGraw-Hill, 1988); Samuel C. Certo and J. P. Peter, *Strategic Management: Concepts and Applications* (New York: Random House, 1988); Arthur A. Thompson, Jr., and A. J. Strickland III, *Strategic Management: Concepts and Cases*, 4th ed. (Plano, Tex.: Business Publications, 1987).

14. H. Igor Ansoff, *Corporate Strategy* (New York: McGraw-Hill Book, 1965), 109.

15. Jonathan B. Levine, "Why National Came to the Fairchild Fire Sale," *Business Week*, September 14, 1987, 38–39.

16. Keith H. Hammonds, "Cullinet's Comeback Trail Is Full of Thorns," *Business Week*, September 19, 1987, 132.

17. John Keller et al., "Hello Anywhere: The Cellular Phone Boom Will Change the Way You Live," *Business Week*, September 21, 1987, 84–92.

18. Resa King, "American Brands Is Breaking Its Cigarette Habit," *Business Week*, September 14, 1987, 90–94.

19. Donald F. Heany, "Businesses in Profit Trouble," *The Journal of Business Strategy* 5 (Spring, 1985): 4–13.

20. Jo Ellen Davis and Richard A. Melcher, "One Swallow Could Make Pickens' Summer," *Business Week*, September 14, 1987, 37.

21. "United Once More," *Time*, June 22, 1987, 46–47.

22. Marilyn A. Harris, Gordon Bock, Anne R. Field, and Geoff Lewis, "How IBM Is Fighting Back."

23. Ian C. MacMillan, "Preemptive Strategies," *Journal of Business Strategy* 4 (Fall, 1983): 16–26.

24. Pandai Ghemawat, "Building Strategy on the Experience Curve," *Harvard Business Review* 63 (March–April 1985): 143–149.

25. George S. Yip, "Diversification Entry: Internal Development versus Acquisition," *Strategic Management Journal* 3 (October–December 1982): 331–345.

26. William K. Hall, "Survival Strategies in a Hostile Environment," *Harvard Business Review* 58 (September–October 1980): 75–85.

27. Anne Sigismiend Huff, "Industry Influences in Strategy Reformulation," *Strategic Management Journal* 3 (April–June 1982): 119–131.

28. Carolyn Y. Woo and H. C. Cooper, "The Surprising Case of Low Market Share," *Harvard Business Review* 60 (November–December 1982): 106–113.

29. Kathryn Rudie Harrigan, "Barriers to Entry and Competitive Strategies," *Strategic Management Journal* 2 (October–December 1981): 395–412; Kathryn Rudie Harrigan, "The Effects of Exit Barriers upon Strategic Flexibility," *Strategic Management Journal* 1 (July–September 1980): 165–176.

30. George S. Yip, "Who Needs Strategic Planning?" *Journal of Business Strategy* 6 (Fall, 1985): 30–42.

31. M. Briance Mascarenhas, "Planning for Flexibility," *Long Range Planning* 14 (October, 1981): 78–82.

32. A. D. Chandler, *Strategy and Structure* (Cambridge, Mass.: MIT Press, 1962).

33. Norman Berg, "Corporate Role in Diversified Companies: A Working Paper," in Bernard Taylor and Keith MacMillian, eds., *Business Policy: Teaching and Research* (New York: Halstad Press, 1973), 298–347; D. J. Hall and M. A. Sais, "Strategy Follows Structure," *Strategic Management Journal* 1 (April–June 1980): 149–165; Robert A. Pitts, "Strategies and Structures for Diversification," *Academy of Management Journal* 20 (June 1977) 298–347.

34. "Who's Excellent," *Business Week*, November 5, 1984, 76–79.

35. Thomas J. Peters and R. H. Waterman, *In Search of Excellence: Lessons from America's Best-Run Companies* (New York: Harper & Row 1982), 103–106.

36. Richard Pascale, "The Paradox of 'Corporate Culture': Reconciling Ourselves to Socialization," *California Management Review* 27 (Winter 1988): 26–41.

37. Jae H. Song, "Diversification Strategies and the Experience of Top Executives of Large Firms," *Strategic Management Journal* 3 (October–December, 1982): 377–380.

38. Richard P. Rumelt, "Strategy, Structure and Economic Performance," Division of Research, Harvard Business School (Boston 1974); Richard P. Rumelt, "Diversification Strategy and Profitability," *Strategic Management Journal* 3 (1982): 359–369.

39. Seymore Tilles, "How to Evaluate Corporate Strategy," *Harvard Business Review* 41 (July–August 1963): 111–121.

40. George A. Steiner, J. B. Miner, and E. R. Gray, *Management Policy and Strategy: Texts, Readings, and Cases*, 3d ed. (New York: MacMillan, 1986), 150–154.

Case for Discussion

Lessons from Hollywood

Few businesses are more costly or risky than the movies. The average movie takes 18 months to make and costs over $20 million to produce and $6.6 million to promote. It must be launched in a highly competitive, glutted market where little brand loyalty exists. In addition, the product's usefulness or appeal cannot be tested before full production. The break-even point for a film may be as much as three times the cost of producing it, or as much as $60 million for each film.

How then does any firm succeed in an environment where only 30 percent of the new products can hope to be profitable after exhausting all channels (e.g., home video, network and pay TV, and foreign releases)? According to *Fortune*, the answer lies in three common attributes: being a division of a larger corporation, having the ability to produce a succession of hits, and having competent and enduring management. Industry leaders such as Warner Brothers, Paramount, and Disney all have these attributes. However, they have used different strategies to capture a combined 45 percent share of the film entertainment market.

Source: "Lessons from Hollywood Hit Men," *Fortune*, August 29, 1988, 78–82.

Warner Brothers builds its strategy around film stars with drawing power such as Chevy Chase, Barbra Streisand, Goldie Hawn, and Clint Eastwood. Each year Warner tries to locate a movie that will provide a vehicle for this stable of stars with audience appeal. Paramount Pictures also focuses on the people side of the business but expands its strategy to include actors, directors, and producers. Paramount signs these industry megatalents to "lucrative, long term, multimovie contracts." Adopting a different strategy, Walt Disney Studios, under the Touchstone label, places the story over the stars. Films such as *Willow* and *Who Framed Roger Rabbit?* use unknown actors in unique stories or with novel cinematography.

In a business in which the product is intangible and the market whimsical, the strategic manager faces complex and turbulent business conditions. Profit is still the bottom line, and movie executives are accountable to stockholders. One way to contend with these complexities is to formulate a strategy that takes advantage of environmental opportunities and draws on the firm's capabilities. In the filmmaking business, opportunities are difficult to assess and capabilities are short-lived. However, it is a dynamic and exciting challenge for the brave strategic manager.

Discussion Questions

1. Conduct an environmental assessment for the movie executive of one of the three firms mentioned in the case. Be sure to indicate which firm you have chosen.

2. Conduct a capabilities analysis for the strategic manager of Walt Disney Studios. Limit your analysis to what you know about Disney and its strengths.

3. Compare the three strategies mentioned in the case to the strategies described in this chapter. How can any or all of the strategies in this case be classified using the master strategy categories in Table 4.2?

4. If you were the senior strategic manager of one of the also-ran movie companies, what strategy would you recommend to crack the dominance of the three firms described in this case?

5. Which strategy of the three firms mentioned in the case presents the best long-term prospects for the firm over the next 20 to 30 years? Which strategy involves the least risk?

Appendix 4.1

Types of Strategies

This supplement provides an expanded discussion of the strategies that were presented in the chapter and when they might be appropriate for an organization.

Generic Strategies

Cost Leadership

Cost leadership as a strategy is one of the "generic" strategies introduced by Michael Porter. To use this strategy effectively, a firm must be the cost leader in its market. According to Porter, "Cost leadership requires aggressive construction of efficient-scale facilities, vigorous pursuit of cost reductions from experience, tight cost and overhead control, avoidance of marginal customer accounts, and cost minimization in areas like R&D, service, sales force, advertising, and so on."[1]

A cost leadership strategy is based on gaining a strong competitive advantage through economies of scale, scope, and technology. Economies of scale are created by using large volume to increase operational efficiencies in the production of a good or service. Scope economies include scale but also include the benefits of large volume on administrative and marketing efficiencies. Porter cautions that the firm must sufficiently differentiate its product or service to maintain adequate profit margins. If it fails to do this, then the product acts like a commodity, and profitability declines to unacceptable levels.

Differentiation

The second of Porter's generic strategies is differentiation. Organizations that adopt this strategy attempt to develop ways to make their product or service appear unique. The desired result of differentiation is increased demand.

Differentiation can be based on the product itself, the distribution system, the service provided after the sale, or the marketing program used. What is important is that the users of the product or service perceive it as unique or superior on some dimension that they value. The basis for differentiation will vary across markets.

Products that have features or characteristics that are unique or are protected by patents are most suited for this strategy. However, occasionally a firm can create the perceptions of uniqueness for a commodity product. For example, Clorox bleach has been successful at creating the impression that it is a superior cleaning bleach, even though all bleaches consist of the same chemical compound.

Focus (Niche)

The third of Porter's generic strategies is a focus, or niche, strategy. Porter suggests that there are two types of focus strategies, cost and differentiation. When a firm adopts a focus strategy, it selects a specific, recognizable segment or segments of a total market and concentrates its product development and marketing efforts on that market niche. The niche is specific in that it is only a portion of the total market that is large or small enough to match the organization's capabilities and needs.

If cost is the basis for the niche strategy, then the firm must function as the cost leader in its niche. Thus, the previously discussed requirements for a cost leadership strategy apply here. The same is true for the enterprise that uses a differentiation focus strategy.

The Japanese have been especially adept at using a focus strategy to enter U. S. markets. They typically target the low-price and low-profit niche of a market that has been neglected or abandoned by U.S. firms. The Japanese supplier becomes firmly entrenched in its niche and builds a reputation for quality and service within that niche. Having accomplished this, the Japanese competitor has a base for launching entries into larger, more profitable niches.

Master Strategies

Internal Growth

Internal growth master strategies include vertical integration, market penetration, market development, and product diversification.

Vertical Integration Vertical integration through continuous growth is the internal development of inputs or outputs for the firm that were previously obtained from outside sources. Internal development of inputs is backward vertical integration, while development of outputs (captive distributorships or sales outlets) is forward vertical integration. For example, strategic managers at IBM selected backward vertical integration when they decided to create an internal capability to produce the semiconductors and integrated circuits the company used in computer manufacturing.

A vertical integration strategy is not limited to materials for manufacturing. General Motors used it as a source of personnel by creating the General Motors Institute to provide engineers for its various divisions.

Internal vertical integration can decrease the organization's dependence on suppliers or channels of distribution. Therefore, it can be a particularly effective strategy when dependence on external sources threatens to hinder the firm's performance. For example, if the organization's suppliers are subject to strikes that cause a shutdown of its operations, then vertical integration may be necessary. Or, on the output side, safety or quality requirements may force the firm to develop its own distributorships rather than sell through independent distributors. However, internal vertical integration must be undertaken carefully, for it introduces the risks related to starting any new venture.

Market Penetration (Concentration) A master strategy of market penetration or concentration leads to new ways to capture a larger share of the existing market. This typically involves intensified sales or promotion coupled with decreased price to pull customers away from competitors. This strategy can work for public-sector firms as is evidenced by the competition for recruits for the voluntary military services. The U.S. Army awarded a $100 million contract to an ad agency to design a new recruiting campaign for 1988 and beyond. The Army's master strategy is to attract potential enlistees from the other branches of the military.

A market penetration strategy involves relatively little risk, as customers are already familiar with the product. It is merely a matter of convincing customers that they should prefer a firm's product or service over that of competitors. However, a market penetration strategy can have hidden costs and should be considered only if the firm believes that the strategy is cost effective. If the product is in a mature market dominated by a single firm, then the cost of overcoming the leader's competitive advantage may be too great. Market penetration strategies are most effective as an internal growth strategy when the firm operates in high-volume, low-margin product-markets with product life cycles that are either very short or very long.

Market Development A firm can also grow internally by a market development master strategy, which creates new markets for existing products. It is a relatively inexpensive strategy that typically involves few major risks and requires only minor modification to the product or service to present it to a new market. However, not all products or services are transferable to other markets.

Market development as a master strategy is typically limited to general-purpose, commodity-type products. In some cases, firms with highly specialized products or services attempt to use a market development master strategy. However, they often have to make expensive modifications to the product or service to introduce it to the new market. An example is the four-wheel-drive vehicle introduced to the U.S. market by Isuzu Motor Company under the brand name Trooper. The same vehicle had been sold in other countries for several years, and Isuzu believed that it could be introduced in the United States with only slight cosmetic changes. The results of this attempt at market development were mixed. The company did determine that there was a potential market for such a vehicle, but also determined that Trooper must have a larger engine, better sound system, and more comfortable seats before it would be suitable for the U.S. market. As Isuzu found, a market development master strategy must be carefully reviewed to determine whether the potential benefits are greater than the costs of entering the market.

Product Diversification Product diversification is the development of a new product for entirely new markets. Strong emphasis on research and development can produce innovations that are unrelated or only remotely related to existing products. These new products or services may require new operations, marketing, and management capabilities. Therefore, great risks and costs may be associated with this internal growth strategy. However, the firm maintains direct control of the new product or service.

If the new markets materialize, the payoffs can be great due to the firm's advantage of being the "first to market." For example, the desire to reduce the cost of check processing led Valley National Bank to develop the Check Safekeeping Program. This program was designed to eliminate the returning of canceled checks to customers. The result was a substantial savings in processing costs and freed check-processing facilities for other uses. Thus, Valley National Bank could utilize these facilities to introduce a new check-processing service that it sold to other banks. In addition, the program was so successful that it created a demand for information on the program. This spawned a new product: seminars on the Check Safekeeping Program. Participants were charged a fee, and a new product (training) was introduced to a new market (other bankers).

External Growth through Merger and Acquisition

Businesses may adopt a master strategy of external growth via vertical integration, horizontal integration, horizontal diversification, concentric diversification, or conglomerate diversification.

Vertical Integration External vertical integration involves building the firm's capabilities to provide its own sources of input and output through the acquisition of or merger with a firm that supplies these resources. The acquisition of a supplier of a critical raw material or subassembly can reduce the firm's vulnerability to interruptions in the flow of the critical input. Likewise, the acquisition of a source of distribution can assure the firm of a reliable customer. A case in point is the recent purchase of the Kentucky Fried Chicken fast-food chain by PepsiCo. This guaranteed that Pepsi products would be dispensed in all Kentucky Fried Chicken outlets.

Robert Buzzell, of Harvard, offers advice to strategic managers who are considering vertical integration as a master strategy. He outlines the pluses and minuses of vertical integration that are summarized in Table 4.1A. Furthermore, he cautions the manager to look for the following pitfalls when considering vertical integration through acquisition or merger:[2]

- Beware of increased investment: When a firm is acquired for the sole purpose of reducing dependence on other sources, it often adds assets without a commensurate increase in return.
- Evaluate the cost-benefit of alternatives to ownership: A firm may be able to increase reli-

Table 4.1A Pluses and Minuses of Vertical Integration

Pluses	Minuses
Reduces transfer costs	Typically involves large capital outlays for acquisitions
Improves reliability of sources of input and output	Creates an unbalanced condition in which the capacities of the acquired firms do not match the capacities of the acquiring firm
Improves coordination of the stages of production and operations	Reduces flexibility because the firm can no longer maintain alternate suppliers
Stimulates product innovation because the firm has control of sources of supply and distribution	May result in a decrease in the efficiencies of specialized administration and marketing functions
Creates higher entry barriers for potential entrants	

Source: Robert D. Buzzell, "Is Vertical Integration Profitable?" *Harvard Business Review* 61 (January–February 1983): 92–102.

ability of sources and reduce dependence through long-term contracts or joint ventures rather than acquisition.

- Avoid partial vertical integration: Research shows that the most benefit is derived from highly integrated operations. Therefore, managers should avoid "gradual, piecemeal" vertical integration.
- Carefully analyze the firm's needs: Make sure that the percentage of the acquired firm's capabilities that are needed is sufficient to justify the acquisition. If only a small percentage of the acquired firm's capacity is needed, then either its capabilities are underutilized, which increases cost, or it must sell the overcapacity in the marketplace. In the latter event, the acquiring firm is thrust into an unfamiliar product-market and may not be an effective competitor.
- Question any reports that vertical integration reduces raw material costs: Unless the organization can monopolize critical resources through vertical integration, it is still subject to the price conditions that exist in the open market. Vertical integration seldom results in a cornering of a market for a resource.

Horizontal Integration Horizontal integration uses merger and/or acquisition of a competing firm as the means to gain a larger share of the market. This is a popular form of external growth that minimizes the risks associated with acquisition because the organization is purchasing a firm in a familiar product-market.

Businesses choose to pursue a horizontal integration master strategy for several reasons. Such a strategy immediately increases market share, which allows the firm to take advantage of economies of scale and scope. It also reduces the firm's dependence on the competitive element of its task environment by giving the firm direct control over a competitor. It quickly provides the necessary capabilities to firms that lack the time or expertise to capture substantial market share in product-markets through internal development. Finally, horizontal integration gives the firm rapid access to channels of distribution.

These were some of the reasons why the May Company, a major retailing firm, acquired Associated Dry Goods for a reported $2.5 billion. The acquisition removed a major competitor from the market for May and moved it into the ranks of the top five retailers in the United States. In addition, it instantly increased revenue and provided hundreds of new retail locations for the company.

Horizontal Diversification Horizontal diversification involves the acquisition of a new yet unrelated product or service for use by the organization's current customers. Safeway grocery stores have started selling shoes, clothing, and sporting goods to keep customers in the store longer. Sears sells insurance and other financial services in its stores, while in Europe most large department stores sell groceries. One of the earliest examples of this strategy was the automobile industry. All three major auto manufacturers horizontally diversified into auto loans to facilitate the sale of cars.

One of the reasons that a firm would adopt a horizontal diversification strategy is to expand its product or service offerings to increase the customer's perceived costs of switching to a competitor. If the user of the firm's product believes that convenience or quality makes looking elsewhere too expensive, then the organization has two sales to that customer rather than one.

The downside of this strategy is that the unrelated product-market may require unique capabilities that the firm does not possess. For example, when Anheuser-Busch acquired Eagle Snacks, it was faced with new technologies for food processing and packaging. To date, Eagle is not a major competitor in the snack food industry.

Concentric Diversification Concentric diversification involves the acquisition of a firm with a new but related product for new markets. This master strategy allows the organization to take advantage of some capabilities that currently exist in the firm while developing new customer bases. It also may involve entering markets that are counter to the business cycles of the firm's present products. This master strategy is typically pursued by organizations that have a unique capability that functions as a competitive strength.

Honda capitalized on its reputation for quality and its existing dealer network for motorcycles to enter a very mature automobile market in the United States. Honda's managers believed that products such as automobiles were similar enough to the company's motorcycles to allow its competitive strengths to carry over. Honda once again used this strategy to introduce its all-terrain vehicles to U.S. markets. In both cases, the company developed new markets for related transportation products. The strategic managers at Honda felt that their strengths in motorized transportation vehicles would decrease the risks associated with growth in the highly competitive U.S. market.

Conglomerate Diversification Organizations that pursue a conglomerate diversification strategy are in the business of buying and selling businesses that add new products to their portfolio or mix of products. Therefore, this master strategy is limited to the corporate level of strategy development, where the primary criterion for selecting a strategy is portfolio management. As they buy and sell businesses, organizations experience immediate growth or decline in revenues and operating profits. However, the overall effect is an increase in assets.

Businesses pursue a conglomerate diversification strategy at the corporate level for several reasons:

- The firm wishes to maintain a balanced portfolio in terms of cash users and cash generators.
- The firm wishes to balance the age or life cycle stages of the products or businesses in its portfolio.
- The firm wishes to increase the return on its investment over what it can obtain on its current businesses or in securities.
- To exit a decaying industry, the firm wishes to explore new product technologies, product-markets, or both.
- The firm wishes to capture new technologies that may evolve as substitutes for its existing products.

Conglomerate diversification carries substantial risk for the enterprise. In theory, this strategy should spread the risk of maintaining profitability over a portfolio of product-markets. However, research appears to indicate that conglomerate firms are generally less profitable than firms of similar size employing more related strategies. One possible explanation is that successful, well-managed firms are expensive to acquire and take longer to generate positive returns on the acquiring firm's investment. Also, the culture of the acquired firm typically changes after acquisition, and the high performance that made it an attractive acquisition target is difficult to maintain under the new culture. Nevertheless, a well-managed conglomerate diversification strategy can provide the firm with a balanced mix of businesses for long-term profitability while assuring the availability of short-term cash to build promising new businesses.

Rejuvenation Strategies

A master strategy for rejuvenation consists of retrenchment or turnaround, and often combines the two.

Retrenchment Retrenchment is a master strategy for negative growth and is undertaken in response to a decline in profitability. The conditions that have caused the profit slide are primarily internal to the firm rather than competitive or economic in nature. The industry or product-market may be growing while the firm is in a state of decline. Or the market may be decreasing, but the firm is declining more rapidly. The main cause of the decline is that the demands in the firm's environment have become too volatile for the capabilities of its managers. Either the strategic and operational management capabilities are stretched too thin, or the environment has changed in a direction that exceeds management's capabilities.

When the firm's managers recognize this, they adopt a retrenchment strategy of cost and asset reduction. The organization typically attempts to return to its basic or core business that best suits the size and capabilities of the management team. The intention is to pull back to markets in which the managers feel capable enough to solidify the firm's profitability and regroup for another attempt at better managed growth.

Turnaround Following a period of retrenchment, a firm should be in a position to start on a gradual turnaround toward growth. Turnaround strategies involve conservative moves to capitalize on the strengths that were consolidated during the retrenchment strategy. The strategic manager tries to breathe new life into the organization by reversing the decline in revenues and profits. Once the retrenchment is complete, sales generally level off or increase slightly. Profits will turn positive as unproductive assets are eliminated. More competitive service and pricing will gradually increase revenues, which will further improve profits. All of these events will help improve the morale of employees, which will further enhance productivity.

The benefits of turnaround are to provide a profit base from which to launch the new growth strategy. However, expenditures for fixed assets and expensive ventures into new high-risk technologies should be avoided until the organization has returned to a sound financial condition.

Stabilization Strategies

Some master strategies are designed to carry the organization through periods of extreme instability in its task environment. These strategies help the firm to maintain its revenue stream during periods of economic downturn or protect it from hostile takeover attempts. Stabilization strategies are transient strategies that allow the firm to survive these malevolent environmental conditions until a growth strategy is again feasible. The two primary stabilization strategies used today are a maintenance strategy and a defensive strategy.

Maintenance During an economic downturn, a firm often adopts a maintenance strategy, which consists of fortifying the firm's market share and profits at the expense of growth. The firm must attempt to decrease costs to maintain profitability while lowering price, increasing promotions, or emphasizing a secondary business to maintain market share and gross revenues. The firm attempts to maintain its necessary productive capacity in preparation for the eventual upswing. This strategy is strictly a short-term measure to protect the competitive viability of the enterprise.

Strategic managers must take caution not to continue with a maintenance strategy when an economic recovery starts. The lower operating costs and continued profitability of the firm may tempt the manager to persist with this conservative strategy. However, if the firm fails to compete aggressively when the market enters a growth period, competitors will take this opportunity to grab market share.

Defense

According to a special report in *Business Week*, "deal mania" was operating in the United States during the middle 1980s. In the words of that report, "The tempo is frantic, and the future prosperity of the U.S. is at stake."[3] Corporate raiders such as Carl C. Icahn and T. Boone Pickens, Jr., are well known and feared by corporate CEOs. In this period of frequent acquisitions and takeovers, a stabilization master strategy to defend the firm from unfriendly suitors has become increasingly familiar. The defensive master strategy is based on restructuring the organization in both an operational and financial sense to decrease its attractiveness as a takeover target. The goal of this strategy is to reach a stock price at which acquisition of the firm is no longer feasible. Several tactics have been used to accomplish this goal, including stock buybacks, leveraged buyouts, and the sale of assets.

Stephen Lofthouse tells the strategic manager how to develop a defensive stabilization strategy to resist takeover. He suggests that when the strategic manager is faced with the need to adopt a defensive master strategy, he or she should follow these guidelines:[4]

1. If the odds of being acquired are significant, be prepared in advance for a possible takeover attempt.
2. Conduct an analysis to determine whether the firm is a likely takeover target.
3. Determine the value of the firm using the valuation methods popular with corporate raiders.
4. Implement steps to restructure the firm before the takeover attempt by improving economic performance.
5. Have environmental scanners active to detect an imminent bid.
6. Become familiar with the laws and regulations that govern the legality of takeover attempts.
7. Plan in advance what actions the firm will take after the bid.

These steps emphasize that the strategic manager must always be prepared with a master strategy to defend the firm from an unfriendly takeover. A manager who chooses to wait until the takeover attempt is made may fail to maintain managerial control of the enterprise.

Termination Master Strategies

Master strategies that deal with the selling or closing of all or part of the firm's operations and assets are labeled termination strategies. The adoption of such a strategy is an admission that the organization as currently structured cannot compete effectively in its markets. The two types of termination master strategies, divestment and liquidation, represent degrees of termination of the firm's activities. The divestment strategy represents an attempt to streamline the organization to improve its competitive posture. Liquidation discontinues the firm's existence with a minimum negative impact on its constituents: stockholders, employees, and the community.

Divestment A firm can pursue a termination master strategy of divestment by selling a subsidiary, division, or product line to another organization or to its employees. (Of 38 recent $1 billion deals, eight were leveraged buyouts in which the management and employees of a firm acquired all of its outstanding stock.) This strategy reduces the size of the organization, generates cash for other ventures, or divests unprofitable SBUs. The result is a decrease in the revenues, profits, and assets of the total organization. One unusual use of resources generated from divestment is reported by James L. Keleksen, CEO of J. I. Case Company, a manufacturer of farm equipment. Keleksen states that he would sell a division to generate enough cash to maintain Case's 8 percent dividend yield.[5]

It is important for the strategic manager to design and implement a divestment strategy effectively in order to maximize the firm's return from the divestment. As Harowitz and Halliday state in their prescriptions for a successful divestment, "The sellers usually leave money on the table."[6] That is, the selling company seldom gets the best price for its divested subsidiary.

Liquidation Liquidation is the final strategy that a firm can pursue. This strategy involves selling all of the assets of the firm for their tangible worth and ceasing operations under the existing ownership. The organization may actually continue to operate but under new ownership, or it may sell its assets for market or salvage value and disband its productive capability.

Liquidation does not always mean that the firm has been unsuccessful or ineffective. It could be that a privately held firm is no longer of interest to its owners, and it is sold for retirement income or investment in another venture. The long-term strategy of the firm's founder may have been to build the organization to a specific value and then liquidate.

Regardless of the reason for liquidation, this master strategy must be carefully planned and executed. An orderly transfer of ownership or ceasing of operations is important so that the managers can obtain the maximum possible return from the liquidation.[7] The choice of a liquidation strategy by the strategic manager as part of the formal process of strategy formulation will allow the organization to locate the most advantageous conditions and price for the sale of its assets. It will also permit the dissolution of contracts under the most favorable terms and the cordial discontinuation of relationships with the firm's constituents. Last, it will make possible a more effective discharge or transfer of employees.

Ancillary Strategies

Consolidation

A consolidation strategy is the closing of a facility and ceasing operations at one of the organization's several locations. It is usually prompted by the obsolescence of the facility or a decline in the demand for the products or services the facility provides. If all strategic managers were excellent long-term planners, many consolidations might be avoided. However, the product produced by the facility often has reached the decline stage of its life cycle, and it may not be cost effective to convert the facility to another product or the facility may have become obsolete.

One extreme example of the latter case is the nuclear power industry. The scheduled life of most nuclear power plants built in the United States during the 1960s and 1970s is 20 years. However, what other use could a nuclear power-generating facility serve after it is obsolete? Therefore, both market conditions and technology as well as shortsighted strategic management practices can result in the need for a consolidation strategy.

Cooperation

Cooperative strategies involve gaining access to needed resources or customers by entering into formal cooperative agreements with other organizations. These agreements can enable the firm to pursue opportunities that would otherwise be closed to it. For example, oil companies typically cooperate with other firms in the purchase of an expensive, high-risk oil lease. This allows them to continue to explore for new sources of crude oil while maintaining risk levels that are acceptable to stockholders.

Cooperative agreements are useful for gaining access to resources and markets the firm could not penetrate on its own. However, entering into a cooperative agreement creates a commitment that the organization must honor and removes absolute control of the situation from the organization's managers. Before choosing to engage in a cooperative agreement strategy, strategic managers must therefore weight the benefits of cooperation against the vulnerabilities created by the agreement.

Joint Venture A firm pursues a joint venture strategy when it joins with another organization to commit resources to the same project. Two or more firms will engage in a joint venture strategy to take advantage of an environmental opportunity or gain access to needed resources. This strategy is chosen when it is mutually beneficial for all organizations involved. The typical motivation for a joint venture is to reduce the risks associated with a venture by combining the strengths of several firms to undertake an activity that is beyond the capability of one firm. For example, a firm with a new technology to transform a mature product-market into a growth mode may seek a joint venture with an established firm to quickly overcome the industry's entry barriers.

The second primary reason for a joint venture strategy is the entry into foreign markets or production. Most countries outside of the United States have laws or policies that prohibit the exploitation of its human and natural resources. These countries attempt to control the export of their resources or capital by requiring that firms doing business in the country have a specified amount of national ownership. Therefore, a U.S. firm that wants to conduct business in one of these countries must enter into a joint venture with nationals of that country.

Regardless of the reason for entering into a joint venture, it can be an effective cooperation strategy to reduce financial risks associated with major new ventures or to combine strengths with another company in order to obtain a competitive advantage.

Agency Agreements Agency agreements are cooperative strategies that consist of one firm acting on the behalf of another firm to obtain a valued resource that would otherwise be unobtainable. One organization agrees to act as an agent to represent another firm in a transaction.

Agency agreements usually relate to two types of transactions, buying and selling. For example, an import-export company, sometimes referred to as a trading company, acts as an agent for large U.S. retailers to purchase foreign apparel. Independent insurance agents represent several insurance companies in sales transactions. They represent both the customer and the company in the transaction and match the buyer's need with the correct insurance product.

Credit Agreements Credit agreements are cooperative arrangements between two organizations in which one firm assists another in obtaining a line of credit that would be unavailable without the guarantee of the original firm. The guarantee usually carries a fee, which is determined as a percentage of the face amount of the line of credit. This strategy is frequently used by small commercial land development firms that, due to their limited assets and short earnings record, would be unable to secure sufficient capital on their own.

Management Agreements Under a management agreement, one organization agrees to manage a facility owned by another. Management agreements are common in the hospitality and commercial real estate industries. Many investors enter into agreements with other firms to manage resort properties that have been purchased as investments. The same is true of large apartment complexes where investor groups have no experience in managing such investments. However, this strategy is not limited to these two industries. The Department of Defense frequently hires defense contractors to manage repair facilities for sophisticated military equipment. Before Chrysler acquired American Motors Company, it signed an agreement to manage and operate a portion of AMC's Kenosha, Wisconsin, assembly facility for the manufacture of its Chrysler Fifth Avenue cars.

Cooperative agreements can provide an organization with access to resources and capabilities that would not be cost effective to obtain under any other strategy. Thus, these agreements allow organizations to pursue opportunities that would otherwise be out of their grasp.

Notes

1. Michael E. Porter, *Competitive Strategy* (New York: The Free Press, 1980): 35.
2. Robert D. Buzzell, "Is Vertical Integration Profitable?" *Harvard Business Review* 61 (January–February, 1983): 92–102.
3. "Why National Came to the Fairchild Fire Sale," *Business Week*, September 14, 1987, 38-39.
4. Stephen Lofthouse, "Strategy and Tactics for Resisting Take-Over," *Long Range Planning* 17 (August 1984): 38-50.
5. Jo Ellen Davis, "Does Tenneco Have Too Much Riding on Tractors?" *Business Week* (December 1, 1986): 118–120.
6. Howard Harowitz and D. Halliday, "The New Alchemy: Divestment for Profit," *The Journal of Business Strategy* 5 (Fall, 1984): 112–116.
7. Ian C. MacMillan, "Preemptive Strategies," *Journal of Business Strategy* 4 (Fall, 1983): 16–28.

Appendix 4.2

Steiner and Miner's Questions for Strategy Evaluation

Is the Strategy Consistent with the Environment?

- Is your strategy acceptable to the major constituents of your company?
- Is your strategy in consonance with your competitive environment?
- Do you really have an honest and accurate appraisal of your competition? Are you underestimating your competition?
- Does your strategy give you a dominant competitive edge?
- Is your strategy vulnerable to a successful strategic counterattack by competitors?
- Are the forecasts upon which your strategy is based really creditable?
- Does your strategy follow that of a strong competitor?
- Does your strategy pit you against a powerful competitor?
- Is your market share (present and/or prospective) sufficient to be competitive and make an acceptable profit?
- If your strategy seeks an enlarged market share, is it likely to be questioned by the Antitrust Division of the Department of Justice or the Federal Trade Commission?
- Is it possible that other federal government agencies will prevent your achieving the objectives sought by your strategy?
- Is your strategy in conformance with moral and ethical codes of conduct applicable to your company?

Source: Reprinted with permission of Macmillan Publishing Company, a Division of Macmillan, Inc. from *Management Policy and Strategy: Texts, Readings and Cases*, 3d ed., by George A. Steiner, J. B. Miner and E. R. Gray, pp. 150–154. Copyright © 1986 by Macmillan Publishing Company.

Is the Strategy Consistent with Your Internal Policies, Styles of Management, Philosophy, and Operating Procedures?

- Does the strategy/policy really fit management's values, philosophy, know-how, personality, and sense of social responsibility?
- Is your strategy identifiable and understood by all those in the company with a need to know?
- Is your strategy consistent with the internal strengths, objectives, and policies of your organization?
- Is the strategy under evaluation divided into appropriate substrategies that interrelate properly?
- Does the strategy under review conflict with other strategies in your company?
- Does the strategy under review exploit your strengths and avoid your major weaknesses?
- Is your organizational structure consistent with your strategy?
- Does your policy/strategy make the greatest overall contribution to the performance of your company?
- Is the strategy likely to produce a minimum of new administrative problems for your organization?

Is the Policy/Strategy Appropriate in Light of Your Resources?

Money

- Do you have sufficient capital, or can you get it, to see the strategy through to successful implementation?
- What will be the financial consequences associated with the allocation of capital to this

strategy? What other projects may be denied funding? Are the financial substrategies associated with this funding acceptable?

Physical Facilities

▪ Do you have sufficient capital, or can you get it, to see the strategy through to successful implementation?

▪ What will be the financial consequences associated with the allocation of capital to this strategy? What other projects may be denied funding? Are the financial substrategies associated with this funding acceptable?

Managerial and Employee Resources

▪ Are there identifiable and committed managers to implement the strategy?

▪ Do we have the necessary skills among both managers and employees to make the strategy successful?

Are the Risks in Pursuing the Strategy Acceptable?

▪ Has the strategy/policy been tested with appropriate analysis, such as return on investment, sensitivity analysis, the firm's ability and willingness to bear risk, etc.?

▪ Does your strategy balance the acceptance of minimum risk with the maximum profit potential consistent with your company's resources and prospects?

▪ Do you have too much and too large a proportion of your capital and management tied into this strategy?

▪ Is the payback period acceptable in light of potential environmental change?

▪ Does the strategy take you too far from your current products and markets?

Does the Strategy Fit the Product Life Cycle and Market Strength/Market Attractiveness Situation?

▪ Is the strategy appropriate for the present and prospective position in the market strength/attractiveness matrix?

▪ Have you considered all the characteristics in the matrix that are pertinent to properly evaluating your strategy?

▪ Is your strategy in consonance with your product life cycle as it exists and/or as you have the power to make it?

▪ Are you rushing a revolutionary product to the market?

▪ If your strategy is to fill a niche not now filled in the market, have you inquired about the niche remaining open to you long enough to return your capital investment plus a required profit?

Can Your Strategy Be Implemented Efficiently and Effectively?

▪ Overall, can the strategy be implemented in an efficient and effective fashion?

▪ Is there a commitment, a system of communications and control, a managerial and employee capability, that will help to assure the proper implementation of the strategy?

▪ Is the timing of implementation appropriate in light of what is known about market conditions, competition, etc.?

▪ If the company culture is not congenial to implementing the strategy, should the culture be changed? If so, how?

Are There Other Important Considerations?

▪ Have you tried to identify the major forces inside and outside the organization that will be most influential in insuring the success of the strategy and/or in raising problems of implementation? Have you given them the proper evaluation?

▪ Are all the important assumptions realistic upon which your strategy/policy is based?

▪ Has the strategy been tested with appropriate analytical tools?

▪ Has the strategy been tested with appropriate criteria such as past, present, and prospective economic, political, and social trends?

Part Two

Implementation and Control

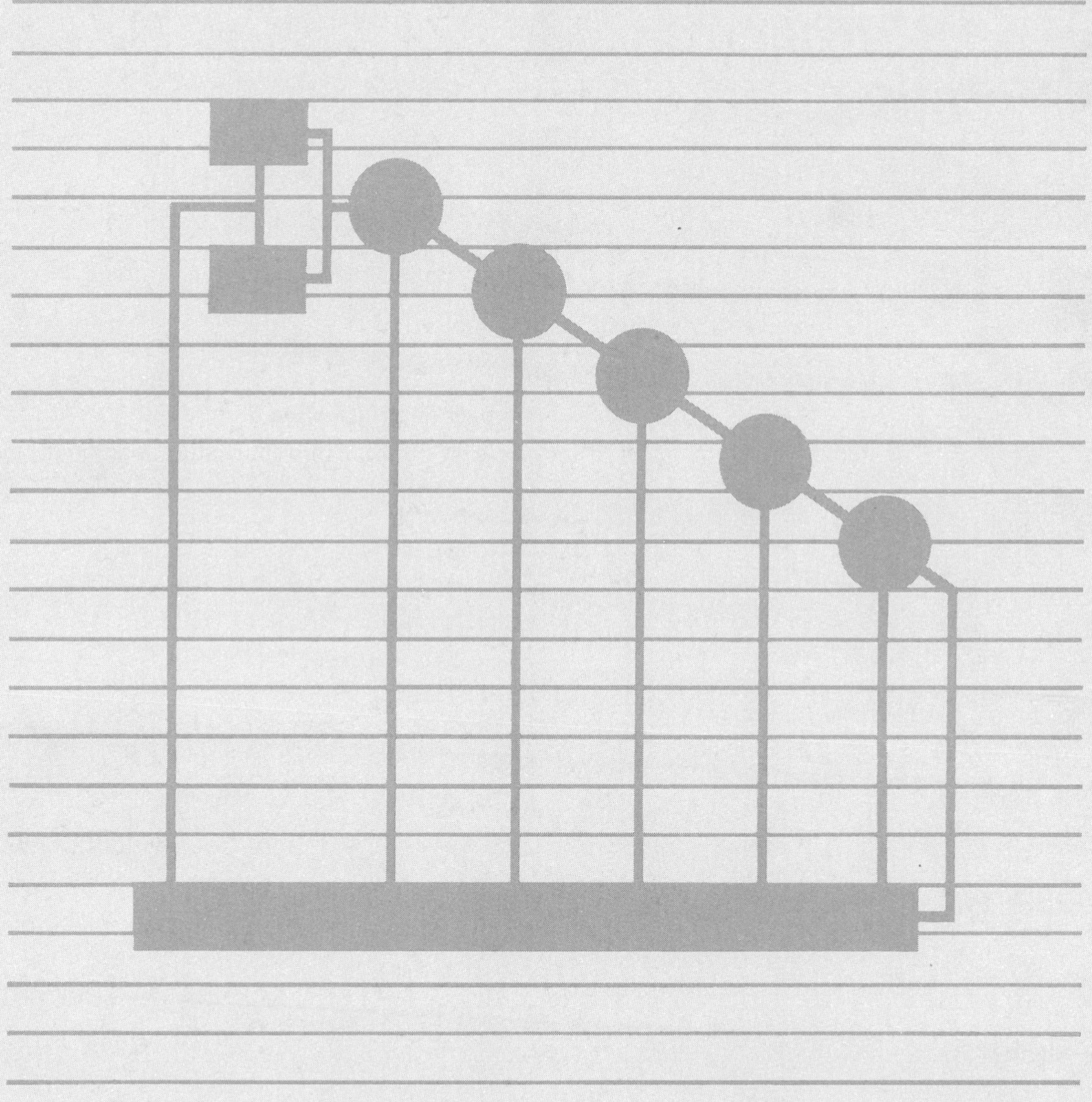

Chapter 5

Implementing Strategies through Plans, Functional Strategies, and Budgets

Three things are to be looked to in building: that it stand in the right spot; that it be securely founded; that it be successfully executed.

—Johann Wolfgang von Goethe, *Elective Affinities*, Book 1, Chapter 9 (1808)

Learning Objectives

- To learn the importance of implementation in achieving a strategy.
- To obtain an overview of what is involved in implementing strategy.
- To understand how plans are used to implement strategy.
- To show how functional planning is used to implement corporate, business, and SBU strategies.
- To demonstrate some of the key decisions that functional managers must make in developing plans.
- To understand the role of budgeting in the implementation of strategy.

AN organization's strategy determines not only the activities its managers choose to carry out, but also the organization's very structure and style of doing business. All of the management processes should support the organization's strategy. If no change in the strategy is called for, management should nevertheless assess its processes to see if they are the best choices for implementing the strategy. If a change in strategy is to occur, many management processes will likely need to change. For example, when AT&T's managers adopted strategies appropriate to the company's shift from a regulated monopoly to the open and tough competition of telecommunications and computing, the managers also had to change AT&T's functional strategies, organization structure, and culture.

This chapter and the two that follow focus on the implementation aspect of strategic management. This chapter will introduce the major activities involved in implementing a strategy. Following an introduction of the implementation process is a discussion of the role of plans, functional strategies, and budgeting in translating a strategic plan into action. In Chapter 6, the focus is on appropriate structural arrangements for particular strategies. Chapter 7 addresses company culture, leadership, and motivation issues associated with achieving strategies.

The Implementation Process

What management does to carry out the planned strategy is called **implementation**. It involves adjusting and redesigning administrative systems so that they facilitate the execution of the strategy. Although the formulation of strategy primarily involves the upper levels of an organization, implementation can reach to all levels of the firm. A quality-control inspector, for example, may have his or her job duties changed as the plant tries out new quality standards required by a strategy. Implementation can involve changes throughout the whole organization as employees take actions to carry out the strategy. Sales territories may be changed, measurements of performance altered, management personnel switched, new products generated, or pricing policies revised.

This does not mean that every change in strategy results in wholesale change throughout the organization. The change may be confined to one division or to subunits within particular functional departments such as marketing or research and development. Nor does it mean the changes must occur all at once. In fact, they are likely to be programmed in over a period of time. But regardless of the extent of change, management must provide for a program to carry out the activities that will make the strategy succeed.

The Importance of Implementation

The importance of linking strategy to what happens in carrying it out has been recognized by John M. Hobbs and Donald F. Heany. They point out the importance of linking strategy with the detailed operating plans and controls at lower levels and recommend five ways to achieve a more effective linkage:[1]

1. Make sure an ambitious strategy will not overload the functional departments.

2. Contain the shock waves generated by new strategy by defining the key issues and insulating some parts of the business from them.

3. Give personal attention to some of the key areas in coupling strategy to operating plans.

4. Keep the planning process going and participants involved until development of a list of the specific tasks required to carry out the strategy, the milestones necessary to track progress of the new strategy, and the assignments of each person responsible for each major program.

5. Concentrate on communicating the strategy to lower levels so they really understand the changes that must be made.

The longer a strategy has been in place and the larger the organization, the more likely the organization's systems are to be congruent with one another. Larger firms are more likely to have elaborate and formal administrative systems. The systems developed for planning, control, reward and motivation, leadership, organization structure, and budgeting are adjusted and tuned over time until they are well matched. A major change in strategy therefore can create much disturbance in the organization because numerous changes will be required and because change in one system may require change in another system. New procedures and working relationships must be developed. Employees will need to change how and with whom they work. It takes time and experience to discover what no longer works and what adjustments are needed.

Many persons in the organization will welcome the changes that accompany a change in strategy, but others will resist or be confused by them. Others will become frustrated if management cannot decide on firm policies and procedures. An example is when a policy or procedure is established, but then management changes its position.

Mere selection of a strategy will not guarantee its success. The firm must provide for achievement of the planned strategy. The best strategy may fail to reach its full potential because of lack of attention to implementation. One study of presidents and division general managers found that over half of their companies experienced problems while implementing a strategic change. Ten problems were experienced most frequently:[2]

1. Implementation required more time than was planned.
2. Major problems were not anticipated.
3. Activities were ineffectively coordinated.
4. Crises developed and diverted attention from implementation.
5. Problems arose because of uncontrollable environmental factors.
6. Involved employees were not capable enough.
7. Department managers did not provide adequate leadership and direction.
8. Lower level employees received inadequate training.
9. Key implementation tasks were inadequately defined.
10. The information system was insufficient for control activities.

The Strategic Application "Johnson & Johnson Uses Its Credo to Guide Behavior" describes how Johnson & Johnson has tried to avoid such shortcomings in implementing its strategy for social responsibility.

A company's administrative systems need to match its strategy. For example, a company diversifying into several unrelated product lines can have difficulties unless it changes to a multidivisional organization structure, develops or hires general managers for each division, employs controls to measure investment returns, and rewards employees based on their performance on such measures. Delta Airlines was slow to recognize the value of computers and an information system that would allow it to keep track of ticket prices in different markets. Consequently, the company was slow

STRATEGIC APPLICATIONS: SOCIAL RESPONSIBILITY

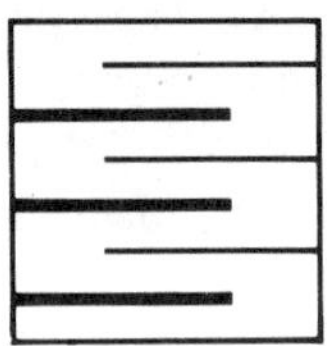

Johnson & Johnson Uses Its Credo to Guide Behavior

How does a company get its employees to behave ethically? Getting employees to do the right things, make the right decisions, and treat customers fairly cannot be guaranteed, but Johnson & Johnson thinks it has found a way to improve its chances: involvement of top-level executives, strict enforcement of ethical codes, and the right balance between centralized management controls and mutual trust.

A large company with multiple divisions, Johnson & Johnson must allow the units autonomy and initiative, but to guide the behavior of all employees, the company uses its Credo. A one-page statement of values, it includes the company's philosophy on such topics as respecting employees as individuals, making high-quality products, and earning a sound profit. To keep the Credo current, top managers review it twice a year. James Burke, CEO, has credited the Credo with helping the company through its difficulties with the Tylenol tamperings in 1982 and 1986.

Source: J. Byrne, "Businesses Are Signing Up for Ethics 101," *Business Week*, February 15, 1988, 56–57.

to match competitors' lower prices and then often lowered prices too much. Hewlett-Packard encountered problems related to the organization's structure and culture. HP had developed a culture emphasizing entrepreneurship, innovation, technology, and engineering. Its divisions were kept small and decentralized to facilitate this emphasis. When it tried to move into new product areas that required the divisions to cooperate, it had trouble achieving the needed cooperation. Now HP is more heavily emphasizing marketing and has centralized many of its efforts.

Implementation Activities

Implementation activities can involve almost every facet of managing and running an organization. For each facet, implementation includes planning, organizing, leading, motivating and rewarding, and controlling.

Planning Once strategy is formulated, the manager should develop detailed plans to tell others in the organization which objectives and activities to accomplish, who is responsible, when the activities must be performed, and the resources that are to be allocated. This requires translating the strategy into major programs and projects, functional strategies and policies, and budgets. At each level in the organization, managers must refine plans formulated at higher levels into plans suitable for their responsibilities and for the levels below them. Later this chapter discusses the use of planning to implement strategy.

Organization The responsibility and authority for activities, programs, and projects to accomplish a strategy must be allocated among persons and organizational units.

In addition, these activities and responsibilities must be coordinated and controlled so they all come together properly. This is the major function of the organization's structure.

For organization structure to facilitate the firm's strategy, it must be appropriately matched to the strategy being employed. Some structures are ill suited for implementing certain strategies but work well with others. One example of a mismatched organization structure is use of the functional organization to facilitate unrelated diversification.

Only a few basic structural patterns exist, but the number of possible modifications to these structures provides the executive with several choices. For example, firms with unrelated products normally find that divisional structures work best for organizing their activities, but divisional structures are expensive when a firm is just beginning to diversify. The single-product firm using a functional organization structure can still gain many of the advantages that go with the divisional structure by employing product teams within its functional structure. The firm can coordinate and control its activities without having to adopt a divisional structure. Once its scale of operations can economically justify a change, it can adopt a divisional structure. Chapter 6 discusses the matching of the firm's structure to its strategy.

Corporate Culture An organization's culture is an important factor in the implementation of its strategy. The appropriate culture can facilitate the implementation of strategy by reinforcing and supporting it. If culture and strategy are incongruent, the culture can interfere with implementation. The shared values and beliefs of a company's members produce rules of conduct and behavior about what is an acceptable way to do things in the company. A strategy is most likely to succeed when it is aligned with a supportive culture, because resistance is minimized and the strategy can be absorbed into the culture. Culture can shape behavior in detailed ways not possible with other implementation procedures. For example, treating customers in the right way becomes part of normal acceptable behavior. There appears to be no ideal culture that supports all strategies. Rather, each company should seek alignment of culture and strategy by adjusting either the strategy or the culture to the other.

Leadership The top managers' leadership is of central importance in implementing strategy. Through their emphasis and commitment, CEOs, group executives, and division managers convey the importance of the strategy and the seriousness of the firm's commitment to carrying it out. Their behavior sets an example for other managers and professionals.

These leaders are constantly in contact with people inside and outside the organization. They receive information and impressions, but they also convey information and intentions, move toward decisions, and work their own agendas. They are able to fill in the gaps unanticipated by formal systems of plans, structures, controls, and rewards. At the hub of an extensive network of contacts, the executive can learn what is working and what is not and can make modifications. He or she can provide inspiration and demonstrate a personal commitment to the strategy. The executive can seek support for his or her own agenda and cooperation among the managers.

He or she can build a coalition of supporters within the organization that can be used in implementation. Through influence, communication, and example, top managers set the tone, induce others to follow, set standards for performance, and reinforce the intent and practice of the organization.

The selection and development of persons for key positions also is an important aspect of implementation. Different strategies impose different task demands and require different skills and personalities to carry them out. The persons in these key positions can shape strategy in their units in significant ways. The person should match the strategy. Chapter 7 will address the matching of executives to strategy.

Motivation and Reward Through overall strategy, functional strategies, budgets, participation in planning, and leadership, managers are told what needs to be done to accomplish the strategy as well as their role in it. Control systems provide feedback on managers' progress so that, working with their superiors, they have the opportunity for corrective action. The organization uses all these systems to convey to its members what should be done and what is expected of them. But the organization needs to reinforce its expectations and provide for motivating and rewarding the behavior it needs.

A system for measurement and reward of performance tells members what behavior is important. It can focus behavior, and it can encourage members through incentives and reward of good performance. To do this, the firm must be able to define the results desired and the performance needed to achieve results. It must also be able to measure performance accurately and in a timely and useful manner. Reward systems can then be linked to controls. The organization must provide the rewards sought by general managers, and the award must depend on the performance needed. For example, if a firm emphasizes short-term performance in its reward system, executives may neglect the long-term strategic plans because the firm has told them the short term is more important.

The primary reward system that most firms use to reward general managers is its compensation plan. Such plans use a number of different ways of compensating managers, including salary, bonuses, and retirement plans. In recent years, executive compensation plans have been criticized for insufficiently linking rewards to performance and for failing to emphasize long-term results. Chapter 7 will review several compensation plans that can be powerful tools in implementing strategy. The compensation plan is an important tool for the executive in building support for strategy.

Control Control is treated separately from the implementation process, but is previewed here because it is the next logical stage in the model of strategic management. The organization needs controls to assess whether it is merging strategy into the firm's activities and whether the strategy is affecting performance. A firm must develop ways to measure whether it is making progress in achieving its strategy as well as to monitor the environment and the set of assumptions upon which its strategy is based. Systems can be established to collect and collate information that can show deviations from the plan. When they interpret this information, executives can take any necessary corrective action.

Good controls for strategic purposes should have certain characteristics that are common to both operating and strategic controls. These characteristics are described in Chapter 8. However, strategic control is different from operating control. The controls that are in place to monitor, measure, and evaluate ongoing operations are usually insufficient for strategic control. Strategic control requires separate control systems tailored to the programs, budgets, structures, motivational needs, and resources of the strategy. Strategic controls, for example, are much more focused on external sources and on future events and tend to depend more on qualitative information. Chapter 8 describes, evaluates, and recommends a number of different strategic controls.

The organization will not accomplish strategic purposes simply because it has a good strategy. Translating a strategy into action requires the firm to ensure that its systems facilitate the implementation of the strategy. Changes in behavior are often required, and the firm will usually have to develop plans to operationalize the strategy, adjust its organization structure and culture, provide for leadership and motivation, and design control systems.

Implementing Strategy through Planning

To translate an organization's strategy into action, managers must couple the strategic planning process with functional or operations planning. Managers can accomplish this by establishing a set of objectives and plans that tell each part of the organization which operations it must carry out each year if strategic goals are to be met. Long-term objectives can be broken down into annual objectives, and business strategies can be translated into functional strategies for key departments. To help managers at all levels make decisions that are congruent with the organization's objectives and strategies, the firm can establish policies. To keep strategic efforts focused and coordinated, the firm can use programs. Finally, so that strategic and operating activities can both be carried out, managers allocate resources through budgets.

Implementing the organization's strategy begins with a process of moving from general to specific strategies, from a long-range to a shorter-range view. As Figure 5.1 shows, corporate goals and strategies are converted into medium-range objectives and strategies for a division. These in turn form the basis for functional strategies, which are carried out as specified by objectives, single-use plans, and standing plans.

Multiproduct firms with several divisions or strategic business units will establish strategies for each division or SBU. These strategies are, in most cases, analogous to the mission, goal, and strategy of a single-product firm at the corporate level. Each division or SBU must develop its strategy from the corporation's strategy. Because each division or SBU is dealing with a different product and industry, its set of conditions will be unique, leading to a separate strategy. Each division or SBU must develop its own objectives, standing plans, and single-use plans for each function. These objectives and plans form the functional strategies of such functions as marketing, production, and research and development. The finance function is usually an exception because many of its strategies apply to all divisions. The setting of

Figure 5.1 From Corporate Strategy to Functional Strategy

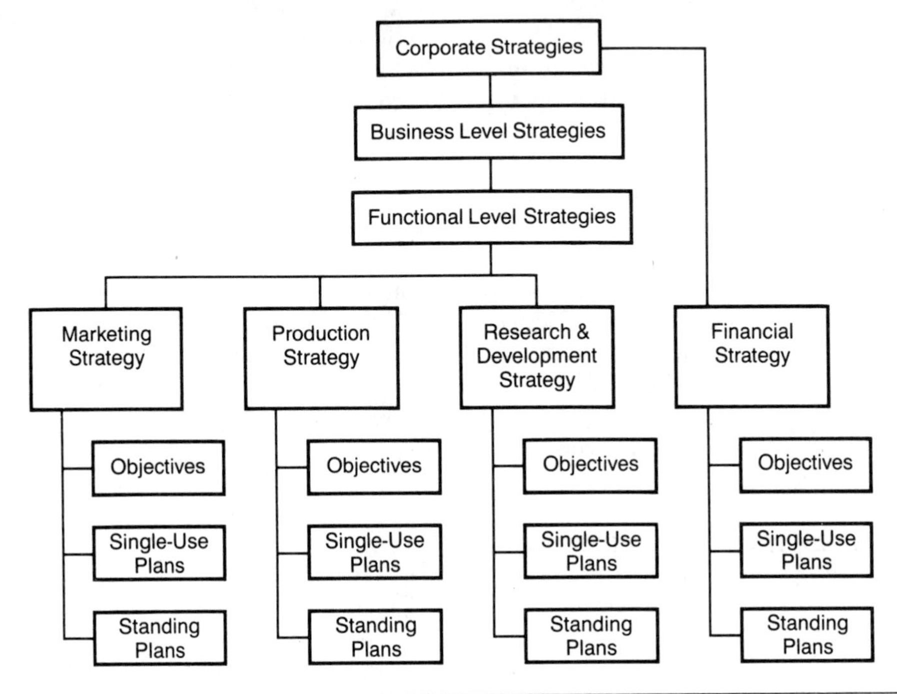

financial strategies tends to remain at the corporate level because its objectives and plans are corporate-wide concerns. In some companies other functional strategies may be determined at the corporate level and imposed on the divisions to ensure uniformity. The development of functional strategies for a single-product firm is similar to that for multiproduct firms except the functional strategies may be developed directly from the firm's master strategy.

Objectives

A goal is a desired state of affairs that a company attempts to achieve. An organization has many types of goals, ranging from the firm's strategic goals and mission to specific objectives such as *cutting scrap by 10 percent this month.* Corporate goals and mission were discussed in earlier chapters; this section will focus on objectives.

The specific results that an organization must produce by a specific date in order to carry out its mission and achieve its strategic goals are its **objectives**. They are what most people think of as goals. A firm has many objectives, and they are more concrete than the organization's strategic goals. In addition, each subunit within an organization has its own set of objectives. The results of a study in which top managers were asked what objectives they considered to be very important are shown in Figure 5.2.

Figure 5.2 A Ranking of Important Objectives by Top Managers

1. Organizational efficiency
2. High productivity
3. Profit maximization
4. Employee welfare
5. Organizational growth
6. Industrial leadership
7. Organizational stability

Note: Ranking is based on the number of managers rating the objective as very important.
Source: Adapted from George England, "Organizational Goals and Expected Behavior of American Managers," *Academy of Management Journal* 11 (June 1967): 107–111.

Multiple Objectives Normally an organizational unit has numerous objectives. One reason for this is the requirements imposed by certain groups outside the firm. For example, a firm may be required by law to pursue such strategic goals as equal employment opportunity or fair trade practices. Such imposed goals will take the form of specific objectives at some level of the organization.

For a firm to achieve numerous objectives simultaneously is difficult. Some objectives may conflict with others, causing the firm to seek trade-offs between them. Sometimes this can be done by assigning higher priorities to some objectives than to others. Two objectives that frequently come into conflict are organizational growth and profit maximization, because growth is often achieved at the expense of profits. In such a case, management should decide which objective should have priority.

One way of resolving conflicts between equally desirable objectives is to set a performance level for one that acts as a constraint on the other. Thus, a sales manager might say, "We will pursue every possible customer in the district as long as our sales expenses do not exceed 5 percent," or a division manager might say, "We will pursue a 15 percent annual growth rate as long as the return on investment can be maintained at 15 percent." Another way of resolving such conflicts is to pursue higher priority objectives until satisfactory levels are achieved and then turn to lower priority objectives. In other words, achievement of one objective triggers efforts to achieve another.

Each functional manager in an SBU or division must establish objectives for his or her own unit to ensure that the unit's activities will contribute to the firm's objectives. This process is repeated for each subunit within the organization, resulting in a hierarchy of objectives for every level of the organization. This hierarchy is sometimes termed a **means/end chain** because each unit's objectives are linked to those of the level above it. Managers at each level start with a problem or objective (that is, an end) and ask which activities or alternative ways (that is, means) are available to achieve the objective or solve the problem. After evaluating the alternatives, managers select the one that is most likely to contribute to meeting the objective. Starting from the end, each new means becomes a new objective; this generates a "chain" of means and ends.

Consider the following example. An SBU might set itself the strategic goal of increasing its profitability. It has three basic alternatives: cut costs, increase revenue, or do both in some combination. Several kinds of costs can be cut, including administrative costs, production costs, and sales costs. Suppose the SBU's managers decide to cut production costs. Now there are several more alternatives. The managers may decide to cut back on maintenance by 25 percent or shut down inefficient equipment or lay off people in some staff positions or consolidate certain managerial positions. Each of these alternatives becomes a means of cutting costs. If the managers choose to shut down inefficient operations, they must ask which sites will be shut down, when to do it, who will be involved, and so forth. In other words, they must determine additional means to achieve the objective. For example, a troubled USX found that to achieve its strategic goal of profit the steel division needed to reduce costs and increase productivity. The program to cut costs and improve productivity led to shutting down inefficient operations and reducing employment. By 1988, the company had cut steelmaking capacity from 34 million tons to 19 million tons. Employment was reduced from 75,000 employees to 20,000 employees. The man-hours to produce a ton of steel had been cut by one-third. With the increase in productivity the steel division returned to profitability.[3]

Most businesses that carry out a procedure like the one just described do not do so explicitly or all at once. In practice, each level of the organization develops its own objectives on the basis of the objectives established by the next higher level.

Management should pay special attention to ensuring that the objectives of subunits are compatible with one another. Often a unit sets objectives that are appropriate for it but that conflict with those of another unit. For example, the production department may want to maintain a steady flow of materials in and out of production, while the sales department wants to launch several sales campaigns, each of which will create a peak in demand for the product and upset the production department's schedule. When functional units need to coordinate their actions and the units are highly interdependent, managers should closely examine the objectives of each unit for indications of potential conflict.

Statement of Objectives An explicit statement of objectives allows management to determine whether the objectives are compatible with the firm's strategy. Because of tradition, apathy, politics, or inappropriate controls and rewards, operating objectives may differ from strategic goals. Sometimes operating objectives gradually displace official objectives so that the activities themselves become more important than their contribution to the SBU's goals and objectives. An example is the case of a unit that is so concerned with making sure employees conform to procedures and rules that compliance with rules becomes more important than operating results. Explicitly stating objectives and examining activities designed to achieve them can prevent such "goal displacement." At the same time, however, the process of determining objectives should be flexible enough to allow for adaptation when conditions change. The longer the planning horizon and the more uncertainty that accompanies goal setting, the greater will be the need to allow for changing conditions.

The Role of Personal Values and Internal Politics The preceding discussion implies that objectives are the product of a dispassionate and rational problem-solving process. Objectives are also influenced by other factors besides management decision processes. For example, they may be affected by the philosophy of the organization's founders. The founders choose the industry and markets in which the firm will compete and put up the capital. Long after the firm has been established, the values of the founder define the kinds of business the firm will conduct and, hence, the nature of its objectives.

Internal politics and the value systems of participants also play a role in determining the objectives that the organization will pursue. All organizations are made up of groups and individuals who have special interests and therefore may or may not support the objectives chosen by upper management. Yet, if the company is to meet its objectives, each manager needs the support of key personnel and at least the compliance of the rest. Lack of support can have serious consequences. Champion International, for instance, went through several presidents trying to bring about the integration of Champion Paper and U.S. Plywood. Managers from each company did not want to give up their own company's identity or surrender control over their own operations.

To a great extent, objectives represent the desires of members of the organization, or at least the dominant members of the organization. Coalitions often form among members who see one set of objectives as more advantageous to them than another set. Members of a sales group may feel that the firm should enter a new market because such a move may open new sales territories for them or perhaps lead to promotions to regional or district sales management. A group of R&D personnel may want the company to develop a new product because of the importance they attach to using certain new technologies. A group of professors may want a new doctoral degree program to be added to the curriculum because it will lead to more research opportunities and greater prestige for them; an opposing group may believe that such a program would take resources away from undergraduate degree programs.

When such coalitions exist, they can be expected to lobby and bargain for organizational support of the objectives they favor. If a manager attempts to resolve the differences between competing groups, a kind of bargaining situation may develop. The bargaining may lead to extraction of policy commitments as the price of continued support and participation by some members of the organization. It is easy to see how this process can result in multiple objectives that are sometimes inconsistent.

The value systems and preferences of key participants also play a role in the formulation of objectives. We all develop a set of values and beliefs so that what one person considers important another may not. Moreover, we not only place different values on various possible outcomes, but we also develop different beliefs about cause-and-effect relationships. For example, one manager may believe that the way to obtain higher performance from subordinates is to be fair but firm. Another may believe that higher performance results from allowing employees to find their own way and rewarding them when they perform well. Still others may believe that a happy work force is a productive work force. Such values and preferences can affect the choice of objectives. Thus, one regional sales manager may place a high value on good relationships with customers and believe that higher sales can be generated by providing the best possible service. Another may believe that charging the lowest possible fair price is more important than cultivating good customer relations. The sales strategies favored by these two managers can be expected to differ accordingly.

Standing Plans

The greater the interdependence among units, employees, and tasks that is required in order to carry out the firm's day-to-day activities, the greater is the need for coordination and communication among them. This need can be met through careful planning. In addition, whenever tasks must be sequenced, planning helps to coordinate them and either improves communication or minimizes the need for communication. Functional-level plans specify how available resources will be used in carrying out strategies, achieving objectives, and coordinating functional activities. The functional plans have a shorter time horizon than do objectives and are much more concerned with current operations.

For the sake of convenience, plans can be classified into two categories: standing plans and single-use plans.[4] If a unit's activities undergo relatively little change or its operations consist of a repeated cycle of activities, these activities can be coordinated through **standing plans** such as policies, schedules, standard operating methods and procedures, and rules.

Policies An organization's **policies** are general guidelines that establish limits or boundaries for decision making and help channel the thinking of management. Usually they permit some freedom in arriving at decisions; in some cases they simply indicate the steps to take in reaching a decision. An example of a policy at McDonald's is described in the Strategic Application "McDonald's Wants No Chlorofluorocarbons."

Policies vary in scope. A particular policy may apply to the whole company; an example would be a statement that purchases over $10,000 require two vendor bids. Or a policy may apply to a particular function in one division; for example, the statement that any deviation from pricing policy must be approved by the marketing manager. Policies at the top of the unit or firm are generally broader in scope than those at lower levels. In fact, at the upper levels it is often difficult to distinguish between strategy and policy, because policies are used to elaborate and implement strategies.

Many policies are not affected by changes in strategy, but others need to be changed when strategies change. Managers need to continually reevaluate policies to ensure that they are not working at cross-purposes with functional strategies and objectives. Managers also must create new policies that will channel decisions toward new objectives.

Methods and Procedures McDonald's outstanding success is often attributed to the fact that customers know what to expect at any McDonald's store, regardless of its

STRATEGIC APPLICATIONS: SOCIAL RESPONSIBILITY

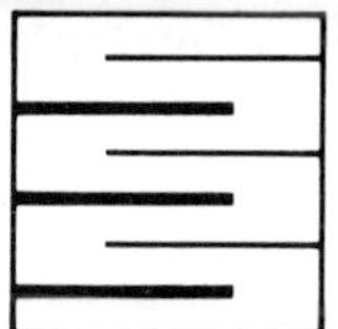

McDonald's Wants No Chlorofluorocarbons

According to many experts, chlorofluorocarbons (CFCs) have been depleting the earth's ozone layer. CFCs are used in producing foam containers, and McDonald's until recently was one of the largest users of these containers. Long a leader in social responsibility with such activities as its Ronald McDonald houses, McDonald's is now setting goals and rules for its suppliers. In 1987 it announced its desire for an environmentally sound packaging policy and the goal to be free of CFCs in its production processes by the end of 1988. McDonald's told its U.S. suppliers that it wanted no containers with CFCs in them. Suppliers responded peacefully, with several indicating they were developing alternative processes.

McDonald's reached its goal in December 1988, leading the fast food industry in voluntarily eliminating CFCs in packaging materials. Now the company is working to improve its packaging further by reducing solid waste.

Source: Stuart Gannes, "A Down-to-Earth Job: Saving the Sky," *Fortune*, March 14, 1988, 133–141; and "McDonald's Won't Give a Break to CFC Foam Blowing Agents," *Chemical Marketing Reporter*, August 10, 1987, 5, 21.

location. This is partly a result of McDonald's objectives and policies, but it is the use of a set of standard **methods** and **procedures** throughout the firm that allows the many different McDonald's stores to achieve this consistency.

Methods differ from policies in that they are more detailed, narrower in scope, and more complete. To achieve standard methods, one needs standard conditions. For example, an information system requires a standard vocabulary and a standard way of recording and accumulating information so that any given piece of information means the same thing at all locations.

Procedures indicate in detail how to perform a sequence of steps or actions. When more than one person is involved, a clearly stated set of procedures helps coordinate their efforts. When an activity is new or unfamiliar, a set of procedures leads the person through the task. This makes it possible for actions to be consistent even when personnel change. Within a typical company, numerous sets of procedures govern activities ranging from recruiting personnel and handling cash to starting up and shutting down equipment.

In very large companies, establishing standard methods and procedures can be a full-time job for specialized employees such as industrial engineers and systems analysts. Because developing and changing procedures can be very costly, a manager must be sure that procedures are needed, that they are worth their cost, and that they are flexible enough to adapt to changing conditions.

Rules A **rule** is a statement that some particular action should or should not be taken. These are statements that purposely leave no room for interpretation, such as "All products to be shipped to the Navy will be inspected by the resident naval inspector prior to shipping" or "Smoking is permitted in designated areas only."

The rigidity of rules can produce consistency, but it may also produce inaction by inhibiting the use of common sense. Also, people who resent the rules may create unnecessary difficulties by playing by the rules when such rigidity actually interferes with achieving corporate objectives. These problems can be prevented by the following means:

- Indicating how much flexibility is permitted
- Involving members in the formulation of rules
- Constantly trying to improve and update standing plans
- Training employees in their responsibilities
- Assuring employees that they may discuss proposed exceptions with a manager

Single-Use Plans

In situations that do not recur and for activities that do not fit into the organization's normal operations, activities are coordinated through **single-use plans**. For example, a firm is not usually prepared to handle the construction of a new plant through its functional departments, but plans are needed specifically for this activity. In other cases, the implementation of a new strategy may require a special plan, or the nature of the business may be such that management is continually overseeing new projects. Some firms operate on a project basis and develop special organizational forms such as matrix and project organizations. These, however, are special cases. Most organizations require single-use programs and projects if the organization is to adapt to these situations.

Programs and projects consist of the steps necessary to accomplish a particular set of objectives. Programs and projects are similar, but programs include more activities and may contain several subprograms and numerous projects. Both are used to handle unique activities that are too complex to be handled by existing units in the course of their regular operations.

As in the case of policies, the scale and scope of a program or project can be large or small. A program to modernize the firm's production equipment could affect the entire organization and include subprograms containing several projects for each plant. Or a project could consist of the recruitment, hiring, and training of new salespeople to introduce a new product line. Figure 5.3 presents some guidelines for planning a program or project.

Because programs and projects deal with nonrecurring situations, often over extended periods, it may be difficult to determine the steps required and to realistically estimate time and costs. Nor is there assurance that the objectives of the program or project will remain the same. Under these conditions, management must be prepared to modify programs and projects. It is also necessary to provide for feedback on the progress of a project or program so that revisions can be made if objectives are not being met. One way to maintain this flexibility is to postpone the development of detailed schedules for some portions of a program until later stages, when more is known about its nature and direction. A manager can also establish trigger levels of

Figure 5.3 Guidelines for Planning a Program or Project

1. Determine the steps necessary to achieve the objectives.
2. Spell out the relationships among the steps and establish priorities and sequences.
3. Estimate the time required for each step, reevaluate sequencing if necessary, develop a time schedule, and establish definite dates for completion.
4. Determine the necessary resources, such as funds, persons, and materials.
5. Determine who will be responsible for each step and assign responsibility. Determine the level of authority necessary to carry out responsibility, and delegate it. Communicate these assignments to all affected and to others in the organization with whom they will be working.
6. Develop a control chart to track progress, as well as the information system needed to aid corrective action.

performance so that certain projects are triggered at specific levels—for example, when step 5 has been 60 percent completed, step 6 will be initiated.

Programs are often made up of subprograms and projects that draw upon many different units within the organization. This complicates planning, coordination, execution, and control. Each subunit may place the highest priority on its own subprograms, regardless of the priority in the program as a whole. Most organizations therefore place one person in charge of the entire program. This employee may be a full-time program manager or may oversee the program in addition to performing his or her regular job. Each program or project in each subunit may also have a contact person. Whatever organizational form is used, someone needs to pay attention to the whole program so that activities can be coordinated and the program can be carried out alongside the firm's continuing operations.

Functional Strategies

All of the objectives, single-use plans, and standing plans intended to carry out organizational strategy within a function form **functional strategies**. These strategies are the means by which the functional units of an organization intend to accomplish their objectives. They are a type of operational strategy, used to implement the organization's strategy. Here, however, the focus is on the functional level of the organization.

The process of formulating functional strategies and the character of those strategies are similar in many ways to the formulation and nature of the corporate strategy. Nevertheless, there are several important differences.[5] Functional strategies cover a much shorter time span than corporate or business-level strategies. They are much more specific and action oriented. Finally, they require much more active participation by lower levels of management.

As the example in Figure 5.4 shows, the functional strategies are derived from the organization's corporate strategy. This example does not indicate the degree of detail that would be required to carry out the corporate strategy, but it does indicate the elaboration of objectives, policies, and other plans at the functional level.

Figure 5.4 Role of Functional Strategies at General Cinema Corporation

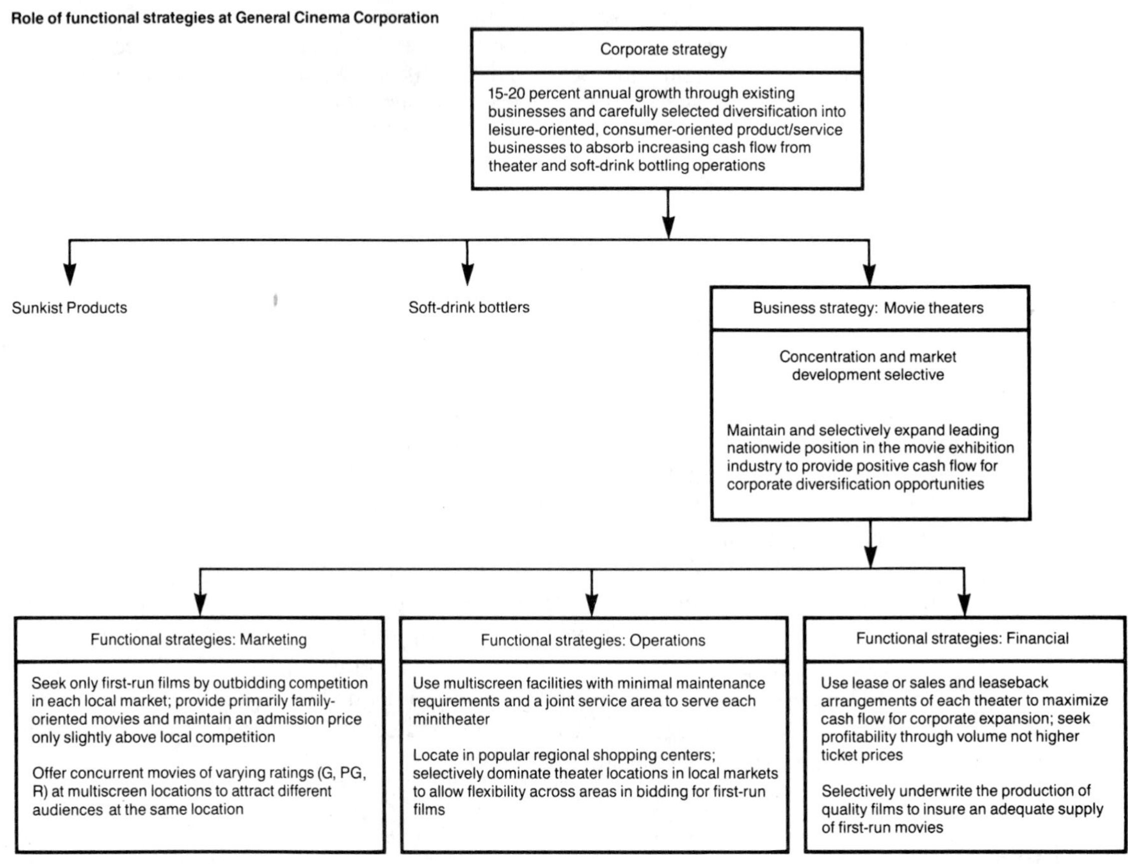

Role of functional strategies at General Cinema Corporation
Corporate strategy
15-20 percent annual growth through existing businesses and carefully selected diversification into leisure-oriented, consumer-oriented product/service businesses to absorb increasing cash flow from theater and soft-drink bottling operations
Sunkist Products
Soft-drink bottlers
Business strategy: Movie theaters
Concentration and market development selective
Maintain and selectively expand leading nationwide position in the movie exhibition industry to provide positive cash flow for corporate diversification opportunities
Functional strategies: Marketing
Seek only first-run films by outbidding competition in each local market; provide primarily family-oriented movies and maintain an admission price only slightly above local competition
Offer concurrent movies of varying ratings (G, PG, R) at multiscreen locations to attract different audiences at the same location
Functional strategies: Operations
Use multiscreen facilities with minimal maintenance requirements and a joint service area to serve each minitheater
Locate in popular regional shopping centers; selectively dominate theater locations in local markets to allow flexibility across areas in bidding for first-run films
Functional strategies: Financial
Use lease or sales and leaseback arrangements of each theater to maximize cash flow for corporate expansion; seek profitability through volume not higher ticket prices
Selectively underwrite the production of quality films to insure an adequate supply of first-run movies

Source: John A. Pierce II and Richard B. Robinson, *Strategic Management: Strategy Formulation and Implementation*, Third Edition, 1988, p. 335. © 1988 Richard D. Irwin, Inc. Reprinted with permission.

Strategies can be developed for any functional area of the firm, but certain areas are especially important to ensure that they achieve implementation of corporate strategies. Although the key functional departments vary according to the nature of the firm's business, a typical firm must plan for marketing, research and development, production, and finance.

Marketing

The function of marketing is to deliver the organization's product or service to customers who need or desire it, in such a way as to achieve the organization's objectives. Philip Kotler has described marketing management as:

> the analysis, planning, implementation, and control of programs designed to bring about desired exchanges with target markets for the purpose of achieving organizational objec-

> tives. It relies heavily on designing the organization's offering in terms of market's needs and desires and using effective pricing, communication, and distribution to inform, motivate, and service the market.[6]

The role of marketing management, thus, is to deliver the proper product or service at the right price at the right time at the right place while promoting it to the right customer.

Market Segmentation A key issue in marketing is the choice of a target market or markets. Increasingly, companies are using market segmentation in making this choice. **Market segmentation** is the division of a market into groups of customers on the basis of their needs and the way they use the product.

Segmentation has several benefits. It allows the firm to target marketing strategies at new markets. The company can plan market and product development better and penetrate the market more fully if it can target groups of customers with clearly defined characteristics. Also, segmentation enables the firm to make better use of its resources by focusing only on the customers for whom the product is intended. The firm avoids wasted promotional efforts, so each dollar spent achieves a better return. Finally, segmentation makes possible better decisions about price, product, promotion, and channels of distribution, all of which can be aimed at specific market segments.

Selecting an appropriate basis for segmenting the market is a key issue. Markets are often segmented on the basis of four types of characteristics: geographic, demographic, psychographic, and behavioral.[7] Geographic characteristics include region, county, and city of residence; population density; and climate. Demographic characteristics include age, sex, income, and education. Using such bases to subdivide the market, the marketer can look for characteristics as well as differences among consumer groups and thereby develop a detailed picture of potential customers. Sometimes this information uncovers a significant opportunity, as shown in the Strategic Application "Kellogg Finds a New Market Segment."

STRATEGIC APPLICATIONS

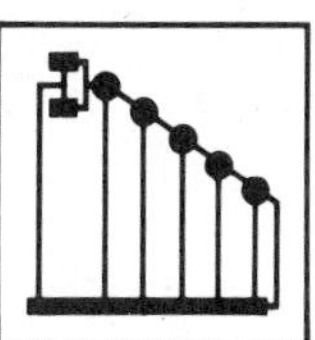

Kellogg Finds a New Market Segment

The cereal business in the late 1970s was stagnant. Most companies in the industry undertook diversification, but Kellogg Company, for the most part, stuck to cereal because the company believed it had found a new market segment—nutrition-conscious adults. Young adults wanted more fiber and no fat or cholesterol.

Kellogg developed a line of adult cereals to appeal to this segment. The cereals were differentiated from the competition by the absence of sugar and preservatives. Today adult cereals account for 40 percent of the industry, and Kellogg has half of this segment.

Source: R. Fannin, "Crunching the Competition: Kellogg Co.," *Marketing & Media Decisions*, March 1988, 70–75.

Product Positioning Once it has identified potential market segments, the firm is in a better position to decide how to meet the needs of its target market. It also has to decide how best to serve that market. The company must learn how competitors are serving the market and develop a plan for establishing an optimal position for its own product in that market. This is called positioning. One expert has described it as follows:

> Positioning refers to the customer's perceptions of the place a product or brand occupies in a given segment. In some markets, a position is achieved by associating the benefits of the brand with the needs or life-style of a customer group. . . . More often, positioning involves the differentiation of the company's offering from the competition by making or implying a comparison in terms of specific attributes such as price or performance features.[8]

This comparison may be based on a positioning of competitors' products as mapped in the example in Figure 5.5. The firm determines the attributes on which customers base their judgments of product similarities as well as their preferences for particular products. Using these attributes, one can indicate where competitors' products are positioned in a given market segment. The extent to which one product competes with another is shown by the closeness of their locations on the map. The relative size of the market for a given set of attributes is shown by the size of the appropriate quadrant or cell, or indicated by a note appended to the chart. Each

Figure 5.5 Perceptual Map of Product Positioning of Textbook Publishers

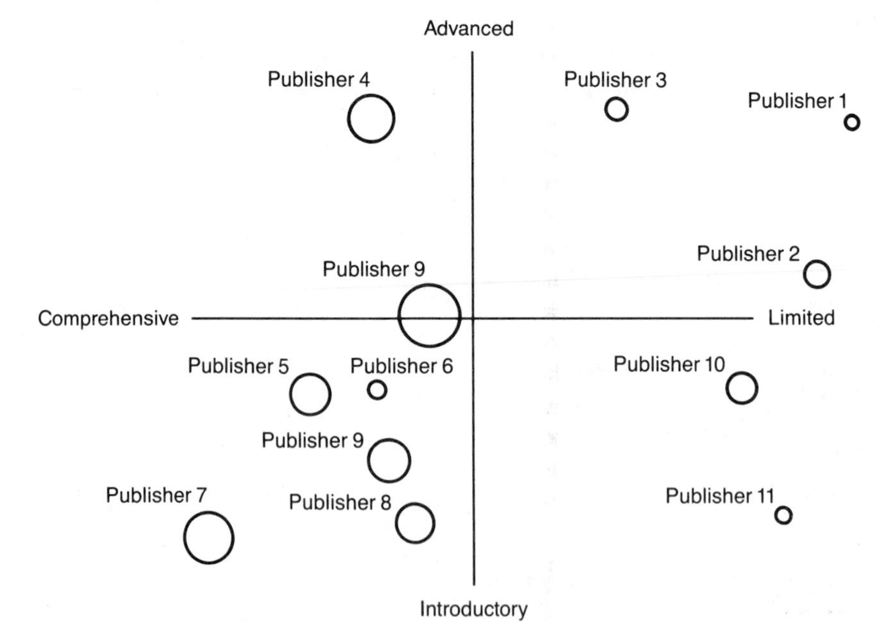

Comprehensive/Limited refers to number of disciplines. *Advanced/Introductory* refers to course level of targeted market.

product's market share can be indicated by the size of the circle showing the product's position or with color coding.

The mapping technique is not precise enough to provide hard-and-fast decision rules, but the following guidelines can be used in deciding where to position a product:

1. Look for where the organization's brand, product, or service can be most competitive in serving the target market.
2. Look for niches in the market that are not being served or that are underserved.
3. Consider the relative strengths of possible competitors.
4. Consider whether the organization's competitive strengths are well matched to the opportunities provided by the open niches.
5. Keep in mind that positions in the middle usually indicate a product or brand or service that customers cannot clearly distinguish from others.

Marketing Mix Once a market segment has been chosen and the product or brand or service defined, the firm can turn its attention to developing the marketing mix. The **marketing mix** is a set of decisions about four key elements: price, promotion, place (distribution), and product.

Price Pricing is an important element of marketing strategy because it affects product image, customer demand, and profitability. Therefore, well-defined price objectives should be established. Depending on the company's overall business strategy, pricing can be used for a number of purposes. For example, during the introduction stage of the product life cycle, a high price may be set in order to project a high-quality image or to skim the market. Later the price may be lowered in order to penetrate the market more fully and gain higher market share. During the maturity stage, the price may be stabilized while promotion is used to maintain market share. When a product is being harvested, the price is set at a level that will maintain market share and cash flow.

These examples should clearly demonstrate that pricing decisions are intertwined with decisions in other functional areas. Production costs typically require a minimum price if the business is to break even. Expected sales volume is important in setting price, and expected price is important in planning for new facilities and predicting operating cost. The interrelationships among these factors are illustrated by the case of a Korean manufacturer that planned to build a plant to produce computer chips expected to sell for $25. This seemed reasonable when the retail price was $50. However, by the time the plant began production, the forces of supply and demand had lowered the price of chips to $2.

The relationship between marketing and production is crucial when a business adopts a low-cost strategy. When the firm follows a strategy that is based on differentiating the product from those of competitors or is aimed at specific niches, pricing is somewhat less critical. Even in such cases, however, it cannot be ignored: accumulated costs always serve as a floor for pricing strategy.

Pricing strategy usually takes one of three approaches. A competitive approach sets prices on the basis of actions and prices of competitors in the market. The price is set at or below the competitors' price. The leaders in a particular market may set prices while smaller competitors follow suit. Or, when a patent is about to run out, the company may lower its prices to discourage competition after the barrier to entry has been removed.

A cost-oriented approach to pricing involves adding a specific markup to total cost. In a variation on cost-oriented pricing, IBM seeks to maintain a specified price/performance relationship for its entire line of mainframe computers. It allocates costs to each model in the line so that the customer must choose the computer that fits its performance requirements. A buyer cannot gain more performance per dollar by choosing one size over another. This policy led to prices for the largest computers being set at a level that did not reflect actual cost. The artificially high price allowed Amdahl to find a niche in the market for large computers.

Finally, a market-oriented approach bases prices on customer demand. Prices are set to achieve a particular market objective. When customer demand for the product is sensitive to the price of the product, pricing can be used to manipulate customer demand. For example, a company can set the price at a level that permits it to gain market share. Another example is the company with an innovative product that can charge higher prices until the demand slows. Polaroid was able to charge higher prices whenever it introduced a new version of its camera. A company that holds a patent on its new product may be able to maintain its price for an extended period.

Pricing also includes determining the type and structure of discounts to be offered, if any. Cash discounts may be used to improve the cash flow and reduce the amount of cash tied up in accounts receivable. Quantity discounts can aid in planning for production and inventory levels by encouraging long, smooth production runs. The firm can use other discounts to adjust for differences in shipping distances, seasonal variations in demand, and variations in utilization rates. For example, telephone companies charge lower prices at nonpeak times.

Promotion Promotion combines four basic tools—personal selling, publicity, advertising, and sales promotion—to communicate with customers in a particular market segment. Numerous factors influence the relative emphasis placed on each of these means of promoting the product and how each is used. For example, personal selling may include finding prospects, selling the product, describing its benefits, providing service, and gathering information about customers. If the product is new and innovative, greater emphasis may be placed on finding prospective customers and describing the benefits offered by the product or service. In the steel industry, some companies emphasize servicing the customer and solving customers' problems. For many food-processing businesses, personal selling is less important than massive advertising aimed at creating a "pull" for the product.

Advertising can be used to persuade potential customers to buy the product or to reinforce existing preferences by providing information. The primary decisions to be made are how much to spend, how to allocate the budget, which media to use, the content of the message, the means of presentation, and the schedule to follow. Promotion policies and plans should be coordinated and should be consistent with other marketing plans and plans of other functions. For example, a company producing at full capacity does not need to advertise to increase demand for the product. However, it may want to advertise to maintain its name awareness.

Publicity, an aspect of public relations, is the securing of "free" (that is, unpaid for) space in the media. It can be an extremely effective way of getting a message to customers at little cost. Many organizations prepare publicity or information releases for the media, which report them as news. In the case of Chrysler Corporation, for example, the public's fascination with Lee Iacocca has given the company quite a bit of publicity. Similarly, IBM gains a great deal of publicity through magazines that serve users of IBM personal computers. Sometimes media publicity can be more important than any other form of promotion in moving a product; this was true for the book *In Search of Excellence.*

Sales promotions can also play a significant role in promoting a product. These include samples, dealer bonuses, and sales contests.

Distribution Distribution places the product in a location where it will be available when and where customers need it. Perhaps the most important decision about distribution is which channels to use to move the product to the customer. The selection of distributors, sales representatives, warehouses, transportation modes, and so forth is influenced by several factors. The number of potential customers and whether they are widely dispersed or concentrated may determine whether the company employs salespeople or uses the services of sales representatives. Product characteristics such as the service requirements of customers and the perishability of the product also affect channel decisions. When a product is highly perishable (for example, daily news), channels must permit rapid distribution to many customers.

Distribution decisions are also influenced by characteristics of the company, especially its financial strength, its size, and its experience with particular channels. A large, financially secure company can employ techniques that allow both extensive and intensive coverage of the market, even though this requires a larger investment in inventory. A company may choose to carry the costs of its inventory through the entire channel, with title passing directly to the customer, so that it can have more control over territory, price, and service. Other factors, such as the channels that competitors employ and the strengths and weaknesses of intermediaries, are important considerations as well. A firm's distribution channels can give it an important competitive advantage. Caterpiller is one firm that has achieved a distinct advantage from its distribution network.

Product Decisions about the firm's product are central to the formulation and implementation of strategy at all levels. At the functional level, these decisions are tied to market segmentation and positioning. One must know the characteristics of the target market for which the product is designed and the position sought for the product. Management must determine which product to emphasize and which ones are most profitable. It is also necessary to decide whether the firm should offer new products or trim its offering. Generally, a firm that is pursuing a growth strategy will expand its product line, whereas one that is harvesting profits will cut back on its product offerings.

As with the other elements of marketing mix, the decisions related to the product should be coordinated with decisions about other elements, as well as with other functional plans. The marketing department needs to take the lead in providing information about the product characteristics needed by customers in the target market, and it should time its marketing efforts to coincide with new-product development. It also needs to provide accurate forecasts for use in setting production schedules and should adjust its activities to these schedules.

For many companies, especially customer-oriented ones, marketing is a critical function. It is a major link with the firm's environment, especially customers, and is usually given the primary responsibility for generating revenue. Strategic decisions often revolve around markets and products, and the marketing department usually takes the lead in moving into new markets. Thus the development of marketing objectives, strategies, and plans is critical to the implementation of the organization's overall strategy.

Production and Operations

Production and operations is the function that acquires inputs such as materials, knowledge, and people and transforms them into the products or services that the organization markets. This function is typically associated with manufacturing, in which a physical product results from shaping, assembly, or fabrication operations, but even nonmanufacturing organizations have production functions. In a hospital, for example, the provision of health care to patients through examinations, testing, surgery, and so forth is a production function. The imparting of knowledge to students in a university can also be considered a production function.

The production and operations strategy should be derived from, and designed to achieve, the overall strategy of the company or SBU. The Strategic Application "Northern States Power Seeks to Control Pollution" shows a company that has been able to integrate its corporate social responsibility objectives with its production strategy. There is no universal production system that will fit any strategy. Instead, the organization's overall strategy makes specific demands on its production function, and the production system must be designed to meet those demands.

The plan that tailors the production system to the overall strategy is the firm's production strategy. The firm's overall strategy cannot be formulated without careful consideration of the capabilities of its production system. Failure to do so may turn a competitive advantage into a disadvantage. Consider the case of a company that produces custom-designed forklifts. Its plant has the flexibility to produce a wide variety of forklifts, and the layout is designed around different production processes, with final assembly in a single location. This production system would become a liability if the firm were to decide to produce standard models, because it could not achieve the necessary volume and efficiency with its existing layout.

Too often, the role of the production function is limited to efficient operation and the provision of acceptable quality and customer service. One observer has commented:

STRATEGIC APPLICATIONS: SOCIAL RESPONSIBILITY

Northern States Power Seeks to Control Pollution

In recent years, federal legislation has brought strict regulations on the emissions of electric utilities, and these companies have found it costly to meet the standards. Northern States Power (NSP) generates 56 percent of its power from coal, which has meant costly cleanup activities. The company has spent nearly $1 billion on pollution controls and reduced its sulfur dioxide emissions by 53 percent while doubling the amount of coal used.

NSP has a history of developing new technologies in anticipation of pollution requirements. Company policy is to exceed every environmental requirement. NSP began using low-sulfur coal years before it was needed. The company put scrubbers on big plants in 1973, and in 1981 it put an experimental dry-scrubber system on an old plant, although neither action was required. In 1986 NSP was the first large commercial plant to use the "fluidized bed," a system that burns coal mixed with limestone to stop the sulfur before it escapes. Through good foresight, a responsible attitude, and policies to implement its objectives, NSP has sought to change before it is in trouble and has change forced on it.

Source: S. Weiner, "Profit without Pollution," *Forbes*, May 18, 1987, 46.

> The view prevails that a plant with reasonably modern equipment, up-to-date methods and procedures, a cooperative work force, a computerized information system, and an enlightened management will be a good plant and will perform efficiently.[9]

These are certainly desirable qualities, but by themselves they are insufficient, and they do not reflect the numerous choices that executives must make.

For example, management must ask what will be required of the production system if the company follows a particular competitive strategy. Different competitive strategies vary in their requirements for product reliability and quality, as well as in cost levels and scheduling. These factors, coupled with technological constraints, may force management to make compromises in choosing a production strategy. The influence of competitive strategy on production system decisions is illustrated in Table 5.1. Managers should choose among the alternatives on the basis of the firm's competitive strategy as well as what will make a good, efficient plant.

Research and Development

The product is often the focus of strategy in a company like 3M, which seeks to maintain technological leadership in bonding and coating products. But even firms that produce commodities cannot allow their products to become obsolete. Production processes themselves must be kept up to date. Every product and service must continually be improved, replaced, or renewed. Similarly, the processes used to produce the product must be improved or replaced.

The research and development function is responsible for developing and improving the company's product and production processes. Its activities must be co-

Table 5.1 Strategic Considerations in Choosing Production Strategy

Decision Area	Choice	Low-Cost Strategy Consideration	Differentiation Strategy Consideration
Product line	Few or many customer options	Strategy argues for standardized product with few models and options.	What is the key value stressed? Exceptional quality might argue for few customer specials, but custom design may require many.
Design changes	Freeze design or allow many engineering design changes	Standard product offers chance for long product runs but enough change must be allowed to lower product cost. Must get far out on experience curve to maintain cost advantage.	Similar to above; i.e., achieving quality may require allowing change only when new design is well tested.
Plant location	Locate near markets or materials or labor	Strategy favors whichever will provide lowest cost.	Cost may be deciding factor, but if service is the key value, then location near markets may be the choice. Skilled labor may be a deciding factor.
Plant size	One large-scale or several smaller plants	Larger-volume plant may be able to use more specialized equipment and gain more experience-curve effects. Scale needed depends on industry. Delivery costs may be more important than production costs.	Economies of scale are still important, but size and location of market, service, or delivery may preclude one large plant.
Equipment	General- or special-purpose	Low cost means volume production of standardized product, thus special-purpose equipment.	When the key value is built into the product with unique features, special equipment and tooling are likely to be needed.
Inventory size	High or low levels	Volume production requires sustained production and thus enough inventory to avoid shutdowns. Advanced techniques like just-in-time inventory needed to minimize investment.	Unique products may allow for manufacturing to order or longer delivery, but a service emphasis may need larger inventory.
Quality control	High reliability and quality or low cost	Maintain reliability and quality at chosen level, but then emphasize low cost.	High-quality or unique features are likely to require greater emphasis on quality control.

ordinated closely with those of the marketing department to ensure that the product will meet customers' needs. R&D activities must also be coordinated with those of the production department so that the product can be manufactured to given standards within specified cost constraints. Most important, the R&D department must derive its own objectives and plans from the overall strategy of the firm or that of the SBU and division it serves.

Several key choices must be made in establishing goals and policies for research and development. These define the emphasis and nature of the R&D function.

Focus The focus for R&D defines the extent to which it should be targeted at specific applications. In the United States and Japan, most research is focused on areas in which one can imagine a use for the results. Such targeted research may include basic research, but usually it is explicitly focused on developing a product for a specific application. Generic or untargeted research, on the other hand, may be called for when knowledge in a given area is expanding rapidly and a firm cannot protect its competitive position with targeted research alone. In the words of one expert, what is important is to be "working at the forefront of technical areas centrally important to the parent company. Is [R&D] producing results of near-term value and laying the groundwork for future advances?"[10]

Market-Driven versus Technology-Driven R&D Research and development must be linked to marketing, but this does not mean that markets cannot be developed for new technologies. Companies like 3M and Dow Corning have been successful in creating new markets for their technological discoveries. They also have based their R&D projects on a knowledge of market needs and requirements. It may be acceptable to allow considerable uncertainty in predicting how an existing market will respond to a new product; identifying potential markets toward which to target a new product also is subject to much uncertainty. Marketing and R&D personnel need to be prepared to identify possible markets for products emerging from R&D, as well as to identify markets for which new products could be developed.

A company's competitive advantage may be its expertise in a particular area of technology. In such cases, maintaining this advantage requires more generic research and a continuing search for potential markets. Nevertheless, targeted research is still appropriate as the company seeks additional markets. It is not a matter of choosing between approaches but of balancing them. Frequent communication among managers, marketing, customers, and R&D personnel can help the company more fully exploit both its generic and its targeted research.

Centralized versus Decentralized R&D A firm with several divisions needs to decide whether each division should conduct its own research and development or whether R&D should be centralized. Locating the R&D units in the divisions preserves the authority of division managers and holds them accountable for performance. It also promotes a close connection between R&D and the division's strategy, plans, and programs and may help R&D better target its efforts. Moreover, if the technological base of each division is different, centralization may provide little in the way of synergy or economies of scale.

When divisions are following varying strategies, the role of R&D can be quite different. A unit that seeks market leadership based on low cost may need research focusing on process improvements that increase efficiency. A unit using a technology that is undergoing rapid change and for which most applications are still speculative will more heavily emphasize generic research. Under such conditions, there is probably little to be gained by having the R&D units located together.

When an organization maintains a corporate R&D center, scientists may be under less pressure to concentrate on short-term projects that promise an immediate payoff.

Some technologies may be applicable to several products and would benefit from concentration of research efforts and the greater variety of personnel that could be employed by a corporate research center. Concentration of talent, equipment, and resources may produce a critical mass that would not be possible if R&D were spread out among several divisions. It also makes possible the formation of interdisciplinary teams and the application of technologies that would be unavailable in a single division. Also, the larger scale of the corporate unit means that it can make available equipment, facilities, and services that decentralized units could not afford.

The decisions involved in locating resources and facilities are not obvious ones. Some companies have solved the problem by establishing corporate R&D units in various units that concentrate on generic research, while R&D units in various divisions focus on targeted programs. Others, believing that division managers may be tempted to sacrifice research quality for the sake of improved short-term performance, locate all R&D in a central facility. Sometimes coordinating mechanisms such as project, product, or small-business teams that cut across divisions can provide the required balance.

Internal versus External Research The development of products and processes need not take place within the organization. A firm may not have the resources to pursue an important technology. Perhaps it needs a particular technology but is far behind other researchers in the field. Maybe another company has already developed a product or process that would meet the organization's needs. Rather than spend the time and resources to develop the technology itself, the firm may decide to buy it. It could purchase the patent or even the company that developed the technology. In some cases, the company may be able to acquire a license to use the technology. Other possibilities are to contract out all or part of the research to a private lab or a university and to enter into a joint project. These alternatives may save the company years of effort and sometimes are the only way to enter a new market or catch up with the competition.

Finance

Financial strategies are concerned with providing the funds to implement the overall strategy and operate the firm. These strategies include policies and plans for acquiring capital, allocating funds for investment projects and operations, managing working capital, and paying out dividends.

Working Capital The level of working capital can play an important role in an organization's strategies as well as its day-to-day operations.[11] Insufficient working capital may cause the firm to go to financial markets or use short-term loans, trade credit, and the like to support its strategic actions. Moreover, some strategies require specific levels of working capital if they are to be implemented properly. The policies used to manage accounts receivable or inventories can be crucial to the success of certain strategies. For example, the credit terms that the organization offers should be at least competitive within the industry, and they can be manipulated to increase sales. Favorable credit policies can sometimes facilitate introduction of new products, expansion into new territories, and entry into new markets.

Management of the amount and timing of cash flow also is important. A cash flow budget allows the company to control the amount of cash that will be available for implementing a strategy. By forecasting sales revenues, collection periods, seasonal influences, and payment schedules, the firm can determine the cash flow required to support particular strategic actions.

Financial officers are concerned with efficient use of working capital as well as with providing funds. However, if they overemphasize efficient cash management, they can stymie the implementation of some strategies. Efficient use of working capital should be viewed as a means of achieving the organization's objectives, not as an end in itself.

Dividend Policy Decisions about whether to pay a dividend and how much to pay affect the funds available to finance corporate growth and strategic actions. The level of dividends paid out to shareholders affects the value of the company's stock to investors and, hence, the cost of capital to the firm. Retained earnings can be used to finance projects and therefore are an important source of funds for implementing strategy. Paying out too much to stockholders may slow the firm's rate of growth and eventually lower the price of its stock. On the other hand, insufficient dividends can make the stock less attractive to investors. In sum, policies regarding retained earnings, equity, and debt financing are interrelated, and decision makers must consider the effects of those policies on the use and availability of funds.

Investment Allocation From the standpoint of strategy implementation, perhaps the most critical area of financial strategy is the allocation of capital for investment. Many strategic changes require investment in facilities, equipment, programs and projects, acquisitions, training programs, or new personnel. Funds from the firm's capital structure and earnings must be allocated to these investments in ways that are commensurate with the firm's objectives. Sources and uses of funds are typically matched under conditions of scarcity, and the decision maker therefore is forced to choose from among competing investments. In addition, management often must commit funds for several years without knowing whether better opportunities will be available in the future. Many firms handle this situation by establishing criteria that any investment project must meet before funds will be committed. Typical criteria include hurdle rates such as a 20 percent return on investment.

Allocation of capital is generally handled centrally. The treasurer and the chief financial officer have considerable influence over the funding of investment opportunities through the formulation and implementation of financial policies. Managers responsible for operations or product-market strategy seem to have little influence on financial policy.[12] This can have negative consequences. For example, because financial managers tend to identify with investment bankers and securities analysts, they often become risk averse. The criteria used to evaluate investment projects reflect this aversion to risk and the decision criteria employed by these professionals outside the company. Such criteria may unnecessarily curtail spending and constrain investment.

Another potential problem is that, over time, financial policies become more than guidelines; they assume the status of goals to be pursued. Under such conditions, corporate strategy can become subordinated to financial policy. One writer on this theme, Richard R. Ellsworth, believes that to realize the full potential of corporate strategy, top management must regain control over the formulation of financial policies. Ellsworth suggests four steps to that end:[13]

1. Identify the underlying assumptions of the existing financial policies. Analyze alternative policies together with the company's business opportunities and the degree of risk it is willing to assume.
2. Encourage financial officers to integrate the needs of firm strategy and the concerns of financial policy. Through selection, training, communication, and incentive compensation, the firm can encourage its financial officers to align their personal interests with improved performance by the firm as a whole.
3. Include operations managers in the process of formulating financial policies.
4. Prevent financial policies from becoming corporate goals, and do not represent them as goals to those outside the company.

A company must establish its investment criteria in light of its own circumstances and strategy. In addition, it must balance competing, often conflicting priorities while reconciling the demand for funds with the available supply. There are a number of constraints on corporate goals and policies, including the nature of capital markets, industry and economic conditions, and the nature of competitive markets.[14] For example, speed, flexibility, and quality are becoming important criteria in investment decisions. When competitors can bring out products faster or of better quality, the company's existence may be threatened. Increasing numbers of companies are using criteria that are hard to account for but contribute to gains in business.[15] In the past, accounting systems have often not been designed to facilitate financial decision making. The Strategic Application "CAM-I Is Developing a New Accounting System" indicates how some companies are beginning to redesign their systems to support strategic and financial decisions. By carefully integrating corporate strategy with financial policy, a company can avoid imposing artificial constraints on itself in addition to the constraints it cannot avoid.[16]

Capital Acquisition Capital acquisition is concerned with the organization's financial structure. The firm must choose from among various possible sources of funds to finance its activities. It must also decide what proportion of the required funds will come from each source.

Businesses can obtain additional funds in several ways. A firm can sell off assets or divest part of its business, reinvesting the receipts in one of its remaining SBUs. It can move earnings from a "cash cow" to a new product or project. Or it can borrow funds from outside the firm. Whatever sources the company uses, it must develop objectives, policies, and plans to provide funds for new strategies while maintaining a sound financial structure.

The mix of debt, equity, and earnings can affect the firm's ability to reach its financial goals and fund its strategies for both the short and the long term. The financial

STRATEGIC APPLICATIONS

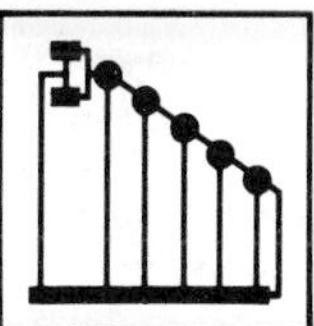

CAM-I Is Developing a New Accounting System

Computer Aided Manufacturing-International Inc. is working in conjunction with Big Eight accounting firms and several dozen large companies to redesign accounting systems. The company's backers argue that traditional accounting systems, especially cost accounting, do not reveal the real costs of shifting jobs overseas and the true costs associated with a product, nor do they allow for quantifiable improvements in quality, improved scheduling, and flexibility.

One of CAM-I's aims is to change the way business calculates costs. For example, one proposal is to identify all costs associated with the product from development to marketing as product costs. Called "life-cycle accounting," the proposal is controversial with conservative accountants, but others believe it is necessary if U.S. business is to stay competitive. The consortium expects to introduce computer software for its proposals by 1990.

Source: Kevin Kelly, "That Old-Time Accounting Isn't Good Enough Anymore," *Business Week*, June 6, 1988, 112.

structure can also constrain strategic choices. For example, inability to provide sustained financing for a project may prevent the firm from undertaking that project. Some of the influences on the financial structure of a firm are listed in Table 5.2.

Financial policies can also influence strategy formulation. First the choices made about the company's financial structure may preclude some strategic choices. A company with a conservative attitude toward debt financing may find its expansion opportunities limited. If forced to rely on internally generated funds when its industry is growing rapidly, the company may find its market position declining. Second, financial policies affect the choices among competing projects when budgets are allocated by establishing the rate of return expected from investment projects. Projects

Table 5.2 Some Factors Affecting Financial Structure

Factor	Nature of Effect
Growth Rate of Sales	Firm's ability to trade on equity is affected.
Sales Stability	Greater stability allows less risk in incurring debt.
Competitive Structure	Competitive pressures affect profit margins.
Asset Structure	Firms with large amounts of fixed assets tend to use more long-term mortgage debt. Firms with large amounts of current assets tend to use more short-term debt.
Management Attitudes	Management's risk preference and desire to maintain control will affect preference for stock and debt.
Lender Attitudes	Lender's risk preference and conservatism can influence financial officer's choices.

Source: J. Fred Weston and Eugene F. Brigham, *Managerial Finance,* 2d ed. (Hinsdale, IL: The Dryden Press, 1966), 262–264.

that could save delivery time to the customer may not be accepted because managers are unable to demonstrate the required rate of return. The result can be the undermining of a key marketing strategy—improved customer service.

Resource Allocation: Budgeting

A company's resources must be allocated to the units that will carry out the corporate or business strategy. For example, if an SBU is to increase sales by 30 percent and market share by 10 percent in two years, additional financial and human resources must be allocated to it. The SBU will also need additional physical resources such as inventories and equipment, and it may even need additional plant capacity. Other required resources may include research, recruitment of skilled personnel, or a new communications and information system. Thus, a firm's strategic plans may call for a wide variety of resources. These resources must be identified, acquired, and allocated.

The formal system for allocating resources within an organization is the **budget**. Most large companies and many small ones have a well-developed budgeting process. The strategic and operational planning process specifies the costs and revenues to be allocated to each activity, that is, the budget for each activity and program. The budget thus shows how the corporation intends to allocate its resources in pursuing its goals. It also represents the firm's priorities for the use of its resources during a given period.

Budgets, of course, allocate resources in terms of money. Budgeting principles assume that the need for other resources can be represented by requests for money to pay for those resources (such as salaries for additional personnel or the cost of new equipment). However, money does not always guarantee the required nonmonetary resources. For example, it may not be possible to buy the services of a scientist who is dedicated to pursuing a specific line of research. Other professionals may be interested primarily in working at a particular location, opportunities for promotion, or discretion over their work. Thus, obtaining the money to pay for needed resources does not necessarily mean that the firm or SBU will be able to acquire those resources. The situation in most companies has been described by Yavitz and Newman:

> Few companies, however, have formalized their allocation processes for nonfinancial resources. Those that do, such as large construction companies or consulting firms, typically work on a series of big projects and have a matrix organization. For most other companies, the allocation of nonfinancial resources for strategic purposes calls for special treatment—often informal bargaining by division managers.[17]

Despite these limitations, money remains the most useful medium for requesting and allocating resources. Therefore, all strategies are eventually translated into budgets.

Budget Formulation

Developing a budget is an integral part of strategic planning as well as implementation. The specific process varies from one company to another, but it usually begins while the company is formulating its strategy and developing the programs to carry it out. Figure 5.6 presents the basic steps in the budgeting process.[18]

The issue of resource allocation enters the picture when strategic business plans are prepared and submitted to top management for approval. These plans include projections of the amount of resources required to implement them. In reviewing the plans, management makes a rough allocation of funds. Following tentative approval by top management, the SBUs or divisions revise and elaborate on the respective plans. Functional managers then develop detailed proposals for the programs and

Figure 5.6 Steps in Developing a Strategic Budget

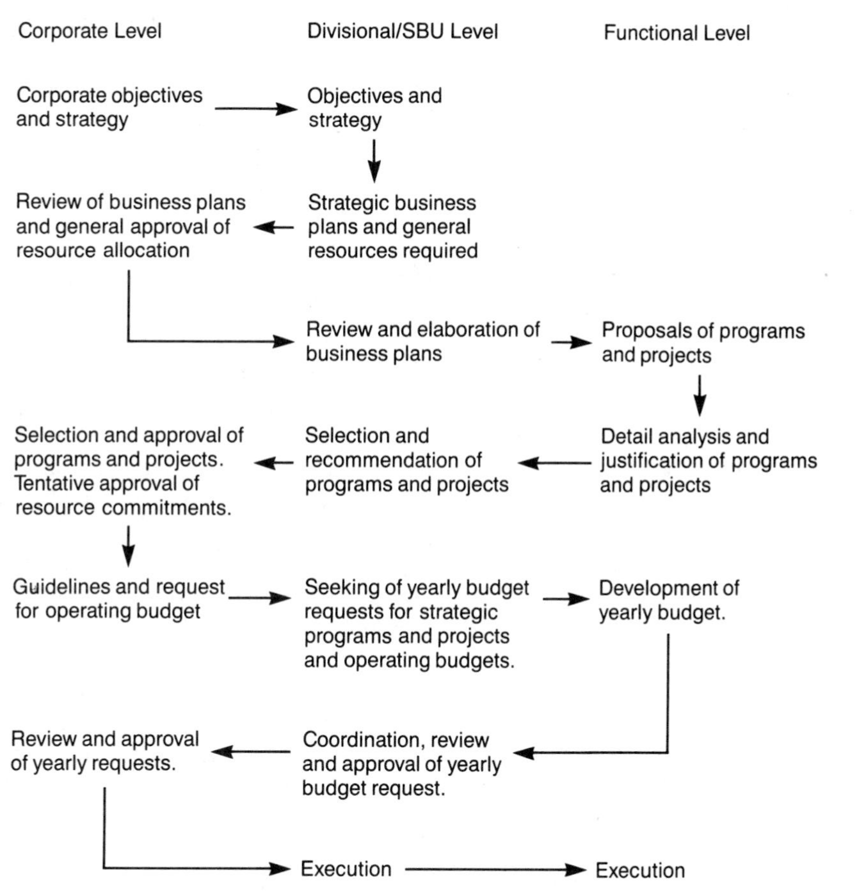

Sources: 1. Richard F. Vancil and Peter Lorange, "Strategic Planning in Diversified Companies," *Harvard Business Review*, January–February, 1975, in Richard F. Vancil and Peter Lorange, *Strategic Planning Systems* (Englewood Cliffs, N.J.: Prentice-Hall, 1977): 22–36; 2. Charles H. Roush, Jr., "Strategic Resource Allocation and Control," 20-1–20-25, in William D. Guth, ed., *Handbook of Business Strategy* (Boston: Warren, Gorham & Lamont, 1985); and 3. William F. Glueck and Lawrence R. Jauch, *Business Policy and Strategic Management*, 4th ed. (New York: McGraw-Hill, 1984): 316–318.

projects, giving special attention to capital expenditure projects needed to carry out their unit's business plan. Managers at the SBU or division level choose among the various programs proposed to them and recommend certain ones to top management, specifying the resources needed for each. At this point, top management makes a somewhat firmer commitment to particular programs.

Next the division develops an operating budget for the coming year. Each department within the division is asked to submit a departmental budget. The budget requests of all the functional departments involved in a particular program or project must be coordinated. The division or SBU's management reviews and approves these budgets and submits them to top management, which will approve resource allocations for the next year. By this stage, a program may have been reviewed several times, each in increasing detail.

Once the budgets have been approved, the divisions, SBUs, and functional departments begin carrying out their plans. The budgets now become a set of standards that can be used to compare the unit's actual progress with the goals established for it. Thus, the budget serves as a control device. Chapter 8 will examine this use of budgets in more detail.

Capital and Expense Budgets

The corporate budget may include budgets for sales, capital, production, overhead, cash expenses, and other categories. From the strategic management perspective, the capital and strategic expense budgets have the greatest impact.

The purpose of capital budgeting is to identify, analyze, and select capital-investment projects. Much of the analysis consists of an evaluation of alternatives in order to determine which opportunities fit the overall strategy and will contribute to the achievement of strategic goals while meeting previously established economic criteria. Capital budgets are reviewed at several levels of management and ideally derive from corporate objectives as a part of the process of formulating business plans and determining general resource requirements. As the capital budget moves through the budgeting process, it becomes more specific and concrete. Although strategic and economic criteria are both applied throughout the process, the emphasis is on strategic fit in the early stages and on economic criteria in the later stages.

Capital budgets often commit funds for extended periods. A new plant may be expected to have a useful life of 10 to 20 years and will require an operating budget as well. The longer the planning period, the more uncertain is the future and the more difficult is rational planning. In addition, some programs require new allocations each year over a period of several years. Thus, capital allocations are significant because they commit the firm to a specific course of action.

Capital funds are often difficult to obtain, and the amount needed usually is much greater than the amount available. The budgeting process establishes the level of funds for new capital projects as well as for replacement, improvements, and maintenance of present capital assets. Because of the considerable competition for available funds, most firms are cautious in the capital budgeting process (see the discussion earlier in the chapter of functional financial strategy). They usually forecast and schedule capital needs for the next five years as well as on a yearly basis. Proposals are reviewed several times by the board of directors, the chief executive officer, or a committee of top management.

Linkage of Resource Allocation to Strategy

To be completely rational throughout the budgeting process is difficult. One reason is that not all proposals are submitted at the same time; as a result, they cannot be evaluated and compared together. Not all projects fit into the planning cycle. Some develop out of unforeseen opportunities. Others stem from failures and breakdowns. Still others are a result of commitments made when a given program was first approved.

Furthermore, the benefits of many projects, especially strategic ones, are difficult to estimate in terms of economic criteria. Some projects are necessary to sustain a strategy or support another project. For example, some laboratory equipment may be needed to perform tests. By itself, the equipment will generate no savings or revenues. It may even increase total costs. But if the development of a new product is to proceed, the equipment must be purchased.

The amount of uncertainty connected with different proposals can vary considerably. When the firm is replacing, improving, or maintaining existing operations, it is easier to determine the likely economic returns. Longer term, more uncertain projects may suffer by comparison if economic criteria are the primary basis for selection.

The strategic fit of a proposal is not always easy to determine. How close a fit is required? Economic criteria based on analytical techniques such as discounted cash flow are well developed, but there is no comparable way to evaluate strategic fit. The subjective judgment of experienced executives becomes pivotal in such decisions.

Personal values also may bias decisions. As noted earlier in the chapter, every executive has a unique set of attitudes, values and cause/effect belief systems. Some proposals match those systems more closely than others. For example, an executive may believe that sales promotions and advertising are the critical factors in generating new sales. This executive will tend to look favorably on any proposal in this area. Or an executive who came up through the production department may believe that production has been shortchanged in the past and will tend to favor proposals that call for more modern equipment.

Company politics also can play a role in the budgeting process. Coalitions may form to lobby for proposals when several departments are involved or the project is in the joint interest of several parties. There may also be political debts to be paid for favors received in the past.

Faced with conditions of scarcity, the generally conservative attitude of financial managers, the difficulty of allocating capital on a rational basis, and the often complex process of building budgets, a company's top executives can find it difficult to integrate the allocation of capital with strategic management. They can review divisional, SBU, and functional plans and later capital proposals for omissions as well as for strategic fit. But what else can they do?

Boris Yavitz and William Newman have suggested several devices to tighten the linkage between capital spending and strategy.[19] One of these is to place specific constraints on the allocation of capital. These constraints can be used to override other criteria or to eliminate proposals from consideration. For instance, when Sherwin-Williams decided to shift its target market from professional painters to ordinary consumers, it could have denied all proposals that were not aimed at consumers. Similarly, a company may decide to focus its sales efforts on the largest markets and hence may create a policy that forbids new investment in territories outside the targeted markets, regardless of the potential return on investment.

Another device suggested by Yavitz and Newman is requiring that each capital allocation proposal include a written statement of the impact the proposed expenditure will have on the execution of current strategy.[20] If the proposed expenditure will not make a significant contribution, it is rejected. Economic and other criteria are still considered, but this approach forces managers to think through the connection between their plans and the company's strategic plans and objectives. This promotes greater emphasis on strategic fit in screening proposals.

When a strategy is formulated, a series of steps to achieve the desired goal are laid out. Each major step can require a program. Programs, and often subprograms, may require new resources and, hence, new capital investment. Yavitz and Newman recommend that approval of a program include approval of the necessary investment. Exactly how the funds will be obtained can be determined when capital proposals are reviewed. The program statement should include the key assumptions about maximum dollar cost and environmental conditions. Later, if it appears these assumptions will not be met, the program is reviewed again. Every program has milestones, such as when a contract will commit the dollars to a supplier. Significant milestones can be a turning point for the program, so these are appropriate times at which to review the program before moving ahead.

A fourth device suggested is a system used by Texas Instruments. Under this system, a budget and temporary organization are established for each strategic program. This arrangement concentrates authority to act and to spend money in a new venture unit, thereby merging strategic programming and capital investing.[21] The Texas Instruments system of budgeting and accounting for strategic funds separately is described in more detail in Chapter 8.

These devices can more closely tie the allocation of capital to strategy and achieve a closer fit. The same devices can be used in allocating dollars for other strategic expenses. The focus is on assuring that managers who are under pressure for immediate results actually use the funds for strategic purposes. For example, funds allocated for training sales managers to introduce a new product should be spent for that purpose and not be diverted to sustain current operations. This can best be achieved by budgeting and controlling strategic funds separately.

In sum, the budgeting process is critical to the implementation of strategic plans. It translates abstract plans into concrete resources. Without the necessary resources, plans cannot move forward. A budget will not ensure that plans will be carried out or that they will succeed. Instead, it constitutes a commitment by the organization to the activities it considers significant, and hence it is an essential step in implementing strategy.

Summary

This chapter described the process of implementing the organization's strategy. It is top management's responsibility to demonstrate what must occur to achieve the strategy. Plans, functional strategies, budgets, organization structure, leadership patterns, organization culture, motivation and reward systems, and control systems must all be tailored to the strategy.

To implement strategy, managers must couple strategic planning with planning for operations. This link is formed by objectives and plans at the divisional and functional levels. Strategies at these levels should be selected to support corporate strategies. Functional strategies are typically selected for marketing, production and operations, research and development, and finance.

Managers provide the resources needed to carry out these plans by establishing budgets. The budgeting process also provides another opportunity for review and evaluation, in which the linkage between strategy and planned action can be reinforced before resources are allocated and the firm becomes committed to action. The budgeting processes of setting objectives, calling for proposals, and reviewing proposals allow top management to seek optimal fit between overall strategy and plans for action.

Questions

1. Your company has just completed a lengthy review of corporate strategy. Many people at a number of levels in the organization were involved, and the strategy changes deemed necessary by management are fairly well understood throughout the organization. What must management now do so that the planned strategy will be carried out?

2. What is the difference between business or SBU strategy and functional strategies? Describe the kinds of plans that are needed to provide for the implementation of SBU strategy. If SBU strategy is not changed, is there any need to review or change functional strategies? Why or why not?

3. How do standing plans, single-use plans, and functional strategies relate to the implementation of SBU strategy? At which phase of the product life cycle is each of the following functional strategies most important: production, research and development, marketing, finance?

4. Why is the budgeting process so important to the implementation of strategy? Assuming that everyone understands the objectives of the company's strategy, why is it still so difficult to allocate the resources necessary to implement the strategy? Describe techniques that can be used to achieve a better integration between the allocation of capital and strategic management.

Notes

1. John M. Hobbs and Donald F. Heany, "Coupling Strategy to Operating Plans," *Harvard Business Review* 50 (May–June 1977): 119–126.

2. Larry D. Alexander, "Towards an Understanding of Strategy Implementation Problems," *Proceedings, Southern Management Association* (November 1982), 147.

3. Adapted from S. W. Angrist, "World Class at Last," *Forbes*, January 25, 1988, 108.

4. William H. Newman, Charles E. Summer, and E. Kirby Warren, *The Process of Management*, 3d ed. (Englewood Cliffs, N.J.: Prentice-Hall, 1972), 420. Much of the material on standing and single-use plans is based on Ronald Simpson and Cyril P. Morgan, *Administration of Real Property* (Arnold, Md.: Building Owners Management Institute, 1982), 2:1–2:20.

5. Lloyd L. Byars, *Strategic Management* (New York: Harper & Row, 1984), 197.

6. Philip Kotler, *Marketing Management: Analysis, Planning and Control*, 4th ed. (Englewood Cliffs, N.J.: Prentice-Hall, 1980), 22.

7. Ibid., 256.

8. George S. Day, *Strategic Market Planning: The Pursuit of Competitive Advantage* (St. Paul, Minn.: West, 1984), 93.

9. Wickham Skinner, "Manufacturing—Missing Link in Corporate Strategy," *Harvard Business Review* 48 (May–June 1969): 136–145.

10. Roland W. Schmitt, "Successful Corporate R&D," *Harvard Business Review*, 63 (May–June 1985): 124–128.

11. Working capital equals current assets minus current liabilities. Current assets usually consist of cash, marketable securities, accounts receivable, and inventories. Current liabilities consist primarily of accounts payable.

12. Richard R. Ellsworth, "Subordinate Financial Policy to Corporate Strategy," *Harvard Business Review* 61 (November–December 1983): 170–182.

13. Ibid., 175–176.

14. Gordon Donaldson, "Financial Goals and Strategic Consequences," *Harvard Business Review* 63 (May–June 1985): 57–66.

15. Otis Port, Resa King, and J. Hampton, "How the New Math of Productivity Adds Up," *Business Week*, June 6, 1988, 103–114.

16. Chapter 8 addresses the use of financial measures to exercise control over strategic programs. The student may also find the material in Appendix B, "Financial Analysis," helpful in assessing and developing financial strategies.

17. Boris Yavitz and William H. Newman, *Strategy in Action* (New York: The Free Press, 1982), 187.

18. This section draws on the following sources: Richard F. Vancil and Peter Lorange, "Strategic Planning in Diversified Companies," *Harvard Business Review* 53 (January–February 1975): 81–90; Charles H. Roush, Jr., "Strategic Resource Allocation and Control," in *Handbook of Business Strategy*, ed. William D. Guth (Boston, Mass.: Warren, Gorham and Lamont, 1985), 20-1–20-25; and John C. Camillus and John H. Grant, "Operational Planning: The Integration of Programming and Budgeting," *The Academy of Management Review* 5 (July 1980): 369–379.

19. Yavitz and Newman, *Strategy in Action*, 194–199.

20. Ibid., 196.

21. Ibid., 199.

Case for Discussion

Mountain Camping

Mountain Camping was the second firm Jim Cascade started. While serving in the mountain division of the U.S. Army, he had discovered an ability to design and sew backpacking gear. After leaving the service he began to manufacture backpacking tents, sleeping bags, and packs. The products quickly gained a reputation for high quality, durability, and functionality. His business grew quickly, at a compounded rate of 15 percent a year, but could not keep up with the demand. The gear was sold through mountaineering stores and sporting goods stores that catered to backpacking, bicycling, and other outdoor sports.

This first company had trouble raising working capital as well as meeting the demands placed on Jim's management systems and his personal ability to manage the enterprise. Eventually he agreed to be acquired by one of the leading diversified firms in the sporting goods industry. When he could no longer accept what the parent company was doing with the business, and realized he was not happy working for someone else, he left the firm. Two years later he started another company similar to the first.

Wanting his second company to be a success, Jim was determined not to repeat his mistakes. Above all he wanted to remain in control and able to manage the company. He limited the product line to backpacks and tents. He refused to sell to large-volume sporting good chains. He believed that if he could limit outlets for the product to those who sold the best, and if he made the best, he could keep the business to a size he could manage.

This background colored all the functional strategies of the company. In marketing, the product was positioned as top of the line and sold only to mountaineering and some bicycling and skiing shops. Price to the dealer was also top of the line and almost what the traffic would bear. The company provided service and repair on its equipment for a reasonable charge if the customer returned the product. The company used the best materials available and constantly searched for and tested the newest materials that were appropriate. The location allowed Jim to hire experienced workers for cutting and sewing the product. Each backpack or tent was made from start to finish by one worker, who was expected to repair any product that was returned. Rejects of finished products were very low.

Organized as a corporation, Mountain Camping had been so successful that it had been able to finance all its own working capital needs. Jim Cascade held 55 percent of the common stock, with the rest distributed among local businessmen and employees. A local bank held the 12 percent mortgage on his plant. Jim felt he had done it right this time and had everything under his control.

Mountain Camping then began to experience a slight softening in product demand. A larger firm in the industry with a wider product line had been trying to expand into the same niche. The quality of its products was good, although not as good as those sold by Mountain Camping. The larger company offered a wider line at a 15 percent lower price to the dealer. Jim always had known what was going on in his industry and particularly with his niche and customers. For the first time he could see competition ahead.

Discussion Questions

1. Under what conditions would Jim have to consider changing his strategy?

2. What changes might he have to make in his strategy? Would they require changes in his functional strategies? If so, what changes would he need to make?

3. If the changes should conflict with his personal values, which should prevail—his values or the strategies?

Chapter 6

Implementing Strategy through Organization Structure

Total grandeur of a total edifice,
Chosen by an inquisitor of structure
For himself. He stops upon this threshold
as if the design of all his works takes form
and frame from thinking and is realized.

—Wallace Stevens, "To an Old Philosopher in Rome," 1950, St. 16

Learning Objectives

- To understand the role of organization structure in implementing a firm's strategy.
- To appreciate the advantages and disadvantages of each structural choice.
- To show that the appropriate structure results from fitting the organization's structure to the firm's strategy.
- To provide a model to facilitate the appropriate fit.
- To demonstrate that an executive has several choices depending on the organization's own situation.

IN seeing that the organization's strategies are implemented and its objectives are accomplished, a major tool for executives is the organization structure and processes. For example, Kodak's recent lethargy has been partly attributed to an insular, tradition-bound management that insisted on doing everything the way Kodak's former CEO, George Eastman, did it. The company was organized along functional lines, and the manufacturing and marketing functions operated as separate fiefdoms. Decisions waited until issues percolated to the top. The new chairman, Colby H. Chandler, is trying to revitalize Kodak by reorganizing its photographic division. To help promote innovation, speed decision making, and establish clear profit goals, he broke the division into 17 SBUs such as cameras and film, photo finishing, and consumer electronics. He pushed responsibility for key decisions down from executive staff to managers of business units.

To implement the organization's strategies, an executive can choose from among several organization structures. The first section of this chapter will review the major structural patterns and their modifications. The second portion of the chapter discusses the importance of choosing the proper structure for implementing a strategy. Whether a structure will work properly in facilitating strategic accomplishment depends on its match to the strategy followed. The chapter therefore provides guidelines for achieving a good fit.

Structural Patterns

The term **structure** has been used to identify many aspects of an organization. It usually includes the overall pattern of formal work relationships and involves a relatively continuous pattern of interrelated parts. It is the organization's anatomy. We prefer to think of organizations as systems as well as structure and will use the following definition: **Organizational structure** is the relatively enduring allocation of work roles and administrative mechanisms that creates a pattern of interrelated work activities and allows the organization to conduct, coordinate, and control its work activities.

The way an organization groups its activities into departments provides a pattern for the organization structure. The patterns that result have been used as the basis for naming organization structures. In this section we will describe the principal overall organization patterns used, so that we can relate them to the implementation of strategies.

Functional Structure

The underlying idea of functional organizations is to group like or similar activities so that employees can specialize. An example of a company using a functional structure is Cullinet Software, which develops and markets integrated computer software. Cullinet is organized according to its four major functions: (1) finance, administration, and strategic planning; (2) product development and technical support; (3) customer support and services; and (4) marketing.

In practice, most functionally organized groups are formed around similar and related occupational skills as indicated by the organization chart in Figure 6.1. Other organizations, especially service and government organizations, may be grouped based on a special activity or purpose needed to carry out the organization's mission. A small business organization may be too small to have extensive occupational specialization and so will organize around a step in the process of bringing the product or service to the customer. Many times these methods will be combined in some fashion that reflects the organization's size and unique characteristics. In general, as the organization grows, one pattern will tend to dominate at the top management level, and the other will be employed at lower levels as needed. The organization may also employ other bases for grouping jobs into departments such as product, customer, and location within the functional departments, but these are usually subordinate to the primary functional groupings that report to the chief operating officer and are

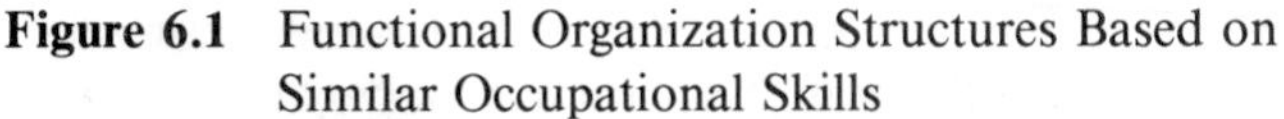

Figure 6.1 Functional Organization Structures Based on Similar Occupational Skills

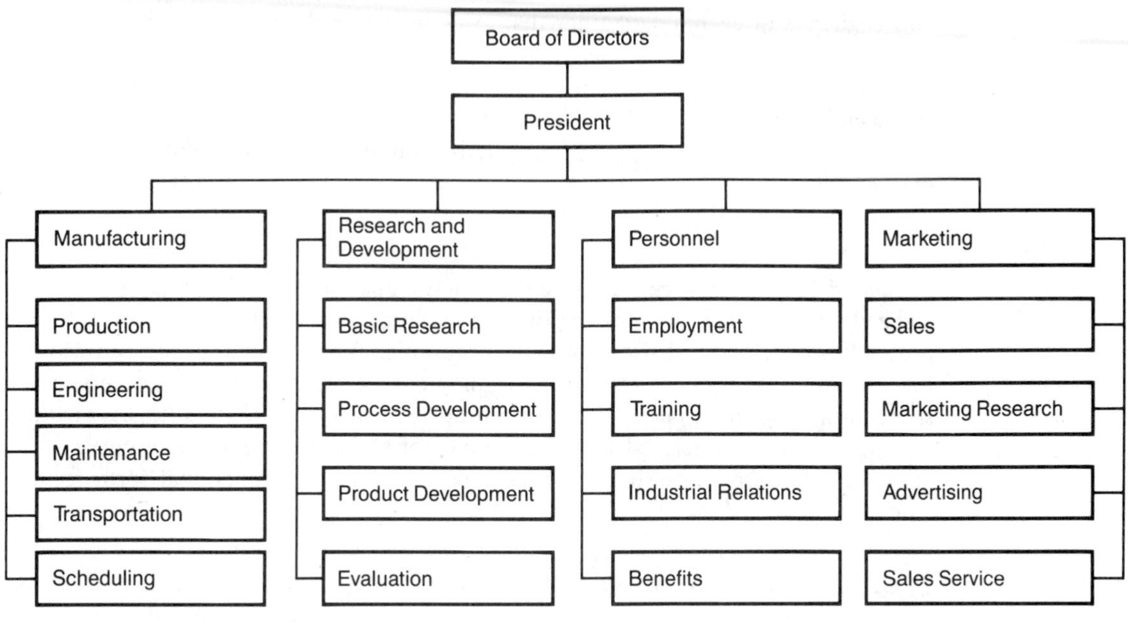

responsible for the primary activities relating to the organization's goals. Because the functional form that is built around occupational specialties is the form most often employed, we will base the remainder of our discussion on it.

In its pure form, the functional structure brings together under one executive all the related occupational activities for that function. The manufacturing vice president would be responsible and accountable for planning, organization, control, and leadership of all personnel and activity relating to manufacturing. The other areas such as marketing and finance would be similarly organized. This allows all similar work to be coordinated under one chain of command. As long as the firm remains in a single business or relatively few highly related businesses, members can concentrate on bringing their specialized knowledge to bear on the product-market.

Advantages The functional structure has certain characteristic advantages compared to other forms of structure. It does a better job of promoting specialization, achieving coordination and control within the function, and efficiently using the organization's resources. Whether these advantages are realized depends on the firm's situation and management's ability to exploit them.

Specialization The functional organization promotes specialization. Grouping all related work together allows the firm to employ professional specialists in specific areas.

It can obtain greater depth and variety of specialists because it avoids duplication and concentrates the specialists in one function. If a firm can employ only four engineers but needs the skills of both mechanical and electrical engineering, it can employ two engineers in each area (rather than, say, asking each engineer to handle all engineering tasks related to a specific product). Furthermore, Hitt, Ireland, and Palia have demonstrated that the importance of a particular function varies according to the overall strategy of the firm.[1] The functional structure allows the firm to strengthen the function critical to its strategy. Specialization also promotes the development of expertise within the function. A specialist has a clear career path in the firm and can work with and for other specialists.

Economic Use of Resources Because the functional structure provides one set of specialized staff and facilities to support production and sale of all the organization's products and services, it uses resources economically. The organization can acquire the minimum amount of resources, be they engineers, information systems, office space, or management talent. The concentration of specialists allows the organization to reap the benefits derived from economies of scale and the learning curve when efforts are focused on a single product-market. Thus, the functional form is very efficient.

Coordination and Control within Functions Because all of the activities associated with each category of work are the responsibility of a single executive, there is a clear chain of command and communication for the function's work. The vice president of marketing, for example, is in charge of all marketing personnel and activity. This function therefore has a common point of decision making, facilitating coordination of all marketing decisions and the uniform application of marketing policies throughout the company. Also, if the nature of a firm's strategy or the nature of the industry requires a distinctive competence in one function, say marketing, this is more easily promoted.

Functional vice presidents are usually a part of the top management team and participate in strategic planning. Because a company with this structure is usually in a single product-market business, corporate and business-level planning involve the same persons or an overlap of persons that can link the two. Strategic, tactical, and operating planning can be parts of the same process.

Disadvantages Most companies can use the functional structure quite successfully. In fact, until the early 1950s, it was the primary structure employed even by the Fortune 500 firms. However, small firms, many firms in processing industries, and single product-market firms are the organizations most likely to find it a good match for their needs. With increasing size, product-market diversity, and geographic dispersion, the firm using a functional structure will encounter difficulties in dealing with diversification, assigning responsibility for total performance, and achieving control and coordination between the functions. Nevertheless, many divisions of large multidivision companies use the functional structure as the primary structure *within a division.*

Diversification The primary disadvantage of the functional structure is inability to handle increasing diversification. The functional organization begins to lose its advantages as it becomes more diversified in terms of products and markets served. Different products require knowledge of additional technologies and bring the firm into contact with different environments. Specialists and managers can no longer focus on a single product and market. Because they must spread their efforts over several products, they can no longer specialize as much. Because the functional structure is focused on the kind of work rather than the product or service, coordination of the different specialists becomes more critical and requires additional techniques. The greater the diversification in terms of products and markets, the more difficult it is for the structure to adjust.

Performance Responsibility No single functional department is totally responsible for the organization's product or service. Only at the top, where the functional departments have a common reporting relationship, is there an executive responsible for all the activities related to the product's performance.

This is not a major problem or at least not a unique problem until the firm begins to diversify or grows large; there are techniques to solve many of the problems. Large divisions can have the same problem, so there is no comparative disadvantage as long as each serves a single product-market.

But when a firm starts selling different products in different markets, the responsibility for the development, manufacturing, and marketing of each product becomes more difficult to establish. Each department focuses on its functional contribution to the product but not on the product; the product has no champions.

Coordination and Control between Functions The coordination of product efforts can suffer when there are many products. While coordination and control within the function may be promoted, coordination and control between functions is not so easily facilitated. Functional specialists have different goal, time, structural, and interpersonal orientations, which can lead to difficulties in coordination and possible conflict.[2]

Responsibility for the total picture, resolution of conflict, and decisions that require coordination between the functions tend to be forced upward in the hierarchy. As the organization grows, the vertical distance that problems must travel gets longer, delaying decision making. When a company introduces more product lines and enters more markets, it increases product-market diversity and encounters more uncertainty from the environment. These changes increase the volume of coordinating decisions to be made, and executives get overloaded. At IBM no one function is responsible for corporate citizenship programs. They employ corporate staff units to coordinate the programs described in the Strategic Application "IBM Committed to Corporate Citizenship."

Divisional Structure

A structure that better equips the organization to handle diversity of markets and products is the divisional structure. Perhaps the best way to initially picture the

STRATEGIC APPLICATIONS: SOCIAL RESPONSIBILITY

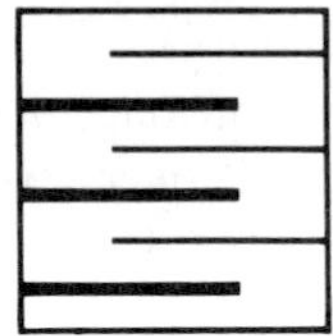

IBM Committed to Corporate Citizenship

At IBM certain programs are coordinated across division and functional departments by units at corporate headquarters. One such program is what IBM calls corporate citizenship. IBM strives to be a positive influence on the communities in which it operates, and the company is committed to affirmative action.

In 1987 the company hired nearly 8,000 employees, of which about 21 percent were minorities and 40 percent were women. Women hold more than 18 percent of the company's management positions, and minorities hold approximately 12 percent. IBM also has a minority purchasing program at multiple locations throughout the country. Each location has an annual dollar goal in purchases from minority-owned and woman-owned companies. Each location is free to choose its own suppliers to fill its quota but must report on its progress twice a year.

IBM supports and sponsors programs designed to help the disadvantaged develop marketable skills. The company currently sponsors 137 job-training centers in the United States. These centers teach basic data- and word-processing skills. In the summer of 1987, IBM headed a program in New York City aimed at youth unemployment. "Summer Jobs '87" put more than 41,300 low-income youths to work.

IBM has also shown concern for the physically disabled. The company established a National Support Center for Persons with Disabilities in Atlanta, Georgia. This center provides individuals, professionals, and community agencies with information about computers and computer-related devices that can assist disabled people.

IBM sponsors programs to encourage and support employees in their efforts to benefit their communities and society as a whole. The IBM Fund for Community Service provides supplemental funding and equipment for special projects of organizations in which IBM employees or their spouses are involved.

Source: M. R. Moskowitz, "Company Performance Roundup," *Business and Society Review* (Fall 1985): 65.

divisionalized company is to visualize several functional organizations reporting to a common executive. Each division is a self-contained functional organization; it has its own functional departments and resources so that it can operate independently in its own separate product-market. The executive in charge is responsible for the company's investment in facilities, equipment, and people and is expected to yield an acceptable return on investment. The division can be operated as a profit center or as an investment center. In other words, a number of separate companies are pulled together under the umbrella of a corporate headquarters as shown in Figure 6.2.

This picture helps describe the structural arrangement, but it is not completely accurate. The divisions are somewhat linked to the corporation. Each division is accountable to corporate headquarters, but how autonomous it is varies from company to company. In some companies the corporate headquarters may concentrate on corporate planning and leave the business-level planning to the division. In other cases all business-level plans may have to be approved by headquarters.

Organizations also have corporate-level offices to perform various functions. Functions that are not vital to the division but that are important to the total corporation may be centralized at headquarters. Examples might be accounting or public

Figure 6.2 Boise Cascade Corporation Organizational Chart

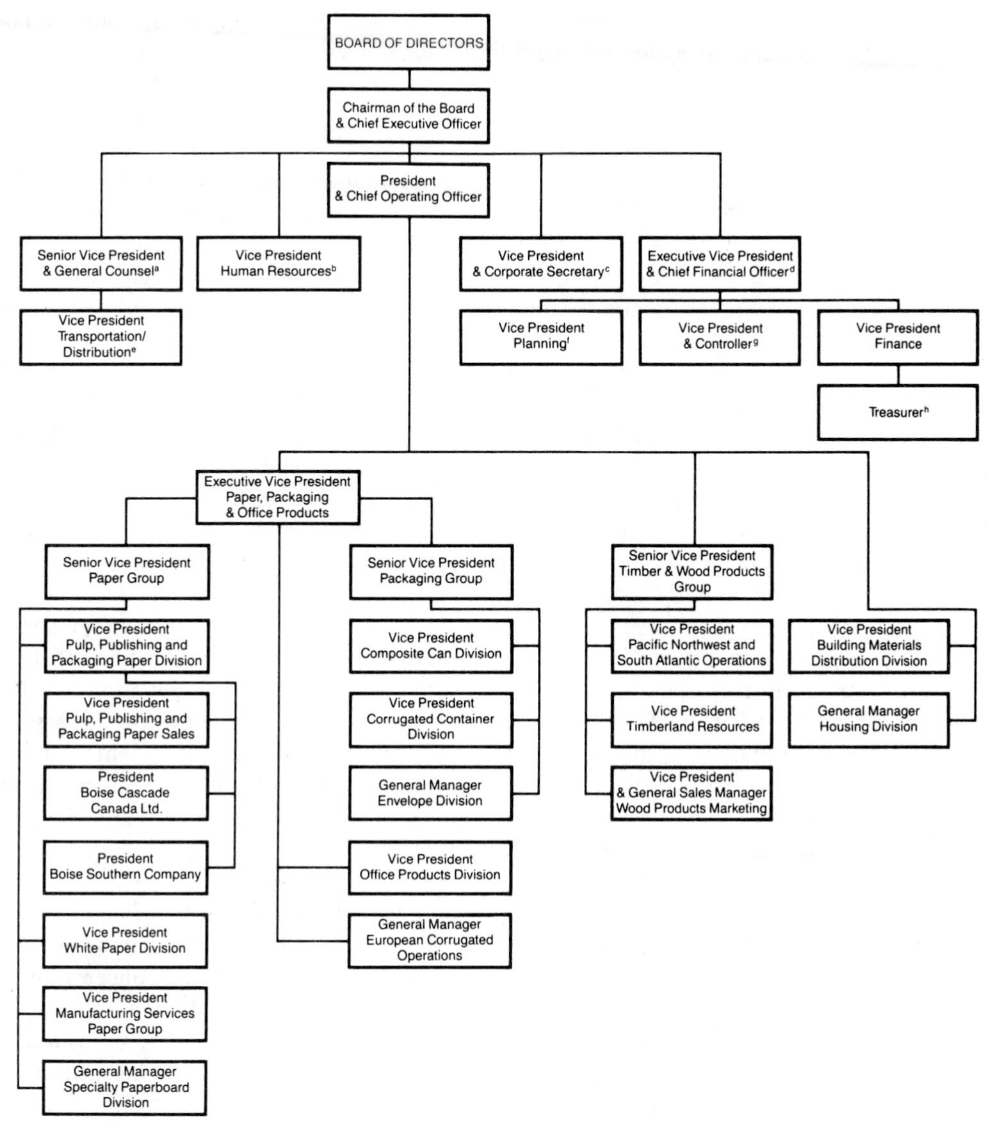

Source: 1980 Statistical Information, Boise Cascade Corporation.

[a]Governmental Affairs, Legal, Records Management

[b]Compensation and Benefits, Employment Services, Equal Employment Opportunity, HR Strategic Planning, Labor Relations, Medical Services, Personnel Administration, Personnel Development, Safety

[c]Board Liaison, Contributions, Corporate Communications, Investor Relations, Shareholder Services

[d]Industrial Security, Internal Audit, Retirement Funds, Risk Management, Tax

[e]Energy Services, Procurement Management, Transportation/Aviation

[f]Corporate Development, Economic Forecasting, Information Services, Planning

[g]Accounting/Control, Budgeting, Financial Reporting

[h]Corporate Credit, Real Estate, Treasury

relations. Other functional units assist the divisions as well as the central executives. A corporate planning staff may help top management in corporate-level planning but also provide planning information and assumptions to the division managers.

Although the typical pattern is for each division to be structured around occupational specialties, this need not be the arrangement. Some companies, such as Safeway and AT&T before it divested its operating companies, have used geographical areas as the basis for their division. Such companies often have single product lines and find that because of geographic dispersion of their operations or the need to adjust to different customer demands, they must focus on geographic region rather than or as well as on the product. The geographic form in divisionalized companies has advantages and disadvantages similar to the product form except that it accommodates numerous locations and markets, while the product form focuses on the products.

Divisionalized companies appeared very early in this century, with AT&T employing a geographic structure. Later in the 1920s, Du Pont used a product division form as it became increasingly diversified. After World War II and especially in the 1950s, more and more of the largest firms began to adopt the structure as they saw its viability in managing their diversified operations. A strong majority of the largest firms use the product division form for their primary structure, so we will primarily focus on the product division form.

Advantages The functional structure encounters problems when the organization diversifies into different markets or begins marketing different products. The divisional structure has been the principal way to respond. It allows the firm many of the advantages of the functional form but also permits concentration on a particular product-market. A divisional structure facilitates diversification, control and evaluation, and motivation. Depending on the scale of operations necessary to achieve appropriate specialization and economies of scale, it may even retain the most important advantages of the functional structure.

Diversification The divisional structure allows each division to concentrate on a relatively narrow product or market. Everyone's work is focused on making that product-market succeed. There is a clarity of purpose, and employees can concentrate on what they do well.

From the corporation standpoint, it is easier to acquire firms. A corporation can buy another business and operate it as a separate division. While integration into the company's way of doing business is not assured, it is facilitated. In some conglomerates, a newly acquired business can operate as a division of its new parent company with very little change in its operations. Similarly, at least organizationally, the company can divest itself of businesses without having to disturb the other divisions.

At the corporate level, management can concentrate on managing a portfolio of products and allow division management to concentrate on strategy at the business level. Of course, this is not always as easy as it sounds, because the company may choose not to operate its divisions as completely autonomous units. For example, research and development, treasury, finance, public relations, and long-range planning may have been centralized so that such functional work for a unit would need to be integrated into or divested from these corporate departments.

Control and Evaluation The divisional structure helps top management identify the results of each division's actions. Generally, each division has considerable autonomy and the means to compete in its business area. The firm can evaluate how well the division is performing in comparison with other companies and with other divisions of the company. Because division managers have complete responsibility for bottom-line results in their division, the company can tell whether they are performing up to par. The corporation can use such indicators as return on investment or assets to measure how well the division is performing. In addition, knowing how well the company is competing in a particular business provides better information for strategic planning.

Improved Motivation Motivation of managers, at least at the top of the division, is facilitated because the company can identify their performance in unambiguous terms, the managers have a clear focus for their work, and the managers have greater and more complete responsibility for the result. Performance in the marketplace is up to the division executive. If the division does well or poorly, the executive and everyone else will know. Such a structure thus provides a fertile training ground for future top management.

Disadvantages No organization is perfect for every situation, and the divisional form is no exception. Because it uses the functional form as its building blocks, it is subject to the same disadvantages, but its ability to create new divisions allows it to accommodate new products and markets. The divisional structure also has several potential problems of its own, such as the loss of economies of scale and coordination between divisions.

Economies of Scale Perhaps the major problem that a divisional form can encounter is the inability to achieve all the economies of scale. Each division must have certain capabilities and resources if it is to function as a competing organization. This can result in a need for more resources than would be required in the functional structure because resources are duplicated. Each division may need its own sales service department, for example, instead of a single one in a functional organization. With the specialists and resources spread over several divisions, no division may be able to achieve the economies of scale to be truly competitive.

The level at which economies of scale are achieved may vary with each resource, so the level of operations required to achieve acceptable economies may differ for division, manufacturing process, or functional department. If a division can achieve a large enough scale of operations, then these limitations are no longer important. It is also possible for the headquarters to centralize certain operations that require large size for economies. But the more unrelated the products and markets, the less likely this is to occur. Such centralization would also lessen the division manager's ability to be truly accountable for division performance.

Coordination Coordination of activities around a specific product is facilitated, but coordination across divisions is not. In designing the organization structure, the divisions should be formed so that they are independent of other divisions. Enhancing the divisions' independence lessens the need to coordinate their activities.[3] Placing the activities that need close coordination together within the division facilitates coordination.

Coordination among the divisions is seldom a major need, but in some cases, interdependence is unavoidable. For example, the product of one division may be a required part for another. This is the usual case in a vertically integrated company. In an integrated steel company, the steel division depends on the coal, limestone, and iron ore divisions for raw materials. The buildings and drainage products divisions depend on the steel division for their major materials. The divisions have little incentive to cooperate with one another unless doing so will improve their own performance. Furthermore, a manager who is being held accountable for division performance is likely to resent interference from corporate staff who are seeking conformity to their policies.

Even when the divisions are independent in accomplishing their own tasks, the corporation may need to coordinate their behavior. What is good for the division is not always good for the company, and vice versa. If one of the divisions is dumping pollution into groundwater, the whole company gets sued and receives the negative publicity. If one division sues another division's customer, the latter division can lose the customer's business. Transfer pricing can also be a problem when one division is more powerful than another. Where the divisions must cooperate, special attention is required.

The comparative advantages and disadvantages of the functional and product divisional forms of organization are summarized in Table 6.1. The differences are

Table 6.1 Advantages and Disadvantages of Major Organizational Structures

	Structure	
Characteristic	**Functional**	**Divisional**
Specialization	+	−
Efficient use of resources	+	−
Economies of scale	+	−
Coordination within function	+	−
Control of function	+	−
Diversification	−	+
Responsibility for total performance	−	+
Control of product	−	+
Coordination of product	−	+
Decentralization	−	+

\+ = relative advantage.
− = relative disadvantage.
Note: This comparison assumes that companies are the same size and that the functionally organized firm has a narrow product line whereas the divisionally organized firm has multiple product lines.

not absolute but allow some comparison of advantages and disadvantages when a company faces a choice. In practice, most organizations are a hybrid of these two forms or have modified them to fit their particular situation. The Strategic Application "Volvo Modifies Its Organization" is an example of how Volvo modified its structure.

Modifications of the Basic Structures

If a division or a firm using the functional structure diversifies to the extent that it loses its ability to respond competitively, good opportunities can be ignored or missed. A division or functional organization can attempt to solve this problem by forming project groups to guide the early development of the product and the processes to produce it. It could also appoint a product manager or "champion" to coordinate and guide the product until it is successful or to manage its marketing. This would improve the attention the product-market receives, but the product would still need to be produced and sold by functional specialists. This approach may be unsatisfactory if unrelated diversification is extensive. Therefore, several modifications to the basic organization structures have evolved to address such problems until diversification becomes extensive enough to necessitate the creation of new divisions.

Project Teams

One modification is the use of project teams. A project team consists of several specialists. The team members are brought together to accomplish a one-time task with a specific purpose. The task is usually one that requires special emphasis or is

STRATEGIC APPLICATIONS: INTERNATIONAL

Volvo Modifies Its Organization

Pehr Gyllenhammar, CEO of Volvo, directed the company through a period of steady growth. At the same time, he took it into such unrelated markets as groceries, biotechnology industries, and chemicals. Although the automobile business contributes 90 percent of Volvo's profit, he thinks this industry has reached its peak and the real profits will come from his diversification efforts. Gyllenhammar's experiments with automobile assembly lines have become famous and resulted in a flattening of the organization's structure and increased decision making at lower levels. In its automotive business, Volvo has given its product divisions primary profit responsibility, but its production and marketing are separate units reporting to central headquarters. Volvo has modified the product division structure by retaining centralized control over the production and marketing functions. Throughout Europe, these two functions are set up on a geographic basis.

Source: E. F. Jackofsky, J. W. Slocum, Jr., and S. J. McQuaid, "Cultural Values and the CEO: Alluring Companions?" *Academy of Management Executive* 2 (February 1988): 39–49.

new and unfamiliar. Often the work of numerous specialists is required, and their work must be closely coordinated because the tasks are highly interdependent.

A typical task for a project team would be construction of a new plant to produce a new product. Although the firm will hire a contractor to construct the plant, members of the firm will also need to be involved. Some will need to communicate with the contractor, and others will need to oversee the operation and coordinate its progress with company personnel. The company's process engineers will need to be involved, and manufacturing, purchasing, and marketing people will need to be preparing for operations when the plant is ready. The normal structure of a firm is unprepared to carry out such a task, and the task would likely distract from employees' regular duties. The best solution is to form a temporary project team. Some members may work full time at it, and others may be brought in only as needed: when the task is finished, members can return to regular assignments.

In some industries, such as construction and government contracting, the project team structure is similar to the product divisionalized company, with the project taking the role of the product. The members of the team come together temporarily, although perhaps for several years, and move to other projects or back to their functional units when the project no longer needs them.

A project team can also be used to oversee the development of a new product or process. The talent and skills needed to develop the innovation can be pulled from research, manufacturing, marketing, and other functions to form a team to develop the product. Once the product and the manufacturing and marketing plans have been developed, the product can be turned over to the regular functional departments. A company with a divisional structure might form a new division or product group to assume responsibility for the product.

The project team benefits the organization by emphasizing a project for a limited time, pulling together the resources for a specific task, and bypassing the regular operating structure. However, if a firm frequently needs such groups to conduct its business, this need is probably a signal to reevaluate the firm's basic structure.

Product Teams

Like project teams, product teams are a means to tightly coordinate and concentrate attention on a particular task, but they differ in that they are more permanent and primarily emphasize product coordination and management. Organizations use product teams to guide a product from its early inception through product development and eventually to market introduction. These teams see that the product receives the attention it requires to become and remain successful.

For example, Xerox once felt it had lost some of its entrepreneurial vigor. Wayland Hicks, head of the company's business systems group, commented, "Nobody said, 'My job is to get a product into the market that will sell and make a profit for us.' No one really had that degree of accountability, and if he did, he didn't have the control of the resources or the authority to make it happen."[4] One of the places Xerox wanted to improve was in its development and delivery of new products. The company created small product-delivery teams and cut the delivery time of a new machine by 30 percent and labor costs by 40 percent. This action better coordinated efforts and sharpened the focus on the product.

The use of product teams varies a great deal. In a few cases, a product team is put together to develop a product. Once the product is developed, the functional departments assume responsibility for it, and the team members return to their regular assignments. The product team manager functions as a coordinator of the team members and "champion" of the product. In most cases, the team stays together as a small-business team to manage a product throughout its life cycle. The team operates very much as a product division except without separate manufacturing and marketing resources. The team must negotiate for resources and attention from the company and functional departments.

An example of an organization structure using product teams is the abbreviated organization chart in Figure 6.3. The product teams—called small-business teams—are each made up of a scientist from the research center and a representative from each of marketing, manufacturing, and the product development center. The company has a small-business team for each of its product lines (approximately 16). This chemical company is a subsidiary of a larger company, which has one research center for the whole firm. The chemical company subsidiary is run like a division and essentially uses the functional structure within itself, but these small-business product teams guide and coordinate products from development to mature business. The small-business teams must propose budgets and are overseen by several committees within the division.

This arrangement may be varied to suit the company's strategy. In firms like Procter & Gamble, the team is marketing oriented with concern for market planning and research, sales, pricing, packaging, and so on. Another variation is to allow the scientist who develops the product idea to become an entrepreneur. The scientist champions the product, puts together a team, and may even carry the product through to head the division formed around it.

Functional and divisional companies can both use this modification to improve their competitiveness and stay close to the product and market. However, the more unrelated the markets served and the technology for producing the product, the more strain that will develop in the marketing and manufacturing departments. Once the products become significant portions of the company's product mix and marketing and manufacturing departments can no longer handle the diversity, the company will feel pressure to form a separate division.

Product Groups and SBUs

Companies like General Electric, Texas Instruments, and Westinghouse operate in many areas of business and can have dozens of different products and markets. The sheer diversity and number of divisions can cause the top manager problems in strategic planning and control as well as overseeing operations. The span of control becomes too large. The solution for some multidivision companies is to combine

Figure 6.3 Product Teams for Product Coordination

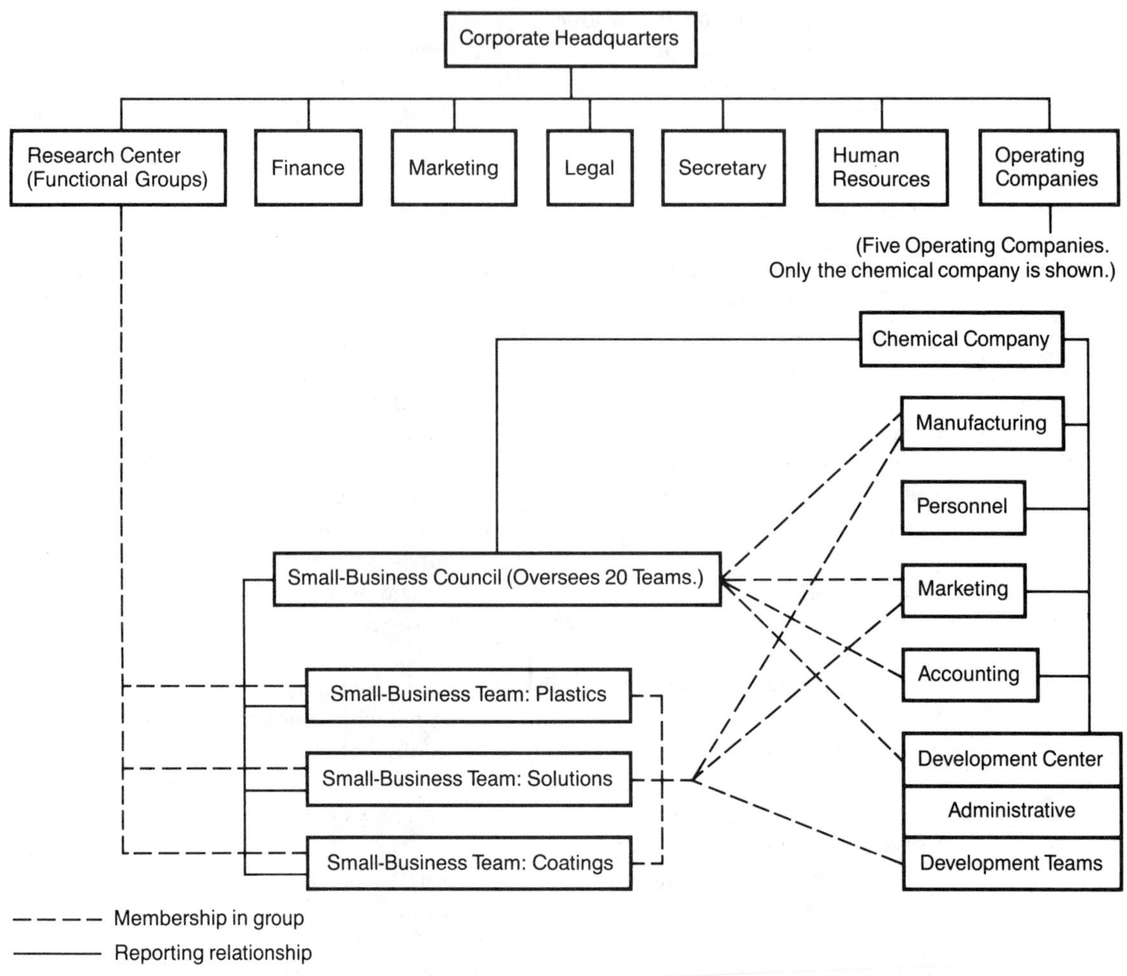

several divisions into product groups or SBUs, each under one executive. When this additional layer of management is added, the CEO can manage the divisions through the group vice president. This is what Westinghouse did in the 1950s as shown in Figure 6.4. This company grouped 67 divisions into five product groups. General Electric, Union Carbide, General Foods, and Texas Instruments have adopted similar structures, although with varying details in how they operate.

The groupings are usually based on some strategic element common to the divisions. Westinghouse seems to have used customer/market and product relatedness. Other common criteria are technology, strategic mission, and global orientation.

Figure 6.4 A Product Divisionalized Company Using Product Groups

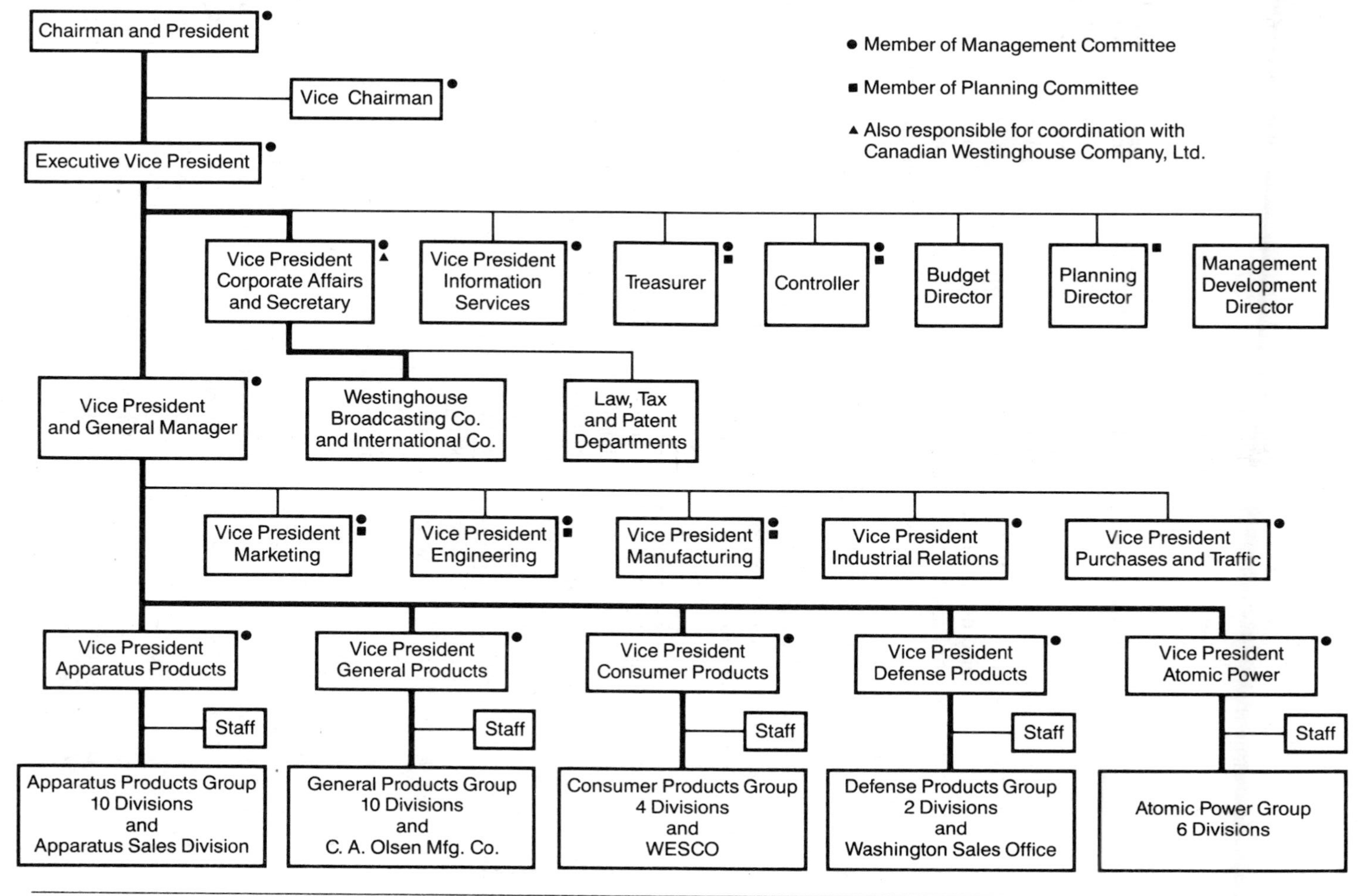

Creating product groups benefits the company by balancing the strengths of independent operations for products and markets with the efficiency of shared resources in such areas as advertising, manufacturing, warehousing, or sales. This is particularly true if several divisions share key customers or operate in the same business sector (such as consumer food products). Putting divisions into groups also helps the company achieve coordination.

Group executives can spot the areas where efficiency can be obtained and see that the divisions cooperate. Through planning and coordination, they can ensure that resources are shared and facilities are fully utilized. When the units are interdependent, group executives can help resolve conflicts between the units. They can consolidate advertising and sales-promotion efforts where appropriate to gain leverage with agencies and media. When the divisions operate in a common business sector, they can also do much of the work required for strategic planning, such as environmental monitoring and forecasting. The group executive's role in the organization can range from simply limiting the span of control to carrying full strategic and profit responsibility.

Often the creation of product groups is based a great deal on strategic planning considerations. Companies identify business sectors or areas that are common to several of their product-markets. Union Carbide, for example, identified 150 strategic planning units among its 15 groups of divisions. The planning units were then recombined into nine new aggregate planning units. General Electric and General Foods are other examples of companies that used a similar process.

When product groups are linked to strategic planning, the groups are called strategic business units, or SBUs. Often each strategic planning unit is a separate division, and the divisions composing the SBU serve a common market segment with their separate products. Much of the strategic planning process can be undertaken at the SBU level. When the SBU is used in this fashion, it frees the division managers to concentrate on carrying out the programs and reaching the profit objectives.

Sometimes the organization structure does not coincide with the planning structure. In General Electric, for example, an SBU can be either a group, a division, or a department.[5] A case prepared by R. F. Vancil on Texas Instruments provides an excellent example of how the planning structure and the organization can diverge but still work effectively.[6] TI has four groups: components, equipment, materials, and services. Each of the groups comprises several divisions. Below the division level, there are 77 product customer centers (PCCs). The PCCs are operated like a small business with short-term profit responsibilities. The strategic planning system cuts across the operating organization structure. Managers at TI act as both strategic and operating managers. A strategy manager is expected to identify and pull together the actions, methods, and arrangements needed for a strategic plan from across several groups, divisions, and PCCs. A strategy manager can be a PCC-level manager or a division manager. A division manager can have responsibility for managing an objective or a strategy. Along with the dual planning system (strategic and operating) is a dual budgeting and control system for the two sets of plans.

Matrix Organizations

A firm may need the economies of scale and specialization possible in a functional organization. This is especially true for firms operating in competitive, highly technical fields. A firm may also need the project/product coordination that can be obtained from product emphasis. If the scale of the operation were large enough and the life cycle long enough, the firm could obtain the benefits of both through product divisions. But when this is not the case, a matrix organization may be the answer.

The matrix organization is a structure and management system that equally and simultaneously emphasizes two or more of the basic structural patterns within the same organization. Typically this has meant both functional and project or product structures, but in recent years, managers have shown an interest in using a geographical dimension to accommodate global marketing. In any case, a matrix organization allows for scale of operation and retention of expertise without duplication while facilitating project/product coordination and control.

An example of a matrix organization structure appears in Figure 6.5. In this organization, a functional manager heads a department of specialists, including electrical engineering, systems analysis, and marketing. The members of these groups will perform work for several of the projects and subprojects such as laboratory testing. Other members are assigned to projects headed by a project manager. The functional manager and the project manager both report to a common general manager—in this case, the division general manager. The members of the functional departments assigned to projects report to the functional manager *and* to the project manager.

Unlike the structures previously discussed, a matrix organization may give many members dual assignments and bosses. The electrical engineer may have a home base in the electrical engineering department but work full time on a project, may be assigned later to another project, or may even return to the electrical engineering department.

The project manager is responsible for the progress of the project and for achieving project objectives. The project manager has to seek the cooperation of other units and decide on priorities and trade-offs. The functional manager provides technical service and expertise and performs some of the project's work.

In practice, organizations vary as to how much they emphasize either the project or the functional side of the organization. At one end of the continuum, the functional managers have the most power and control, and the project manager monitors progress and relies on persuasion. At the other end of the continuum, the functional manager maintains a pool of personnel to supply project managers, who control project progress. The most obvious reason for this variance in emphasis is that the nature of the business and industry in which the firm competes requires a stronger emphasis on one than another. For example, a firm that is in a high-technology field with a strong need for technical specialists but that lacks product diversity and competitive pressure to bring the products/projects quickly to market may tend toward a functional emphasis. In contrast, a firm that is performing contracts for the Defense Department and experiences pressure to meet deadlines and control costs may need to emphasize

Figure 6.5 A Matrix Organization Structure

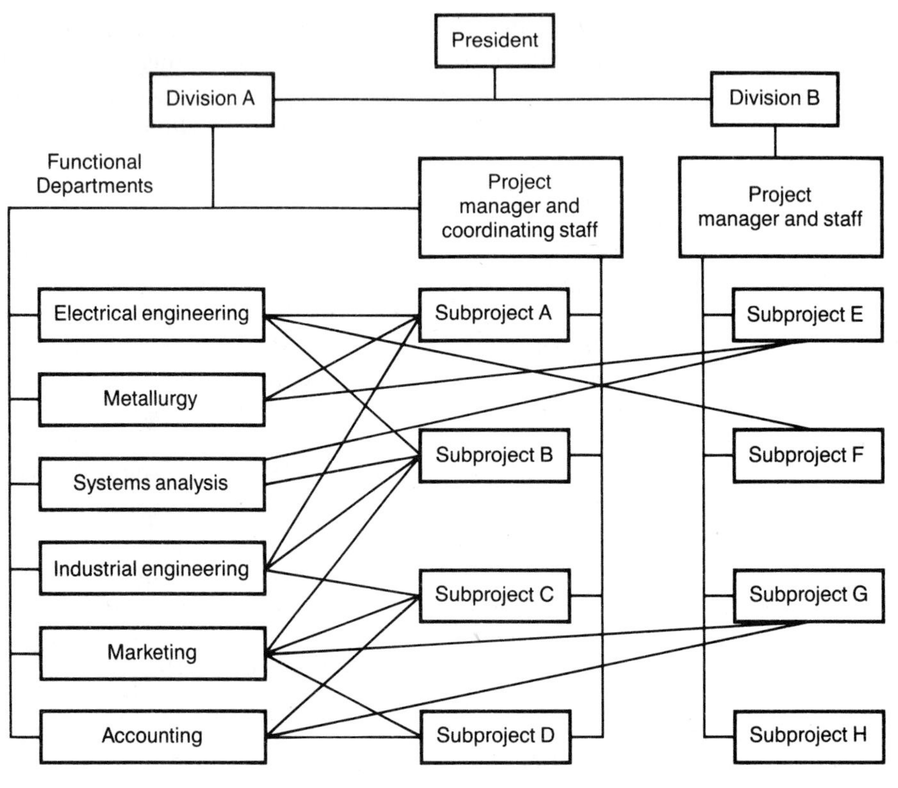

the project side. The balance of pressures experienced by a firm can shift over time. For example, the U.S. government has changed demands on defense contractors from technical performance to reduction of costs and finally to reduction in demand for the project/product.[7] The Strategic Application "Organizing Multinational Corporations" describes how the changing environment of multinational corporations may lead to a type of matrix structure.

The matrix organization is more than another structural variation. It requires different management systems.[8] Strong conflict may arise among members of this dual management system, and they must learn new interpersonal skills. The presence of two emphases can require dual career ladders, dual budgets and information systems, dual reward criteria, and dual planning systems.

Although the matrix almost always grows from one of the other structural patterns, the requirements for properly implementing and operating it can stifle its effectiveness. Several companies have tried it and then abandoned it.[9] Sometimes the structure did not fit the business, but even when it did, some firms have abandoned it. Galbraith and Kazanjian have cited two major reasons for these failures. First, the structure

STRATEGIC APPLICATIONS: INTERNATIONAL

Organizing Multinational Corporations

The business of multinational corporations adds to the complexity of designing an organization structure. Their strategy has led them to seek growth in foreign countries, and now they must deal with new governments, cultures, and often remote locations. How can such an organization differentiate its structure to adapt to this new diversity and ensure that foreign businesses can be integrated with the rest of the company?

Source: Stanley M. Davis, "Trends in the Organization of Multinational Corporations," in *Managing and Organizing Multinational Corporations*, ed. Stanley M. Davis (New York: Pergamon Press, 1979), 231–248.

According to Stanley Davis, the basic pattern of organization is clear. When the focus of a company is primarily on its domestic business but it has some foreign operations, the company will group these foreign activities into an international division. When the foreign business becomes substantial so that the company begins to see itself as a global business, the company will adopt either a worldwide product or geographic structure (divisions), depending on which of these features is most salient for its business. The functional form is seldom used.

Once the company significantly diversifies in both products and markets, the structure becomes inadequate, and another change is needed. The structure that allows simultaneous emphasis on markets and products is the global matrix organization. Its features are similar to the matrix organization described in this section, but projects and functions are displaced by markets and products.

was not implemented properly. The matrix structure requires collaborative and participative processes to work, but some of the firms did not use these processes in implementing it. Other companies did not let their structure evolve to a matrix, but imposed it before the company had the management systems to support it. The second reason for failure is that the business conditions faced by the firm changed so that the matrix structure was no longer the most appropriate organization structure for the conditions. In some cases, the time-to-market cycle decreased so much that the company required product divisions that were less efficient but faster responding.

The matrix organization allows a firm to use both the functional and the product/project structures, but it is not simply a combination of these forms. It has its own character and requires managers to operate differently than they would in either of the other two. Managers need a dual focus and the ability to fully utilize human talent and physical resources. Also, the scale of operation should be small enough that a product division could not achieve as effective a result.

Strategy and Organization Structure

The importance of organization to accomplishing purposes and objectives is well established, and its use can be traced to ancient times.[10] It seems only logical to believe that organization structure has played a role in the implementation of strategy. That its specific role has not been well documented until recent years is probably because writers have given little attention to strategy until recently. The geographic organization of AT&T's operating companies was important in maintaining service and a monopoly in the telephone industry. Du Pont and General Motors are cited as early users of the divisional structure in maintaining their strategies. But the greatest interest in the role of structure in implementing strategy has developed since World War II.[11] Perhaps this is because few organizations used anything but the functional structure before that time.

In the 1950s and 1960s, there was a strong trend in American industry toward diversification, both internally generated and through acquisition. There was also a strong shift among the largest firms from the use of the functional organization structure to the use of the divisional organization structure. One of the first to recognize the trend and address the implications of diversification for the organization structure was Louis A. Allen.[12] In discussing when to change from a functional to a divisional structure, Allen said:

> When the enterprise is small and operating under personal, centralized leadership, the advantages of the functional type organization heavily outweigh its disadvantages. However, as the company grows in size and diversity, the drawbacks tend to increase almost geometrically.[13]

Allen attributed the need to change from a functional to product divisional structure to growth and diversification as well as the engineering, manufacturing, and marketing characteristics of the product. But it was Alfred D. Chandler's work that propelled the interest in the link between strategy and structure.[14]

Structure Follows Strategy

Chandler studied the historical development of 70 of the largest American companies, including firms such as Du Pont, General Motors, and Sears.[15] His study revealed a pattern of structural evolution as firms pursue growth. Chandler's thesis that structure follows strategy is illustrated in Figure 6.6, which shows how changes in growth strategy lead to administrative problems and a structural response to solve the problems.

In Chandler's model, companies start as a single unit with a single function in a single industry. For example, the firm might be a retail store located downtown selling hardware, or it might be a plant located in Delaware producing explosives. Its initial growth pattern is simply expansion of volume.

With success comes continued growth through extending sales to other geographic areas. Increased volume and the need to coordinate with the different sales locations causes a need for and allows the firm to begin specialization and standardization. The firm is now a functional organization, and it can grow very large while the functions are elaborated and the owner becomes a general manager over the functions. The firm is still in the same industry but has multiple functions and multiple locations.

The next growth strategy the company is likely to pursue is vertical integration. A manufacturing plant might integrate forward by establishing warehouses. A beer producer might integrate backward by growing its own hops. Or a tire manufacturer

Figure 6.6 Chandler's Model: Structure Follows Strategy

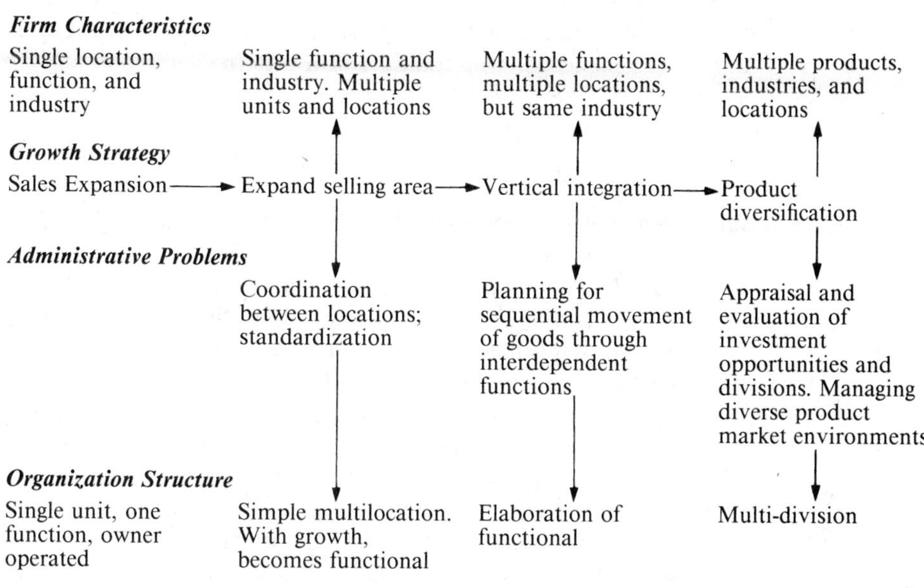

might establish its own retail stores. Through vertical integration, a firm can gain control over another step in the sequence of bringing a product to the customer and may increase the predictability and efficiency of its operations as well as capture the value added by that step in the sequence. The vertical integration observed by Chandler was in the same industry and increased the number of functions of the firm. But this move brings with it additional administrative problems, which are chiefly concerned with balancing the sequence of operations through the vertically integrated firm. Solving these problems requires specialists in forecasting demand, scheduling movement through operations, and inventory control, as well as such service functions as transportation and maintenance.

As the markets for the firm's primary products plateau or begin to decline, the firm uses a diversification strategy to seek additional growth through different products or services. The firm might try to use its resources in new industries. A meat packer might begin to produce soap, a petroleum company might move into petrochemicals, or a rubber company might use its knowledge of chemistry to develop plastics or rubber-plastic compounds. The administrative problems created by this growth strategy are how to deal with the different product-market environments and how to appraise and evaluate the different opportunities. Because the functional structure does not handle diversity well, the structural response is the multidivisional structure. With this structure, the company can separate investment opportunities. Each division can respond to a different set of product-market environments and demands, and the central office can concentrate on comparing opportunities and strategic concerns. The changes that Chandler observed from one stage to another occurred only after administrative problems led to economic inefficiencies. In addition, the change did not occur until the leader who took the firm into the corresponding growth strategy had left the firm. The Strategic Application "The Apple Computer Story" provides a current example of a similar pattern.

Chandler's work seems to have stimulated other studies on the relationship between strategy and structure. In a study by Wrigley[16], firms from the Fortune 500 followed one of four strategies: (1) remaining in a single-product business; (2)operating in a business dominated by a single product; (3)obtaining at least 30 percent of sales from related businesses; or (4) obtaining at least 30 percent of sales from businesses unrelated to the main business. Wrigley found that the more diversified the strategy, the more the multidivisional structure was used. In addition, the firms that were dominated by a single product but had other products used a functional structure for the main business and a divisional structure for other products.

In a more comprehensive and often cited study of strategy, structure, and performance, Rumelt found that firms that are in a single business or are dominated by their main business use the functional structure. Firms characterized by diversification use the multidivisional structure. Product diversification leads to or is accompanied by a change to a product divisional structure, because if a firm does not switch, it will suffer inefficiencies.[17] Other studies of companies in Europe show similar results but indicate that competitive pressures are necessary to encourage adoption of product divisions.

STRATEGIC APPLICATIONS

The Apple Computer Story

For an excellent example of the steps in Chandler's model, consider the Apple Computer story. Beginning in the late 1970s, Apple helped to create the personal computer market. The formation of Apple Computer Company took place in 1977. Just three years later, Apple was worth $2 billion. In 1980 Apple was organized into divisions.

Source: L. Butcher, *Accidental Millionaire* (New York: Paragon House, 1988), 147–165.

Continued rapid growth and inexperienced management led to problems. In 1981 IBM announced its intentions to enter the personal computer market. Apple looked upon IBM with arrogance, running an ad in *The Wall Street Journal* with the headline "Welcome IBM, Seriously." The arrogance was ill-fated. By 1982, cracks in Apple's armor had begun to show as IBM gained market share. Up to this point, Apple had been managed very loosely. It was apparent that professional management was needed.

Enter John C. Scully to take the job of president and CEO in 1983. Many changes were to come in short order, including the realignment of nine divisions into three. Only two years later, a change that shocked Silicon Valley was to come, the dismissal of one of the company's founders and its then chairman of the board, Steven Jobs.

Diversification and Structure

Of all the generic strategies, the decision to grow through diversification seems to have the greatest impact on an organization's structural pattern. This is especially true at the corporate level, but diversity has a major impact at lower levels as well—for example, the use of product management teams within a division or a predominately functional firm. Diversification has long been thought to influence the structure employed by firms. But what kind of diversity is important enough to encourage a firm to change its structure? A firm is considered diversified if it operates in several different businesses at once.[18]

Hill and Hoskinson write of three major categories of corporate diversification: vertical integration, related business diversification, and unrelated diversification.[19] Each type may use the multidivisional form, but for different economic reasons. Firms following vertical integration are seeking economies of scale, economies from tighter integration of the two companies, and control over suppliers or customers. Related diversifiers expect to gain economies through common use of such factors as resources, channels of distribution, or technological processes. Unrelated diversifiers expect to achieve economies by treating the set of businesses as an internal capital market, spreading risk, and pooling and redistributing cash to businesses that can generate the best return. Both vertical and related diversifiers require tighter coordination between the divisions to achieve the economies.

Hoskinson tested these propositions by comparing the performance of 62 firms after they adopted a divisional form with their performance before this organizational change.[20] The unrelated diversifiers improved their rate of return and lowered their risk. The vertically integrated firms lowered their risk but did not increase their return. The performance of the related diversifiers actually went down, although they outperformed the other two types. The unrelated diversified firms gained the most from their change of structure.

It is the difference in the nature of the product produced and the market served that pressures organizations into strategic modification and structural adaptation. Developing and manufacturing different products or services require different bases of technological knowledge. The chemistry of steel and paper manufacture is different, and knowledge and techniques of producing silicon wafers do not transfer to producing PVC chemicals. If these products can be sold to the same customers or to different customers using the same techniques and channels, the firm would have high product diversity but low market diversity. In contrast, if a company's products are developed from a similar technological base and produced with similar techniques but are marketed to different customers, the firm has high market diversity but low product diversity. Maximum pressure to establish separate organizational units is experienced with a combination of high product diversity and high market diversity.

The concept that seems to best capture this type of diversity is relatedness. Researchers have used this concept in their studies, and it has been used to recommend matching structure with strategy.[21]

The more related a company's products are in terms of production and marketing, the less the company will need to organize them into separate groups. Siemens, A.G., one of the world's largest electrical and electronic equipment producers, provides an interesting example of a company whose changed market focus resulted in more relatedness. Siemens is a diversified company with six relatively autonomous product groups, including computers and telecommunications. As the market for office automation developed, the technological base as well as the manufacturing and marketing techniques for computers and telecommunications equipment became closely related. Siemens decided that to compete effectively, it needed to merge its computer and telecommunications divisions.

Relatedness can exist at several organizational levels. At the corporate and SBU level, the organization must decide whether there is enough diversity to justify separate divisions, but the same issues arise at the divisional level. A division can go through the same process of growth that an independent functional business does.

Scale of Operation and Structure

Scale of operation has a powerful influence on the matching of structure with relatedness. Scale of operation influences whether a firm can efficiently employ a particular organization structure. Several studies already cited have indicated that size in combination with diversification is important to the movement from a functional structure to a divisional structure.[22] Sufficient scale of operation allows the firm to shift to a divisional structure without losing the advantages connected to specialization. Scale also minimizes the impact of duplicating resources, because costs may be spread over many units.

What is important here is not the absolute size, but rather that the scale of operation be sufficient to gain the economies required for effective and efficient competition. This consideration includes whether the organization can reach sufficient size in the future. That is, to gain coordination benefits at present with the expectation it will soon obtain sufficient size, the company may wish to switch to a divisional structure before all the economies of scale can be achieved.

An organization's structure is not quickly or easily changed, and the transformation costs can be high. Therefore, the timing and stability of the change are important. A business that lacks sufficient scale may be wise to consider postponing the change or using one of the modifications to basic structure discussed earlier.

The required scale of the unit could depend on the attractiveness of the business area. The size of market competitors, for example, affects how large the unit must be to compete effectively. Sun Microsystems wants to diversify from its scientific computer market to become a leader in the computer industry. Part of its plan is to introduce a new era of open architecture in the computer industry and offer a new user-friendly operating system based on AT&T's Unix system. This plan will bring Sun into direct competition with the giants of the computer hardware business—IBM and Apple—and the giant of the software business—Microsoft. A small operation like Sun cannot develop and market a new industry standard, so the company's solution was to try not to go it alone. Sun signed an agreement with AT&T to develop a new standard version of Unix, and AT&T bought 20 percent of Sun's stock and the rights to use Sun's unique microprocessor chip. Sharing resources with AT&T was necessary to give Sun a scale of operation it could not afford on its own.

Combining Scale and Relatedness

By considering the organization's scale and its technological and market relatedness, managers can decide which organization structure will be most effective for achieving the organization's strategy. Figure 6.7 presents a model that combines these characteristics into a three-dimensional matrix. The organization's location in the matrix determines which structure is most appropriate.

Organizations in cell 1 have technology and market relatedness, but the scale of operations is insufficient. This is the typical condition found in Chandler's study. The company markets one or a few similar products in essentially the same way. The structure of such a firm is a simple one and in the beginning is essentially undifferentiated; the firm has too little volume to allow much specialization. It may be able to gain some advantages of specialization by using sales agents or wholesalers, or it may be able to contract for services with a lawyer, bookkeeper, or CPA firm. It may also be able to gain expertise by including experts on its board of directors, employing consultants, or utilizing the Small Business Administration and banking services. A major organizational problem is to grow large enough to afford the personnel needed to handle the work load. With growth will come the need to coordinate and control activities, and elements of a bureaucracy will appear.[23] The appropriate structure is the simple structure until growth allows a simple bureaucracy. With continued development, the organization will look more and more like a functional structure.

In cell 2, there is market and technology relatedness and sufficient scale of op-

Figure 6.7 A Model for Structural Choice

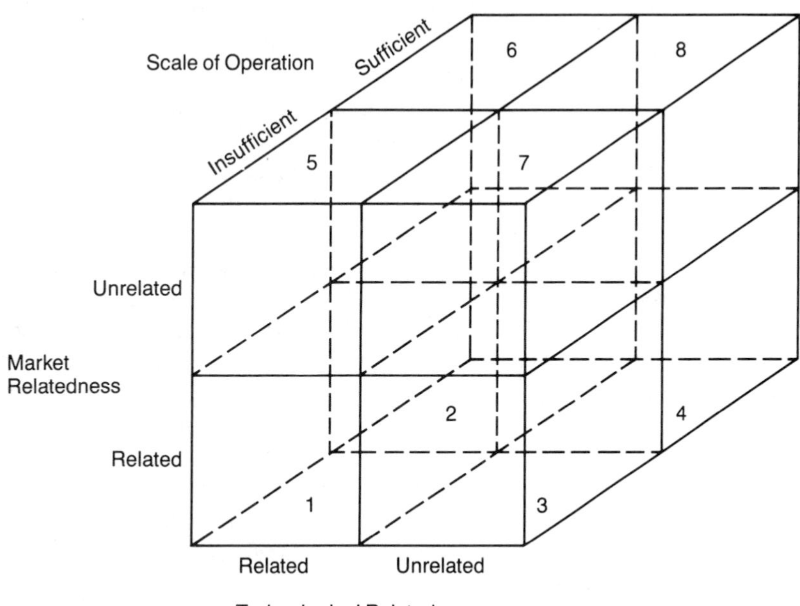

erations to support a functional organization structure. Micropolis Corporation is an example of a firm in this cell. The company is a manufacturer of high-performance Winchester disk drives for micro- and minicomputers. With similar technology and marketing largely aimed at original equipment manufacturers, this company uses a functional structure. Firms in single or very similar product-markets can grow very large with this form. They can fully use specialists, capital, and resources.

In cell 3, the marketing channel and techniques are quite similar, but the development and manufacturing characteristics are relatively unrelated. Also, the scale of operations is insufficient. The conditions in cell 4 are the same, except that the scale of operations is sufficient. An example is a firm that is in both consumer paper products such as diapers and napkins as well as detergents. It could use separate divisions that both manufacture and market the products or it could manufacture in separate facilities, but use one marketing function or division to distribute the products. The technological base of these products is different but both are being sold through the same channels to the consumer.

Under conditions of sufficient scale a product divisional form may be the right choice. This would permit competitive response and focus on the product. In cell 3 the scale is insufficient to justify a full product division structure. However, it may be that scale is sufficient to support establishing separate manufacturing divisions that transfer the goods to the marketing division to market all the products. This would allow attention where diversity exists, but minimize the costs connected with marketing.

Another possibility when scale does not justify separate divisions is to use product development groups to manage the product. A firm in cell 3 or 4 must manage the technological diversity. The range of choice is from full divisional to separate development and manufacturing units to using product teams. The choice depends on the scale of operation the firm can generate. Perhaps the volume for one of the products is enough to establish a separate division for it.

In cells 5 and 6, the technology is related, but the marketing of the product is unrelated. Scale of operation is insufficient in cell 5 and sufficient in cell 6. Again, the scale of operations required can greatly affect the choice of structure. Capital-intensive industries may have so much invested in the manufacturing process that there is no question of having separate facilities. An automobile manufacturer does not need to have a separate division to sell to government. If the marketing of the products is different enough and the scale of operations is large enough, a divisional structure may be appropriate. When scale is insufficient, there are other possibilities. An appropriate choice might be a functional structure that organizes its sales and marketing by customer and centralizes its research and development and manufacturing. Or the company might use sales agents to reach some classes of customers.

Another, and perhaps special, case of unrelatedness in market factors is when the lack of relatedness stems from geographical differences. The differences may be in customer preference, in which case the product will require some alteration. If the scale of operation required is not large and transportation costs are significant, the company can locate plants regionally if the alterations cannot be made in the central plant. Sales and manufacturing could be organized into geographic divisions. When the differences derive from dealing with global markets, the scale of operation will again modify a firm's choices as described in the international chapter.

In cells 7 and 8, technological and marketing characteristics are both unrelated. The conglomerate company is the classical case. When the scale of operations is sufficient to support it (cell 8), the obvious choice is the multidivision structure. Another choice for such firms is what has been called the holding company structure.

The holding company is similar to the multiple-product divisional structure. The divisions operate either as separate subsidiaries or as divisions with substantial autonomy. Headquarters provides little coordination, and the businesses are managed as a portfolio. In recent years, there has been a trend in the electric utility industry to diversify out of the industry to avoid the heavy regulation of utilities. To facilitate this type of move, many utilities have chosen the holding company structure. An example is Pinnacle West Capital Corporation, which in 1987 had two major subsidiaries: Arizona Public Service Company, an electric utility, and MeraBank, a federal savings bank. In addition, Pinnacle owns three smaller subsidiaries: Suncor Development Company (land development), Malapai Resources Company (uranium), and El Dorado Investment Company (venture capital).

When the scale of operations is insufficient (cell 7), the firm that chooses to divisionalize or use a holding company structure will incur added costs of managing its diversity. If a firm has insufficient scale but needs to divisionalize to manage unrelatedness, it needs to become large enough to support an appropriate structure. Until it can gain sufficient scale of operation, it must find some way to manage its great diversity. It can incur the extra costs, but that is not a desirable alternative. One possibility is to use the small-business teams described on pages 206–207. The team serves the function of a product division, but within a functional structure.

Groups, SBUs, Scale, and Relatedness Relatedness and scale affect the grouping of divisions into groups and SBUs. But grouping is also affected by the preexistence of a multidivision structure. When a firm has diversified and grows, it may develop so many divisions that the span of management becomes large and managers have difficulty planning, coordinating, and controlling the divisions. The administrative response may be to establish another layer of management between headquarters and the divisions. The divisions grouped together are then accountable through their group executive.

To facilitate these groupings, there should be some relatedness in the products and markets of the divisions. (Because the divisions have been previously formed, the firm probably believed there was sufficient scale to support a divisional structure.) Relatedness is relative, and if the firm is grouping divisions for administrative control, the group may be loosely related—for example, consumer products. But if the firm is reorganizing for purposes of strategic planning, the marketing and/or the technological factors should be related. Because SBUs are usually formed on the basis of some strategic business factors, SBUs would be possible choices if relatedness is present on one of the dimensions. The Strategic Application "Magna International" provides an example of a company that forms SBUs for another reason.

STRATEGIC APPLICATIONS

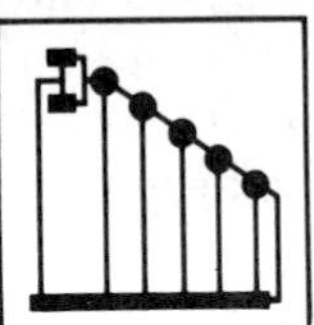

Magna International

Most Magna International plants, which make parts for new cars, employ fewer than 200 people. If a plant gets more work than it can handle, Magna starts a new facility. The number of small plants reflects not only Magna's management philosophy but also a strategy for growth. Magna has grown by creating more and more small divisions rather than bigger and bigger divisions. Magna's chairman and CEO, Frank Stronach, chose this philosophy because he believes it encourages entrepreneurship and because it is easier to hold someone accountable for any problems that arise.

The head person in each division is called a general manager and acts much like a president. Each general manager has financial, marketing, manufacturing, and shipping responsibilities, as well as many others. In many respects, the company's managers run their units like private businesses. Plants with similar product lines find themselves bidding against each other. Although the plants submit competitive bids for a job, only one bid from Magna goes out to the customer.

Source: John Case, "How to Grow without Getting Big," *Inc.*, December 1986, 108–114.

The degree of relatedness required for strategic planning may be different than the degree required for organization structure. As discussed earlier in the chapter, Texas Instruments uses such a dual structure. General Electric also has used separate structures. The planning structure and the organizational structure might not coincide when economies can be gained by shared production and product development, but the business targets are disparate, requiring separate strategic marketing plans. Like product teams and project teams, planning structure can cut across organization structure to provide the planning and coordination required to handle diversity.

Matrix Structures, Scale, and Relatedness The use of a matrix structure is also influenced by the combinations of relatedness and scale. Matrices are used when the organization needs a dual focus on the functional structure's advantages of technical expertise and efficiency and the product divisional advantages of product focus and coordination. Other considerations in the use of a matrix structure are the need to share resources because of pressure for efficiency and the need to handle large amounts of information because a task is complex and the environment uncertain. Matrices usually evolve when an organization is already using coordination devices such as product or project team management.

The matrix occupies the middle ground between the functional and divisional structures. If an organization has sufficient scale, it will use a product division. If it is too small, it will use product or project teams to gain the dual focus. If the scale does not justify a division but the diversity cannot be handled by the functional structure, the organization uses a matrix.

Vertical Integration

A firm that practices vertical integration may still be committed to its basic business, but it is entering a new business. For example, when Armco Steel acquired its coal and limestone mines, it obtained two of the three basic raw materials to produce steel. However, the extraction of raw materials has a different technological base than the manufacturing of steel. If the acquisition is operated only for the benefit of the primary business, the supplier becomes essentially another step in the production process. But if the supplier is of sufficient scale, it could be operated as a manufacturing division or profit center. If the acquired supplier is large enough to supply the primary business and still conduct business with other firms at a profit, then it will probably be operated as a separate division or as a subsidiary but with little autonomy. In other companies, such as Chevron Corporation, a giant integrated oil company, some subsidiaries service only the parent firm, and others conduct business with outside customers as well.

Firms that integrate backward usually do so because they need to control their supplier or gain economies to benefit their primary business. This means there is pressure to rationalize and integrate the new business into the primary business. Where conditions permit, the primary business will try to make the new business a part of its functional structure rather than operate it as a separate division or as an autonomous unit within a holding structure.

The greater the unrelatedness and the greater the scale of the supplier's operations, the more difficulty the primary business will have in absorbing the acquired firm and the more pressure there will be to operate it as a separate unit such as a profit center or division. Firms may integrate backward more than one stage, and the more stages they acquire, the more unrelatedness they will experience.

Firms that integrate forward may be seeking greater control over the outlets for their products or additional economies or new outlets for their products. Movements toward the consumer tend to entail a different kind of competition. Products become more differentiated, and greater variety is possible. A few of the factors that become more important are marketing skills, advertising, product innovation, and position.

A firm is likely to seek outlets that are major users of its product. When Armco established its Armco Drainage and Metal Products division, it established a big user of its product, but not the only user. The division took the firm into a different business—fabrication of products for construction and buildings. When Armco acquired National Supply, it entered into the oil-drilling supply business. In the process of integrating forward into the fabrication of steel, it acquired more unrelatedness in markets and technology, although it was hardly a conglomerate.

The reasoning applied to backward integration applies here as well. The greater the unrelatedness and the larger the scale, the more pressure to operate the business as a separate unit such as a division, profit center, or subsidiary.

Single-Business Strategy (Market Penetration or Horizontal Integration)

Another business strategy that may be employed by a division within a company as well as an independent single-business firm is to concentrate on one product or line of business. This strategy corresponds to cell 2 in the matrix described earlier. Firms like McDonald's and Holiday Inn have been able to grow in industries where the product life cycle has not reached decline. In other cases, the firm can continue to grow by taking market share away from competitors more economically than it can diversify.

Firms following this strategy generally use the functional structure. Once they are past the introduction stage of the product life cycle and the shakeout of competitors and products begins, these firms act to strengthen or increase their markets rather than change their technology. The products are becoming standardized, and the pressure on technology is to improve processes and lower costs of production. The firm may try to attract more users to its product or may promote more uses for the product. The resulting need to develop new marketing plans could lead to different channels and marketing techniques and even the need to customize the product. But for the most part, these changes can be handled by adjustments within the functional structure. For example, the marketing function may reorganize sales by customer categories or may employ brand managers to coordinate marketing activities aimed at a brand or customer. If the expansion includes new geographical territories, this simply means a new sales territory in most cases. In a service industry like hotels, the units or districts might be treated as profit centers for control of operations, but this does not have to change the organization's basic structure.

Acquiring and Divesting Units (External Growth and Termination)

Some strategies involve divesting or abandoning businesses. Others involve changing the mix of the company's portfolio of businesses by acquiring and divesting businesses. By their very nature, such strategies usually mean the firm is diversified to some degree. When this is the case, the divisional or holding company form is at an advantage because the firm can relatively easily decouple the unit. The unit already exists as a separate business, and the more autonomously it has been operated, the more easily the firm can abandon or divest it. But a unit within a functional structure is never autonomous, because it cannot operate without the other functional units. The functionally organized company can sell off plants and other major assets, but they are more difficult to disengage.

A company may seek an acquisition for several reasons, including diversification and vertical integration, discussed previously. The firm may also be seeking to increase its capacity within its own business by acquiring markets and increasing its own efficiency and scale. In this case, the firm acquired will relate to the primary business, and management will try to merge the two into one structure as did Chevron with Gulf. Staff units may be consolidated under one system, as Chevron and Gulf did in data processing, and the duplication of units may be rationalized. If the advantage sought is leverage in advertising or finance, this area may be centralized while the rest of the acquired business operates as a division. When the firm seeks economies of scale, it can merge the units into one or operate them separately while centralizing the desired function. But unless the company is already diversified or seeking to diversify, its tendency will be to merge the units into one.

Summary

This chapter showed the use of organization structure as a tool to implement a firm's strategy. To achieve a good match between strategy and structure, an executive must understand what each structure can and cannot do, as well as the demands the strategy will make on the structure. Given certain strategies, some structures work better than others.

The primary structural choices available are the functional, divisional, and matrix structures. Also, a number of modifications can be made that will allow the primary structure to be adapted to the firm's strategies and operations. These modifications include project teams, product teams, and product groups and SBUs.

The main factors affecting selection of an appropriate structure are sufficient scale of operations to support a structure and the extent to which the firm's business involves market and technological unrelatedness or diversity. The strategies of diversification, vertical integration, and single-business concentration influence relatedness and scale, and in this way they influence the match between structure and strategy.

Questions

1. Define functional organization structure and divisional organization structure. What are their relative advantages and disadvantages? When is it more appropriate to use a divisional structure than a functional structure?

2. Describe modifications that can be made to the basic organization structures to allow them to better deal with their limitations. To what kinds of problems or situations would each modification be best suited?

3. How can a company with dozens of divisions be organized so that corporate headquarters can plan, oversee, and control all of the divisions? Because of independent products and markets, a company may grant autonomy to its divisions, yet the company could be more efficient and effective if planning were integrated and resources were shared. Which organization structure allows companies to achieve simultaneous autonomy and integration?

4. Describe a matrix organization. What can it do that makes it different from functional and divisional structures?

5. What role does organization structure play in implementing corporate strategy?

6. Describe the effect on organization structure of (a) related diversification and (b) unrelated diversification. How do scale of operation and relatedness act in combination to influence a company's choice of a good organization structure?

Notes

1. M. A. Hitt, R. D. Ireland, and K. A. Palia, "Industrial Firms, Grand Strategy and Functional Performance: Moderating Effects of Technology and Uncertainty," *Academy of Management Journal* 25 (June 1982): 265–298.

2. Paul R. Lawrence and Jay W. Lorsch, *Organization and Environment* (Boston: Graduate School of Business Administration, Harvard University, 1967), 23–53.

3. James D. Thompson, *Organizations in Action* (New York: McGraw-Hill, 1967), 51–65.

4. "Culture Shock at Xerox," *Business Week*, June 22, 1987, 106, 108, 110.

5. Peter Lorange, *Corporate Planning* (Englewood Cliffs, N.J.: Prentice-Hall, 1980), 70.

6. Richard F. Vancil, "Texas Instruments Incorporated," in *Strategic Planning Systems*, eds. Peter Lorange and Richard F. Vancil (Englewood Cliffs, N.J.: Prentice-Hall, 1977), 338–361.

7. Jay R. Galbraith and Robert K. Kazanjian, *Strategy Implementation: Structure, Systems and Process*, 2nd ed. (St. Paul, Minn.: West, 1986), 77–81.

8. Stanley M. Davis and Paul R. Lawrence, *Matrix* (Reading, Mass.: Addison-Wesley, 1977), 103–128.

9. Galbraith and Kazanjian, *Strategy Implementation*, 150–154.

10. See, for example, Arthur L. Stinchcombe, "Social Structure and Organizations," in *Handbook of Organizations*, ed. James G. March (Chicago: Rand McNally, 1965), 142–193.

11. A number of authors have questioned whether structure always follows strategy and have argued that structure can limit, influence, or constrain strategy. The interest here is in using structure to implement strategy. For further reading on this issue, see J. R. Montanari, "Management Discretion: An Expanded Model of Organizational Choice," *Academy of Management Review* 3 (April 1978): 211–219; D. J. Hall and M. A. Salas, "Strategy Follows Structure," *Strategic Management Journal* 1 (January–March 1980): 149–163; and R. J. Litschert and R. W. Bonham, "A Conceptual Model of Strategy Formulation," *Academy of Management Review* 3 (April 1978): 211–219.

12. Louis A. Allen, *Management and Organization* (New York: McGraw-Hill, 1958).

13. Ibid., 84.

14. Of course, the strategy of a firm is not the only significant influence on organization structure. Other well-developed theses argue for the importance of contextual factors such as environment, size, and technology. However, the thrust of this book is on strategy formulation and implementation, and in that context organization structure is viewed as a tool or mechanism for implementing strategy. For these other views, see J. D. Ford and J. W. Slocum, Jr., "Size, Technology, Environment and the Structure of Organizations," *Academy of Management Review* 2 (October 1977): 561–575; and John H. Jackson, Cyril P. Morgan, and Joseph G. P. Paolillo, *Organization Theory: A Macro Perspective for Management*, 3d ed. (Englewood Cliffs, N.J.: Prentice-Hall, 1986), 56–102, 165–284.

15. Alfred D. Chandler, *Strategy and Structure* (Cambridge, Mass.: MIT Press, 1962), 7–52.

16. Leonard Wrigley, *Divisional Autonomy and Diversification* (unpublished doctoral dissertation, Harvard Business School, 1970), vi–90.

17. O. W. Williamson, *Markets and Hierarchies: Analysis and Antitrust Implications* (New York: Free Press, 1975), 136–150.

18. Robert A. Pitts and H. Donald Hopkins, "Firm Diversity: Conceptualization and Measurement," *Academy of Management Review* 7 (October 1982): 620–629.

19. Charles W. L. Hill and Robert E. Hoskinson, "Strategy and Structure in the Multiproduct Firm," *Academy of Management Review* 12 (April 1987): 331–341.

20. Robert E. Hoskinson, "Multidivisional Structure and Performance: The Contingency of Diversification Strategy," *Academy of Management Journal* 30 (December 1987): 625–644.

21. Wrigley and Rumelt in the works we have cited previously have both used the concept of relatedness. Galbraith and Kazanjian in *Strategy Implementation* have also employed this concept in relating structure to strategy.

22. Organization size has its own impact on organization structure and causes problems independently. Here we are interested in its impact in combination with relatedness. For a discussion of the other impacts of size on structure, see Jackson, Morgan, and Paolillo, *Organization Theory*, 201–228.

23. There is some indication that these elements may appear at relatively small size, for example, eight to ten employees. See Frederick T. Evers, Joe M. Bohlen, and Richard D. Warren, "The Relationship of Selected Size and Structure Indicators in Economics Organizations," *Administrative Science Quarterly* 21 (June 1976), 326–342.

Case for Discussion

Genuine Office Products

The Genuine Office Products Company began as a wholesale operation selling a variety of office supplies to retail stores. Over time the business encompassed the whole country and the volume of sales justified acquiring several manufacturers of office items such as pencil sharpeners, staplers, and tape dispensers. All the products were distributed through one marketing division, but there were separate manufacturing divisions for each major product that the company made. Most items distributed by the company were still purchased from outside manufacturers.

Both the marketing division and the manufacturing divisions were operated as profit centers. The manufacturing divisions sold their product to the marketing division, but marketing was allowed to seek outside suppliers as well. At first, this arrangement worked well enough. If the marketing division found lower prices from an outside supplier, it notified the manufacturing division and could usually negotiate a better price from the manufacturing division. The vice president of purchasing sat in on these negotiations and could mediate in the dispute. As a result, if the item was manufactured within the company, invariably marketing bought the item from the respective manufacturing division.

Last year, Jim Stemming became the new head of the marketing division. Aggressive and ambitious, he brought in several of his own people and decided to change the way the division was operated. He thought that products supplied by manufacturing divisions were often lower in quality than products from outside sources and were overpriced. The manufacturing divisions were making their own profits look good at the expense of his division, in his opinion. Disputes between manufacturing and marketing increased and negotiations over price became tougher.

The Stapler Division had been under pressure from Stemming to improve the quality of the striking rod and the quality of the chrome finish. Head of the Stapler Division, Jane Woods, had been willing to make the required changes, but the price to marketing would increase by $.80. Stemming said he could get the same product from an outside supplier for only $.25 more. Frustrated with Stemming, Woods had made a proposal to the company president that would allow the manufacturing divisions to sell their products to other office supply companies.

The president and CEO was tired of the infighting and wanted to find a way to end it.

Discussion Questions

1. Is the conflict between marketing and manufacturing detrimental to the organization? If you think it is not, how would you convince the president?

2. What criteria should be used to select a solution?

3. Is the organization structure at fault in this case? How would you change the structure?

4. Can the problem be solved without changing the structure of the organization?

Chapter 7

Implementing Strategy through Culture, Leadership, and Human Resource Management

Leadership and learning are indispensable to each other

—John Fitzgerald Kennedy, remarks prepared for delivery at the Trade Mart in Dallas, November 22, 1963.

Learning Objectives

- To explain the need to align human factors with strategy so they support its implementation.
- To show how corporate culture can support a strategy and why and how to change it if it does not.
- To discuss the role that leadership plays in implementation.
- To provide an understanding of the supportive role human resource management can play in implementing strategy.
- To understand the key roles of staffing and rewarding in implementing strategy.

GOALS, functional strategies, and structural arrangements are important in aligning a company's systems with its strategy, but they are not enough. Managers also must pay attention to human factors. Although others have stressed human factors in implementing strategy, probably none have done more to popularize the importance of human factors and social systems than Thomas J. Peters and Robert H. Waterman, Jr.[1] They assert that effective organizational change results from the interaction among the organization's strategy, structure, goals, systems, skills, staff, and style.

Previous chapters have discussed the first five of these factors. This chapter will consider strategy implementation through staff and style. Specifically, the focus will be on three people-oriented factors that need to be aligned with strategy: corporate culture, leadership, and human resource systems.

Corporate Culture

The United States has a culture that is different from that of Japan, Iran, India, or Mexico. We all recognize that in such diverse countries, things are done in different ways. People have different histories, traditions, views of what is important, and standards of behavior. Less recognizable is that companies also have cultures that can distinguish them. In part, this is because we share a common culture. That is, a company's culture is embedded in the national and even regional culture, and we tend to take for granted what is common. But companies have different origins, participate in different industries, contain different occupations, have experienced different leaders and strategies, and so forth, and so they have distinctive histories and social systems. The Strategic Application "Japanese Leadership" describes ways in which these cultural patterns, combined with each organization's unique experiences, form corporate cultures.

Corporate culture reflects the dominant values, norms, and beliefs of the organization's members. The culture of an organization has been seen as the way a group maintains the integrity of its social structure, as the informal social organization, and as a personality-like pattern.[2] Common to these views is the concept of culture as a social system that brings order by giving meaning to members' experience.

Shared values and beliefs are a source of this common meaning. Norms or rules of conduct develop to define acceptable behavior. Kathleen L. Gregory has summarized how the common meaning becomes shared:

> People interact as if they shared culture. Through trial and error, sometimes through conversation and negotiation, they confirm whether or not their meanings are similar enough to get through social interaction appropriately. . . . From a base of shared culture, people can negotiate new apparently shared meanings, and do, as a matter of course.[3]

With the shared meaning comes a pattern of acceptable attitudes, beliefs, and behaviors about how one does things, what is important and what is not, and how to solve problems. In a strong and consistent culture, the pattern may permeate the company's decision making, structure, and administrative systems. The personnel evaluation and reward system may use criteria that reflect the company culture. For example, managers and professionals who do not follow the acceptable values may not get promoted. Persons who find the culture unacceptable may self-select themselves out of the situation. A scientist who wants to develop new ways to solve problems may not fit a culture that values using well-established techniques, and may seek a research lab that better fits his or her value system. Over time the company may develop a strong, consistent culture in which the various parts reinforce the cultural pattern.

The culture is strengthened, reinforced, and transmitted through the telling of stories and the development of symbols, rituals, and myths. For example, Frito-Lay sells potato chips and pretzels and has a strong majority of the market share in the industry. Although the company is good at many things, it emphasizes its sales force and its service level.[4] At Frito-Lay and among its customers, stories abound of sales-

STRATEGIC APPLICATIONS: INTERNATIONAL

Japanese Leadership

American management practice and lore give great credit to the leadership of executives in any organizational achievement. The leader is seen as a strong individual who directs and inspires followers toward company objectives. Individual responsibility and action are emphasized. The ideal leader takes charge and energizes members of the group. Perhaps this derives from a culture that values individuality and requires strong leaders to move a collection of individuals in a new direction.

However, in Japanese management, the conception and role of the leader is quite different. In Japanese companies, task and responsibility are not assigned to individuals, but are shared by the whole group. The group's performance is important, rather than that of the manager or even individuals within the group. Collective performance is emphasized, and members share responsibility. Individual names and positions are not even shown on the organization charts. Only units are shown. Responsibility is assigned to the units in brief and vague terms.

The emphasis on collective responsibility means that the role of the leader is to create the right social environment for the group so it can obtain its objectives. Harmony among group members and a united group are seen as forming the appropriate environment. On the other hand, hierarchal status is meticulously and rigidly defined, and members are expected to adhere to it. The relative status of each organizational unit and person is carefully defined in relation to that of other persons and units in the hierarchy. Status is largely determined by educational level and seniority, and the reward system is based on seniority, not performance.

Top management is heavily involved in day-to-day operations, and members often see themselves as representatives of their groups rather than adopt a total company view. Almost no companies employ outsiders on the board of directors, and the board consists of full-time operating executives from inside the company. Usually, the chairman and president control appointments to the board. Because independent auditors are not used, there is no independent body to check on performance, and power is concentrated in these two officers. Junior board members are appointed by them and are quite aware of who controls their appointment and their status, which also limits the expression of independent judgments.

Source: M. Y. Yoshino, *Japan's Managerial System* (Cambridge, Mass.: M.I.T. Press, 1968), 85–117.

people going to an extraordinary effort to service customers, helping to clean up and restock stores after hurricanes and accidents, making long and costly trips to restock a $30 order. Told and retold, such stories can become legends that convey what is valued.

The concept of corporate culture is elusive because it has been given so many different meanings.[5] But there is a growing recognition that companies have an identifiable culture. Most of us, although we may have difficulty describing them, recognize differences among organizations in the way things are done, what is considered important, and employee attitudes. The difference may be in the way they treat customers, how they accomplish activities, or how they are described by their employees. Such differences are a part of their culture.

The Importance of Culture

Strong corporate cultures have been cited as a reason for continued excellence, superior financial performance, and the ability to adapt and innovate. Often high performance is attributed to some core value that is dominant in the company. IBM, for example, is said to be a customer service-oriented company. Of course, IBM is excellent at other things as well, but one story indicates the value placed on customer service:

> In a decision to purchase a major computer system one person [an IBM customer] described the decision. Many of the others [bidding on the job] were ahead of IBM in technological wizardry, he noted. And heaven knows their software is easier to use. But IBM alone took the trouble to get to know us. They interviewed extensively up and down the line. They talked our language, no mumbo jumbo on computer innards. Their price was fully twenty-five percent higher. But they provided unparalleled guarantees of reliability and service. They even went so far as to arrange a back-up connection with a local steel company in case our system crashed. Their presentations were to the point. Everything about them smacked of assurance and success. Our decision, even with severe budget pressure, was really easy.[6]

At IBM the corporate culture thus supports and reinforces the company's strategy. Another example illustrates what can happen when the culture and strategy are not aligned. Johnson & Johnson, makers of such products as Band-Aids, had been consistently successful and predominately market oriented. The company was also decentralized, having 170 divisions, each with its own president and considerable autonomy. When it started a move into more sophisticated medical technology markets, Johnson & Johnson believed this move required closer coordination and communication in such areas as packaging, purchasing, and distribution. But the cooperation necessary to carry out the new strategy was alien to the old culture. Units have been resisting change, and managers have been leaving. The entrepreneurial companies Johnson & Johnson has acquired have not adjusted well to the new financial and control systems nor to the new operating policies and practices. The old way of doing things has not fit the requirements of the new strategy.[7]

The first example indicates that an appropriate corporate culture can strengthen and support company strategy. The second example indicates that the wrong corporate culture can interfere with the implementation of company strategy. These are two powerful reasons for considering culture when deciding on strategy and in planning for its implementation.

Culture and Strategy

There is little doubt that culture is important in shaping attitudes, values, and beliefs and that the social system shapes the behavior of members. But how does this affect the success of a strategy? Although many observers of and participants in business think culture is important for strategy to succeed, culture by itself cannot assure success. The strategy itself may be the wrong one for market and company conditions. When the wrong strategy is chosen, culture is unlikely to be able to overcome the effects of the choice and may even intensify poor performance by reinforcing the mistaken strategy.

When the right strategy is aligned with a culture that does not support it, the company will likely experience resistance to change, and its success will be problematic. Exxon's Petrochemical Division (Canada) provides an example.[8] Top management thought a fundamental change in the business required a different strategy. The managers agreed that the company must develop products that focused on a market niche. They intended to remain in their core business of supplying basic products, but also entered into joint ventures and joint development agreements with many of their customers. One year later, nothing was changing. A study indicated that culture was at the root of the problem. Many of the company's norms directly conflicted with the new strategy.

When a company's culture runs counter to its strategy, the company faces two choices. It can choose a strategy that fits the culture, or it can change the culture to better fit the strategy. A strategy is most likely to succeed when there is **cultural alignment**, that is, when the right strategy is aligned with a supportive culture. When the two are aligned, resistance to the strategy is minimized, and the patterns of how things are done and what is important incorporate the strategy. At the action level, culture influences how employees serve customers, deal with suppliers, support other functions, solve problems, structure their units, employ controls, reward others, and practice management. It defines acceptable behavior in detailed ways that the company's functional strategies, organization structure, human resource systems, budgets, and control usually do not. Ideally, therefore, culture and strategy become as one, pulling in the same direction.

Jay Barney has said that culture can be the source of sustained competitive advantage if it meets three conditions.[9] First, the culture must enable the firm to do things and behave in ways that lead to such results as lower cost and higher sales and margins. The culture also must have attributes that are not common to the cultures of many other companies. Finally, the culture must not be subject to imitation. Barney argues that when a culture is common and can be copied, other firms will change their cultures, thus negating the uniqueness.

This raises the question of whether there are cultures that are valuable and rare and that cannot be copied. Barney suggests there are and that these firms should nurture these attributes. He also suggests that firms without them should not attempt to imitate other firms, because doing so can only result in normal economic returns. However, imitation can gain short-run advantages and at least will improve the firm's position. An alternative is for the firm to seek to develop its own unique culture. Or, instead of seeking competitive advantage from its culture, the firm can make the culture supportive of the organizational factors such as strategy and structure.

Besides being valuable, rare, and inimitable, what attributes does a desirable culture have? There are two ways to answer this question. One way is to assume the existence of a set of characteristics common to successful companies. Knowing such characteristics would simplify the task of shaping the culture.

Exemplary of efforts to discover a set of characteristics is the work of Peters and Waterman, reported in their highly popular book, *In Search of Excellence.* They describe eight basic attributes that most of their excellent companies believed in and were strongly committed to:

1. A bias for action—The companies are analytical in decision making, but their bias is to experiment and try out ideas.

2. Closeness to the customer—They work with and listen to their customers to improve quality, service, and reliability. Many of their new products come from the customer.

3. Autonomy and entrepreneurship—They foster product champions and innovators and turn them loose to make mistakes.

4. Productivity through people—Every member of the organization is seen as a source of improvement. Everyone is a part of the team.

5. Hands-on, value-driven approach—The company is clear about what it stands for and what is important. The top executives promote and foster these values through hands-on involvement with its members.

6. Sticking to the knitting. They stay reasonably close to the business they know. When they do branch out, it is into areas and skills they know about.

7. Simple form, lean staff—They keep their priorities clear and their structures stable, simple, and flexible. They minimize corporate staff by decentralizing it.

8. Simultaneous loose-tight properties—They are at the same time centrally controlled and allow autonomy, entrepreneurship, and innovation from members. They are unbending about their culture—the beliefs and values—but as long as members stay within the bounds of the values, they are free to perform.

These attributes both spring from and are a part of the excellent companies' cultures. The companies are intensely committed to these attributes.

The Peters and Waterman work has been criticized in several ways. Daniel Carroll criticized the work for not being specific about how the companies were analyzed and how the authors identified the eight attributes.[10] There is also a question about whether the excellent companies chosen for study were in fact excellent. *Business Week* has since reported that many of these companies have run into trouble.[11] Furthermore, Michael A. Hitt and R. Duane Ireland found no performance differences between the Peters and Waterman companies and a sample of 162 representative firms from the Fortune 1000.[12] Nor did they find any difference among the two sets of firms in their use of the excellence attributes. Only one of the attributes—innovation, autonomy, and entrepreneurship—was related to performance. Hitt and Ireland conclude from their research:

> These data suggest that the excellent firms identified by Peters and Waterman may not have been excellent performers, and they may not have applied the excellence principles to any greater extent than did the general population of firms. Additionally, the data call into question whether these excellence principles are, in fact, related to performance.[13]

It would appear that the eight attributes do not provide a universal culture that leads to excellence.

Other models have been proposed as a basis for developing a culture. Theory Y, Theory Z, and participative management are only a few examples that could be used as a basis for certain aspects of culture such as interpersonal relations. But it has not yet been demonstrated that these theories are any more able to support all types of strategies than the attributes identified by Peters & Waterman are. This lack of information does not negate the concept that culture is important to the implementation of strategy, but it does suggest that the alignment of culture with strategy may need to be unique for each company.

Aligning Culture and Strategy

Alignment can result from changes in strategy or culture or both. To decide what should be changed, management must decide where the pressure for change is coming from. A change in strategy resulting from consideration of corporate strengths may bring the strategy into alignment with an existing culture. Schwartz and Davis, for example, cite the incompatibility of North American and Rockwell as a case in which changing the strategy would be useful in aligning strategy and culture.[14] More typical is the situation in which changes in the environment and competition pressure management to reformulate strategy.

Not all changes in strategy will dictate a change in culture, but significant reformulation will typically find the culture out of alignment. Faced with a need to change strategy, what steps can top management take to assure that its corporate culture will support the new strategy?

Understand the Strategy Management should begin by understanding its strategic plan, including the strategy, goals, functional strategies, and programs. This information dictates the new behaviors that will be required of the organization's members. It is also important for communicating the reasons for the change as well as the new behaviors required.

Unless management has a clear, shared vision of what will be required, there is little chance of developing a program to align culture with strategy. For example, what does it mean in terms of employee behavior to say, as did AT&T's chairman, "We will become a marketing company"? Does it mean increased emphasis on customer service? Or that the customer will come first? If the customer does not come first now, how will employees have to behave for that to happen? Perhaps it means meeting customer-requested delivery dates 99 percent of the time. The ability to specify such behaviors will clarify the changes in culture.

Also, managers should determine whether the company's culture will support a strategy when they are formulating the strategy. During formulation of strategy, management will evaluate the organization's internal strengths and weaknesses and its distinctive competencies. The culture embodies certain of these skills and competencies. Management may not be able to foresee all the cultural attributes needed to support its strategy, nor the one that may conflict with it, but explicitly looking at the strategy in these terms will help. The information gained will provide an early check on whether change will be required.

Understand the Culture The second step in aligning culture and strategy is to thoroughly know the company's culture. Such knowledge makes it possible to determine if change is needed and the extent of any change required. For example, Bank of America conducted interviews in 1983 to assess its culture. Management found that the bank's culture had changed in the 1960s and 1970s to one that was unprepared to face the problems and opportunities created by deregulation. They discovered that one of their shared beliefs was "Don't risk failure."[15] A complementary belief was to make any investment pay off in the short run. Both beliefs were thought to discourage innovation and experimentation such as installation of automatic teller machines. Unfortunately innovation and experimentation were both attributes management believed necessary for the bank to cope with changes occurring in the banking industry.

Determine What Must Change Next, management must compare the strategy and its required behaviors with the present culture. The goal is to discover where the gaps are and to determine which values, beliefs, and behaviors need to be changed. Is the culture in conflict with the strategic behaviors? How big is the gap? How many beliefs are in conflict? Are values and beliefs widely shared, or are they local to a few key functions or divisions? Are there a few key values and beliefs to be changed, or must a whole culture be reshaped? The more drastic the change, the more difficult the task will be, the more intensive the effort required, and the longer the change process will take.

If the executive knows the culture and the strategic behavior required, asking questions like these will help in developing the targets for change. Bank of America, for example, decided to focus on four areas: place the customer first; respect, recognize, and reward customers and employees; make the most of technology; and "share our strategy, strengthen our team."

Changing a culture can be slow and can be costly in time and resources. It may also disturb the established way of doing things, leading to frustration and loss of motivation for many members. Some will leave. This step should allow executives to determine how big a change is needed, assess the costs of the change, and decide whether to proceed. If the cost is too high, the company may have to decide whether it has the skills and resources to make the strategy work. If not, it may have to reevaluate the appropriateness of the strategy and whether the company could alter the strategy to better fit its skills and resources.

An alternative is to determine whether the company can manage *around the culture.*[16] If the strategic change does not involve the whole company, it may be best to isolate or localize the change required. For example, if the strategy involves moving into a new and different product-market, the company may be able to set up an autonomous division or subsidiary. It can select new leaders and employees with appropriate values and skills. It might even allow these people to develop their own goals, structures, systems, distinctive competence, and management style. The division can then build its own culture so that it is aligned with the strategy without disturbing the parent company's culture or being burdened by it. However, there still may be conflict if the parent tries to impose its own integrative systems; the more autonomous the division, the greater chance that a separate culture will emerge. Some hotel and retail chains have used this approach in entering new market segments. If the changes are needed and the company cannot manage around the culture, it will have little choice but to change the culture.

Change the Culture Finally, management must develop a plan for changing the culture. Kurt Lewin specifies three phases of change: unfreezing, change, and refreezing.[17] In Table 7.1 Lewin's phases are used to summarize change activities for each phase. A plan of change should provide for these three phases.

The present culture is initially maintained because it is meeting the needs of employees. The pressure for change is held in check by the pressure to maintain the culture. To unfreeze the culture, management must therefore increase the pressure for change. The external conditions that stimulated the change in strategy can be used to convince members of the need to change. Unfreezing is furthered by creating discontent with the company's ability to meet the challenge using its present strategy and organizational capabilities. Some companies, like Honeywell and Bank of America, have used survey feedback methods to indicate the inadequacy of the present culture. Creating a need for change is important to developing a readiness to receive and become committed to a new way of doing things.

The role of top executives in communicating the need to adapt also is important. Through speeches, informal and working contacts, and programs, executives communicate the dissatisfaction with the status quo, the need to change, and the expectation for change. Some, like Lawrence Rawl at Exxon, are rabble-rousers and dissidents. Others press for incremental change. For example, when John F. Welch was appointed CEO of General Electric, he thought the company too cautious and wanted more innovation. He pushed the idea that employees needed to take more risks and must not allow their budgets to control them. In word and deed, he has championed the idea that the old management system was strong, but that GE also has to become more entrepreneurial and innovative.

Table 7.1 Changing Culture with the Lewin Model

Phases of Change	Change Activities
Unfreezing	Environmental changes
	Discontent with present strategy
	Adjustment of strategy to the environment
Change	Development of new models of behavior
	Communication and change of new models through: Functional plans Structure Leadership Culture change Rewards Staffing Controls
Refreezing	Adherence to changes
	Persistent leadership
	Alignment of implementation factors
	Success of new systems in producing results

Once the company is unfrozen, management must provide a new model (culture) for its members. Top executives need to communicate the new strategy and their goals and vision of the future, as well as what will be required to get there. This requires a clear picture of the values, beliefs, and behaviors that will be important. At Bank of America, the top management team took about a year to complete its review and develop key values.[18] The process was systematic, but other companies, like Exxon under Lawrence G. Rawl, have plunged ahead, reshaping the culture to fit the CEO's views.[19]

Many of the organizational factors used to implement strategy can be used to help put the culture in place and reinforce its values and beliefs. For example, Lawrence Rawl wanted to concentrate Exxon on what the company knew best: energy and chemicals businesses.[20] He also wanted to cut costs. He was dissatisfied with the way the company's bureaucracy complicated decision making and forced consensus. He cut back on corporate staff, consolidated units, cut organization levels, and shrank the business as well as the number of employees. He also cut down the size and number of reports, reduced committee agendas, and streamlined the budget review process. Such changes emphasized his lean, tough-minded, and operations-oriented style. At Exxon, organization structure, administrative systems, and leadership were major tools for **reshaping culture**.

This example also illustrates how many aspects of the organization can be tied together in establishing a new culture. Some of the means available to executives in transforming cultures, with examples of how they can be used, are the following:

- *Staffing* Focus on gaining commitment from key managers. Fill key positions with leaders who exemplify the important values. If you want action over analysis, for example, you should put action-oriented people in the important jobs.
- *Structure* Use a structural pattern that emphasizes the important values and beliefs. For example, if the customer comes first, make the structure reflect that value. If entrepreneurship is valued, make sure the units where it is expected have the autonomy to exhibit it.
- *Controls* Measure and evaluate the firm's progress in changing cultural values. What is measured and evaluated conveys what the organization gives priority to. If delivery to the customer is important, then measure the firm's success in that area.
- *Rewards* Promotion, pay, praise, and other awards should go to those who demonstrate the behaviors sought. Rewards signal what is really important and reinforce for everyone what the values are to be in the future.
- *Leadership* Leadership, especially from the top, can reflect the important parts of the culture through example and persistent championing. Leaders should be out front, visible, and showing what is important. Commitment from top management is perhaps the key factor in change.
- *Goals and Plans* Values and beliefs can be seen in the goals and plans at all levels, because goals and plans incorporate the desired results. If customer service is important, it should be seen in the expectations for those who deal with customers.

Because the culture is shared beliefs and values of people in the system, these are what must change. Changing the goals, plans, structure, and administrative systems conveys expectations and assures that all aspects of the organization are pulling together, but it is people who hold the beliefs and values.

Changing a strong culture can be very difficult. It requires the commitment of time and resources and perhaps most importantly the persistence of top management.

Leadership

One person alone cannot change the organization's goals, plans, structure, culture, and administrative systems. The transformation that must occur in the company to implement strategy requires the efforts of many people. The chief executive officer must exert **leadership** to see that these efforts are made. Changes in strategy that involve movement in a new direction will require someone to define the path, mobilize resources, and show personnel how to get there. In changing corporate culture, the CEO plays a vital role in demonstrating values and his or her commitment to the changes in culture. Other top executives also are critical in implementing strategic changes.

The experience of Joseph F. Alibrandi, CEO of Whittaker Corporation, provides an illustration.[21] In 1970, when Alibrandi joined the company, Whittaker Corporation faced bankruptcy. Half of its debt was due within one year. Its stock was selling for $5.50 a share, down from $73.00 in 1968. A conglomerate, it had acquired 142 costly businesses. Alibrandi first assessed the company's strengths and then sold 93 unprofitable business units for cash. He moved the cash into units where the company had strengths it could turn into a large market share. By 1982 the company had become a major force in all its business areas and had set sales and net earnings records for five years in a row.

In the beginning, Alibrandi's major obstacle was "to get a lot of people who clearly felt they were on a sinking ship to believe we could save it."[22] To persuade his people and present his strategy, he held a weekend meeting of the entire management team. He was able to overcome their initial skepticism, but he recalls, "If I had not been able to sell the plan, it would never have worked, no matter how sound the strategy."[23] Alibrandi is known for his ability to evaluate people and what motivates them and then to energize them to work for him. He likes to meet and talk with people and will meet with anyone who has a contribution to make. He uses every opportunity to get his message across, often using a tour of company operations to talk with workers.

This example shows many of the attributes of leaders who are able to transform their companies. Leadership that implements strategy and moves companies in different directions has an agenda for change that is exercised consistently and persistently over an extended period. At times successful leaders may be dramatic and seize on events to pursue their agenda, but for the main part, they exercise leadership in the context of their position and other managerial activity.

Roles of the General Manager

What do chief executive officers and other general managers do that makes their roles so central in implementing strategy? There are thousands of leadership studies, but relatively few have focused on general managers.[24] Yet few people interested in strategy doubt that general managers have a valuable role to play in formulating and implementing strategy. This section will try to clarify some of the important roles a general manager plays, because it is in these roles that he or she finds the opportunity to persuade, set an example, and provide a vision of where the company needs to go.

Leaders seek commitment and support for their strategy. They also motivate and energize their followers. Their efforts to implement the strategy are not separate from their other leadership acts, but are folded into the many contacts and events in which they are constantly involved. The agenda and priority may change as the program for implementation unfolds, but the roles leaders play and the activities they engage in allow them to exert leadership throughout the implementation process.

The Mintzberg Study A good beginning for understanding the opportunities available for providing leadership is Mintzberg's study of five chief executives, which focused on the activities of general managers.[25] Mintzberg combined his findings with other empirical studies to describe ten roles all managers perform. These findings are summarized in Table 7.2.

Mintzberg argues that these roles stem from the manager's being placed in charge of an organizational unit. This authority gives the manager a special status. The ten roles form an integrated whole, but not every manager places equal emphasis on each role. Differences in environment, job, person, and situation contribute to forming individual priorities. Mintzberg concludes that level and functional area account for more difference than the other variables. For example:

> The higher the level of the manager in the hierarchy, the more unstructured, unspecialized, and long-range the job, the more complex, intertwined, and extended in time the issues handled, the less focused the work.[26]

In addition to the ten common roles, Mintzberg found several common characteristics of the executive's work.[27] Executives must perform a great deal of work, and the rate never lets up. Even when an executive is off duty, his or her mind is never far from work-related problems, because the job is never finished.

Also, the executive's pattern of work can be described as brief, variable, and fragmented. The important and unimportant activities are interspersed. A scheduled meeting on a complex issue might take an hour, but most activity is characterized by less than 15 minutes, and the executive is frequently interrupted. Knowing his or her worth to the organization, the executive seems to prefer this pattern.

The executive also "gravitates toward the more active elements of his work activities that are current, specific, and well-defined, and those that are nonroutine."[28] He or she prefers current information that comes from the telephone and unscheduled meetings to routine reports. Time tends to be scheduled around definite, concrete, and specific issues rather than general issues. If the executive is engaging in reflective

Table 7.2 Mintzberg's Summary of the Ten Roles of Executives

Role	Description	Identifiable Activities from Study of Chief Executives	Recognition in the Literature
Interpersonal			
Figurehead	Symbolic head; obliged to perform a number of routine duties of a legal or social nature	Ceremony, status requests, solicitations	Sometimes recognized, but usually only at highest organizational levels
Leader	Responsible for the motivation and activation of subordinates; responsible for staffing, training, and associated duties	Virtually all managerial activities involving subordinates	Most widely recognized of all managerial roles
Liaison	Maintains self-developed network of outside contacts and informers who provide favors and information	Acknowledgments of mail; external board work; other activities involving outsiders	Largely ignored, except for particular empirical studies (Sayles on lower- and middle-level managers, Neustadt on U.S. Presidents, Whyte and Homans on informal leaders)
Informational			
Monitor	Seeks and receives wide variety of special information (much of it current) to develop thorough understanding of organization and environment; emerges as nerve center of internal and external information of the organization	Handling all mail and contacts categorized as concerned primarily with receiving information (e.g., periodical news, observational tours)	Recognized in the work of Sayles, Neustadt, Wrapp, and especially Aguilar
Disseminator	Transmits information received from outsiders or from other subordinates to members of the organization; some information factual, some involving interpretation and integration of diverse value positions of organizational influences	Forwarding mail into organization for informational purposes, verbal contacts involving information flows to subordinates (e.g., review sessions, instant communication flows)	Unrecognized (except for Papandreou discussion of "peak coordinator" who integrates influencer preferences)
Spokesman	Transmits information to outsiders on organization's plans, policies, actions, results, etc.; serves as expert on organization's industry	Board meetings; handling mail and contacts involving transmission of information to outsiders	Generally acknowledged as managerial role

(continued)

Table 7.2 *(continued)*

Role	Description	Identifiable Activities from Study of Chief Executives	Recognition in the Literature
Decisional			
Entrepreneur	Searches organization and its environment for opportunities and initiates "improvement projects" to bring about change; supervises design of certain projects as well	Strategy and review sessions involving initiation or design of improvement projects	Implicitly acknowledged, but usually not analyzed except for economists (who were concerned largely with the establishment of new organizations) and Sayles, who probes into this role
Disturbance Handling	Responsible for corrective action when organization faces important, unexpected disturbances	Strategy and review sessions involving disturbances and crises	Discussed in abstract way by many writers (e.g., management by exception) but analyzed carefully only by Sayles
Resource Allocator	Responsible for the allocation of organizational resources of all kinds—in effect the making or approval of all significant organizational decisions	Scheduling; requests for authorizations; any activity involving budgeting and the programming of subordinates' work	Little explicit recognition as a role, although implicitly recognized by the many who analyze organizational resource-allocation activities
Negotiator	Responsible for representing the organization at major negotiations	Negotiation	Largely unrecognized (or recognized but claimed to be nonmanagerial work) except for Sayles

Source: Excerpt from *The Nature of Managerial Work* by Henry Mintzberg, pp. 92–93.

planning, he or she is doing it on the run and in bits and pieces upon receiving and manipulating information.

The executive's work heavily involves communication, especially the verbal media. A strong majority of his or her time is spent in verbal communication, with unscheduled meetings and the telephone used for brief contacts, and scheduled meetings used for longer formal contacts.

The executive maintains a position as a hub in an extensive network of contacts. Externally he or she is in contact with clients, government and trade officials, suppliers, peers from other organizations, and experts for outside information. Much contact time is with such external persons. Executives spend very little time with their superiors, but a great deal of time with subordinates and a significant amount of time with staff relationships.

The executive's job is a blend of duties and rights. Much of what the executive does is in reaction to requests from others. Subordinates request meetings and authorizations, problems come up, and the telephone rings. Much of this activity has been generated by earlier activities.

The Kotter Study In a more recent study, Kotter also looked at general managers' jobs.[29] The focus of the study was 15 general managers from nine different corporations in the United States. Most of these managers were division general managers or division presidents, and their organizations ranged in size from a few hundred to over 10,000 employees.

Kotter recognizes the differences and variety among general management jobs but believes that all the jobs can be described in terms of their responsibilities and relationships. Key challenges and dilemmas are associated with the job responsibilities and job relationships Kotter found. Kotter's organization of information and terminology is different from that of Mintzberg, but there are fundamental similarities. For example, both say that general managers must decide how to employ resources, handle large amounts of information, and motivate and control subordinates.

Kotter also found considerable variation in job demands. Some general manager jobs emphasize either long-run or short-run responsibilities. Some place more importance on lateral relationships. For example, an autonomous divisional manager, one who has rather complete management responsibility for profit and loss of a business, has less long-run responsibility and less demanding lateral relationships than the group general manager who has several division managers reporting to him or her. But a source of even greater variation is differences in such factors as age and size of the organization and the manager's level of performance. For example, larger organizations have many more decisions, issues, and activities; general managers of this type of organization have less detailed information for decision making in comparison to those of smaller organizations. They also have to work through more people and bureaucracy to implement their decisions than those in smaller divisions.

The general managers studied by Kotter seem to approach their jobs in a similar way. Building on their knowledge of the business, using their relationships with others and their own skills, they begin setting **agendas** for their responsibilities. The agendas are goals and plans and the actions needed to implement them. The managers use these working agendas in persuading others, conveying their vision of the company, establishing priorities and values, and gaining commitments and allies. They develop a network of cooperative relationships with others in the organization upon whom they depended to implement their agenda.

Kotter also found considerable similarity in the daily behavior of general managers. Kotter's description of how general managers use their time is particularly revealing:

> Specifically they typically spent the vast majority of their time with other people, discussing a wide variety of topics. In these conversations the GM [general manager] usually asked numerous questions, yet they very rarely could be seen making big decisions. These conversations often contained considerable amount of joking and non-work related issues. Indeed, in many of these discussions the substantive issue involved was relatively unimportant to the business. The GMs rarely gave orders, but they often tried to influence others. Their time was seldom planned in advance in any detail and was usually characterized by brief and disjointed conversations.[30]

Like Mintzberg's findings, Kotter's show general managers' emphasis on oral communication and brief, often fragmented interactions. The manager exercises leadership during brief episodes. The communication must be concise and easy to grasp. No time is set aside for leadership per se; rather, leadership occurs during daily interaction. The general manager uses his or her network of supporters to implement his or her agenda. Kotter concludes that what appears to be unprofessional behavior in fact derives from the nature of the job and is understandable, efficient, and effective. Chief executive officers and general managers spend considerable time cultivating a **network of persons** who provide information. This information helps them understand the environment and the organization; identify problems; plan solutions; and establish goals, strategies and policies. Managers allocate resources and implement their agenda by communicating, motivating, controlling, and gaining the cooperation of a network of key people. General managers implement strategy by persuading and questioning. They use every opportunity to win support for their goals and plans, but do it in brief episodes with concise and easy-to-grasp ideas.

Transformational Leadership

The leader's ability to significantly change an organization in a new direction has been called **transformational leadership**.[31] **Transactional leadership**, in contrast, involves making minor adjustments in the organization's mission, structure, and human resource management. Noel M. Tichy and David O. Ulrich have described the transactional leader as defensive, in search of a quick fix, and blindly seeking the "latest solution."[32] Bernard Bass characterizes this pattern of leadership as an exchange process in which the followers' needs are met if their performance meets the leader's expectation; that is, subordinates meet job requirements because of rewards and punishments.[33] Transactional leaders can gain compliance and some degree of commitment and loyalty, and so transactional leadership may work well enough for relatively minor adjustments in strategy. It does not provide enough energy when transformations are required.

Transformational leaders create a higher order of commitment, performance, and change. They inspire and energize followers to an enthusiastic pursuit of the company's mission. They do this by providing a vision, gaining support and commitment, and shaping culture.

Providing a Vision Transformational leaders are able to generate a **vision** of what the future can be like for the company. This vision is not the mission or goals, although it may include them and they should reflect it. Rather, it is a mental image of the company's character, its direction, and what it will become.

The important ability is to imagine the future, articulate it, and convey it in such a way that people understand the direction they are going. In the words of John Carter, president and CEO of The Equitable, "The fundamental role of a leader is to articulate a vision for the company, fertilize it, and then communicate it in such a way that whether employees agree with it or not, they understand that the vision is created with their own best interests and the company's in mind."[34]

The Strategic Application "Monsanto Leadership and Public Disclosure" is an

STRATEGIC APPLICATIONS: SOCIAL RESPONSIBILITY

Monsanto Leadership and Public Disclosure

With so much news about companies hiding the fact that they are selling unsafe products or generating toxic waste, it is refreshing to hear of a company that discloses the negatives. Monsanto, a St. Louis-based chemical and drug producer, has begun a program of public disclosure to do just that. The company surprised the industry and environmental activists by announcing it would begin to publicize information about its toxic products to residents in all its plant communities. Monsanto didn't have to do this: It is not required by state or federal regulations. But as the president of Monsanto, Richard J. Mahoney, said in an interview with *The Washington Post*, "If my neighbor said to me 'What are you making in there anyway?', how could I say anything but, 'Come on in and I'll show you.' "

Source: M. R. Moskowitz, "Company Performance Roundup," *Business and Society Review* (Spring 1985): 76.

example of how the president of one company acted on his vision of the company as a responsible citizen.

Gaining Support and Commitment The leader's vision is not enough. Followers must accept it and commit themselves to it. The leader uses every opportunity to articulate it and build support for it. Some will support the vision because they believe in the cause, others because it is the "wave of the future," still others because of the charismatic and intellectual qualities of the leader.[35] Like the managers in Kotter's study, the leader constantly works his or her agenda. Alibrandi at Whittaker, for example, conveyed his vision with the presentation of his ten-year plan, but he also continued to articulate it at every opportunity through speeches, dialogue, and example.

The example provided by top management and other key leaders is important in gaining support. Because actions are interpreted as indications of what is really important, they send signals that guide followers.[36] When the company restructures to emphasize new product-markets, it sends a signal as to what it considers important. Every action that an executive takes to align the company's functional strategies and policies or administrative systems with a vision is a signal that the leader is committed. The leader's commitment generates commitment in followers. These kinds of changes also help to institutionalize the transformation as it unfolds, so that the pattern of behavior becomes enduring.

Robert H. Waterman, Jr., has emphasized that, in addition to communication and example, it is important for leaders to turn causes into action: "The most motivating causes focus on quality, products, service, and the customer—making the work people do seem worth the effort—and on people quality, helping people believe in their individual worth."[37]

An example of turning a cause into action is the program developed by Alibrandi at one of Whittaker's plants. He had championed and promoted the link between productivity and rewards at every opportunity, but he also developed a program for employees that encouraged them to increase productivity. If employees could maintain quality while cutting costs or increase production while maintaining costs, they were allowed to keep 80 percent of the savings.[38] Word and deed went together to generate commitment.

Shaping Culture Many observers agree that one of the primary roles of a leader is to promote, shape, and protect the values of the organization.[39] The utility of values and beliefs is that they tell members the right way to approach and solve problems. Values and beliefs also explain why a certain activity is important and help to promote it. They tell members how things should be done in the organization. Values tell employees what is important, and beliefs tell them that if they do it a certain way, they will get a certain result. For example, the use of task forces to solve problems is a natural way of doing things at IBM. Every employee knows how to form and use them to solve problems. Similarly, at The Equitable, participation, speaking one's mind, and consensus building are valued as the way to approach problems.[40]

What the leader does and says helps to shape the company's culture. How leaders spend their time, what they pay attention to, and what they reward promote values and beliefs. When J. C. Penney personally inspected his company's stores and the cleanliness of their sidewalks, he was telling employees that attractive, inviting stores are important to the business. Executives can be quite unaware that they are shaping the culture, but many do so consciously by promoting their agendas at every opportunity over a period of years.

Human Resource Systems

Human resource systems provide the people, skills, and systems to facilitate and reinforce the behavior required. The importance of human resource management to strategy implementation can be seen in the statement of Reginald H. Jones, former CEO of General Electric: "When we realized that they [GE's SBUs] were going to have quite different missions we also realized we had to have quite different people running them."[41] This statement recognizes the need to match a company's human assets with its strategy. To put quite different people in charge requires changing the person assigned to the job or changing the behavior of the person in the position. The task of human resource management is to provide the support to top management to do either. It does this through systems for planning, staffing (selection and placement), appraisal, compensation, and rewards. Figure 7.1 shows how the human resource components reinforce each other to provide an integrated service to strategic management.

Planning

If human resource management is to play a major role in strategic implementation, it must be linked to strategic management early in the process. Top executives need

Figure 7.1 Integration of Human Resource Components with Strategic Management

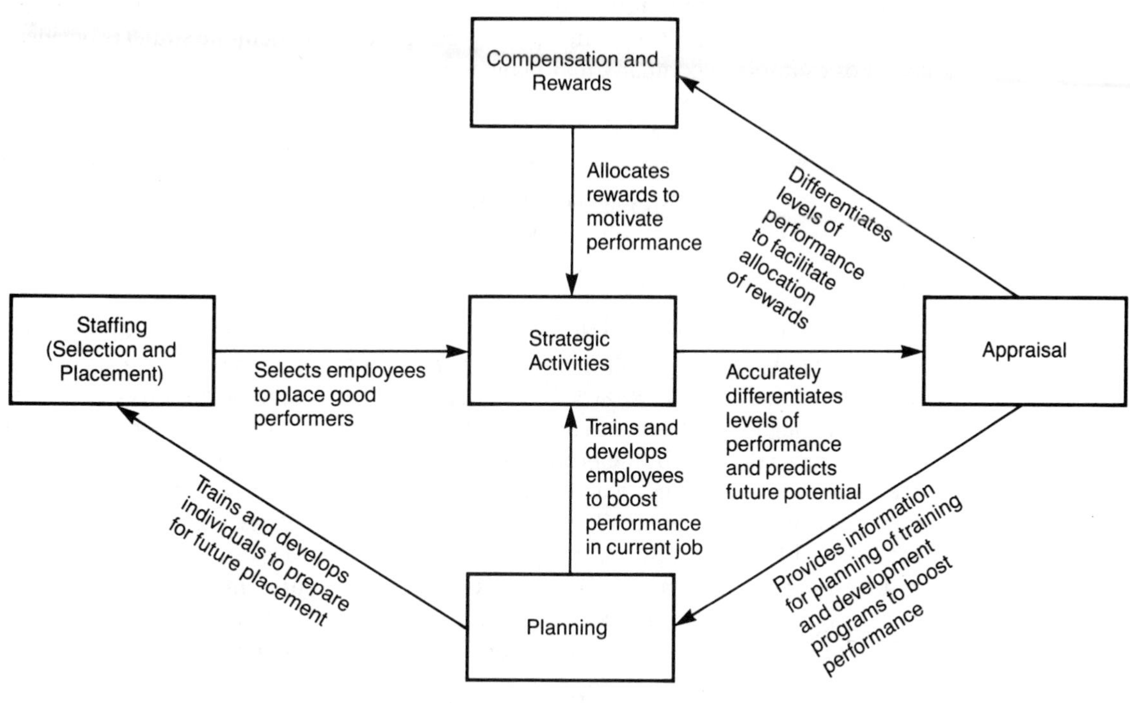

Source: Noel M. Tichy, "Managing Change Strategically: The Technical, Political, and Cultural Keys," p. 78. Adapted, by permission of publisher, from *Organizational Dynamics*, Autumn/1982. © 1982 American Management Association, New York. All rights reserved.

to understand the value of considering human resource factors in the strategic management process. In companies like IBM, Whirlpool, and Merck, **human resource planning** is conducted as a part of business planning. Many, like Hewlett-Packard, include among their company goals specific people objectives.

Inclusion of human resource planning integrates the company's functional plans and activities into strategic plans in a manner consistent with the thrust of business plans. It also makes valuable contributions to the premises of the strategic plan. For example, knowledge of the company culture may help in assessing the feasibility of a strategy. Knowledge of the skills available within the company and of the outside labor market provides a basis for assessing the cost of alternatives. Human resource planning also contributes to environmental scanning with information such as trends in education, labor markets, and laws and regulations. Internal information on productivity, absenteeism, turnover, employee relations, and persistent people problems also may be valuable. These are only a few examples of the contributions human resource planning can make to identifying and assessing the company's environment: its strengths, weaknesses, opportunities, and threats.

Perhaps the primary value of including human resource management in strategic planning is to assure that human resource management understands the intent of top managers as it develops its own functional strategy to implement the strategic business plan. For example, a company that plans to incorporate increased electronic controls in its products, as did Whirlpool in the 1980s, will be affected by demographic changes. A growing shortage of electrical and computer engineers brought the company into strong competition for graduate engineers and required more use of paraprofessionals. Knowing future product plans can allow human resource management to develop plans for recruiting and retaining the needed employees.

Staffing

Staffing involves recruiting, selection, and placement of persons with appropriate competencies needed to fulfill their roles. This activity can be particularly significant in the implementation of strategy. Many strategic moves involve growth either internally through expansion or externally through acquisition. As the firm grows, it will need new talent to fill the positions. Human resource management must forecast what skills will be needed, where the jobs will be, how many will be required, and when personnel must be available. It must determine if these requirements can be met from within the company and, if not, whether programs can develop the skills or the company must recruit new people. Human resource management can also develop systems to plan the careers of individuals so they will receive the experience and training needed to prepare them for openings that may occur.

Selecting Persons to Implement Strategy Of particular interest in the implementation of strategy is to have the right people placed in key positions. General managers, vice presidents, and division presidents can be selected for their ability to implement specific strategies. Criteria can include experience, education, or personal qualities. In addition, because persons in these positions will significantly shape the strategy as they follow their own preferences, one of the ways to shape strategy is to put persons with known preferences in key positions.[42] The head of an SBU, for example, will have considerable influence over which projects are proposed, how budgets are prepared, the functions and products that will be emphasized, and whom he or she selects for key positions. For a discussion of how two large companies matched top-level hiring decisions with their strategies, see The Strategic Application "Exxon and TRW Select Their CEOs."

One way to match persons to strategy requirements is to use their functional background. If strategy is based on company strength and distinctive competence in certain functional areas, then this background of key executives may be important to carrying out the strategy.[43] For example, a firm that wishes to grow through product innovation and related diversification and that uses internal product development to do so is likely to have competence in R&D and marketing.

At the corporate level, it has been argued that the functional experience of the CEO is related to how a firm pursues diversification. A firm following a strategy of unrelated diversification might be more likely to have a CEO with a background in finance, accounting, or law, because this strategy is usually accomplished through

STRATEGIC APPLICATIONS

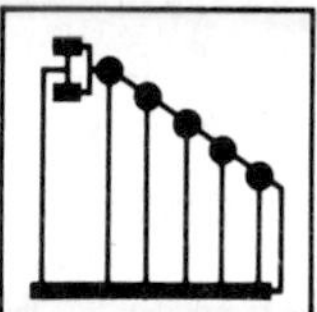

Exxon and TRW Select Their CEOs

Exxon, one of the largest companies in the world, was starting to fall behind competitors in some areas. Many competitors were cutting out fat and restructuring. In contrast, life at Exxon was formal, gentlemanly, and secure. As one observer put it, Exxon "hired quality people and gave them comfortable, high paying jobs in a protected environment that oozed arrogance."

When it came time to replace the aristocratic Clifton C. Garvin as chairman, the board chose Lawrence G. Rawl. His aversion to bureaucracy and inclination to dissent and question were well suited to the company's needs. He cut costs, focused the company on the energy business, and cut bureaucracy. His blunt, direct style focused on the inside workings of the company. The directors picked him because they knew he could get the job done.

TRW had different needs. A conglomerate with diverse businesses, it needed a chairman and CEO with flexible skills. TRW also was a possible takeover candidate and was running into legal difficulties with the Defense Department and General Accounting Office. To take on these challenges, TRW's board picked a lawyer, Joseph T. Gorman. Known as hard working and well prepared, Gorman seeks information until he can make an informed decision. His flexibility and legal background are suited to handling the diverse businesses and expected legal problems.

Source: John A. Byrne, "The Rebel Shaking Up Exxon," *Business Week*, July 18, 1988, 104–111; and Stephen Phillips and David Giffiths, "The Legal Eagle Who Will Rule the Roost at TRW," *Business Week*, March 21, 1988, 100–104.

acquisition, and managing the acquisition of a portfolio of businesses emphasizes financial skills, negotiations, and legal issues. One study reported that firms having CEOs with finance, accounting, or law backgrounds tended to use acquisition for diversification, but firms using internal diversification had CEOs with production or marketing backgrounds.[44] However, another study did not find any relationship between CEO background and means of diversification, but did find that when CEO experience and strategy were matched, the companies achieved better performance on certain financial measures.[45] This may mean that whether matching a person's background to strategy pays off depends on which particular objectives the firm wants to achieve with its strategy.

In matching general managers' backgrounds to strategy at the SBU or divisional level, it makes sense that a growth strategy seeking a larger market share would call for strong marketing skills. Similarly, a strategy to milk a cash cow product or division calls for cost control and maximizing cash flow. Techniques and experience might be best supplied by persons with accounting/finance or production backgrounds. A low-cost competitive position might call for the same skills. Other individual and background characteristics that have been suggested as important in obtaining a good fit between person and strategy include background characteristics such as education and age, whether the person comes from within the company, personality factors such as willingness to take risk, and managerial skills needed for organizational development.

Our discussion so far has focused on the CEO or general manager, but these positions may not be the only ones of importance in implementing strategy. In many cases the important match may be a team with the needed qualities. Increasingly, companies are making use of teams or multiple executives to run their affairs.[46] Sharing responsibilities and the task makes it less critical that any one person have all the necessary qualities. General Electric, International Harvester, Du Pont, and Xerox are just a few of the companies using this approach in one form or another.

Randall S. Schuler and Susan E. Jackson have suggested a way to link strategy and needed behaviors.[47] Using Michael Porter's three competitive strategies, they infer that each strategy needs a different set of role behaviors to implement it. Each of the strategies and its matching set of behaviors are described in Table 7.3. The role of human resource management would be to locate persons who can play these roles and help develop the culture and human resource systems to shape such behavior.

Developing Employees The optimum source of talent for the future of the company is found in its current employees. The company can provide for the human resources it will need in the future by investing in their development today. Training and development can be linked to strategic implementation by providing the training required for new skills and behaviors that will be needed to implement the strategy. The development activities might range from managerial training in the cultural

Table 7.3 Required Role Behaviors for Three Strategy Types

	Strategy Type		
Type of Role Behavior	**Innovation**	**Cost Reduction**	**Quality Enhancement**
Creativity versus predictability	Highly creative	Relatively repetitive and predictable	Relatively repetitive and predictable
Length of focus	Longer term	Rather short-term	Long-term or intermediate
Cooperation versus independence	Relatively high level of cooperative, interdependent behavior	Primarily autonomous or individual activity	Modest amount of cooperative, interdependent behavior
Degree of concern for quality	Moderate	Modest	High
Degree of concern for quantity of output	Moderate	High	Modest
Concern for process versus concern for results	Equal	Primarily for results	Primarily for process
Degree of risk taking	Relatively high	Low	Low
Orientation toward change	High tolerance for ambiguity and unpredictability	High comfort with stability	Commitment to the goals of the organization

Source: Adapted from Randall S. Schuler and Susan E. Jackson, "Linking Competitive Strategies with Human Resource Management Practices," *Academy of Management Executive* 1 (August 1987): 207–219. Adapted with permission.

values desired to teaching the use of new telecommunications equipment to improve customer service. Other development activities include teaching employees how to service new products or providing language and cultural training for employees being sent overseas.

Helping employees prepare for placement in future roles can motivate them. It can also ensure that the company will have talented persons when replacements are needed. One textile company, for example, identified 40 individuals with potential for top management and general manager positions. It assigned a full-time development officer to counsel and work with these future executives. The development officer planned activities such as off-site workshops, university educational programs, and individually tailored work experiences to prepare these employees for their future roles. A company that decided investing in its young employees is the most socially responsible thing to do is described in the Strategic Application "Burger King Invests in Its Own."

One question is whether the requirements in the future will match the talent developed. In a long-term, stable strategy, the future matchup is easier to achieve, because the future needs are easier to predict. But the future is not always so predictable. Witness the change that occurred under chairman Lawrence G. Rawl at Exxon. Employees prepared for a career in a slow-moving, protected environment. When Rawl changed the norm of expected behavior by making the company leaner and more focused, these employees needed to adopt new skills and attitudes.

In the short term, a change in strategy can upset the career plans of individuals and the development activities of human resource management. But if human resource management is included in strategic management, it can develop plans in light of strategic considerations. Also, much of the experience, education, and talent the company has invested in will be transferable. Technical skill and knowledge may become obsolete or inappropriate, but people can relearn.

STRATEGIC APPLICATIONS: SOCIAL RESPONSIBILITY

Burger King Invests in Its Own

After 14 years of sponsoring a float in the Orange Bowl parade, Burger King dropped out. The company announced it would instead use the funds to expand its contributions to support education in its headquarters city of Miami, Florida.

Burger King's charitable budget had been approximately $250,000. This change made that budget at least $2 million, the bulk going to educational programs. According to the announcements, most of the money would go to high school students who work at Burger King. For each student/worker who maintains a C average, Burger King would deposit $500 in an education trust fund for every six months he or she worked.

Source: M. R. Moskowitz, "Company Performance Roundup," *Business and Society Review* (Winter 1985): 74.

Appraisal and Reward

Appraisal and reward of performance tell members what behavior is important. They also reinforce the proper behavior, focus behavior, and provide encouragement through incentives.[48] However, if the system is deficient, it may shape behavior in inappropriate or even counterproductive directions. To avoid this, management must define the behavior relevant to achieving and implementing strategy, accurately measure it, and reward executives for the proper performance.

The criteria used to appraise performance must reflect strategic goals and plans. For example, if part of a company's strategy is to penetrate new markets, one of the criteria for evaluating performance of division and marketing managers might be the market share achieved in target markets. For territory managers and salespersons, a performance criterion could be the extent to which they meet sales goals. Another criterion might be the number of new customers, and salespersons might be rated on sales calls to new customers.

For this to happen, managers at each level should translate the strategic goals and plans into performance criteria that are consistent with the strategic plan. Managers must communicate to each person what he or she should be doing for the unit to contribute to the overall strategy.

Executive Compensation

A key part of implementation is the executive compensation system used to motivate behavior. In most theories of motivation, the underlying assumption is that rewards should be tied to performance in order to achieve the best performance.[49] Unfortunately, reward and performance are not always clearly connected, and there is no one best compensation system to use in making the connection. Executives are expected to produce both short-term operating results and actions that lead to implementation of long-run strategies. Often actions that will produce superior operating results can detract from strategic results. In one case, a company was under contract to pay a bonus based on net profits. The division manager neglected plant maintenance nearly to the point of ruining the production facility. Likewise, achieving maximum results from a division can come at the expense of cooperation with other divisions that would maximize results for the whole firm.

Compensation plans can be powerful tools in implementing strategy when management is astute in developing them. A good plan should achieve several goals:

- Define proper performance behavior
- Be difficult to manipulate
- Allow for executive control of the basis of performance
- Measure performance on relevant results
- Use readily understandable measures and permit easy conversion of measures to incentives
- Tie compensation to performance

Designing reward systems that will compensate executives for all the behaviors required is difficult. Most compensation systems are aimed at several objectives, such as retaining executives, meeting competitive industry rates, and seniority, as well as rewarding performance. Table 7.4 summarizes the use of compensation packages for executives. The table shows that the majority of U.S. companies offer their top executives a bonus, which is typically 20 percent of their total compensation. Much of an executive's compensation is not directly related to performance or achievement of strategy. Stock options (a right to buy stock at a set market price), for example, may be granted over a five- to ten-year period and exercised many years later when the current price is high. This may provide a huge bonus unrelated to the individual's current performance. Currently, more than 40 percent of a typical chief executive's total pay comes from options and other long-term incentive plans tied to a company's stock price.[50]

Criticisms Executive compensation plans have received considerable criticism. The criticism has been directed at the poor association between reward and performance and the lack of emphasis on long-term results. For example, consider the following observations:

- Over a recent ten-year period, compensation for senior management of companies in the Standard and Poor's 400 increased 10 percent in real dollars while total shareholder value decreased 2 percent in real dollars.[51]

Table 7.4 Compensation Packages for Top Management

	Direct Cash—Performance Related		**Deferred Cash—Partially Performance Related**	**Noncash—Not Performance Related**	
	Base Salary	**Bonus**	**Stock Options**	**Fringe Benefits**	**Perks**
CEO					
Frequency of Use	100	55–85%	70–85%	100%	100%
Feasible Range	100	Up to 60% of base	Unlimited	—	—
Percent of Total Compensation	40%	20%	15%	20%	5%
Top VP					
Frequency of Use	100%	55–85%	70–85%	100%	100%
Feasible Range	80%	Up to 40% of base	Unlimited	—	—
Percent of Total Compensation	50%	15%	8%	24%	3%

Source: A. Nash, *Managerial Compensation: Highlights of the Literature,* Work in America Institute Studies in Productivity No. 15 (Scarsdale, N.Y.: Work in America Institute, 1980), 25.

- Texaco's CEO earned the third highest compensation among the large oil companies in 1981, while the firm's performance was one of the worst.[52]
- Executives are not infrequently granted packages offering sizable severance pay (golden parachutes) in case they fail to prevent a takeover by another firm.
- Annual bonus plans usually provide a greater percentage of total compensation than long-term incentives for CEOs and profit-center managers, thus rewarding them primarily for one-year earnings.[53]

A heavy emphasis on short-term performance such as return on investment or profits can discourage investment. Long-term strategic programs can be neglected in favor of annual results. By not investing in working capital, R&D projects, or capital assets, managers can make their current returns look good but detract from the future. In addition, firms typically use accounting measures to evaluate performance, but strategy and performance are best assessed in terms of the creation of economic value for the stockholder.[54]

There are also problems when only financial targets are used to measure strategic progress. Not only are appropriate measures difficult to use at the divisional level, but progress toward a strategy cannot be measured by financial targets alone. Progress on a product development program may not show up in earnings until several years after it is completed. In addition, R&D expenditures are treated as expenses rather than as an investment, which can encourage cost cutting if an executive wants to show short-term profits. Are there to be no rewards for this work for four to eight years? Even if that is the case, measurement is still needed to control this part of the strategy. In many cases, a strategy-oriented objective-setting process or one that measures progress toward milestones is as appropriate as financial targets in setting compensation.

Problems and concerns such as these have led to several **compensation plans** that try to overcome such obstacles. In recent years, companies have been looking for ways to connect rewards to earnings as well as long-term performance. Walt Disney Company, for example, pays its CEO an annual bonus of 2 percent of any net income the company earns over a 9 percent return on equity. Other compensation plans that have been adopted in an effort to overcome some of these criticisms include the weighted factors plan, multiyear evaluation, separate strategic and operations evaluation, and economic value performance.

Weighted Factors Plan Paul J. Sonich describes a company that wanted to tie long-term strategy to operations. The executive committee had identified programs to achieve specific strategic objectives and had established priority funding for them. The plan was almost defeated by the short-term orientation of the company's managers. The managers' bonuses were determined by the return on assets and budget performance of their strategic business units. The managers had no enthusiasm for the long-term programs. The company categorized the SBUs as high-, medium-, and low-growth SBUs. The performance of high-growth units was judged on market share, sales growth, designated future payoff, and progress toward strategic projects. Low-growth units' performance was judged on their return on assets and cash generation.

The medium-growth units were judged on a combination of these factors. One year later, management's behavior had adapted to the new system.[55]

Diversified firms, with a portfolio of businesses following different strategies, need a way to adjust their plans to the different strategies of each unit. Units with high-growth strategies can be treated differently than mature, cash-generating units, for example. Performance measures such as cash flow, market share, product development, strategic development programs, return on assets, or even creation of shareholder value can be applied to all units but adjusted to each situation by weighting each factor differently according to its importance for each unit's performance. This is called a weighted factors plan.

An example of how to weight factors appears in Table 7.5. In this example, increasing market share is much more important to the performance of a unit pursuing high growth than it is to a unit with a mature product. The unit with a mature product is expected to generate cash for the company; the high-growth unit is not expected to generate cash but to use strategic funds to further its growth. Thus, the weights of the factors reflect the different objectives and strategies.

Multiyear Evaluation To encourage a long-term perspective in decision making and performance, companies can use multiyear periods in their evaluation. They set goals for multiyear periods, typically three to five years, and give rewards for achieving targeted goals over these periods. Typical of such rewards would be a deferred stock plan or an option to buy stock at a given price. A cash bonus could be another type of reward for reaching a multiyear goal.

Each year, as the firm works out a new business plan, it can extend the multiyear period and therefore maintain a constant long-term interest for the manager. In this case, the firm must find a reasonable way to determine how to weight and convert

Table 7.5 Weighted Factors Method Adjusted for Strategy

Strategy Category	Key Factors	Weight (%)[a]
Cash cow	Return on equity	40
	Use of strategic funds	10
	Cash generation	40
	Product development	10
Star	Return on equity	15
	Use of strategic funds	45
	Cash generation	5
	Product development	35
Dog	Return on equity	45
	Use of strategic funds	5
	Cash generation	50
	Product development	0

[a]Weights assigned are arbitrary for illustration.

the goal achievement into real or imaginary stock. For example, over a three-year period, the firm may accumulate rights for the manager to purchase stock in an account. The purchase price of the stock might be set at a level equal to its price at the start of the period. Options could be granted each year, with a bonus at the end of the period if the manager reaches the long-term goal. This approach requires the company to decide when and how to vest the executive's "ownership" in the firm.

Separate Strategic and Operations Evaluation In many companies, executives must focus on current operations with a short-term time span and also on strategic concerns, which are more long-term. Lumping current operations together with investments in the future gives a manager some incentive to use strategic funds to make current operations look good. If funds for current operations run short because of a crisis or underfunding, managers are under pressure to use the funds targeted for strategic plans to finance current operations. Of course, this misplaced incentive would be aggravated if the performance evaluation is based on short-term criteria.

To discourage executives from focusing only on short-term operations, companies separate evaluation of strategic performance from evaluation of current operations. One such approach is to separate the funds designated for maintaining current operations from those to be used for strategic development. The organization can treat other development costs, such as R&D costs, similarly. Separating the funds and performance evaluation for the long term and the short term encourages the manager to invest in the future while still managing for maximum current performance.

A variation on this approach calls for measuring progress toward strategic targets separately from the results of current operations, and separately determining incentive awards for current operations and strategic progress.[56] The strategy can be translated into strategic thrusts, which can be separated into programs. Programs by nature incorporate a set of steps, schedules, and assignments. These can form the basis for measuring progress, and an executive's contribution can be assessed before the strategic change is complete. By using such measures, the company can assess strategic progress over a shorter period and tie it to incentives such as bonuses.

The Union Pacific Corporation has developed a new plan to encourage its top 23 executives to focus on strategy. The company puts cash into a reserve account when its stock price reaches certain levels and remains there for 60 days. At the $100 a share level, it puts in $17 million. At $120 a share, the amount is an additional $22.7 million. If the targets are reached, the money will be paid out after five years as bonuses. Union Pacific's stock was at $65 in April 1988. The company hoped its strategic incentive plan would encourage executives to become more entrepreneurial.

Economic Value Performance It has been argued that the most valid basis for evaluating strategic progress is the extent to which the strategy creates economic value for stockholders. If this is so, the creation of economic value is a logical way to evaluate executive performance. However, this approach is not typical of executive compensation plans, as indicated by the fact that CEOs receive raises of less than 6 cents for each $1,000 of increased shareholder wealth.[57] Nevertheless, Rappaport has proposed that executive compensation plans based on creation of economic value overcome the major problems found in many compensation plans such as reliance on short-term performance criteria.[58]

Management can increase economic return by increasing earnings, increasing real return on equity, or both. The economic return is calculated for each year. Then the average economic return for a base period is compared to the average economic return for a performance period to determine the increase. For example, the period 1983 through 1986 could be the base period, and 1987 through 1990 the performance period. The average economic return per share is calculated for each period. Any increase for the performance period over the base period indicates the extent to which management has increased economic value.

Value contribution tables can be created to convert performance into incentives for executives. Units can be assigned to a position, SBU, or executive based on its impact on the economic return, position within the company, and so forth. The compensation can be made contingent on achieving three- to five-year goals, and the amount per share or unit can be set before the period used for evaluation or by the market price per share at the end of the period. The compensation can be based on the extent to which actual contribution meets the targeted contribution.

This incentive plan seems to work best with top managers because it best fits their responsibilities. However, it is often possible to measure economic return for subsidiaries and divisions. To the extent they are autonomously managed, return is an appropriate measure of performance and a useful incentive.

Plans based on creation of economic value have the major advantages of tying compensation to the same criteria used to select and evaluate strategies and providing an incentive to select and implement strategies in the best long-term interests of the company. Such plans should also be subject to less gaming by executives trying to manipulate the numbers.

Whatever approach the company uses in designing a compensation system, top management should remember that compensation is not the only reward that executives seek. Greater challenge, the opportunity for promotion, and the chance to prove one's ability are only a few of the incentives that strongly motivate functional executives and general managers. Promotions may be the strongest signal a company can give to aspiring employees as to the behavior that it considers important. The great effort that Lee Iacocca expended in revitalizing Chrysler cannot be explained by compensation alone. Nor can compensation explain the frustration and willingness to speak out that Ross Perot experienced in his brief tenure at General Motors. Total reliance on compensation systems may eventually lead to failure because the firm cannot reward all behaviors that are important to the firm, nor can it serve as a source of all the powerful motivations of an executive.

Also, provision of rewards is only part of the **performance review process**. The process provides the opportunity to review performance and provides feedback on correct and incorrect actions. This can be a chance to counsel and coach managers on how to improve their performance. The reviewer can gain information that may help improve strategic plans or identify what can be done to help the manager improve performance. The entire performance review process is one more opportunity for an executive to improve and to work his or her agenda in the ongoing effort to implement strategic plans.

Summary

The implementation of a strategy, especially a significantly different one, depends on the way the organization's members behave. Human factors through which a company can implement its strategy include organization culture, leadership patterns, and human resource management systems. Successful implementation requires that all these forces be aligned with the strategy.

Corporate culture provides a common set of beliefs and values that help to shape the behavior of company members. When the culture is supportive, the behavior of members is consistent with that required to make the strategy work. Culture defines and reinforces behavior in detailed and often subtle ways that the conscious, rational, and formal corporate systems cannot replace. But these systems can be used to shape the culture. To shape corporate culture, top executives must first understand the company strategy and the present corporate culture. They must also define the kind of behavior that is required to support the new strategy and determine what must be changed to develop a supportive culture. The company can then plan a program to develop the desired culture.

Leadership is critical in implementing strategy. Executives must provide leadership consistently and persistently in the context of their position and responsibilities. Successful leaders work their agenda at every opportunity as their roles bring them into interaction with others. Major change in strategy requires transformational leadership. Such leaders provide a vision of what the company's future can bring. They turn the company vision into causes and develop programs to turn the causes into actions. They also promote, shape, and protect the corporate culture through how they spend their time, what they consider important, what they pay attention to, and what they reward.

Human resource management systems provide, develop, and reward the people needed to carry out the company's strategy. To provide the kind of support top management needs in implementation, human resource management should be integrated into the strategic management process at the planning stage. Early integration allows human resource management to create programs to develop, staff, and motivate the needed personnel. Correspondingly, top management should assume major responsibility in selecting managers to carry out the strategy as well as in coaching and motivating their performance.

Questions

1. Why is corporate culture important in the implementation of corporate strategy? If the company's culture does not match its strategy, how can the culture be adapted to the strategy?

2. What is the role of leadership in implementing strategy? In other words, what do managers do when they provide leadership to carry out strategy?

3. Are an aligned culture and good leadership enough to motivate people to change their behavior in ways that will help to implement a strategy? Why or why not? If not, what else is required?

4. If a company's strategy is going to require its employees to behave in new ways, what can the company do to obtain the different behavior? What role do human resource management systems play in obtaining the behavior needed to implement a strategy?

5. How can executive compensation systems encourage or discourage the implementation of strategy?

Notes

1. Thomas J. Peters and Robert H. Waterman, Jr., *In Search of Excellence: Lessons from America's Best-Run Companies* (New York: Harper & Row, 1982). See also Howard Schwartz and Stanley M. Davis, "Matching Corporate Culture and Business Strategy," *Organizational Dynamics* 10 (Summer 1981): 30–48; and Noel M. Tichy, "Managing Change Strategically: The Technical, Political and Cultural Keys," *Organizational Dynamics* 11 (Autumn 1982): 59–80.

2. Kathleen L. Gregory, "Native View Paradigms: Multiple Cultures and Culture Conflicts in Organizations," *Administrative Science Quarterly* 28 (September 1983): 359–376.

3. Ibid.

4. Peters and Waterman, *In Search of Excellence*, 164–165.

5. Linda Smircich, "Concepts of Culture and Organizational Analysis," *Administrative Science Quarterly* 28 (September 1983): 339–358.

6. Peters and Waterman, *In Search of Excellence, xx.*

7. "Changing Corporate Culture," *Business Week*, May 14, 1984, 130–138.

8. Alan L. Wilkins and Nigel J. Bristow, "For Successful Organization Culture, Honor Your Past," *Academy of Management Executive* 1 (August 1987): 221–229.

9. Jay B. Barney, "Organizational Culture: Can It Be a Source of Sustained Competitive Advantage?" *Academy of Management Review* 11 (July 1986): 656–665.

10. Daniel Carroll, "A Disappointing Search for Excellence," *Harvard Business Review* 61 (December 1983): 78–88.

11. "Who's Excellent Now," *Business Week*, November 5, 1984, 76–88.

12. Michael A. Hitt and R. Duane Ireland, "Peters and Waterman Revisited: The Unending Quest for Excellence," *Academy of Management Executive* 1 (May 1987): 91–98.

13. Ibid., 95.

14. Schwartz and Davis, "Matching Corporate Culture and Business Strategy," 30–48.

15. Robert N. Beck, "Visions, Values, and Strategies: Changing Attitudes and Culture," *Academy of Management Executive* 1 (February 1987): 33–41.

16. This approach has been suggested in both of the following writings: Schwartz and Davis, "Matching Corporate Culture and Business Strategy"; and John A. Pearce II and Richard B. Robinson, Jr., *Strategic Management*, 2d ed. (Homewood, Ill.: Irwin, 1982), 348–349.

17. Kurt Lewin, "Group Decision and Social Change," in *Readings in Social Psychology*, eds. E. E. McCoby, T. M. Newcomb, and E. L. Hartley (New York: Holt, Rinehart and Winston, 1958), 197–211.

18. Beck, "Visions, Values, and Strategies."

19. John A. Byrne, "The Rebel Shaking Up Exxon," *Business Week*, July 18, 1988, 104–111.

20. Ibid.

21. Tony Velocci, "Bringing a Company Back from the Brink," *Nation's Business*, March 1982, 77–78.

22. Ibid., 78.

23. Ibid.

24. R. M. Stodgill, *Handbook of Leadership* (New York: The Free Press, 1974).

25. Henry Mintzberg, *The Nature of Managerial Work* (New York: Harper and Row, 1973).

26. Ibid., 130.

27. Ibid., 28–53, 169–173.

28. Ibid., 35.

29. John P. Kotter, *The General Managers* (New York: The Free Press, 1982). Kotter was also interested in the background and personality of the general managers, their behavior on the job, and the results of their behavior.

30. Ibid., 127.

31. James McGregor Burns, *Leadership* (New York: Harper & Row, 1978), 10–40.

32. Noel M. Tichy and David O. Ulrich, "SMR Forum: The Leadership Challenge—A Call for the Transformational Leader," *Sloan Management Review* 26 (Fall 1984): 59–68.

33. Bernard M. Bass, "Leadership: Good, Better, Best," *Organizational Dynamics* 13 (Winter 1985): 26–40.

34. W. Warner Burke, "A Conversation with John Carter," *Academy of Management Executive* 1 (November 1987): 337.

35. Bass, "Leadership: Good, Better, Best."

36. Thomas J. Peters, "Leadership: Sad Facts and Silver Linings," *Harvard Business Review* 57 (November–December 1979): 164–172.

37. Robert H. Waterman, Jr., *The Renewal Factor* (New York: Bantam Books, 1987), excerpted in *Business Week*, September 14, 1987, 120.

38. Velocci, "Bringing a Company Back from the Brink."

39. See Philip Selznick, *Leadership in Administration* (Evanston, Ill.: Row, Peterson, 1957); Peters, "Leadership: Sad Facts and Silver Linings"; and Tichy and Ulrich, "The Leadership Challenge—A Call for Transformational Leadership."

40. Burke, "A Conversation with John Carter."

41. C. Frombrun, "An Interview with Reginald Jones," *Organizational Dynamics* 10 (Winter 1982): 46.

42. Boris Yavitz and William H. Newman, *Strategy in Action* (New York: The Free Press, 1982), 162.

43. M. A. Hitt, D. R. Ireland, and K. A. Palia, "Industrial Firm's Grand Strategy and Functional Importance: Moderating Effects of Technology and Uncertainty," *Academy of Management Journal* 25 (July–September 1982): 265–298; and M. A. Hitt and D. R. Ireland, "Corporate Distinctive Competence Strategy, Industry and Performance," *Strategic Management Journal* 6 (1985): 273–293.

44. J. H. Song, "Diversification Strategies and the Experience of Top Executives in Large Firms," *Strategic Management Journal* 3 (October–December 1982): 377–380.

45. Richard Reed and Margaret Reed, "Internal and Acquisitive Diversification: CEO Experience and Synergy Effects," Unpublished working paper, Washington State University, Pullman, Wash.

46. Stanley C. Vance, *Corporate Leadership: Boards, Directors and Strategy* (New York: McGraw-Hill, 1983).

47. Randall S. Schuler and Susan E. Jackson, "Linking Competitive Strategies with Human Resource Management Practices," *Academy of Management Executive* 1 (August 1987): 207–219.

48. There are many considerations in determining compensation for executives. Here we focus only on performance and strategy implementation.

49. Gerardo Rivera Ungson and Richard M. Steers, "Motivation and Politics in Executive Compensation," *Academy of Management Review* 9 (April 1984): 313–323.

50. John A. Byrne, Keith H. Hammonds, Ronald Grover, James B. Treece, and Jo Ellen Davis, "Who Made the Most—and Why," *Business Week*, May 2, 1988, 50–56.

51. Louis J. Brindisi, Jr., "Why Executive Compensation Programs Go Wrong," *The Wall Street Journal*, June 14, 1982, 20.

52. C. Loomis, "The Madness of Executive Compensation," *Fortune*, July 12, 1982, 42–52.

53. Alfred Rappaport, "How to Design Value-Contributing Executive Incentives," *Journal of Business Strategy* 4 (Fall 1983): 49–59.

54. Alfred Rappaport, "Corporate Performance Standards and Shareholder Value," *Journal of Business Strategy* 3 (Spring 1983): 28–38.

55. Paul J. Stonich, "Using Rewards in Implementing Strategy," *Strategic Management Journal* 2 (July–September 1981): 345–352.

56. Yavitz and Newman, *Strategy in Action*, 179–181.
57. John A. Byrne, "Executive Pay: Who Got What in '86," *Business Week*, May 4, 1987, 50–58.
58. Rappaport, "How to Design Value-Contributing Executive Incentives."

Case for Discussion

Rooster Industries

Rooster Industries, which bears its founder's nickname, has operations in several distinct but technologically related industries with total annual sales of $800 million. All its products use microelectronic circuits, which it acquires from other manufacturers. It performs forming and assembly operations itself. Its own manufacturing of parts—about 40 percent of the end value—involves the shaping of metal and the injection molding of plastics. Each product line is sold to quite different customers.

The company has one manufacturing facility, which produces all the products. The development and marketing functions are handled by three separate divisions, each formed around separate product-markets. The products are sold through transfer pricing to the business divisions. The divisions have always been closely coordinated with manufacturing to provide service to the customer. The company's products have an enviable reputation for quality but are not always seen as being at the leading edge of technology or innovation. All the divisions work closely with their customers to solve customers' problems and they have a high customer retention rate.

The oldest division is the commercial division. It has a dominant market share within the U.S. market, which is growing moderately. The division expects growing competition from Japanese producers. It contributes 65 percent of the company's sales and about 60 percent of its profits. The defense division has recently experienced rapid growth, but its history over the past ten years has been one of moderate but sporadic growth. The new-technology division has experienced rapid growth in an expanding market. There has been a growing demand from its customers for products not within its current portfolio or based on the company's basic technological expertise. In all divisions' markets, the barriers to entry are too low to stop a determined competitor.

The company's strategy has been essentially the same for ten years: to provide the best-quality product at the lowest price to all customers in the industries in which the company competes. Manufacturing has emphasized automation to produce the lowest cost at the defined level of quality. Divisions emphasize delivery and service to the customer. The company has always been rather paternalistic toward its employees. The average employee finds it a comfortable place to work.

Almost all of top management have come from the ranks of the commercial division or manufacturing. None of the founding family members are currently involved in the company. The general manager of the commercial division will retire next year. The president and CEO is 62 and plans to retire at age 65 in accordance with company policy. He is currently negotiating to acquire a $50 million firm engaged in the development of genetically engineered products directed mainly at chemical and biological waste. Recently the president has become concerned about his successor and who will replace the retiring commercial division manager.

Discussion Questions

1. What kinds of issues face this company in the next five years?

2. What types of leaders would make the best match for each of the soon-to-be vacant positions?

3. What kind of executive compensation plan would you develop for this company?

Chapter 8

Control of Strategy

We are all controlled by the world in which we live, and part of that world has been and will be constructed by men. The question is this: are we to be controlled by accidents, by tyrants, or by ourselves in effective cultural design?

—Burrhus Frederic Skinner, Cumulative Record [3rd], 1972, Chapter 1.

Learning Objectives

- To understand the process of control and why it is important.
- To distinguish strategic control from operational control.
- To learn principles of strategic control and corrective action.
- To know how to select and use the appropriate responsibility center.
- To learn how an organization can use budgets for strategic control.
- To learn how strategic planning techniques can be used for control.

CONCEPTUALLY, strategic control is the final part of the strategic management process. The process is cyclical, and strategic control feeds back into strategic planning. Practically, strategic control is therefore the basis for a new cycle of strategic management.

This chapter brings into focus the control stage of the strategic management process. First the chapter describes the actions involved in control and how the organization uses control. Then the discussion shifts specifically to the nature of strategic control and the qualities that differentiate it from the control of ongoing operations. The remainder of the chapter presents ways to implement and use strategic control techniques.

The Use of Control

An essential part of successfully implementing strategy is the exercise of control. Not only can strategy fail because the strategy itself is poor, but it can fail because economic, political, technological, and social forces in the environment have changed.

In addition, the actors in the system cannot always be depended upon to behave in the firm's best interest. They may not understand what is expected, or they may lack the information or ability to do what is expected. They may also be unwilling. Because events and activities cannot always be expected to go according to plan, the organization must exercise control.

The Control Process

The process of **control** involves what a manager does to ensure that actions conform to planned activities. A simple control system is the temperature control in a building. A thermostat records the temperature in the building, compares it to a preset standard, and switches the heating or cooling system off or on. Thus, when there is a deviation from the plan (the desired temperature), an action is taken to bring performance back into conformance with the plan. A more complex control is the budget system. Plans are converted into resource requirements and allocated to units, projects, and programs in the firm. Expenditures that deviate from this plan call for reviews by managers, who decide what action should be taken.

The control process is highly interrelated with the other management functions. It is particularly close to planning because plans—strategic and operational—are the foundation upon which controls are based. By monitoring actions and performance, management can determine the extent to which the plans are being achieved. If there are deviations, management must determine the reasons for the deviations and decide what corrective action is needed to bring the organization back on course. Management may decide to change the plans or to renew its effort to keep the company on course. The information on progress thus may become feedback for new planning.

The control process can be broken down into a few steps that are always involved:

1. *Establish standards and measurements of performance.* Determine clear standards for measuring the outcome of plans and ways that these can be measured. Goals and objectives should point the way to standards.

2. *Measure performance.* Collect and collate the information needed to determine whether deviations from plans are occurring. The information should also facilitate the manager's decision concerning any needed corrective action.

3. *Interpret information and take corrective action.* Compare performance with standards; if deviations are occurring, determine why. Here the manager must investigate the difficulties, decide how to solve the problem, and implement a solution.

The Need for Control

The need for control is a logical extension of the need for strategy and planning. Control is needed to assess whether strategy is being merged into the firm's activities and whether strategy is affecting the firm's performance. Control should tell the firm if the correct strategy was selected and if it is being executed properly. A strategy can fail because it was the wrong one for the company's situation. A strategy, even if correct, can also fail because it is not properly executed. **Control systems** provide the information to identify and correct such weaknesses. Two major reasons for strategy failure are environmental change and human considerations.

Environmental Change A firm can appropriately match its strategy to its situation and conditions but find that its projected future has changed. Most companies evaluate and forecast their environment when formulating strategy. But many of these companies do not repeat this process until they reevaluate their strategy or until a major environmental change forces them to reconsider their premises and assumptions. These companies may be surprised to find themselves conducting business in an altogether different environment than the one they had expected.

Any sector of the environment can change in a way that affects strategy implementation. For example, Avon Products found that in the social sector of the environment, changes in demographics, culture, values, and preferences can change customers and employees.[1] In the 1960s Avon Products was one of the highly sought-after growth stocks. The company had achieved an attractive record of growth in sales with a simple formula: add sales representatives. With more representatives, sales went up, profits went up, and stock prices went up. Throughout the 1970s and continuing today, however, the world changed. Women went to work in growing numbers. Not only were fewer women at home when the Avon representative called, but fewer women—the traditional Avon representatives—were interested in doing the commission-only sales work. Avon had to find a new way to reach the customer.

Monitoring the sectors of the environment most important to the company's strategy can allow the company to reevaluate the premises and assumptions upon which its strategy is based. The more important an environmental force is to the strategy, the more it should be monitored and evaluated. A major question is, what will be central in the future? Are changes occurring that will have a major effect on strategy, perhaps by omission, that may render it ineffective? Dynamic changes can have a wrenching effect.

Human Considerations A changing environment and imperfect strategies are by themselves enough to call for a strong system of controls, but yet another condition argues for the need for control. As several writers have emphasized, human considerations are also critical. Merchant makes the point well:

> The key point is that if all personnel could always be relied upon to do what is best for the organization, there would be no need for a control system. But individuals are sometimes unable or unwilling to act in the organization's best interest; so management must take steps to guard against the occurrence, and particularly the persistence, of undesirable behaviors and to encourage desirable behaviors.[2]

People may be unable to act in the organization's interest for several reasons. They may simply not understand what the firm expects from them or may lack the abilities, knowledge, or experience to do what is expected. In response to these shortcomings, many management techniques not normally thought of as controls nevertheless serve the purpose of control. Personnel training and selection, policies and procedures, performance reviews, organization culture, management by objectives, and participative management are just a few techniques that may help people see more clearly what is expected.

A situation at Lotus Development Corporation provides an example.[3] Lotus had been the largest software company in both sales and profits. But in 1987 and 1988

Lotus developed an embarrassing problem. The company would announce a product revision or a new product and its shipping date, but when the date came, the company could not deliver. Delays in meeting schedules became common. In response, W. Frank King, hired as senior vice president of the Software Products Group, stopped premature announcements of products and canceled one major product. He then imposed a new discipline on software development. With many new products and 700 software developers, King needed a way to control the process. He required daily and weekly meetings for code writers and program testers. Schedules were made of what each programmer would do each day, and the entire Software Products Group began to hold monthly meetings. King created new positions to see that all new products shared standard features and systems. He was also updated each day on the software errors discovered by quality testers. The software developers liked his approach, and the company's problem appeared to be under control.

Even when people know what is expected and have the prerequisites to perform, they may not because they are unwilling or even perverse. Employees do not naturally seek what the organization wants. They have their own set of desired outcomes. Whether individuals will be willing to work toward the firm's goals depends somewhat on whether they can meet their own needs while doing so and whether they perceive a connection between meeting personal needs and company objectives.

How Much Control

In general, the more control management exerts, the greater its effectiveness. However, the kinds of control techniques and the looseness of their application change according to such factors as the stability of the environment, the technology employed by the organization, the organization's diversity, and the competitiveness of the industry. The design and operation of control systems incur cost, which should be less than the losses prevented. But gains and losses cannot be measured solely in terms of dollars. A strategic control system that is so lean it does not provide information about changes in the environment may lead to opportunity losses (or faulty investments). The effect of a changing environment is discussed in the Strategic Application "Bell & Howell in South Africa," which describes how Bell & Howell was led by societal expectations to divest a business.

Too much control or poorly designed controls can also lead to behavioral dysfunctions. A heavy imposition of controls can entangle employees in red tape and dull their motivation and creativity. Too much control can cause managers to overcomply with, resist, or sabotage the system.[4] A salesperson may sabotage the control, for example, by reporting many more contacts with new customers than were actually made. Such situations are not uncommon. The Boy Scouts of America reported that its drive to increase membership resulted in reports of increased membership considerably greater than actual membership.[5] Likewise, Armco Inc., which diversified into insurance, thought it had strict underwriting controls but in fact found that one of its subsidiaries, Universal Reinsurance, reported a reserve surplus of $40 million when it actually had a $77 million deficit.[6] No one at corporate headquarters knew the insurance business or how to control it.

STRATEGIC APPLICATIONS: INTERNATIONAL

Bell and Howell in South Africa

Some important issues seem to go unnoticed for years; others gain such a strong following you can't help but notice. One such issue of late is the practice of apartheid in South Africa. While there is much debate on the correct response, there can be no debate that public pressure has caused a variety of responses.

Bell & Howell is a textbook distributor and producer of microimage systems and mail-handling devices. The company also used to be in the photographic business, but the threat of boycotts in the United States caused Bell & Howell to divest its South African audiovisual and mail-sorting operations. The operations were sold even though they generated $1 million of profit in 1984. A company representative explained, "We saw the possibility of a school system or a state refusing to adopt our textbook as the recommended textbook, or our microfilms."

Source: M. R. Moskowitz, "Company Performance Roundup," *Business and Society Review*, Spring 1986, 125.

Good Control Characteristics

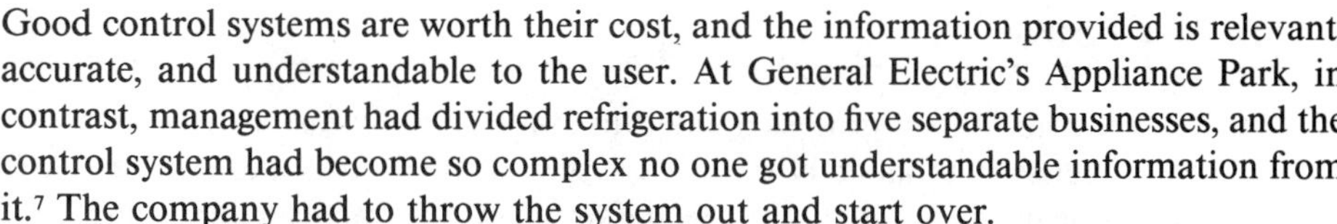

Good control systems are worth their cost, and the information provided is relevant, accurate, and understandable to the user. At General Electric's Appliance Park, in contrast, management had divided refrigeration into five separate businesses, and the control system had become so complex no one got understandable information from it.[7] The company had to throw the system out and start over.

The information also must be received on time and must help the manager take corrective action. A chemical company began a major expansion program for a commodity by building a new plant. Estimates of volume, unit costs, and construction costs were accurate at the time they were made. For the program to be a success, these critical success factors had to meet their targets. But the construction took too long and overran planned investment. When finished, the plant could not produce at the planned volume. Entry was delayed, and investment and unit costs were so high and volume so low that unit costs did not allow the company to compete in a commodity market. The company's strategy failed because the company lacked controls that provided the type of information needed to project what would happen to its strategy.

The controls should fit the needs of different users and give them an incentive to take corrective action when needed. The results of a control system must be understood by the users, so the information should be clear, simple, and objective. Managers should be able to see the connection between the information provided and the performance expected. During a consulting project, a manager asked the consultant to read a report the manager received monthly. The report focuses on the materials used in producing the unit's product. Numerous ratios and figures indicated the amounts used relative to units produced. The report also compared the manager's unit to other, like units. This manager had only the vaguest idea what the report was about and what to do with it. She asked the consultant what the figures meant. The consultant started to explain in some detail the different results, but seeing the blank look on the manager's face, she said that essentially it meant the manager had the best-performing unit in the organization. The manager was considerably relieved but never referred to the report again.

The positive influence of appropriate controls can be seen in a statement attributed to Irwin Miller, former CEO of Cummins Engine Company:

> Facts are friendly. Facts that tend to reinforce what you are doing and give you a warm glow are nice, because they help in terms of psychic reward. Facts that raise alarms are equally friendly, because they give you clues about how to respond, how to change, where to spend the resources.[8]

The system should be designed so that all the essential dimensions of unit or program performance are measured. There should be a strong association between the level of performance achieved and what the firm rewards. For example, if the organization controls for and rewards performance based simply on return on investment (ROI), that is what it will get—along with declining maintenance, declining R&D productivity, and lack of investment in new equipment.

Strategic Control

The control process applied to strategic concerns is **strategic control**—the process of ensuring that activities necessary to achieve goals and strategies are carried out. Strategic control involves keeping strategic movements on track and gathering information for the evaluation of strategy. It is concerned with whether assumptions about the future are still valid and whether a gap is developing between strategy and the actual future unfolding. In addition, strategic control monitors whether programs and functional strategies are actually leading to the goals sought.

The Nature of Strategic Control

Strategic control and **operational control** share the same basic steps and processes. However, strategic control differs from operational control because of the length of time involved, its external focus, its greater impact on the firm, the uniqueness of its task, and the qualitative and creative nature of the control techniques involved. There is no distinct demarcation line between strategic control and control of ongoing operations. Strategic control makes use of operational control and subsumes it. Operational control contributes to strategic control but cannot by itself provide strategic control. The Strategic Application "Hanson Trust" discusses a company that has adapted the nature of its controls to its changes in strategy.

Timing Often the length of time to fully implement a strategy and achieve strategic goals involves two or often five to ten years. For example, a firm following a strategy of internal growth through new products might expect to spend three to ten years

STRATEGIC APPLICATIONS

Hanson Trust

In 1964 the Wiles Group Ltd. was a relatively small British company operating agricultural services. A year later, James Hanson became chairman, and the company embarked on a series of related diversifications. As the strategy, size, and structure of the firm have changed, so have the nature and location of its strategic control.

In 1969 the company changed its name to Hanson Trust Ltd. and acquired low-technology firms—companies in construction equipment distribution, brick manufacturing, and engineering—and began making them more efficient, a process sometimes referred to as rationalization. The rationalization approach to improving efficiency was appropriate to increasing profits, because the company was operating relatively stable industries and marketing products in the mature stage of their life cycle. Strategic control was concerned with maintaining momentum of their strategy and focused on measuring and assessing whether the company's improvements in efficiencies were working. Operational controls were important to tracking the company's attempts at improving efficiency in each function of the company, especially production. Strategic control was concerned with internal results of efficiency programs, such as market penetration, prices, and profits.

In 1973 Hanson entered the United States, and by 1984 U.S. sales reached $1.7 billion. By 1984 Hanson was no longer following a strategy of related diversification, but described itself as "an industrial management company." Diversification had become unrelated, and the acquired firms larger. Hanson retains the management of acquired firms and, after streamlining the operations, lets each new unit run as a profit center. Managers of the 150 profit centers have considerable authority, but their capital expenditures are closely supervised. Central staff is kept lean, concentrating on financial control of the conglomerate and search for new acquisition candidates. Strategic management at the corporate level focuses on maintaining and enlarging Hanson's portfolio of businesses and on financial control of the divisions. Managers of profit centers are responsible for strategy and control of their businesses.

Source: Richard Reed and James M. Lohan, *Anatomy of a Takeover: Hanson's Battle for SCM* (Unpublished case study, Department of Management and Systems, Washington State University, Pullman, 1986).

before it knows their market acceptance. A target market may change or disappear, and new competitors may enter the market during this period of time.

In strategic control, review and assessment tend to be triggered by events rather than deviations from a set of standards. Management is often unaware that changes are occurring until some event signals the beginning of a change or the change itself. The formation of OPEC as a cartel to control oil prices would have triggered reviews by energy companies. The entry of IBM into the personal computer market caused reviews by many small competitors. The dependence on events to trigger review means the company must rely more on sensitive observers than on quantitative measures.

External Focus Much of the information employed in strategic control comes from a variety of diverse external sources. Much of this information is qualitative, discrete, and imprecise. Because the environment is so large, diverse, complex, interdependent, and uncontrollable, the information comes from many sources and is hard to measure, monitor, and evaluate. The entry of one particular competitor into a market may be much more important than whether 15 new firms have started up. A case in point is IBM's entry into the personal computer market. The deregulation of the trucking and telecommunications industries is another example of discrete, qualitative information that could have great impact but for which it is difficult to predict the consequences precisely.

Impact The impact of strategic control is great because of the amount of resources committed to carrying out the strategy and the potential loss or gain connected with the strategy. Committing the firm to a strategy often involves betting the whole firm on the outcome. The longer time frame and the episodic nature of control can mean a longer time before a firm knows if its plans are out of control. In August 1985, Hanson Trust bid $755 million to take over SCM Company.[9] In January 1986, after SCM's attempts to avoid a takeover and two court rulings, the price had risen to $927.5 million. Such a large investment would require years to recover. In the same vein, attempts to develop new products internally may span a time frame of three to ten years.

Task Neither the process of strategic control nor the problems it addresses are routine. Consequently, mechanisms for monitoring, evaluating, and taking corrective action are harder to set up, and corrective action is difficult to preprogram. In trying to control strategies, managers know less about what problems to expect and what to do to solve them.

The more a company moves away from what it knows well, the more uncertainty it will face. When the successful steelmaker Armco used a strategy of unrelated diversification to spread its risk, it entered businesses it did not know or understand. It acquired insurance companies that were losing money and that took big risks for low premiums. Lacking understanding of the business, Armco could not control it.[10]

Reliance on Qualitative and Creative Skills Strategic control relies relatively heavily on human problem solving. Managers largely use qualitative information from diverse sources to evaluate, reach judgments about, and select alternative corrective actions. Problem identification and problem solving are more intuitive and creative and less subject to formal analysis. Creativity is a key skill for seeing patterns in diverse information and for developing alternative courses of action. The more unusual the problem, the less managers can rely on previous ways of solving a problem.

Strategic Change and Control

Chief among the influences on the nature of strategic control is the extent to which the company is changing its strategic direction. Lorange and his colleagues posit that there are two basically different strategic planning situations—maintaining the momentum of the company's present strategy and seeking to move in an entirely new direction.[11] The kind of strategy developed will affect the kind of strategic control system a company must employ. According to Lorange et al., the appropriate control systems for the two planning situations are momentum control and leap control.

Momentum Control Momentum or "peacetime" control tries to maintain the firm's present strategic direction. The environment may be peaceful, or it may be subject to major change, but the firm is not subject to any major discontinuities. It can see its way through any change by maintaining its momentum. Changes in environmental forces stem from the past and the present, so the firm can anticipate its future environment simply by extrapolation.

Strategic control helps maintain momentum by the traditional techniques of developing standards for performance and measuring deviations, monitoring changes in environmental assumptions, and deciding whether any changes in strategy are necessary.[12] Techniques such as revenue, profit, investment, and cost centers and the annual strategic planning review are used as the primary basis for steering the company.

Leap Control The organization should use **leap control** when the environment is not continuous. The future environment of the firm will break with the past; planners cannot extend the present and past into the future. Such an interruption calls for strategies that break with the past and "leap" off into a new direction. Maintaining momentum will not get the firm where it wants to go and may not even allow it to survive under future conditions. Because of the lack of continuity, it is harder to foresee the future and thus even to be specific about goals. How to achieve this leap in strategy becomes a major issue for strategic planning and control. The problems are less structured, more uncertain, and less clear.

The kinds of control techniques used in momentum control are less useful. They may still be employed, but they should be directly related to the new strategic goals. In fact, with leap control, it is difficult to differentiate between the strategic planning techniques and the techniques employed for strategic control. For example, as described later in this chapter, a strategic issues management system can become an instrument of control as well as a planning technique.[13] Strategic issues management can be used to compare the company's assumptions with the positions that seem to be developing. Strategic control overlaps with strategic planning because the planning process is dynamic until the organization can return to momentum conditions. Leap control, for the most part, relies on human assessment and evaluation. This argues for widespread participation in the process, greater sharing and acceptance of planning assumptions, and sensitivity to the factors that should be monitored. The Strategic Application "Gulf & Western Breaks with the Past Again" provides a discussion of momentum and leap control at Gulf and Western, a company that has undergone several breaks with the past in the last 30 years.

Facilitating Corrective Action

For strategic control to be most effective, needed corrective actions should occur before the company gets too far off course. The company cannot wait until all the results are in; it needs to be forewarned of approaching problems. The controls used should allow a forecast of future results and give the company time to correct its course. Newman has suggested two types of controls that permit such action: screening and steering.[14]

STRATEGIC APPLICATIONS

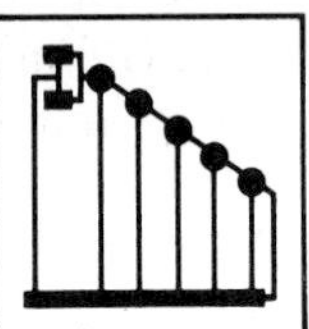

Gulf & Western Breaks with the Past Again

The many conglomerates that were formed in the 1960s gave new meaning to diversification and fostered new financial planning control mechanisms. One of the most successful was Gulf & Western. Its leader at the time, Charles Bluhdorn, had observed that investors sought out companies showing consistent growth in earnings. He therefore envisioned the company as a portfolio of disparate businesses, so that one business experiencing a down business cycle would be offset by another business on the upside of its cycle. Earnings could continue steadily upward; the conglomerate would attract capital. This strategy was a discontinuous break with its past for Gulf & Western as well as a break from the business practice of the time.

The strategy worked well for Gulf & Western until the 1980s. Its businesses included over 11 disparate product groups and its products ranged from auto parts and racetracks to sugar, cement, and zinc. Management then decided that the environment dictated another change in strategy. Like many American companies, Gulf & Western was experiencing economic downturns, but there were other radically changing conditions such as "rapid technological gains, deregulation, tougher world wide competition," outsourcing, and the splintering of markets. Gulf & Western began restructuring to refocus on a much narrower set of businesses: entertainment, publishing, and financial services. The new strategy was not as radical as the 1960s break with the past, but it did represent a significant alteration in how management related the company to the environment.

Source: Martin S. Davis, "Two Plus Two Doesn't Equal Five," *Fortune*, December 9, 1985, 171–179.

Screening Control Control through **screening** is essentially a yes/no or go/no-go control. Specific conditions must be met, specific conditions satisfied, or specific approval given before action can continue. For example, after drafts and blueprints are prepared for a new plant, the CEO may be required to approve the project before it can continue. Before the company proceeds with a marketing effort, the program may have to be reviewed to see that it meets assumptions about market size and prices.

Screening is a common type of control that can be employed throughout the organization in operational as well as strategic control. In strategic control, it might be used when a program reaches a milestone. For example, launching a new program to capture the market in a new country may require a yes/no screen before an advertising campaign begins.

Steering Control An organization uses **steering control** when it is trying to move a program or project to its target. The company has a goal or standard it is attempting to reach, and it is trying to correct any deviations before the action is complete. Rather than wait until the company reaches the wrong destination, management tries to make corrections en route. This requires timely and accurate information that will allow management to predict where the project is headed on the present course.

An example of a company whose control system failed to provide timely information is Apollo Computer. Apollo, which produces workstations for scientists and engineers, was the market leader until Sun Microsystems gained that position. Apollo was on its way to recovery with new products and needed credibility with customers and investors. But in the spring of 1988 it suffered unexpected losses. The loss was a surprise because those in charge of Apollo's European operations had not reported that Siemens, a major customer, was cutting back its orders.

Controls that can track industry and market conditions before they are problems allow a company to steer itself. The company can institute steering controls by monitoring strategic thrusts, monitoring key external variables, and reassessing at milestones.[15]

Monitor Strategic Thrusts In developing a strategy, an organization selects its domain and tries to employ its differential advantage over competitors in serving this domain. The steps it takes in securing its domain and differential advantage are its strategic thrusts. These are the key programs or moves that will advance the firm to where it wants to be. Thrusts are then fleshed out and broken down by detailing plans and resources.

For example, a company preparing to enter a new market may need to develop a new manufacturing process, build a new plant, prepare a promotion campaign, and staff and train plant and marketing personnel. Each of these activities may consist of several projects. Management must closely monitor, evaluate, and coordinate the progress of these projects in order to bring the program on line. The company must also continue to monitor and evaluate the market, competitors, and other elements of the environment, because changing competitive conditions may make even a successfully run program noncompetitive. To do this requires controls that monitor the programs of the thrust. Feedback from measuring these early programs should go to the managers in charge as well as to the strategic manager. Schedules and progress can be monitored, and the strategic manager can check for consistency across the detailed programs. These early data may be hard to evaluate, but they give some basis for reevaluating strategy at an early stage. A strategic thrust such as "becoming the quality leader in our industry by 1995" can be translated into more detailed moves such as automating 90 percent of production by 1993, which in turn can be translated into steps for process engineering and construction.

For American Express a key thrust was to develop cooperation among its businesses, and one program was to promote cross-selling of products among its different divisions—for example, stockbrokers would sell life insurance. The CEO required senior executives to identify such opportunities and include them in their annual strategic plans. He made it company policy to evaluate all managers and professional employees on their contributions to this program. A system of bonuses was established to reward those who contributed. In addition, a monthly report was initiated to update top executives on the status of each project. Managers who are making progress are therefore quite visible, and so are those who are not. This technique integrates planning, motivation, and control around a strategic thrust, making strategic control all the more effective.[16]

Monitor Key External Variables The development of a strategy requires predicting the state of the key factors in the environment that are crucial to the success of the strategy. These predictions may allow for change in the factors, and they may be flexible. For Philip Morris, the key factors in the environment have been those related to the cigarette business. Although Philip Morris is more than a tobacco company, it has depended heavily on tobacco for profits to fund its efforts to diversify out of the dying cigarette business. Thus anything that threatened this business has been a threat to the company's survival. The actions of federal and state governments as well as important precedents in the courts have been key external variables for Philip Morris to monitor and evaluate.

A company must identify which premises are most decisive for its strategy and begin monitoring the critical factors to detect changes in course. Because the firm cannot monitor everything that could affect it, it must concentrate on the factors that are key to the success of its strategy. For example, changes in affirmative action laws and legal precedents may be important to the company but may not be crucial to premises that will affect its strategy. The personnel department should monitor these changes and incorporate what is important in its operation. On the other hand, changes in tax laws affecting depreciation and the decline of prices in the market of a cash cow expected to fund the strategy may change the economics of key programs. Sometimes monitoring of changing conditions is not enough to allow the organization to adapt to a changing environment. The Strategic Application "Japanese Companies in South Africa" provides an example of a government strategy that failed because it could not control the key success factor. Competitors did not respond as expected and, constrained by political pressures, the government did not respond to the changes that occurred.

Sometimes these key variables are peculiar to the individual firm, but many can be identified from an examination of its industry. Other important factors may be those the firm considered when it formulated its strategy. Certainly the firm should monitor key factors that affect the company's domain, differential advantage, and major thrusts. These factors can often be identified by asking what-if questions about them: What if the cost of capital increases by 10 percent? What if growth in the market declines to 10 percent annually? How would our strategy be affected? Key factors such as major competitors, customers, or suppliers are also important to watch. These factors are the subject for strategic review in the planning process, but it is often important to monitor them regularly.

Careful analysis does more than identify key variables to watch. It begins to sensitize the company controllers to the ways changes in the key variable may affect the firm. The impact of these changes must be evaluated and tied to the strategy.

Reassess at Milestones and Alerts Steering control should include the opportunity to reassess the entire situation and strategy. The company can provide for this with annual strategic reviews and assessments tied to strategic planning efforts. Watching the progress on strategic thrusts and monitoring key external variables can provide much of the information required. From the internal perspective, a company can assess its progress on key programs as in the American Express example cited earlier. Is the organization completing the thrusts according to schedule? What is the projected total cost based on information to date? How do these costs compare to projected costs? Will more or less funding be needed? Are the new projected returns acceptable? From the external perspective, management wants to know if assumptions and fore-

STRATEGIC APPLICATIONS: INTERNATIONAL

Japanese Companies in South Africa

In the United States companies have come under increasing pressure to divest their assets in South Africa and to reduce or halt trade with South Africans. Pressure has been applied by state and local governments, colleges, and religious groups through refusal to invest in the stocks of companies holding assets in South Africa. Recently the U.S. government has restricted trade by U.S.-based companies. Critics of this policy have argued that companies can serve as a force for change if they remain in South Africa providing jobs, economic presence, training, and a cadre of black skilled and professional workers, and applying internal pressure on the South African government. Critics have also charged that leaving South Africa has little effect because the place of U.S. companies is quickly taken by foreign competitors. Congress responded by passing the 1986 Comprehensive Anti-Apartheid Act calling for sanctions against countries who assume the trade forsaken by U.S. companies. As a result of these efforts many U.S. companies have pulled out of direct investment and curtailed or abandoned trade with South Africa.

In 1987, U.S. trade with South Africa was about $3 billion, a decline of 20 percent from the year before. In contrast, Japanese trade with South Africa increased about 14 percent to over $4 billion, and Japan became South Africa's largest trading partner. This occurred in spite of restrictions on business with South Africa. Japan bans direct investment, exports of computers to South African security forces, and the import of South African steel. It also restricts commercial loans to South Africa.

How then does Japan's attempt to control trade result in an increase? One reason is that there are few critics of apartheid in Japan. Because there is almost no U.S. ownership of Japanese stocks, no pressure is exerted by the investors who have pressured U.S. companies. Also, Japan's Ministry of International Trade and Industry has no further plans to limit trade, nor will Japan's leading businesses commit to additional restraints. Another factor is the method used by Japanese companies to export their products to South Africa. For example, instead of exporting cars, the automobile companies export the parts. Licensing agreements with local companies allow them to assemble the cars in South Africa. Toyota sold 87,000 cars to South African buyers in that way in 1987. Other companies and products are handled in much the same way, allowing them to circumvent the restrictions.

Source: Ted Holden, Alan Fine, Steven J. Dryden, and Elizabeth Weiner, "Japan's Embarrassment of Riches in South Africa," *Business Week*, February 1, 1988, 44.

casts are still valid. Are the forecasted opportunities still there? Are any possible threats developing? What are the company's current strengths and weaknesses compared to those of competitors? Is the company's differential advantage still holding, and will it in the future?

This is the time to reconsider the soundness of the strategy. If only corrections in course are required, it is time to fine-tune the thrusts. It is also time to examine consistency between thrusts, programs, and strategy, as well as between corporate and business-level strategy.

As indicated early in this chapter, strategic control responds more to events than periodic reviews. This is especially true of full-scale reassessments, because they can be arduous and expensive. But because they must be done, the time to do so is when a milestone is near, when an alert is sounded from the environment, or when too much time has elapsed since the last reassessment. A milestone is a significant event in the progress of the key program. It might be the signing of a contract with a supplier or for a new plant. Certainly any major commitment of new resources would qualify. Or a milestone might be a new phase of a major project connected with a program. Monitoring the environment may uncover a key event. Perhaps a competitor that has been cash poor and that was not expected to be a threat in a thrust for best quality in the industry suddenly announces a merger with a larger, cash-rich firm. For example, the acquisition of B.F. Goodrich by Hanson Trust might give it the backing to compete in the tire industry. These are all good times for deciding whether reassessment is in order.

Some companies will conduct the reassessments every couple of years even if events or milestones do not call for it, because even small changes can accumulate over time. Reassessment is a major step to ensure that management reviews the total picture.

Strategic Control Techniques

Every important strategic objective should have a measure that management uses to track progress toward it. For example, a key performance area for General Electric is market share, which the company monitors for each product using the percentage of available business that GE has captured. For productivity, GE uses the payroll cost and the depreciation cost of goods produced to measure labor and equipment efficiency. The financial appendix in this book reviews numerous measures of a company's position that can be used for control purposes.

The number of control techniques available to measure strategic progress and evaluate unit performance is as vast as the number of objectives. The following discussion focuses on some commonly used techniques: responsibility centers, budgeting systems, and strategic planning controls. For the most part, the techniques are aimed at gauging each unit's contribution to the company's financial performance.

By themselves, such measures are inadequate. Just as an investor needs to know more than earnings per share to estimate a stock's value, an executive needs more than a financial indicator to see if a unit is meeting its objectives. For example, in controlling a program to introduce a new product line, management must know whether the projects are on schedule. To evaluate advertising agency performance, General Foods uses changes in market share and sales volume.

Responsibility centers and budgets are simply numerical representations of objectives. Objectives are translated into financial terms that units must achieve for the company to meet its goals. Properly supplemented with other well-chosen indicators like market share and product leadership, and critically reviewed by top management, these techniques allow management to maintain control while implementing strategy.

Responsibility Centers

Most businesses have corporate goals for the level of profits and returns on investment they expect to receive. These goals are the bottom line for strategic management.

They are also the basis for controlling the performance of organization units, that is, how well these units are contributing to the corporate goals. Stripped of all the details, the responsibilities of each unit can be evaluated with four indicators: costs, revenues, profits, and investment. These four financial indicators are the basis for **responsibility centers** and can be used at several organizational levels.

The choice of which type of responsibility center to use depends on the kind of contribution expected from the unit and the scope of what the unit can control. A division or SBU in a multidivision company can usually be assigned responsibility for profit and investments. However, a functional department in a single-product firm may be able to control only its own costs. A company structured around divisions or SBUs or a division with SBUs can use all four indicators. When the focus is on the SBU or a division, responsibility centers coincide with the organizational unit, and the responsibility for costs, revenues, and investment is more easily fixed. Most companies would prefer to monitor performance using some form of investment center, but usually this is possible only when evaluating divisions or SBUs. In the case of functional departments, the responsibility for total performance is not so easy to fix; profit and investment responsibility may be used only at the corporate level. Some units, like production, can have a large influence on costs but no direct responsibility for producing revenues. Other units, like marketing, are responsible mostly for generating revenue but have little control over costs.

The nature of the business will affect which function and which aspects of those functions are critical to the company's competitive success. Major responsibilities and organizational structure affect what a unit can be held accountable for and which key variables to measure in monitoring and evaluating. For example, in some manufacturing departments, by-products are sold to other firms, allowing the company to treat this subunit as a profit center although manufacturing as a whole is treated as a cost center. In other cases, several SBUs may share plant operations but not customers and marketing, making it difficult to decide whether the SBUs should be assigned profit and cost responsibility.

Business strategy affects the emphasis placed on the four types of responsibility centers. For instance, a conglomerate typically treats its companies or divisions as investment centers, but it is also concerned with revenue growth, market share, and cash flow. A company that pursues a low-price strategy will give more emphasis to cost control.

The responsibility centers discussed here are typical of how firms assign responsibility to a unit when there is a clearly defined set of activities for which the manager can be held accountable. The thrust is to measure the financial impact of the manager's performance.[17] Table 8.1 shows some typical organization units and the responsibility centers used.

Expense Centers An **expense center** is a unit that has a separate budget and whose manager has some discretion over the costs generated. Although the unit generates costs, it does not generate revenue. Some expenses are associated with operations, allowing standard amounts of direct labor and materials to be attributed to each unit produced. This is typically the case in manufacturing. Other expense centers are associated with departments in which unit costing is not practical. In most admin-

Table 8.1 Typical Use of Responsibility Centers

Resources (Inputs)	→	Typical Unit (Responsibility Center)	→	Performance Measure (Output)
(For example, assets, budget, personnel, objectives)		Personnel		Expense
		Sales		Revenue
		Product Division or SBU		Profit or Investment
		Company or Subsidiary		Investment

istrative units, like marketing research, the outputs or products are difficult to measure. The size of budget required to perform the unit's service is a matter of judgment.

Control is exercised by measuring differences between the planned (budgeted) and actual expenses. The planned expense represents the objectives for the unit. Variance from the planned level indicates that costs are not being controlled and provides an opportunity for review and change. Control is also exercised in setting the planned level of expenditure, because this level sets the standard for comparing performance.

For control to be most effective, each expense item should be reported and evaluated separately. Items that the unit can control should be separated from the uncontrollable items. Although both categories of items are important, the controllable expenses are most likely to reflect unit performance. Thus, the unit with the most influence over an item should be held accountable for it.

Meeting expense objectives may seem like a simple basis for control, but fixing responsibility is not always easy. At IBM, for example, account representatives are responsible for any IBM equipment in place with one of their customers. If a piece of IBM equipment is removed because it does not operate effectively, which department should be responsible for the expenses of removing it? Should the repair service department be responsible because they couldn't keep it operating? Perhaps manufacturing is at fault for designing and producing a faulty piece of equipment. If sales is accountable for making everything go right for the account, maybe the expense should be assigned to that department. What about the hidden expenses, like the commission that was paid to the representative who sold the equipment and serviced the account? For expense centers to work well, a company must be able to fix responsibility for the expenses, and the responsibility must be clearly known. In IBM's system, the account representative *would* be liable for at least the commission.[18]

Revenue Centers Sales forecasts are critical to all planning, and so every firm makes such a forecast a major part of the firm's environmental assessment. These forecasts are readily assigned to the various sales units and become standards the units are expected to achieve. The sales department, regional sales offices, and related units are evaluated by how much revenue they generate. Sales-related expense centers may be held responsible for sales training and advertising, but these costs are usually relatively small when compared to total costs. Because the unit has little ability to control costs, the manager is expected to live with the expense budget while maximizing sales revenue. Thus, for revenue centers, it is easy to state and measure the desired objective, but it is more difficult to define how the objective should be achieved and thus difficult to have standard costs.

Although the manager is not held accountable for product costs and perhaps not even price, it is too simple to imply that he or she completely controls revenue generation. Everything that happens to the product in the process from design to production costs and quality can affect the product's cost, price, and attractiveness. These relationships should be considered in setting a sales budget and determining standards for measurement.

In contrast to expense centers, which are designed to measure efficiency (output/input), **revenue centers** are designed to measure effectiveness (goal achievement). Profit requires control over both costs and revenues. However, it is often impossible to set up a system in which every manager is responsible for both revenue and cost. If the controls are to be fair and the manager's efforts in the best interest of the whole company, considerable thought must be given to designing measures that will be appropriate and controllable and that encourage managers to pursue goals that are congruent with the company's goals. For example, if a unit is responsible only for expenses, it may cut costs so much that the quality of the product suffers or delivery times fall behind schedule. As a result, declining sales and lost customers may injure strategy even though the cost centers exceeded their objectives. The major problem with revenue and expense centers is that they direct attention to only one factor in producing profits. The system must be designed so that all the centers contribute in an optimal way to the objectives.

Profit Centers In **profit centers**, the focus is on the difference between revenues and expenses. The unit is responsible for both and is evaluated on the amount of profits it returns. Thus, profit centers should overcome some of the problems linked to revenue and expense centers.

In a single-product company, the one obvious place revenues and expenses come together is at the level of the president. In multidivision companies and ones with multiple SBUs, the managers may have considerable autonomy in controlling cost, price, and volume. Under such circumstances, it is relatively easy to set up profit centers and expect managers to run them for a profit.

It is also possible to create other profit centers in most organizations. A manufacturing plant, for example, might "sell" its output to another division or to a marketing department. The plant can then generate revenue as well as costs. For years Union Carbide had a division that marketed by-products and products that did not fit into another division's mission. Many of these products could be sold to consumers, but the industrial chemical divisions did not have the channels or marketing organization to exploit the opportunities. It seemed logical to sell such products to other divisions or to create a separate division to market these products. There are many opportunities to create profit centers in this way and thereby gain more complete control over the center's performance.

If the whole company is treated as a profit center or the divisions operate independently of each other, the situation is not particularly complicated. Products are sold in the marketplace to other firms, and the marketplace determines the price. If a subunit of the whole organization is treated as a profit center, some mechanism is required to charge another unit for the product or service being sold or purchased. The typical way of doing this is to use **transfer pricing**.

One way to determine the price is simply to use the unit cost of the product up to the time it is transferred. But this provides no incentive for manufacturing to control the costs.

The units involved might attempt to negotiate a price. Manufacturing will want the price to be as high as possible to increase its profits; marketing will want the price to be as low as possible for the same reason.

In other situations, transfer prices may be partially or wholly based on what the product or service could be sold for in the open market. This method could be used when a profit center is already selling the product to other firms. Weyerhaeuser established its computing center as a profit center; other company units can decide whether or not to use it. If the other units think they can get better service or a lower price from another company, they are free to do so. The computing center must prove its worth within the company.

Profit centers do solve some of the control problems associated with cost or revenue centers, but they can have their own control problems. A major concern for the company using profit centers is to assure that total company profits are maximized. When a company unit is given enough autonomy to manage profits, it may optimize its profit at the expense of another unit. The company as a whole may be suboptimizing unless it puts other constraints on its profit centers. A star product, for instance, may have great potential for profits but be starving for cash to expand while a cash cow product has more cash than it needs. It is also possible for a profit center to show profits in the short run to the detriment of long-run profits. It may neglect its assets by cutting preventive-maintenance expense or neglecting training of personnel to show a profit.

The pursuit of profit should not be unconstrained. The company should review how the center produced the profits, its capital budgets, and whether its actions have been detrimental to its future profit potential. It is also important that the company control the use of profits generated by the center. The profit center's plan for profit must be integrated with the company's strategic plan.

Investment Centers The **investment center** is concerned with the efficient use of assets in generating profits. A firm that has invested $100 million in a business to generate $1 million in profits is much less efficient than a firm that makes a $1 million profit on a $20 million investment. The use of investment centers holds managers accountable for all the factors involved in generating a profit as well as their use of assets in producing income.

The investment center can be used at the corporate, division, or SBU level, because the structure lends itself to control over profits and investment. Investment centers can also be used wherever the company can identify a group of assets that can be managed to produce a profit.

Although the company can review strategic plans and the capital budget to control what assets are used and how they are used, the strategic plan invariably calls for an expected rate of return on the company's investment. This measure is an important indicator of how efficiently managers are using the company's assets while implementing its strategy. If the company also has an information system that provides the details of how the return was achieved, it has a very powerful system to control the use of investments.

Return on investment (ROI) was originally developed by DuPont as part of a reporting system for the financial control of decentralized divisions in its multidivision company. The indicator was widely adopted throughout the business world.[19] Figure 8.1 shows how Du Pont derived ROI. Each of the ROI components was analyzed

Figure 8.1 The Calculation of Return on Investment (ROI)

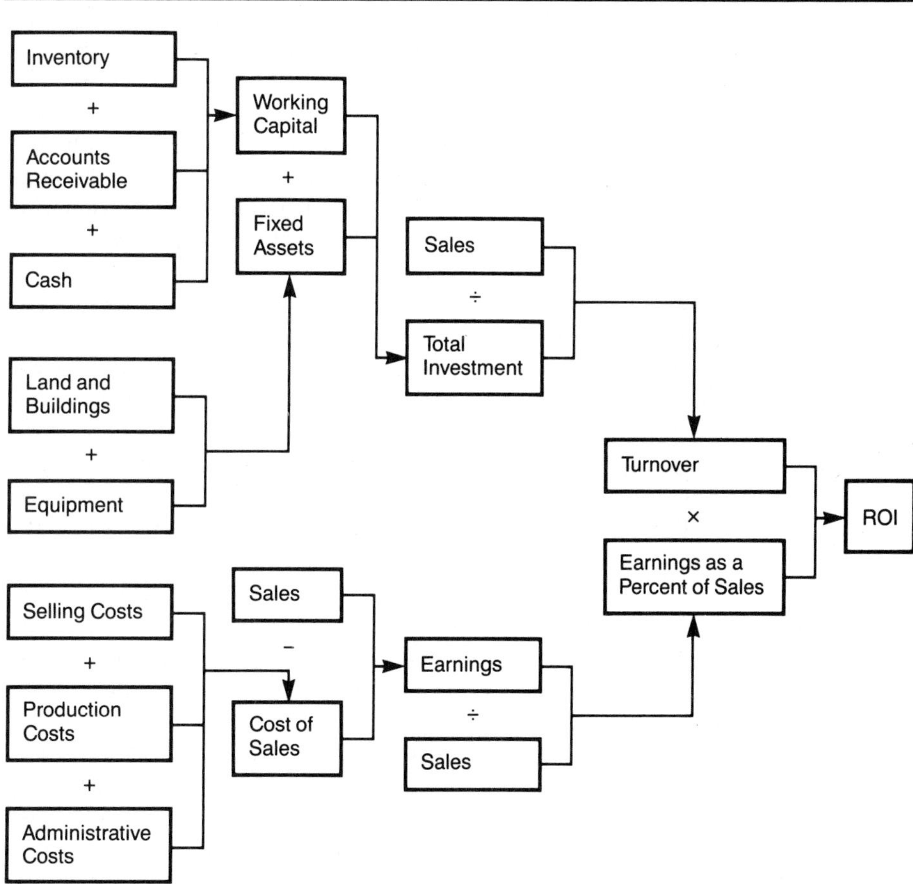

and reviewed in sessions with division managers so that every aspect of financial performance could be evaluated.

The use of ROI to measure performance has several advantages. Among those cited by Dearden in his review of ROI are the following:[20]

- Everything that affects the financial status of a unit shows up in the ROI figure. This provides a single comprehensive figure.
- ROI measures how well the unit's manager uses the company's assets to generate profits. This is an incentive to use the investment to its fullest and to acquire more assets only when they will improve the ROI. It also provides a good basis for comparing the accuracy of proposals for capital investment.
- It provides a common denominator to use in comparing investment centers with each other as well as in comparing investment alternatives.

ROI does draw attention away from one-dimensional criteria such as sales or costs and causes the manager to examine the combination of factors that lead to success.

Investment centers are subject to many of the same difficulties associated with the other responsibility centers. A primary reason is that cost, revenue, and profits are components of ROI. Although the combination of components in investment centers overcomes some of the limitations that stem from lack of control and goal incongruence, it cannot correct them all. For one thing, the manager does not and probably should not completely control his or her own center. The manager's discretion to choose depreciation policies or to make any investment he or she chooses will be constrained in most companies, at least at the division and SBU levels.

Also, in giving the manager the added responsibility for the use of assets, the company provides a whole new set of investment-related factors that the manager can manipulate. The manager can trade off increases and decreases in one factor for those in another. If the increased responsibility is to be meaningful, the manager must have some discretion as to how the variables are combined. The question is whether the increased discretion of managers leads to more or less control for the firm as a whole.

ROI measures must be reviewed with care because managers may be able to manipulate them. Because profit is a component of ROI, the investment center can manipulate it to make the unit's ROI look good. The manager can also manipulate the ROI in the way that he or she uses assets. To maintain a 10 percent rate of return after taxes, an increase in assets of $1 requires an increase in pretax profits of 15 cents (assuming a 34 percent tax rate) or a 15-cent reduction in costs. Conversely, a reduction in assets would maintain the same rate of return with lower profits or higher costs.[21] That is, anything the manager does to reduce the asset base without additional profits or sales will improve the return. The manager could also improve ROI by selling the assets and leasing them back. But for a company that wants to dominate its market, getting rid of assets may work counter to its strategy.

ROI also falls short as a performance measure when one division is to serve as a cash generator to fuel the cash needs of other divisions. In this case, it probably would be useful to have a goal for how much cash should be generated. Reducing assets would generate cash in the short run and decrease the asset base, but the cash generation cannot be sustained. In fact, a leaseback arrangement might even be a net cash user because of lease payments. Also, loss of depreciation will reduce after-tax working capital and funds flow. What if a division is expected to increase its market share? Such a strategy would usually call for increased sales attempts and prompt deliveries. This strategy could be undermined if the manager cuts his or her investment base by reducing inventories.

Because ROI is so sensitive to the impact of capital investment, a manager is unlikely to invest in assets unless they can be expected to generate a return equal to the required ROI. This is part of the intended impact of the technique. But ROI is a short-term measure, based on a year's activities, and the productivity of investment is sometimes delayed. This can discourage investment in an otherwise good project.

The effect of depreciation on the value of an asset can also discourage new investment. Depreciation lowers the value of a capital asset on the books of the company, which means the investment part of the formula will decrease over time.[22] In fact, ROI will increase automatically if nothing else in the equation changes. Therefore older assets (with more accumulated depreciation and probably a lower purchase price) will cause the investment to be lower and ROI higher. Managers may therefore be reluctant to invest in new plant and equipment. If managers continue to use obsolete assets merely to keep ROI high, their ROI performance looks good in the short term, but they are hampering the company's ability to carry out its strategy in the long term.

Another difficulty in using this technique is the question of what assets the manager should be responsible for. If a manager cannot buy, sell, or significantly change the assets in any way, should he or she be held accountable for a return on them? Some companies answer this question by including in the asset base only assets over which the manager can exert significant control. Other companies, especially those that employ other control measures as well, conclude that as long as the rules are the same for all units, responsibility can extend to all assets.

These examples are only a sampling of the difficulties that can arise in using ROI as the sole basis for control. Despite the inherent problems associated with using ROI, most companies use it to measure performance.[23] Perhaps the usage can be attributed to its seeming simplicity and the ready availability of information.

Economic Value Creation Attempts to measure and evaluate the performance of investment centers have caused some to question whether management has been evaluating the wrong performance. The rationale is that companies should use the same criteria for both allocating investment and evaluating the performance of management. This approach establishes a tighter and clearer connection between strategy, investment, and control. The primary criterion for planning and control with this approach is **economic value creation**.

A widely used method of evaluating economic value creation is to consider shareholders' value. This measure can be used in much the same way as ROI to track the progress of units and their contribution to strategy. This approach is most likely to be used in evaluating strategies in the formulation and decision stages, but it is also appropriate for tracking the progress of strategies and units. Measures of shareholder value are most easily applied at corporate and divisional levels, but they can be adapted to other investment centers if the company can apportion its income, debt, assets, and related measures to the various centers.

Shareholder value is a more sophisticated approach than ROI because it can better compare the economic and financial performance of units with that of competitors. It also takes into account the risk characteristics of a business and the cost of capital invested in the business. Improving ROI may not contribute to shareholders' value. Similarly, a firm can be making a profit but really be losing shareholder value, because profits are based on accounting figures that do not always reflect economic returns.

Management can increase the shareholders' value by concentrating on businesses, strategies, and projects that offer the greatest spread between return on equity and cost of equity. The firm is creating shareholder value only when return on equity is greater than the cost of equity. When a return is less than the cost of equity, the firm's strategy should be to minimize growth (because growth will worsen the situation) or to disinvest from the unprofitable business. The spread between return and cost also serves as a basis for choosing among projects, programs, and even businesses.

Businesses may be compared with competitors as well as with other divisions or SBUs within the firm. When a shareholder value measure is used at levels below the corporate level, some adjustments may be required, because market value is determined by value attached to company shares. Managers do not know how the market would evaluate separate divisions or SBUs, so they must estimate the value. If all the divisions were equal in contributing cash flows and in risk characteristics, the return could be apportioned evenly, but this is rarely the case. The cost of equity can be adjusted by using risk premiums of comparable firms. The **return on equity** can be estimated in several ways. One way is to allocate a portion of the firm's equity and debt to each unit and then to calculate its equity cash flow as follows:

$$\frac{\begin{array}{c}\text{Business Profits}\\ \text{after Taxes}\end{array} - \left(\begin{array}{c}\text{After-Tax}\\ \text{Interest}\\ \text{for}\\ \text{Unit}\end{array} + \begin{array}{c}\text{Retained}\\ \text{Earnings for}\\ \text{Reinvestment}\\ \text{in Unit}\end{array}\right)}{\text{Equity Cash Flows from Unit}}$$

Another way is to ignore the debt structure; then measure becomes a return on assets rather than return on equity.[24]

A firm can also examine which businesses are or are not contributing to shareholders' wealth and identify candidates for disinvestment or liquidation.[25] Because this indicator better reflects long-term performance, it may capture the total performance of a unit more accurately than ROI and, for the most part, it can be used for controlling performance in much the same fashion. But one must recognize that numerous assumptions go into the model used. The projected cash flows depend to a great extent on outsiders' projections of the future of the company and to some degree reflect a comparison with other companies. Although the market may be efficient in the long run, it may not be efficient for shorter periods for one particular company. The actual cash flows greatly depend on management's strategic action. The market does seem to reward long-term performance, but future cash flows result to a great extent from actions already taken and planned and resources already committed.

Using creation of shareholder value as a performance standard is better suited to helping management choose how to allocate resources. It employs criteria that allow more congruence between evaluation of performance (control) and strategic choice (planning) and avoids many of the difficulties associated with other criteria used in responsibility centers. But it is also more difficult to employ with many units, because it is more complex and because obtaining the information to calculate it is harder below the SBU level. Therefore, responsibility centers are likely to continue to be widely employed.

Multiple Measures Each primary criterion used to assess the performance of a responsibility center has potential problems. Much of the difficulty stems from oversimplifying the performance of a unit by focusing on a single measure to represent what is really a rather complex issue (progress toward strategic goals). The need to maintain both strategic and operational control is complicating, because these two types of control are not always served equally well by the same technique. **Multiple control techniques** are therefore required.

At the same time, it is impossible to measure all the relevant variables. Not only is it too costly, but management can handle only a limited amount of information. Computers can help process and reduce the information, but at some point management must make a decision. The choice of what to measure must be influenced by what is important to the particular business and to its strategy and key thrusts. Camillus concludes that five types of measures will describe the operations of any responsibility center:[26]

1. Input measures—resources used and costs incurred
2. Workload measures—volume of work and activity
3. Output measures—volume of goods and services provided
4. Effectiveness measures—degree of goal accomplishment
5. Efficiency measures—ratio of output to input or effectiveness to workload

Table 8.2 combines these types of measures with the types of responsibility centers to show examples of measures that can be used in control of the centers. The examples in the table are meant to be suggestive, not inclusive.

Responsibility centers are a way of assigning major responsibilities for a unit's contribution to a firm's strategy and operations. The fact that the center is seen as a cost center or an investment center does not mean it is allowed to ignore other contributions expected by the firm. However, what the firm measures is likely to get attention, particularly if the reward system is linked to these results.

Table 8.2 Responsibility Center Measures

Type of Measure	Responsibility Center Type: Cost	Revenue	Profit and Investment[a]
Input	Direct labor Direct material Indirect labor Supplies Inventory machine time Work hours	Units available Dollar value of goods Salaries Advertising Number of salespeople	Accumulated costs Staffing Overhead Plant and equipment Investment
Work Load	Units-in-process Rejects Units produced Meeting hours Outside contacts	Customer calls Miles traveled Number of sales orders Ad copy placed Number of promotions Bids made	Worker hours Units produced Overtime Customers contacted Requests for service
Output	Finished units Quality level Orders written	Units sold Sales in dollars New customers	Sales in dollars Units delivered Order delays Sales backlog New products
Effectiveness	Lost-time accidents Minor accidents Units returned by customer Percentage of production goal met Unit backlog	Percentage of sales goal Market share New-area penetration Sales returns Customer retention Value added	Growth rate Market share Return on investment Return on value added Value added Shareholder value created Progress on programs
Efficiency	Machine and capacity utilization Units per hour/worker Customers per day Copies per employee	Dollars per sale Sales per call Sales per salesperson Average delivery delay Percentage of expenses to sales	Sales per customer Expenses to sales Product costs to sales R&D to sales Personnel turnover Assets per employee Accounts receivable turnover Inventory turnover

[a]Because profit centers and investment centers both tend to be used with complete units, similar indicators can often be used. However, some are more appropriate for one than the other.

Budgeting Systems

As described in Chapter 5, a **budget** is a plan that projects the use of resources and how the organization intends to allocate these resources. Budgets represent management's priorities for the period for the use of the firm's resources. In other words, budgets are numerical or quantitative representations of strategic goals and objectives.

The budget is a plan, but it is also a control device. Having formulated its plans and translated them into budgets, management provides standards and measurements based on the planned levels of objectives that each function, program, or unit is expected to meet. The responsibility center is designed around one aspect of the budget, such as cost, revenue, profit, or investment, but managers are still expected to meet the budget. The control exercised by the budgeting process and the corrective action that results from deviance from the budget are key aspects of maintaining the progress of the organization or unit toward its goals and objectives. Conforming to or achieving the budget is typically rewarded as good management performance.

Budget Variance Reporting Almost every organization employs budgets and expects its managers to live within their budget levels. Therefore most firms issue monthly reports on the units' status with respect to budget items.[27] These reports typically show the budgeted amount, the actual amount used, and the percentage of variance for the month and the year to date. The reporting of variance is meant to facilitate control by indicating deviations from the plan. Table 8.3 shows an example of such a report.

The use of variances in reviewing performance has led to criticism. When managers participate in establishing the budgeted targets, are held accountable for staying

Table 8.3 New Budget Variance Report Form Incorporating a Mechanistic Forecast

	Current Month			Year to Date			Year-End Results	
	Budget	Actual	Variance	Budget	Actual	Percent of Budget	Budget	Mechanistic Forecast
Net sales	140,000	118,326	(15%)	450,000	425,261	95%	1,950,000	1,852,500
Marginal Contribution Percent				20%	18.7%			
Marginal Contribution	28,000	22,326	(20%)	90,000	79,328	—	390,000	346,417
Less Total Expenses	22,000	23,894	(8%)	68,500	77,278	—	270,000	304,778
—Salaries and Wages	10,000	11,050	(10%)	30,550	34,152	112%	120,000	134,400
—Accommodation	3,000	3,000	—	9,000	9,550	106%	38,000	40,208
—Data Processing	5,000	6,123	(22%)	16,000	19,250	120%	65,000	78,000
—Data Processing	4,000	3,721		12,950	14,326	111%	47,000	52,170
Net Profit	6,000	(1,568)	—	21,500	2,050	—	120,000	41,639
	1	2	3	4	5	6	7	8

Mechanistic forecast net sales = column 6 × column 7.
Mechanistic forecast marginal contribution = Actual year-to-date marginal contribution percent (row 2/column 5) × mechanistic sales forecast (row 1/column 8).
Mechanistic forecast total expenses and net profit is calculated in column 8 in the usual manner.
Source: F. Grant Schutte, "Budgetary Control Systems for the Eighties," *Journal of General Management* 5, (Spring 1980): 10. Reprinted with permission from the Journal of General Management, Greenlands, Henley-on-Thames, OXON R69 3AU-UK.

within them, and are rewarded for achieving the budget, they may engage in "budgeting games," submitting targets they are confident of reaching.[28] Such games can reduce the effectiveness of budgets for planning and control.

One way to preserve the control aspect of the variance reporting system is to add a mechanistic forecast of year-end performance to the variance report, as shown in the right-hand column of Table 8.3.[29] Year-end performance is forecast given the current level of performance. Line managers then prepare a "Bridge of Profit Statement." They start with the mechanistic forecast, analyze it, and update it by "adjusting for anything they think will more accurately reflect year-end results and by estimating the impact of the financial results of past management action during the remainder of the financial year."[30] Then each manager is expected to develop new programs to improve performance.

Review sessions are still held, but the focus is not on explaining variances. Instead, the focus is on updating and evaluating new programs. Managers' performance is judged on the action programs developed, not on meeting the budget. This behavior can be judged during the review sessions held with the managers. This approach reportedly has four positive results: (1) it causes planning and control to become a dynamic, ongoing activity; (2) the culture of the organization becomes more innovative and action oriented; (3) the management team is more motivated; and (4) performance improves.

Strategic Budgets The typical budget system is oriented to financial reporting, which in turn is geared to the fiscal year. The typical budget period is, in practice, one year. In contrast, strategic planning may cover considerably longer periods, so that carrying out a strategy can require several budgeting periods. The successful execution of strategy will require expenditures over several years, not only for capital assets, but for activities that will be expensed in the current year. The typical budget contains funds for strategic commitments as well as the normal operational budget, although the latter may be the dominant component. For example, the budget may contain funds for developing new sales promotions or training salespersons, expenses that are a part of the strategic plan. Normally the two funds are combined. The budget is simply increased by some amount to handle these strategic additions.

Operational control tends to center a manager's attention on short-term financial results—showing a profit, meeting a cost or revenue goal. Other demands on the manager are managing current operations, meeting deadlines, and responding to current pressures. Consequently, the manager pays attention to what is most pressing. It is easy to use strategic funds to support today's operations. The typical budget does not reveal this activity, however, and the strategy eventually suffers.

To motivate managers to pursue strategic objectives, the budget may separately identify strategic funds. In the words of Hax and Majluf, these funds are "expenses required for the implementation of strategic action programs whose benefits are expected to be accrued in the long term, beyond the current budget period."[31] Strategic funds have several uses:

Tangible Assets: The company may invest in new plant and equipment, office space, acquisitions, and the like.

Working Capital: Strategic commitments can cause the need for changes in working capital. For example, inventories may need to be increased to provide better service or in anticipation of entry into a new market.

Development Costs: These are expenses over and above the needs for existing business but required by strategic commitments. Examples might be sales promotion for a new product or the cost of management development.

One firm that has successfully developed a system that assures attention to the strategic dimension is Texas Instruments.[32] In the TI system, budgets and accounts are kept for ongoing current operations. However, TI also budgets for and separately tracks strategic funds for each new venture. The budgeting system is part of a whole system of planning, organization, leadership, and control. Senior executives allocate resources between the operations and strategic needs and rigorously review progress in strategic development, the appropriateness of the business objective for current conditions, and any actions to modify strategic programs. They also meet for progress reviews with managers at the strategic and tactics level. The almost continuous review and updating allows for revised budget allocation.

If a firm can accumulate costs by different projects or programs, it can account for operating and strategic funds separately. Then its profit and loss statements and budgets can report the separate uses and improve control.

Strategic Planning Controls

Conceptually strategic control is seen as the end of the strategic management cycle, but it is often difficult to tell when strategic control ends and a new cycle begins with strategy formulation. The information obtained from measuring, monitoring, and evaluating, and the results of corrective action, can be used to reevaluate strategy and undertake new planning efforts. Techniques that can be used in strategic control as well as strategic planning are strategic planning controls. The focus of these techniques can be to watch for deviation, but they can also lay the foundation for a new cycle of strategic management.

Periodic Planning Review Strategic planning—beginning with determination of the firm's mission and goals and continuing through the formulation of strategies, strategic thrusts, action programs, and budgets—is repeated at periodic intervals. A part of this process is a review of the environment to determine the validity of assumptions and forecasts and to review progress toward strategic goals. For many organizations, the most effective control technique may be to consciously repeat this scanning of the environment, assessment of performance, and examination of the organization for internal trends. In other words, a control cycle should be built into the periodic strategic planning process as a way to test the validity of the chosen strategy. The longer the period between reviews, the more likely deviations are to occur. But when the environment is not particularly dynamic, this technique can be very effective.

Strategic Issue Management When a company initiates strategic planning, it is usually an annual activity. Strategic planning is completed and revisions undertaken during the next year's annual planning cycle. Much time, expense, and effort can go into this activity, and top management can quickly find it burdensome. Strategic plans are developed for the long term and often take years to fully implement. When this is the case, a comprehensive annual review and revision is not required. Firms begin to undertake comprehensive reviews only every couple of years. However, the longer the time between reviews, the more likely changes are to have an important impact on the strategic plan.

To satisfy both concerns, firms begin to focus attention on a review of the progress made in the last planning cycle, taking care to zero in on components of the plans that have encountered difficulty. To this is added a review of key external issues. The focus of this activity, known as strategic issue management (SIM), becomes strategic issues. A strategic issue is "a forthcoming development, either inside or outside of the organization, which is likely to have an important impact on the ability of the enterprise to meet its objectives."[33]

In many cases, firms combine strategic issue management with the strategic planning system. In other cases, they have separated it from the annual planning cycle. SIM seems to be particularly relevant when the organization encounters many surprises, the environment is turbulent, and the signals from the environment are too weak to be recognized by the typical control systems. For example, Sun Oil has a Future Issues Committee whose purpose is to scan the environment, identify issues, and make the organization aware of their impact well before their effect is directly visible.[34]

SIM is a system to identify and correct deviations that may occur in the planning thrusts of a firm as a result of new strengths, weaknesses, opportunities, or threats. It is a continuous surveillance of possible key issues and the analysis of their pragmatic impact on the organization's performance. The organization can then determine what response to take and focus action on these issues. The American Council of Life Insurance has a program to look for changes in public needs. The organization regularly reviews numerous publications in fields ranging from science and economics to government and politics to see what trends may be emerging that would affect members. The council wants its members to be aware of critical strategic issues that affect their performance well before these are formulated into a public agenda for legislation. Anticipating these trends gives members a long lead time to formulate strategies.[35]

Implementing SIM requires some means of scanning the environment. Part of the usefulness of SIM is that it focuses on only a few issues, but the environment can be much broader. To find the issues it should focus on, the aforementioned insurance group uses 100 volunteers to survey the literature. Another way is to focus on the strategic thrusts that have not met expectations during strategic planning review. Or the organization may examine the key assumptions that are the foundation of the strategic plan.

A way to combine all three approaches would be to assign the responsibility for SIM to a group of senior managers representing a cross-section of the organization. The managers can divide into groups that look for developing trends within the firm, trends in strategic plan performance, and trends relating to key environmental sectors. Some of the responsibility may be delegated to staff or some other study group, but the senior managers should remain accountable and participate fully in analyzing the information. This process will identify numerous possible issues from which the senior executives must distill the ones that will potentially have the greatest impact and urgency.

Once the issues are identified and studied, a task force or project team can be formed to take action. One action may be to integrate the findings and proposals into the strategic plan. Other actions may require more immediate changes such as modifications in programs and operating plans. The task forces are frequently expected to follow up on their study through the implementation stage partially because the executives responsible for areas where changes are needed may be wedded to the status quo.

Normative Models Another type of control technique is to compare the strategies employed against a **normative model**. Management compares the appropriateness of a strategy against a norm derived from empirical research, case studies, or theory. This approach is probably best used in conjunction with other strategic control approaches, because it does not actually measure the progress of the strategy being employed. It can also be used as a check during the strategy formulation stage or during comprehensive reviews.

The norm is the suggested strategy with which the firm can compare its own strategy. Several models propose a set of strategies and suggest the conditions under which a firm should follow the strategy to obtain a particular performance result. By assessing the organization's situation and desired results, management can determine the appropriate strategy for connecting the two. This approach is similar to the prescriptive models of strategy formulation discussed earlier in the book.

Several normative models have been presented earlier in this text. The literature is too extensive to review here, but we will give several brief examples. The Profit Impact of Marketing Strategies (PIMS), which began in 1972, now has a data base of several thousand businesses. The PIMS study was able to identify strategic variables—such as investment intensity, market position, and quality of product or service—that could be used to predict return on investment, market share, or profits. For a fee, an organization can even submit data to have a prediction run for a strategy. A company can see if it fits the norm or if its strategy differs from the way other companies have achieved their results. Of course, violating the norm does not assure failure, but it may be a caution to critically evaluate why the company is doing it differently. The PIMS model has been subjected to criticism, and a company considering its use should be aware of its limitations.[36]

The Boston Consulting Group model (see Chapter 3) is also popular. It suggests strategies for businesses depending on how the business is categorized in terms of market share and market attractiveness.

Numerous other models can serve as normative comparisons or at least suggest the basis for critical questioning. For example, Harrigan has proposed a model for selecting strategies in declining industries, and Hofer has suggested a means of picking the right turnaround strategy.[37] The work of Michael Porter provides another framework for matching strategy to a variety of factors.[38]

One final caution is in order. The questioning should not continue forever. No strategy will succeed if it is constantly in doubt and if the makers cannot gather support for its validity. The normative models can serve as a basis for critique, reevaluation, and comparison, but the decision makers must determine themselves what is appropriate for their situation.

Summary

Control is what a manager does to ensure that actions conform to planned activities. It begins with the establishment of standards and performance measures based on goals and objectives. Information is collected to determine whether deviations from plans are occurring. Based on this information, management determines the reasons for any deviation and attempts to correct the problems. A good control system should offer benefits that are worth the cost of the system. The system should focus on factors that are critical to success. The information should be relevant to the user's needs. The system should facilitate corrective action. The information should be timely and understandable. The system should be adaptable to the needs of the users. Controls should be motivational, linking rewards to performance.

Strategic control is the control process applied to strategic concerns. It is concerned with the future of the firm and has an external focus. It is geared to events rather than to periodic reviews. Because of the time frame and the amount of resources involved, strategic control has a great impact on the company. The task of strategic control is less routine than operational control. It requires relatively great reliance on the creativity of the manager. The nature of strategic control varies with the firm's situation. When a firm's future can be projected from its past, the firm can use momentum control—trying to maintain the firm's present strategic direction into the future. When the environment can no longer be expected to be continuous, the firm needs leap control, which controls strategies that break with the past. Under these conditions, it is often difficult to separate strategic control from strategic planning.

One way of initiating strategic control is to use screening and steering controls. Of these, the most applicable is steering control, which tries to correct deviations before the results of the plan are known. Key steps in steering control are identifying the major thrusts required to achieve the domain and differential advantage; monitoring their progress; monitoring key external variables; reassessing the entire situation and strategy at milestones and key events; and evaluating the strategic management process.

Firms use several techniques to control their strategies. Responsibility centers group responsibilities for strategic activities so that performance can be evaluated. The typical centers are expense centers, revenue centers, profit centers, and investment centers. Some companies attempt to evaluate economic value creation of their responsibility centers, and many companies use multiple measures. Budgets are perhaps the most commonly employed control technique. When budgets are used for strategic control, they require certain modifications such as separating strategic funds from operating funds. Additional techniques are associated with strategic planning but can be used for strategic control. These techniques evaluate the validity of the strategic plans and steer the firm to its objectives. Strategic control at this level is subject to more uncertainty and requires more judgment from decision makers at the top.

Strategic control is the last stage of the strategic management process. Although we have discussed the strategic management process sequentially, all the stages of the process need to be integrated for strategic management to work well.

Questions

1. What is the role of control in the achievement of strategic objectives? Why is control needed?

2. Compare strategic control with operations control. How does leap control differ from momentum control? How is steering control practiced?

3. Describe the types of responsibility centers. When is each most appropriately used? If you were a CEO, which one would you prefer to use in controlling strategy?

4. How can budgets be used as a technique to control strategy?

5. Are strategic planning controls considered planning techniques or control techniques? When would you use each of them?

6. How can strategic controls be used to aid in strategic planning? How can they be used to aid in implementing strategy?

Notes

1. "CEO Interviews: Hicks B. Waldron, Avon Products," *Wall Street Transcript*, May 12, 1986, 81, 864, 81, 876–81, 877; and A. Dunkin, "Big Names Are Opening Doors for Avon," *Business Week*, June 1, 1987, 96–97.

2. Kenneth A. Merchant, *Control in Business Organizations*, (Marshfield, Mass.: Pitman Publishing, 1985), 5.

3. Keith H. Hammonds, "Teaching Discipline to Six-Year-Old Lotus," *Business Week*, July 4, 1988, 100–102.

4. See, for example, Chris Argyris, "Human Problems with Budgets," *Harvard Business Review* 31 (January–February 1953), 97–110; Melville Dalton, *Men Who Manage* (New York: Wiley, 1959), 194–215; and Edward E. Lawler, "Control Systems in Organizations," in *Handbook of Industrial and Organizational Psychology*, ed. Marvin D. Dunnette (Chicago: Rand McNally, 1976), 1247–1287.

5. Cortland Camman and David Nadler, "Fit Control Systems to Your Managerial Style," *Harvard Business Review* (January–February 1976): 65.

6. Gregory L. Miles and John A. Byrne, "Smeltdown at Armco: Behind the Steelmaker's Long Slide," *Business Week*, February 1, 1988, 48–50.

7. Robert H. Waterman, Jr., *The Renewal Factor: How the Best Get and Keep the Competitive Edge* (New York: Bantam Books, 1987), excerpted in *Business Week*, September 14, 1987, 100–120.

8. Ibid., 105.

9. Ibid.

10. Miles and Byrne, "Smeltdown at Armco."

11. Peter Lorange, Michael F. Scott Morton, and Sumantra Ghoshal, *Strategic Control* (St. Paul, Minn.: West, 1986), 14–18.

12. Ibid., 63.

13. Ibid., 104.

14. William H. Newman, *Constructive Control* (Englewood Cliffs, N.J.: Prentice-Hall, 1975), 6–9.

15. Based on Boris Yavitz and William H. Newman, *Strategy in Action* (New York: The Free Press, 1982), 206–220.

16. Monci Jo Williams, "Synergy Works at American Express," *Fortune*, February 16, 1987, 79–80.

17. This discussion of responsibility centers draws on the conceptual framework of Robert N. Anthony and John Dearden, *Management Control Systems* (Homewood, Ill.: Irwin, 1980), 181–196; and Richard F. Vancil, "What Kind of Management Control Do You Need?" *Harvard Business Review* 51 (March–April 1973): 75–86.

18. Example adapted from Thomas J. Peters and Robert H. Waterman, Jr., *In Search of Excellence* (New York: Harper & Row, 1982), 162.

19. C. A. Kline, Jr., and Howard C. Hessler, "The Du Pont Chart System for Appraising Operating Performance," in *Readings in Cost Accounting, Budgeting, and Control*, rev. ed., ed. William E. Thomas (Cincinnati, Ohio: Southwestern, 1969), 751–775.

20. John Dearden, "The Case against ROI Control," *Harvard Business Review* 47 (May–June 1969): 124–134.

21. Ibid., 136.

22. For a discussion of the impact of using different methods of valuing fixed assets, see Ibid. and Lorange, Morton, and Ghoshal, *Strategic Control*, 72–75.

23. J. S. Reece and W. R. Cool, "Measuring Investment Center Performance," *Harvard Business Review* 56 (May–June 1978): 28–49.

24. The discussion on the technicalities of calculating has been necessarily brief throughout this section. The reader is encouraged to consult more thorough treatments such as William E. Fruhan, *Financial Strategy* (Homewood, Ill.: Irwin, 1979), 35–62; and Arnoldo C. Hax and Nicolas S. Majluf, *Strategic Management* (Englewood Cliffs, N.J.: Prentice-Hall, 1984), 211–242.

25. For several interesting techniques that build on the basic model to analyze firms within an industry as well as between units in a firm, see Hax and Majluf, *Strategic Management*, 209–242.

26. John C. Camillus, *Strategic Planning and Management Control* (Lexington, Mass.: Lexington Books, 1986), 103–119.

27. Richard L. Daft and Norman B. Macintosh, "The Nature and Use of Formal Control Systems for Management Control and Strategy Implementation," *Journal of Management* 10 (Spring 1984): 43–66.

28. Carolyn Conn, "Budgets: Planning and Control Devices?" *Managerial Planning* 29 (January–February 1981): 36–38; and Charles C. Gibbons, "The Psychology of Budgeting," *Business Horizons* 5 (June 1972): 48–49.

29. F. Grant Schutte, "Budgetary Control Systems for the Eighties," *Journal of General Management* 5 (Spring 1980): 3–18.

30. Ibid., 10.

31. Hax and Majluf, *Strategic Management*, 25.

32. Richard F. Vancil, "Texas Instruments Incorporated," in *Strategic Planning Systems*, eds. Peter Lorange and Richard F. Vancil (Englewood Cliffs, N.J.: Prentice-Hall, 1977), 338–361.

33. H. Igor Ansoff, *Implanting Strategic Management* (Englewood Cliffs, N.J.: Prentice-Hall, 1984), 337–351.

34. Lorange, Morton, and Ghoshal, *Strategic Control*, 103.

35. J. C. Camillus and D. K. Datta, "Designing Sensitive Systems: Integrating Strategic Planning and Issues Management" (Paper presented at the 44th Annual Meeting of the Academy of Management, Boston, 1984).

36. Articles providing a good introduction to the literature on PIMS are Carl R. Anderson and Frank T. Paine, "PIMS: A Reexamination," *Academy of Management Review* 3 (July 1978): 602–611; and Vasudevan Rasmanujam and N. Venkatraman, "An Inventory and Critique of Strategy Research Using the PIMS Database," *Academy of Management Review* 9 (April 1984): 138–151.

37. Kathryn Rudie Harrigan, "Strategies for Declining Industries," *Journal of Business Strategy* 1 (Fall 1980): 20–34; and Charles W. Hofer, "Turnaround Strategies," *Journal of Business Strategy* 1 (Summer 1980): 19–31.

38. Michael E. Porter, *Competitive Strategy* (New York: The Free Press, 1980); and Michael E. Porter, *Competitive Advantage* (New York: The Free Press, 1985).

Case for Discussion

The Washtuchna Casket Company

The Washtuchna Casket Company mass-produces over 200 models of metal caskets, which it sells directly to funeral directors in the United States, Europe, and Japan. The U.S market represents 85 percent of its business. The funeral directors pay from $600 to $2,200 per unit. Last year, sales were $120 million, with an operating profit of $22.8 million.

Manufacturing caskets is a lot like making car bodies. The company hires many engineers from the automobile companies and employs many similar techniques. Fit of parts, finishes, and corrosion protection are important to buyers, and the company has worked hard on these qualities to please customers. Washtuchna's manufacturing plant is highly automated so that no human assistance is needed for many processes, including sanding, welding, stamping, and painting. All production is done in one plant, which can produce 330 caskets a day. The company uses just-in-time inventory control and has reduced steel inventories to four days. Washtuchna has increased the number of units produced by 35 percent since 1982.

The casket industry is heavily influenced by the death rate. In the United States, death rates per 1,000 have declined by 7 percent in the past 20 years. In addition, cremations and foreign competition have increased. The growth rate of industry sales has declined.

Discussion Questions

1. What are the critical success factors likely to be for Washtuchna Casket Company?
2. Briefly describe the kind of strategy that is likely to succeed for this company.
3. What kind of control system will be needed to achieve this strategy? Be as specific as possible.

Part Three

Strategic Issues

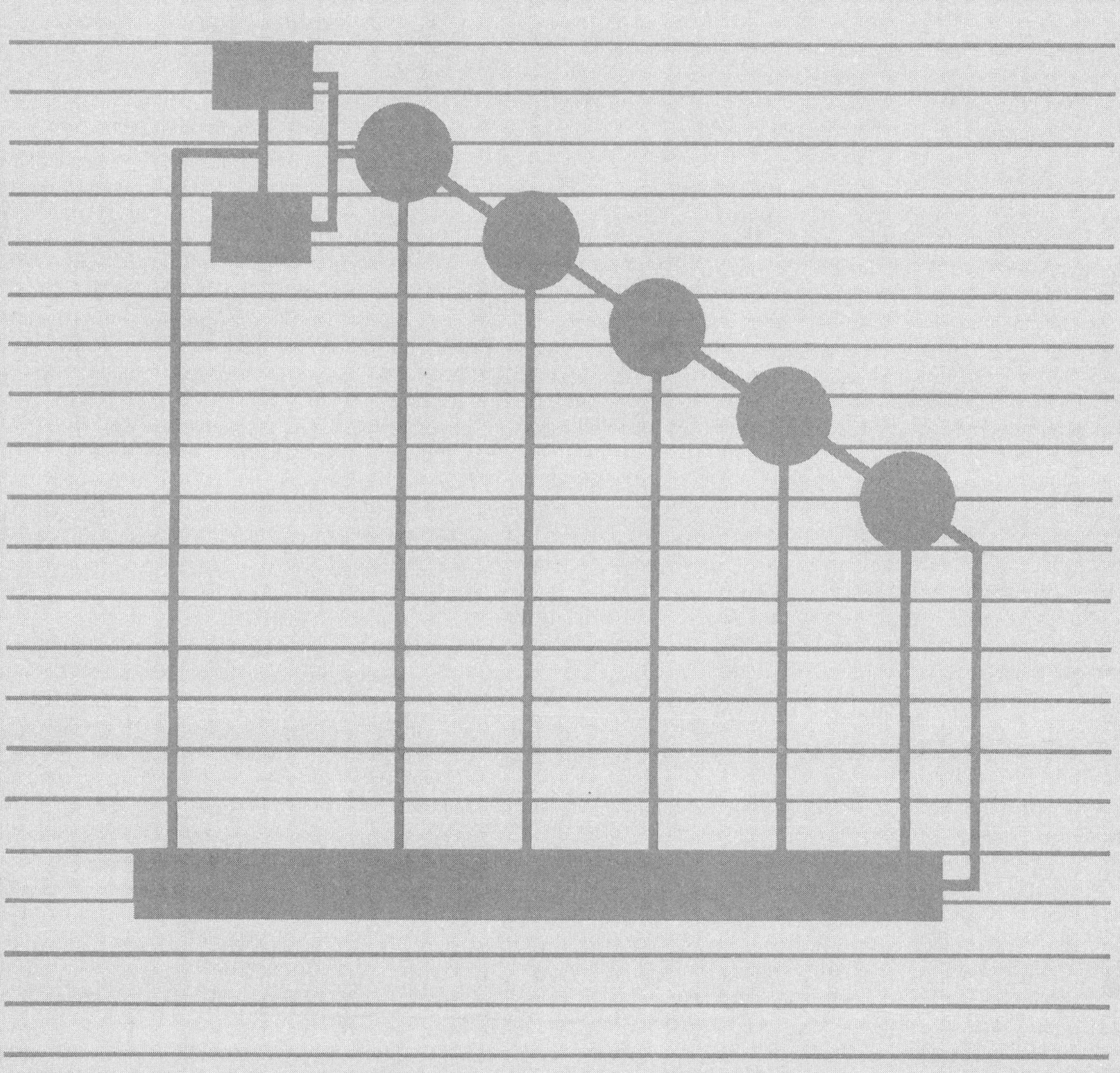

Chapter 9

Special Cases of Strategic Management: Entrepreneurial and Not-for-Profit Organizations

He that will not apply new remedies must expect new evils: for time is the greatest innovator.

—Francis Bacon, *Essays* [1625]

Learning Objectives

- To recognize the similarities and differences among private sector firms, entrepreneurial ventures, and public sector organizations.
- To learn about entrepreneurship.
- To gain an understanding of the psychological, personality and demographical factors that are common among successful entrepreneurs.
- To learn what successful entrepreneurs do and how they do it.
- To understand the unique strategic requirements of public sector organizations.
- To learn how to conduct environmental assessments and capabilities analyses in public sector organizations.
- To gain insight into the strategic options available to the public sector manager.

THE United States is one of the most innovative countries in the industrialized world. It has traditionally led in new-product innovation even during periods when it trailed other countries in productivity and quality. In addition, the United States has always had an unusual capacity to create new jobs. But where do the new jobs come from, and who creates them? The answer lies in the country's entrepreneurial spirit and the small, entrepreneurial firms that it generates.

How important are small businesses to the U.S. economy? Over 93 percent of the 19 million businesses in the United States are considered small by the criteria established by the Small Business Administration. These firms account for over 50 percent of the gross product originating (GPO) and employ approximately

60 percent of the work force.[1] According to one estimate, over 100 million Americans directly or indirectly depend on small businesses for their livelihood.[2] Small, entrepreneurial firms have provided nearly half of the major innovations in recent years.[3]

Considering the importance of small, entrepreneurial organizations to the economy, future managers should be aware of the management processes in these types of firms. Most managers who become top-level executives start in small, entrepreneurial firms as founders or one of the initial cadre of employees.

Another type of organization is extremely important to the economies of most countries and has special strategic management requirements: the not-for-profit organization. Like the entrepreneurial firm, the not-for-profit organization faces unique environmental demands and has constraints on its capabilities that are not considerations for most larger, established for-profit companies. Whereas entrepreneurial ventures are greatly influenced by the founder, not-for-profits are subject to the demands of their sponsors or funding governments.

This chapter considers both not-for-profit and entrepreneurial organizations because they are similar in four areas that make them different from private sector, for-profit firms. These four areas are types of environmental demands, importance of internal capabilities, influence of management on strategic decisions, and the source of their mission. Each of these areas will be discussed in the chapter.

Entrepreneurship and Strategic Management

Entrepreneurship is the practice of entrepreneurial behavior through the creation and operation of a new venture. Entrepreneurs and entrepreneurial ventures are frequently confused with small-business owners and small-business ventures. Carland, Hoy, Boulton, and Carland help resolve this confusion by providing concise definitions for each type of enterprise.[4]

A **small-business venture** is any business that meets the SBA criteria for a small business, is independently owned and operated, and does not engage in innovative marketing or operations. An example of a small business is the grocery store that never grows beyond a neighborhood market and ceases to operate when the owners retire. It follows that the small-business owner is an individual or small group (typically a family)

> who establishes and manages a business for the principal purpose of furthering personal goals. The business must be the primary source of income and will consume the majority of one's time and resources. The owner perceives the business as an extension of his or her personality, intricately bound with family needs and desires.[5]

In contrast, an **entrepreneur** is an individual who establishes and manages a venture in order to make a profit and see it grow. The entrepreneur is an innovator and uses varying degrees of sophisticated strategic planning and management. The entrepreneurial firm uses principles of strategic management and innovation to create and maintain a competitive advantage.[6] McDonald's Corporation and Apple Computers are examples of entrepreneurial firms that were built on the drive and strength of their founders. McDonald's success was based on marketing innovation, whereas Apple is noted for its technological innovation.

One of the most famous modern entrepreneurs is Donald Trump, the New York real estate developer and casino owner. Starting with the help of his developer father, Trump at 28 initiated an innovative and risky venture to build a grand hotel in New York City. He has been in the vanguard of the New York real estate boom ever since. Trump now completes about one major development project every year and is still not satisfied. He intends to become a force in the gambling industry and an international business tycoon. Trump typifies the modern entrepreneur and perfectly fits the definition.[7]

What Makes an Entrepreneur

Most managers and management experts agree that the entrepreneur is different from other people. Chapter Appendix 9.1 lists characteristics that have been associated with entrepreneurship. These characteristics generally fall into three categories: psychological factors, personality factors, and demographic factors. The discussion here is limited to a few characteristics that have been most consistently related to entrepreneurial activity.

Psychological Factors The three psychological factors associated with most entrepreneurs are high need for achievement, internal locus of control, and high propensity toward risk. These factors either singularly or in combination have been related to entrepreneurship in several studies.

McClelland discovered that the *need for achievement* was high in individuals who started their own businesses.[8] In other words, entrepreneurs displayed traits related to high achievers. They set challenging but attainable goals, and they require frequent and timely feedback about performance.

Locus of control refers to the individual's belief that his or her destiny is controlled from within or by external events. Most entrepreneurs have an internal locus of control; that is, they feel they have control over events that affect their success. They can use initiative and drive to create opportunities and exploit them. Other people may be more likely to believe that events beyond their control determine their fate. They believe that luck or being in the right place at the right time holds the key to their success.

Entrepreneurs are *risk takers*. They are willing to risk money, reputation, security, and status on starting a new venture. An example is Donald D. Iverson, president and founder of Iverson Technology Corporation, a firm that produces computer security devices for government and industry. Before starting his current successful business in 1981, he ran a string of computer-related businesses.[9] Like many entrepreneurs, Iverson searched for new ventures and had little concern for the risks involved.

Considering the internal drive, self-confidence, and tolerance for risk that an individual must have to abandon the security of a large company to start a new venture, it is easy to understand why entrepreneurs have these characteristics. However, this does not mean that all persons with these traits will be successful entrepreneurs. Other skills that managers acquire through experience and training are also necessary to start and successfully operate a new venture.

Personality Factors Some experts have attempted to describe the makeup of an entrepreneur by focusing on personality characteristics. Three personality factors that are often related to entrepreneurship are opportunism, ambition, and self-confidence. Research has shown that entrepreneurs display high levels of these personality characteristics.

Smith identified two basic types of entrepreneurs, who differed in their view of the environment and reaction to it.[10] The first type he labeled **opportunistic**. Such an entrepreneur perceives a broad range of environmental impacts, exhibits breadth of education and training, and has a high level of social involvement. In addition, he or she is flexible and future oriented. The opportunistic individual seeks and plans for the growth of the enterprise. The opposite of such an entrepreneur is the **craftsman** entrepreneur. This individual has a narrow perspective of the environment, received relatively little formal education, and shuns social involvement. The craftsman also is more rigid in his or her beliefs and tends to plan from day to day. According to some authors, the *opportunistic* entrepreneur is more likely to be the founder of a successful entrepreneurial venture than is the craftsman entrepreneur.[11]

Ambition has long been associated with entrepreneurship.[12] The energetic and ambitious person is thought to be more willing to devote the time and effort necessary to create an entrepreneurial venture. An example of a person with the ambition and drive needed to be a successful entrepreneur is Bill Gates, the young founder of Microsoft. In just 12 years, he built his software company from a back-room start-up operation to the second largest producer of computer software.

Recently, he took on IBM and convinced the company to use a Microsoft product as the main software in their new generation of PCs. IBM had intended to develop their own software for the new line of PC products, but the ambitious Gates argued to win a trial period in which he worked with IBM engineers and tailored his product to IBM's needs. The payoff was IBM's exclusive endorsement of the Microsoft product. A less ambitious and energetic David would not have challenged the IBM Goliath.[13]

Entrepreneurs usually need *self-confidence* to believe that they can successfully start a new venture. Statistics on business start-ups that are still viable after only three years are alarming. Approximately 95 percent of the businesses started in the United States fail by their third year. Yet thousands of new businesses are started every year, and many of these by individuals who have failed at previous start-ups. These persistent risk takers have the confidence to believe that they can defeat the odds and be one of the 5 percent that survive and prosper over the long term. For example, the founders of Autodesk Inc., a commercial graphics software company, overcame meager start-up capital and industry tradition to become one of the hottest growth companies in the United States. They had the confidence in their product and approach to avoid the traditional expensive, captive sales force and developed a network of dealers, like those used in the automobile industry. These dealers have become the heart of the Autodesk distribution system and their primary sales vehicle, helping to make Autodesk a $52 million company in only a few years.[14]

Demographic Factors Some characteristics related to entrepreneurship are associated with the demographic context of the individual's personal and professional development. Factors such as the entrepreneurial predispositions of parents, age, education, and previous work experience are thought to indicate a tendency toward entrepreneurship. These factors describe the personal and professional setting in which an individual forms mental and emotional preferences. Therefore, providing an entrepreneurial environment during a person's formative years is thought to develop the suitable psychological and personality characteristics. This leads some people to believe that society can actually nurture entrepreneurship in the population.

Whether or not entrepreneurs can be developed, it is important to understand the characteristics that are associated with entrepreneurship. Because new ventures and small businesses are important to the economy, it is in the best interests of the nation to recognize and encourage the formation and growth of new businesses. The founders of today's new ventures may be the strategic managers of tomorrow's major corporations.

What Entrepreneurs Do

One of the major distinctions between small-business owners and entrepreneurs is the use of strategic management practices by entrepreneurs.[15] As strategic managers, entrepreneurs make many of the same decisions as their counterparts in large organizations. The strategic management tasks are typically performed by the one or a few founders of the firm rather than a staff of planners, but the same factors are considered. Entrepreneurial strategic managers must formulate, implement, and control strategy for their venture, just as managers of established firms do.

As the definition of an entrepreneurial firm suggests, much of its success is based on the activities of the strategic manager of the venture. According to some authors, the primary competitive activities of entrepreneurs fall into five categories:[16]

1. Introduction of new goods
2. Introduction of new methods of production
3. Opening of new markets
4. Opening of new sources of supply
5. Industrial reorganization

Entrepreneurs perform one or more of these activities because they recognize that they have a distinctive competence in that area and can capitalize on it.[17]

The entrepreneur's distinctive competence can be based on the creation of a new product like the personal computer at Apple. Or it could be the development of an innovative method of production or distribution. Ken Kucera, the cofounder of Swallowtail Inc.—a new computer software venture—found that the software that increases the capacity and speed of the hard disk on a PC was in demand but also was difficult to protect from unauthorized copying. Kucera discovered a method of incorporating the software into an integrated circuit board for installation into a PC. This novel way to produce and package Swallowtail's product allowed the firm to market its software without fear of illegal duplication.

Another way to look at the activities of entrepreneurs is suggested by Gartner.[18] He says that the primary behaviors of entrepreneurs are to locate business opportunities, accumulate resources, produce a product or service, market products or services, build an organization, and respond to government and society. You can see that many of these activities are performed by strategic managers of large firms. Therefore, successful entrepreneurs must be effective strategic managers as well as creators and innovators.

Because entrepreneurs are strategic managers in the true sense, they are also responsible for strategy formulation in their new enterprise. Bracker and Pearson observed varying levels of sophistication in strategy formulation in small, entrepreneurial firms.[19] The lowest level was the total absence of any structured planning process. Somewhat more sophisticated were firms that relied on the intuitive development of plans based on the experiences of the founders. At a higher level of sophistication, firms generate formal, short-range operational plans and budgets. At the highest level of sophistication in strategy development, the firm develops formalized, written, long-range strategic plans based on environmental assessment. Successful firms were more likely to have a higher level of sophistication in their strategy formulation.

However, entrepreneurs seldom have the expertise, time, and inclination to engage in sophisticated strategy development. More often than not, strategy formulation is unstructured, irregular, and uncomprehensive. Using the terms described in Chapter 4, it is more incremental than synoptic.[20] Given this lack of sophistication, it is understandable why such a large percentage of start-up businesses fail.

Importance of Strategy Formulation to Entrepreneurial Organizations

Evidence strongly favors the view that structured planning of some kind benefits small, entrepreneurial organizations. Of several research studies reviewed, all but one showed some improvement from using planning in the small firm.[21] Some firms improved their ability to evaluate the consequences of their actions. Others enjoyed greater profitability and new product success. Still other firms reported that more structured planning led to greater growth in terms of personnel, sales, and assets.[22] Finally, Bracker and Pearson report test results showing "young firms with long planning histories outperformed old firms with short planning histories with regard to revenue growth and entrepreneurial compensation."[23] Likewise, the Strategic Application "DeBenedetti's Strategy Builds an Empire" illustrates how the international entrepreneur Carlo De Benedetti effectively formulated and executed strategy to build one of the largest conglomerate empires in Western Europe.

STRATEGIC APPLICATIONS: INTERNATIONAL

De Benedetti's Strategy Builds an Empire

An entrepreneur of international status is Carlo De Benedetti, CEO of Olivetti. Well known as a European entrepreneur, De Benedetti took over the reins of a faltering Olivetti in 1978 and devoted all of his energies to reviving this nearly bankrupt typewriter manufacturer.

In 1984, having successfully turned Olivetti around, he returned to his entrepreneurial interest. He turned over the operational responsibilities of Olivetti to others and started to develop his master plan for creating an empire. Through effective strategic management and shrewd entrepreneurship, De Benedetti has assembled a series of holding companies with products that range from pasta to high fashion and from auto parts to financial services. For this entrepreneur, strategy formulation on a grand scale was crucial for the success of his many entrepreneurial ventures.

With his strategic plan as a guide and the help of a small group of assistants, De Benedetti used one of his holding companies to raise more than $750 million to acquire stakes in companies as diverse as Yves St. Laurent designer products and Valeo, a manufacturer of auto parts. Together his one French and two Italian groups control eight companies, of which only five are industrial. In 1984 De Benedetti purchased a firm with one of the most respected names in pasta—Buitoni—in only one week. This combination of effective strategy formulation and agile operations has given De Benedetti a reputation as one of Europe's premier entrepreneurs.

Source: "DeBenedetti's Double Life," *Business Week*, August 24, 1987, 42–47.

Unique Features of Strategic Management in Entrepreneurial Firms

If managers of entrepreneurial ventures cope with many of the same problems and issues as senior executives of major firms, how does strategic management differ for the small firm? Five characteristics appear to be unique to the strategic management process in small, entrepreneurial organizations. Figure 9.1 shows these characteristics as they affect the entrepreneur-manager.

Strategic management of an entrepreneurial venture typically focuses more on the short term. Because innovation is the key to success for the entrepreneur, the new product, production or distribution system, or marketing approach that forms the basis for the new business will be only partially developed at start-up. As the business matures, the innovation will be refined and replaced by other innovations. This process of frequent change and adaptation requires a shorter planning horizon. In addition, because most entrepreneurs initially must be creators as well as strategic and operational managers, they seldom have the luxury of the time and resources for an elaborate long-term strategy. Many successful entrepreneurial ventures were well into the growth stage of their original product's life cycle before they had the time to concentrate on developing longer range strategies.

Because entrepreneurs are frequently experts in the areas in which they innovate but not in strategically managing a new firm, they typically lack the knowledge and experience to be effective strategic planners. Therefore, successful entrepreneurs are more likely to use outside consultants to help them with strategy formulation. A

Figure 9.1 Strategic Management in Small Entrepreneurial Firms

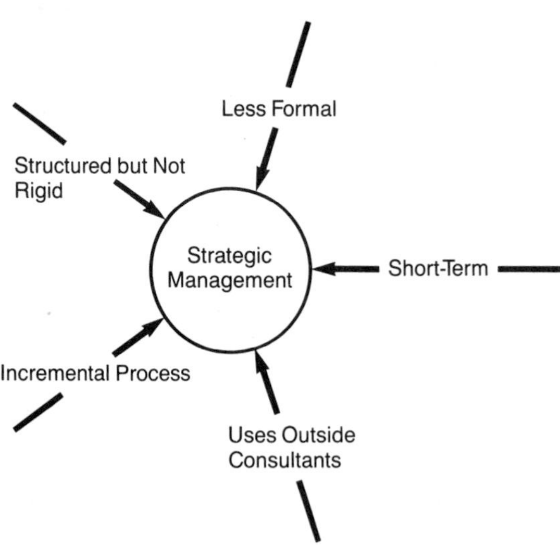

number of sources of outside help are available, including seminars, books, and planning kits from the Small Business Administration (SBA) and private firms such as some of the larger accounting firms. The SBA offers direct assistance to the small venture through seminars and consultants. Another source of inexpensive consulting help is local business colleges that require students of business, under the guidance of their instructor, to conduct strategic analyses and develop strategic recommendations for local small businesses. All of these sources of consulting help are relatively inexpensive.

Another characteristic of strategic management in small, entrepreneurial firms is its incremental rather than rational, synoptic nature. The logical, incremental approach to strategy development was discussed in Chapter 4. Because most small, entrepreneurial ventures have limited start-up capital, they do not have slack financial resources to adapt to drastic shifts in their environments. Therefore, small changes in the firm's markets can produce a substantial shift in strategy. Such rapid strategy shifts as a consequence of competitors' reactions to the firm's initial success make strategy appear to develop through an incremental process.[24]

A dramatic example of how rapidly the fortunes of an entrepreneurial venture can change involves Beeba's Creations Inc. The company's founder, A. C. Waney, brought his firm from $3.2 million in sales in 1984 to $94 million just three years later. His innovative skill lies in recognizing hot new styles for teenagers and using factories in Turkey and Sri Lanka to make copies under store brand labels. Waney was forced to adjust his strategy when his company posted a loss during one quarter of $124,000 because a delivery of casual shorts arrived too late to be in fashion.[25] Not all industries are as volatile as the fashion industry, but the vulnerability of small firms to environmental shifts makes an incremental approach to strategy development most effective.

Strategy formulation in successful entrepreneurial firms is structured at the operational and strategic levels. This means that organizations have written, short-term action plans that include budgets. In addition, some organizations have short-term strategic plans that use environmental assessment to determine strategy. Whether the plans are operational or strategic, the important requirement is that they be written and structured, though not rigid. They should also be specific enough to direct the competitive actions of the firm.

Last, research has shown that strategy development is less formal in entrepreneurial organizations than in larger firms. Because entrepreneurial managers have less time to devote to formal planning, they tend to conduct informal meetings rather than instituting formal processes that would occupy large amounts of employees' time. In many cases the entrepreneurs doing the planning are busy refining their innovation to meet changes in market demands and lack the administrative training to initiate a formal planning system. However, in successful firms, these entrepreneur/managers do develop short-range plans and put them in writing.

The Strategic Management Process in Entrepreneurial Firms

In small, entrepreneurial organizations, as in larger firms, the strategic management process consists of a series of choices. However, because of the short-term and incremental nature of strategic management in new ventures, the choices originate with the entrepreneur's innovation and focus on specific short-range and operational issues that are not a part of strategic management for the larger firm. Figure 9.2 illustrates the process that an entrepreneur might use in the strategic management of a new venture.

Innovation and Business Conditions Analysis The process of creating a new venture starts in the mind of the entrepreneur; from a mere idea, it becomes a decision to act on that idea, and then grows to a start-up business. The transformation of an idea into a new business may take only a few weeks or several years. The innovation may be in the form of a new product, service, operations process, or form of distribution. The Strategic Application "John Fanning Innovates in the Personnel Business" describes how John Fanning, founder of Uniforce Temporary Personnel, used an innovative method to distribute temporary services.

Once the entrepreneur has refined the innovative idea enough to check its feasibility in the market, he or she can initiate an analysis of the attractiveness of the business conditions for the new venture. This environmental assessment consists primarily of analyzing potential markets to determine the feasibility of the new venture. Issues that should be addressed include the anticipated size of the potential market or market niche that the entrepreneur will pursue. Within the chosen market niche, what share of the market does the entrepreneur expect? What competitive forces will the venture face, and how vulnerable is it to these forces? Specifically, who or what are the firm's competition? Who are the buyers, where are they located, and

Figure 9.2 Strategic Management Process in Entrepreneurial Ventures

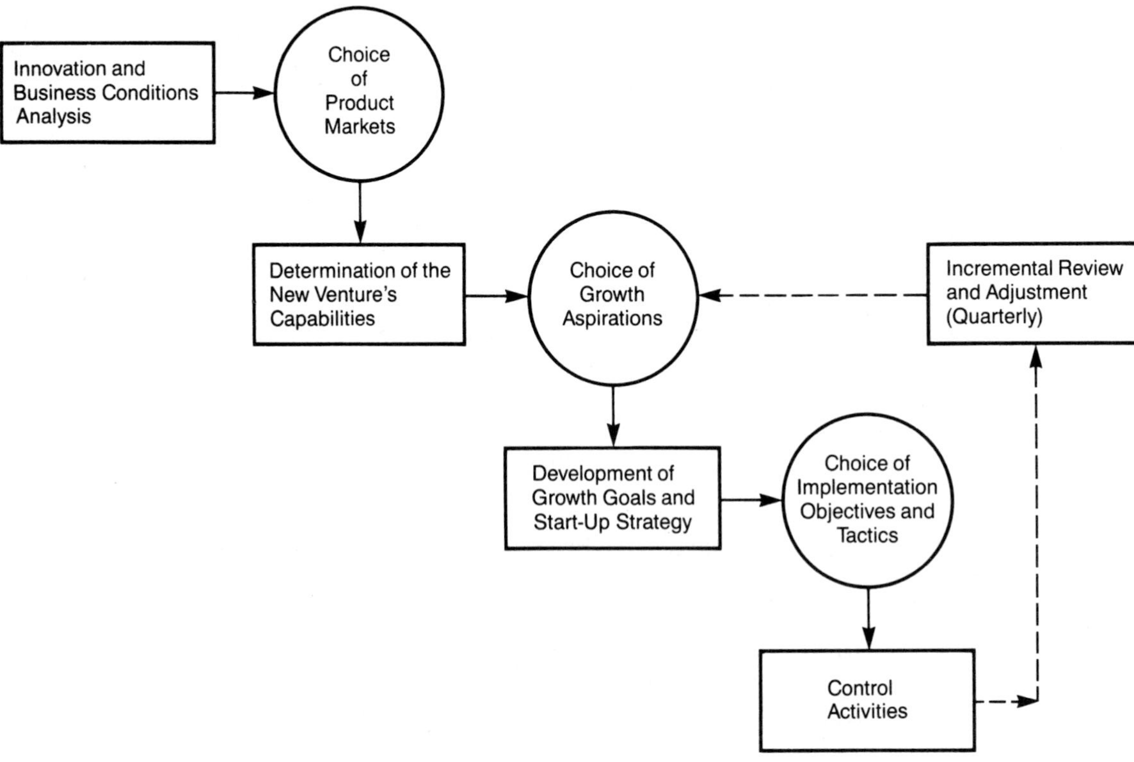

how many are there? How will the firm distribute to its buyers? Does the firm depend on suppliers that have a reputation for being reliable? Does it have a patent or other protection from larger firms that may enter the market if it successfully develops? Is the firm's innovation completely novel, so that a market must be created, or will the product compete or substitute in an existing market?

A thorough market analysis is the foundation of an effective plan for development of the new venture. Like the senior manager of a larger firm, the entrepreneur needs to understand the environment in which he or she plans to conduct business in order to decide which markets to enter with the new product or service. In analyzing potential markets, the entrepreneur should ask questions such as those listed in Table 9.1.

Choice of Domain and Determination of the New Venture's Capabilities Newly created organizations have not yet developed stable cultures. They are typically started by one or a few founders who intend to build a highly profitable business. Entrepreneurial organizations can have any geographical orientation but are primarily regional at their outset. Therefore, organizational factors have minimal impact on the selection of a

STRATEGIC APPLICATIONS

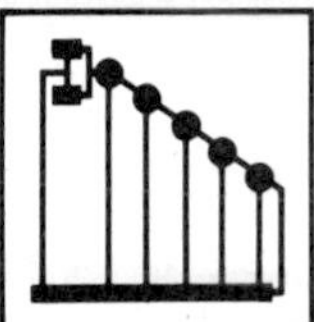

John Fanning Innovates in the Personnel Business

John Fanning sold his share of a successful personnel agency that carries his name to start a new venture in the business of temporary services. This was a fairly risky undertaking for Fanning, even though he had a successful record of new business start-up. Manpower Inc. and Kelly Services Inc. were the major players in the temporary services business, and both had a large share of the market. Fanning had to come up with an innovation that would allow ample growth without competing head-on with the industry giants.

The innovative spark came in the form of an initial penetration strategy and a novel distribution method. Fanning decided to locate his outlets in areas that had been mostly neglected by the big players. Uniforce, Fanning's firm, has opened most of its approximately 60 offices in small towns that the other temporary services firms have avoided. This has allowed the company to build a solid reputation and experience base up to annual sales of $60 million. Fanning is now ready to enter larger markets and compete directly with Kelly and Manpower.

The most important innovation credited to Fanning, however, is his decision to franchise 83 percent of Uniforce's locations. The use of franchising to engender an entrepreneurial spirit and drive in the owner-managers of these locations has resulted in a highly motivated work force that is dedicated to making the firm a success. Thanks in part to this innovation, the company achieved an average 63 percent growth in earnings between 1983 and 1987.

Source: "Will Success Be Merely Temporary?" *Business Week*, May 25, 1987, 86.

market and task environment for the entrepreneurial firm. However, environmental and personal factors exert strong influence on this selection process.

The process of domain selection and the constraints on that process vary with the type of entrepreneur and level of capitalization of the entrepreneurial organization. Some entrepreneurs are active founders of the venture and participate in product development and operational management of the new firm. Others are passive entrepreneurs, who only supply the start-up capital for the new venture. For example, some new firms are created by venture capitalists who have pooled their money to find an investment with large, long-term returns. These entrepreneurs will look for a product or service to meet that goal. If their combined investments are large, the new venture can operate in a national market and have sophisticated technological requirements. If the total pool of investment funds is limited, then the geographical scope of the venture's domain will be more modest. More typical for new businesses is the entrepreneur who develops a product or service idea that he or she desires to produce and market. In this instance, the product characteristics drive much of the process of selecting a domain.

The selection process for most entrepreneurial firms consists of the steps listed in Table 9.2. The unique features of the selection process for the entrepreneurial organization are located in steps 2, 6, and 9. Step 2 emphasizes the importance of the available capital as a criterion for selection of the initial markets. Step 6 considers only the personal constraints and preferences of the entrepreneur. Step 9 involves

Table 9.1 Format for Market Analysis

Industry Description and Outlook

What industry are we in?

How big is it now? How big will it be in five years?

Ten years?

What are its chief characteristics?

Who are or will be the major customers? Specifically, are they Fortune 100, 500, or 1000 companies, or are they small proprietorships?

What are or will be the major applications of our product or service?

What are the major trends in the industry?

Target Markets

What are the major segments we will penetrate?

For each major application, what are the following:

a. Requirements by the customer or regulatory agencies?
b. Current ways of filling these requirements?
c. Buying habits of the customer?
d. Impact on customers of using our product or service?
   —User economics. (How much will it save them per year? What return on investment will they get?)
   —Other impacts. (Will they have to change their way of doing things? Buy other equipment? Change work habits? Modify organizational structure?)
e. How will these segments and applications change over the next three to five years?

Competition

Which companies will we compete with (including those like us who are not yet in the market)?

How do we compare with competitive companies?

What competition will we meet in each product or service line?

How does our product or service compare with others (especially in the eyes of the customer)?

What is the market share of each existing competitor?

Do we threaten the major strategic objectives or self-image of competition, or just financial results? (for example, will competition seek to destroy us at any cost?)

Do we interface with important, noncompetitive equipment whose manufacturer might still be reluctant to support our product due to warranty, liability, or image considerations?

---

evaluating all organizations and agencies in the task environment rather than a limited list as recommended for established organizations. Because the new strategic manager has no experience with many of the organizations in the firm's task environment, a thorough evaluation is a necessary help in selecting the organizations and agencies that can increase the probability that the new enterprise will survive for the first critical three years.

The most important influence on domain selection for the entrepreneurial organization is the personality and preferences of the founder(s). As described earlier, entrepreneurs are innovative, independent, ambitious, and achievement-oriented risk takers who like to control their own destiny.[26] Generally, entrepreneurs give up secure positions in large, established organizations, are confident, and form strong opinions. These opinions carry over to their beliefs about their capabilities and the potential

Table 9.1 *(continued)*

Reaction from Specific Prospective Customers

Which prospective customers have we talked to?

What was their reaction?

Have they seen or tested a realistic prototype of the product or service?

If so, what was their reaction?

Marketing Activities

What are our plans for:

a. Marketing strategy (one-stop shopping, specialization, market share objective, image)?
b. Distribution (direct, retail)?
c. Promotion (advertising, conventions, etc.)?
d. Pricing (demand pricing or cost-based pricing, volume discounts, changes in pricing over time)?
e. Sales appeals?
f. Geographical penetration (domestic, Europe, Far East, etc.)?
g. Field service or product support?
h. Setting priorities among segments, applications, marketing activities? The limited human resources in a new venture cannot be all things to all people, regardless of the opportunities.

Selling Activities

How will we identify prospective customers? Consider not just the companies, but the relevant decision makers who can spend either discretionary or budgeted funds.

How will we decide whom to contact and in what order?

What level of selling effort will we have (for example, the number of salespeople)?

What efficiency will we have (for example, how many calls per salesperson)?

What conversion rates will we be able to obtain (for example, how many calls per demonstration; how many demonstrations per sale)?

How long will each of these activities take in person-days? In elapsed time?

What will our initial order size be? What is the likelihood and size of repeat orders?

Based on these assumptions, what is the sales productivity of each salesperson?

What is the commission structure for the salespeople?

Does it have increasing or decreasing rates for exceeding quota? What will the average salesperson earn per year, and how long will he or she have to wait to receive commissions (for example, sales cycle milestones)?

What evidence do we have to back up our answers to these estimates?

---

for their new product or service. They also influence the selection of feasible markets for the new venture. As steps 6 through 9 of the selection process indicate, the selection of product-markets in which the firm will operate determines to a great extent its domain. Therefore, the domain of the new organization is a function of the entrepreneur's personal preferences regarding product-markets.

As discussed in earlier chapters, the preferences of the strategic manager are determined by several personal factors. Two of the main personal factors are functional perspective and prior professional experience. Thus, the entrepreneur will be inclined to stay in technical and commercial areas with which he or she is familiar. Likewise, the entrepreneur's prior professional experience will dictate how the new enterprise is organized and operated. These influences will directly affect the size of the new firm's domain.

Table 9.2 Domain Selection in Entrepreneurial Firms

Step	Description
1	Select the product–markets that offer the most opportunity for the new product.
2	Calculate the level of capitalization required to enter the product–markets selected in step 1.
3	Select the product–markets that are consistent with the level of capitalization available to the new venture.
4	Evaluate the threats for each product–market remaining from step 3. —Check for any terminal threats. —Describe the remaining threats.
5	Select the product–markets with no terminal threats and the fewest nonterminal threats.
6	Consider all personal constraints and preferences of the founders regarding each product–market.
7	Select the product–markets that offer the greatest opportunities and meet the personal constraints of the founder(s).
8	List all of the organizations and agencies in the newly determined task environment from step 7.
9	Evaluate all of the organizations and agencies in the task environment to determine which of these should be included in the firm's domain.
10	Select the organizations and agencies that will become part of the entrepreneurial firm's business domain.

Once the initial selection of a domain is made, the entrepreneur should determine the new firm's internal capabilities to compete effectively in the chosen market. The entrepreneurial organization is typically concerned only with analyzing internal capabilities at the single-business level. Figure 9.3 illustrates the strategic capabilities analysis for the entrepreneurial venture. It differs in several fundamental ways from the strategic capabilities analysis for the established organization.[27] The process for the entrepreneurial firm emphasizes the importance of the founder's capabilities in determining the firm's ability to secure funding and acquire needed resources.

The first stage of the analysis stresses the acquisition of equity and working capital as an essential capability for the entrepreneurial enterprise. The other types and locations of capabilities as discussed in Chapter 3 also pertain to the newly formed organization. However, many of these capabilities are located only in the combined experiences of the founders. Therefore, a profile of founders' capabilities is added to the analysis. The current demands on the new business are usually minimal. However, the demands on the founders can be extensive. Lack of experience in many facets of business requires the new strategic manager to learn how to conduct business as well as develop the organization's operations processes.

The time, experience, and personalities of the founders are the most important and limited capabilities of many new organizations. This is reflected in the second stage of the process.

Strategic choices will also differ for the new firm. An important decision is whether to use the scarce resources of the founders or to acquire those resources through new employees or consultants. The second major choice of the new manager is the method and source of funding. The following choices are typical sources of funding:

Figure 9.3 Strategic Capabilities Analysis for the Entrepreneurial Firm

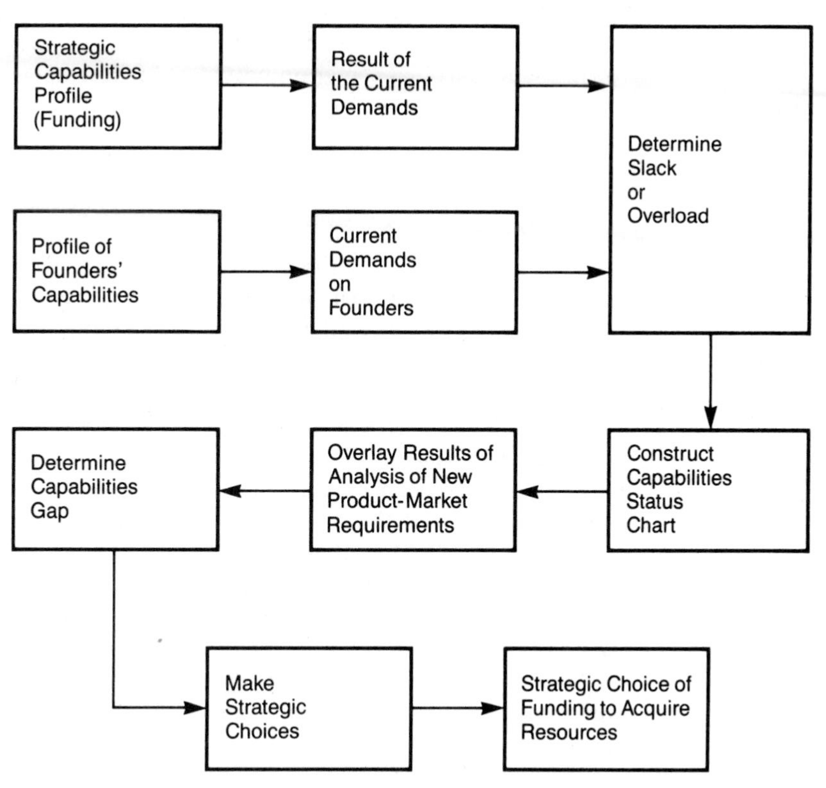

Personal savings

Loans from friends and relatives

Guaranteed loans from government agencies (for example, Small Business Administration, state agencies, or local municipalities in the form of cash, tax incentives, or land grants)

Commercial bank loans

Venture capital firms

Limited stock offerings

Because the typical entrepreneur has obligations to family or a primary employer, the paramount need is obtaining funding to acquire the capabilities that the entrepreneur does not possess or to buy his or her full-time attention to the new venture.

Choice of Growth Aspirations The domain selected for the new venture determines to a great extent the business conditions that the firm will face. In addition, the start-up nature of the new business and its small size limit the mission statement to an expression of the growth aspirations of the founders. This stage distinguishes the small, entrepreneurial venture from the small (mom-and-pop) operation that has conservative growth aspirations that center on providing an acceptable standard of living for their founders. The growth aspirations of the entrepreneurial business should accurately reflect the market potential of the product or service and the capabilities of the founders.

Development of Growth Goals and Start-up Strategy Strategic or growth goals for the new enterprise are based on the growth aspirations of the founders. These aspirations should be formally stated as goals in order to communicate the expectations of the founders to all employees and to direct the initial activities of the firm. Growth goals are typically stated in terms of sales, revenues, or profits. However, asset and employee growth may be more important for the manager during start-up, to allow for plowing profits back into the firm to stimulate future profit growth. Regardless of the goals selected, they should be short term (12 to 18 months) to afford the new venture the flexibility to respond to changes in its business conditions.

Strategy formulation at the start-up of the entrepreneurial firm should follow the steps outlined in this and preceding chapters. New ventures typically must develop a business plan to present to a funding institution or venture capital firm to obtain funding for the new enterprise. The business plan starts with a description of the proposed new venture and a detailed environment and market analysis. Next, it discusses the capabilities of the founders to create and manage the new venture. This is followed by a presentation of specific objectives and strategies to meet the overall strategic goals of the new business. For the new venture, strategic goals are usually limited to financial goals of profitability and cash management. The last part of the business plan is a detailed discussion of exactly how the firm will implement its strategies and control its activities. This final section usually includes several years of pro forma financial statements to verify the profits and cash flows projected in the strategic goals. Chapter Appendix 9.2 outlines in more detail the format of a business plan. This format is based on interviews with entrepreneurial managers who have succeeded with their own business plan.

Why use a detailed, formal process of strategy formulation in small or entrepreneurial organizations? After all, the environments that these firms face are probably less uncertain and dynamic than those of larger firms. Also, there are fewer employees to guide toward strategic goals. The rationale for recommending a formal strategic management process is that the new venture is actually more dependent on a limited number of customers, suppliers, and other constituents than is the larger firm. This means there is less tolerance for error in the small firm, so it is more important that managers know where they are going and how they intend to get there. Research evidence supports this view.[28]

Choice of Implementation Objectives and Tactics Growth goals and start-up strategies must be translated into specific objectives to guide the actions of the entrepreneur/manager. Because the founder of the new venture must frequently act as strategic and operational manager combined, he or she can help assure effective implementation by translating the more general growth goals into objectives that are specific and precise. These objectives should specify time horizons and allowable ranges for deviations. The objectives should be communicated to and understood by other members of the organization. If operating objectives are developed correctly, the steps to effective implementation are much easier to recognize.

Two additional aspects of implementation are the organizational and communication processes in the entrepreneurial enterprise. Organizational processes are the method of structuring the working relationships and the management style of the entrepreneur. Previously mentioned research indicates that the more successful small entrepreneurial firms are less formally structured. The rules that specify who interacts with whom are flexible, and the need to accomplish the job takes priority over formal reporting requirements. The founders of the firm typically spend long hours in meetings with workers to solve problems and make decisions. Structures are flat, and several employees may have direct access to the head of the organization. This less rigid structure is necessary because the new product or service is probably still undergoing development. A more formal structure might stifle the final stages of innovation that are important to bring the new product to market.

Likewise, communication channels must remain open and rich.[29] Rapid and accurate information flow is necessary during product development and organization start-up. The final preparation of the product for introduction to the market takes place as the product is being produced. Initial versions of products seldom look exactly like their later cousins. The original Apple computers were almost custom-built, for example; practically every machine was unique. In addition, the entrepreneur is probably not an experienced administrator and may need help from others in the organization to maintain administrative control. In a small, entrepreneurial insurance company, the head of personnel was the individual who persuaded the CEO to start strategic planning, because the CEO lacked the experience to develop a formal strategic plan.

Control Activities

Control activities are more important for the small, entrepreneurial organization than for larger firms. Because over half of new businesses fail in their first year, the typical entrepreneur has only a short time to introduce and market the new product. He or she must be keenly aware of the feedback from the marketplace and internal operations to quickly modify the product or internal processes to respond to market demands. This requires effective control of the quality and quantity of operations and the product. In addition, entrepreneur-managers are typically short of start-up capital. Thus cash flow, variable costs, commercial and administrative expenses, and sales efforts must all be controlled. New ventures cannot afford to learn of mistakes when the start-up capital is gone and corrective action is too costly.

The entrepreneur's difficulty in planning is greater if the shortage of start-up capital has caused an incomplete assessment of the marketplace. When the initial activities of a new venture are based on limited or inaccurate information, the organization must remain flexible to adjust strategies and activities to account for new information gained from the start-up process. This need explains the success of an incremental strategic management process in small firms,[30] and the particular importance of strategic control.

The controls established by the entrepreneur provide feedback about the performance of the organization and product. Typically, the market analysis for the innovation is overly optimistic, and the entrepreneur's growth aspirations must be corrected once the product has been on the market for a while. Likewise, the new venture's capabilities may not meet the original estimates. For example, the quantity or quality of a new process may take longer than expected to reach acceptable levels. The founders of the new venture may not be as capable of managing a growth firm as they thought. Any change in environmental conditions that causes an adjustment in the business plan must start with a modification of the aspirations, strategies, and goals of the entrepreneur.

Other Entrepreneurial Issues

The previously described characteristics of entrepreneurs are also found in managers in all types of organizations. Recently, several larger organizations have attempted to capture the entrepreneurial spirit in their managers by establishing small, entrepreneurial units within the structure of the large organization. The name given to this practice is **intrapreneurship**. IBM and other larger firms have established such units under the label of "independent business units" and staffed them with engineers, managers, and scientists in the hope of promoting the creativity and innovation associated with entrepreneurial firms. The benefits to the organization can be a higher level of innovation and new-product development, and increased satisfaction leading to greater commitment on the part of their scientists and managers. The benefits to the individual are the freedom and responsibility similar to that of starting one's own entrepreneurial venture without the risk of personal capital.

Incubator Organizations Some larger firms also contribute to the entrepreneurial spirit by acting as **incubator organizations**. These organizations are typically in high-technology industries in which new products are being developed daily and spin-off products frequently appear. A highly innovative scientist, engineer, or manager may develop a product or process that is marketable but out of the mainstream of the larger firm's business. The product or service may be related to the larger firm's main product line, or it could use similar technology but be unrelated to the major firm's primary product focus. The creator of the new product may turn over his or her new idea to the larger firm, running the risk that the innovation will never be developed, or he or she can decide to become an entrepreneur, attempting to produce and market the product or service.

Incubator organizations play an extremely important role in society. These high-tech organizations typically define the state-of-the-art technology for that industry. The individuals who work in these organizations are aware of the directions in which the industry is going and the unmet needs that currently exist in the market. Therefore, incubator organizations function as the breeding ground for new and spin-off ideas that further the growth and maturity of an industry and its products. Large high-tech firms such as IBM, INTEL, Motorola, and Bell Labs are excellent examples of incubator organizations.

Why New Businesses Fail The alarming failure rate of new businesses is attributable to several factors related to the start-up and operation of the new venture. One reason why new businesses fail at start-up is undercapitalization. The entrepreneur may try to fund the start-up out of personal savings or personal loans and fail to gather enough capital to start the firm in a way that will ensure its success. Another problem at start-up is the failure to conduct a thorough market assessment and capability analysis before launching the new product or service. Entrepreneurs typically overestimate the size of their markets and their ability to fulfill the needs in the marketplace. A third cause of failure associated with start-up is an absence of a well-developed business plan.

Once the new venture has survived the start-up process, it faces another period of vulnerability. One of the primary reasons new firms fail in their second or third year is that cash flows are not properly managed. When the new venture grows to a size that the founders can no longer directly manage, they may lose sight of the costs associated with bringing on additional employees and improving the facilities to produce a more sophisticated or expanded product line. Sales may be increasing at the projected rate, but costs may be increasing faster. Soon costs exceed revenues.

Many of the causes of failure can be corrected through effective strategic management. Developing a thorough and well-thought-out business plan for the new venture will help the entrepreneur avoid many of these pitfalls. If this plan is prepared in accordance with the principles discussed in this chapter, the manager will have a plan that not only guides the activities of the employees, but also is flexible enough to respond to changes in business conditions.

Strategy Development in the Not-for-Profit and Public Sector

The mission of the not-for-profit firm is established by the charter that it receives from its sponsors. Consequently, the manager of a not-for-profit cannot alter the firm's mission as easily as a manager in the private sector can. With the charter of the organization mandated, strategy development starts with a review of the not-for-profit's environment or its relevant publics. Unlike managers of private sector firms, the not-for-profit's manager cannot choose the task environment. Rather, it is dictated by the organization's charter, which typically specifies the constituents with whom the not-for-profit must interact.

The strategic management process in a not-for-profit organization follows the stages in Figure 9.4. Several of the stages are similar to strategic management in the private sector. Therefore, this discussion will focus on the unique features of strategic management in not-for-profit and public sector firms.

Figure 9.4 Strategic Management Process in Not-for-Profit Firms

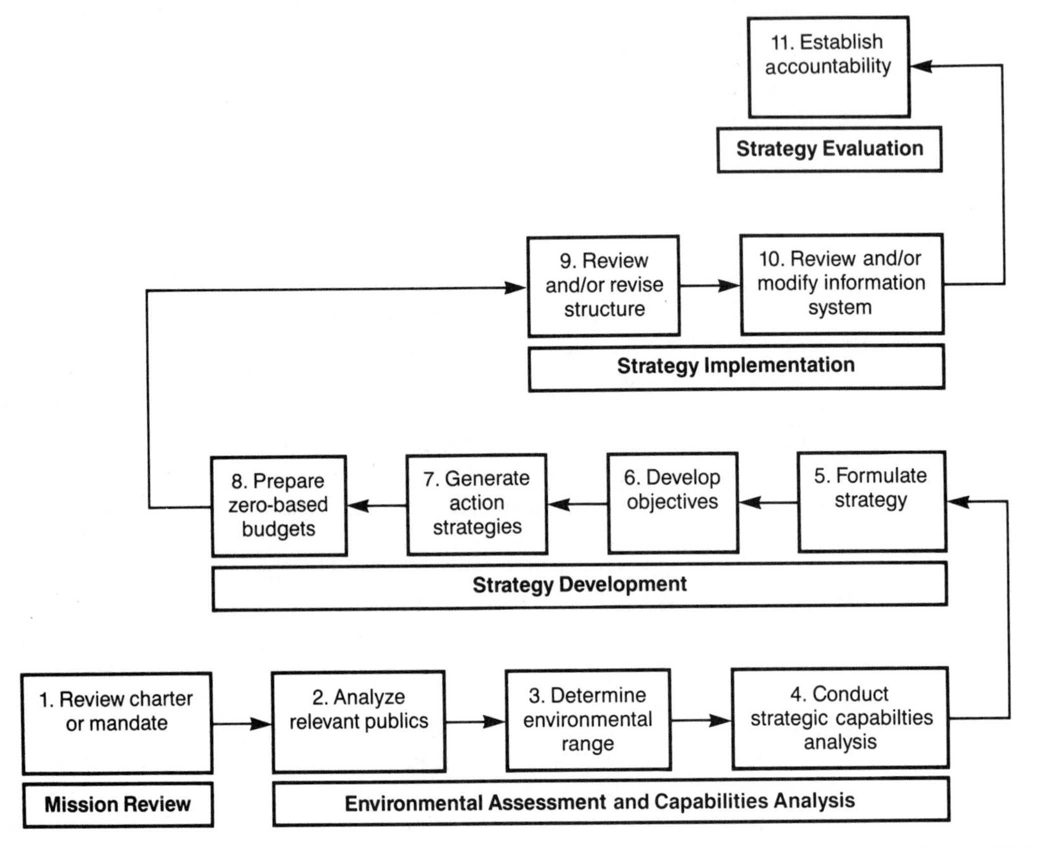

Environmental Assessment

Not-for-profit organizations face an increasingly difficult environment. Efforts made by legislators to balance the federal budget, deregulate many industries, and privatize many government functions have drastically reduced the level of government funding for many not-for-profits. These and other recent developments have dramatically increased the importance of environmental assessment for organizations in this sector of the economy. Not-for-profits that were already diversified in their approaches to fund-raising have merely focused more on private sources of funding. However, organizations that depended entirely on federal funding have either quickly changed or ceased to exist.

More so than those in the private sector, managers of not-for-profits must be aware of the political cycle. The government sector is a dominant part of the environment of most not-for-profits. If the organization does not directly depend on government funding, as with a federal or state agency, then it is indirectly dependent through tax legislation regarding contributions to not-for-profits. Every two, four, or six years via the election process, the strategic direction of the political environment is subject to change. However, the impact of that change on the not-for-profit continues throughout the administration's term of office. Therefore, these organizations must regularly assess the political environment.

Although the governmental element is extremely important to the not-for-profit, other environmental elements and stakeholders are also important. Strategic managers of not-for-profits must assess all other relevant elements and stakeholders (commonly referred to as publics) to produce a prioritized list of elements, publics, and issues that are critical to the organization. One modification of the private sector assessment is the relevant publics or advocate and adversary (A&A) analysis. This useful analysis method is comparable to the opportunity and threat analysis discussed in Chapter 2.

The not-for-profit manager initiates the A&A by listing all of the advocates and adversaries considered relevant to the success and survival of the organization. Next, as in the O&T analysis, the manager lists the issues that relate to each advocate or adversary. Each issue that is rated as critical or very important by managers involved in the assessment should be separated and ranked, based on its urgency. Critical issues that must be handled immediately are ranked higher than issues that can be dealt with later.

The list may include two possible types of adversaries that the not-for-profit may encounter. The first type, **intruders**, consists of any other not-for-profit organization or issue that has the potential to divert funding from the organization. For example, state universities are not-for-profits that depend on the state legislature for appropriations. Recently, the strategic manager (president) of a major state university found that the governor's favorite project was diverting monies from the general fund that also funded the university. Had the president been scanning for this intruder, he might have been able to formulate a strategy to protect the university's appropriations.[31] The second type of adversary, **private sector substitutes**, consists of private firms that perform functions previously performed by not-for-profits in the public sector. Two typical examples are waste collection and airport management. As many not-for-profits have learned, they must scan the private sector as well as competing not-for-profits to be aware of potential threats to their funding.

The results of the A&A analysis give not-for-profit managers a clear picture of the sources of support and competition that affect their funding. With the results of this analysis, the managers can formulate strategies to nurture the organization's advocates and guard against its adversaries, thus protecting its funding sources.

Determining the Not-for-Profit Environmental Range Just as one dominant factor influenced the selection of the product-market for the entrepreneurial organization, one factor is dominant for selecting the environmental range of the not-for-profit organization. **Environmental range** refers to the needs of the local, regional, or national society addressed by the not-for-profit. The most important factor in the process of selecting an environmental range is the charter or mandate under which the organization operates. The purpose and mission of the not-for-profit are determined by the members of society who **sponsor** the organization. In other words, the not-for-profit organization's environmental range is established by the charter. Therefore, the manager has discretion in selecting the not-for-profit's environmental range only if he or she is one of its sponsors. The director and strategic manager of the not-for-profit rarely has much influence on range selection.

The not-for-profit's strategic manager can, however, influence the operational aspects of the firm's range. He or she can select other firms in the task environment that the firm interacts with on issues that do not threaten the organization's charter. For example, according to its charter, the Federal Bureau of Investigation of the United States is forbidden to conduct espionage operations outside of the borders of the United States. Although the director of the FBI lacks the discretion to expand the scope of the FBI's charter beyond the U.S. border, he or she can select the organizations from which to purchase supplies and materials for the daily operation of the organization. Also, the director can determine which legislators to lobby for funds to support the agency. These operational issues involve the selection of organizations and individuals in the firm's environmental range but do not directly violate its charter.

The not-for-profit organization is seldom pursuing opportunities for expansion into new domains. Therefore, it must concentrate on maintaining the support of its sponsors, whether they are contributors, as for charities, or the citizenry for public or governmental agencies. The primary means available to the not-for-profit to ensure continued support is to consistently fulfill a valued need of its sponsors. This requires that the organization maintain the capability to meet these needs.

Strategic Capabilities Analysis for Not-for-Profits The strategic capabilities analysis recommended for the not-for-profit firm is the SWAA (strengths, weaknesses, advocates, and adversaries) analysis. The SWAA analysis is similar to the SWOT analysis in the for-profit sector. However, the unique environment of the not-for-profit organization makes the use of advocates and adversaries more appropriate. The environmental assessment provides a list of the external advocates (sponsors, patrons, legislators, general public) who can support the not-for-profit's request for resources. This assessment can also isolate the organization's adversaries—those who threaten or compete for resources.

Next, the organization must conduct an accurate audit of its internal strengths and weaknesses. Strengths might include existing management and personnel, as well as the not-for-profit's history of cost effectively fulfilling a need. For some not-for-profits, strengths may include plant and equipment (for example, a historic theater for an acting company or surgical facilities for a not-for-profit hospital). Internal weaknesses could be poor control or accountability procedures that prevent the not-for-profit from building arguments that it is carrying out its charter cost effectively. Additional weaknesses could be in the areas of personnel, operations, or other functional areas.

From the results of the SWAA analysis, the organization can then generate a service differential assessment. Like the SWOT analysis, the service differential assessment is designed to combine the results of the environmental assessment and internal capabilities analysis to indicate the appropriate orientation of the organization's strategy. The relevant dimensions are shown in Figure 9.5. The horizontal axis indicates the organization's determination of its ability to effectively satisfy the demands of its sponsors after comparison of its strengths and weaknesses. The vertical axis represents funding attractiveness; it is based on the not-for-profit's assessment of its publics and their need for its service and the support available from its advocates. The not-for-profit should locate itself in one of the four cells of the matrix and formulate its strategy accordingly.

If the organization determines that it has low funding attractiveness to its sponsors and lacks adequate resources to provide its service effectively, it will be moved to **back-drawer** status for funding.

Not-for-profits that are in the position of providing a service currently being vocally demanded by the public (for example, law and order in the 1980s and environmental protection in the 1970s) but that are too new or underfunded and understaffed to provide adequate service will find themselves **celebrities** in the not-for-profit arena. (Actually, it appears that environmental protection may reemerge as a celebrity in the 1990s under the new administration.) These organizations are in an advantageous position for future funding.

Not-for-profit **stars** are the organizations that have secured the support of their relevant publics and the funding of their sponsors. These not-for-profits are attractive for funding because they can only enhance public perceptions of the sponsors who support them. For example, the YMCA has high funding attractiveness because it is highly visible in most communities and typically is able to satisfy its sponsors' humanitarian and recognition needs. Stars should exercise caution not to lose their funding attractiveness through operational inefficiencies.

Figure 9.5 Service Differential Assessment

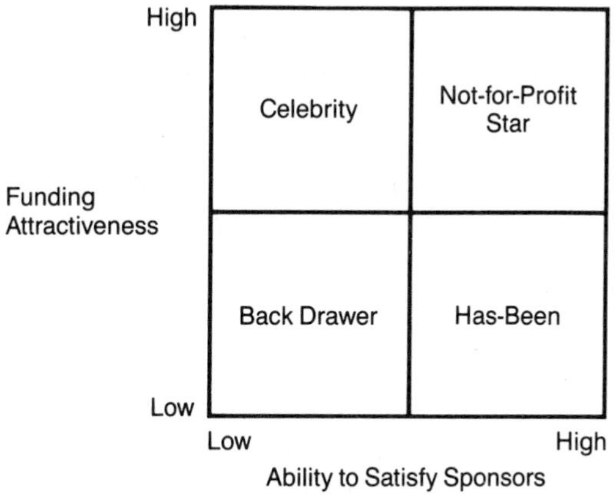

Source: Adapted from John R. Montanari and J. S. Bracker, "The Strategic Management Process at the Public Planning Unit Level," *Strategic Management Journal* 7 (1986), 251–265. Copyright 1986 John Wiley & Sons, Ltd. Reprinted by permission of John Wiley & Sons, Ltd.

Last, the not-for-profit may find itself in the position of having substantial ability to satisfy the sponsors' needs but having lost its attractiveness to its publics. Perhaps the organization no longer provides a necessary service to its publics, or it may have been so incompetent at providing its service that the public has lost interest in supporting its efforts. If this is the case, then it will be labeled a **has-been**. The has-been not-for-profit is viewed as an unnecessary endeavor and will soon experience a funding shortfall.

Strategy Development

The first step in strategy development is to design a strategy that defines in general terms how the not-for-profit intends to fulfill its charter and attract an equitable share of the funding from its sponsors (private donors or government appropriations). Through the strategy, the not-for-profit specifies the activities that it will pursue during the next planning cycle.

The not-for-profit has four alternative strategies recommended by the service differential assessment. The first of these four strategies relates to the organization that finds itself in the back-drawer category. In this case, the not-for-profit will focus its strategy on either preparing to phase out or developing ways to increase its funding attractiveness to sponsors. The back-drawer not-for-profit is limited to a termination or retrenchment and turnaround strategy.

The not-for-profit celebrity might adopt a strategy of interorganizational linking, in which the not-for-profit enters into a cooperative agreement with an organization that has slack capabilities to serve.[32] This strategy is similar to cooperative ancillary strategies in the for-profit sector. One example of this strategy is the informal linking of the Environmental Defense Fund, a not-for-profit environmental protection organization, with the Environmental Protection Agency to promote waste management. Since waste management is rapidly becoming the premier business-related social issue of the 1990s, the Environmental Defense Fund can be considered a not-for-profit celebrity. The Strategic Application "Waste Management Creates a Celebrity" discusses this important social issue and the not-for-profit organizations that have gained celebrity status because they address it.

Stars in the not-for-profit sector are the most vulnerable, because there is intense competition for their funding resources. Not-for-profit stars will concentrate their strategy on maintaining this favorable position while guarding against a celebrity organization that could provide a service that would directly compete for funding. Therefore, the star organization must develop a combination of a maintenance and a defensive strategy with an eye out for growth through incremental increases in its charter.

The strategy for the has-been not-for-profit must focus on improving funding attractiveness to sponsors. The primary means of doing this is to regain the support of its publics and rebuild a strong advocate base. This strategy is sometimes referred to as "strategic piggybacking." Choosing this strategy means that the not-for-profit develops a new activity that is indirectly related to its current charter and is capable of returning it to celebrity status as the Strategic Application on waste management

STRATEGIC APPLICATIONS

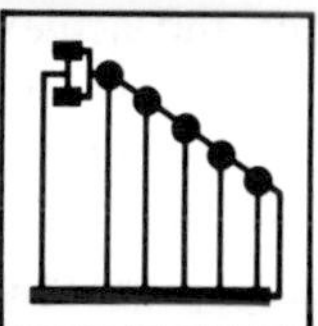

Waste Management Creates a Celebrity

A social issue that promises to be a major social demand on business in the 1990s is waste management. The United States generates over 150 million tons of waste each year, or 3.5 pounds per person per day. Half of the cities in the United States are projected to exhaust their current landfills by 1990. Much of this waste is produced by U.S. industry. In addition, over 300 million tons of hazardous waste flow from plants and processing facilities each year. The oceans can no longer absorb the huge amounts of waste dumped by coastal communities.

The Environmental Defense Fund (EDF) is working with the Environmental Protection Agency to attack the problem. The EDF provides information, lobbying, and grass-roots support, while the EPA has enforcement powers to put teeth into the EDF social agenda. This informal "piggybacking" or linking arrangement appears to be paying off. 3M Company's worldwide operations now have a program for waste reduction—Pollution Prevention Pays. Another industry giant, Monsanto Company, has pledged to chop hazardous air emissions 90 percent by 1992.

The attention that U.S. business is starting to pay to social outcries for waste management is coming just in time. In the summer of 1988, the EPA directed its officials to make waste management a priority. This federal government acknowledgment of the social issue promoted by the EDF puts it in the forefront of the waste abatement movement. As this social issue has come of age, the EDF is a not-for-profit in the limelight.

Source: "Garbage, Garbage, Everywhere," *Time*, September 5, 1988, 81–82.

shows.[33] The choice of the appropriate strategy for the current conditions facing the not-for-profit can assure its continued existence and sponsorship.

Consensus on a strategy permits the strategic manager to develop specific functional objectives to serve as guides to action and standards for evaluation and control. The same factors that contribute to the development of effective objectives for private sector firms apply to the not-for-profit. Also, as in the private sector, the functional objectives lead to operational strategies. However, in the not-for-profit, the operational strategies may be somewhat limited by the organization's charter or the desires of sponsors. These limitations may appear in the form of laws or the perceptions of what is "acceptable" to sponsors.

The last step in strategy development is to prepare a budget. A zero-based method is recommended for use by the not-for-profit.[34] This does not mean that the strategic manager should use a formal zero-based budgeting technique as President Carter attempted to use with the federal government. A better approach is a tailored technique that reviews the previous budgets from a zero base to verify that only line items that relate to current objectives and strategies are included in the budget. Because budgets are numerical representations of functional objectives and operational strategies, they should reflect the previous stages of the strategy development process for the not-for-profit.

Strategy Implementation

Just as in the private sector, not-for-profit strategy implementation refers to all of the activities that the organization performs to carry out its strategies and achieve its objectives. One of the most important activities that an organization engages in is developing an organizational structure that facilitates the accomplishment of strategy. Initially the not-for-profit organization should review its existing structural arrangement to determine if it is consistent with the objectives that have been established. If environmental conditions have changed, the manager will probably need to modify the organization's structure to be consistent with the dictates of the new strategy. For example, a not-for-profit facing a large number of dynamic publics would not be well served by a rigid, nonresponsive organization structure.

Many designs for organization structure are available to the not-for-profit. These designs range from a high-control and low-responsive, rigid design to the highly responsive and lower-control design called a matrix structure.

A rigid design clearly defines lines of authority and responsibility, and therefore allows for a more direct administrative and supervisory control. However, this design, typically referred to as centralized, has low responsiveness to changes in environmental conditions. Some experts say that a centralized structure is more appropriate for not-for-profits.[35] They argue that the nature of services provided by many not-for-profits (such as art and environmental protection) makes it difficult to establish performance standards and specific goals. Therefore, decision making should be focused at the top of the organization.

The task force design is more responsive because it incorporates the development of a special unit called the task force when environmental changes occur. The task force is created to respond to new developments in the environment. Membership in the task force is temporary and is typically an additional duty of the manager and task force members. A task force merely makes recommendations to the responsible manager regarding the problem. The manager maintains the responsibility for solving the problem.

A still more responsive organization design is the project team or project management design. This design is also temporary, but it is normally associated with projects or issues of longer duration and of sufficient importance to the firm to warrant placing several members of the firm on the project team full time. The project management design is more responsive than the task force because project teams are responsible for actually solving the problem or issue rather than merely recommending ways to handle it. Both of these designs typically appear in conjunction with other designs.

The most responsive design is also the one with the lowest control: the matrix management organization design. This is a permanent design that is developed to accommodate rapid change in the not-for-profit's environment. In a matrix structure, all work that enters the organization is classified as a project, and revolving project teams with changing membership handle work as it arrives in the organization. The makeup of the project team depends on the abilities needed for completing the project. Coordination is maintained through linking mechanisms or positions such as project managers.

The criteria for selecting a structural design are that it should be consistent with the demands of the strategies developed and consistent with the talents and skills of the individuals who must function within the structure. For example, if the not-for-profit is a public sector agency responsible for providing the same service to a large number of individuals, then a more rigid bureaucratic design may be appropriate. However, if the organization is involved with relatively few major projects—for example, NASA and the space shuttle—then a more responsive or flexible design is more appropriate to accommodate the changes in environmental conditions.

Besides structure, implementation depends on the existence of an effective and efficient information system. The key to successful implementation of any plan is to make the requirements of that plan known to all who must fulfill those requirements. Furthermore, the same individuals must receive rapid feedback when actions or activities do not adhere to the plans. In larger not-for-profit firms, communication of objectives takes place through the management information system. In some organizations, this information system is formalized and computerized. In other organizations, it is informal, using the grapevine or indirect communication between the managers and the employees.

The nature and type of information system that the organization uses depends to some extent on the strategy the organization selects. Strategies that require quick response on involved and important issues will probably require a less formal, more personal management information system. Strategies that use the same methods and procedures with many publics can utilize a more formal computerized information system. Also, some information, such as data analysis and legal requirements, can be communicated through a more formal information system, whereas observations and judgments may need to be communicated through less formal channels.

As suggested by several management experts, there are additional ways to facilitate strategy implementation.[36] The presence of a strong and forceful leader can add direction to the organization's charter and help translate it into action. Another way to implement strategy is to develop a "mystique" that provides a set of principles to guide the actions of organizational members.[37] Thus, plans are implemented through members having the same values as the manager. The not-for-profit manager can also establish rules and procedures that ensure members act in accordance with plans. Last, a strong "working" board of directors helps monitor and manage the not-for-profit in a manner consistent with its strategy.

Strategy Evaluation and Accountability

The final stage of strategic management in the not-for-profit organization is the evaluation of the activities that organizational members perform to accomplish objectives. In a not-for-profit organization, evaluation has two aspects, control and accountability. Strategic control, according to Schendel and Hofer, looks at whether the strategy developed is being implemented as planned and whether the results produced by the strategy are what were intended.[38]

To determine whether activities are proceeding according to plan, managers use two types of control: strategic control and operational control. Strategic control refers to whether the conditions that caused a particular strategy to be developed still exist. The manager cannot control environmental conditions, but he or she can be aware of changes in these conditions in order to adjust the organization's strategy. Therefore, the first aspect of strategic control is to verify that a change in environmental conditions has not rendered the strategy inappropriate. The second aspect of strategic control is to verify whether the assumptions used to interpret the environmental information are still appropriate.[39] In developing its strategy for fund raising and research for the disease of polio, the March of Dimes assumed that a cure for polio would not be discovered in the short term. However, fortunately, a cure for polio was discovered. The sponsors of the March of Dimes had to either discontinue the organization because the need no longer existed or change the charter of the organization to address another need of the general public. The sponsors decided to change the charter, and the March of Dimes is now concerned with birth defects of all kinds.

Operational control determines whether the specific objectives established for the current planning cycle are being met by the members of the organization. The organization's managers determine the results of the organization's actual activities and compare them with planned activities. If a gap exists, corrective action must be taken to get back on target, or plans must be adjusted to reflect current environmental conditions.

The second purpose of evaluation in the not-for-profit is to establish accountability for deviations from plans. If the organization is operating efficiently but the public no longer views the organization's service as necessary, the strategic management of the not-for-profit must be accountable for the necessary corrective action. If the organization is not functioning efficiently but the society still perceives a need for the service, then the managers can modify the operational activities of the members of the organization. Therefore, accountability means establishing the individual or individuals who are accountable for taking corrective action to direct the not-for-profit organization back to the accomplishment of its objectives.

Summary

Entrepreneurial and not-for-profit organizations are vitally important to the economy of the United States. Practically all of the growth in employment over the previous decade has been attributable to increases in the number and size of small organizations and the growth of the public sector. Future strategic managers must therefore understand the unique characteristics of strategic management in entrepreneurial and not-for-profit organizations.

Entrepreneurship is the practice of entrepreneurial behavior through the creation and operation of a new venture. Entrepreneurial ventures must be distinguished from small businesses, because only the former contribute substantially to economic growth and employment. The distinguishing characteristic of an entrepreneurial venture is that the entrepreneur establishes the organization to grow and make a profit. To achieve these goals, the entrepreneur needs to adopt strategic management principles.

The entrepreneur displays psychological, personality, and demographic characteristics that combine to describe an independent, ambitious, and achievement-oriented individual. In addition, the entrepreneur typically has a high need to control his or her own destiny and is comfortable with a moderate amount of risk. These individuals are recognized for developing innovative products or services, operations processes, and marketing and distribution systems that give them a unique initial advantage in the marketplace. Entrepreneurs are also strategic managers and planners. While they do not necessarily use the formal, sophisticated processes developed for larger firms, entrepreneurial organizations that use written plans to communicate the aspirations and directions of their founders have been shown to have higher performance than those that do not plan.

The process of strategic management in small, entrepreneurial firms resembles that of private sector for-profit firms but is unique in several ways. Strategic management in the entrepreneurial firm starts with the creation or innovation of the entrepreneur. The new manager then checks business conditions and chooses the domain(s) in which the firm will conduct business. Once he or she has determined the capabilities of the new organization, growth aspirations and strategies are made more specific by establishing growth goals and operating objectives. Last, implementation tactics and control activities are developed. This entire process evolves incrementally.

Strategy development in not-for-profit firms also differs from that in private sector organizations. The main differences are in the use of advocates and adversaries in the environmental assessment and the constraints imposed by the not-for-profit's charter. The charter is the reason for the creation of the not-for-profit and the source of its continued sponsorship. The managers of the not-for-profit may not change the charter, but they may select a strategy suitable for carrying it out.

Questions

1. Select four small firms (gross revenue of less than $5 million) in your local area. Two of these firms should be small businesses, and two should be small, entrepreneurial firms. Why did you select each firm for the category in which you placed it?

2. Locate two individuals in your community who have started their own businesses. Arrange an interview with each one, and try to determine if they have the psychological, personality, and demographic characteristics of an entrepreneur. Describe your conclusions and how you arrived at them.

3. What are the hallmarks of a small, entrepreneurial organization that is strategically well managed? In other words, what do entrepreneur/managers do, and what are the characteristics of the strategic management process?

4. Compare and contrast the strategic management process in small, entrepreneurial firms with the process used in not-for-profit organizations. How do they differ? Why?

5. If the charter established by the sponsors of a not-for-profit is the purpose or mission of the organization, how can a not-for-profit or public organization expand its charter? Select one not-for-profit and one public organization to discuss how their managers could expand their charters.

Notes

1. Small Business Administration. *The State of Small Business: A Report to the President.* U.S. Government Printing Office, Washington, D.C., 1989.

2. Jeffrey S. Bracker and J. N. Pearson, "Planning and Financial Performance of Small Mature Firms," *Strategic Management Journal* 7 (November–December 1986): 503–522.

3. Richard B. Robinson and J. A. Pearce II, "Research Thrust in Small Firm Strategic Planning," *Academy of Management Review* 9 (January 1984): 128–137.

4. James W. Carland, F. Hoy, W. Boulton, and J. C. Carland, "Differentiating Entrepreneurs from Small Business Owners: A Conceptualization," *Academy of Management Review* 9 (April 1984): 354–359.

5. Ibid., 358.

6. Ibid.

7. James R. Norman, "Trump: Behind the Hype," *Business Week*, July 20, 1987, 92–97.

8. D. McClelland, *The Achieving Society* (Princeton, N.J.: Van Nostrand, 1961).

9. Maria E. Recio, "Keeping Top Secrets inside the Computer," *Business Week*, May 25, 1987, 85.

10. N. R. Smith, *The Entrepreneur and His Firm: The Relationship between Type of Man and Type of Company* (East Lansing, Mich.: Michigan State University, 1967).

11. Bracker and Pearson, "Planning and Financial Performance of Small Mature Firms"; N. R. Smith and J. B. Miner, "Type of Entrepreneur, Type of Firm and Managerial Motivation: Implications for Organizational Life Cycle Theory," *Strategic Management Journal* 4 (October–December 1983): 325–340.

12. Carland, Hoy, Boulton, and Carland, "Differentiating Entrepreneurs from Small Business Owners."

13. Richard Brandt, "The Whiz Kid," *Business Week*, April 13, 1987, 68–75.

14. Jonathan B. Levine, "The Pack Leader Still Acts 'Like a Hungry Rat,'" *Business Week*, May 25, 1987, 84.

15. Carland, Hoy, Boulton, and Carland, "Differentiating Entrepreneurs from Small Business Owners."

16. Ibid.; J. A. Schumpeter, *The Theory of Economic Development* (Cambridge, Mass.: Harvard University Press, 1934); K. H. Vesper, *New Venture Strategies* (Englewood Cliffs, N.J.: Prentice-Hall, 1980).

17. Vesper, *New Venture Strategies.*

18. William B. Gartner, "A Conceptual Framework for Describing the Phenomenon of New Venture Creation," *Academy of Management Review* 10 (October 1985): 696–706.

19. Bracker and Pearson, "Planning and Financial Performance of Small Mature Firms."

20. Robinson and Pearce, "Research Thrust in Small Firm Strategic Planning."

21. Ibid.

22. J. Chicha and P. A. Julien, *The Strategy of SMBs and Their Adaptation to Change* (Trois-Rivières, Quebec: University of Quebec, 1979); Robinson and Pearce, "Research Thrust in Small Firm Strategic Planning."

23. Bracker and Pearson, "Planning and Financial Performance of Small Mature Firms."

24. James Brian Quinn, *Strategies for Change* (Homewood, Ill.: Irwin, 1980).

25. "Keeping Teens Decked Out in Whatever's Hot," *Business Week*, May 25, 1987, 88.

26. See Carland, Hoy, Boulton, and Carland, "Differentiating Entrepreneurs from Small Business Owners"; Gartner, "A Conceptual Framework"; C. Borland, "Locus of Control, Need for Achievement and Entrepreneurship" (Unpublished doctoral dissertation, University of Texas at Austin, 1974).

27. Ingolf Bamberger, "Portfolio Analysis for the Small Firm," *Long Range Planning* 15 (December 1982): 49–57.

28. Bracker and Pearson, "Planning and Financial Performance of Small Mature Firms."

29. Richard L. Daft and R. H. Lengel, "Information Richness: A New Approach to Managerial Behavior and Organization Design," in *Research in Organizational Behavior*, vol. 6, ed. B. Staw and L. L. Cummings (Greenwich, Conn.: JAI Press, 1984): 191–233.

30. Robinson and Pearce, "Research Thrust in Small Firm Strategic Planning."

31. John R. Montanari and J. S. Bracker, "The Strategic Management Process at the Public Planning Unit Level," *Strategic Management Journal* 7 (May–June 1986): 251–265.

32. Thomas L. Wheelen and J. P. Hunger, *Strategic Management and Business Policy*, 2d ed. (Reading, Mass.: Addison-Wesley, 1986): 363–366.

33. R. P. Nielsen, "Piggybacking for Business and Nonprofits: A Strategy for Hard Times," *Long Range Planning* 17 (April 1984): 96–102.

34. See John V. Pearson and R. J. Michael, "Zero-Base Budgeting—A Technique for Planned Organizational Decline," *Long Range Planning* 17 (October 1984): 103–110; James C. Weatherbe and J. R. Montanari, "Zero Based Budgeting in the Planning Process," *Strategic Management Journal* 2 (January–March 1981): 1–14.

35. Wheelen and Hunger, *Strategic Management and Business Policy.*

36. Ibid.

37. Nielsen, "Piggybacking for Business and Nonprofits."

38. Dan E. Schendel and C. W. Hofer, eds., *Strategic Management: A New View of Business Policy and Planning* (Boston: Little, Brown and Company, 1979): 1–23.

39. G. Schreyogg and H. Steinmann, "Strategic Control: A New Perspective," *Academy of Management Review* 12 (January 1987): 91–103.

Case for Discussion

Entrepreneurship: Sometimes a Case of David and Goliath

Three "Davids" who have taken on three of the largest industrial "Goliaths" are Michael Kelly, David Draper, and Ed Butcher. Each of these entrepreneurs in his own way has tried to break into the U.S. automobile industry, which is dominated by General Motors, Ford, and Chrysler. Their comments help tell the story:

> "It's ego. It plays as big a part as the pocketbook."
>
> —Michael E. Kelly, CEO of New Avanti Corporation

> "I don't understand the blind commitment of people who want to build their own car."
>
> —David L. Draper, chief executive of C&C Inc.

> "I've been laughed out of banks. I've been thrown out of banks by lawyers. And believe it or not, the dream still lives on."
>
> —Ed Butcher, President of Owosso Motor Car Company

These are entrepreneurs in the true sense of the word. Kelly fell in love with the Studebaker Avanti some 25 years ago. Recently, he rescued from bankruptcy, for $775,000, the company that makes the auto using the original 1963 body style. He attracted $10 million of additional start-up venture capital and was in the car business. The new Avanti Corporation now sells about 500 cars through 50 dealers for $35,000

Source: "Three Men Who Put Their Dreams on Wheels," *Business Week*, August 29, 1988, 72–73.

to $55,000 and has become profitable. Kelly doesn't plan to challenge the big three automakers directly but does have plans to expand the present market.

David Draper started installing sunroofs in cars in 1976. Today, 150 new Ford Mustangs are delivered to his plant every day. He manages four assembly lines, three of which turn hardtop automobiles into convertibles. He feels that the large auto manufacturers cannot profitably make fewer than 50,000 cars of a particular type. In Draper's opinion, his company is in the right place at the right time. The surge in demand for unique cars has fragmented the market to the point that the numbers favor his firm. This entrepreneur is so confident that he is expanding into making one-time-only and experimental vehicles such as Pontiac's Banshee and Laforza Automobiles Inc.'s newly conceived top-line utility vehicle.

Ed Butcher is the founder of the Owosso Motor Car Company, which produces the Pulse. This "autocycle" is technically a motorcycle with two enclosed seats and two extra side wheels on winglike outriggers. The vehicle accelerates from 0 to 60 miles per hour in 6.7 seconds and costs between $14,995 and $25,000. Butcher has modest aspirations for his car company and expects to sell no more than 10,000 vehicles in any year. However, that doesn't mean that he is passive about his company. Butcher is an optimist who knows there is a place for his automobile (motorcycle? autocycle?).

Discussion Questions

1. Which psychological or personality factors were evident in the entrepreneurs discussed in this case?

2. Which strategies from the master strategies discussed in Chapter 4 has each entrepreneur appeared to pursue?

3. Which entrepreneurial venture has the highest likelihood for financial success? Why?

4. Would you invest in Michael Kelly's new Avanti Corporation? If so, why?

5. Which of the three men described in the case most closely represents the classic entrepreneur? Discuss your rationale for your answer.

Appendix 9.1

Characteristics Associated with Entrepreneurship

The Individual

Risk bearing
Initiative
Desire for responsibility
Source of formal authority
Risk taking
Ambition; desire for independence; responsibility; self-confidence
Drive/Mentality; human relations; communication ability; technical knowledge
Need for achievement; autonomy; aggression; recognition; innovation/independence
Need for power
Internal locus of control
Personal value orientation
Self-confidence; goal orientation; moderate risk taker; internal locus of control; creativity
Energy/Ambition; positive reaction to setbacks
Need to control; responsibility seeking; challenge taking
Growth orientation; independence orientation
Previous work experience
Entrepreneurial parents
Age; education

The Environment

Availability of venture capital
Presence of experienced entrepreneurs
Technically skilled labor force
Accessibility of suppliers
Accessibility of customers or new markets
Governmental influences
Proximity of universities
Availability of land or facilities
Accessibility of transportation
Attitude of the area population
Availability of supporting services
Living conditions
High occupational and industrial differentiation
High percentages of recent immigrants in the population
Large industrial base
Larger urban areas
Availability of financial resources
Barriers to entry
Rivalry among existing competitors
Pressure from substitute products
Bargaining power of buyers
Bargaining power of suppliers

Source: James W. Carland, F. Hoy, W. Boulton, and J. C. Carland, "Differentiating Entrepreneurs from Small Business Owners: A Conceptualization," *Academy of Management Review* 9 (April 1984): 356; and William B. Gartner, "A Conceptual Framework for Describing the Phenomenon of New Venture Creation," *Academy of Management Review* 10 (October 1985): 702.

Appendix 9.2

Contents of a Business Plan for a New Venture

I. Title page
II. Plan overview
III. Executive summary
  A. Management data
    1. Business mission
    2. Officers with titles
    3. Directors
    4. Employees (number by function)
    5. Consultants (if appropriate)
  B. Pro forma five-year financial summary of operations
    1. Sales broken down by type
    2. Cost of sales broken down by major categories
    3. Gross margin (dollars and percentage)
    4. Operating expense broken down by major functional cost centers
    5. Operating margin
    6. Other income and/or expenses
    7. Profit before taxes
    8. Taxes
    9. Net income
    10. Cumulative net income
  C. Pro forma five-year summary of financial position (balance sheet)
  D. Gantt chart of accomplishments (two-year minimum)—schedule of activities with start and stop dates
  E. Future prospects and direction
IV. Table of contents and list of exhibits
V. The firm's mission
  A. Business focus
  B. Strategic posture
  C. Functional orientation
  D. Product–market orientation (niche)
VI. The firm's environment
  A. Opportunity
    1. National, regional, or local economic conditions
    2. Competitive conditions
    3. Supplier conditions
    4. Others (for example, facility availability)
  B. Threats
    1. Economic constraints
    2. Competitive constraints
    3. Supplier constraints
    4. Others (for example, government intervention)
  C. Thorough market analysis
VII. The firm's capabilities
  A. Physical resources
  B. Major investors
  C. Management experience
  D. Human-resource competencies
  E. Technology advantage
  F. Proprietary right
  G. Distribution networks
  H. Location
  I. Others
VIII. Overall strategic goals
  A. Return on investment
  B. Return on equity
  C. Total sales
  D. Gross and net profit
  E. Total debt
IX. Operational objectives (suggestions)
  A. Financial
    1. Stock price
    2. Price/earnings ratio
    3. Debt/equity ratio
    4. Cash management
    5. Level of net working capital
  B. Marketing
    1. Sales by type and area
    2. Pricing
    3. Advertising
    4. Sales commissions
    5. Sales force composition

6. Sales force salaries

C. Production
   1. Variable manufacturing costs
   2. Facilities improvements
   3. Productivity
   4. Production levels
   5. Inventory levels
   6. Production workweek
   7. Allocation of finished products

D. Personnel
   1. Individual assignments
   2. Administrative duties
   3. Organization structure
   4. Training
   5. Profit sharing

X. Functional strategies

XI. The management team—a brief biographical sketch and statement of how each individual's talents will facilitate the accomplishment of objectives

XII. Results
   A. Amount of capital requested and justification
   B. Return to the investor (financial and other)
   C. Pro forma sources and uses statement for five years into the future

Chapter 10

Strategic Management in the International Arena

Insufficient attention is paid to the "international component" of the curriculum. Our interview discussions with deans and faculty members—and certainly our own personal biases on this point—would lead us to this conclusion.

—Don Hellriegel,
"Presidential Address: The State of the Academy,"
1988 Annual Academy of Management Meeting.

Learning Objectives

- To understand why companies enter the international arena.
- To review the choices available to a company when entering a foreign market.
- To know which aspects of the environment the international business must particularly scan and assess.
- To learn how to manage political risks in foreign markets.
- To understand the strategic choices available in meeting international market and product needs.
- To understand financial management considerations unique to international business.

BUSINESS has probably never been more competitive nor more international than it is today. Since the early 1970s exports have continued to rise, but imports have risen more rapidly. By 1984 the foreign trade deficit exceeded $100 billion and grew to about $171 billion in 1987.[1] Led by exports growing four times faster than imports, the trade deficit began to shrink in 1988 and is predicted to become a surplus by 1992.[2] The United States plays a central role in international business and international competition has a major impact on the success of U.S. business.

The U.S. market is large and attractive. Therefore, even businesses that have not become involved in exporting or conducting foreign operations find their domestic markets exposed to international competition. Firms that export goods to foreign markets are feeling strong competition from other international competitors. European car makers, for example, must compete with Japanese car makers at home and abroad. Increasingly competition has become global, with multinational corporations as major players.

Foreign markets often represent attractive new markets and profit opportunities. In 1987, 100 U.S. multinational corporations generated more than $1 billion in revenues. Coca-Cola alone generated 74 percent of its operating profits from the 26 percent of its assets located outside the United States. Exxon, Mobil, IBM, Dow Chemical, and Merck are examples of companies that generate more than 50 percent of their revenues from foreign operations.[3]

The strategic management process in an international company is essentially the same as that discussed in previous chapters, but the issues, complexity, and focus are different. There is considerable variety in the extent to which firms do international business, ranging from the Washington State chicken grower and processor who wants to sell the product in the Far East to the giant Japanese trading company Mitsubishi, which conducts a global business in many products. This chapter focuses on large multinational corporations to better illustrate the differences in choices for strategic management in international operations.

Becoming an International Company

Reasons for Going International

Why seek out international markets? Why incur the extra effort required to engage in international competition? To some extent, the reasons are the same as those for expanding into new territory domestically. But in the context of international business, firms expand into international markets for four basic reasons: greater sales and profits, cost advantages, global financial opportunities, and protection of domestic markets.

Increased growth opportunities in foreign markets provide additional sales and profits.[4] Parker Pen Company, for example, has used international expansion as an effective means of increasing revenues. Locating manufacturing and marketing operations in many countries has allowed Parker Pen to grow without having to significantly diversify lines of business, technology, or products. Parker capitalizes on its technological expertise and long-developed reputation worldwide.[5] The extra volume can provide smaller unit cost. If the company enters several markets, it can reduce the risk of being in any one market. Many growth opportunities come in new geographic or political arenas. While the economic growth rates in many of the more mature industrial economies, such as those of Germany, the United States, and the United Kingdom, have declined, other economies have shown increasing demand and provided new opportunities.

Competitive cost advantages are available to companies that seek out foreign locations with cheaper labor, cheaper raw materials, or investment and tax advantages. With trade liberalization, most national markets and national industries are exposed to competition.[6] For example, Ford can assemble the Fiesta in Spain at a lower labor cost and export the car to Italy and France. Multinational corporations, particularly those with an integration strategy (described later in the chapter), can gain competitive advantage by exploiting the scale and experience they gain from serving an expanded market. This raises the barriers to entry faced by competitors. In addition, multinationals can benefit from the economic reality that while free trade has created a relatively efficient market for goods, costs of production factors vary from one country to another. The company that has access to the least costly factors of production can therefore achieve the greatest spread between costs paid and prices charged.[7]

The development of global financial systems has facilitated the growth of international enterprise.[8] The International Monetary Fund, the World Bank, and such international financial institutions as Japan's Dai-Ichi Kangyo Bank, Germany's Deutsche Bank, and the American Bank of America and Citicorp have provided funds and found investors from around the globe. Multinational corporations can spread their risk and take advantage of differences in tax structure, cost of capital, exchange rates, and government incentives.

For some firms, the best way to protect their domestic markets is to attack in the competitor's own markets. Forcing the competitor to defend its own markets prevents it from consolidating efforts and resources on the market it is trying to enter. IBM, General Electric, Intel, Texas Instruments, and Cincinnati Milacron have found this approach to be an effective means of countering attacks from foreign competitors.[9]

These reasons for entering international markets apply to a greater or lesser degree depending on the exact nature of a firm's international involvement. A firm that is exporting to one or two markets may not be able to take advantage of differences in tax structure or government incentives, but a company that does business on a global scale probably can.

Entering Foreign Markets

With the development of better transportation, communication, trade, and financial systems, the world has become smaller, and more and more companies have decided to go international. There are several ways a company can enter foreign markets. These options are not mutually exclusive, and so the company may use one option in one market and another one in a different market. Typically, the company has already established itself in an industry and enters international competition by exporting or licensing its products to selected markets. Such a move adds geographic dimensions to marketing, but the company is still fundamentally a domestic firm selling to foreign markets. Later it may locate manufacturing or even complete business units in the markets it serves. Eventually the firm may have operations in multiple countries and may even treat each country as a strategic business unit.

Exporting Most firms enter international business by exporting. This can be a good way to test a new market or to minimize risk in building a foreign market. The company can get all the functions it needs to transport, distribute, sell, and service the product in the foreign market. It may also contract for some or all these services by using the services of an agent, export management company, or foreign sales representative.

Exporting is not generally the best option for firms that depend on foreign markets. Nor does it allow the firm to exploit differences in labor and materials costs. A company that needs the foreign sales but that has most of its operations in one country can be hurt by changes in the value of the home country's currency. For example, if the value of the dollar increases relative to the foreign market currency, purchasing American goods will be less desirable. If the currency increases in value, as it did in the United States in the early 1980s, the exporter will be at a cost disadvantage.

Licensing. With little investment, a company can gain access to foreign markets through licensing. The licensing company grants a foreign firm the right to produce or sell its products or use its patents, trademark, copyright, technical knowledge, designs, or processes. The licensee pays a fee or royalty for the right.

Licensing works well when there are certain barriers to entry. When the licensing company cannot afford the investment required or the government makes entry difficult, this can be the mechanism to open the market. The licensee may gain valuable knowledge and experience that can accelerate its development as a competitor. One company that has effectively used licensing on its patents is IBM, which has over 9,000 U.S. patents and over 23,000 international patents covering a vast range of high technology products. The licensing fees help increase the return on IBM's huge R&D investments. These fees can also benefit IBM in price wars against rivals that use its patents.[10]

Joint Venture A rather common way to gain entry to foreign markets is to join with a target market firm by using the ancillary strategy of a joint venture. A company can quickly acquire expertise in doing business in the target country by using and learning the expertise of the foreign partner. Such a joint venture may reduce the political risks of doing business in the country and speed up the entry.

Developing such relationships carries risks. The partner may acquire the firm's technological knowledge, and the companies have to share control of the venture. Coca-Cola pulled out of India rather than give up majority control and risk revealing its secret formula.[11] On the other hand, Pratt & Whitney, an engineering design firm, has used joint ventures to its advantage. An example is the venture named International Aero Engines, formed in 1983. Italy's Fiat, Britain's Rolls-Royce Ltd., Japan's Aero Engines, and West Germany's Motoren-und-Turbinen Union all shared the heavy start-up costs. The operation is based in the United States, but with the partners' aid in selling overseas, IAE has booked more than $1.6 billion in orders for its V2500 engine.[12]

Acquisition A company may use an external growth strategy and buy out a firm in the host country or one already doing business there. Typically the acquired firm is in the same or related business, so the company gains a distribution network as well as expertise in the host country and its products. The acquiring firm gains entry and retains control of the operation. Acquisition is a quick way to enter and may allow the company to more rapidly gain the benefits of economies of scale.

With these advantages, it is not surprising the acquisitions market is becoming increasingly active. For example, the Perrier Group, a French company, began exporting bottled water to the United States, but quickly found the fastest way to increase its market share was to acquire local companies.[13]

Many countries restrict foreign ownership, however, making this approach sometimes difficult to use. For example, Canada and Mexico restrict ownership to some degree. Mexico restricts foreign firms to a minority interest in their Mexican operations. In a country like the United States, where ownership is relatively unrestricted, acquisition can be an easy way to gain access to markets. Japan's Fujitsu Ltd. acquired Fairchild Semiconductor Corporation to avoid the trade agreement between the United States and Japan governing the sale of semiconductors.[14]

Direct Investment If country regulation permits, a company can build and develop its own capabilities in the target market. This approach may take longer in gaining entry to the market, but it allows the firm to select exactly what it wants and to maintain control of the operation and technical knowledge. The firm following an integration strategy, discussed later in this chapter, can usually design and tailor its total company facilities better. By building specialized plants in different countries, an integrated firm can increase product volume at each plant and increase economies of scale. Some countries require that a certain percentage of the value added to the product be added in that country. Such a policy may become a significant factor in entry considerations to the point that a company wishing to enter the country's markets must build plants in the country.

Environmental Scanning

When a company begins doing business internationally, it subjects itself to a new environment. Additional social, economic, political, and technological forces may affect the company in ways quite different from the way those forces affect it in its own country. In addition, the environment created by the interplay of these forces may be different in each geographic target market. Confronted with differing environments, a firm must find ways to accurately assess the environments, so that it can adjust its strategy as necessary.

The task of scanning the environment is fundamentally the same for an international company as for a domestic one. The major differences are that the firm must scan more environments and that the environments are unfamiliar. In addition, the specific aspects of the environment that are relevant to company strategy and operation may differ among countries. Such conditions complicate the task but also increase its importance.

Social Forces

Perhaps the most important social forces are those that affect market segmentation, product position, and the four Ps of marketing: product, place, price, and promotion. Will the product be desired, by whom, and by how many? Will its image and presentation have to be changed? The demand for the same product around the globe may be one of the biggest factors allowing for global competition.[15] Many companies, including Coca-Cola, have succeeded with standardized products around the world. Other companies have had to modify their products. For example, although Japanese automakers have done well with standardized cars, they still must make modifications like larger seats, a different location for steering, and pollution controls for the U.S. market.

Even if cultural differences do not force changes in the product, they may affect other practices. Language differences may be important, for heterogeneity of language within countries may be associated with potential conflict, instability, and consumption patterns.[16] As a practical matter, diversity of language can complicate how a company conducts business within a region or country. Which language will it use? Must it employ managers who are multilingual? Must it use different versions of advertising?

Unfortunately attention to language does not guarantee perfection in overcoming this barrier. Consider the surprise Coca-Cola got when PepsiCo started entering China markets. Coke had arrived first, making what the company thought was an exclusive deal with a central government trading company in 1978. However, in the Chinese-language version of the agreement, "exclusive" became "priority." When local and provincial governments were given more autonomy, Pepsi grabbed the chance to enter regional markets.[17]

Other cultural differences such as education, religion, values, and social organization, may change business practice. For example, Islamic law forbids paying or charging interest. Hinduism prohibits eating beef. In northern India, people prefer wheat, while those in southern India want rice. In countries with lower education and training levels, the firm may have difficulty employing local workers for some positions in the business. In the United States communities expect businesses to take an active interest in communities and public affairs. Japanese companies have found that corporate social responsibility programs are helpful in building community acceptance. The Strategic Application "Japanese Companies Do Good Works in the United States" gives several examples of their efforts.

Economic Forces

The economic policies and situations of a country can strongly affect the kind and degree of risk a company will incur, as well as how it conducts its operations. Many of the same market factors that affect domestic strategic planning are applicable. Examples include market size, growth rate of the market, and the inflation rate.

Other factors are unique to international business. A country subject to high inflation rates may require closer management of current assets. For example, it does not pay to hold cash or notes when inflation is high, because they will buy less the longer they are held. Credit terms must also be more restrictive, or the payment will be less than the credit granted. Any devaluation of the country's currency can drastically affect the company's assets and profit. An exporter would find that devaluation reduces customers' ability to purchase the product. Also, a centrally planned economy may be more inclined to regulate prices, entry, and conditions of trade. In such economies, it is often hard to distinguish economic from political forces.

STRATEGIC APPLICATIONS: SOCIAL RESPONSIBILITY

Japanese Companies Do Good Works in the United States

Given the international nature of business, it's not surprising to find companies doing good in their foreign markets. The decision to act seems not to be based on the location of the company's headquarters, but rather on the importance of the foreign market to the company's revenues.

Japanese-owned Subaru of America, for example, set up a charitable foundation in the United States. During its first six months of operation, the foundation reportedly gave grants of nearly $200,000 to more than 100 nonprofit groups.

Matsushita, the Japanese electronics giant, also set up a foundation in the United States. Original funding of $10 million was provided "as a token of gratitude to the American people." The foundation was established to give grants of $500,000 a year to improve education in such fields as language instruction and leadership training. It also supports an exchange program for Japanese and American scholars, business people, labor leaders, and artists.

The Japanese trading company Sumitomo gave $1 million to the graduate school of business at Columbia University. The purpose was to establish the Center on Japanese Economy and Business.

Source: M. R. Moskowitz, "Company Performance Roundup," *Business and Society Review* (Summer 1985): 83; (Winter 1985): 72; (Summer 1986): 75.

Technological Forces

The importance of technology depends somewhat on the degree of sophistication required to produce and maintain the product. Are skilled and professional staff required to make and maintain the product? Are they available? Can they be trained? Caterpillar Tractor built an extensive field distribution system to finance users, sell the product, carry spare parts, and service and repair its machines. The company built this system around the world over a 40-year period since World War II. This system, along with Caterpillar's scale of production, is its main competitive advantage, but such distribution systems are not quickly or easily set up. If the supporting technology in a country is unsophisticated, careful planning and creative solutions may be required.

In some countries, the primary reason for allowing companies to enter is to gain higher employment, increase the skill level of workers, and acquire the firm's technical know-how. In such a situation, the firm must decide how willing it is to expose its technology.

According to Vernon, demand for a product moves from the country that develops it to other developing countries over time.[18] Later, production location follows the shift in demand. With higher demand and lower production costs, competitive advantage shifts to the new country, and the innovating country becomes an importer of the product. The producing firm needs to decide whether this process is inevitable for its product or whether the firm can delay the process. If it cannot delay the process, then it must eventually move its operations overseas or get out of the business.

Political Forces

One of the most important forces in a target market are the political and legal ones. The law and politics of governments and potential intervention can greatly affect the conditions of doing business in a country. Political forces can affect the form of entry into the market, as when ownership is limited to licensing or a joint venture. The government may restrict the removal of profits from the country. Other laws may govern relationships with workers or unions, such as the ratio of foreign to domestic workers or the payment of overtime. The specifics of the laws and policies will vary from country to country, and their accumulation will make some countries more or less attractive as markets or as a base of operations. Table 10.1 is a checklist of some of the political and economic conditions with which a firm should be concerned.

Specific laws or policies are important, but of more concern are the stability of the country, its general attitude and climate toward business, especially foreign business, and the extent to which it protects domestic business from competition. A company needs to know how much political risk it is exposed to via intervention by a country. Intervention can take the form of standard regulations, discriminatory actions, or targeted interventions.[19]

Standard regulations are regulations that apply to all firms. They are seldom particularly harsh.

Discriminatory actions are directed at a specific group of companies, such as foreign-owned companies, and attempt to prevent or require some action that may be unique to this group of companies. They are intended to give an advantage to domestic organizations. For example, Malaysia requires that rubber plantations be under majority control of Malaysians.[20] In the United States, companies operating in certain high-technology fields and in defense fields may not trade certain products with Soviet block countries. For the group of companies involved, the action can be quite restrictive.

Targeted intervention is the severest type of government action, but it affects only a few firms.[21] It may require a foreign firm to reinvest all its profits in the host country. A harsher form might be the expropriation of facilities or ownership. International law recognizes expropriation as a right if the government promptly compensates expropriated firms at fair market value in convertible currencies.[22] Government takeovers of companies have occurred most frequently in Latin American countries that have recently changed to leftist governments and in the extractive or service industries. Larger firms and ones that have entered joint ventures with the host government are also at higher risk.[23] The risk of losing investment is not limited to less developed or politically unstable countries. In the early 1980s, when the socialists gained control, France forced many foreign-owned companies to sell much of their stock to the government.

In light of these risks, monitoring political forces should assume a major role in strategic planning and strategy formulation. A good assessment of the amount of political risk can help decision makers determine whether to enter a market, judge the adequacy of projected financial return, choose among alternative markets, identify how the firm can reduce the risk if it decides to enter, and choose a form of entry.

Table 10.1 A Checklist for General National Business Conditions

Government
Stability of government
Form of government
Government role and participation in industry
Attitude toward private enterprise
Attitude and policies toward foreign investment
Industrial strategy and plans
Administrative procedures for dealing with foreign firms
Policies of major alternative governing groups

Economic
Domestic economic growth (historic and future outlook)
Per capita gross national product
Population growth
Income distribution
Record of inflation
Availability of local capital
Rate of interest

General Legislation
Legislation governing foreign investment
Restrictions on repatriation of capital, earnings, royalties, license fees
Trade and investment treaties with other countries
Pollution and product legislation
Bookkeeping and records requirements
Corporate tax rates
Tax differences relative to domestic firms
Sales taxes, property taxes, local taxes, etc.
Tax treaties
Trade and investment treaties
Company contributions to national health insurance, retirement schemes

Regulations and Conditions of Work
Regulations of governing union rights and practices
Hours of work
Provisions for shift work
Severance pay and other requirements
Type of unions (e.g., craft, planwide)
Labor productivity record
Special skills
Work permits
Laws governing compensation of employees and managers
Regulations governing nationality of managers
Availability of special skills

Logistics
Availability and competence of suppliers and subcontractors
Raw materials, fuel
Transport system and costs
Insurance
Land (zoning requirements)
Communications (national and international)

Investment Incentives
National
Local

Cultural
Educational level
Attitude to new products and techniques
Familiarity with industrial methods and practices
Technological sophistication

Living Conditions (Foreign Personnel)
Education and health facilities
Housing
Sports and cultural attractions
Personal taxation provisions
Cost of living

Source: James Leontiades, *Multinational Corporate Strategy* (Lexington, Mass.: Lexington Books, 1985), 115. Reprinted with permission.

Obtaining good information about political and other forces is difficult. Many large multinationals maintain corporate staff groups to monitor conditions in countries where they do business. Bank of America, for example, uses experts for each country. Information in periodicals such as *The Economist* is not tailored to a specific company and industry, nor does it allow comparative assessment between countries.

Table 10.2 The *Euromoney* Country Risk Ratings

Rank 1986	Rank 1985	Country	Index	Rank 1986	Rank 1985	Country	Index
1=	11=	Belgium	100.00	36=	27=	Malaysia	65.00
1=	1=	Germany, West	100.00	36=	18	Saudi Arabia	65.00
1=	1=	Japan	100.00	38	25	Kuwait	63.00
1=	1=	Netherlands	100.00	39	33	Thailand	62.00
1=	1=	Sweden	100.00	40	50	Bulgaria	61.00
1=	1=	Switzerland	100.00	41	35	Greece	60.00
1=	1=	United Kingdom	100.00	42	37	Indonesia	59.00
1=	1=	United States	100.00	43	48	UAE	57.00
9	1=	Canada	98.00	44	42	Algeria	55.00
10	14	Norway	97.00	45	56	Turkey	54.00
11=	11=	Austria	95.00	46	45	Jordan	53.00
11=	16=	Denmark	95.00	47=	38	Cyprus	52.00
13=	11=	Luxembourg	94.00	47=	40	Oman	52.00
13=	17	France	94.00	47=	36	Tunisia	52.00
15	15	New Zealand	93.00	50=	51	Barbados	51.00
16	1=	Australia	92.00	50=	57	Papua New Guinea	51.00
17	10	Finland	87.00	52	73	Pakistan	50.00
18	22	Ireland	86.00	53=	72	Malta	49.00
19=	24	Spain	84.00	53=	62	Solomon Islands	49.00
19=	29	USSR	84.00	55	59	Fiji	44.00
21	23	Italy	83.00	56=	53=	Egypt	43.00
22	19	China	78.00	56=	64	Gabon	43.00
23	21	Hong Kong	75.00	56=	70	Panama	43.00
24	26	Iceland	74.00	59	47	Colombia	42.00
25	32	Korea	73.00	60=	61	Israel	41.00
26	44	Portugal	71.00	60=	31	South Africa	41.00
27	43	Qatar	70.00	62	81	Mauritius	40.00
28=	49	Hungary	69.00	63=	74	Romania	39.00
28=	46	India	69.00	63=	65	Sri Lanka	39.00
30=	39	Bermuda	68.00	63=	58	Burma	39.00
30=	20	Singapore	68.00	66=	93	Kenya	38.00
30=	30	Taiwan	68.00	66=	62	Nauru	38.00
33=	41	Czechoslovakia	67.00	66=	67	Syria	38.00
33=	34	Germany, East	67.00	66=	53=	Trinidad and Tobago	38.00
35	27=	Bahrain	66.00	70	86	Poland	37.00

A number of firms now provide risk assessment services that a company can use in its strategic planning. Ratings based on access to international credit, shown in Table 10.2, are provided by *Euromoney* magazine. Services like Frost and Sullivan, Business International, Business Environment Risk Information, and Beri-Forelend are other sources of political risk ratings. The information available from these services, if

Table 10.2 *(continued)*

Rank 1986	Rank 1985	Country	Index	Rank 1986	Rank 1985	Country	Index
71=	68	Cameroon	36.00	94=	97	Guatemala	23.00
71=	90	Swaziland	36.00	94=	78	Senegal	23.00
73	88	Brazil	35.00	97	89	Costa Rica	22.00
74	77	Zimbabwe	34.00	98=	107	Chile	21.00
75=	69	Botswana	33.00	98=	113	Peru	21.00
75=	66	Congo	33.00	98=	112	Lesotho	21.00
77=	55	Mexico	31.00	98=	98=	Libya	21.00
77=	60	Paraguay	31.00	98=	87	Zaire	21.00
77=	82	Venezuela	31.00	103=	117	Guyana	20.00
80=	109	Ecuador	30.00	103=	98=	Iraq	20.00
80=	83	Jamaica	30.00	103=	108	Lebanon	20.00
82=	79	Argentina	29.00	103=	106	Zambia	20.00
82=	76	Cuba	29.00	107	102	Liberia	19.00
82=	85	Morocco	29.00	108	91	Bangladesh	18.00
82=	63	Yugoslavia	29.00	109=	95=	Mauritania	17.00
86	105	Uruguay	28.00	109=	100=	Niger	17.00
87=	92	Ivory Coast	27.00	109=	111	Nigeria	17.00
87=	110	Tanzania	27.00	109=	115	Uganda	17.00
89=	75	Angola	26.00	113=	113=	Bolivia	16.00
89=	84	Ghana	26.00	113=	118	Ethiopia	16.00
89=	71	Mozambique	26.00	113=	104	Haiti	16.00
92	80	Philippines	25.00	116	95=	Honduras	13.00
93	100=	Malawi	24.00	117	103	Iran	10.00
94=	94	Dominican Republic	23.00	118=	119	El Salvador	6.00
				118=	115	Sudan	6.00

Method of ranking: This year we have stuck to the same set of criteria we used in 1985. Although new instruments have been introduced which allow countries to tap new markets, they haven't changed the overall evaluating structure. We have, however, added one layer to the process. The rankings, once they had been compiled, were shown to political risk insurers and top syndicate managers in the Euromarkets for their comments, which confirmed the changes we've noted in the way the market views country risk.

In this year's table, the key criteria we used were: access to bond markets (Yankee and Euro-bonds and FRNs), the Euroloan and Euronote markets, trade finance, political risk and a country's payment record.

The weighting was: access to markets, 20%; access to trade finance (forfaiting), 10%; payment record (whether on time or late), 15%; difficulties in rescheduling, 5%; political risk, 20%; selldown, a good measure of over-subscription or otherwise of an issue, 30%. Thus, low cost funds alone are not the arbiter of a country's credit standing.

Source: *Euromoney* (September 1986) pp. 364–65. Reprinted with permission.

tailored to a company's needs, might well be the best alternative for a company new to strategic planning in an international setting or considering entry into these new markets.

The conclusions reached from such assessments can then be included when rating the attractiveness of a market or country. To rate the attractiveness of countries, Ford Tractor has used a weighted scale that includes several economic and political factors as well as market size and growth.[24]

Assessing political risk is particularly important when a firm is selecting target markets, because the firm has greatest control at this time. It can still avoid the negative aspects of political risk. It can make an informed decision as to whether to avoid the risk and how much risk it is prepared to assume.

Managing Political Risks

The risk of intervention by a host government is a significant problem for the foreign-owned business. The threat can never be eliminated, but it can be planned for in strategic management. The first line of defense is thoroughly scanning and assessing the environment of the prospective host country before deciding on entry. In addition, a company can take several steps to manage the risk:

1. Reduce the risk before entry by negotiating the environment.
2. Reduce the risk after entry by establishing appropriate management policies.
3. Reduce losses if exit is required.

Negotiation of the Environment One way a company can negotiate its environment is to obtain a concession agreement before it invests in the country. A concession agreement documents the rights and responsibilities for the company and the host country. As in the example in the Strategic Application "Occidental Petroleum Cuts a Deal," the terms of the agreement depend on the benefits each party can offer. Some countries, including Japan and Norway, require an agreement before permitting foreign investment. But a concession agreement is not always honored by a succeeding government.

STRATEGIC APPLICATIONS

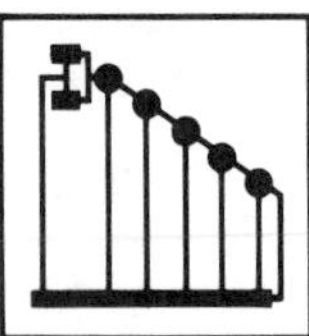

Occidental Petroleum Cuts a Deal

One company that has been active in pursuing international petroleum reserves is Occidental Petroleum Corporation. It claims to be sitting on what looks like the biggest new oilfield since the North Sea and Mexico offshore. Cano Limon, as the oil field is called, is the company's 2.7-million-acre contract in Colombia.

The Colombian venture is a 50–50 partnership with Ecopetrol, the Colombian national oil company. Industry observers say Occidental Petroleum got a favorable deal with the Colombian government. The government receives a 20 percent royalty on its half of production, plus 40 percent in taxes. In comparison, the U.S. Windfall Profits Tax can run much higher than 40 percent.

How did Occidental strike such a deal? The Cano Limon field is a difficult prospect. The field is in a floodplain, under water eight months a year. To get the oil to market, Occidental must build a $400-million, 286-mile pipeline over the Andes to the Caribbean port of Covenas.

Source: J. Cook, "Armand's New Elephant," *Forbes*, June 17, 1985, 66–67.

The agreement can address any subject the parties believe could cause disagreement. It could, for example, specify how conflicts and disputes will be handled. It might also address the method of taxation or how transfer prices will be handled. Divestment is another condition that has been required for entry or has been forced on firms later. A company can try to preplan a divestment and even negotiate the plan into the concession agreement. Preplanning might forestall more severe intervention by the host country.

Another way to reduce risk before entry may be to obtain insurance.[25] Many industrialized countries in the West have programs to protect investments in less-developed countries. In the United States, the program is the Overseas Private Investment Corporation. Such programs usually provide insurance and guarantees.

Management Operating Policies Because a company cannot anticipate all of its or the host country's concerns, it may not capture all these concerns in a concessionary agreement. Therefore, after a company has invested, it can reduce the risk of intervention by adopting operating policies that recognize the needs and priorities of the host country. Some of the operating policies may make it difficult for the host country to operate the facilities should the government decide to confiscate.

Many of the issues addressed by operating policies are concerned with allowing the company to maintain control over decisions about operations and reducing the ability of the host country to intervene.

Achieving a balance satisfactory to both parties is difficult. The most successful approach is likely to be adapting to the country's concerns while maintaining the company's ability to run its operations effectively and efficiently. However, as the parties jockey for position, hostile relationships may escalate.

Exit Tactics If the government confiscates a company's assets, management still has alternatives that can reduce the economic damage. Hoskins has described these in terms of four phases that follow confiscation.[26] These phases are rational negotiation, political and economic power tactics, legal remedies, and concession.

At the rational negotiation phase, the company usually has some warning of the impending confiscation. The company can use the warning to persuade the government of the advantages to be gained by continuing operations. The company can also offer concessions for continued operations. It might, for example, offer to invest more capital or concede certain terms negotiated in its prior concession agreement.

If the situation escalates to the use of political and economic power tactics, the company might seek to have its own government intercede. Economically it might seek to weaken the country's bargaining position by withdrawing resources (such as technological know-how) so the local operations cannot sustain themselves. A wise choice of operating policies can strengthen the company's position. For example, when Belco Petroleum's Peruvian oil-producing properties were expropriated, the company located refineries elsewhere and separated the producing locations from the transportation of oil to the refineries and to markets.[27] Although the producing properties were expropriated, the other properties were not, so Peru needed to cooperate with Belco. Similarly, companies that integrate operations across nations risk losing only one part of their operation, and the part located in one country may be of little use to the country by itself. In effect, companies limit their dependency on any one country. However, such power tactics risk toughening the host country's position.

When companies turn to legal remedies, they often begin by seeking redress in local courts. Such action is less visible and usually is more efficient. The company also can seek redress in its own country's courts for claims against the host country's property. It may also claim damages with its own country's insurance and guarantee program. In addition, the company may seek arbitration through the International Centre for Settlement of Investment Disputes. This service is available to members when parties consent to its jurisdiction. Consent might be given in the concessionary agreement. A number of developing countries belong to the group, although most Latin American countries do not.

Eventually management may have to concede and seek to salvage as much as it can. The best deal may be to continue a relationship with the country, perhaps by operating the business even if the company no longer owns it.

Strategic Choices

The primary distinguishing characteristic of an international firm is the market it serves. Because the market is located in a different environment and is geographically separated from the firm's domestic business, the firm must often focus its strategy differently to serve that market.

Primary Market Choices

The primary strategic choices concerning markets involve decisions about the markets to target and about the segments of the industry in which to compete. Internationally this can mean whether to compete across the full range of products in the industry or in some segment of it and whether to compete globally or concentrate on fewer national markets. Table 10.3 combines these choices and summarizes the conditions when each is appropriate.

In a **multinational industry strategy**, the company perceives the market as a worldwide one that it can serve with essentially the same products. Obvious candidates for this strategy are makers of soft drinks like Coke and Pepsi as well as cigarette companies like RJR Nabisco. These products have worldwide appeal. Product concepts like color television and fast foods also lend themselves to this approach, known as *globalization*. The strategy is appropriate if the company has the resources to sustain it and can use its scale of operations and the worldwide availability of production factors to achieve cost or value advantages. These competitive advantages make it difficult for local firms to compete. To achieve integration and competitive advantage, the firm must conduct centralized planning and management.

In contrast, the **national industry strategy** sees each country or region as a distinct market, requiring differences in the product. The company often responds to these fragmented markets by establishing fairly autonomous operations for each country.

Table 10.3 Market Choices for International Competition

Market Choice	Appropriate Conditions
Multinational industry	Firm has current and potential customers. A dominant market position is possible in a full range of products. Firm has the resources to support the strategy globally.
National industry	Current and potential customers want significant variation in product. Economic constraints limit global competition. A dominant position over a full range of products is possible nationally. Firm has the resources to support the strategy in national markets.
Multinational segment	Firm has current and potential customers. Segment is defensible against firms with a global focus. Strategic market segment exists.
National segment	Dominance in the industry is not available to the firm. Firm lacks resources to obtain dominance. Conditions for multinational industry exist for segment, and segment is defensible.
National protected	National market is protected from world competition. National government is willing to grant protection to develop local industry.

Source: Adapted by permission of the publisher from Thomas N. Gladwin, "Multinational Corporate Strategies," in *Handbook of Business Strategy*, W. D. Guth, ed., pp. 13–1 to 13–23. Copyright 1985 Warren, Gorham & Lamont, Inc., Boston, Massachusetts.

Each separate market may be treated as a separate SBU or subsidiary. Lacking uniform markets and products, the firm cannot gain the same advantages of scale as the multinational company, but it will have certain scale advantages over a purely local company. For example, it will be able to easily transfer its know-how and technology across national lines. Unlike the uniformity of the multinational industry strategy, markets and products vary in the national industry strategy. To remain flexible and respond to differences, the firm requires more decentralized planning and management.

The **multinational market segment** is similar to the multinational industry market except that the focus is on a segment of the industry. The company views market and customer needs as homogeneous, and it chooses to compete in a niche or narrow band of products within the industry. For example, while Ford competes across a broad spectrum of the industry, Jaguar concentrates on the high-quality, high-performance segment.

A **national segment strategy** is like the national industry strategy except that it focuses on only a segment of the industry.

In all of these segment strategies, it is particularly important that the niches be distinct and defensible against companies with large operations. Honda, for example, turned a segmented industry into a global one with its marketing and economies of scale.[28]

A **national protected strategy** differs from the other strategies in that it responds not to differences in the product or market, but to political constraints. The firm is able to concentrate on a national market because the market is protected by tariffs or some government action. The government may intend to develop a local industry for locally used products by limiting imports and protecting the industry from foreign competition. A firm may gain access to the market by helping to develop the business, perhaps by agreeing to eventual divestment, contracting to build and manage the facility, or employing and training locals. Japan is rather well known for protecting selected industries from competition domestically until the industry is developed enough to compete internationally.

Global Business Strategies

One of the most important choices multinational companies face in today's competitive environment is whether to respond to individual country markets or to build a company whose operations are integrated cross country borders. Several authors have emphasized the changing pattern of competition and the need to develop a multinational business strategy to respond to the globalization of markets.[29] In a study of conditions that influence the strategic choice of firms in European markets, Doz concluded that the available strategic choices depend on the economic characteristics of the industry, the capabilities and policies of nations, and the firm's current competitive posture in the industry.[30] The choice between national responsiveness and global integration is not clear-cut but involves how much to emphasize one or the other.

National Responsiveness A multinational corporation using a national responsiveness strategy has a national subsidiary for each national market. Each subsidiary is fairly autonomous, and the manager is allowed to respond to the market independently. The markets are often protected with tariff barriers, and business conditions may be negotiated with the government. Corporate headquarters tends to decentralize managing authority and operations except for such functions as research and development and finance. Activities involving coordination of several subsidiaries also may be performed at headquarters. The subsidiary can call upon other subsidiaries or headquarters for expertise in such areas as new-product development, process engineering, and management. The corporation can spread profits, financial risk, and research and development costs over a large volume. Each subsidiary produces a relatively complete product line for its own market.

Because the nationally responsive firm has a large scale of operations, ability to spread cost has tremendous advantages over the strictly domestic firm. It can better share purchasing opportunities and central services. In addition, it can coordinate its competitive actions to better respond to competitors and strengthen its position in different markets. It can use its strong position in other countries to subsidize entry into a new market. Or it might attack a competitor in its home country. If the competitor must compete at home, it may have difficulty using enough resources to successfully enter a foreign market. Goodyear did this to Michelin; to counter the French tire company's entry into the U.S. market, Goodyear launched its own attack in Europe.[31] This action forced Michelin to defend its own market and increased the cost of gaining market share in the United States.

Multinational Integration If a company chooses a strategy of multinational integration, it integrates its operations across national borders. Each national subsidiary may distribute the product or product line, but no single subsidiary produces the whole line or the whole product. Manufacturing plants are specialized by product, component, or process so that the complete line of products is produced in more than one country. Engines for a car may be produced in Germany, frames and steerage in France, and bodies in Italy, while the car may be assembled in each country or in one location.

The driving force behind this strategy is the need to lower cost. The company attempts to rationalize its operation so that products or parts are produced where the lowest costs can be achieved. With maturing of industries, the transfer of technology, and the lowering of trade barriers has come global competition. At the same time, global markets have arisen for standardized products.

A special case of multinational integration has occurred in the way many Japanese companies have dealt with U.S. markets. In the past, many companies, including Toyota and Sony, preferred to manufacture their products in Japan because of lower costs and scale and control of operations. As the dollar weakened in comparison to the yen, many of these companies found their exports to the United States cut as much as 50 percent. In addition, the U.S. government increased pressure to curtail imports into the United States and threatened additional trade barriers. Many Japanese companies responded by setting up manufacturing operations and establishing their own supplier networks in the United States. These plants are part of a global network, supplying other plants in other countries as well as U.S. buyers. Finished products including Honda cars have even been shipped back to Japan.[32]

Specializing plants by product or process enables the firm to obtain larger production volumes and employ more efficient manufacturing methods. Although such plants in the United States are often capital-intensive facilities like computer-automated plants, this strategy can also allow companies to locate labor-intensive operations in countries with relatively low labor costs. Experience and scale economies go beyond the volume economies obtained within a country. Because of its scale of operations, know-how, and freer trade, the integrated firm can more easily take advantage of the differences throughout the world in cost of supplies and labor. Barriers to entry into the business are thereby raised, and the cost of remaining in the industry is increased for the nonintegrated firms. A national government will also find it more difficult to confiscate operations and control the product, because it can obtain control over only one part of the product or process. As companies seeking lower cost positions change plant locations they can cause economic dislocation for workers, other companies, and communities as well as public relations problems for themselves. The Strategic Application "American Companies Take Jobs Abroad" provides two examples of this problem.

The very nature of the specialization and integration across borders can pose difficulties for the integrated strategy. Because units are interdependent, disruptions in one location can cause breakdowns for the whole system. For example, if no engines are coming out of Germany, no cars will be built. Also, governments can have power over a whole system rather than just the subsidiary in the country. A government

STRATEGIC APPLICATIONS

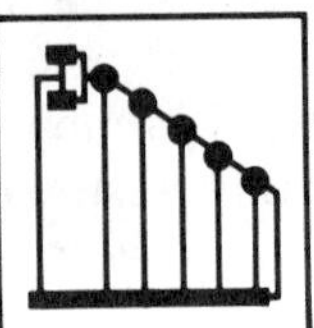

American Companies Take Jobs Abroad

As companies adjust to international competition, new social concerns have arisen. For instance, when a company decides to move some of its operations to a foreign land to lower costs, what happens to the displaced employees? This is exactly the situation that Atari, the maker of computers and video games, faced in 1983. The company was moving some of its production from California to the Far East, and 537 workers were suddenly told they no longer had a job. The word came without even a single day's notice. The group of workers sued and settled out of court with the company's then parent, Warner Communications, for four weeks' pay.

Numerous companies have located plants across the U.S. border with Mexico. In 1965 the U.S. government began sponsorship of a program to create jobs for Mexico. Parts made in the United States were shipped to these plants and the finished product shipped back to the United States. More than 350,000 people are employed in these plants. The workers are low skilled and very underpaid even by Mexican standards. Some Americans charge that the companies exploit Mexican labor. American labor unions are angry that the U.S. companies have transferred jobs to Mexico.

In 1988, the U.S. government passed a law regulating the closure of plants and requiring prior notification of intent to close a plant.

Source: M. R. Moskowitz, "Company Performance Roundup," *Business and Society Review* (Fall 1986): 67; Stephen Baker, Todd Vogel, and Adrienne Bard, "Will the New Maquiladoras Build a Better Mañana?" *Business Week*, November 14, 1988, 102, 106.

may use its power to disrupt the system to bargain for local concessions. Management of the system is more complex because decision makers must seek optimum results for the whole system, not just one subsidiary. With greater integration and interdependence comes the need for greater—usually more costly—coordination. Finally, the system will have less capacity to respond to national markets. The strategy assumes that the various markets have a uniform demand for the product and forfeits the ability to respond to national differences. If conditions change or the company has calculated wrong, it is in a poor position to respond.

Integrated operations dictate integration of management. The higher degree of coordination required is best obtained by more planning at headquarters and less discretion for the subsidiaries. Particularly in functions closely allied to manufacturing—such as transportation and research and development—and also in any function requiring significant integration, management decision making is more centralized in the multinationally integrated firm than it is in a company following a strategy of national responsiveness.

Multifocal Strategy The multifocal strategy lies between national responsiveness and multinational integration. A mixture of both, it seeks the relative merits of each in policy decision. Responsiveness to local markets where necessary may lead the firm to use local plants, while also seeking integration to the extent conditions and national governments allow. For example, 70 percent of Sony's sales come from outside Japan. A strong yen, rivals with lower costs in developing countries, and increasing protectionist and competitive pressure in the United States and Europe led to lower sales and earnings. Sony responded by moving 20 percent of its manufacturing operations overseas, but the company did so selectively. Televisions are now made in San Diego, California, and in Bridgend, Wales, but all Walkman products are still made in Japan because of a special automated plant. Sony also diversified into industrial products.[33]

A company may be willing to accept less than optimum cost in order to gain entry to a market. The multifocal strategy may result when a firm tries to integrate while trying to maintain a favored position with a national government. L. M. Ericsson of Sweden, like most major international makers of telephone equipment, produced its equipment locally to get lower labor costs and to respond to the desire of governments of less-developed countries to produce locally. When switching technology went from mechanical to electronic, the industry became global. The movement threatened Ericsson's relationship with many of its customers. The company responded with modular technology and software that could be adapted to diverse small systems at reasonable cost. Ericsson has a centralized R&D function and a partly integrated manufacturing system, but the autonomy of each subsidiary depends on the maturity of its market.[34]

The mixed nature of the multifocal strategy requires the integration of corporate and subsidiary managers. At the same time, the shared decision making needs to respond to fluid and often ambiguous conditions. The management process necessary to achieve such decision making is more complex and situational.

Which strategy is the most favorable to pursue depends on numerous factors having to do with the structural characteristics of an industry, the forms of government intervention, the relative bargaining power of the firm and governments, and the competitive posture of the firm. These conditions are to some degree situational and difficult to summarize. For example, when the economies of scale required to compete exceed the scale of operation possible within one country, the choice of a multinational integration strategy it favored. However, when the distribution of the product requires intensive local selling and servicing, the national responsiveness strategy is the more favorable choice.[35]

Financial Management as a Strategic Tool

The strategic management of international business relies heavily on several financial issues. The company can lessen its exposure to devaluation of currency by managing foreign exchange. Countertrading can be a major strategic management tool in opening new markets and can be required as a condition of doing business in a country. Tax and profit planning also have important implications for strategic management decisions.

Foreign Exchange

When a company does any business in a foreign country, it must be concerned with the valuation of the country's currency. Even companies with no foreign sources, sales, or debt may be affected by changes in foreign exchange rates. If the company competes with a British luggage manufacturer that is the market leader, the British company will consider its cost in pounds when setting its dollar price. If the pound weakens relative to the dollar, the dollar-equivalent costs of the British company's product will be less, giving the British company a competitive advantage.

The value of each currency can change almost daily. Because the exchange rate is subject to change, it exposes a company to risk. For example, if Boeing has contracted with Britain's Securicor to deliver Boeing 747s in 1992, it may lose money if the dollar rises in value relative to the pound. In the currency markets, Boeing can limit this risk by selling pounds for dollars for delivery up to one year later, thus locking in the revenue in terms of the dollars it will receive. Foreign exchange management thus becomes a significant task for companies with substantial foreign business in many different companies.

Exchange rates can affect the balance sheet. It may be to the firm's advantage to borrow capital from local sources in local currency or to defer capital expenditures in dollars.

Exchange rates may also affect how and when a company takes profits out of a country and its accounting practices. The impact on revenues of some companies can be considerable. Travel agencies and airlines that depend on tourist travel by Americans to Europe have seen their fortunes rise and fall with the strength of the dollar. As the dollar changes in its ability to buy more or less, the willingness of tourists to travel also rises and falls.

The ability of a company to minimize its exposure varies with the nature of its overseas involvement and the particular countries with which it is involved. Some countries do not allow their currency to float.

Besides the techniques discussed so far, several other ways are available to manage the risk related to exchange rates:[36]

- A company can carefully locate its foreign operating sites in many countries or otherwise structure its businesses to offset its exposure. However, this may lead to lower economies of scale.
- A company may minimize the total corporate exposure by selecting a portfolio of businesses that have offsetting operating exposures from operating in different countries.
- A company can plan its product and sourcing so that it has the flexibility to increase its production and sourcing in countries where the currency is greatly undervalued.

The case of one Japanese firm illustrates several of these strategies. Like many Japanese firms, Canon faced a major economic problem when the value of the yen increased 88 percent compared to the dollar. About 70 percent of its sales were exports, much of it to the United States. With the increase in the value of the yen, the price of Canon products became too high for many markets. The company decided to cut its profit margin from 3.9 percent to 1.4 percent, although this led to a 71 percent decline in profit for 1986. At the same time, it started to shift its production out of Japan into Southeast Asia, Europe, and the United States. In addition, it fought the effect of the rising yen with innovation, heavy spending on R&D, introduction of new products, and by improving existing products. Despite the increasing value of the yen, Canon's profit grew more than 10 percent in 1988.[37]

Countertrade

Throughout the history of commerce, traders have been willing to barter one good for another. Today the practice is called countertrading, and companies as well as nations are still trading goods for goods instead of for monetary payment. Countertrading has increasingly become a fact of doing business internationally. Many countries insist on countertrading because they do not have the cash or credit to pay for goods. As an example, First Interstate Trading Company, a subsidiary of First Interstate Banking Corporation, agreed to a countertrade with Peru whereby the bank would provide loans and accept commodities such as fabric in return. First Interstate benefited by reducing its unsyndicated loans and Peru was able to reduce its debt liabilities and increase exports.[38] Other countries find that they can use the distribution systems of large multinational corporations, which they lack, to get their goods to market.

While most companies prefer cash, some have found their willingness to barter has opened markets to them that competitors cannot penetrate. For example, General Electric won out in a $150 million contract for power plant turbines in Romania because the company would use its global distribution network to open markets for Romanian goods. GE also gained contacts and goodwill within the Romanian government.

Countertrading is not for every company. It requires trading know-how, networks and contacts, and much coordination between the organization's divisions and functions. The volume of business must be large enough to cover the costs and the willingness to assume the risk. Yaffie has suggested several guidelines for companies considering countertrading:[39]

1. The company should decide whether it has the desire and necessary resources for doing business by countertrading. If the firm does not have or cannot acquire the needed capabilities, it should either avoid countertrading, hire a trading company, or use the countertrade division of a bank such as Bank of America or Citibank.

2. The cost of selling the country's goods should be included in the selling price to it. The company may have to search for customers for the goods and sell them at discount. The cost of negotiating sales, transporting the goods, and so forth can also be great. If the firm can get the country to pay up front, it will lower its exposure to loss.

3. The firm should know the bartering country's government, policies, and regulations. Knowing who to deal with and what is permissible cuts time and cost. Experience with all regulations, not just those involved in direct negotiations, can save costly mistakes and erroneous assumptions.

4. The firm should know the product it is bartering for. Does the firm have the expertise to import and distribute the product? Can it match the product's characteristics with customer needs? Are there industry standards and specifications that will ensure its quality for users?

5. The firm should know the process of negotiating a barter with the country it is dealing with. This may avoid premature concessions and loss of opportunity. All terms should be presumed negotiable.

Tax Planning

Tax implications can affect choices such as entry, capital investment, relationships between subsidiaries and headquarters, and the country network used in achieving an integration strategy. Tax planning may therefore become a part of any major strategic management decision. For multinational firms subject to many varieties of tax codes, the primary concern is to minimize the firm's total tax bill without restricting its economic potential or limiting its opportunities.[40]

When a U.S.-owned company earns profits in another country, how should it be taxed and by which country? To reduce its overall tax bill, a company will try to shift reported profits from countries with a high tax structure to one with a low tax structure. The company can divert profits by moving the goods through other companies. It can use transfer pricing by under- or over-pricing materials and supplies transferred between subsidiaries. It can also use a domestic international sales corporation, to which some countries grant tax breaks on exports. The company might also reduce profits in a country through fees, royalties, and interest it charges the subsidiary. For example, it might charge a high royalty for the use of patents. Prices charged for supplies can have the effect of increasing cost and lowering profits.

Summary

Today businesses have many reasons to consider the world their market. Foreign markets provide additional growth opportunities. They can allow companies to lower costs because of increased economies of scale as well as lower labor and material costs. A company may be able to gain tax benefits and other financial incentives through foreign governments and financial institutions. In addition, companies cannot avoid foreign competition by staying at home. For many firms, the best way to compete is to go international. Once a firm decides to go international, it has many options. A company can export its products, license them to foreign companies, enter into joint ventures with foreign firms, acquire a firm, or develop its own capability in the target market.

When a company ventures into a foreign market, it places itself into a new and unfamiliar environment. It must learn to scan and assess these new social, economic, political, and technological forces. Social forces can change the market segments, positioning, and functional plans regarding price, promotion, distribution, and even product characteristics. A few of the important economic considerations are market size, market growth, and the inflation rate. Technological development of the country affects whether the company can manufacture on site and its willingness to expose its know-how and products to the country. Perhaps of greatest concern is the political stability of the country, particularly the threat of intervention by the host country through regulation, discriminatory action, or expropriation. Although this risk can be lowered, it can never be abolished.

When a company enters the international arena, it must make many strategic choices. Primary among these choices are the market to serve and the segments in which to compete. The company must decide whether its market is worldwide or whether each individual country or region is a distinct market. It must also decide whether to serve the chosen market with a wide range of products or to concentrate on some segment(s). Later the company may have to decide whether it can serve the world with a standardized product, set up subsidiaries for each national market, or seek multinational integration of its operations.

The international arena forces a company to handle different currencies and tax laws. Fluctuating values of the currencies can expose the company to considerable risk, over which the company has no control, though it can manage and minimize the risk through various strategies. Countertrading is also important in world trade, because many countries wish to trade in goods and contracts rather than in currency. Finally, tax codes vary across countries, and management must seek to minimize the firm's worldwide tax bill.

Questions

1. Why would a company decide to do business in the international arena? What methods are available for entering foreign markets?

2. If your company decides to go international, which political forces would you consider important in making strategic decisions? What steps could you take to manage the political risk to which your company would be exposed?

3. Compare a multinational industry focus and a national industry focus. What is meant by a multinational integration strategy? When is this strategy appropriate? How does a multifocal strategy differ from it?

4. Why must you learn to manage the risk related to exchange rates if your company does any business in foreign countries?

5. How can the willingness of your company to engage in countertrading be helpful? What kind of concerns should you have and what guidelines might be helpful should you decide to negotiate a countertrade?

Notes

1. Alan Murray, "The Budget Albatross," *The Wall Street Journal*, January 20, 1989, R16–17.

2. William J. Holstein, Steven J. Dryden, Gail Schares, Ted Holden, and Jonathan B. Levine, "Made in the U.S.A.," *Business Week*, February 29, 1988, 60–62.

3. "The 100 Largest U.S. Multinationals and the 100 Largest Foreign Investments in the United States," *Forbes*, July 25, 1988, 240–250.

4. Thomas L. Wheelen and J. David Hunger, *Strategic Management and Business Policy*, 2d ed. (Reading, Mass.: Addison-Wesley, 1986), 260.

5. Y. H. Godiwalla, "Multinational Planning—Developing a Global Approach," *Long Range Planning* 19 (April 1986): 110–116.

6. Yves Doz, *Strategic Management in Multinational Companies* (New York: Pergamon Press, 1986), 2.

7. Ibid., 3.

8. David C. Shanks, "Strategic Planning for Global Competition," *Journal of Business Strategy* 5 (Winter 1985): 80–89.

9. Craig M. Watson, "Counter-Competition Abroad to Protect Home Markets," *Harvard Business Review* 60 (January–February 1982): 41–42.

10. M. W. Miller, "IBM Is Raising Licensing Fees on Its Patents," *The Wall Street Journal*, April 11, 1988, 2.

11. "The Mouse That Roared at Pepsi," *Business Week*, September 9, 1987, 42.

12. R. W. King, A. Borrus, and J. Heard, "UTC Adds Westland to Its Growing Foreign Arsenal," *Business Week*, February 24, 1986, 88–89.

13. John Rossant, "Perrier's Unquenchable U.S. Thirst," *Business Week*, June 29, 1987, 46.

14. Richard Brandt, "Japan Buys a Piece of Silicon Valley," *Business Week*, November 10, 1986, 45.

15. Several authors have argued that change has produced a global market wherein corporations sell the same product everywhere. Theodore Leavitt, "The Globalization of Markets," *Harvard Business Review* 61 (May–June 1983): 92–102, is particularly persuasive in presenting the argument.

16. Vern Terpstra and Kenneth David, *The Cultural Environment of International Business* (Cincinnati, Ohio: South-Western Publishing, 1985), 175–209, 219–245.

17. L. Kraar, "Pepsi's Pitch to Quench Chinese Thirsts," *Fortune*, March 17, 1986, 58–64.

18. R. Vernon, "International Investments and International Trade in the Product Cycle," *Quarterly Journal of Economics* 80 (May 1966): 190–207; and R. B. Reich, *The New American Frontier* (New York: Time Books, 1983), 117–139.

19. Thomas N. Gladwin, "Multinational Corporate Strategies" in *Handbook of Business Strategy*, ed. W. D. Guth (Boston, Mass.: Warren, Gorham and Lamont, 1985), 13–1 to 13–23.

20. "Uniroyal Sells a Unit for Over $71 Million to Malaysian Concern," *The Wall Street Journal*, December 24, 1984, 12.

21. Gladwin, "Multinational Corporate Strategies."

22. David K. Eiteman and Arthur I. Stonehill, *Multinational Business Finance*, 3d ed. (Reading, Mass: Addison-Wesley, 1982), 291.

23. Ibid.

24. John K. Ryans, Jr., and William L. Shanklin, *Strategic Planning* (New York: Random House, 1985), 279, citing Gilbert D. Harrell and Richard O. Kiefer, "Multinational Strategic Market Portfolios," *MSU Business Topics* 29 (Winter 1981): 5–15.

25. Eiteman and Stonehill, *Multinational Business Finance*, 312–313.

26. William R. Hoskins, "How to Counter Expropriation," *Harvard Business Review* 48 (September–October 1970): 102–112.

27. "Belco Nationalized in Peru," *Oil and Gas Journal*, January 6, 1986, 47–48.

28. Thomas Hout, Michael E. Porter, and Eileen Rudden, "How Global Companies Win Out," *Harvard Business Review* 60 (September–October 1982): 98–108.

29. Ibid.; Leavitt, "The Globalization of Markets"; and Gary Hamel and C. K. Prahalad, "Do You Really Have a Global Strategy?" *Harvard Business Review* 63 (July–August 1985): 139–148.

30. Doz, *Strategic Management in Multinational Companies*, 5–6.

31. Hamel and Prahalad, "Do You Really Have a Global Strategy?"

32. William J. Holstein, "Japan, U.S.A.," *Business Week*, July 14, 1986, 45–54.

33. Larry Armstrong, Christopher Power, and G. David Wallace, "Sony's Challenge," *Business Week*, June 1, 1987, 64–69.

34. This example draws from Hout, Porter, and Rudden, "How Global Companies Win Out"; and Doz, *Strategic Management in Multinational Companies.*

35. For a more in-depth treatment, consult Doz, *Strategic Management in Multinational Companies,* 26–27.

36. Donald R. Lessard and John B. Lightstone, "Volatile Exchange Rates Can Put Operations at Risk," *Harvard Business Review* 64 (July–August 1986): 107–114.

37. Mare Beauchamp, "From Fuji to Everest," *Forbes,* May 2, 1988, 35–36.

38. Kathryn Rosenblum, "First Interstate Tries Barter," *Euromoney,* April 1987, 10–13.

39. David B. Yaffie, "Profiting from Countertrade," *Harvard Business Review* 62 (May–June 1984): 8–16.

40. Gladwin, "Multinational Corporate Strategies," 13–23.

Case for Discussion

Adapting to the New Europe

Jean-Paul Descarpentries was CEO of a large French electronics firm, St. Cloud Electronics. In its specialized niche it was the largest in France with 35 percent of the market and second in Spain with 20 percent. St. Cloud did not compete across the broad spectrum of electronics, however, and did not rank among the largest electronics firms worldwide. Its return on investment was about half that of major German and Japanese competitors.

The company had been content to view its market as France and Spain. Protected from foreign competition by government regulations and trade barriers, it had shown modest and steady growth. But the future promised change for St. Cloud as well as most other European companies. The governments of 12 European nations were seeking to forge their countries into one large market. Changes in financial, economic, and trade regulations were beginning to lower barriers and open markets to competitors throughout Europe. At a minimum these changes would mean more competition from European companies.

Monsieur Descarpentries did not think St. Cloud could compete with the larger companies on the basis of cost. He was sure some would enter the niche dominated in France and Spain by St. Cloud, because they already sold comparable products in other countries. If the New Europe did not protect its market from U.S. and Japanese firms, his company might not survive. The changes then beginning to occur were significant and were scheduled to go into full effect in 1992. Monsieur Descarpentries knew he must decide how to adjust his company's strategy to its changing environment.

Discussion Questions

1. What are the major pieces of information the company needs in order to predict what will happen to its markets?

2. What will be the impact on St. Cloud of the New Europe?

3. What are the major alternatives available to Jean-Paul?

4. Give your recommendations for strategic actions the company should take over a period of five years.

Chapter 11

Social Issues in Strategic Management

English civilization—the humanizing, the bringing into one harmonious and truly humane life, of the whole body of English society—that is what interests me.
—Matthew Arnold, *Ecce, Conventimur ad Gentes*

Learning Objectives

- To consider social responsibility as an important aspect of matching the organization to its environment.
- To determine the position the company should take in deciding whether to become socially responsible.
- To understand the role social responsibility plays in a firm's performance and management behavior.
- To understand the questions a firm should address when it decides to incorporate social responsibility into its strategic actions.
- To provide a systematic approach for integrating social responsibility into the strategic management process.

WHEN *Consumer Reports* rated the Suzuki Samurai "not acceptable" because it was likely to tip over, public attention turned to the safety of light trucks. Not only did Suzuki Motor Company experience a sudden slump in sales, but all makers of light trucks faced increasing scrutiny of their products. In recognition that off-road vehicles, pickups, and vans are now being used as passenger cars, the federal government considered legislation to require that these vehicles meet the safety standards imposed on automobiles.[1]

Automakers have strengthened the roofs of most light trucks; however, industry lobbyists have tried to persuade the government that most other modifications are unnecessarily costly. Automakers fear that if light trucks are treated as cars, they might be required to meet automobile emissions and mileage rules. Should the industry put its fears aside and consider safety first? Such issues are the topic of this chapter.

The chapter begins by defining the concerns of social responsibility. It then considers various arguments for and against assuming social responsibility and describes attempts to measure the relationship between social responsibility and performance. The remainder of the chapter discusses some approaches to integrating social responsibility into the organization's strategy.

Focusing on Social Responsibility

A major activity in strategic management is scanning the environment for trends in economic, social, political, and technological forces. One aspect of the social forces is social responsibilities.

Definition of Social Responsibility

As are many controversial subjects, social responsibility is often hard to define. Table 11.1 provides a sampling of proposed definitions. The discussion here will be based on the following definition: **Social responsibility** is the posture a firm takes in its attitudes, policies, and actions with respect to the duties, obligations, and expectations for which society believes the business should be held accountable in the conduct of its affairs or pursuit of its purpose.

This definition is meant to reflect a more neutral position than some stated in Table 11.1 and to recognize that the behavior of firms can represent a negative to positive continuum with respect to societal expectations. Social responsibility should

Table 11.1 Perspectives on Social Responsibility

Author	Perspective
Sheldon (1920s)	Management's primary responsibility is service to society and community.
Henry Ford (1920s)	What is good for business is good for society. Service comes first, but it means increased productivity and profit.
Levitt (1950s)	Pursuing social programs is undesirable because of the possible domination of business values.
Henry Ford II (1960s)	Corporations should help solve major social problems, such as helping disadvantaged minorities and preventing environmental damage.
Carr (1960s)	Ethics are irrelevant to business. Business should attend to performing within the limits of the law.
Friedman (1970s)	To do more than make a profit, use resources efficiently, and obey the law is irresponsible.
Drucker (1980s)	The greatest need today is for capital formation. Anything else is antisocial activity.
Barry (1980s)	Society's expectation that business behave in a socially responsible way has never been greater.
Willard (1980s)	It is not sufficient to act within the law; business must also not inflict harm and injustice.
Business Roundtable (1980s)	The long-term viability of the corporation depends upon its responsibility to society.

be viewed not only in terms of the behavior for which society will hold a firm accountable but also in terms of behavior that exceeds or falls short of societal expectations. Society's expectations include behaving legally, and also avoiding harm and being just. This definition implies that society or its agent will sit in judgment on a business that does not fulfill its responsibilities.

Importance of Social Responsibility

Why should businesses be concerned about social responsibility? There are several reasons. First, numerous groups in society are quite interested in telling a business or industry what it should do. Advocates of environmental protection, withdrawal of investments from South Africa, and support for the fine arts, as well as businesspeople who believe that assumption of social responsibility is necessary to protect free enterprise, are just a few examples of groups in society that press businesses to take positions favoring their ends. Because businesses control so many resources and employ so many people, their decision to support an issue can tremendously affect the success of a movement. Consequently, the leaders of these movements have learned that they can gain great leverage and achieve significant change by focusing change efforts on the leaders of business organizations. For example, the Interfaith Center on Corporate Responsibility provides church groups with information on corporate social performance and coordinates campaigns to pressure companies for change. Gulf & Western and Nestlé are just two companies that have been targets of this group's efforts.[2] Thus, whether or not a company wishes to be concerned about social responsibilities, it will receive pressure from many sources. If the firm considers social concerns during the strategic planning process, it will be better prepared to decide whether to take a proactive or reactive position.

A second reason for focusing on a firm's social responsibility is the public concern and often dissatisfaction with the behavior of some firms or their representatives. Headlines announce the sale overseas of products illegal in the United States, illegal and unethical behavior in some brokerage firms, unsafe products and subsequent attempts to avoid responsibility, and bribery to obtain business. The Strategic Application "RJR Nabisco Exports Contaminated Tobacco" is one example of such behavior. Every reader can add examples while reading a local newspaper or *The Wall Street Journal.* These incidents can be interpreted in several ways, but they certainly have caught the public's attention. Will such behavior affect the responses of the public and government toward business? Can such incidents be lessened? No society can function unless most of the participants play by the rules most of the time. If not enough businesses behave in acceptable ways, the system will break down.

A third reason for concern about social responsibility is the increasing body of literature, both within and outside the field of strategic management, that addresses topics such as social responsibility, business ethics, and public policy. Businesspeople, politicians, scholars, and news organizations have all addressed the issue. Although this chapter cannot review all this material, it can introduce the topic to provide a basis for evaluating this literature.

STRATEGIC APPLICATIONS: INTERNATIONAL

RJR Nabisco Exports Contaminated Tobacco

When Japan finally agreed to lift its 20 percent to 25 percent tariff on U.S. cigarettes, sales increased substantially. Japan was already the U.S. tobacco industry's largest export market. But backlash and an end to boom times may follow a disclosure that RJR Nabisco's tobacco unit exported Winston Lights cigarettes contaminated with the weed killer dicamba to Japan. RJR won't say if it knew the tobacco was contaminated before buying it. Although RJR officials say they immediately notified the Japanese subsidiary to stop distributing the cigarettes after they confirmed USDA test results that the tobacco was tainted, the real issue is quality: regardless of whether illnesses occurred, demand could cool considerably for U.S. tobacco products in general. U.S. officials launched a criminal investigation to see if RJR misled government inspectors and tried to sell something in Japan that they could not legally sell in the United States.

Source: Steven J. Dryden, Neil Gross, and Scott Ticer, "Tainted Tobacco Could Poison a Hot Market," *Business Week*, June 15, 1987, 45–49.

Finally, socially responsible activities may provide opportunities to an astute business. If there are problems in the environment, for example, the company that finds a solution may obtain a new product or service, a better use of resources, or some other advantage. Plastics are a major contributor to solid waste and were once thought to be nonrecyclable and nonbiodegradable. Pressured by mandatory recycling laws, however, businesses are finding ways to develop infrastructures for the collection and sorting of plastics so they may be recycled and are developing products that break down when acted on by bacteria or ultraviolet light.[3] Similarly, the recycling of aluminum cans has helped both the environment and the aluminum companies, and has improved the industry's public image as well. Helping companies assess their impact on the environment has generated new businesses for other companies and consulting firms.

Social responsibility is perhaps no more important to business than the other elements of a firm's environment. But business organizations must be mindful that they are **social institutions**. They perform a function for and have a purpose in society. For society, the business system is not an end in itself; it must function within and for society. Douglas S. Sherwin, managing partner of Sherwin, Davidson and Associates and chairman of the board of Duraco Products, has stated this concern well:

> American society has purposefully left a place for businesses among its institutions to secure economic performance in the production and distribution of goods and services. . . . Society always has this strategy on trial; it continuously compares it with alternative strategies for securing economic goods and monitors it for negative effects that business's economic behavior might have on other social goods it values. The signs are that society is nowhere near satisfied.[4]

In the long run, the business community cannot afford to ignore social responsibility.

Social Responsibility and Business Ethics

Ethics is a concern for right and wrong or good and evil behavior. **Business ethics**, then, can be thought of as a concern with establishing a pattern of thought and action that guides businesspersons in the conduct of their affairs.[5]

Business ethics can be codified into law, but not all business conduct has been or is likely to be codified. Most people would agree that laws should be followed, but there is disagreement about whether all behavior allowed or required by law is in fact ethical. That is, in some cases business behavior may be legal but not ethical. For example, a U.S. company may legally sell products overseas that cannot be legally sold in the United States for sound safety reasons. The company doing business internationally must also decide which country's laws to follow and whether the home country's laws should be applied to its conduct in another country. For example, are 'grease payments' to facilitate a transaction in a foreign country unethical?

To answer such questions, business ethics can be examined at three levels: the social system, the organization, and the individual. The focus of this book is primarily on the organization level. Business executives decide the strategic positions of the company, however, and therefore decide how they will relate the company to the larger society. This is what social responsibility is about: the ethical position the company will take in its strategic position toward society.

Assumption of Social Responsibility

General agreement that a firm is answerable, even accountable, to the society in which it is embedded does not mean that firms will willingly assume the responsibility. Nor does it mean that there will be a consensus as to what those responsibilities should be. In fact, there are many views.[6]

Views against Assumption of Social Responsibility

Several arguments oppose businesses assuming a proactive strategy of social responsibility. Some of these arguments use an economic justification, while others derive their support from a philosophical rationale—particularly one based on political philosophy.

Perhaps the best-known economic position is that espoused by Milton Friedman. His argument is that the function of business is economic—to use resources efficiently and to maximize profits. The market is the mechanism to allocate scarce resources. When a manager uses resources to pursue social responsibilities, the market is not at work, but rather social and political considerations.

According to this view, the executive has not only substituted his or her judgment for the market, but has interfered with the social and political judgments concerning which issues should receive attention. The executive is an employee of the owners of the business and has a fiduciary role with respect to stockholders. Executives therefore should use the owners' assets as the owners wish: to maximize profits. When executives spend resources on social concerns, they are diverting profits and distorting their own role, as well as violating the owners' trust. Friedman believes that for an executive to be socially responsible is to give away other people's money:

> Insofar as his actions in accord with his "social responsibility" reduce returns to stockholders, he is spending their money. Insofar as his actions raise the price to customers, he is spending the customers' money. Insofar as his actions lower the wages of some employees, he is spending their money.[7]

Closely associated with this position is the belief that diverting resources to social responsibilities will weaken the competitive position of the firm. Of course, government may force business to undertake programs that government is unable to undertake. This is the case when government finds it unpopular to raise taxes but requires businesses to spend money on social programs. Such action essentially becomes a hidden tax. For example, Massachusetts passed a law requiring companies to contribute $1,680 a year to a state fund to subsidize health insurance for workers.[8] In addition, if owners cannot use their own property for their own benefit, their economic freedom will be undermined, and the loss of political freedom will follow.[9]

Another opposition argument is also rooted in economic concerns. It is that social responsibility programs are exceedingly costly.[10] The thrust of this position is that such programs should be subjected to a cost-benefit analysis but usually are not. Programs concerning employee and product safety, air and water pollution, chemical waste cleanup, consumer protection, equal opportunity, and comparable worth may be mandated by law or voluntarily enacted without benefit of cost-benefit analysis. After a point, increasing the benefits received may require a disproportionate increase in cost. For example, to move from 90 percent assurance that a product will not fail to a 95 percent assurance may double the cost of the product. Because the company competes in a market, perhaps internationally, it risks being priced out of the market. Will the customer assume the cost of safety, quality, and other social benefits?

Economic concerns are not the only basis for attacking socially responsive behavior. Some argue that it is not the role of business to usurp government's role in deciding social issues, because businesses do not have the charter, perspective, or competence in these matters. Some believe that when executives enter the realm of social matters, they leave behind the hard-decision criteria of efficiency with which they are so familiar and enter a world in which they have no special capabilities. A similar position is taken by Theodore Levitt, who fears, "The corporation would eventually invest itself with all-embracing duties, obligations and finally power—ministering to the whole man and molding him and society in the image of the corporation's narrow ambitions and its essentially unsocial needs."[11] When do corporate concern and action become an intrusion into areas where businesses have no responsibility? Have companies such as the ones in the Strategic Application "Programs to Encourage Good Health and Living" gone too far when they promote healthy employee behavior? The view that business will become too prominent in solving societal problems worries those who see it as a way for the elite to preserve their power, as well as those who prefer a socialist solution. Others argue that many social problems are the result of competition, greed, or the pursuit of profits. These values make it impossible for businesses to truly behave in socially responsible ways.[12]

STRATEGIC APPLICATIONS: SOCIAL RESPONSIBILITY

Programs to Encourage Good Health and Living

What may at the outset appear as a luxury or a waste of stockholder profits may have hidden benefits, such as motivating employees. Consider these three programs to motivate good health and good living:

Du Pont's Waynesboro, Virginia, plant offered free gifts to help motivate employees to use their seat belts. Usage increased from 25 percent to 90 percent. The company also went from 394 lost workdays from auto accidents to just 51 lost workdays.

Flexcon Company of Spencer, Massachusetts, offered a $30 gift certificate to employees each week to provide an incentive to quit smoking. Those who already were nonsmokers were automatic winners. Over one six-month period, 22 percent of the company's smokers decided to kick the habit. The company hopes for a reduction in health care costs.

Comsat of Washington, D.C., also uses a program to motivate better health. To encourage lower paid employees to join the professional staff members in its fitness center, the company uses a sliding-fee scale. Side benefits might include better relations and understanding between the two groups.

Source: M. R. Moskowitz, "Company Performance Roundup," *Business and Society Review* (Winter 1986): 64.

Views Favoring Assumption of Social Responsibility

The arguments favoring assumption of social responsibilities have a pragmatic orientation. Business must respond because to do so is in its self-interest, because society demands it, because such behavior is necessary to avoid government regulation, or because it is good business.

The Committee for Economic Development has taken the position that it is in the enlightened self-interest of corporations to become involved in solving any social problem.[13] The belief of this organization is, "People who have a good environment, education and opportunity make better employees, customers and neighbors for business.[14]

The Business Roundtable also supports involvement as being in the long-term self-interest of corporations and society.[15] Business is embedded in and interdependent with society. Therefore business and society both benefit from business's involvement in producing a better environment. Clorox, for example, pledged $1.5 million to endow a youth center in its hometown of Oakland, California, because of concern for the quality of life.

A related but separate view is that it is good business practice to become involved. In the long run, a good environment will lead to less cost and more profits. A deteriorating environment and a sluggish economy will not support prosperous businesses. Others argue that many investors are attracted to the socially responsible firm as being a less risky investment. Social responsibility therefore improves the firm's stock price, cost of capital, and earnings.[16]

A third argument is that if business does not assume responsibility, government (on its own or at the behest of an activist group) will intervene with regulation or by deciding the framework for solution. This undermines business and is to be avoided because regulation is generally more expensive than social programs likely to be pursued by business. Firms that take a proactive stance to responsibility also are able to be more flexible and autonomous in making decisions and meeting competition than they would be if they were subject to regulation.[17]

A good example of this is the growing effort to deal with hazardous wastes.[18] Companies are finding it more effective and cheaper to avoid making the waste rather than to try to dispose of it. For example, Borden's chemical unit has become the darling of environmentalists by demonstrating that companies can reduce toxic discharges. A program at Borden's Fremont, California, plant eliminated 98 percent of toxic chemicals from waste discharges. Other companies that are saving millions through successful programs are 3M and Dow Chemical.

Companies that remain uninvolved also miss the opportunity to participate in defining and structuring the problem and in determining how the problem will be solved. For example, socially responsible companies might address whether businesses will be involved in carrying out a program or whether a government agency will conduct the program. Or they can help decide whether the program will be a voluntary one or will be required and controlled by a government agency.

Another view is that society wants and expects businesses to assume responsibility for many problems. Business is an institution that society has created and allows to exist to fulfill an economic function. Society desires other social goods as well as economic ones; these include clean air, security, and freedom. If business does not satisfactorily fulfill its function or conflicts with other social goods, society may consider disenfranchisement. A company that once could "let the buyer beware" may now have to ensure product safety. A firm that once could discharge pollutants must now comply with new clean air standards. Because business is franchised by society, has a concentration of resources and a large impact on society, and can be regulated by society, society expects a great deal from business. To anticipate these expectations and act on them is in the interest of business.

Most of these arguments contain an element of pragmatism; that is, the business will be better off if it behaves responsibly. But another view is that the firm should behave responsibly because that is the right thing to do. Even here one can argue that doing the right thing is a way of fulfilling a personal self-image or avoiding punishment from a deity. This position suggests that socially responsible behavior of companies grows out of the personal values and belief systems of business leaders. Although the leaders of companies are constrained by their role in the firm, their behavior is also affected by their own attitudes, values, and cause–effect belief system. Their power and choice of action may be enough to start the company on a tradition of **social action programs**. Once established, the tradition may continue. Notable executives who have led their firms in that direction include Calvin Verity and Charles Hook of Armco Steel, William Norris of Control Data, and Walter Haas of Levi Strauss.

To determine individual motives is difficult, but it does appear that individual executives are often behind a company's support of some social program. The self-interest arguments in support of social responsibility may be rationalizations used to support actions a leader or firm has already decided are the right thing to do. Because the leader and firm are supposed to be rational and because economic self-interest is a widely held expectation, the self-interest rationale may be used to persuade and justify actions.

The case for and against the assumption of social responsibilities does not clearly favor one position or another. Those who have already made up their mind can find a position to justify their decision. Those who are searching for the best or most correct answer are not likely to find it among these arguments. Nor will the business-person be free from criticism regardless of the position he or she chooses.[19] If these philosophical positions do not give a business a clear-cut choice, perhaps a guide can be found in the behavior of firms.

Social Responsibility, Performance, and Management

In practice, is social responsibility related to economic performance? If such programs are in the self-interest of business, as some arguments contend, shouldn't there be some indication that companies practicing social responsibility outperform firms that do not? If investors do prefer more socially responsible firms, the financial performance of the firm should indicate this preference. If Friedman's arguments are correct, however, firms that practice social responsibility should be less efficient and perform more poorly. If company executives believe it is in the company's long-run self-interest, there should be some indication that they have included social responsibility in their goal structure or provided a means to accomplish the programs.

Economic Performance

A number of studies have looked for a relationship between social responsibility and the economic performance of a company. If social responsibility is good business or in the self-interest of a firm, there should be a positive relationship between these two characteristics. If it is not good business or if the company must pay a price to be socially responsible, there should be a negative relationship. Perhaps the most comprehensive review is Arlow and Gannon's comparison of seven studies.[20]

Each study seems to approach the examination of the relationship a little differently, and the studies reach no consensus. However, of the seven, only one study found a negative association. In that study, executives and graduate business students ranked firms on their degree of social responsibility and related that to the percentage change in the companies' stock price per share between 1974 and 1975. The negative relationship supports the argument that companies pay a price for their social responsiveness. In the other six studies, three of the results were in the positive direction, supporting the argument that social responsiveness is good business or in the self-interest of the firm. The other three studies found either no relationship or no difference.

Before too much is made of these studies, it may pay to examine them more closely. First, the studies used different measures for social responsibility. One study simply asked students and executives to rank the firms on their degree of social responsibility. How reasonable is it to expect that the persons doing the ranking have enough valid information about 45 to 50 firms to be able to rank them accurately? Another study assumed that the firms responding to their survey would be more socially responsible than other firms in the Fortune 500. Other studies examined the annual reports of firms. The measures used to compose the rating of social responsibility differ, and what was actually measured may have differed as well. The measure of performance also differed across the studies, although the measures were often related to common stock. Here the question is not so much whether the measure is accurate as whether one should expect it to change as a result of socially responsive behavior. Even if one believes the results support assuming social responsibilities, one must remember that the results can also support the interpretation that it is only the efficient and effective firms that *can* support social programs. In other words, something else could have led to the performance.

Other reviewers have reached essentially the same conclusion. Aldag and Bartol reviewed more than 100 studies and concluded that there was no clear trend relating social responsibility to profits.[21] In light of these problems, it seems that, at best, the results might be interpreted as meaning that social responsibility is not dysfunctional to firms. A more cautious approach is to conclude that the results are inconclusive and that a strong case for social responsibility leading to better economic performance remains to be proven.

Managerial Action

A possible explanation for why the effects of social responsibility do not show up strongly in economic performance is that executives do not undertake actions that bolster social programs in their own companies. Despite the policy statements of groups like the Business Roundtable and the Committee for Economic Development, acceptance of social responsibility as an action program may not be widespread.

There is not much evidence concerning these issues. Gallup Poll surveys rate the ethical standards and honesty of professions, but this is the public's opinion and not that of executives, nor does it indicate what managers actually do.[22] One survey by Holmes of 180 corporations indicates that 41 percent of the executives agreed that a firm is responsible for making a profit and for solving social problems even if a profit is unlikely.[23] In a poll of *Harvard Business Review* readers, almost half of the readers believed executives do not use "the great ethical laws" at work.[24]

However, in their review of the literature, Arlow and Gannon conclude that social responsibility is important to business executives and that they do seem committed to acting on it.[25] As an example, General Motors has been issuing an annual accounting of its performance and positions related to various issues in the public interest. GM's 1988 report yields a brief sampling of its activities, including sponsorship for 10 Presidential Young Investigator Awards, support for Historically Black Colleges and Universities and the United Negro College Fund, awards to preeminent cancer scientists, sponsorship of the National Concerto Competition, and underwriting of performing arts.[26]

Perhaps more important than what companies say is what they actually do. A wide range of social action programs have been reported. In the early 1970s, the

Committee for Economic Development compiled a list that includes the categories of responsibilities shown in Table 11.2. A survey using the CED list asked large corporations to indicate which programs they had committed substantial time and money to. Many companies had committed to every program on the list. The programs receiving the highest number of significant commitments were in employment and advancement opportunities for minorities (86 percent of the companies) and in providing financial aid to schools (84 percent of the companies). Other programs to which 60 percent or more of the companies were committed included pollution control, support of the arts, and civil rights.

The data on how many companies are involved and the extent of their involvement are unclear. One should not expect every company to be involved and committed, nor should one expect each company to have a social program in each Committee for Economic Development category except where required by law. Companies that are selective and match their strengths and interests to programs may be most effective in meeting social objectives.

The presence of social responsibility in the hierarchy of goals pursued by firms also has been taken to indicate the commitment of firms. The fact that financial and economic goals dominate in the goal structure does not necessarily indicate that social goals are unimportant to these companies. After all, the primary function a company fulfills for society is economic. Goals may be pursued sequentially, so that once higher ranked goals are reached, attention turns to other goals.[27] In other cases, the social responsibilities may be considered a constraint. For example, a firm may seek to maximize timber production as long as pollution does not exceed a certain level.

Table 11.2 A Sampling of Social Action Programs

Encouraging minority entrepreneurship
Training and developing disadvantaged minorities
Aiding urban renewal
Improving the level of education
Avoiding pollution
Developing technology and practices for pollution control
Conservation of resources
Protecting the environment and renewing resources
Low-income housing
Ensuring a basis for a sound economy: jobs, foreign competition, etc.
Product safety
Economic growth
Efficient management
Ensuring civil rights and justice
Behaving responsibly in foreign markets

Sources: William C. Frederick, "Corporate Social Responsibility in the Reagan Era and Beyond," *California Management Review* 25 (Spring 1983): 145–157; Committee for Economic Development, *Social Responsibilities of Business Corporations* (New York: CED, 1971) 35–46; and Committee for Economic Development, *Public-Private Partnership: An Opportunity for Urban Communities* (New York: CED, 1982).

Companies do seem to recognize social responsibility as important and have committed significant resources to social programs. Pressure from interest groups may have forced some companies to initiate social programs, but others have done so willingly. The Strategic Application "Voluntary and Involuntary Housing Efforts" provides several illustrations of this. How widespread and effective the commitment has been is unclear. We can say only that the company that chooses to become involved will not be lonely and that there is substantial precedent for involvement.

Social Responsibility and Strategy

A company that has decided to assume social responsibility needs to make it part of the company's strategy. As the Strategic Application "Syntex Tries to Do It Right but Comes Up Short" shows, careless implementation of efforts to be socially responsible

STRATEGIC APPLICATIONS: SOCIAL RESPONSIBILITY

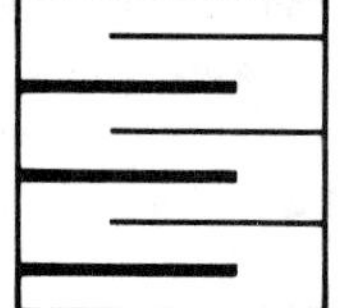

Voluntary and Involuntary Housing Efforts

Social activists in many parts of the country have pressured banks to provide loans for low-income housing. The activists use a provision in the Community Reinvestment Act that allows them to file objections when banks file for approval of mergers. Rather than risk disapproval or bad publicity, banks agree to make loans for projects. It is estimated that such efforts generated over $5 billion for low-income housing in a three-year period in the late 1980s.

Using a different tactic, cities across the country have been forcing developers to fund public works with "linkage" laws. The cities link approval of a project to the agreement of the developer to fund some public project. Boston, for example, requires the developer to provide $5 for housing and $1 for job training for every square foot of the project over 100,000 square feet. Other cities may require a park, the donation of the builder's expertise, or jobs for minorities.

In contrast, some housing efforts are voluntary. No housing other than subsidized housing had been constructed in the Harlem district of New York City for 25 years until 1986. The third largest life insurance company in the United States, Equitable Life, committed $2.6 million in construction financing for a private housing development in central Harlem. The project involves the renovation of two apartment buildings and a conversion into residential condominiums for middle-income families.

The publisher of *Better Homes & Gardens*, Meredith Corporation, has set up a foundation to help homeless families. The magazine will be used to spearhead the project, which calls for the construction of housing in three to five cities and assistance programs for the homeless in 20 more cities. The company has set a goal of $10 million to be raised from readers and advertisers. Meredith also hopes to receive donations of needed equipment from its advertisers of building materials and home furnishings.

Source: M. R. Moskowitz, "Company Performance Roundup," *Business and Society Review* (Summer 1986): 74 and (Winter 1988): 69; Catherine Yang, Michael Oneal, and Richard Anderson, "The 'Blackmail' Making Banks Better Neighbors," *Business Week*, August 15, 1988, 101; and John Schwartz, Sue Hutchinson, and Lynda Wright, "Giving Something Back," *Business Week*, September 5, 1988, 46–47.

STRATEGIC APPLICATIONS: SOCIAL RESPONSIBILITY

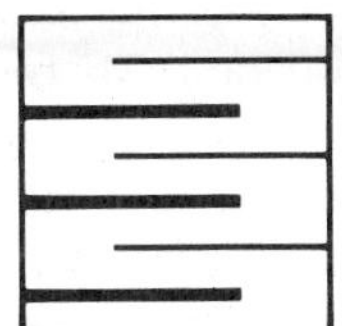

Syntex Tries to Do It Right but Comes Up Short

In response to complaints from nutritionists that baby foods contained too much sodium, Syntex removed salt from its infant formulas in 1978. The lack of salt had an unwanted side effect: a dramatic reduction in chlorine (salt is sodium chloride), which is needed to regulate fluid levels. When the problem was brought to Syntex's attention, the company promptly withdrew the formulas from the market.

That response was the right thing to do, but it was not enough to escape liability. Over 20,000 infants were fed the formulas, and at least 247 suffered health problems, ranging from minor illness to death. At the time, federal law did not specify chloride levels in infant formula, but the problem was still seen as Syntex's fault, because the mistake arose due to lack of testing. Syntex settled nearly 200 lawsuits brought by parents who fed the formulas to their children.

Even though a company is trying to be a good corporate citizen, trying to respond to the public's desires, it must still act on its own best judgment. As this case illustrates, even what appears to be in the public's best interest may not be. The corporation is responsible for making sure.

Source: M. R. Moskowitz, "Company Performance Roundup," *Business and Society Review* (Winter 1986): 67.

can have dire consequences. The firm must develop strategic goals related to social responsibility, create a strategy for meeting the goals, select programs to carry out the strategy, and provide for implementation of the strategy and programs. Social responsibilities can be incorporated into the company's plans and activities through essentially the same basic steps used in formulating overall strategy and providing for the implementation of plans. For example, environmental scanning and forecasting can use many of the same techniques and procedures.

What kind of **strategic posture** does a company wish to take in meeting social responsibilities? There are no clear guidelines for determining a firm's mission in this area. As in other areas of strategy formulation, a mission can define the scope of the firm's activities. This focuses attention, resources, and decision making. As a result, the firm can develop objectives and programs closely allied to its business goals, strengths, and opportunities, and it can protect itself from threats and weaknesses.

Principles

The mission can be defined with a set of principles. One general model suggests that socially responsible actions can be evaluated along two dimensions: legality and responsibility.[28] Combined, these two dimensions provide four alternative postures: legal/responsible, legal/irresponsible, illegal/responsible, and illegal/irresponsible. There are several guiding principles a company can use to decide which posture it wishes to adopt when confronting its social responsibilities.

The first principle, derived from the Hippocratic oath, is for the organization to avoid engaging in any behavior that is known to cause harm. The principle applies to normal business activities as well as social programs. When an advertising agency offered to provide Microsoft with trade secrets about the Lotus program, Microsoft decided this was a violation of law and business ethics. Microsoft believed employees and agents should bring to the company their experience and expertise, not proprietary and confidential information. It told its competitor of the action, and Lotus sued the agency.

Although this is an admirable rule of conduct, many company actions could unintentionally cause harm. A company product may be shown to cause or be associated with harmful health effects. If the company sells such a product because it did not know of its effects, has the company followed the principle? In the earlier example of Syntex, the company withdrew its baby formula when it learned of its harmful effect, but suits contend the company should have known. What if an analysis shows that a company's actions are doing more good than harm? What if the product is used in unintended ways? When does the user assume responsibility for its harmful effects? On the other hand, Johns-Manville Corporation is alleged to have known of the harmful effects of asbestos, but suppressed evidence to protect company officers and shareholders and chose to fight suits. Forced into Chapter 11, shareholders now own only 6 percent of the company. Another asbestos company, Raybestos, a subsidiary of Raytech, is scrambling to avoid bankruptcy from claims by reorganizing into a holding company with wholly owned subsidiaries.[29] Should the shareholders have a higher claim on executive action than the victims of asbestos? The principle derived from the Hippocratic oath leaves many questions unanswered, but it is probably a good guide to use in determining the company's posture.

The second principle is that the company should be accountable for its actions that affect society. Does the company in the course of its business generate costs to society? Should society be asked to bear those costs? The company should be responsible for such costs or should at least share responsibility for reducing negative effects. If the business passes on the cost for environmental, health, or safety problems—because society either sanctions this behavior or is passive to it—the company should be responsible for actions to solve the resulting problems.

A third principle argues that a company should exercise a degree of social responsibility that is proportionate to the amount of its power in society and the extent of its impact on society. Because large companies have greater influence and impact on society, more should be expected of them. If a company's impact is large, the programs it undertakes should be significant.

These principles argue that a company's strategic responsibility mission should be legal and responsible. Furthermore, the mission should cause no harm, encourage accountability for the company's impact on society, and do so commensurate to the company's size and impact. These principles also suggest that the nature of a company's business should be reflected in its social responsibility mission, as that will provide some direction for the kind of impact it will have on society. For example, a large farm corporation should be concerned with soil conservation and pollution, a mining company with safety and environmental issues, and a firm in a company town with its impact locally.

Extent of Proactivity

Another approach to setting the scope and strategic posture is for the firm to decide on the extent to which it wants to be **proactive** in its activities.[30] The more proactive the firm wants to be, the more its strategy calls for influencing its environment, anticipating problems, and using policies and programs to address the problems. A consumer products firm, for example, knows it must be concerned with product safety and rigorously tests its products. It may take an active position with safety regulatory bodies. It may also have vigorous programs for affirmative action and equal employment opportunity. Firms with a less proactive posture try to forecast changes in legislation and public opinion. Their purpose is to be prepared to react quickly, but not to take the lead. At the other extreme is to be **reactive**. The reactor waits till the issues are very clear or are forced on it. Once it sees what other companies are doing, it follows. This strategy costs little and calls for little planning. In general, it translates into, "Keep it legal, but don't volunteer."

The degree of proactivity firms choose is loosely related to their size. Larger firms have more resources to support proactivity. Their impact on the environment is likely to be greater, so public expectations may be greater, and they are likely to be subject to greater scrutiny. More self-interest may be involved for larger firms, but there is no inherent reason that prevents a proactive stance by any firm. Probably just as important in determining proactivity is the value system of the firm's leaders. A firm could also take a proactive stance in areas of its greatest concern and a less proactive stance in other areas.

Domain Models

Firms also may define the scope of social responsibility by using a model that directs the strategy toward a portion of the company's domain. In effect, this approach gives top priority to a particular segment of a firm's environment. Seven models an executive can use to select the company's emphasis in determining its social responsibilities are summarized in Table 11.3.

The criteria for selecting among the models can be the extent to which a model agrees with the executive's own views. Another basis for selection could be a priority ranking of the significance of each domain segment to the company's business mission. For example, if a company believes that its employees are the most important segment for achieving its business mission, it would rank the household model as its first priority.

Of course, a company need not be confined to this listing of models. By examining its own business mission, goals, and strategies, it can easily identify the stakeholders that are most relevant to its domain. One large construction company directs its efforts toward getting managers involved in community activities on and off the job, even to the extent of providing time off with pay. The company also has a highway cleanup program and one for youth employment. The company has other programs, but these three are most connected with its mission and have its highest priority. Likewise, the high-tech Japanese firms described in the Strategic Application "Hitachi America Wins Friends" focus many of their social responsibility efforts in areas that may help them maintain their technological advantage.

Table 11.3 Models of Business Social Responsibility

Title	Description
Austere	Concentrates on maximizing stockholder wealth.
Household	Focuses on interests of employees, who are seen as having a claim equal to that of stockholders. Employees are the most important asset.
Vendor	Focuses on the best interests of customers.
Investment	Seeks to foster an environment in which business will prosper by pursuing social programs. Long-term profits and survival are sought through enlightened self-interest.
Civic	Recognizes that the franchise for business derives from society. Feels a responsibility to help the community to achieve its goals.
Artistic	Sees a relationship between a humane society and the creativity and innovation needed in the business world.
Eclectic	Selects from and combines attributes of the other models.

Sources: George A. Steiner, John B. Miner, and Edmund R. Gray, *Management Policy and Strategy*, 2d ed. (New York: Macmillan,1982), 86; and Clarence C. Walton, *Corporate Social Responsibilities* (Belmont, Calif.: Wadsworth, 1967), 122–149.

STRATEGIC APPLICATIONS: INTERNATIONAL

Hitachi America Wins Friends

In Japan, Japanese companies don't undertake public works. As their operations in the United States have grown, however, they have learned to influence the American public with lobbying and the use of investment, philanthropy, and social responsibility programs. Hitachi America Ltd. provides an example.

One of its attempts to win influence and change its image was to set up the Hitachi Foundation with well-known Americans as chairman and president. The largest Japanese foundation in the United States, it has funded such programs as minority business start-ups and public television programs on education and the environment. The company has also set up community action committees at each company location. In Norman, Oklahoma, Hitachi gave $30,000 to the local library, and its top manager directs the local American Red Cross. The company also set up a cooperative research program with the University of Oklahoma. Its efforts seem to be paying off in the support of local political leaders.

Other Japanese companies also are spending heavily in the United States because it is their biggest customer. In 1988 they spent an estimated $140 million on corporate philanthropy, $30 million on research contracts with U.S. universities, and $50 million on lobbying in the nation's capital. Some view the research contracts with universities and think tanks as an investment to gain access to the minds of the best American scientists. At MIT for example, Japanese companies have endowed 16 chairs at $1.5 million each. For another $4 million a year, they receive access to the research. At other universities, they are paying for and sharing research laboratories.

Sources: William J. Hostein and Amy Borrus, "Japan's Clout in the U.S.," *Business Week*, July 11, 1988, 64–66; Amy Borrus, James B. Treece, Pam Ellis-Simons, and Elizabeth Ehrlich, "Japan Digs Deep to Win the Hearts and Minds of America," *Business Week*, July 11, 1988, 73–75; and Todd Mason and John Hoerr, "Hitachi: Winning Friends and Influencing People in Oklahoma," *Business Week*, July 11, 1988, 74–75.

Integrating Responsive Management

A systematic approach to integrating a firm's management of its social responsibility efforts is the **marketing approach to responsive management (MARM).**[31] The major tenet of this approach is that corporate social policies and behavior can be analyzed as a "product" that the firm implicitly offers to its various publics and is, therefore, the focus of an exchange process between the firm and society.

The concept of social responsibility as a product follows from the notion that society is the set of actual or potential markets for all of the goods and services offered by the firm. The range of products of the firm could be extended to include all social goods or services typically associated with socially responsive activities—such as safety, hiring practices, pollution control, or support of colleges and social programs.

Viewing social programs as products allows management to consider these programs in a familiar context using economic considerations. This approach does not argue that moral justifications for these programs should be discounted. Rather, it argues that in addition to considering whether the programs are doing something for society, management can evaluate whether they are justified on the basis of cost effectiveness. Viewed as a product, social responsibility begins to take on properties associated with more conventional goods and services. The programs can be managed based on their role in the company's business operations and for their impact on the success of the firm in the marketplace. In viewing the programs as products, the firm is concerned with determining the kind of organizational activities that will have the greatest positive impact on fulfilling society's goals, values, and needs.

Formalizing this process for business firms means the adopting of what other types of organizations do implicitly. The planning and behavior of many public and nonprofit organizations exemplify an MARM orientation. For example, local governments must at some point be responsive to their environments, or new officials are empowered.

Social Responsibility and the Marketing Concept

The marketing approach to responsive management is predicated on using the marketing concept in contrast to a selling or production concept. Table 11.4 describes these philosophies in terms of social responsibility.

The MARM philosophy focuses on providing long-run social benefit as a key to attracting and holding customers and societal support. The market-oriented philosophy espouses that a key task of the organization is to determine the needs, wants, interests, and moral expectations of target publics and to adapt the organization to delivering the desired satisfactions more effectively and efficiently than its competitors.

The firm should apply an integrated marketing approach that first identifies the various publics of the firm and then addresses the important social morality needs of these groups within the framework of the four Ps of marketing (product, price, place/distribution, and promotion). This philosophy is based on the notion that the

Table 11.4 Dimensions of Responsibility with Three Marketing Philosophies

	Philosophies		
Dimensions	**Selling Concept**	**Production Concept**	**Marketing Concept**
Focus	Protecting the reputation of the firm	Focusing on a limited number of preestablished areas of social responsibility	Providing long-run social benefit as a key to having customer and social support
Premises	Public(s) is cynical in its view of the firm. Public(s) can be induced to alter opinions and attitudes toward the firm by promotional techniques.	Society does not attach much importance to social responsibility behaviors beyond minimum mandated. Public's expectations of the firm are economic, not social in nature.	Publics can be segmented depending on their social responsibility interests and needs.
Means	Public indoctrination by means of corporate advertising, PR, publicity, and promotional techniques	Implementation of socially beneficial activities that are required by law or commonly practiced in the industry	Integrated marketing approach indentifying specific publics: addresses important social needs and interest within the framework of four Ps of marketing mix
Ends	Societal support occurring as a result of blind conditioning process	Societal support occurring as a result of compliance with existing norms	Societal support occurring as a result of a firm's recognition and anticipation of societal needs and interests
Implications	Lacks normative reference; may be biased or deceptive	Subjects firm to lack of strategic control. Invites government regulation and interference	Strategic control maximized over sociopolitical environment Assures continued legitimization of firm in societal role Opportunity to achieve industry preeminence

Source: Keith B. Murray and John R. Montanari, 'Strategic Management of the Socially Responsible Firm: Integrating Management and Marketing Theory," *Academy of Management Review* 11 (October 1986): 820. Reprinted with permission.

company's publics can be grouped into different segments depending on their social responsibility interests and needs, and that these publics will support the organizations that satisfy their societal interests.

The MARM Model

The MARM model outlines an approach to identifying the relevant societal issues confronting a particular firm and the specific sequence of events through which it applies the model. An illustration of the MARM model is shown in Figure 11.1.

An additional tenet of the MARM theoretical framework is that it assigns managerial accountability for social responsibility activities to the marketing department

Figure 11.1 The Marketing Approach to Responsive Management

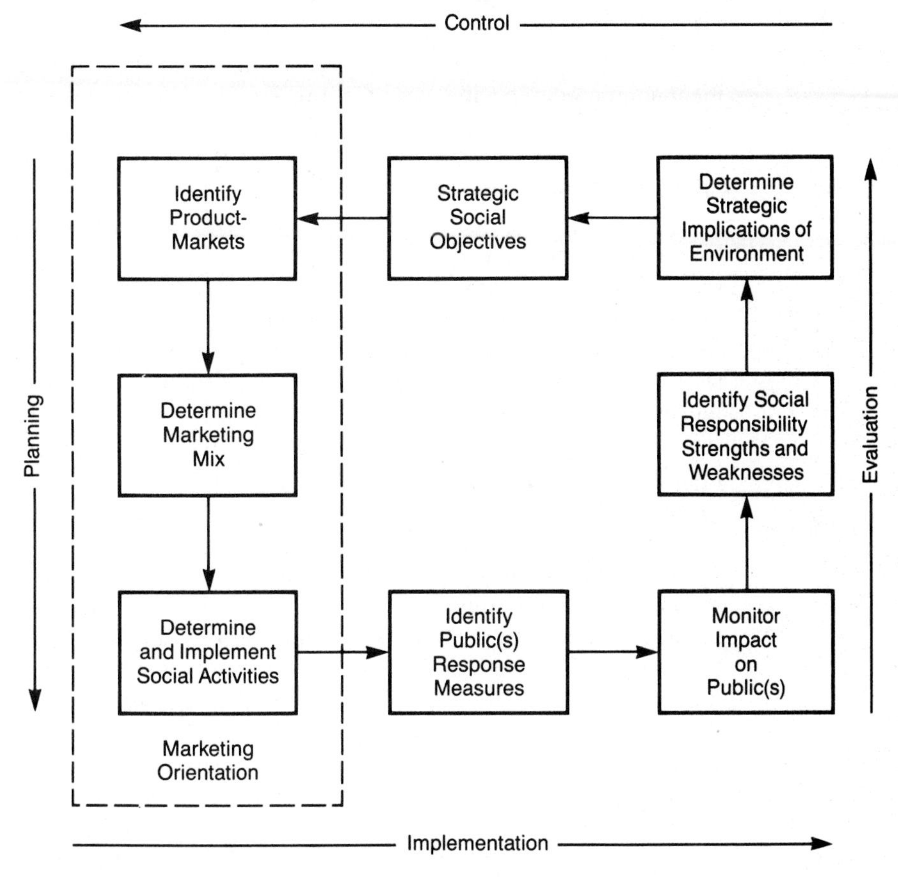

Source: Keith B. Murray and John R. Montanari, "Strategic Management of the Socially Responsible Firm: Integrating Management and Marketing Theory," *Academy of Management Review* 11, no. 4 (1986): 822. Reprinted with permission.

of the firm, rather than to the staff departments that traditionally have taken it on as an additional duty. Under the marketing umbrella, social responsiveness assumes a marketing orientation.

Identifying Product-Markets First, the firm must identify relevant societal values, attitudes, needs, desires, and interests, as well as the firm's important publics. Referred to as social responsibility product-markets, these publics may be conceptualized as social interest groups. Relevant social product-market groups also may be composed of a cross-section of the population–individuals unified by similar values, attitudes, or interests about specific social issues.

In a general context, identifying social responsibility product-markets involves segmenting the sociopolitical environment into distinct expectation and value groups, such as employees, environmental groups, consumer action organizations, community residents, or socially conscious investors. This identification process is carried out in a number of ways, including the use of marketing research, general and historical information available to the firm, and managerial judgment.

This step in the MARM model recognizes that the firm operates in an environment composed of a wide variety of important and overlapping publics with differing social morality expectations that have varying degrees of strategic importance to the firm. At this stage, it is important for management to identify social responsibility product-markets as thoroughly as possible.

Determining the Marketing Mix After identifying relevant markets for the firm's social responsibility activities, management must specify the marketing mix variables to be associated with each relevant public. The product variable defines the specific social responsibility activities that will address the needs, desires, and wants of each relevant market segment. The firm's offerings should focus on important social morality issues that the firm can address and may include such actions as energy conservation, supporting local charities, engaging in fair hiring practices, sponsoring community employee health programs, or contributing to educational institutions. Initially, all economic, legal, and discretionary company responsibilities should be reviewed for each relevant group.

Decisions about distribution—that is, the channels for delivering the socially responsive activity—should be based on which and how many of the firm's organizational units are instrumental in providing various offerings. Corporate executives and line management may be the most appropriate vehicles for delivering certain activities, while operating units and staff personnel may be more appropriate for others. In the case of corporate management, delivery may require policy decisions or investment strategies, such as a hiring policy or investment in pollution control equipment. Typically, a combination of several organizational units will deliver socially responsible activities. In any case, it is important to identify these organizational units, so that coordination issues can be addressed and managed.

Although social responsibility product offerings are not sold in the same sense that the firm's business products or services are sold, it is nonetheless possible to associate costs with each social responsibility offering. Management should assess the price that the firm "pays" (short-term opportunity costs or forgone profits) and that the customer "pays" (higher prices for goods). Only in this manner can management properly determine the relative value of these programs in terms of satisfying the firm's objectives. For example, the Northern States Power Company produces electric power for 1.2 million customers in five states. It has spent nearly $1 billion on pollution controls. In the process, it has reduced sulfur dioxide emissions by 53 percent since 1973, even though the utility is burning about twice as much coal. Despite the expenditure, profits have more than doubled. James Howard, president and CEO, says a company must be environmentally responsible to have a hope for success or longevity.[32]

Furthermore, objectives should be associated with the social responsibility demands of the specific public. Although it is not currently possible to determine precisely the perceived value to the public of a special social program, market research techniques can assess public attitudes toward the firm before and after it has announced and implemented a socially responsive endeavor. This information will provide baseline data to evaluate the costs and benefits of future projects.

With regard to promotion, the firm's social responsiveness should be translated into public information that will reinforce and be consistent with the firm's commitment to the well-being of its relevant publics. In addition, relevant segments of the public should be aware of the programs available to meet their needs and thus be able to avail themselves of the programs.

Determining and Implementing Programs After the firm has identified relevant product-markets and the appropriate marketing mix elements associated with each, it can determine what will constitute the firm's social responsibility activities. Management should establish this set of activities on the basis of technological feasibility, management capabilities, cost effectiveness, and strategic relevance. Thus, the MARM model assists company executives in managing social responsibility activities that address the interest of relevant publics in the context of their relevance to the firm.

The conventional notion persists that implementing social responsibility activities is essentially an isolated event, occurring at a fixed point in time. In contrast, the MARM model calls for ongoing management involvement with this strategic issue. In addition, the MARM model shifts the operational responsibility for social responsiveness to the marketing unit of the firm, rather than to the planning or personnel functions. This shift makes someone permanently responsible for these types of strategic decisions and assigns them to an operating unit rather than to a staff unit. The actual delivery of the "product" is assigned to the organizational unit most instrumental in providing the company's product or service. The marketing unit and the providing unit can coordinate programs and budget proposals.

The firm must monitor the impact of its activities on key publics. This requires accurate measures of public response to socially responsible activities. A range of market research methods and survey techniques could provide this valuable information to management. Another benefit of ongoing data collection is the ability to evaluate continuously the relative position of the firm in the sociopolitical environment.

In the final analysis, monitoring and evaluation lead to the control phase of social responsibility management. If management receives continuous input regarding the firm's effectiveness in addressing the social responsibility expectations of key publics, it can alter the product mix. These alterations are necessary because of the dynamic nature of the firm's societal environment, which will influence the firm's social responsibility objectives.

Clearly, business cannot provide for all societal needs and values. Nonetheless, it is advantageous that firms explicitly recognize these social expectations and address the inherent conflict and trade-offs that accompany a responsive approach to management.

Summary

Companies today must decide how they will respond to society's expectations for their behavior. Through government and pressure groups, society demands that business take a position on many issues. Leaders in the business community also have called upon businesspeople to behave more responsively. In addition, many companies are discovering business opportunities in the solution of societal problems. There is ample reason for an executive to weigh the company's role with respect to social responsibility.

Although many companies feel pressure to respond to society's expectations, there is no clear consensus as to a firm's real responsibilities. Several arguments oppose business becoming involved in societal issues. Other positions argue for business involvement. The debate may not clearly favor one position or the other, but one can find sufficient rhetoric on the issue to support either position. Nor is the performance of socially responsible firms a sufficient guide. Firms that practice social responsibility may not consistently perform better than other firms, but in general they do not have worse records. The executives and their team must decide, much as they decide about business mission strategy. In the midst of uncertainty and ambiguity, they must take a position and lead their firm forward.

Once a firm decides to assume social responsibility, it needs to incorporate this decision into its process of strategic management. The incorporation of social responsibilities into the company's plans and activities can follow essentially the same basic steps and processes as are used in formulating and implementing strategy. The differences include the lesser size and scope of the firm's commitment to social programs as opposed to business units. However, the process of formulating strategy, developing programs and policies, making organizational assignments, and evaluating and controlling are all necessary to the strategic management of social responsibility.

Questions

1. As the executive in charge of coordinating and directing the firm's social responsibility programs, you have been asked to address the annual meeting of stockholders. You are expected to provide an update on the programs and defend the use of company funds and effort on the programs. A group of stockholders is expected to protest the expenditure of company funds on these programs. They see this activity as a diversion of funds from investment in the company, as unnecessary expenditures, and not in the stockholders' best interest. What will you say to them?

2. Your company has decided to formalize its involvement in socially responsible programs. It has asked you to develop a set of goals, policies, and programs to be presented to the Chief Executive Officer for his approval prior to presentation to the Board of Directors. What steps would you take to develop the plan?

3. Your company has been engaged in social responsibility programs for over thirty years. Its programs range from helping the local community in community chest drives to programs for energy conservation and pollution control. It now wants to have better coordination and direction of the programs, but does not want to stifle the entrepreneurial spirit of those who have developed and run the programs. How would you go about achieving the company's objectives?

Notes

1. Jim Treece, "If It Has Wheels and Carries People, Shouldn't It Be Safe?" *Business Week*, June 20, 1988, 48.
2. Oliver Williams, "Who Cast the First Stone?" *Harvard Business Review* 62 (September–October 1984): 151–160.
3. Jaoni Nelson-Horchler, "Recycling: Plastics' New Weapon," *Industry Week*, July 4, 1988, 54–56; and Elliott Lee, "Opposition to Plastic Packaging Is Intensifying As the Nation's Solid-Waste Problem Grows Acute," *The Wall Street Journal*, November 25, 1987, 40.
4. Douglas S. Sherwin, "The Ethical Roots of the Business System," *Harvard Business Review* 61 (November–December 1983): 192.
5. Kenneth E. Goodpaster, "Toward an Integrated Approach to Business Ethics," *Thought* 60 (June 1985): 161–180.
6. Many authors have developed cases for and against the assumption of social responsibility. We are particularly indebted to the following works, which have organized these positions: George A. Steiner and John F. Steiner, *Business, Government and Society: A Managerial Perspective*, 4th ed. (New York: Random House, 1985), 230–244; Dan R. Dalton and Richard A. Cosier, "The Four Faces of Social Responsibility," *Business Horizons* 25 (May–June 1982): 19–27; and Henry Mintzberg, "The Case for Corporate Social Responsibility," *The Journal of Business Strategy* 4 (Fall, 1983): 3–15.
7. Milton Friedman, "A Friedman Doctrine: The Social Responsibility of Business Is to Increase Its Profits," *The New York Times Magazine*, September 13, 1970, 33, quoted in Mintzberg, "The Case for Corporate Social Responsibility."
8. Gary S. Becker, "If It Smells Like a Tax and Bites Like a Tax . . . ," *Business Week*, August 22, 1988, 16.
9. Steiner and Steiner, *Business, Government and Society.*
10. Dalton and Cosier, "The Four Faces of Social Responsibility."
11. Theodore Levitt, "The Dangers of Social Responsibility," *Harvard Business Review* 36 (September–October 1958): 44.
12. M. Tumin, "Business as a Social System," *Behavioral Science* 9 (April 1964): 120–130; and William C. Frederick, "Corporate Social Responsibility in the Reagan Era and Beyond," *California Management Review* 35 (Spring 1983): 49–58.
13. Committee for Economic Development, *Social Responsibility of Business Corporations* (New York: CED, 1971), 17–49.
14. Ibid., 26.
15. Business Roundtable, *Statement on Corporate Responsibility* (New York: The Business Roundtable, October 1971).
16. E. H. Bowman, "Corporate Social Responsibility and the Investor," *Journal of Contemporary Business* 2 (Winter 1973): 21–43; and E. H. Bowman and Mason Haire, "A Strategic Posture Toward Corporate Social Responsibility," *California Management Review* 18 (Winter 1975): 49–58.
17. Steiner and Steiner, *Business, Government and Society*, 239.
18. Eric Jay Dolin, "Industry Is Going on a Waste-Watcher's Diet," *Business Week*, August 22, 1988, 94–95.
19. Dalton and Cosier, "The Four Faces of Social Responsibility."
20. Peter Arlow and Martin J. Gannon, "Social Responsiveness, Corporate Structure, and Economic Performance," *Academy of Management Review* 7 (April 1982): 239.

21. Ramon J. Aldag and Kathryn M. Bartol, "Empirical Studies of Corporate Social Performance" in *Research in Corporate Social Performance and Policy*, vol. 1, ed. Lee Preston (Greenwich, Conn.: JAI Press, 1978), 165–192.

22. Mintzberg, "The Case for Corporate Social Responsibility."

23. S. L. Holmes, "Executives' Perceptions of Corporate Social Responsibility," *Business Horizons* 19 (May–June 1976): 34–40.

24. S. N. Brenner and E. A. Molander, "Is Ethics of Business Changing?" *Harvard Business Review* 55 (January–February 1977): 57–71.

25. Arlow and Gannon, "Social Responsiveness, Corporate Structure, and Economic Performance."

26. *General Motors Public Interest Report 1988* (Detroit, Mich.: General Motors Corporation, May 18, 1988), 56–61.

27. For a more complete discussion of the goal-setting process, see Max D. Richards, *Setting Strategic Goals and Objectives*, 2d ed. (St. Paul, Minn.: West Publishing, 1986), 24–43.

28. Dalton and Cosier, "The Four Faces of Social Responsibility."

29. James R. Norman, "How Raytech Means to Sidestep Manville's Fate," *Business Week*, August 24, 1987, 56–60.

30. Fred Luthans, Richard M. Hodgetts, and Keith R. Thompson, *Social Issues in Business*, 4th ed. (New York: Macmillan, 1984), 466–483.

31. This section is substantially based on Keith B. Murray and John R. Montanari, "Strategic Management of the Socially Responsible Firm: Integrating Management and Marketing Theory," *Academy of Management Review* 11 (October 1986): 815–827.

32. Steve Weiner, "Profit without Pollution," *Forbes*, May 18, 1987, 50–52.

Case for Discussion

Southern Agriculture: Saint or Sinner?

Sharon Smith heads a subsidiary of a large conglomerate, Western World Enterprises. Her company, Southern Agriculture, is headquartered in the United States but has operations in several Latin American countries. The foreign operations grow and process sugarcane, bananas, and pineapple. Each of these products is the basis for a separate division. Only the banana division has operations in more than one country.

Western World Enterprises purchased Southern Agriculture for $60 million in 1985. Included were a quarter-million acres of planted and undeveloped land in San Bernardo. Since 1985, SA has acquired real estate, hotels, and other enterprises. Collectively the company holds physical assets in San Bernardo worth more than $500 million. Its annual payroll exceeds $100 million.

Sharon has been the president of Southern Agriculture for three years. She was hired from another U.S. agriculture firm where she was manager of the sugarcane division. She was happy to join SA because of its reputation in its industry as an efficiently run operation that receives the support of its corporate parent. SA enjoys good relations with its host countries as well as a reputation for being a good corporate citizen, at least among those in the government and industry. One of the reasons

---

Source: Oliver Williams, "Who Cast the First Stone?" *Harvard Business Review* 62 (September–October, 1984): 151–160. This is a real company but certain facts such as names, figures, and locations have been changed.

Sharon left her former firm was its lack of social concern, although the primary reason was the more challenging position with SA. The former firm gave little more to employees than low wages and steady jobs. The owners would not support the programs she proposed for improving living conditions. She was aware that SA was different.

In the early 1970s, the San Bernardo government had requested SA to establish a free zone several miles from its main plant. SA operates the free zone as a nonprofit corporation, using the revenues for social programs or plant maintenance of free zone installations. Over the years companies located in the zone because of low wages (now about $0.80 per hour), freedom from trade restrictions, and a 20-year tax exemption. Now 23 companies and 30 plants employ over 9,000 local workers.

In 1975 SA set up the Southern Agriculture San Bernardo Foundation for the purpose of improving living conditions in the country. The foundation has spent over $15 million on community development projects aimed at improving education, health, and recreation. SA has also spent over $30 million around its own plant areas on churches, schools, libraries, and health clinics. Recently it launched a new program designed to improve living conditions in the workers' camps that existed in the remote areas before SA took ownership.

Sharon believes this is an impressive record for her company, although she knows that life is not easy for many workers, especially those who work the farms in remote areas. SA has built a modern medical center in the town near the main plant. It provides free care to SA workers and their families. But it is hard for the 50,000 people living in the camps to reach the medical center. Sharon proposed building multiservice health clinics throughout SA property, and the first two have just been finished. The company has also built more than 3,000 houses and 140 schoolrooms for workers in the camps. Sharon believes that SA's workers are much better off than others in the country. Their wages are 15 percent higher, and their living conditions much better.

Sharon and her corporate parent feel the company practices good social responsibility. Still, the critics never let up. When she is angry and frustrated with them she privately calls them Marxists. But now she is trying to be objective as she reviews the company's progress and its critics' charges. She knows that next month the Center for Social Justice and Corporate Responsibility will introduce a new shareholders' resolution attacking the corporation's operation in San Bernardo. What began as a way for churches to make informed investment decisions has become a group of religious activists. As shareholders, they participate in stockholder meetings.

Last year the SJCR resolution was a statement condemning her operation, including low wages, poor living conditions, and exploitation of the workers. There was no mention of any of the company's social programs. What was even more upsetting, none of the SJCR people had even visited her operation. In the hallway after the meeting, one approached her and charged that she was a modern-day Scrooge. She enumerated the company's programs and progress, but she is convinced the activists did not listen. They seem sure she is wrong and they are right. Sharon doesn't want to continue to face this year after year.

Discussion Questions

1. How should Sharon prepare for the stockholders' meeting?

2. Is Southern Agriculture being a good corporate citizen?

3. What goals do you think the religious activists are trying to obtain? Why do they continue to pursue this issue so persistently?

4. What can Sharon do to improve the situation?

5. Should socially responsible behavior in this situation be determined by Sharon Smith? employees of Southern Agriculture? management in Western World Enterprises? the San Bernardo government? industry standards? citizens of San Bernardo? stockholders of Southern Agriculture? members of SJCR? the U.S. government?

Chapter 12

Strategic Management in the Future

We should all be concerned about the future because we will have to spend the rest of our lives there.

—Charles Franklin Kettering, former chairman of General Motors
Seed for Thought, 1949

Learning Objectives

- To learn about the increasing demands on strategic managers.
- To understand expected changes in the firm's competitive environment over the next several decades.
- To gain insight into how the organization must change to adapt to its new, more complex environment.
- To understand how the firm will have to adapt its strategic management to accommodate environmental and organizational changes.

NOTHING is as certain in today's dynamic business arena as change. Stock markets around the world crashed on October 19, 1987, but the expected recession did not follow.[1] Unlike 1929, the 1987 crash was not the start of a downward spiral into a depression; by October 1988 most stocks had recovered their precrash values and markets were more active than ever before. In the wake of deregulation of the airline industry, two once healthy, major airlines, Continental and Eastern, filed bankruptcy under the same CEO, Frank Lorenzo.[2] The savings and loan industry in the United States is in disarray. Taxpayers are paying the bills for bailing out the S&Ls. However, the S&L problems have created an opportunity for full-service banks as customers flood to move their deposits to more secure institutions.[3]

These events vividly illustrate the turbulent and complex business environment faced by organizations today. This turbulence will only increase as businesses become more diversified, international, and interrelated. Organizations in the private sector increasingly depend not only on other organizations in the private sector but also on U.S. government agencies, foreign governments, and even foreign special-interest groups. Correspondingly, organizations in the public sector are increasingly dependent upon private sector organizations to provide the technology, training, personnel, and skills necessary to run complex global economies. Managers must be prepared to strategically manage their organizations under conditions of dynamic change.

These conditions make strategic management especially important, because it is a dynamic process that accommodates, even encourages, change and adaptation. Tomorrow's strategic manager must have some sense of what the future may hold and how to adapt the organization and its strategic activities to that future.

Future Environmental Changes

Managers are operating in a more dynamic business environment than ever before in our history. According to Toffler,

> instead of being routine and predictable, the corporate environment has grown increasingly unstable, accelerated, and revolutionary. Under such conditions, all organizations become extremely vulnerable to outside forces or pressures. . . . It [the organization] needs 'managers of adaptation' equipped with a whole set of new nonlinear skills.[4]

What this means is that modern managers must be willing to drop established products and processes and venture into unknown areas of their business. Social, political, and technological revolutions make every aspect of the firm's environment subject to catastrophic change.[5] Some of these changes provide the manager with opportunities, while many are threats to avoid. Increasing productivity, emerging economies, and American innovativeness are opportunities that will open new markets for future business. However, declining manufacturing capabilities in the United States,[6] projected shortages of skilled employees,[7] moderate to level growth, and increased competitiveness of emerging economies provide threats that can negate these opportunities if tomorrow's strategic managers are not extremely capable. These environmental conditions pose a tremendous challenge.

Changes in Competitors

Beginning in the 1980s, managers saw the end of the domestic economy for most industrialized nations. Many foreign firms have grown large and powerful enough to saturate their domestic markets and have turned to the United States and Canada, the largest consuming populations in the world, for their future growth. In addition to an extremely high standard of living, large markets, and substantial discretionary income, these economies exist in stable political environments. This combination of attractive features has encouraged many foreign manufacturers to target the American marketplace. The result is a dramatic increase in competition, both from foreign organizations and from domestic firms that have had their primary markets invaded by foreign competitors.

Although experts disagree, some events and trends are on the horizon that could greatly affect the competitive arena in which American firms operate. The United States has continued to hold its own as a dominant economic world power through the 1980s. However, Japan has outstripped the United States in average annual GNP growth for over two decades. China is slowly emerging as an economic threat and in 1992 the European Community will remove internal trade barriers and unite as an economic force.[8] Increasingly attractive U.S. markets and the appearance of powerful foreign competitors threaten the economic dominance that U.S. firms have enjoyed since World War II.

As American firms move into the 21st century, competition will intensify. Other industrialized countries are gaining advantages over American technology in areas such as computers and rocketry, so they will begin to compete in areas that were previously the exclusive domain of the United States. Already, for example, West Germany has the capability to launch satellites into outer space in direct competition with the National Aeronautics and Space Administration. Also, Japan is poised to exploit the upcoming marriage of personal computers with photographic-quality video images and digital audio with their lead in high-definition television (HDTV). According to Stephen S. Cohen, Director of the Berkeley Roundtable on the International Economy (BRIE), "Consumer electronics is undergoing a revolution that will eliminate the barriers" between devices.[9] Computers will be able to perform animation, edit music, dub home videos with commercial films, and carry out a host of other audiovisual tasks.

An additional competitive threat that has recently started to concern American managers is the influx of goods from emerging economies. Countries such as Taiwan, South Korea, South Africa, and India have become major competitors by exploiting their competitive advantage in labor-intensive products. South American countries have severely weakened the copper mining industry in the western United States. Energy exploration and development in the United States has been severely hampered by relatively inexpensive sources of energy from the Middle East and from the British Isles. China's emergence as an economic contender is uncertain but the Chinese have a history of entrepreneurship that could resurface in the 21st century. These are but a few examples of the intense competition that could continue to come from emerging economies.

The number and intensity of competitive threats operating on the organization give rise to concern for the future of American business as we know it. How does tomorrow's strategic manager prepare for this onslaught of foreign competition in areas of traditional American strength? Two concepts will help the manager deal with a globally competitive business environment. One is competitive advantage, and the other is comparative advantage. Competitive advantage, according to Michael Porter, derives from building the organization's strength in areas in which competitors have recognizable weaknesses.[10] The firm achieves such an advantage by creating a positive price or benefit differential compared to that of competitors. In contrast, comparative advantage typically accrues to nations or regions of the world and suggests that countries should concentrate on producing the goods or services that they are best equipped to provide. Sources of comparative advantage could be land, labor, capital, or raw materials (including energy) that a nation or region can provide in the most efficient and effective manner and at the lowest price. When combined with an intelligent assessment of the future, these ideas can prepare the organization for what lies ahead.

For example, some experts on the future suggest that America's comparative advantage lies in becoming almost a total service economy.[11] Others suggest that America is rapidly moving from being an industrialized society to being an information society.[12] That is, the majority of the U.S. population will be employed in creating and transmitting information and data rather than manufacturing a good or providing a service. Still others suggest that this is the dawn of an era when Americans all become "prosumers"—consumers who become competitors by actively participating in producing the good or service that they consume. Such an era would gradually start with individuals providing their own services such as preliminary medical self-diagnoses or banking by computer at home and using personally owned robots to perform services that were previously purchased. If any of these projections come true, strategic managers will formulate and implement strategy in dramatically different ways.

These futurists' projections are already beginning to occur. Originally IBM, the world's largest manufacturer of mainframe computers, concentrated on making computer hardware. However, over the past decade, IBM realized the profit potential of producing software to support its computer systems. Now software accounts for a large portion of IBM's gross revenue. The IBM of the future may manufacture all of its computers under license to offshore manufacturers and concentrate on developing software packages that allow inexperienced computer users to program their own systems for a variety of complicated tasks. Or IBM could focus on developing expert systems that will convert voice instructions to software that will support the user's needs. Such a change in IBM's thrust would represent a shift in all three of the directions previously mentioned. The resulting IBM would be information oriented, would primarily provide a service through its American organization, and would take advantage of consumers' becoming prosumers.

Changes in Input Sources

The nature and availability of input sources will change dramatically over the next 40 to 50 years. The factors of production (land, labor, capital, and energy) will adapt to reflect the changing conditions in businesses and society. As America moves toward being a service economy, new factors will become important in selecting the location of a business. As Figure 12.1 shows, the population growth of the southern and western portions of the United States will continue, as individuals use climate and quality-of-life considerations as primary reasons for relocating.[13] Service organizations will tend to follow this flow of labor from the northern industrialized cities to the southern and southwestern service-oriented locations in the economy. This change will become even more important through the next three to four decades, as those born during the post–World War II baby boom mature and age and the availability of entry-level labor—whether skilled, unskilled, or professional—becomes more critical.

In the year 2015 the majority of the population bulge caused by the post–World War II baby boom will have reached the ages of 50 to 60. As shown in Figure 12.2, the population groups that follow are relatively stable and smaller than the baby boom population. At the same time, as fewer and fewer jobs in the service sector lend

Figure 12.1 U.S. Regional Populations 1987 and 2010 (Projected)

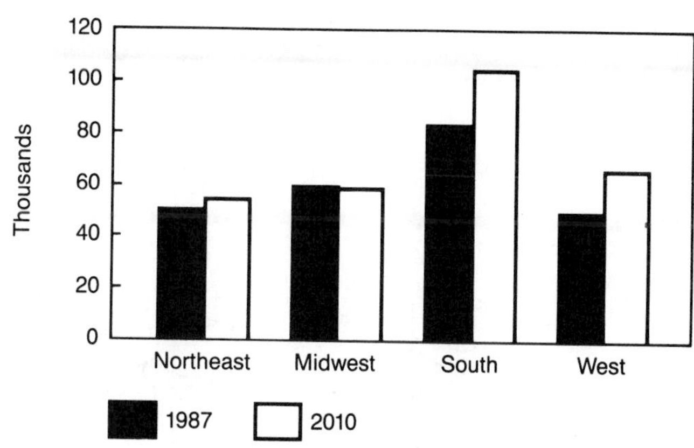

Source: U.S. Census Bureau Estimates as of 1988 (numbers in 000s)

themselves to increases in productivity through the substitution of capital for labor, more and more jobs will be created. Figure 12.3 shows that the number of new jobs created is expected to increase 10 percent over the next decade. This will produce a compression situation; fewer employees will be available for more jobs. As a result, a smaller percentage of the working population must produce output for a larger percentage of the graying population.

In addition, immigration from other countries, which appears to have leveled off at approximately 25 percent of the growth in the U.S. population, has occurred predominately in the Sunbelt states. Therefore, the combination of migration and immigration to the South and Southwest will encourage more firms to move to take advantage of the remaining available labor pool in these states.[14]

The land component of production also will change dramatically. The decreased emphasis on mass transportation in terms of rail and water, combined with increases in the number and usage of truck and continuous-flow forms of transportation (such as solids through pipelines), will lead businesses to place less importance on proximity to rail and water transportation in deciding where to locate a facility. In addition, the decreasing population will place less and less demand on the construction industry for new housing. Once the population shifts primarily to the South and Southwest and construction has saturated that market, the demand for residential construction should decline. Thus, although there will always be a premium on land as a component of production, that premium will decline as the demand for new land decreases.

The demand for agricultural land in America will also decrease as more and more foreign countries develop their own capabilities to produce enough food to feed their populations and export to other countries. For example, after many years of food shortages, China used new technology to develop the capability to feed its population. The European Community can now export grain and other products. Over the past several years, the USSR has decreased its need for foreign wheat. All of these devel-

Figure 12.2 Age and Sex Composition of the U.S. Population

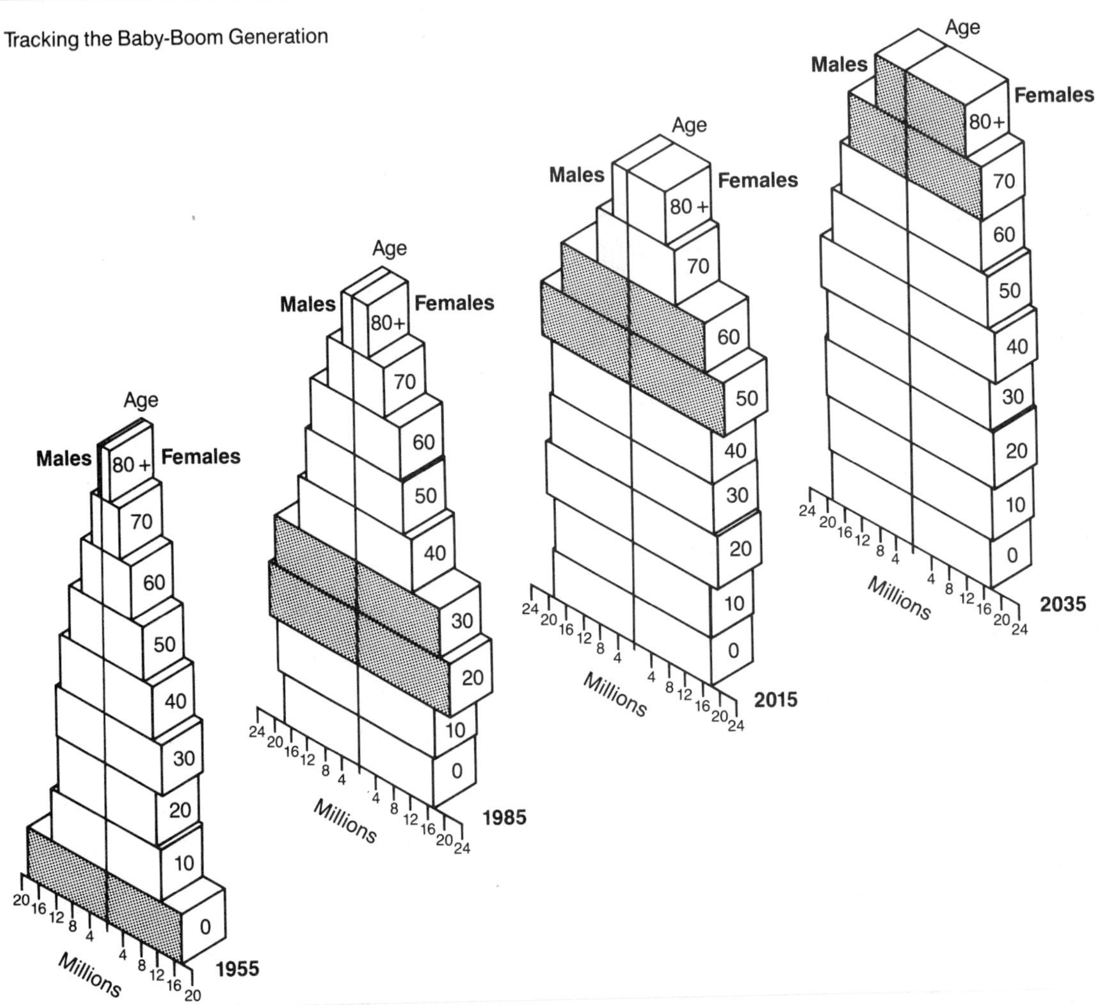

Source: U.S. Bureau of the Census

opments, combined with the increased productivity of land in the traditional food-exporting nations such as the United States and Canada, have resulted in an abundance of food in most regions of the world. There will continue to be hunger in some regions, but unfortunately these areas are probably incapable of purchasing the output of exporting countries. Therefore, land will cease to occupy the position of importance that it has occupied in the past.

The availability of capital will continue to be important to maintaining mature businesses and stimulating new businesses. As international financial markets merge,

Figure 12.3 Millions of Jobs in the U.S. Economy

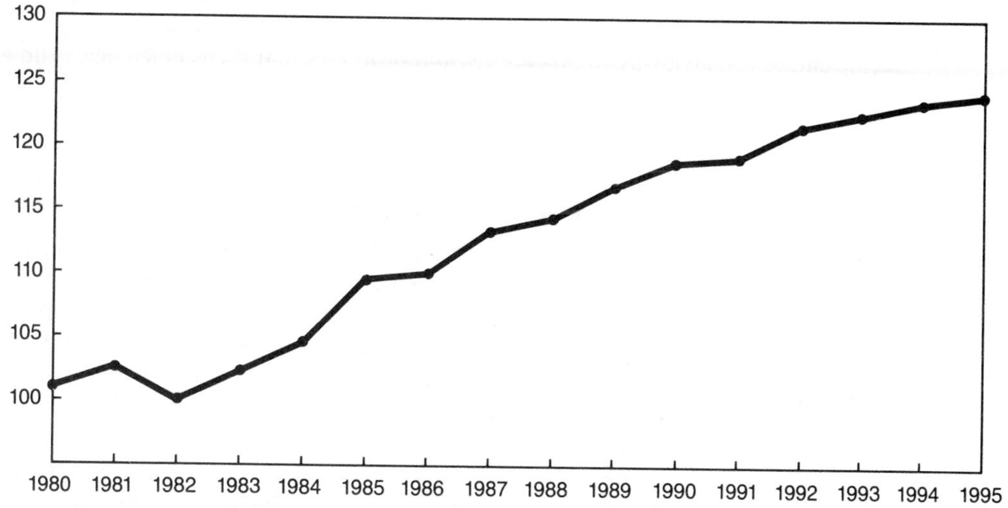

130
125
120
115
110
105
100

1980 1981 1982 1983 1984 1985 1986 1987 1988 1989 1990 1991 1992 1993 1994 1995

Source: Data from U.S. Bureau of the Census

more foreign capital will become available to countries such as the United States and Canada. The rapid transfer of information and the interconnectedness of financial markets have resulted in a capability to transfer funds at the speed of light. This new capability allows foreign investors to buy stocks in companies in the United States, Canada, and around the world with the confidence that their investments will be treated with the same care as those of domestic investors. Thus, capital will tend to flow more easily across borders and follow the world's successful economies.

Capital movement across national borders also depends upon the stability of national economies. Therefore, a dramatic change in the economic conditions in a country could cause capital to flow away from that country. Because the United States is now a net debtor, the country's stability has become more critical than ever for U.S. business.

The last major input source is energy. The availability and cost of resources continues to be a problem for future executives, regardless of their industry. Managers generally recognize that the era of a single energy source such as fossil fuels is rapidly coming to an end. Meanwhile, much of the work on alternative energy sources such as synthetic fuels or transportable electric energy for automobiles has declined substantially due to a relatively recent abundance of fossil fuels. Thus, once oil reserves are depleted and until an alternative universal fuel is found, energy will be obtained on a local or regional basis, using energy sources that are abundant in that particular area. For example, Norway has the least expensive electricity in any industrialized nation, because it has an abundance of waterfalls that produce hydroelectric power. Other parts of the world have easily accessible geothermal energy, and still others are located near coalfields or natural gas wells.

Energy management in the future will require a completely different perspective on the part of those that supply and use energy in their businesses. Suppliers and users of energy will find that economies of scale and scope based on large volume efficiencies will give way to procedures and processes that allow efficiencies and economies at much lower volumes. Such processes and procedures will be based on flexibility and convertibility.

Flexibility refers to the firm's ability to change processes and procedures in response to changes in the demand of the firm's customers or clients. The use of easily programmable industrial robots means that manufacturing firms can enjoy economies of scale with smaller quantities. This means that the low production costs associated with long production runs using expensive dedicated machines will be available on much shorter runs with the use of robots. In addition, robots can be inexpensively and quickly reprogrammed to manufacture a different product. This combination of low-cost automation through robotics and ease of reprogramming give to smaller organizations the cost efficiencies usually attainable only in large firms.

Convertibility is an ability to change processes or procedures in response to changes in the source of inputs that the firm uses in its operations. An example of high convertibility is found in the power generation industry. New electric generating plants can be quickly converted from coal to oil to gas depending on the relative cost of each fuel. The result may therefore be smaller, more efficient and effective facilities that use many alternative sources of input energy.

Changes in Markets

For the first decade in its history, the United States has a chronic problem with the balance of trade. This means that the United States as a country imports more goods than it exports to other countries. The trade imbalance is occurring even as American workers are becoming more productive than their foreign competition, which should make U.S. goods more attractive to foreign consumers.[15] However, the United States has lost part of its world export market, while Canada, Japan, Western Europe, and several newly industrialized countries have been the beneficiaries of this loss.[16]

The increasing role of foreign businesses will continue to bring about fundamental and revolutionary changes in the marketplace. Tom Peters argues that the building of the international marketplace is essentially complete.[17] The next stage for the marketplace will therefore be fragmentation, not uniformity. More and more niches will emerge, requiring what Peters calls "localized marketing." As mentioned earlier, many of these niches will involve consumers doing much of their own production or manufacturing in the confines of their own home or office.

Not only is the market itself changing, but so is the customer. According to the Population Reference Bureau, the "proportion of population over age 65 will increase from the 1985 level of 12 percent to about 21 percent in 2030." Increasing life expectancy will also mean that those over 65 can expect to live longer. Between the years 2030 and 2050 the proportion of the population over age 85 is projected to double. Figure 12.4 shows the dramatic increase in senior citizens through the century from 1950 to 2050. Not only will the number of elderly increase but this graying of

Figure 12.4 The Aging of the U.S. Population, 1950–2050

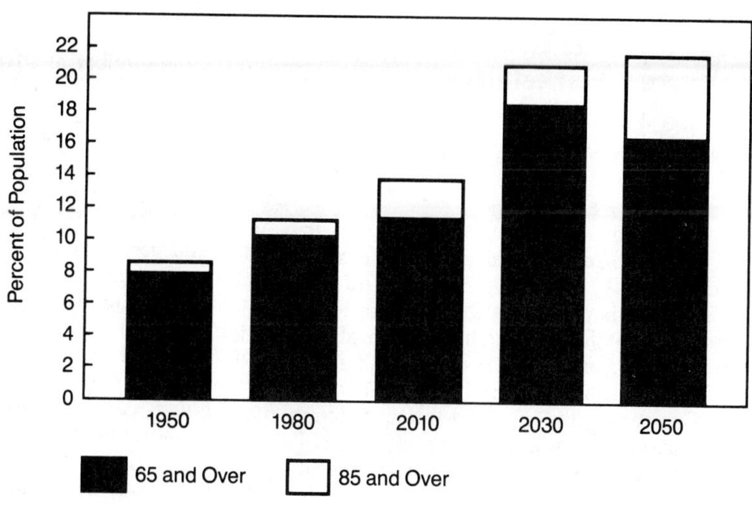

Source: U.S. Bureau of the Census

America will also affect consumer tastes. The Strategic Application "The Graying Marketplace" provides some examples of this development.

These changes in customers and markets will lead to new products and services that are directed toward smaller niches and specific customers. The beginning of the trend is apparent with the tremendous success of the home entertainment industry in the United States. There are other examples as well. Gourmet meals can be ordered by telephone and delivered to the door. Mobile health spas drive up to the front of the house.

In addition, products will be more specialized and personalized for niche markets that in the past would have been uneconomical to serve. For example, Audi was able to introduce and successfully market its Quattro four-wheel drive 4000 and 5000 automobiles in areas that experience severe weather conditions, although the company did not even attempt to market those cars in other parts of the country. Increases in the flexibility of printing processes allows major newspapers to adjust their advertising for different suburbs or regions of a major city. Modern transportation technology allows *The Wall Street Journal* to adjust its editions for the various parts of the world. These examples suggest that new products will have to be designed with flexibility that enables the organization to take advantage of more fragmented market niches.

Distribution systems also will change fundamentally. Domino's Pizza became successful by delivering a pizza to people's doors within 30 minutes. Now practically everything from pet grooming to fine wines to ski maintenance can be obtained by delivery directly to the consumer's door. Furthermore, as localized or regional facilities are established to meet more fragmented market tastes, major distribution systems

STRATEGIC APPLICATIONS: INTERNATIONAL

The Graying Marketplace

Life expectancy has risen since 1960 by 5 years to as much as 12 years in industrialized countries such as Japan, Norway, Sweden, England, and the United States. This means that by the year 2020, almost one-third of the population in industrialized countries will be 55 or older. The senior population is thus growing as an international force in the marketplace. Companies like General Motors, Proctor & Gamble, Honda, and Sharp Electronics are designing special features into their products to appeal to the senior citizen. For example, General Motors is considering larger control buttons and visual displays as a convenience to older drivers. Sharp Electronics is developing a VCR that talks viewers through the programming steps.

Perhaps more obvious than new design features is the number of advertisements directed at the senior market. Domestic firms like AT&T are showing more seniors using their products. International cruise lines are directing messages to active senior citizens in an attempt to tap this growing travel market. Honda shows couples over 50 in advertisements emphasizing room and comfort over speed and performance.

International firms recognize that 50-plus consumers in the United States today are healthier and better educated than they were in the past and control 75 percent of the nation's wealth. Moreover, having made most of the major initial purchases (e.g., house, car, and children's educations), this group accounts for half of the nation's discretionary income.

In the next half century products for seniors—for example, bath lotion for older skin, phone-receiver amplifiers, grab bars for showers, nonslip bathmats, simple-use appliances, and easy-access transportation—will proliferate. These products will be promoted by novel approaches such as sponsorship of Senior Olympics, special clubs for seniors like the Over the Hill Gang sponsored by Copper Mountain Ski Area, and advertisements in popular senior magazines and catalogs such as *Comfortably Yours.*

Source: Joan O'C. Hamilton, "Gray Expectations: A New Force in Design," *Business Week*, April 11, 1988, 108; and Walecia Konrad and Gail DeGeorge, "U.S. Companies Go for the Gray," *Business Week*, April 3, 1989, 64–67.

will no longer be as appropriate. Centralized manufacturing with long-distance transportation will be replaced by smaller, localized, yet efficient production facilities with less sophisticated and less costly transportation. For example, the popularity of mail-order selling has resurged over the past decade. Direct ordering without going through a distributor or a sales representative is occurring more and more, as interconnected personal computers or minicomputers directly link customers with businesses. Factory warehouses and outlets are becoming a popular mode of distribution. Teleshopping, with entire television channels devoted to offering goods for sale, has become very popular over the past several years.

Changes in Government

Public initiatives such as California's Proposition 13 and the initiatives that followed in 20 other states to curb government spending, frequent mass marches on the nation's capital,[18] and citizens calling for more ethical conduct by legislators[19] are evidence of a fundamental shift from a representative form of democracy to a more participative democracy.[20] Higher involvement on the part of citizens is prompted by a growing interest in politics and the advent of advanced information technology that will allow a more participative form of government.

Technology has already improved communication between elected officials and their constituents. The C-Span television network is dedicated to providing continuous coverage of U.S. Senate and House deliberations. Many states have developed their own television networks dedicated to covering deliberations on state and local legislation. Such coverage is a clear sign that Americans are beginning to take greater interest in the individuals who initiate and pass legislation that directly affects them.

Spurring the new interest in participatory government is the growing use of modern information technology to bring all citizens directly into the legislative process through public initiatives and referenda.[21] Initiatives appear directly on a voter's ballot through direct citizen action, while referenda are means for citizens to approve legislative action by their elected representatives.

Modern technology could facilitate citizen participation through a television voting process that used dedicated public channels and telephone voting to allow citizens to view debate on proposed legislation and register a straw vote on issues that they would like to see put on a ballot for a formal vote. Or citizens could directly express their opinions to their representatives by indicating through a signaling device on their televisions which legislation they would like that individual to support. This procedure would make individual legislators more responsive to the wishes of the citizens that they represent and give the entire legislative body directions as to which issues the citizenry feels are important.

The new participative form of government can present opportunities to future businesses. Firms that manufacture home-voting devices for attachment to an individual's television set will have an opportunity to gain a competitive advantage in producing and marketing these products. Companies that are in the business of transmitting information to individual legislators in their chambers will find an opportunity in providing that service.

These developments can also pose threats to businesses. At particular risk would be organizations that have neglected their social responsibility to their surrounding communities or to the nation. Individual citizens will be able to quickly call for legislatures to sanction socially irresponsible activities of these organizations.

Change in Technologies

Perhaps the area of most dramatic change in the environment is technological change. The analysis of technological change and technological forecasting have become extremely important considerations for the strategic manager. Many analysts attribute the tremendous fluctuations in the stock market to the technological advances in the stock exchange. Programmed trading, which uses computers to automatically trade large volumes of stocks when prices reach a specified level, create selling and buying volumes unheard of in earlier decades.

Some technological innovations that could alter the way firms do business are appearing on the horizon. Superconductivity could dramatically affect the transportation industries by making feasible magnetic trains that can travel as fast as airplanes, using less energy. Superconductivity can reduce the need for large-scale power plants.[22] Robots with two arms, two video-camera eyes, and a delicate sense of touch will replace seamstresses in the apparel industry and assemblers in the automobile industry.[23] By the year 2000, silicon chips could contain 1,000 times more transistors than they do today, making high-definition flat-screen television, lightning-fast supercomputers, and real-time telecommunications possible.[24] Chips will be not only more powerful and faster but more specialized. Experts project that by the year 1995 over 700,000 custom designs for new chips will be needed. This drastically changes the nature of the semiconductor industry. Large production runs will be replaced by shorter product life cycles and smaller production runs. The firms that can produce full customized chip designs at competitive prices will be the winners.[25]

Many future technological developments will be based on computers. According to George Heilmeier, senior vice president and chief technical officer at Texas Instruments, research and development personnel are working on the following projects:[26]

- A symbolic processing engine, which will allow expert systems and artificial intelligence programs to be included in a standard personal computer, giving the user access to the decision-making power of a vast network of experts in a particular area
- Improvements on the speech understanding capability of today's computers
- An "image understanding box," which consists of an intelligent computer sensing system that will recognize images in complex environments, including human faces
- An "automatic programming box," which lets the user tell the computer what he or she wants it to do, and the computer can determine for itself how best to do it

However, technological innovations that are forecast for the near future are not always successful. Consequently, the strategic manager of the future must be aware of technological innovation and must use technological forecasting to the firm's best advantage. At the same time, he or she must take care not to become enamored with technology for technology's sake or to neglect the human worker's role in the firm.

John Naisbitt suggests that most innovations are developed to make the human being more efficient but frequently dehumanize the employee's work. These high-tech innovations should be accompanied by a "high-touch" technology that can help substitute for the loss of social interaction and sense of accomplishment that results from applying the technology.[27] As an example, Naisbitt points to the introduction of the television and videocassette recorder, which allow families to have their entertainment in the home. This high-tech innovation in home entertainment was accompanied by an increase in the use of self-help support groups that allow people to interact because they cannot interact at traditional gatherings such as community dances or theater. Such trade-offs may account for the slow acceptance of such ideas as home-based banking and robotics.

Some experts argue that the United States has invested in capital equipment but neglected human capital. A drop in the overall literacy rate in the United States (80 percent today as compared with 90 percent in 1851 and 95 percent in modern Japan) and an increasing gap between required job skills and applicant skills are just a few signs of the neglect.[28]

U.S. managers have begun to appreciate the importance of recognizing the human side of the productivity equation and combining high-tech with high-touch techniques in manufacturing. According to *The Wall Street Journal*, tomorrow's factory will be a more efficient reflection of today. Improved training and "back to basics" for employee involvement and commitment are the keys to putting the worker's touch back into the higher tech factory. Firms such as GenCorp Inc., Huffy Corporation, and Caterpillar are using a combination of new production methods, imaginative management, a more participative work atmosphere, and modern computer-controlled equipment rather than full automation.[29,30] The long term may see fully automated plants controlled by robot managers but, for the short term, high tech and high touch are still joined in the workplace.

The future manager must consider technological innovations in light of how they fit into the total technical and social milieu of the user. For example, technological innovations that deprive employees of the opportunity to interact with others will probably encounter a great deal of resistance when introduced into the workplace. Innovations that reduce individuals to mere automatons who follow directions provided by a computer will also meet resistance and possible sabotage. A new piece of equipment or a new office automation device cannot simply be ergonomically appropriate. Rather, the manager must consider its effect on the employee's ability to receive social gratification from the job and feel that he or she is a contributing member of the organization.

The need for high-tech, high-touch technology will also provide opportunities for organizations that are astute enough to read the signals. Service organizations that monitor high-tech advances will be wise to look for opportunities in high-touch areas. A company using technologies that reduce the need for an operations manager to spend extensive time in meetings with other functional managers must be sure to substitute other mechanisms to fulfill the manager's social and recognition needs. Technologies that are aimed at prosumers should be accompanied by opportunities for them to experience social interaction and recognition from other facets of their lives.

Future Organizational Changes

The organization itself will change in many ways over the next 25 years. Employees' expectations for the organization are going through dramatic changes today and will continue to do so in the future. The role of the organization and its managers will change, along with how new managers are selected to replace existing ones. In addition, the level of employee commitment to the organization will change. Organization structures will change to accommodate the more dynamic and turbulent environments of an international economy. Last, the cultures of organizations will become more fluid and responsive to changing business conditions. All of these changes place new demands on the strategic manager.

Changes in Employees' Expectations

At the end of World War II, with the dominance of the United States as an industrial nation established, status and worth were attributed to those who managed large corporations and provided the country's international prominence. Until the 1980s this continued to be the primary source of status and of recognition in the business world. Henry Ford II, Lee Iacocca, Ross Perot, and others who emerged as CEOs of major corporations were the primary business heroes prior to the 1980s.

Today the popular press frequently acclaims successful entrepreneurs rather than CEO's of large corporations. Executives such as Bill Gates, founder of Microsoft, and Steven Jobs, father of Apple Computer and now NEXT Inc., have become entrepreneurial role models for the next generation of American executives.[31]

What does this mean for the expectations that employees bring to the organization? Entry-level managerial positions will no longer serve as training grounds to socialize the firm's future executives. Rather, these jobs will serve as incubators for creating a new generation of entrepreneurs. Employees will expect less from the organization and consequently return a lower level of dedication to it. Salaries as a form of compensation will cease to be a major issue for the new professional. Rather, the opportunity to learn a broad range of managerial skills and to gain product knowledge useful in starting a new enterprise will become important incentives. This means that organizations must expect that the best and brightest of their employees will turn over within a few years after they are originally hired.

Managers can try to counteract this turnover by designing radically new organizations that provide the challenge and independence desired by entrepreneurially oriented executives. One company's approach to this is described in the Strategic Application "Multilevel Management at Diedre Moire Corporation." The period of socialization and indoctrination will be substantially shortened. As the strategic application shows, responsibility will be given sooner to this group of highly educated and confident junior executives. More and more attention will be given to the challenge of the job itself rather than to the challenge of achieving a high level in an organizational hierarchy. Status and worth will be awarded according to the type of job one occupies and one's success at that job rather than to organizational rank.

Considering that 25 percent fewer college graduates are expected by the year 2000, these developments are important for the firm. If large organizations are to survive and prosper, they must pay particular attention to the needs and desires of the future young executive. The strategic manager's challenge is to design organizational systems for implementing long-term strategies through flexible and convertible organizational units and to provide challenge and status to the junior executive in charge.

Changes in Staffing and Succession

As general population growth levels off and the number of employees available for entry-level positions declines, the organization will experience many new problems in staffing and succession of top-level managers. New and different types of workers will need to be attracted to the organization. Women, who made up only 40 percent

STRATEGIC APPLICATIONS

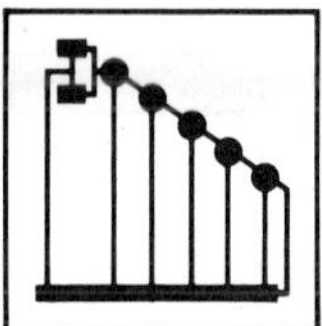

Multilevel Management at Diedre Moire Corporation

Steven Reuning, the 31-year-old CEO of Diedre Moire Corporation, developed a multilevel management system that rewards managers for hard work and puts responsibility for promotions squarely in their hands. Earlier, frustrated with the dead-end nature of jobs in professional recruiting firms, Reuning had left a recruiting position to start his own firm. He soon realized that talented employees were leaving his firm in search of challenge, independence, and self-determination elsewhere.

Reuning's multilevel management system offers entry-level employees, called consultants, a commission on the client fees they generate. Once they are able to sustain a certain level of fees for six consecutive months, consultants qualify for promotion to group leader.

Group leaders, who comprise the second level, hire and train consultants and collect an override commission on their commissions. In time, one or more of these consultants may be promoted to group leader; if an employee that you hire achieves group leader, the first group leader then collects an override on the sales of everyone in the new group.

The third level is floor leader. Promotion to this level requires that a group leader (1) have a minimum of five consultants working under him or her, (2) attain a specified monthly minimum for three consecutive months, and (3) have two consultants who have achieved group leader and are themselves supervising at least two consultants. A floor leader receives all group leader commissions and overrides plus a 1 percent commission on the sales of any group headed by a floor leader whom he or she hired and trained.

At the last level, a qualified floor leader may become an office manager–partner with a 50 percent ownership of a branch office. The office manager–partner may take half of his or her consultants to the new branch.

The multilevel management system was developed to recognize the differences among employees. Each can control his or her level of effort, compensation, and promotion. The result is that Diedre Moire Corporation has a substantially lower turnover rate than other firms in the industry. Steven Reuning has found a way to design organization systems to meet the needs of entrepreneurially oriented employees.

Source: Tom Richman, "Up from Drudgery," *Inc.*, January 1988, 79–82.

of the work force in 1975, today make up over 45 percent and are expected to continue to be attracted in larger numbers to the workplace. Figure 12.5 shows the dramatic growth in working women through the year 2000. This will require that organizations provide benefits that have, to date, not been part of an organization's benefits program. Benefits such as subsidized child care and flex time will be common. These changes will be necessary to provide women time to maintain their family commitments as well as participate as contributing members of the work force.[32,33]

Minorities will also be attracted to the work force in larger numbers. Figure 12.6 shows the growth of minority workers in U.S. firms over the next decade. This huge pool of underutilized labor will be recruited into the organization in substantial numbers. New challenges will be present, such as providing transportation for minorities working in firms in outlying locations but living in inner cities. Training must become a top priority for organizations to bring skill levels of the newly employable minorities up to levels that will allow the organization to remain competitive. Many firms will

Figure 12.5 Women in the Work Force

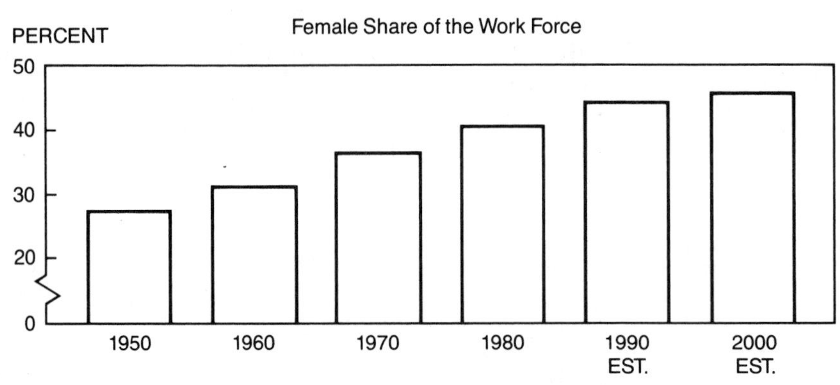

Source: Bureau of the Census, Labor Department

need to change their organization's culture to accept and embrace the influx of new types of employees.

Some experts suggest that the United States may actively seek immigrants for many low-skill jobs.[34] Movement in that direction has begun with the amnesty provided to illegal aliens from Mexico and other South and Central American countries. Immigrants in more professional categories will also be used to supplement the declining population of U.S.-born workers. For example, the health care industry is slated to hire 20,000 foreign nurses on five-year visas over the next several years to alleviate the shortage of American nurses. Figure 12.6 shows that substantial growth in the U.S. labor force for both males and females will occur in the immigrant population.[35] A study reported in *The Wall Street Journal* suggests that U.S.-born workers should not fear this influx of immigrants. Results show that a large immigrant population has no impact on the earnings or employment levels of U.S.-born citizens.[36] Importing workers to fill the many new jobs that will be created in the United States (see Figure 12.3) may be the only way to maintain America's international competitiveness.

An increased presence of women, minorities, and immigrants in the work force means that the complexion of the organization and its staffing will change over the next several decades. Because these different groups need different benefits, organizations should consider converting to a cafeteria-style benefit program. For example, employees who have children may elect to take part of their benefit package in child-care subsidies. Inner-city minorities may take part of their benefit package in additional training to develop their skill levels so that they can become more employable and promotable. Figure 12.7 compares the skills required to the skills available in new jobs created between 1985 and 2000. Immigrants may take part of their benefit package in the form of periodical transportation to their homeland so that they can

Figure 12.6 Composition of the Labor Force, 1985–2000

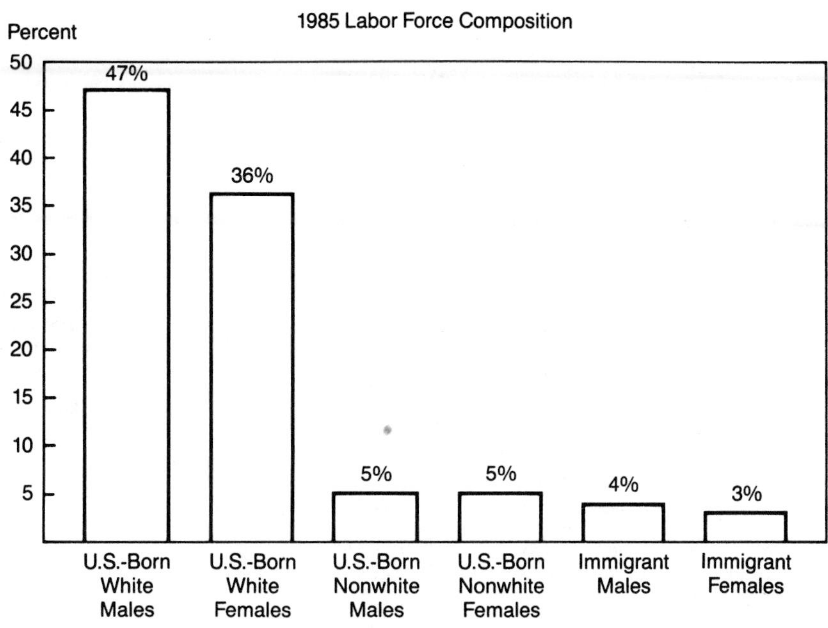

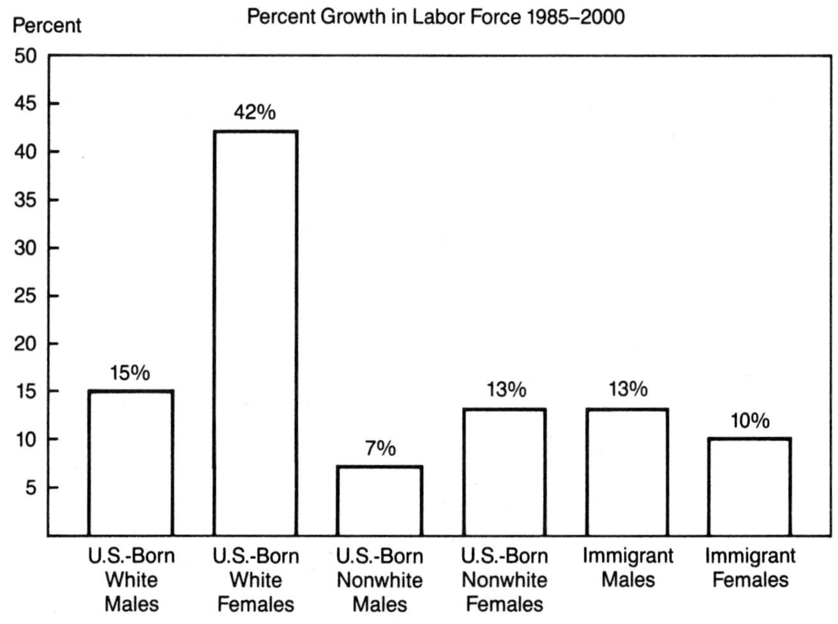

Source: Hudson Institute

Figure 12.7 Skills Required vs. Skills Available, 1985–2000

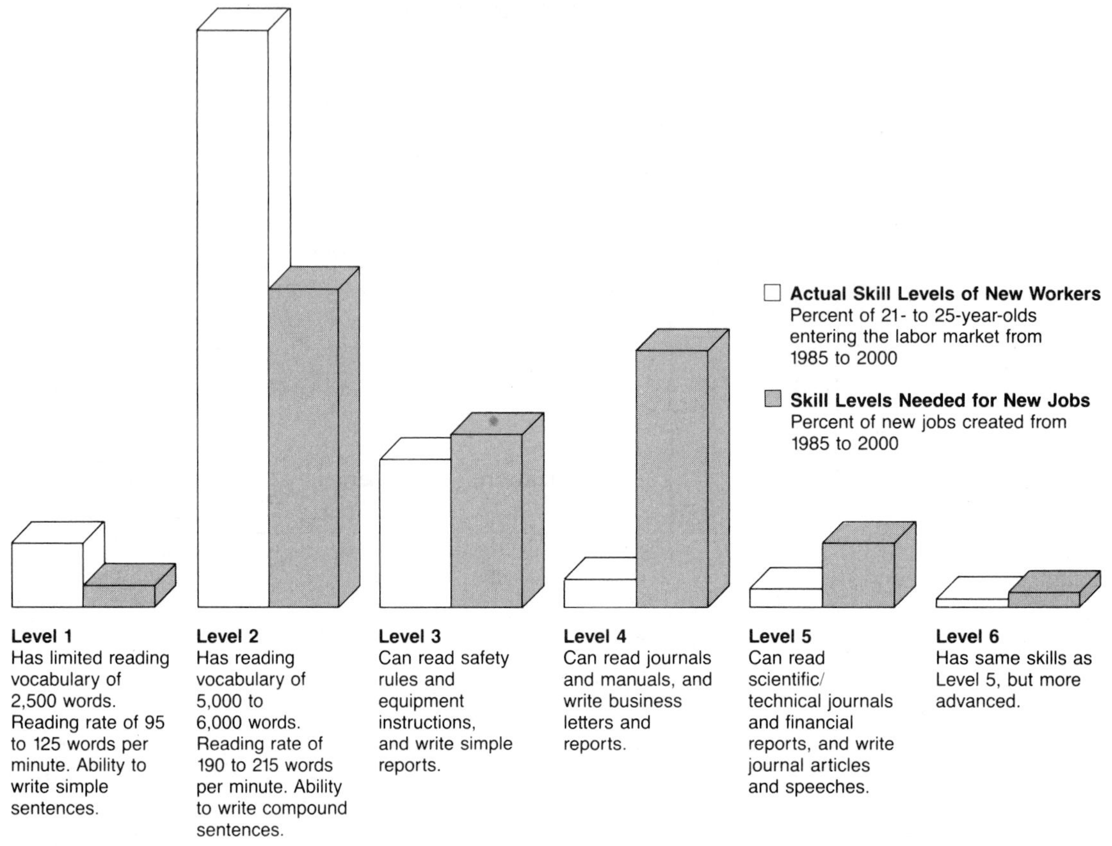
Actual Skill Levels of New Workers
Percent of 21- to 25-year-olds entering the labor market from 1985 to 2000
Skill Levels Needed for New Jobs
Percent of new jobs created from 1985 to 2000
Level 1
Has limited reading vocabulary of 2,500 words. Reading rate of 95 to 125 words per minute. Ability to write simple sentences.
Level 2
Has reading vocabulary of 5,000 to 6,000 words. Reading rate of 190 to 215 words per minute. Ability to write compound sentences.
Level 3
Can read safety rules and equipment instructions, and write simple reports.
Level 4
Can read journals and manuals, and write business letters and reports.
Level 5
Can read scientific/ technical journals and financial reports, and write journal articles and speeches.
Level 6
Has same skills as Level 5, but more advanced.

Source: "Where the Jobs Are Is Where the Skills Aren't," Chart—"The Looming Mismatch Between Workers and Jobs," pp. 104–108. Reprinted from the September 19, 1988 issue of *Business Week* by special permission, copyright © 1988 by McGraw Hill, Inc. Data from Hudson Institute and Labor Department.

maintain contact with their families. All of these benefits will be in addition to the standard benefits of health care and retirement.

Without the traditional worker, businesses will need to provide new incentives and new ways of arranging their organizations. For example, as more people move away from metropolitan areas, and to smaller communities,[37] more firms will locate facilities in outlying areas. Many individuals will want to work at home and communicate with the organization via computer, coming to the office only once or twice a week for social interactions. According to LINK Resources, a market research firm, nearly 14 million American workers are staying home for at least part of a workweek and maintaining ties with the office as telecommuters.[38]

In the future, adult education will be more widely available through the use of the computer. College courses for credit are currently available from many institutions at work sites through computer and television hookups. It is only a minor technological development to move these courses into the person's home through use of a personal computer.

Because of the shortage of skilled employees, future organizations will use more consultants than they did in the past.[39] The manager can expect that many of the functions previously performed by captive organizational units will be contracted out to organizations providing these services more efficiently and inexpensively. Many firms now purchase payroll services and equipment maintenance from other organizations. However, in the future, traditional staff functions such as marketing, advertising, sales, and controlling may be available from outside consultants as well. Management in the future will be primarily responsible for the long-range management of the firm and for directly providing the product or service to clients and customers. Very few staff functions will be performed in-house. This change will be brought about not only by the shortage of employees for entry-level and staff positions but also by the growing interest in entrepreneurship and independence discussed earlier.

As Figure 12.7 shows, organizations may experience a shortage of technical personnel. There is currently an acute shortage of engineering professors in colleges of engineering across the country. In addition, little increase in enrollment is expected in engineering colleges in the United States and Canada. The declining population of college-age individuals through the year 2000 will result in a real decline in enrollment in technical programs.[40] This means that organizations may be forced to hire engineers from outside the organization and will have to make more effective use of artificial intelligence and computer-aided design/computer-aided manufacturing to perform many of the functions currently performed by the firm's engineers.

Staffing executive positions and preparing for the succession of top-level decision makers will also be a problem for future organizations. In an attempt to increase productivity and cut overhead during the 1980s, many firms have reduced their middle-level management staff to minimum levels.[41] This reduction in the ranks of middle managers has reduced short-term operating costs at the expense of adequate preparation to move middle managers into top positions.[42] Also, as discussed previously, middle managers will view entrepreneurs as their role models and leave large organizations to pursue opportunities in their own smaller businesses. Entrepreneurs will lack the training and the skills to strategically manage large organizations in international or global marketplaces. These conditions will create a shortage of potential strategic managers for existing large firms and for entrepreneurial firms that are successful and grow to dominate national and global markets.

Organizations of the future that want to ensure the availability of capable strategic managers will need to nurture these managers from the very beginning of their careers. Potential chief executive officers will have to be targeted at the very early stages of their careers and be given sufficient challenges and independence to encourage them to stay with the large firm. This will mean placing them in charge of their own profit centers and giving them the independence to make strategic decisions and overcome challenges with little help from corporate headquarters. Procedures such as assessment centers, innovation centers, and independent business units are vehicles to provide this responsibility to budding young executives and determine their ability to function in a strategic capacity. Only in this manner will organizations be able to breed the next generation of CEOs.

Changes in Employee Commitment

Tomorrow's young professionals will no longer consider advancement in the organization the primary measure of success in American society. Therefore, employees' commitment to the organization will diminish. Several factors previously discussed will reduce employee commitment. A decreasing supply of entry-level employees, increased interest in entrepreneurship, and the advent of computer offices in the home all will make tomorrow's employee more independent and more disengaged from the organization. A constant criticism of top students graduating from professional schools of engineering and business is that they have expectations for advancement and challenge that most organizations are incapable of delivering in the early stages of their career. Current young professionals lack the patience that characterized new employees of the past.

Tomorrow's managers are being trained in today's educational institutions to make strategic decisions and take action. They expect that their new jobs will provide similar challenges and responsibilities. However, these expectations remain unfulfilled in most large organizations. Entry-level professionals are placed in training programs that require them to get to know their organizations. This is little more than an extensive socialization process that can last up to two years. Tomorrow's youth, disenchanted with large organizations, will resist going through such an extensive orientation.

The commitment of tomorrow's young professionals will be based on the challenges and excitement associated with the position. Strategic managers of the future must therefore develop programs that present challenges and responsibilities to this more mobile group of young executives. Dynamic changes in the firm's marketplace provide excellent opportunities for today's managers to offer these challenges. If current senior managers insist on retaining all of these challenging decisions and activities for themselves, high turnover and low employee commitment will result.

Changes in Organization Structures

Because organizations will face more turbulent environments and employees will have different expectations and commitments regarding the organization, the traditional bureaucratic or rigid organization structures that dominate most of today's firms will be incompatible with the needs of tomorrow's organizations. Businesses will need a more organic, flexible, and responsive structure that will accommodate tomorrow's smaller, more adaptive, and highly convertible organizations.

The organization structure of the future will have to emphasize coordination of diverse activities rather than control of individual actions. Control of the quality and consistency of operations processes (such as manufacturing and quality control) will be maintained through extensive use of robotics and computers. Artificial intelligence

(AI) systems, which apply the judgment of many experts to solving a problem, will help maintain consistency of the organization's operating decisions. Problems and issues that cannot be automated or solved with AI systems will dominate the decision-making activities of a more diverse and independent group of employees. Therefore, organizations will ensure coordination of activities through more flexible structures that use employee commitment to guarantee that employees' actions are consistent with the goals of the organization.

The informal organization structure can be used to maintain coordination in more flexible formal structures. Improved communication and better distribution of information will help verify that the informal structure supports the goals of the formal structure. This emphasis on less formal structural arrangements is a high-touch method to coordinate the activities of diverse employees in a high-tech arena. Quality circles, collateral teams, task forces, strategy implementation committees, and communication from top executives are just some of the procedures that can help keep the organizational team of the future pulling in the same direction.

The formal organization structure will change dramatically as well. The traditional organizational chart will be inappropriate to represent the diverse pattern of relationships in the organization structure of the future. Organization designs of the future will look more like networks similar to the one shown in Figure 12.8. These networks will represent specific functions the organization must coordinate for its overall success. Strategic decision makers, rather than being at the top of a hierarchy, will be at the center of the organizational network. This network will specify the types of interactions that are necessary for coordination, as well as indicate the information flows that must be provided to the individuals in the network. Furthermore, decision responsibility, not formal titles, will be the basis for identifying individual positions in the network.

As you can see from Figure 12.8, all employees are responsible for contributing to the overall success of the organization. An individual's performance will be evaluated primarily on the basis of his or her contribution to the organization's success. Because individuals will not regularly be in an office environment but will be performing much of their work at home on computers, traditional performance evaluation factors such as personality, attitude, dress, and charisma should be less important in assessing an individual's contribution to the firm.

Organization structures of the future will directly reflect the external and internal environments that the organization faces. The rapid change in future markets, competitors, suppliers, and customers will be mirrored in the expectations and commitments of the employees. This, combined with the additional use of consultants, will make direct bureaucratic control of the organization impossible. Control must be replaced by coordination of activities and dedication to the challenges of the job and goals of the organization.

Changes in Organization Culture

With so many changes in the internal workings of the organization, it is only natural to expect the culture of the organization itself to change. Remember, by culture we

Figure 12.8 Future Organization Structure

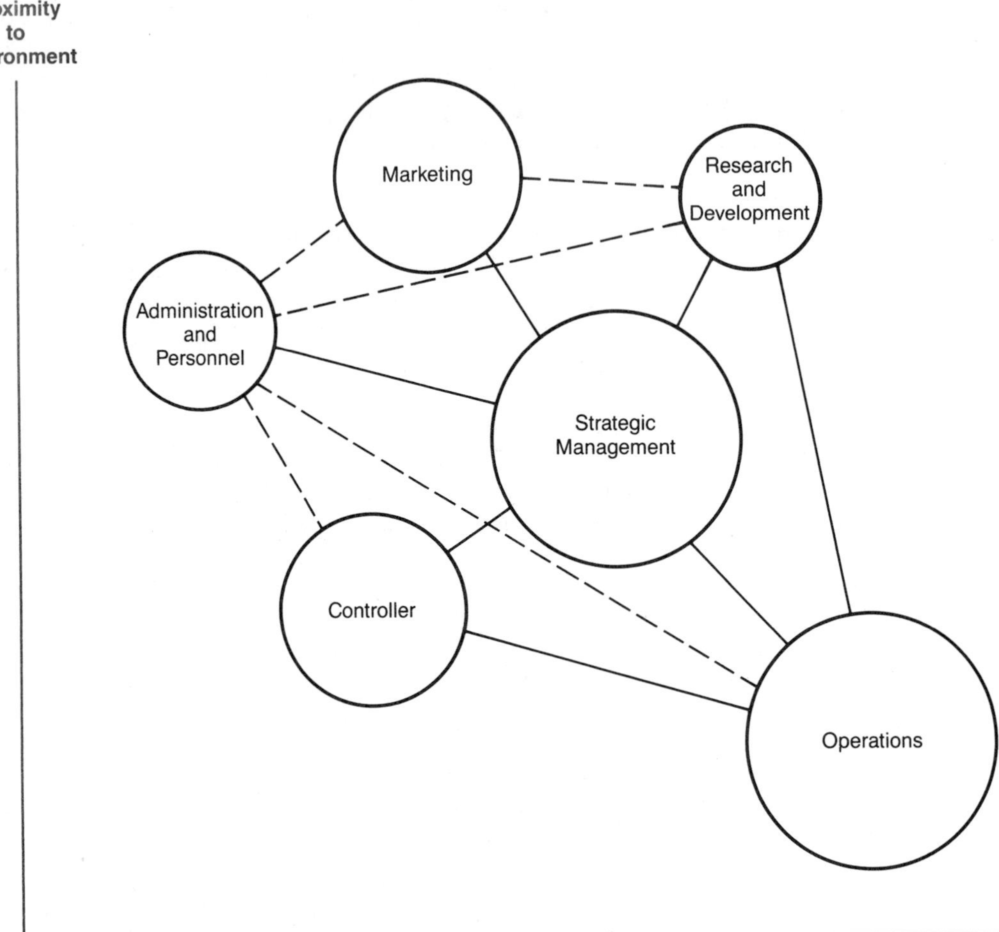

- Proximity to Environment:
  How direct the interactions are between the functional unit and the environment
- Contribution to Profitability:
  The contribution that the unit makes to organizational profitability
- Size of the Circle:
  The strategic importance of the functional unit
- Types of interactions:
  ——— Direct transaction
  — — — Coordination transaction

mean the rites, rituals, ceremonies, symbols and traditions that make an organization unique and rally organizational members toward the accomplishment of organizational goals. For example, traditional status symbols of large offices and expensive office furniture will no longer be meaningful indicators of a person's level of authority and responsibility. The current status symbol of a personal computer on one's desk will cease to be an indication of position, because every employee will have a personal computer. This computer will be linked into an organizational network that will schedule appointments, provide necessary information to perform one's job, transmit the results of analyses to other units, and use expert systems or artificial intelligence programs when needed. In addition, practically every employee will have a computer at home. Status will instead be determined primarily by the importance and the challenge of an individual's job and his or her contribution to the overall success of the organization. As one telecommuter says, "If you do the job well, then it doesn't matter where you work."[43]

Cultural change within an organization will no longer be an unconscious evolutionary process that results from the activities of an incumbent. Rather, it will be recognized as a necessity to accomplish a given objective. The primary cultural tradition that will remain is the acceptance and embracing of change to accommodate variation in the organization's business conditions. Therefore, today's culture of stable symbols, rites, rituals, ceremonies, and traditions will be replaced by a culture of acceptance of change and of organizational flexibility and convertibility.

Future Demands on Strategic Management

Current strategic managers recognize that they must set an initial direction for the firm to pursue. Strategic managers of tomorrow will also set the firm's direction, but the direction and the process used to progress in that direction will substantially change. Strategic managers of the future will be more adaptive, flexible, and responsive, as will the strategic management processes that they use to guide their organizations.

Change in Focus

American firms will change their focus from short to long term. However, their long-term orientation will be in terms of developing organizational processes and systems to remain flexible and responsive. The organization will be lean so that, although threats will bend the organization, it will be able to survive and rejuvenate.

This type of flexibility requires a change in the organization's specific strategic focus. Today's strategically well-managed organizations focus on environmental assessment and organizational capabilities. Environmental opportunities are recognized, organizational capabilities are matched with these opportunities, and the organization exploits the opportunities to be successful.

In contrast, organizations of the future will focus on specifying an environmental niche and organizational reflection. Organizations will become adept at discovering environmental niches and defining those niches clearly enough to easily convert to providing the product or service that can fill that niche. Organizational reflection refers to the continual monitoring of organizational flexibility and responsiveness to verify that the organization is capable of responsive action when a new environmental niche is discovered. This change in focus will be difficult for many managers, because it does not reward the building of empires but rewards astute environmental surveillance and rapid deployment of resources.

Change in the Strategic Management Process

The length of the strategic planning cycle will change. Planning cycles of 5, 10, or 15 years will no longer be feasible, even for the most traditional of industries. Planning cycles will be limited to 1, 2, or 3 years to enable the firm to be flexible enough to recognize, exploit, and abandon a market niche as it appears and dies. The role of the strategic manager also will fundamentally change. The strategic manager will not be the primary individual to select the niches for the organization to pursue. Instead, junior executives trained as specialists will be responsible for recognizing and exploiting niches within their own organizational area. As Michael Porter says, the areas in which organizations can gain a competitive advantage are top management, human resource management, R&D, procurement, inbound logistics, operations, outbound logistics, marketing and sales, and service.[44] Different managers of these organizational areas will select niches in which they have competitive advantages in any of the above stages of the value chain. The future chief executive officer must maintain the overall responsiveness, adaptability, and convertibility of the organization without getting involved in the operational management of the specific areas of the organization.

The stages of the strategic management process also will change. For most organizations, environmental analysis will become the location and specification of environmental niches. Assessment of the organization's capabilities will primarily involve determining its flexibility, adaptability, and convertibility. The choice of the domain in which the organization operates will be a rapid succession of niche selections. The domains will be much smaller and of shorter duration than the domain of firms operating in today's environment. The choice of the mission and strategic goals of the organization will remain essentially as they are today. The strategies available in the next 40 to 50 years will be different. Merger and acquisition will cease to be a primary means of growth for organizations. Acquiring large firms for the purpose of gaining assets only decreases the flexibility and responsiveness of the organization. Therefore, organizations will typically grow internally by taking advantage of the entrepreneurial spirit of the executives entrusted with the various areas of the organization. Rejuvenation strategies will diminish in importance as maintaining the size and integrity of large organizational units ceases to be an indicator of success. Rather, market niches that are no longer viable will simply be abandoned, and the organizational processes will be converted to the product or service for another market niche.

The first signs of a new form of strategy are evident in the world semiconductor industry. When a new semiconductor product is introduced, firms rush to produce large quantities to take advantage of the economies of scale and maintain a competitive price structure for this product. Very shortly new technology introduces a new product that makes its precursor obsolete almost overnight. Again, managers frantically rush to produce these chips and integrate them into computers. This has been repeated for several generations of chips, and experts in the computer industry anticipate that it will continue for several more generations with shorter product life cycles and more custom designed chips. Firms move from niche to niche and totally abandon the previous product as it becomes obsolete, making little attempt to salvage the product by finding alternative uses. This particular mode of strategic management will spread to other industries in the future.

Change in Techniques

Techniques used to provide information to the strategic manager and to assist him or her in making strategic choices will become more sophisticated. As Toffler suggests,

> in a period of rapid change, strategic planning based on straight line trend extrapolation is inherently treacherous. (Trends are either spotted too late, or they reverse themselves, or they convert to something qualitatively new.) This criticism of simple trend projection becomes doubly true if the trends are limited to economic and demographic factors. What is needed for planning is not a set of isolated trends, but multidimensional models that interrelate forces—technological, social, political, even cultural, along with economic.[45]

What this indicates for managers is that today's techniques will soon be obsolete.

The development of techniques such as artificial intelligence and expert systems will gain acceptance and be in common use by the year 2000. Because of the deemphasis of centralized decision making and the emphasis on coordination and flexibility, managers will have to continually reassess their strategic assumptions. A technique developed by Mason and Mitroff to help managers systematically reassess their strategic assumptions, labeled the Strategic Assumption Surfacing Technique (SAST),[46] will gain additional acceptance. Also, strategic control as described in this text will become more prevalent. Control of the premises upon which the effectiveness of a strategy is measured will be an important aspect of tomorrow's management. Management also will more frequently use surveillance control to assess environmental occurrences that can threaten the organization. Finally, to assure that the firm can take advantage of environmental niches when they arise, it will develop techniques to analyze its responsiveness to assess the firm's capability to be flexible, adaptive, and convertible.

Many of the techniques described in this text are based on the changes projected in this section. Other techniques are yet to be developed. However, the strategic manager of today can be assured that new techniques will be necessary to survive the dynamic conditions of tomorrow's business world.

Change in the Result

The outcome of the strategic management process also will be altered in the future. Tomorrow's stockholders, strategic managers, and organizational members will have to be satisfied with lower return on investment and profitability as competition becomes more intense. As markets become more global, organizational constituents will have to lower their expectations for returns from the organization. The results of the organization will in many cases be measured by its contribution to society and to the community as well as by the challenges it provides its employees. The Strategic Application "State-Sponsored Gaming: Dr. Jekyll or Mr. Hyde?" describes how state-sponsored gaming may be a short-term growth business with long-term negative social consequences.

The primary measure of success will be organizational survival. In tomorrow's competitive environment, only the effective adapters will survive. Organizations that fail to adapt and convert to meet the demands of specific environmental niches will cease to exist. This economic contraction will strain the profitability of American firms and result in profits that are more consistent with some Asian and European firms. The leveling out of international and organizational performance will turn the burden of organizational success to the firm's strategic managers rather than the financial markets.

STRATEGIC APPLICATIONS: SOCIAL RESPONSIBILITY

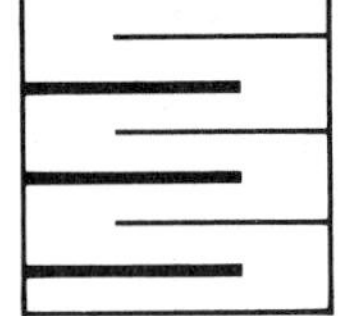

State-Sponsored Gaming: Dr. Jekyll or Mr. Hyde?

State lotteries experienced 229.7 percent growth during a five-year period in the late 1980s. By the beginning of 1989 over $17 billion was being wagered annually in state-sponsored gaming. Gambling fever has helped many economically depressed states cope with budget deficits and an intense antitax movement. States spend vast amounts on market research and advertising to entice citizens to become gamblers. But what are the long-term social consequences of building state budgets on uncertain gambling revenues and creating a nation where luck, not hard work, is the key to financial success?

Many state executives argue that gambling is a harmless form of recreation that may help citizens cope with the frustrations of a complex modern society. Critics feel that legalized gambling gives the wrong message to teenagers. Like Wall Street's obsession with short-term speculation rather than long-term real economic growth, state-sponsored gaming may be telling tomorrow's workers that education, skill, and hard work are not as important as fate and luck.

In the long term, states with lotteries and the firms that support them may be judged not on their profitability but on their social responsibility. The cost of providing state services without a lottery may seem unnecessarily high. However, the cost of rebuilding a work ethic in a society may be staggering.

Source: Chris Welles, "America's Gambling Fever: Everybody Wants a Piece of the Action—But Is It Good for Us?" *Business Week*, April 24, 1989, 112–120.

Forward to the Future

This text has attempted to describe a strategic management process for today's business conditions. In this last chapter, we have been bold enough to project trends for the future in the organization's environment and in its internal operations. Our purpose was to prepare future managers for the demands of tomorrow's strategic management. The picture that we have painted in this chapter may appear to be full of challenges. Indeed, the next 40 to 50 years should be an exciting time for competent managers. The challenges are many and substantial. The next generation of strategic managers will manage their organizations in a more competitive and dynamic business environment and will utilize employees with substantially different expectations. These changes will require that the strategic manager of tomorrow be creative and meet these challenges with new ideas, systems, processes, and techniques.

We have attempted to start you on a course for the future. Two statements seem apparent—the past is certainly no guarantee of the future, and the year 2000 will be more difficult than today for the strategic manager. However, new strategic tools are being developed daily to provide the manager with the skills to meet these challenges. We sincerely hope that this text has provided you with the knowledge and the confidence to use this insight in your future as strategic managers.

Good luck, and forward to the future.

Questions

1. Explain how the material presented in this chapter will help you, as a future strategic manager, in assessing tomorrow's business environment.

2. Discuss two factors highlighted in this chapter that will make capabilities analyses more important for the firm of the future.

3. If government is more participative in the future, how might tomorrow's firm become more proactive toward its political environment?

4. Discuss some of the reasons why organizations in the year 2010 must be smaller and more adaptive.

5. Suppose that you were the CEO of a medium-sized firm that marketed a line of casual sports clothing nationwide. What would you need to do to pursue an internal growth strategy with a strategic goal of a 10 percent growth rate?

Notes

1. Thomas McCarroll and Raji Samghabadi, "A Shock Felt round the World," *Time*, November 2, 1987, 20–36.

2. Aaron Bernstein, "Back to You, Frank," *Business Week*, April 24, 1989, 24–26.

3. Catherine Yong, Douglas Harbrecht, and Howard Gleckman, "The S&L's Last Stand Against Congress," *Business Week*, July 3, 1989: 30–31.

4. Alvin Toffler, *The Adaptive Corporation* (New York: McGraw-Hill, 1985), 1–2.

5. Kenyon Degreene, *The Adaptive Organization: Anticipation and Management of Crisis* (New York: Wiley, 1982), 167–181.

6. Otis Port and John W. Wilson, "Making Brawn Work with Brains," *Business Week*, April 20, 1987, 56–60.

7. Aaron Bernstein, Richard W. Anderson, and Wendy Zellner, "Help Wanted: America Faces an Era of Worker Scarcity That May Last to the Year 2000," *Business Week*, August 10, 1987, 48–54.

8. Karen Elliott House, "The '90s and Beyond: For All Its Difficulties, U.S. Stands to Retain Its Global Leadership," *The Wall Street Journal*, January 23, 1988, A1 and A8.

9. Lois Therrien, "High-Definition TV Is Rallying a Digital Revolution," *Business Week*, January 30, 1989, 64–66.

10. Michael E. Porter, *Competitive Advantage* (New York: The Free Press, 1985), 3.

11. Alvin Toffler, *The Third Wave* (New York: William Morrow, 1980), 243–260.

12. John Naisbitt, *Megatrends: Ten New Directions Transforming Our Lives* (New York: Warner Books, 1982), 11–38.

13. Kimberly A. Crews, *U.S. Population: Charting the Change* (A Population Learning Series Student Chartbook) (Washington, D.C.: Population Reference Bureau, 1988), 3.

14. David Snyder, "Future Forces and the Future of Human Services" (Presentation to the Texas Department of Human Services, December 13, 1985).

15. Stephen Koepp, "Taking on the World," *Time*, October 19, 1987, 46–47.

16. Ibid.

17. Tom Peters, "Localized Marketing: An Emerging Trend," *Denver Post*, October 16, 1987.

18. Eloise Salholf, Ann McDaniels, and Sue Hutchinson, "Pro-Choice: 'A Sleeping Giant' Awakes," *Newsweek*, April 24, 1989, 39, 40.

19. John M. Barry, "Is Wright Getting a Fair Shake," *The Washington Post*, April 30, 1989, C5.

20. Naisbitt, *Megatrends*, 159–188.

21. Ibid., 164–175.

22. Emily T. Smith and Jo Ellen Davis, "Our Life Has Changed: The Lightbulb, the Transistor, Now the Superconductor Revolution," *Business Week*, April 6, 1987, 94–99.

23. "This Steel-Collar Seamstress Has a Velvet Touch," *Business Week*, April 3, 1989, 110.

24. William D. Marbach and Richard Brandt, "Taming Space and Time to Make Tomorrow's Chips," *Business Week*, March 13, 1989, 68–70.

25. Otis Port, "Custom Chips for Sale, No Job Too Small," *Business Week*, March 6, 1989, 99–102.

26. George Heilmeier, "Silver Bullet Opportunities," *Computers and People*, September–October 1986: 17–27.

27. Naisbitt, *Megatrends*, 39–53.

28. Aaron Bernstein, "Needed: Human Capital," *Business Week* (Special Report), September 19, 1988, 100–108.

29. Ralph E. Winter, "Delayed Future: Upgrading of Factories Replaces the Concept of Total Automation," *The Wall Street Journal*, November 30, 1987, 1, 8.

30. Gregory Stricharchuk and Rick Wartzman, "Business Bulletin: Factory of the Future," *The Wall Street Journal*, September 1, 1988, 11.

31. Richard Brandt, "Steve Jobs Gets the Keys to the Office PC Market," *Business Week*, April 10, 1989, 80, 81.

32. Elizabeth Ehrlich and Susan B. Garland, "For American Business, A New World of Workers," *Business Week*, September 19, 1988, 112–114.

33. Elizabeth Ehrlich, "The Mommy Track," *Business Week*, March 20, 1989, 126–134.

34. Michael Goldfarb, "U.S. in Future May Need Immigrants to Boost Work Force," *The Washington Post*, August 17, 1982, B3.

35. Elizabeth Ehrlich and Susan B. Garland, "For American Business, A New World of Workers," 112–114.

36. Alan L. Otten, "Workers Shouldn't Fear the Arrival of Immigrants," *The Wall Street Journal*, February 13, 1989, B1.

37. Andrew Pollack, "Electronic Trend: Do the Work at Home," *The New York Times*, March 12, 1981, A1, D6.

38. John Schwartz, Dory Tstantfir, and Karen Springen, "Escape from the Office: High-Tech Tools Spur a Work-At-Home Revolt," *Newsweek*, April 24, 1989, 58–60.

39. William H. Jones, "$30 Billion a Year Goes for Consulting," *The Washington Post*, June 6, 1979, D1.

40. Otis Port, "Making Brawn Work with Brains," 56–60.

41. "The Shrinking of Middle Management," *Business Week*, April 25, 1983, 54–61.

42. John A. Byrne, Wendy Zellner, and Scott Ticer, "Caught in the Middle: Six Managers Speak Out on Corporate Life," *Business Week*, September 12, 1988, 80–88.

43. John Schwartz, Dory Tstantfir, and Karen Springen, "Escape from the Office," 58–60.

44. Porter, *Competitive Advantage*, 36–53.

45. Toffler, *The Adaptive Corporation*, 19.

46. Richard O. Mason and I. I. Mitroff, *Challenging Strategic Planning Assumptions: Theory, Cases and Techniques* (New York: Wiley, 1981), 35–57.

Case for Discussion

Executive Profile in Year 2010

Experts agree that future CEOs must be more globally oriented and computer literate than their 1990 counterparts. Ed Dunn, Whirlpool corporate vice president, has suggested that the next century's senior executive must have "multienvironment, multicountry, multifunctional, maybe even multicompany, multiindustry experience."

Dow Chemical's chairman, Paul Orrefice, has set up a worldwide panel of senior executives to try to determine the skills and knowledge necessary to lead Dow into the 21st century. Preliminary indications are that tomorrow's business leader will:

- Have experience in several business disciplines
- Have exposure to more than one industry
- Have a global orientation and experience running foreign operations
- Be comfortable exchanging information electronically
- Have an ability to think and act quickly in response to rapidly changing business conditions
- Have a more collegial working style that allows for sharing of the responsibility for setting the firm's strategic direction
- Be able to work more skillfully with government agencies and regulators

---

Source: Amanda Bennett, "Going Global: The Chief Executives in Year 2000 Will Be Experienced Abroad," *The Wall Street Journal*, February 27, 1989, A1.

The problem becomes where to find someone with all of these qualifications and how to prepare him or her for the top job. Today's managers must generate answers to these questions.

Discussion Questions

1. Given the demographic information provided in Chapter 12, how would you locate tomorrow's CEO?

2. Compare the qualifications of tomorrow's senior executive as outlined in this case with the type of challenges that firms must provide to future employees. Is there a match? If so, why? If not, why not?

3. Develop a personal career strategy for acquiring the skills you would need as a CEO in the year 2015.

Appendix A

Strategic Case Analysis

Both the format and the focus of the case analysis presented here stress strategic-level analysis. The approach is applicable to historical cases such as those in this text as well as real-world strategic situations. The format is not the only one acceptable for student case analyses; in fact, most instructors have a preferred case analysis format.

For this presentation, we have selected the short case on Holiday Inns Inc. reproduced at the end of the appendix. Any case provides only limited information, and some interpretation and interpolation are required. However, here we have attempted to limit our analyses to the facts of the case. This limits, to some degree, the richness of the analysis. Before proceeding with the analysis, please turn to page 421 and read the Holiday Inns case.

Introduction

Set the stage by describing relevant characteristics of the case; for example, industry, main thrust of the case, products(s), your assumptions, and so on.

- Describe the firm's position on the product or firm life cycle.
- Describe the strategy level the case is focused on.
- Discuss the firm's competitive portfolio (business or product-markets).

Case Analysis Holiday Inns Inc. (HI) is the world's largest hospitality company. Its primary thrust is lodging with interests in hotels, casino gaming, and restaurants. The case is written on HI as it existed in 1984. It focuses on HI's attempts to segment the lodging market into upscale business traveler hotels, budget hotels, standard Holiday Inn hotels, and gaming hotels.

The lodging industry appears to be in the mature stage of its life cycle. HI's attempts to segment the market are aimed at increasing the company's market share. Because the case concentrates on the lodging part of HI's business and mentions little of the gaming operation, the case is focused on the business level of strategy development.

Although it is difficult to determine from the case, Crowne Plaza, Embassy Suite, and Hampton Inn hotels appear to be question marks using the BCG portfolio analysis. Gaming seems to be the star of HI's current businesses. Exhibit A.1 on p. 422 shows that gaming is the only business to realize an increase in revenues in 1982. The traditional Holiday Inn hotels are probably cash cows.

Environmental Assessment and Capabilities Analysis

Conduct a SWOT (strengths, weaknesses, opportunities, threats) analysis. Strengths are the positive internal capabilities of the organization that give it a strategic advantage in achieving its objectives. Weaknesses are the internal liabilities or limitations that the organization currently possesses that prevent it from effectively achieving its objectives. Opportunities are usually external factors that an organization can exploit to give it a strategic competitive advantage. Threats are external factors that have the potential of adversely affecting the organization's effectiveness and/or survival. The SWOT analysis helps locate problems associated with exploiting opportunities, protecting against threats, building on strengths, and correcting weaknesses.

Case Analysis A SWOT analysis for Holiday Inns might consist of the following:

Internal Strengths: market leadership, broad product line, industry's largest reservation system, strong financial position, excellent reputation and name recognition, and properties in the prime gaming locations.

Internal Weaknesses: low operating margins due to competitive pricing strategy, expensive remodeling and construction campaign underway, decreasing operating income in all business segments except gaming, and concentration in hospitality industry.

External Opportunities: Greater segmentation in the lodging industry, increase in business travel, growth in gaming market, and foreign markets.

External Threats: clouded economic picture, mature product-market, increased competition in all market segments, massive federal budget deficits, and possibility of a collapse of hospitality market due to world recession caused by business downturn.

Strategic Problem Definition

Clearly state your view of what the primary strategic problem is and label it as such. Next, briefly discuss the causes and effects of the strategic problem as stated in the case.

Case Analysis An interpretation of the strategic problem might be: "How can HI reduce its vulnerability to a decline in the hospitality market?" This vulnerability was caused by the reversal of HI's previous diversification strategy, which culminated with the divestment of Delta Steamships. Strategic management's strategic choice to concentrate in the hospitality business created a situation in which the effect of an economic downturn that curtails business travel will be a rapid decline in HI's profits.

Generation of Strategic Alternatives

List at least three alternative solutions to the problem you have stated. We assume that you have reviewed many alternatives and the three that you present are the three best.

Case Analysis Three possible alternatives that would reduce HI's vulnerability to a downturn in the hospitality business are the following:

- Return to a diversification master strategy involving acquisition of new but related product lines for new and existing customers that would be countercyclical to the hospitality business.
- Develop a cost leadership strategy that reduces HI costs to the point that a decline in occupancy to recession levels will continue to generate profits.
- Develop a conglomerate diversification master strategy that provides a mix of businesses that will generate a profit even in the event of a hospitality market collapse.

Evaluation of Alternatives

Include the following three subsections in this section:

- Evaluation criteria: You should use the same criteria to evaluate each alternative (you want to compare apples to apples).
- Evaluation method: You may use a quantitative technique (e.g., payoff matrix) if you wish. However, a well-developed pros versus cons analysis can also be used. Remember to use the same criteria to determine whether each alternative is a pro or a con.
- Presentation and discussion of results: Here you should present a table that summarizes the results of your alternative analysis. For example, you might use a pros versus cons analysis for which the table would consist of the alternatives on the horizontal axis and the criteria on the vertical axis. The cells would contain the word *pro* or *con*. Next, develop a method to compile these data and discuss the rationale for the results.

Case Analysis The criteria that one would use to evaluate the alternatives depend, to a large extent, on the information in the case. For our illustration here, we will use these criteria:

- Efficacy: Does the alternative solve the strategic problem over the long term?
- Cost: Does HI have the financial resources to implement this alternative?
- Acceptability: Is this alternative acceptable to HI management or will it be resisted if chosen?
- Efficiency: How should HI's stated criteria be weighted?
- Consequences: What are the chances that negative consequences will evolve from the choice and implementation of this alternative?

Analyses Method One way to evaluate alternatives is to use a payoff matrix. This would be set up as shown in Matrix A.1.The numerical evaluation indicates that the second alternative is the strategy that will be most appropriate to recommend to HI for the situation described in the case. The presentation of the table with a complete explanation of the scale used and how the scores were determined will give a clear illustration of the evaluation procedure used.

Recommendations

Present your recommendations to solve the strategic problem and discuss how they will address/alleviate the effects of the strategic problem. The discussion should include the impact of your recommendations on the firm's actions, structure, process, and performance.

Case Analysis Here we would recommend that HI management adopt a cost leadership strategy that reduces costs to a point that will maintain profitability during a downturn in the hospitality market. This strategy has only a moderate ability to solve the problem (3 on a scale of 5) because it depends on an accurate prediction of the bottom of the market slide. If the hospitality business falls below projections, HI has no contingency to draw upon. However, this alternative is well within HI's financial capabilities and will be readily embraced by management. Finally, it is associated

Matrix A.1 Payoff Matrix

	Criteria			
Alternative	**Efficacy (3)**	**Cost (1)**	**Acceptability (2)**	**Calculation**
Horizontal or Concentric Diversification Master Strategy (0.6)	5	4	3	(3 × 5) + (1 × 4) + (2 × 3) = 25 (25 × 0.6) = 15
Cost Leadership Strategy (0.8)	3	5	5	(3 × 3) + (1 × 5) + (2 × 5) = 24 (24 × 0.8) = 19.2
Conglomerate Diversification Master Strategy (0.3)	5	4	2	(3 × 5) + (1 × 4) + (2 × 2) = 23 (23 × 0.3) = 6.9

Efficacy, cost, and acceptability are evaluated on a numerical scale: 1 = "no" answer to the question asked in the criterion; 2 = "probable no" answer to the question asked in the criterion; 3 = neither "no" nor "yes" to the question asked in the criterion; 4 = "probable yes" to the question asked in the criterion; 5 = "yes" answer to the question asked in the criterion.
Efficiency is indicated by the numerical weight in parentheses (3–1) under the criterion. These weights were determined by subjective analysis of the case.
Consequences are indicated by the probabilities shown in parentheses under each alternative. They are determined by calculating $(1 - p)$, where p is the subjective probability that negative consequences will be associated with the alternative.

with only a slight probability of negative consequences from employees or the marketplace.

The discussion of the impact of the recommendations on the firm's actions, structure, process, and performance is an opportunity for the case analyst to integrate material from previous business courses and apply that knowledge to this aspect of the analysis. It should be thoughtful speculation regarding the impact of a recommendation on the critical dimensions of the organization's operations and performance.

Suggestions for Implementation

Present ways in which the recommendations can be implemented in the organization. For example, what should key managers do now, six months from now, and so on? How can the chief executive know the plan is working?

This is a general outline of how the organization might go about implementing the recommendations. This section encourages the case analyst to deal with the practical realities of introducing change into an organization. For example, cost leadership strategy, if implemented by HI, might precipitate some employee layoffs and changes in cost reporting procedures. These changes can be difficult for managers to implement.

Holiday Inns Inc. (1984)*

Holiday Inns Inc. (HI), headquartered in Memphis, Tennessee, is the world's largest hospitality company, with interests in hotels, casino gaming, and restaurants, having sold its Delta Steamships subsidiary in 1982. For the first half of 1983, 64.6 percent of operating income came from hotels, 32.9 percent from gaming, and 1 percent from restaurants. First-half net income and sales were at respective annual rates of $123 million and $1.5 billion. More detailed financial information is provided in Exhibits A.1 and A.2.

The Holiday Inn hotel system includes 1,744 hotels with 312,302 rooms in 53 countries on five continents and produces an estimated $4 billion in annual revenues. Licensed, or franchised, hotels account for 86 percent of total Holiday Inn hotels, 81 percent of total rooms, and 6 percent of HI sales. Franchisees pay $300 a room initially plus a royalty of 4 percent of gross room revenues and a fee for marketing and reservation services of 2 percent of gross room revenues. The company's reservation system is the largest in the hotel industry.

In 1982, less than 3 percent of Holiday Inn customers dropped in without room reservations, down from 95 percent in the 1950s. In 1981, the company started to deemphasize highway locations. Virtually all new Holiday Inn hotels are placed near airports, industrial parks, and similar sites.

---

*(This case was prepared by Arthur Sharplin, McNeese State University, Lake Charles, LA. Connie Shum provided research assistance. Reprinted with permission. The case portrays neither the effective nor the ineffective handling of an administrative situation. Rather, it is to be used as the basis for classroom discussion.)

Exhibit A.1 Holiday Inns Inc. and Consolidated Subsidiaries Statements of Income (in thousands, except per share)

	Three Quarters Ended		Fiscal Year Ended	
	September 30, 1983	October 1, 1982	December 31, 1982	January 1, 1982 (Restated)
Revenues				
Hotel	$ 667,644	$ 651,740	$ 840,698	$ 853,645
Gaming	449,239	360,608	472,792	388,148
Restaurant	71,016	70,865	100,584	96,366
Other	4,183	7,624	11,224	13,616
Total revenues	1,192,082	1,090,837	1,425,298	1,351,775
Operating income				
Hotel	143,552	132,280	150,205	170,944
Gaming	98,576	63,647	74,595	56,291
Restaurant	3,486	2,714	5,029	6,547
Other	2,741	3,424	4,999	10,826
Total operating income	248,355	202,065	234,828	244,608
Corporate expense	(22,058)	(17,860)	(24,487)	(25,736)
Interest, net of interest capitalized	(31,725)	(38,738)	(50,965)	(65,540)
Foreign currency translation gain (loss)	—	—	—	1,889
Income from continuing operations before income taxes	194,572	145,467	159,376	155,221
Provision for income taxes	85,612	58,187	62,157	56,515
Income from continuing operations	108,960	87,280	97,219	98,706
Discontinued operations				
Income from operations, net of income taxes	—	(22,100)	4,671	38,652
Loss on disposition, plus income taxes Payable of $5,505	—	—	(25,910)	—
Net income	$ 108,960	$ 65,180	$ 75,980	$ 137,358
Income (loss) per common and common equivalent share				
Continuing operations	$ 2.86	$ 2.23	$ 2.50	$ 2.68
Discontinued operations	—	(.58)	(.56)	.98
Total income (loss)	$ 2.86	$ 1.65	$ 1.94	$ 3.66
Average common and common equivalent shares outstanding	38,055	38,305	38,216	39,449

Exhibit A.2 Holiday Inns Inc. and Consolidated Subsidiaries Balance Sheets (in thousands, except share amounts)

	December 31, 1982	January 1, 1982 (Restated)
Assets		
Current assets		
Cash	$ 49,945	$ 39,655
Temporary cash investments, at cost	32,544	20,181
Receivables, including notes receivable of $12,618 and $31,927, less allowance for doubtful accounts of $18,925 and $15,080	73,008	91,782
Supplies, at lower of average cost or market	21,871	23,424
Deferred income tax benefits	13,510	11,190
Prepayments and other current assets	18,101	9,775
Total current assets	208,979	196,007
Investments in unconsolidated affiliates, at equity	108,480	46,535
Notes receivable due after one year and other investments	44,186	49,214
Property and equipment, at cost		
Land, buildings, improvements, and equipment	1,635,310	1,496,491
Accumulated depreciation and amortization	(367,434)	(313,947)
Subtotal	1,267,876	1,182,544
Excess of cost over net assets of business acquired, amortized evenly over 40 years	54,314	55,787
Deferred charges and other assets	24,172	31,275
Net assets of discontinued operations	—	111,297
Total assets	1,708,007	1,672,659
Liabilities and shareholders' equity		
Current liabilities		
Accounts payable	77,867	66,375
Long-term debt due within one year	31,267	30,478
Accrued expenses	123,283	133,256
Total current liabilities	232,417	230,109
Long-term debt due after one year	436,356	581,465
Deferred credits and other long-term liabilities	33,938	34,851
Deferred income taxes	62,334	53,857
Shareholders' equity		
Capital stock		
Special stock, authorized—5,000,000 shares; series A—$1.125 par value; issued—491,541 and 576,410 shares; convertible into 1.5 shares of common stock	553	648
Common stock, $1.50 par value; authorized—60,000,000 shares; issued—40,218,350 and 32,909,606 shares	60,327	49,364
Capital surplus	294,517	161,188
Retained earnings	671,609	626,310
Cumulative foreign currency transaction adjustments	(3,804)	—
Capital stock in treasury, at cost; 3,036,081 and 2,439,500 common shares and 72,192 series A shares	(78,660)	(63,170)
Restricted stock	(1,580)	(1,963)
Total shareholders' equity	942,962	772,377
Total liabilities and shareholders' equity	$1,708,007	$1,672,659

Business travelers account for about 60 percent of Holiday Inn room nights occupied. The company is launching two new hotel chains aimed at the upscale business traveler. The first, Crowne Plaza hotels, offers fine dining, complimentary morning newspapers, continental breakfasts, 24-hour maid service, bellmen, and free HBO movies. Rates are $15 to $20 higher than the average rate of $44 at existing company-owned Holiday Inns. Crowne Plaza hotels are now located in Rockville (Maryland), San Francisco, Miami, and Dallas. Four more will open in Stanford (Connecticut), Houston, and New Orleans by year-end. The second new chain, Embassy Suite hotels, is targeted primarily at the business traveler near the upper end of the lodging market who stays three or four days instead of the usual two, and will pay for specialized service. Each suite will offer a separate living room with a wet bar and the option of one or two bedrooms. The company plans to have six all-suite hotels in varying stages of development in 1984.

In December 1983, the company announced plans to develop a new budget hotel chain, called Hampton Inn hotels, to include 300 company-owned and franchised units within five years. The first will open in Memphis, Tennessee, in 1984. Room rates at these hotels will average about $30. They will feature rooms for smokers and nonsmokers, free television and movies, local telephone calls, continental breakfasts, and arrangements for children under 18 to stay free with their parents.

The Holiday Inn hotel group spent $60.1 million in 1982 to upgrade and renovate company-owned hotels. Old franchises were eliminated at the rate of about one a week, as minimum operating standards were raised. So drastic was the pruning that, even with 569 new hotels in the past eight years, there has been a net gain of only 45 in the number of Holiday Inns. At the end of 1982, there were 48 Holiday Inn hotels under construction worldwide. The Holiday Inn sign is being replaced with a new rectangular one bearing the chain's name topped with an orange and yellow starburst on a green background.

In March 1983, Roy E. Winegardner, chairman, and Michael D. Rose, president and chief executive officer, briefed stockholders on Holiday Inn's preparations for the future. Some excerpts from their comments follow:

"With the disposition of our steamship subsidiary, Holiday Inns Inc. is now strategically focused on the hospitality industry. We also introduced a new sign and logo for our Holiday Inn hotel system, better reflecting the range of property types and level of product quality that will characterize the Holiday Inn hotel system in the decades ahead. Recognizing the increasing segmentation of the lodging market, we also began construction on two new hotel products. We also embarked on an aggressive expansion plan for our core Holiday Inn hotel brand. This represents the most aggressive company hotel development effort in recent years, and reflects our continuing belief in the long-term strength of the lodging market and of our Holiday Inn brand within the large moderate-priced segment of that market.

"Our company has prospered with the growth of Atlantic City, as our Harrah's Marina facility there has proven to be the most profitable hotel/casino in that market on a pretax, preinterest basis. We entered into a joint venture to build a new 600-room hotel and 60,000-square-foot casino on the Boardwalk. We believe this should contribute to Harrah's ability to achieve the same brand leadership position in Atlantic City that it now enjoys in Northern Nevada.

"As a result of [a competitive] pricing strategy, operating margins suffered in our hotel business. However, this approach enabled us to maintain occupancy levels despite the fact that occupancies declined throughout the rest of the hotel industry. At Perkins Restaurants Inc., our restaurant subsidiary, this pricing strategy paid off, contributing to substantially higher customer count and improved unit profitability. We also made the decision to dispose of a number of restaurants and hotels which were not performing to our financial standards.

"In addition to strengthening our market position, we also strengthened our balance sheet. The company's 9⅝-percent convertible subordinated debentures were called for redemption on March 2, 1982. The result was conversion to $143 million of additional equity, which provides the basis for significant new debt capacity to fund our future expansion. Consistent with our stated intention to reduce floating rate debt, we issued $75 million in fixed-rate, 10-year notes in August. In 1982 we commissioned an update of an independent study of the appreciated value of the company's tangible assets and certain contract rights. This study indicated that the net market value of these assets approximated $2.5 billion. [This] appraisal reflects the value of the company's franchise and management contract income streams as well as the appreciation of our real estate assets. [We have] also made substantial progress in improving the productivity of our most important resource, our people. We undertook a thorough review of staffing levels and programs to assure that we were bringing sufficient resources to bear on those things that matter the most, and not expending time or money on those efforts that yield more limited returns. As a result, we have eliminated significant overhead costs and focused our attention more clearly on those things that are most critical to our success in the future. We deliberately increased our expenditures on training and development. We believe that in our businesses, people represent the greatest opportunity for competitive advantage.

"As we look ahead, the economic picture remains clouded. We cannot accurately predict the impact of the unprecedented massive federal budget deficits on our economy. We remain confident in our ability to manage our businesses effectively under both good and difficult economic conditions."

Appendix B

Financial Statement Analysis

The Purpose of Financial Analysis

The primary purpose of financial analysis is to help in evaluating management performance by appraising financial condition, efficiency, profitability, and risk. Each analyst may have a different point of view in conducting the appraisal. For example, possible creditors may be concerned with the company's liquidity or ability to cover interest payments as they try to decide whether to extend credit to the firm. Investors want to know whether the firm represents a good investment. The executive wants to know how the firm looks to outsiders like banks, investors, and bondholders, but also needs to know how well it is doing compared to competitors and to past performance. Most of these analysts are concerned with projecting how well the firm will perform in the future, and for this purpose they use financial statement analysis.

The financial statements most frequently used to provide information for analysis are the balance sheet, the income statement, and the sources and uses of funds statement. They indicate the state of the firm at a particular time, such as the end of the year or quarter (balance sheet), or for a particular period of time, such as one quarter or one year (income statement and uses and sources of funds statement). The balance sheet indicates the assets controlled by the company and how the company financed their acquisition. A balance sheet for the Cascade Corporation is shown in Exhibit B.1. The income statement indicates sales generated, the expenses incurred in generating the sales, and the earnings obtained from the sales over a period of time. Exhibit B.2 is an income statement for Cascade Corporation. These two statements will be the primary sources of information used in the analysis performed later in the appendix. The sources and uses of funds statement employs information from both the balance sheet and the income statement to provide a summary of where funds were obtained and where the company used its funds. Exhibit B.3 is the source and use of funds statement for Cascade Corporation.

The data on which financial statement analysis is performed is historical. The basic assumption is that past performance is a reliable predictor of how management will perform in the future. The assumption may be reasonably sound for well-entrenched firms with good management teams in fairly stable environments. In other cases, the assumption could easily mislead an analyst. In a rapidly changing industry past performance may not be a good predictor of the future. For example, Microsoft, a software company, produces MS-DOS, the operating system used in many personal computers. This operating system accounts for over 50 percent of Microsoft's revenues. The company has been highly dependent on its relationship with IBM and is now developing an OS/2 operating system for IBM's new personal computers. If Microsoft

Exhibit B.1 Balance Sheet for Cascade Corporation, 1983–1987 (in $000)

	1987	1986	1985	1984	1983
Assets					
Cash	$ 776	$ 205	$ 8,394	$ 7,733	$ 2,438
Marketable Securities	10,100	8,600	NA	NA	NA
Receivables	16,945	13,784	12,411	11,096	893
Inventories	20,246	19,452	16,890	17,110	19,497
Raw Materials	3,421	3,512	3,122	2,045	3,742
Work in Progress	3,578	3,968	3,452	3,497	3,255
Finished Goods	13,247	11,972	10,316	10,568	12,500
Notes Receivable	NA	NA	NA	NA	NA
Other Current Assets	726	522	571	464	356
Total Current Assets	48,793	42,563	38,266	36,403	32,984
Property, Plant, and Equipment	29,465	49,897	42,439	22,211	24,829
Accumulated Depreciation	NA	23,250	20,426	NA	NA
Net Property and Equipment	29,465	26,647	22,013	22,211	24,829
Investment and Advances to Subsidiaries	NA	NA	NA	NA	NA
Other Non-Current Assets	NA	NA	NA	NA	NA
Deferred Charges	NA	NA	NA	NA	NA
Intangibles	NA	NA	NA	NA	NA
Deposits and Other Assets	350	614	400	565	404
Total Assets	$78,608	$69,824	$60,679	$59,179	$58,217
Liabilities					
Notes Payable	$ 5,249	$ 3,123	$ 2,269	$ 2,931	$ 4,101
Accounts Payable	6,305	6,645	5,050	4,773	2,685
Current Long-Term Debt	1,154	2,602	1,891	3,298	1,331
Current Portion Capital Leases	NA	NA	NA	NA	NA
Accrued Expenses	5,725	5,205	5,184	4,977	2,736
Income Taxes	1,183	946	1,262	908	769
Other Current Liabilities	NA	NA	NA	NA	NA
Total Current Liabilities	19,616	18,521	15,656	16,887	13,016
Mortgages	NA	NA	NA	NA	NA
Deferred Charges/Income	4,169	3,599	2,613	2,553	2,273
Convertible Debt	NA	NA	NA	NA	NA
Long-Term Debt	7,501	6,587	7,333	7,138	10,388
Non-Current Capital Leases	NA	NA	NA	NA	NA
Other Long-Term Liabilities	NA	NA	NA	NA	NA
Total Liabilities	31,286	28,707	25,602	26,578	25,677
Minority Interest (Liabilities)	NA	NA	NA	NA	NA
Preferred Stock	NA	NA	NA	NA	NA
Common Stock Net	1,549	387	387	387	387
Capital Surplus	2,045	2,045	2,045	2,045	2,045
Retained Earnings	46,454	43,772	39,575	35,734	34,506
Treasury Stock	686	686	686	1,220	1,220
Other Liabilities	−2,040	−4,401	−6,244	−4,345	−3,178
Shareholder Equity	47,322	41,117	35,077	32,601	32,540
Total Liabilities and Net Worth	$78,608	$69,824	$60,679	$59,179	$58,217

Source: Cascade Corporation 10K reports, 1983–1987.

Exhibit B.2 Income Statement for Cascade Corporation, 1983–1987 (in $000)

	1987	1986	1985	1984	1983
Net Sales	$98,682	$86,664	$84,090	$67,708	$63,045
Cost of Goods	63,840	56,222	55,003	45,391	44,330
Gross Profit	34,842	30,442	29,087	22,317	18,715
R&D Expenditures	NA	NA	NA	NA	NA
Selling, General, and Administrative Expense	19,748	16,738	15,609	13,980	14,914
Income before Depreciation and Amortization	15,094	13,704	13,478	8,337	3,801
Depreciation and Amortization	4,619	3,854	3,701	4,006	4,037
Nonoperating Income	−253	−164	−347	−160	−396
Interest Expense	482	353	263	812	1,168
Income before Taxes	9,740	9,323	9,167	3,359	−1,800
Provision for Income Tax	4,095	3,700	3,900	1,455	−1,620
Minority Interest (Income)	NA	NA	NA	NA	NA
Investment Gains/Losses	NA	NA	NA	NA	NA
Other Income	NA	NA	NA	NA	NA
Net Income before Expense Items	5,645	5,623	5,267	1,904	−180
Expense Items and Discount Operations	NA	NA	NA	NA	NA
Net Income	$ 5,645	$ 5,623	$ 5,267	$ 1,904	$ −180
Outstanding Shares[a] (000)	3,002	751	751	774	713
Earnings per Share	1.88	7.49	7.01	2.46	−.25

[a]Three-share dividend declared May 1986.
Source: Cascade Corporation 10K reports, 1983–1987.

failed to land the contract for the new OS/2 operating system or if the system did not perform well, the company's future performance would decline rapidly.

The projection of future performance from historical financial statements can be a valuable tool in evaluating a firm's situation. It can point out potential problems for the firm and suggest additional analysis to be performed. The analyst with good judgment who corroborates the data with additional information can learn much about the firm, gaining clues as to how it is managed and how performance can be improved. A mechanical analysis will not provide this insight. Data must be analyzed in the context of the company's situation, the nature of the industry, and the economic conditions the company faces. Several ratios may be needed to understand the results of one. For example, return on investment can be arrived at as follows:

$$\text{ROI} = \text{Turnover} \times \text{Operating Profit as a Percent of Sales}$$

By probing deeper we can see:

$$\text{Turnover} = \frac{\text{Sales}}{\text{Total Investment}}$$

Exhibit B.3 Sources and Uses of Funds for Cascade Corporation, 1985–1987 (in $000)

	1987	1986	1985
Annual Sources			
Income/Loss before Expense Items	$ 5,645	$ 5,623	$ 5,267
Depreciation and Depletion	4,619	3,864	3,701
Deferred Income Taxes	506	848	199
Minority Interest—Subsidiaries	NA	NA	NA
Other Funds from Operations	NA	NA	NA
Total Funds—Operations	10,770	10,335	9,167
Funds Used for Extraordinary Item	NA	NA	NA
Sale of Property, Plant and Equipment	NA	NA	NA
Issue Long-Term Debt	107	NA	1,049
Sale of Stock	NA	NA	NA
Other Sources of Funds	922	900	165
Total Sources of Funds	$11,969	$11,235	$10,381
Annual Uses			
Dividends	$ 1,801	$ 1,426	$ 1,426
Capital Expenditures	5,197	6,521	4,435
Increase in Investment	NA	NA	NA
Decrease Long-Term Debt	NA	1,642	622
Purchase of Stock	NA	214	NA
Acquisitions	NA	NA	NA
Other Uses of Funds	264	NA	804
Total Uses of Funds	$ 6,734	$ 9,803	$ 7,287
Increase/Decrease in Working Capital	$ 5,135	$ 1,432	$ 3,094

Source: Cascade Corporation 10K reports, 1985–1987.

and

$$\text{Operating Profit as a Percent of Sales} = \frac{\text{Operating Profit}}{\text{Sales}}$$

Breaking out the components of ROI allows us to understand which components contributed to the ratio and trace the causes of good or poor performance. Each of these components can also be broken down until we can see which component is responsible for changes in the ratio.

As another example, return on equity is an important measure of the rate of return on common stockholders' investment. Normally it can be arrived at, provided there is no preferred stock, using this formula:

$$\text{ROE} = \frac{\text{Net Income}}{\text{Equity}}$$

It can also be seen as deriving from three other ratios:

$$\text{Total Asset Turnover} = \frac{\text{Sales}}{\text{Total Assets}}$$

$$\text{Financial Leverage} = \frac{\text{Total Assets}}{\text{Equity}}$$

$$\text{Net Profit Margin} = \frac{\text{Income}}{\text{Sales}}$$

Now the same ROE can be found as follows:

$$\text{ROE} = \frac{\text{Sales}}{\text{Total Assets}} \times \frac{\text{Total Assets}}{\text{Equity}} \times \frac{\text{Income}}{\text{Sales}}$$

The first formula suggests that, to increase ROE, management must increase net income and/or decrease equity. The second formula suggests that management could improve ROE through increasing asset turnover, by using its assets more efficiently, by increasing financial leverage, by changing the capital structure, or by improving the profit margin.

Using Ratios

Ratios are used in most financial analysis for strategic decision making. They allow the analyst to put the results in context and make comparisons. For example, knowing a company earned \$50,000 in net income last year means very little in itself. The net income figure could reflect a good or bad performance depending on such considerations as the amount of sales required to produce it, the total equity invested, the amount of debt employed, the industry, performance of the company's major competitors, and the state of the economy. The use of a ratio also allows comparison of numbers of quite different sizes. A \$50,000 net income of one company, for example, may represent a much better performance than \$100,000 net income of another company because the second company has three times the asset base of the first. The use of ratios helps the analyst make meaningful interpretations of how management has obtained and used the resources of the company.

The ratios obtained must be put into perspective if they are to be meaningful. The results will vary with time, industry, and economic conditions. A firm with a profit margin that does not change during an economic expansion may be showing signs of weakness while the same profit margin may indicate strength if obtained during an economic contraction. Most firms are affected by business cycles, although some are more severely affected than others. Learning how a firm performs through a business cycle can lead to better predictions of future performance.

Perhaps the most common comparisons sought by an analyst are the company's figures relative to its industry. Firms in the same industry are most frequently the company's competitors and face similar conditions, especially when there is a rela-

Exhibit B.4 Sample Trend Analysis of Financial Ratios

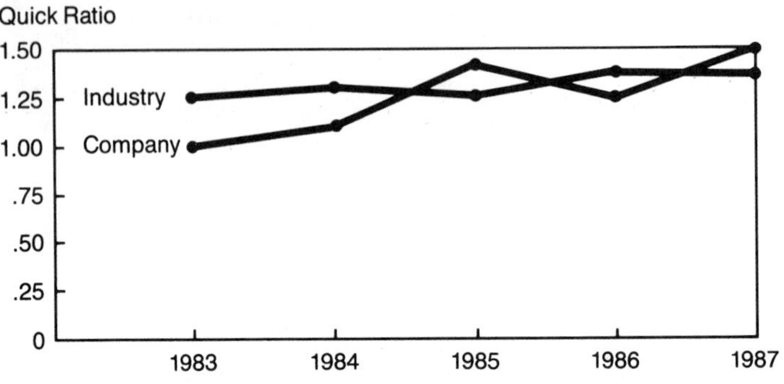

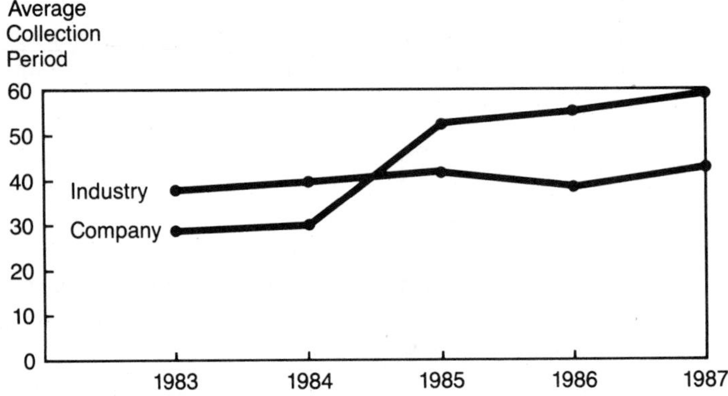

tively homogenous or standardized product, for example, lumber. The technology and production processes may be similar. The "economics of the industry" may implore rather common uses of capital and lead to such characteristics as labor or capital intensity. The firms may also be subject to similar demand characteristics. When firms are subject to similar conditions a more meaningful comparison of management performance can be made. Nevertheless industry comparisons are subject to a couple of caveats. The less homogenous the industry, the less meaningful will be the comparisons. If firms produce different products for different clientele, their demand curves may be significantly different. Firms of quite different size may use different production processes and compete on a different scale. In addition a particular firm may be not typical of the industry norm. In cases in which comparison to an industry average would be misleading, a better comparison would be to selected firms in the industry that are similar in product, service, size, or clientele.

Often a more meaningful comparison is to be found in the trend of a firm's performance. Is it improving or becoming worse? Has the firm recognized its problems or is it heading toward trouble? Here the analyst needs to track the ratios over time. Comparisons can be made with past performance. Here again the most meaningful information may be obtained when the analyst can relate the trend of the firm to economic conditions of the time period considered and to the trends of the industry and firm's competitors. Simple graphs plotting the performance of key ratios for the firm along with the industry norm and key competitors can vividly show the comparisons. Exhibit B.4 is an example of how such a comparison might look.

A sampling of relevant sources of information needed for these comparisons can be seen in Exhibit B.5. From such sources an analyst can obtain or construct ratios for the industry and key competitors as well as the company being analyzed. Com-

Exhibit B.5 A Sampling of Sources of Information Used in Financial Ratio Analysis

Source	Description
Economic	
Business Conditions Digest	Contains leading, coincident, and lagging indicators based on time series that allow analysts to predict trends and identify business cycles. Published by the Department of Commerce.
Industry	
Standard & Poor's Industry Survey and S&P Analysts Handbook	Cover the major domestic industries with the industry's prospects and trends. Latest developments and statistics for industries. Handbook has income and balance sheet items and ratios.
Trade associations	Often provide extensive statistics. Each trade association is established by members of the industry.
Dun & Bradstreet's Industry Norms and Key Business Ratios	Provides industry averages for 14 different ratios for 800 types of business. Data are grouped by Standard Industrial Classification number and broken down by size.
Robert Morris Associates, Annual Statement Studies	Provide industry averages for 16 different ratios. Data are grouped by SIC number and by size.
Individual Company	
Annual reports	Published by publicly held companies. Often available in university libraries.
Security and Exchange Commission 10K Reports	Required annually by publicly held companies. Available from the companies.
Moody's Manuals	Provide financial information for numerous companies.
Standard & Poor's Value Line	Provides financial information for numerous companies.
Compustat	A databank on computerized tape from Standard & Poor's data. The tapes contain 20 years' data for about 120 banks, 1,000 OTC companies, 2,200 industrials, 175 utilities, and 500 Canadian companies. Complete balance sheet and income statements. An analyst can use the data to construct industry ratios. Frequently available at universities.
Compact Disclosure	A databank for microcomputers that contains balance sheet, sources and uses of funds statement, income statement, calculated ratios, and a president's report to the stockholders. Typically carries data for five years or more. Available in many libraries.

prehensive reviews of the many sources of information available on the economy, industries, and individual firms include Jugoslav S. Milutinovich, "Business Facts for Decision Makers: Where to Find Them," *Business Horizons,* March–April 1985, 63–80; David M. Brownstone and Gorton Carruth, *Where to Find Business Information: A Worldwide Guide for Everyone Who Needs the Answers to Business Questions* (New York: Wiley, 1979); Oscar Figueroa and Charles Winkler, *A Business Information Guidebook* (New York: AMACOM, 1980); and Paul Wasserman, C. C. Georgi, and J. Woy, *Encyclopedia of Business Information Sources, 4th ed.* (Detroit: Gale Research, 1980).

Calculating Financial Ratios

The balance of this appendix is devoted to the most common financial ratios used in financial analysis. The calculation of each ratio is demonstrated using data from the Cascade Corporation in 1987. The primary business of the firm is indicated by its Standard Industrial Classification (SIC) code: 3537, Industrial Trucks and Tractors. Exhibit B.6 provides a summary list of the ratios and gives the formulas employed. It also provides a format for a worksheet that could be used to record ratios for both the company and the industry for a period of five years.

Liquidity Ratios

Liquidity ratios indicate the firm's ability to meet its future short-term obligations. The focus here is on whether the company's most liquid assets are adequate for paying its potential short-term obligations.

Current Ratio. The current ratio is the most well-known measure of liquidity. Current assets such as cash, inventories, and accounts receivables are matched against current liabilities such as accounts payable. The current ratio is calculated as follows:

$$\frac{\text{Current Assets}}{\text{Current Liabilities}}$$

For the Cascade Corporation the current ratio for 1987 was:

$$\frac{48{,}793}{19{,}616} = 2.49$$

A popular guideline for the ratio is 2 or 3 to 1; however, the ratio will vary by industry. An industry with a stable cash flow such as a public utility may not need as high a ratio as a retailer who has a high investment in inventory and accounts receivable, which are subject to rapid change in value. The composition of the assets should also be considered because they may affect the firm's ability to turn the assets into cash as needed. Inventories or accounts receivables that are slow to turn over may impair the firm's ability to meet short-term obligations. Conversely, a firm with a high current ratio may have the ability to meet obligations to short-term creditors, but may not be wisely using its current assets to generate business.

Acid Test or Quick Ratio. This ratio represents the ability of the firm to meet its short-term obligations without sale of its inventories. Inventories may not turn over quickly or they may be obsolete. Other current assets that are of questionable or unknown liquidity should also be deducted for this test. It is a more severe test than the current ratio because it concentrates on the most liquid of assets. It is calculated as follows:

$$\frac{\text{Liquid Current Assets}}{\text{Current Liabilities}}$$

When inventories are the only nonliquid asset, the formula can be written in this way:

$$\frac{\text{Current Assets} - \text{Inventories}}{\text{Current Liabilities}}$$

For the Cascade Corporation the quick ratio for 1987 was:

$$\frac{48{,}793 - (20{,}246 + 726)}{19{,}616} = 1.42$$

The typical guideline is 1 to 1. Again, volatile industries require higher figures. Assets such as cash, marketable securities, and receivables are considered to be current and liquid. If the asset is of suspect liquidity a conservative approach would be to exclude it.

Because receivables and inventories can be a major portion of current assets, the liquidity of the receivables and inventories can be a concern. Three ratios to be considered under efficiency ratios can be used to shed light on the liquidity: accounts receivables turnover, average collection period, and inventory turnover.

Efficiency Ratios

Efficiency ratios indicate how management is performing in using the assets and capital of the firm.

Total Asset Turnover. This ratio is a measure of the volume of business generated by the asset base. It indicates how efficiently company management is using all the assets of the firm to generate sales. It is calculated with the formula:

$$\text{Total Asset Turnover} = \frac{\text{Net Sales}}{\text{Average Total Net Assets}}$$

Net assets are found by subtracting depreciation on fixed assets from gross assets. (The average is calculated by adding together the amounts for the beginning and the end of the year and dividing by 2.) Total net assets are listed as simply total assets on the Cascade balance sheet. For the Cascade Corporation the 1987 total asset turnover was:

$$\frac{98{,}682}{(78{,}608 + 69{,}824)/2} = 1.33$$

Exhibit B.6 Financial Analysis Worksheet

Ratio	Formula	Company Year					Industry				
		1	2	3	4	5	1	2	3	4	5
Liquidity Ratios											
Current Ratio:	$\frac{\text{Current Assets}}{\text{Current Liabilities}}$										
Quick Ratio:	$\frac{\text{Current Assets} - \text{Inventories}}{\text{Current Liabilities}}$										
Efficiency Ratios											
Total Asset Turnover	$= \frac{\text{Net Sales}}{\text{Average Total Net Assets}}$										
Fixed Asset Turnover	$= \frac{\text{Net Sales}}{\text{Average Net Fixed Assets}}$										
Equity Turnover	$= \frac{\text{Net Sales}}{\text{Average Equity}}$										
Inventory Turnover	$= \frac{\text{Net Sales}}{\text{Average Inventory}}$										
Accounts Receivable Turnover	$= \frac{\text{Net Annual Sales}}{\text{Average Accounts Receivables}}$										
Average Collection Period	$= \frac{365}{\text{Annual Turnover}}$										

Profitability Ratios

Gross Profit Margin $= \dfrac{\text{Gross Profit}}{\text{Net Sales}}$

or

$= \dfrac{\text{Net Sales} - \text{Cost of Goods Sold}}{\text{Net Sales}}$

Operating Profit Margin $= \dfrac{\text{Earnings before Interest and Taxes}}{\text{Net Sales}}$

or

$= \dfrac{\text{Operating Profit}}{\text{Net Sales}}$

Net Profit Margin $= \dfrac{\text{Net Income}}{\text{Net Sales}}$

Expense Analysis (Percentage of Sales) $= \dfrac{\text{Expense Item}}{\text{Net Sales}}$

Expense Analysis (Percentage of Costs) $= \dfrac{\text{Expense Item}}{\text{Total Costs}}$

Common Size Income Statement $= \dfrac{\text{All Income Statement Items—Individually}}{\text{Net Sales}}$

Exhibit B.6 *(continued)*

Ratio	Formula	Company Year 1	2	3	4	5	Industry 1	2	3	4	5
Return on Total Assets	$= \dfrac{\text{Net Income}}{\text{Average Total Assets}}$										
Return on Total Capital	$= \dfrac{\text{Net Income + Interest}}{\text{Average Total Assets}}$										
Return on Total Equity	$= \dfrac{\text{Net Income}}{\text{Average Total Equity}}$										
Return on Common Equity	$= \dfrac{\text{Net Income} - \text{Preferred Dividend}}{\text{Average Common Equity}}$										
Return on Equity	$= \text{Equity Turnover} \times \text{Net Profit Margin}$ or $= \text{Total Asset Turnover} \times \text{Financial Leverage} \times \text{Net Profit Margin}$										
Equity Turnover	$= \dfrac{\text{Sales}}{\text{Equity}} = \dfrac{\text{Sales}}{\text{Total Assets}} \times \dfrac{\text{Total Assets}}{\text{Equity}}$										
Financial Leverage	$= \dfrac{\text{Average Total Assets}}{\text{Average Equity}}$										
Growth	$= \text{Earnings Retention (1 − \% of payout)} \times \text{Return on Equity}$										
Earnings per Share	$= \dfrac{\text{Net Income} - \text{Preferred Stock Dividends}}{\text{Number of Common Shares Outstanding}}$										

Business Risk

Business Risk

$$= \frac{\text{Standard Deviation of Operating Earnings (OE)}}{\text{Mean Operating Earnings}}$$

$$= \frac{\sqrt{\sum_{i-1}^{n} (OE - \overline{OE})^2/N}}{\sum_{i-1}^{n} OE/N}$$

Sales Variability

$$= \frac{\text{Standard Deviation of Sales (S)}}{\text{Mean Sales}}$$

$$= \frac{\sqrt{\sum_{i-1}^{n} (S_t - \overline{S})^2/N}}{\sum_{i-1}^{n} S_t/N}$$

Operating Leverage

$$= \sum_{i-1}^{n} \left| \frac{\% \Delta OE}{\% \Delta S} \right| / N$$

Exhibit B.6 *(continued)*

Ratio	Formula	Company Year 1	2	3	4	5	Industry 1	2	3	4	5
Financial Risk											
Proportion of Debt:											
Total Debt to Total Capital	$= \frac{\text{Total Debt}}{\text{Total Capital}}$										
Debt to Capital	$= \frac{\text{Total Long-Term Debt}}{\text{Total Long-Term Capital}}$										
Debt to Equity	$= \frac{\text{Total Long-Term Debt}}{\text{Total Equity}}$										
Debt Coverage:											
Interest Covered	$= \frac{\text{Income before Interest and Taxes}}{\text{Debt Interest Charges}}$										
Earnings Decline Coverage	$= 1 - \frac{\text{Coverage Ratio}}{\text{Reciprocal}} \times 100\%$										

Fixed Asset Turnover. This ratio indicates how efficient the company is in using its plant and equipment in generating sales. The ratio is found by the formula:

$$\text{Fixed Asset Turnover} = \frac{\text{Net Sales}}{\text{Average Net Fixed Assets}}$$

For the Cascade Corporation the 1987 fixed asset turnover was:

$$\frac{98{,}682}{(29{,}815 + 27{,}261)/2} = \frac{98{,}682}{28{,}538} = 3.46$$

Both the fixed asset and the total asset turnover ratios should be compared to industry ratios because there is considerable variation among industries. Capital intensive industries may yield low ratios (1 to 1) whereas those that are low capital intensive may yield much higher figures (between 7 and 10 to 1). Old depreciated plants would also contribute to a high ratio as would the use of leased equipment and plants. Thus it is possible for a firm to have a high ratio and look efficient when in fact it has neglected the fixed asset base.

Equity Turnover. Another measure of efficiency is to see how well management is using the firm's capital to generate sales. Different components of capital can be used to determine the dollar amount of sales generated for each dollar of respective capital component. Of these ratios perhaps the most interesting is equity turnover. The interest is in how many dollars of sales are generated for each dollar of owner (shareholder) equity. Owner equity excludes long-term debt, current liabilities, and preferred stock in this ratio calculation. It can be found with the formula:

$$\text{Equity Turnover} = \frac{\text{Net Sales}}{\text{Average Equity}}$$

For the Cascade Corporation the 1987 equity turnover was:

$$\frac{98{,}682}{(47{,}322 + 41{,}117)/2} = \frac{98{,}682}{44{,}220} = 2.23$$

Changes and trends in this figure need to be interpreted along with other capital figures such as the proportion of debt. For example, a firm may rely on increasing debt to finance increased sales, which would make it look efficient in its use of owner equity, but would also increase the financial risk.

Inventory Turnover. This ratio indicates whether a firm has excessive inventory, how liquid the inventory is, and how efficient the firm is in moving inventories into sales. It is computed using the following formula:

$$\text{Inventory Turnover} = \frac{\text{Net Sales}}{\text{Average Inventory}}$$

The 1987 inventory turnover for Cascade Corporation was:

$$\frac{98{,}682}{(20{,}246 + 19{,}452)/2} = \frac{98{,}682}{19{,}849} = 4.97$$

Because inventories are carried at cost, the use of cost of goods sold is preferable to net sales although the services reporting ratios use net sales.

Again, good judgment must be used when interpreting the figures. The results vary by industry, although 9 is about "typical." Supermarkets have a low profit margin, but depend on high turnover of inventories. On the other hand, some furniture stores have a low inventory turnover, but have a high profit margin because of a 200 percent to 300 percent markup. Other furniture stores use the supermarket approach. The nature of the strategy, the industry, and the products can make a major difference in this ratio. When the ratio is out of line with the industry average, the analyst should look for the reasons. The ratio may be either too high or too low. A ratio that is high for the industry might indicate inadequate stocks to support sales, shortages, and a loss of customers. A low ratio might indicate the firm is carrying too much inventory, is not planning production and sales wisely, or is incurring excessive carrying costs.

Accounts Receivable Turnover. The turnover of accounts receivable can indicate the quality of the asset for liquidity, but it can also be an indicator of management's performance. It tells the analyst the average collection period on sales. It is calculated as follows:

$$\text{Accounts Receivable Turnover} = \frac{\text{Net Annual Sales}}{\text{Average Accounts Receivables}}$$

For the Cascade Corporation the 1987 accounts receivable turnover was:

$$\frac{98{,}682}{(16{,}945 + 13{,}784)/2} = \frac{98{,}682}{15{,}365} = 6.42$$

A ratio that is too low may indicate a tight credit policy that means a loss of sales. If the ratio is too high, management may have established a credit policy that is too loose. Management may be failing to collect debts, may be extending credit too easily, or may be tying up too much capital in accounts receivables.

Average Collection Period. The average collection period can be found as follows:

$$\text{Average Collection Period} = \frac{365}{\text{Annual Turnover}}$$

In 1987 the average collection period was:

$$\frac{365}{6.42} = 56.8 \text{ days}$$

This figure gives the average length of time in days that it takes to collect on sales. Again, the figure must be related to the industry, the current trend, and the firm's credit policy. Comparisons can be distorted by differences in credit policy among firms and whether the firm sells for cash as well as on account. For example, cash sales will make the ratio appear stronger because receivables will be smaller in relationship to sales.

Profitability Ratios

Profitability ratios are measures of the firm's ability to generate profits from its sales and its capital. The ratios will vary widely across industries. Within industries comparisons can give some indication of how well the firm has been managed overall. However, a high return on sales may not mean a high return on investment if sales volume is relatively low or investment relatively high. Thus, returns on both sales and capital should be examined.

Gross Profit Margin. Gross profit margin is the total margin available to cover operating expenses and provide a profit. It gives some indication of the firm's basic cost structure. When compared over time with industry margins it can give a good indication of the firm's relative cost and price position. It is found with the formula:

$$\text{Gross Profit Margin} = \frac{\text{Gross Profit}}{\text{Net Sales}}$$

or

$$\text{Gross Profit Margin} = \frac{\text{Net Sales} - \text{Cost of Goods Sold}}{\text{Net Sales}}$$

The Cascade Corporation's gross profit margin in 1987 was:

$$\frac{34{,}842}{98{,}682} = 35.3\%$$

Operating Profit Margin. Operating profit margin indicates the firm's profitability without the effect of interest or taxes. It can be found as follows:

$$\text{Operating Profit Margin} = \frac{\text{Earnings before Interest and Taxes}}{\text{Net Sales}}$$

The operating profit margin for the Cascade Corporation in 1987 can be found by picking up the figure for income before taxes and adding back in the interest expense:

$$\frac{9{,}740 + 482}{98.682} = 10.36\%$$

Some analysts use the variability of the operating profit margin over time to indicate business risk.

Net Profit Margin. The net profit margin is the after-tax profit per dollar of sales. Net income is earnings after taxes but before preferred and common stock dividends are subtracted. Net profit margin is found with the following formula:

$$\text{Net Profit Margin} = \frac{\text{Net Income}}{\text{Net Sales}}$$

In 1987 the net profit margin for the Cascade Corporation was:

$$\frac{5{,}645}{98{,}682} = 5.72\%$$

The net profit margin will vary considerably across industries, but the average for U.S. companies is about 5 percent. Below-normal profit margins may indicate relatively low prices, relatively high costs, or a combination of the two.

Income and Expense Analysis. The profitability ratios already discussed can give an indication of the overall cost–price structure and the ability to generate profits. However, a more detailed analysis of the firm's sources of expense and income is often useful. Are certain expenses increasing over time relative to other firms in the industry? If there is an increase or decline in gross profit margin, what is the source of the change? In addition to helping answer questions such as these, a more detailed analysis that looks at all expenses and income items as a percentage of sales allows a comparison of the firm's efficiency of operations with the efficiency of other firms. Such ratios can be used to compare performance from one period to another and in management control activities. The particular ratio used depends on the needs of the analyst. For example, one analyst may be interested in R&D costs as a percent case of sales, particularly in such high-technology industries as pharmaceuticals. If the percentage of R&D expenses is too low, it may be cause for concern that the firm is not investing in its future. However, if other pharmaceutical firms are selling for relatively low prices, the firm may be showing good management by acquiring another firm. Rather than developing products through its own R&D, the company acquires a firm—and thus its products. Often this can be done more cheaply than developing a new product through R&D. Another example might be to examine administrative costs by determining the percentage of total costs or the percentage of sales. If administrative costs are creeping up when compared to past periods and to industry averages, the firm should be examined more closely for inefficiency or increased bureaucracy. For the Cascade Corporation an analysis of selling, general, and administration expenses as a percentage of sales gives the following:

$$\frac{19{,}748}{98{,}682} = 20.01\%$$

Another measure related to sales is the firm's sales growth relative to the industry's sales growth. This measure will indicate the change in market share. If it is calculated for each competitor in the industry, relative market share can be seen. Market share is important in many strategic decisions and can be an important indicator of management's performance.

The discussion of income and expense analysis has focused thus far on the selective use of percentages for a particular purpose. Another approach is to prepare common size income statements such as the one for the Cascade Corporation in Exhibit B.7. Each item on the income statement is shown as a percentage of sales. The selling, general, and administrative expenses as a percentage of sales, which was calculated earlier to be 20.01% for Cascade, can be read directly from the common

Exhibit B.7 Common Size Income Statement for Cascade Corporation, 1983–1987 ($000)

	1987		1986		1985		1984		1983	
Net Sales	$98,682	100.00%	$86,664	100.00%	$84,090	100.00%	$67,708	100.00%	$63,045	100.00%
Cost of Goods	63,840	64.69	56,222	64.87	55,003	65.40	45,391	67.03	44,330	70.31
Gross Profit	34,842	35.30	30,442	35.12	29,087	34.59	22,317	32.96	18,715	29.68
R&D Expenditures	NA	0	NA	0	NA	0	NA	0	NA	0
Selling, General, and Administrative Expense	19,748	20.01	16,738	19.31	15,609	18.56	13,980	20.64	14,914	23.65
Income before Depreciation and Amortization	15,094	15.29	13,704	15.81	13,478	16.02	8,337	12.31	3,801	6.029
Depreciation and Amortization	4,619	4.680	3,854	4.447	3,701	4.401	4,006	5.916	4,037	6.403
Nonoperating Income	−253	−0.25	−164	−0.18	−347	−0.41	−160	−0.23	−396	−0.62
Interest Expense	482	0.488	353	0.407	263	0.312	812	1.199	1,168	1.852
Income before Taxes	9,740	9.870	9,323	10.75	9,167	10.90	3,359	4.961	−1,800	−2.85
Provision for Income Tax	4,095	4.149	3,700	4.269	3,900	4.637	1,455	2.148	−1,620	−2.56
Minority Interest (Income)	NA	0	NA	0	NA	0	NA	0	NA	0
Investment Gains/Losses	NA	0	NA	0	NA	0	NA	0	NA	0
Other Income	NA	0	NA	0	NA	0	NA	0	NA	0
Net Income before Expense Items	5,645	5.720	5,623	6.488	5,267	6.263	1,904	2.812	−180	−0.28
Expense Items and Discount Operations	NA	0	NA	0	NA	0	NA	0	NA	0
Net Income	5,645	5.720	5,623	6.488	5,267	6.263	1,904	2.812	−180	−0.28
Outstanding Shares[a] (000)	3,002		751		751		774		713	
Earnings per Share	1.88		1.87	0.001	1.75		0.65		−0.06	

[a]Three-share dividend declared May 1986.
Source: Cascade Corporation 10K reports, 1983–1987.

size income statement. When this is done for several years, trends can be spotted. When they are compared to trends of other firms or the industry as a whole, management can better understand the firm's performance.

Return on Total Assets. Ratios related to the rate of return generated by the firm's assets are generally considered a better indication of management's success and the firm's efficiency and profitability than are the profitability ratios related to sales and expense. Return on total assets, sometimes called return on investment, is an indicator of the after-tax returns per dollar of assets. Because the firm may buy and sell assets and the capital employed may change, an average figure for total assets should be used. Thus the formula is:

$$\text{Return on Total Assets} = \frac{\text{Net Income}}{\text{Average Total Assets}}$$

The return on total assets for the Cascade Corporation in 1987 was:

$$\frac{5{,}645}{(78{,}608 + 69{,}824)/2} = \frac{5{,}645}{74{,}216} = 7.61\%$$

Total assets are financed by creditors as well as stockholders. To reflect the earnings available to all investors, interest paid on debt can be added to net income to find out how productive total assets are, as indicated by the following modification:

$$\text{Return on Total Capital} = \frac{\text{Net Income} + \text{Interest}}{\text{Average Total Assets}}$$

The 1987 return on total capital for the Cascade Corporation was:

$$\frac{5{,}645 + 482}{(78{,}608 + 69{,}824)/2} = \frac{6{,}127}{74{,}216} = 8.26\%$$

Return on Equity. Return on equity (ROE) is a measure of how well management has earned profits using the owners' investment. It is the rate of return earned on the capital provided by the stockholders after paying all other suppliers of capital. It is calculated as follows:

$$\text{Return on Total Equity} = \frac{\text{Net Income}}{\text{Average Total Equity}}$$

The return on total equity for the Cascade Corporation in 1987 was:

$$\frac{5{,}645}{(47{,}322 + 41{,}117)/2} = \frac{5{,}645}{44{,}220} = 12.8\%$$

Total equity is all shareholder equity including preferred stock. If the analyst is interested in common equity only, it would be calculated as follows:

$$\text{Return on Common Equity} = \frac{\text{Net Income} - \text{Preferred Dividend}}{\text{Average Common Equity}}$$

For the Cascade Corporation in 1987 the return on common equity was:

$$\frac{5{,}645 - 0}{(47{,}322 + 41{,}117)/2} = \frac{5{,}645}{44{,}220} = 12.8\%$$

Common equity is found by subtracting the par value of preferred stock from total equity. Because the Cascade Corporation has no preferred stock, common equity and total equity are the same.

ROE can be broken down into several subcomponent ratios.

$$\text{ROE} = \text{Equity Turnover} \times \text{Net Profit Margin}$$

or

$$\text{ROE} = \frac{\text{Net Income}}{\text{Equity}} = \frac{\text{Sales}}{\text{Equity}} \times \frac{\text{Net Income}}{\text{Sales}}$$

These two components indicate two ways to improve ROE. Management can increase the company's equity turnover by using equity more efficiently. Equity turnover can also be broken down into additional components for examination:

$$\text{Equity Turnover} = \frac{\text{Sales}}{\text{Equity}} = \frac{\text{Sales}}{\text{Total Assets}} \times \frac{\text{Total Assets}}{\text{Equity}}$$

Management can also increase the company's net profit margin because

$$\text{Net Profit Margin} = \frac{\text{Net Income}}{\text{Sales}}$$

Because total assets divided by equity is a measure of financial leverage, management can manipulate three components in improving ROE. The formula is rewritten as follows:

$$\text{ROE} = \text{Total Asset Turnover} \times \text{Financial Leverage} \times \text{Net Profit Margin}$$

$$\text{ROE} = \frac{\text{Sales}}{\text{Total Assets}} \times \frac{\text{Total Assets}}{\text{Equity}} \times \frac{\text{Income}}{\text{Sales}}$$

The only component of this formula not previously calculated is financial leverage:

$$\text{Financial Leverage} = \frac{\text{Average Total Assets}}{\text{Average Equity}}$$

Financial leverage for the Cascade Corporation in 1987 was:

$$\frac{(78{,}608 + 69{,}824)/2}{(47{,}322 + 41{,}117)/2} = \frac{74{,}216}{44{,}220} = 1.68$$

Thus, using figures already calculated for total asset turnover (1.33) and net profit margin (5.72), the ROE for the Cascade Corporation in 1987 was:

$$\text{ROE} = 1.33 \times 1.68 \times 5.72 = 12.8\%$$

By breaking down ROE the analyst can sometimes determine the actions management has taken as well as actions that can be taken to improve ROE. For example, management can increase equity turnover by using more debt capital. However, this would also increase financial risk and likely increase the required rate of return on equity.

Growth The growth of a company is usually important to its strategic goals. Expected growth affects the price buyers are willing to pay for the company's stock. It also affects lender decisions because earnings growth provides protection to debt holders. Earnings growth also affects a firm's ability to finance the investments required to carry out its strategy. It is generally assumed that the more a company reinvests in itself, the more it will grow. We can look at growth by focusing on (1) the percentage of earnings retained for reinvestment and (2) the rate of return earned on equity retained. The indicator is as follows:

$$\text{Growth} = \text{Earnings Retention} \times \text{Return on Equity}$$

Earnings retention is found by subtracting the percentage of payout from 1. Again, trends are important in estimating future growth. If the growth rate is declining, expected return on equity should decline, whereas an increasing rate would predict an increase in return on equity. Based on figures in the sources and uses of funds statement, the earnings retention for the Cascade Corporation in 1987 was:

$$1 - (1{,}801/5{,}645) = 1 - .319 = .681$$

The growth rate for Cascade Corporation in 1987 was:

$$.681 \times 12.8 = 8.72\%$$

Earnings per Share Earnings per share shows the earnings available to owners of common stock and is found as follows:

$$\text{Earnings per Share} = \frac{\text{Net Income} - \text{Preferred Stock Dividends}}{\text{Number of Common Shares Outstanding}}$$

Earnings per share for the Cascade Corporation in 1987 was:

$$\frac{5{,}645 - 0}{3{,}002} = 1.88$$

Risk

The uncertainty of returns and income is important to strategic analysis of a firm. The volatility of sales, operating earnings, and earnings available to stockholders can be important to assessing risk. If another firm is an acquisition or merger candidate, the risk connected with the volatility of its sales and earnings may be an important consideration. Business and financial risk can also affect the alternatives available to a firm in financing the company; that is, its capital structure.

Business Risk Business risk is concerned with the uncertainty of future earnings. A firm's earnings vary because its sales and production costs vary. The products and customers in some industries lead to more variability in sales and costs over time. For example, capital goods like machines and tools have a more volatile history than retail soft goods or grocery products.

Business risk can be gauged by looking at the variability of the company's operating earnings over time. The more variable the operating earnings over time, the more uncertain are the future earnings and the greater is the business risk. The coefficient of variation of operating earnings is used here because it allows comparison of companies of different sizes. Data for at least five to ten years should be used for a meaningful measure.

$$\text{Business Risk} = \frac{\text{Standard Deviation of Operating Earnings (OE)}}{\text{Mean Operating Earnings}}$$

$$= \frac{\sqrt{\sum_{i=1}^{n} (OE_t - OE)^2/N}}{\sum_{i=1}^{n} OE_t/N}$$

The business risk for the Cascade Corporation is based on minimum data points, but for illustration is:

$$\frac{4{,}220.46}{10{,}882.80} = .388$$

Business risk can be broken into its two components: (1) sales variability and (2) operating leverage.

Sales Variability. The most powerful component of earnings availability is greatly affected by the general economic environment and the company's industry. Machine tools or steel, for example, are more affected by the economic cycle and are a more cyclical industry than groceries. The former will have a greater sales variability. The sales variability can be found using the coefficient of variation of sales. Sales are substituted for operating earnings in the previous formula. The basic formula is as follows:

$$\text{Sales Variability} = \frac{\text{Standard Deviation of Sales (S)}}{\text{Mean Sales}}$$

$$= \frac{\sqrt{\sum_{i=1}^{n} (S_t - \overline{S})^2/N}}{\sum_{i=1}^{n} S/N}$$

The sales variability for the Cascade Corporation was:

$$\frac{13{,}028.52}{80{,}037.80} = .163$$

Operating Leverage. The mix of costs from producing goods or services affects the variability of a company's operating earnings. Production costs may be viewed as variable and fixed cost. If all production costs were variable, the total production costs would vary directly with sales, and operating earnings would be a constant proportion of sales. But because of fixed or relatively fixed production costs (such as plant, machinery, and management), earnings will not remain a constant proportion and will vary more than sales. In periods of decline earnings will decline more than sales, whereas during expansion periods earnings will increase more than sales. Thus the greater the fixed production costs, the more variable will be the operating earnings relative to the sales variability. Operating leverage is determined by comparing the percentage of change in operating earnings to the percentage of change in sales for several years:

$$\text{Operating Leverage} = \sum_{i=1}^{n} \left| \frac{\%\,\Delta\ \text{OE}}{\%\,\Delta\ \text{S}} \right| / \text{N}$$

The operating leverage for the Cascade Corporation was:

$$\frac{19.94}{4} = 4.99$$

Financial Risk. In addition to business risk there is the risk to the owner derived from the use of debt obligations because the payment on debt capital comes prior to earnings available to common stock. If there were no debt, the only risk would be to that of business risk. The use of fixed debt obligations produces an effect similar to that of fixed production costs on operating earnings variability. That is, during favorable business conditions earnings on equity will be relatively larger than for operating earnings, whereas during unfavorable times the earnings available will be relatively less. Financial risk is measured by looking at the proportion of debt and the coverage of interest and fixed charges.

Proportion of Debt. The greater the proportion of long-term debt in a company's capital, the more volatile will be earnings available to common stock and the greater the chance of defaulting on the bonds. In other words, the higher the proportion of debt, the greater the financial risk will be. As financial risk increases, the interest rate demanded becomes higher and equity capital becomes more difficult to obtain. The level of acceptable financial risk is affected by the company's business risk. Companies with stable earnings have lower business risk and can tolerate higher debt ratios; an example is public utilities. Several ratios may be used to examine proportion of debt.

$$\text{Total Debt to Total Capital} = \frac{\text{Total Debt}}{\text{Total Capital}}$$

Total debt includes both current liabilities and long-term liabilities. It is most useful when the company utilizes considerable short-term borrowing. The total debt to total capital for the Cascade Corporation in 1987 was:

$$\frac{31{,}286}{78{,}608} = 39.8\%$$

A second ratio for examining proportion of debt is the following:

$$\text{Debt to Capital} = \frac{\text{Total Long-Term Debt}}{\text{Total Long-Term Capital}}$$

Long-term debt includes all long-term fixed obligations. Long-term capital includes all long-term debt, total owner equity, and preferred stock. The Cascade Corporation long debt to long capital for 1987 was:

$$\frac{31{,}286 - 19{,}616}{78{,}608 - 19{,}616} = 19.78\%$$

A third ratio is:

$$\text{Debt to Equity} = \frac{\text{Total Long-Term Debt}}{\text{Total Equity}}$$

Total equity includes preferred stock, common stock, and retained earnings and is essentially the book value of equity. The Cascade Corporation long-term debt to equity in 1987 was:

$$\frac{31{,}286 - 19{,}616}{47{,}322} = 24.66\%$$

Coverage Ratios. Coverage ratios indicate the adequacy of earnings to pay the interest on debt obligations. The greater the coverage, the smaller the financial risk will be.

$$\text{Interest Covered} = \frac{\text{Income before Interest and Taxes}}{\text{Debt Interest Charges}}$$

The interest coverage for the Cascade Corporation in 1987 was:

$$\frac{9{,}740}{482} = 20.21$$

This ratio indicates how many times fixed interest charges could be covered by earnings available to pay the charges. It can also be used in another ratio to determine the extent to which earnings can decline before the company can no longer meet its interest charges. This can be found as follows:

$$\text{Earnings Decline Coverage} = 1 - \text{Coverage Ratio Reciprocal} \times 100\%$$

$$\left[1 - \frac{1}{N}\right] \times 100$$

For example, if the ratio yields a 3, then 1 minus 1/3 equals .67; means earnings could decline 67 percent and the company could still pay its charges. The earnings decline coverage for the Cascade Corporation in 1987 was:

$$\left[1 - \frac{1}{20.21}\right] \times 100 = 95.05\%$$

Exhibit B.8 provides the calculated financial ratios for the Cascade Corporation for the years 1983 through 1987.

Exhibit B.8 Calculation of Financial Ratios for Cascade Corporation, 1983–1987

	1987	1986	1985	1984	1983
Current Ratio	2.4874	2.2980	2.4441	2.1556	2.5341
Quick Ratio	1.4182	1.2196	1.3288	1.1149	1.0088
Total Asset Turnover	1.3296	1.3281	1.4031	1.1534	
Average Net Assets (000)	74,216	65,251	59.929	58,698	
Fixed Asset Turnover	3.4579	3.4893	3.7217	2.8206	
Average Net Fixed Assets (000)	28,538	24,837	22,594	24,004	
Equity Turnover	2.2316	2.2748	2.4850	2.0788	
Average Equity (000)	44,220	38,097	33,839	32,570	
Inventory Turnover	4.9716	4.7693	4.9464	3.6991	
Average Inventory (000)	19,849	18,171	17,000	18,303	
Accounts Receivable Turnover	6.4227	6.6168	7.1544	11.295	
Average Receivables (000)	15,365	13,097	11,753	5,994.5	
Average Collection Period	56.830	55.162	51.017	32.315	
Gross Profit Margin	0.3531	0.3512	0.3459	0.3296	0.2968
Operating Profit Margin	0.0987	0.1075	0.1090	0.0496	−0.028
Net Profit Margin	0.0572	0.0648	0.0626	0.0281	−0.002
Percent of Sales Example: Selling, General, and Administrative Expense	0.2001	0.1931	0.1856	0.2064	0.2365
Return on Total Assets	0.0761	0.0861	0.0878	0.0324	
Return on Total Capital	0.0826	0.0915	0.0922	0.0462	
Return on Total Equity	0.1276	0.1475	0.1556	0.0584	
Average Total Equity	44,220	38,097	33,839	32,570	
Return on Common Equity	0.1277	0.1475	0.1556	0.0584	
Return on Equity	0.1277	0.1475	0.1556	0.0584	0
Financial Leverage	1.6783	1.7127	1.7710	1.8021	
Growth	0.0870	0.1101	0.1135		
Earnings Retention	0.6810	0.7463	0.7292		
Dividends (000)	1,801	1,426	1,426	NA	
Earnings Per Share	1.8804	7.487	7.013	2.459	−0.252
Debt to Capital	0.3980	0.4111	0.4219	0.4491	0.4410
Long-Term Debt to Long-Term Capital	0.1978	0.1985	0.2209	0.2291	0.2801
Long-Term Debt to Total Equity	0.2466	0.2477	0.2835	0.2972	0.3890
Interest Covered	20.207	26.410	34.855	4.1366	−1.541
Earnings Decline Coverage	95.051	96.213	97.131	75.826	164.88

Source: Cascade Corporation 10K reports, 1983–1987.

Part Four

Cases

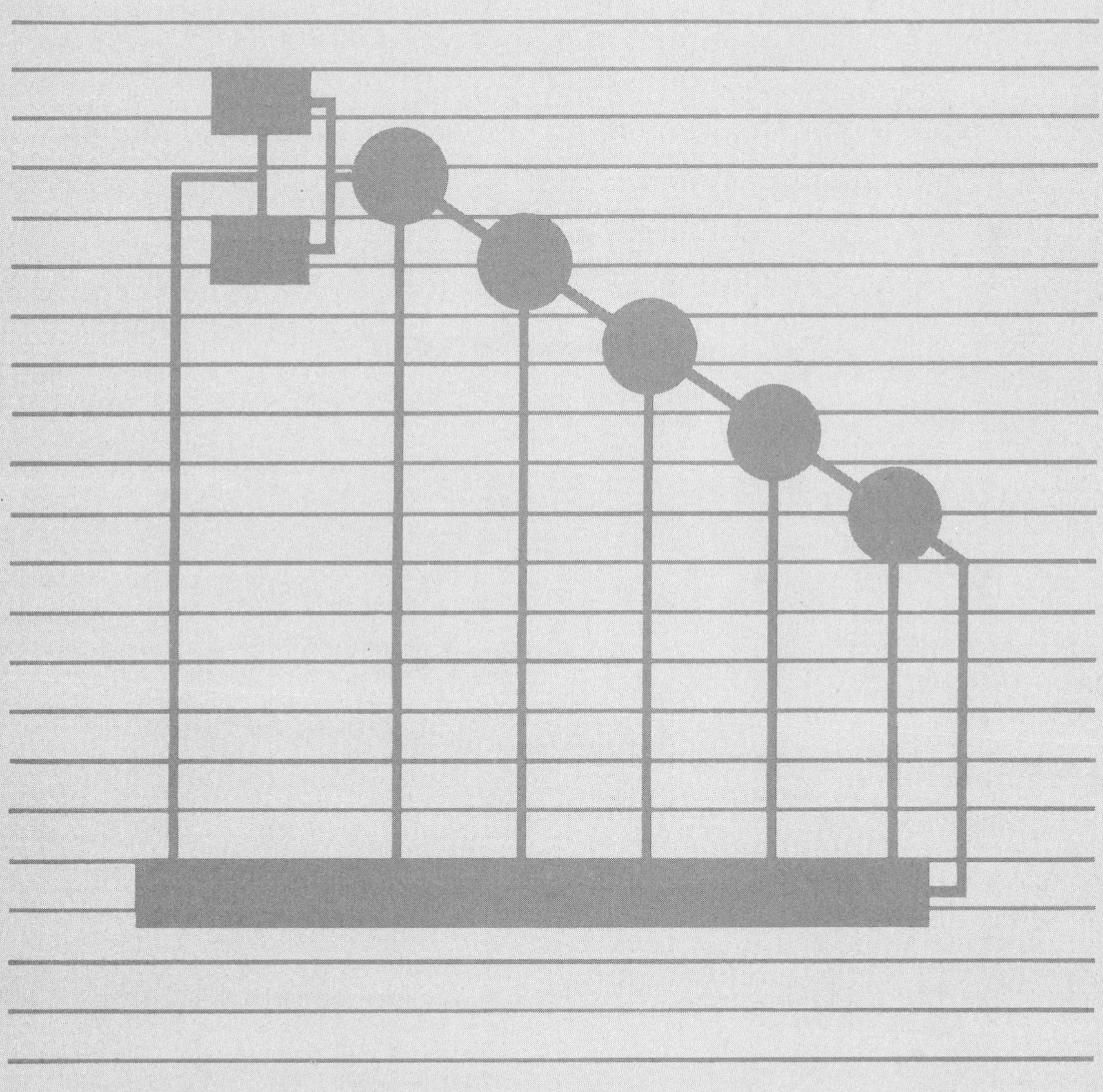

Case 1

Industry Note on the Commercial Aircraft Manufacturing Industry

Three of the four giants of the commercial aircraft industry have their roots in the World War I era. In 1916 William Edward Boeing began building seaplanes in Seattle. The same year, the Loughead brothers founded Lockheed in Santa Barbara, California. In 1924, the Douglas Corporation became a late entry into the fledgling aircraft manufacturing industry. Until 1953, Douglas Corporation was the industry giant, having produced the most successful family of propeller planes ever built, the DC-3 through the DC-7. In 1954, however, the industry environment changed abruptly when Boeing Corporation convinced the United States government that the proposed long range strategic bomber, the B52, should be jet powered.

The Beginning of the Commercial Jet Age

The U.S. government's acceptance of Boeing's proposal to equip the B52 with jet engines ushered in the commercial jet age. Boeing used the knowledge gained from producing the B52 and the KC135 (jet tanker) to launch the Boeing 707 in the early 1960s. The rapid success of these aircraft gave Boeing immediate industry dominance, relegating Douglas and Lockheed to second and third positions in the growing commercial aircraft industry. Also contributing to Boeing's position was the fact that Douglas Corporation and Lockheed had gambled unwisely. Both companies concluded that the time saved flying coast to coast on a jet aircraft was not worth the additional costs to the airlines. This miscalculation put Douglas, formerly number one, in a catch-up position. Douglas did not introduce its first jet liner for several years after Boeing; the DC-8 was delayed with production problems and suffered cost overruns. By the late 1960s Douglas was on the verge of collapse. Fortunately, the McDonnell Corporation, primarily a military aviation firm, became interested in a merger, and the two companies formed McDonnell Douglas Corporation.

Lockheed experienced major problems with its turboprop Electra, which was plagued by crashes in its first years of operation. Further, the plane reportedly experienced vibrations, causing it to become structurally unstable. After this fiasco, Lockheed management decided to sit out the first round of the jet powered commercial aviation battle.

The Market for Commercial Aircraft in the 1960s

Commercial airlines began to realize that the corporation that offered a family of planes, including short-to-long range aircraft, was the most viable producer. During the 1960s, Boeing became the only such producer.

Manufacturers of commercial airplanes face an enormous expense in developing a new aircraft. Like many industries, the aircraft industry relies on a highly skilled work force to ensure success. However, few other industries are as capital intensive or as involved with such a high volume of new technologies. Thus two factors set the airplane industry apart from others: the major costs incurred in developing a new plane and the monumental amount of moneys risked.

The aircraft industry is often compared to the automobile industry; however, Ford Motor Corporation was reported to have lost over $300 million on the Edsel and yet it remains a viable healthy organization today. On the other hand, Glenn Martin Company, General Dynamics, and Lockheed are no longer in commercial aircraft because each manufactured one unsuccessful plane. Through 1988 a total of 26 commercial jet-powered aircraft have been introduced in the marketplace, but few have been profitable.

In the late 1960s the enormous growth in profitability of commercial airlines began to decay. Even though forecasts indicated a slowing in growth of passenger miles, airlines were purchasing new jet aircraft. Major carriers bought aircraft they could not operate successfully. For example, Pan Am, the inaugural flyer of the 747, applied competitive pressure to force TWA, its major U.S. competitor for international flights, to purchase 747s—even though TWA could not justify the size of the plane.

The market in the 1960s saw an environment that demanded a twin-aisle, wide-body, two-engine, fuel-efficient aircraft that could carry between 200 and 280 passengers. Both Lockheed and McDonnell Douglas worked feverishly to produce such a plane. Their entrants, the L-1011 and DC-10, respectively, were among the most technologically complete planes ever built. They were also major failures. Lockheed is reported to have lost over $1.5 billion on the development of the L-1011, while McDonnell Douglas lost hundreds of millions as well as the confidence of the flying public because of the tragic DC-10 crashes in Turkey and Chicago. At a time when commercial producers could ill afford further competition, a consortium of European countries founded Airbus Industrie.

A major contributor to the loss of profitability of commercial airlines was fuel costs. Fuel rose from about 11 cents a gallon in the 1960s to over a dollar a gallon in 1981. The spiraling costs of operating an airline, the deregulation in 1978, and the recession of the early 1980s combined to send the airlines into a tailspin. This sharp downturn in the fortunes of commercial carriers ushered in one of the most difficult periods in the history of commercial aircraft manufacturers.

The Differences between Defense and Commercial Markets

Though military and commercial planes may appear to be similar, the commercial aircraft industry has a longer road to profitability. It takes many years and often the sale of hundreds of planes before initial R&D costs are recovered. For example, Lockheed had to sell 400 L-1011s before realizing any profit. In the military aircraft industry, however, R&D costs are often recovered immediately because the federal government assumes these costs. The defense industry provides an immediate customer that orders large quantities and pays on time. Conversely, commercial aircraft customers stagger orders over the plane's projected life. Because the manufacturer has no guarantee on the reliability of future orders, it is less inclined to use the learning curve economies of scale. On the other hand, dependence on the military does have drawbacks. The most notable is the often irrational method for selecting contractors. Some observers suggest that the best design among competing entries often loses out because of political considerations. Other differences include the military priority of performance over reliability, whereas most commercial airlines stress reliability for safety. Thus these two criteria involve different design parameters for the two markets.

The Bonanza Market: 1985 to 1995

In early 1985 both U.S. and foreign commercial air carriers prepared to purchase new aircraft needed to replace their aging, loud, fuel-inefficient jets. Boeing estimated that over 8,000 new jet airliners would be sold by Western manufacturers from 1989 through 2004 (Exhibit 1). This estimate is 1,500 more aircraft than Boeing's 1987 estimate. Of this $100 billion increase in business, more than $90 billion was on order by 1988.

The gloom of earlier years turned into a manufacturer's bonanza. In the first four months of 1989 Boeing received orders in excess of $17 billion. Its sales for all of 1988 were $30 billion. In a single week Airbus received orders and options for more than $7 billion. McDonnell Douglas also benefited from large orders by Delta and American. Aircraft sales for 1988 are presented in Exhibit 2.

This wild growth according to industry analysts is attributable primarily to three factors. First, growth in air travel is fueling the sales boom. RPMs, the number of passengers carried on a flight times the distance, will grow at a rate of 5.4 percent a year. This will double the current market by the year 2005. Seventy percent of all new aircraft purchased will accommodate this growth. The second factor is the replacement of old aircraft. Renewed concerns about geriatric jets falling from the sky and noise regulations are forcing replacements. Airlines want to use new, more efficient jets to serve new marketplaces also. Finally, the stretched-out delivery dates for new aircraft are forcing airlines to make their purchases quickly or be shut out of the market.

Exhibit 1 Actual and Estimated Commercial Aircraft Sales, 1970–2004

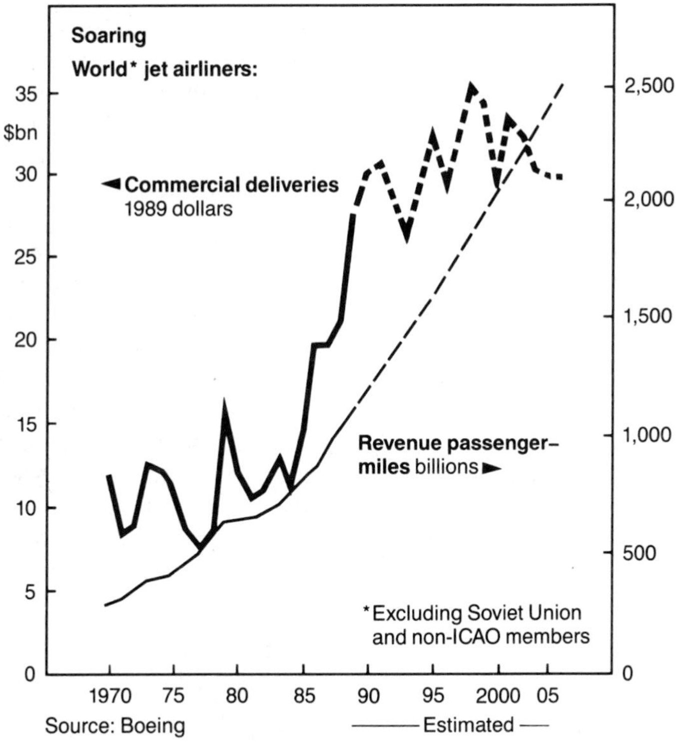

Source: The Boeing Company

Exhibit 2 1988 Commercial Jetliner Firm Orders (through September)

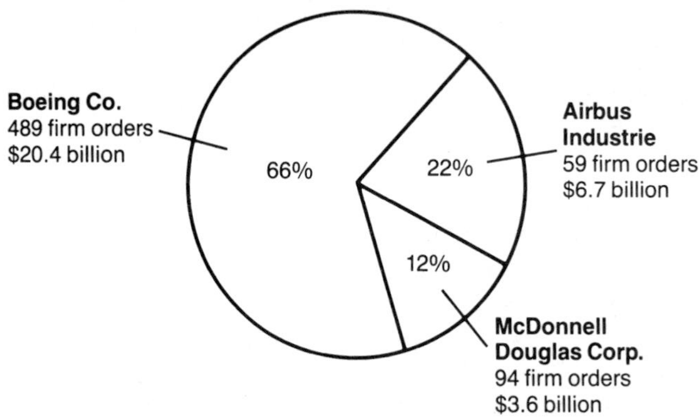

Source: Prudential-Bache Securities

As an example, Cathay Pacific placed an order for Airbus 330s on April 3, 1989 but will not take delivery until early 1995.

Because many airlines are strapped for cash, leasing firms are also increasing their purchases. GPA Group Ltd. of Ireland in 1989 ordered $17 billion worth of aircraft to be delivered over a ten-year period. Of the 308 planes, 182 valued at $9.4 billion will be supplied by Boeing.

Competitive Pressure among Manufacturers

Even with the strong demand, some doubt exists about whether the three major commercial aircraft builders—Boeing, McDonnell Douglas, and Airbus—can all successfully compete during the 1990s.

Competitive pressures in the airline industry have drastically thinned the ranks of airframe and engine manufacturers. Of the six major companies that remain viable, four are American. Airframe manufacturers include Boeing, Airbus Industrie, and McDonnell Douglas. Engine manufacturers are Pratt & Whitney, General Electric, and Rolls Royce. The two American engine manufacturers (GE and Pratt & Whitney) are larger than the American airframe manufacturers; this increases the pressures on aircraft producers because of vulnerability to these suppliers.

The engine totals one-third of the cost of a jetliner. To develop a completely new jet engine may cost hundreds of millions of dollars and take as long as five years in research time. Nonetheless, airframe manufacturers still sell their planes with a choice of two or three types of engines. These engine options increase engineering and development costs for the airframe manufacturers and affect the profitability of the aircraft. For example, Airbus Industrie offers Pratt & Whitney engines on its A300–600 series. This limits the flow of profits to Europe from an aircraft sale because one-third of the revenue is engine related and would revert to Pratt & Whitney.

The 150-Seat, Narrow-Body Aircraft Market

Delta Air Lines initiated the idea of the 150-seat aircraft in the mid-1970s. This plane would fly more frequently to more places, which would create a need for more, not necessarily larger, aircraft. Most carriers prefer long-haul, wide-body aircraft, but the shorter high-frequency flights—less than two hours in duration and about 800 miles in distance—constitute 75 percent of all scheduled flights. Certainly, the market for the 150-seater appears to exist. However, the cost of developing such an airplane is staggering. One calculation shows that it would cost Boeing, the world's most efficient aircraft manufacturer, almost $2 billion to get this plane off the ground.

Despite staggering start-up costs, Airbus Industrie began development of a 150-seat market with reengineered existing aircraft. Nor have American companies abandoned the concept of a 150-seat aircraft. Their strategy is to update existing designs. Even though their entries to the marketplace lack the fuel efficiency of the A320, they are $1 million to $5 million less expensive and immediately available. In the early 1980s Boeing announced its intent to produce a new 150-seat aircraft by the year 1992. According to industry sources, this plane will be more cost effective than the A320. Boeing's message was clear; the A320 would be an inferior design by the year 1992. McDonnell Douglas also chose to build a new derivative of its successful MD-80 series that flew on Propfan-powered engines. However, changing factors in the marketplace caused Boeing to shelve its all-new 7J7. McDonnell Douglas also put its new Propfan-powered plane on hold.

The Trend Toward Larger Aircraft

A major factor in the current buying spree of commercial airlines is a move toward larger aircraft. Boeing estimates that almost 90 percent of all aircraft delivered after 1995 will have more than 170 seats, compared to 120 to 170 seats for the preceding few years. All three major airframe manufacturers are studying ways to meet this demand.

The cramped space at many airports has caused airlines to rethink plane size for their hub and spoke system. Both Delta and American have lost business travelers to other airlines when flights on 727s and 737s were sold out. Thus Airbus and McDonnell Douglas consider the junior jumbo, with a range of up to 8,000 miles and seating of 270 to 330 passengers, to represent a major market niche for the future. Both manufacturers are developing and taking orders for such planes. Airbus expects its long-haul 330 will compete with Boeing's 767ER and its A340 mini-jumbo will not only compete with the 747 series but will establish itself as the market leader in the mini-jumbo niche.

In a move that surprised some in the industry, American Airlines in early 1989 ordered 75 Fokker 100s and took option on another 75. This deal has a value of close to $3 billion. The aircraft seats 95 to 97 and is part of a strategy at American to fill the low end of its capacity range.

American Airlines had identified 100 markets for the 100-seat airplane. According to chairman Robert Crandall, "With the Fokker 100, we can bring larger numbers of passengers into our hubs, where they in turn will fill connecting flights, allowing those flights to operate at higher load factors."[1] He cited three reasons for selecting the Fokker 100 over the MD-87 or Boeing 737–500: The aircraft is available in 1991, the agreement limits the airline's vulnerability to a recession, and the aircraft will pay for itself once it enters service.

Product Line Decisions

Product line decisions take place in a dynamic environment, even for products with such long lead times as commercial aircraft. For example, within a short while after the idea of the 150-seat airplane was conceived in the early 1980s, a great deal of new information became available and the environment changed considerably.

Some of the issues driving the fleet-planning decisions for airlines are engine-noise restric-

[1]James T. Mckenna, "American Fokker 100 Order Caps Carrier's Growth Plan," *Aviation Week and Space Technology,* March 27, 1989, 88–89.

tions at domestic airports, new engine and avionics technology, and aging fleets. The engine-noise issue has been controversial for at least a decade. The very popular 727 series and the 737–100 and 737–200 aircraft have Pratt & Whitney JT8D engines in almost all their configurations, and they exceed noise limits at most domestic airports. The FAA has authorized installation of "hush kits" on these engines to allow the airlines to continue operating during the staged restrictions on engine noise. However, by 1992, when Stage III is implemented, even the hushed engines will not meet noise standards. These airplanes will have to be replaced. No replacement engine is currently available or planned.

New engine and avionics technology will be also necessary for the airlines to remain competitive in their operations beyond the year 2000. General Electric and Pratt & Whitney are both developing new engines that are more fuel efficient as well as much quieter than the engines on the Boeing 767 and the Airbus 320.

Airbus

The Airbus consortium is presently comprised of Aero Spatiale (France), 37.9 percent, and CASA (Spain), 4.2 percent. Fokker (Netherlands) and Belairbus (Belgium) are associates participating only in the larger A310 (220 seats).

Interestingly, until 1978 the Airbus was a typical European airplane; it was well produced but a commercial failure. However, when Eastern Airlines purchased 24 A300s, Airbus's fortune began to change. Soaring fuel costs and stiff competition among airlines had created a demand for a large, fuel-efficient airplane. Only Airbus had such a plane. Up to 1978, only 38 had been sold, but by the end of 1979 sales totaled over 300 planes. This was the highest figure for any European commercial aircraft. Airbus has since followed Boeing's strategy by introducing a family of aircraft (Table 1). Conventional wisdom in the industry argues that an aircraft manufacturer must offer a family of aircraft in order to sell any single model.

Table 1 Airbus Current Family of Planes

	General Data			Dimensions and Weights		
Name	**Primary Mission**	**Crew**	**Passengers**	**Wingspan, ft.**	**Wing Area, sq. ft.**	**Max. Length, ft.**
A300B4/C4	Medium-haul/convertible	3	220-345	147.1	2,800	175.9
A300-600	Medium-haul	2	230-375	147.1	2,800	177.4
A300-600C	Convertible	2	230-375	147.1	2,800	177.4
A300-600R	Medium-long haul	2	230-345	147.1	2,800	177.4
A310-200 Standard	Medium haul	2	210-280	144.0	2,357	153.1
A310-200 Option	Medium-haul	2	210-280	144.0	2,357	153.1
A310-300	Medium-long haul	2	210-280	144.0	2,357	153.1
A310-200C	Convertible pax/cargo	2	210-280	144.0	2,357	153.1
A320-200	Short-medium haul	2	140-179	111.3	1,318	123.3

[a]A330 and A340 are scheduled for introduction in the early 1990s, will be part of the Airbus family.
Source: "Leading International Aircraft, Spacecraft, Weapons," *Aviation Week & Space Technology,* March 20, 1989, 153.

Airbus is government supported and, by French law, not required to publish financial statements. However, many industry experts believe the company's orientation toward economic efficiency differs dramatically from its American counterparts. The underlying objective of Airbus may be employment of its own 180,000 direct and indirect employees. Industry experts suspect that Airbus Industrie is selling planes below cost; in that case, the government would be fostering employment through subsidies. If Airbus's financial statements were in the public domain, the demands for efficiency could cause significant layoffs and production slowdowns. Thus the very fact that Airbus does not openly report financial figures may be the method by which the company is able to preserve its existence. Boeing estimates that Airbus will not break-even in sales until 2001.

Airbus has been very successful in marketing its family of jets to both European and Asian carriers. It has capitalized on the theme "buy European." In addition, sales to air carriers in the Middle East (particularly Kuwait and Lebanon) have been brisk.

Airbus has developed a strategy of negotiating with government leaders instead of airline executives. For the many countries in which air carriers are state owned, the ultimate decision to purchase a plane becomes an upper level governmental policy decision. Thailand's purchase of A310s is an example. Airbus presently holds a 75 percent share of the market in new sales in South America; almost 80 percent in Europe, the Middle East, and Africa; and 70 percent in Asia.

Airbus's recent success is a result of shrewd planning. The consortium targeted market niches not occupied by Boeing, the first being junior jumbo jets with ranges approaching 8,000 miles (similar to the Boeing 747) but with a capacity of only 300 seats. The second is the 150-seat passenger jet replacement market. Airbus has 134 orders for junior jumbo jets and a remarkable 450-plus orders for the 150-seat A320.

Table 1 *(continued)*

Dimensions and Weights				
Max. Height, ft.	**Empty Weight, lbs.**	**Gross Weight, lbs.**	**Powerplant: Number, Make, and Model**	**Max. Speed, mph.**
54.2	195,100	363,760	2 GE CF-6-50C2 tf. or 2 P&W JT9D-59A tf.	M.86
54.2	195,500	363,760	2 GE CF6-80C2, or 2 P&W 4000	M.82
54.2	196,300	375,400	Same as A300-600	M.82
54.2	194,600	375,300	2 GE CF6-80C2 tf. or 2 P&W PW 4000	M.82
51.9	174,800	305,560	2 CF6-80C2 or 2 P&W 4000	M.84
51.9	174,800	313,100	Same as A310-200 std.	M.84
51.9	175,600	330,690	Same as A310-200 std.	M.84
51.9	176,800	305,560	Same as AP310-200 std.	M.84
38.6	87,100	162,000	2 CFM56-5 or IAE V2500	M.82

Airbus Industrie members in March 1989 approved a significant reorganization plan, designed to move the airframe manufacturer toward profitability and to increase its competitiveness. The changes involved the structure and size of the supervisory board, the structure of senior management, and the creation of an executive board. The supervisory board, which has responsibility for strategic decisions concerning current and future programs, shrank from 17 to 5 members. A new position of financial director was created to ensure full open accounting.

The newly created executive board has responsibility for Airbus's operations. Jean Pierson, managing director, will coordinate the firm's commercial needs with the industrial and financial capabilities of its four partner companies.

McDonnell Douglas

Historically, McDonnell Douglas has generated most of its revenue outside the sales of commercial aircraft. Defense contracts have been the company's lifeblood. However, February 1989 brought an order from American Airlines for 150 planes valued at $7 billion. The company had taken orders for 203 MD-80 jets and 43 MD-11 long-range trijets in 1988. This compared with 138 orders for commercial aircraft in 1987.

McDonnell Douglas held 23 percent of the commercial aircraft market with revenues of $4.9 billion and earnings of just $127 million in 1988. This low return (2.6 percent), according to McDonnell Douglas sources, is a function of high production costs, inability to meet some deliveries, or missed performance schedules.

The company restructured the Douglas aircraft division in 1989. A management team dedicated to bringing about fundamental changes and improvements in the production process was put in place. Newly elected president of McDonnell Douglas, Robert H. Hood, said, "Growth is always hard to deal with if you don't have the proper systems in place. You can't just throw people at a problem." The company planned to deliver 135 commercial aircraft in 1989. Although it had no plans to boost production, an unplanned increase could result from a new quality management structure.

McDonnell Douglas, in its MD-80, a derivative of the DC-9, has developed a counterpart to the Boeing 737–300 and Airbus A320 in the 150-seat market. McDonnell Douglas's strategy assumes that new, high-technology aircraft cannot compete successfully with derivative reengined aircraft that match the efficiency levels of newly developed equipment. The reengined aircraft has a lower purchase price, less technical risk, and is available currently.

McDonnell Douglas designed its MD-11 series for the 270- to 400-seat market. By early 1989 the firm had orders and options totaling 250 for the mini-jumbo jets. In September 1988 Delta picked the MD-11 over Boeing and Airbus planes for its expansion of its Pacific routes. American placed a large order in early 1989 for MD-11s and, like Delta, will use them to expand its Asian network.

The MD-11 may be stretched to add 70 seats. Another possible configuration would include a lower lobe "panorama deck" and seat close to 600. A new wing has been discussed to regain the range that would be lost because of the proposed changes.

McDonnell Douglas has made a commitment to its role in the commercial aircraft industry with the MD-80 series. The MD-83 (Super 83), a derivative of the original design, has a 2,500-mile range and features high-technology engines and a seating capacity of 169 in an all-economy configuration. McDonnell Douglas has boasted that this plane has a lower cost per seat than either Boeing or Airbus planes. This family of aircraft, according to McDonnell Douglas, comes within 10 percent of the operating costs of the newly developed aircraft.

The MD-80 series spearheaded a long-awaited McDonnell Douglas turnaround. MD-80 sales have been made to foreign carriers such as Scandinavian Airlines and China Air, and orders and options from various sources totalled 885 by early 1989; 568 MD-80 series planes had been delivered.

The strength of the commitment McDonnell Douglas has made to the MD-80 series has been expressed in the creative financing packages offered to commercial airline carriers. For example, the company leased 20 MD-80s to American Airlines and picks up the major maintenance and training costs associated with the sales. Similar arrangements were made with TWA and Texas Air.

McDonnell Douglas's family of planes is presented in Table 2.

Boeing

Boeing is the world's largest aircraft producer, operating primarily in two industries: transportation equipment and related services and missiles and space. Through 1988 the company had manufactured almost 58 percent of all jet airliners ever made outside the Soviet Union. Its market share is projected at 58 percent of the commercial market. America's largest exporter, Boeing holds close to 75 percent of the North American medium- to long-range market. However, its overall market share declined from a high of 63 percent to as low as 51 percent in 1987.

Orders in 1987 were for 461 aircraft valued at $20 billion. In its best year ever, Boeing booked orders for 636 commercial aircraft valued at $30 billion in 1988. Its market share also jumped from a low of 51 percent to 56 percent. The firm was at a record production rate of 32 planes a month. Its backlog of jets exceeded 1,000.

Technology is a major factor for continued success of Boeing's derivative models and for newly developed aircraft. At one time some industry watchers believed that Europe lagged behind the United States in technological innovation. This gap, if it ever existed, has been closed by Airbus.

In addition, the $2 to $3 billion estimated by Boeing for introducing a new aircraft only scratches the surface of total costs. Nonrecurring cost of investment and an expansion of existing plant capacity, needed to implement programs, machinery, labor, and so on, could inflate costs far beyond initial investment projections. Therefore, Boeing feels it must be sure about the size and duration of the market before it embarks on a new aircraft development program. Potential major carriers have given conflicting signals about the characteristics of this new market or the potential size of the market.

Before 1967, Boeing had identified a market for a 200-seat airplane that had the capacity of flying 800 miles or more and for longer than two hours. The project team assigned to this potential aircraft was initially dubbed "the 747 project." Then the 150-seat market was identified and Boeing assigned project team 7N7 to design the aircraft. Now the 100-seat market is hot and so is the over-170 market.

Boeing worked closely with the major airlines in "feeling out" a product it could produce to satisfy a majority of the demand requirements such as number of aisles and body size. However, Boeing was unable to obtain a consistent description of the demand characteristics for this new dynamic market. This is one possible reason that Boeing has used its derivative models rather than developing entirely new planes.

Boeing is committed to satisfying the variety of tastes and needs of commercial aircraft buyers. Table 3 lists the models that the commercial airplane division is actively developing. It does not include all the models that the company is contemplating.

The 737–400 is Boeing's major competitive entry in the Airbus A320 150-seat market. The plane contains such features as longer fuselage, improved stability, increased tail and wing spans, new fuel efficient engines, reinforced wings, advanced tires and brakes, improved aerodynamics and avionics. Its 737–500 will compete in the 100-seat market, while its 757 competes in the 170–220 market and 767 and 747 variations compete in the wide-body marketplace.

Table 2 McDonnell Douglas Family of Planes

Model designation	Popular Name or Subtype Designation	Flight Crew	Passengers	Cargo Capacity, lb.	Wingspan, ft.	Wing Area, sq. ft.	Maximum Length, ft.
DC-8	Series 30[a]	3	116-176	20,850	142.3	2,758	150.5
DC-8	Series 40[a]	3	117	20,850	142.3	2,758	150.5
DC-8	Series 50[a]	3	116-189	20,850	142.3	2,884	150.5
DC-8	Super 61[a]	3	259	66,665	142.3	2,884	187.4
DC-8	Super 62[a]	3	189	42,580	148.4	2,927	157.4
DC-8	Super 63[a]	3	259	66,665	148.4	2,927	187.4
DC-9	Series 10[a]	2	85	9,000	89.4	934	104.4
DC-9	Series 20[a]	2	85	9,000	93.3	1,001	104.4
DC-9	Series 30[a]	2	110	13,425	93.3	1,001	119.3
DC-9	Series 40[a]	2	120	15,285	93.3	1,001	125.6
DC-9	Series 50[a]	2	135	15,510	93.3	1,001	133.5
MD-81	—	2	155	18,795	107.8	1,209	147.9
MD-82	—	2	155	18,795	107.8	1,209	147.9
MD-83	—	2	155	15,195	107.8	1,209	147.9
MD-87	—	2	130	14,195	107.8	1,209	130.4
MD-88	—	2	155	—	107.8	1,270	147.9
DC-10	Series 10	3	250-380	4,618[b]	155.5	3,550	182.3
DC-10	Series 15	3	250-380	4,618[b]	155.3	3,550	180.6
DC-10	Series 30	3	250-380	4,618[b]	165.3	3,647	181.6
DC-10	Series 40	3	250-380	4,618[b]	165.3	3,647	180.6
MD-11	—	2	321-405	5,630[b]	169.3	3,618	200.8
MD-11ER	—	2	277	4,670[b]	169.5	3,648	182.3

[a]Production terminated.
[b]Cubic feet of cargo space.
[c]P&W = Pratt & Whitney; R-R = Rolls Royce; GE = General Electric.
Source: "Leading International Aircraft, Spacecraft, Weapons," *Aviation Week & Space Technology,* March 20, 1989, 150.

In facing the competition from Airbus, Boeing has also been creative in new areas of financing, that is, leasing, trade-ins, price cutting, discounts, offering free training and support services, and taking competitors' planes as trade-ins. The tax incentives created by leveraged leases now help Boeing finance foreign aircraft sales at rates several points below those offered by commercial banks. When loan levels for the Export-Import Bank were cut in 1983, these deals became even more popular. In 1983 Boeing delivered twelve 747s to foreign airlines through leveraged lease financing. The total value of this deal was about $1 billion.

Congress has proposed cutting the 10 percent investment tax credit and five-year accel-

Table 2 *(continued)*

Maximum Height, ft.	Empty Weight, lb.	Typical Gross Weight, lb.	Max. Landing Weight, lb.	Powerplant: Number Make, and Model[c]	Maximum Speed, mph.	Best Cruise Speed, Mach or mph.
43.3	26,525	315,000	207,000	4 P&W JT4A-9, -11	600	544
43.3	24,369	315,000	207,000	4 R-R R, Co. 12	600	544
43.3	34,854	325,000	207,000	4 P&W JR3D-3B	600	544
43.0	48,897	328,000	240,000	4 P&W JT3D-3B	600	580
43.3	41,903	350,000	240,000	4 P&W JT3D-7	600	586
42.3	53,749	355,000	258,000	4 P&W JT3D-7	600	583
27.5	51,000	90,700	81,700	2 P&W JT8D-1 or 7	576	.76-.80
27.5	56,000	98,000	95,300	2 P&W JT8D-9 or 11	576	.76-.80
27.5	59,000	108,000	98,100	2 P&W JT8D-9	586	.76-.80
27.5	62,500	114,000	102,000	2 P&W JT8D-11 or 15	586	.76-.80
27.5	65,150	121,000	110,000	2 P&W JT8D-15 or 17	586	.76-.80
29.6	78,421	140,000	128,000	2 P&W JT8D-209 or 217A	576	.76-.80
29.6	78,549	149,500	130,000	2 P&W JT8D-217A	576	.76-.80
29.6	80,503	160,000	139,500	2 P&W JT8D-219	576	.76-.80
30.5	73,157	140,000	128,000	2 P&W JT8D-217C	576	.76-.80
29.6	78,000	149,500	130,000	2 P&W JT8D-217C	576	.76-.80
58.1	243,000	440,000	363,500	3 GE CF6-6D	593	0.82
58.1	248,500	455,000	363,500	3 GE CF6-50C2F	593	0.82
58.1	267,200	572,000	403,000	3 GE CF6-50C2	593	0.82
58.1	271,000	572,000	403,000	3 P&W JT9D-59A	593	0.82
57.8	277,300	602,500	430,000	3 P&W PW4360 or 3GE CF6-80C2-DF1	588	0.82
57.8	264,500	602,500	410,000	3 P&W PW4360 or 3 GE CF6-80C2-DF1	588	0.82

erated depreciation on equipment leased to foreign users. This, Boeing fears, will present a threat to sales of its commercial aircraft and initiate large decreases in cash flows.

Financing arrangements for aircraft purchasers are a key part of the competition for the non-U.S. market. If the Export-Import Bank budget is reduced sharply, Boeing fears it will have to fund more financing incentives to attract foreign buyers. This represents a major portion of company sales.

Finally, through creative efforts to sell additional aircraft, Boeing has become an industry giant in the free world. Boeing frequently takes trade-ins of used aircraft toward the purchase of new ones.

Outlook for the Future

No one can tell what sort of aircraft most passengers will choose over the next few decades: quieter aircraft, slower aircraft with sleeping

Table 3 Boeing Family of Planes

Model Designation	Popular Name or Subtype Designation	Flight Crew	Passengers	Cargo Capacity, lb.	Wingspan, ft.	Wing Area, sq. ft.	Maximum Length, ft.
707-320B[a]	Intercontinental	3	165	1,700[2]	145.8	2,892	152.9
707-320C[a]	Intercontinental	3	165	1,700[2]	145.8	2,892	152.9
727-100[a]	—	3	94	900[2]	108.0	1,560	133.2
727-200[a]	Advanced	3	145	1,525[2]	108.0	1,560	153.2
737-100	—	2	103	650[2]	93.0	980	94.0
737-200	Advanced	2	120	875[2]	93.0	980	100.2
737-200	Advanced[b]	2	120	640[2]	93.0	980	100.2
737-300	—	2	141	1,068[2]	94.8	980	109.6
737-300	—	2	141	1,068[2]	94.8	980	109.6
737-300	—	2	141	853[2]	94.8	980	109.6
737-400	—	2	159	1,375	94.8	980	119.6
737-400	—	2	159	1,160	94.8	980	119.6
747-100B	Superjet	3	452	6,190[2]	195.7	5,500	231.9
747SR	Superjet	3	550	6,190[2]	195.7	5,500	231.9
747-200B	Superjet	3	366-452	6,190[2]	195.7	5,500	231.9
747-300B	Stretched upper deck	3	400-490	6,190[2]	195.7	5,500	231.9
747-200C	Convertible	3	366-452	5,990[2]	195.7	5,500	231.9
747SP	Superjet	3	276-343	3,860[2]	195.7	5,500	184.7
747-400	Advanced Superjet	2	412-509	6,030[2]	211.0	5,650	231.9
757-200	—	2	186-220	1,790[2]	124.8	1,951	155.3
767-200	—	2	174-290	3,070[2]	156.1	3,050	159.2
767-200ER	—	2	174-290	3,070[2]	156.1	3,050	159.2
767-300	—	2	204-290	4,030[2]	156.1	3,050	180.3
767-300ER	—	2	204-290	4,030	156.1	3,050	180.3

[a]Production terminated.
[b]High gross weight structure.
[c]P&W = Pratt & Whitney; R-R = Rolls Royce; GE = General Electric; CFM = CFM International S.A.
[d]GE, R-R engines optional.
Source: "Leading International Aircraft, Spacecraft, Weapons," *Aviation Week & Space Technology*, March 20, 1989, 150.

berths, aircraft with greater operational flexibility, or "economy" aircraft. This uncertainty adds to that already facing commercial airframe manufacturers in today's volatile aircraft market.

A major question in the manufacturers' battle to fill the marketplace remains: Can the market support three competitors? All three aircraft manufacturers are utilizing their fullest resources and talent to gain that elusive edge needed to win customers and market share. However, one

Table 3 *(continued)*

Maximum Height, ft.	Empty Weight, lb.	Typical Gross Weight, lb.	Max. Landing Weight, lb.	Powerplant: Number, Make, and Model[c]	Maximum Speed, mph.	Best Cruise Speed, Mach or mph.
42.4	138,518	336,000	247,000	4 P&W JT3D-7	600	.8-.83
42.4	146,400	336,000	247,000	4 P&W JT3D-7	600	.8-.83
34.0	87,600	170,000	142,500	3 P&W JT8D-1, 7 or 9	600+	.8-.84
34.0	98,300	191,500	154,500	3 P&W JT8D-15A	600+	.8-.84
37.0	62,000	111,000	101,000	2 P&W JT8D-7 or 9	586	.73-.78
37.0	60,660	116,000	103,000	2 P&W JT8D-15A	586	.73-.78
37.0	62,445	128,600	107,000	2 P&W JT8D-17A	586	.73-.78
36.5	69,730	125,000	114,000	2 CFM 56-3-B1	566	.745
36.5	69,730	135,500	114,000	2 CFM 56-3-B1	566	.745
36.5	70,780	139,000	114,000	2 CFM 56-3-B2	566	.745
36.5	73,170	139,000	121,000	2 CFM 56-3-B2	566	.745
36.5	74,170	150,500	124,000	2 CFM 56-3C	566	.745
63.2	373,300	750,000	564,000	4 GE CF6-45A2[d]	640	M.84
63.2	356,400	600,000	525,000	4 GE CF6-45A2[d]	640	M.84
63.5	374,100	833,000	564,000	4 P&W JT9D-7R4G2[d]	640	M.84
63.5	380,000	833,000	574,000	4 P&W JT9D-7R4G2[d]	640	M.85
63.5	386,500	833,000	630,000	4 P&W JT9D	640	M.84
65.4	333,300	700,000	475,000	4 RR RB.211-524D4	640	M.85
63.5	390,200	870,000	630,000	4 GE CF6-80C2[d]	630	M.85
44.5	125,940	240,000	198,000	2 RR RB 211-535E or 2 P&W PW2037	593	M.8
52	176,100	315,000	272,000	2 P&W JT9D-7R4 or GE CF6-80A	594	M.8
52	179,900	351,000	278,000	2 P&W JT9D-7R4 or GE CF6-80A	594	M.8
52	190,200	351,000	300,000	2 P&W JT9D-7R4 or GE CF6-80A	594	M.8
52	196,100	400,000	320,000	2 P&W 4000 or GE CF6-80C2	594	M.8

factor may be overlooked. Ultimately, the winners of this race will be the commercial airlines and the consuming public. The advent of U.S. deregulation of this industry has allowed free market principles to work. The results are evident in lower fares and better service.

The same can be said of the fierce competition between the airframe manufacturers. For some time, Boeing has been the principal supplier and leader in producing commercial aircraft. This fact alone worried many commercial carriers, especially foreign airlines, who were apprehensive of being dependent on American-made aircraft. This fact, not entirely by itself but with a host of other factors, presents a distinct advantage to Airbus.

Any commercial airline CEO would agree that the most important factors needed for the business are high load factors and at least two competing aircraft suppliers. As in all free market competition, concessions relating to cost, financing, and special incentives are more readily obtained from the suppliers where there is competition. For example, since the 747 has no real competition, Boeing is less likely to offer creative pricing or special financing arrangements. Conversely, the 767 and A310, two relatively similar aircraft, are more vigorously marketed. Often manufacturers make concessions that may not be economically sound. Boeing's sale of 767s to TWA or Airbus's lease of A300s to Pan Am are two good examples. In both cases, these aircraft giants probably incurred losses to make the deal. Boeing provided TWA a guarantee that its 767 would meet specific fuel-burn requirements, probably with the knowledge that its quoted figures were beyond the capability of the aircraft. Airbus, at least in the assessment of industry analysts, leased A300s to Pan Am below cost.

The question of what the Boeing corporation will do remains. The age distribution of the commercial carriers' short- and medium-haul fleets supports Airbus Industrie's belief that the A320 is the right plane for the right time. According to Interavia, by 1988 110 Boeing 727s would be 20 or more years old, 200 will be between 15 to 19 years old, while over 420 will be 10 to 14 years old. The youngest 727 will be at least 16 years old by the year 2000. Airbus's strategy is not just to fill the replacement market for the 727 but to offer A320 to replace more than 1,500 DC-9 and 737–200 aircraft that will also be obsolete by the 21st century.

The battle for this market and the others not only exists in the manufacturing end of the industry but is related to the commercial airlines, engine manufacturers, and all the industry's support services. A loser or winner in one area will cause ripple effects in related areas, resulting in other winners and losers. The race is more costly than it seems at first glance, because American and European jobs, as well as the survival of many companies, are at risk. Many companies are betting their future on commercial aviation.

Case 2

Boeing's Commercial Jet Aircraft Business

The Current Marketplace

Maker of half the airliners produced since the jet age began, Boeing is flying high. The year 1988 was the best ever for its commercial airplane division. The company sold close to $30 billion worth of jetliners. This amounted to a staggering 636 jets, up from the 1978 record of 461 planes and the 1987 record of orders valued at $19.9 billion. A breakdown of company performance for five years is given in Table 1.

Much of Boeing's recent success is attributable to chairman Frank Shrontz (profiled in Exhibit 1). Serving under him, Dean Thornton is president of the commercial airplane division. Nine other key executives in the division and the positions they hold are shown in Exhibit 2, the organization chart for commercial airplanes.

To stay on top in an industry that exists at the boundary of technology, massive amounts of money are needed to develop aircraft. Dean Thornton has pointed out, "Hell, if we wanted to maximize earnings, we'd just cancel research."[1] No research would mean no new products or refinements to existing ones. This formula for short-term gain would lead to sure demise over time.

The Family of Planes

Boeing's dominance in the commercial aircraft industry was achieved through the strategy of offering a family of planes. Boeing airliners range from the narrow-body 737 and 757 series to the wide-body 767 and 747. Within each of these plane types, numerous configurations are available.

In 1987, the 737 surpassed the 727 as the most successful jet plane of all time with more than 1,800 units sold. Within the 737 series there are five configurations, four of which were being produced in 1988, when the 737–200 was phased out. Its replacement is the 737–500. This plane, which seats 100, has advanced avionics and all the sophistication of the larger 737–300 and 737–400. The 737 series enables operators to meet market requirements ranging from 100 passengers to nearly 170 on planes with a high degree of commonality. Flight crews can be cross-qualified on all versions. Airlines benefit from increased flexibility, reduction of inventory, and better usage of manpower.

Boeing's 757, its most fuel-efficient airplane, seats 180 to 220 passengers. This large, highly efficient plane fits well into the hub-and-spoke systems of numerous airlines. It gained renewed interest in 1988. In its first ten years, only 239 planes were sold. In 1988 Boeing took orders for 161 of the 757s. The plane is most effective on highly traveled congested routes that don't warrant a wide-body version but need 170-plus seating. A new all-cargo version is suitable for air delivery service because it can operate at night from the most noise-sensitive airports.

After what British Airways described as "a most careful study," the airline picked the wide-body 767–300 over the Airbus 300. The extended-range 767ER has been ordered by

---

This case represents neither effective nor ineffective handling of an administrative situation. Rather, it is to be used as a basis for classroom discussion.

[1]"The Higher the Flight, the Farther the Fall," *The Economist,* May 3, 1986, 23.

Table 1 Five Year Summary (Dollars in millions except per share data)
(Per share data restated for 1985 three-for-two stock split)

	1988	1987	1986	1985	1984
Operations					
Sales (including other operating revenues)*					
Commercial	**$ 12,170**	$ 10,623	$ 11,060	$ 9,002	$ 6,114
U.S. Government	**4,792**	4,882	5,384	4,743	4,328
Total	**16,962**	15,505	16,444	13,745	10,442
Net earnings	**614**	480	665	566	390**
Per primary share	**4.02**	3.10	4.28	3.75	2.67**
Percent of sales*	**3.6%**	3.1%	4.0%	4.1%	3.7%
Cash dividends paid	**$ 237**	$ 217	$ 186	$ 157	$ 136
Per share	**1.55**	1.40	1.20	1.04	.93
Other income, principally interest*	**378**	308	304	184	153
Research and development expensed	**751**	824	757	409	506
General and administrative expensed	**880**	793	606	477	420
Additions to plant and equipment	**690**	738	795	551	337
Depreciation of plant and equipment	**541**	486	433	356	337
Salaries and wages	**5,404**	5,028	4,374	3,442	3,011
Average employment	**147,300**	136,100	118,500	98,700	86,600
Financial position at December 31					
Total assets	**$ 12,608**	$ 12,566	$ 10,910	$ 9,153	$ 8,423
Working capital	**1,856**	2,246*	2,819	2,349	2,130
Long-term customer financing	**1,039**	392	195	514	541
Cash and short-term investments	**3,963**	3,435	4,172	3,209	1,595
Total borrowings	**258**	270	277	34	299
Long-term debt	**251**	256	263	16	284
Long-term deferred taxes	**205**	189*	219	326	322
Stockholders' equity	**5,404**	4,987	4,826	4,364	3,695
Per share	**35.27**	32.75	31.12	28.12	25.34
Common shares outstanding (000's)	**153,233**	152,273	155,095	155,189	145,837
Firm backlog					
Commercial	**$ 46,676**	$ 26,963	$ 20,084	$ 18,637	$ 15,949
U.S. Government	**6,925**	6,241	6,304	6,087	5,562
Total	**$ 53,601**	$ 33,204	$ 26,388	$ 24,724	$ 21,511

*Restated to conform to 1988 presentation.
**Exclusive of cumulative DISC adjustment to federal income tax provision. Net earnings after cumulative DISC adjustment were $787 or $5.39 per share.

Cash dividends have been paid on common stock every year since 1942.

Table 1 *(continued)*

Year ended December 31,	1988	1987	1986
Revenues			
Commercial transportation products and services	**$11,369**	$ 9,827	$ 9,820
Military transportation products and related systems	**3,668**	3,979	4,882
Missiles and space	**1,457**	1,063	1,126
Other industries	**468**	636	616
Operating revenues	**16,962**	15,505	16,444
Corporate income	**378**	308	304
Total revenues	**$17,340**	$15,813	$16,748
Operating Profit*			
Commercial transportation products and services	**$ 585**	$ 352	$ 411
Military transportation products and related systems	**(95)**	60	367
Missiles and space	**124**	119	55
Other industries	**(28)**	(34)	(9)
Operating profit	**586**	497	824
Corporate income	**378**	308	304
Corporate expense	**(144)**	(147)	(100)
Earnings before taxes	**$ 820**	$ 658	$ 1,028
Identifiable assets at December 31			
Commercial transportation products and services	**$ 4,558**	$ 5,170	$ 3,533
Military transportation products and related systems	**2,923**	2,846	2,285
Missiles and space	**684**	548	434
Other industries	**319**	362	364
	8,484	8,926	6,616
Corporate	**4,124**	3,640	4,294
Consolidated assets	**$12,608**	$12,566	$10,910
Depreciation			
Commercial transportation products and services	**$ 243**	$ 218	$ 200
Military transportation products and related systems	**188**	170	136
Missiles and space	**52**	42	34
Capital expenditures, net			
Commercial transportation products and services	**$ 326**	$ 286	$ 332
Military transportation products and related systems	**241**	316	356
Missiles and space	**62**	72	82

*The implementation of SFAS No. 87 (see Notes 1 and 9) increased 1987 operating profit by $33 for commercial transportation products and services, $24 for military transportation products and related systems, $4 for missiles and space and $4 for other industries.

Exhibit 1 Profile of Frank Shrontz

You'd think Boeing chairman Frank A. Shrontz would be on easy street. A $54 billion order backlog will keep Boeing plants humming into the mid-1990s and send its earnings up. Yet the giant planemaker suffers from an embarrassment of riches. Customers are fuming over production delays on the new 747–400 jets they've ordered. And in the clamor over air safety, Boeing Company has come under intense scrutiny from regulators and the traveling public. Shrontz' biggest challenge is ensuring that the No. 1 planemaker keeps its reputation for quality and safety.

The pressures on the composed and urbane Shrontz, 57, come just as earnings are taking off. Thanks to a five-year buying binge by airlines, the Seattle company's profits are expected to jump 50 percent this year [1989] to $918 million, on a 29 percent gain in revenue, to $22 billion. Profits next year should rise 25 percent, and revenues 7 percent. "We have plenty of business," says Shrontz, a 30-year Boeing veteran. "Our big job is to execute."

Shrontz will have his hands full getting 747 production back on schedule. Because the company is overcommitted, it's running several months behind in delivering the jumbo jets—Boeing's first missed deliveries in 20 years. The company's top brass is busy negotiating concessions with irate airlines.

Employees are none too happy, either. Boeing has increased its work force 83 percent in the past five years, to 155,000, but it's still so short of manpower that it took the unusual step in early March of "borrowing" 760 Lockheed Corporation workers for its 747 production line. When labor negotiations start this fall, Boeing's unions will grouse most about excessive overtime.

As production pressures increase, Shrontz will have to be more vigilant about safety and quality. Boeing's image has slipped because of miswirings and plumbing problems on 59 of its jets and several crashes involving its planes. Although investigators may exonerate Boeing, the Federal Aviation Administration has stepped up its oversight of production and quality control.

Shrontz' problems on the military side are more commonplace: Business is just too slow. And while the former Assistant Defense Secretary would love to restore profitability to Boeing's military transport business, which last year [1988] lost an estimated $60 million, shrinking defense budgets may block his way. Defense and space will probably drop to 22 percent of Boeing's sales by 1991, from 29 percent last year. In the face of numbers like that, Boeing's backlog doesn't look so bad after all.

Source: Maria Shao, "Frank Shrontz," 129. Reprinted from April 14, 1989 Top 1000 Special Bonus Issue of *Business Week* by special permission, copyright © 1989 by McGraw-Hill, Inc.

American, Canadian Airlines, SAS, and LTU. The 767ER has a range of almost 6,000 miles and can carry up to 290 passengers.

The 747 is the mainstay of the free world's international airlines and Boeing's cash cow at over $110 million per plane. It enjoyed outstanding years in 1987 and 1988. Sales of this plane alone accounted for over $17 billion. In 1988 Boeing rolled out its new 747–400, with a range of 8,000 miles and passenger capacity of 400 to 600. However, production problems slowed the delivery of this advanced jetliner. Boeing officials conceded that earlier delivery positions played a role in the American Airlines $7.4 billion order for MD-11s and MD-80s.

Many people still remember the expense involved in developing this successful plane. In the years 1969 through 1971, development of this plane and the cancellation of the SST supersonic transport almost bankrupted Boeing. "It's like living on the damn San Andreas fault all the time. The fact that it hasn't moved for ten years doesn't mean a thing," observed Boeing's economist Tom Craig. In a drastic retrenchment the airline cut its work force by over 60,000 workers.

Marketing Strategy

Boeing works closely with its customers in planning new or derivative product offerings. As with any product line, but especially for one that requires the tremendous resources required to produce an airliner, it is imperative that new products meet the needs of customers. Domestically, Delta and American have been the primary sources of market information. United more recently has also been a prime source of information. Among European airlines, SAS, British

Exhibit 2 Organization Chart for Boeing Commercial Airplane Division

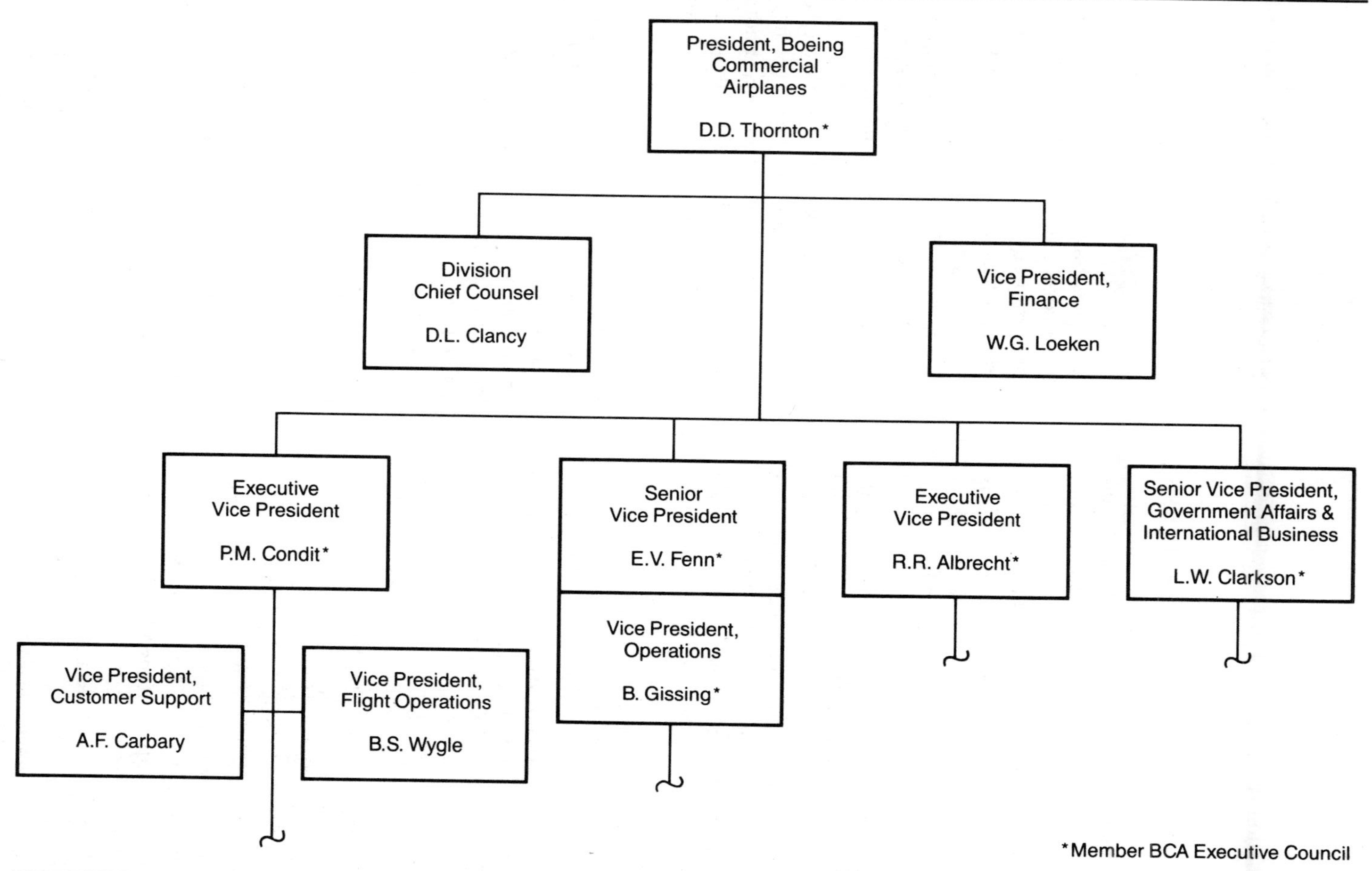

Source: The Boeing Company

Airways, and Lufthansa provide input. In the Orient, Japan Airlines and to a small extent Singapore Airlines are the sources of primary market information.

Boeing gives the market what it wants, not what its engineers think the market wants. European state-owned aircraft makers in the past have tailored their products to the needs of state-owned airlines. These planes often became unsuitable for other airlines with different route networks or passenger requirements. Good examples are the Trident and the BAC 1–11 designed to fulfill the workhorse role of the 727. These planes were tailored to British European Airlines and sold only 351 units compared to the 727's 1,832.

Almost a decade ago the input from the market indicated a need for a 150-seat airplane. Delta had expressed a strong interest in a short-haul airplane that would carry 150 passengers between its many destinations on the East Coast. Delta also was the champion of the twin-aisle configuration that is now standard on all wide-body aircraft.

Market information emerged that indicated that two or more niches could be served with new products that resided on either side of the 150-passenger mark. For example, in its fleet planning meetings with Boeing, SAS presented a plan for a fleet of airplanes having three different configurations: 75 to 95 passengers, 120 to 140 passengers, and 160 to 180 passengers. SAS also indicated a desire to fill those configuration needs with only two airplane types. Similar needs have been expressed by domestic companies as well. Delta has purchased McDonnell Douglas MD-88 (142-passenger) aircraft to fill their 150-seat need. American has also purchased MD-80 series planes, Fokker 100s for the 95- to 100-seat market, and Boeing 757s for the 170- to 220-passenger configuration. It appears the demand for a new 150-seat plane, widely believed by some at the start of the decade to be the plane of choice to replace the 727, has changed.

Boeing does have the 146-passenger 737-400 to compete head to head with the Airbus A320. It has the same engines as the A320 and has technically equivalent avionics. A foreshortened version of the 737, the 737–500, became available in the summer of 1989. This 737-lite will compete in the 100-seat market.

Boeing is positioned to compete in all segments of today's marketplace. In the "Boeing first and better" days, Boeing airplanes commanded a premium price because there was no genuine competition for its products. Also, in exchange for substantial input to the final configuration of the airplane, airlines would prepay up to 25 percent of their committed purchases, which helped finance development of new planes. However, Airbus has taken a market-driven position in the marketplace. Through government subsidizing of interest rates and exchange rate fluctuations, it competes on price. The selling of aircraft now revolves around lease buy-backs, recession insurance, trading in of used planes, and other deal making or breaking issues that fall squarely on financial concerns.

The Future

The market for aircraft is difficult to define, because conflicting signals are given by the airlines. The threat is that the characteristics and the potential size of the new market are not very well defined. What is known is that 8,000 jets may be purchased between 1989 and 2004. Of these the majority, or close to 70 percent, will handle the explosive growth experience worldwide in air travel. The rest will replace the aging fleet of the world.

Boeing is facing a volatile aircraft market requiring huge investments. Even when a product is established, airlines tend to order little by little, so Boeing is unable to make any long-term plans for a large number of planes. The company cannot take advantage of either learning curves or economies of scale. Large orders are more frequent with the military, but the military sector is a function of the Administration in power.

Moreover, military budgets are the first targets for cuts and searches for abuse.

A possible threat is the flying public's loss of confidence in a Boeing product. A series of incidents that have involved older planes could incite the consumer to avoid airlines using Boeing planes, similar to the experience of the airlines flying the DC-10.

The greatest potential competition in the next century could come from Japan. The Japanese would like to erase a multibillion-dollar deficit in aerospace trade and become a front runner in this technology. One way for the Japanese to achieve this goal is to acquire technology and thus enter the airline market through cooperation with foreign firms.

Cooperation is a fashionable management technique in the aerospace industry. International cooperation, however, is difficult and nearly always more expensive. Political motives also play an important role, because partners may look for different benefits. Some examples of cooperation are the tactical fighter produced by Brazil and Italy; a commuter plane produced by the United States and Sweden; Concorde, produced by France and Great Britain; and a commuter series produced by Indonesia and Spain. Numerous joint productions between France and Germany also helped the German aerospace industry to develop after World War II. McDonnell Douglas had been planning to license its MD-80 to China for production, but the negotiations took place prior to the 1989 violence.

The Japanese are willing to push the cooperation between Japan and Boeing. Boeing was willing to share in the costs and the risk of developing a new 150-seat aircraft called the 7J7 with Japan Aircraft Development Corporation. This company is composed of Mitsubishi Heavy Industries (manufacturer of the Zero during World War II), Kawasaki Heavy Industries, and Fuji Heavy Industries. All of these companies are presently engaged in home designs or in license production. They have facilities and money, but each needs technology and expertise.

For the 150-seat aircraft, the Japanese company was willing to provide 25 percent of the development costs in exchange for more management, technical, and marketing responsibilities. The Japanese wanted the plane to be ready by 1989 to compete with the A320, which was introduced in 1988.

In February 1985, however, Boeing postponed the development of the 150-seat aircraft. Boeing's position was that the agreement made in March 1984 was not a joint venture but simply an agreement to study the possibilities of a new plane. The studies would have considered the 150-seat aircraft and a 100-seat aircraft.

Boeing's 747–400 program, as mentioned earlier, is behind schedule with only one of three engine combinations certified and only one aircraft delivered. The company will be at a record 34 planes per month by 1992. According to executive vice president Philip Condit, "Whatever we do, we do it carefully and logically—we won't try to do it all at the same time. At these high rates, we must stay in control, or we won't be able to meet our commitment."[2] Industry experts have indicated that investments in technology that have been unbalanced toward engineering will be applied more to manufacturing. The industry is in a phase in which there are no radical new technology breakthroughs. Condit believes that the primary attributes airlines are seeking are operating economies across the board and reasonable first cost.

The commercial airplane division's president has summed up his feelings about Boeing: "This is a hell of a company and it's got a hell of a group of people. We fight and we make love and it's fun to work here. You look at a company making toothpaste, or a new kind of bread. . . . We've got something to be proud of."[3]

---

[2]Richard G. O'Lone, "Commercial Airframe Makers Take Conservative Approach," *Aviation Week and Space Technology,* March 20, 1989, 198.

[3]"The Higher the Flight, the Farther the Fall," *The Economist,* May 3, 1986, 26.

Case 3

The Kellogg Company and the Ready-to-Eat Cereal Industry

You take care of the outside.
We'll help take care of the inside.
1985 ad for Kellogg's All Bran

Advertising campaigns for Kellogg products in the 1980s stress the healthy, nutritious quality of cereal flakes—corn, bran, wheat, oats—a Kellogg theme that began almost a century ago. Dr. John H. Kellogg and W. K. Kellogg sought to develop a cereal that could replace meat in the diets of the patients at the Battle Creek sanitarium that the Kelloggs managed. The product of their efforts, Corn Flakes, became popular enough with the patients that the Kelloggs formed two companies that became the Kellogg Company in 1899.

Eighty-six years later Kellogg is one of the largest food companies in the world, with annual sales exceeding $2.5 billion and earnings greater than $250 million. Kellogg has established a position in the ready-to-eat (RTE) cereal market almost twice as large as either of the two nearest competitors, General Mills and General Foods. "Kellogg knows the cereal business better than anyone else" said William Wason of Brown Brothers Harriman & Co., "and the management has had the wisdom to stick with what they know." In December 1985, Kellogg was named one of the five best managed companies in the United States by *Dun's Business Month* (Dec. 1985). Kellogg won this acclaim because of its performance throughout the 1970s and early 1980s, the darkest time in the industry's history, and the progress Kellogg made in recovering during 1984 and 1985.

This case was prepared by Joseph A. Schenk, Dan S. Prickett, and Stanley J. Stough. Address reprint requests to: Joseph A. Schenk, Management Department, University of Dayton, 300 College Park, Dayton, OH 45469–0001.

The Ready-to-Eat Cereal Industry

The RTE cereal industry is composed of firms that are engaged in the manufacture and sale of prepackaged, processed foodstuffs made primarily of grain products. The user does not have to prepare the product prior to use, and it can be eaten in dry form or with the addition of other substances, such as milk and sugar. Advantages of the product from a consumer perspective include convenience of use and easy satisfaction of nutritional requirements. Consumption of the products takes place primarily at breakfast, but they are also used as between-meal snacks. The first products in the market were introduced by W. K. Kellogg, Wheat Flakes in 1894 and Corn Flakes in 1898.

The $4 billion RTE cereal industry is composed of several large companies that dominate the market. Led by Kellogg, the industry includes General Mills, General Foods, Quaker Oats, Ralston Purina, and Nabisco. Table 1 lists the market share performance of the major competitors as of 1984.

The significance of cereals within the product lines of the competitors changes as a result of competition and developments within the companies themselves. Although cereals represent more than 75% of Kellogg sales, cereals are

Table 1. The Ready-to-Eat Cereal Industry: Market Share Data[a]

Company	1976	1977	1978	1979	1980	1981	1982	1983	1984
Kellogg	42.6	42.5	42.0	41.5	40.9	39.3	38.5	38.5	40.3
General Mills	20.8	20.5	20.4	22.2	22.4	23.0	23.1	23.2	23.1
General Foods	15.7	16.8	16.0	15.4	15.0	15.0	16.0	16.1	13.3
Quaker Oats	8.9	8.9	8.7	8.6	8.6	8.6	8.9	8.9	8.6
Ralston Purina	4.9	3.4	5.7	5.6	6.2	6.1	5.6	6.1	6.3
Nabisco	4.0	4.2	4.2	4.1	3.8	3.9	3.8	3.8	4.2
All others	3.1	3.7	3.0	2.6	3.1	4.1	4.1	3.4	4.2

Source: Advertising Age: Aug. 5, 1985, p. 42; Jun. 14, 1982, p. 62; May 25, 1981, p. 62; Aug. 28, 1978, p. 217.
[a]All figures are percentages.

estimated to constitute no more than 13% of General Foods sales and 7% of General Mills sales. Kellogg sales and estimated operating profits by division are listed in Table 2.

Vigorous competition in the RTE cereal industry requires intensive and decisive actions to expand investments in research, in the development of new products, and in marketing. Marketing plans generally center on facing the competition squarely and forcefully. Budgets for advertising and promotions have increased substantially in recent years, both to give additional support to established products and to successfully support new product introductions. Market shares for the top ten products in the industry are listed in Table 3. Selected information regarding each major competitor is presented below.

General Mills

General Mills managed to increase its market share significantly during the 1976–1981 period. Since then market share has stabilized, and General Mills has been able to maintain a share position in the industry at about 23%. Recent new product activity included the national roll-out of

Table 2. Kellogg Company: Operating Profit at Year End December Estimated by Division ($ millions)

	1982	1983	1984	1985	1986 (estimated)
Net sales	$2,367	$2,381	$2,602	$2,930	$3,250
Operating profits					
Domestic RTE Cereals	238.0	255.0	311.0	395.0	450.0
Mrs. Smith's	29.0	28.5	31.5	36.9	43.0
Salada	9.0	10.0	11.0	12.5	14.0
Fearn	13.8	15.5	17.0	19.0	21.0
International	107.9	105.4	96.7	95.0	110.0
Total operating income	397.7	414.4	467.2	558.4	638.0
Net income	227.8	242.7	250.5	281.3	320.5

Source: Prudential-Bache Securities, Inc., Apr. 2, 1986.

Table 3. Cold Cereal's Top Ten in Market Share[a]

Brand (company)	1983 Pounds	1983 Dollars	1984 Pounds	1984 Dollars
Corn Flakes (K)	6.8	4.7	6.8	4.7
Frosted Flakes (K)	5.2	4.8	5.6	5.2
Cheerios (GM)	5.5	5.8	5.2	5.5
Raisin Bran (K)	4.6	4.1	4.5	4.0
Chex (RP)	4.3	4.4	4.3	4.6
Shredded Wheat (N)	4.0	3.1	4.0	3.3
Rice Krispies (K)	3.6	3.9	3.5	3.8
Raisin Bran (GF)	3.0	2.5	2.7	2.1
Cap'n Crunch (Q)	2.9	3.5	2.7	3.2
Honey-Nut Cheerios (GM)	2.3	2.6	2.6	2.9
Total	42.2	39.4	41.9	39.3

Source: Advertising Age, Aug. 5, 1985, p. 42.
Abbreviations: K = Kellogg; GM = General Mills; GF = General Foods; Q = Quaker Oats; N = Nabisco; RP = Ralston Purina.
[a]All figures are percentages.

E.T.'s, which failed to produce significant sales, reflecting a decline of consumer interest in licensed properties. Cinnamon Toast Crunch, Fiber One, Bran Muffin Crunch, and S'More's Crunch are all expected to perform well after national roll-out in early 1986. General Mills' brands and the market share performance of each brand for the period 1982–1984 are shown in Table 4.

General Mills has concentrated its efforts on its snack food, yogurt, and restaurant businesses. It has divested some toy operations and repurchased 7 million shares of its own stock (44 million shares outstanding). General Mills net sales and operating profit by segment are listed in Table 5.

General Foods

Throughout the 1970s, General Foods relied on coffee—Maxwell House, Sanka, Yuban, and Brim—for approximately 40% of its total revenue (*New York Times,* Sep. 15, 1985). Since then, it has made major acquisitions. Currently, the company gets 40% of its revenues from packaged groceries, 28% from coffee products, and 18% from processed meats (*Economist,* 1985). Coffee is still General Foods' largest single product, and it holds a 38% share of the coffee market (Philip Morris, 1986). In fiscal year 1985, General Foods achieved total revenues of $9 billion and the RTE cereal sales accounted for $512 million of total sales (Drexel, Burnham, & Lambert, May 20, 1985).

Sales of Post Toasties and Grape Nuts are eroding. Raisin Bran and Honey Nut Crunch Raisin Bran are reported to be performing well in the health-conscious market segment (*New York Times,* Sep. 15, 1985). Table 6 lists General Foods' RTE cereal products and market share performance for the 1982–1984 period.

Most of General Foods' development in the 1980s has consisted of creating or acquiring product lines to enter new markets, particularly convenience, low-calorie foods. Acquisitions include Oscar Meyer, Entenmann's bakery, Ronzoni, and Orowheat. New products developments include Crystal Light, Pudding Pops, Sun Apple, Lean Strips, and Crispy Cookin' French Fries, of which only Crystal Light and Pudding Pops had met with success as of the end of 1985.

Table 4. General Mills' Ready-to-Eat Cereals: Market Share Data[a]

Brand	1982 Pounds	1982 Dollars	1983 Pounds	1983 Dollars	1984 Pounds	1984 Dollars
Cheerios	5.6	5.9	5.5	5.8	5.2	5.5
Honey Nut Cheerios	2.1	2.4	2.3	2.6	2.6	2.9
Total	1.7	2.4	1.9	2.6	2.1	2.8
Lucky Charms	1.7	2.2	1.6	2.1	1.7	2.1
Trix	1.5	1.9	1.5	1.9	1.5	1.9
Wheaties	2.5	1.9	2.3	1.7	2.0	1.4
Golden Grahams	1.3	1.3	1.3	1.3	1.3	1.3
Crispy Wheats 'n Raisins	1.1	1.3	1.1	1.3	1.0	1.1
Licensed Products	0.4	0.5	1.1	1.3	0.7	1.0
Monsters, etc.	0.7	1.0	0.6	0.9	0.5	0.8
Cinnamon Toast Crunch	—	—	—	—	0.6	0.7
Cocoa Puffs	0.7	1.8	0.7	0.8	0.6	0.7
Buc Wheats	0.5	0.6	0.4	0.5	0.3	0.4
Others	0.3	0.2	0.5	0.4	0.6	0.5
Total	20.7	23.1	20.8	23.2	20.7	23.1

Source: Advertising Age, Aug. 5, 1985, p. 42.
[a]All figures are percentages.

Table 5. General Mills: Operating Profit at Year End May, by Segment ($ millions)

	1983	1984	1985	1986 (estimated)
Net sales	$4,082	$4,118	$4,285	$4,550
Operating profits				
Consumer foods	269.4	275.3	265.6	300.0
Restaurants	80.0	70.0	91.5	97.0
Specialty retailing and other (loss)	10.4	19.8	(1.7)	23.0
Total operating profit	359.8	365.1	355.4	420.0
Net income (loss)	245.1	233.4	(72.9)	182.9

Source: Prudential-Bache Securities, Inc., Apr. 2, 1986.

Simultaneously, General Foods has divested its pet foods division and the Burger Chef restaurant chain and repurchased 11% of its stock. In 1985, Philip Morris acquired General Foods to integrate its food operations into the tobacco products company. General Foods sales and operating profits by segment are listed in Table 7.

Quaker Oats

In the 1960s, Quaker Oats acquired many diverse businesses. By the 1980s, Quaker Oats had divested its restaurants and chemical products units and was concentrating on acquiring packaged foods and specialty companies including Brookstone (tools), Jos. A. Bank (clothiers), Eye-

Table 6. General Foods' Ready-to-Eat Cereals: Market Share Data[a]

	1982		1983		1984	
Brand	**Pounds**	**Dollars**	**Pounds**	**Dollars**	**Pounds**	**Dollars**
Post Raisin Bran	3.1	2.8	3.0	2.5	2.7	2.1
Grape-Nuts	2.9	2.4	2.5	1.9	2.2	1.5
Super Sugar Crisp	1.4	1.6	1.5	1.6	1.4	1.4
Honeycombs	1.1	1.5	1.2	1.5	1.1	1.3
Post Fruit & Fibre	1.5	1.7	1.3	1.4	1.3	1.4
Pebbles	1.2	1.4	1.2	1.4	1.1	1.3
Smurf Berry Crunch	—	—	1.0	1.1	0.5	0.6
Post Toasties	1.3	0.9	1.2	0.9	1.0	0.8
Alpha-Bits	0.8	0.9	0.8	0.9	0.7	0.8
Bran Flakes	0.8	0.8	0.8	0.8	0.8	0.8
Honey-Nut Crunch Raisin Bran	0.3	0.3	0.7	0.7	0.2	0.2
Raisin Grape-Nuts	0.8	0.8	0.6	0.6	0.4	0.4
Fortified Oat Flakes	0.6	0.5	0.6	0.5	0.5	0.4
C.W. Post Hearty Granola	0.2	0.2	—	0.1	0.1	0.1
Others	0.4	0.2	0.1	0.2	0.3	0.2
Total	16.4	16.0	16.6	16.1	14.3	13.3

Source: Advertising Age, Aug. 5, 1985, p. 42.
[a]All figures are percentages.

Table 7. General Foods: Operating Profit at Year End March, by Segment ($ millions)

	1983	**1984**	**1985**	**1986 (estimated)**
Net sales	$8,256	$8,599	$9,022	$9,500
Operating profits				
Packaged groceries	427.8	470.5	419.3	451.0
Coffee	131.1	107.9	127.2	135.0
Processed meats	90.1	96.9	104.2	115.1
Food services and other	38.4	39.9	51.2	55.0
Total operating income	686.6	715.2	701.9	756.1
Net income	288.5	317.1	302.8	316.4

Source: Prudential-Bache Securities, Inc., Oct. 1, 1985.

lab (eyeware retailing), and Stokely Van Camp (pork and beans, Gatorade). In addition, Quaker Oats repurchased 5% of its own shares in March 1985. The 1980s witnessed an aggressive Quaker Oats expanding its operations throughout its product lines.

Quaker Oats has bundled its product development (20 new products and line extensions since 1983) under the Quaker umbrella and has pushed those lines in which it has a leadership position: hot cereals, granola bars, and Gatorade. Spending $200 million in 1985 for advertising, Quaker Oats has shown a 16% growth in advertising expenditures and a 31% growth in merchandising expenditures since 1984.

As a result of this strategy and increasing new product development at Kellogg, General Mills, and Ralston Purina, Quaker Oats has allowed its share of the RTE cereal market to erode from 8.9% in 1983 to 8.6% in 1984. Halfsies and Cap'n Crunch have lost market share, whereas Life and 100% Natural have maintained their sales levels. Quaker Oats RTE cereal brands and market share performance are listed in Table 8, and Quaker Oats net sales and operating profits by segment are shown in Table 9.

Ralston Purina

Ralston Purina led the RTE cereal industry in restructuring through the use of share repurchase. Ralston Purina has acquired almost 40 million shares of its own stock, and, through divestiture of its Foodmaker division, can acquire more. Ralston Purina acquired Continental Baking in 1984, which added the Hostess brands to the Ralston Purina product lines.

Ralston Purina is expected to focus on its pet food operations and the Hostess lines for the foreseeable future. New product activity in 1985,

Table 8. Quaker Oats' Ready-to-Eat Cereals: Market Share Data[a]

	1982		1983		1984	
Brand	**Pounds**	**Dollars**	**Pounds**	**Dollars**	**Pounds**	**Dollars**
Cap'n Crunch	3.2	3.8	2.9	3.5	2.7	3.2
Life	2.5	2.3	2.4	2.2	2.4	2.2
100% Natural	1.6	1.5	1.6	1.5	1.5	1.4
Halfsies	—	—	0.7	0.7	0.2	0.3
Corn Bran	0.7	0.6	0.7	0.6	0.6	0.6
Others	0.9	0.7	0.6	0.4	0.9	0.9
Total	8.9	8.9	8.9	8.9	8.3	8.6

Source: Advertising Age, Aug. 5, 1985, p. 42.
[a]All figures are percentages.

Table 9. Quaker Oats: Operating Profit at Year End June, by Segment ($ millions)

	1983	1984	1985	1986 (estimated)
Net sales	$2,611	$3,344	$3,520	$3,650
Operating profits				
U.S. and Canadian grocery	193.8	219.5	250.0	272.0
International grocery	49.1	32.9	49.7	60.0
Fisher-Price	29.6	43.6	47.1	50.0
Specialty retailing	15.8	12.7	15.2	18.0
Total	288.3	308.7	362.0	400.0
Net income	119.3	138.7	156.6	174.2

Source: Prudential-Bache Securities, Inc., Apr. 2, 1986.

greatest in company history, brought extension of the Chuck Wagon line with three new dog food products, expansion of the dog treats line with Waggles and T-Bonz, and new cat foods. New products in cereals include Sun Flakes, Rainbow Brite, and Cabbage Patch. Ralston Purina's RTE cereal products and market share performance for the 1982–1984 period are presented in Table 10. Ralston Purina's net sales and operating profits by segment are listed in Table 11.

Nabisco

Since 1983, Nabisco has introduced 140 new products and line extensions globally. This aggressive posture indicated a recognition by Nabisco of the importance of the international market, which accounts for 40% of its normalized operating income.

In 1985, Nabisco was acquired by R. J. Reynolds, a tobacco products company. The com-

Table 10. Ralston Purina's Ready-to-Eat Cereals: Market Share Data[a]

	1982		1983		1984	
Brand	**Pounds**	**Dollars**	**Pounds**	**Dollars**	**Pounds**	**Dollars**
Chex	4.2	4.0	4.3	4.4	4.3	4.6
Donkey Kong	—	—	0.7	0.7	0.6	0.6
Cookie Crisp	0.6	0.6	0.5	0.7	0.4	0.7
Others	0.3	0.2	0.3	0.2	0.6	0.4
Total	5.9	5.6	5.9	6.1	5.9	6.3

Source: Advertising Age, Aug. 5, 1985, p. 42.
[a]All figures are percentages.

Table 11. Ralston Purina: Operating Profit at Year End September, by Segment ($ millions)

	1982	1983	1984	1985	1986 (estimated)
Net sales	$4,803	$4,872	$4,980	$5,864	$5,350
Operating profits					
Pet food	227.0	263.5	303.0	350.0	399.0
Seafood (loss)	(11.0)	14.5	9.5	10.0	11.5
Cereals	38.5	43.5	41.5	45.5	50.0
Continental baking	—	—	—	84.0	94.0
Other consumer goods	3.7	5.5	1.6	6.6	8.0
Agriculture	96.6	105.6	92.5	74.9	82.0
Restaurant	46.7	58.5	61.4	47.2	0.0
Diversified operations	27.1	33.6	35.9	24.2	30.0
Total operating income	428.6	524.7	545.4	642.4	674.5
Net income	69.1	256.0	242.7	256.4	371.0

Source: Prudential-Bache Securities, Inc., Apr. 2, 1986.

bined R. J. Reynolds and Nabisco advertising budget weighs in at $1 billion. This financial strength is to be applied, among other things, to joint product marketing. For example, Del Monte coupons may come with Shredded Wheat. It is hoped that this mixed marketing approach will boost sales of product lines throughout the combined companies.

Nabisco's major product in the RTE cereals market is Shredded Wheat. Shredded Wheat held a 3.3% dollar market share in 1984 (4.0% in pounds). All Nabisco RTE cereal products held a total market share of 4.2% on a dollar basis (4.9% on a poundage basis) (*Advertising Age,* Aug. 5, 1985).

Industry Challenges

The RTE cereal industry emerged from the 1970s facing continuing challenges from the Federal Trade Commission (FTC). Founded in 1914 to combat monopolies, the FTC is charged with preventing unfair methods of competition and unfair or deceptive acts or practices that affect commerce. For almost a decade, the FTC had pursued the RTE industry leaders on two issues: children's television programming and advertising, and the operation of an oligopolistic "shared monopoly."

Children's Television and Advertising

As early as 1970, consumer groups pressed for greater regulation of children's television and advertising (*Federal Register,* vol. 49). A group called Action for Children's Television (ACT) prodded the FTC to establish minimum requirements for age-specific programming for children. In 1971, ACT petitioned the FTC to ban all vitamin advertising on programs intended for children. (One third of advertising on TV programs for children had been for vitamin products.) To avoid further pressure, the manufacturers voluntarily complied with the petition (Ward, 1978).

From 1971 through 1974, the Children's Television Task Force studied the state of children's television and recommended that licensees increase the amount of television programming created for children, particularly programs of educational and informational content. The task force recommended that selling, promotion, or endorsement of a product by the host of the program be prohibited, and that program content be clearly distinguished from commercial messages.

The ACT and other watchdog groups increased their efforts to influence the FTC in the late 1970s, with the result that the FTC introduced proposals for regulations to limit advertising on programs whose primary audience was children. Despite efforts toward self-regulation by industry groups such as the Children's Advertising Review unit of the National Council of Broadcasters and the Codes of the National Association of Broadcasters (Ward, 1978), the FTC banned all commercials on shows aimed at children of a very young age and commercials for highly sugared foods on programs directed at older children. The regulation also required advertisers to devote money to public service announcements to promote good dental and nutritional habits.

In 1980, Congress limited the scope of the FTC's attempts to regulate children's advertising to matters of deception and "unfair" or misleading advertising (Dewar, 1980). By October 1981, the FTC dropped its pursuit of the broadcasters and advertisers with respect to "Kid Vid" issues (*Federal Register,* vol. 46). The ACT continues to monitor television and file complaints to the FTC on those companies that ACT believes exploit the innocence of youth. The ACT has filed against Quaker Oats (1982), General Mills (1983), and General Foods (1983), charging unfair or deceptive advertising by each company (*Associated Press,* Jul. 18, 1983).

In 1983, Kellogg was brought to court in Canada to force the company to cease advertising to children. Kellogg claimed that such a ban would limit the company's ability to release new products and thus freeze competitors' present market shares. The availability of U.S. television in Canada obscures any verification of Kellogg's claim. However, Kellogg and other companies marketing products aimed at children, including games, toys, and foods, were restricted from advertising to children on Canadian television. The Canadian court stated that ads are presumed to be intended for children if they include "themes related to fantasy, magic, mystery, suspense or adventure," if they depict authority figures, role models, heroes, animals, or "imaginary or fanciful creatures," or if they rely on cartoons, children's music, or attention-getting technical devices (Lippman, 1983). Products of interest to children can be presented on Canadian television only if addressed to adults in a mature fashion.

Shared Monopoly

In the ten years that followed the FTC's initial complaint against Kellogg, General Mills, General Foods, and Quaker Oats, 243 days of testimony produced more than 36,000 pages of transcript and 60,000 pages of documents. The FTC charged the industry leaders with operating a "shared monopoly" that resulted not from conspiracy or collusion but from the collective power of the few firms (Kiechel, 1978).

The concept of shared monopoly arose from a study by a Massachusetts Institute of Technology economist, Richard L. Schmalensee. He argued that the cereal companies crowded the supermarket shelves with a large number of brands that left little space for new entrants. The flood of products into the market invited competition among those brands with similar characteristics—crunchiness, flavor, sweetness—but not competition between all brands on the market. The profusion of brands ensured that only existing firms could afford to compete; a new entrant would be required to invest $150 million in development with little assurance that it could gain the 3–5% share necessary to gain scale economy in production (Sebastian, 1979).

Specifically, the FTC charged the companies with the following practices (FTC vs Lonning & Kellogg).

Brand Proliferation. "The four companies introduce a profusion of ready-to-eat cereal brands into the market," that fill the "perceptual space" of the consumer with over 200 brands on the supermarket shelves.

Aggressive Marketing. "The brands are promoted by intensive advertising aimed primarily at children, which . . . conceals the true nature of these cereals." For example, Honey and Nut Corn Flakes implies significant sweetening by honey; in fact the flakes contain more brown sugar, white refined sugar, vegetable oil, salt, and malt flavoring than honey (Sebastian, 1979).

Product Differentiation. The four companies produce "basically similar" ready-to-eat cereals that are artificially differentiated through trivial differences.

In addition to creating barriers to entry into the RTE cereal market, the companies were also accused of other unfair methods of competition in advertising and product promotion. The charges included:

1. Cereal advertising is false and misleading. This issue, also raised by ACT, pits the claims of nutrition and health against the high sugar content of many cereals. The sugar content has been blamed for health and dental problems.

2. Kellogg's program of shelf-space allocation, a program emulated by other cereal manufacturers, controls the exposure of breakfast food products. Kellogg records the sales of cereals in the supermarket and recommends brand selection and shelf-space allocation to the supermarket manager.

3. The companies made numerous acquisitions to eliminate competition in the RTE cereal market. These acquisitions have enhanced the shared monopoly structure of the industry.

4. The companies have exercised monopoly power by refusing to engage in price competition or other consumer-directed promotions.

The FTC claimed that the results of these acts were artificially inflated prices, excessive profits, and an absence of price competition. Government economists used the concept of shared monopoly to explain the reluctance of large consumer-products companies, such as Procter and Gamble, to enter the lucrative, albeit competitive, cereal market.

The FTC hoped to apply shared monopoly or oligopolistic behavior restrictions to other industries after establishing the validity of the concept in a landmark decision with references to the RTE cereals industry case. Any industry in which relatively few companies hold 90% market share (examples include telecommunications, oil, automobiles, and computers) would then be vulnerable to FTC action (Cowan, 1981; *Time,* Oct. 5, 1981).

Demographic Changes

Another basic challenge facing the industry has been a slowdown in the rate of growth of cereal consumption, brought about, in part, by the aging of the U.S. population. The U.S. median age is now 30 and is forecasted to reach 35 by the year 2000. The total population is expected to grow by less than 1% per year during the 1980s, primarily because of a slowdown in the U.S. birthrate.

Age-group populations do show different growth rates. Several changes expected in the 1980–1990 decade are listed below.

- The 15–24 year age group will decrease by 17% or 7.1 million.
- The 25–34 year age group will undergo a strong 14% increase.
- The 35–54 year age group will undergo the largest increase of all age groups, 25%.
- The 55–64 year age group will shrink by 2%.
- The over-65 age group will show the second largest increase, up by 20% (*Newsweek,* Jan. 17, 1983).

These demographic trends pose a threat to companies that sell a significant portion of their production to the youth market. The greatest consumers of RTE cereals are children under the age of 13. In the 1970s, the industry had experienced a decline in the population of this group. Tables 12–15 provide additional data on demographic changes facing the industry and on consumption of RTE cereal products.

Despite the challenges faced by the industry, the 1980s held some promise for the RTE cereal makers. Grain prices were weakening, with strong gains in production continuing through mid-decade. Moreover, cereal companies were able to levy 5% and 6% price increases while maintaining cereal at the lowest cost-per-serving of any breakfast food.

Kellogg's Business Situation

For Kellogg, the end of the 1970s and the beginning of the 1980s was an era of severe problems. The company retained its market leadership po-

Table 12. Age Distribution Changes and Composite Percentage Change

Age (yr)	1970–1980	1980–1985	1985–1990 (estimated)
<5	−8.7	32.1	7.6
5–13	−16.3	1.2	25.6
14–17	2.3	−11.6	−11.3
18–21	16.6	−9.9	−6.1
22–24	21.6	2.3	−14.3
25–34	38.5	13.8	3.1
35–44	8.6	24.8	16.6
45–54	−1.5	−2.2	12.7
55–64	12.3	3.7	−4.4
65+	22.8	10.7	9.2
Total	8.1	7.4	6.6

Source: U.S. Bureau of Census.

Table 13. Ready-to-Eat Cereal Consumption: Percent of Total Consumption by Age Group

Age (yr)	1984	1983	1982	1981	1980	1979	1976	1972
<13	31.0	31.5	31.5	31.6	31.8	31.9	32.2	36.1
13–18	13.9	13.9	13.8	13.8	13.8	13.9	14.0	12.9
19–49	28.9	28.1	28.0	28.2	28.1	28.0	27.9	25.7
50+	26.2	26.5	26.7	26.4	26.3	26.2	25.9	25.3
Total	100	100	100	100	100	100	100	100

Source: Drexel, Burnham, & Lambert Brokerage House Report, "Kellogg Co.," Apr. 8, 1985.

Table 14. Pounds Per Capita Ready-to-Eat Cereal Consumption by Age Group

Age (yr)	Pounds
<6	11.5
6–11	14.3
12–17	13.4
18–24	7.0
25–34	5.6
35–49	5.8
50–64	7.7
65+	11.3

Source: Kellogg Company publication.

Table 15. Ready-to-Eat Cereals: Consumption and Tonnage Shipped

Year	Pounds consumed per capita	Percent change in year-to-year tonnage
1971	6.76	3.00
1972	7.75	9.30
1973	8.30	15.20
1974	8.62	7.20
1975	9.03	5.40
1976	9.06	5.80
1977	8.89	1.00
1978	9.07	0.20
1979	9.07	1.30
1980	9.13	2.80
1981	9.26	2.40
1982	9.30	2.10
1983	9.41	2.30
1984	9.74	4.20

Source: Drexel, Burnham, & Lambert Brokerage House Report "Kellogg Co.," Apr. 8, 1985.

sition, but their erosion of market share in the United States was a growing concern.

Domestic Sales

The introduction of generic and private-label brands contributed to a loss of Kellogg market share. Kellogg's position in the industry weakened as its market share dropped from a high of 43% in 1972 to a low of 38.5% in 1983. Consumers appeared to switch to the less-expensive generic brands as the rate of inflation grew to double digits in the 1970s. The cost of this share erosion was substantial: each percent of the RTE cereal market is valued at approximately $40 million.

Kellogg executive Arnold Langbo stated that Kellogg was particularly vulnerable to the generic and private-label inroads in the RTE cereal market. He observed, "The whole philosophy or principle of the private label is to copy the leading products in the market" (Johnson, 1983).

Kellogg fought the invasion of generic and private-label cereals with aggressive price decreases, recovering 1.8% of market share in 1984 as generic goods dropped 10% in tonnage shipped. Kellogg's two primary competitors held 36.4% of the market, considerably less than Kellogg's 40.3% share. In 1984, General Foods market share dropped 2.8% to 13.3%; General Mills held constant at a 23% share. Sales trends for several of Kellogg's products are presented in Table 16. Market share performance of the Kellogg brands for the years 1982–1984 is presented in Table 17.

Table 16. Kellogg's Principal Products' Sales Trends ($ millions)

Product	1983	1984	Change (%)
Corn Flakes	$141.3	$162.5	15.0
Rice Krispies	144.1	141	−2.2
Raisin Bran	134.3	151.9	13.1
Special K	70.3	82.9	17.8
Fruit Loops	88.9	103.6	16.5
Frosted Flakes	188.8	217.9	15.4
Total	767.5	859.7	12.0

Source: Drexel, Burnham, & Lambert, Inc.

Research and Development

In addition to price decreases, Kellogg increased its efforts in research and development (R & D) advertising, and new product introduction. With an R & D budget of $6.5 million in 1978, Kellogg began to develop cereals to appeal to different segments of the cereal market. By 1981, Kellogg was investing $20 million a year in research. Kellogg built two advanced research centers and acquired Agrigentics, a research company exploring improvements in grain development. Kellogg's efforts in research produced the first flaked cereal with no sugar or preservatives, Nutri Grain in 1981, the first cereal to combine two grains with identity separation, Crispix in 1983, and the first cereals to fully enrobe fruit, Raisin Squares and OJ's in 1984 (Patent numbers: 4,178,392, 4,103,035, and 3,952,112).

Advertising

In 1984, Kellogg increased its advertising budget by 49% to $160 million, an aggressive move when compared to the 16% increase (to $52 million) of General Foods, and the 1% decrease in advertising by Post. As General Foods limited its primary advertising on its top five (of 14) leading brands, Kellogg was able to devote considerable push to its new products (*Forbes,* Oct. 7, 1985). Kellogg advertising themes for selected products are presented in Table 18.

Kellogg was able to take advantage of reports connecting a high-fiber diet with a reduced risk of colon cancer and they positioned their new All Bran cereal as a cancer-preventative tool. Kellogg advertised, "At last, some news about cancer you can live with." By the end of 1984, $250 million of Kellogg's sales came from bran cereals: All Bran, Bran Buds, Cracklin' Oat Bran, Fruitful Bran, Kellogg's Bran Flakes, Kellogg's Raisin Bran, and, in 1985, All Bran with Extra Fiber (Tracy, 1985).

The advertising campaign sparked controversy among industry, medical, and government groups. Officials at the FTC hailed the campaign as "the type of advertisement that we believe should be encouraged" (Kronhelm, 1985; Wollenberg, 1985). The Food and Drug Administration, however, protested that Kellogg was making medical claims for its product and considered seizing all boxes of All Bran from the shelves (Marwick, 1985). The National Food Processors Association petitioned the FDA to allow its member manufacturers to tout the health benefits of their products as long as the labeling was truthful and could be substantiated.

"Everyone has his opinions of advertising, but we didn't think anyone would misinterpret our commercials," explained Kellogg Vice President of Public Affairs, Peggy Wollerman. "Our goal is to communicate recommendations of the National Cancer Institute's findings that maintaining a high-fiber diet is a direct means of reducing the risk of cancer" (Rotenberk, 1984). The Kellogg advertisement had been cleared by Kellogg and National Cancer Institute scientists and lawyers for accuracy, and it had been passed by lawyers for the three television networks.

Table 17. Kellogg's Ready-to-Eat Cereals: Market Share Data[a]

	1982		1983		1984	
Brand	**Pounds**	**Dollars**	**Pounds**	**Dollars**	**Pounds**	**Dollars**
Frosted Flakes	5.2	4.8	5.2	4.8	5.6	5.2
Corn Flakes	6.8	4.7	6.8	4.7	6.8	4.7
Raisin Bran	4.7	4.2	4.6	4.1	4.5	4.0
Rice Krispies	3.9	4.2	3.6	3.9	3.5	3.8
Fruit Loops	2.2	2.8	2.2	2.8	2.3	2.9
Special K	1.5	2.1	1.7	2.3	1.9	2.5
Bran Products	2.7	2.0	2.8	2.1	3.1	2.3
Frosted Mini-Wheats	1.8	1.8	1.8	1.8	1.9	1.9
Apple Jacks	1.0	1.5	1.0	1.5	1.0	1.5
Sugar Smacks	1.3	1.3	1.3	1.3	1.2	1.3
Sugar Pops	1.1	1.3	1.0	1.2	1.1	1.2
Product 19	0.8	1.1	0.8	1.1	0.9	1.1
Nutri-Grain	1.0	1.0	1.0	1.0	1.2	1.1
Crispex	—	—	0.7	0.7	0.5	0.5
Honey & Nut Corn Flakes	0.6	0.7	0.6	0.7	0.5	0.6
Marshmallow Krispies	0.5	0.7	0.5	0.7	0.4	0.6
Cocoa Krispies	0.5	0.7	0.5	0.7	0.6	0.8
Frosted Rice	0.6	0.8	0.5	0.6	0.4	0.4
Fruitful Bran	—	—	—	—	0.7	0.6
C-3PO	—	—	—	—	0.5	0.6
Apple Raisin Crisp	—	—	—	—	0.5	0.6
Raisin Squares	—	—	—	—	0.3	0.3
Most	0.3	0.4	0.3	0.4	0.2	0.3
Raisins Rice & Rye	0.5	0.6	0.3	0.4	0.1	0.1
Others	1.2	1.4	1.0	1.3	0.8	1.4
Total	38.5	38.5	38.5	38.5	40.5	40.3

Source: Advertising Age, Aug. 5, 1985, p. 42.
[a]All figures are percentages.

Until 1970, the FDA prohibited manufacturers from making any health claims on behalf of food products. In the following years, the FDA relaxed its standard for claims of "low calorie" and "low cholesterol." If a product is claimed to be useful in the treatment of a disease, it is considered a drug and the manufacturer must prove the efficacy of its claims (Cowart, 1985).

New Marketing Developments

Kellogg's move into the adult market in the late 1970s and early 1980s signaled a new direction for the cereal industry. Kellogg's strategy included promoting vitamin-enriched, whole grain, and sugarless cereals to the 25–49 year age group, high fiber to the 65+ age group, and C-3POs and OJs to the under 17 market (*Business Week,* Jan. 8, 1977).

Recognizing sociological changes in the United States, Kellogg introduced all-family cereals to enhance the convenience of shopping. Kellogg also introduced Smart Start, a cereal aimed at the working woman (*Business Week,* Nov. 26, 1979). Key to Kellogg's development

Table 18. Kellogg's Cereal: Products and Advertising Themes

Product	Themes
Special K	Thanks to the K, Staying in Shape Never Tasted so Good—Can't Pinch an Inch
Product 19	Flaky, Bumpy, Crispy, Crunchy *Vitamins*—100% of Your Daily Allowance of 10 Vitamins
Fruitful Bran	Bushels of Taste!—Fiber Rich
Nutri-Grain	Whole Grain Goodness . . . No Sugar Added—Dedicated to the Ones We Love
Apple Raisin Crisp	New Great Taste—New, Big, Juicy Chunks of Real Apple
Frosted Flakes	Gr-r-reat Taste—Tony the Tiger—The Taste Adults Have Grown to Love
Raisin Bran	Two Scoops of Raisins—Fiber Rich—Here is the Goodness of Fiber
All Bran	High Fiber—The Highest Fiber Cereal Ever
Rice Krispies	More Vitamin Nutrition than Old Fashioned Oatmeal—Snap! Crackle! and Pop!—The Talking Cereal Talks about Nutrition
Corn Flakes	The Original and Best—Provides 8 Essential Vitamins and Iron—How 'bout these Kellogg's Corn Flakes Now?—The Surprise is the People Who Eat Them
Just Right	High Nutrition . . . Uncompromising Taste—Kellogg's Just Right Cereal
Bran Flakes	Fiber-rich *Bran Flakes*—We'll Help Take Care of the Inside, You take Care of the Outside
Fruit Loops	Natural Fruit Flavors with 100% U.S. RDA of Vitamin C—All Natural Flavors: Orange, Lemon, Cherry—Delicious Natural Fruit Flavors with a Full Day's Supply of Vitamin C

Source: Kellogg advertisements.

and marketing were the themes of health, diet, convenience, and taste (Brody, 1985). Numerous surveys and surveying organizations, including the Bureau of Labor Statistics, have recorded significant social demographic changes in the last 15 years. A few of the changes that Kellogg and the other cereal companies had to address are listed below.

- In 1985, the numbers of families with school-age or preschool-age children increased by 460,000; the number of employed mothers increased by 765,000 to 18.2 million.
- In 1985, the median family wage and salary earnings increased 4.6%. Since 1982, the median family earnings increased 16% compared to a consumer price increase of 11% over the same period (*New York Times,* Feb. 19, 1986).

In the 1980s, breakfast has become a more significant part of the American diet, with 89% of the populace eating breakfast each day. Frozen breakfast foods were also becoming an important part of the breakfast food industry. In 1985, sales of all frozen foods totalled $849.3 million, 15% more than in 1984. In part, this increase was caused by the fact that more than 44% of American homes now had a microwave oven, making cooking at home easier. Sales of frozen breakfast entrees tripled from 1979 to 1985: sales of frozen pancakes increased 390%; frozen toaster items increased 1000%. Moreover, between 1978 and 1984, the number of Americans eating breakfast at a restaurant increased 45.7% compared to the overall restaurant increase of only 6.3% (Callahan, 1986).

Despite the decline in the population of children under 13 years of age, competition in breakfast food market segment continued without any slackening of intensity. As consumers of the greatest per capita amounts of cereal, children have long been the focus of cereal company advertising. Although Tony the Tiger has represented Kellogg's Sugar Frosted Flakes for many years, General Mills broke new ground in products for children with the first licensed character, Strawberry Shortcake. This was a move to link the cereal with other commercial media. Other RTE cereal companies followed quickly. The RTE cereal companies' licensed character products now include General Mills' ET, General Foods' Smurf Berry Crunch, Ralston Purina's Donkey Kong, Rainbow Brite, and Gremlins, and Kellogg's C-3PO's.

The benefit of tying a cereal to an established figure from television, movies, comics, or toys (character licensing) is a quick gain in market share through exposure in a good trial period. Although traditional cereal products have existed for more than 30 years, the licensed-character cereals may have a life cycle of only 6–18 months. "The first licensed characters did well for about a year. Now their life span is about six months," said Nomi Ghez of Goldman Sachs & Co. (Spillman, 1985). The editor of *New Products News,* Martin Friedman, stated, "the characters that have been created by cereal companies go on forever, and the others don't" (Hollie, 1985). To seek a license for a character, Kellogg depended on assurances that the character would continue, that the character had personality and integrity, and that the character would not alienate adults.

By 1986, the cereal companies had less interest in developing licensed-character products because of a general decrease in the popularity of the characters with consumers (Friedman, 1986).

International Operations

By 1980, Kellogg measured sales in 130 countries from 19 manufacturing locations (Kellogg Annual Report, 1982). Kellogg International was divided into four divisions: Canada; United Kingdom and Europe; Latin America; and Africa, Australia, and Asia. International sales accounted for 30% of Kellogg's total sales. In France, Kellogg planned to target all segments of the population in hopes of replacing the croissant with cereal. In Japan, Kellogg has targeted children to establish the habit of eating cereal (*Dun's Business Month,* Dec., 1985). Financial results for several geographic operating segments are detailed in Table 19.

Federal Trade Commission Case Revisited

In addition to the problems created by the introduction of generic and private-label brands, Kellogg management also attributed the previously mentioned loss of market share to the inability of top management to concentrate on operating the business. The Chairman of the Board, William E. Lamothe, estimated in 1982 that 40% of top management time had been spent on the FTC litigation (*Business Week,* Dec. 6, 1982).

For Kellogg, losing the FTC case would have been significant. If the FTC had won the case, it would have divided Kellogg into five separate operating companies organized around its major product lines. Additionally, the FTC would have required Kellogg to license its brands to smaller, regional manufacturers. Kellogg argued that such actions would place Kellogg at a competitive disadvantage in the RTE market and would produce inconsistent quality within Kellogg's brands.

As the trial entered the 1980s, Kellogg changed its passive strategy of litigation, becoming an aggressive champion of the industry's positions. Kellogg sponsored intense letter-writing campaigns to congressional representatives from districts in which Kellogg maintained facilities. As a result, the FTC received numerous inquiries from congressional representatives regarding the efficacy of continuing the case further (*Business Week,* Nov. 26, 1979).

In 1981, Kellogg created Project Nutrition, a teaching unit for secondary grade school children, as well as nutrition inserts for children's television. Kellogg also provided cereals in 33,000 school breakfast programs. In 1982, Kellogg introduced Fitness Focus, a physical education program for high schools. Kellogg be-

Table 19. Kellogg Company: Geographic Operating Segments ($ millions)

	1985	1984	1983	1982	1981
Sales					
United States	$2,074.9	$1,789.6	$1,560.0	$1,514.3	$1.454.0
Canada	177.6	178.9	176.0	169.0	170.2
Europe	474.9	425.9	437.8	453.0	435.9
Other	202.7	208.0	207.3	230.8	261.2
Total	2,930.1	2,602.4	2,381.1	2,367.1	2,321.3
Net Earnings					
United States	222.7	194.7	170.5	163.0	150.7
Canada	11.7	11.6	27.6	15.2	13.1
Europe	38.8	35.0	38.6	36.9	34.0
Other	7.9	9.2	6.0	12.7	7.6
Total	281.1	250.5	242.7	227.8	205.4
Assets					
United States	833.6	731.6	677.1	639.0	606.9
Canada	262.7	247.5	192.3	143.4	130.2
Europe	337.9	223.3	195.4	199.0	197.5
Other	158.9	148.6	139.8	153.7	178.0
Corporate	133.0	316.1	262.6	162.3	166.5
Total	1,726.1	1,667.1	1,467.2	1,297.4	1,279.11

Source: Kellogg Annual Reports.

lieved that the program would enhance its image as a producer of health-related foods, an image that could benefit Kellogg in its case against the FTC as well as in its position in the market.

Procedural errors in the handling of the case by the administrative judge and the FTC raised challenges from Kellogg and the other cereal companies. Judge Harry R. Hinkes decided in 1978 to retire from the judiciary in order to gain full pension benefits, some of which he would lose if he postponed his retirement. The FTC, fearing a considerable delay and possible dismissal of the case, offered the judge a salary to stay on the case. The impropriety of such an arrangement, alleging a possible conflict of interest, was raised by Kellogg as grounds for dismissal. A new judge was appointed to continue the suit in 1981. Later, in 1982, the FTC dropped its suit (*Federal Register,* vol. 47).

Following the collapse of the FTC lawsuit against its four largest companies, the RTE industry witnessed increased competitive rivalry. This increased rivalry manifested itself in new product releases and advertising, and in corporate-development activities including acquisitions, divestitures, and share repurchases.

Diversification. The slowing growth rate in the cereal industry compelled Kellogg to look toward diversification for continued growth and comparable rates of returns for reinvestment of its retained earnings. In 1970, Kellogg entered the frozen food industry with the acquisition of Fearn International. In 1976, Kellogg acquired Mrs. Smith's Pie Co. and in 1977, it acquired Pure Packed Foods. Products such as Eggo waffles, salad dressings, LeGout soups, Salada Tea, Whitney Yogurt, Mrs. Smith's Pies, and pickles entered Kellogg's lines. Kellogg consolidated its frozen food operations under the Mrs. Smith's label in 1980 to gain greater efficiencies in manufacturing, warehousing, transportation, and marketing as well as a stronger product identity in the marketplace (Prokesch, 1985). By 1984, 25% of Kellogg's sales were noncereal (Blyskal, 1984). Table 20 presents net income contributions of several elements of Kellogg, and Table 21 presents sales and operating income for several segments of the company.

Despite LaMothe's declaration that Kellogg was "gung ho" on diversification, Kellogg lost in three attempts to acquire Tropicana and in attempts to acquire Binney and Smith, manufacturers of Crayola crayons, and Seven-Up. Kellogg believed in each case that the price was too high for the company. "Today we are kind of

Table 20. Kellogg Company: Net Income Contributions

Product/division	1981	1982	1983	1984	1985 (estimated)	1986 (estimated)
Domestic cereals	$121.0	$135.7	$138.0	$169.9	$206.0	$231.0
Canadian operations	11.0	13.0	13.8	9.4	10.0	12.0
Salada	12.1	13.0	14.0	15.0	16.0	18.0
Fearn International	9.0	9.5	10.5	11.6	12.0	14.0
Mrs. Smith's Pie Co.	8.7	7.0	8.0	8.9	10.0	11.0
Kellogg International	41.6	49.6	44.6	39.2	42.0	50.0
Total	203.4	227.8	228.9	254.0	296.0	336.0

Source: Drexel, Burnham, & Lambert, Inc., Oct. 7, 1985.

Table 21. Kellogg Company: Estimated Sales and Operating Income ($ millions)

	1979	1980	1981	1982	1983	1984	1985
Sales							
RTE cereals	$1,426	$1,687	$1,802	$1,792	$1,755	$2,000	$2,260
Salada	128	140	154	165	182	180	190
Fearn International	118	132	145	165	177	165	180
Mrs. Smith's Pie Co.	157	172	200	218	239	222	235
Other	18	19	20	27	50	35	35
Total	1,847	2,150	2,321	2,367	2,381	2,602	2,900
Operating Income							
RTE Cereals	240	297	331	343.7	370	408.2	510
Salada	12	12	13	14	16	14	15
Fearn International	8	9	10	11	12.5	11.5	13
Mrs. Smith's Pie Co.	19	20	22	24	27.5	25	28
Other	2	2	2	3	4	4.5	5
Total	281	340	378	395.7	430	463.2	571

Source: Merrill, Lynch, Pearce, Fenner, & Smith brokerage house report: "Kellogg Co.," Oct. 31, 1985.

glad we did [lose]," said LaMothe, "There is no embarrassment in losing. The big embarrassment is to win by paying too much and then never being able to make a return to your shareholders" (*Dun's Business Month,* Dec. 1985).

Capital Projects. Productivity improvements were made at many Kellogg manufacturing facilities in the late 1970s and 1980s, culminating in a $100 million expansion and improvement in the Battle Creek plant in 1985, the largest single capital expenditure in the company's history. Kellogg's ability to improve productivity is demonstrated by the 50% increase in revenues per employee that the company enjoyed between 1979 and 1985 (Drexel, Burnham, & Lambert, Oct. 7, 1985). Early in 1986, Kellogg ended a long practice of public tours of the Battle Creek facility because of a desire to protect proprietary information. Several Kellogg capital projects for the years 1980–1983 are listed in Table 22.

Preventing Takeover. Matching Kellogg's rates of return in an acquisition candidate is difficult. Moreover, the consumer-products companies such as Kellogg are attractive takeover targets

Table 22. Kellogg Company: Capital Projects

Year	Location	Project
1980	Rexdale, Ontario	Frozen food manufacturing facility
	Wrexham, England	Expanded capacity for Super Noodles
	Valls, Spain	New cereal plant
	Rooty Hill, Australia	Expansion of frozen food plant
	Queretro, Mexico	New corn milling operation
	Sao Paolo, Brazil	Expansion of cereal plant
	Maracay, Venezuela	New office building, processing, and packing
	Guatemala	Expansion of grain storage
	Arlington, TN	Pure Packed dry materials warehouse
	McMinnville, OR	Expansion of Mrs. Smith's plants
	San Jose, CA	Expansion of plant
	Blue Anchor, NJ	Mrs. Smith's facility
	Milpitas, CA	Eggo salad dressing plant
1981	Battle Creek, MI	Expanded for Nutri-Grain cereal
	Lancaster, PA	Increase capacity for cereal
	Battle Creek, MI	Advanced technology facility for research and development
	South Korea	New processing plants
	London, Ontario	Advanced technology center
	Manchester, England	Expansion of packing facility
	Bremen, West Germany	Purchased land
1982	London, Ontario	Expansion of plant
	Seoul, South Korea	Plant completed
	Manchester, England	Conversion of packing line
	Sao Paolo, Brazil	Expansion of facilities
1983	Pottstown, PA	Expansion of office space, storage Warehouse

Source: Kellogg Annual Reports.

themselves because of their high returns. To reduce the risk of a takeover, Kellogg purchased 20% of its own stock in 1984, an "investment in our own business," said LaMothe. The effect of the stock repurchase added $500 million of debt to the Kellogg balance sheet. Before the transaction, Kellogg enjoyed only $19 million of debt against $1 billion in equity. The 20% block of stock had been held by the Kellogg Foundation. Any potential sale of the stock, said LaMothe, was a "cloud we didn't think was good to leave hanging out there in today's time" (Willoughby, 1985).

Kellogg's competitors employed a range of strategies in response to the same takeover challenge. Ralston Purina also acquired blocks of its own stock, continuing this strategy through mid-decade. In 1985, R. J. Reynolds acquired Nabisco Brands, itself a result of a merger between Nabisco and Standard Brands. Phillip Morris acquired General Foods. Table 23 lists several recent acquisitions of established brands.

Some of the largest companies in the food industry have been built through a series of acquisitions: Beatrice and Sara Lee Corporation are both the products of acquisitions. Traditionally, regional brands were acquired to take advantage of a larger, national sales force, as well as the financial strength of the parent company. When product lines of the two companies overlapped, the strength of the broader product line commanded greater influence in attracting shelf space in the supermarket, and greater discounts in advertising rates (Brown, 1985).

For Reynolds and Phillip Morris, acquisition of food products carried other benefits. Slower sales of cigarettes and pending lawsuits and legislation about smoking are expected to eventually erode profitability in the cigarette industry. The higher than average returns of the cereal and food companies, with a strong brand image of health and nutrition, is an attractive inducement for investment.

According to Marc C. Patricelli of Booz Allen & Hamilton Inc., 19 of 24 RTE cereal brands retained their leadership position from 1923 to 1983. "So if a company buys a leader, and if they run it correctly, they are buying an annuity, because brand leadership is sustainable" (Brown, 1985). Kellogg's financial performance and dominance in the cereal industry makes it an appealing target for merger or acquisition. Tables 24–26 give financial information on Kellogg.

Table 23. Recent Acquisitions of Established Brands

Buyer	Acquisition	Brands
Procter and Gamble	Richardson-Vicks	NyQuil, Vidal Sassoon, Clearasil
Phillip Morris	General Foods	Jell-O, Maxwell House
Monsanto	G.D. Searle	Nutrasweet, Metamusil
Brown-Forman	California Cooler	California Cooler
Greyhound	Purex' Cleaning	Purex Bleach, Brillo
Sara Lee	Nicholas Kiwi	Kiwi shoe polish
Nestlé	Carnation	Carnation Milk, Friskies pet food
Ralston Purina	Continental Baking	Hostess Twinkies, Wonder Bread
R.J. Reynolds	Nabisco Foods	Oreo cookies, Life Savers, Ritz Crackers, Shredded Wheat
Beatrice Foods	Esmark	Wesson Oil, Playtex
R.J. Reynolds	Canada Dry	Canada Dry soft drinks
Quaker Oats	Stokely-Van Camp	Gatorade, canned goods

Source: Brown (1985).

Table 24. Kellogg Company: Consolidated Balance Sheet ($ millions)

	1985	1984	1983	1982	1981
Current Assets					
Cash and temporary investments	$ 127.8	$ 308.9	$ 248.8	$ 159.8	$ 163.7
Accounts Receivable	203.9	182.5	157.1	140.7	158.9
Inventory					
Raw materials	135.6	119.7	115.7	128.8	129.4
Finished goods and work in progress	110.3	101.4	101.1	98.9	101.8
Prepaid expenses	40.5	39.0	40.4	35.9	28.4
Total current assets	618.1	751.5	663.1	564.1	582.2
Property					
Land	25.6	25.6	26.3	25.1	24.0
Buildings	321.2	277.7	274.1	263.4	263.8
Machinery and equipment	903.2	762.4	692.7	677.6	620.6
Construction in progress	280.4	215.7	143.7	83.5	90.0
Total property	1503.4	1281.4	1136.8	1049.6	998.4
Less accumulated depreciation	494.5	425.4	393.6	367.4	340.0
Net property	1035.9	856.0	743.2	682.2	658.4
Intangible assets	28.3	30.5	29.0	33.6	32.2
Other assets	43.8	29.1	31.9	17.5	6.3
Total assets	1726.1	1667.1	1467.2	1297.4	1279.1
Current Liabilities					
Current maturities of debt	34.8	340.6	20.0	6.5	16.5
Accounts payable	189.7	127.4	116.8	99.1	104.5
Accrued liabilities					
Income tax	29.4	51.4	85.0	81.9	77.4
Salaries and wages	41.8	38.7	36.2	31.4	29.9
Promotion	71.3	60.2	66.4	45.0	30.9
Other	46.4	45.8	36.3	43.7	41.7
Total Current Liabilities	444.3	664.1	360.7	307.6	300.9
Long-term debt	392.6	364.1	18.6	11.8	88.2
Other liabilities	12.3	9.5	9.2	11.0	9.8
Deferred income tax	193.9	142.2	100.8	82.3	69.9
Shareholder's Equity					
Common stock	38.4	38.4	38.2	38.2	38.2
Capital in excess of par value	44.5	40.8	34.4	32.9	32.5
Retained earnings	1288.5	1118.4	991.5	872.8	761.6
Treasury stock	−576.8	−577.8			
Currency translation adjustment	−111.6	−132.6	−86.2	−59.2	−22.0
Total equity	683.0	487.2	977.9	884.7	810.3
Total liabilities and equity	1726.1	1667.1	1467.2	1297.4	1279.1

Source: Kellogg Annual Reports.

Table 25. Kellogg Company: Consolidated Earnings and Retained Earnings ($ millions)

	1985	1984	1983	1982	1981	1980
Net sales	2930.1	2602.4	2381.1	2367.1	2331.3	2150.9
Interest revenue	7.2	27.7	18.6	21.3	18.2	18.7
Other, net	−2.8	3.9	18.1	2.1	0.0	0.0
Total revenue	2934.5	2634.0	2417.8	2390.5	2339.5	2169.6
C.O.G.S.	1605.0	1488.4	1412.3	1442.2	1447.8	1385.2
S, G, & A Exp.	766.7	650.8	554.4	529.2	501.1	435.7
Interest Exp.	35.4	18.7	7.1	8.2	12.0	10.4
Total	2407.1	2157.9	1973.8	1979.6	1960.9	1831.3
EBT	527.4	476.1	444.0	410.9	378.6	338.3
Income taxes	246.3	225.6	201.3	183.1	173.2	154.3
Net earnings	281.1	250.5	242.7	227.8	205.4	184.0
Retained earnings, Jan. 1	1118.4	991.5	872.8	761.6	665.1	583.5
Dividends	−111.0	−123.6	−124.0	−116.6	−108.9	−102.4
Retained earnings, Dec. 31	1288.5	1184.4	991.5	872.5	761.6	665.1

Source: Kellogg Annual Reports.

Conclusion

"The question is not whether this is a mature market," said LaMothe, "it's whether we can be inventive enough. . . . [Americans now have] the highest level of per capita [cereal] consumption in U.S. history. A lot of areas are close to 13 pounds. Why not make the whole country average 13?" (Willoughby, 1985). Kellogg's challenge is to increase the market for cereals, both domestic and foreign, by increasing consumption. In the United States, middle-aged and older Americans are the target segments. According to LaMothe (*Dun's Business Month,* Dec. 1985):

Dr. Kellogg and Mr. Kellogg were going on either intuition or their basic beliefs coming out of a Seventh Day Adventist background, where they believed that meats were not healthful for the diet . . . We think that it (cereal) has a tremendous future . . . The whole grains . . . healthy lifestyle . . . avoidance of major disease in the Western World . . . more grains, fruit and vegetables. Where else can you get such nutrition for 20 cents a serving? There will be 6 billion people on the face of the earth by the year 2000 and grains will continue to be the most efficient way for most people to get their calories and nutrition. We are going to help feed them, that's what Kellogg is all about.

Table 26. Kellogg Company: Changes in Consolidated Financial Position ($ millions)

	1985	1984	1983	1982	1981	1980
Source of funds						
Net earnings	281.1	250.5	242.7	227.7	205.4	184.0
Depreciation	75.4	63.9	62.8	55.9	49.1	44.7
Deferred tax/other	54.9	62.6	12.0	27.1	10.4	12.0
Total funds provided by operations	411.4	377.0	317.5	310.7	264.9	240.7
Changes in working capital components						
Accounts receivable	−21.4	−25.4	−16.4	18.2	−9.2	−17.0
Inventory	−24.8	−4.3	10.9	3.5	26.1	−19.2
Prepaid expenses	−1.5	1.4	−4.5	−7.5	−3.7	−7.1
Current debt maturity	−305.8	320.6	13.5	−10.0	−10.0	5.7
Accounts payable	62.3	10.6	17.7	−5.4	−1.5	−9.8
Accrued liability	23.7	−27.9	21.9	22.1	25.2	46.2
Net change	−267.5	275.1	43.1	20.9	26.9	−1.2
Funds provided by operations and changes in working capital	143.9	652.1	360.6	331.6	291.8	239.5
Long-term debt	31.5	348.1	1.5	0.0	7.9	0.4
Common stock	3.7	6.7	1.1	0.4	0.0	0.0
Property disposal	4.3	12.0	38.0	5.3	2.9	5.0
Tax-lease benefits	1.2	3.1	6.2	12.0	0.0	0.0
Other	7.9	0.9	0.5	3.1	0.5	1.4
Total source of funds	192.1	1022.9	407.9	352.4	303.1	246.3
Use of funds						
Property	245.6	228.9	156.7	121.1	146.4	122.9
Cash dividends	111.0	123.6	124.0	116.6	108.9	102.4
Treasury stock purchases	0.0	577.9	0.0	0.0	0.0	0.0
Investment in tax leases	0.0	0.0	11.6	14.2	0.0	
Long-term debt reduction	2.8	2.7	3.6	75.7	0.4	2.8
Other	23.8	14.7	10.5	13.9	6.4	1.1
Total use of funds	383.2	947.7	306.4	341.5	262.1	229.2
Exchange rate effect on working capital	10.0	−15.1	−12.5	−14.9	−9.1	0.0
Increase in cash and temporary investments	−181.1	60.1	89.0	−4.0	31.9	17.1

Source: Kellogg Annual Reports.

References

Advertising Age, Aug. 5, 1985, p. 42.

Associated Press, "FTC Accused of Sanctioning Bad Advertising Practice," Jul. 18, 1983.

Blyskal, Jeff (1984) "Branded Foods," *Forbes,* Jan. 2, p. 208.

Brody, Jane E. (1985) "America Leans to a Healthier Diet," *New York Times,* Oct. 13, p. 32, section 6.

Brown, Paul B., et al. (1985) "NEW? IMPROVED? The Brand Name Mergers," *Business Week,* Oct. 21, p. 108.

Business Week, Industrial Edition, Jan. 8, 1977, p. 46.

Business Week, Industrial Edition, Nov. 26, 1977, p. 80.

Business Week, "Too Many Cereals for the FTC," Mar. 20, 1978, p. 166+.

Business Week, "Still the Cereal People," Nov. 26, 1979, p. 80+.

Business Week, "Kellogg Looks Beyond Breakfast," Dec. 6, 1982, p. 66+.

Callahan, Tom (1986) "What's New With Breakfast; Morning Meals, Fresh from the Freezer," *New York Times,* Feb. 16, p. 17, section 3.

Cowan, Edward (1981) "F.T.C. Staff is Rebuffed on Cereals," *New York Times,* Sep. 11, p.D1.

Cowart, V. (1985). "Keeping Foods Safe and Labels Honest; Food Safety and Applied Nutrition," *Journal of the American Medical Association,* 254, 2228–2229.

Dewar, Helen (1980) "FTC Curbs are Adopted by Senate," *Washington Post,* Feb. 8, p.A1.

Drexel, Burnham, & Lambert, Brokerage House Report, "Kellogg Co.," Apr. 8, 1985.

Drexel, Burnham, & Lambert, Brokerage House Report, "General Foods," May 20, 1985.

Drexel, Burnham, & Lambert, Kellogg Company, Research Abstracts; Food Processors, Oct. 7, 1985.

Dun's Business Month, "Kellogg: Snap, Crackle, Profits," Dec. 1985, p.32+.

The Economist, "Philip Morris/General Foods: Chow Time for the Marlboro Cowboy", Oct. 5, 1985.

Federal Register, Federal Trade Commission, "Children's Advertising", 46 FR 48710.

Federal Register, "Childrens Television Programming and Advertising Practices," 49 FR 1704.

Federal Register, Federal Trade Commission, "Kellogg Company, et al; Prohibitive Trade Practices, and Affirmative Correction Actions," 47 FR 6817.

Federal Trade Commission v. J. E. Lonning, President, and Kellogg Company, a Corporation, Appellants, 539 F2nd 202.

Forbes, Oct. 7, 1985, p.126.

Friedman, Martin (1986) "Cereal Bowls Spill Over with Nuttiness," *ADWEEK,* Feb. 10.

Hollie, Pamela G. (1985) "New Cereal Pitch at Children," *New York Times,* Mar. 27, p.D1.

Johnson, Greg (1983) "Who's Afraid of Generic Cereals?" *Industry Week,* May 16, p.33.

Kellogg Company Annual Reports, 1981, 1982, 1983, 1984, 1985.

Kiechel, Walter III (1978) "The Soggy Case Against the Cereal Industry," *Fortune,* Apr. 10, p. 49.

Kronhelm, William (1985) "Should Food Labels Carry Health Claims, FDA's Policy Challenged," *Associated Press,* May 15.

Lippman, Thomas W. (1983) "Quebec's Ad Ban No Child's Game; Advertisers, TV Try to Adjust," *Washington Post,* Apr. 17, p.G1.

Marwick, C. (1985). "FDA prepares to meet regulatory challenges of 21st century," *Journal of the American Medical Association,* 254, 2189–2201.

Meadows, Edward (1981) "Bold Departures in Antitrust," *Fortune,* Oct. 5, p.180.

Newsweek, "A Portrait of America," Jan. 17, 1983, pp. 20–33.

New York Times, Sep. 15, 1985, section 3, p.1.

New York Times, "More Mothers are Working," Feb. 19, 1986, p. C4+.

Patent Number 3,952,112, "Method for treating dried fruits to improve softness retention characteristics," Fulger et al., April 20, 1976.

Patent Number 4,103,035, "Method for retaining softness in Raisins," Fulger et al., July 25, 1978.

Patent Number 4,178,392, "Method of Making a ready-to-eat breakfast cereal," Gobble et al., December 11, 1979.

Philip Morris Co., Press Release, Apr. 24, 1986.

Prokesch, Steven (1985) "Food Industry's Big Mergers," *New York Times,* Oct. 14, p.D1.

Prudential-Bache Securities, Inc., Oct. 1, 1985.

Prudential-Bache Securities, Inc., Apr. 2, 1986.

Rotenberk, Lori (1984) "Ad Exec Blasts JWT's All-Bran Ad," *ADWEEK* (Eastern edition), Oct. 29.

Sebastian, John V. (1979) "A Slight Taste of Honey," *Business Week,* Reader's Report, Dec. 17, p. 10.

Spillman, Susan (1985) "It's a Kid's Market," *USA Today,* Oct. 7.

Tracy, Eleanor Johnson (1985) "Madison Avenue's Cancer Sell Spreads," *Fortune,* Aug. 19, p.77.

Ward, S., "Compromise in Commercials for Children," *Harvard Business Review,* Nov. 1978, p. 128+.

Willoughby, Jack (1985) "The Snap, Crackle, Pop Defense," *Forbes,* Mar. 25, p. 82.

Wollenberg, Skip (1985) "Reagan's Cancer Diagnosis Sparks Prevention Ads," *Associated Press,* Jul. 29.

Case 3 Update*

To Our Stockholders:

A broad increase in consumption of ready-to-eat cereal products helped make 1987 another record year and one of substantial growth for Kellogg Company. Sales increased for the 43rd consecutive year, earnings improved for the 36th consecutive year, and dividends were raised for the 31st consecutive year, with a per-share increase from $1.02 to $1.29. A further increase of the quarterly dividend, to $0.38 per share, was announced in January 1988.

Consumer recognition of the importance of diet to good health and longevity continues to grow worldwide. This trend strongly favors nutritious, grain-based, ready-to-eat cereal products.

Traditionally, cereal consumption has been highest among children under 17 and adults over 50. In recent years, however, consumption increases in the 18–49 age group have represented not only a commitment by young adults to better health and fitness, but also an additional opportunity for long-term growth of our business.

Cereal consumption growth in more recently developed international markets has been very encouraging, with growth rates in several major countries currently exceeding 20 percent.

Marketplace competition in 1987 was more intense than ever before, challenging Kellogg Company to be even more innovative and aggressive in responding to the needs of consumers.

To strengthen our leadership position and our prospects for long-term growth, we continue to invest heavily in new technologies, product research and development, and effective marketing support programs.

Particularly noteworthy in 1987 was our substantial investment in modernizing and expanding our production facilities. Among major projects, we made significant progress in updating our Sydney, Australia facility; we began a further expansion of our Manchester, England plant; and we continued the work on our major addition to the Battle Creek, Michigan cereal plant. This new Battle Creek facility began producing cereal ahead of schedule in February 1988.

In January 1988, we announced the start of an additional expansion project in Battle Creek and plans to construct a new cereal production plant in Memphis, Tennessee.

Kellogg Company's strong financial condition provides great flexibility as we continue to invest in our business and seek new growth opportunities. In recognition of this strength, three major rating agencies—Moody's, Standard & Poor's, and Duff & Phelps—currently assign their highest debt rating to Kellogg Company.

Management Reorganization and Changes

In December 1987, Kellogg Company consolidated its U.S. subsidiary operations into Kellogg North America. This expanded division also includes our U.S. Food Products Division and our Canadian operations, Kellogg Salada Canada Inc. Concurrently, Horst W. Schroeder, president of Kellogg North America, was named group executive vice president, Kellogg Company.

We believe that bringing together all of our U.S. and Canadian operations provides greater synergisms within our organization and positions us to take better advantage of growth opportunities in all lines of our business.

In October 1987, Dr. Theodore Cooper, chairman of the board and chief executive officer of The Upjohn Company, was elected to the Kellogg Company Board of Directors.

Earlier in 1987, Walter T. Redmond, former vice chairman and chief administrative officer of Kellogg Company; Paul J. Kehoe, former vice

*Excerpts from Kellogg Company 1987 annual report, pp. 3, 16–17, 20–22.

chairman; and Gerald D. Robinson, former president and chief operating officer, retired from the Board of Directors. Also during 1987, W. Lawrence Romans was named corporate vice president-internal auditing.

In January 1988, Louis R. Somers, senior vice president-finance, retired from Kellogg Company and, in February 1988, Robert L. Burrows, vice president-materials planning, announced his plans to retire in March 1988. Concurrent with Mr. Somers' retirement, John R. Hinton was named vice president-finance and Jay W. Shreiner was named corporate treasurer.

No investment is more important than our continuing commitment to the growth and well-being of our most valuable asset, Kellogg employees. Their skills and dedicated performance have made us the leader in our business and provide strong encouragement as we face the challenges of the future.

William E. LaMothe
Chairman of the Board
Chief Executive Officer

Robert L. Nichols
Vice Chairman

Eleven-Year Summary (dollar amounts in millions, except share data)

Summary of Operations

	Net Sales	% Increase	Pretax Earnings	% Increase	Net Earnings	% Increase	Per Common Share Data: Net Earnings	Per Common Share Data: Cash Dividends	Per Common Share Data: Book Value	Average Shares (000's) Outstanding	Shareholder's Equity
10-year Compound Growth Rate	9%		10%		11%		14%	9%			
1987	**$3,793.0**	**14%**	**$665.7**	**13%**	**$395.9**	**24%**	**$3.20**	**$1.29**	**$9.82**	**123,668**	**$1,221.4**
1986	3,340.7	14%	586.6	11%	318.9	13%	2.58	1.02	7.27	123,481	898.4
1985	2,930.1	13%	527.4	11%	281.1	12%	2.28	.90	5.54	123,275	683.0
1984	2,602.4	9%	476.1	7%	250.5	3%	1.68	.85	3.96	149.380	487.2
1983	2,381.1	1%	444.0	8%	242.7	7%	1.59	.81	6.39	152.934	977.9
1982	2,367.1	2%	410.9	9%	227.8	11%	1.49	.76	5.79	152,878	884.7
1981	2,321.3	8%	378.6	12%	205.4	12%	1.34	.71	5.30	152,864	810.3
1980	2,150.9	16%	338.3	20%	184.0	14%	1.20	.67	4.81	152,860	735.8
1979	1,846.6	9%	281.6	4%	161.5	12%	1.06	.65	4.28	152,846	654.2
1978	1,690.6	10%	271.7	4%	144.4	5%	.94	.60	3.87	152,808	590.9
1977	1,533.4	11%	261.4	4%	137.6	6%	.90	.56	3.52	152,622	537.0

Other Information and Financial Ratios

	Property, Net	Capital Expenditures	Depreciation	Total Assets	Number of Employees	Financial Ratios: Current Ratio	Financial Ratios: Pretax Interest Coverage (times)	Financial Ratios: Return on Average Equity	Financial Ratios: Debt to Total Capital	Working Capital	Long-term Debt
1987	**$1,738.8**	**$478.4**	**$113.1**	**$2,680.9**	**17,762**	**.9**	**14**	**38%**	**27%**	**$(51.5)**	**$290.4**
1986	1,281.1	329.2	92.7	2,084.2	17,383	1.1	13	40%	31%	43.2	264.1
1985	1,035.9	245.6	75.4	1,726.1	17,082	1.4	11	48%	38%	173.8	392.6
1984	856.0	228.9	63.9	1,667.1	17,239	1.1	26	27%	59%	87.4	364.1
1983	743.2	156.7	62.8	1,467.2	18,293	1.8	64	26%	4%	302.4	18.6
1982	682.2	121.1	55.9	1,297.4	19,290	1.8	51	27%	2%	256.5	11.8
1981	658.4	146.4	49.1	1,279.1	20,260	1.9	33	27%	11%	281.3	88.2
1980	582.2	122.9	44.7	1,181.9	21,285	2.0	34	26%	12%	276.3	82.7
1979	509.0	80.9	40.5	1,049.8	20,818	2.1	28	26%	15%	258.0	84.6
1978	474.0	86.7	36.3	941.9	20,905	2.1	29	26%	16%	222.3	84.0
1977	422.1	75.9	31.9	839.0	20,405	2.2	29	27%	17%	206.7	80.3

Kellogg Company and Subsidiaries Consolidated Earnings and Retained Earnings
Year Ended December 31

(millions)	**1987**	**1986**	**1985**
Net sales	**$3,793.0**	$3,340.7	$2,930.1
Interest revenue	**14.1**	11.7	7.2
Other revenue (deductions), net	**(8.4)**	(31.0)	(2.8)
	3,798.7	3,321.4	2,934.5
Cost of goods sold	**1,939.3**	1,744.6	1,605.0
Selling and administrative expense	**1,162.5**	948.7	766.7
Interest expense	**31.2**	41.5	35.4
	3,133.0	2.734.8	2,407.1
Earnings before income taxes	**665.7**	586.6	527.4
Income taxes	**269.8**	267.7	246.3
Net earnings—$3.20, $2.58, and $2.28 a share	**395.9**	318.9	281.1
Retained earnings, beginning of year	**1,481.5**	1,288.5	1,118.4
Dividends paid—$1.29, $1.02, and $.90 a share	**(159.5)**	(125.9)	(111.0)
Retained earnings, end of year	**$1,717.9**	$1,481.5	$1,288.5

See notes to financial statements.

Kellogg Company and Subsidiaries Changes in Consolidated Financial Position Year Ended December 31

(millions)	1987	1986	1985
Source of funds			
Net earnings	**$395.9**	$318.9	$ 281.1
Depreciation	**113.1**	92.7	75.4
Deferred income taxes and other	**40.5**	31.2	54.9
Funds provided by operations	**549.5**	442.8	411.4
Changes in components of working capital:			
Accounts receivable	**(57.6)**	(13.6)	(21.4)
Inventories	**(45.5)**	(19.5)	(24.8)
Prepaid expenses	**(41.1)**	(8.1)	(1.5)
Current maturities of debt	**15.8**	100.8	(305.8)
Accounts payable	**49.1**	73.1	62.3
Accrued liabilities	**102.1**	68.2	23.7
Net change	**22.8**	200.9	(267.5)
Funds provided by operations and changes in working capital	**572.3**	643.7	143.9
Issuance of long-term debt	**52.4**	22.6	31.5
Issuance of common stock	**8.8**	4.8	3.7
Property disposals	**10.2**	4.1	4.3
Other	**9.5**	13.5	8.7
Total source of funds	**653.2**	688.7	192.1
Use of funds			
Additions to properties	**478.4**	329.2	245.6
Cash dividends	**159.5**	125.9	111.0
Purchase of treasury stock	**22.6**		
Reduction in long-term debt	**29.1**	151.3	2.8
Other	**30.6**	15.4	23.8
Total use of funds	**720.2**	621.8	383.2
Effect of exchange rate changes on working capital	**(4.9)**	3.4	10.0
Increase (decrease) in cash and temporary investments	**$(71.9)**	$ 70.3	$(181.1)

See notes to financial statements.

Kellogg Company and Subsidiaries Consolidated Balance Sheet at December 31

(millions)	**1987**	**1986**
Current assets		
Cash and temporary investments	**$ 126.2**	$ 198.1
Accounts receivable, less allowances of $2.6 and $2.3	**275.1**	217.5
Inventories:		
Raw materials and supplies	**161.9**	147.7
Finished goods and materials in process	**149.0**	117.7
Prepaid expenses	**89.7**	48.6
Total current assets	**801.9**	729.6
Property		
Land	**34.7**	29.7
Buildings	**568.3**	439.0
Machinery and equipment	**1,427.2**	1,172.6
Construction in progress	**387.8**	213.1
Accumulated depreciation	**(679.2)**	(573.3)
Property, net	**1,738.8**	1,281.1
Intangible assets	**77.4**	28.0
Other assets	**62.8**	45.5
Total assets	**$2,680.9**	$2,084.2
Current liabilities		
Current maturities of debt	**$ 151.4**	$ 135.6
Accounts payable	**311.9**	262.8
Accrued liabilities:		
Income taxes	**113.5**	72.2
Salaries and wages	**56.3**	51.0
Promotion	**151.9**	101.2
Interest	**30.0**	25.6
Other	**38.4**	38.0
Total current liabilities	**853.4**	686.4
Long-term debt	**290.4**	264.1
Other liabilities	**69.3**	16.4
Deferred income taxes	**256.4**	218.9
Shareholders' equity		
Common stock, $.25 par value—shares authorized 165,000,000; issued 154,015,283 and 153,744,802	**38.5**	38.4
Capital in excess of par value	**58.1**	49.3
Retained earnings	**1,717.9**	1,481.5
Treasury stock, at cost—30,607,683 and 30,182,783 shares	**(598.2)**	(575.6)
Currency translation adjustment	**(4.9)**	(95.2)
Total shareholders' equity	**1,211.4**	898.4
Total liabilities and shareholders' equity	**$2,680.9**	$2,084.2

See notes to financial statements.

Case 4

Financial Services Industry Reference Note

Introduction

If an industry is defined as a group of companies whose products are largely substitutable, the Financial Services Industry, per se, did not exist prior to the mid 1970s. Before that, each type of financial intermediary or institution was considered by consumers, regulators, and the institutions themselves to constitute a distinct, separate industry which had only minimal competition from other types of intermediaries. However, all types of financial intermediaries are basically similar because their (asset) portfolios consist of primary securities (claims against business and individuals) and their liabilities consist of secondary securities (claims against financial intermediaries).

The differences among intermediaries principally arose from the laws and regulations which (1) required some of them to invest in particular types of primary securities and (2) restricted the types of secondary securities they could issue.[1] The bulk of these laws and regulations, especially those separating commercial and investment banking were passed as a response to the collapse of the country's financial system during the Great Depression. Legislators believed that if they limited the powers of depository institutions and surrounded them with protective regulations, the overall banking system would be much safer.

A New World

The period from 1973 to 1985 was a traumatic one for all of the major financial intermediaries. They all found they suddenly were operating in a changed and constantly evolving environment. This note concentrates on the commercial banking and investment banking segments of the industry. However, other financial intermediaries experienced many of the same changes. Table 1 shows the major asset restructuring which occurred during this dramatic decade.

Trends

1973 saw an end to the fixed currency exchange rates which had long been used in international transactions. Then, as governments sought to control inflation by controlling money supply and worried less about money's price (interest rates), huge exchange rate fluctuations began taking place. With few exchange controls, differences in interest rates between countries were magnified into exchange rate shifts by movements of capital seeking higher returns. In the mid 1980s more than $200 billion of foreign exchange was traded every day.[2] Then another shock hit the monetary community. From the end of 1973 through the end of 1982 the U.S. inflation rate, stimulated by the oil price shocks of 1973/74 and 1979/80, was never less than 5%, ranging from 5¾% to over 15% (See Table 2).

Suddenly, interest rates capped by the government's Regulation Q at 5% for savings ac-

Table 1 Assets of Financial Intermediaries (Billions $)

	1973	%	1983	%
Commercial Banks	832.7	46.5	2,341.8	41.6
Savings and Loan Assns.	264.4	14.8	806.5	14.3
Mutual Savings Banks	106.7	6.0	193.5	3.4
Credit Unions	18.9	1.1	82.0	1.5
Life Insurance Cos.	252.4	14.1	654.9	11.6
Other Insurance Cos.	25.7	1.4	249.1	4.4
Private Pension Funds	126.5	7.1	607.8	10.8
Finance Cos.	73.2	4.1	202.7	3.6
Securities Brokers & Dealers	22.6	1.3	214.8	3.8
Mutual Funds	46.5	2.6	113.6	2.0
Money Market Mutual Funds	—		162.5	2.9
Real Estate Investment Trusts	19.9	1.1	7.6	0.0
Total	1,789.5		5,629.0	

Source: Statistical Information on the Financial Services Industry, 3rd ed., 1984.

Table 2 Inflation Rates (1st Quarter)

	'74	'75	'76	'77	'78	'79	'80	'81	'82
% Change in U.S. Consumer Price Index (CPI)	10	11	6.5	5.8	6.5	9.5	14.5	11.3	7.5

Source: Statistical Information on the Financial Services Industry, 3rd Ed., 1984.

counts made no sense. During the peak inflation period of 1978–1982 savings deposits fell by 25% while money market mutual funds grew by 152%, reaching a peak of $233 billion in November of 1982.[3] And on the average, paper assets failed to preserve their owners' wealth, let alone make them richer. From 1968 to 1980, the average change in CPI was 8%. Common stocks, as measured by the S&P 500 Index, returned about the same %, and so did short-term money market instruments. Long-term high-quality corporate bonds actually lost 4% of their value each year in real terms. Real estate, on the other hand, increased in value by 250% from 1970 to 1980 while the CPI rose only 112%. Individuals consequently increased their mortgage debt half again as fast as they raised their total assets. Between 1970 and 1980 tangible assets as a % of total householder assets rose from 30 to 40%. Adjusted for inflation, householders' direct holdings of stock fell 30% over the same period.[4] (See Table 3 for statistics on ownership of various financial instruments in 1983.)

As the federal debt rose along with federal spending (from $243 billion in 1960 to $1.63 trillion by 1983[5]) all segments of the financial services industry were obliged to increase their proportion of total assets represented by government securities. The existence of huge federal deficits also brought greater uncertainty about the future to financial markets in general, further increasing upward pressures on money

Table 3 Ownership of Various Financial Instruments, 1983 (Estimated Values in Billions of Dollars)

Institution	Total Assets	Common Stocks Amount	Common Stocks %	Corporate Bonds Amount	Corporate Bonds %	Mortgages Amount	Mortgages %	U.S. Treasury/Agency Bonds Amount	U.S. Treasury/Agency Bonds %	Municipal Bonds Amount	Municipal Bonds %	Open Market Paper Amount	Open Market Paper %	Loans Amount	Loans %
Mutual savings banks	193	3	—	22	4	99	8	34	3	2	1	7	3	6	1
Savings and loans	814	—	—	—	—	531	40	125	10	—	—	9	4	26	2
Credit unions	106	—	—	—	—	6	1	32	3	—	—	—	—	52	5
Life insurance companies	654	70	3	226	37	151	11	51	4	11	2	29	11	—	—
Property/casualty insurance	230	50	2	26	4	—	—	30	2	89	19	—	—	—	—
Corporate pensions	419	265	12	69	11	5	—	64	5	—	—	—	—	—	—
State/local pensions	319	69	3	119	19	16	1	88	7	3	1	—	—	—	—
Endowments	98	75	4	16	3	2	—	3	—	—	—	2	1	—	—
Municipal bond funds	87	—	—	—	—	—	—	—	—	87	18	—	—	—	—
Mutual funds	125	73	3	12	2	—	—	7	—	—	—	5	2	—	—
Money market funds	161	—	—	—	—	—	—	30	2	—	—	72	29	—	—
REIT/mortgage banks	26	—	—	—	—	20	2	—	—	—	—	—	—	—	—
Broker/dealers	50	3	—	4	1	—	—	10	1	2	—	—	—	—	—
Foreign investors	370	131	6	38	6	—	—	168	13	—	—	33	13	—	—
Commercial banks	1,636	—	—	11	2	333	25	270	21	164	35	16	6	806	69
Households	4,652	1,413	66	76	12	157	12	494	38	113	24	46	18	—	—
State/local governments	78	—	—	—	—	—	—	88	7	—	—	—	—	—	—
Finance companies	247	—	—	—	—	—	—	—	—	—	—	—	—	225	19
Business corporations	114	—	—	—	—	—	—	17	1	—	—	35	14	61	5
Totals	10,379	2,151	100	618	100	1,320	100	1,511	100	471	100	254	100	1,175	100

Source: From *Inside Investment Banking* by Robert C. Perez. Copyright © 1984 by Praeger Publishers. Reprinted by permission of Praeger Publishers.

costs. Monetary policy makers struggled with problems of defining M1 (the basic money supply indicator including all checkable deposits) let alone controlling it as capital markets became increasingly volatile and global in nature. The demand deposit turnover rate in New York City rose from 243 in 1973 to approximately 1200 in 1982 and the income velocity of M1 rose from 5.02 to 6.39 over the same period.[6] Since quasi-checks could now be written on deposits in mutual funds, some believed they should be included in the calculation of M1. Money could be transferred easily into and out of Eurodollars by commercial banks, raising further questions about the nature of money supplies and their control by governments.

Interest and currency exchange rates were so volatile that a new financial futures market opened which operated like a commodities futures market and allowed both speculation and hedging. By 1981 financial intermediaries and others were writing 8 million interest rate futures contracts and more than 5 million currency exchange rate contracts per year.

Technology Changes

Technologically, the financial services world had changed dramatically. Computer and memory costs and performance improved so rapidly that electronics technologies spread quickly from back-room operations to products with which the customer interacted directly—such as Automatic Teller Machines (ATMs) and International Cash Management systems on corporate treasurers' desks. Advances in technology made it possible for a group of banks in the New York Clearing House to create CHIPS (Clearing House International Payments System) and handle 20 million transfers worth $60 trillion annually with same day settlements.[7] Electronics also made it possible for the National Association of Securities Dealers to create their automatic quotation and electronic national market system which in 1983 handled an annual volume of 3.7 million trades of 4.4 billion shares from multiple market makers.[8] Electronic communications integrated the world's capital markets into a single global system, and electronic funds transfer (EFT) systems increased the flow of funds, the complexity, and the velocity of financial world transactions to the point where the use of electronic technology in all financial services sectors became a necessity.

Demographic Changes

Demographically, the 1970s and early '80s witnessed the coming of age of the "baby boom" generation and the beginning of the so-called "graying" of America as the number of people over 65 rose dramatically in comparison with those under 20. Two-income families became the norm and education levels in the general population rose steadily.

These demographic changes along with high rates of inflation in the late '70s/early '80s forced individuals and corporations to become much more sophisticated and value conscious financially. Individuals moved their money from low yield savings accounts and insurance policies into newly created money market funds whose returns exceeded inflation. And corporations hired highly trained financial staffs to explore alternatives to high cost external financial services. They began self-insuring for certain risks, setting up or acquiring their own financial subsidiaries, preparing their own securities issues, using EFT to maintain zero-balance checking accounts, and issuing commercial paper and tapping the Eurobond market rather than relying on bank loans.

Deregulation and New Competitors

In 1977 Merrill Lynch introduced its revolutionary Cash Management Account (CMA) which provided consumers with the services of a checking account, money market fund, and credit card as well as those of a traditional securities trading account. CMA typified both the consumer's growing sophistication and demands for convenience, and the development of "hybrid" money instruments which cut across the regulatory barriers between different segments of the financial services industry. Providers of financial services began invading each other's turf wherever a loophole or ambiguity in the laws permitted. There was a growing recognition that many of the barriers, especially geographic ones, established in the past had been made irrelevant by electronic funds transfer technologies, communications advances (like satellites and 800 numbers), the unregulated Euromarket, extensive private and business use of credit cards, and the ingenuity of companies both within and outside the industry to find chinks in the old regulatory armor.

Commercial banks and savings and loans were unable to respond effectively to the new competitive environment because of various regulations limiting (1) the interest rates they could pay on deposits, (2) the types of assets they could hold, and (3) their geographic markets. (Insurance companies and investment banks while regulated were not hampered by such limitations.) In the mid 1970s prompted by soaring inflation, regulators began a gradual process of "deregulation." Major milestones in that process included the Depository Institutions Deregulation and Monetary Control Act of 1980, the Garn-St. Germain Depository Institutions Act of 1982, and the July 1985 Supreme Court decision upholding the legality of regional interstate banking. (See the section on Commercial Banking for more details.)

In their efforts to compete in new areas many formerly specialized financial firms acquired or merged with firms already in those markets, creating "financial supermarkets" such as the Sears Financial Network, Shearson/Lehman/American Express, and Prudential/Bache. Although many people questioned their ability to gain the benefits of synergy, these large, diversified financial service companies became formidable competitors. Competition among financial service providers was no longer based on old perceptions about a particular institution's or intermediary's traditional role, but on the quality of its products and services, its efficiency in pricing, its innovative use of technology, and its convenience and rendering of personal support services.[9] The following sections offer some pertinent facts about major segments of the new industry.

Keeping Up with Inflation?

Inflation and interest rates have enormous impact on pension funds. High inflation rates rapidly erode the purchasing power of fixed retirement benefits. For example, a 9% inflation rate could drop the value of a retiree's benefits by 58% at age 75 and by 82% at age 85.[10] Approximately 70% of all companies surveyed by the *Institutional Investor* in November 1983 said they had upgraded benefits to help retirees keep up with inflation, but they could make no promises for the future. More than 70% had raised their actuarial assumptions to reflect higher inflation and interest rates, but less than 50% said that the total return on their pension fund investments had kept up with the inflation rate over the past decade.[11] Pension funds increasingly acquired such inflation hedged assets as real estate and guaranteed investment contracts. Through the early 1980s, inflation driven salary increases as well as ERISA requirements had led to rapidly rising pension costs for companies. However, by 1983 these costs began leveling off.

Commercial Banking

Commercial banks made up the largest segment of the Financial Services Industry with assets of $2.25 trillion in January 1985.[12] Although their share of deposits relative to other depository institutions had not changed much since 1973, their share of total financial assets had dropped while that of insurance companies, pension funds, finance companies, real estate investment trusts, open-ended investment companies, money market funds, and securities brokers and dealers grew.

The structure of commercial banking changed substantially from 1970–1983. Although the number of banks grew only moderately (13,976 in 1973 to 14,473 in 1983), average assets per bank soared. More importantly, the Bank Holding Company (BHC) became the dominant form of banking organization. (See Table 4.) Although small banks dominated the number of institutions, the largest banks dominated the banking system. In 1980, those BHCs with consolidated assets of over $1 billion had 41.3% of all branches, 60.3% of all employees, and 69.2% of all assets.[13]

A BHC form of organization has many advantages. Perhaps the most significant are: (1) certain tax-related benefits, (2) the ability to supplement funds through sale of commercial paper, and (3) the capacity through subsidiaries to engage in nonbank activities on an interstate basis. In 1985 one-bank holding companies were permitted in all states. Three states prohibited multi-bank holding companies, and 15 others placed restrictions on them. The nonbank activities of BHCs were regulated by the Fed under the proviso that such activities must be "so closely related to banking . . . as to be a proper incident thereto." As of 1983, there were more than 10,000 interstate nonbank subsidiaries of BHCs and the largest BHCs operated in as many as 40 states.

Other changes in the banking structure included a tendency for states to liberalize their branching laws—allowing county-wide if not state-wide branching. Partly as a result of liberalized branching laws and partly in an effort to collect low-cost deposits, banks steadily expanded their branch networks, increasing the average number of branch offices from 1.91 in 1973 to 2.82 in 1983.

Table 4 Comparative Statistics—Holding Companies 1969–1980

	1969	1980
% of total domestic assets held by subs of BHCs		
Total	19.0	74.1
Multi-Bank	—	35.7
One-Bank	—	38.4
# of Multi-Bank Holding Cos.	86	361
# of banks controlled by Multi-Bank Holding Cos.	723	2,426
# of One-Bank Holding Cos.	1,352	2,544

Source: "Developments in Banking Structure, 1970–1981," *Federal Reserve Bulletin,* February 1982.

Bank Regulation

Commercial banks, like S&Ls, had a dual system of regulation—federal regulators overseeing federally chartered national banks and state regulators overseeing state chartered banks. In addition, the Federal Deposit Insurance Corporation (FDIC) examined member banks (which held 99% of all bank deposits and included many state chartered banks). The Federal Reserve Board regulated BHCs and the activities of state chartered banks that were held by BHCs. National banks, granted a charter by the Office of the Controller of the Currency (OCOC), were required to be members of the Federal Reserve System while state banks might elect not to be. The Federal Reserve System (Fed) was made up of a Board of Governors and 12 Federal Reserve Banks of which member banks were shareholders. (See Exhibit 1.)

The Fed's primary activities were the management of monetary policy and the supervision and regulation of its members. Member banks were required to deposit with the Fed "reserves" which were specified minimum percentages of each bank's demand and time deposits. No interest was paid on these funds but they could be used to provide a secondary source of liquidity for member banks in the form of "discount paper." The level of these reserve requirements determined how far member banks could "expand" credit to their customers.

Membership in the Fed provided a bank with free access to the check clearing and collec-

Exhibit 1 The Federal Reserve System: Relationships to Instruments of Credit Policy

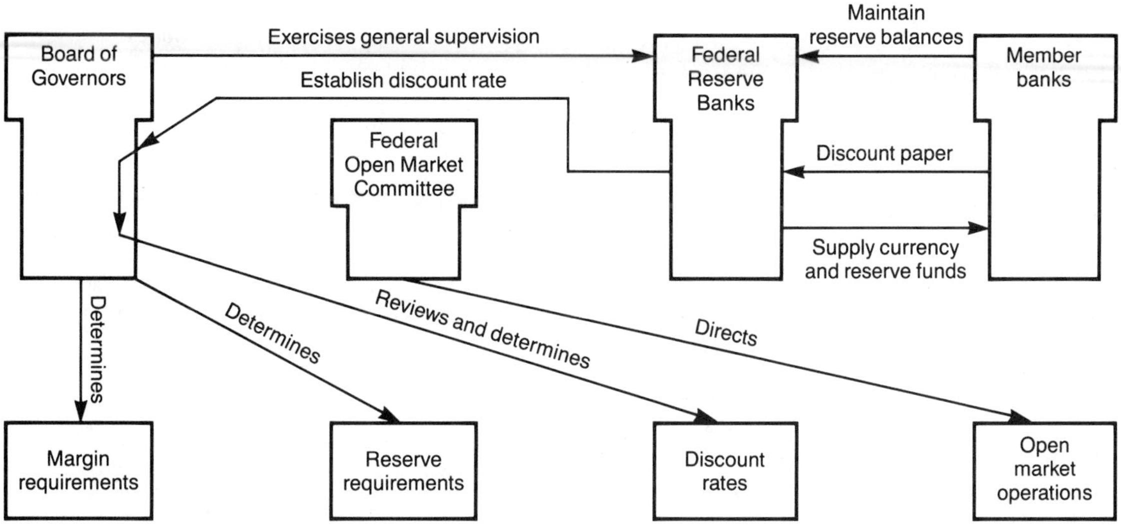

Source: Benton E. Gup, *Financial Intermediaries: An Introduction,* Houghton-Mifflin Co. 1976.

tion, wire transfer, and securities storage systems run by the Fed as well as access to its low-rate discount funds. Non-member banks could obtain access to some of these services through relations with a "correspondent" member bank. However, since state non-member banks were often subject to less onerous reserve requirements, there were certain disincentives to membership. In fact, over the decade of the '70s the number of member banks had fallen steadily. The Fed felt that this hindered its conduct of monetary policy, despite the fact that the Fed could "create" money through the banks or withdraw it from circulation through its Open Market Operations.

The Depository Institutions Deregulation and Monetary Control Act of 1980 (DIDMCA) changed many of these relationships. It made all depository institutions (banks, S&Ls, savings banks, and credit unions), whether members or not, subject to the Fed's reserve requirements (although these were reduced from past levels). It then required the Fed to charge for all its services at full market rates and to offer them to all depository institutions. The Fed had to compete with major banks and other enterprises for its share of those services—like clearing—which were not its exclusive domain. By mid 1985 a subsidiary of General Electric, Automatic Data Processing, Inc., GM's Electronic Data Systems, and NCR were competing with the Fed in processing payments between banks—automated clearinghouse businesses.[14]

Deregulation

During the period 1980 to 1985 there were three areas of banking which underwent "deregulation." The DIDMCA mandated the gradual removal of interest rate ceilings which allowed banks to compete more effectively for deposits during periods of high inflation/high interest rates. The Act also put banks and other depository institutions on a par in terms of reserve requirements.

Then, faced with increasing competition from nonbank competitors, major BHCs began to press vigorously on the Fed to loosen its definition of allowable "non-banking" activities. In 1982 the Bank of America applied for and received permission to acquire a discount brokerage firm, and in 1983 it acquired 24.9% of an insurance company. Citicorp tried but failed to obtain permission for a specialized securities subsidiary but was successful in winning approval for a data processing-oriented subsidiary. State banking commissions went even further in expanding permissible activities. In 1985, some states allowed banks to enter certain non-banking activities including: real estate development (13 states), travel agencies (12 states), management consulting (10 states), insurance underwriting (8 states), and various areas of investment banking (4 states).[15]

Finally, there was an inexorable movement towards some form of interstate banking. In May 1983, the Chairman of the Federal Reserve Board himself stated that "interstate banking exists de facto for everything but that portion of retail banking and other services that require a building."[16] But for BHCs to expand beyond the highly competitive business of lending to large corporations into consumer and small business banking they needed to be able to offer full-service banking. And the increasing use of technology requiring huge systems and investments demanded a large customer support base. Other competitors such as brokerage firms could sell services on a national level. The Bank Holding Company Act of 1970 allowed a state to permit an interstate bank acquisition/merger if it saw fit. By September 1985, 22 states had passed legislation allowing interstate mergers in specific circumstances. (See Table 5.)

In June 1985 the Court unanimously ratified interstate banking on a regional basis and thereby "unleashed a process of consolidation that makes nationwide banking a virtual certainty by the end of the decade."[17] In response, the House Banking Committee approved legislation to permit nationwide interstate banking after a five-year transition period. The bill would prohibit mergers that would result in one institution controlling more than 1% of the nation's deposits and mergers among the nation's 25 largest banks in terms of assets. The Senate Banking Committee had not acted but was unlikely to go along with the House bill.

Table 5 States Allowing Interstate Bank Mergers

Circumstances	States	
National, nonreciprocal	Alaska Arizona	Maine
National, reciprocal	New York	Washington
Regional, nonreciprocal	Oregon	
Regional reciprocal with national trigger	Kentucky Nevada	Ohio Rhode Island
Regional, reciprocal with no national trigger	Connecticut Florida Georgia Idaho Indiana Maryland	Massachusetts North Carolina South Carolina Tennessee Utah Virginia

Source: "Banking Deregulation Benefits Many People But Stirs Some Worry," *Wall Street Journal,* September 30, 1985. With permission of the *Wall Street Journal.*

The dual system of bank regulation was threatened by worries that (1) individual states might be too liberal in defining allowable bank activities and geographic expansion limits, and (2) individual states would be regulating entities that crossed state lines.

Reregulation

While federal and state regulators generally pursued a course of deregulation, the regulations which remained were more strictly enforced and bank supervision was increased overall. In addition, there were two instances where regulation was increased and loopholes closed. The Fed had permitted BCHs to offer discount brokerage services, but in July 1985 the SEC extended its regulations to cover those services. It required banks to segregate those activities in separate subsidiaries and register them with the SEC. And the existence of so-called "limited-service" or "nonbank" banks was jeopardized by moves to close the loopholes which had enabled them to arise. A "limited-service" bank was a bank which either made commercial loans or accepted deposits but not both. Such banks fell outside of the legal definition of a commercial bank and thus were exempt from the BHC Act or other federal regulations which prohibited bank ownership across state lines or ownership by nonbanking companies. More than 100 such banks had been chartered by BHCs and other non-bank competitors.

Payments Systems

In the mid '80s banks, which had maintained a virtual hegemony over third-party payments (check clearing and collection) systems, faced new competitors. Savings and Loan Associations, Savings Banks, and credit unions (the so-called "Thrifts") in 1980 began offering checking account services through NOW Accounts and share-draft accounts. Money market funds and brokerage firms (through their Cash Management Accounts) also began to offer checking and other financial transaction services. Initially, all these financial intermediaries chose to handle transactions through commercial banks. However, the Thrifts had direct access to the Fed's check collection and clearing services if they so chose.

Should the banks' pricing of payment services make it economical, new competitors could also enter this business. The volume of check processing handled by banks and by the Fed had grown from 59 billion in 1973 to almost 86 billion in 1983.[7] Domestic interbank transfers via the Fed's wire system had also grown significantly from 14.8 million transfers worth $30.8 trillion in 1977 to 38 million transfers worth $89.5 trillion in 1983.[7] The emergence of telephone bill paying, home banking, preauthorized payments, Automated Clearing House transactions (such as direct payroll deposits), and direct debit or point-of-sale systems—and their possible control by non-bank competitors—would also influence the future of the payments system. The development of direct debit systems would particularly affect bank credit card systems (like Master Card and Visa) which were currently paper-based systems. These systems embraced 132.5 million cards used at 4.2 million merchant outlets for a gross volume of $83.7 billion in 1983 (up from 55.8 million cards, 2.2 million outlets, and $13.9 billion in 1973).[7]

Cheap Funds?

With cheap funds from deposits readily available, bankers used to focus primarily on the loan aspects of their businesses. The 1970s quickly changed that view. Funds for loans were not necessarily easily accessible, especially at low prices. "The volatile behavior of interest rates, combined with the increasing sensitivity of both corporate and retail customers to interest rate changes made accurate control of both sides of a bank's balance sheet indispensable."[18] Asset-liability management emerged as a critical banking activity. Even with NOW Accounts and the removal of Regulation Q rate ceilings, banks had to compete hard for funds against many new competitors—both other depository institutions and other types of intermediaries. Banks' cost of funds had risen significantly—interest-free checking deposits fell from more than 17% of all funds raised in 1978 by the five largest BHCs to just over 9% in 1982.[19] (See Table 6.)

And obtaining deposits became ever more costly. Inflation drove up banks' operating costs, and they had to make major investments in new technologies to compete. The cost of maintaining large branch networks often became a burden as electronic funds transfer (EFT) systems increasingly offered economies both for front and back office operations. (See Exhibit 2.)

Perhaps most importantly, all financial intermediaries had to deal with the fact that in-

Table 6 Assets and Liabilities of FDIC-Insured Commercial Banks

		1973		1983
Distribution of Assets (%)				
Commercial and Industrial Loans		19.1		22.4
Cash and Due from Deposit. Institutions		14.0		14.6
Real Estate Loans		14.3		14.4
Loans to Individuals		12.1		9.6
State/Local Securities		11.0		6.8
U.S. Treasury Securities		6.6		7.2
Federal Funds and RPs		4.1		4.0
Other U.S. Gov't Agency and Corporate Securities		3.3		3.3
Other Assets		15.6		17.9
Total Assets		$832.7		$2,341.8
Distribution of Liabilities (%)				
Deposits				
Demand	37.1		16.6	
Savings	—		19.7	
Time	44.7		29.1	
Total Domestic		81.9		65.5
In Foreign Offices		—		13.2
Total		81.9		78.7
Other Liabilities and Subordinated Notes and Debentures		11.8		15.3
Equity Capital		6.4		6.0

Source: Statistical Information on the Financial Services Industry, 3rd Ed., 1984.

terest rates (and therefore their cost of funds) had become extremely difficult to predict. The average cost of deposits (and thus the relative attractiveness of any specific deposit product) depends on (a) anticipated inflation rates, (b) the desire and will of the government to control monetary supply, (c) individual corporate appetites for debt financing, (d) the level of anticipated federal deficits, (e) interactions with trade deficits and the relative economic performance of other economies hence the attractiveness of other countries' currencies, (f) the performance of other financial markets, etc.

Less Lending/More Guarantees

The joint trends of internationalization and securitization of capital markets had changed the world of commercial banking dramatically. As the *Economist* commented, most of the banks' large customers, especially those with good credit ratings, had discovered ways to raise money preferable to fixed-priced bank loans. Since the early 1970s, such companies have increasingly chosen to issue commercial paper (selling their own securities directly to investors, cutting out the "turn" made by bankers). By 1985 the market for commercial paper was worth over $230 billion. The unregulated Eurobond market, in which "blue-chip" borrowers could raise money at lower rates than the American treasury pays on treasury bonds, was taking away other loan customers. The annual compound growth rate in Eurodollar bonds from 1979 to 1983 was 32.2% with total volume going from $12.6 billion to

Exhibit 2 Economies of Scale

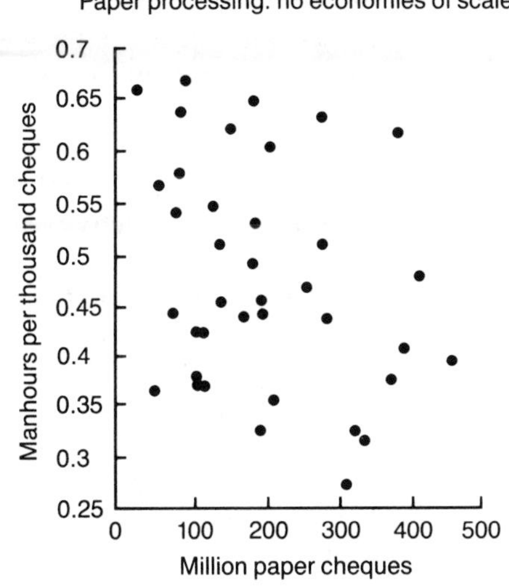

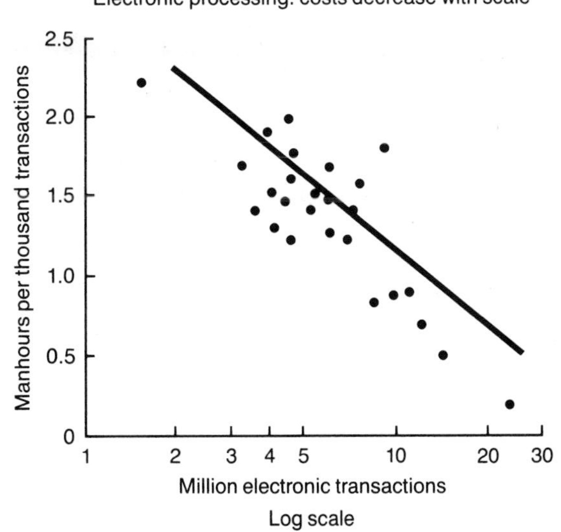

Big is better when screens replace paper

Source: Boston Consulting Group in "A New Awakening: Survey of International Banking," *Economist,* March 24, 1984.

$38.4 billion—exceeding the total value of bonds issued in the U.S.[20] Back in 1980, new bank loans far outstripped the volume of new bond offerings. But the Organization for Economic Cooperation and Development (OECD) recently estimated that for the first half of 1985 new international bond issues would total $80.1 billion and new international bank credits only $44.6 billion.[21]

Even companies with lower-quality credit ratings found alternatives to high-cost bank loans and private placement bonds. In the growing "junk" or high-yield bond market, companies with credit ratings from B to BBB could issue and readily sell bonds with compensatingly higher yields. Inflation and the realization that even on a risk-adjusted basis their yields may be higher have made junk bonds popular with high risk investors. In the U.S., some $14 billion of junk bonds were issued in 1984,[22] when they became an especially popular instrument for use in hostile takeovers.

As banks found fewer opportunities to make profitable commercial loans and became locked in to their huge loans to LDCs (see discussion later), they began "guaranteeing" more through standby loans, Note Issuance Facilities (NIF), and swaps. NIFs are medium-term loans financed by selling short-term paper. Underwriting banks guaranteed the availability of funds to the borrower by buying any unsold notes at each roll-over date or by providing a stand-by credit line. NIFs were significantly less profitable than ordinary stand-by loans. In 1983 use of this device totaled $2.7 billion but by the first half of 1985 it had soared to $23 billion.[23] By 1982 volatile interest and currency exchange rates had led to the creation of the swaps market. In a swap two companies obtain financing in the market in which they are best rated and then swap their interest obligations, splitting the interest savings. For example, a medium sized U.S. company that wanted fixed rate funds might find them very expensive in this country, while a large foreign corporation might be happy with cheaper U.S. floating-rate money at costs below its domestic wholesale money markets. In effect, instead of borrowing long-term fixed-rate money from its U.S. banks, the medium sized company would borrow at floating rates (much less profitable for the banks) and use the proceeds to perform a swap with the foreign company.[22] In a swap, banks must cover lost interest but not the principal, if someone defaults. *Euromoney* estimated that close to $20 billion of long-term currency and interest rate swaps were completed in 1983, and the *Economist* stated that over 80% of Eurobond issues had a swap transaction linked to them. By the end of 1984, swaps amounted to about $80 billion.[23]

Competitive pressures forced down bank fees for such "guarantees" and often margins became extremely thin. Since this type of business did not count as assets on banks' balance sheets, many of them used it as a way to grow without having to add capital. Regulations requiring banks to set aside capital for off-balance-sheet business seemed likely.

International Banking

International banking, both by U.S. banks and by their foreign competitors, had been greatly affected by (1) some countries' moves to allow foreign institutions a bigger role in their domestic financial markets, (2) the growth of international markets, such as the Eurocurrency markets, and (3) increases in the integration of domestic markets with international markets.

Foreign Operations of U.S. Banks

In an attempt to provide services to their largest customers (who were increasingly international or multinational in scope) and to expand their sources of funds and profits, U.S. banks looked more and more to international operations. By the early 1980s, 30–40% of all bank profits came from these operations, with the figure for many of the biggest money center banks exceeding 50%. International banking in the U.S. had its origins in the 1919 Edge Act which "permitted banks to establish Edge Act Corporations (EACs) to engage in international banking activities and to acquire foreign banks by the establishment of subsidiary EACs."[24] EACs were used not only to move overseas but also to establish interstate networks of international banking services within the U.S., a trend which was accelerated by a 1979 ruling of the Fed explicitly excluding EACs from interstate branching rules. By 1983 there were 168 interstate EAC offices majority owned by U.S. banks.[7]

Although the aggregate impact of U.S. banks' overseas operations is very significant, only about 1% of U.S. banks have overseas branches or affiliates. By 1983 163 banks had 900 overseas units holding $476.2 billion in assets. However, ownership of more than 80% of these overseas branches and affiliates and 90% of all overseas banking assets was held by only 20 U.S. banks.[24] Nevertheless, many banks participated in international syndicated loans and in the interbank lending market. While U.S. banks went international primarily to service their U.S.-based customers, they soon diversified their foreign lending to include loans to foreign local firms, foreign banks, and foreign governments. And because their overseas EAC subsidiaries were not covered by the Glass-Steagall regulations which prohibited investment banking activities, U.S. banks became quite active in the Eurobond market and the capital markets of some foreign countries.

As world oil prices increased in the late 1970s, loans to Less Developed Countries (LDCs) by U.S. banks grew from $47 billion in 1977 to nearly $100 billion by 1982 with close to 50% of that amount in loans to only 3 countries (Mexico, Brazil, Argentina).[24] Non-OPEC LDCs' international bank debt also rose to 125% of their total exports.[7] Several large U.S. banks loaned more to LDCs than their total equity. As oil prices fell, an international debt crisis developed which was still being resolved in the mid 1980s. Although actual default had been avoided, the implications for participating U.S. banks were enormous. Their original and later work-out agreements locked them into continuing participation in LDC loans which might not ever be repaid. And the ensuing crisis brought new disclosure requirements and increased regulatory scrutiny in this area of banking.

International Banking in the U.S.
As foreign banks followed their own multinationals into the U.S. market, U.S. assets held by foreign banks grew from $24 billion in 1972 to more than $300 billion in 1983.[7] In the mid 1980s over 300 foreign banks had offices in various states. Prior to the passage of the International Banking Act (IBA) of 1978 foreign banks were only regulated by the states that chartered them; consequently they could offer many services their U.S. competitors could not. The IBA made all branches, agencies, and commercial lending subsidiaries of foreign banks subject to the U.S. Bank Holding Company Act—and thus to federal regulation and supervision (although many ongoing activities were "grandfathered").

On U.S. banks' home turf, Japanese, Australian, British, West German, Canadian and other foreign rivals grabbed big portions of the corporate loan market at least in part because they were willing to compete on a price basis. U.S. offices of foreign banks had made $12.8 billion of loans to companies in the U.S. in 1973 or 7.6% of total U.S. business loans. By 1983 they had made $84.5 billion of loans, capturing 18.3% of the total.[25] In addition, foreign banks helped drive down fees on standby letters of credit guaranteeing municipal-bond issues and guarantees of commercial paper.

In an effort to discourage further development of "offshore" banking operations, as of 1981 any U.S. depository institution, EAC, or U.S. office of a foreign bank was permitted to establish—through a relatively simple segregation on its books—an International Banking Facility (IBF). These units could accept foreign-source deposits and make overseas loans with the same freedom as an overseas subsidiary. By 1983 there were 400 IBFs having aggregate assets of almost $160 billion.[24] And in response to the Japanese trading companies success, the 1982 Export Trading Company (ETC) Act allowed banks to own and finance ETCs with approval from the Fed. Bank-owned ETCs were permitted to engage in all aspects of international trade, including financing, marketing coordination, order processing, and providing transportation support services. These support activities were especially useful to the "middle market companies" banks were assiduously trying to woo as loan customers, as these companies ventured more into international markets.

The Banks Respond
As banks lost much of the lending business they used to do with major U.S. and multinational companies, they had begun to market heavily to the next hierarchical level—the "middle market." Success in this market required a different type of relationship management. And since only the "lead" bank was likely to make good returns, ability to provide full-service banking was essential.

Another development in commercial lending was the creation of a genuine secondary market for loans. Banks wanting to increase equity-to-loan ratios transferred (sold) loans to a bank that needed something to do with its money. Corporate bonds and corporate loans thus became very similar, although bonds were still a more liquid, tradeable instrument. As the secondary market grew, it became ever harder to distinguish between lending for resale and underwriting corporate bonds, an activity forbidden to commercial banks by the Glass-Steagall Act of 1933.

As commercial banks' opportunities to earn profits from lending out cheap deposited funds steadily decreased, they were caught in another squeeze. Non-interest costs rose by an average of nearly 15% a year in 1979–82. By contrast, net interest income increased by an annual average of only 10.6% in the same period despite high inflation rates.[18] Fee income became an increasing percentage of banks' profits. Part of the apparent increase in fee income came from explicit charges for services which had been cross-subsidized in the past—such as check and credit card processing costs. Most fee business, however, was based on highly specialized skills or on offering the customer something new and different rather than on the continuing relationships banks were used to. Increasingly the push for fee income coincided with another trend—i.e., measuring bank performance on the basis of return on assets (which can be ballooned by fee income) rather than return on equity (which is most effectively fueled by asset growth).

Increasingly, commercial banks have pushed into obviously profitable investment banking activities. They began (1) participating fully in the Euromarket and other capital markets through Edge Act Corporations; (2) acting as agents in the "private placement" of commercial paper and "shelf-registered" corporate securities (see *Investment Banking* below); (3) offering retail discount brokerage services; (4) offering "corporate finance" advice and specialized services in areas like mergers and acquisitions, venture capital, and leveraged buyouts; (5) participating in Euromarket foreign exchange hedging and underwriting; (6) trading in interest rate futures and mortgage-backed securities, and (7) managing such stock related programs as dividend reinvestment and employee or payroll stock purchase plans. Glass-Steagall, however, continued to bar commercial banks from both major corporate securities underwriting and the high-volume industrial revenue bond business. Thus it was still impossible for a U.S. bank to offer a complete product and service system to corporate clients.

Investment Banking

Investment banks' primary public capital-raising services are: (1) originating and managing a new financing issue; (2) underwriting (contracting to purchase an issuer's securities at a fixed price, thus assuming market risks); (3) distributing securities to institutional and individual investors. Related services and activities include corporate financial services such as consulting on corporate capital structures, advising on mergers and acquisitions, and handling certain secondary-market activities like brokerage, market making, and arbitrage. Many investment banks also provide private placement services and offer some venture capital potentials. Recently, investment banks have also begun offering consumer-oriented products like Cash Management Accounts, mutual funds, or deferred annuities through their retail brokerage outlets.

The Way It Was

In the early 1970s corporations felt dependent on their primary investment banker for financial and market expertise and tended to maintain a long-term relationship with one firm—a partner of which often sat on their Boards of Directors. Capital markets tended to be local or national (rather than international) in scope due to communications and other structural limitations. The secondary securities market was dominated by the New York Stock Exchange (NYSE) whose members maintained fixed commission rates on trades and were prohibited from trading outside of the exchange. Investment banks were almost entirely organized as partnerships and as such had limited and unpredictable levels of capital. The majority of investment banks' revenues came from commissions (66% in 1972).[26]

The industry was broken down into three major segments: originators, regionals, and national distributors. Originators normally had small, elitist professional staffs, low overhead, and a minimal presence in the secondary markets. They tended to maintain long-term, stable relationships with corporate clients. For the latter, they designed securities issues, handled the registration and regulatory hurdles of the SEC, negotiated a gross spread from which they took a 20% management fee, and syndicated regional and national distribution firms to underwrite and sell those securities not sold directly to large institutional investors. Distributors had regional or national networks of retail outlets to deal with many small or local investors. They played major roles in secondary markets, handled very little (if any) origination, and were dependent upon originators for supplies of newly issued securities. The entire industry was regulated by the SEC, with membership in the exchanges and the National Association of Securities Dealers (NASD) involving additional restraints.

The bull market of the '60s with its high volume of trading on the secondary markets offered distributors expanded opportunities. Some of them began to integrate vertically and to "manufacture" by developing their own mutual funds, real estate deals, and tax shelters. As their staffs grew, they began to compete on the origination of new issues. Eventually many of the larger distributors converted from partnerships to corporations and sold their stock to the public. This gave them the capital base they needed to aggressively compete in other areas.

Open competition for underwriting developed, and firms began locating professionals in regional offices to call on current or potential corporate clients. Many active large corporations came to realize that their bankers, particularly originators, were dependent on them—rather than the other way around. They began to develop their own internal financial and market expertise and to shop around for investment counselors when needed. Dividend reinvestment programs and the trend toward stock-for-stock corporate mergers (versus registered secondary offerings) also increased corporate clients' independence.

"May Day" and Its Aftermath

The Securities Industries Amendments Act of 1975 increased competition further by mandating an end to fixed commission rates on May 1, 1975—"May Day." The Act also eliminated the NYSE rules that prohibited members from using other exchanges and mandated the creation of an electronic network to form a national market. The Act, particularly the national market notion ("a linking of all markets . . . through communications and data-processing facilities"), was designed to: foster efficiency, enhance competition, increase the availability of market information, and facilitate the offsetting and execution of investors' orders.[27]

The unfixing of commission rates led to dramatic changes in U.S. capital markets. The NYSE's portion of total shares traded fell from 65% to 50% between 1975 and 1983; its percentage of share values traded dropped from 75% to 70% over the same period.[28] NASD's Automatic Quotation System (NASDAQ) garnered market share with its introduction in 1982 of an electronic National Market System which utilized multiple market makers rather than specialists for each stock traded. NYSE contributed to a more national marketplace by introducing a Composite Quotation System (consolidated tape) and by participating in the national clearance and settlement system started in 1980. Finally an Intermarket Trading System was introduced to permit orders received in any market to be displayed instantaneously with orders in the same stock on all of the other markets and NASD's Computer Assisted Execution System was connected up to the NYSE's Intermarket Trading System in May 1982.

Negotiated commissions led to huge cuts of up to 75% in the rates for large institutional trades. Turnover of institutional portfolios rose dramatically pushing average daily shares traded on the NYSE from 18.5 million to 102 million by 1984. Able to negotiate lower commission rates and unencumbered by tax considerations, pension fund managers sought to lock in short-term profits often because of the greater scrutiny of their performance created by ERISA. A growing proportion of individual savings were being channeled through institutions such as life insurance companies, pension funds and mutual funds. And as institutional trading increased, so did the dominance of institutional investors in the market. By 1984 50% of all NYSE trades involved 10,000 shares or more and were made primarily by institutional investors.[29] The exchanges could handle the greater volume only because of the application of new technologies and the development of block trading mechanisms off the trading floors and off the specialists' books.

This increased portfolio turnover among institutions changed many corporations' attitudes about having their shares held mainly by institutions. Large block trades could cause big short term swings in a company's stock price. And desires for short-term stock gains made some institutions impatient about longer term investments and eager to accept tender offers in takeover situations. Corporate clients' disenchantment with institutional investors for equity issues often forced old style originators to co-manage new issues with a distribution firm that could reach the retail market.

New Retail Products

While the institutional brokerage business was less attractive, it was still essential. Institutions still purchased over 90% of all debt offerings. Many investment firms, however, began looking more closely at their retail customers who had suddenly become relatively more profitable. The emergence of "discount brokerage" firms who cut retail commission rates by offering only trade execution services increased competition for retail customers. By 1984 these discount brokerages had captured a 20% share of the retail market. Studies revealed that 1% of all households produced 45% of all retail brokerage revenues and that these customers viewed themselves as having a relationship with their particular broker, not the firm.[30] Full-line investment houses began to exploit this relationship by developing and marketing new products like Merrill Lynch's Cash Management Account (CMA) and money market mutual funds. By 1981 broker/dealer money-market funds held the largest share of total fund assets with about $90 billion.[31]

These products helped diversify firms away from commission revenues. Other new products helped to bolster sagging commission incomes. Stock options which were first traded in 1973 had mushroomed to 55 million contracts by 1981. The market for commodities futures and later financial futures also grew rapidly, and by 1981 commissions on these products made up 20% of larger firms' commission revenues.[32] Some insurance related products (like deferred annuities or even term insurance) were added to enhance the commissions needed to give distributors a national presence and a competitive advantage over other financial service providers.

Changing Revenue Mix

In addition to shrinking commissions, investment banks were faced with other changes in their revenue bases. (See Tables 7a and 7b.)

Underwriting revenues were cut by high inflation rates. Tax considerations and high inflation made debt more attractive to corporations than equity issues. In 1979 79% of all underwritten public offerings were bonds—only 15% were equities. Margins on underwriting major debt issues were only 25% of those for equity issues.

As finance costs shifted and more creative instruments became available, the fastest growing revenue source for investment bankers became Merger and Acquisition (M&A) activities. In 1973 dollar values of acquisitions were $16.7 billion; by 1983 they had soared to $73.1 bil-

Table 7a Changes in Investment Banking Revenues

Mix of Revenues (%)

	1970	1974	1980
Commissions	48	48	36
Trading and Investment	19	15	23
Underwriting	12	10	8
Margin Interest	8	12	13
Other	13	15	20
Total ($ billions)	$4.8	$5.1	$16.0

Source: Based on material from Paul A. Masson, *Report No. 696, Trends in Corporate Financial Services.* Copyright © 1984 by Business Intelligence Program, SRI International.

Table 7b Changes in Investment Banking Revenues

Revenue Growth Index

	1973	1977
Public Underwriting	100	199
Private Placement	100	251
Mergers & Acquisitions and other fees	100	391
Municipal Financing	100	290

Source: Reprinted by permission of the Harvard Business Review. An exhibit from "The Transformation of Investment Banking," by Samuel L. Hayes III (January/February 1979). Copyright © by the President and Fellows of Harvard College; all rights reserved.

lion.[33] In 1984 they were $120 billion, but the actual number of mergers had only risen from 2,300 in 1975 to 2,550 in 1984.[34] Investment banks earned fees for arranging mergers, fighting off mergers, arranging divestitures, arbitraging, or establishing fair prices for friendly transactions of this sort. Fees were normally based on a % of the deal's dollar value and could run as high as 5% on a single transaction. Although there was heavy competition for M&A services, corporations tended to be somewhat price insensitive in such a vital strategic area. Since M&A business involved no capital risk, large commercial banks and even several public accounting firms became competitors for this business. But investment banks had some competitive advantages, and with their combination of analytical staffs and traders they were able to engage in profitable—but risky—arbitrage or trading activities whenever they were not being retained by either of the parties involved.

Another growing source of revenues was municipal underwriting. The bulk of profits in this field came not from underwriting general obligation bonds—which faced thin margins and highly competitive commercial bidding—but from underwriting negotiated revenue bond issues which, like other tax-exempt bond financings, were growing rapidly.

The private placement market also became a more important part of investment bankers' portfolios as the SEC eased its rigid (Regulation A) requirements for such securities in the late 1970s and early '80s. Private placements do not have to follow the costly and time consuming procedures of a public offering, but must be presented to only a few knowledgeable and financially competent investors as defined by SEC rules. In the mid 1980s, 70% of all private placements used a financial intermediary—93% of the time an investment bank. However, since fees for private placements compared favorably with those for management of public bond underwritings and involved no capital risk, commercial banks began competing for this business with corresponding pressures on margins. On the buyers' side, life insurance companies dominated the private placement bond market. However, in recent years, insurance companies had sought the more liquid portfolios that publicly traded bonds offer. And the supply of private placements bonds had been held down by the surge in publicly traded junk bonds issued by companies who otherwise might have used the private market.

The internationalization of the world's capital markets brought other, dramatic changes to the economics of investment banking.

Internationalization

In the world's capital markets, borders had begun to be irrelevant. Computerized quotes and satellite communications had made global markets possible. Big institutional investors had increased their overseas involvement in search of fresh investments. Savvy corporate treasurers had discovered that by tapping foreign markets they could often lower their capital costs and broaden their investor base. In 1985 some 500 companies were listed on at least one stock exchange outside their home country and international markets like the Eurobond markets were booming.

Interconnections among capital markets meant that innovations or changes in one market were gradually being reflected in others. The Eurobond market offered companies both lower costs and new ways of doing business which allowed them to decrease the time required to arrange and present a new financing issue—critical because of the growing volatility of interest rates and capital markets in general. Corporate treasurers could dispense with the time and expense of formal underwriting procedures. Instead, banks bid competitively to buy an issue, with the successful bank taking the whole issue directly onto its books and reselling pieces of it as quickly and as profitably as possible. This was known as a "bought deal." The SEC gradually changed key requirements to make the U.S. capital markets more attractive. In 1978, the SEC: (1) instituted abbreviated registration statements that allowed large companies to disclose information in a prospectus by reference to other publicly available documents (10Ks, etc.) and (2) provided for "selective SEC review" of certain documents which cut clearance times from several weeks down to 48 hours. Large companies, which had strong enough internal finance staffs to design and register issues using this abbreviated process, began pressing investment banks to bid for their business on the same competitive "bought deal" basis they used in the Eurobond market.

SEC Rule 415 in March 1982 accelerated this process further. Rule 415 allowed large, well capitalized companies to register all the securities they planned to issue over the following two years at one time, and then sell some or all of them "off the shelf" as funds needs or market conditions dictated. From 1982 to 1984, 50–60% of all debt issues and 10% of all equity issues used this technique. Rule 415 meant that a company did not have to choose a managing underwriter before registering an issue; it could simply list a number of acceptable possible managers and encourage those firms to bid for its business, often on a bought deal basis. The advent of shelf registration heated up competition in the capital markets since commercial banks could place shelf registered issues without actually underwriting them, and some corporations were even contemplating doing their own private placements.

The negotiated rates of the U.S. markets were being forced on exchanges in other countries by powerful institutional investors—as evidenced by the unfixing of commission rates in London and Australia. To compete with the Eurobond markets the U.S. removed the withholding requirements for foreign purchasers of U.S. bonds. The result was an increasingly comparability in rates for Eurodollar bonds and U.S. Treasurys.

Abroad—especially in the fast growing unregulated Euromarket—investment banks faced both new foreign competitors and large U.S. commercial banks free from Glass-Steagall restrictions. But currency volatilities and the internationalization which meant increased foreign trading and ownership of U.S. securities made it imperative for investment banks to operate on a global level both to serve their corporate clients and to take advantage of arbitrage opportunities for their own account. As foreign exchanges in London and Tokyo opened up their memberships and let foreign brokerages in, major U.S. investment firms were faced with difficult decisions about how fast and where they should expand their operations.

Resulting Structural Changes

As bought deals became more common and negotiated spreads shrank, the underwriting side of investment banking became highly concentrated. Only certain firms had the capital base, distribution, and trading systems to handle bought deals. By 1984 two-thirds of all new issues were underwritten by 5 firms.[34] Syndicate sizes shrank along with spreads and regional firms were increasingly squeezed out of underwriting, which they wanted badly because of its higher profit potentials. Regional distributors were also forced to automate their back-offices to deal with the high trading volumes and growing array of new products. Many either merged with national firms or went out of business. This heightened the competition between old style originators and national distributors.

Trading gained in relative importance and the nature of corporate/banker relationships shifted away from long-term stable ties and toward a transaction basis. The banks competed by developing innovative financing techniques and many new firms (boutiques) emerged pursuing niche or specialist strategies. Specialists and traders gained more power within investment banks. As competition increased in underwriting and other activities proliferated, investment banks rapidly expanded the size of their professional staffs. From 1966 to 1977 while revenues grew by 135% on an inflation adjusted basis, staffs grew by 345%.[35]

Many of these changes were reflected in the balance sheets of investment banks. (See Table 8.)

Table 8 Assets and Liabilities of New York Stock Exchange Member Firms

	1973	1978	1983
Distribution of Assets (%)			
Long Positions in Securities and Commodities	37.6	54.6	67.6
Receivables from Customers and Partners	37.1	29.8	15.4
Receivables from Other Brokers and Dealers	12.9	9.5	11.4
Bank Balances, Cash and Other Deposits	4.3	1.8	1.4
Land and Other Fixed Assets	1.1	0.6	0.9
Secured Demand Notes	1.9	0.5	0.1
Exchange Memberships	0.7	0.2	0.1
Other Assets	4.4	3.1	3.1
Total ($ billions)	$22.6	$53.9	$214.8
Distribution of Liabilities (%)			
Money Borrowed	38.8	47.8	48.7
Short Positions in Securities and Commodities	4.8	12.3	18.0
Payables to Other Brokers and Dealers	11.5	8.7	9.5
Other Accrued Expenses and Accounts Payable	7.4	9.5	8.0
Capital	16.6	8.1	6.6

*NYSE member firms account for over 90% of total industry assets.
Source: Statistical Information on the Financial Services Industry, 3rd ed., 1984, pp. 121 and 164. © American Bankers Association. Reprinted with permission. All rights reserved.

Notes

1. Benton Gup, *Financial Intermediaries: An Introduction,* Houghton-Mifflin, 1976.

2. "The World is Their Oyster," *Economist,* March 16, 1985.

3. George Benson, *Financial Services: The Changing Institutions and Government Policy,* Prentice-Hall, 1983, pages 252–3.

4. "No Longer a World Apart: A Survey of Wall Street," *Economist,* June 20, 1981.

5. A.D. Little, *Financial Services: A Business in Transaction,* April 1984.

6. Op.cit., Benson, *Financial Services: The Changing. . . .*

7. American Bankers Association, *Statistical Information on the Financial Services Industry,* 3rd Ed. 1984.

8. National Association of Securities Dealers. *1983 NASD Fact Book.*

9. "Banks and Nonbanks: Who's in Control?" *The Bankers Magazine,* September/October 1984, p. 14.

10. "The Future of Private Pension Plans," *Pension World,* August 1980.

11. "An Inflation Scoreboard," *Institutional Investor,* November 1983.

12. "Domestic Financial Statistics," *Federal Reserve Bulletin,* April 1985.

13. McKinsey & Company, Inc., "Discussing the Impact of Deregulating the Commercial Banking Industry," Report to the Office of the Controller of the Currency, June 1982.

14. "Fighting the Fed," *Fortune,* July 8, 1985.

15. "Federal Lawmakers and Regulators Fear States are Going Too Far in Expanding Banks' Powers," *Wall Street Journal,* July 31, 1985.

16. *Federal Reserve Bulletin,* May 1983.

17. "Nationwide Banking: A Welcome Mat, Not a Slammed Door," *Business Week,* June 24, 1984.

18. "A New Awakening: Survey of International Banking," *Economist,* March 24, 1984.

19. "The Revolution in Financial Services," *Business Week,* November 28, 1983.

20. *Euromoney Yearbook 1983,* Credit Suisse—First Boston, Section 1.3.

21. "European Bankers Struggle to Compete in Fast Moving Underwriting Markets," *Wall Street Journal,* August 7, 1985.

22. "The World is Their Oyster," *Economist,* March 16, 1985.

23. Banking Heads for a New Patch of Thin Ice," *Business Week,* July 29, 1985.

24. K. Cooper and D. Fraser, *Banking Deregulation and the New Competition in Financial Services,* Ballinger Publishing Co., 1984, p. 92

25. "Bargain Loans," *Wall Street Journal,* June 26, 1985.

26. NASD, *The Financial Services Industry of Tomorrow,* November 1982, p. 17.

27. L. Goldberg and L. White (Eds.), *The Deregulation of the Banking and Securities Industries,* D.C. Heath and Co., 1979.

28. Securities Industry Association, *Securities Industry Yearbook 1984–85.*

29. "Wall Street is Finding . . . It Enjoys Unfixed Rates," *Wall Street Journal,* April 22, 1985, p. 1, 18.

30. SRI, *Success in the New Financial Services Industry,* July 1983.

31. Investment Company Institute, *Mutual Fund Fact Book, 1982.*

32. "No Longer a Business Apart: A Survey of Wall Street," *Economist,* June 20, 1981.

33. Robert Perez, *Inside Investment Banking,* Praeger Publishers, 1984.

34. "The World is Their Oyster: A Survey of International Banking," *Economist,* March 16, 1985.

35. "Transformation of Investment Banking," *Harvard Business Review,* January/February 1979.

Case 5

The American Express Company

American Express company executives, meeting in their new fifty-one-story headquarters in the financial district of lower Manhattan, look to the future with a certain optimism. As the chairman and CEO, James D. Robinson, III, put it, "We are extremely active in two of the world's greatest growth industries: financial services and tourism."[1] A trusted name since 1850, AMEXCO looks to the second half of the eighties and into the nineties with a corporate philosophy and values anchored in entrepreneurship, quality, integrity, and service. A brief history of the company appears in Appendix A.

Flushed with the apparent success of its major acquisitions, AMEXCO's total assets had tripled from 1982 to nearly $62 billion by the end of 1984. This international financial supermarket (Exhibit 1) employs 77,000 people in more than 2,000 offices spread throughout 131 countries. Much of its incredible growth has occurred in only 3 years, "faster than expected because of profound changes in insurance, banking and securities wrought by the interplay of higher interest rates, technology and deregulation."[2]

During this period of expansion, AMEXCO revenues doubled to almost $13 billion with net income increasing from $466 million to $610 million (Exhibit 2). Through 1982 AMEXCO enjoyed its thirty-fifth consecutive year of increased earnings. This ended in 1983 with an 11 percent decrease in net income primarily attributed to problems at Fireman's Fund. By the end of 1984, AMEXCO showed respectable growth in net income of 18 percent.

The competition has a very healthy respect for the strength of AMEXCO. Dee Hock, former managing director and CEO of VISA International, commenting on combat with AMEXCO, said:

> They [AMEX] are rough, tough, smart competitors with tons of money. There is very little they will not do to achieve their objectives. The advantage of American Express is that James Robinson can say, "To the left, march" and they do. I couldn't think of doing that. Each of our institutions [members] is totally independent.[3]

George Ball, president and CEO of Prudential-Bache Securities Inc., was quoted in April 1984 as saying, "Four years ago [AMEX] was a plastic card company, but with the addition of Lehman, AMEX is a fully fleshed-out financial services confederation of the type that will be dominant in tomorrow's marketplace."[4] Herbert E. Goodfriend, an analyst with Prudential-Bache, calls American Express "unquestionably the premier company in the financial services industry."[5]

---

[1]"American Express: Financial Powerhouse," *Dun's Business Month,* December 1983, p. 39.

[2]Arlene Hershman, "The Supercompanies Emerge," *Dun's Business Month,* April 1983, p. 44.

[3]Leonard A. Schlesinger, Robert G. Eccles, John J. Gararro, *Managing Behavior in Organizations* (New York: McGraw-Hill, 1983), p. 479.

[4]"The Golden Plan of American Express," *Business Week,* April 30, 1984, p. 118.

[5]"American Express: Financial Powerhouse," p. 38.

Exhibit 1 The American Express Company (December 1984)

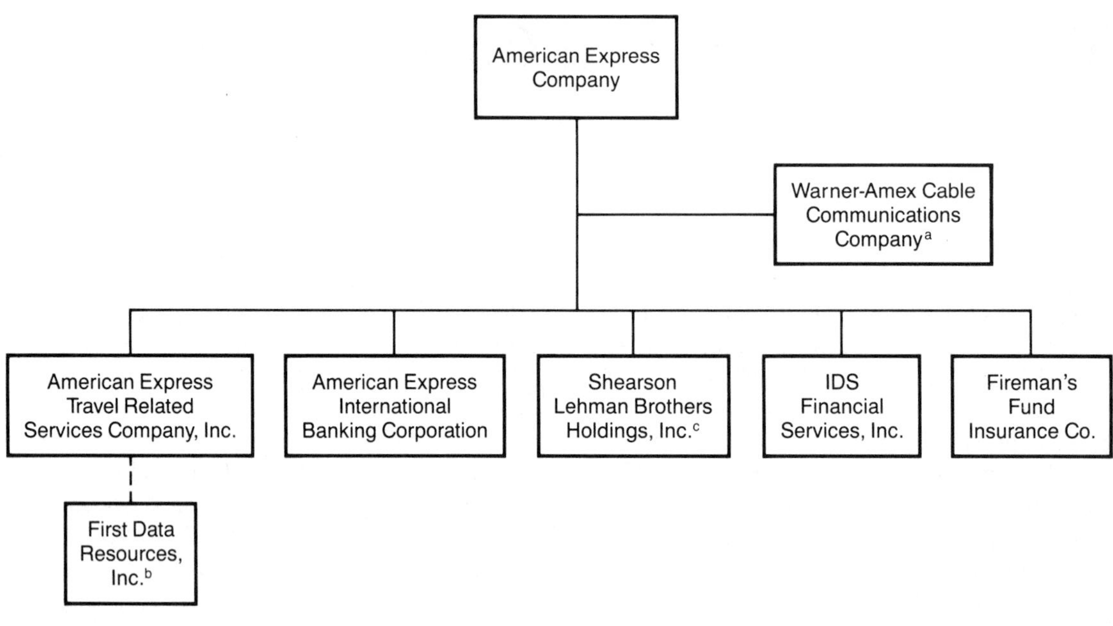

Source: Constructed from information contained in American Express Company 1984 Annual Report.
[a]AMEXCO owns 50 percent.
[b]TRS owns 75 percent of capital stock of the largest third-party processor of debit and credit cards in the United States.
[c]Includes fourteen major subsidiaries of which Shearson Lehman Brothers, Inc. is the principal.

The financial services supermarket is considered to operate in one or more of five major businesses. They include banking, credit cards, insurance, real estate, and securities. AMEXCO is looking for ways to enter the domestic U.S. banking business; Citicorp wants to enter the securities business. Sears, Roebuck, and Co. and Bank America are both involved in all five major businesses. Prudential-Bache and Merrill Lynch, the other two principal financial supermarkets, like AMEXCO, lack domestic banking operations.[6] AMEXCO currently outstrips all the others in the travel-related services industry. Exhibit 3 shows six companies that have major positions in a number of critical financial-services businesses (at end of 1982).

According to a 1984 survey conducted by the *American Banker,* people rate American Express products and services higher than those of any other top financial services firm in the United States. The same survey indicates that the American Express name is best known among consumers.[7]

AMEXCO's Major Companies

Assembled under the American Express corporate roof are five major companies. They include American Express Travel Related Services Company, Inc. (TRS), American Express International Banking Corporation (AEIBC), Shearson Lehman Brothers, Inc. (SLAX), IDS Financial

[6]"The Supercompanies Emerge," p. 45.

[7]*American Express Company 1985 Annual Report,* p. 4.

Exhibit 2 Consolidated Summary of Selected Financial Data

	1984	1983	1982	1981	1980
Operating results					
Revenues	$12,895	$ 9,770	$ 8,093	$ 7,291	$ 6,426
Percent increase in revenues	*32%*	*21%*	*11%*	*13%*	*26%*
Expenses	12,159	9,253	7,339	6,586	5,830
Income taxes	126	2	173	181	130
Net income	610	515	581	524	466
Percent increase (decrease) in net income	*18%*	*(11)%*	*11%*	*12%*	*23%*
Assets and liabilities					
Time deposits	$ 5,470	$ 4,071	$ 2,127	$ 1,784	$ 1,120
Investment securities					
Carried at cost	13,449	12,766	7,163	6,446	6,026
Carried at lower of aggregate cost or market	315	211	81	148	166
Carried at market	8,566	1,709	948	917	1,235
Accounts receivable and accrued interest, net	14,802	11,497	9,204	8,191	6,825
Loans and discounts, net	7,089	6,642	4,379	3,929	3,811
Total assets	61,848	43,981	28,311	25,252	22,731
Customers' deposits and credit balances	13,262	12,511	6,810	6,218	5,818
Travelers checks outstanding	2,454	2,362	2,177	2,468	2,542
Insurance and annuity reserves	8,831	7,667	4,323	4,110	3,856
Long-term debt	3,839	2,643	1,798	1,293	1,293
Shareholders' equity	4,607	4,043	3,039	2,661	2,430
Common share statistics					
Net income per share	$ 2.79	$ 2.53	$ 3.02	$ 2.79	$ 2.59
Cash dividends declared per share	$ 1.28	$ 1.26	$ 1.125	$ 1.025	$ 1.00
Average number of shares outstanding	217	203	192	188	180
Shares outstanding at year-end	217	213	191	188	185
Number of shareholders of record	*51,211*	*45,753*	*36,580*	*36,611*	*34,735*
Other statistics					
Number of employees at year-end					
United States	*59,420*	*53,740*	*48,533*	*43,315*	*39,475*
Outside United States	*17,027*	*16,716*	*15,472*	*14,994*	*15,556*
Total	*76,447*	*70,456*	*64,005*	*58,309*	*55,031*
Number of offices at year-end					
American Express offices worldwide	*1,472*	*1,356*	*1,160*	*1,066*	*1,046*
Representative offices	*810*	*797*	*760*	*782*	*782*
Total	*2,282*	*2,153*	*1,920*	*1,848*	*1,828*

Note: Data in millions, except per share amounts and where italicized.
Note: Operating results for the year ended December 31, 1983 do not include the effect of the acquisition of Investors Diversified Services, Inc., accounted for as a purchase as of December 31, 1983. Where applicable, amounts and percentages for 1984 include the effect of the acquisition of Lehman Brothers Kuhn Loeb Holding Co., Inc., accounted for as a purchase as of May 11, 1984.
Source: American Express Co. 1984 Annual Report.

Exhibit 3 The Six Financial-Services Leaders

	Banking	Credit cards	Insurance	Real estate	Securities
American Express Co. Assets: $30 billion Revenue: $8.1 billion Net income: $581 million	—	(1)	(2)	(3)	(1)
BankAmerica Corp. Assets: $122.5 billion Revenue: $4 billion Net income: $451 million	(1)	(1)	(3)	(1)	(2)
Citicorp Assets: $130 billion Revenue: $5.2 billion Net income: $723 million	(1)	(1)	(3)	(1)	—
Merrill Lynch & Co. Assets: $20.7 billion Revenue: $5 billion Net income: $309 million	—	(3)	(2)	(2)	(1)
Prudential Insurance Co. of America Assets: $76.5 billion Revenue: $18.5 billion Net income: $2.13 billion	—	(3)	(1)	(2)	(1)
Sears, Roebuck & Co. Assets: $36 billion Revenue: $30 billion Net income: $861 million	(2)	(1)	(2)	(2)	(1)

(1) = Major factor in this industry.
(2) = Medium-sized factor in this industry.
(3) = Small factor in this industry.
Source: "The Supercompanies Emerge," *Dun's Business Month*, April 1983, p. 44.

Services Inc. (IDS), and Fireman's Fund Insurance Companies (FF). Additionally, AMEXCO owns 50 percent of Warner AMEX Cable Communications. Appendix B presents 1982–1984 financial data by service category. Appendix C presents 1983–1984 financial data by subsidiary. Following is a discussion of each of these companies.

American Express Travel Related Services Company

Perhaps the oldest name in travel is TRS, the flagship organization of AMEXCO. The company was founded in 1850 and became a separate company under the AMEXCO banner in 1983. Annual growth in revenues exceeded 18 percent from 1982 to 1984. TRS is in the process of modernizing and is emerging as the most customer-responsive travel and credit card service company in the world with great profit potential.

TRS has grown and developed a great deal since its early days as a small package and funds freight company. Currently, TRS is best known for its worldwide network of travel offices, charge card, and traveler's cheques (without which you do not leave home). In addition, TRS offers direct mail merchandise services, publishing (*Travel and Leisure* and *Food and Wine*), and data processing services. TRS is also moving into communications, providing AMEX card members access to MCI. This is primarily a billing service providing MCI long-distance dialing through what AMEXCO calls "Expressphone."

In 1985, TRS launched "Project Hometown America" which raises money for local communities by contributions from American Express Card purchases, AMEX traveler's cheques, purchases of travel packages, and new card applications. TRS continues to utilize extensive advertising which, among other things, features tie-ins with major hotels, resorts, car-rental companies, and Eastern and United Airlines.

TRS operates 1,200 offices in more than 131 countries. Overseas travel has been popular due to the strength of the American dollar and TRS has capitalized on this opportunity. In 1984 and early 1985, TRS acquired new travel companies in Pittsburgh, Denver, and thirty-eight locations in the United Kingdom.

While the proliferation of plastic money and automatic teller machines (ATM) have eaten into the traveler's cheque market, AMEXCO still sold $15.1 billion in 1984, an increase of 9.1 percent over 1983. The average outstanding traveler's cheque's volume in 1983 was $2.6 billion, up 8.3 percent. It is on these outstanding cheques, or "float," that TRS makes its profit, which in 1982 was $76 million before taxes. In 1962 the traveler's cheque float accounted for 80 percent of AMEXCO's total income. Twenty years later, it was responsible for only 11 percent of the total income. (Credit cards accounted for 24 percent of income; Fireman's Fund, 36 percent; and Shearson, 18 percent in 1982.) It is the lessons learned from managing the traveler's cheque float that make AMEXCO's management of cash balances anywhere within the corporation masterful.[8]

By the end of 1984 there were more than 20 million American Express Cards in force throughout the world, an increase of 17 percent over 1983. Credit card charge volume grew 24 percent to $47.6 billion during the same time. One out of every four cardholders lives overseas and the card is issued in twenty-eight currencies. In 1984, 125 mainland Chinese establishments accepted the card compared to 14 in 1983.

In August 1984, the platinum card ($250 fee, by invitation only) was offered in addition to the green card (offered since 1958) and the gold card (first offered in 1981). In 1984, AMEXCO added major retailers such as the May Company and the J. C. Penney Company as establishments that accept the American Express Card. TRS also acquired Health Carecard, Inc., a company whose product combines medical record keeping with payment capabilities.

The American Express Card differs from other plastic cards in distinct ways. It must be paid in full monthly (unless special arrangements have been made in advance) and the annual fee is more than other cards. (In 1985 the green card fee increased by 30 percent to $45.) These facts, coupled with economies of scale in billing and extensive experience in managing moving cash balances, make the American Express Card unique and highly profitable.

Another segment of TRS is direct marketing. When American Express began in 1974 to include product inserts in its 5 million monthly bills, it did not envision a merchandise services division of $185 million in sales just 10 years later. The growth of TRS's direct mail business is largely the result of its sophisticated use of customer segmentation based on the exact purpose for which each cardholder uses the card. Particular product mailings are targeted with precision to those customer groups with the greatest potential buying interest in that product. The merchandise services division has six target customer segments:

The frequent traveler, to whom it sells products and services to make business and travel more enjoyable

The upscale male consumer, to whom it sells

[8]Priscilla S. Meyer, "Cheques and Balances," *Forbes*, March 14, 1983, p. 50.

state-of-the-art electronics for home entertainment and personal productivity

The upscale female consumer, to whom it sells products related to home design and household invention

Business executives of small- to medium-sized companies, to whom it sells products for the office that will increase chances for success

Portions of each of the above, to whom it offers new products on a test basis

Portions of each of the first four groups, to whom it offers various services, including magazine subscriptions at discounted prices[9]

A key to the merchandise services division's success is its strategy of offering exclusive merchandise. Whenever possible, TRS strives to be the sole source of the merchandise it offers. More than 90 percent of the noncatalog merchandise offered is exclusive. TRS seeks manufacturers who will modify certain aspects of a product just for AMEXCO. As a result, TRS sold 18,000 IBM electric typewriters in 1983 and 42,000 Gucci watches in 1982 and 1983.[10]

The strengths that TRS has identified as its basis for its marketing approach are:

The prestige attached to owning an American Express card

The excellent customer service provided by AMEXCO

A vast, affluent cardmember customer base (over 11 million in the United States)

AMEXCO's orientation toward business

AMEXCO's adeptness at packaging goods and services

A very strong overall quality image

Strong information processing skills[11]

The goals of the merchandise services division are: to continue to use the strong name recognition of American Express to generate sales to new customers; to provide the best service available in direct merchandising, with new, quality products tailored to the customers' needs; and to go outside the AMEXCO cardmember base to allow customers to pay for merchandise by Visa, MasterCard, or other credit cards.[12]

In publishing, TRS saw new highs in both ad pages and revenues in 1984. With almost a million paid subscribers, *Travel and Leisure* saw an increase of 23 percent in advertising revenues over 1983. *Food and Wine,* with 600,000 paid subscribers, saw an 18 percent increase in advertising revenues over 1983.

Since 1984, TRS has owned 75 percent of the capital stock of First Data Resources, Inc. This data processing company is the largest third-party processor of debit and credit cards in the United States. It is this acquisition that gives AMEXCO its economies of scale in processing transactions.

Historically TRS has exhibited a great deal of support for the arts. From 1979 through 1984 TRS sponsored fifty projects, in one hundred cities, over five continents, to bring the arts closer to the people (at a cost of $20 million in 1984).[13] In AMEXCO's opinion, it has been worth the investment. AMEXCO has gained recognition within these communities and increased opportunities to attract potential customers and financial institutions. The "Project Hometown America" mentioned earlier is an extension of AMEXCO's charitable, goodwill efforts, while it offers potential tax advantages.

American Express International Banking Corporation

Growing out of a need to provide the travel-hungry American tourist financial services

---

[9]Larry Jaffee, "AMEX Targets Mailings Precisely to List Segments," *Direct Marketing,* May 1984, p. 78.

[10]Ibid., p. 79.

[11]Ibid., p. 78.

[12]Ibid., p. 86.

[13]Susan Bloom, "Beauty and the Bottom Line," *Business Quarterly,* Fall 1984, p. 86.

abroad after World War I, AEIBC was founded in 1919 as the American Express Company, Incorporated. In 1968, the name was changed to American Express International Banking Corporation.

By 1980 AMEXCO was itching to get rid of its overseas bank, AEIBC. The bank, under the direction of Richard Bliss, had been attempting to establish itself as a big investment banking concern in London. In 1981 Robert F. Smith, formerly AMEXCO's treasurer, took over as vice-chairman of the bank. Smith quickly changed the direction of the bank by slashing its operating costs and paring down its attempt to offer every service imaginable. The bank began to focus on trade finance and private banking for wealthy individual clients. AEIBC evolved into a deal-making organization with trade-related transactions involving export credit guarantees from Western governments.

The big improvement in AEIBC performance through 1983 was clearly a result of sheer cost-cutting. Total operating expenses fell from 63 percent of net financial revenue in 1981 to 52 percent in 1983. Also figuring prominently in the improvement was the acquisition of the Trade Development Bank (TDB) in Switzerland in March 1983. At $800 million in shareholders' equity, the combined bank has more than twice the equity of the old AEIBC. That, in turn, reduced AEIBC's Latin American debt from four times equity to a more manageable, yet still concerning, two times equity.[14]

To acquire the TDB, AMEXCO paid more than 50 percent over the book value of TDB stock. Many believe that AMEXCO paid the premium price to obtain the services of Edmond J. Safra, Lebanese-born banking genius and owner of TDB.[15] Safra needed U.S. government approval to become CEO of AEIBC (a condition of sale). Although the sale was made in January 1983, Safra did not set foot in AMEXCO's corporate offices in New York throughout the year. While waiting for U.S. approval, AMEXCO top executives visited and called Safra frequently (he has controlling interest in other U.S. banks) at his TDB office in Geneva to get the benefit of his advice and banking instincts.[16] Safra continued running TDB and in 1984 was elected to AMEXCO's board of directors.

As a result of these moves, the AEIBC was a welcome member of the AMEXCO family in early 1984. The former wallflower is a highly profitable bank with $13 billion in assets.[17] The AMEXCO hierarchy sees a great potential for marketing Shearson/American Express Inc. services through the AEIBC. 1984 was a year of record profits for AEIBC, even though it was a year that will be remembered as one of the most difficult in international banking. Net income in 1984 increased 15 percent to a record $156 million after a 126 percent increase to $136 million from 1982 to 1983.

Today, with 82 offices in 39 countries, AEIBC includes international private banking, trade financing operations, correspondent banking (more than 2,000 active correspondent bank relationships worldwide), treasury and foreign exchange services, equipment financing (American Express Leasing Corporation), and military banking for the U.S. Armed Forces overseas.

Citicorp has been a pioneer among the major financial supermarkets in pushing for changes in the law that would permit it, a leader in domestic banking, into the insurance field.[18] Citicorp has made inroads in this regard in South Dakota. If Citicorp is successful on a national basis, the door would be open for AMEXCO, if they so choose, to move into the domestic banking in-

---

[14]"AMEX's Bank: A Wallflower Suddenly Blossoms," *Business Week,* January 9, 1984, p. 101.

[15]Gwen Kinkead, "The Mystery Man American Express Is Banking On," *Fortune,* December 12, 1983, p. 142.

[16]Ibid.

[17]"AMEX's Bank: A Wallflower Suddenly Blossoms," p. 101.

[18]Carol J. Loomis, "Fire in the Belly at American Express," *Fortune,* November 28, 1983, p. 87.

dustry either as a separate AMEXCO company or as a division of AEIBC.

Fireman's Fund Insurance Company

Since 1863, when it was founded in San Francisco, Fireman's Fund Insurance Company has grown to be a leading provider of insurance protection for individuals, groups, businesses, and institutions, offering a broad range of property, liability, life, accident, and health insurance. Acquired by AMEXCO in 1968, FF products are offered through more than 10,000 independent agents and brokers throughout the United States.

In 1979 and 1980 the property and casualty industry experienced serious trouble due to price-cutting on many types of policies. In 1981, under the leadership of Fireman's Fund CEO Myron Dubain, FF cut a deal with the Insurance Company of North America to swap certain casualty policies. The swap allowed both companies to discount the loss reserves required on their newly acquired policies, without disclosing a change in accounting practices on their financial statements or to their respective boards of directors. This accounting sleight-of-hand increased FF's reported pretax profits by $66 million in 1981–1982, but resulted in a negative cash flow due to an additional $30 million tax bill[19] (Exhibit 4).

In 1982, Edwin F. Cutler became FF's CEO with guidance from AMEXCO to further increase profits. From January to September 1983, FF dropped its premium prices and generated a 13 percent increase in written premiums while the insurance industry average was only about 4 percent.[20]

In the third quarter of 1983, a sharp rise in claims forced FF to add $10 million to its loss reserves, which resulted in a fourth-quarter after-tax net loss of $10 million.[21]

A *Fortune* article in November 1983 exposed the paper profits of 1981–1982 and seriously undermined the credibility of FF's and AMEXCO's financial statements.[22]

In December 1983 Cutler was removed as CEO and replaced by acquisition and financial

Exhibit 4 Fireman's Fund Net Income

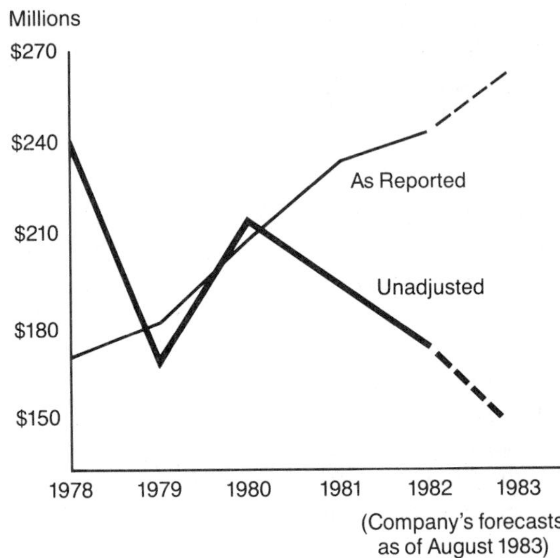

The dollar gap between "reported net income" and "unadjusted net income" at Fireman's Fund in the 1978–83 period was recapped in an August 1983 memo from Edwin F. Cutler, then chairman of the American Express subsidiary, to his boss, James D. Robinson III, chairman of the parent. Unadjusted profits were those earned on the subsidiary's basic insurance business, which as time went on felt increasing cyclical pressure. But "special items" added to or subtracted from those profits allowed Fireman's Fund to report figures that showed the smooth uptrend American Express loves to see. Cutler's memo forecast a further gain for reported profits in 1983. But a subsequent spike in claim costs and a $230-million addition to reserves blitzed 1983 profits. Reported net income for 1983 was $30 million; unadjusted net income was not announced.

Source: "The Earnings Magic at American Express," *Fortune*, June 25, 1984, p. 58.

[19]Carol J. Loomis, "How Fireman's Fund Stoked Its Profits," *Fortune*, November 28, 1983, pp. 99–104.

[20]Carol J. Loomis, "How Fireman's Fund Singed American Express," *Fortune*, January 9, 1984, p. 80.

[21]Ibid.

[22]Loomis, "How Fireman's Fund Stoked Its Profits," pp. 99–104.

wizard Sanford Weill, an executive with no prior insurance experience. FF simultaneously announced a reduction in its work force of 14,000 by more than 10 percent through retirement and attrition in an effort to reduce costs.

In December 1983, AMEXCO's board of directors added $230 million to FF's loss reserves which contributed to a drop in AMEXCO earnings from $700 million to $520 million for 1983. A public announcement by AMEXCO on December 12, 1983 regarding FF's financial problems caused a single-day drop in AMEXCO stock from $32 to $29 per share.[23] FF's performance, or lack thereof, was the principal reason why AMEXCO had its first downturn in earnings in 36 years.

In the first quarter of 1984, Sandy Weill cut 1,200 employees from the payroll, estimating a $40–50 million annual saving. Weill announced a three-step strategy to become the low-cost producer in the industry: lay-offs and cost cutting, combined with increased efficiencies in decision making due to more autonomy at lower levels; top management compensation tied to performance; and a revamping of FF's data processing system.[24]

The first quarter of 1984 saw a modest $10 million profit, but in the second quarter 1985 FF reported a quarterly loss of $71.7 million on revenues of $1 billion. Once again AMEXCO felt compelled to add $187 million to FF's loss reserves.[25]

By July 1985, Sandy Weill was replaced as CEO of Fireman's Fund by John J. Byrne, former CEO at Government Employees Insurance Company.[26] In December 1985, FF changed executive vice-presidents, with James Ridling, formerly of Crum and Foster, replacing Donald McComber. As the year closed, AMEXCO owned 41 percent of FF.[27]

Shearson Lehman/American Express

Synergy—the art of making one plus one equal three—was the underlying impetus behind the broad concept of creating financial supermarkets, which, in turn, led to the stampede of acquisitions of large brokerage firms by giant outsiders in 1981. As part of the stampede, AMEXCO acquired the prestigious Wall Street brokerage firm Shearson at a price of approximately $1 billion. The merger was, to some degree, a response to the Prudential-Bache merger. Sandy Weill, Shearson's CEO at the time, did not want to risk being left behind by the entry of the largest U.S. insurer into the securities business. The merger between AMEXCO and Shearson was brought about by the two firms' belief that the barriers of tradition and regulation separating banking, brokerage, and insurance would eventually evaporate.[28]

In 1984 Shearson, under the leadership of their new CEO, Peter Cohen, purchased the 134-year-old investment bank of Lehman Brothers Kuhn-Loeb. This acquisition provided AMEXCO with additional strength in investment banking and fixed-income trading. As a result, SLAX wields this investment banking strength with a broadbased, soundly capitalized trading capacity and a global distribution network with over 5,000 professional financial consultants in 354 offices located in forty-four states and fifteen countries. Through these consultants, SLAX offers stocks, bonds, options, futures, commercial paper, certificates of deposit, insurance, and tax-advantaged investments as well as investment banking, pension and investment management, real estate, and mortgage banking services.

Mergers such as this have had the effect of moving retail brokers closer to becoming finan-

[23]Loomis, "How Fireman's Fund Singed American Express," p. 80.

[24]Mary Row, "Can Sandy Weill Turn Fireman's Fund Around," *Institutional Investor,* May 1984, pp. 110–112.

[25]Carol J. Loomis, "The Earnings Magic at American Express," *Fortune,* June 25, 1984, p. 60.

[26]"A New Chief for Fireman's Fund," *Business Week,* August 5, 1985, p. 38.

[27]"Who's News," *Wall Street Journal,* December 19, 1985, p. 14.

[28]Anthony Bianco, "How A Financial Supermarket Was Born," *Business Week,* December 23, 1985, p. 10.

cial consultants, although the SLAX brokers can now refer their clients with specific problems to the specialists who may reside in one of their sister companies and who also fall under the AMEXCO umbrella. This is due in large part to AMEXCO's purchase of such firms as Balcor (the nation's largest real estate syndicator) and Investors Diversified Services and Ayco (both well-known financial planning firms).[29]

Among the mergers' by-products, none seems to have benefited the brokers more than the reputation of AMEXCO. SLAX staff members acknowledge an overnight surge in client confidence. "Once Shearson teamed up with American Express, we got the credibility we needed."[30] Other beneficial side effects include the infusion of capital by AMEXCO (which has enabled many of the brokers to obtain desktop computers, which improves their service to the client); the ability to attend workshops on specific products and selling skills; and stepped-up advertising campaigns to enhance their visibility.

The effect of these advantages can be seen in the year-end summary of activities for SLAX for 1984. The company managed over 300 underwritings in U.S. and international markets. The corporate finance division represented clients in more than 70 completed mergers, acquisitions, and divestitures with an aggregate transaction value of over $12 billion. The public finance division managed tax-exempt financings of $28 billion for state and local governments in 1984. Shearson also recognized a 135 percent rise in revenues in the fixed-income sector and an 8.4 percent increase in revenues from the sale of tax-advantaged investments.

However, there have been certain drawbacks to the merger. The presence of AMEXCO has diminished the informal atmosphere that previously existed at Shearson. "A certain impersonality has emerged, it is no longer the closely knit firm it once was."[31] The bureaucratic system of the conglomerate is also frustrating to the Shearson staffers: "It takes six weeks to get some requests through."[32] Along with the abundance of products has come an abundance of paperwork. Equally as frustrating is the fact that the parent company, as of March 1984, had not yet released the names of its 9 million green-card holders to the brokerage firm. This single source of potential clients could easily double or triple Shearson's client base.[33]

Despite these drawbacks, it is the consensus of the brokerage community that the full effects of the mergers will not be felt for some time. They are convinced that these mergers will give rise to a new breed of broker, one able to deal with a larger client base by supplying a wider range of financial services.

IDS Financial Services, Inc.

IDS Financial Services, Inc. (IDS) was established in 1894 to help people and businesses manage money and achieve their financial goals. Through its sales force of more than 4,400 representatives, IDS offers sound financial plans and the products and services to fulfill those plans. Among its offerings are investment certificates, mutual funds, life insurance, annuities, unit investment trusts, IRAs, limited partnerships, and management and fiduciary services for pension and employee benefit plans. IDS has traditionally concentrated on the lower end of the investing public (incomes in the $25,000–$75,000 range).

IDS was acquired by AMEXCO in January 1984 as part of its multibrand approach to providing financial services.[34] In addition to adding the American Express name to the IDS banner, this merger has also resulted in more training opportunities for the IDS sales force and a con-

[29]Andrew Marton, "What Have the Megamergers Meant for Brokers," *Institutional Investor,* March 1984, pp. 147–150.

[30]Ibid., p. 148.

[31]Ibid.

[32]Ibid.

[33]Ibid.

[34]"The Golden Plan of American Express," p. 119.

tinual flow of new and upgraded products. With AMEXCO's support, IDS has launched its most aggressive advertising campaign ever in an attempt to provide the company with further exposure.

Investors were apparently not impressed by AMEXCO's purchase of IDS. In fact, AMEXCO's stock plummeted from $45 to $28 in the year after the announcement of the merger. This was a much greater drop than that of the stock market averages during the same period. However, at the end of 1985, AMEXCO's stock was up to approximately $52.

Warner Amex (W-A)

In the late seventies, "gripped with doubts about its competitive position in checks and cards,"[35] AMEXCO sought acquisitions in the communications arena. After trying to buy the McGraw-Hill publishing company and looking at others in the field, AMEXCO settled on 50 percent of Warner-AMEX, a cable TV company that has grown to be the sixth largest cable operator in the United States.

W-A owns 104 cable television systems in twenty-one states serving 1.2 million subscribers, but has done poorly with big-city franchises. In its first 5 years of co-ownership, AMEXCO has contributed more than $300 million to W-A's operations.[36] In 1983, AMEXCO's share of operating losses was close to $40 million. In 1984, Drew Lewis, W-A CEO, reduced pretax losses to $94 million with net losses falling from $99 million to $25 million. Looking to 1985 and beyond, W-A owns almost two-thirds of MTV Network which also includes the VH-1 and the Nickelodeon Children's channels. W-A also owns 19 percent of the Showtime Movie channel.

The Cable Company Policy Act of 1984 provided for rate deregulation after 2 years, which will allow cable operators to function in a more competitive market, which may contribute to greater economic stability in the industry. In 1984 W-A sold cable systems in Pittsburgh, Chicago, St. Louis, and twenty smaller locales as well as its regional sports programming service and its security division. Contract modifications in its urban franchises in Milwaukee, New York City, and Dallas were also a part of the cost-containment strategy launched in 1984.

According to Drew Lewis:

> This year [1984] marked a turning point for Warner-Amex. The foundation for the future is now in place and Warner-Amex is moving forward toward its goal of profitability. The cable industry is entering an era of realism and its future is bright. Warner-Amex is well positioned for a key role in that future.[37]

The Financial Supermarkets

Deregulation has given rise to many investment alternatives. Americans spent $200 billion in 1982 for financial services with an estimated margin of 25 percent.[38] These facts, coupled with tax breaks for IRAs and capital gains, stimulate demand and encourage supplies of financial services to enter the market. A major barrier to expansion into the financial supermarket category has been the legal restrictions on combining banking operations with insurance or investment banking, or interstate branching by security brokers with investment banking.

As the supermarkets emerge, there is competition to become the low-cost financial service provider. ATMs and 800 telephone numbers make personal banking more efficient and easier for most types of financial transactions. Technology with its inherent efficiencies makes pursuit of a low-cost strategy more feasible. Other ways to pursue a low-cost strategy include the use of service representatives (rather than more expensive account executives) to handle walk-in low-margin investment clients, selling to indi-

[35]Loomis, "Fire In the Belly At American Express," p. 88.

[36]Ibid.

[37]*American Express Company 1984 Annual Report,* p. 47.

[38]Hershman, "The Supercompanies Emerge," p. 44.

viduals at the workplace (corporate benefit programs), and vertical integration.[39]

The supercompanies plan to go after the middle-income families earning $20,000 to $50,000 a year. The company that can profitably serve the middle-income investor is going to make a potload of money, as this market group contains the most people. Further strategies will be to have a broad and diversified base of revenues to overcome the large cycles of financial services. Furthermore, geographic diversification will be necessary to cover costs and enjoy the economies of scale of mass marketing. One method of mass marketing is the national ad campaigns that have just begun. These mass marketing strategies will be aimed at reaching as many people as possible and trying to gain national recognition for each company as a full-service financial provider. Banks have the inside track here as cash and checks are the centerpiece of financial transactions.[40]

AMEXCO considers itself to be in the financial and travel-related service industries. While each of its corporate companies is a separate profit center, AMEXCO attempts to capitalize on its corporate synergy by using multiple distribution channels that target select market segments with strong brand-name products and services. Cross marketing, another synergy of the financial supermarket, allows an AEIBC customer in West Germany, for example, to buy securities or real estate in the United States through SLAX.

In terms of vertical-integration economies, AMEXCO owns Balcor, a firm that puts together and manages real estate syndications which can then be sold through SLAX account executives to potential investors. Another economy of scale is its low-cost, high-speed data processing capability (First Data Resources, Inc.) on which AMEXCO spends $300–400 million annually for hardware and software improvements. A clear goal is for AMEXCO to be the low-cost processor of financial transactions.[41]

As a financial supermarket, AMEXCO competes on many levels within international, national, and regional markets. In the industry, AMEXCO competes with the other financial supermarkets on a corporate basis. This competition includes Sears Roebuck, Prudential-Bache, Bank America Corporation, Citicorp, and Merrill Lynch. To a lesser degree, AMEXCO competes with potential financial supermarkets such as Travelers, Transamerica, Aetna, and Security Pacific Bank. On a regional basis, AMEXCO competes with growing financial empires such as First Interstate Bancorp.

Looking at the leaders (AMEXCO, Sears, Prudential, and Merrill Lynch), it is clear that all are spending money as never before in efforts to revamp their business identities. The strategy for these firms is twofold: first, to make consumers comfortable with once unheard-of combinations of merchandise the supermarkets now offer (e.g., risky tax shelters and riskless life insurance or, in Sears' case, stocks and socks) and, second, to distinguish each firm from its competitors.[42]

Achieving the first goal (one-stop shopping) will take time. A recent sampling survey revealed that most respondents did not see many benefits in one-stop financial shopping. The survey results indicated that younger adults are more receptive to the idea than older ones.[43]

In terms of differentiation, Merrill Lynch ("to be all things to some people") has said frankly that it is after affluent households with incomes over $50,000.[44] This involves courting young professionals, who may not have big incomes now, but seem likely to at some point in the future. Sears is capitalizing on its image of trustworthiness and is using a celebrity spokes-

[39]Ibid., p. 49.

[40]Ibid., pp. 44–50.

[41]Ibid., p. 50.

[42]Geoffry Colvin, "Would You Buy Stocks Where You Buy Stocks?" *Fortune,* July 9, 1984, p. 50.

[43]Ibid., p. 130.

[44]Ibid.

man, Hal Holbrook, to convey that image in TV advertising ($3.1 million in first-quarter 1984).[45]

American Express is trying to cover all the bases. The company offers its credit card in three versions—green, gold, and the ultraexclusive platinum card—with the intent to intercept investors at three levels of wealth.

IDS Brokerage firm has always concentrated on the lower end of the investing public (incomes in the $25,000–$35,000 range). For the middle and upper range, there is Shearson. And then for the corporate client, Shearson has the investment banking firm of Lehman Brothers.[46]

American Express ads reflect its multibrand approach. There is intentionally no similarity between IDS ads and those for Shearson Lehman. It is too early to judge the effectiveness of the IDS ("IDS doesn't cater to get-rich-quick schemes") or the Shearson ads ("for the serious investor").[47]

Prudential's advertising is aimed at households with annual incomes of at least $50,000.[48]

The Outlook

Synergy was touted as the motivation behind the rash of acquisitions and mergers among the financial giants in the early 1980s, but, halfway through the decade, analysts claim that "when it comes to the financial supermarkets' synergy, one plus one well might end up equaling one."[49]

The torrid pace of AMEX's diversification drive is, however, straining its ability to control its far-flung operations. "Their management team has been assembled mostly by purchase," says Walter B. Wriston, CEO of Citicorp. "I don't think there's any question that if a team has played together for 10 years, you have a better chance on Saturday afternoon than the all-star team that was assembled that morning."[50]

Sanford Weill, who brought Shearson into the AMEXCO family in 1981 and started to turn FF around in 1984, left AMEXCO in 1985. The leadership position at FF has been anything but stable with five CEOs in 6 years. Lewis Gerstner, Jr., CEO of the TRS, is rumored to be unhappy with decisions being made at New York corporate headquarters.[51] Weill's protégé, Peter Cohen, CEO at Shearson Lehman at thirty-six, may not sit well with some of AMEXCO's older executives. If AMEXCO has a major weakness, it may be in senior management, which is often accused of buying its talent rather than grooming it, notwithstanding the fact that such notables as Henry Kissinger and Edward Safra have recently been added to the AMEXCO board of directors. Could the problems at Fireman's Fund mean the beginning of the end of AMEXCO's involvement in insurance? Down to only 41 percent ownership, AMEXCO could be looking to cut bait altogether if and when the price is right.

Warner-Amex has yet to see black ink. How long will AMEXCO dabble in the communications/entertainment industries without a winner?

Visa, MasterCard, and others (including possibly Sears' new entry, Discover) pose a challenge to the AMEX card's dominance. They have erased all vestiges of complacency at TRS.[52]

IDS margins have been considered thin and visibly low. An announcement in December 1985 indicated that AMEXCO was pumping $65 million to expand IDS's business lines, giving IDS capital of more than $900 million.[53] In the same announcement, AMEXCO added $175 million to AEICB, which apparently is now a successful member of the AMEXCO family.

---

[45]Ibid., p. 133.

[46]Ibid., p. 131.

[47]Ibid., p. 133.

[48]Ibid., p. 131.

[49]Bianco, "How a Financial Supermarket Was Born," p. 10.

[50]"The Golden Plan at American Express," p. 118.

[51]Ibid., p. 120.

[52]"The Golden Plan of American Express," p. 119.

[53]"Business Briefs," *Wall Street Journal,* December 20, 1985, p. 8.

Will AMEXCO, regulations permitting, expand into domestic banking? Will AMEXCO's success in direct marketing take it into retail sales to compete with Sears through acquisition of a retailer such as J. C. Penney or Montgomery Ward? Can AMEXCO make greater use of First Data Resources to further cut internal costs or sell data processing services at a profit?

Are there economies to be gained, as well as synergistic effects, by placing IDS under SLAX management? Would such a move reduce internal competition for investors in AMEXCO's three-tiered investment strategy (Lehman—wealthy corporate, Shearson—middle income, IDS—small investor)? Or, conversely, is this too broad a front on which to attack?

Appendix A: History of Growth of AMEXCO

1850: American Express evolves from the merging of three small freight companies for delivery of small packages and funds by rail and horseback. American Express agents are expected to foil the efforts of masked bandits.

1891: The first traveler's checks are introduced by American Express.

1900: American Express opens the first overseas travel office in Paris.

1919: The American Express Company, Incorporated (known as the "Inc Company") is formed to provide financial services for post–World War I American travelers.

1958: The famous green travel and entertainment charge card is introduced.

1968: The international banking operation known as the Inc Company changes its name to the American Express International Banking Corporation (AEIBC).

American Express acquires the Fireman's Fund Insurance Company.

1981: Shearson investment firm is added to the growing AMEXCO financial empire.

1983: AMEXCO buys the Geneva-based Trade Development Bank and joins it to AEIBC.

AMEXCO formally establishes the American Express Travel Related Services Company, Inc., as one of the five major entities of AMEXCO.

IDS Financial Services, Inc. (a leader in financial planning) joins the AMEXCO corporate family.

1984: Shearson/American Express acquires Lehman Brothers, Kuhn, Loeb Holding Co. Inc. to join the AMEXCO financial conglomerate as Shearson Lehman Brothers, Inc.

Appendix B: Financial Performance by Service Category

The company is principally in the business of providing travel related services, international banking services, investment services, investors diversified financial services and insurance services throughout the world. Travel Related Services principally consists of the American Express Card and Travelers Cheque operations. The results of the company's 50 percent interest in Warner Amex are included in "Other and Corporate." Tables 1, 2, and 3 present certain information regarding these industry segments at December 31, 1984, 1983 and 1982 and for the years then ended (millions).

Appendix C: American Express At-A-Glance

This appendix contains excerpts from the American Express 1984 Annual Report, wherein American Express explains its different activities, with accompanying data.

1. American Express: Top Rated by Independent Study. American Express products and services hold the confidence of millions of people. They look to American Express brand names for better ways to make, use and protect their money. In a survey in 1984, the *American Banker* found that people rate American Express products and services higher than those of any other top financial services firm in the United States *(continues page 546)*.

Table 1 1984 Data

	Travel Related Services	International Banking Services	Investment Services	IDS Financial Services	Insurance Services	Other and corporate	Adjustments and eliminations	Consolidated
Revenues	$ 3,620	$ 1,548	$ 2,280	$1,576	$4,025	$ 82	$ (236)	$12,895
Pretax income (loss) before general corporate expenses	$ 625	$ 193	$ 168	$ 95	$ (114)	$ 16	$ (18)	$ 965
General corporate expenses	—	—	—	—	—	(229)	—	(229)
Pretax income (loss)	$ 625	$ 193	$ 168	$ 95	$ (114)	$ (213)	$ (18)	$ 736
Net income	$ 387	$ 156	$ 103	$ 62	$ 43	$ (125)	$ (16)	$ 610
Assets	$12,542	$13,768	$22,735	$6,411	$7,735	$1,239	$(2,582)	$61,848

Insurance services comprises the following:

	Property-Liability					
	Commercial Lines	Personal lines	Investment income	Total	Life and other	Total insurance services
Revenues	$ 2,017	$ 817	$ 429	$3,263	$ 762	$ 4,025
Pretax income (loss)	$ (558)	$ (40)	$ 404	$ (194)	$ 80	$ (114)

Table 2 1983 Data

	Travel Related Services	International Banking Services	Investment Services	IDS Financial Services	Insurance Services	Other and corporate	Adjustments and eliminations	Consolidated
Revenues	$ 2,889	$ 1,437	$1,826	—	$3,784	$ (6)	$ (160)	$ 9,770
Pretax income (loss) before general corporate expenses	$ 445	$ 183	$ 326	—	$ (242)	$ (17)	$ (10)	$ 685
General corporate expenses	—	—	—	—	—	(168)	—	(168)
Pretax income (loss)	$ 445	$ 183	$ 326	—	$ (242)	$ (185)	$ (10)	$ 517
Net income	$ 301	$ 136	$ 175	—	$ 30	$ (117)	$ (10)	$ 515
Assets	$10,226	$13,287	$9,060	$5,410	$7,057	$1,095	$(2154)	$43,981

Insurance services comprises the following:

	Property-Liability					
	Commercial Lines	Personal lines	Investment income	Total	Life and other	Total insurance services
Revenues	$1,925	$ 783	$ 437	$3,145	$ 639	$3,784
Pretax income (loss)	$ (609)	$ (95)	$ 452	$ (252)	$ 10	$ (242)

Table 3 1982 Data

	Travel Related Services	International Banking Services	Investment Services	Insurance Services	Other and corporate	Adjustments and eliminations	Consolidated
Revenues	$2,516	$1,025	$1,318	$3,356	$ 14	$ (136)	$ 8,093
Pretax income before general corporate expenses	$ 363	$ 101	$ 228	$ 220	$ (5)	—	$ 907
General corporate expenses	—	—	—	—	(153)	—	(153)
Pretax income	$ 363	$ 101	$ 228	$ 220	$ (158)	—	$ 754
Net income	$ 247	$ 60	$ 124	$ 244	$ (94)	—	$ 581
Assets	$8,445	$7,681	$6,351	$6,513	$ 784	$ (1,463)	$28,311

Insurance services comprises the following:

	Property-Liability					
	Commercial Lines	Personal lines	Investment income	Total	Life and other	Total insurance services
Revenues	$1,947	$ 640	$ 348	$2,935	$ 421	$3,356
Pretax income (loss)	$ (95)	$ (22)	$ 328	$ 211	$ 9	$ 220

	Who consumers know (%)[1]
American Express	75
Prudential Insurance	72
Bank of America	70
Merrill Lynch	66
Beneficial Finance	55
Sears Roebuck	54
Citicorp	53
Chas. Schwab	21

2. Travel Related Services. Travel Related Services began the American Express tradition of reliable service in 1850 by moving freight. Today, it moves people and their buying power around the world. People know the quality of the American Express Card, Travelers Cheque and Travel Services. *(See Table A)*

3. International Banking Services. At American Express International Banking Corporation, the accent is on "international." The Bank helped American Express expand internationally following World War I. Today, 82 offices in 39 countries offer export financing, private banking and other select services. *(See Table B)*

4. Investment Services. Shearson Lehman Brothers Inc. evolved from strategic acquisitions—most recently, Lehman Brothers. Today, Shearson Lehman melds this investment banking franchise with strong trading and distribution capabilities.[2] *(See Table C)*

5. IDS Financial Services. IDS Financial Services Inc. and its subsidiaries have earned people's trust, through outstanding financial advice and services, since 1984. The 4,400 representatives of IDS provide financial plans and products that stand the test of time.[3] *(See Table D)*

6. Insurance Services. Fireman's Fund Insurance Companies was born in San Francisco in 1863 to provide protection against the frequent fires that ravaged the city. Today, Fireman's Fund is an industry leader in developing new products and new approaches to marketing. *(See Table E)*

[1]Multiple responses permitted. Adapted from the *American Banker.*

[2]Note: Investment Services 1984 amounts include the effect of the acquisition of Lehman Brothers Kuhn Loeb Holding Co., Inc., accounted for as a purchase as of May 11, 1984.

[3]Note: The acquisition of IDS Financial Services was accounted for as a purchase effective December 31, 1983. Therefore, revenues, pretax income and net income for 1983 are not presented.

(Table A)

(Millions, except percentages)	1984	1983	Percent increase
Revenues	$ 3,620	$ 2,889	25%
Net income	$ 387	$ 301	29
Card charge volume	$47,638	$38,356	24
Travelers Cheque sales	$15,116	$13,862	9
Total assets	$12,542	$10,226	23
Average Travelers Cheques outstanding	$ 2,634	$ 2,437	8
Cards in force	20.2	17.3	17
Return on average shareholder's equity	25.3%	24.1%	

[1]Multiple responses permitted. Adapted from the *American Banker.*

(Table B)

(Millions, except percentages)	1984	1983	Percent increase (decrease)
Net income from International Banking Services	$ 156	$ 136	15%
Loans and discounts	$ 6,272	$ 6,290	—
Reserve for loan losses	$ 165	$ 162	2
Total assets of American Express International Banking Corporation	$13,875	$13,309	4
Customers' deposits and credit balances	$10,517	$10,328	2
Shareholder's equity of American Express International Banking Corporation	$ 897	$ 819	10
Primary capital to average assets	7.64%	7.05%	
Return on average assets	1.15%	1.04%	
Return on average shareholder's equity	17.81%	17.67%	

(Table C)

(Millions)	1984	1983	Percent increase (decrease)
Revenues	$ 2,280	$ 1,826	25%
Pretax income	$ 168	$ 326	(49)
Net income	$ 103	$ 175	(41)
Total assets	$22,735	$ 9,060	151
Total capital, including subordinated debt, of Shearson Lehman Brothers Inc.	$ 1,896	$ 1,057	79
Assets managed and/or administered	$64,939	$47,144	38

(Table D)

(Millions)	1984	1983	Percent increase (decrease)
Revenues	$ 1,576	—	—
Pretax income	$ 95	—	—
Net income	$ 62	—	—
Individual life insurance in force	$13,818	$11,424	21%
Assets owned and/or managed:			
Assets managed for institutions	$ 3,080	$ 3,650	(16)
Assets owned and managed for individuals:			
Owned assets	$ 6,411	$ 5,410	19
Managed assets	$ 9,812	$ 9,162	7

(Table E)

(Millions, except percentages)	1984	1983	Percent increase
Fireman's Fund Insurance Companies			
Revenues	$ 4,025	$ 3,784	6%
Net income	$ 43	$ 30	42
Total assets	$ 7,735	$ 7,057	10
Shareholder's equity	$ 1,485	$ 1,304	14
Return on average shareholder's equity	3.1%	2.2%	
Property-Liability Companies			
Premiums written	$ 2,834	2,781	2
Underwriting ratio	121.1%	126.0%	
Loss and loss expense ratio	86.4%	86.5%	
Expense ratio	32.2%	36.6%	
Policyholder dividend ratio	2.5%	2.9%	
Life Companies			
Premiums written	$ 655	$ 539	21
Life insurance in force	$23,133	$15,493	49

Case 5 Update*

This report is dedicated to the men and women of American Express whose initiative, creativity and commitment to service and excellence enable us to be—and stay—ahead of the curve.

Ahead of the pack. State of the art. Cutting edge. There are a lot of ways to put it. At American Express, we say "ahead of the curve." Which, quite simply, means being proactive, innovative and entrepreneurial—a leader in everything we do. It means anticipating customer demands for greater choice in credit cards and devising creative approaches to dealing with the debt burdens of developing nations; providing flawless service face-to-face and unrivaled efficiency in our operating centers; building globe-spanning data networks and creating eye-catching advertising. being ahead of the curve is the basis for American Express' 137-year history of success and our growing preeminence worldwide in financial and travel services.

Who We Are

American Express Company

American Express Company, founded in 1850, is a diversified financial and travel services company. Through its four principal operating units—American Express Travel Related Services, IDS Financial Services, Shearson Lehman Hutton and American Express Bank—the Company is a leader in the payment systems, travel, data based services, personal financial planning, asset management, brokerage, investment banking and international banking industries.

American Express' goal is to be the best financial and travel related services company in the world by applying shared values to anticipate and fulfill the requirements of its customers. These values encompass a never-ending search for excellence through:

- Outstanding people who embrace entrepreneurship and flexibility in managing change;
- Premium products with strong brand names provided through carefully targeted marketing channels;
- Individual and corporate commitment to community involvement and citizenship; and
- Above all, consistent and uncompromising *quality* in all that we do.

Travel Related Services

American Express Travel Related Services (TRS)—the foundation of the modern American Express Company—markets some of the world's most distinguished brand names: the American Express Card, Gold Card, Platinum Card, Optima Card, Corporate Card, American Express Travelers Cheques and American Express Money Orders.

Its direct marketing arm offers premium merchandise, life insurance, credit lines from American Express Centurion Bank and publications, including *Travel & Leisure, Food & Wine* and *New York Woman* magazines.

The company's network of over 1,400 travel offices serves millions of people around the world each year. In addition, TRS' Travel Management Services helps businesses schedule travel and control travel and entertainment expenses.

The First Data Resources Inc. (FDR) subsidiary provides data processing for a wide variety of industries. It is one of the largest third-party processors of debit and credit card transactions in the United States, and offers billing services for securities systems and cable television companies. FDR also supplies billing and management services to hospitals and doctors.

*Source: Excerpts from American Express Company 1987 annual report, pp. 1–3, 5–9, 51–55.

IDS Financial Services

IDS Financial Services is the industry leader in personal financial planning. Its nearly 6,200 financial planners meet face-to-face with more than 1.2 million clients throughout the United States, providing detailed programs designed to help those clients attain their personal financial goals, and products and services needed to make those programs work.

IDS products include investment certificates, mutual funds, life insurance, annuities, tax-exempt investments, limited partnerships and unit investment trusts. IDS also provides management and fiduciary services for employee benefit and pension plans, consumer banking and tax preparation services, and financial planning for the employees of client companies.

IDS maintains rigorous qualification standards for its representatives and acts as an industry leader in promoting uniform regulation of financial planning throughout the United States.

IDS measures itself by its success in helping clients manage their income and balance sheets. It has achieved broad-based recognition not only for its investment performance but also for its integrity and creativity.

Shearson Lehman Hutton

Shearson Lehman Brothers enhanced its industry position in the first quarter of 1988 when it acquired The E. F. Hutton Group. The combined firm—Shearson Lehman Hutton—will have approximately $4.2 billion in capital, over $95 billion in assets under management for others and will serve nearly three million households in the United States through a network of almost 12,000 Financial Consultants in over 600 offices.

Throughout the world, Shearson Lehman Hutton applies proven creativity and expertise to meet a broad diversity of financial needs for corporations, institutions, governments and individuals. The firm delivers one of the most comprehensive arrays of investment banking, merchant banking, investment advisory, asset management, securities trading and real estate services available from a single source. Its state-of-the-art data processing technology contributes to Shearson Lehman Hutton's leadership in productivity and service.

Through its worldwide facilities in investment banking and brokerage, Shearson Lehman Hutton provides quality service that sustains long-term client relationships.

American Express Bank

American Express Bank, incorporated in 1919, maintains a network of 103 locations in 42 countries. Through two subsidiaries—the Trade Development Bank, Geneva, and American Express Bank (Switzerland) A.G., Zurich—the Bank offers private banking services for high net worth individuals, including asset management, discretionary accounts, trust and estate planning, and investment services for securities and precious metals. The Bank's global office network offers corporate, governmental and institutional clients, including central banks, a broad range of treasury, foreign exchange, investment and correspondent banking services.

American Express Bank is committed to provide exceptional service to all clients at all times. To meet that pledge, the Bank selectively adds new services to meet growing client needs in constantly changing global financial markets. The Bank continues to build on its unique competitive advantages: a strong balance sheet, an extensive branch network and the singular ability of its bankers to provide clients a broad range of quality personalized services.

Letter to Shareholders

On a consolidated basis, 1987 was a disappointing year. Earnings from continuing operations of $533 million were down from $1.1 billion in 1986, and per share net dipped to $1.20 from $2.48.

But 1987 was a year unlike any other in recent history. It was a year the stock market experienced a one-day 508-point plunge, banks added billions to reserve for troubled loans, and changes in ways of doing virtually everything in financial services came fast and furious.

Managing change, particularly in periods of high volatility, is what leadership is all about, of course. We've said that before, but 1987 was the test. Happily, we passed.

Travel Related Services, the core of our Company, continued to demonstrate its remarkable talent for adding value and utility to the American Express Card, Travelers Cheques and its other businesses. TRS' net income rose 16 percent to a record $655 million.

IDS Financial Services, our newest major operating unit, turned in its best year ever, too, lifting earnings 21 percent to $124 million.

Shearson Lehman was buffeted by adverse market forces, the strains of rapid growth and consolidation within the industry. The sale of 18 million shares of Shearson Lehman common stock to the public and two other major strategic alliances—one with Nippon Life Insurance Company, which purchased a 13 percent voting interest in Shearson Lehman, the other with E. E. Hutton, which became part of Shearson Lehman early in 1988—turned Shearson Lehman Hutton into what many see as the prototype investment firm of the future.

Additions of $950 million to credit reserves caused American Express Bank to report a loss in 1987. However, as a result of the reserve additions and a capital infusion from American Express, the Bank now has one of the strongest balance sheets in its industry and is more clearly focused on private banking and other fee-generating businesses.

The bottom line reads like this: despite being hit with everything but the proverbial kitchen sink, American Express earned more than half a billion dollars in 1987. The Company also ended the year in a strong position, well prepared for the challenges and opportunities we'll face in 1988 and the years beyond.

Much of that strength comes from TRS, which has shown earnings increases every year for the past two decades. Earnings during the last 10 years have grown at a compound annual rate of better than 17 percent. Cynics—and we have our share—might scoff, saying that American Express has always had charge cards and Travelers Cheques locked up and that the rising economic tide of the past decade carried all boats higher.

The facts are somewhat different. The past 10 years have seen recession and growth, sky-high interest rates, periods of galloping inflation, a strong dollar, a weak dollar, the emergence of tenacious overseas competitors, the decline of others, and a stock market that experienced its most violent swings in history.

It also was a period in which all members of the financial services business encroached on each other's turf: dozens of banks began issuing travelers checks during the decade, and one of the largest acquired Diners Club and Carte Blanche, two big names in the card business.

So much for locks and rising tides.

How'd we do it? Well, we don't want to give away trade secrets, but it boils down to a set of basics that are followed by all our business units:

- Assembling the smartest, most entrepreneurial people we can find, giving them the resources and freedom to do their thing and holding them accountable for results.
- Remembering we are market driven, which means listening and responding to customers.
- Constantly reminding ourselves that our goal is to deliver high-quality, prestigious products and services to carefully targeted market segments that want and appreciate them.

Not very original, but with the right commitment, it's a formula that works. It worked last year when American Express Company's revenues rose to a record $17.8 billion, up from $16.7 billion in 1986.

Earnings were considerably less robust, as the gains at TRS and IDS were overtaken by shortfalls elsewhere. American Express Bank incurred a loss of $625 million, the result of the $950 million addition to reserves that was made to reflect the status of developing nation debt and provide the Bank flexibility in managing its balance sheet. Shearson Lehman's 1987 earnings of $101 million were less than one-third the $341 million of 1986, reflecting the turmoil in world financial markets. Our share of Shearson Lehman's 1987 earnings was $89 million.

Earnings also reflected a $200 million after-tax net gain from rule changes required by the Financial Accounting Standards Board and a $142 million after-tax gain from the sale of the Shearson Lehman stock. (Earnings in 1986 included an after-tax gain of $88 million from the sale of common stock of Fireman's Fund Corporation.) Absent these nonrecurring items and the Bank's addition to credit reserves, American Express' consolidated income from continuing operations would have totaled $1.1 billion in 1987 and $1.0 billion in 1986.

Other statistical benchmarks also were mixed—some very impressive, others so-so. We ended 1987 with $71 billion of assets owned and managed, up 20 percent from 1986. Assets managed and/or administered for others soared 47 percent to $211 billion.

Return on equity from continuing operations was 11 percent in 1987, compared with 23 percent in 1986.

A record 27.1 million American Express Cards were in force at year-end, up 14 percent from a year ago. Travelers Cheque sales rose 16 percent in 1987, reaching a new high of $19.9 billion.

We split our stock 2-for-1. The quarterly dividend was increased from 18 cents to 19 cents a share. And shareholders' value was further augmented by the continuation of stock repurchase programs begun in 1985; since then, some 50 million shares of American Express common stock have been repurchased.

The operating highlights of 1987—TRS' successful introduction of the Optima Card, the American Express Gift Cheque and the "Membership Has Its Privileges" advertising campaign, IDS' dramatic progress as the country's leading financial planner, Shearson Lehman's acquisition of E. F. Hutton, and the swaps and debt sales that significantly reduced American Express Bank's cross-border term loans—are described in detail on the following pages.

They add up to an impressive list of accomplishments, one that was capped, fittingly enough, early in 1988 when American Express was cited in a *Fortune* magazine poll as the most admired firm in the diversified financial services industry. The citation speaks volumes about the American Express employees worldwide whose dedication, skills and plain old hard work made us No. 1 and—in keeping with the theme of this report—have kept us out front and constantly ahead of the curve.

But this is hardly the time to rest on laurels. Everywhere we turn we see intensifying challenges from well-heeled companies. Domestically, they are the familiar institutions that have branches on most downtown corners, plus others in shopping malls and elsewhere. It's no secret, meanwhile, that the world is fast becoming an integrated global market, nor that many of the banks, insurance companies and financial services firms in Japan and Europe outrank us in terms of assets.

We never set out to be the biggest, of course, only the best. We have no doubt of our determination and ability to remain a leader, extend that leadership and further distance ourselves from the competition.

Our goal remains simple—to be the world's top provider of travel and financial services. We have the financial wherewithal to make it happen. And we have a road map to get us there. It consists, among other things, of:

- A decentralized, entrepreneurial approach to business;

- The application of state-of-the-art technology to enhance productivity, develop new products and deliver superior service;
- Recognizing the diverse corporate cultures within American Express and how this diversity fosters innovation; and
- Contributing to the well-being of the communities in which our employees and customers live through a broad sweep of philanthropic and volunteer service activities.

The glue that binds all this together is a commitment to quality in everything we do. It's what's gotten American Express where it is today and it's the "patent protection" that will keep us ahead of the curve of the future.

James D. Robinson III
Chairman and
Chief Executive Officer

Louis V. Gerstner Jr.
President

March 1, 1988

Staying Ahead of the Curve

The United States of the mid-19th century had a broad frontier and a need for capital to fuel commercial growth. Funds transport was risky. Banks charged up to 10 percent to cover the cost of special couriers and insurance. These conditions gave rise to a new business, the express industry, whose economies of scale vastly reduced the cost of moving money safely. The industry's leading entrepreneurs included Henry Wells, William G. Fargo and John Butterfield—the founders of American Express Company.

The early 1880s ushered in the greatest immigration in American history and new needs for secure, transportable and easy-to-use financial instruments. Money orders sold by the U.S. Post Office required completion of complicated forms. "Persons who cannot read or write have to blunder about until some outsider takes pity and writes out their application for them," noted American Express executive Marcellus Fleming Berry. To solve the problem, Berry devised and patented a money order that was easy to use, easy to purchase and resistant to forgery.

In 1890, Berry's inventive mind put American Express well ahead of the curve of another historic trend: the growing eagerness of Americans to travel abroad. His innovation, the Travelers Cheque, had first-year sales of just over $9,000. By 1900, however, volume topped $6 million.

"The greatest rendezvous for Americans which has ever existed in Europe"—that was the goal of William Swift Dalliba, American Express Company's first representative in Europe, as he scouted for office space in Paris at the turn of the century. The site selected, 11 Rue Scribe, was the forerunner of today's global network of American Express Travel Service Offices. This facility quickly fulfilled Dalliba's vision as the spot for tourists to meet, conduct financial transactions and pick up their mail.

In August 1914, American Express was one of the few financial institutions in Europe prepared for the coming of war. The month before, European Director General Dalliba had ordered American Express offices to build up cash reserves. When World War I broke out, American Express was able to redeem not only its own Travelers Cheques but also the financial paper of other institutions. The Paris office proved so effective in meeting the financial, communications and travel needs of Americans that the U.S. embassy directed tourists seeking emergency help to 11 Rue Scribe, not vice versa.

Two decades later, American Express was ahead of the curve at another calamity, the Great Depression. When depositories across the United States closed their doors during the Bank Holiday of 1933, the Company's offices remained open and continued to cash American

Express Travelers Cheques—demonstrating the unequaled dependability of the Cheque.

The end of World War II, coupled with advances in air transport and telecommunications, prompted a global boom in tourism and business travel. American Express responded with a greatly expanded travel office network and, on October 1, 1958, a brand-new product—the American Express Card—that enabled users to charge travel and entertainment outlays. The American Express Card has since earned the loyalty of millions of Cardmembers and gone on to become one of the world's great venture capital success stories.

In more recent years, as technological advances have increased global economic interdependence and financial volatility, American Express has remained in the vanguard of change by selectively expanding its quality services to meet customer needs. Whether building its capabilities as an asset manager (through the landmark 1981 acquisition of Shearson Loeb Rhoades) or attaining preeminence in financial planning (via the 1984 acquisition of Investors Diversified Services), American Express has stayed well ahead of the curve.

The past year was no exception.

Transnational Alliance. American Express initiated the first strategic partnership between U.S. and Japanese financial services providers, when Nippon Life Insurance Company purchased a 13 percent voting interest in Shearson Lehman Brothers and established a series of cooperative ventures with the Company.

The Optima Card. American Express introduced its first revolving credit product, the Optima Card, with an interest rate far below that charged by most credit cards.

Developing Nation Debt. The debt problems of developing nations demand creative solutions. In Mexico, American Express converted a portion of its loans into investments in major tourist development projects.

Asset Management Leadership. Few companies equal American Express in its control of every phase of mutual fund operation, from investment to distribution to service. Based on 1987 industry rankings of top investment managers, the Company stands second in the United States in assets under management.

Technological Expertise. American Express has earned wide recognition for the Authorizer's Assistant, an "artificial intelligence" computer system that automates routine card charge authorizations to provide significant gains in productivity.

American Express is one of the world's largest users of computers and telecommunications, operating 19 major information processing centers and 15 worldwide data and voice networks, and over 120 mainframe central processing units, 170 minicomputer systems and 46,000 individual work stations. The First Data Resources Inc. subsidiary helps clients maximize the value of their data bases and perform transactional services.

At times, customer needs demand the resources of two or more subsidiaries. American Express makes such partnerships a success. In the past five years, over 260 joint operations by subsidiaries have been tested, and a significant majority has worked.

American Express will continue to evolve to meet the changing needs of a dynamic world. Whether safeguarding funds across the wilds of 19th-century America or, today, helping people and assets move swiftly around the world, American Express has stayed in front for 137 years. In the years to come, it will continue to do business in the same place . . . ahead of the curve.

Consolidated Statement of Income—American Express Company

Year Ended December 31, (millions, except per share amounts)	1987	1986	1985
Revenues			
Commissions and fees	**$ 8,455**	$ 7,477	$ 6,020
Interest and dividends	**6,084**	5,915	4,431
Life insurance premiums	**786**	1,149	1,059
Annuity premiums	**1,382**	967	860
Other	**1,061**	1,230	530
Total	**17,768**	16,738	12,900
Expenses			
Compensation and employee benefits	**3,721**	3,438	2,573
Interest	**4,899**	4,776	3,415
Provisions for losses and benefits:			
Annuities	**1,810**	1,371	1,238
Life insurance	**666**	941	860
Investment certificates	**99**	109	107
Banking, credit and other	**1,818**	951	693
Occupancy and equipment	**957**	789	636
Advertising and promotion	**877**	696	528
Communications	**515**	472	415
Taxes other than income taxes	**270**	242	197
Printing and supplies	**223**	199	154
Other	**1,226**	1,212	930
Total	**17,081**	15,196	11,746
Pretax income from continuing operations	**687**	1,542	1,154
Income tax provision	**154**	426	458
Income from continuing operations	**533**	1,116	696
Discontinued operations (net of income taxes):			
Loss from operations	—	—	(2)
Gain on disposal	—	140	—
Net income	**$ 533**	$ 1,256	$ 694
Income (loss) per common share:			
Continuing operations	**$ 1.20**	$ 2.48	$ 1.52
Discontinued operations	—	0.31	(0.01)
Net income per common share	**$ 1.20**	$ 2.79	$ 1.51

Consolidated Balance Sheet—American Express Company

December 31, (millions of dollars)	1987	1986
Assets		
Cash	**$ 3,130**	$ 2,650
Time deposits	**5,395**	4,989
Investment securities—at cost:		
U.S. Government and agencies obligations	**1,994**	2,817
State and municipal obligations	**5,428**	4,862
Corporate bonds and obligations	**13,566**	9,137
Foreign government obligations	**910**	900
Investment mortgage loans and other	**1,269**	768
Total (market: 1987, $23,166; 1986, $19,421)	**23,167**	18,484
Investment securities—at lower of aggregate cost or market (cost: 1987, $2,402; market: 1986, $1,406)	**2,265**	1,396
Investment securities—at market:		
Preferred stocks	**267**	525
Common stocks	**668**	962
Bonds and obligations	**9,039**	10,729
Commercial paper, bankers' acceptances and time deposits	**4,530**	3,058
Other	**1,435**	1,287
Total	**15,939**	16,561
Securities purchased under agreements to resell	**19,160**	12,626
Accounts receivable and accrued interest, less reserves: 1987, $941; 1986, $829	**26,529**	22,685
Loans and discounts, less reserves: 1987, $800; 1986, $223	**11,394**	11,634
Land, buildings and equipment—at cost, less accumulated depreciation: 1987, $875; 1986, $617	**2,571**	2,172
Assets held in segregated asset accounts	**1,811**	1,304
Other assets	**5,073**	4,801
	$116,434	$99,302

Consolidated Balance Sheet—American Express Company *(continued)*

December 31, (millions of dollars)	1987	1986
Liabilities and Shareholders' Equity		
Customers' deposits and credit balances	**$ 26,308**	$22,446
Travelers Cheques outstanding	**3,602**	2,990
Accounts payable	**9,792**	8,414
Securities sold under agreements to repurchase	**21,485**	18,573
Securities and commodities sold but not yet purchased—at market	**5,950**	4,835
Insurance and annuity reserves:		
Fixed annuities	**5,900**	4,849
Life and disability policies	**1,969**	1,554
Investment certificate reserves	**1,753**	1,507
Short-term debt	**16,902**	14,620
Long-term debt	**10,639**	8,400
Liabilities related to segregated asset accounts	**1,786**	1,280
Other liabilities	**5,794**	4,959
Total liabilities	**111,880**	94,427
Shareholders' equity:		
Money Market Preferred shares—authorized 600 shares of $1.66⅔ par value; issued and outstanding 600 shares in 1987 and in 1986, stated at liquidation value	**300**	300
Common shares—authorized 600,000,000 shares of $.60 par value; issued and outstanding 420,802,173 shares in 1987 and 430,555,204 shares in 1986	**252**	258
Capital surplus	**1,516**	1,474
Net unrealized security gains (losses)	**(41)**	11
Foreign currency translation adjustment	**35**	46
Deferred compensation—Stock Ownership Plan	**(80)**	—
Retained earnings	**2,572**	2,786
Total shareholders' equity	**4,554**	4,875
	$116,434	$99,302

Consolidated Statement of Shareholders' Equity—American Express Company

Three Years Ended December 31, 1987 (millions)	Total	Money Market Preferred Shares	Common Shares	Capital Surplus	Other	Retained Earnings
Balances at December 31, 1984						
As previously reported	**$4,607**	**$225**	**$130**	**$1,224**	**$(56)**	**$3,084**
Adjustment for 2-for-1 stock split			130	(130)		
Cumulative impact of changes in accounting policies	(740)					(740)
As restated	**3,867**	**225**	**260**	**1,094**	**(56)**	**2,344**
Net income	694					694
Change in net unrealized securities gains	14				14	
Foreign currency translation adjustments	21				21	
Repurchase of common shares	(136)		(4)	(18)		(114)
Dividend Reinvestment Plan	54		2	52		
Acquisition of minority interest of First Data Resources Inc.	85		2	83		
Issuance of Money Market Preferred shares	75	75				
Issuance of common stock in exchange for warrants	47		2	45		
Other changes	100		4	94		2
Cash dividends:						
Money Market Preferred	(17)					(17)
Common	(291)					(291)
Balances at December 31, 1985	**4,513**	**300**	**266**	**1,350**	**(21)**	**2,618**
Net income	1,256					1,256
Change in net unrealized securities gains	20				20	
Foreign currency translation adjustments	58				58	
Repurchase of common shares	(871)		(18)	(84)		(769)
Issuance of common stock in exchange for warrants	145		6	139		
Other changes	72		4	69		(1)
Cash dividends:						
Money Market Preferred	(14)					(14)
Common	(304)					(304)
Balances at December 31, 1986	**4,875**	**300**	**258**	**1,474**	**57**	**2,786**
Net income	533					533
Change in net unrealized securities gains (losses)	(52)				(52)	
Foreign currency translation adjustments	(12)				(12)	
Repurchase of common shares	(478)		(9)	(57)		(412)
Deferred compensation	(80)				(80)	
Other changes	106		3	99	1	3
Cash dividends:						
Money Market Preferred	(14)					(14)
Common	(324)					(324)
Balances at December 31, 1987	**$4,554**	**$300**	**$252**	**$1,516**	**$(86)**	**$2,572**

Consolidated Statement of Changes in Financial Position—American Express Company

Year Ended December 31, (millions)	**1987**	**1986**	**1985**
Financial Resources Provided By			
Income from continuing operations	$ 533	$ 1,116	$ 696
Add items not requiring funds:			
Provision for losses and benefits	3,495	2,153	2,201
Depreciation, amortization, deferred taxes and other	64	267	322
Minority interest in subsidiary	12	—	—
Deduct net gain from:			
Sale of Shearson common stock	(142)	—	—
Sale of Fireman's Fund Corporation units, warrants and common stock	—	(88)	(52)
Funds provided by continuing operations before dividends	3,962	3,448	3,167
American Express cash dividends declared	(338)	(318)	(308)
Funds provided by continuing operations after dividends	3,624	3,130	2,859
Increase in:			
Short-term debt	2,282	4,219	2,460
Long-term debt	2,239	3,001	1,543
Travelers Cheques outstanding	612	311	225
Accounts payable	1,378	36	3,707
Securities sold under agreements to repurchase	2,912	8,613	2,163
Securities and commodities sold but not yet purchased—at market	1,115	306	1,531
Customers' deposits and credit balances	3,862	6,243	2,941
Other liabilities and other items	723	562	1,218
Common shares	111	223	288
Money Market Preferred shares	—	—	75
Proceeds from sale of Shearson common stock	574	—	—
Proceeds from sale of Shearson preferred stock to Nippon Life	508	—	—
Proceeds from sale of 50% interest in Warner Amex Cable Communications Inc.	—	450	—
Proceeds from sale of Fireman's Fund Corporation units, warrants and common stock	—	386	910
	$19,940	$27,480	$19,920
Financial Resources Used For			
Increase (decrease) in:			
Cash and time deposits	$ 886	$ (329)	$ 750
Accounts receivable and accrued interest	4,758	5,452	5,593
Securities purchased under agreements to resell	6,534	4,881	2,830
Investment securities	4,930	12,041	6,111
Loans and discounts	776	2,621	2,295
Other assets	899	1,245	544
Purchases of land, buildings and equipment	679	698	1,081
Purchases of Life Operations from Fireman's Fund Corporation	—	—	330
Repurchase of common shares	478	871	136
Acquisition of minority interest, including goodwill, of First Data Resources Inc.	—	—	250
	$19,940	$27,480	$19,920

Case 6

The John Hancock Mutual Life Insurance Company

John G. McElwee, Chairman of the Board and Chief Executive Officer of the John Hancock Mutual Life Insurance Company,[1] asked himself three questions in the spring of 1984 as he prepared the company for the 1990s and beyond: "What is it you want the institution to be? What do you think the world will be like? How do we prepare for that in terms of what business the company will be in and what it will need in terms of talent?" A move to financial services came out of that analysis and, more specifically, an analysis of what McElwee saw as his six criteria: economy, demographics, attitudes and lifestyles, competition, technology, and government action. In McElwee's view, however:

> Nobody *really* knows what the financial services industry (FSI) will be. We all admit to that. We are all trying to be flexible. We know we all are not doing everything right, and the jury is still out as to which companies will have the right combination and the wisdom and courage to remedy the situation as it evolves. When will this happen? When will the paradigm of the new FSI be in place? In my view it won't be before 1990.[2]

The John Hancock Mutual Life Insurance Company began its move into financial services in 1968. This case offers some background on the financial services industry, the insurance industry, and the nature of the issues and problems facing the company in 1984.

Trends in the Industry

The late 1970s and early 1980s saw a significant trend toward the provision of fuller financial services being offered by numerous financial-based institutions:

The FSI is a huge amalgam of firms ranging in size from the CitiCorp with well over $130 billion in assets to many small credit unions with a few hundred thousand dollars of assets. In

[1]See Appendix A for biographical sketches.

This case was prepared by Raymond M. Kinnunen, Associate Professor of Business Administration, with the assistance of L. Jake Katz, Research Assistant, with the cooperation of the John Hancock Mutual Life Insurance Company and its Chairman, John G. McElwee and the support of the Instructional Development Fund at Northeastern University. It is intended to be used as the basis for class discussion rather than to illustrate either effective or ineffective handling of an administrative situation.

The research and written case information were presented at a North American Case Research Symposium and were evaluated by the North American Case Research Association's Editorial Board.

[2]From Gregory L. Parsons, *The Evolving Financial Services Industry: Competition and Technology for the '80s*, 9–183–077, pp. 1–3. Copyright © 1982 by the President and Fellows of Harvard College. Reprinted by permission of the Harvard Business School.

1980, there were over 40,000 individual firms competing in the FSI with a mix of products including savings accounts, life insurance policies, pension management services, and stock brokering. The size of the FSI as measured by financial assets under control was nearly $4 trillion in 1980, and was experiencing nearly 11% growth [See Exhibit 1].

Historically, the various segments of the FSI have been primarily defined by government regulation. In fact, this is the reason many firms in the FSI are considered institutions rather than firms in the economic sense. The institutional segments of the FSI have been controlled and defined by their relationships to regulatory agencies. For example, banks are regulated at the federal, state, and local levels by various agencies. Securities firms are regulated only at the federal level by the Securities and Exchange Commission (SEC). Insurance companies, since 1946, have been regulated by state agencies. The result is an industry where products have been defined by regulation and customer markets have been given access to those products only through specific institutions. Until fairly recently, a customer went to a bank for a loan, to an insurance company for an insurance policy, and to a securities firm to trade stock. In this regulated environment, which defined the channels between customers and the financial products, the FSI was, on average, very profitable. Between 1975 and 1980, the banking industry reported annual profit growth of 18%, the life insurance industry reported 30% annual profit growth, and the securities industry reported 7% profit growth (for a scale of measurement, all U.S. industry reported 12% profit growth during that time).

Competition in the FSI has not been very intense compared to other industries; in fact, the common view of many financial institutions has been that the main objective is not to compete, but to provide public services. This view has been allowed and reinforced by: a) the regulatory environment, b) the web of relationships among financial institutions which required a large degree of coordination and cooperation and c) the historical values and culture which preside in most financial institutions. (The "lean and mean" operation has not been the role model for most financial organizations.) Regulations, severely limiting the dimensions of competition, have sought to create a sort of economic DMZ (demilitarized zone) between the customers and financial markets, reasoning that unlimited competition, by nature, causes behavior and results which are not in the best interest of the customer. The regulatory thinking assumed that unbridled competition would certainly mean more failures of weak and poorly run institutions. This would, over time, create a more efficient marketplace, but the result on the customer of a failing institution could be devastating. Also, it was expected that competition would drive institutions to more predatory and less benign behavior towards their customers and competitors as the scramble for profits intensified.

Traditionally, different types of institutions offered different types of products and services. Banks have concentrated on offering transaction

Exhibit 1 Assets

Company	Dollar Amount of Total Assets*
Prudential	$66,707,209
Metropolitan Life	55,731,371
Equitable Life of New York	40,285,559
Aetna Life	28,551,098
New York Life	22,549,386
John Hancock	21,710,494
Travelers	17,440,305
Connecticut General	15,660,054
Teachers Insurance and Annuity	13,519,897
Northwestern Mutual	13,252,835

*Figures do not include assets of subsidiaries.
Source: *Best's Insurance Management Reports,* October 1983.

products, and many kinds of loan products to individuals and corporations. Savings and loans (thrifts) have provided savings products and specialized mortgage lending to individuals. Securities firms have tended to specialize to a degree, with different firms offering "wholesale" products to corporations such as underwriting and other investment banking activities (e.g., Goldman Sachs and Salomon Brothers) and other firms specializing in "retail" brokerage and trading for consumers (e.g., Merrill Lynch, Shearson and E. F. Hutton). Insurance companies have generally specialized in either life insurance products (e.g., Prudential, Metropolitan and New York Life), or property and casualty insurance (e.g., State Farm, AllState, INA). To a degree they have also been involved in mortgage and commercial lending. Traditionally, most insurance companies have served both individual and corporate customers. Finance companies have concentrated on consumer lending and mortgage lending primarily to individuals. As noted above, a dominant reason in the traditional product/institution relationship has been regulation, but institutional thinking has also greatly influenced how the industry has defined itself.[3]

Consolidations Hindered by Sales Force Organization

While the level of merger and acquisition activity within the financial services industry over the last decade seemed to suggest an inevitable fusion of services under one roof, companies found that sales personnel trained to move one service were not necessarily well suited at uncovering client needs for another. For example, Merrill Lynch, the largest marketer of securities, found it inefficient to have their stockbrokers selling insurance policies. "Meanwhile, Merrill has begun experimenting with a more specialized approach to selling. Convinced that the average broker is unable to sell insurance, Merrill last June [1983] began installing life insurance specialists in 32 branches. It plans to hire 100 more this year."[4]

David Koehler, President of Financial Learning Systems, a firm training both securities and insurance personnel to sell new products and to prepare for licensing exams, cites five major barriers insurance agents face when selling non-insurance products. These barriers include: (1) licensing (state licensing exams are relatively easy for the insurance industry but fairly rigorous exams exist for securities); (2) product knowledge (the level necessary for agents to be comfortable selling securities may be underestimated); (3) skills to sell the product (different skills are required to sell a life insurance policy than a mutual fund); (4) commissions (to get a similar dollar-for-dollar commission, an agent has to sell a fund possibly 50 times the "value" of a life policy); and (5) attitude (life agents are accustomed to selling "guaranteed" products).[5]

Others in the industry acknowledge these barriers but conclude that the lines between agents and brokers are becoming blurred. Because of competition, the agent has diversified his product line while the broker has added more service through financial planning.[6]

To make matters more complex, some feel that both agents and brokers will be competing with other brokers selling products based more on price than on service.[7] The vast majority of consumers' liquid assets are held in depository institutions which gives the banking industry an advantage. One way for insurance companies to

[3]Ibid.

[4]"Merrill Lynch's Big Dilemma," *Business Week*, January 16, 1984, p. 62.

[5]Stephen Piontek, "Securities Products Face Agents with Problems," *National Underwriter, Life and Health Insurance Edition*, July 17, 1982, pp. 28–36.

[6]Ibid., p.3

[7]Ibid., p. 43.

compete with banks is to offer transaction accounts. To do this, however, they must acquire a bank image.[8]

Total Lines of Services

Standard and Poor's Industry Surveys note the following in regard to the trend toward full service:

> The emergence of alternative products, along with general deregulation of the financial industry, has intensified competition in the life insurance industry. The successful life insurance company will be one that adapts quickly to the changing environment. The competitiveness of life insurance will increasingly depend not only on innovations in products and services, but also importantly on the quality of marketing and distribution systems.
>
> Insurers are aware of the need for more effective marketing strategies and some already are making changes. One approach that is taking hold is the combination of insurers and other major financial institutions to form broad-based financial services conglomerates. The goal here is to bring together a variety of financial products and services, provide one-stop access to the consumer, and allow cross-marketing of product and service combinations as financial services packages. This approach to market expansion is evidenced by such recent acquisitions as Bache Group Inc. by Prudential Insurance Co. of America and Shearson Loeb Rhoades by American Express (which owns Fireman's Funds Insurance Co.) among others.[9]

Theodore Gordon, president of the Futures Group, summed it up this way:

> The whole marketplace for insurance is becoming very dynamic. It will be increasingly difficult in the future to tell the difference between a brokerage house, an insurance company, a bank, and a large-scale credit card company. To some degree, the functions of these institutions already overlap.[10]

Are Synergistic Benefits Possible?

A May 1982 article in *Institutional Investor* questions the effects of mergers that result in extended financial services:

> While it is too early for a verdict on that, however, there's another critical question at stake here. These firms have also been trumpeting the *synergistic* benefits that are supposed to flow from these mergers. American Express, for example, hopes to sell a wide variety of financial services through its credit cards, opening up vast new vistas for Shearson. Sears can envision its millions of customers buying Dean Witter products at its stores. And the Pru can look forward to its agents selling Bache products nationwide. Bache chairman Harry Jacobs Jr. perhaps best sums it up when he says, "We expect the merger to extend the range of services both firms provide."
>
> Yet, amid all the euphoric talk, no one has really stopped to ask whether these future synergistic wonders will actually come to pass, whether synergy on such a grand scale can really work in the financial services business. Will the vaunted synergy ever materialize to any *significant* extent? Will the diverse parts of these financial services conglomerates truly mesh and spur each other on to new heights—boosting sales, cutting costs and adding up to more than the sum of the parts?
>
> Actually, there's plenty of evidence to suggest these companies may be in for a tougher time of it than most people suspect. For one thing, there's the nagging fact that dozens of previous attempts to create synergy in the financial services industry have, at best, been somewhat disappointing. It was fashionable in the early 1970s, for example, to suppose that retail brokers could sell life insurance as a sideline, thereby increasing their earnings and those of their firms. As it turned out, however, these brokers either lacked the skills to

[8]Barbara E. Casey, "Customer is Key to Insurance-Banking Rivalry," *National Underwriter, Life and Health Edition,* July 17, 1982, pp. 8–9, 36.

[9]*Standard & Poor's Industry Surveys,* July 7, 1983 (Vol. 151, no. 27, sec. 1), *Insurance & Investments Basic Analysis,* p. 155.

[10]Theodore J. Gordon, "Life Insurance Companies in the 80's: A Quiet Revolution," *Resources,* July/August 1981, p. 3.

sell insurance or were too busy with stocks to bother with it. No precise figures are available, but Securities Industry Association statistics indicate that Wall Street firms gathered revenues of less than $500 million from insurance in 1980, compared with their total revenues of $16 billion.[11]

The article goes on to detail the experience of Continental Insurance.

> Continental Insurance made little progress toward the synergy that was supposed to accrue from its consumer finance subsidiary and its Diners Club credit card operations—both of which have since been sold. Other than the relatively minor business of travel life insurance, Continental found it difficult to sell policies via the credit card. It was hard, says one Continental official, to design a home insurance application form to mail out with bills because it entailed asking so many detailed questions. Nor was it really feasible to sell insurance through consumer finance outlets—local Continental agents would have been annoyed by the competition. Reports Continental chairman John Ricker sadly: "One-stop financial shopping is a buzzword returning to our vocabulary. I am skeptical, not by nature, but by experience. Continental has tried the full financial services approach, and it didn't work."[12]

Robert Beck of Prudential is quoted later in the same article with this view:

> "I don't think previous attempts have *all* been failures," is the way Prudential chairman Beck shrugs it off. Or perhaps a better way of putting it is that they're persuaded that times have changed dramatically since their previous efforts to achieve financial services synergy were made. Notes American Express chairman Robinson, "The environment today is 100 percent different than it was when those (previous) relationships were formed." For one thing, he notes, "there's a trend toward constructing hybrid financial products," begun by Merrill Lynch's CMA account—a trend Robinson thinks multifacted houses may be able to exploit.[13]

Consumer Base

The customer base is also an important factor when it comes to offering financial services.

> Sears Roebuck and Company, American Express Company and Prudential Life Insurance Company currently sell their services to some 50 million Americans. The three companies intend to bombard these clients with new financial services products. But according to conventional wisdom in the financial services business, it's not really the quantity of customers that counts, but the quality—how rich the customers are. . . . It's generally assumed that servicing well-heeled folk will be more profitable in years to come than pushing financial products at people of moderate means.[14]

"Well-heeled" is typically defined as meaning an annual family income of $50,000 or more; there are an estimated 3.2 million households in this group. Some experts fear that, with a large number of big as well as small institutions competing, few will make a profit. Given those estimates "the supercompanies plan to concentrate on the vast middle market of families earning $20,000 to $50,000 a year."[15]

Current Actions

The supercompanies (Sears Roebuck and Company, Prudential-Bache Securities, Bank America Corp., American Express, CitiCorp, and Merrill Lynch and Co.) continue to expand into new businesses as fast as the law and technology permit (Exhibit 2 compares some financial and product data on the supercompanies with those of the John Hancock). Some large insurers are acquiring small securities firms, money man-

[11] Neil Osborn, "What Synergy," *Institution Investor,* May 1982, p. 50.

[12] Ibid., p. 52.

[13] Ibid., p. 52.

[14] Ibid., p. 54.

[15] Arlene Hershman, "The Supercompanies Emerge," *Dunn's Business Month,* April 1983, p. 46.

Exhibit 2 Financial Industry Major Competitors Comparative Data

Financial Data (all figures in millions of dollars)	**American Express**	**BankAmerica**	**Citicorp**	**Merrill Lynch**	**Prudential**	**Sears**	**John Hancock***
Revenues	7,800	13,112	18,258	4,590	13,200	29,180	4,422
Net Income	559	425	774	220	Not Comparable	735	NC
Assets	27,700	120,498	128,430	20,940	62,500	34,200	**23,714
Customers' deposits	5,700	93,208	77,359	3,930	—	2,300	—
Customers' credit balances	1,200***	—	—	2,700	740	200	—
Money market funds	17,200	—	—	48,900	5,000	9,000	1,125
Commercial loans	4,200	48,800	60,411	400	1,560	—	2,000
Consumer loans	1,000	25,100	22,029	5,000	3,900	4,250	1,900

What They Do	**American Express**	**BankAmerica**	**Citicorp**	**Merrill Lynch**	**Prudential**	**Sears**	**John Hancock**
Securities brokerage	•			•	•	•	•
Securities trading	•	•	•	•	•	•	•
Cash management services	•			•		•	•
Investment management	•	•	•	•	•	•	•
Commodities brokerage	•			•	•	•	
U.S. corporate underwriting	•			•	•	•	
International corporate underwriting	•	•	•	•	•	•	
U.S. commercial banking		•	•				
International commercial banking	•	•	•	•			
Savings and loan operations			•			•	
Small loan offices		•	•			•	
Credit card, charge cards	•	•	•			•	
Traveler's checks	•	•	•				
Foreign exchange trading	•	•	•	•	•	•	
Leasing	•	•	•	•	•		•
Data processing services	•	•	•	•			•
Property-casualty insurance	•				•	•	•
Life, health insurance	•			•	•	•	•
Mortgage insurance						•	•
Mortage banking	•	•	•	•		•	•
Real estate development	•				•	•	•
Commercial real estate brokerage				•		•	
Residential real estate brokerage				•		•	
Executive relocation services				•		•	

Source: *The New Financial Services*, Alliance of American Insurers, Shaumburg, Ill., 1983 (reprinted with permission of Prudential-Bache Securities).
*Source: John Hancock Internal documents.
**Not including subsidiary assets.
***Total assets under management $37 million.

Exhibit 3 Financial Services Announcements The First Half of 1983

Travelers owns Securities Development Corporation (securities clearing subsidiary).
President of American Express joins Travelers (hiring said to be influenced by his financial services background).
Equitable Life and First National Bank of Chicago to market cash management services.
Prudential to buy Capital City Bank of Hopeville, Georgia.
Sears to have Dean Witter offices in 100 stores by the end of 1983, 150 by the end of 1984, and eventually 400.
CIGNA buys automatic Business Centers, commercial payroll processing centers.
Kemper's regional brokerage houses earned $8.3 million in 1982.
Nationwide to offer insurance in offices of Banc One.
John Hancock's Independent Investment Associates to offer financial services for corporations and institutions.
Prudential to have 30 joint offices with Bache by the end of 1983.
Travelers to offer insured cash management services through its trust company.
Hartford to buy 24 percent of Minneapolis brokerage firm.
Aetna Life & Casualty buys majority interest in Federal Investors.
Mutual of Omaha plans to acquire investment banking and brokerage firm of Kilpatrick, Pettis, Smith, Polian, Inc.
J.C. Penney to buy First National Bank of Harrington, Delaware.
Merrill Lynch to buy Raritan Valley Financial Corporation, a New Jersey savings and loan.
Kemper announces intention to buy a savings and loan.
Chairman of Manufacturers Hanover says much of the euphoria about financial supermarkets may be exaggerated.

Source: Bull, Robert A. "Insurance and the Financial Services Industry," *United States Banker*, August 1983, p. 118.

agers, and mortgage bankers. Alexander Clash, President at New York's John Alden Insurance Company, expressed one view that acquisitions are a cheap form of R&D and added, "Buying a foothold in every conceivable financial service is a way of participating in every business because no one is sure what the hot areas will be in 1990."[16]

Obviously, there are considerable mixed feelings in the financial services community concerning recent changes. Movement continues to take place even in light of the questionable results companies may achieve when they offer one-stop financial services, in effect becoming financial supermarkets (see Exhibit 3). Part of the reason for this trend may be the estimated $200 billion that Americans spent on financial services in 1982, reportedly earning suppliers of those services $42 billion.[17]

The decade of the 1980s promises to be an exciting one for the huge American financial services industry, which has, until now, been fragmented. Some uncontrollable factors, such as interest rates, the economic climate, the regulatory climate, and the role of technology, will also affect the industry. Many experts believe that technology (especially computers and telephones), with its costs and unpredictable product breakthroughs, will play such a large part in product cost and delivery that the big competition to worry about may not be other companies in the financial services industry but AT&T and IBM.[18]

[16]Ibid., p. 47.

[17]Ibid., p. 44.

[18]Ibid., p. 50.

The John Hancock Mutual Life Insurance Company[19]

The John Hancock Company began in 1862 when John Hancock started selling life insurance. By 1864 the company had over $500,000 of insurance in force. In less than ten years, the company's insurance in force grew to nearly $20 million. In the early part of the twentieth century, the company pioneered a number of products, including group life insurance. The John Hancock Company prospered during the boom years following World War I and continued to grow through the Depression. As late as the mid-1960s, the company was still primarily a seller of insurance. A hundred years after its founding, the company's pool of capital had been invested in nearly every imaginable sector of the economy, both private and public.

In December 1983, in an internal bulletin to all home office employees, the John Hancock Mutual Life Insurance Company announced a definitive merger agreement with the Buckeye Financial Corporation of Columbus, Ohio. The merger agreement provided for the acquisition of Buckeye by the John Hancock subsidiary for approximately $28 million in cash, equal to $13.50 per share of Buckeye common shares on a fully diluted basis. Buckeye, a savings and loan holding company in Columbus, Ohio, is the parent of Buckeye Federal Savings and Loan Association. Buckeye Federal, a federally chartered savings and loan association, conducts its business through 19 offices located throughout central Ohio. With assets of approximately $1.2 billion as of September 30, 1983, Buckeye Federal is one of the largest savings and loan associations in Ohio and is the largest mortgage lender in central Ohio. In April 1982, less than two years prior to this merger agreement, the Hancock had acquired Tucker Anthony Holding Corporation, the parent of Tucker Anthony and R. L. Day Inc., a regional brokerage house with 30 offices in the Northeast.[20] These two announcements were the latest of a number of financial services subsidiaries (most developed internally) that had been added since 1968. In a letter dated December 23, 1968, and addressed to home office associates, then-President Robert E. Slater discussed the concept of subsidiaries:

> We think of them (the subsidiaries) as a device through which we can develop markets and new products and, as a corollary, other new avenues toward increased compensation for our sales forces. They also provide investment vehicles to enhance the return on total investable funds. Life insurance is still our main business—by a very wide margin—but in the larger view we can use these subsidiaries to augment or supplement our life insurance sales with the marketing of a wide array of financial services.

Background on the Insurance Industry

Today in the United States the insurance industry is divided into three major categories: life, health, and property and casualty. The life and health areas are further divided into group and individual categories. In 1981 new purchases of life insurance in the United States amounted to $812.3 billion.[21]

Commercial life insurance companies are divided into two categories: stock and mutual companies.[22] A company that has stockholders is a stock company, whereas a mutual company is owned by its policyholders. Just over 2,000 life insurance companies were doing business in the

---

[19]Historical facts on the company were taken from *A Bridge to the Future; One Hundredth Anniversary 1862–1962,* copyright 1962, John Hancock Mutual Life Insurance Company, Boston, Mass.

[20]"Hancock to Acquire Tucker Anthony at up to $47 Million," *Wall Street Journal,* April 15, 1982, p. 16.

[21]Sources of factual data on the insurance industry were: *1983 Life Insurance Factbook* (Washington, D.C.: American Council of Life Insurance, 1983), and S. S. Hubner and Kenneth Black, Jr., *Life Insurance,* 9th ed. Englewood Cliffs. N.J.: (Prentice Hall, Inc., 1976).

[22]For data on the top ten insurance companies, see Exhibit 29.1.

United States and accounted for 43 percent of the life insurance in force in 1982.

Stock companies seek to earn the highest possible profits for their shareholders. Policy owners do not benefit from any gains the stock company enjoys nor are they hurt by any losses the company suffers. Because they are not directly affected by the company's financial experience, their policies are called nonparticipating. Because no dividend is expected, the premium paid by a stock company must meet capital and surplus requirements as well as other requirements established by its home state. Having met these requirements and having had its stock subscribed, a stock company may begin doing business. Because a stock company is owned by its shareholders, the first responsibility of the directors is to those shareholders. Because shareholders can vote on major issues and elect the board of directors, control of the company rests with the owners of a majority of the stock. Shareholders may sell their stock or buy more shares at prevailing market prices.

Mutual insurance companies are owned by policyholders. Management's first obligation is to create profit for policyholders, who have the right to vote for directors. When funds available exceed solvency requirements, the directors may pay policyholders a dividend, although such payment is not mandatory. The cost of a policyholder's premium less the dividend paid determines the final cost of the insurance coverage. Because the policyholder may benefit from the favorable financial experience of a mutual company, that policy is called participating. Owners of mutual companies are numerous and scattered and have proportionately small ownership positions. For these reasons, control of a mutual company remains largely with management.

By the end of the 1960s, the rising inflation rate caused a number of people to seek new investment vehicles that offered higher returns than life insurance. The public's attention turned to the stock market. Many viewed life insurance as a high-opportunity cost versus returns they imagined were available through stock market investments. A number of investment firms answered that market's desire by offering mutual fund shares. The public sank dollars into a new breed of mutual fund called money market funds. Securities firms (such as Merrill Lynch) and fund operators (such as Fidelity) invested billions of dollars in low-risk securities offering record levels of income. Banks began offering certificates of deposit (CDs) with very high returns. The insurance industry found itself fighting not only for new business but to retain the reserves that they already held.

To grow and, indeed, to survive, traditional insurance institutions like John Hancock found themselves forced to compete with higher-yielding instruments offered by the federal government, municipal governments, and brokerage houses.

John Hancock Subsidiaries Inc. (JHSI)

In 1980, the structure of the John Hancock Company was changed to incorporate the existence of ten subsidiaries in the form of a downstream holding company (see Exhibits 4 and 5). Exhibit 6 describes the products and services offered by the subsidiaries. Selective financial data on the parent company and the subsidiaries can be found in Exhibits 7 and 8.

Stephen Brown, Executive Vice-President of Financial Operations of the John Hancock Mutual Life Insurance Company and President and Chief Executive Officer of John Hancock Subsidiaries Inc., had worked for the Hancock for 22 years when he became president of the holding company in 1981. Brown offered the following explanation on the origins of the holding company and its operations. Initially when the individual companies were started (the first in 1968), they became part of an existing department of the company. For example, Hanseco, which offered a line of casualty insurance, operated as a part of the Marketing Department and was expected to attract more revenue to the

Exhibit 4 John Hancock Mutual Life Insurance Company, Boston, Massachusetts, Organization Chart, Effective April 1, 1983

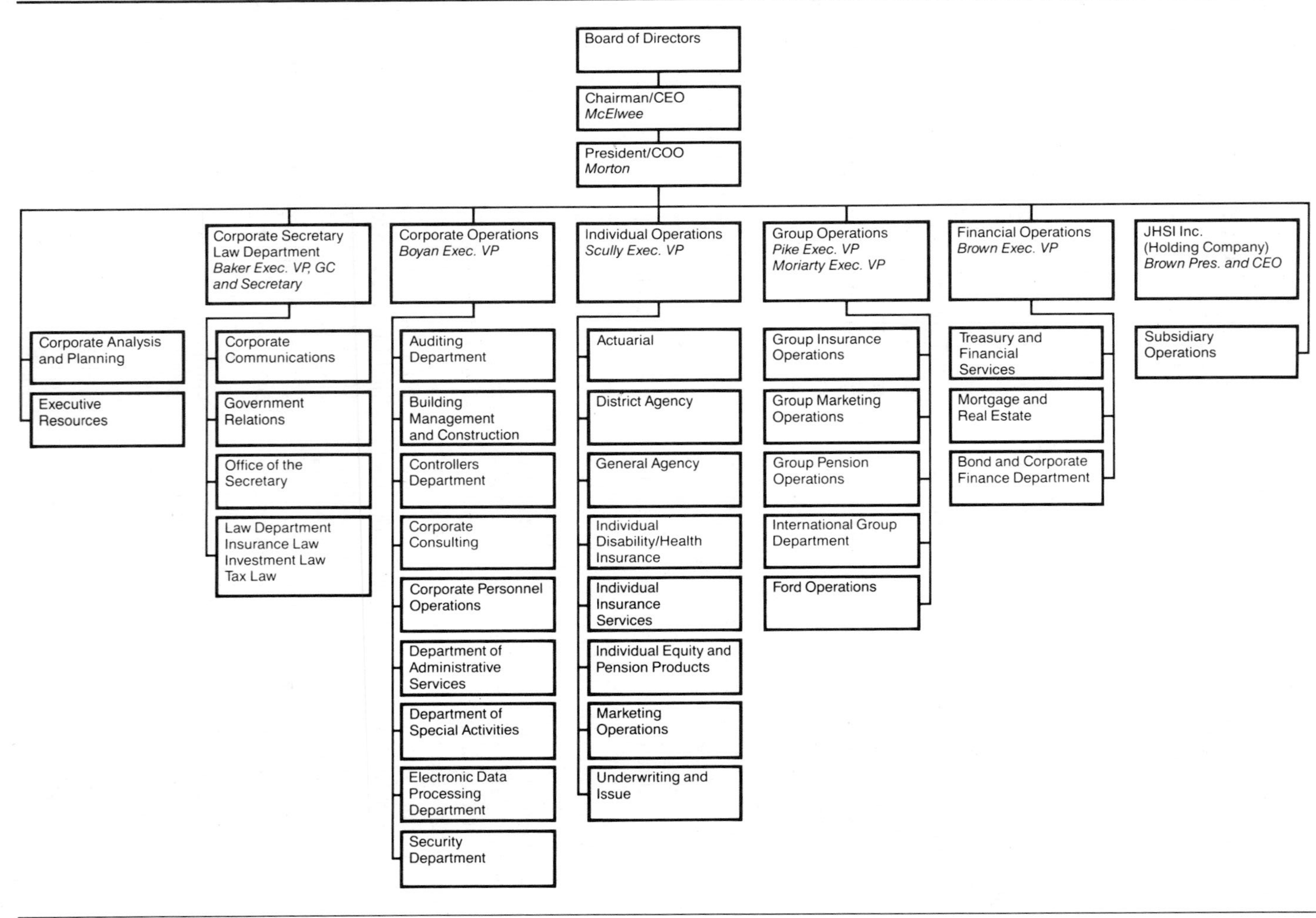

Exhibit 5 Subsidiary Organization Chart

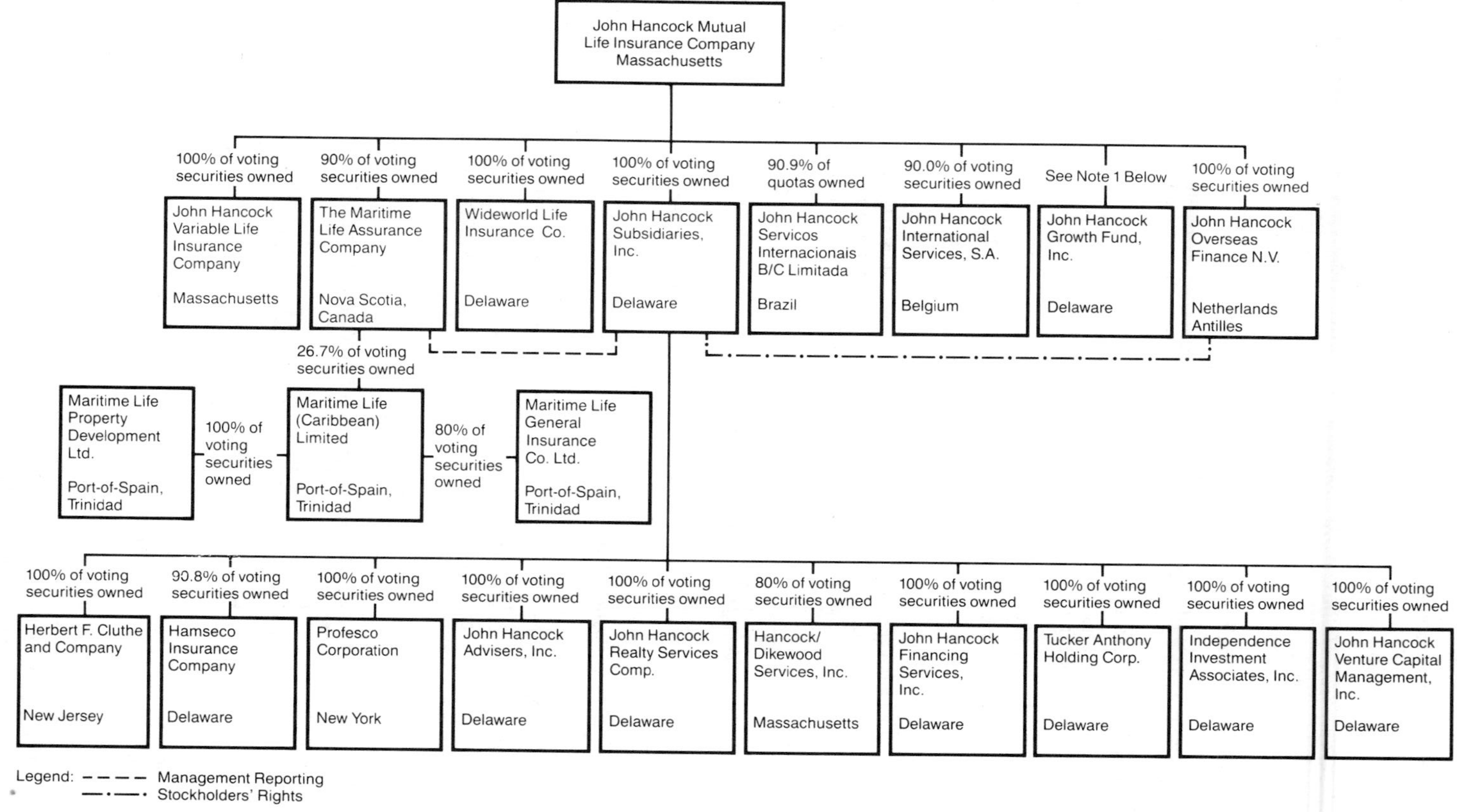

Exhibit 6 Subsidiaries of John Hancock Mutual Life Insurance Company (JH)

John Hancock International Services S.A., Brussels, Belgium

1968 Incorporated in Belgium. Established to enable the International Group Department of John Hancock to perform the international employee benefit services expected by multinational companies that participate in the John Hancock International Group Program (IGP).

Maritime Life Insurance Co., Halifax, Nova Scotia

1969 Acquired by JH. Reports to Life Company through JH Subsidiaries, Inc. for management reporting purposes. Offers a full range of life insurance products in Canadian markets.

John Hancock Servicos Internacionalis S/C, Ltda., Sao Paulo, Brazil

1973 Organized in Brazil. Established to enable IGP to deliver the same financial results to clients with subsidiaries in Brazil as in all other IGP countries, and to enable funds to be transferred out of Brazil.

John Hancock Variable Life Insurance Co., Boston, Massachusetts

1979 Incorporated in Massachusetts. Provides a vehicle for John Hancock agents to sell individual variable life insurance and universal life insurance products.

John Hancock Overseas Finance N.V., Curacao, Netherlands Antilles

1982 Incorporated in Netherlands Antilles. Raises funds outside the United States and lends such funds to John Hancock and its affiliates.

John Hancock Subsidiaries, Inc., Boston, Massachusetts

1979 Incorporated in Delaware; commenced business in 1980. A downstream holding company organized to provide a means of centralizing the reporting responsibility for the following subsidiaries as a group to coordinate their financial planning and the development of unified policies and strategies.

Subsidiaries of JHSI

Herbert F. Cluthe and Co., Springfield, New Jersey

1968 Acquired by JH.

1980 Acquired by JHSI. Develops total financial plans and group and pension programs for business and trade associations.

John Hancock Advisers, Inc., Boston, Massachusetts

1968 Incorporated in Delaware.

1980 Acquired by JHSI. Manages the portfolios of six open-end investment companies: John Hancock Growth Fund Inc.; John Hancock U.S. Government Securities Fund Inc.; John Hancock Bond Fund Inc.; John Hancock Tax-Exempt Income Trust; John Hancock Cash Management Trust; and John Hancock Tax-Exempt Cash Management Trust, shares of which are sold by its subsidiary broker-dealer, John Hancock Distributors Inc.

Exhibit 7 John Hancock Companies—Assets Under Management ($ in millions)

	1972	1973	1974	1975	1976
General account	$10,377	$10,737	$11,232	$12,071	$13,098
Separate account	818	710	591	730	898
Guaranteed benefit separate account	0	0	0	0	0
Subsidiaries (estimated)*	283	488	462	633	708
Pension advisory accounts	0	0	0	0	19
Total assets under management	$11,478	$11,935	$12,285	$13,434	$14,723

*Subsidiary assets are net of John Hancock parent equity holdings and contain estimated components.

Source: John Hancock Mutual Life Insurance Company Annual Reports.

Exhibit 6 *(continued)*

John Hancock Realty Services Corp., Boston, Massachusetts

1968 Incorporated in Delaware.

1980 Acquired by JHSI. Invests in income-producing real estate; provides commercial real estate brokerage, mortgage placement and servicing, and appraisal services through its sudsidiary, John Hancock Real Estate Finance Inc. Operations are conducted nationwide through a series of regional offices.

Profesco Corporation, New York, New York

1968 Acquired by JH.

1980 Acquired by JHSI. A nationwide organization of franchised specialists providing complete financial services to the professional and business communities.

HANSECO Insurance Co., Boston, Massachusetts

1971 Incorporated in Delaware.

1980 JH ownership transferred to JHSI. In addition to providing a vehicle for John Hancock agents to sell personal lines of Sentry Insurance, the company is actively involved in the reinsurance business through three wholly-owned subsidiaries.

Hancock/Dikewood Services Inc., Albuquerque, New Mexico

1979 Incorporated in Massachusetts.

1980 Acquired by JHSI. Provides data processing and systems analysis services to health care providers. The company also offers a full range of management services to health maintenance organizations and associations.

John Hancock Financial Services Inc., Boston, Massachusetts

1980 Incorporated in Delaware. Provides equipment leasing and financing (tax- and nontax-oriented) and related financial services to the agricultural, professional, and general commercial markets on a national scale.

Independence Investment Associates Inc., Boston, Massachusetts

1982 Incorporated in Delaware. Provides investment management and advisory and counseling services, principally to pension funds and other institutional investors.

John Hancock Venture Capital Management Inc., Boston, Massachusetts

1982 Incorporated In Delaware. Serves as general partner and manager of the John Hancock Venture Capital Fund, a limited partnership with $148,000,000 of committed capital.

Tucker Anthony Holding Corp., Main Offices: Boston, Massachusetts, and New York, New York

1982 Incorporated in Delaware. A holding company offering, through its subsidiary Tucker Anthony & R.L. Day Inc., a broad range of financial services, including stocks and bonds, money management, corporate finance, and tax-advantaged investments.

1977	1978	1979	1980	1981	1982	1983
$14,101	$15,212	$16,207	$17,263	$17,824	$18,336	$18,708
937	1,016	1,111	1,377	1,448	1,754	2,066
0	0	0	121	671	1,633	2,766
838	1,014	1,269	1,625	2,365	5,400	6,013
24	83	133	161	203	269	398
$15,900	$17,325	$18,720	$20,547	$22,511	$27,392	$29,951

Exhibit 8 Consolidated Summary of Operations and Changes in Policyholders' Contingency Reserves, John Hancock Mutual Life Insurance Company and Subsidiary

	Year Ending December 31,		
	1983	1982	1981
Income			
Premiums, annuity considerations, and pension fund contributions	$2,489.5	$2,573.4	$2,435.6
Investment income	1,818.1	1,668.1	1,491.2
Separate account capital gains (losses)	118.4	132.9	(106.9)
Other	(346.1)	(562.6)	(552.5)
	4,079.9	3,811.8	3,267.4
Benefits and expenses			
Payments to policyholders and beneficiaries:			
Death benefits	513.3	447.0	405.1
Accident and health benefits	423.9	444.5	496.4
Annuity benefits	182.9	25.0	11.6
Surrender benefits	248.9	90.1	79.1
Matured endowments	15.2	11.6	11.3
	1,384.2	1,018.2	1,003.5
Additions to reserves to provide for future payments to policyholders and beneficiaries	1,560.2	1,599.3	1,187.6
Expenses of providing service to policyholders and obtaining new insurance:			
Field sales compensation and expenses	308.9	292.5	285.6
Home office and general expenses	310.6	279.0	262.5
State premium taxes	30.5	32.2	30.2
Payroll and miscellaneous taxes	27.6	25.2	22.7
	3,622.0	3,246.4	2,792.1
Net gain before dividends to policyholders and federal income taxes	457.9	565.4	475.3
Dividends to policyholders	390.5	326.7	314.2
Federal income taxes	36.0	70.1	50.2
	426.5	396.8	364.4
Net gain	31.4	168.6	110.9
Net capital gain or loss and other adjustments	(52.6)	(50.2)	40.4
Less amounts allocated for:			
Increase (decrease) in valuation reserves	(1.2)	(1.2)	1.2
Additional provision for prior years' federal income taxes		13.9	30.0
Other adjustments	16.0	7.0	15.8
Increase (decrease) in policyholders' contingency reserves	(36.0)	98.7	104.3
Policyholders' contingency reserves at beginning of year	1,002.8	904.1	799.8
Policyholders' contingency reserves at end of year	966.8	$1,002.8	$ 904.1

Exhibit 8 *(continued)*

	Year Ending December 31,	
	1983	1982
Assets		
Bonds	$ 6,551.5	$ 6,590.2
Stocks:		
Preferred or guaranteed	190.6	197.1
Common	431.3	361.1
Investment in affiliates	342.5	319.4
	964.4	877.6
Mortgage loans on real estate	6,542.0	6,527.3
Real estate		
Company occupied	161.4	148.6
Investment properties	636.2	530.6
	797.6	679.2
Policy loans and liens	2,041.2	1,890.4
Cash items:		
Cash in banks and offices	40.0	12.4
Temporary cash investments	558.8	789.8
	598.8	802.2
Premiums due and deferred	388.8	341.1
Investment income due and accrued	362.8	344.3
Other general account assets	460.9	283.7
Assets held in separate accounts	4,832.1	3,386.2
Total assets	$23,540.1	$21,722.8
Obligations		
Policy reserves	$11,659.7	$11,442.2
Policyholders' and beneficiaries' funds	4,596.4	4,649.3
Dividends payable to policyholders	429.0	359.5
Policy benefits in process of payment	161.2	99.3
Other policy obligations	161.6	148.3
Indebtedness to affiliate–	74.7	74.4
Commercial paper outstanding–	72.6	0
Mandatory securities and other asset valuation reserves	389.3	272.3
Federal income and other accrued taxes	109.5	148.8
Other general account obligations	101.9	158.1
Obligations related to separate account business	4,817.4	3,367.8
Total obligations	22,573.3	20,720.0
Policyholders' contingency reserves		
Special contigency reserve for group insurance	92.6	87.8
General contingency reserve	874.2	915.0
Total contingency reserves	966.8	1,002.8
Total obligations and contingency reserves	$23,540.1	$21,722.8

company by giving insurance agents a larger package of securities to offer. At that time the major objective of a new addition was synergy—or—as Brown described it, "putting more dollars in the agency force." Profit and growth were secondary.

In January of 1980, when the holding company (John Hancock Subsidiaries Inc.) was established, management was charged with the responsibility of overseeing the subsidiary companies and reporting to the Board of Directors of the life company. As control mechanisms, the holding company was to submit to the board quarterly financial statements and yearly presentations on its overall strategy. In addition, various Board committees on organization, finance, compliance, conflict of interest, and auditing could also ask for reports. The individual subsidiaries submitted strategic plans to the board of the holding company. In 1980 the objectives for the subsidiaries had become first profit, followed by growth, and then synergy; and the subsidiaries were expected in the long run to return 15 percent on investment. Brown noted that before this time "profit and return on investment" were not commonplace expectations in the company.

In Brown's view, the major reasons for changing the structure to a holding company were for tax purposes (some subsidiaries were profitable and others were not) and to form more consistent planning and control systems throughout the subsidiaries. Although there were some in the company who felt that various departments should continue to control the subsidiaries, the outcome of the restructuring, according to Brown, was that "there are now clear controls in place with the subsidiaries operating autonomously from day to day."

Each subsidiary has its own board of directors. The holding company decides on the directors and reviews the minutes of meetings. Major capital requirements and any significant change in the type of business performed by a subsidiary also requires approval by the holding company. Personnel selection and compensation are left completely to the subsidiaries. Subsidiaries are welcome, but not required, to use the staff facilities at the life company (for example, EDP, Accounting, Public Relations). Brown stated that, on the average, he visits the subsidiaries once a month. With the major objectives of profitability, growth, and synergy clearly stated, the approach used to run the subsidiaries is, according to Brown, "Now, go do it!"

Mr. Brown commented on the future of the John Hancock:

> Profit and return on investment were not common words in the company. In the long run I see us adopting GAAP (Generally Accepted Accounting Principles) instead of statutory accounting and defining profit centers throughout the Life Company as we do in the Holding Company. This is a step toward becoming in the long run a stock company where we can purchase with stock as opposed to cash and offer stock incentives to management and tie a bonus to profits and growth. If in the long run this is where we are headed, the only way to do it is the profit center concept.

The addition of the holding company in 1980, along with the different systems used to measure performance, added a new dimension to the John Hancock and its way of operating. This became clear as people discussed the changes that had taken place inside the Hancock over the past 16 years and the future in the changing financial services industry.

Structure, Culture, and Systems

A major concern in the company was the fact that two different entities operate under the name John Hancock Mutual Life Insurance Company. Furthermore, two distinct cultures evolved as a result of defining the subsidiaries as profit centers in 1980 and evaluating them based on profit and return on investment. That change in structure and systems in essence created a new way of operating and, to some extent, a new breed of manager.

Phyllis Cella was president and chief executive officer of Hanseco, a subsidiary spawned in 1971 from within the Hancock and staffed originally with Hancock employees. The expressed purpose of starting Hanseco was to provide products for the Hancock agents. In 1983, Hanseco had approximately $750 million in assets under its management. Up until 1980 they had operated within the Hancock structure. Cella described some of the thinking that went on inside Hanseco as the subsidiary grew. In the beginning:

> Hanseco was run according to the Hancock style, and we were all on the Hancock payroll. As we got bigger and began to understand our own business, we began to change that. Having grown up in it you learn how to deal with it, but you also understand how time consuming it is and that you don't always get the answer you want because it is a bureaucracy. Even before the Holding Company officially was formed, we saw ourselves as running a company that was now different from and, in our minds, separate from the John Hancock, even though we were still on the John Hancock payroll. In our minds the paycheck was the only connection. When the world turned [introduction of the subsidiary structure] and the primary objective now became profit, it strengthened the fact that you really are a completely separate entity—it has now been blessed—and you are your own employer.

In 1984 Hanseco had its own payroll that was processed, not on the John Hancock computers, but by the First National Bank of Boston. The subsidiary set its own salaries and had its own retirement plan. According to Cella, the attitude at Hanseco was: "If I can get it cheaper downtown, then I'm going to do that—it's my bottom line. There are still people in the organization that don't understand or accept that fact that maybe we will buy their services—but maybe we won't. There is no question that there now exists two different cultures."

Hanseco's 40th-floor offices are a modular arrangement as opposed to the traditional open concept of the Hancock. Cella's office was on the outside corner of the glass building overlooking the Charles River and the Boston Common. She remarked that she had consciously chosen the modular design and had had to fight for it.

> Once you get a taste of it (the profit center concept), I don't think it would be possible to go back and work in the other framework—not at this level or an officer level. Partly because of the size—we still have only 225 employees but are growing every day—but partly because of the need. We all participate very heavily in this organization—all of the officers. We have eight officers, so it is not hard to get eight people together, hammer things out, let everyone have his say, have everyone really go at it, and wide open. How do you do that in the Hancock? You don't—it is impossible. It is much more fun here. A bigger challenge, a lot more sleepless nights than you ever had in the other big organization, but you cannot match the excitement and satisfaction of it and the gratification when it works.

Although officers of the life company were quite aware of the differences, some, like Frank Irish, Vice-President, Corporate Analysis and Planning, viewed the subsidiaries "as indistinguishable from the parent company from the point of view of management control. Standards should be applied equally to subsidiaries and parent company. A lot of my efforts have been designed to achieve this goal, and I think we are close to that."

In response to the issue of transforming units of the life company into profit centers, Irish went on to say: "I can only say that we are very seriously considering it. We obviously can. We know we can." He also had some doubts, however, as to whether the change would accomplish what the Hancock wanted and if, in fact, that change was consistent with their policyholders. "When managing a participating insurance business you are not supposed to be profit maximizing—so why have a profit center concept. There is a conflict."

Phyllis Cella felt as Steve Brown did: "Theoretically, they (the units of the life company) ought to be profit centers and have a bottom line." There was some concern, however, from a practical point of view as to the difficulty of actually getting to the bottom line of some of the units within the life company that really do not have income.

There was also some concern among middle managers within the Life Company concerning the somewhat different nature of the business conducted within the holding company and the way the holding company managers were being compensated. As Irish commented:

> What is at this point different about the subsidiaries is their attitude toward things like personnel policies, tenure, compensation, that sort of thing. Not only have they been decentralized, but in theory the subsidiary personnel are working in a more highly rewarded, more risky business than the parent company. . . . I'm not sure how top management views it—and I usually know top management. I know how many middle managers view it—very critically. Subsidiary managers are paid better and have more freedom and have greater opportunities. That's how some people view it, and it's a problem we are going to have to work with. I don't know what the answer is. . . . The other is that you are generally dealing with the kinds of operations where you need risk takers. . . . I think the problem is perhaps made worse by the obvious fact that, despite the statements about profit responsibility, some of the subsidiaries have not produced an adequate rate of return.

Becoming a Stock Company

A related issue was the Hancock's financial restructuring to a stock company. Although this issue was much broader, it related directly to the existing culture within the Hancock. As noted previously, Steve Brown saw the Hancock, in the long run, taking on the structure of a stock company. On that particular issue, Frank Irish pointed out that the thinking had been dominated in the past by having to generate capital internally and that that way of doing things takes away certain possibilities in the way of financial dealings. However, there is less pressure in a mutual company to sacrifice long-term objectives for short-term profit growth.

Irish went on to say that there are other advantages and disadvantages to both forms of business. Some feel mutual companies have more leeway in pricing their products. By adjusting the dividends, mutual companies may much more closely reflect the actual cost of the service provided than their stock company counterparts. Stock companies are constrained to charge whatever the market will bear to achieve the highest possible level of profit for their stockholders.

As insurance companies extend themselves into broader areas of financial service, there is a tendency for firms to make use of holding companies for the management of their subsidiaries. Stock companies typically employ upstream holding companies. An upstream holding company is perched at the top of a corporate organization. The shareholders own it and it owns the subsidiaries. Mutual companies are constrained to use downstream holding companies. A downstream holding company is positioned midway down the corporate hierarchy and is wholly or partially owned by the mutual company. Because the parent mutual company is governed by state insurance laws, the management of a downstream holding company is often more complex than that of an upstream holding company.

As noted earlier, a stock company can raise capital by selling stock. A mutual company does not have this equity option. It may earn revenue from its operations, receive income from its investments, and acquire debt. A stock company may use its stock to acquire other organizations and in merger situations. Frank Irish contends that many of the older and larger mutual companies were able to experience immense growth because at their outset they were not pressured by shareholders to achieve high levels of profitability. Instead, management chose to pursue growth as the company's main objective.

It is possible for a mutual company to convert into a stock company and vice versa. Both processes are complicated, time consuming, and expensive. Conversion from a mutual company to a stock company would typically require the calculation of a policyholder's share of the company and transference of that share to shares of stock. In some instances a stock company, usually motivated by the fear of a takeover, may attempt to mutualize. This conversion would require approval by the company's board, the state insurance commissioner, the stockholders, and the policyholders. All the stock must be purchased and canceled by the company before it can mutualize. According to the *1983 Life Insurance Fact Book,* "In the past 16 years, five companies have converted from the status of a mutual company to a stock company and two stock companies have converted to mutual."[23]

Phyllis Cella commented on moving from a mutual to a stock company:

> I think that it is essentially a good idea, because then the whole company has to have a bottom line. Right now mutuals do have a net gain from operations. A stock company has a very different attitude and culture because they have the stockholder that wants a rate of return. But just doing it is not the answer. Just because you become a stock company doesn't suddenly make everything perfect. The old culture is still there.

The Future

Given the recent announcement of a merger agreement with Buckeye Financial Corporation and the 1982 purchase of Tucker Anthony in addition to the other ten subsidiaries, the Hancock has taken some major steps toward competing in the FSI. The strategic thrust behind such moves was that they would result in synergies along such dimensions as offering more products for the sales force, developing multiple service relationships with individual customers, and management synergy—they "knew how to manage financial services."

For E. James Morton, President and Chief Operations Officer and Vice-Chairman of the Board, the question of measuring performance in the life company was at the heart of what he considered one of the Hancock's major problems. What had been done in the past could not be readily identified as bottom-line. They essentially had no measures of profit and had only inconsistent measures of growth. Size as indicated by assets under management had also become difficult to measure. According to Morton: "We have always had some kind of measures that we have tried to be tough about. But I'm not sure they have been the right ones and the ultimate kinds of measures. And they haven't been the kinds of measures that you can really compensate people on."

Morton had some reservations about moving to the profit center concept. He noted that at times they had the feeling that they were a generation behind and that the profit center idea was becoming outmoded. He referred to management journals that indicated that managers spent too much time worrying about short-term results, thus sacrificing long-term objectives.

Part of the problem of moving to the profit center concept was the method of accounting used in mutual life insurance companies. Morton felt, however, that another big piece of the problem was attitude:

> Maybe the attitude was not so bad in the days when all we were was a mutual life insurance company being operated with the primary purpose to supply insurance at cost to our policyholders. But now that we are trying to compete in a broader financial services industry we can't do that anymore. We have to operate with the same kinds of efficiencies as our competition.

Morton felt that they had to change the way management and essentially all of the employees of the company look at what the objectives are.

> If we do that, we are going to benefit our policyholders a lot more than perhaps we have in the

[23] *1983 Life Insurance Factbook,* (Washington, D.C.: The American Council of Life Insurance, 1983), pp. 88–89. Of the seven companies that converted, the council has identified six. Those converting from mutual to stock were: National Heritage Life-Insurance (1966), Brooking International Life Insurance (1966), Viking Life Insurance (1972), West States Insurance Company (1973), and Equitable Beneficial Mutual Life Insurance Company (1977). Farmers and Traders Life Insurance converted from stock to mutual in 1974.

> past. We will be forced to cut costs, run things efficiently, be market-driven, and expand the base that expenses can be spread over, resulting in lower consumer costs. We think we are headed in the right direction. But that is not to say that for the first 100 years things were done the wrong way. The times have changed.

Demutualizing, or moving to a stock company, is a very complex issue because of having to deal with 50 state insurance commissions and agreeing on whether a mutual company has equitably treated its existing policyholders.

For Jack McElwee, this was also a complex issue but one that he related to the future environment of the Hancock.

> A lot of people feel that it is too complex but you can't possibly afford to feel that way. If the reality of the future is that only a corporation which is the form of a stock company will be able to survive, then you'd better find a way to be a stock company, or at least have all the legal and regulatory characteristics that a stock company has.

Even though the future of the FSI is questionable, there should also be all kinds of opportunities. McElwee noted that capitalizing on those opportunities means "managing ourselves properly. That's what this exercise is all about—it's called management."

Jim Morton expanded on the role of the John Hancock in the FSI:

> I am not sure what one-stop financial shopping means. What we hope to do is attract clients. If we attract a client in one piece of the organization, we hope to make that client a target for the other pieces of the organization. I think it would be unrealistic to think that there are going to be a lot of people that get all their financial services from us. We want to see a lot of cross-selling. We want to have plenty of clients in all the sectors and hopefully the rest will take care of itself.

Morton felt that to succeed in the FSI, the important step is to fill out the product line. He went on to say:

> That is why we so badly need a bank. If we can't buy the bank, let's find that out in a hurry because we have to make other arrangements. There is no way we can be a large financial services organization without offering banking services. If you can't do it by owning a bank, you have to do it some other way.

Morton went on to discuss the future of the John Hancock:

> We want to end up with an organization that, when people look at it they say, "That's a financial services organization." And if you ask the man on the street, "What is the John Hancock?" he will say that "it is a financial services organization where I can go to do almost anything. I can buy stocks and bonds, house insurance, securities, and tax shelters. I can also get a mortgage for my house and banking services. Furthermore, I get a statement on everything once a month." . . . That is what we would like to be in 1990, and I think we have a reasonably good chance of doing it. There will be maybe 50 large financial organizations at that time and that is the list we want to be on. In order to do that we have to internally become customer-driven, profit-oriented, entrepreneurial, and all those good things you are supposed to be if you are a healthy, growing business. We know what we need to do. The trick is to do it.

It was also clear to Jim Morton that in the next five to ten years the composition of the businesses of the Hancock was also going to change. The assets in the nontraditional ventures were going to become bigger than those in the traditional ventures. According to Morton, "If we succeed in buying the bank that is another billion dollars of assets. Clearly, the nontraditional ventures are where the growth is."

To complicate management tasks in the environment of an evolving FSI, McElwee also had to deal with what he considered an intriguing question, namely, "What is beyond the financial services industry?" To this end he recently put together a study group focusing on the time frame of 2025 and the major questions of "What are the directions that the Hancock should move?" and "To what extent do those directions influence what we do in the way of financial services today?"

Appendix A

Officers

John G. McElwee

John G. McElwee was elected chairman and chief executive officer of John Hancock Mutual Life Insurance Co. effective January 1, 1982. McElwee entered the John Hancock administrative training program in 1945 and subsequently served as administrative assistant and in a series of line management responsibilities prior to his election as second vice-president in 1961. He became executive vice-president and secretary in 1974. McElwee then served as president and chief operations officer from January 1, 1979, to his election as chairman. He has been on the Board of Directors since March 1976.

E. James Morton

E. James Morton was elected president and chief operations officer of John Hancock Mutual Life Insurance Co. effective January 1, 1982. Morton entered the company as an actuarial student in 1949. He subsequently held a variety of line assignments within the actuarial area prior to his election in 1967 as vice-president and actuary. In 1971, he was elected senior vice-president, technical operations, and in 1974 executive vice-president, corporate operations. Morton has been on the Board of Directors since March 1976.

Stephen L. Brown

Stephen L. Brown was elected executive vice-president of financial operations of the John Hancock Mutual Life Insurance Co. in December 1981, to the Hancock Board of Directors in January 1982, and served as president and chief executive officer of John Hancock Subsidiaries Inc. until February 1984. Brown joined the company in 1958. He subsequently held various assignments within the actuarial department and was elected second vice-president in 1970 and vice-president in 1973. In 1975, he became vice-president at the Treasury Department and in 1977 was named senior vice-president and treasurer.

Phyllis A. Cella

Phyllis A. Cella of Boston is president, chief executive officer, and director of Hanseco Insurance Co., a subsidiary formed for the reinsurance of Sentry Insurance Co. policies sold by John Hancock representatives. She is also chairman of the board of Hanseco (U.K.) Insurance Company Ltd. and a director of John Hancock Subsidiaries Inc. Cella joined the parent company as a statistician. She advanced to statistical consultant in 1963 and served as assistant to the senior vice-president of field management and marketing from 1968 to 1970, when she was named general director of special projects and research. Cella was elected second vice-president in January 1972, vice-president in February 1975, and senior vice-president in December 1979.

Frank S. Irish

Frank S. Irish was promoted to vice-president, corporate analysis and planning, at John Hancock Mutual Life Insurance Co. in January 1979. Irish joined the company in 1963 as an assistant actuary. He was promoted to associate actuary in 1966 and in 1971 joined the Corporate Analysis and Planning Department in that capacity. Irish was elected second vice-president, corporate analysis and planning, in 1972.

Case 6 Update*

To Our Policyholders and Customers

Nineteen eighty-seven . . . fulfilling the promise. This year, more than any other year in the history of John Hancock, was a year of measuring up to the promises made over the past ten years. Promises of a responsive, thoughtful and customer-driven organization that would deliver to the marketplace those products and services our customers needed—and delivering them in a competitive, yet quality-conscious way.

"Real life, real answers" has been the continuing theme in our advertising and our marketing. We have assessed the real-life requirements of the financial services marketplace and have, in 1987, driven toward fulfilling those needs with real answers.

In real life, the lives we all live, there were events that shaped our way of doing business. There were events that shook the financial services world. And events that clearly pointed toward pressing needs among the many publics that we serve.

The continuing plight of many senior citizens, who are living longer and facing destitution rather than dignity after many years of hard work, the shocking stock market tumble of October 19th, the growing concern over the spread of AIDS, and the globalization of American business. Diverse events on the surface, yet linked together in our awareness of the real world we live in.

ProtectCare, a new insurance product that is specifically geared to the senior market, was introduced in 1987. Expectations are high that this product will distinguish John Hancock as an industry leader in the provision of long-term health care coverage.

*Source: Excerpts from John Hancock Mutual Life Insurance Company 1987 annual report, pp. 2–3, 24–27.

To say we were unaffected by the events of October 19th would be unrealistic. Yet, because of John Hancock's approach to the funds under our management, our diversified strategy for investments lessened the impact of the stock market crash on Hancock customers.

John Hancock introduced AIDS Case Management, a humane, caring program that provides our employee benefits customers with a cost-effective way of helping those stricken by this catastrophic disease. And does it with compassion.

To remain competitive in a spreading global marketplace, John Hancock is now the majority owner in a life insurance company in Indonesia, P.T. Asuransi Pensiun Bumiputera John Hancock. Augmenting our presence in Asia, we completed establishment of a fully operational regional office in Hong Kong, John Hancock International Services (Hong Kong) Ltd. And as of January 1, 1988, our regional office in Brussels, originally established to coordinate activity of the International Group Program®, also will be involved in acquisitions. In addition, John Hancock Advisers formed a wholly owned subsidiary, John Hancock Advisers International, Ltd. (London), which provides international investment advice for its mutual funds. We also introduced an international index fund for pension clients.

There were other promises to keep in 1987. John Hancock undertook a major restructuring of its internal organization. Three marketing sectors were established with direct-line responsibility for those areas given to sector presidents, and the post of Chief Financial Officer was created. A reevaluation of our personnel requirements was necessary. In the first quarter of 1987, through a voluntary retirement program, 696 employees left the Company. Additional work force reductions over the year brought that number to 964.

The increased emphasis on profit center and cost center management brought about further reductions in expenses. There emerged, in 1987, a heightened sense of responsibility; an individual sense that each Hancock employee mattered and could contribute. And those contributions would be felt and recognized immediately.

Responding to Our Customers' Needs

ServiceLine, initiated in 1986 on a test basis, was continued throughout 1987. ServiceLine puts John Hancock management personnel in direct contact with customers who call the home office for assistance. Your President and members of the Management Committee, as well as other senior managers, have spent time speaking directly to, and handling inquiries of, customers who call.

We have increased the tempo of management training at John Hancock. Since 1985, more than 1,300 managers from the home office and field organizations have attended a week long Management Training Program that stressed the responsibility of the individual to our customers and prospects. The second phase of this ongoing program is already under way. Called The Excellent Manager Program, it will continue to stress individual responsibility and responsiveness to the needs of our customers.

1987 Results

Assets under management increased more than 9 percent to nearly $46 billion in 1987. Earned Product and Service Income (PSI), a comparative measure of each product's value and contribution to growth, totaled $1.6 billion for the entire complex, of which our non-life subsidiaries accounted for $462 million.

The further development and implementation of the GAAP (Generally Accepted Accounting Principles) system took place throughout the Company. GAAP results have helped us compare ourselves to other diversified financial services companies, not just life insurance companies. Through this comparison, we are able to evaluate our strategies in the real world of financial services. It has helped us focus on the needs of our customers and the viability of the products and services we offer them. It has proven very valuable in restructuring the Company, as well as evaluating the products and services being delivered.

Hancock as a Corporate Citizen

Just as we must evaluate ourselves as a profitable provider of financial services to our customers, we grade John Hancock as a corporate citizen and member of our communities. We have continued to support the improved quality of the Boston public schools system through HEART (Hancock Endowment for Academics, Recreation and Teaching) with a self-perpetuating grant of $1 million. The youngsters of Boston and the surrounding communities have benefited from the running and fitness clinics established in conjunction with our sponsorship of the Boston Marathon. In all, John Hancock contributed $3 million to 1,500 community charities and services nationwide in 1987.

Because of our concern about the spread of AIDS, the Company has taken an active role in education about this fatal disease. Of these efforts, Larry Kessler, Executive Director of the AIDS Action Committee of Massachusetts, said, "I applaud John Hancock's leadership in the corporate community advocating education and support for persons with AIDS." Hancock has contributed to seven Boston health and human services organizations for their respective AIDS education programs; we cosponsor an annual 10-kilometer AIDS "Walk for Life" that raised $750,000 in 1987; conducted forums to help educate employees on AIDS prevention, many during the Company's observance of AIDS Employee Education Month; and held a community forum bringing teenagers together with experts who answer their questions.

Responding to the Real World

In 1987 we took major internal restructuring steps that brought your Company to a state of readiness to deal with the real world problems and opportunities in our marketplace. Not just for 1987 but for many years to come. We now have a new organization, a new line of customer responsive products coming into being, and a renewed sense of purpose. We are becoming a part of the real life of our customers by providing them with real answers through better products and services than ever before.

E. James Morton
Chairman of the Board and
Chief Executive Officer

Stephen L. Brown
President and
Chief Operations Officer

Consolidated Statement of Financial Position
John Hancock Mutual Life Insurance Company and Subsidiary

	Year ended December 31 (In millions)	**1987**	**1986**
Assets			
	Bonds	$ 9,365.8	$ 9,471.3
	Stocks:		
	Preferred or guaranteed	95.3	134.0
	Common	103.1	241.2
	Investments in affiliates	415.0	436.7
		613.4	811.9
	Mortgage loans on real estate	8,687.7	8,563.4
	Real estate:		
	Company occupied	193.6	193.6
	Investment properties	1,271.9	1,151.1
		1,465.5	1,344.7
	Policy loans and liens	2,256.1	2,301.4
	Cash items:		
	Cash in banks and offices	131.8	370.0
	Temporary cash investments	942.2	465.5
		1,074.0	835.5
	Premiums due and deferred	398.1	359.7
	Investment income due and accrued	458.9	483.0
	Other general account assets	955.1	796.7
	Assets held in separate accounts	2,936.3	2,840.8
	Total Assets	$28,210.9	$27,808.4

Obligations and Policyholders' Contingency Reserves

	Year ended December 31 (In millions)	1987	1986
Obligations			
	Policy reserves	$20,374.6	$19,863.9
	Policyholders' and beneficiaries' funds	2,323.8	2,232.0
	Dividends payable to policyholders	409.9	456.2
	Policy benefits in process of payment	201.8	171.1
	Other policy obligations	225.6	220.2
	Long-term debt—Note 3	103.3	180.4
	Mandatory securities and other asset valuation reserves	473.0	426.2
	Federal income and other accrued taxes—Note 2	.0	158.3
	Other general account obligations	177.1	274.6
	Obligations related to separate account business	2,911.0	2,820.4
	Total Obligations	27,200.1	26,803.3
Policyholders' Contingency Reserves			
	Special contingency reserve for group insurance	119.2	113.4
	General contingency reserve	891.6	891.7
	Total Contingency Reserves	1,010.8	1,005.1
	Total Obligations and Contingency Reserves	$28,210.9	$27,808.4

Certain 1986 amounts have been reclassified to permit comparison.
The accompanying notes are an integral part of the consolidated financial statements.

Consolidated Summary of Operations and Changes in Policyholders' Contingency Reserves
John Hancock Mutual Life Insurance Company and Subsidiary

Year ended December 31 (In millions)	1987	1986	1985
Income—Note 8			
Premiums, annuity considerations and pension fund contributions	$4,916.8	$4,571.1	$4,388.0
Investment income—Note 5	2,320.7	2,276.3	2,178.8
Separate account capital gains (losses)—Note 2	(117.2)	100.5	277.7
Other—net	(1.9)	(27.6)	(188.2)
	7,118.4	6,920.3	6,656.3
Benefits and Expenses—Note 8			
Payments to policyholders and beneficiaries:			
Death benefits	679.7	635.2	608.2
Accident and health benefits	453.8	402.5	427.3
Annuity benefits	692.6	580.3	480.6
Surrender benefits and annuity fund withdrawals	3,418.5	2,787.2	2,163.2
Matured endowments	21.2	23.4	20.7
	5,265.8	4,428.6	3,700.0
Additions to reserves to provide for future payments to policyholders and beneficiaries	738.4	1,253.2	1,688.5
Expenses of providing services to policyholders and obtaining new insurance:			
Field sales compensation and expenses	364.2	351.7	329.9
Home office and general expenses	319.0	352.9	311.4
State premium taxes	35.3	35.0	28.2
Payroll and miscellaneous taxes	34.1	34.7	32.1
	6,756.8	6,456.1	6,090.1
Gain before dividends to policyholders and federal income taxes	361.6	464.2	566.2
Dividends to policyholders	357.3	410.7	394.8
Federal income taxes (credits)	(135.9)	(63.9)	89.1
	221.4	346.8	483.9
Net Gain	140.2	117.4	82.3
Other increases (decreases) in policyholders' contingency reserves:			
Net capital losses and other adjustments—Note 6	(177.4)	(124.1)	(93.5)
Valuation reserve changes	(3.7)	.5	(3.1)
Prior years' federal taxes	(12.7)	63.2	(73.6)
Other reserves and adjustments—Note 4	59.3	(9.5)	1.0
Net Increase (Decrease) in Policyholders' Contingency Reserves	5.7	47.5	(86.9)
Policyholders' Contingency Reserves at Beginning of Year	1,005.1	957.6	1,044.5
Policyholders' Contingency Reserves at End of Year	$1,010.8	$1,005.1	$ 957.6

Certain 1986 and 1985 amounts have been reclassified to permit comparison.
The accompanying notes are an integral part of the consolidated financial statements.

Consolidated Statement of Changes in Financial Position
John Hancock Mutual Life Insurance Company and Subsidiary

Year ended December 31 (In millions)	1987	1986	1985
Additions			
From operations:			
Net gain	$ 140.2	$ 117.4	$ 82.3
Summary of operations items not affecting cash and temporary cash investments:			
Increase in aggregate reserves for all policies	503.3	1,399.9	1,542.6
Increase (decrease) in policyholders' and beneficiaries' funds and general liabilities	(34.3)	(336.9)	186.3
(Increase) decrease in premiums due and deferred and investment income due and accrued	(20.6)	34.9	48.3
Provision for depreciation	45.8	43.9	33.2
Accrual of discount and amortization of premium on bonds and mortgage loans—net	(39.1)	(45.7)	(47.0)
Total from Operations	595.3	1,213.5	1,845.7
Proceeds from issuance of long-term debt	.0	98.5	.0
Net carrying value of long-term investments upon disposal:			
Bonds	3,362.6	2,127.0	1,936.9
Stocks	392.0	248.4	293.0
Mortgage loans on real estate	934.2	778.3	590.5
Real estate	111.6	77.8	88.2
Policy loans and liens	359.0	325.4	316.5
	5,159.4	3,556.9	3,225.1
Net capital gains (losses) realized for general account upon disposal of long-term investments	(58.8)	78.8	(58.7)
	5,695.9	4,497.7	5,012.1
Deductions			
Acquisition of long-term investments:			
Bonds	3,192.2	2,126.7	2,584.5
Stocks	301.2	213.3	261.7
Mortgage loans on real estate	1,093.4	1,404.7	1,278.6
Real estate	244.8	279.8	256.4
Policy loans and liens	313.7	373.4	407.1
	5,145.3	4,397.9	4,788.3
Other—net:			
Increase in other assets	103.8	36.5	169.5
Increase in assets held in separate accounts	95.5	248.6	355.4
Repayment of commercial paper	75.0	.0	.0
Miscellaneous	37.8	80.4	22.4
	5,457.4	4,763.4	5,335.6
Increase (Decrease) in Cash and Temporary Cash Investments	238.5	184.3	(323.5)
Cash and temporary cash investments at beginning of year	835.5	651.2	974.7
Cash and Temporary Cash Investments at End of Year	$1,074.0	$ 835.5	$ 651.2

Certain 1986 and 1985 amounts have been reclassified to permit comparison.
The accompanying notes are an integral part of the consolidated financial statements.

Case 7

Circle K Corporation

Introduction

The convenience industry, ranging from established convenience stores, food and gas chains, to home cleaning, pest control, and lawn care, is making life a little easier. Ambitious entrepreneurs and major corporations are discovering that people are willing to buy time with good money.

As the proportion of two-income families in the United States approaches 50 percent, time has become a precious commodity for most people. In fact, what used to be a time crunch has become a time famine, and despite the diverse selection of products and services being offered by this industry, the real product may be personal time.

Demographic shifts and sharp rises in two-income families and households headed by singles are powerful factors that create the healthy growth in the convenience industry. Chase Econometrics predicts that by the 1990s more than 50 percent of all families will have dual incomes. Also by 1990, 31 percent of all families will earn more than $35,000 a year in inflation-adjusted dollars.

Most individuals, although insistent upon quality, are increasing the value they place on convenience. What is perhaps most telling about the swing to convenience is that the mature members of the industry aren't resting on their laurels; they're trying to make themselves even more convenient.

This case portrays neither the effective nor the ineffective handling of an administrative situation. Rather, it is to be used as the basis for classroom discussion.

The Convenience Store Industry

The convenience store industry is enthusiastic about its potential. Sales in 1988 topped $72 billion compared to under $19 billion a decade earlier. This industry was the sector of retailing with the best growth record in the 1980s, and analysts predicted the industry would double in size over a 15-year period beginning in the late 1980s, when about 505 million people shop in the nation's 80,000 convenience stores each day. An average 4,000-square-foot store churned out about $500,000 in annual revenue.

The traditional customer base has been blue-collar males from 18 to 34 years old. Fifty-seven percent of convenience store customers are male and 52 percent are under 35 years old. Many chains are making a concerted effort to appeal to women, a group that has not traditionally been a substantial part of their customer bases. To woo this customer, stores are adding more fast foods, including freshly prepared dishes, more health and beauty items, and better services. Also, convenience stores are beginning to give supermarkets and other fast food retailers a better run for their money. Convenience stores in the late 1980s accounted for 8 percent of total food dollars, up substantially from the 3.8 percent of ten years before.

By accepted definition, convenience stores are 1,200–4,000 square-foot retail outlets providing staple groceries, snacks, gasoline, and various other products and services. The industry was born 60 years ago, in Oak Cliff, Texas, when the Southland Ice Company began supplementing its ice business by selling bread, milk, and eggs.

Significant growth did not come until the late 1950s and early 1960s, however, when America began its move to the suburbs. At that time, convenience stores arose in response to four suburban phenomena: (1) the growth of the supermarket and the resultant inconvenience of shopping at increasingly larger stores; (2) the creation of suburban shopping centers along heavily traveled roads; (3) the decline of the "mom and pop" grocery store; (4) and the need to conserve personal time because of the increasing amount of time spent commuting to work.

Convenience stores developed first where populations were most mobile—in areas with mild climates. That is why today, most c-stores (as they are commonly called in the industry) are concentrated in the South and Southwest.

The convenience store industry is the seventh largest major retail sector in the United States. Total industry sales in the late 1980s amounted to 8 percent of all retail food, 5 percent of all fast food, and 20 percent of all gasoline being sold through over 70,000 convenience stores. Membership in the National Association of Convenience Stores is over 900.

Because of the maturity of the retail industry, there are fewer opportunities for unit store growth. Convenience store retailers are now driven to obtain earnings growth through gaining market share from regional convenience store chains, g-stores, and potential expansion of in-store gross margins through improvements in product mix. As market share growth is now the key factor in the convenience store industry, success will depend on improved sales per store, a well-conceived merchandise mix, and a broader demographic appeal.

C-store chains will likely in the future concentrate more on consolidating the industry. Three trends seem to reflect this shift in the industry. First, through more sophisticated product mixes the larger, more marketing-oriented chains will be more successful at promoting higher product lines. Marketing and advertising will assume a much more important role as the industry continues to improve its mix of merchandise. Second, a more mature competitive marketplace has forced tighter prices. Finally, the larger chains in an effort to sustain store growth have become more actively involved in acquisitions.

As convenience retailing becomes more product driven the larger, more merchandising-intensive chains will be able to gain market share from competitors. Market share will shift from small, less sophisticated operators to the major chains.

Because the barriers to entry are quite low, major oil companies have started to enter the business as they have seen their market share drastically reduced due to gasoline sales at c-stores. The other primary competitors of Circle K are: The Southland Corporation, National Convenience Stores, Convenient Food Mart Inc., Dairy Mart Convenience Stores, and Casey's General Stores.

Charismatic Leadership at Circle K

Karl Eller has turned Circle K into an exciting company that is aggressively expanding. He has extensive management experience from his tenure as a chief managerial officer at Columbia Pictures and Gannett Company and from building a small outdoor advertising company into a media conglomerate. He has the reputation of being tough, aggressive, and flamboyant.

His efforts have led to a fairly well-defined company mission and a dynamic, adaptive company. The company mission statement is provided in Exhibit 1.

Chairman Eller's letter to shareholders for 1988 is presented in Exhibit 2. He discusses the highly competitive marketplace Circle K operates in, the results of operations, and what to expect in the future.

Circle K, since Eller joined it as CEO in 1983, has significantly increased its marketing efforts. He brought a professionalism to the company in this area that it had previously lacked.

Exhibit 1 Circle K Corporate Mission Statement

Introduction
We believe our primary business is not so much retail as it is service oriented. Certainly, our customers buy merchandise in our stores. But they can buy similar items elsewhere, and perhaps pay lower prices.

But they're willing to buy from Circle K because we give them added value for their money. That added value is service and convenience.

Our Mission
As a service company, our mission is to: Satisfy our customers' immediate needs and wants by providing them with a wide variety of goods and services at multiple locations.

Our Customers
We will not place a limit on the conveniences we offer customers. They buy at Circle K much differently than at a supermarket. They come to our stores for specific purchases, which they make as quickly as possible. They want immediate service and are willing to pay a premium for it.

Our Stores
We will build our stores at locations most accessible to our customers. We will organize our merchandise to (1) facilitate quick purchases and (2) encourage other purchases. We will maintain our stores so they will always be brightly lit, colorful, clean, and comfortable places for our customers and our employees.

Our Goods and Services
We will not be one store—but a dozen stores in one.

We are a gas station, a fast-food restaurant, a grocery store, drugstore, liquor store, newsstand, video rental shop, small bank—and more. While other convenience stores may limit their selection to the most profitable items, we will maintain a competitive edge by providing our customers with as many different products and services as possible—even those items infrequently purchased.

Our People
We will educate the people who work in our stores to understand that our customers are most interested in quick, responsive service. We will emphasize to our people that courtesy and friendliness are imperative in building customer loyalty—and they will be instructed to greet customers as they enter our stores, thank them when they leave. Our sales people will be well-groomed at all times and assume responsibility for the cleanliness and appearance of their store.

Our Future
We are a giant distributing company. No other company possesses the operational capacity to deliver such a variety of goods and services to so many different and diverse locations.

We will endeavor to enlarge our customer base by understanding and anticipating their wants and needs.

Environmental and sociological influences continually alter shopping behaviors. As a result, next year's merchandise mix may be slightly different from this year's. And in ten years, it may be greatly different.

By responding quickly to changing consumer demands, we believe our growth to be virtually unlimited.

Source: Annual Report, Circle K Corporation, 1986, 4–5.

Company History

The Circle K Corporation is the second largest player, in terms of gross annual sales and number of stores, in the convenience store industry. Circle K's stores are in competition with local and national convenience food chains, local and national grocery and gasoline chains, supermarkets, drugstores, fast-food outlets, and other similar retail establishments. However, each unit competes only in the immediate surrounding neighborhood, and the ability of each unit to compete is largely dependent upon location, access, area population growth, and individual service.

The company operates 4,665 modern stores in 26 states. It also has licensed and joint venture operations in 12 foreign countries that amount to over 850 stores. At the end of fiscal 1988, Circle K had approximately 24,544 employees.

Exhibit 2 Letter to the Shareholders

Circle K is again pleased to report increases in both revenues and net earnings for fiscal year 1988. These results were achieved despite the highly competitive convenience store environment and the less than vigorous economies in some of our operating areas.

These increases were accomplished by maintaining our competitive edge through aggressive marketing, continued control of operating costs and a lower income tax rate.

Included in Circle K's net income is a non-recurring cumulative effect change in accounting principles of $5,500,000 or $.08 per share fully diluted. The effect of that change increased the Company's net earnings to $60,411,000 or $1.04 per share fully diluted.

For the year ended April 30, 1988, net earnings before the accounting change increased 11% to $54,911,000 compared to $49,430,000 last year. Our fully diluted earnings per share were $.96 versus $.85 last year, up 13%, and revenues for the year were $2,656,722,000, 15% better than the $2,316,784,000 of the previous year.

Our fourth quarter net earnings were $14,018,000 compared to $10,721,000 last year. Fully diluted earnings per share for the quarter increased 37% to $.26 versus $.19 the year before. Revenues for the fourth quarter were $669,318,000, an increase of 11% over revenues of $603,843,000 in the comparable quarter last year.

Gasoline sales are an integral part of Circle K's operations. During fiscal 1988 we sold more than a billion gallons of gasoline. Gas revenues of $964,602,000 represented 36% of our total revenues for the year. Not only do gasoline operations provide profits on their sales, but they also attract additional customers into our stores enabling us to increase merchandise sales.

We continue to test not only new food items which we produce in our Phoenix commissary, but also items from vendors which show promise. For example, the Dunkin' Donut™ program, tested last year, is a great success and is being expanded as rapidly as possible. Other branded programs such as tea and coffee, soft ice creams and juice items are creating favorable reactions from consumers.

We engaged in promotional campaigns in cooperation with vendors including the successful Hulk Hogan promotion in the summer of 1987 and the "Crocodile" Dundee™ II Thirstbuster™ advertising program in the summer of 1988.

We aggressively promote sales of state-run lottery game tickets. A new lottery was added in Florida in January of 1988 and with more than 800 stores in Florida, lottery ticket sales became a significant revenue producer.

We continue to upgrade the appearance and functionality of our stores. During fiscal 1988 we remodeled 490 stores and built 252 new stores. Of those, 44 were moved to major intersections replacing mid-block or secondary locations. We believe that a clean, modern and highly visible store is one of our most effective marketing tools as we continue to make a strong effort to attract the new, upscale customer.

The most financially threatening problem your Company has faced during the past five years was resolved on April 25, 1988 in a U.S. District Court in San Diego when a jury exonerated Circle K and other defendants of any blame or liability in what became known as "the Nucorp litigation," a lawsuit which was filed in 1983.

Circle K management had contended from the beginning that the lawsuit was without merit and completely unwarranted. Naturally, we are pleased with the jury's verdict, that the Company was exonerated and not assessed any damages. In July 1988 a motion by attorneys for the plaintiffs for a new trial against Circle K was denied. While the plaintiffs' time to file an appeal has not yet expired, we believe there is no basis for a successful appeal.

On April 5, 1988 we completed the acquisition of 473 7-Eleven stores, most of which were in the southeastern United States. The acquisition moved us into our 26th state, South Carolina, and significantly increased our presence in Louisiana, Georgia, Tennessee and North Carolina. It also added more stores to our operations in Texas, Alabama and Florida.

In May we signed a definitive agreement to acquire the 538 stores and the gasoline marketing operation of The Charter Company. That acquisition is expected to be completed in early October. While the majority of Charter's stores are in the southeast, the acquisition also provides us with more than 100 stores in the economically attractive New England area.

Our International operation continues to expand. In October 1987, we created a joint venture with Rupert Murdoch's News Corporation, PLC. Circle K sold 50% of its then wholly-owned United Kingdom subsidiary to News Corporation and signed a licensing agreement with the new joint venture for further expansion in Europe and Scandinavia. In January 1988, the UK joint venture acquired 45 stores in the Greater London area to bring the number of stores in the United Kingdom to 177 at year end.

Exhibit 2 *(continued)*

In the wake of the October 19 stock market crash, Circle K purchased 771,800 shares of its common stock in the open market. In early November we offered shareholders the opportunity to exchange common shares, at $12 per share, for a new issue 13% Junior Subordinated Debenture due 1997. The exchange was completed in December 1987 with approximately 6,000,000 shares tendered and accepted.

We continued to develop stronger division, district, zone and store managers, promoting from within where qualified personnel were available, retaining good management personnel from acquired companies and by hiring experienced field management from the industry. On December 28, Larry Zine, Vice President of Financial Reporting, became Senior Vice President and Chief Financial Officer of the Corporation, replacing Bill J. Farmer who resigned to pursue personal business interests.

Many positive things were accomplished during the year just ended. Consequently, we're optimistic about the Company's prospects for the future and we enter the new fiscal year with renewed dedication to the continued improvement of the Company's operating results and the enhancement of your investment.

Karl Eller, Chairman of the Board
Robert M. Reade, President

Source: Annual Report, Circle K Corporation, 1988, 2–3.

Despite its retail emphasis, Circle K's primary business is providing service. The mission of Circle K is to satisfy customer's immediate needs and wants by providing them with a wide variety of goods and services at multiple locations. This mission is accomplished by building stores in locations that are most accessible to customers; by organizing merchandise so as to facilitate quick purchases and encourage other purchases; and by maintaining stores that are brightly lit, colorful, clean, and comfortable. Circle K is determined not to be only one store—but a gas station, fast-food restaurant, grocery, drugstore, liquor store, newsstand, video rental shop, small bank, and more.

The company was started in 1951 in El Paso, Texas, when Fred Hervey purchased three small neighborhood markets called Kay's Drive-In Grocery Stores. He took the K from Kay's Drive-In and enclosed it in a circle, forming an old-fashioned cattle brand as the symbol of the company. The company is incorporated in Texas as the Circle K Corporation. In the 1960s and 1970s Circle K began a rapid expansion program throughout Arizona, New Mexico, California, Colorado, Idaho, Montana, and Oregon. In 1979 the company entered into a licensing agreement with UNY Co., LTD of Nagoya, Japan, giving UNY exclusive rights to operate and franchise Circle K stores in Japan. In September 1980, Circle K acquired approximately 13.2 percent of Nucorp Energy Inc. for $23.5 million cash and entered into an agreement with Nucorp to participate in oil and gas exploration and development activities. In July 1982, Nucorp experienced financial difficulties and filed for relief under Chapter 11 of the federal bankruptcy code. Circle K in January 1983 sold its Nucorp stock, which resulted in a $3.7 million loss for financial reporting purposes and a $27.8 million tax-purpose loss, representing one of the biggest blunders in the company's history.

In July 1983, Fred Hervey announced his retirement as chairman of the board and appointed Karl Eller as the new chief executive officer and board chairman. Eller was formerly the president of Columbia Pictures Communications and was an entrepreneur who built up Combined Communications and sold it to Gannett for $367 million.

Continuing its expansion in December 1983, Circle K purchased UtoteM Inc. and its 960 stores. That expanded Circle K into an additional seven southern states. Then, in October

1984, the company acquired 435 Little General Stores from General Host Corporation. That acquisition pushed Circle K into an additional four states, giving the company operating stores in 25 states throughout the Midwest, West, and the Sunbelt. In December 1984 Circle K penetrated the northern California area by acquiring 21 Day-N-Nite convenience stores. In July 1985 Circle K purchased 446 Shop & Go Inc. stores for $167 million, and 186 stores were purchased for $51.8 million in March 1986 from National Convenience Stores Incorporated. In early 1988 the firm completed its acquisition of 473 7-Eleven stores, 90 closed stores, convenience store sites, stores under construction, and other related assets for $147.5 million plus the assumptions of capital leases and inventories at cost. Circle K was also negotiating with Charter Company to acquire 538 stores, 100 of which are in the New England area. This deal was valued at over $120 million dollars, $70 million of it in cash alone.

In addition to its aggressive acquisition program, Circle K has engaged in an active new-store construction program. The company is on the leading edge of the store location upgrade that is taking place throughout the industry. More than half of the traditional service stations that were operating in the United States in 1976 have closed. Virtually all of those stations were on prime corners. Circle K is aggressively seeking those prime locations. New locations are selected on the basis of high traffic volumes and, where possible, have a minimum of 12 gasoline hoses and full canopy coverage. In fiscal 1988 the company spent $269 million on land, buildings, and equipment.

Numerous new store locations were in various stages of development in 1988, all within the states in which the company operated. Construction time takes approximately 120 days, although the time may be longer in some cases due to adverse weather conditions, zoning, environmental requirements, or other factors. New stores opened in fiscal 1988 totaled 252.

Circle K limits its investment in land and buildings in the belief that its capital may be more profitably utilized in store operations. Typically, the company will acquire the real estate, erect the building, and enter into a sale and leaseback agreement with the purchaser. Most of the leases provide for the payment of a fixed rental, or a percentage of gross sales in excess of the fixed rental, real estate taxes, and insurance premiums. Store leases usually have initial terms of from 7 to 25 years. Circle K has to provide for payment of real-estate taxes, repairs, maintenance, and insurance in most cases. Circle K has the right to renew almost all its leases for additional periods. In fiscal 1988, Circle K paid aggregate store rentals of $68.885 million. This is an increase of more than $30 million from 1986. Future minimum rental commitments were expected to total close to $85 million a year from 1989 through 1993.

A summary of the results of ten years of operations, consolidated balance sheets for 1988 and 1987, and a statement of cash flows are presented in Tables 1a, 1b, and 1c.

Foreign Operations

Since 1979, Circle K has made great strides in foreign operations. It provides consultation on location, design, merchandising, employee training, and management of convenience stores in Japan. Circle K Japan operates approximately 675 stores that have the same identity as Circle K in the United States.

Besides its operations in Japan, in January 1985 Circle K entered into a joint venture with UNY and Li & Fung Ltd. of Hong Kong for the purpose of opening Circle K stores in other areas of the Far East. By the late 1980s Circle K has 50 stores in operation in Hong Kong, 10 in Indonesia, 5 in Taiwan, and 5 in Australia. Also in 1985 the company entered into a joint venture and licensing agreement with Imperial Brewing and Leisure Ltd. In July 1986, Circle K purchased the interest of Imperial and opened three stores in London. The company opened approximately 100 stores in England in fiscal 1987. In addition, it purchased 84 Sperrings convenience stores in the greater London area for approximately $30 million. Circle K (U.K.) was sold to News Corporation Limited owned by billionaire Rupert Murdoch. A 50/50 joint venture between the two firms was launched. The venture was granted licensed expansion rights to Norway, Sweden, Denmark, Finland, Holland, Belgium, France, West Germany, Spain, and Italy.

Earlier in May 1986, Circle K entered into a licensing agreement with Shell Canada Products Ltd. covering the operation of Circle K convenience stores at selected Shell locations in Canada. In less than three years, 75 stores were operating in Canada.

Facilities and Vertical Integration

Phoenix, Arizona, is the international headquarters for the Circle K Corporation. In 1985, the company moved into its new 43,000-square-foot office building at Seventh Street and McDowell. Also in Phoenix is the 58,000-square-foot administrative office building located at 40th Street and Broadway. The company owns and leases approximately 80 other administrative offices located in various states throughout its operating areas.

Other than the brief encounter with Nucorp Energy, Circle K has made tremendous strides toward becoming vertically integrated. The company is involved in the manufacture and distribution of many products including sandwiches, burritos, ice, soda pop, and various other flavored beverages. In 1983 Circle K opened an 18,500-square-foot commissary in Phoenix, which produces more than 180,000 sandwiches a day. The commissary supplies all of its stores with its Deli-Fresh line of ready-to-eat sandwiches and supplies the Deli-Pride line of sandwiches to supermarkets, military installations, and other convenience stores. Suppliers of the Deli-Fresh line include Oscar Mayer, Louis Rich, Hormel, Kraft, Durkee, and others. The commissary utilizes a flash-freeze process to manufacture and distribute the sandwiches for the Phoenix market. More than 30 varieties of self-serve, ready-to-eat sandwiches and Mexican food products are available in Circle K stores throughout the country. New items introduced in 1986 included a french bread pizza, a steak fajita burrito, and a turkey and swiss cheese sandwich. Besides sandwiches, Circle K distributes through its commissary: cookies and cakes, nuts, some brands of candy, pie slices, and various other snack items.

Circle K operates a 72,000-square-foot beverage plant in Phoenix. Within the past few years, the company's Polar Beverage division moved into contract packaging and expanded into the noncarbonated-drink market with private label citrus punches, fruit drinks, mixers, bottled water, and Hi Spark'l soft drinks. The company's Polar Beverage bottling plant produces more than 1.5 million cases of soft drinks and natural juice products.

In addition to its commissary and beverage plant, Circle K has operated a 50,000-square-foot ice plant in Phoenix for the production and distribution of its Sparkle Ice. The plant is capable of producing 640,000 pounds of ice per day. Other warehouses, distribution centers, and ice plants are located in Tucson, Albuquerque, Tampa, Hearne, Port Neches, and Houston.

Circle K also owned and operated two outdoor advertising companies: The Bauman Company in El Paso, Texas, and Idaho Outdoor Advertising Inc., headquartered in Boise, Idaho. Apparently this sideline did not fit into the corporate scheme of vertical integration and was sold in late 1986. However, Circle K does have plans to lease billboard space above its stores where local zoning permits.

In a shift of corporate strategy that had some analysts thinking that the company was on the market to be purchased, Circle K decided to divest nonstore assets such as its ice plant, bottling plant, and food commissary. In August 1988 the company sold its commissary for an after-tax

Table 1a Summary of Operations

SUMMARY OF OPERATIONS

The Circle K Corporation and Subsidiaries

	1988	1987	1986	1985
Sales	$2,613,843,000	$2,289,444,000	$2,111,267,000	$1,682,164,000
Other income and (expense)	42,879,000	27,340,000	20,249,000	14,164,000
Gross revenues	2,656,722,000	2,316,784,000	2,131,516,000	1,696,328,000
Cost of sales	1,893,058,000	1,649,496,000	1,551,538,000	1,252,684,000
Operating and administrative expenses	627,553,000	537,374,000	467,079,000	362,315,000
Interest and debt	56,608,000	41,566,000	36,560,000	21,772,000
Total cost of sales and operating expenses	2,577,219,000	2,228,436,000	2,055,177,000	1,636,771,000
Operating profit	79,503,000	88,348,000	76,339,000	59,557,000
Income (loss) Nucorp Energy, Inc.	—	—	—	—
Gain on sale of assets	8,198,000	5,948,000	—	—
Special litigation	—	—	(6,736,000)	—
Earnings before income taxes	87,701,000	94,296,000	69,603,000	59,557,000
Federal and state income taxes				
Current	7,696,000	35,473,000	18,926,000	18,648,000
Deferred	25,094,000	9,393,000	11,455,000	7,236,000
Estimated taxes	32,790,000	44,866,000	30,381,000	25,884,000
Net earnings before cumulative effect of accounting change	54,911,000	49,430,000	39,222,000	33,673,000
Cumulative effect on prior years of change in accounting for deferred taxes	5,500,000	—	—	—
	$ 60,411,000	$ 49,430,000	$ 39,222,000	$ 33,673,000
Earnings per common share before cumulative effect of accounting change				
Primary	$1.04	$0.93	$0.85	$0.82
Fully diluted	$0.96	$0.85	$0.74	$0.71
Earnings per common share				
Primary	$1.15	$0.93	$0.85	$0.82
Fully diluted	$1.04	$0.85	$0.74	$0.71
Cash dividends per common share	$0.28	$0.28	$0.25	$.245
Primary Shares	49,322,062	49,184,843	41,376,454	36,291,826
Fully dilutive shares	70,036,337	69,402,798	64,852,198	53,287,312

All share and per share information included herein reflects the two-for-one stock split on September 15, 1986 and the three-for-two stock split on October 15, 1985. In fiscal 1987, the Company changed from the LIFO method to the FIFO method of inventory valuation. Information contained herein has been restated to give effect to the change.

ADDITIONAL STATISTICS

	1988	1987	1986	1985
Stores opened and acquired	825	284	798	517
Stores closed	255	149	95	33
Net store increase during year	570	135	703	484
Stores at end of year	4,077	3,507	3,372	2,669
Total assets	$1,535,784,000	$1,136,500,000	$ 855,798,000	$ 583,843,000
Current assets	$ 379,513,000	$ 358,869,000	$ 277,123,000	$ 180,014,000
Current liabilities	$ 280,607,000	$ 169,449,000	$ 187,875,000	$ 115,200,000
Working capital	$ 98,906,000	$ 189,420,000	$ 89,248,000	$ 64,814,000
Current ratio	1.35	2.12	1.48	1.56
Net property and equipment	$ 708,314,000	$ 451,845,000	$ 345,715,000	$ 252,512,000
Long-term debt	$ 844,065,000	$ 536,616,000	$ 382,936,000	$ 269,416,000
Redeemable preferred stock	$ 47,500,000	$ 47,500,000	$ 50,000,000	$ 50,000,000
Stockholders' Equity	$ 283,521,000	$ 310,013,000	$ 200,102,000	$ 124,833,000
Book value per common share	$ 6.56	$ 6.23	$ 4.66	$ 3.44
Number of employees	24,544	20,983	19,342	16,657

Table 1a *(continued)*

1984	1983	1982	1981	1980	1979
$1,028,853,000	$747,844,000	$726,793,000	$644,457,000	$533,103,000	$438,559,000
6,299,000	5,885,000	9,021,000	3,402,000	3,308,000	2,633,000
1,035,152,000	753,729,000	735,814,000	647,859,000	536,411,000	441,192,000
783,148,000	573,099,000	556,840,000	484,250,000	385,109,000	320,647,000
205,946,000	149,732,000	141,331,000	126,673,000	115,340,000	96,949,000
7,949,000	5,644,000	7,528,000	6,757,000	4,259,000	3,968,000
997,043,000	728,475,000	705,699,000	617,680,000	504,708,000	421,564,000
38,109,000	25,254,000	30,115,000	30,179,000	31,703,000	19,628,000
—	(3,675,000)	(31,862,000)	567,000	—	—
—	—	—	—	—	—
—	—	—	—	—	—
38,109,000	21,579,000	(1,747,000)	30,746,000	31,703,000	19,628,000
12,800,000	(1,576,000)	10,673,000	12,847,000	14,642,000	8,978,000
4,873,000	7,399,000	2,425,000	1,367,000	113,000	(28,000)
17,673,000	5,823,000	13,098,000	14,214,000	14,755,000	8,950,000
20,436,000	15,756,000	(14,845,000)	16,532,000	16,948,000	10,678,000
—	—	—	—	—	—
$ 20,436,000	$ 15,756,000	$(14,845,000)	$ 16,532,000	$ 16,948,000	$ 10,678,000
$0.56	$0.47	($0.48)	$0.56	$0.58	$0.37
$0.54	$0.46	($0.48)	$0.54	$0.56	$0.35
$0.56	$0.47	($0.48)	$0.56	$0.58	$0.37
$0.54	$0.46	($0.48)	$0.54	$0.56	$0.35
$.245	$.245	$0.24	$.225	$.195	$.165
33,896,058	33,319,582	30,946,684	29,556,228	29,363,574	29,174,070
41,031,216	34,673,874	32,293,716	30,907,360	30,907,062	30,913,446
995	20	25	22	64	77
31	10	8	28	22	24
964	10	17	(6)	42	53
2,185	1,221	1,211	1,194	1,200	1,158
$ 415,778,000	$180,584,000	$168,142,000	$190,315,000	$151,882,000	$138,727,000
$ 123,250,000	$ 80,160,000	$ 70,680,000	$ 72,543,000	$ 62,858,000	$ 53,622,000
$ 99,637,000	$ 54,280,000	$ 42,478,000	$ 50,764,000	$ 42,813,000	$ 42,273,000
$ 23,613,000	$ 25,880,000	$ 28,202,000	$ 21,779,000	$ 20,045,000	$ 11,349,000
1.24	1.48	1.66	1.43	1.47	1.27
$ 189,388,000	$ 91,560,000	$ 86,817,000	$ 82,798,000	$ 78,597,000	$ 74,859,000
$ 157,007,000	$ 40,548,000	$ 55,615,000	$ 63,675,000	$ 45,789,000	$ 45,215,000
$ 50,000,000	$ —	$ —	$ —	$ —	$ —
$ 93,535,000	$ 71,668,000	$ 63,950,000	$ 72,528,000	$ 62,688,000	$ 50,817,000
$ 2.69	$ 2.15	$ 1.92	$ 2.45	$ 2.12	$ 1.74
12,461	6,714	6,518	6,244	6,545	6,049

Source: Annual Report, Circle K Corporation, 1988, 15–16.

Table 1b Consolidated Balance Sheets

CONSOLIDATED BALANCE SHEETS
The Circle K Corporation and Subsidiaries

April 30:	1988	1987
ASSETS	*(in thousands)*	
Current Assets:		
Cash and short-term investments (Note 14)	$ 44,216	$ 24,785
Receivables	34,446	25,666
Inventories (Notes 1 and 3)	191,000	160,150
Properties held for sale (Note 1)	80,000	140,875
Federal income tax receivable (Note 9)	26,139	1,246
Prepaid expenses	3,712	6,147
Total current assets	379,513	358,869
Property, Plant and Equipment		
(Notes 1, 2, 4 and 8)	902,500	600,348
Less—Accumulated depreciation and amortization	194,186	148,504
Net property, plant and equipment	708,314	451,844
Deferred Interest Promissory Notes Due From Affiliate (Note 14)	35,289	31,616
Long-Term Receivables (Note 1)	65,193	15,043
Intangibles, net (Notes 1, 2 and 5)	247,092	235,235
Other Assets (Note 2)	100,383	43,893
	$1,535,784	$1,136,500

The accompanying notes are an integral part of these consolidated financial statements.

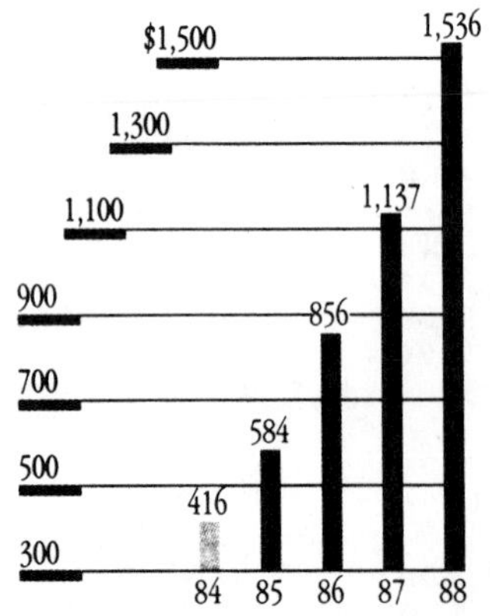

WORKING CAPITAL
CIRCLE K CORPORATION
(IN MILLIONS)

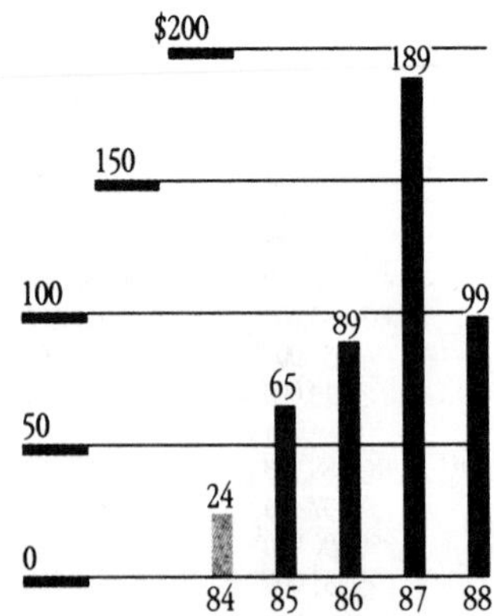

Table 1b (continued)

April 30:	1988	1987
LIABILITIES AND STOCKHOLDERS' EQUITY	*(in thousands)*	
Current Liabilities:		
Due to banks (Note 6)	$ 60,000	$ 10,000
Accounts payable	112,144	84,564
Other current liabilities (Note 7)	108,463	74,885
Total current liabilities	280,607	169,449
Long-Term Debt (Notes 2 and 6)	844,065	536,616
Deferred Income Taxes (Note 9)	38,133	40,381
Other Liabilities and Deferred Revenue (Note 8)	41,958	32,541
Commitments and Contingent Liabilities (Notes 8, 15 and 16)		
Mandatory Redeemable Preferred Stock, at redemption value (Notes 10 and 11)	47,500	47,500
Stockholders' Equity (Notes 2, 6, 10, 11 and 13):		
Common stock, $1 par value	50,003	49,750
Additional paid-in capital	165,040	163,182
Common stock warrants	2,300	2,300
Retained earnings	138,563	94,967
Equity adjustment from foreign currency translation	5,449	—
Less—Treasury stock at cost	(77,834)	(186)
Total stockholders' equity	283,521	310,013
	$1,535,784	$1,136,500

The accompanying notes are an integral part of these consolidated financial statements.

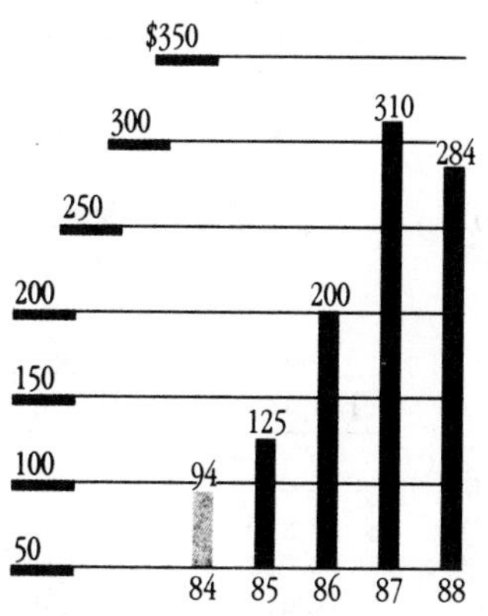

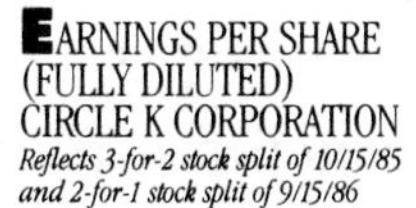

EARNINGS PER SHARE
(FULLY DILUTED)
CIRCLE K CORPORATION
Reflects 3-for-2 stock split of 10/15/85
and 2-for-1 stock split of 9/15/86

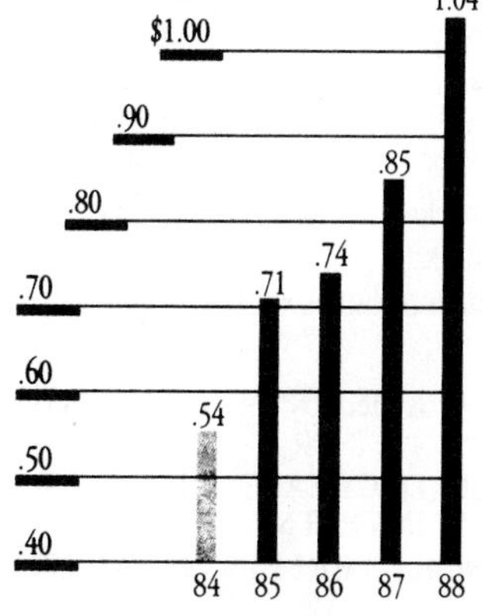

Source: Annual Report, Circle K Corporation, 1988, 18–19.

Table 1c Consolidated Statements of Cash Flows for Year Ended April 30

	1988	1987	1986
		(in thousands)	
CASH FLOWS FROM OPERATING ACTIVITIES:			
Net earnings	$ 60,411	$ 49,430	$ 39,222
Adjustments to reconcile net earnings to net cash—			
Depreciation and amortization	65,659	51,680	40,846
Provision for deferred income taxes	25,094	9,393	11,455
Deferred revenue	(7,720)	(3,418)	(2,787)
Cumulative effect on prior years of change in accounting for income taxes	(5,500)	—	—
Gain on sale of assets	(8,198)	(5,948)	—
Current payments of Federal and State Income Taxes	(28,439)	(38,358)	(43,997)
Increase in receivables	(8,780)	(13,185)	(1,352)
Increase in inventories	(30,850)	(24,396)	(24,595)
Increase in accounts payable	27,580	7,423	16,089
(Increase) decrease in other current assets and liabilities, net	(8,122)	39,468	29,189
Net cash provided by operating activities	81,135	72,089	64,070
CASH FLOWS FROM INVESTING ACTIVITIES:			
Acquisitions			
Property, plant and equipment	(121,203)	(40,184)	(154,921)
Intangibles and other assets	(26,297)	(39,725)	(63,679)
Cash used for acquisitions	(147,500)	(79,909)	(218,600)
Purchases of property, plant and equipment	(233,087)	(144,570)	(66,443)
Additions to properties held for sale	(35,852)	(119,546)	(84,343)
Proceeds from sale of property, plant and equipment	101,406	119,837	125,657
Increase in long-term receivable	(10,000)	—	—
Proceeds from sale of 50% interest subsidiary	23,399	—	—
Other	(10,527)	(10,468)	(1,729)
Net cash used by investing activities	(312,161)	(234,656)	(245,458)
CASH FLOWS FROM FINANCING ACTIVITIES:			
Increase (decrease) in due to banks, net	50,000	(42,000)	52,000
Proceeds from long-term debt	280,969	478,768	443,991
Repayments of long-term debt	(50,741)	(249,850)	(298,072)
Proceeds from exercise of warrants and options	2,045	1,781	1,591
Dividends—			
Common stock	(13,015)	(12,959)	(9,876)
Preferred stock	(3,800)	(3,950)	(4,000)
Treasury stock purchases	(8,658)	—	—
Other	(6,343)	(4,349)	(6,605)
Net cash provided by financing activities	250,457	167,441	179,029
NET INCREASE (DECREASE) IN CASH AND SHORT-TERM INVESTMENTS	$ 19,431	$ 4,874	$ (2,359)
CASH AND SHORT-TERM INVESTMENTS, BEGINNING OF YEAR	24,785	19,911	22,270
CASH AND SHORT-TERM INVESTMENTS, END OF YEAR	44,216	24,785	19,911

Source: Annual Report, Circle K Corporation, 1988, 22.

gain of $14.4 million and in October 1988 sold its ice plant for an after-tax gain of $6.4 million.

Company officials have hired the investment banking firm of Wasserstein Peralla to assist management in developing and implementing strategies to enhance shareholder return on investment. According to CEO Eller this could include expansion domestically or internationally, financial restructuring, mergers, or other alternatives that will serve shareholder interest.

Product Mix

In terms of its product mix, Circle K operates on the premise that providing customer convenience is the key to success. Today a typical Circle K store, within its 2,600-square-foot-area, offers more than 3,200 consumer items including nationally advertised brand items, such as health and beauty aids, tobacco products, soft drinks, fast foods, groceries, and where permitted, liquor. Out of Circle K's product mix, 68 percent of total sales in 1988 were generated by the consumption of gas (36 percent), alcoholic beverages (16 percent), and tobacco products (17 percent). In-store items represented 64 percent of the company's total sales during fiscal 1988.

Circle K believes that there are two main product categories for the future: gasoline and fast food.

Convenience stores were the unintentional winners following the OPEC gas shortages of the 1970s because they bought out thousands of full-service station lots on prime corners, increased the number of hoses, and added all kinds of other merchandise. Convenience stores now sell one out of every five gallons of gas. Gasoline sales accounted for 36 percent of total sales for Circle K in fiscal 1988 ($964 million) while total sales increased to $1.65 billion. Pure gasoline sales represent low-margin business (between 6½ to 8 cents per gallon). Yet industry analysts show that 40 percent of the gas customers buy something else at the store (usually a higher gross-profit item), which dramatically changes the economics of the individual sale of gasoline.

Currently, Circle K sells gas at 74 percent of its locations. The company purchases gasoline from several major and independent refiners. Arrangements are also in place to purchase exchange barrels when the economics of the spot market prevail.

Because of the 40 to 70 percent profit margins, fast food has become a desirable product mix in the convenience store industry. Circle K's fast-food program is recognized by analysts as the best in the convenience store industry. Sales of fast foods were second only to gasoline in 1988 store merchandise. In-store fountain service has also been dramatically upgraded. The Thirstbuster accounts for 25 percent of the total fountain drink volume. Circle K has added Lipton iced tea as its exclusive fountain tea drink and the "slush puppie" as its fountain slush drink. Maxwell House and Folger's replaced the generic coffee previously sold in Circle K stores.

Circle K's agreement to market the sale of branded doughnuts, including Winchell's and Dunkin' Donuts has been very successful. Under the agreement, Circle K stores will display the doughnuts in cases bearing their brand names and the cases will be serviced two to three times a day.

To compete directly with the fast-food chains, Circle K is test marketing a drive-through-only hamburger operation with Hooker's Hamburgers. The franchisee, Hooker's, puts up the capital, paying Circle K rent plus a royalty of 3 percent of revenues. There have also been negotiations with McDonald's on the feasibility of opening a restaurant/convenience store complex on a joint site.

In addition to the major product mixes already described, Circle K has expanded its services with videocassette and quick-cash debit card programs. In February 1986, Circle K signed five-year agreements with two videocassette suppliers—Stars to Go and Consolidated Video Systems—to implement their "Quick Flick" videocassette program. The suppliers provide each store with a library of 200 different titles (20 percent of which change monthly) and a display case with a built-in video monitor. Circle K pays the suppliers a minimum of $700 a month per store and gets 30 percent of the rental revenue. On cassettes alone, the average Circle K store nets a little over $1,000 a month. Research shows that 55 percent of the movie renters are new customers, and 45 percent are women, which could help change the traditional customer base for the industry. Also, as Karl Eller has pointed out, customers are drawn into the store twice. Customers are spending about $8 (excluding the rental) on the first visit and $3 on the second. According to the National Association of Convenience stores, that figure is much higher than the average purchase of about $2.

Circle K's quick-cash debit card program, introduced in 1984, enables check guarantee cardholders to make purchases and/or obtain up to $40 in cash at participating Circle K stores without writing a check. Also, the company has introduced automatic teller machines into some test market stores. Future considerations for additional product offerings include airline ticket dispensers and dry-cleaning facilities. Circle K derives additional revenue from electronic video games in the stores and the sales of money orders and lottery tickets.

Circle K Corporation has a large number of products within its overall product mix; however, certain products account for a significant proportion of total corporate sales. Those product groupings, followed by estimates of the total portion of sales they contribute, are briefly discussed in the following paragraphs.

Gasoline (36 percent of total sales). Consumption is expected to moderately increase as the population increases. However, per capita usage is expected to decrease somewhat in the upcoming years. The majority of Circle K stores sell gasoline (approximately 74 percent of all stores).

Tobacco (17 percent of total sales). Overall tobacco consumption is expected to gradually decline in the coming years. Tobacco products are sold at all store locations, subject to local zoning restrictions and guidelines.

Alcohol (16 percent of total sales). Overall alcohol consumption is expected to see some decrease in the coming years. Some local governments are beginning to pass restrictions concerning the common-site sale of gasoline and alcohol. Circle K sells alcohol at stores where local ordinances allow its sale.

Groceries (15 percent of total sales). This category contains a large number of separate items, for example, milk and produce. Any one item does not represent a significant portion of total sales. Expected growth is minimal.

Fast Foods (9 percent of total sales). This category includes fountain drinks and deli items. The company is planning to expand its participation in this portion of its business because forecasts indicate significant growth opportunities in this area.

Health and Beauty Aids (HBA) (3 percent of total sales). This category contains a large number of separate items, none of which represents a significant portion of total sales. Expected growth is minimal.

Videos (1 percent of total sales). Even though this represents a relatively small portion of overall revenue, videos do much to increase walk-in traffic and increase sales of all other products in the company's product mix. The expected growth in the video rental business is substantial, and Circle K has aggressively installed video rental programs in many of its stores. The implementation is expected to be systemwide.

Convenience Services (less than 1 percent of total sales). Again, this represents a very small portion of overall revenue, but the walk-in traffic that is generated results in increased sales in other product areas. To date, Circle K has done little in the area of convenience services. The sale of lottery tickets and featuring ATMs and debit cards have been about the extent of services that have been offered; however, the company is testing the selling of airline tickets and dry-cleaning services in some of its stores.

Case 8

The Lodging Industry

Total receipts for the lodging industry approximated $29.4 billion in 1983. This represented a 6-percent increase over the 1982 figures. For 1984 the industry was expected to top $31 billion.

What the Industry Does

In very basic terms the lodging industry takes care of travelers' (housing) needs while they are away from home. However in today's society the needs of travelers are very different from those of 1794 when the City Hotel opened in New York City. The City Hotel was proported to have been the first building constructed in the United States specifically for hotel purposes.

Today's travelers are often business travelers who typically occupy more than 60 percent of all lodging rooms, with the remaining 40 percent split almost equally between personal and convention travelers. Business travelers' needs include the basic lodging room plus meal services and communication facilities. However additional needs related to meeting rooms, special stenographic, material-duplicating, and special communication needs, as well as recreational and entertainment, are also frequently desired.

This case portrays neither the effective nor the ineffective handling of an administrative situation. Rather, it is to be used as the basis for classroom discussion.
Source: The Lodging Industry from *Strategic Management and Organizational Policy*, Third Edition, by James M. Higgins and Julian W. Vincze, pp. 610–614, copyright © 1986 by The Dryden Press, a division of Holt, Rinehart and Winston, Inc., reprinted by permission of the publisher.

The convention travelers' needs also include the basics of lodging room, meal services, and basic communication facilities. However the obvious additional needs relate to standard convention activities such as meeting rooms (both small and large), exhibit halls, and banquet rooms. But additional expectations may also include appropriate social gathering facilities as well as significant leisure and recreational amenities.

The personal travelers' needs are often more basic and relate to lodging rooms and meal services, unless the location is a destination resort. However destination resorts are expected by the personal traveler to provide extensive leisure and recreational facilities as well as socializing facilities. Personal travel has grown steadily in recent years. Several factors which have encouraged this growth in personal travel include rising disposable personal income, stable gasoline prices, expanded leisure time, and increasing numbers of single-person households. In addition the deregulation of the airline industry, with the resultant fare-reduction situations and the establishing of no-frills regional carriers, have also increased personal travel.

Personal travel is generally viewed as being quickly affected by changes in the economy whereas business travel more typically follows the turns in the economy by three to six months.

Food and beverage sales account for approximately one-third of total lodging revenues. Gross profits are usually about 20 percent, which is substantially narrower than those on room rentals, and although food and beverage sales per room have risen over the last ten years, this rise has been at a slower pace than room rates.

Innovation in the Industry

Instead of travel to the same location, business people may now hold conferences in different cities using satellite communication. Because an estimated 40 percent of hotel revenues come from corporate business meetings, many hotels originally feared this development. Recently, however, more than one-eighth of the nation's largest hotels have been linked to a teleconferencing system. These hotels are expecting teleconferences to attract new customers and to increase the bar, catering, and meeting room revenues, although it may indirectly hurt the primary room revenues.

Another innovation that has been introduced are in-room computer terminals that provide the occupant with access to a computer that can receive telegrams and telexes, and supply economic news, shopping information, entertainment tips, and even job listings. Users gain access to the computer through the use of a credit card number and will be charged for their time at the terminal on the basis of sliding rates similar to those for long distance calls. Some industry observers predict that within the next few years thousands of rooms may be equipped with these terminals.

Major Subdivisions

More than 50,000 lodging locations are currently operating in the United States. However the industry is fragmented, ranging from small roadside motels to mammoth resort hotels containing 3,000 or more rooms. The lodging industry is usually subdivided into four distinct categories: convention/commercial, resort, roadside, and airport.

Lodging chains may operate through a management contract of a franchise system or have full or partial ownership of their properties. On a franchised system the properties are neither owned nor managed by the lodging company—the company receives an initial fee and a percentage of gross room receipts in exchange for the use of the company's name, reservation services, national advertising, and other considerations. Most of the national chains are franchise operations.

The management contract method has grown in importance over the years. With this method, the facility is managed for its owners for a fee based on gross room rentals.

Factors in Successful Lodging Enterprises

Although a variety of factors influence the operation of every lodging enterprise, the following six are considered the key success factors: an effective reservation system, actual locations chosen, the amenities/facilities available at each physical location, friendliness/efficiency of staff, pricing policies, and aggressive marketing, including customer groups targeted plus advertising and special promotional activities.

It may seem unnecessary to detail the importance of an effective reservation system; however, no other single factor can cause the equivalent ill will in potential customers than lost reservations, incorrect dates, errors in requested room types, and so on. Even if adjustments at the check-in registration can be affected in order to accommodate the customer, the impact is still the same—a negative start to the guest's stay at that location. A negative which may never be overcome.

In a similar manner it seems intuitively logical that the actual physical location chosen for a lodging enterprise would be extremely important to the success of its operations. For example, a resort hotel in Florida located on the beach would be expected to have a more advantageous location than one situated three or four blocks further inland. However locational factors are much more complex than this simplistic example. Various factors must be included in the location decision analysis process. These factors include, but are not limited to, the following: (1) the type of lodging enterprise planned (airport versus midtown commercial); (2) the physical amenities to be included in the actual operation (lounges, cafes, swimming pool, exercise facilities); (3) the types of customer groups expected to be chosen as the dominant group targeted for marketing efforts (business versus personal versus convention traveler); (4) the proximity of the physical location to other desirable amenities and services (for example, golf courses, gourmet restaurants, or afterhours social activities), including proximity to business centers, transportation facilities, convention centers, exhibition halls, and so forth.

A third success factor includes the actual facilities available at each location site, both in-room facilities such as bed sizes, bath and dressing room configurations, cable, color television, and desks and furnishings; and also overall facilities such as swimming pools, tennis courts, exercise rooms, cafes, restaurants, lounges, meeting rooms, recreational and duplicating services, computer hookups, and so on. The list can be very lengthy and is continuing to expand with changing lifestyles and technology.

Several lodging chain operators have quickly suggested that the friendliness and efficiency of the lodging staff is an extremely important success factor. This friendliness and efficiency must be a pervasive staff attitude. It must begin at the initial guest/staff contact point, be in the doorman or reception desk clerk or wherever, and continue through all other guest/staff contact situations for the duration of the guest's stay.

The final few success factors of pricing policies, advertising, and special promotional activities are all related to an aggressive marketing program as an important key to success. Pricing has recently become far more segmented and competitive than in the past. Convention and business as well as other group pricing is only the beginning of the pricing policy variables currently practiced at many enterprises. A basic variable of room amenities and location becomes much more complex when factors related to the type of guest, the length of stay, the days of the week in residence, the frequency of visits, and so forth, are included in a pricing formula approach. In addition these pricing policies must be established to be compatible with and coordinated to other marketing activities such as advertising themes and special promotion programs and activities. To summarize, what is necessary for success in today's highly competitive lodging industry is a well-designed and coordinated aggressive marketing program which stresses promotional activities such as media advertising in conjunction with a relatively sophisticated approach to multiple pricing policies.

In the future all segments of the lodging industry are expected to become more aggressive as they compete in the market. Special promotions will be offered to encourage short stays during holiday periods and weekends. Hotels that cater to a balanced mix between business, convention, and pleasure travelers are expected to fare better than others.

Major Competitors in Integrated Hotels

Listed below are a number of organizations which operate multiple locations and which have thousands of lodging rooms available nightly:

- Best Western Inc.
- Friendship Inns
- Budget Motels and Hotels
- Days Inn of America
- TraveLodge International/Trusthouse Forte Inc.
- Quality Inns

However these organizations are either specialized or concentrated in their types of operations and therefore are not considered major competitors in the integrated hotel segment of the lodging industry.

The major competitors operating in the integrated hotel segment are firms such as:

- Holiday Inns Inc.
- Ramada Inns Inc.
- Sheraton Corp.

- Hilton Hotels Corp.
- Hyatt Hotels Corp.
- Marriott Hotels Corp.

These firms are integrated from the standpoint of operating several types of lodging destinations from resorts to airport to convention to business and commercial locations. And, in addition, a number of these firms have also moved into new areas such as all-suite and mid-priced locations. All are diversified in their operations. Exhibit 1 provides details regarding some of these major competitors.

Occupancy Rates

In 1982 the economic downturn adversely affected occupancy levels. This downturn moderated room-rate increases and lowered profit margins. However, despite an increase in the number of rooms available, economic recovery in 1983 and 1984 boosted pleasure and business travel.

An important factor in determining the profitability of any lodging enterprise is the occupancy rate. The break-even occupancy level for a hotel is determined by the property's initial cost, the manner in which the initial cost was financed, the ability of management to control operations costs, the actual occupancy rate, and the average price per room. The average industry occupancy rate in 1983 was 66.5 percent and grew approximately 6.6 percent from 1982. But with economic recovery 1984 was expected to have an even stronger showing.

The average price per occupied room was just over $56 in 1981. In 1982 it rose to $62, and fluctuated around $68 in 1983. In 1984 room rates continued to rise; however the increase was less than the double-digit raises of previous years

Exhibit 1 Competitors in Integrated Hotels*

Name	Properties		
	Number of Hotels	Number of Rooms	Occupancy Rate
Hilton Hotels Corp.	N/A	88,864	60%
Holiday Inns Inc.	1,707	310,337	70.2
Marriott Corp.	131	55,000	69.5**
Ramada Inns Inc.	593	93,592	63.0

Name	Financial Highlights (in thousands)				
	Revenues	Net Income	Earnings Per Share	Return on Equity	Main Businesses
Hilton Hotels Corp.	$ 682,928	$112,637	$4.20	18.7%	Hotels and casinos (international)
Holiday Inns Inc.	1,585,080	124,399	3.28	12.5	Hotels, restaurants, and casinos (international)
Marriott Corp.	3,036,703	115,245	4.15	20.0	Hotels, contract food services and restaurants (international)
Ramada Inns Inc.	573,831	12,597	.38	5.2	Hotels and casinos (international)

*1983 figures.
**Estimated by author.
Source: 1983 annual reports.

when several lodging chains boosted rates in line with changes in the Consumer Price Index.

Construction

The construction rate of new hotel facilities is not expected to grow in the near future, mainly because interest rates remain high. In the latter part of the 1970s and the early 1980s, most lodging chains curtailed construction programs. The reasons included: rising building costs, high capital costs, an oversupply of rooms stemming from overbuilding in previous years, and declining occupancy rates for many hotels brought about by unfavorable economic conditions. In recent years the emphasis has been on renovation of older rooms and eliminating marginal locations. When new construction resumes, airport and downtown locations are predicted to have top priority.

Industry Outlook

As the lodging industry enters the mature phase of its life cycle, several analysts believe that major market segmentation strategies will be utilized by the national chains. These segmentation strategies, which have been identified as budget-priced operations, all-suite operations, premium full-service operations, and so forth are necessary if the national chains are to retain their market share percentages and insure future profits. Meanwhile, the smaller industry competitors are intent on creating a marketing niche for themselves—a niche that separates their operations from the other competitors in the industries. In fact, the all-suite hotel and the budget-priced operations were started by small competitors searching for a marketing niche to give themselves a competitive advantage.

References

Moody's Handbook of Common Stocks. Fall 1984.

Standard and Poors, *Industry Surveys, 1984.*

Travel Weekly, May 31, 1983.

U.S. Industrial Outlook, 1984.

Value Line Investment Survey, 1984.

Case 9

The Restructuring of Ramada Inc.

History

The Ramada chain was started by a Chicago restaurateur, Marion Isbell. When in his 40s, Isbell sold a Chicago-based food service business and retired to Arizona. He grew restless in retirement and soon began building roadside motels around Phoenix and Flagstaff, using the name Ramada.

By 1959 Isbell and his partners owned 14 motels and were encouraged by the rapid expansion of Holiday Inn. In 1962, the partners began competing directly with Holiday Inn as both firms developed units along the interstate highway system. Like Holiday Inn, Ramada established design, construction, and purchasing divisions, so that the company became a one-stop shopping center for hotel developers and operations. Potential franchisees could look to Ramada for help in site selection, building site designs, and the provision of everything needed for operation (e.g., supplies and a reservation network).

In addition to the franchise network, Ramada was also building inns on its own as fast as the highway system expanded. By 1969, however, the interstate system was completed and new sites became harder to find.

In the 1970s, Ramada expanded its operations through the purchase of existing hotels and resorts and attempted to diversify by getting into the car rental business and into the ownership and management of campgrounds. However, the company was not successful in either venture. At this time Ramada also expanded overseas into Europe and entered into hospital management in California.

In 1974 Bill Isbell, Marion Isbell's son, assumed control of the company. At about the same time, the Arab oil embargo raised energy prices, which adversely affected the tourism industry. Ramada's earnings fell from $15.3 million in 1973 to $1 million in 1975. Instead of continuing to expand and/or diversify, the company began to streamline its operations. Ramada renovated its units and encouraged its franchisees to do likewise. The refurbishing program occurred at an opportune time. As the program was being completed, industry sales rose and Ramada's earnings were in excess of $17.5 million by 1980.

Also in the 1970s, Ramada became interested in owning and operating a casino. The company purchased a 7 percent stake in Del Webb, which operated the Mint and the Sahara in Las Vegas. Del Webb also owned casinos in Reno, Lake Tahoe, and Laughlin, and had purchased a site in Atlantic City. Due to its ownership position, Ramada expected to gain a seat on Del Webb's board of directors. One was never given and, subsequently, Ramada sold the stock in Del Webb for a sizable profit. Soon thereafter, Ramada purchased the Ambassador Hotel in Atlantic City, which had become defunct. Ramada's intention was to completely renovate the hotel. Unfortunately for Ramada, New Jersey officials were encouraging new construction rather

---

This case portrays neither the effective nor the ineffective handling of an administrative situation. Rather, it is to be used as the basis for classroom discussion.

than renovations. Eventually, Ramada was able to renovate the Ambassador but, due to government delays and the effects of the salty ocean air, the project was far over budget.

During the time that Ramada was waiting for regulatory approval on the Ambassador Hotel, Nevada gaming officials approached the company to purchase the Tropicana. The Tropicana had a history of trouble and the Nevada regulators hoped that Ramada would stabilize the hotel/casino operations. Ramada bought the Tropicana Hotel and Casino in 1979. The Atlantic City casino, now called Tropicana Hotel and Casino, opened in 1981.

Between 1976 and 1982, Ramada decreased its chain by 35 percent, selling the units to raise cash to enter the gaming business or to get rid of unprofitable properties. Earnings from the Atlantic City casino hit an all-time high, with revenues from the hotel/casino greater than the revenues of the entire hotel division in 1982. Ramada continued with its system of selling older hotels and replacing them with newer properties.

Changes under CEO Snell

President and chief executive officer Richard Snell was elected Chairman of the board for Ramada in 1981. Snell was for 25 years associated with the Phoenix law firm of Snell & Wilmer. He was elected president of Ramada in 1982. Bankers drafted Snell to manage the financially distressed company, for which he served as legal counsel until 1981. According to various sources, he joined Ramada reluctantly and expected to leave in a few months. The company's nervous bankers persuaded him to stay on until the company was healthy.

In his first three years as CEO he sold 69 hotels, cut staff, and pumped up Ramada's balance sheet. Long-term debt had reached 79 percent of total capital in 1982. This was mostly a function of costs overruns at the Atlantic City casino hotel. Snell arranged a sale–lease back of the facility and reduced debt in 1985 to 58 percent. His feelings on Ramada's performance for 1987 and 1988 are presented in Exhibit 1, a letter to shareholders. Results of Ramada Inc.'s operations are presented in Tables 1a through 1e.

Exhibit 1 Annual Letter to Shareholders from the Chairman of the Board

In last year's letter to you I expressed confidence that our plan to reposition Ramada's hospitality products would lead to appreciable earnings gains as we moved toward the end of the decade. At the same time, I was cautious in my assessment of the company's 1987 prospects. As things turned out, that caution was well-deserved for the reasons discussed further on.

Nonetheless, 1987 was a year of significant progress toward our goal of transforming Ramada from a company whose product mix had low growth prospects into one whose upgraded mix offers excellent growth potential. Our development programs, notably those in hotels and gaming, will soon be far enough along to make measurable contributions to income. But the nature and timing of these programs were such that they diluted earnings of the two groups in 1987.

In the hotel group, the operating results for 1987 were about as expected. The year-over-year decline in operating income was occasioned by the planned sale of older hotel properties that had limited growth opportunities. In their stead, we have been opening hotels in markets selected to broaden our representation and to provide higher levels of profit. But the immaturity of most of these hotels, in relation to start-up expense and fixed costs, limited their profit contribution.

Within the gaming group, we anticipated that the huge expansion project at the Atlantic City Tropicana would have a disruptive effect on casino and food and beverage operations at the property. That situation proved to be worse than we had expected and contributed to a decline in the property's, and the gaming group's, performance for the year.

A disappointment in 1987 was the contribution from the restaurant group. Marie Callender's, operating in an industry characterized by intense compe-

Exhibit 1 *(continued)*

tition, experienced severe pressure on revenues and margins which produced weak full-year earnings.

These circumstances, along with a higher tax rate and an extraordinary loss, contributed to lower net income in the year just ended.

While 1987 was not a banner year from a financial standpoint, it was not without some important achievements that have moved Ramada into position to attain significantly improved results from its three business units beginning in 1988.

Our hotel group made tremendous progress in extending the reach of the company's lodging products and more clearly defining the market niches of our hotel brands.

Owing to aggressive domestic and international development programs, we added more new Ramada and Renaissance rooms to the company's worldwide hotel system than in any other year in Ramada's history.

Through the mid-year acquisition of the Rodeway inn chain we added several thousand more rooms. Equally important, the Rodeway purchase gave us a strong foothold in the economy, limited-service lodging tier, sharpened the focus of our brand strategy and provided a new product for expansion through franchising.

The year just ended saw our activity on company-developed hotel projects move into full swing. The opening of several new domestic and international properties contributed to an improving image for Ramada's lodging products and further anchored our presence in the global marketplace.

In 1987, our gaming group moved within sight of its goal of establishing a portfolio of highly profitable, themed casinos in the primary U.S. gaming markets.

The Las Vegas Tropicana, the first property to be themed as part of a major expansion two years ago, came into its own and delivered an impressive operating performance in 1987.

During the year, the gaming group also guided the $200 million expansion of the Atlantic City Tropicana through its first year of construction on budget and on schedule for opening by early 1989, and perhaps sooner given the progress to date. This project will clearly position the Tropicana, to be renamed TropWorld when the expansion is completed, as one of the first of a new generation of gaming megafacilities in the Atlantic City market.

Through an active program of geographic expansion, the gaming organization completed its entry into a third gaming jurisdiction, Reno, Nevada, and began construction on a fourth gaming property, a hotel casino in the dynamic and fast-growing Laughlin, Nevada, market.

The restaurant group devoted considerable resources to the tasks of seizing new development opportunities for Marie Callender's and implementing measures to respond to the competitive pressures in its industry.

The group made measurable progress against its development agenda, opening a number of new Marie Callender's restuarants in both established territories and new markets. In the face of a tough competitive environment, Marie Callender's management assigned a top priority to sales and marketing initiatives to increase on-premises sales at individual restaurants.

Throughout the Ramada organization, we remained on course toward our goal of positioning Ramada's hotel, gaming and restaurant properties as the service leaders in their industries. In 1987, our business units embarked on a number of programs to strengthen service delivery. Noteworthy among these efforts is the hotel group's "You're Somebody Special" program through which employees at company-operated and franchised hotels are working together to give our guests the finest service available in our markets.

With the programs and plans I've discussed, we enter 1988 confident in our ability to realize substantially higher levels of profitability in the years immediately ahead, assuming reasonably decent economic conditions. Our development programs are now nearing the point where they will make an important contribution to earnings. We also expect a reorganization completed last year to provide real savings in corporate expense and business unit overhead. Future income should also benefit from other expense reduction measures already taken and a lower effective tax rate.

The thousands of employees who represent Ramada and its hospitality products around the world are fully committed to achieving higher levels of performance and, in the process, enhancing the value of your investment in our company.

Richard Snell
Chairman of the Board and President

Annual Report, Ramada Inc., 1987, 3–6.

Table 1a Financial Highlights, 1984–1988

FINANCIAL HIGHLIGHTS
Ramada Inc. and Subsidiaries

For the Five Years Ended December 29, 1988
(in thousands, except per share data and number of shareholders)

	1988	1987 (Restated)	1986 (Restated)	1985 (Restated)	1984 (Restated)
Revenue	$476,645	$407,622	$383,712	$344,163	$334,023
Operating income	$ 39,961	$ 30,686	$ 37,970	$ 31,296	$ 44,422
Corporate expense	(10,236)	(10,871)	(14,532)	(13,957)	(17,361)
Interest expense (net of capitalized interest)	(24,813)	(18,103)	(12,951)	(12,367)	(18,443)
Other, net	(6,692)	(9,898)	(8,163)	(3,269)	(4,410)
Income/(Loss) from continuing operations before income taxes and extraordinary items	(1,780)	(8,186)	2,324	1,703	4,208
(Provision)/Benefit for income taxes	15	1,422	(3,087)	(1,750)	(3,653)
Income/(Loss) from continuing operations before extraordinary items	(1,765)	(6,764)	(763)	(47)	555
Discontinued operations	(3,898)	13,041	11,038	13,840	4,150
Extraordinary items	563	(1,365)	—	3,414	4,116
Net income/(loss)	$ (5,100)	$ 4,912	$ 10,275	$ 17,207	$ 8,821
Earnings per share:					
Income/(Loss) from continuing operations before extraordinary items	$ (.04)	$ (.17)	$ (.02)	$ —	$ .02
Discontinued operations	(.10)	.32	.29	.37	.11
Extraordinary items	.01	(.03)	—	.09	.11
Net income/(loss)	$ (.13)	$ .12	$ .27	$ .46	$ .24
Dividends declared: None					
Weighted average shares outstanding	39,751	39,727	38,705	37,209	37,205
Position at end of year:					
Total assets	$705,035	$663,142	$535,933	$471,576	$450,983
Long-term debt	$275,863	$258,584	$131,276	$109,448	$117,872
Shareholders' equity	$295,659	$300,326	$301,532	$268,706	$248,753
Equity per share	$ 7.43	$ 7.56	$ 7.59	$ 7.22	$ 6.69
Number of shareholders of record (at February 1 of the subsequent year)	30,536	34,389	37,346	39,990	44,801

Source: Ramada Inc. 1988 Annual Report, p. 1.

Table 1b Consolidated Statements of Operations, 1986–1988

RAMADA INC. AND SUBSIDIARIES

Consolidated Statements of Operations

For the Years Ended December 29, 1988, December 31, 1987 and January 1, 1987
(in thousands, except per share data)

	1988	1987 (Restated)	1986 (Restated)
Revenue:			
Casino	$358,295	$302,565	$289,053
Rooms and related services	68,677	58,645	51,049
Food and beverage	68,537	60,477	56,440
Other	22,436	21,076	21,492
	517,945	442,763	418,034
Less promotional allowances	(41,300)	(35,141)	(34,322)
Net revenue	476,645	407,622	383,712
Operating expenses:			
Casino	127,991	117,878	109,547
Rooms and related services	41,222	35,036	30,629
Food and beverage	63,660	55,924	51,948
Other operating expenses	96,217	74,852	68,718
Property operations	23,670	19,287	18,172
Lease rentals	59,331	55,582	51,141
Depreciation and amortization	24,593	18,377	15,587
Total operating expenses	436,684	376,936	345,742
Operating income	39,961	30,686	37,970
Corporate expense	(10,236)	(10,871)	(14,532)
Interest expense, net	(24,813)	(18,103)	(12,951)
Equity in unconsolidated partnerships' losses	(5,982)	(5,958)	(5,455)
Minority interests	(710)	(3,940)	(2,708)
Income/(Loss) from continuing operations before income taxes and extraordinary items	(1,780)	(8,186)	2,324
(Provision)/Benefit for income taxes	15	1,422	(3,087)
Income/(Loss) from continuing operations before extraordinary items	(1,765)	(6,764)	(763)
Discontinued operations	(3,898)	13,041	11,038
Extraordinary items	563	(1,365)	–
Net income/(loss)	$ (5,100)	$ 4,912	$ 10,275
Earnings per share assuming no dilution:			
Income/(Loss) from continuing operations before extraordinary items	$ (.04)	$ (.17)	$ (.02)
Discontinued operations	(.10)	.32	.29
Extraordinary items	.01	(.03)	–
Net income/(loss)	$ (.13)	$ .12	$ .27
Weighted average shares outstanding assuming no dilution	39,751	39,727	38,705

The accompanying Financial Review is an integral part of these financial statements.

Source Ramada Inc. 1988 Annual Report.

Table 1c Consolidated Balance Sheets, 1987 and 1988

RAMADA INC. AND SUBSIDIARIES

Consolidated Balance Sheets

December 29, 1988 and December 31, 1987
(in thousands)

	1988	1987 (Restated)
ASSETS		
Current assets:		
Cash	$ 23,875	$ 38,730
Accounts and notes receivable, net	28,129	26,391
Refundable income taxes	12,015	—
Inventories	5,388	3,355
Prepaid expenses and other	5,488	5,356
Total current assets	74,895	73,832
Net assets of discontinued operations	179,902	217,025
Property and equipment:		
Buildings and equipment, net	237,301	56,550
Land	63,281	71,728
Construction in progress	4,894	112,871
Leased under capital leases, net	20,143	21,704
	325,619	262,853
Investments and long-term receivables:		
Investments in and advances to unconsolidated partnerships	20,904	22,368
Notes receivable and other investments	76,719	69,345
	97,623	91,713
Other assets	26,996	17,719
	$705,035	$663,142
LIABILITIES AND SHAREHOLDERS' EQUITY		
Current liabilities:		
Accounts payable and accruals	$ 35,410	$ 40,865
Accrued payroll and employee benefits	23,490	14,557
Accrued interest payable	13,496	6,932
Current portion of long-term debt	28,100	18,915
Total current liabilities	100,496	81,269
Long-term debt, net	275,863	258,584
Other long-term liabilities	23,701	16,235
Deferred income taxes	7,044	4,906
Contingencies and commitments		
Minority interests	2,272	1,822
Shareholders' equity:		
Common stock	3,978	3,973
Paid-in capital	224,556	224,245
Foreign currency translation adjustments	1,443	1,291
Retained earnings	65,682	70,817
Total shareholders' equity	295,659	300,326
	$705,035	$663,142

The accompanying Financial Review is an integral part of these financial statements.

Source: Ramada Inc. 1988 Annual Report.

Table 1d Consolidated Statements of Cash Flows, 1986–1988

RAMADA INC. AND SUBSIDIARIES

Consolidated Statements of Cash Flows

For the Years Ended December 29, 1988, December 31, 1987 and January 1, 1987
(in thousands)

	1988	1987	1986
CASH FLOWS FROM OPERATING ACTIVITIES:			
Cash provided by continuing operations before extraordinary items	$ 13.458	$ 14.101	$ 15.493
Extraordinary items	563	(1.365)	—
Items not using/(providing) cash:			
Decrease in deferred mortgage expense		1.015	—
Tax benefit of capital loss carryforward	(563)	—	—
Cash used by extraordinary items	—	(350)	—
Cash provided by continuing operations after extraordinary items	13.458	13.751	15.493
CASH FLOWS FROM INVESTING ACTIVITIES:			
Payments on notes receivable	610	928	66.352
Proceeds from sales of property and equipment	12.000	—	—
Reduction in invested funds	6.603	131.111	3.602
Purchases of property and equipment	(129.111)	(107.071)	(27.815)
Increase in invested funds	—	(96.519)	(44.313)
Additions to other long-term assets	(13.504)	(8.528)	(14.741)
Cash used in investing activities	(123.402)	(80.079)	(16.915)
CASH FLOWS FROM FINANCING ACTIVITIES:			
Proceeds from issuance of common stock	316	157	21
Net borrowings under line-of-credit agreements	(30.000)	11.000	29.000
Proceeds from issuance of long-term debt	108.067	130.127	91
Principal payments on long-term debt	(19.900)	(13.922)	(12.173)
Redemption of Ramada New Jersey Holdings Corporation preferred stock	(295)	(18.918)	—
Cash provided by financing activities	58.188	108.444	16.939
Cash flows from discontinued operations	36.901	(27.135)	(31.742)
Net increase/(decrease) in cash	(14.855)	14.981	(16.225)
Cash at beginning of year	38.730	23.749	39.974
Cash at end of year	$ 23.875	$ 38.730	$ 23.749

The accompanying Financial Review is an integral part of these financial statements.

Source: Ramada Inc. 1988 Annual Report.

Table 1e Financial Review, 1985–1987

Revenue and operating income by industry segment are as follows (in thousands):

	1987	1986	1985
HOTEL			
Revenue:			
Room and related services	$121,504	$136,453	$138,210
Food and beverage	58,319	65,863	63,534
Other	46,823	37,584	36,462
	226,646	239,900	238,206
Cost and expense:			
Room and related services	35,438	40,152	41,251
Food and beverage	49,216	51,797	49,621
Other (including undistributed operating expenses and fixed charges)	129,737	127,188	128,942
	214,391	219,137	219,814
Operating income (excluding gains on property dispositions)	$ 12,255	$ 20,763	$ 18,392
GAMING			
Revenue:			
Casino	$302,565	$289,053	$272,470
Room and related services	45,225	39,232	27,391
Food and beverage	38,756	35,317	24,330
Other	20,297	19,770	17,623
	406,843[a]	383,372[a]	341,814[a]
Cost and expense:			
Casino	117,878	109,547	110,328
Room and related services	35,036	30,629	25,299
Food and beverage	55,924	51,948	43,485
Other (including undistributed operating expenses and fixed charges)	168,098	153,618	133,755
	376,936	345,742	312,867
Operating income	$ 29,907	$ 37,630	$ 28,947
RESTAURANT			
Revenue:			
Food and beverage	$104,542	$ 58,895	
Other	8,517	4,459	
	113,059	63,354	
Cost and expense:			
Food and beverage	73,539	41,140	
Other (including undistributed operating expenses and fixed charges)	30,758	15,104	
	104,297	56,244	
Operating income	$ 8,762	$ 7,110	

[a]Total promotional allowances netted against revenue were $35,141, $34,322 and $39,020 in 1987, 1986 and 1985, respectively.
Source: Ramada Inc. 1988 annual report.

Reasons behind the Restructuring

In a marked shift of corporate strategy, Ramada management decided in October 1988 to shed its hotel and restaurant divisions leaving it with only its four casino hotels. This sale of assets moved Ramada closer to its objective of managing assets instead of owning them. Financial factors, a potentially damaging lawsuit by the firm's second largest shareholder, takeover threats, and a major deal that fell through may have led to the decision.

Results of operations in the hotel and restaurant group had been disappointing. The hotel group had a pretax profit of $749,000 for the first half of 1988 compared to $6.8 million the year before. Restaurant pretax profit fell from 5.3 million to 2.1 million.

Management felt increased pressure to reorganize when the Pritzker family offered Ramada $371 million for the company. The Pritzkers, who owned 7.2 percent of the company, indicated if the company refused to discuss a sale they might attempt a hostile takeover. Rumor had it that the Pritzker family had talked internally and with third parties about a possible acquisition or restructuring of Ramada. The Pritzkers owned Hyatt Corporation, and with its casino in Lake Tahoe they could expand gaming operations into Las Vegas, Reno, Laughlin, and Atlantic City.

Ramada operated in three areas of the hospitality industry before its restructuring began: hotel, gaming, and restaurants. Ramada's hotel group operated a system of midpriced domestic and international hotels, restaurants, and resorts. Further, Ramada licensed the use of the Ramada name and provided services to its licensees. The company's activities in the gaming group consisted of four casino hotels, three in Nevada and one in Atlantic City. Ramada was consequently divided into three divisions—hotel group, gaming group, and restaurant group.

The hotel group conducted its business through a network of company-owned, leased and licensed hotels located throughout the U.S., Puerto Rico, and over 20 foreign countries. The hotel group was run by Jerry Manion, an executive vice president. He was the fourth president of the hotel group in six years. Prior to his joining Ramada in February 1985, Manion was president of Economy Motor Inns. In addition, he was senior vice president, director of franchise, for Quality Inns International from 1977 to 1980. Manion discussed Ramada's goals in an interview reproduced in Exhibit 2.

April 1989 marked the completed sale of the hotel group.

The restaurant group was established in 1986 through the acquisition of Marie Callender's, a California-based chain of family-style restaurants. Tom Martin was the executive vice president in charge of the restaurant group. Prior to heading up the restaurant division, Martin served in various executive positions with Ramada. In 1979 Martin was appointed senior vice president and chief financial officer, and in 1982 he was appointed executive vice president, finance and administration.

Ramada announced in March 1989 that the restaurant group had been sold to Wilshire Restaurant Group Inc. Marie Callender's is a midpriced restaurant operation that has 152 franchised or company-owned restaurants. These units were primarily concentrated in California and other western states. Operating income had been deteriorating steadily since Ramada purchased Marie Callender's. Management attributed this to the tough industrial market the group was in.

Former owner and founder of Marie Callender's, Donald Callender, had been suing Ramada. He claimed the units had been mismanaged. According to Callender, the deal to sell the chain didn't "pass the smell test." He further stated that the Wilshire group had an "inside track" because it promised to "keep all the incompetent management" Ramada had installed at Marie Callender's. Michael Hayes, chairman of Hayes Financial, indicated that Wilshire had

Exhibit 2 An Interview with the Hotel Group President about Ramada's Goals

Jerry Manion, president of the Ramada Hotel Group, discussed [Ramada's] goals with the hotel editor of *Travel Weekly*.

TW: Let's talk about the overall state of the company. Analysts have said that Ramada has been underperforming for years; that its profitability is low and its development is behind that of its major competitors. What is your estimation of the company's financial health?

Manion: It's true that the company has been under-performing in the past number of years. I think everybody realizes we had serious problems. Since the new management took over in 1981 under [chairman] Richard Snell, the company has been in a restructuring position.

In the past several years, we have come out of the doldrums and are now back in the mainstream of the hospitality industry.

We have development going throughout the world—probably more in the international area than any other company has been able to achieve in the last four years.

In the U.S., we have a considerable number of developments, not only company investment in our new Ramada Inns, but also in the franchising opportunities. We have put together probably the finest franchising development teams in the industry. This started about three years ago and is now producing quite well.

We have restructured the management of the hotel group, the marketing areas, the financial areas and the franchise operations area, which was and is responsible for the quality of our product.

We have eliminated several hundred Ramada properties from our system over the past four or five years.

We have been replacing those on a steady basis, a very slow, direct program where we look for properties that can be financially successful for the owners and for Ramada.

We are not looking for numbers. We are looking to be a very healthy company again, and we are very rapidly achieving that.

TW: What were your goals when you took over? How far have you gone toward realizing them?

Manion: My goal was really to restructure Ramada, bring it back as a well-performing hotel company.

Ramada has always been a large company; it has probably been the third largest hotel company for a number of years and still is.

However, it was not a performing company.

Franchise relations were at an all-time low when I joined the company. The health of the company-owned properties, the management group for the company-owned properties, the attitude of the employees left a lot to be desired. There wasn't a service attitude to any great degree.

I think that when the company got very successful and then went into various other areas that had nothing to do with the travel industry, it lost sight of what its main objective was: to run a fine hotel company.

While we are heavily franchised, we can help the licensees make money in their own investments.

TW: What were the reasons for the slump, in terms of the company's performance?

Manion: It didn't happen overnight. It built over a number of years from about mid-1970.

I believe that in '74, when the crash hit the hospitality industry, Ramada found itself injured considerably.

And there was a change in management where Marion Isbell, the founder of the company, stepped aside and his son took over. It's apparent the company started going downhill at that time and was not able to reverse itself.

It then invested in the gaming business, buying the Tropicana in Las Vegas and then starting the Tropicana in Atlantic City.

Those two ventures caused some serious financial distress from operating losses in Las Vegas and a tremendous overbudget drain in Atlantic City to finish that property.

That, along with the fact that the money was being taken out of the other hotels to feed these investments, continued to take Ramada on a downward slide.

Our properties weren't renovated. If you don't put money back into a hotel every year, it becomes tired very, very quickly because of the massive use.

The company also lost direction in terms of the quality control of its licensee group. The licensees had a negative attitude toward Ramada as things continued to go downhill, and this continued to build. It is just a domino effect.

Finally, in '81, the board saw fit to make a management change, at which time Dick took over to see if there was a way to save the company.

It takes a considerable amount of time to change a company of this size and scope. It's also very difficult

Exhibit 2 *(continued)*

to grab 500 licensees and say, "OK, guys, we're back in the boat now. Get behind us and spend the money to renovate your properties, and let's get it rolling immediately."

You just can't turn the switch that fast. It's a matter of working individually with owners to help them find ways to invest in their property to bring it back.

Ramada invested $65 million in the company-owned properties we elected to keep. We completed that renovation in about three years.

All of the company properties have been totally refurbished. They are all first class operations. Most of the licensee properties have now been totally renovated.

Today we only have 30 properties in our licensee group that do not meet our minimum standards. We still have a number of properties, roughly 100, in some phase of renovation.

These will soon be completed, and 30 properties is not a disastrous number for us.

At the same time the operational reorganization of the company has been going on. We have eliminated a tremendous amount of bureaucracy.

TW: You have eliminated positions?

Manion: Yes, in our headquarters here in Phoenix. Ramada, at one time, had a tremendous number of company-owned properties. As these were sold, the headquarters was not shrunk in size.

In January '85, we had roughly 700 people at our headquarters. We dropped that down to just less than 400 people over the 2½-year period since I arrived.

We eliminated positions that were not necessary. The people were all pretty good, but the jobs weren't necessary for the products we had.

TW: So it was really a streamlining?

Manion: It was a reorganization to take away what you might call interference in the operation of the company.

There were so many people here that when a licensee called to have a question answered no one knew who to give it to. This we eliminated.

We gave each of the executives who were responsible for major functions the authority to make decisions. We made them viable executives who could utilize their ability to bring the company around.

Within a year from the time I arrived, we had brought a service attitude to all areas of our operations. We had put together some of the basic framework to start rebuilding in terms of marketing and advertising and the product we had to offer.

We have come out with our "new concept" Ramada Inns. We had five open and six more under construction, with another 15 under contract ready to start.

At this stage of the game, Ramada is prepared to take on this over-built industry we are operating in and survive. As our new product comes on line and as those new products mature, the profits on them will [have an] impact on the bottom line of Ramada.

This year the hotel group has exceeded its budget and its bottom-line profit performance for the first time—considerably so—and we anticipate this will continue.

TW: Do you think, as some people have said, that Ramada is a takeover target? There have been rumors, and the Pritzker family, owners of Hyatt Hotels, has purchased a 6 percent stake in the company. Are you nervous about that purchase? Do you view it as a threat or is it viewed merely as an investment?

Manion: I think Ramada is a takeover target. It's a very healthy company today, and in the next three or four years we are going to see the return of our efforts to rebuild this organization.

We are at the threshold of really showing improved bottom lines. So therefore, I think Ramada is a good target.

It is a company I think a lot of people would like to have their hands on.

Ramada is an international hotel company with representation in most of the major markets today with fine new properties, inns, hotels and Renaissance properties.

We have over 100 properties right now operating internationally. That has grown from 32 in 1984—tremendous growth. We will open 18 more properties internationally this year. So the future is very good for Ramada.

Do the Pritzkers want to own it? I don't know. They have said they want to invest in our stock, and that very likely is what they are doing. We have had no other contact with them on that.

TW: Your strategy now is to transform the company from one that owns property into a management company. Is this an outgrowth of the effort to reduce your debt?

Manion: It happens to be what most other hotel companies are doing to get out of asset management.

The returns are much higher in a nonasset com-

(continued)

Exhibit 2 *(continued)*

pany where you do not have to invest huge sums of monies into your facilities.

The effort is to use other people's money to build the properties and take a reasonable management fee or the licensee franchise fee and supply those investors with what they need to manage a hotel, run the international marketing organization, the reservations system, support systems, etc. That gives you your best return on your investment.

TW: Will you still own a certain number of hotels?

Manion: Yes. As a matter of fact we are building a number of company-owned properties right now.

These properties are 150 to 180 rooms and run $10 million to $12 million.

TW: These are residential-style properties, similar to the Courtyard by Marriott?

Manion: Yes. We took advantage of a lot of their research and improved it in some areas. But yes, they are very similar.

TW: They are also similar to Howard Johnson's Park Square Inns and Hilton's Hillcrest. Why the decision to build this sort of property? It's got a lot of competition.

Manion: We have always been in the midpriced market. That's what we know best. This property fits that market.

Marriott is actually after our market. They found it to be a very profitable type inn to build, what the traveling public is looking for today, and they started building it.

We, of course, came along a little later. We were not able to venture into these new developments at that time, partially because of the financial problems the company had gone through.

But in 1984 our new concept inn was conceived and we opened our first one in 1986 in Naperville, just outside of Chicago. We now have five open with another five under construction.

So, the reason we did it? It's our market, the midprice market. And we also needed to come up with a new so-called prototype that licensees could build and develop themselves. We needed to make it cost effective so that in today's market—a very overbuilt market and a very difficult time in which to finance new hotels—we can have one that has a good chance of getting financing and of being profitable.

TW: Marriott gave its property a different name. Hilton did the same and so did Howard Johnson. How do you at Ramada market your new inn as something new and appealing, when it still bears the Ramada Inn name?

Manion: Ramada has, as I said, always been in the midprice market. Marriott is trying to get into that market. The Marriott name didn't fit the midprice market, so I am sure that's why they chose a different name.

But we market this as Ramada Inn. We have, while we are developing this, totally rehabbed and rebuilt our Ramada system so that our properties out there are viable, long-term investments.

The existing Ramada Hotels that are in the field have been refurbished; are first class. They compete with anyone else in the market on an equal or better basis and they compete with this hotel.

TW: I understand the company's philosophy is keep everything under the Ramada umbrella.

How does Rodeway [purchased last year] fit in with that philosophy of keeping the same name? This would be a first for Ramada wouldn't it, in terms of having a segment under a different name?

Manion: That is correct. It is a first for Ramada in having something that doesn't have the Ramada name on it.

We chose it because, in our decision to go into the limited service tier, we did not want to confuse the Ramada customer who is used to having a midprice inn or hotel right here, knowing roughly what they are going to get and what they are going to spend and then ending up with another Ramada Hotel down the road that is a limited service, no restaurant, no meeting space, much lower price.

So we say, let's keep them separate, and we looked for a chain that had a name that could fit into the tier. We also wanted to pick up a company that had some distribution so we weren't starting from scratch.

TW: What are your plans for Rodeway?

Manion: Our plans are to take the Rodeway company and make it very aggressive and hard hitting in the marketing area of the limited service tier; to expand it as a franchise company, and to give it the necessary support it hasn't had in the past because of its financial problems.

Exhibit 2 *(continued)*

TW: In terms of your development, is it true you are dropping franchise licenses at a faster rate than you are picking up new license agreements? Does that pose a problem for the company's growth at this time?

Manion: Ramada basically held its own with no growth for three or four years as we eliminated a lot of not only franchise properties but company-owned properties that no longer fit with what we were trying to bring the company back to. So there was a rather stagnant number of properties and number of rooms for three to four years.

In 1986, we increased for the first time the number of rooms in the system. And in 1987, we increased it considerably over the previous year. We now have open and operating in Ramada, roughly 110,000 rooms.

If you will look back to past years, you will find that the replacement properties we brought in have usually been larger properties, particularly in the national marketplaces. So that most properties on the average are coming in roughly at 200 or more rooms where it was much lower before.

So while we have the same number of properties, roughly, the number of rooms was continuing to grow.

We will probably always be at a base of about 30 company-owned properties in the U.S., give or take 3 or 4 over one year or the other, and roughly 30 properties in the international marketplace, not wholly owned international but joint ventures or leases.

TW: In light of the Tax Reform Act and its effect in slowing development, last October's stock market crash and the overbuilt nature of many markets, what do you think the prospects are for development at this time?

Manion: The climate for development right now is not good. But at the same time, that doesn't mean it's not good for the hotel industry. We were tremendously overbuilt. We are still overbuilt. That's not going to change in a period of a year or two.

However, the fact that it is more difficult to develop means there will be fewer properties built and therefore those properties that are in existence will have a chance to come into a more profitable structure. This way they can survive and give the service that is necessary to satisfy the traveling public.

Source: Robin Amster, "Manion Sees New Vitality and Worldwide Role for Ramada Inns," *Travel Weekly*, March 10, 1988. Reprinted with permission from Travel Weekly.

no plans for management changes and hoped to keep on Thomas Martin as CEO.

Proceeds of the sale were to go toward a $7 cash dividend payment to shareholders. Though the terms were not announced, financial analysts estimated that Ramada would fetch no more than $60 million for Marie Callender's Pie Shops Inc. Ramada purchased the chain for $57 million and 2.5 million shares of stock in 1986.

Gaming Group Potential

The gaming group competes in the gaming industry with the operation of four casinos. It is headed by Paul Rubeli, who is also an executive vice president. Rubeli joined Ramada in 1979 as group vice president, industrial operations, and was named executive vice president, gaming, in 1982. Prior to joining Ramada, Rubeli was an industrial engineer. Despite his relative lack of experience in gaming, Rubeli is highly thought of not only in Ramada but also in the gaming industry.

The casino group for Ramada continued to be a major factor. The newly expanded Atlantic City hotel and casino was in 1985 the largest in the city. It features a 90,000-square-foot casino and 1,000 hotel rooms. This $200 million addition to the Atlantic City casino hotel included a two-acre theme park (indoor), a 508-room guest tower, a 26,000-square-foot convention center, and 37,000 square feet of additional casino space. The completion of the expansion plus the improved infrastructure of Atlantic City (Atlantic City is expanding its airport, widening the freeway system, and implementing a street traffic control system) should greatly improve Ramada's gaming revenues.

In 1984 Ramada invested over $70 million to expand and transform its Las Vegas Tropicana into a world-class resort and convention center. This work, completed in 1986, included a new 806-room guest tower and a five-acre tropical theme water park.

The Ramada casino in Reno, Nevada, incorporates a 1950s theme into an existing gaming facility. The building consists of a 35,000-square-foot casino but does not include hotel rooms. The casino opened in 1987 and was named Eddie's Fabulous 50's Casino.

In addition, Ramada owns a casino in Laughlin, Nevada, which it developed into a 406-room hotel, a 30,000-square-foot casino, five restaurants and lounges, and a 1,500-car parking facility in 1988. It was named the Ramada Express Hotel and Casino.

Some analysts felt that Ramada could quadruple its net income in 1989 and 1990 through its gaming group, which had been labeled the jewel in Ramada's crown.

Case 10

The Marriott Corporation, 1984

J. W. Marriott, Jr., President and CEO of Marriott Corporation, glanced at the calendar clock on his desk and reminded himself that the date was January 7, 1985. But his mind really wasn't on this day's events. Instead he was thinking about the future. He wondered what lay ahead for Marriott in the next five years, and especially in 1985.

J. W. was principally concerned with the overbuilding in the lodging industry and the provisions of the proposed 1985 Tax Act. He could readily recall grimacing at the headlines "U.S. Lodging Industry Is Staggered by Room Glut and Building Boom" which had appeared in *The Wall Street Journal.* The article had confirmed Marriott's own market research. He vividly remembered the quote attributed to Tom Herring, Sr., the president of the American Hotel and Motel Association: "We're on a collision course with disaster if we don't do something about the overbuilding." He had chatted with Tom several times recently and knew that Tom meant what he said. Perhaps more ominous were the proposals by the U.S. Treasury Department to virtually eliminate business deductions for travel. A lot of empty hotels would result. (Exhibit 1 contains the proposed changes in the tax laws.) J. W. did not really believe that the proposed revisions would pass, but he felt that you never could tell about such things. He wanted his firm to be prepared for the most likely scenarios.

The Marriott Corporation

The Marriott Corporation is a diversified company organized into four divisions: Hotels and Resorts, Contract Food Services, Restaurants, and, until 1983, Theme Parks/Cruise Ships. Annual sales surpassed $3 billion in 1983 and were estimated to exceed $3.5 billion in 1984 as shown in Exhibits 2 and 3. Marriott has facilities in 49 U.S. states as well as 25 countries, and employs more than 109,000 people who make an estimated 6 million customer contacts yearly.

Founded in 1927 by J. Willard Marriott, who is still chairman, the company began as a small root beer stand. Marriott is dedicated to taking special care of people away from home. The primary objective of Marriott is "to be the premier company in lodging, food service and related areas." 1984 had been one of Marriott's most memorable years of operation, filled with major events which had made it a very successful year as Exhibit 2 reveals.

Distinctive Aspects

One reason for Marriott's success is the relationship between guests and employees. The company provides an environment which stimulates pride and performance. Employees are encouraged to have the hospitable and friendly

---

This case was written by Julian W. Vincze. Source: "The Marriott Corporation, 1984" from *Strategic Management and Organizational Policy,* Third Edition, pp. 615–626, by James M. Higgins and Julian W. Vincze, copyright © 1986 by The Dryden Press, a division of Holt, Rinehart and Winston, Inc., reprinted by permission of the publisher.

This case portrays neither the effective nor the ineffective handling of an administrative situation. Rather, it is to be used as the basis for classroom discussion. The incident upon which this case is based is hypothetical.

Exhibit 1 Lodging Industry Braces for Tax Changes

The U.S. Treasury has proposed limiting deductions for out-of-town business trips and for business meals. In addition the Treasury would completely eliminate entertainment expense deductions for such items as club dues, cruise ship travel, and tickets to professional sports events.

If the Treasury's plan becomes law, the proposal is to limit out-of-town business travel expenses to a maximum of $150 per day, and for some areas (cities) of the country this would be a maximum of $100 per day. These maximums do not include the costs incurred in traveling to the destination city from the traveler's home base of business. Instead the limits per day are for lodging, meals, and other business expenses incurred at the destination city.

These limits are very restrictive, says a spokesperson for the restaurant industry. For example, the Florida Restaurant Association says that the meal limits proposed by the Treasury at $10 for breakfast, $15 for lunch, and $25 for dinner, "aren't realistic because they don't take regional differences into account."

Sources: Vicki Vaughan, "Industry Braces for Tax Overhaul," *Central Florida Business*, 7–13, 1985, pp. 10–15.

Exhibit 2 Income Statement

Marriott Corporation and Subsidiaries
Income Statement

	1984	1983	1982	1981
	(in thousands except per-share amounts)			
Sales				
Hotels	$1,640,782	**$1,320,535**	$1,091,673	$ 860,134
Contract food services	1,111,300	**950,617**	819,824	599,050
Restaurants	772,855	**679,375**	547,403	446,475
Theme Parks	—	**86,176**	82,453	94,655
Total sales	$3,524,937	**$3,036,703**	$2,541,353	$2,000,314
Operating Income				
Hotels	161,245	**$ 139,706**	$ 132,648	$ 117,561
Contract food services	90,250	**73,300**	51,006	45,552
Restaurants	76,220	**61,634**	48,492	38,533
Theme Parks	—	**13,041**	20,004	17,714
Total operating income	$ 327,715	**$ 287,681**	$ 252,150	$ 219,360
Interest expense, net	48,691	**55,270**	66,666	52,024
Corporate expenses	42,921	**34,309**	31,801	28,307
Income before Income Taxes	240,613	**198,102**	153,683	139,029
Provision for income taxes	$ 100,848	**$ 82,857**	$ 59,341	$ 52,893
Net income	$ 139,765	**$ 115,245**	$ 94,342	$ 86,136
Earnings per share				
Primary	$ 5.18	**$ 4.15**	$ 3.46	$ 3.21
Fully diluted	$ 5.18	**4.15**	$ 3.44	$ 3.20

Source: Annual reports.

Exhibit 3 Marriott Corporation and Subsidiaries Balance Sheet

	1984	1983 (in thousands)	1982
Assets			
Current assets			
Cash and temporary cash investments	$ 22,656	$ **92,279**	$ 89,811
Accounts receivable	242,341	**169,630**	167,173
Inventories, at lower of average cost or market	111,722	**95,806**	89,071
Prepaid expenses	53,330	**43,655**	36,617
Total current assets	$ 430,049	$ **401,370**	$ 381,672
Property and equipment, at cost			
Land	141,714	**171,984**	153,528
Buildings and improvements	245,367	**373,593**	419,634
Leasehold improvements	658,815	**716,461**	564,284
Furniture and equipment	415,634	**475,003**	446,133
Property under capital leases	77,566	**86,539**	89,297
Construction in progress	668,845	**388,025**	200,808
Total property and equipment	2,207,941	**2,211,605**	1,873,684
Depreciation and amortization	(375,108)	**(419,823)**	(379,457)
Total property and equipment less depreciation and amortization	$1,832,833	**$1,791,782**	$1,494,227
Other assets			
Investments in and advances to affiliates	268,177	**68,412**	42,961
Assets held for sale	230,760	**81,312**	27,979
Cost in excess of net assets of businesses acquired	26,742	**26,380**	26,929
Other	116,058	**132,172**	88,880
Total other assets	641,737	**308,276**	186,749
Total assets	$2,904,669	**$2,501,428**	$2,062,648
Liabilities and shareholders' equity			
Current liabilities			
Short-term loans	$ 7,486	$ **8,895**	$ 9,155
Accounts payable	252,806	**194,499**	183,043
Accrued wages and benefits	129,452	**111,420**	91,145
Other payables and accrued liabilities	152,654	**149,308**	116,903
Current portion of debt and capital lease obligations	31,588	**29,799**	27,898
Total current liabilities	$ 573,986	$ **493,921**	$ 428,144

(continued)

Exhibit 3 *(continued)*

Debt			
Mortgage notes payable	632,923	**491,999**	182,455
Unsecured notes payable	420,860	**509,144**	627,854
Total debt	$1,053,783	**$1,001,143**	$ 810,309
Capital lease obligations	61,504	**70,468**	79,016
Other long-term liabilities	259,694	**60,009**	61,420
Deferred income taxes	280,142	**247,683**	167,754
Shareholders' equity			
Common stock	29,419	**29,422**	29,424
Capital surplus	145,756	**140,882**	135,589
Deferred stock compensation and other	3,141	**4,160**	6,671
Retained earnings	622,283	**494,585**	389,524
Treasury stock, at cost	(125,039)	**(40,845)**	(45,203)
Total shareholders' equity	675,560	**628,204**	516,005
Total liabilities and shareholders' equity	$2,904,669	**$2,501,428**	$2,062,648

Source: Annual reports.

spirit that has become a Marriott trademark.

The Marriott Corporation became the largest chain of company-operated hotel rooms in America in 1984. They have a strong management training and development system and controls which help maintain an unsurpassed reputation.

The strategic planning, market research, and business development staffs work closely with senior operating executives to develop new opportunities. These new opportunities include the Host and Gino's acquisitions, as well as the internal developments. (See Exhibit 4.)

Marriott is one of the largest developers in the country utilizing another key skill—real estate expertise. Each year they develop hotels and restuarants valued at over $1 billion. These are designed and constructed through a fully integrated internal department.

Marriott's management is characterized as strong, stable, and aggressive. The top 100 executives average 12 years of company experience.

Financial Policies

Creative, sophisticated financial skills have been used to repurchase the company's stock, to dispose of nearly $200 million in underproductive assets, and to finance $3 billion in hotels since 1978.

Financial policies which are followed by Marriott and which are important to shareholders involve cash flow, cost of capital, debt maturity, and working capital. These financial policies are important because Marriott's ambitious capital investment and acquisition programs are financed by a combination of retained discretionary cash flow, incremental debt on an expanding asset base, and sales of hotels with management agreements. Careful management of Marriott's highly liquid hotel assets and debt structure has enabled the company to maintain targeted leverage and to minimize capital costs. (Exhibit 5 details discretionary cash flow.) Marriott bases target debt levels on cash-flow coverage of four times interest expense. Marriott's coverage objective is reported to be what lenders

Exhibit 4 Acquisition of Host and Gino's

Host International Inc.

Purchase date:	March 3, 1982.
Purchase price:	Reported at $204,725,000.
Type of business:	Operator of bars and shops in airports (nationwide).
Base of operations:	California.

Gino's Inc.

Purchase date:	February 5, 1982.
Purchase price:	Reported at $112,725,000.
Type of business:	Restaurant operations with a total of 308 locations.
	108 Rustler Steak Houses included in purchase resold in 1983.
	180 of the units acquired were updated and turned into Roy Rogers units (this conversion began in May of 1982 and was estimated to take 20 months).
Base of operations:	Mid-Atlantic market (Baltimore north to northern New Jersey).

Source: The Marriott Corporation 1983 Annual Report, *Business Week*, February 1, 1982.

require to provide the company with debt financing at prime rates.

Despite aggressive expansion, Marriott financing techniques maintained coverage at targeted levels. Total capital spending of $800 million in 1984, $499 million in 1983, and $667 million in 1982 (including Gino's and Host acquisitions) was financed primarily from internal cash-flow and hotel dispositions.

The ability to grow aggressively, yet maintain planned coverage, demonstrates that Marriott's high discretionary cash flow ($8.85 per share versus EPS of $4.15), combined with the declining capital intensity of the company's hotel business, has allowed Marriott to expand hotel rooms 20 percent annually without commensurate capital requirements. As a result, investment capacity has been released to fund additional corporate growth such as the 1982 Host and Gino's acquisitions.

Marriott's objective is to minimize the cost of capital by optimizing a mix of fixed and floating interest rate debt obligations. Marriott believes operating cash flows have a high correlation with inflation and short interest rates. Therefore the desired optimal debt structure requires a significant quantity of floating rate debt to minimize capital cost and risk. In addition, the company requires that construction in progress be financed in the traditional manner with floating rate debt. Excluding construction financing, long-term debt with floating interest rates averaged 58 percent of total debt capitalization in 1983, compared to 60 percent in 1982.

Marriott has followed a policy of avoiding new commitments of nonprepayable, fixed-rate, long-term debt since 1980. Rather than speculate on fixed interest rates at relatively high levels, the company has matched capital costs with cash

Exhibit 5 Discretionary Cash Flow vs. Net Income ($ in millions)

Year	Cash Flow	Net Income
1984	$278	$140
1983	246	115
1982	192	94
1981	157	86
1980	125	72
1979	118	71

Source: Annual reports.

Exhibit 6 Debt Maturity Schedule ($ in millions)

Year	1984	1983	1982	1981	1980	1979
1	$ 26	$ 25	$ 23	$ 16	$ 9	$ 9
2	36	36	28	17	18	18
3	50	43	36	22	18	24
4	58	50	42	40	34	27
5	72	62	48	43	38	35
Total	$242	$216	$177	$138	$117	$113
Funds provided from operations	**$330**	**$294**	**$231**	**$187**	**$150**	**$141**

Source: Annual reports.

flows, thus attempting to minimize capital cost and risk.

Debt maturity remains within Marriott's conservative policy limits, which require that total debt amortizing in the subsequent five-year period not exceed funds provided from operations of the prior year. The company has met this policy constraint by wide margins since 1979, as shown in Exhibit 6.

Marriott has no requirement for positive working capital, since it principally sells services (rather than goods) for cash. Therefore, the company maintains relatively low receivable and cash balances. Negative working capital is a source of interest-free financing. As a result of a company-instituted program to aggressively reduce current asset investment, Marriott increased its negative working capital to $93 million at year-end 1983. Exhibit 3 contains a traditional balance sheet.

Lodging

The Hotels and Resorts Division, with annual sales in excess of $1.5 billion, continues to be Marriott's largest and fastest growing. The lodging operations include locations in the United States, Mexico, Central America, the Caribbean, Europe, and the Middle East.

In 1983 sales increased by 21 percent and the trend continued with a 24 percent increase in 1984. Occupancy rates also continued to be among the highest in the industry (up 3 percent in 1983), while average room rates increased by approximately the same rate as inflation.

Marriott is noted for its aggressive marketing program. This program, begun in 1982, stresses strong ties with the airlines' frequent-flier programs but also utilizes extensive promotions at the individual hotel level, the keystone of which is the emphasis on selling skills in all levels of customer-contact employees.

The corporation has excellent employee relations. Marriott reinforces its employees' positive attitudes with recognition and development programs, but also believes in internal promotion/advancement opportunities and the need for strong technological support systems. In 1983 approximately one-third of all new managers were originally hourly paid personnel.

Marriott concentrates ownership of its hotels among outside investors while retaining long-term management contracts. In fact, over 75 percent of Marriott-operated hotels are owned by outside investors. Marriott is also a leader in financing hotel growth utilizing various methods, including private syndications, management agreements, and traditional financing. In fact it has developed and financed more than $4 billion in hotels since 1970 with $800 million in 1984 alone.

Contract Food Services (CFS)
Contract Food Services revenues amount to approximately one-third of Marriott's annual sales. CFS sales increased 16 percent in 1983 and 17 percent in 1984, while operating profit rose 30 percent in 1983 and 23 percent in 1984. CFS is the world's leading airline caterer, serving more than 150 airlines (from 80 flight kitchens located in the U.S. and abroad).

Since 1982, through its Marriott/Host facilities, CFS has been a major operator of airport terminal cafeterias, snack bars, full-service restaurants, gift shops, and newsstands. These airport operations at 39 domestic locations are viewed as complementing CFS's airline catering business and thereby broadening Marriott's ability to serve airline passengers.

A third area of CFS's activities involve providing quality meals and food-service assistance to more than 275 business, educational, and health care facilities nationwide. CFS's services range from management supervision to facilities design, and even to turnkey operations. CFS also manages education and conference center facilities for corporate clients.

In addition CFS does operate a few nonairport merchandise shops and turnpike restaurants. However CFS's strategic growth is attributed primarily to these factors: its relatively large size and depth of experience; its productivity (low costs); and its reputation for quality in operations management, procurement capabilities, and organizational depth.

Restaurants
Marriott's Restaurants Division operates or franchises over 1,800 popularly priced restaurants in 47 states, Canada, and Japan. In 1983 a sales gain of 24 percent was reported with a 27 percent increase in operating income. The sales increase was attributed to gains in both customer counts and average amount of checks, plus the addition of 100 company-operated and franchised units. The increased income was attributed to relatively stable food and labor costs throughout the year. The two largest restaurants (chains) are Roy Rogers and Big Boy.

The Roy Rogers (RR) chain was founded in 1968 and provides premium quality fast-food at more than 500 locations, primarily in the Middle Atlantic region. RR features a varied menu offering roast beef sandwiches, burgers, chicken, salad, and breakfast items. Approximately one-fourth of RR's locations are franchised.

The Big Boy (BB) chain includes more than 1,200 restaurants, making it larger than any of its direct competitors. Although founded in California more than 40 years ago, BB now is located nationwide. Most BB restaurants are franchised but more than 200—operating under the name Bob's Big Boy—are company-owned. During 1983 the Big Boy franchise system received new emphasis via cooperative national programs in marketing, menu development, and procurement, in order that Big Boy might retain its company-perceived leadership in family restaurants.

In addition to Big Boy and Roy Rogers, Marriott operates several other theme restaurants. Over 50 speciality restaurants are in operation in California or the East Coast under the Charley Brown's/Charley's Place dinner house concept or the Casa Maria Mexican restaurant concept.

Theme Parks and Cruise Ships
Marriott's fourth division until 1983 included two Great America theme parks and three Sun Line cruise ships. In total about 5 million people annually were customers of this division. The 1983 sales revenues increased about 5 percent over the prior year but operating income declined some 35 percent.

Located in Gurnee, Illinois (between Chicago and Milwaukee), and in Santa Clara, California (near San Francisco), the theme parks were designed to have strong family appeal. Thrill and family rides, as well as games, stage shows, and restaurants were offered. Attendance rose 9 percent in 1983 due to lower admission prices and aggressive marketing. However 1983's attendance was still 10 percent below the 1981 figure. Both parks were sold during 1984.

The city of Santa Clara purchased the California park for $101 million. The Gurnee park sold for approximately $114.5 million. Neither park will be operated by Marriott in the future.

The three Sun Line Ships—the Stella Oceanis, the Stella Maris, and the Stella Solaris—offer a combined total of about 140 cruises per year. Cruises are offered on the Caribbean, Aegean, and Mediterranean Seas.

Theme Parks and Cruise Ships by the end of 1984 was no longer considered a separate operating division or a "primary business line."

Remarks to Shareholders—1984 Results

J. W. had asked his secretary to bring him a copy of his "Remarks to Shareholders" from the 1983 annual meeting and, as he held the document up to look at it, his memory focused on that day (May 10, 1984).

He remembered beginning his remarks by noting the construction of the New York Marriott Marquis which, at 1,900 rooms, will be Marriott's largest hotel. However, the construction list included Boston's Copley Place and Fort Lauderdale's Beach Resort (both of which opened in 1984) as well as the Atlanta Marriott Marquis (which, with the New York Marquis, was due to open in 1985), the Orlando World Center Resort (1986), and the San Francisco–Yerba Buena Center (1988). These five added a total of over 6,000 more rooms. In fact, by including the international expansions and acquisitions, especially the Vienna, Austria, 1984 opening, the planned additions to hotel rooms totaled 26,000 by 1988.

However the real theme of his remarks had centered on the phrase about Marriott's "five special strengths–(which) are the basis for our growth strategy." J. W. scanned the copy and recalled these five distinctive strengths as:

First, our values and systems.
Number two is our leadership position.
The third strength is our business synergy.
The fourth strength is our technical skills.
Number five, we have a strong management team.

But here, J. W. paused! In his own mind the question formed—are these still our special strengths? Or, does Marriot have more than five special strengths? He didn't want to take the time now to answer these questions, but J. W. knew he would have to come back to answer these questions very soon.

Instead J. W. scanned his copy to recall how he had worded the "strategy for growth." After noting the most visible growth mechanism—"the expansion of our existing business"—which was exemplified in hotel room additions, other operations' "selective expansions" were highlighted in general terms. But perhaps the most important major growth strategy was: "acquisition and development of new businesses . . . to develop, test, and expand a number of new, yet related business opportunities."

Two specific new opportunities for 1984 had been cited, Courtyard Hotels and American Resorts Group.

Courtyard Hotels. In fact the decision to move forward from a testing of the Courtyard concept into a major expansion mode had occurred in June of 1984, shortly after the annual shareholders' meeting. A statement had been released that Marriott planned to expand Courtyard nationwide. Over the next 18 months between 20 and 30 Courtyards in: (1) New Jersey/New York; (2) Washington D.C./Baltimore; (3) Chicago/Milwaukee; and (4) northern California were planned. The total investment over five years would be between $1 and $2 billion. The statement also noted that, by the 1990s, Marriott could have more than 300 Courtyard locations with more than 5,000 rooms.

The Courtyard hotel concept had developed from Marriott's research (over several years) into the moderate-price segment of the lodging market. The moderate segment's current price range was considered to be between $30 and $60 per night and was referred to as the "largest part of the lodging market." Marriott had found that these customers viewed the following factors as important:

1. An attractive, comfortable, and functional room.

2. A relaxed, secure environment.

3. A relatively simple restaurant with good food.

4. A well-managed operation.

5. Friendly, helpful staff.

6. All the above at "affordable" prices.

To meet these customer needs, Marriott had designed a small 130- to 150-room operation that required "very few employees." The targeted customer group was focused "on the transient guests . . . not the group business of a traditional hotel."

Testing of Courtyard had occurred in Atlanta, Augusta, and Columbus, Georgia, and because of the favorable results, expansion into states adjoining Georgia was planned as well as the eventual nationwide expansion noted above.

American Resorts Group. The second example of new opportunities, American Resorts Group, was viewed as an extension of Marriott's lodging and management skills. American Resorts Group is a leading developer of vacation ownership condominiums in the time-share industry. Marriott's initial venture into the time-share industry was a 120-unit resort on Hilton Head Island in South Carolina named Monarch at Sea Pines.

J. W. knew he would have to carefully explain to the shareholders why Marriott had moved into the time-share industry. He was well aware of the many negative stories about the time-share industry which had appeared in the press recently. J. W. recognized that some shareholders were likely to hold a poor opinion of the time-share industry and perhaps even the basic concepts of time-sharing. It was even probable that some shareholders could have personally experienced a less-than-successful time-share investment, or at least have close relatives or friends who were unhappy about a time-share investment. He knew he had to think through this "new-opportunity" explanation with more than ordinary care for shareholders' sensitivities.

Recent Developments

As J. W. was pondering the ways of explaining these already-announced new opportunities which Marriott had acted upon, he also realized that other more recent developments had not yet received full disclosure. Three items immediately came to mind.

First there was the sale of the 24-unit Casa Maria Mission restaurant operation to El Torito Restaurants Inc., a subsidiary of W. R. Grace and Company. This divestiture was expected to be completed in early 1985 and was generally reviewed as consistent with Marriott's longer-term strategy related to the purchase of Host in 1982. Casa Maria was acquired as a part of Host in 1982 and since Host's acquisition, many locations which were considered peripheral to the Restaurant Division's main activities had been sold.

A second development related to a new approach to financial management of Marriott's assets. In August of 1984 a wholly-owned but indirect subsidiary had been established to purchase nine existing Marriott hotels for $305 million. The new company would continue to operate these hotels as an integral part of the Marriott Hotels and Resorts Division (via management agreement with Marriott). Interests in Chesapeake Hotel Limited Partnership were offered in private placement to accredited investors in 440 units of $100,000 each.

The third development concerned a recent decision that Marriott would build all-suite hotels. Construction of the first Marriott Suites hotel was announced to begin in the spring of 1985, with about a dozen expected to open in 1988. This new hotel product was designed to compete directly with companies already in the all-suite market. Marriott Suites would be located in suburban areas, and possibly in downtown areas of medium-sized cities. Each would contain 200 to 250 suites as well as limited meeting space.

A few other developments also had occurred. For example, during 1984 Marriott had substantial numbers of its own shares on the open market, 1,475,000 shares during the first six months of the year. Also Marriott had reported "exploring entry into the life care community development." In an approach similar to that used for the Courtyard hotel concept, Marriott had issued a statement that a test of the concept would occur with "two or three life care communities" being established "over the next four years." A decision to proceed on a larger scale would then occur. A typical Marriott life care development was expected to accommodate approximately 300 to 400 people in a complete retirement community. Services offered would include lodging, food service, recreational facilities, and limited health care facilities.

Summary of Items to Be Explained

At this point J. W. paused and mentally summarized the items which he felt needed to be explained to shareholders:

1. Full expansion of Courtyard hotels concept (moderate price customer segment);

2. Movement into time-share vacation ownership—American Resorts Group;

3. Continued expansion of major hotels with ongoing construction program;

4. Sales of the two Great America theme parks;

5. The sale of Casa Maria Mexican restaurants and the continued expansion of Big Boy and, to a lesser extent, Roy Rogers Restaurants;

6. The testing of Marriott Suites concept in hotels;

7. The purchase on the open market of Marriott's own stock; and finally

8. The continuation of funding the hotel expansion program through creative financial arrangements, i.e. the Chesapeake Hotel Limited Partnership.

However, in addition to these eight items, J. W. knew he also had the traditional explanation of operating results for 1984 to explain. He knew the stockholders would be pleased with the 1984 financial results but the future role of Marriott in the lodging industry was the key issue.

References

"Bill Marriott's Grand Design for Growth: Upscale and Down in the Lodging Market." *Business Week,* October 1, 1984, pp. 60–62.

Carmichael, Jane. "Full Speed Ahead." *Forbes,* July 5, 1982, pp. 90–94.

Celis, William, III. "U.S. Lodging Industry Is Staggered by Room Glut and Building Boom." *The Wall Street Journal,* November 26, 1984, p. 37.

"Expansion at Marriott Hits a Financial Snag." *Business Week,* June 7, 1982, p. 28.

Form 10-K, Marriott Corporation, Securities and Exchange Commission.

Gamrecki, John. "The 'New Breed': Marriott Design Transformed." *Hotel and Motel Management,* June 1982, pp. 22–23.

Karmin, Monroe W., and Morse, Robert J. "Higher Taxes? Who Would Pay." *U.S. News and World Report,* December 10, 1984, pp. 20–24.

Kordsmeier, Joseph G. "Kordsmeier Analyzes Industry's Growth," pp. 207–208.

Marriott Corporation 1983 and 1984 Annual Reports.

"Marriott's New Deals Defy the Recession." *Business Week,* February 1, 1982, pp. 21–22.

Mikesell, Lillie A. "Marriott International Headquarters." *Buildings,* August 1980, pp. 35–39.

Moody's Handbook of Common Stocks, Fall 1984.

Travel Weekly, 25th Anniversary, Vol. 42, No. 46, May 31, 1983.

Vaughan, Vicki. "Industry Braces for Overhaul." *Central Florida Business,* January 7–13, 1985, p. 15.

Weiser, Mort. "The Rise of Hotel Chains and Expansion of Markets," pp. 189, 192.

Case 10 Update*

To Our Shareholders

In 1987, Marriott Corporation reaffirmed its commitment to be a leading lodging and food service company.

As in earlier years, this resulted in strong financial performance. In 1987, sales grew 24% to over $6.5 billion. Return on equity was 22%, while earnings per share increased 19% to $1.67.

Marriott's sales and earnings have doubled over the past four years. Net income has increased over the past 20 years at a compound rate of 20%. Return on equity has remained above 20% since 1980.

We intend to remain a premier growth company. This means aggressively developing appropriate opportunities within our chosen lines of business—lodging, food service and related businesses. In each of these arenas, our goal is to be the preferred employer, the preferred provider and the most profitable company. We believe that treating our employees in a way that creates extraordinary customer service and value is central to achieving these overall goals.

Commitment to Superior Service

Marriott has two main goals in planning its future growth: to maintain its leadership in established businesses, and to become a leader in related new business. Superior service is vital if we are to achieve these objectives.

Continued Success in Established Businesses. In 1987, we continued successful operation and expansion of our existing lodging, contract services and restaurant businesses. Despite operating in highly competitive markets, each of our established businesses performed well.

Our lodging group continued to expand its market presence. We opened 14 full-service hotels and 40 moderate price Courtyards in 1987, in addition to acquiring the Residence Inn system. There now are over 100,000 Marriott-affiliated hotel rooms at 361 properties throughout the world, more than triple the number in 1980.

Despite rapid growth, service quality has remained high. In 1987, for the third consecutive year, Marriott was rated the top hotel system in a survey by *Business Travel News,* a leading trade publication. In addition, Courtyard was rated higher than all other moderate price hotels, and ahead of several more expensive chains.

Our contract services group posted solid gains in 1987. In the mid-1980s, we became the leading food service management company in the United States through three acquisitions, culminating with the purchase of Saga Corporation in 1986. Saga was the largest acquisition in Marriott's history, adding more than 900 quality food service accounts and 3,000 talented managers to our food and services management division. In 1987, we focused on retaining profitable accounts and developing more effective ways to attract new accounts.

Our airport operations and airline catering divisions continued to lead their industries, remaining very competitive by providing quality service and products. Host International has introduced food courts and expanded fast food facilities at a number of airports, to provide travelers with more convenience and a wider variety of choices. Despite cost-cutting pressures from clients, Marriott rates highly as an in-flight caterer with both airline officials and flight attendants.

Our restaurant group performed well in 1987. Big Boy rolled out three new dinners for its food bars and improved its market presence

---

*Source: Excerpts from Marriott Corporation 1987 annual report, pp. 2–4, 41–44, 54–55.

through 96 units it added, remodeled or converted from other concepts. The Roy Rogers division increased sales by continuing to enhance food quality and customer service. Our travel plaza operations generated higher sales by converting restaurants to branded concepts, and by acquiring several new units.

Excellent Service in New Arenas. In 1987, we made progress toward leadership in the large moderate price sector of the lodging industry by continuing to expand Courtyard and acquiring Residence Inn. Since its introduction in 1983, Courtyard has become a significant force in its market segment and will total 110 properties by the end of 1988. Residence Inn complements Courtyard; it has an excellent service reputation, good unit economics and operates in a different market segment. With over 100 units open, Residence Inn has a strong market presence. We expect it to double in size by the early 1990s.

In late 1987, we entered the economy segment of the lodging market by opening our first two Fairfield Inns. Four more will be added in the first quarter of 1988. We intend to open 20 Fairfield Inns by the end of 1988 and will pursue aggressive development in years to come.

We also opened the first Marriott Suites hotel in 1987 and will open the first of our smaller full-service hotels in the first quarter of 1988. Marriott Suites enables us to capitalize on the company's reputation for quality service in the growing full-service suites segment. Our new smaller Marriott hotels allow us to offer a full-service product in emerging markets.

We made excellent progress in developing lodging-related service businesses by starting construction on our first two lifecare retirement communities. We continue to believe that this arena, which we call "senior living services," offers promising opportunities.

In July 1987, we acquired Quornden Company, a leader in facilities management—which involves services ranging from housekeeping to plant operation. Facilities management provides us with ways to leverage our skills and existing customer base in food and services management.

Dispositions. We disposed of several businesses in 1987 that did not offer sufficient opportunities to sustain competitive advantage. In November, we sold the franchise rights for the Big Boy system. Family restaurants continue to present very attractive prospects for Marriott, and sale of the franchise system allows greater flexibility to pursue new opportunities in this segment. We continue to operate 214 Big Boy units which along with over 100 Howard Johnson restaurants will be converted to a new Marriott concept.

During the year, we also sold the restaurants acquired with Saga which did not fit our restaurant strategy. We sold two Sun Line cruise ships because the cruise market is relatively small, volatile and not a strong fit with our skills.

Performance through People

To become the preferred lodging and food service company, we rely on our people and their operating, development and financial skills. In 1987, our employees again enabled us to provide demonstrably superior service in virtually all of our businesses.

People are the most important resource of a service company. Throughout the company, Marriott employees share a level of commitment to customer service that we believe is unmatched by our competitors.

We recognize the challenge of rapid growth in labor-intensive businesses. The number of Marriott employees worldwide has nearly doubled in the last four years and will increase another 20% by 1990. We continue to honor a long-standing commitment to treat our people fairly and with respect, and we try hard to be responsive to their changing needs. By becoming the preferred employer in our industries, we will continue to attract top quality people in a competitive labor market.

Through centrally designed and tested operating procedures, we maintain high quality services and products while controlling costs and productivity. With combined purchases of food and supplies exceeding $2 billion each year, we help to maximize economies of scale for our businesses.

Marriott is one of the 10 largest commercial real estate developers in the country, developing over $1 billion of properties annually. Our fully integrated development process—from feasibility through construction—has enabled us to create new products such as Courtyard, Fairfield Inn and senior living services, while continuing to develop existing businesses aggressively.

Our development is supported by exceptional financial strength and innovative financing strategies. Funds provided from continuing operations increased to $473 million in 1987 and have grown at an annual rate of nearly 21% since 1980. Our financing techniques allow us to adapt to constantly changing market conditions. In 1987, we syndicated 70 Courtyards and three Marriott hotels for $890 million. We retained profitable long-term operating agreements on these properties while virtually eliminating our capital investment.

Commitment to Growth

We will pursue profitable new opportunities while remaining committed to the fundamental strategies that have served us so well. By the early 1990s, we plan to add 100,000 more rooms to our lodging group. We will continue to test new businesses with significant lodging, food and service components. And we will continue to pursue acquisitions that provide economic means of entry and expansion in our chosen businesses.

Marriott celebrated its 60th anniversary in 1987. The long, successful history of our company shows our continuing achievements in highly competitive markets as well as in difficult economic times. We believe that 1988 will be a good year for our company, and we are optimistic about the long-term prospects for our businesses.

We think Marriott will remain a sound investment. Over the past nine years, we have demonstrated this confidence by repurchasing the company's common stock when we believed it to be undervalued in the marketplace. We intend to continue this practice in the years ahead. In 1987, we purchased 13.6 million shares for $429 million; most were acquired after the October 19 drop in stock market prices.

The combination of aggressive growth and service excellence is central to our continuing success. Through these means, we will pursue our goal of being the preferred employer, the preferred provider and the most profitable in each of our chosen businesses.

We are grateful for the support of our investors, and for the loyalty and dedication of our employees.

J. W. Marriott, Jr.
Chairman of the Board and President

March 16, 1988

Income Statement

Marriott Corporation and Subsidiaries Fiscal years ended January 1, 1988, January 2, 1987 and January 3, 1986	1987	1986	1985
	(in millions, except per share amounts)		
Sales			
Lodging	**$2,673.3**	$2,233.1	$1,898.4
Contract Services	**2,969.0**	2,236.1	1,586.3
Restaurants	**879.9**	797.3	757.0
Total sales	**6,522.2**	5,266.5	4,241.7
Operating Expenses			
Lodging	**2,409.4**	2,017.4	1,712.6
Contract Services	**2,798.4**	2,081.2	1,467.7
Restaurants	**797.5**	718.2	678.8
Total operating expenses	**6,005.3**	4,816.8	3,859.1
Operating Income			
Lodging	**263.9**	215.7	185.8
Contract Services	**170.6**	154.9	118.6
Restaurants	**82.4**	79.1	78.2
Total operating income	**516.9**	449.7	382.6
Corporate expenses	**(74.5)**	(71.7)	(54.2)
Interest expense	**(90.5)**	(60.3)	(75.6)
Interest income	**47.0**	42.5	42.9
Income before Income Taxes	**398.9**	360.2	295.7
Provision for income taxes	**175.9**	168.5	128.3
Net Income	**$ 223.0**	$ 191.7	$ 167.4
Earnings Per Share	**$ 1.67**	$ 1.40	$ 1.24

The accompanying notes are an integral part of these financial statements.

Balance Sheet

Marriott Corporation and Subsidiaries **January 1, 1988 and January 2, 1987**	**1987**	**1986**
	(in millions)	
Assets		
Current Assets		
Cash and temporary cash investments	**$ 15.6**	$ 26.7
Accounts receivable	**493.6**	450.7
Due from affiliates	**125.8**	98.2
Inventories, at lower of average cost or market	**186.5**	171.3
Prepaid expenses	**97.6**	81.0
Total current assets	**919.1**	827.9
Property and Equipment		
Land	**469.5**	348.3
Buildings and improvements	**323.6**	402.9
Leasehold improvements	**1,064.9**	874.4
Furniture and equipment	**680.0**	591.8
Construction in progress	**690.2**	537.3
	3,228.2	2,754.7
Accumulated depreciation and amortization	**(650.1)**	(547.3)
	2,578.1	2,207.4
Investments in and Advances to Affiliates	**495.1**	484.5
Assets Held for Sale	**501.2**	386.4
Intangible Assets	**528.5**	403.2
Other Assets	**348.5**	269.9
	$5,370.5	$4,579.3

The accompanying notes are an integral part of these financial statements.

(continued)

Balance Sheet *(continued)*

Marriott Corporation and Subsidiaries January 1, 1988 and January 2, 1987	1987	1986
	(in millions)	
Liabilities and Shareholders' Equity		
Current Liabilities		
Accounts payable	**$ 508.6**	$ 440.8
Accrued payroll and benefits	**225.0**	211.9
Other payables and accrued liabilities	**342.7**	331.9
Current portion of long-term debt	**46.4**	32.9
Total current liabilities	**1,122.7**	1,017.5
Long-Term Debt	**2,498.8**	1,662.8
Other Long-Term Liabilities	**212.1**	193.7
Deferred Income	**289.5**	316.8
Deferred Income Taxes	**436.6**	397.5
Shareholders' Equity		
Common stock, 147.1 million shares issued	**147.1**	147.1
Additional paid-in capital	**87.7**	60.1
Retained earnings	**1,150.2**	948.9
Treasury stock, at cost, 28.3 and 16.5 million shares, respectively	**(574.2)**	(165.1)
Total shareholders' equity	**810.8**	991.0
	$5,370.5	$4,579.3

Changes in Financial Position

Marriott Corporation and Subsidiaries
Fiscal years ended January 1, 1988, January 2, 1987 and January 3, 1986

	1987	1986	1985
		(in millions)	
Operations			
Net income	**$ 223.0**	$ 191.7	$ 167.4
Add expenses not requiring current outlay of working capital:			
Depreciation and amortization	**167.1**	141.1	111.9
Deferred income taxes	**54.7**	73.6	71.7
Other	**28.0**	23.9	22.4
Funds provided from operations	**472.8**	430.3	373.4
Financing Activities			
New financing	**1,498.1**	1,358.9	751.2
Maturities and prepayments of debt	**(662.1)**	(888.4)	(696.9)
	836.0	470.5	54.3
Investing Activities			
Investments in property and equipment	**(1,166.8)**	(1,031.9)	(936.9)
Investments in and advances to affiliates	**(26.4)**	(130.8)	(115.9)
Acquisitions of businesses	**(378.6)**	(826.6)	(140.5)
Proceeds from hotel dispositions and syndications, net of tax	**475.2**	846.0	864.4
Disposals of other property and equipment	**326.9**	36.8	206.7
Other	**(139.0)**	238.0	(325.9)
	(908.7)	(868.5)	(448.1)
Capital Transactions			
Issuances of common stock	**36.4**	22.9	20.9
Cash dividends	**(21.7)**	(17.8)	(14.7)
Purchases of treasury stock	**(428.8)**	(64.7)	(4.2)
	(414.1)	(59.6)	2.0
Change in Working Capital	**$ (14.0)**	$ (27.3)	$ (18.4)
Summary of Change in Working Capital			
Cash and temporary cash investments	**$ (11.1)**	$ (20.1)	$ 24.1
Receivables, including due from affiliates	**70.5**	158.0	148.5
Inventories	**15.2**	23.6	36.0
Prepaid expenses	**16.6**	26.3	1.4
Accounts payable and accrued liabilities	**(91.7)**	(221.5)	(220.7)
Current portion of long-term debt	**(13.5)**	6.4	(7.7)
Change in Working Capital	**$ (14.0)**	$ (27.3)	$ (18.4)

The accompanying notes are an integral part of these financial statements.

Financial History

Marriott Corporation and Subsidiaries (dollars in millions, except per share amounts)	1987	1986 (53 Weeks)	1985	1984
Summary of Operations				
Sales	6,522.2	5,266.5	4,241.7	3,524.9
Earnings before interest expense and income taxes	489.4	420.5	371.3	297.7
Interest expense	90.5	60.3	75.6	61.6
Income before income taxes	398.9	360.2	295.7	236.1
Income taxes	175.9	168.5	128.3	100.8
Income from continuing operations*	223.0	191.7	167.4	135.3
Net income	223.0	191.7	167.4	139.8
Funds provided from continuing operations**	472.8	430.3	372.3	322.5
Capitalization and Returns				
Total assets	5,370.5	4,579.3	3,663.8	2,904.7
Total capital***	4,247.8	3,561.8	2,861.4	2,330.7
Long-term debt	2,498.8	1,662.8	1,192.3	1,115.3
Percent to total capital	58.8%	46.7%	41.7%	47.9%
Shareholders' equity	810.8	991.0	848.5	675.6
Return on average shareholders' equity	22.2%	20.6%	22.1%	22.1%
Return on average total capital (before interest expense and income taxes)	13.2%	12.2%	14.1%	14.8%
Per Share and Other Data				
Earnings per share:				
Continuing operations*	1.67	1.40	1.24	1.00
Net income	1.67	1.40	1.24	1.04
Cash dividends	.17	.136	.113	.093
Shareholders' equity	6.82	7.59	6.48	5.25
Quoted market price at year-end	30.00	29.75	21.58	14.70
Shares outstanding (in millions)	118.8	130.6	131.0	128.8
Hotel rooms:				
Total	102,893	77,730	67,034	60,873
Company-operated	81,244	64,502	55,920	50,930
Employees	210,900	194,600	154,600	120,100

*The company's theme park operations were discontinued in 1984.

**Funds provided from continuing operations consist of income from continuing operations plus depreciation, deferred income taxes and other items not currently affecting working capital.

***Total capital represents total assets less current liabilities.

1983	1982	1981 (53 Weeks)	1980	1979	1978	5-Year Compound Growth Rate	10-Year Compound Growth Rate
2,950.5	2,458.9	1,905.7	1,633.9	1,426.0	1,174.1	21.5%	20.4%
247.9	205.5	173.3	150.3	133.5	107.1	19.0%	18.5%
62.8	71.8	52.0	46.8	27.8	23.7		
185.1	133.7	121.3	103.5	105.6	83.5	24.4%	21.0%
76.7	50.2	45.2	40.6	43.8	35.4		
108.4	83.5	76.1	62.9	61.8	48.1	21.7%	20.9%
115.2	94.3	86.1	72.0	71.0	54.3	18.8%	19.0%
272.7	203.6	160.8	125.8	117.5	101.2	18.4%	19.4%
2,501.4	2,062.6	1,454.9	1,214.3	1,080.4	1,000.3		
2,007.5	1,634.5	1,167.5	977.7	891.9	826.9		
1,071.6	889.3	607.7	536.6	365.3	309.9		
53.4%	54.4%	52.1%	54.9%	41.0%	37.5%		
628.2	516.0	421.7	311.5	413.5	418.7		
20.0%	20.0%	23.4%	23.8%	17.0%	13.9%		
14.9%	15.1%	17.6%	18.0%	17.7%	14.5%		
.78	.61	.57	.45	.34	.25	22.3%	25.0%
.83	.69	.64	.52	.39	.29	19.3%	23.0%
.076	.063	.051	.042	.034	.026	22.0%	
4.67	3.89	3.22	2.49	2.58	2.28		
14.25	11.70	7.18	6.35	3.48	2.43	20.7%	29.0%
134.4	132.8	130.8	125.3	160.5	183.6		
54,986	49,432	40,419	30,169	26,284	22,658	15.8%	18.3%
45,909	41,126	33,088	23,704	20,956	17,987	14.6%	18.1%
109,400	109,200	81,800	67,300	65,700	63,600	14.1%	14.2%

Case 11

The Airline Industry

Since the first scheduled passenger service of the 120-mile distance between Los Angeles and San Diego, the airline industry has undergone dramatic changes. Today, the U.S. airline industry employs more than 355,000 people, operates over 4,500 aircraft, and serves over 380 million passengers.

Tremendous growth has occurred in the industry, as evidenced in Table 1. Flying, once a glamorous experience, has become today's mass transportation. Since 1975, the number of available seat-miles (one airline seat transported one mile) has increased by 80 percent, and the number of passengers has increased 85 percent. Capacity utilization has improved, with load factors rising from 53.7 percent to 61.4 percent. With the exception of a slight dip in 1982, passenger revenues have steadily increased.

Net operating profit has followed a more erratic course, with the 1978 record profits exceeding $1 billion in sharp contrast to the red ink that flowed in the 1981–83 time period. The industry returned to profitability in 1984, and earned profits in excess of $860 million in 1985.

This industry note will concentrate on domestic operations of passenger airlines, and as such, will not focus on air cargo or international operations. International operations are subject to regulation by both the U.S. and foreign governments, thus adding a degree of complexity beyond the scope of this discussion. Although a secondary source of revenue for the scheduled passenger airline, air cargo remains a somewhat unique operation served by a small group of specialized carriers.

The Competitors

Airlines are classified into three principal groups—majors, nationals, and regionals. The majors (sometimes referred to as trunks) have annual revenues exceeding $1 billion. Nationals are those carriers with annual revenues between $75 million and $1 billion. Regional airlines' revenues are less than $75 million.

The term *national* is somewhat misleading, as the operating territory of these airlines is normally regional. The nationals typically operate shorter segments and may serve smaller cities than the majors do. Aloha, Braniff, and Southwest are examples of national carriers.

Selected 1985 statistics are provided in Table 2 on the top 12 airlines in operating revenues (airlines with more than a billion dollars in revenues).

The intense competition which has occurred since deregulation has contributed to the erratic performance of several major carriers. Table 3 on page 646 compares the net operating profit or loss for 11 major carriers between 1985, 1986, and the first quarter of 1987.

The Pre-Deregulation Era

Government action has impacted the structure of the industry since its earliest days. In the industry's infant days, postal service air mail subsidies served to promote development. In the 40

This case was developed by Patricia P. McDougall, Georgia State University.

Table 1 1975–1985 Highlights—U.S. Scheduled Airlines

	1975	1976	1977	1978
Traffic—scheduled service:				
Revenue passengers enplaned (000)	205,062	223,318	240,326	274,719
Revenue passenger-miles (000)	162,810,057	178,988,026	193,218,819	226,781,368
Available seat-miles (000)	303,006,243	322,821,649	345,565,901	368,750,530
Revenue passenger load factor (%)	53.7	55.4	55.9	61.5
Passenger revenue ($000)	12,353,501	14,265,947	16,273,355	18,806,247
Freight and express revenue ($000)	1,309,779	1,497,123	1,718,529	1,986,820
Mail revenue ($000)	303,022	320,121	390,762	386,639
Charter revenue ($000)	489,856	572,580	644,381	578,285
Total operating revenues ($000)	15,355,921	17,501,215	19,924,800	22,883,955
Total operating expenses ($000)	15,228,042	16,779,282	19,016,760	21,519,092
Operating profit ($000)	127,879	721,933	908,040	1,364,863
Interest expense ($000)	402,041	371,634	373,206	538,642
Net profit ($000)	(84,204)	563,354	752,536	1,196,537
Revenue per passenger-mile (c)	7.6	8.0	8.4	8.3
Rate of return on investment (%)	3.1	8.5	10.2	6.5
Operating profit margin (%)	0.8	4.1	4.6	6.0
Net profit margin	(.5)	3.2	3.8	5.2
Employees	289,926	303,006	308,068	329,303

Source: Air Transport Association of America, Washington, D.C.

Table 2 Top 12 Airlines in 1985 in Operating Revenues

Airline	Total operating revenues ($000)	Passengers (000)	Break-even*	Net profit (loss) ($000)
American	$5,859,334	41,229	47.8	$ 322,640
United	4,920,132	38,101	56.5	(88,223)
Eastern	4,815,070	41,766	56.8	6,310
Delta	4,738,168	39,805	44.9	156,775
Trans World	3,860,695	20,871	60.0	(193,092)
Pan American	3,156,988	13,040	54.4	40,474
Northwest	2,650,008	14,538	51.5	72,961
USAir	1,749,126	19,278	47.7	109,850
Republic	1,734,397	17,442	NA†	177,006
Continental	1,731,054	16,143	NA	64,280
Piedmont	1,366,641	18,053	46.6	66,710
Western	1,306,546	11,908	51.4	67,134

*Percent of capacity that must be sold to cover all expenses.
†NA = not available.
Source: *Air Transport 1986* (the Annual Report of the U.S. scheduled airline industry).

1979	1980	1981	1982	1983	1984	1985
316,863	296,903	285,976	294,102	318,638	344,683	380,024
262,023,375	255,192,114	248,887,801	259,643,870	281,829,148	305,115,855	335,897,966
416,126,429	432,535,103	424,897,230	440,119,206	464,537,979	515,323,339	546,994,334
63.0	59.0	58.6	59.0	60.7	59.2	61.4
22,791,390	28,048,689	30,722,629	30,549,719	32,744,618	36,939,345	39,235,809
2,211,321	2,431,926	2,596,850	2,437,703	2,592,567	2,859,419	2,680,715
452,021	610,996	653,996	688,675	653,129	712,070	889,575
520,916	1,160,524	1,175,154	1,085,537	1,075,428	1,112,050	1,279,812
27,226,665	33,727,806	36,662,555	36,407,635	38,953,672	43,825,047	46,664,414
27,026,610	33,949,421	37,117,325	37,141,070	38,643,262	41,673,536	45,238,150
199,055	(221,615)	(454,770)	(733,435)	310.410	2,151,511	1,426,264
618,446	967,719	1,209,461	1,384,084	1,482,352	1,540,377	1,588,306
346,845	17,414	(300,826)	(915,814)	(188,051)	824,668	862,715
8.7	11.0	12.3	11.8	11.6	12.1	11.7
6.5	5.3	4.7	2.1	6.0	9.9	9.8
0.7	(0.7)	(1.2)	(2.0)	8.0	4.9	3.1
1.3	1.3	(0.8)	(2.5)	(0.5)	(1.9)	1.8
340,696	340,696	360,517	330,495	328,648	345,079	355,113

years between 1938 and 1978, the Civil Aeronautics Board (CAB) was given broad power in regulating entry, exit, subsidy allocation, route structure, pricing, mergers and acquisitions, and quality of service. Unlike other regulatory agencies such as the Interstate Commerce Commission, the CAB had the explicit responsibility not only for the regulation of the air transport industry, but also for its promotion and development. The CAB was not given responsibility for safety, as this was and still is, the province of the Federal Aviation Administration (FAA) formed in 1958. Since the formation of the Department of Transportation in 1966, the FAA has been housed within the DOT.

Under regulation, airlines operating in interstate markets were required to obtain a certificate from the CAB that they had been found "fit, willing, and able" to provide air transportation. In its 40 years of regulation, the board did not approve a single one of scores of proposals to form new carriers to serve major markets. The only significant entry into scheduled service came when the board certified the local service carriers after World War II. Although several local service airlines were later permitted to serve major markets, they initially were granted certificates only to replace the trunks in providing subsidized service to smaller communities.

During regulation, a carrier's route map was among its most valuable assets. Route competition was tightly controlled by the CAB through issuance of route certificates. Some routes were highly competitive, while others were protected and became the virtual property of one or two carriers. In assigning routes, the CAB often sought to maintain the status quo of the industry. A financially weak carrier was often awarded a profitable route. This type of action maintained

Table 3 Major Carrier Performance

Carrier	Net profit (loss) ($000) 1985	1986	1987—1st quarter
American	$322,640	$ 529	$25,210
Continental	64,280	(13,626)	(97,835)
Delta	156,775	(6,375)	27,076
Eastern	6,310	(110,626)	2,098
Northwest	72,961	(16,445)	(25,981)
Pan American	40,474	(125,274)	(87,690)
Piedmont	66,710	(6,918)	5,662
TWA	(193,092)	(169,363)	(54,813)
United	(88,223)	(107,284)	(35,120)
USAir	109,850	(10,360)	18,701
Western	67,134	10,883	(15,795)

Source: U.S. Department of Transportation.

competition and avoided bankruptcies. When an airline was forced to service unprofitable routes, the CAB often assigned a more profitable route as well.

Mergers were also used to maintain status quo in the industry and to avoid disruption in passenger services. Financially weak carriers were often allowed to merge in order to avoid bankruptcy.

Since deregulation virtually removed competition on pricing and routes, the various carriers competed principally on scheduling convenience and service.

Deregulation

Limited competition and the refusal of the board to permit new carriers into the industry provoked complaints from entrepreneurs who wanted to enter the industry, and from critics who argued that the industry had developed into an oligopoly that charged consumers higher prices than were necessary and offered few price or service options. Proponents of deregulation cited the lower fares of smaller, unregulated intrastate operators such as Southwest Airlines operating in Texas, and Air California and Pacific Southwest Airlines operating in California.

In light of the protected environment to which carriers had become accustomed, it was not surprising that the Airline Deregulation Act of 1978 transformed the industry. The act removed almost all market entry barriers and price controls. However, the government did retain control of safety and controlled air traffic through the Federal Aviation Administration (FAA).

With deregulation new airlines entered the industry, and with the aid of a deep recession, recruited experienced airline personnel and purchased aircraft at bargain prices. Unencumbered by union wage contracts, the new entrants operated on a lower cost basis, and in turn were able to cut fares below those of the majors. A major shakeup of the industry followed.

Costs

Labor. As shown in Table 4, labor represents the single largest expense. During regulation, fare increases were typically passed on to the consumer in fare increases. Following deregulation, the new entrants operated with significantly lower wage costs. This disparate situation was created by a number of conditions. The new entrants entered the industry at a time when there was a surplus of airline personnel, the new entrants

Table 4 Principal Elements of Airline Operating Expenses

	Percent of total operating expense	
	1982	**1983**
Labor	35.8%	36.6%
Fuel	27.8	25.0
Traffic commissions	6.2	6.9

were encumbered with union wage contracts, and their employees had no seniority. The starting pay of an airline pilot at a new airline was about $30,000, whereas the average union pilot's wage was about $71,000 per year. New entrant People Express was able to operate on a cost basis of 5.3 cents per seat mile, compared to an 11 cents average for major carriers.

Airlines with comparatively low operating costs became the industry's price leaders, forcing the higher cost carriers to lower costs so they could reduce prices. Western Airlines and Pan American both received 10 percent wage cuts from its employees, with workers receiving company stock in exchange. Some airlines drastically cut their work forces and sought higher productivity. For example, United pilots increased their flying time 15 percent. More extreme measures occurred at some airlines. With Continental's bankruptcy in 1983, Chairman Lorenzo reduced pilots' salaries of $89,000 to $43,000 and flight attendants' salaries dropped from $29,000 to $15,000.

As airline executives attempted to rachet down wages, the controversial two-tier wage system developed. The economic recovery and resultant expansion in the industry changed a labor surplus into a tight labor market, and by the mid-1980s, the two-tier systems began to be modified or eliminated. New entrants were forced to increase wages to retain their personnel. Industry giants, as well, found themselves subject to wage competition. A 29-day strike by United pilots in 1985 prevented the carrier from achieving its objective of permanent lower wages. American, finding its pilot salary scales lagged United, hastened to match United. American abandoned its two-tier wage scale for mechanics and proposed to abandon it for flight attendants.

Fuel. Fuel costs represent the second most significant cost to the carrier. Carriers have attempted to reduce fuel costs through the purchase of more fuel efficient aircraft, speed reduction, and weight reduction. Lighter seats and carpets, the elimination of 125 to 450 pounds of exterior paint, a change from glass to plastic minibottles, and carrying a reduced quantity of drinking water have all contributed to weight reduction. Even small reductions in speed bring large fuel savings. For example, a reduction of 14 miles per hour on a DC-8 in a flight from Chicago to Los Angeles saves 164 gallons of fuel, but adds only 4 minutes of flight time.

Following deregulation, fuel costs skyrocketed. The average price per gallon in 1978 was $.392; in 1979 it rose to $.578. It continued to rise in 1980 to $.894, and by 1981 was $1.042. For some airlines, fuel costs escalated to more than one third of operating expenses. The reaction of some major carriers of purchasing more fuel efficient aircraft and selling off older, less fuel efficient aircraft, created a glut of airplanes. New entrants purchased these aircraft at fire-sale prices and were able to offset their higher fuel costs with lower labor costs. People Express purchased seventeen 737s for only $62 million. That same amount would have purchased only four new 737s.

The drop in fuel costs since the early 1980s and the fuel conservation measures have benefited the industry. From June 1985 to June 1986, aviation fuel costs plummeted 35 percent to $.52 a gallon—one half the 1981 cost. Each one cent change in the price of jet fuel affects operating costs by about $100 million.

Barriers to Entry

Hub and Spoke System. In the hub and spoke system an airline uses connecting flights to and from smaller spoke cities to generate traffic for flights from hubs in larger cities. This ability to feed passengers from one flight to another has allowed large airlines to dominate traffic at major airports, reaping economies of scale and enormous market clout. For example, US Air, Inc., in Pittsburgh and TWA in St. Louis control more than 80 percent of the flow through these hubs.

The spoke flights may be flown by the carrier's own planes, or increasingly, major carriers are linking with smaller, commuter lines to generate traffic for flights from hubs in larger cities. The advantages of the system are numerous: a large number of points are connected without having to schedule individual flights between them; lightly traveled point-to-point segments are avoided; the passenger is retained in the system for a longer distance without interlining; and the carrier has a centralized location for maintenance, control, and crew base.

Facilities. Sufficient facilities (air traffic control personnel and airports) have not kept pace with the increased air traffic following deregulation. The 1981 Professional Air Traffic Controllers Organization (PATCO) strike added additional pressure to the system. New entrants and airlines wishing to expand often find that established carriers already control terminal facilities such as ticket counters and gates at congested airports. Landing slots may be allocated by the FAA.

Antitrust immunity has been granted to establish airlines for meetings to allocate slots and gates. With demand exceeding supply, agreements have been difficult to reach, and their allocations have not pleased new entrants and small commuters. No easy solution is seen in the short term as additional airports and massive additions to the air traffic control system require a long lead time.

Computer Reservation Systems. The unfairness of computer reservation systems (CRS) have long been argued by the small carriers. These systems handle approximately 90 percent of flights booked by travel agents. The systems are available to all carriers for a fee. In response to charges that the systems offered unfair advantages to the host company in methods of display and ticketing, the CAB adopted anti-bias rules in 1984. Even so, Delta Air Lines complained to the Transportation Department that American Airlines, who owns the largest CRS, had "abused its CRS market power to the detriment of air transportation."[1] American has denied the charge.

Five CRS systems are currently in operation. These are owned by American, United, TWA-Northwest, Texas Air, and Delta. American's Sabre and United's Apollo, together, account for about 70 percent of the market. The CRSs have become an important source of revenues for their owners. Some of the systems have been extended to other kinds of reservations, such as hotels and rental cars.

Frequent Flier Programs. Frequent flyer programs have probably become the most widely used and successful marketing effort in the industry. These plans offer points for various totals of mileage which can then be traded for free airline tickets. The plans are designed to build carrier loyalty among customers. Since the programs were introduced in 1981, airlines have issued about 30 million memberships. Julius Maldutis, an airline analyst with Salomon Brothers, estimates that if the rewards were claimed, the potential lost revenue would amount to over $300 million for the industry. Triple award programs increase the potential for lost revenue to $940 million. As seen in Table 5, the potential revenue lost to American, the program's innovator and largest member, is $190 million.

Wall Street analysts, who try to predict the financial performance of the industry, contend that the airlines don't have a consistent method of accounting for the value of frequent-flier re-

[1]"Is Deregulation Working?" *Business Week,* December 22, 1986, p. 53.

Table 5 Frequent-Flyer Programs

Airline	Membership (millions)	Extra potential revenue loss* (millions)
American	6.3	$190
Continental/Eastern	3.0	170
Delta	4.0	140
Northwest	3.0	90
Pan Am	1.0	30
TWA	4.0	15
United	6.0	215
USAir/Piedmont	3.0	90
Total	30.3	940

*Includes direct losses (cost of meals, baggage handling, etc.) and potential lost ticket sales if members cashed in their miles.
Source: Salomon Brothers, Inc., estimates.

wards. One of the Financial Accounting Standards Board (FASB) proposals for measuring frequent flyer liabilities called for airlines to set aside 10 percent of their revenues to cover potential losses from the reward programs. Such an accounting change could have a devastating impact on earnings.

Code Sharing—New Opportunity for the Commuters and Regionals

Deregulation allowed the major carriers to abandon lower-density routes they were previously required to serve, thus abandoning service to many smaller cities. This created opportunities for the commuter and regional carriers. In the first five years following deregulation, they increased their service from less than 175 cities to over 850 cities. Airplanes belonging to this group typically accommodate about 19 passengers, although a small percentage hold more than 30 passengers. The number of cities they serve has remained fairly constant since this time, as the majors have, for the most part, completed their route abandonments.

Recent growth for the commuters and regionals has resulted primarily from marketing agreements with major carriers. Table 6 lists some of the larger airlines and their partners. The commuters or regional airline feeds traffic from smaller cities into the major's hub airport, and in return the smaller airline code-shares the major's flight schedule. In code-sharing the smaller carrier's flight schedule is listed with that of the

Table 6 Major Airlines' Code-Sharing Agreements (as of March 1987)

Major airline	Partners
American Airlines	Air Midwest, AV Air, Chaparral, Command Airways, Executive Air Charter, Metro Airlines, Simmons Airlines, Wings West
Continental Airlines	Air New Orleans, Britt Airways, Colgan Airways, Emerald Airlines, Gull Air, Mid Pacific Air, PBA, Presidential Airways, Rocky Mountain Airlines, Royale Airways, Trans-Colorado
Delta Air Lines	Atlantic Southeast, Business Express, Comair, Skywest
Eastern Air Lines	Air Midwest, Atlantis Airlines, Aviation Associates, Bar Harbor, Britt Airways, Metro Airlines, Precision Valley Aviation
Northwest Airlines	Big Sky Airlines, Express Airlines, Fischer Brothers, Mesaba Aviation, Simmons Airlines
Pan American	Air Atlanta, Pan Am Express (Ransome), Presidential Airways
Piedmont Aviation	Brockway Air, CCAir, Henson Aviation, Jetstream International
Trans World Airlines	Air Midwest, Piedmont, Resort Air, Resort Commuter
United Airlines	Air Wisconsin, Aspen Airways, Westair Commuter
USAir	Air Kentucky, Chautauqua Airlines, Crown Airlines, Pennsylvania Airlines, Pocono Airlines, Southern Jersey Airways, Suburban Airlines

Source: *Travel Weekly*.

Table 7 Concentration among Carriers Increasing

1986 Rank	Company	Market share	1985 Rank	Company	Market share
1.	Texas Air System	19.6%	1.	American	13.3%
2.	United	16.4	2.	United	12.5
3.	American	14.1	3.	Eastern	10.0
4.	Delta	11.7	4.	TWA	9.6
5.	NWA	10.1	5.	Delta	9.0
6.	TWA	8.2	6.	Pan Am	8.1
7.	USAir	7.1	7.	NWA	6.7
8.	Pan Am	6.0	8.	Continental	4.9
9.	Southwest	2.0	9.	People Express	3.3
10.	America West	0.9	10.	Republic	3.2
	Others	3.9		Others	19.4

Source: Department of Transportation and S&P.

larger carrier in the commuter reservation system. The smaller carrier may also benefit from shared advertising and the handling of flights at the larger airline's gate. The larger carrier benefits by the added development of their hub operation at a minimal cost. Passengers can be carried beyond the major hub airport without the cost of providing support operations at the smaller city.

Airline Oligopoly—The Reconcentration of the Industry

The fierce competition by new entrants which followed deregulation appears to be about over as the industry returns to the conditions which brought on regulation in the first place. With more than half of the airlines operating in 1978 and two thirds of the new entrants having failed, the industry is dominated by six megacarriers controlling 80 percent of the market, versus 73 percent in 1978. Ten airlines control 96 percent of the market. Airlines consultant Lee Howard of Airline Economics, Inc., predicts a share of more than 90 percent by 1990. Market shares of the 10 largest carriers for 1985 and 1986 are shown in Table 7.

Industry analysts cite the following seven major factors as contributing to this reconcentration:

1. Hub and spoke development by major national airlines.

2. Marketing alliances between large and regional/commuter airlines.

3. Control of traffic by such mechanisms as computerized reservation systems and code-sharing.

4. Innovative marketing plans such as bonus miles for frequent flyers.

5. Control of airport access gates, landing slots, ticket counters, and hangars.

6. Mergers and acquisitions.

7. Bankruptcies.[2]

As indicated from Table 8, 19 of the 36 scheduled carriers operating before deregulation are no longer in operation, having either been acquired, merged, or declared bankrupt. The operating percentages of the other categories are

[2]Frank A. Spencer and Frank H. Cassell, "Airline Oligopoly Reemerges from Deregulation," *Airline Pilot* 56, no. 5 (1987), pp. 10–14.

Table 8 Airline Attrition under Deregulation, October 1978–December 31, 1986

Category	Total	No longer operating	Currently operating	Percent operating
Certified prior to regulation	36	19	17	47%
Former intrastate	4	3	1	25
Former supplemental charter	10	10	0	0
Former commuters	59	38	21	36
New entrants	119	84	35	29
Former all cargo	6	5	1	17
Total	234	159	75	32%

Source: Frank A. Spencer and Frank H. Cassell, "Airline Oligopoly Reemerges from Deregulation," *Airline Pilot* 56, no. 5 (1987), p. 13.

even lower. Of the four former intrastate carriers, only one remains in operation. All 10 of the former supplementals have ceased operation. Thirty-eight of the 59 former commuters have disappeared. Of the new entrants, 84 of the 119 have fallen from the industry. The six all-cargo lines have been reduced to one.

Rampant merger activity characterized the industry in the 1980s. The 22 mergers shown in Table 9 represent over $7 billion spent in pursuing concentration. Texas Air, which has accounted for much of the activity, has combined Continental Airlines, New York Air, Eastern, People Express, and Frontier Airlines to become the largest airline in the free world.

The increased importance of the hub and spoke system has been an impetus for merger activity, as a merger is often viewed as the cheapest and most efficient manner to enter a market dominated by a competitor's hub. Delta's acquisition of Western added a valuable western hub in Salt Lake City to Delta's major hub in Atlanta.

Declining Service, Concern for Safety, and Reconcentration Foster the Move toward Re-regulation

The American public's increasing concern with flight safety and the declining quality of service has made re-regulation at some minimum level more amenable. Complaints by passengers to the Department of Transportation, flight delays, and the bumping of passengers from overbooked flights have increased.

Reports of near midair collisions involving at least one commercial airliner jumped 48 percent in 1987. Airline pilots filed 487 reports of near collisions with the Federal Aviation Administration (FAA) in 1987, compared with 329 in 1986. Sixty-six of these were classified as critical; that is, the planes passed within 100 feet of each other.

Many pilots believe the air traffic control system has not fully recovered from the 1981 Professional Air Traffic Controllers Organization Strike, and that the federal government has failed to provide sufficient facilities to handle the increased traffic. FAA officials dismiss the charges that the system is not back up to standards. The FAA is quick to note that despite the record number of near miss reports, the actual number of in-flight collisions dropped from 27 in 1986 to 21 in 1987.

Unprecedented fines have been levied by the FAA on American Airlines, Continental, and Eastern Air Lines for maintenance violations. To correct faulty maintenance practices which earned Eastern $9.5 million in fines in 1985, the airline increased its spending on maintenance to

Table 9 Merger/Acquisition Activity, 1980–1987

Year	Companies	Price ($ millions)
1980	Pan Am-National	373.7
	Republic–Airwest	38.5
1981	Texas Air–Continental (50 percent)	80.8
1985	Southwest–Muse	61.8
	People Express–Frontier	309.0
	United–Pan Am Pacific Routes	750.0
	Texas Air–Continental (19 percent)	81.1
1986	Northwest–Republic	884.0
	Texas Air–Eastern	607.5
	Trans World–Ozark	224.0
	People Express–Britt	36.0
	People Express–PBA	UNK
	Delta–Western	860.0
	Alaska–Jet America	19.8
	Texas Air–People/Frontier (September 16)*	298.0
	Texas Air–Rocky Mountain Airways	3.0
	American–AirCal (November)	225.0
	Alaska–Horizon	68.0
	USAir–PSA	400.0
1987	USAir–Piedmont	1,600.0
	Total	7,365.2

*Note: Texas Air later reduced its offering for People Express from $138.4 million to $113.7 million, a decrease of about $25 million. A proposed $146 million merger of Frontier and United Airlines was aborted because of lack of agreement on Frontier pilot pay after absorption into United.
Source: Frank A. Spencer, "The Creeping Shadows of Re-regulation," *Airline Quarterly*, April 1988, p. 8.

$500 million in 1987. Maintenance problems on aircraft may entail serious safety concerns which are not apparent to the consumer. For instance, American was fined for a leaky toilet, a problem more than merely hygienic. Water escaping to the outside of the plane formed a chunk of ice that knocked off an engine in midflight.

Calls for some form of reregulation are being heard from diverse quarters. Alfred E. Kahn, former chairman of the CAB and considered to be deregulation's granddaddy, has expressed serious concerns about anticompetitive side effects of deregulation. In a June 1987 speech, Robert Crandall, chairman and president of American Airlines, suggested that the government should allocate airport capacity. New entrants, as well, are beginning to suggest a return to regulation as they find it more and more difficult to protect themselves in the concentrating industry. Code-sharing is seen by many of the commuters as a form of domination by the majors in which the commuter airline is forced to lose its independence in order to survive in an oligopolistic market. Environmentalists want greater regulation in noise and particulate emissions.

Just as the industry appears to be returning to some stability, many industry analysts predict that the Department of Transportation or Congress may be forced to return the airline industry to some form of regulation.

Case 11 Update*

Airline Industry, 1988

Fundamentals for the airline group appear to be reasonably positive, at this juncture. Indeed, we're optimistic that the industry has evolved to the point where the fare structure will no longer be as vulnerable to collapsing as it once was. Still, earnings prospects are mixed. 1988 is shaping up as a record year. But next year may well be another story, given our forecast of a mild recession in the June and September interims.

In our view, there are currently few interesting investment opportunities within the Air Transport Industry. A number of these stocks, however, are suitable for inclusion in risk-tolerant portfolios that are focusing on capital gains to the early Nineties.

The Evolving Marketplace

The airline group has endured tumultuous times since deregulation occurred a decade ago and, for the most part, industrywide profitability has been disappointing over this period. Two external factors were responsible for a good deal of the poor bottom-line performance—the sharp rise in fuel prices and the walkout by the air traffic controllers. But throughout this evolution—which is still ongoing—industry players have grappled with the problem of fares. This shouldn't have been surprising; ticket prices, as well as market entry and/or withdrawal, had previously been controlled by the federal authorities. Suddenly, not only were carriers freed to set fares and redeploy assets at their own discretion, but restrictions on the number of players in the marketplace were also removed.

Indeed, the post-deregulation era was initially characterized by a rash of new entrants which weren't burdened with seniority and unionized work forces; and these upstart carriers were able to profitably price their services below those of the major airlines. Thus, in order to maintain market share, the established companies found they had to slash prices. The resulting lower fare structure, plus the surge in fuel prices, pushed the industry into the red. But the older players fought back by seeking ways to differentiate their service and reduce costs. This led to the development of hub-and-spoke flying (to carry more passengers from origin to destination by offering connecting opportunities at a central location), and frequent flyer programs (to establish a base of loyal customers). Ploys used by one airline to distinguish itself from its competitors were quickly copied by the other carriers, however. Seats became pretty much a commodity product, and fare discounting ran rampant.

The combination of declining oil prices, a strong economy, and a lengthy strike by United's pilots (which proved to be a boon for all other industry players) helped the bottom line in '84 and '85. But consistent profitability remained elusive, and the established carriers finally realized that market share couldn't be secured by pricing alone. The strategy eventually embraced was one of "critical mass". The theory here was that maximizing revenues required control of a reasonably good flow of traffic which, in turn, necessitated a wide base of loyal customers. In order to build the latter, an airline had to be able to satisfy a great proportion of travelers' needs, and this pretty much required an extensive domestic route network. So, the industry entered a phase of consolidation, as the now-major carriers scrambled to expand their domain by acquiring more vulnerable players as quickly as possible.

*Source: Marilyn M. McKellin, "AIR TRANSPORT INDUSTRY," *Value Line Investment Survey*, September 30, 1988, pp. 251–252. Copyright © 1988 by Value Line, Inc.; used by permission.

Composite Statistics: Air Transport Industry*

1984	1985	1986	1987	1988	1989	© Value Line, Inc.	91-93E
39743	42803	38885	46684	**55000**	**58000**	Revenues ($mill)	**75000**
57.8%	55.3%	57.9%	60.0%	**58.0%**	**57.0%**	Load Factor	**57.0%**
11.7%	10.3%	10.7%	10.4%	**10.5%**	**11.0%**	Operating Margin	**12.0%**
2455.0	2693.5	2773.7	2848.3	**2775**	**2950**	Depreciation ($mill)	**3700**
827.8	438.3	39.6	129.8	**1000**	**1250**	Net Profit ($mill)	**1750**
45.0%	47.9%	NMF	NMF	**30.0%**	**33.0%**	Income Tax Rate	**34.0%**
2.1%	1.0%	.1%	.3%	**1.8%**	**2.2%**	Net Profit Margin	**2.3%**
10919	13734	15402	16827	**21000**	**22000**	Long-Term Debt ($mill)	**25000**
8851.4	10704	11432	13199	**13750**	**14700**	Net Worth ($mill)	**19750**
7.1%	4.4%	2.6%	3.1%	**5.5%**	**6.0%**	% Earned Total Cap'l	**6.5%**
9.4%	4.1%	.4%	1.0%	**7.5%**	**8.5%**	% Earned Net Worth	**9.0%**
8.3%	2.4%	NMF	NMF	**6.5%**	**7.5%**	% Retained to Comm Eq	**8.0%**
23%	47%	NMF	NMF	**20%**	**16%**	% All Div'ds to Net Prof	**15%**
12.8	42.8	NMF	NMF	Bold figures are Value Line estimates		Avg Ann'l P/E Ratio	**11.0**
1.19	3.48	NMF	NMF			Relative P/E Ratio	**.90**
.8%	.8%	.8%	.7%			Avg Ann'l Div'd Yield	**.7%**

*Excludes Airborne Freight, Air Express Int'l, British Airways, Emery Air Freight, Federal Express, KLM, Tiger Int'l.

By now, merger mania has just about run its course, and a vastly different marketplace has emerged. To better understand the change the industry has undergone, consider this: Of the carriers covered by Value Line in the early 1980s, Eastern, Frontier, Ozark, Pacific Southwest, People Express, Piedmont, Republic, and Western are no longer independent. Indeed, about 80% of the market is now dominated by six companies—*AMR, Delta, NWA, Texas Air, UAL,* and *USAir.* Importantly, fare restructuring has been one of the major consequences of this transformation. To be sure, discount traffic still accounts for about 90% of the total. But the majors that survived deregulation have all developed sophisticated computerized systems to maximize revenues by coordinating flight demand and the sale of reduced-fare tickets. The absence of new entrants, and the fact that marginal carriers have either been grounded or acquired, has also helped the industry to establish restrictions that make it difficult for the typically price-insensitive business traveler to qualify for the discount fares.

At this juncture, a return to the destructive fare wars of the early '80s appears unlikely. That's not to say that discounting will abate. Indeed, we think the cut-rate ticket is here to stay. But, given that the industry is dominated by only a half-dozen megacarriers, it seems probable that a reasonable fare structure will prevail. That's largely because fewer players frequently mean less competitive pressures. Witness Northwest's near-monopoly in its major markets at Minneapolis-St. Paul, Detroit, and Memphis, USAir's dominance at Pittsburgh, and the benefits *Delta* is reaping from the problems of its main competitor—Eastern. Additionally, our optimism is in part due to the fact that the individual carriers are focusing more on profits these days; but it also assumes that *Texas Air* continues with its strategy of upgrading service and attempting to raise revenue per passenger mile at Continental.

We're further encouraged because quality of service—as measured by the now-publicized reports of on-time performance and number of passenger complaints—is fast becoming a major weapon in the airlines' marketing arsenals. Though better service does take its toll on the cost side of the ledger, we think such a move away from price-only considerations will be a definite positive over the longer haul.

How Fundamentals Are Holding Up

There are four critical variables for the airline group—yield (revenue per passenger mile), traffic, fuel prices, and labor-related expenses. As discussed above, the yield picture is looking reasonably bright. The other major factor that influences these companies' revenues is traffic. Gains in revenue passenger miles are running at good levels in view of the recent upturn in yields. Moreover, we don't look for a marked weakening over the next year or so since comparisons will not be against a particularly strong base. The story on the expense side doesn't give rise to too much concern either. True, there will be substantial—but manageable—capacity additions next year, as United ramps up its expansion plans and Airbus and McDonnell Douglas catch up on aircraft deliveries to American. And for the time being, we're not estimating any spike up in jet fuel prices over the near term. As usual, on the labor front there are pluses and minuses. The recent spate of takeovers has exacerbated these issues. *NWA's* negotiations with its pilots are stalled, as the groups from Northwest and Republic struggle to come up with a combined seniority list. *USAir* faces similar difficulties as it seeks to assimilate the work forces of PSA and Piedmont. *UAL* has yet to resolve differences with its pilots. *Pan Am* seems to be making little headway in getting its unions to accept more competitive contracts. Finally, Eastern's unions have taken their grievances to both the FAA and the courts. We doubt that *NWA* or *USAir* will face serious difficulties in reaching satisfactory

Figure 11A Relative Strength (Ratio of Industry to Value Line Comp.)

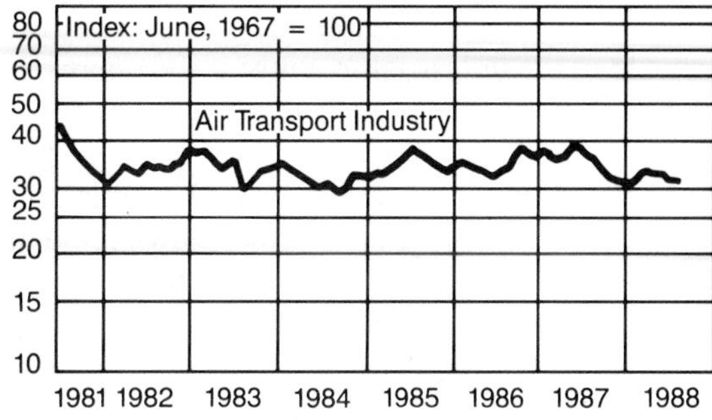

Source: "AIR TRANSPORT INDUSTRY," *Value Line* (Sept. 30, 1988): 251.

settlements. We're less optimistic about the situation at *UAL*. As far as Eastern is concerned, we think management's current proposal will be rejected and that at some point mediators will start the clock ticking on a 30-day cooling off period. If so, odds would seem to favor a strike by machinists. On the plus side, *AMR* and *Delta*, along with regional carriers like *Southwest*, have no potentially confrontational labor discussions looming on the horizon. On balance, then, though we foresee employee-related expenses gradually drifting up as the two-tier wage scale is eventually merged into one, we don't see any sharp departure from the status quo in the near term.

Earnings Prospects This Year and Next

Postings in the past couple of quarters have generally been stronger than had been expected. We think the better results are due to a number of factors—some of which are discussed above. Higher yields, in our opinion, are the major reason for the improvement. Though discounting ebbs and flows, the pricing structure is such that the typical all-important business traveler has difficulty qualifying for a reduced-fare ticket. As we've mentioned, this happy situation is probably the result of a somewhat less competitive marketplace. Yield management systems are also playing a big role in limiting the damages of promotional fares. We think the recent strength shown in the industrial sector of the economy is another reason for the good growth most of these companies are enjoying. Economic expansion is now being led by gains in industrial production, and corporate profits are on the upswing. Such a scenario suggests that travel for business purposes—more often than not at full-fare—is on the rise. On the whole, we now expect 1988 to be one of the airline sector's best ever.

Prospects of a mild recession along about mid-1989 dampen our enthusiasm for next year. Although at this juncture we only expect a modest downturn in the second and third interims, this could well be enough to trigger deeper fare discounts, particularly in view of the industry's planned capacity additions. To be sure, we think the staying power of the group's major players, plus the yield management expertise that all six have demonstrated, will prevent the degree of erosion in revenue per passenger mile that characterized the early Eighties. Still, the downward pressure on yield and traffic that would be precipitated by even a mild recession would not go unnoticed. Accordingly, we aren't looking for more than modestly improved share net next year from most of the airlines under review here. An exception, in our opinion, would be *NWA*, which should have most of its post-merger difficulties behind it. *Texas Air's* losses should narrow substantially, too, assuming that the impasse with Eastern's employees can be satisfactorily resolved before midyear.

Investment Considerations

The Air Transport Industry remains in the lower third of Value Line's industry rankings for relative market performance in the upcoming six to 12 months. That's not to say, however, that there are not investment opportunities here. Indeed, we think a number of these equities offer 3- to 5-year capital gains potential that's greater than that of the typical issue. In selecting long-term holdings, however, we recommend that investors focus on the stocks of companies that can be characterized by the following: a strong domestic route system or market niche, solid finances, some flexibility in capital spending plans, a management team with a proven track record, access to a computerized reservations system, an efficient fleet, and a history of reasonably good labor relations. At present, the companies that appear to fit this bill are *AMR, Delta, NWA, Southwest,* and *USAir.*

Case 12

Delta Air Lines, Inc.

Introduction

Delta Air Lines Inc. is a major truck air carrier providing scheduled air transportation for passengers, freight, and mail over a network of routes throughout the United States and abroad. Delta's route structure crisscrosses the continental United States and serves Alaska and Hawaii. In addition, Delta operates flights to Canada, Bermuda, the Bahamas, Puerto Rico, England, Germany, France, Ireland, Japan, Korea, Mexico, and Taiwan. Service over most of Delta's routes is highly competitive. As an air carrier, Delta is subject to federal regulation pursuant to the Federal Aviation Act of 1958, as amended (primarily concerning international transportation), as well as many other federal, state, and foreign laws and regulations.

Delta is presently one of the largest airlines in the world and is considered to be one of the most profitable and best-managed airlines. The story of Delta Air Lines goes back to the birth of aviation.

Company History

The name of the company was St. Petersburg–Tampa Airboat Line when its first commercial flight took place in 1914. The line consisted of a single small flying boat that carried two passengers at a time. Designed as an alternative to steam engine trains, the first "Delta" flight was slower than the train.

This case portrays neither the effective nor the ineffective handling of an administrative situation. Rather, it is to be used as the basis for classroom discussion.

Analyzing Delta is impossible without considering Collett Everman Woolman, the man who created the company. Born in 1899 in Indiana, he had been interested in aviation since boyhood. At the age of ten, he visited France to attend the first air show in the world.

Delta was created on November 18, 1928, and chartered a few weeks later, on December 3. Because the company began in the Mississippi delta region, the name Delta Air Service was chosen. At age 30, Woolman became the first vice president. The company's capital consisted of 800 shares at $100 per share.

Delta inaugurated passenger service little more than six months later, in June 1929. The first trip was a 90-mile-per-hour jaunt from Dallas, Texas, to Jackson, Mississippi. Prior to this, however, Delta had served the south as the world's first crop-dusting organization, as a division of Huff Daland Manufacturing Company of Ogdensburg, New York. C. E. Woolman was an active member of this group and aided in the break in 1928 to form Delta.

In 1930 the company changed its name to Delta Air Corporation and sought an award from the U.S. Post Office for the southern airmail route. Unfortunately, a rival airline received the award, and Delta was forced to remain primarily in the crop-dusting business. Four years later, however, all airmail routes were submitted for rebid and Delta won the route from Dallas/Fort Worth to Birmingham and beyond to Atlanta and Charleston. After only six years, the company's climb to prominence had firmly begun.

In 1941 Delta was awarded routes from Atlanta to Savannah, Georgia, and from Atlanta to

Knoxville, Tennessee, and Cincinnati, Ohio. This new mileage necessitated a reevaluation of company goals, and Delta management decided to move the general offices and the main overhaul maintenance from Louisiana to Altanta.

For the next few years, as World War II began and ended, few routes were added in the airline industry. With the return of peace, however, considerable expansion took place. In December 1945 Delta's routes were expanded once again, this time north to Chicago and south to Miami.

In 1953 Delta obtained a smaller, fairly new airline in a merger, thus increasing its routes even further. By 1955 Delta was able to link the South and Southwest with the Northeast travel markets, when the Civil Aeronautics Board awarded the company 1,075 miles of new routes into the New York/Washington, D.C., area. A year later, in 1956, the first pure jet service was offered by Delta and by Northeast, which flew primarily the northeastern states. At this time, Northeast introduced Boeing 707 flights between New York and Miami. Over the next few years, both airlines increased their lines to become major transcontinental air carriers, flying to California, Nevada, and Montreal. In 1969, flights even began to Bermuda. Three years later, the two companies merged, exchanging one-tenth of one Delta common share for one Northeast common share. Although the CAB limited the merger agreement, in 1976 Delta was finally awarded the Los Angeles–Miami flight that had belonged to Northeast prior to the merger.

In a move that shook the industry, Delta Airlines agreed on September 9, 1986, to acquire Western Air Lines for $860 million. This merger created the fourth largest airline in the United States. "It truly makes Delta a national carrier," said David Garrett, Jr., Delta's chairman at the time.[1] According to Helane Becker of Drexal Burnham Lambert, "The advantage of the Western deal is in the national route system it creates."[2] It allowed Delta to expand domestically and internationally. The merger boosted Delta's hub-and-spoke system with a major presence in Salt Lake City and Los Angeles. It was expected that Delta would have to do something if it were going to compete with American, Texas Air, and United. The acquisition of western by Delta took its place among the flurry of airline mergers and acquisitions after deregulation, as summarized in Exhibit 1.

Through the years, Delta has been characterized as the airline that makes the most money, although not the largest airline or the line with the most passengers. With earnings considerably better than other trunk airlines, Delta is among the most profitable and steadiest airlines in the United States. Delta also has the best cumulative net income in the industry for the 1980s.

Delta has not only survived such difficulties as the fuel crisis, the PATCO (air traffic controller) strike, and deregulation, but has been productive and consistent, committed to success. Delta has always wanted to have the best fleet and most fuel-efficient planes in the industry. Aided by management's financial conservatism, the company has developed important borrowing power, which allows it to improve its fleet whenever necessary.

Because of these assets, Delta was able to add overseas routes between Atlanta and Frankfort in 1979, to Paris in 1985, and to Honolulu in 1986.

Route System Characteristics

With all its assets, Delta has an expansive route system. One of the shortest flights is Atlanta to Birmingham—100 miles–and one of the longest is the intercontinental flight to Europe. In addition, the company's route system allows it to be profitable in both winter and summer months.

[1]John T. Barr, "Delta Comes Out Swinging," *Business Week,* September 22, 1986, 24.

[2]"Fewer Airlines are Flying High," *U.S. News & World Report,* September 22, 1986, 60.

Exhibit 1 Airline Mergers and Acquisitions since Deregulation

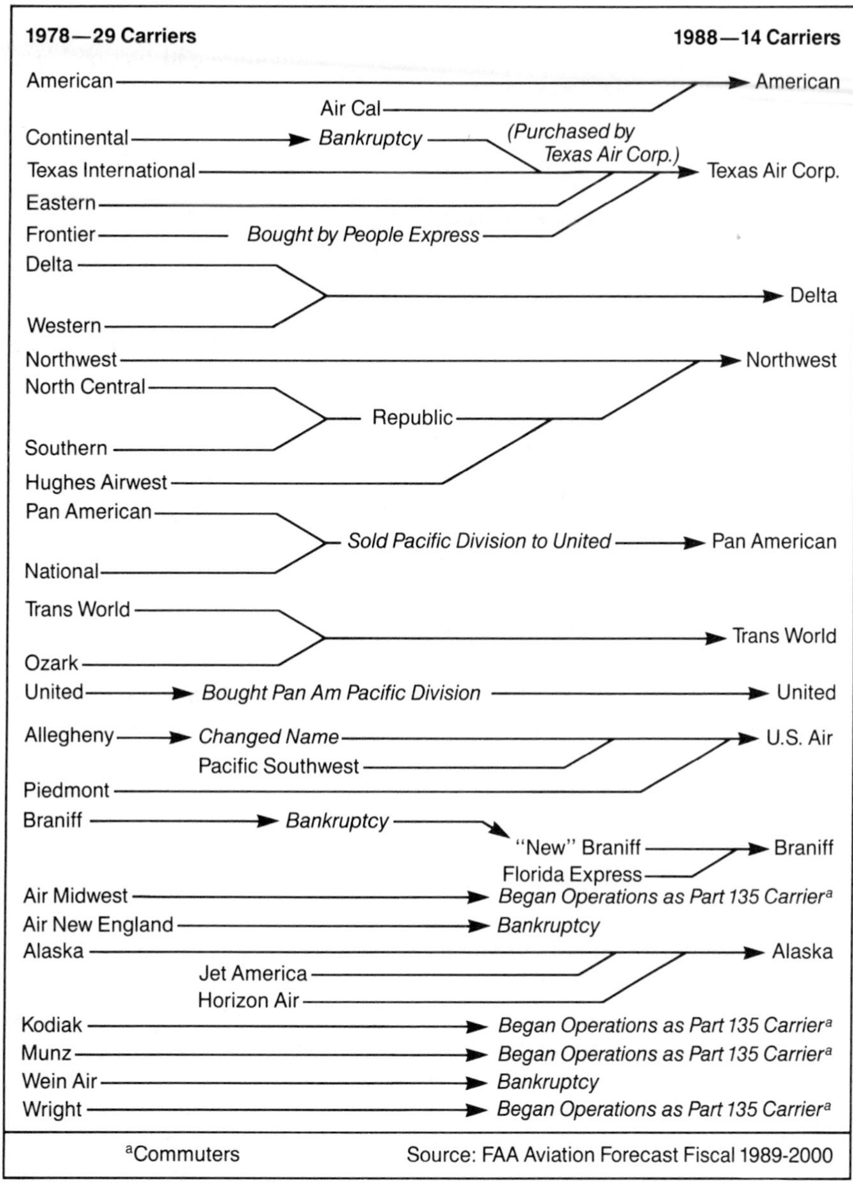

[a]Commuters.
Source: FAA Aviation Forecast Fiscal 1980–2000.

The North–South routes aid the winter profits, and the East–West routes aid the summer profits. A complete list of cities served by Delta is given in Table 1.

Although Delta has always been a prime example of the benefits of a hub-and-spoke system, recent FAA developments forced the company to increase its point-to-point systems. Delays and limitations caused by the lack of air-traffic controllers had stretched the hub-and-spoke system to its limits and required an alternative method of routing.

Fleet Management

Another success factor for Delta has been an equipment acquisition policy intended to keep the fleet efficient, young, and closely matched to the corporate mission.

During the years of C.T. Woolman's management, Delta purchased the majority of its planes from Douglas Aircraft. When both of these gentlemen died, so did the close relationship between the two companies. Delta thus became one of the first airlines to operate a Boeing 707.

Delta's equipment acquisition policy had always been flexible, geared toward specialization rather than commonality in the fleet composition. Various mergers over the years, however, had brought in a wide variety of planes. In the mid-1970s Delta was finally able to reduce its fleet to four types: B727, DC8, DC9, and L1011. After trying several other planes and reselling them in a matter of years, Delta began focusing on fuel efficiency to narrow its fleet. This proved a successful method, but also served to compromise Delta's ability to shift to larger aircraft at times.

Delta had also planned to purchase a new 200-seat aircraft in the early 1970s. However, inflation and fuel price controls made it unwise economically for manufacturers to produce such an aircraft. To take care of its expanding needs, Delta purchased more than 100 B-727s, designed in the early 1960s, and 42 Douglas 204-seat DC-8s. At a cost of $1.6 billion, Delta managed to pay only a fraction of the cost of new aircraft, instead re-engining these older planes to correct the noise and fuel problems.

By 1980, Delta was again able to pursue its quest for a smaller new-technology aircraft with lower costs per mile. Because of its interest in fuel economy, Delta was willing to wait a year for the certification of a Pratt & Whitney 2037 high-bypass engine with still greater fuel savings. For this reason, Delta purchased only 60 Boeing 757s, which seated 187 passengers. Although the upgraded 767 carried more passengers and was a newer plane, Delta intended these planes for a shorter mission—to fill the gap until the newer plane was ready.

By early 1982 Delta realized they had too many wide-body planes and that they needed to do something about this quickly. Delta replaced B-727-200s with B-757s and anticipated operational savings from the two-crew, twin-engine transport that will justify a capital cost exceeding $4 billion through the mid-1990s. The 187-seat 757 is 70.5 percent more fuel efficient than the 148-seat 737 on the basis of available seat miles per gallon on a 500-mile trip.

When purchasing the 757, Delta required aircraft cost efficiencies that would exceed the original 1980 Boeing proposal by 10 percent. Real performances were 14 percent more efficient. For the engines, Delta negotiated normal guarantees for reliability, costs, fuel-efficiency deterioration rate, and total performance. Delta also obtained a special guarantee from Pratt & Whitney that the PLO 2037 would be kept at a higher efficiency level than the 757 engines operated by its competitors.

The B-757 is used on Delta's shortest route—between Atlanta and Birmingham—which is 100 miles. On this route, capacity has often exceeded the 148 seats offered by the 727–200. The 757 is welcomed on this short route, but also on long flights such as those to Orlando and Boston.

The savings in cost with the B-757 are also to be associated with the B-767. Operating both aircraft is a cost-saving measure, because the two

Table 1 Cities Served by Delta in 1988

System Route Map

Delta serves 132 domestic cities in 42 states, the District of Columbia and Puerto Rico, and also operates flights to 23 international cities in 11 foreign countries. During fiscal 1988, Delta inaugurated service to Dublin, Ireland, and Seoul, Korea. On July 1, 1988, the Company initiated service to Taipei, Taiwan.

Domestic Service

ALABAMA
- Birmingham
- Mobile/Pascagoula, MS
- Montgomery

ALASKA
- Anchorage
- Fairbanks
- Juneau

ARIZONA
- Phoenix
- Tucson

ARKANSAS
- Little Rock

CALIFORNIA
- Burbank/Hollywood
- Fresno
- Long Beach
- Los Angeles
- Oakland
- Ontario
- Orange County
- Palm Springs
- Sacramento
- San Diego
- San Francisco
- San Jose

COLORADO
- Colorado Springs
- Denver

CONNECTICUT
- Hartford/Springfield, MA

DISTRICT OF COLUMBIA
- Washington

FLORIDA
- Daytona Beach
- Ft. Lauderdale
- Ft. Myers
- Jacksonville
- Melbourne
- Miami
- Orlando
- Pensacola
- Sarasota/Bradenton
- Tallahassee
- Tampa/St. Petersburg/Clearwater
- West Palm Beach

GEORGIA
- Atlanta
- Augusta
- Columbus
- Savannah

HAWAII
- Honolulu, Oahu
- Kahului, Maui

IDAHO
- Boise
- Idaho Falls

ILLINOIS
- Chicago

INDIANA
- Ft. Wayne
- Indianapolis

KENTUCKY
- Lexington
- Louisville

LOUISIANA
- Baton Rouge
- Monroe
- New Orleans
- Shreveport

MAINE
- Bangor
- Portland

MARYLAND
- Baltimore

MASSACHUSETTS
- Boston

MICHIGAN
- Detroit

MINNESOTA
- Minneapolis/St. Paul

MISSISSIPPI
- Jackson

MISSOURI
- Kansas City
- St. Louis

MONTANA
- Billings
- Bozeman
- Butte
- Great Falls
- Helena
- Kalispell
- Missoula

NEBRASKA
- Omaha

NEVADA
- Las Vegas
- Reno

NEW JERSEY
- Newark

NEW MEXICO
- Albuquerque

NEW YORK
- New York

NORTH CAROLINA
- Charlotte
- Greensboro/High Point/Winston-Salem
- Raleigh/Durham

NORTH DAKOTA
- Bismarck

OHIO
- Cincinnati
- Cleveland
- Columbus
- Dayton
- Toledo

OKLAHOMA
- Oklahoma City
- Tulsa

OREGON
- Portland

PENNSYLVANIA
- Philadelphia
- Pittsburgh

PUERTO RICO
- San Juan

SOUTH CAROLINA
- Charleston
- Columbia
- Greenville/Spartanburg

SOUTH DAKOTA
- Rapid City
- Sioux Falls

TENNESSEE
- Chattanooga
- Knoxville
- Memphis
- Nashville

TEXAS
- Amarillo
- Austin
- Dallas/Ft. Worth
- El Paso
- Houston
- Lubbock
- San Antonio

UTAH
- Salt Lake City

VIRGINIA
- Norfolk/Virginia Beach/Williamsburg
- Richmond

WASHINGTON
- Pasco/Richland/Kennewick
- Seattle/Tacoma
- Spokane

WYOMING
- Casper
- Jackson Hole

International Service

BAHAMAS
- Nassau

BERMUDA
- Hamilton

CANADA
- Calgary, Alberta
- Edmonton, Alberta
- Montreal, Quebec
- Vancouver, B.C.

ENGLAND
- London

FRANCE
- Paris

IRELAND
- Dublin
- Shannon

JAPAN
- Tokyo

KOREA
- Seoul

MEXICO
- Acapulco
- Guadalajara
- Ixtapa/Zihuatanejo
- Mazatlan
- Mexico City
- Puerto Vallarta

TAIWAN
- Taipei

WEST GERMANY
- Frankfurt
- Munich
- Stuttgart

Source: Annual Report, Delta Air Lines, Inc., 1988, 28.

Table 2 Delta Fleet in 1988

3. Aircraft Purchase and Sale Commitments:

At June 30, 1988, the status of the Company's current fleet and aircraft purchase commitments was as follows:

Aircraft Type	Current Fleet Owned	Leased	Total	Orders	Options
B-727-200	108	23	131	—	—
B-737-200	1	60	61	—	—
B-737-300	—	13	13	—	—
B-757-200	15	23	38	22	20
B-767-200	15	—	15	—	—
B-767-300	—	15	15	1	11
DC-8-71	—	7	7	—	—
DC-9-32	31	5	36	—	—
DC-10-10	3	3	6	—	—
L-1011-1	22	—	22	—	—
L-1011-200	1	—	1	—	—
L-1011-250	6	—	6	—	—
L-1011-500	10	—	10	—	—
MD-82	—	6	6	—	—
MD-88	—	16	16	31	57
	212	171	383	54	88

Note: At June 30, 1988, Delta had outstanding commitments to sell three DC-10-10 aircraft.
Source: Annual Report, Delta Air Lines, Inc., 1988, 18.

planes have common cockpits, maintenance, and training systems that permit education and qualification of pilots for both aircraft and flexibility in new assignments.

Technical Characteristics of the Fleet

Delta has long been acknowledged as an innovator. Not only is Delta the only airline to have introduced three different types of aircraft into service (the DC-8, the DC-9, and the Convair 880), but the airline was 13 months ahead of schedule in complying with government regulations regarding reduced engine noise. Delta also made history by operating four of the new-generation wide-body jets: the Boeing 747, the Douglas DC-10, the Lockheed 1011, and the Boeing 767.

Delta's fleet as of June 30, 1988, is described in Table 2. At the start of 1989 Delta placed an order and option for $11 billion of new aircraft. The bulk of this order is for the new MD-11 long-range tri-jet. This three-engine, wide-body plane, which holds up to 400 individuals and has a range of close to 8,000 miles, will be used to expand Delta's international position in the Pacific. According to Julius Maldutis, analyst at Salomon Brothers, Delta has the youngest airline fleet and the lowest consumer-complaint ratio of any major carrier.[3]

[3] "Why the Folks at Delta are Walking on Air," *Business Week*, August 1, 1988, 93.

Employees

Delta employees numbered 54,920 on June 30, 1988, compared to 37,554 five years before. Good relations between Delta management and other employees have been a permanent process for more than 50 years. It is a rule that high-ranking executives must meet every employee every 12 to 18 months. To do this, executives travel to all of Delta's airports. First, employees meet with the executive in the presence of their direct supervisors. In the second meeting, the employee meets with the executive alone. This allows grievances to reach top management so that corrective steps can be taken quickly.

Delta also has a long-standing policy of rotation. Ground employees are shifted to different positions from time to time so that they can become familiar with various tasks. Promotions, including those to executive posts, come from within the organization. This strengthens initiative and enhances morale. Pilots and medical personnel are among the few exceptions to this policy.

During recessions and strikes, Delta has an employee-oriented attitude. Delta employees thus have a sense of job security, which translates into high morale. For example, during the 1973 fuel crisis, Delta had to cut back on flying by 20 percent within 60 days, which meant that about 200 pilots and 400 flight attendants were surplus. They were put to work where they were the most needed—loading cargo, cleaning airplanes, selling tickets, making reservations. They kept their seniority and their medical benefits. Even during the PATCO strike, the airline kept its pilots and attendants at full pay for the first three weeks and some of its low-seniority flight personnel were reassigned to ground duties.

When Delta merged with Northeast, most of the Northeast employees merged with the new company. The same policy was employed by Delta when merging with Chicago and Southern Air Lines. D.P. Hetterman, senior vice president of technical operations, joined Chicago and Southern in 1946 as a mechanic and was promoted to his present position within the Delta family. The same pattern was more recently adopted with Western employees. Delta, unlike other merged airlines, has not experienced costly service problems. Paine Webber analyst Edward J. Starkman said of Delta's merger with Western, "It's probably the best merger we have seen so far."[4]

Delta's paternalistic attitude associated with good salaries has imbued workers with a "non-union" philosophy. Every time that the International Association of Machinists (IAM) signs an agreement with one of Delta's competing carriers, Delta gives its employees a percentage more—up to 5 and 10 cents an hour.

The major advantage in not dealing with unions is that, without union resistance, line personnel may work longer hours and management can better fit the available labor supply to demand. This enhances worker productivity despite high salaries. This important aspect of operating without union constraints has been underscored by the increase in nonunion airlines with vastly lower costs entering existing airline markets.[5] Delta pilots are unionized with ALPA, but they are the most promanagement pilots in the industry. The only other unionized employees are the flight dispatchers, who belong to a small company union.

The promotion from within and the long tenure are evident when executive biographies are analyzed. The current and youngest chairman, Ronald Allen, has spent his entire career at Delta. He joined Delta as a methods analyst. The former chairman of the board and CEO, David C. Garrett, Jr., joined Delta as a reservationist in 1946. Managers from outside are integrated through mergers. Prior to Garrett, W.T. Beebe had joined Chicago and Southern Air

[4]"Why the Folks at Delta are Walking on Air," *Business Week,* August 1, 1988, 92.

[5]Source: "Upstart in the Sky: Here Comes a New Kind of Airline," *Business Week,* June 15, 1981, 81.

Lines in 1947, and became personnel director of the combined company following the merger in 1953.

Delta management has over the years learned to work as a team and by consensus. When Woolman died in 1966, the team was ready to manage, and they maintained the Delta spirit. In contrast, when the founders of Eastern, Pan Am, and United left the airlines, no successors had been groomed. These airlines have had histories of management restructuring, fluctuating earnings, and change in direction.

Delta management is lean. Lines of communication are short; this allows quick decisions and interchangeability among managers. Each manager has well-defined responsibilities, but all are well informed and work as a team; they can make decisions even when one manager is absent. Quick reaction was an invaluable strength during the PATCO strike. Warned about the strike, the management team developed a plan to operate by trying to preserve the hub-and-spoke feed as much as possible. Within two weeks, the operations were stabilized. Communication with employees is also effective and ongoing. In addition to regular meetings, an open-door policy exists.

Management believes strongly in planning, and do whatever they can to stick with the plan. Delta showed a long-term vision of the airline industry when it defined the concept of the 150-seater in 1981.

The Impact of Deregulation

From 1949 to 1969 air-carrier traffic measured in revenue passenger miles increased 280 percent, which amounts to an annual average of nearly 15 percent. This was due to a favorable economic climate, the introduction of long-haul propeller aircraft after World War II, and the introduction of the jet in the 1950s. The industry saw costs falling and profits rising. Because of regulation, there was no price competition. The only competition was in schedules. Airlines added more and more planes, and the average load factor of 59 percent in 1960 dropped to 50 percent in 1969. Observers increasingly made the point that a regulated airline industry was not efficient. In 1978 the deregulation act was passed. It assumes that economic efficiency is improved through increased flexibility in setting fares and routes and the fact that new carriers can begin interstate service.

An immediate result of deregulation was the vulnerability of trunk airlines to local airlines in the new competitive environment. For Delta, Piedmont was a feeder but became a competitor. The rapid growth of the locals enticed the trunks to consolidate their activities around hubs. Delta was in a good position at that time. CEO W.T. Beebe said, "If deregulation does come, no new carrier could successfully take on Delta's entrenched hub-and-spoke operation in the South."[6] Other airlines developed the hub-and-spoke system after deregulation, but Delta was ready before, and this gave Delta a distinct strategic advantage. The prediction of Beebe has proved thus far to be true.

Delta, despite some of its inherent strengths, maintained that deregulation was not in the interest of the consumers or the carriers. This can be assessed as a sign of marketing conservatism. When deregulation came, however, Delta applied its traditional policy of moving from a position of strength and thus benefited from a competitive advantage.

Hub-and-Spoke Route Systems

Delta developed the hub-and-spoke route system to its full efficiency and was ready for a deregulated industry. Delta's jets depart early each morning from its terminal in Atlanta and fly in all directions like spokes on a wheel while other Delta aircraft fly toward Atlanta. The inbound flights are scheduled to land in rapid succession so that 30 or more are at the terminal at the same time. This bunching of flights, or "the big push"

[6]Source: "Delta's Flying Money Machine, *Business Week*, May 9, 1977, 87.

as it is known within Delta, is repeated 10 times a day, giving the airline an awesome service pattern and marketing clout in its territory.

Delta gains on profitability by an efficient scheduling of short flights so that they can interconnect. The hub-and-spoke system is an efficient method of gathering and distributing passengers on flight segments that might otherwise be unprofitable. Delta benefits from greater load factors and higher aircraft utilization rates by using the system. The short-haul routes have been acknowledged as Delta's bread and butter.

The hub-and-spoke system also acts as a feeder for international flights. Delta is able to gather passengers from all over the South who wish to fly to Europe. International flights from Atlanta are a viable alternative to those leaving from Houston or Miami. The same strategy is planned for the Japanese market. Delta estimates that it can funnel 120,000 passengers a year from its hubs through Portland, Oregon, an existing Tokyo gateway.

The hub-and-spoke system may also have problems. It tends to come apart when the weather causes delays. Delta's system can be a horror when bad weather "gums up" the Atlanta airport. The service may lose some of its quality when the airline's ramp-and-baggage people become hurried as they try to patch together new connections. Problems arise also when Delta's on-time performance is marred by holding flights for connections.

As deregulation forced the evolution of new route-structure strategies, the industry's equipment also needed to be changed. The hub-and-spoke system generated increased demand for smaller, short- to medium-haul aircraft that would be economical on the shorter spoke routes.

Marketing

No function of airline management has been affected more by deregulation than marketing. The unrestricted availability of every market to any airline and the complete freedom in pricing airline service have put a great premium on the development of a multifaceted marketing program. In addition to a strong route network, the highly competitive environment in the industry necessitates vigorous marketing efforts to make it work.

Approximately 90 percent of travel-agent-generated reservations are made through computer reservation systems, and American's Sabre and United's Apollo account for about 70 percent of this market. In fiscal 1983, Delta installed a computer reservation system, DATAS II, to improve its competitive position with travel agents. A significant development for the system is that travel agencies can use an IBM PC/XT personal computer as an integral part of the DATAS II reservation system.

During 1984, Delta implemented a highly advanced flight-planning system that computes the most cost-effective flight paths for Delta flights. The system uses current weather information and wind velocities in conjunction with flight information on flight characteristics of Delta's aircraft to compute the fastest and most economical routes.

During 1984, to make its frequent flyer program more attractive, Delta completed a computerized system in which frequent flyer mileage balances were maintained and statements sent to participants who had flight activity during the month. Delta also expanded the program to add new hotels, rental car companies, and other airlines. In 1988 Delta took the offensive in the frequent flyer programs by launching a triple mileage award program with American Express. The company figures it gained an additional 250,000 business travelers. The cost to Delta and the other airlines of frequent flyer programs caused airlines to begin pulling back by the end of the 1980s, however. In addition, several legal and accounting issues have been raised that put the future of the programs in question.

A major program initiated by Delta called the Delta Connection involves the establishment of a close working relationship with some of the nation's most successful commuter airlines.

Delta coordinates its schedules with the commuter, thus optimizing connections with Delta flights.

To avoid the losses caused by uncontrolled discounts, carriers are expected to depend more and more on yield management programs, which are attempts to control the levels of discount and full-fare traffic on a flight basis to avoid yield erosion. Delta came to this policy after sustaining losses. After some hesitation, Delta entered in the fare wars at the beginning of 1982, announcing that it would not be undersold in any domestic market. The average percentage of discount passengers on Delta flights, then at 60 percent, would increase to as high as 100 percent when in direct competition with high-discount operations.

In January 1982, Delta dropped fares from New York to Florida to $114; Pan Am followed with a $77 fare that Delta matched. The fare war was intense at Christmas 1981 between Delta and Air Florida. Delta increased traffic between the North and Florida during the winter seasons. This pushed Delta to cut prices on these routes; Air Florida retaliated but Delta followed. In doing so, Delta revealed how important the Florida market was (25 percent of Delta's business).

As Delta became unable to control the number of seats it offered at discounts—a total of 90 percent of all the tickets sold—it delayed some aircraft deliveries and planned for selective market growth. A key decision was to increase its share of the Dallas/Fort Worth market, and in 1983 Delta's share of the Dallas market rose from 15 percent to 25 percent.

Parallel to this selective growth, Delta seriously entered into the computer age with the yield management system developed by Control Data Corporation. The system monitors every flight's booking patterns so that discounted capacity is kept to a minimum. Discounted seats are either eliminated on routes where these fares do not generate additional volume, or expanded where they generate volume.

The yield management system allows carriers to increase the conditions on discount travel while limiting the number of discount seats and the frequency of offers. Delta published rates that offered 70 percent off the full coach fares in selected markets. But to benefit from these discounts, Delta established many restrictions (purchased in advance, a minimum length of stay, and penalties for refund or reissue of an unused ticket). The advantages of the yield management system are numerous. It allows a more favorable mix of discount and full-fare traffic by saving seats for late-booking, high-yield passengers—shifting group or low-yield traffic to flights that are booking at a slow pace. This system allows the addition of discount seats to achieve incremental revenue gain on slow-booking flights.

Financial Operations

The years 1982 and 1983 were difficult for Delta. Despite an $18 million operating loss in the first quarter of 1982, Delta refused to lay off workers. In fact, employees received an 8 percent raise in September 1982. To show their appreciation for this attitude, Delta employees organized a fund-raising action to buy a Boeing 767 for the company. This represented a gift of $30 million. The plane they purchased was named "The Spirit of Delta."

The losses were Delta's first in 36 years of operation. Previously, Delta had had lean years, but no losses. The company had, unlike other airlines, a regular pattern of profits. In 1986 income per share dropped from an all-time high of $6.50 in 1985 to $1.18. Many analysts believed that American and Piedmont, the latter having once been a feeder airline to Delta, had made large incursions into the South. During this time period Delta's passenger traffic grew slightly. Delta also had difficulty in dealing with the sharp cut in fares offered by new entrants to the marketplace.

Under the direction of new CEO Ronald Allen, Delta leaped back in 1987 and 1988. (Allen is profiled in Exhibit 2.) Delta has benefited significantly from the labor strife and downsizing at Eastern. In June 1988 Delta's passenger traffic rose almost 10 percent, while Eastern's dropped

Exhibit 2 Profile of Robert W. Allen

On a sold-out Delta flight last year, Chairman Ronald W. Allen cheerfully moved from the first-class cabin into the cockpit jump seat to make room for another passenger. But Allen really showed his concern for customer comfort when a passenger got locked inside the plane's lavatory. Allen rescued the man by prying open the door with a couple of table knives. "The No. 1 priority with Delta," declares Allen, "is always customer service."

Allen, who became chief executive officer of Delta Air Lines Inc. last August [1987], is as keen as his predecessors on maintaining the airline's traditions of Southern service and hospitality. In fact, Allen's résumé greatly resembles those of the men who preceded him. He is a native Southerner, an engineer from the Georgia Institute of Technology, and a private sort who has spent his entire career at Delta. But at 46, Allen stands out as Delta's youngest CEO.

Freewheeling

No one executive at team-oriented Delta can be the sole proponent of change. But Allen in particular symbolizes Delta's reawakening. Unlike previous CEOs, who rose through Delta's operational ranks, Allen started as a methods-analyst intern and worked his way through Delta's training, administrative, and personnel departments. In 1983 he was named president and understudy to longtime Chairman David C. Garrett Jr.

Allen, in contrast to the shy and reserved Garrett, is an affable and outgoing manager. Executives say Allen is much more freewheeling, too, especially when it comes to signing off on projects with less predictable payoffs. Delta's latest marketing efforts are the most telling examples. Last year, Allen helped push through a deal worth more than $15 million to become Walt Disney World's official airline, an agreement he repeated with Disneyland this year. "Ron understands marketing clout," says one executive. "And he's willing to spend."

Allen has an all-American background—he married his high-school sweetheart and was on the safety patrol in school. He also has a sly sense of humor, as illustrated by an incident related to the merger with Los Angeles-based Western Air Lines Inc. In April last year, when the two airlines formally combined, former Western Chairman Gerald Grinstein flew to Atlanta. Allen sent a white Cadillac limousine to ferry him in from the airport. But when Grinstein flew in for the first management meeting of the combined companies, Allen dispatched a mud-spattered pickup truck, complete with gun rack and driven by an overall-clad Delta service agent who did a fair imitation of a Southern redneck. "He was sending a message," says Grinstein. "It was time to get down to business."

Source: Scott Ticer, "The Good Ol' Boy in the Pilot's Seat," 93. Reprinted from the August 1, 1988 issue of *Business Week* by special permission,

more than 16 percent. Table 3a gives consolidated financial data for ten years. Performance highlights for 1987 and 1988 are presented in Table 3b.

When considering costs of airlines, the most striking elements are the rise of fuel prices and the cost of new aircraft. Since 1972, fuel prices have increased more than 800 percent, more than 150 percent between deregulation in 1978 and 1981, a climb in constant dollars from 40 cents a gallon in 1978 to $1 in 1981. Fuel represents an average of 40 to 50 percent of the total operating costs as a percentage of total cash operating expenses. However, in the United States fuel prices have been in decline since the second quarter of 1981, when those costs as a percentage of cash operating expenses reached a peak of 31.7 percent. Fuel costs were 30 percent on average in 1981, 27 percent in 1982, and 24.9 percent in 1983. Five years later, Delta Air Lines' fuel costs represented 15 percent of the total of its costs for the year ending June 30, 1988.

The high cost of fuel justifies the acquisition of fuel-efficient aircraft. Relatively low costs caused numerous airlines to delay acquisitions of aircraft. As the cost of fuel appears to be rising, planes are becoming geriatric, and lead times for new aircraft delivery in some cases are over five years, airlines are going on a mass buying spree. Delta's order for close to $11 billion in new aircraft is an example.

The impact of salary on total expense ex-

Table 3a Consolidated Financial Data for Years Ended June 30

Consolidated Summary of Operations For the years ended June 30
(Dollars expressed in thousands, except per share figures)

	1988	1987	1986
Operating revenues:			
Passenger	$6,443,111	$4,921,852	$4,132,284
Cargo	349,775	280,271	240,115
Other, net	122,491	116,049	87,663
Total operating revenues	6,915,377	5,318,172	4,460,062
Operating expenses	6,418,293	4,913,647	4,425,574
Operating income (loss)	$ 497,084	$ 404,525	$ 34,488
Interest expense, net[1]	(65,204)	(61,908)	(55,355)
Miscellaneous income, net	24,992	8,312	7,775
Gain (loss) on disposition of flight equipment	(1,016)	96,270	16,526
Income (loss) before income taxes	$ 455,856	$ 447,199	$ 3,434
Income taxes (provided) credited	(180,851)	(219,715)	2,228
Amortization of investment tax credits	31,821	36,245	41,624
Net income (loss)	$ 306,826	$ 263,729	$ 47,286
Net income (loss) per share*	$6.30	$5.90	$1.18
Dividends paid	$ 58,456	$ 44,397	$ 40,073
Dividends paid per share*	$1.20	$1.00	$1.00
[1]Has been reduced by interest capitalized of	$ 32,329	$ 32,092	$ 23,758

Other Financial and Statistical Data For the years ended June 30

	1988	1987	1986
Total assets	$5,748,355	$5,342,383	$3,785,462
Long-term debt and capital leases	$ 729,493	$1,018,417	$ 868,615
Stockholders' equity	$2,208,823	$1,937,912	$1,301,946
Stockholders' equity per share*	$ 44.99	$ 39.84	$ 32.45
Shares of common stock outstanding at year end*	49,101,271	48,639,469	40,116,383
Revenue passengers enplaned	58,564,507	48,172,626	39,582,232
Available seat miles (000)	85,833,959	69,013,669	53,336,135
Revenue passenger miles (000)	49,009,094	38,415,117	30,123,387
Passenger load factor	57.10%	55.66%	56.48%
Breakeven load factor	52.69%	51.09%	56.01%
Available ton miles (000)	11,249,578	8,999,668	6,934,047
Revenue ton miles (000)	5,556,584	4,327,195	3,371,917
Passenger revenue per passenger mile	13.15¢	12.81¢	13.72¢
Operating expenses per available seat mile	7.48¢	7.12¢	8.30¢
Operating expenses per available ton mile	57.05¢	54.60¢	63.82¢

*Adjusted for 2-for-1 stock split distributed December 1, 1981.
The financial and statistical information presented above reflects the Company's acquisition of Western Air Lines, Inc. on December 18, 1986.

Table 3a *(continued)*

1985	1984	1983	1982	1981	1980	1979
$4,376,986	$3,963,610	$3,347,014	$3,352,173	$3,287,511	$2,733,820	$2,213,024
235,199	239,649	227,146	230,597	213,431	190,490	167,904
71,930	60,472	42,253	34,753	32,384	32,650	46,918
4,684,115	4,263,731	3,616,413	3,617,523	3,533,326	2,956,960	2,427,846
4,318,105	4,052,339	3,823,747	3,625,679	3,359,132	2,864,323	2,218,814
$ 366,010	$ 211,392	$ (207,334)	$ (8,156)	$ 174,194	$ 92,637	$ 209,032
(62,053)	(109,802)	(63,494)	(22,284)	(7,596)	(11,062)	(9,461)
6,863	9,114	15,898	13,665	26,144	6,952	1,959
94,343	129,511	28,229	1,570	30,078	36,091	20,514
$ 405,163	$ 240,215	$ (226,701)	$ (15,205)	$ 222,820	$ 124,618	$ 222,044
(186,624)	(102,625)	109,642	9,652	(101,447)	(54,433)	(104,429)
40,914	38,014	30,329	26,367	25,101	22,973	19,129
$ 259,453	$ 175,604	$ (86,730)	$ 20,814	$ 146,474	$ 93,158	$ 136,744
$6.50	$4.42	$(2.18)	$0.52	$3.68	$2.34	$3.44
$ 27,938	$ 23,857	$ 39,761	$ 37,773	$ 27,832	$ 23,857	$ 20,875
$0.70	$0.60	$1.00	$0.95	$0.70	$0.60	$0.53
$ 22,028	$ 18,263	$ 29,398	$ 38,154	$ 15,539	$ 10,790	$ 6,717

1985	1984	1983	1982	1981	1980	1979
$3,626,840	$3,268,822	$3,246,960	$2,657,880	$2,304,327	$2,042,539	$1,788,325
$ 535,159	$ 670,993	$1,089,796	$ 362,774	$ 198,411	$ 147,901	$ 125,483
$1,287,094	$1,048,907	$ 897,160	$1,023,651	$1,040,611	$ 921,969	$ 852,668
$ 32.21	$ 26.38	$ 22.56	$ 25.75	$ 26.17	$ 23.19	$ 21.44
39,958,467	39,761,154	39,761,154	39,761,154	39,761,154	39,761,154	39,761,154
39,340,850	36,319,567	35,666,116	34,169,927	36,743,214	39,713,904	39,360,368
51,637,084	50,935,173	47,915,817	45,154,885	45,428,277	43,217,372	39,826,891
29,061,618	26,099,115	26,096,996	24,284,804	25,192,531	26,171,197	25,518,520
56.28%	51.24%	54.46%	53.78%	55.46%	60.56%	64.07%
51.57%	48.51%	57.84%	53.91%	52.52%	58.51%	58.02%
6,667,512	6,569,248	6,202,910	5,937,817	6,037,476	5,748,143	5,357,995
3,275,329	2,983,840	2,951,119	2,773,337	2,845,425	2,934,375	2,916,585
15.06¢	15.19¢	12.83¢	13.80¢	13.05¢	10.45¢	8.67¢
8.36¢	7.96¢	7.98¢	8.03¢	7.39¢	6.63¢	5.57¢
64.76¢	61.69¢	61.64¢	61.06¢	55.64¢	49.83¢	41.41¢

Source: Annual Report, Delta Air Lines, Inc., 1988, 24–25.

Table 3b Performance Highlights for Fiscal Years 1987 and 1988

	1988	1987	*Per Cent Change*
Operating Revenues	$6,915,377	$5,318,172	+30%
Operating Expenses	$6,418,293	$4,913,647	+31
Operating Income	$497,084	$404,525	+23
Net Income	$306,826	$263,729	+16
Net Income Per Share	$6.30	$5.90	+ 7
Dividends Paid	$58,456	$44,397	+32
Dividends Paid Per Share	$1.20	$1.00	+20
Stockholders' Equity Per Share	$44.99	$39.84	+13
Average Number of Common Shares Outstanding	48,706,851	44,712,993	+ 9
Debt-to-Equity Position	25%/75%	35%/65%	—
Revenue Passengers Enplaned	58,564,507	48,172,626	+22
Revenue Passenger Miles (000)	49,009,094	38,415,117	+28
Available Seat Miles (000)	85,833,959	69,013,669	+24
Passenger Mile Yield	13.15¢	12.81¢	+ 3
Passenger Load Factor	57.10%	55.66%	+ 3
Breakeven Passenger Load Factor	52.69%	51.09%	+ 3
Cargo Ton Miles (000)	652,833	480,969	+36
Cargo Yield Per Ton Mile	53.58¢	58.27¢	− 8
Total Fuel Gallons Consumed (000)	1,753,538	1,435,801	+22
Average Fuel Price Per Gallon	56.09¢	46.80¢	+20
Revenue Passenger Miles Per Fuel Gallon	27.9	26.8	+ 4
Available Seat Miles Per Fuel Gallon	49.0	48.1	+ 2
Average Seats Per Aircraft Mile	169.0	169.2	—
Cost Per Available Seat Mile	7.48¢	7.12¢	+ 5
Average Passenger Trip Length in Miles	837	797	+ 5
Average Aircraft Flight Length in Miles	640	617	+ 4
Average Aircraft Utilization (Hours Per Day)	8.62	8.37	+ 3

Source: Annual Report, Delta Air Lines, Inc., 1988, 1.

plains why airlines are obliged to gain concessions from their employees in order to satisfy their need for new aircraft. Delta initiated two-track career and wage escalations, giving new entrants less pay for equivalent work for their services. Delta recognizes that labor is the only controllable cost. By 1989, almost 75 percent of all positions at Delta were covered by the two-tier wage system.

An analysis of operating expenses for the major national airlines shows that the breakdown is relatively similar for all airlines. On a 100 percent scale, the flying operating costs (i.e., crew expense, fuel, oil, taxes, insurance) for Delta and Eastern are very similar. Delta has an advantage in maintenance in comparison to Trans World and USAir because of Delta's modernized fleet. If the percentages are similar, a small gain in one expense would give a distinct advantage to the other airlines. The reason is that profits are more and more difficult to achieve and the net income trend line is downsloping.

Case 13

America West Airlines

Introduction

America West Airlines Inc. was incorporated September 4, 1981, and began flight service to five cities with three used Boeing 737-200s on August 1, 1983. By early 1989 the airline had grown to 70 aircraft serving 47 cities. Foremost among the cities served are Phoenix, the airline's base of operations, and Las Vegas. Since October 1984, America West has had the largest market share in Phoenix. From just four gates at its inception, the airline has expanded to 21 gates and 42 percent of all passengers boarded in Phoenix. By contrast, Southwest Airlines, the primary competitor in the Phoenix hub, has just over 21 percent of the market share of enplanements. By the end of 1986, America West had also become the number one carrier in Las Vegas. America West routes are shown in Exhibit 1.

Along the way, the rapid expansion of the America West system has also had a few changes. One of the air carrier's first scheduled destinations, Kansas City, was subsequently removed from the schedule in October 1984. Similarly, flights to Tulsa and Oklahoma City, which were begun in December 1983, were canceled in October 1984. Also in October 1984, America West moved its flight to San Francisco, which had begun only four months earlier, to Oakland. Finally, the service to Palm Springs, which began in February 1984, was discontinued in March 1985. Meanwhile, the airline was expanding to areas in the Midwest having little competition, such as Lincoln, Grand Junction, Durango, Sioux City, Cedar Rapids, Springfield, Pueblo, and Moline/Quad Cities. Many of these routes have low landing fees and gate costs, which serve to make them some of the more profitable destinations flown by America West. The servicing of these various noncompetitive destinations was one of the initial strategies conceived by the airline's management.

Beginning in 1985, America West expanded flights dramatically to Las Vegas, and instituted flights from Las Vegas to a number of other destinations apart from Phoenix. By the end of 1986, this service had created a second hub city, with direct flights to 18 destinations, excluding Phoenix. Together, the Phoenix and Las Vegas airports comprise a newly conceived superhub, whereby schedules are integrated to common cities in order to maximize both direct and connecting services between points on one side of either hub and points on the other side. This is accomplished with more than 20 daily round trips between Phoenix and Las Vegas. Outside of these flights, America West has 167 daily departures from Phoenix and 92 daily departures from Las Vegas. The locations of gates in Phoenix and Las Vegas are shown in Exhibit 2.

America West has little competition on most of its Midwest routes and serious competition on its flights to Denver, New York, and Chicago, but California is by far the most popular destination for Arizona travelers. Therefore, the company focuses on service to and from California as an essential element in its hub and spoke system. Nearly 70 percent of the airline's passengers travel through the Phoenix hub from other destinations, which underscores the importance of linking California with the Midwest. Although

This case portrays neither the effective nor the ineffective handling of an administrative situation. Rather, it is to be used as the basis for classroom discussion.

Exhibit 1 America West Routes in 1989

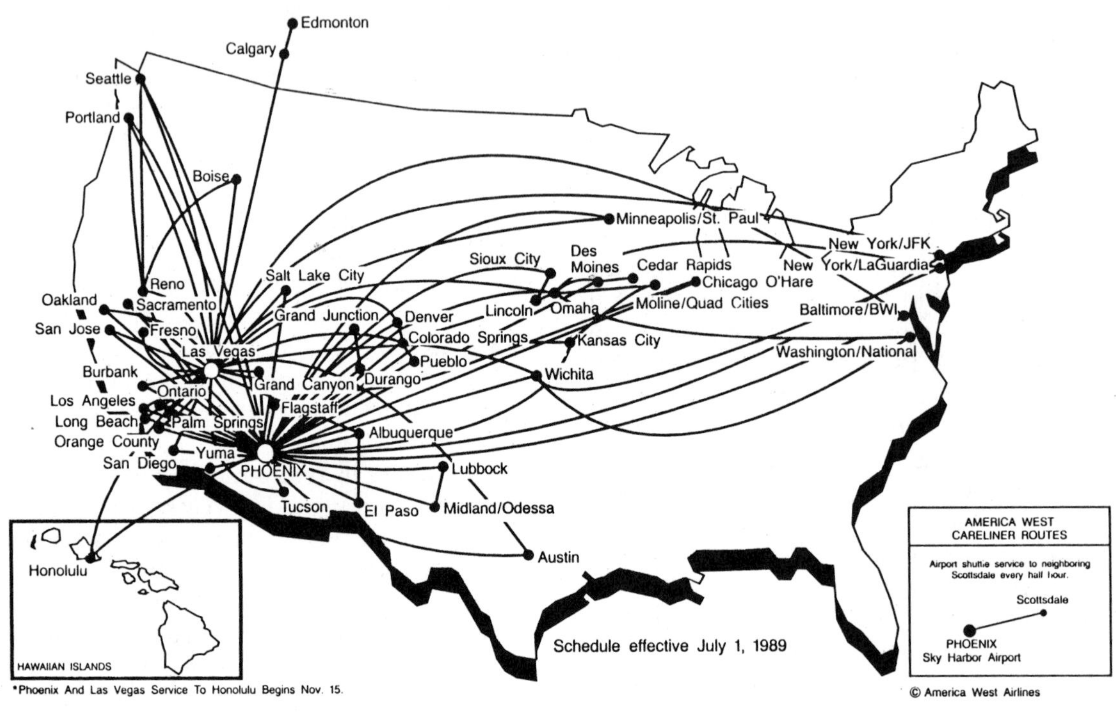

Source: America West Airlines

the California routes are an important ingredient in the success of America West, they are highly competitive and not as lucrative. However, the airline has been successful in these markets as a result of its dominance of the Phoenix market and its overall low costs.

The airline has also experienced success in its Las Vegas and Phoenix flights to New York because there are few direct flights from these cities to New York. The threat of direct competition from a major carrier remains on these routes. America West is inviting competition in the opinion of Gerald Grinstein, former chairman of Western Airlines, who believes that America West has "succeeded so far through anonymity."[1]

[1]Stewart Toy, "This Upstart Could Be Flying a Bit Too High," *Business Week*, June 15, 1987, 76.

A chronological history of America West is presented in Exhibit 3.

Air Fleet

From its inception, America West has centered its aircraft needs on the fuel-efficient, twin-engine, two-pilot Boeing 737. More recently, two-pilot 757s and Boeing de Havilland Dash 8s have been added for short haul routes. The efficiency of these aircraft is enhanced through the use of slim-line seats, which have enabled the company to substantially increase passenger capacity. Through its reliance for most flights on a single plane (the 737), the company has endeavored to minimize parts inventory and maintenance expense. As of February 1989, America West had a fleet of Boeing 737 aircraft, 7 Boeing 757 aircraft, and 3 Boeing de Havilland Dash 8s. The

Exhibit 2 America West's Superhub Gate Connections

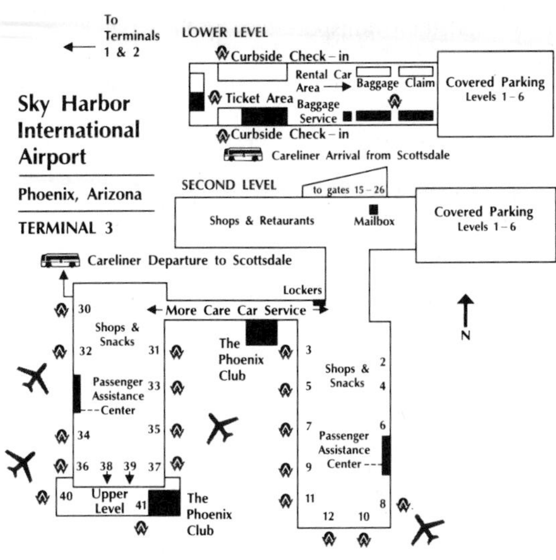

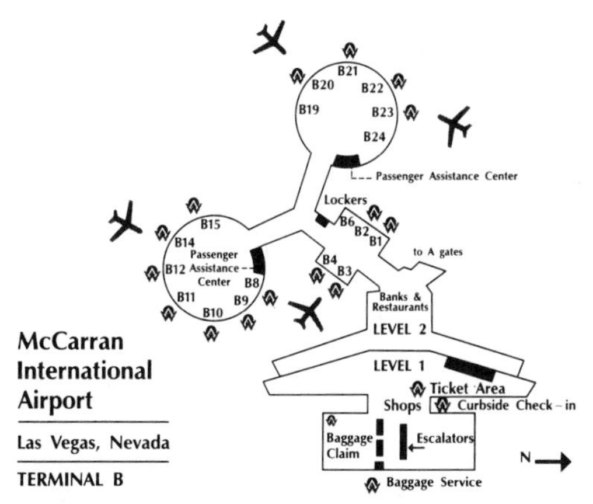

Source: America West Airlines

airline offers both economy and first-class service on its 757s. All other service is economy.

The average age of the fleet is six years, which is young by industry standards. Together with future planned deliveries of new aircraft, America West will have one of the youngest fleets by far in the airline industry.

Initial Marketing Strategy

America West has consistently pursued a well-conceived marketing strategy designed to have broad-based appeal to air travel customers. To attract the individual discretionary traveler, the airline offers consistently low fares and only one seating class on its 737s. To attract the business traveler, America West offers complimentary copies of *The Wall Street Journal* and *USA Today*, assigned seating, complimentary alcoholic beverages, a frequent flier program, larger overhead bins for carryon luggage, interline ticketing and baggage transfer, and the participation in travel agent automated reservation systems. America West believes that it is presently the only airline in its service areas that provides this exact combination of services.

As previously noted, America West's principal route strategy was to link less competitive Midwest markets with California flights through the Phoenix hub. As is evident from the history of the airline, this strategy underwent some revision with the cancellation of flight service to the more competitive Midwest markets of Tulsa, Oklahoma City, and Kansas City. More recently, however, the air carrier began flights to Denver, Chicago, New York, Baltimore, and Washington, which appears to signal a willingness to enter more competitive markets. With the future delivery of more large aircraft, the entry of America West into increasingly competitive markets appears inevitable. In its short history of operations, the airline has altered its initial route strategy, which was committed to serving the western United States, to direct service from Phoenix to various major East Coast destinations. Although these distant destinations will be more competitive, America West will be the only air carrier with direct service from Phoenix.

Current Marketing Strategy

America West's marketing strategy is centered around the motto, "What we serve is you,"

Exhibit 3 Chronological History

Sept. 1981	Incorporated as America West Airlines, Inc.
Nov. 1981	Issued a certificate to engage in domestic scheduled air transportation by the Civil Aeronautics Board
Feb. 1983	First public offering of 2,500,000 shares of common stock at $7.50 with two subsequent equity transactions raising $33 million for preoperating and start-up
Aug. 1, 1983	Revenue service established from Phoenix hub with three Boeing 737s Initiated service at: Colorado Springs, Colorado Kansas City, Missouri (Discontinued 10/28/84) Los Angeles, California Phoenix, Arizona Wichita, Kansas
Aug. 1, 1983	**Phoenix** Daily Departures: 9 Employees: 280 Total Fleet Size: 3 Boeing 737s Cities Served: 5
Oct. 1, 1983	Initiated service at: Omaha, Nebraska Ontario, California
Oct. 30, 1983	Initiated service at: Las Vegas, Nevada **Las Vegas** Daily Departures: 3
Dec. 1, 1983	Initiated service at: Albuquerque, New Mexico Des Moines, Iowa Oklahoma City, Oklahoma (Discontinued 10/28/84) San Diego, California Tulsa, Oklahoma (Discontinued 10/28/84)
Dec. 31, 1983	**Phoenix** Daily Departures: 31 Employees: 806 Total Fleet Size: 10 Boeing 737s Cities Served: 13 **Las Vegas** Daily Departures: 4
Feb. 1, 1984	Initiated service at: Palm Springs, California (Discontinued 3/15/85)
Mar. 13, 1984	Western Savings & Loan Association of Phoenix purchased $15 million of Series B 10.5% convertible preferred stock.
Mar. 30, 1984	Second public offering of 1,000,000 shares of common at $9.50
June 1, 1984	Initiated service at: Austin, Texas Durango, Colorado San Jose, California Tucson, Arizona
July 15, 1984	Initiated service at: San Francisco, California (Switched service from SFO to OAK 10/28/84)
Sept. 14, 1984	Initiated service at: Burbank, California
Oct. 26, 1984	Expansion at Phoenix Sky Harbor Airport from 3 to 9 gates

Exhibit 3 *(continued)*

Oct. 28, 1984	Initiated service at: Oakland, California
Nov. 1, 1984	Initiated service at: Calgary, Alberta, Canada
Nov. 15, 1984	Initiated service at: El Paso, Texas Salt Lake City, Utah
Dec. 8, 1984	Initiated temporary service at: Montrose, Colorado (Special ski flights Saturday only through April 8, 1985.)
Dec. 15, 1984	Initiated service at: Grand Junction, Colorado
Dec. 31, 1984	**Phoenix** Daily Departures: 78 Employees: 1650 Total Fleet Size: 21 Boeing 737s Cities Served: 22 **Las Vegas** Daily Departures: 7
Mar. 15, 1985	Initiated service at: Edmonton, Alberta, Canada
Apr. 1, 1985	Initiated service at: Orange County—John Wayne Airport—Santa Ana, California Sacramento, California
Apr. 11, 1985	Third public offering of 3.8 million shares of common stock at $7.00
July 1, 1985	Initiated Air Cargo Service
July 1, 1985	Opened a Satellite Reservations Center in Colorado Springs, Colorado
July 15, 1985	Initiated service at: Lincoln, Nebraska
Aug. 6, 1985	Public offering of $69,000,000 7¾% Convertible Subordinated Debentures; due 2010
Aug. 23, 1985	Expanded existing corporate office space with an additional building. The new facility, called the Madison I Building, 606 Madison, Tempe, houses the airlines' warehouse, engine shop, purchasing department, quality assurance, technical publications, and sales department.
Nov. 15, 1985	Initiated service at: Pueblo, Colorado
Dec. 5, 1985	Expansion at Phoenix Sky Harbor Airport from 9 to 18 gates
Dec. 31, 1985	**Phoenix** Daily Departures: 118 Employees: 2527 Total Fleet Size: 32 Boeing 737s Cities Served: 26 **Las Vegas** Daily Departures: 16
Jan. 24, 1986	Initiated service at: Sioux City, Iowa
Feb. 15, 1986	Initiated service at: Cedar Rapids, Iowa Scottsdale, Arizona (Complimentary shuttle bus service to and from Sky Harbor)
Mar. 19, 1986	Public offering of $80,000,000 7½% Convertible Subordinated Debentures. Due 2011

(continued)

Exhibit 3 *(continued)*

Mar. 28, 1986	Office space expanded with an additional building at 618 Madison, called Madison II, housing Corporate Marketing, Properties & Facilities, Legal, Air Cargo offices, and Operations Management
Apr. 27, 1986	Initiated service at: Springfield, Missouri (Discontinued 2/29/88)
July 1, 1986	Initiated Las Vegas "Nite Flite" service to seven cities: Albuquerque Oakland Phoenix Los Angeles Ontario Salt Lake City Tucson
July 15, 1986	Initiated service at: Chicago Midway, Illinois (Discontinued 1/5/88)
Sept. 3, 1986	Purchased three de Havilland Canada Dash 8s with options to purchase three additional turboprop airplanes
Sept. 11, 1986	A ground-breaking ceremony held at Sky Harbor commemorating the beginning of construction for the new America West Airlines Technical Support Facility
Nov. 15, 1986	Initiated service at: Denver, Colorado Reno, Nevada
Dec. 15, 1986	Initiated service at: Portland, Oregon Seattle, Washington
Dec. 31, 1986	**Phoenix** Daily Departures: 145 Employees: 4596 Total Fleet Size: 46 Boeing 737s Cities Served: 35 **Las Vegas** Daily Departures: 54
Jan. 15, 1987	Initiated service at: Midland/Odessa, Texas Moline/Quad Cities, Illinois
Feb. 4, 1987	Purchased six Boeing 757 aircraft from the Boeing Company with a commitment for an additional three to be delivered in fall 1989
Feb. 27, 1987	Received delivery of first Boeing de Havilland Dash 8
Mar. 2, 1987	Initiated service at: Yuma, Arizona (Boeing de Havilland Dash 8 service)
May 1–22, 1987	Received delivery of four Boeing 757s
May 16, 1987	Received delivery of two Boeing de Havilland Dash 8s
May 20, 1987	Initiated service at: Chicago O'Hare, Illinois Flagstaff, Arizona (Boeing de Havilland Dash 8 service) Grand Canyon, Arizona (Boeing de Havilland Dash 8 service) Mesa, Arizona (Discontinued 1/31/88 (Complimentary shuttle bus service to and from Mesa, Arizona)
May 20, 1987	Expansion at Phoenix Sky Harbor Airport from 18 to 21 gates
June 1, 1987	Initiated service at: Long Beach, California
June 1, 1987	Opened a Satellite Reservations Center in Reno, Nevada
June 3–12, 1987	Received delivery of two Boeing 757s

Exhibit 3 *(continued)*

July 1, 1987	Initiated service at: New York/JFK, New York Baltimore/Washington International, Maryland
Aug. 11, 1987	Ansett Airlines of Australia invests in 20% of America West's common stock (newly issued shares—3,029,235 shares at $10.50 per share). Total value of stock transaction—$31,806,967
Sept. 15, 1987	Opened new VIP lounge, the Phoenix Club, near Gate 40 in Terminal III at Sky Harbor International Airport. Available to members only, providing separate television and bar areas, a library with a personal computer and copy machine, and a conference room
Nov. 15, 1987	Initiated service at: Lubbock, Texas
Dec. 1, 1987	Initiated nonstop service between: Oakland—Calgary
Dec. 13, 1987	Received delivery of the seventh Boeing 757
Dec. 14, 1987	Grand opening of AmeriWest Vacations (tour packaging division)
Dec. 31, 1987	**Phoenix** Daily Departures: 167 Employees: 7800 Total Fleet Size: 59 Boeing 737s 7 Boeing 757s 3 Boeing de Havilland Dash 8s Cities Served: 45 **Las Vegas** Daily Departures: 102
Feb. 16, 1988	Opening of "Fast Check" drive-through terminals east of Terminal III at Sky Harbor International Airport offering full check-in services. Passengers may proceed directly to the airplane after utilizing "Fast Check."
Feb. 23, 1988	America West Airline's Hangar and Technical Support Facility ribbon-cutting press conference
Apr. 13, 1988	America West unveils new laser baggage system at Sky Harbor International Airport. The $2.5 million system works similar to automated grocery store checkout stands and allows America West to handle baggage with high speed and accuracy.
May 1, 1988	Initiated service at: Minneapolis-St. Paul, Minnesota
May 15, 1988	America West Airlines joins the International Air Transport Association (IATA).
June 23, 1988	America West Airlines is announced as the official carrier for the Phoenix Cardinals (National Football League). America West agrees to charter the Cardinals to all road games and launches a major advertising campaign utilizing the Cardinals as a vehicle to tell the America West story.
June 27, 1988	America West Airlines receives a Federal Aviation Administration (FAA) contract to train FAA pilot-inspectors on the Boeing 737 aircraft. The contract is valued at $894,415.
Sept. 11, 1988	Initiated service at: Kansas City, Missouri
Oct. 16, 1988	Initiated service at: Boise, Idaho Initiated daytime service at: Minneapolis-St. Paul, Minnesota
Dec. 10, 1988	Initiated new service at: Palm Springs, California
Dec. 12, 1988	Opened second luxury lounge (Phoenix Club) at Sky Harbor Airport in Phoenix on the connector between the two America West concourses in Terminal III. The lounge offers complimentary cocktails, beverages, and snacks; two conference rooms, a library

(continued)

Exhibit 3 *(continued)*

	complete with a personal computer, copier, and facsimile machine; free local phone calls; credit card telephones, and separate television and bar areas.
Dec. 13, 1988	America West announced the order of 15 new Boeing 737-300s and 10 new Boeing 757s at an estimated purchase amount of $800 million. Options for 10 Boeing 737-300s and 15 757s were also announced. Delivery date of the 25 firm orders begins in 1992.
Dec. 17, 1988	Initiated new service at: Steamboat Springs, Colorado (3 round trips/week)
Jan. 19, 1989	Announced the signing of a two-year maintenance agreement with Odyssey International Airlines of Canada in which America West will provide the heavy maintenance on Odyssey's 757s. Contract could produce revenue in excess of $3 million.
Feb. 1989	**Phoenix** Daily Departures: 167 Employees: 8000 Total Fleet Size: 60 Boeing 737s 7 Boeing 757s 3 Boeing de Havilland Dash 8s Cities Served: 47 **Las Vegas** Daily Departures: 92 "Nite Flite" cities served: 30
Apr. 4,1989	DOT begins hearing for route authorization to Sydney, Australia.
Apr. 11, 1989	America West filed with the DOT for the authority to serve Tokyo, Japan with service from Honolulu, Hawaii.
May 3, 1989	Announced the offer of $726 million for the Eastern Shuttle and ten Boeing 757 aircraft. Included in the Eastern Shuttle were 21 Boeing 727s. (America West withdrew offer on May 24, 1989.)
May 11, 1989	Announced purchase of four 747-200 aircraft from Amsterdam based KLM Royal Dutch Air to be delivered in the 4th quarter of 1989 and the 1st quarter of 1990.
May 11, 1989	Announced new non-stop service from Phoenix and Las Vegas to: Honolulu, Hawaii (beginning November 16,1989.)
May 25, 1989	Announced new service from Phoenix to: New York LaGuardia, New York (beginning July 1, 1989) Washington National, District of Columbia (beginning July 1, 1989) Both New York LaGuardia and Washington National will be served via Omaha, Nebraska and Wichita, Kansas.
May 31, 1989	Announced new non-stop service from Las Vegas to: Fresno, California (beginning July 1, 1989)
June 1, 1989	Introduced a special new offer, "Passport to Paradise," which provides FlightFUND members with the opportunity to earn a free award certificate and two upgrade discount certificates for a round trip to Honlulu, Hawaii. (Complete details are available upon request.)
June 1989	**Phoenix** Daily Departures: 181 Employees: 9000 Total Fleet Size: 63 Boeing 737s 7 Boeing 757s 4 Boeing de Havilland Dash 8s Cities Served: 46 **Las Vegas** Daily Departures: 104 "Nite Flite"cities served: 31

Source: "Chronological History," America West Airlines, February 1989, June 1989.

which is central to its "More Care" service commitment. The airline has tried to set itself apart from the typical discount airline. Its pricing policy is to offer more low-fare seats than the competition. This is intended to stimulate traffic by developing and increasing air travel among four groups:

1. Frequent business travelers

2. Current passengers who may travel more frequently due to better service at low fares

3. Automobile, bus, and train travelers who may switch to air travel

4. Nontravelers who may fly as an alternate expenditure of discretionary income

The airline's "More Care" strategy is described in Exhibit 4.

America West is currently listed in the APOLLO, PARS, SABRE, and SYSTEM I central reservation systems, but it does not own even a portion of any of these CSRs.

Exhibit 4 "More Care" Service: Amenities Offered by America West to Attract the Frequent Traveler

1. Assigned seating
2. Knowledgeable and well-trained personnel dedicated to the company's goals of personalized service
3. High-quality complimentary alcoholic beverages
4. King-size overhead baggage bins for storage of carryon baggage
5. Quality seats in each aircraft designed for passenger comfort and maximum legroom
6. Interline agreements that provide baggage handling for connecting flights to final destinations
7. Complimentary copies of *The Wall Street Journal* and *USA Today*
8. Efficient ticketing procedures to reduce waiting time at airports and facilitate faster access to flights
9. A frequent flyer program (FlightFUND) whereby credit accrual is measured by the fares paid, as well as actual miles flown. Credit may be gained through the use of various FlightFUND partners.
10. Complimentary round-trip shuttle service between the popular resort area of Scottsdale, Arizona, and Phoenix Sky Harbor International Airport
11. Members-only V.I.P. airport lounges (Phoenix Club) at Sky Harbor Airport. Offer complimentary snacks and beverages, library (complete with personal computer, copy machine, and facsimile machine) and conference room, as well as separate television and bar areas
12. Seatfone Service, an inflight telephone system by GTE Airfone Inc., available on all America West Boeing 757s. These credit card telephones will be available in each seatback in first class and the center seatback of each row in coach.
13. A "Fast Check Drive-Thru" satellite terminal located just east of Terminal III at Phoenix Sky Harbor Airport. Full check-in services are offered without leaving the car.

Source: "Fact Sheet," America West Airlines, March 1989, 6.

Personnel

The management at America West is both young and experienced. The CEO and founder of the firm, 52-year-old Edward Beauvais, was a partner in a consulting firm for ten years prior to founding America West. His specialty was route selection. Beauvais also completed a long-range planning study for the never consummated Continental–Western merger. Prior to 1971, Beauvais served as the assistant vice president of research and development for Bonanza and Hughes Air West. His position prior to that was as an accountant for Frontier Airlines.

The current president of America West is Michael Conway. Conway, who is 43 years old, was named president in 1984 after the company's first president, Michael Roach, resigned. From 1981 to 1984, Conway was the executive vice president of America West. His previous experience was as vice president and controller for Continental Airlines. The other officers are also young and have substantial experience with large airlines.

By April 1989, America West had grown to over 8,000 employees. The airline's labor force is entirely nonunion, which effectively reduces the overall cost of operations. These savings enable America West to cross-utilize staff. For example, most flight attendants double as ticket agents and baggage handlers. In addition to increasing productivity, cross-training increases employee value and encourages promotion from within.

The emphasis placed on employee development is also illustrated by the creation of various employee advisory boards, whereby the staff is able to interact with all levels of management. A further example of employee involvement is the fact that over 16 percent of the issued and outstanding common shares of the company are held by the staff and management of the airline; the percentage of the airline owned by the employees has steadily grown from just over 11 percent at the end of 1983. Much of the stock was purchased voluntarily, but the airline mandates that employees acquire stock at a 15 percent discount from market amounting to 20 percent of their first year's salary. The entrepreneurial culture at America West is emphasized through the payment of annual profit sharing of 15 percent of pretax profits. This amounted to over $1.8 million in 1988.

America West offers its employees an attractive benefit package. In addition to comprehensive medical, dental, and life insurance benefits, the company offers unusually liberal travel benefits. Employer-sponsored child care is the newest of the benefits. The company is attentive to the well-being and interests of its personnel. *Working Mother* magazine rated it one of the top 50 companies in the country from the standpoint of the needs of working mothers.[2] Some comments made by employees about worklife at America West are given in Exhibit 5.

Phoenix Base

An important part of the initial strategy of America West was its decision to be based in Phoenix.

[2]Darla Morgan, "Flying Right," *Arizona Trend*, December 1988, 63.

Exhibit 5 Personal Comments of Employees on America West's Fifth Anniversary

"As one of the very first employees, it has been my distinct privilege and a unique experience to witness the company's growth from the dream to the reality . . . a true caterpillar-to-butterfly story in not-so-slow motion. Our top management has genuine compassion for their fellow employees, and I am proud to work with the thousands of delightful people who make up our company."—*Evelyn Daurio, Director, Human Resources*

"I had come from the coolness of Alaska to listen to 'the man,' Ed Beauvais, despite the 110-degree temperature in Phoenix. This natural leader unfolded the America West business plan with solid, in-depth knowledge, maturity, vision and charisma. The 'risk' I envisioned as part of a start-up airline reversed itself. Now, how could I pass up the opportunity of a lifetime? I didn't . . . based on 'the man' and his presentation, I accepted a captain's position in the first pilot class of 1983."—*Pat Helfrich, Captain*

"As we reach our fifth year of operation at America West Airlines, I can only say how proud and thankful I am to have been a part of starting our airline. The road has been rough at times for all of us, but we have stuck together, sharing pride, positive thinking, love and above all, respect for each other."—*Edward Gonzales, Customer Service Representative*

"In five years, this company has gone from no aircraft and a handful of employees to an airline of substantial proportions. People say that it has changed. In some ways, that is true, but the basic fiber, the thing that holds it all together, is still intact. It has made me realize the awesome power of a right idea coming to fruition at the right time."—*Greg Gibbs, Manager, Aircraft and Facility Appearance*

"I first started as an aircraft technician and then became a supervisor. I am now a shift manager at the new hangar. I am filled with pride as I walk through the hangar door and see how professional and sophisticated we have become."—*Fritz Warnstedt, Shift Manager, Hangar*

"I have found that at America West you can grow as much as you would like, both personally and professionally. There are no limits!"—*Doug Karolak, City Manager/Yuma*

Source: "Welcome Aboard," *America West Airlines Magazine*, August 1988, 7.

Much of the initial success achieved at America West results from the decision to concentrate air service in points to and from its Phoenix base. Phoenix is the ninth largest metropolitan area in the United States and has consistently been one of the most rapidly growing cities in recent years. Between 1983 and 1987 Phoenix was the fastest growing air transportation center among the 20 largest cities in the United States, with passenger levels growing at more than 70 percent (Table 1). It moved up in rank from 14 to 11, surpassing Miami, Las Vegas, and Honolulu. In addition to the obvious benefits of being based in a high-growth area, the generally good weather conditions in Phoenix and the lack of congestion at the airport promote timely and consistent service.

America West at present maintains its headquarters in downtown Tempe, Arizona. The airline opened its new four-plane-bay airline hangar and technical support facility in February 1988. As previously noted, it maintains 21 gates at Phoenix Sky Harbor International Airport. The airline committed to accept all 30 to 35 gates in the new Terminal 4 in Phoenix, scheduled for completion in 1990.

Table 1 Air Transportation Demand in 20 Largest U.S. Cities, 1983–1987

City	1983 O&D Passengers[a]	Passenger Rank 1983	1984	1985	1986	1987	1987 O&D Passengers[a]	Growth Absolute	Growth Percent
New York	41,308,580	1	1	1	1	1	44,098,850	2,790,270	6.8%
Los Angeles	21,081,410	2	3	3	2	2	27,200,860	6,119,450	29.0%
Chicago	19,379,030	3	2	2	3	3	26,179,350	6,800,320	35.1%
Dallas/Ft. Worth	15,430,250	4	4	4	4	5	18,019,620	2,589,370	16.8%
San Francisco	15,263,620	5	5	5	5	4	18,140,940	2,877,320	18.9%
Washington, DC	13,610,370	6	6	6	6	6	17,352,260	3,741,890	27.5%
Boston	13,002,030	7	7	7	7	7	16,982,980	3,980,950	30.6%
Houston	11,580,550	8	8	8	10	9	13,004,100	1,423,550	12.3%
Atlanta	9,293,670	9	10	10	9	8	14,321,270	5,027,600	54.1%
Denver	9,016,800	10	9	9	8	10	12,134,260	3,117,460	34.6%
Miami	8,286,010	11	11	11	13	12	11,053,340	2,767,330	33.4%
Las Vegas	7,324,770	12	15	17	16	15	10,011,800	2,687,030	36.7%
Honolulu	7,006,010	13	14	18	21	23	6,481,970	(524,040)	−7.5%
Phoenix	**6,926,100**	**14**	**12**	**13**	**11**	**11**	**11,818,270**	**4,892,170**	**70.6%**
Detroit	6,875,510	15	13	12	14	14	10,807,880	3,932,370	57.2%
Seattle	6,706,410	16	20	20	12	17	9,052,280	2,345,870	35.0%
Philadelphia	6,174,350	17	17	16	18	16	9,179,700	3,005,350	48.7%
Minneapolis	6,093,870	18	16	15	17	19	8,190,830	2,096,960	34.4%
Tampa	6,016,930	19	19	19	20	20	8,116,020	2,099,090	34.9%
San Diego	5,849,630	20	21	21	19	18	8,643,460	2,793,830	47.8%
	236,225,900						300,790,040	64,564,140	27.3%

[a]Air transportation demand is measured in terms of annual origin/destination (O&D) passengers from the ongoing Department of Transportation 10 percent sample.

Source: "The Economic Impact on Phoenix," America West Airlines Inc., 1988, p. 6.

Aircraft

America West's aircraft fleet as of November 1988 is described in the table that follows. The total number of aircraft was 70, and the average age of the fleet was six years.

Aircraft Type	Status	Number of Aircraft	Average Age (years)	Average Remaining Lease Term (years)
DHC-8	Leased	3	2	8
737-100	Owned	1	19	—
737-200	Owned	6	11	—
737-200	Leased	24	11	8
737-300	Owned	7	1	—
737-300	Leased	22	2	10
757-200	Leased	7	2	17

Source: Proxy Statement, America West Airlines Inc., November 1988, 38.

Financial Data

America West operating and financial highlights for the past several years are presented in Table 2. After America West achieved break-even results in the last quarter of 1984, positive earnings results were achieved until 1987, when the company lost over $45 million. During 1986, the airline expanded to nine new cities and increased its staffing to be poised for further similar expansion in 1987. The result was increasing operating costs as a percentage of sales, despite a 34.1 percent drop in fuel prices from 1984 to 1988. Were it not for a $9.8 million gain from the sale of six used aircraft and the early termination of two leases, America West would have posted a loss for 1986. Also adversely affecting the company during 1986 was a nearly 5 percent decline in passenger yield due to steep industry-wide airfare discounts.

America West's operating efficiencies have made up for the costs resulting from the extremely high leverage of the air carrier. Inclusive of operating lease obligations, effective debt was over 15 times equity in early 1988. Leverage rose to new highs in 1989 as the result of new asset acquisitions. Despite this high leverage, return on equity has been nominal as a result of low earnings levels. Partially offsetting the risk of the higher leverage has been the use of roughly $151 million in convertible subordinated debentures. It should also be noted that the airline has steadily experienced infusions of equity through its employee stock plan. Additionally, the company has consistently maintained large cash balances and a good positive working capital position, which reduces the risk of an immediate liquidity crisis.

Because of America West's high leverage and the increasingly large fixed costs of the infrastructure, the airline appears extremely vulnerable to cyclical economic downturns (which it has never experienced), rising interest rates (nearly $100 million in debt in floating rate obligations on December 31, 1986), and predatory pricing from competing airlines.

Although America West prides itself on its ability to maintain costs below the industry average, operating costs have steadily risen as a percentage of sales as a result of the toll of increasingly rapid expansion. The resulting nominal operating pretax earnings underscore the risks of combining high leverage with rapid expansion.

In 1987 America West received 30 million in cash from Ansett Airlines of Australia. This company, 50 percent owned by billionaire Rupert Murdoch, received a 20 percent stake in America West and a seat on the board. America West subsequently applied to fly to Australia via Hawaii, one of four airlines in contention for this potentially profitable route. Flights from the United States then may feed into Ansett's domestic system. The seat on America West's board is held by Tibor Sallay, New York–based general council for the TNT/Ansett Group. Sallay has commented, "We think it [America

Table 2 America West Operating and Financial Highlights, 1984–1988

OPERATING HIGHLIGHTS	**1988**	**1987**	**1986**	**1985**	**1984**
Revenue Passengers Enplaned	**12,746,499**	11,231,607	7,140,160	5,125,710	2,397,953
Available Seat Miles (000)	**12,200,104**	10,318,096	5,296,100	3,657,560	2,373,833
Revenue Passenger Miles (000)	**7,120,084**	5,785,814	3,233,085	2,283,806	1,247,134
Passenger Load Factor (%)	**58.4**	56.1	61.0	62.4	52.5
Break-Even Passenger Load Factor (%)	**56.7**	59.6	60.2	57.5	56.2
Average Passenger Revenue Per Passenger Mile (¢)	**10.44**	9.66	9.90	10.41	9.71
Average Passenger Revenue Per Available Seat Mile (¢)	**6.09**	5.42	6.05	6.50	5.10
Operating Expense Per Available Seat Mile (¢)	**6.21**	5.92	6.14	6.09	5.52

FINANCIAL HIGHLIGHTS (In thousands except per share amounts)	**1988**	**1987**	**1986**	**1985**	**1984**
Passenger Revenues	**$743,261**	$559,181	$320,179	$237,805	$121,062
Total Operating Revenues	**775,675**	575,447	328,926	241,307	122,565
Operating Income (Loss)	**18,141**	(35,355)	3,957	18,674	(8,564)
Income (Loss) Before Income Taxes and Extraordinary Items	**(12,247)**	(45,675)	3,088	11,436	(15,441)
Income Taxes	**—**	—	1,482	5,313	—
Income (Loss) Before Extraordinary Items	**(12,247)**	(45,675)	1,606	6,123	(15,441)
Extraordinary Items (1)	**21,608**	—	1,421	5,261	—
Net Income (Loss)	**9,361**	(45,675)	3,027	11,384	(15,441)
Per Average Share of Common Stock	**0.51**	(3.85)	0.11	1.01	(3.26)
Cash and Short-Term Investments	**68,448**	26,049	76,600	42,270	5,904
Total Assets	**639,477**	572,255	385,406	237,686	157,515
Long-Term Debt	**384,819**	369,232	254,762	121,269	87,212
Net Stockholders' Equity	**57,983**	45,870	57,933	65,048	28,129
Working Capital (Deficiency)	**(7,606)**	1,583	50,177	29,442	(15,094)

(1) Include gains of $21,608,000 in 1988 resulting from the purchase and retirement as well as exchange of convertible subordinated debentures and, in 1986 and 1985, the utilization of net operating loss carryforwards amounting to $1,421,000 and $5,261,000, respectively.

Source: Annual Report, America West Airlines Inc., 1988, inside front cover.

West] is going to be a good investment. . . . We think its strengths are a modern, up-to-date fleet, employees who are stockholders, very good management. And it fills a niche in Arizona and California that has been missing."[3]

Industry observers quoted in a March 1988 *Business Week* believed that America West had less than a fair chance of survival.[4] America West's management insisted that the reports of the airlines demise were exaggerated. According to CEO Beauvais, "We are not very impressed with [it]. Things are not as bleak as they said,"[5] Helane Becker of Shearson Lehman Hutton wrote in August 1988, "We had all but given up on the company, but management has been able to turn the company around."[6]

The year 1988 marked a return to profitability for America West. Sales reached the $775 million mark and profitability per share reached a new all-time high of 51 cents. This was achieved by slowing expansion, improving load factors, improving on-time performance, and increased employee productivity. Beauvais credited the company's employees: "The support from our employees was a vital factor in turning the airline around. It was tough on them. They did a terrific job—unlike the employees at Eastern who are battling their management every step of the way."[7]

The airline reported first quarter 1989 traffic up 19.8 percent compared to the previous year, while available seat miles remained flat.

Competition from Southwest Airlines

In Phoenix, airfare competition was largely with Southwest Airlines, which serves nearly 50 percent of America West's destinations. Southwest's steep fare discounts seemed intended to raise its market share of Phoenix enplanements while keeping the earnings level depressed for America West. However, in December 1986, Southwest raised the fares on most Phoenix departures by as much as 30 percent. Analysts perceive this move to be the result of a need to increase Phoenix passenger yield while the air carrier is competing with Continental in its Houston market.

Then, in November 1987, Southwest slashed fares in markets in which the airline competed with America West. (A map of Southwest flights is reproduced as Exhibit 6.) Fares were as low as $19 from Phoenix to Los Angeles. In 1988 the airline had 104 departures a day from Phoenix, a 27 percent increase. Highlights of Southwest performance in 1988 and 1989 are presented in Table 3.

Southwest initiated a large advertising campaign in Phoenix criticizing America West. These ads contended that Southwest had lower fares, more accessible gates, and more punctual flights than America West. America West CEO Edward Beauvais said, "This kind of competition is designed to drive us out of business. It's more aggressive and tenacious than most airlines deal with."[8]

Southwest employs a point-to-point method of scheduling instead of the more common hub-and-spoke strategy employed by America West. The point-to-point strategy enables the company to offer a large number of convenient daily departures between nonstop city pairs. This keeps ground time and total flight time to a minimum. The airline feels this best serves the short-flight business traveler.

Other more noticeable differences exist between the two airlines. Southwest is considered a no-frills airline. No meals are served and passengers are not given assigned seats. America

[3]Morgan, "Flying Right," 63.

[4]"The Last of the Upstarts May Be Falling," *Business Week*, March 14, 1988, 35–36.

[5]Morgan, "Flying Right," 62–63.

[6]Morgan, "Flying Right," 63.

[7]Morgan, "Flying Right," 63.

[8]Morgan, "Flying Right," 62.

Exhibit 6 Southwest Airlines Flight Routes in 1989

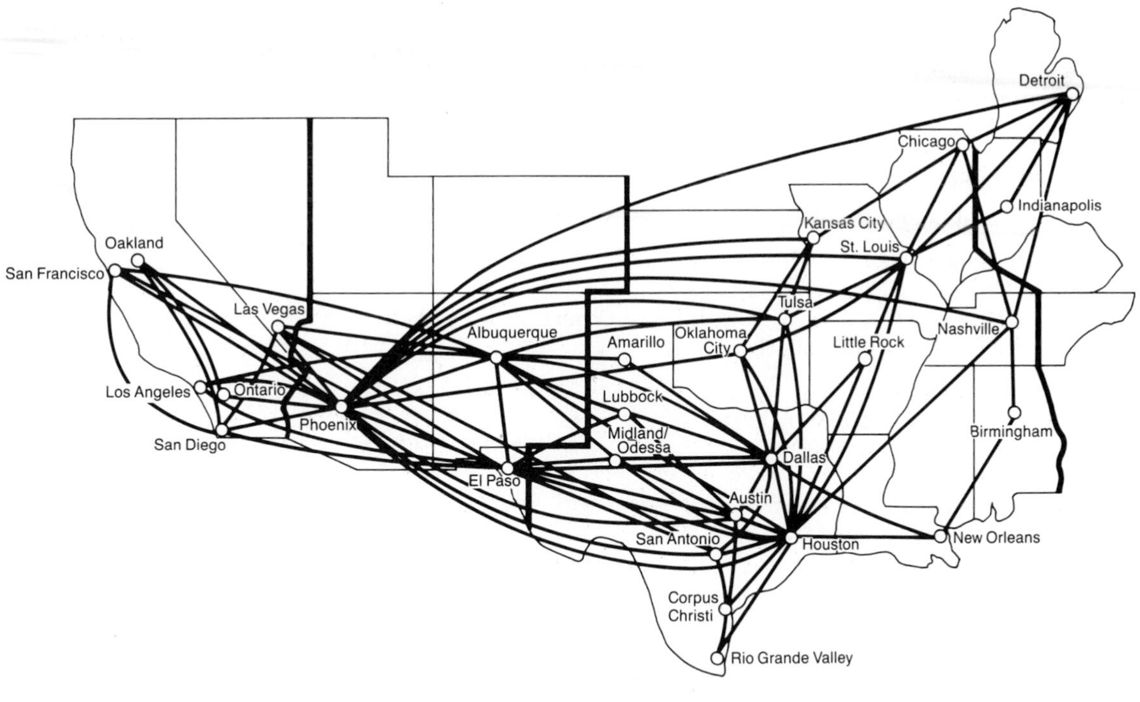

Source: Southwest Airlines

West offers all the traditional services and more, as described in Exhibit 4.

Southwest continues to be a big threat to America West. It earned almost $60 million in 1988. Its debt is low and it has a strong cash position. Growth in Phoenix seems inevitable. Southwest is seeking to increase from 9 gates to 12 in Phoenix. In addition, it has opened a reservation center. Its total work force in Phoenix in 1989 exceeded 1,000.

Even with this increase in direct competition, Ed Beauvais is confident of America West's success: "America West will be one of the greatest stories written in our industry."[9]

---

[9]Morgan, "Flying Right," 62.

Table 3 Southwest Airlines Performance Highlights, 1987–1988

	1988	1987	Percent Change
Operating Revenues (000)	$860,434	$778,328	10.5
Operating Expenses (000)	$774,454	$747,881	3.6
Operating Income (000)	$ 85,980	$ 30,447	182.4
Operating Margin (000)	10.0%	3.9%	6.1 pts.
Net Income (000)	$ 57,952	$ 20,155	187.5
Net Income per Common Share	$1.84	$.63	192.1
Stockholders' Equity (000)	$567,375	$514,278	10.3
Return on Average Stockholders' Equity	10.8%	4.0%	6.8 pts.
Long-Term Debt as a Percentage of Total Invested Capital	39.4%	32.8%	6.6 pts.
Stockholders' Equity per Common Share	$18.15	$16.43	10.5
Revenue Passengers Carried	14,876,582	13,503,242	10.2
Revenue Passenger Miles (RPM) (000s)	7,676,257	7,789,376	(1.5)
Available Seat Miles (ASM (000s)	13,309,044	13,331,055	(.2)
Passenger Load Factor	57.7%	58.4%	(.7) pts.
Passenger Revenue Yield per RPM	10.79¢	9.65¢	11.8
Operating Revenue Yield per ASM	6.47¢	5.84¢	10.8
Operating Expenses per ASM	5.82¢	5.61¢	3.7
Number of Employees at Year-End	6,467	5,765	12.2

Note: Operating income and related operating data include the results of TranStar through June 30, 1987. After that date TranStar decided to cease its operations and liquidate its assets and liabilities and, accordingly, is excluded from operations.
Source: Annual Report, Southwest Airlines Inc., 1988, inside front cover.

Case 14

Exxon Corporation, 1986*

Throughout the 20th century Exxon Corporation ranked as the largest company in the international petroleum industry and as one of the largest corporations in the world. In 1985 Exxon reported revenues of $92.9 billion, net income of $4.9 billion, and total assets of $69.1 billion. These results gave Exxon a worldwide ranking among corporations of all types of number two in sales, number two in after-tax profits, and number one in assets.

Exxon Corporation and its affiliated companies operated in the United States and more than 80 other countries. The company's business interests included exploring for and producing crude oil and natural gas, operating marine and pipeline facilities for transporting both crude and refined products, refining and marketing petroleum-based products, manufacturing petrochemicals, fabricating nuclear fuel, mining coal and other minerals, producing electric motors and electrical equipment, and the generation of electric power in Hong Kong. Over 70 percent of invested capital and over 85 percent of revenues were tied to Exxon's oil and natural gas activities. Exhibits 1 and 2 provide a financial overview.

Company History and Background

Exxon Corporation is the surviving parent company from the legendary breakup of the Standard Oil Company of New Jersey in 1911, then headed by John D. Rockefeller—the man who dominated the oil industry in its early years and who became a symbol for both the sins and the virtues of capitalism. When the Supreme Court ruled in 1911 that the Rockefeller-controlled Standard Oil of New Jersey constituted a monopoly in restraint of trade, the court-ordered remedy was a breakup: Standard Oil (New Jersey) continued on as the largest of 34 new downsized companies.

In 1960 Standard Oil (New Jersey) consolidated a number of divisions into one U.S. subsidiary, Humble Oil and Refining Company. Humble's trademark, Esso, was one of the best known in the world and was widely used by Standard Oil (New Jersey) in many foreign countries. However, since the nationwide use of Esso as a trade mark had been ruled by the courts as inappropriate owing to conflicts with other trademarks established during the Rockefeller era, Humble marketed its products under the Esso brand in some areas, under the Enco (from Energy Company) brand in others, and under Humble in Ohio; retail operations were conducted in 35 states. In 1960 Humble announced its intention to market in all 50 states and to adopt a uniform design for its service stations. In 1972, frustrated by an inability to use any one of the existing trademarks under which to market and advertise nationwide, Standard Oil (New Jersey) and its domestic operating subsidiary, Humble Oil and Refining Company, announced that they would, henceforth, use Exxon as their single primary trademark on a nationwide basis. Subsequently, Standard Oil (New Jersey) became known as Exxon Corporation, and Humble Oil

---

*Prepared by Professor Arthur A. Thompson, Jr., The University of Alabama, with the research assistance of Victor Gray and Miriam Aiken.

Exhibit 1 Financial Summary, Exxon Corporation, 1981–1985 (Dollar Figures in Millions, except per Share Amounts)

	1981	1982	1983	1984	1985
Sales and other operating revenue					
Petroleum and natural gas	$102,418	$ 92,570	$ 83,622	$ 85,415	$ 81,399
Chemicals	7,116	6,049	6,392	6,870	6,670
Coal	204	288	272	327	357
Minerals	83	80	115	97	108
Reliance Electric	1,673	1,561	1,397	1,538	1,667
Hong Kong power generation	604	584	566	608	586
Other and eliminations	1,122	927	1,083	1,018	833
Total sales and other operating revenue	113,220	102,059	93,447	95,873	91,620
Earnings from equity interests and other revenue	1,702	1,500	1,287	1,415	1,249
Revenue	$114,922	$103,559	$ 94,734	$ 97,288	$ 92,869
Earnings:					
Petroleum and natural gas					
Exploration and production	$ 4,117	$ 3,431	$ 4,079	$ 4,789	$ 4,937
Refining and marketing	1,132	1,141	1,156	408	872
International marine	29	(76)	(101)	(63)	(65)
Total petroleum and natural gas	5,278	4,496	5,134	5,134	5,744
Chemicals	238	93	270	430	249
Coal	13	23	37	43	39
Minerals	(97)	(95)	(57)	(52)	(21)
Reliance Electric	29	(32)	(33)	11	30
Hong Kong power generation	36	51	71	88	90
Other operations	(78)	14	44	47	(19)
Corporate and financing	(507)	(323)	(497)	(298)	(508)
Earnings before special items	4,912	4,227	4,969	5,403	5,604
Foreign exchange on debt	(32)	166	85	267	(2)
Facilities restructuring	(54)	(207)	(76)	(142)	(187)
Hawkins provision	—	—	—	—	(545)
Net income	$ 4,826	$ 4,186	$ 4,978	$ 5,528	$ 4,870
Net income per share	$ 5.58	$ 4.82	$ 5.78	$ 6.77	$ 6.46
Cash dividends per share	$ 3.00	$ 3.00	$ 3.10	$ 3.35	$ 3.45
Net income to average shareholders' equity (*percent*)	17.8	14.9	17.2	19.0	16.8
Net income to total revenue (*percent*)	4.2	4.0	5.3	5.7	5.2
Working capital	$ 5,500	$ 3,328	$ 3,556	$ 1,974	$ (1,734)
Total additions to property, plant and equipment	$ 9,003	$ 9,040	$ 7,124	$ 7,842	$ 8,844
Exploration expenses, including dry holes	$ 1,650	$ 1,773	$ 1,408	$ 1,365	$ 1,495
Research and development costs	$ 630	$ 707	$ 692	$ 736	$ 681
Total assets	$ 61,575	$ 62,289	$ 62,963	$ 63,278	$ 69,160
Long-term debt	$ 5,153	$ 4,556	$ 4,669	$ 5,105	$ 4,820
Total debt	$ 8,186	$ 7,303	$ 5,536	$ 6,382	$ 7,909
Shareholders' equity	$ 27,743	$ 28,440	$ 29,443	$ 28,851	$ 29,096
Average number of shares outstanding (*thousands*)	864,926	867,959	861,399	816,169	754,093
Number of shareholders at year end (*thousands*)	776	865	889	839	785
Wages, salaries, and employee benefits	$ 5,832	$ 5,993	$ 5,849	$ 5,550	$ 5,381
Average number of employees (*thousands*)	180	173	156	150	146

Source: *1985 Annual Report.*

Exhibit 2 Consolidated Balance Sheets, Exxon Corporation, 1983–1985 (In Millions of Dollars)

	December 31, 1983	December 31, 1984	December 31, 1985
Assets			
Current assets:			
Cash	$ 2,512	$ 1,384	$ 1,078
Marketable securities	1,584	1,906	1,396
Notes and accounts receivable, less estimated doubtful amounts	7,900	7,366	7,527
Inventories			
Crude oil, products and merchandise	3,598	3,600	3,803
Materials and supplies	1,373	1,102	993
Prepaid taxes and expenses	1,628	1,881	2,558
Total current assets	18,595	17,239	17,355
Investments and advances	1,747	1,743	2,311
Property, plant and equipment, at cost, less accumulated depreciation and depletion	40,868	42,776	48,262
Other assets, including intangibles	1,753	1,520	1,232
Total assets	$62,963	$63,278	$69,160
Liabilities and Shareholders' Equity			
Current liabilities:			
Notes and loans payable	$ 867	$ 1,277	$ 3,089
Accounts payable and accrued liabilities	11,001	10,845	13,359
Income taxes payable	$ 3,171	$ 3,143	$ 2,641
Total current liabilities	15,039	15,265	19,089
Long-term debt	4,669	5,105	4,820
Annuity reserves and accrued liabilities	3,272	3,478	3,319
Deferred income tax credits	9,012	8,948	11,042
Deferred income	315	369	412
Equity of minority shareholders in affiliated companies	1,213	1,262	1,382
Total liabilities	33,520	34,427	40,064
Shareholders' equity	29,443	28,851	29,096
Total liabilities and shareholders' equity	$62,963	$63,278	$69,160

Source: *Annual Reports*, 1984 and 1985.

and Refining became known as Exxon Company, U.S.A.

One of the most important strategic decisions in the company's history also unfolded in 1960 when Monroe J. Rathbone started a five-year stint as Exxon's CEO. Rathbone believed that the demand for oil, rising faster than new discoveries, would one day convert the presently abundant oil supplies into a scarcity and that the Middle East oil-producing countries would be able to charge much higher prices for their crude. Thus, even though Exxon then had more crude than its refined-products markets could absorb, Rathbone persuaded the company's board to approve major outlays for a search for oil outside the Middle East. Rathbone set up a new subsidiary called Esso Exploration and sent geologists and drilling crews into new areas of the world; Exxon's existing subsidiaries were ordered to begin combing their territories for more oil. In the period 1964–67 Exxon spent nearly $700 million on exploration, mostly in non-OPEC areas. Other major oil companies indicated their amusement at Exxon's move by declining to follow suit on any large scale. Mobil, for instance, with the greatest lack of crude oil reserves of any major U.S. company, spent just $267 million for exploration during the same period. Exxon's decision paid off; as of 1977 Exxon had more proven oil reserves outside the Middle East than any other major company. For his role and foresight in engineering Exxon's move, *Fortune* in 1975 named Monroe J. Rathbone to its Business Hall of Fame—he was one of four living executives so chosen (together with 15 other deceased laureates among whom was John D. Rockefeller).

Organization and Management

Exxon first adopted the principle of decentralized management of its operations in the late 1920s. Decentralized approaches were much in evidence in 1986. Generally speaking, strategy formulation, planning, and coordination were functions of Exxon Corporation's senior management and staff. Activities such as drilling wells, running refineries, and marketing products were delegated to local and division managements close to the scene of these activities. Management positions in Exxon's foreign affiliates and subsidiaries were, with few exceptions, staffed by personnel native to the countries where Exxon operated.

Prior to 1966 some 40 subsidiary companies were reporting directly to corporate headquarters in New York. Feeling that this system was becoming unwieldy and inefficient, Exxon reorganized into a smaller number of regional and operating units. The top official in each subunit was given broad responsibility and a sizable staff in an effort to permit quicker response to changing conditions and, further, to reduce the number of people reporting to corporate headquarters. Some subunits had geographic responsibilities for designated parts of the world—the United States, Europe and Africa, Latin America, and the Far East; others had worldwide responsibilities for particular segments of Exxon's business, such as chemicals or research. As of 1986 there were 14 such subunits, each headed by a senior executive: Exxon Company, U.S.A., Esso Middle East, Exxon Chemical Company, Exxon International Company, Esso Eastern, Inc., Esso Europe Inc., Esso Exploration Inc., Esso Inter-American, Inc., Exxon Enterprises, Inc., Exxon Research and Engineering Company, Imperial Oil Limited (70 percent owned by Exxon), Exxon Production Research Company, Reliance Electric Company, and Exxon Minerals Company.

In 1986 the principal link between Exxon and each regional or operating subunit was provided by one of seven senior management officials (either a senior vice president or the corporation president) who were on Exxon's board of directors. The officer-director was designated as the "contact executive" for at least one of the regional or operating subunits. The concept of "contact" responsibilities was, according to Exxon, a significant innovation when introduced in 1943. A contact executive's responsibilities were implicit rather than precisely defined, but the chief role was to provide strategic guidance over the assigned subunits. The contact executive endeavored to stay well informed about the plans of the regional or operating subunits and the problems they faced. On many matters the contact executive had final review authority; on big issues recommendations had to go before Exxon's management committee (composed of all seven officer-directors) or the compensation and executive development (COED) committee. From time to time the contact assignments of the officer-directors were rotated so as to provide new viewpoints and broaden their own experience.

In 1986 Exxon's board chairman was Clifton C. Garvin; he had been board chairman since August 1975 and director since 1968. Garvin began his career with Exxon in 1947. A graduate of Virginia Polytechnic Institute, he joined Exxon as a process engineer at Exxon's Baton Rouge refinery and became operating superintendent in 10 years. Later he moved through a series of positions in Exxon Company, U.S.A., gaining experience in other major functions of the oil business. In 1964 he went to New York as executive assistant to Exxon's president. During the three years prior to his election as a director he headed Exxon Chemical, U.S.A., and Exxon's worldwide chemical organization. Garvin regularly consulted with the corporation's management committee composed of all eight employee directors; he was chairman of this committee and was also chairman of the COED committee which was primarily concerned with the continuity and quality of Exxon's management. The COED committee directly concerned itself with about 200 senior management positions around the world and indirectly kept an eye on another 400 top management jobs in affiliated companies and subsidiary operations. The COED committee met weekly. Garvin had announced that he planned to retire at the end of 1986.

Exxon's president was Lawrence G. Rawl; he served as vice chairman of both the management committee and the COED committee. Rawl started with Exxon as an engineer in Texas in 1952, holding a variety of supervisory jobs in the Southwest United States. Rawl eventually took on U.S. marketing operations and was the number two executive of Exxon's Esso Europe unit. In 1980 Rawl was appointed to the Exxon board; he played a critical role in boosting Exxon's oil production and profits during the 1980s. Rawl was named president in early 1985 and was expected to take over the chairman's position when Garvin retired.

Anthony Sampson, in a book largely critical of the seven biggest international oil companies, said the following about Exxon and its management:

> In the middle of Manhattan, in the line of cliffs adjoining the Rockefeller Center, is the headquarters of the most famous and long-lived of them all: the company known in America as Exxon, and elsewhere as Esso, and for most of its hundred years' existence as Standard Oil of New Jersey or simply Standard Oil. It is a company which perhaps more than any other transformed the world in which we live. For much of its life it was automatically associated with the name of Rockefeller and some links still remain. The family still own two percent of the stock; Nelson Rockefeller once worked for it in Venezuela; and the desk of the founder, John D. Rockefeller I, is still preserved as a showpiece at the top of the building. But Exxon has long ago outgrown the control of a single family.
>
> The tranquil style of Exxon's international headquarters seems to have little in common with the passionate rhetoric of Arab politicians in Algiers. Beside a bubbling fountain and pool on Sixth Avenue, the fluted stone ribs soar up sheer for 53 storeys, and inside the high entrance hall is hung with moons and stars. On the 24th floor is the mechanical brain of the company, where the movements of its vast cargoes are recorded. A row of TV screens are linked with two giant computers and with other terminals in Houston, London, and Tokyo, in a system proudly named LOGICS (Logistics Information and Communications Systems). They record the movement of 500 Exxon ships from 115 loading ports to 270 destinations, carrying 160 different kinds of Exxon oil between 65 countries. It is an uncanny process to watch: a girl taps out a question on the keyboard and the answer comes back in little green letters on the screen with the names of ships, dates, and destinations across the world. From the peace of the 24th floor, it seems like playing God—a perfectly rational and omniscient god, surveying the world as a single market.
>
> Up on the 51st floor, where the directors are found, the atmosphere is still more rarefied. The visitor enters a high two-story lobby with a balcony looking down on high tapestries; the wide corridors are decorated with Middle East artifacts,

Persian carpets, palms, or a Coptic engraving. It is padded and silent except for a faint hum of air-conditioning, and the directors' offices are like fastidious drawing rooms, looking down on the vulgar bustle of Sixth Avenue. It all seems appropriate to Exxon's reputation as a "United Nations of Oil."

But in this elegant setting, the directors themselves are something of an anticlimax. They are clearly not diplomats or strategists or statesmen; they are chemical engineers from Texas, preoccupied with what they call "the Exxon incentive." Their route to the top has been through the "Texas pipeline"—up through the technical universities, the refineries, and tank farms. The Exxon Academy, as they call it, is not a university or a business school, but the giant refinery at Baton Rouge, Louisiana. Watching the Exxon board at their annual meeting, I found it hard to imagine them as representatives of a world assembly. It was true that there were, in 1974, two foreign directors—Prince Colonna, the former commissioner of the Common Market, and Otto Wolff, the German industrialist; and there was also one director, Emilio Collado, with experience of government. But the core of the board was made up of the engineers, enclosed in their own specialized discipline.

Within their own citadel these men seem confident enough with some reason: they are directors of a company that has survived for a century, they have acquired great expertise, and they each earn over $200,000 a year. They move in a world enclosed by the rules of Exxon, which belongs to them. "I think of it as a proprietary relationship," said Garvin in 1973, "Like running a company of which I am the owner. It is not just my duty, but my deep personal desire, to keep it in the best shape possible for the men who will come after me." But once outside their own territory, their confidence easily evaporates. Confronting their shareholders they seem thoroughly nervous, sitting in a row, their fingers fidgeting and their cheekbones working, as they listen to questions about Exxon's African policy, Exxon's salary policy, Exxon's kidnap policy, Exxon's Middle East policy. They know well enough that their company, while one of the oldest, has also been the most hated.

It is in Texas, not New York, that the Exxon men feel more thoroughly at home: and it is the Exxon skyscraper in Houston, the headquarters of Exxon U.S.A., which seems to house the soul of the company. At the top is the Houston Petroleum Club with two entire storeys making up a single room where the oilmen can lunch off steaks and strawberries every day of the year. They like to show visitors the view of which they are justly proud. The flatlands stretch in every direction, broken only by the jagged man-made objects: the domes and tower-blocks in place of cliffs and hills; the curving freeways instead of rivers; the giant roadsigns instead of trees. The glaring gasoline signs stick up from the desolate landscapes like symbols leading to some distant shrine: Exxon, Texaco, Shell, Gulf, Exxon. The fluid which has wrought all these changes is concealed from the view: around Houston there are only a few little pumps nodding in the fields, a few piles of pipelines to indicate the underground riches. But no one needs reminding: it was all done by oil.[1]

Size and Structure of the Petroleum Industry

The business of supplying crude oil and petroleum products in 1985 was not only economically crucial but it was also the largest industry in the world. Worldwide sales of crude oil and petroleum products in 1985 approached $1 trillion, and worldwide petroleum consumption averaged over 50 million barrels per day. Billion-dollar oil companies were commonplace, and no nation was without at least one truly largescale oil company. In 1985 11 of the 20 largest U.S. industrial corporations were primarily petroleum companies—Exxon Corporation, Mobil Corporation, Texaco, Inc., Chevron Corporation, Phillips Petroleum Company, Amoco Corporation, Atlantic Richfield Co., Shell Oil Company, (the U.S. subsidiary of Royal Dutch Petroleum), Tenneco Inc., Sun Company, Inc., and Occidental Petroleum Corporation. Exhibit 3 presents selected statistics for the leading oil companies.

---

[1]Anthony Sampson. *The Seven Sisters* (New York: The Viking Press, 1975), pp. 8–10. Quoted with permission.

Exhibit 3 Exxon's Performance in Comparison with Other Petroleum Companies, 1984

Primary Scope of Operation/ Company	Revenues (in millions)	Net Income (in millions)	Five-Year Growth Rate in Earnings	Return on Equity	Return on Assets	Net Return on Sales	Debt as a Percent of Invested Capital	Debt as a Percent of Net Working Capital
Integrated companies—international:								
British Petroleum	$43,926.0	$1,624.0	−14.7%	11.9%	4.1%	3.7%	22.8%	165.7%
Chevron Corp.	26,798.0	1,534.0	−3.0	10.6	5.1	5.7	43.4	14,910.3
Exxon Corp.	90,864.0	5,528.0	5.2	19.0	8.8	6.1	11.6	258.6
Mobil Corp.	56,047.0	1,268.0	−8.8	9.2	3.3	2.3	40.9	2,723.2
Royal Dutch Petroleum	44,226.0	2,539.0	−9.4	14.6	6.0	5.7	17.3	110.8
Texaco Inc.	47,334.0	306.0	−29.5	1.8	0.9	0.6	41.0	761.9
Integrated companies—domestic:								
Amerada Hess Corp.	8,277.0	170.5	−19.6	6.7	2.7	2.1	40.1	287.1
American Petrofina	2,155.1	45.1	−11.5	7.2	2.9	2.1	39.1	580.6
Amoco Corp.	26,949.0	2,183.0	7.7	17.5	8.5	8.1	17.3	1,053.8
Atlantic Richfield Co.	23,768.0	1,129.0	−0.6	10.9	5.0	4.8	26.9	NM
Kerr McGee Corp.	3,537.0	65.0	−16.5	3.7	1.7	1.8	23.5	286.6
Phillips Petroleum Co.	15,537.0	810.0	−1.9	12.7	5.4	5.2	26.0	NM
Standard Oil Co. (Ohio)	11,692.0	1,488.0	4.6	18.1	8.8	12.7	26.4	NM
Sun Co. Inc.	14,466.0	538.0	−5.1	10.2	4.3	3.7	25.3	3,816.1
Unocal Corp.	10,838.4	700.4	6.9	12.9	7.2	6.5	15.3	417.3

NM = Not meaningful.
Source: Standard and Poor's, *Industry Surveys*.

The petroleum industry spanned a wide range of geographically separate and technically distant activities relating to getting oil from the ground to the final user. The main stages in the process were (1) finding and producing the crude oil, (2) transporting it to the point of processing, (3) refining it into marketable products, (4) transporting the products to regions of use, and (5) distributing them at retail. However, in the search for oil, producing companies were commonly involved in the production, use, and sales of natural gas; many of the major oil companies were suppliers of natural gas.

In the United States roughly 10,000 companies were involved in oil and gas exploration and production. No one firm accounted for more than 11 percent of oil and gas production. Over 80 percent of total U.S. crude oil output came from Texas, Louisiana, California, Alaska, and Oklahoma. It moved mainly through about 70,000 miles of gathering lines and 85,000 miles of trunk pipelines, as well as on oceangoing tankers, river barges, railroad tank cars, and trucks to some 200 operating refineries, with total 1984 capacity of about 15 million barrels/day. In 1984 the U.S. refining industry operated at about 80 percent of capacity. These refineries were operated by approximately 140 companies; in 1984 the top four companies accounted for under 35 percent of refining capacity. In 1985 over 75 pipeline companies were engaged in transporting crude oil and refined products on an interstate basis; additional companies operated intrastate. The top four pipeline companies accounted for less than 30 percent of total volume moved.

Most petroleum products moved from the refinery to the final customer via one or more intermediate storage facilities. Although residual fuel oil, for example, was delivered to large utility and industrial customers directly from the refinery, most products first went to large terminals, located generally at the outlet of a pipeline or on a river, lake, or coastal port, where they could take barge or tanker delivery. By far most of these terminals were owned by refiners, although independent wholesaler-owned terminals took a substantial portion of the distillate and residual oils. Most gasoline and home heating oils were shipped next to local bulk storage facilities. From area bulk plants, the gasoline was transported to service stations and the heating oil to the storage tanks of homes and commercial establishments. However, in the case of gasoline it was not uncommon for the marketing departments of the refinery companies to bypass local bulk plants and ship gasoline directly to their own service stations from large area terminals. This development was made possible by the construction of large-volume retail outlets and the use of increasingly efficient truck carriers.

In 1985 there were over 12,000 wholesale distributors and about 150,000 service stations retailers (down from a peak of 226,000 in 1972). Another 100,000 outlets (convenience food stores, motels, and car washes) retailed gasoline as a secondary activity. The large oil companies owned less than 10 percent of the retail outlets which they supplied; most were owned (or leased) by wholesalers and retail resellers who established their own prices and operating practices.

Exxon's Petroleum and Natural Gas Business

Prior to the 1960s the strategic emphasis at Exxon had always been focused on strengthening the company's position as a major, transnational, fully integrated petroleum enterprise. Its operating scope was worldwide. Even though diversification efforts were begun in the 1960s, in 1986 Exxon was predominantly still an oil company (see the revenue and earnings breakdowns in Exhibit 1). The company was a major factor in all phases of the oil business.

Exploration and Production

Exxon's worldwide production of crude oil and natural gas liquids from internally generated sources declined in 1985 to about 1.7 million barrels a day (one barrel = 42 gallons)—down from the 1976 record high of 5.6 million barrels per day and from 4.0 million barrels per day in 1980. This was due to three factors: (1) weak economic conditions in many of the large industrial nations, (2) stagnating demand for petroleum products stemming from the meteoric climb of prices for petroleum products of the past seven years and growing conservation efforts by users, and (3) the expiration of long-term and special agreements with foreign governments for fixed supply amounts. Exxon in 1985 filled much of its needs for crude oil with purchases on the open market. Exxon was struggling to keep its discoveries of new oil and gas deposits abreast of current production rates from its own wells so as to stabilize its net proved reserves position. Exxon's crude oil reserves totaled nearly 7.5 billion barrels worldwide, and its natural gas reserves were about 45 trillion cubic feet; further statistics are presented in Exhibit 4.

Exxon drilled more than 2,400 wells in 1985, versus about 2,100 in 1984, 1,500 in 1983, 1,725 in 1978, and 1,550 in 1970. At year-end 1981 Exxon had drilling and exploration rights to some 596 million acres, up from 443 million acres in 1970. In 1985 additional exploration acreage was acquired in 15 countries. The company had increased its worldwide oil and natural gas reserves for four consecutive years—only a select group of oil companies were accumulating new reserves at a rate that more than replaced volumes currently produced.

Exxon's exploration teams were considered superior in selecting sites to drill for oil; in recent years Exxon had compiled a 20 percent success rate in finding oil and/or gas on new tracts where it has obtained drilling leases—compared to an industry average of 10 percent. Exxon U.S.A.'s senior vice president of exploration indicated that there was no real alternative to anteing up and accepting the drilling risks of dry holes: "You have nightmares going into these things, but an exploration man has to learn early that it's better to try and fail than not to try and have nothing."[2] To try to reduce the risk of choosing drill sites, Exxon, like other oil companies, sent out seismographic teams to assess the probability to discovery.

Operating and financial results for Exxon's exploration and production activities are highlighted in Exhibit 5.

Refining and Marketing

Exxon was the world's largest refiner with a capacity of roughly 5 million barrels a day. About 30 percent of Exxon's refining capacity was in the United States, and its domestic capacity advantage over other U.S. companies was much less than its size advantage elsewhere.

Total U.S. refining capacity in 1984 was 15.1 million barrels daily (down from 15.9 million barrels in 1983). Worldwide refining capacity was 74.5 million barrels in 1982, down from 76.4 million barrels in 1983. The declines reflected shutdowns of old inefficient refineries.

At Exxon, as well as at other integrated oil companies, the role of refining and marketing had shifted dramatically during the past decade. Prior to the 1973 Arab oil embargo refining and marketing assets were considered a support conduit for transforming crude oil into profit-making capability. Most of the profit in the oil business was made at the wellhead, and refining and distribution operations were only marginally profitable. Beginning with the 1973 embargo, however, major oil companies lost their influence over world crude oil prices and supplies; effective control shifted to the OPEC nations. This reduced the need to protect the profitability of crude oil production via forward integration into refining and distribution. At the same time in the United States the oil and gas depletion allowance was phased out, and a windfall profit tax was imposed on the revenues from crude oil production, both of which limited profitability at the wellhead. In those foreign countries where oil companies were able to retain some owner-

---

[2]Ibid., p. 120.

Exhibit 4 Selected Petroleum and Natural Gas Operating Statistics, Exxon Corporation, 1980–1985

	1980	1981	1982	1983	1984	1985
			thousands of barrels daily			
Net production of crude oil and natural gas liquids and petroleum supplies available under special agreements:						
Net production, Exxon-owned wells						
United States	787	752	740	781	778	768
Canada	116	94	95	90	93	116
Other Western Hemisphere	11	11	10	14	16	18
Europe	155	194	289	370	412	417
Middle East and Africa	56	39	5	5	4	3
Australia and Far East	225	230	228	267	310	330
Total consolidated affiliates	1,350	1,320	1,367	1,527	1,613	1,652
Proportional interest in production of equity companies	351	32	33	32	21	20
Oil sands production—Canada	24	26	18	23	21	29
	1,725	1,378	1,418	1,582	1,655	1,701
Supplies available under long-term agreements with foreign governments	1,802	2,020	1,340	706	489	0
Other supplies available under special agreements	481	398	341	294	226	0
Worldwide	4,008	3,796	3,099	2,582	2,370	1,701
Petroleum product sales:						
Aviation fuels	336	323	330	316	312	326
Gasoline, naphthas	1,453	1,369	1,346	1,344	1,392	1,397
Home heating oils, kerosene, diesel oils	1,428	1,324	1,299	1,280	1,349	1,343
Heavy fuels	1,179	1,051	849	681	685	539
Specialty products	557	534	486	464	466	477
Total	4,953	4,601	4,310	4,085	4,204	4,082
			millions of cubic feet daily			
Natural gas production available for sale:						
Net production, Exxon-owned wells						
United States	3,373	3,065	2,594	2,345	2,485	2,085
Canada	191	186	186	181	168	141
Other Western Hemisphere	78	82	72	70	70	69
Europe	719	799	773	851	1,069	1,086
Middle East and Africa	87	46	—	—	—	1
Australia and Far East	189	251	264	225	215	231
Total consolidated affiliates	4,637	4,429	3,889	3,672	4,007	3,613
Proportional interest in production of equity companies	2,396	2,191	1,860	1,956	1,911	2,048
Supplies available under long-term agreements with foreign governments	104	107	—	—	—	—
Worldwide	7,137	6,727	5,749	5,628	5,918	5,661
			thousands of barrels daily			
Pipeline throughput	3,297	2,740	2,624	2,600	2,694	2,933

Source: *Annual Reports*, 1984 and 1985.

Exhibit 5 Summary of Exxon's Exploration and Production Operations (Millions of Dollars)

	1970	1978	1980	1983	1984	1985
Earnings from operations:						
United States	$ 517	$ 1,202	$ 2,131	$ 1,866	$ 2,012	$ 2,111
Foreign	579	1,282	1,869	2,213	2,777	2,826
Total	1,096	2,484	4,000	4,079	4,789	4,937
Average capital employed:						
United States	2,418	5,871	7,306	11,625	11,907	12,312
Foreign	2,374	4,987	5,095	4,724	4,428	4,812
Total	4,792	10,858	12,401	16,349	16,335	17,124
Capital and exploration expenditures:						
United States	368	1,523	2,395	3,564	4,224	4,638
Foreign	370	1,884	2,818	2,521	2,715	2,923
Total	$ 738	$ 3,407	$ 5,213	$ 6,085	$ 6,939	$ 7,561
Research and development costs	$ 18	$ 61	$ 78	$ 151	$ 174	$ 159

Source: *Annual Reports*, 1979, 1981, 1984, 1985.

ship position in crude oil reserves, taxes imposed by government amounted to 80 percent or more of profits. The upshot was that the major integrated companies like Exxon came to regard refining and marketing investments as "stand alone" assets which were expected to generate returns on capital employed commensurate with alternative investment opportunities.

This "decoupling" of the investment/profitability links between production operations and refining/marketing operations came at a time when refining/marketing activities faced increased worldwide profit pressures. Chief among these were (1) the prospect of no long-range growth in demand for refined petroleum products in industrialized nations, (2) a need to alter refining capabilities to accommodate shifts in the demand mix for refined products and in the patterns of "light" and "heavy" (high-sulfur content) crude oil availability, (3) the possibilities that OPEC countries would acquire existing refinery capacity and integrate forward, and (4) a growing refinery overcapacity.

In the United States the demand for refined products topped out in 1978 at about 19.2 million barrels per day; declines were recorded each of the next six years—down to 16.0 million barrels in 1984: forecasts of U.S. demand to the year 2000 indicated very small amounts of demand growth (see Exhibit 6). The worldwide peak in refined product sales occurred in 1979 with declines registered the following five years. Over the longer term, prospects were for little if any growth in demand in the industrialized free-world nations, but small demand gains were projected to occur in lesser-developed countries.

Exhibit 6 U.S. Demand for Refined Petroleum Products (Millions of Barrels per Day)

	Actual		Projected	
	1980	1984	1990	2000
Total demand	17.0	16.0	16.5	17.0
Gasoline	6.9	6.5	6.2	5.9
Kerosene	1.2	1.0	1.1	1.4
Distillate	3.0	3.0	3.2	3.4
Residual	2.5	1.5	1.7	1.9
Other	3.4	4.0	4.3	4.4

Source: *World Oil.*

The stagnant demand prospects reflected the sharp run-up in the prices of all petroleum products and the conservation effect of more fuel-efficient automobiles, altered driving habits, greater industrial energy efficiency, shifts of electric utilities from fuel oil to coal and nuclear powered generation, and growing efforts of homeowners to use less fuel oil for space heating. Long-term demand was proving to be much more price elastic than short-term demand.

These trends had greatly affected Exxon's refinery capacity utilization. In 1981 Exxon's refinery utilization averaged about 74 percent in the United States, about 61 percent in foreign countries, and about 65 percent overall—well below the 85–93 percent rates typical of previous decades and the levels needed for maximum efficiency. Exxon reacted by closing down its least efficient U.S. refining capacity, and eight refineries in Europe were sold or shut down between 1980 and 1986. In 1985 Exxon's U.S. refineries ran at 80 percent of capacity.

To improve the profitability of its refining and marketing operations, Exxon had undertaken several major cost reduction efforts. The energy efficiency of Exxon refineries had been improved over 25 percent since 1974. Computer automation and job content studies in plants and distribution terminals had been completed. Marginal service station outlets had been eliminated (over 66,000 were closed between 1969 and 1981). Self-service pumps had been installed in most stations. In 1985 the company introduced 120 Exxon Shops to the U.S. motoring public; the shops carried convenience goods, beverages, and automotive items and were entirely self-service outlets staffed only by a cashier. Credit card operations had been tightened and 4 cents per gallon discounts for customers who paid cash at self-service pumps had been instituted to discourage credit card sales and thereby reduce working capital tied up in financing accounts receivable. Exhibit 7 presents selected statistics for Exxon's refining and marketing operations.

International Marine Transportation

In recent years a world tanker surplus combined with slumping crude oil production had made a money loser of Exxon's international tanker operations (*see Table A*).

Responding to the marine division losses during 1985, Exxon sold or scrapped six large crude oil carriers and three smaller vessels, reducing the capacity of fleet tonnage almost 25 percent to 9.7 million tons; these efforts followed on the heels of major fleet reductions between 1981 and 1984.

Chemical Operations

Exxon's chemical plants were primarily in the United States, Canada, and Europe. Products included plastics and polyethylene, solvents and specialty chemicals, petroleum resins, lubricant additives, agricultural fertilizers, and primary petrochemicals. Revenues totaled $6.7 billion in 1985, and earnings from operations amounted to $249 million. Although its petrochemical business was inherently cyclical, Exxon's management felt bullish on the long-term prospects for its petrochemical operations because of Exxon's strong feedstock position and the company's long-standing experience in managing the technologies involved. Several chemical plants in Europe were sold or closed in 1985 to enhance long-term profit prospects.

A profile of the performance of Exxon's chemical operations is shown in Exhibit 8.

Exxon's Strategic Shift to Become an Energy Company

As far back as the 1960s Exxon management began to sense that oil and gas reserves would be inadequate to meet the world's need for energy. It was with this in mind that Exxon started laying the groundwork for a major strategic shift from being just a petroleum company to becoming an energy company.

Exhibit 7 Summary of Exxon's Refining and Marketing Operations (Millions of Dollars)

	1970	1978	1980	1983	1984	1985
Earnings from operations:						
United States	$ 103	$ 294	$ 202	$ 456	$ 161	$ 229
Foreign	187	563	1,702	674	196	643
Total	290	857	1,904	1,130	357	872
Average capital employed:						
United States	2,372	2,741	2,546	2,535	2,380	2,547
Foreign	7,058	5,349	7,541	6,151	5,730	6,297
Total	7,430	8,090	10,087	8,686	8,110	8,844
Capital expenditures:						
United States	315	271	250	363	380	624
Foreign	577	606	947	818	1,003	1,309
Total	892	877	1,197	1,181	1,383	1,933
Research and development costs	33	56	93	113	111	104
			thousands of barrels a day			
Petroleum product sales:						
United States	1,753	1,736	1,503	1,146	1,149	1,123
Foreign	3,931	3,654	3,450	2,939	3,055	2,959
Total	5,684	5,390	4,953	4,085	4,204	4,082
Refinery crude oil runs:						
United States	989	1,426	1,246	958	1,021	1,054
Foreign	4,281	3,001	2,903	2,308	2,199	1,849
Total	5,270	4,427	4,149	3,266	3,220	2,903

Source: *Annual Reports*, 1979, 1981, 1984, 1985.

Table A

	1970	1978	1980	1983	1984	1985
			millions of dollars			
Earnings (losses) from operations	$112	$ (31)	$ 34	$ (126)	$(117)	$(65)
Average capital employed	581	1,676	1,438	1,031	828	640
Average expenditures	162	48	65	14	5	1
Research and development costs	3	4	5	3	2	2
			millions of deadweight tons			
Average capacity, owned and chartered						
Owned vessels	8.1	17.3	16.8	13.3	12.0	11.2
Chartered vessels	10.6	8.9	8.6	2.2	1.5	1.5
Total	18.7	26.2	25.4	15.5	13.5	12.7

Exhibit 8 Summary of Exxon's Chemical Operations (Millions of Dollars)

	1970	1978	1980	1983	1984	1985
Earnings from operations:						
United States	$ 22	$ 154	$ 129	$ 118	$ 204	$ 123
Foreign	23	114	273	152	226	126
Total	45	268	402	270	430	249
Average capital employed:						
United States	410	1,052	1,480	1,890	1,858	1,767
Foreign	865	1,160	1,331	1,889	1,875	1,862
Total	1,275	2,212	2,811	3,779	3,733	3,627
Capital expenditures:						
United States	47	359	260	207	109	146
Foreign	54	111	155	338	194	187
Total	101	470	415	545	303	333
Research and development costs	31	40	72	105	124	133

Source: *Annual Reports*, 1979, 1980, 1984, 1985.

Exxon's strategic move into nonpetroleum energy sources was motivated by two factors: (1) projections that all types of new and existing energy sources would be needed to meet a growing U.S. and world demand for energy and (2) the conviction that Exxon could meaningfully contribute to meeting these needs in a fashion that served both consumers and shareholders. Top management was convinced that the skills needed to develop these energy sources were similar to those Exxon had acquired in its existing business. A senior executive of Exxon described the desirability of diversifying thusly:

> Over many years Exxon has regularly prepared energy supply/demand outlooks for both the United States and the world. In the early 1960s we were projecting that oil and gas demand would continue to grow at about the same rate as the total demand for energy; however, it was not clear just where in the long term these supplies would come from. It appeared to us at that time that domestic production of both oil and gas could peak during the 1970s. We were also aware that there were very substantial reserves of oil and gas located overseas; however, like others, we were becoming increasingly concerned over the national security aspects of increased imports. Thus, we concluded at this early date that there could be substantial future needs for synthetic oil and gas. It also appeared that since coal reserves are so plentiful in this country, a high percentage of the synthetic fuels would be made from coal. . . .
>
> Another important conclusion reached by our appraisals during this period was that use of electricity was going to grow about twice as fast as the demand for total energy. The high projected growth rate for electricity led to our interest in uranium. Looking ahead it appeared to us that nuclear power would play a significant and increasingly important role in meeting the electric utility demand growth. . . .
>
> Another important question which had to be answered before we made a decision to enter either the coal or uranium business was the availability of resources. . . . Our studies indicated that of this amount of potential reserves, approximately 65 percent were not owned or under lease by any company then producing coal. . . .
>
> In the case of uranium, the reserves situation was quite different. Because uranium is difficult to find, it has a very high discovery value. This resource had been much more actively sought af-

ter than coal, and all known reserves were controlled by companies which were already active in the business. We believed, however, that the company's accumulated oil and gas exploration skills would offer a good start toward discovering new reserves . . . most of the known uranium deposits in the United States occur in sedimentary rocks. . . . Since oil and gas occur in a similar environment, we had a great deal of geological expertise which could be applied to uranium exploration. Also, Exxon U.S.A. had an extensive library of geological and geophysical information that had not yet been examined with the objective of locating uranium deposits. Many of the areas of the United States containing known or potential uranium deposits had been explored in the course of our oil and gas exploration efforts. It seemed possible that rock samples and detailed geological information could be reexamined for guides to locating uranium deposits. In addition, the company held mineral leases which covered not only oil and gas but also other minerals, including uranium. For all these reasons, we believed we could contribute to uranium discovery.

In addition to our exploration capabilities, we had other strengths which could be effectively used in establishing a position in the nuclear fuel and coal businesses. For example, we had developed over the years considerable expertise in processing hydrocarbons in our refineries. We believed that much of the research and development work we had done in refining would prove useful in developing processes for converting coal to gas or liquids.

It was determined at an early date that, to be successful, the coal and nuclear fuel businesses would require sizable amounts of front-end capital. Another important factor was that our company had considerable experience in the area of high-risk, capital-intensive, long-lead-time ventures. In short, we concluded that the needs to be met in these energy fuel areas were compatible with the capabilities of our company.[3]

Exxon's corporate strategy became one of using a sizable and growing fraction of the company's cash flow from oil and gas operations to diversify into other energy endeavors and gradually lessen the firm's total dependence on its petroleum-related operations. The strategy was to be implemented over a 10- to 20-year period with heavy investments in other energy sources coming during the 1980s; the strategic objective was to transform Exxon into a well-diversified, full-line energy supplier by sometime in the 1990s. Generally speaking the strategy called (1) for starting up the new energy activities internally rather than via acquisition so as to avoid any antitrust problems or adverse public reaction associated with acquiring existing companies and (2) for energy diversification to be financed by investing an increasing percentage of Exxon's \$8–\$10 billion cash flows in developing new energy businesses. Meanwhile, in the near term, the bulk of Exxon's capital expenditures would be concentrated in protecting the company's long-term position as a leader in the worldwide petroleum industry.

Exxon's Entry into Coal

Exxon's studies revealed that the economically recoverable domestic coal reserves in the United States were in the range of 200 billion tons. When compared to current annual coal production of about half a billion tons, these reserves represented more than a 400-year supply. Since coal was plentiful, it was expected to be a raw material for production of synthetic fuels. Synthetics were believed to be a likely future raw material for Exxon's refineries and chemical plants or to be substitutable as retail products.

Exxon's coal activities became the responsibility of a subsidiary, The Carter Oil Company. The purchase of undeveloped coal reserves began in 1965; bituminous coal reserves were purchased in Illinois, West Virginia, and Wyoming, and lignite reserves were obtained in Arkansas, Montana, North Dakota, and Texas. Coal marketing activities began in 1967. Initially coal from the Illinois reserves offered the best sales

[3]Testimony before Senate Committee on Interior and Insular Affairs, December 6, 1973.

prospects because of its proximity to midwestern electric utilities—power companies with coal-fired generating plants used 75 percent of all the coal consumed in the United States (an average-sized coal-fired plant used 1 to 2 million tons of coal per year). In 1968 a sales contract was negotiated with Commonwealth Edison, a large electric utility based in Chicago, and Monterey Coal Company, a Carter subsidiary, was formed and began development of its first mine in southern Illinois; production commenced in mid-1970. The mine employed about 500 people, had a maximum capacity of about 3 million tons of coal per year, and was one of the largest and most modern underground mines in the country. A second mine was opened in 1977 to supply coal to Public Service Company of Indiana; its capacity was 3.6 million tons per year.

The Carter Mining Company, another subsidiary of the Carter Oil Company, developed Exxon's coal reserves in the West. By 1982 two surface mines were in operation near Gillette, Wyoming. Outside the United States Exxon had coal mining properties in operation or under development in Colombia, Canada, and Australia; in Colombia Exxon was one of the partners in a $3 billion project to construct and operate a coal mine, railroad, and port for coal exporting.

Management was proud of the company's coal mining efficiency. Exxon's underground coal mine productivity in 1975 was 23 tons/man-day; this compared with 17 tons/man-day for all underground mines in Illinois (1974) and less than 10 tons/man-day for all U.S. underground mines (1975). Even so, Exxon's coal business did not become profitable until 1980, 10 years after the first mine was opened in Illinois. Exhibit 9 shows operating statistics for Exxon's coal mining and development business.

Exxon's Entry into Nuclear Energy

As far back as the mid-1960s, Exxon's analysis of the energy situation indicated that use of electricity was to grow about twice as fast as the demand for total energy; Exxon believed that nuclear power would supply as much as 30 percent of the U.S. electric energy supply by the 1990s—an outcome which would greatly increase uranium demand and make diversification into uranium mining and nuclear fuels a profitable business opportunity.

As Exxon saw it, the nuclear fuel business consisted of several distinct activities—uranium exploration, mining, and milling; uranium enrichment; fabrication of enriched uranium into nuclear fuel assemblies; chemical reprocessing of the spent fuel assemblies; chemical reprocessing of the spent fuel assemblies to recover uranium and plutonium for recycling into the fuel cycle, thus reducing requirements for new uranium supply and enrichment services; and ultimate safe storage and disposal of nuclear wastes. Exxon elected to enter only the first three of these segments.

Exploration, Mining, and Milling

Exxon initiated its uranium exploration program in the United States in 1966. By 1977 the company had made two uranium discoveries that had been brought into production and two others that were in varying stages of evaluation. Exxon's petroleum activities played a key role in two of the four discoveries: one discovery was located on a lease which was originally obtained as a petroleum prospect and another resulted, in part, from information gained during geophysical exploration for hydrocarbons. Exxon estimated that in 1977 it had about 5 percent of the uranium reserves in the United States. The reserves that had been assessed as commercially viable were already committed under contract to the utility industry.

Nuclear Fuel Fabrication

During the 1970s Exxon entered into uranium marketing and into the design, fabrication, and sale of nuclear fuel assemblies to electric utilities with nuclear-generating plants. The company also began to provide a range of fuel manage-

Exhibit 9 Summary of Exxon's Coal Mining and Development Operations (Millions of Dollars)

	1970	1978	1980	1983	1984	1985
Earnings from operations after tax:						
Operating mines	$ —	$ 2	$ 22	$ 60	$ 65	$ 59
New business and mine development costs	(1)	(22)	(19)	(23)	(22)	(20)
	$ (1)	$ (20)	$ 3	$ 37	$ 43	$ 39
Research and development costs	$ —	$ 4	$ 2	$ 7	$ 8	$ 3
Average capital employed	$ 24	$ 271	$ 358	$ 792	$ 1,057	$ 1,333
Capital and exploration expenditures	$ 13	$ 87	$ 52	$ 336	$ 397	$ 367
			millions of short tons			
Recoverable reserves	7,000	9,500	10,500	10,566	11,070	11,040
Production	.3	5.2	11.4	20.5	25.1	28.9
Design capacity						
Existing operations	3.0	26.6	36.0	37.9	37.9	37.9
Under construction	—	1.0	9.3	8.3	8.3	9.1
Mines						
In operation	1	4	4	5	5	5
Under construction	—	1	2	1	1	1

Sources: *Annual Reports*, 1978, 1980, 1984, 1985.

ment and engineering services to electric utility firms. Responsibility for these activities was assigned to a newly created subsidiary, Exxon Nuclear, Inc. Exxon Nuclear competed only in the market segment for refueling nuclear reactors. Nuclear reactors were refueled every 12 to 18 months during their 30 to 40 year life. Exxon Nuclear's primary rivals in the replacement fuel market were Westinghouse, General Electric, Combustion Engineering, Inc., and Babcock & Wilcox Co. Exxon Nuclear was the only fuel fabricator not engaged in selling nuclear reactors and supplied about 6 percent of the domestic fuel fabrication market.

Even though Exxon's nuclear operation lost money every year during the 1970s, Exxon continued to be optimistic about the outlook for its budding nuclear fuels business because of continued construction of nuclear plants all over the world. Over 270 nuclear plants were either in operation or under construction at various sites worldwide. However, by early 1982, the outlook for nuclear fuel was reversed. Although Exxon Nuclear had signed contracts with seven utilities for the fabrication of nuclear fuel through 1990, reduced demand projections for nuclear fuel (owing to numerous cancellations in nuclear plant construction and stretchouts in the construction of others) had caused management to begin planning in 1983 for shutdowns of Exxon Nuclear's U.S. mining operations. Moreover, Exxon's uranium exploration had been stopped, developmental engineering work at one mineable deposit was deferred, and a joint venture to develop techniques for separating uranium isotopes with laser beams was ended. The company halted its research activities in nuclear enrichment and reprocessing because of uncertainties in the outlook for profitable investment opportunities.

In mid-1984 the Wyoming uranium mine was closed due to low demand and depressed prices, terminating Exxon's uranium mining operations. In the meantime, both General Electric and Westinghouse had moved to divest their nuclear fuel businesses. So far Exxon had decided to remain in the nuclear fuel fabrication business; since 1969 Exxon Nuclear had provided fuel for more than 40 reactors in the United States, Europe, and the Far East. In the United States in 1985 there were 99 nuclear reactors in operation, and 32 more were under construction; outside the United States there were an additional 244 nuclear units in operation and another 137 under construction. In 1985 Exxon's shipments of nuclear fuel assemblies were up 22 percent.

Exhibit 10 summarizes the recent operating results of Exxon's ventures into uranium mining and nuclear fuel fabrication.

Exxon's Other Diversification Efforts in Energy

Exxon's diversification into other energy areas was motivated by some of the same factors that motivated its diversification into coal and nuclear fuel. As late as 1977 Exxon's total expenditures on these other diversification efforts were small relative to coal and nuclear fuel expenditures. The company's efforts were designed to learn about emerging technologies, to contribute to their development, and to position the company so that a competitive commercial contribution could be initiated when and if market demand led to profit opportunities that appeared to be commensurate with the risks involved.

Oil Shale

Oil shale from deposits in Colorado, Utah, and Wyoming represented a potential source of supplemental liquid and gaseous fuels many times that of the proved domestic reserves of crude petroleum. While considerable shale lands were held by oil companies, the vast majority—about 80 percent—of potential reserves were federally controlled.

Exxon's oil shale activities were relatively limited because of the high-cost economics and because of federal control of most oil shale lands. During the early 1960s Exxon acquired a number of small tracts of patented land and mining claims in the oil shale area of Colorado. These holdings, however, were widely scattered and

Exhibit 10 Summary of Exxon's Uranium Mining and Nuclear Fuel Fabrication Activities

	1970	1978	1980	1981	1982	1983	1984	1985
				millions of dollars				
(Losses) from operations, after tax:								
Operating results	$ (3)	$ (33)	$ (18)	$ (41)	NA	NA	NA	NA
Exploration costs	(1)	(18)	(14)	(9)	NA	NA	NA	NA
Total	$ (4)	$ (51)	$ (32)	$ (50)	$(14)	$23	$20	$119
Research and development costs	$ 1	$ 25	$ 17	$ 14	NA	NA	NA	NA
Average capital employed	$ 7	$201	$229	$203	NA	NA	NA	NA
Capital and exploration expenditures	$10	$ 74	$ 72	$ 42	NA	NA	NA	NA
Revenue	$ 1	$142	$183	$273	NA	NA	NA	NA
				millions of pounds				
Production of uranium concentrates	—	3.3	3.6	3.1	.8	1.4	.4	0
Mines:								
In operation	—	3	3	3	1	1	—	—
Under development	1	—	—	—	—	—	—	—

NA = not available.
Source: *Annual Reports*, 1979, 1980, 1983, 1984, 1985.

would have to be consolidated to form mineable blocks. Exxon's expenditures in oil shale totaled more than $16 million as of 1977. Of this $8.8 million went to acquire oil shale reserves in the early 1960s, $4.9 million was spent on research and $2.8 million on core drilling, administrative expenses, and the like.

During the late 1970s Exxon became a 60 percent partner in the Colony oil shale project in northwestern Colorado. The project (scheduled to begin producing in 1986 with an ultimate production target of 47,000 barrels a day of upgraded synthetic oil) was halted in 1983 when a growing worldwide surplus of crude oil and declines in crude oil prices combined to make the production of synthetic fuel uneconomic; in 1983 Exxon wrote off losses of $106 million on the Colony project. An Australian oil shale project, in which Exxon was a joint venture partner, was halted for reappraisal in 1982.

Solar

Exxon started investigating commercial uses of solar energy in 1970 when a research program was initiated to develop advanced low-cost photovoltaic devices. Throughout the 1970s Exxon and other companies worked at developing applications for photovoltaic devices for use in microwave transmitters and ocean buoys. In 1979 Exxon's Solar Power Corp. recorded a 33 percent increase in unit sales of its solar photovoltaic products. It also obtained government contracts for several major demonstration projects in amounts sufficient to assure that 1980 sales would more than double the 1979 total. In the mid-1980s Exxon's efforts in solar energy were terminated, partly because the paths of solar technology that Exxon was pursuing were found to be less promising than those under development elsewhere; the solar activities were never profitable.

Batteries and Fuel Cells

Recognizing the increasing electrification of energy and the need for efficiently storing solar-generated electricity, Exxon funded research in electrochemistry during the 1970s. Fuel cells (devices that convert special fuels such as hydrogen to electricity) had been under study in Exxon Research and Engineering since 1960. In 1970 Exxon Enterprises entered a joint development effort with a French electrical equipment manufacturer to develop a more efficient power supply for electric vehicles and to replace generators driven by engines or gas turbines. Program costs through 1975 exceeded $15 million, but technical progress as of 1985 had not met expectations. Fuel cell technology had progressed to the point in 1986 where many electric utilities were engaged in constructing and operating small-scale pilot projects utilizing fuel cell technology.

A battery development program was initiated at Exxon in 1972 based on concepts developed by Exxon Research and Engineering Company. Batteries with increased energy densities were viewed as being useful as storage devices to help utilities meet peak electricity demands and as potential power sources for electric vehicles. Company experts felt the technological challenge was to develop new batteries that would store from two to five times more energy per unit weight than conventional batteries and be rechargeable hundreds of times without deterioration. In 1978 Exxon's Advanced Battery Division began selling a titanium disulfide button battery for uses in watches, calculators, and similar products. As of 1986, however, Exxon had not become a major factor in pioneering significant breakthroughs in either batteries or fuel cells.

Laser Fusion

Exxon Research and Engineering Company was one of the sponsors of a program at the University of Rochester begun in 1972 to study the feasibility of laser-ignited fusion of light atoms for the economical generation of power. Out of an estimated program cost of $5.3 million through August 1975, Exxon Research and Engineering Company had contributed about $917,000. This included the cost of Exxon scientists on direct loan to the university. In 1986 Exxon's laser fusion efforts were still in the long-range research and product development stage; the bulk of Exxon's activities were in monitoring results elsewhere.

Hong Kong Power Generation

Exxon's biggest and most profitable nonoil energy venture was launched during the late 1970s and 1980s when Exxon became a 60 percent partner in a $3 billion joint venture with China Light and Power Co. to build and operate two large multiunit coal-fired electric power generation plants in Hong Kong. In 1986 five out of the eight generating units were operational, and construction was continuing on three 677-megawatt units. All of the facilities were managed and operated by China Light and Power. Eight percent of China Light and Power's total sales of electricity were to the People's Republic of China. Operating statistics for Exxon's Hong Kong venture are summarized below:

	Millions of Dollars				
	1981	1982	1983	1984	1985
Revenues	$604	$584	$566	$608	$586
Operation earnings	36	51	71	88	90
Average capital employed				839	1,002
Capital expenditures				328	346

Minerals Mining and Development

For about 10 years Exxon had been a participant in ventures to develop and operate several minerals projects. In 1986 these projects involved two copper mines in Chile, a gold mine in Australia, and a zinc/copper mine. The copper mines in Chile made their first profit from operations in 1985 after incurring losses of $500 million during the past decade. The gold mine in Australia also had a small profit for the year on production of about 35,000 ounces; mining began at midyear. Exxon was a 50 percent owner and was the operator of the gold mine. A profile of recent operating results for the Exxon Minerals division is shown in Exhibit 11.

Exxon's Acquisition of Reliance Electric Company

During 1979 Exxon acquired 100 percent ownership of the Reliance Electric Company of Cleveland, Ohio, at a cost of $1.2 billion. With 31,000 employees and principal operations or subsidiaries in 16 states and 14 foreign countries, Reliance's primary domestic operating organizations were a rotating machinery group that made electric motors; a drives and systems group that made motor controls; a mechanical group that made mechanical power products and components; a weighing and controls group that was composed primarily of the Toledo Scale subsidiary; a telecommunications group, primarily a supplier to the telephone industry; and Federal Pacific Electric, a subsidiary which manufactured and marketed electric power distribution equipment.

Exxon's principal purpose in making the acquisition was to obtain the means for rapid development and marketing of a new energy-saving technology called alternating current synthesis (ACS). The technology held promise for a low-cost, efficient, and reliable means of converting standard utility alternating current electricity into variable voltage and variable frequency electricity with resulting savings in power consumption. The new technology, which grew out of Exxon's research efforts on an electric car, was thought to have the potential for cutting the energy required by a standard industrial electric motor as much as 50 percent (the equivalent of 1 million barrels of crude oil a day)—there were an estimated 20 million electric motors in industrial use. Exxon felt it needed to acquire a

Exhibit 11 Operating Results—Exxon Minerals Division, 1982–1985

	1982	1983	1984	1985
		millions of dollars		
Revenues	$ 80	$ 115	$ 97	$ 108
Earnings (Losses):				
Operating results	(67)	(24)	(16)	1
Mine pre-development & development costs	(23)	(10)	(17)	(9)
Exploration costs	(24)	(23)	(19)	(13)
Total Earnings (losses)	$ (114)	$ (57)	$ (52)	$ (21)
Average capital employed	$325	$338	$352	$359
Capital and exploration expenditures	93	59	71	82
Research & development costs	7	5	4	2
		thousands of metric tons		
Recoverable reserves with contained metal:				
Copper	12,716	12,530	12,819	12,752
Zinc	4,454	4,212	4,212	4,088
Lead	366	353	353	388
Molybdenum	231	212	214	213
Gold (thousands of troy ounces)			354	330
Production:				
Copper			67	77
Gold (thousands of troy ounces)			—	18

well-established electrical equipment manufacturer to manufacture and market the ACS device with a high probability of success. Reliance Electric in 1978 had sales of $966 million and profits of $65 million; about 12 percent of its sales were in electric motors.

Exxon was also interested in Reliance Electric because of Exxon's high-priority research into a new power system for automobiles. In 1979 Exxon had reached the prototype stage in its efforts and had come up with a hybrid car powered by both a battery-driven motor and a small gasoline engine. The electric motor, equipped with the new ACS device, provided the power for acceleration and steep grades; the gasoline engine took over on level stretches and served to recharge the batteries. Exxon felt the new system would be very fuel efficient even on larger cars.

The Reliance Electric acquisition did not produce spectacular results for Exxon. Shortly after Exxon made the acquisition, antitrust violations surfaced in Reliance Electric's Federal Pacific Division and settlement damages ran into the millions. More importantly, development work on the ACS project hit major snags and it was determined that the concept would not be cost effective. An alternative concept was explored, but did not offer a significant competitive advantage over existing products. In August 1981 the whole ACS project was canceled. In 1985 the Federal Pacific unit of Reliance was sold. Reliance's revenues in 1985 were $1.67 billion, up from $1.54 billion in 1984; several new products were introduced. A profile of Reliance's performance since its acquisition is shown below: *(see Table B)*

(Table B)

	Millions of Dollars					
	1980	1981	1982	1983	1984	1985
Revenues	$1,595	$1,673	$1,561	$1,397	$1,538	$1,667
Operating results	1	39	(41)	(51)	15	NA
Business development costs	(7)	(8)	(9)	(7)	(4)	NA
Total operating earnings (loss)	(6)	31	(50)	(58)	11	30
Research and development costs	29	34	36	30	25	40
Average capital employed	1,586	1,566	1,451	1,307	1,230	1,085
Capital expenditures	83	102	98	56	51	49

NA = not available.
Reliance took $60 million of write-offs in 1984.

Exxon Enterprises

A subsidiary, Exxon Enterprises, was started in the early 1970s to become the "new business development arm" of Exxon. By 1981 Exxon Enterprises had invested over $800 million in some two dozen new ventures, either by joining other investors in additional venture-capital deals or by funding new businesses created and run by its own employees. Most of these were fledgling firms far removed from Exxon's traditional business. Only two involved the energy industry—Solar Power and Daystar, both of which made equipment for collecting solar energy and both of which were divested in 1981–82 because they were no longer felt to be attractive investments. Scan-Tron sold scholastic tests that were automatically graded by its own machine; Environmental Data produced instruments for measuring air pollution; Qyx marketed computer-controlled office typewriters; Graftek made graphite shafts for golf clubs and fishing rods; Delphi had developed a way to store voice messages in a computer; Zilog manufactured microprocessors to transmit and process data; Qume made highspeed printers; Vydec produced word-processing display terminals and text-editing systems; and Periphonics made switching computers. Other companies that were a part of Exxon Enterprises included Amtek, Xentex, Qwip, Micro-Bit Corporation, Magnex Corp., Intecom, and Optical Information Systems.

The corporate role of the Exxon Enterprises division was to develop nonenergy options for Exxon's future, mainly in case Exxon's diversification into other energy sources did not prove to be as successful as anticipated, and also to take up slack from the eventual decline of the oil business. Unlike other oil companies such as Mobil and Atlantic Richfield which chose to diversify by acquiring well-established companies, Exxon opted for buying ownership interests in small entrepreneurial companies which were just getting started and which appeared to have products capable of achieving $100 million in sales. The idea was to grow up with a new industry as opposed to entering an established industry. In addition Exxon had a longer time horizon, less aversion to risk, more money, and a greater determination to "stick with the winners" than many other venture capital firms.

In 1980 Exxon Enterprises consolidated its several ventures in the office equipment and office systems field. Fifteen of the small "startup" companies were molded into a new unit called Exxon Information Systems; the combined sales of these companies totaled $200 million in 1979 and nearly all were experiencing rapid growth (though none were profitable). A drive was also launched to recruit senior executives away from other information processing companies—IBM and Xerox in particular. A senior vice president of Exxon Enterprises said, "We intend to be *the* systems supplier to the office market." The strategy was to become a major factor in advanced office systems equipment within three to five years using a "supermarket approach"—offering customers a wide variety of products (typewriters, word processors, fast printers, electronic files, voice-input devices, message units, and so on) with the potential of computer-controlled coordination. Most industry observers predicted that Exxon would try to challenge IBM and Xerox head-on in the office automation market which, by the end of the 1980s, was projected to be a $150–$200 billion industry.

Exxon indicated that revenues would probably have to reach $1 billion before the Exxon Information Systems unit became profitable. Management stated that Exxon was prepared to be patient in integrating the 15 companies into a single systems company and in "growing" the unit into a profitable and high competitive market position. However, the prospects for making EIS profitable got gloomier between 1980 and 1984. By 1984 Exxon had invested more than $600 million in the office systems units, but losses continued to mount—the cumulative total exceeded $250 million. In early 1985 the foreign operations of the Office Systems Division were sold to Italy's Olivetti and the U.S. operations were sold to Harris Corporation's Lanier Business Products unit: the sales price was undisclosed but Exxon did not come close to recovering its $600 million investment. The only company of significance from the original group of Exxon Enterprises companies still owned by Exxon in 1985 was Zilog. Several new companies had recently been added to Exxon Enterprise's business portfolio; the biggest of these was Gilbarco.

Major New Developments: 1981–1986

Between 1981 and 1986 conditions in the worldwide oil and gas market swung sharply from shortage to surplus. Worldwide crude oil supplies were plentiful as end-use demand fell well short of earlier projections. Crude oil prices softened slowly during 1982–84, began a slide from the $34–$38 range to the $25–$30 range in 1985, and crashed temporarily to the $10–$14 per barrel range in early 1986. In 1980–81 it had been widely predicted that crude oil prices would reach at least $50 per barrel by 1985 and perhaps $70–$100 per barrel by 1990.

Efforts to conserve all types of petroleum products, brought on by the sharp run-up of prices in the 1974–80 period and by expectations of further sharp increases to come, were the driving forces in the shift from shortages to surplus conditions. Energy-saving technology of all types was increasingly available and in 1986 automobiles were delivering about double the miles per gallon of the early 1970s. Conditional upon developments in energy-saving technology, on energy prices, and on economic growth rates, it seemed probable that worldwide demand for crude oil in 1990 would not be substantially higher than the 1979 peak of 63 million barrels per day. Supplies of natural gas had also shifted from short to abundant; prices were declining and a surplus of natural gas was expected at least through 1986.

The jolt to enterprises tied to the oil and gas business as the sellers' market turned into a buyers' market was far reaching. The belief that oil and gas prices were destined to rise indefinitely and that investing in drilling and exploration for oil and natural gas were certain payoff propositions had prompted a rush in the late 1970s and early 1980s to invest in oil and gas exploration by all kinds of small companies as well as the major oil companies like Exxon. Banks were willing to finance speculative drilling projects and many independent operators borrowed heavily. Multimillion dollar limited partnerships were formed to drill for new supplies. Du Pont acquired Conoco Oil and U.S. Steel bought Marathon Oil (both multibillion-dollar transactions) because of the lucrative long-term profit prospects in oil. But in 1982 when the glut became highly visible and several OPEC countries turned to price cuts to help them maintain production volumes, the near-term outlook for companies dependent on rising oil prices became desperate. Many oil companies began major restructuring to avoid possible takeover attempts and there were several buy-outs among the oil giants: Occidental Petroleum acquired Cities Service; Texaco bought Getty Oil; Chevron acquired the Gulf Oil Corporation; and Mobil acquired Superior Oil. Capital investments in drilling, coal-based synthetic fuels, and oil shale were cut back drastically. Drilling activity fell off sharply. Financing dried up for the programs of many small independent operators. Long-term contracts to supply oil and natural gas, which buyers had rushed to sign in the shortage era, became unattractive. The budding synthetic fuel business virtually collapsed. Many coal-based synthetic fuels projects, always looked upon as marginally viable and longer range than oil shale, were canceled or downsized. The bulk of the major oil shale projects in the United States were slowed, reduced in size, or halted; two multibillion-dollar Canadian projects were canceled. A $40 billion pipeline to transport Alaskan North Slope gas to the lower 48 states was put on hold. Most oil company exploration and production programs were tailored to maximize cash generation rather than to find reserves which might be recoverable at a profit later if prices rose enough.

Long-term, oil's share of total energy use was still expected to drop from 53 percent in 1980 to 40 percent by the year 2000; natural gas was expected to hold onto its roughly 18 percent share of the energy market. Coal, synthetic fuels, nuclear energy, and solar energy were expected to fill the gap. However, the potential for coal, oil shale, tar sands, coal liquefaction, and coal gasification really depended on (1) how much new oil and natural gas was discovered, (2) the extent to which energy-saving technologies were developed to permit conventional oil and gas to stretch further, (3) how much of the total energy demand would be supplied by nuclear power plants (the accident at Three Mile Island in the United States and the disaster at Chernobyl in Russia raised major safety questions), and (4) the speed with which developments in solar energy technology made solar power a cost effective and almost infinite energy source. Coal was coming under closer environmental scrutiny and there was now a consensus that the use of high-sulfur coal contributed to "acid rain." Tougher, more costly pollution regulations concerning coal use were a virtual certainty before 1990.

Exxon's chairman, Clifton Garvin, reflected on both the successes of 1985 and uncertainty about the future:[4]

> That we were able to do as well as we did in 1985 is attributable to strategies set in motion some time ago. A major emphasis in our planning over the past several years has been to prepare for a more competitive future. We have done this in a variety of ways, all directed toward making Exxon a more productive organization. In refining and marketing, for instance, we have systematically phased out less efficient capacity when it became apparent that it could no longer compete. Current refining capacity, as a result, is down about a quarter from its 1981 level. At the same time, we have upgraded to higher levels of efficiency and productivity those facilities that we have retained. Average sales volume in Exxon service stations is an example. Over the same four-year period this has increased some 30 percent. Emphasis on higher-value products and greater selectivity in geographical market participation have been other elements in our downstream strategy.
>
> In exploration and production our goal has been twofold: to develop and maximize recovery from existing oil and gas fields (about two thirds

[4]Management's letter to the shareholder, *1985 Annual Report.*

of our producing investments have gone for this purpose) and to strengthen our resource bases through cost-effective additions to reserves. In 1985 we drilled a record number of development wells and the largest number of exploration wells in the last quarter of a century. The new discoveries and extensions to existing fields that resulted, along with purchases and revised recovery estimates, more than replaced volumes produced. For the fourth year running we increased our reserve base.

All in all, then, it was a good year for Exxon. But as we all know much has happened since the year ended. Early in 1986 spot crude oil prices experienced their most drastic drop in the modern history of the oil industry. How far this may go, how permanent it may be, and all that it implies for the future remains to be seen. But that there will be far reaching consequences for our industry seems certain. As a result, we are having to rethink our entire strategy. Exploration ventures, capital investments, the lines of business that we are in—all must be reexamined to make sure that they continue to make sense in a radically new environment.

In April 1986 Exxon offered 40,000 employees the option to retire early or resign with compensation, citing the poor outlook for the oil industry due to recent drastic declines in oil prices. The company planned a major reorganization with staff reductions extending to all levels of the corporations. Some divisions faced a 30 to 50 percent reduction in staff, as the company sought a method of coping with $15 per barrel oil.

The company was using portions of its $11 billion annual cash flow to (1) repurchase shares of its stock (a 125 million-share stock buyback campaign had helped boost earnings per share and keep Exxon's stock price in the $50–$65 dollar range), (2) make small acquisitions of distressed U.S. oil properties (about $600 million had been spent since early 1984 to acquire at least 100 million barrels of oil reserves and an undisclosed amount of natural gas), (3) search for new oil reserves in altogether new fields (30 percent of exploration expenditures) and in fields where oil had already been discovered (70 percent of exploration expenditures), and (4) fund the expansion efforts of existing operations. Analysts estimated that Exxon could take on an additional $4 to $5 billion in long-term debt without jeopardizing its AAA bond ratings.

Case 14 Update*

Letter to the Shareholders

Exxon's financial results in 1987 were generally strong, particularly in view of the continuing volatility and uncertainty in energy markets. The year ended with fourth quarter earnings higher than any of the preceding six quarters, although net income for the full year, $4.8 billion, was down 9.7 percent from the near-record level of 1986.

Exxon's exploration and production business results, which were depressed by low crude oil prices in 1986, made a strong recovery in 1987, due to increased liquids production, higher prices, and lower operating costs. Our liquid reserve additions in 1987 equalled 114 percent of our production. We also achieved a second consecutive year of record earnings from our chemicals business. These gains, however, did not fully offset the squeeze on profit margins in our downstream refining and marketing business where the increased cost of crude oil could not be fully recovered in product selling prices.

Our chemical sales increased 19 percent in 1987, benefiting from strong worldwide demand and productivity improvements in our plants. Exxon's margins improved, and most of our chemical units ran at or near capacity during the year.

Among Exxon's other business segments, the adverse effect of lower coal prices was largely offset by increased earnings from copper mining and electric power generation in Hong Kong.

During the year, our shareholders approved a two-for-one stock split, the dividend was increased and per share earnings of $3.43 turned out to be among the highest in recent years. We also repurchased 58 million Exxon shares. Thus, 1987 was a rewarding year for shareholders, despite a volatile financial climate.

Since 1986 had been the year for restructuring our worldwide organization, 1987 became a year for testing the new structure. It turned out to be a tough test, but the new organization produced the benefits we had anticipated. We confirmed that we could operate quite profitably with oil prices well below what they were in the first half of the decade. We demonstrated that we could reduce our costs and operate more effectively without impairing our traditional strengths—something we will not forget in a higher price environment. We estimate that this organizational efficiency added $375 million to our 1987 net income. These efficiencies will remain in place and further benefits will accrue in future years. Finally, the restructured organization has given us the greater flexibility and shorter response time needed to seize and profit from rapidly emerging opportunities during these uncertain times.

All considered, these 1987 results were satisfying and confirmed that our underlying businesses and our new organizational structure are sound and that we are well-positioned for the future.

Exxon's ability to maintain superior corporate performance derives from certain fundamental strengths. We have a very large natural resource base diversified throughout the world. Exxon also has a strong marketing presence, coupled with highly efficient manufacturing facilities in the petroleum and chemical businesses. A range of Exxon-developed technologies serves to keep us in the forefront of the industry; some of them are highlighted in the new Research and

---

*Source: Excerpts from Exxon Corporation 1987 annual report, pp. 2–3, 20, 26–28.

Technology section of this report. Our sound financial position is attested by one of the strongest balance sheets in industry. And, most importantly, we have the capable services of our dedicated employees located in 80 countries.

Our ongoing challenge is to develop opportunities to utilize these underlying strengths to maximize shareholder values. We are pursuing that challenge in a number of ways.

In exploration and production, we are being appropriately selective in targeting our efforts, due to the difficult supply and demand situation. Although oil prices are about half of what they were in 1985, there are a number of opportunities which can be aggressively pursued in a lower price environment, so we are focusing on those. Exxon is also adding to its oil and gas reserves through attractively priced acquisitions—some 450 million oil equivalent barrels last year for about $1.8 billion. Meanwhile, we are continuing to invest in enhanced recovery technologies to ensure that we get all the oil that can be economically produced from maturing fields.

In refining and marketing, we are continuing to invest in those markets where we are competitive and have the opportunity to achieve satisfactory profitability. As product markets evolve, we are continuing to upgrade existing refinery facilities to convert lower-grade products and feedstocks into more profitable transportation fuels, lubricants and specialty products.

Further, we are prepared to disinvest where careful analysis persuades us that a particular business environment is unfavorable.

In chemicals, we are well-positioned in an industry with good growth prospects. Our strategies emphasize quality, higher value-added products, and services tailored to our customers' needs. Facilities that have been operating at or near capacity are being expanded through an ongoing program of low-cost capacity additions. We are also broadening our range of participation to additional chemical markets through carefully selected new investments and acquisitions.

In coal and minerals, we are continuing with the development of our resources. Our aim in these very competitive businesses is to ensure that our operations are among the most cost-efficient in their industries.

In 1987, Exxon's capital and exploration spending in support of these strategies totaled $7.1 billion. At this stage, our plans call for expenditures of about $6.5 billion in 1988. However, to the extent that attractive acquisitions are available, additional funds will be spent again this year.

Looking beyond 1988, the outlook for continuing volatility in oil prices suggests that the years immediately ahead are likely to remain difficult. Our ability to convert change into opportunity will be constantly tested. But knowing that we can continue to compete successfully in a low energy price environment gives us the confidence to maintain our focus on longer-term strategies, while taking advantage of near-term opportunities.

As we see it, some time in the decade of the 1990s world crude oil supply and demand should become better balanced and prices will rise. In this environment, our extensive inventory of heavy oil, remote gas and presently noncommercial resources will become more economic to produce, thereby providing us with a very large investment portfolio in the future. Beyond these resources, we also have sizeable coal and oil shale holdings that will provide the basis for synthetic fuels production. We have already developed improved, second generation synthetic fuel technologies that could be utilized with real crude oil prices in the $30 to $35 a barrel range. And we are pursuing research leads that we expect will lower the cost of synthetics still further.

We believe that our investment program coupled with our research and development efforts position us favorably to take full advantage of the profitable opportunities that lie ahead and will further enhance our position in the industry.

We wish to thank our customers for their business and to commend our employees for their effective efforts in helping to convert another challenging year for the industry into a successful one for Exxon. Our thanks, also, to our shareholders, whose ongoing support contributes greatly to Exxon's underlying strength and stability.

FOR THE BOARD OF DIRECTORS
February 29, 1988

L. G. RAWL, *Chairman*

L. R. RAYMOND, *President*

Financial Review

Financial Summary

	1983	1984	1985	1986	1987
			(millions of dollars)		
Sales and other operating revenue					
Petroleum and natural gas	$83,622	85,415	81,399	65,477	73,197
Chemicals	6,392	6,870	6,670	6,079	7,177
Coal and minerals	387	424	465	542	594
Hong Kong power generation	566	608	586	637	699
Other and eliminations	2,480	2,556	2,500	2,252	416
Total sales and other operating revenue	93,447	95,873	91,620	74,987	**82,083**
Earnings from equity interests and other revenue	1,287	1,415	1,249	1,568	1,252
Revenue	$94,734	97,288	92,869	76,555	**83,335**
Earnings					
Petroleum and natural gas					
Exploration and production	$ 4,079	4,789	4,937	3,060	3,767
Refining and marketing	1,055	345	807	1,934	489
Total petroleum and natural gas	5,134	5,134	5,744	4,994	4,256
Chemicals	270	430	249	470	750
Coal and minerals	(20)	(9)	18	12	(38)
Hong Kong power generation	71	88	90	132	162
Other operations	11	58	11	70	74
Corporate and financing	(412)	(31)	(510)	(551)	(404)
Restructuring	(76)	(142)	(187)	233	40
Hawkins provision	—	—	(545)	—	—
Net income	$ 4,978	5,528	4,870	5,360	**4,840**
Net income per share*	$ 2.89	3.39	3.23	3.71	**3.43**
Cash dividends per share*	$ 1.55	1.675	1.725	1.80	1.90
Net income to average shareholders' equity (*percent*)	17.2	19.0	16.8	17.5	14.7
Net income to total revenue (*percent*)	5.3	5.7	5.2	7.0	5.8
Working capital	$ 3,556	1,974	(1,734)	1,100	95
Ratio of current assets to current liabilities	1.24	1.13	0.91	1.07	1.01
Property, plant and equipment, less allowances	$40,868	42,776	48,262	49,289	53,434
Total additions to property, plant and equipment	$ 7,124	7,842	8,844	5,402	5,787
Total assets	$62,963	63,278	69,160	69,484	74,042
Exploration expenses, including dry holes	$ 1,408	1,365	1,495	1,231	818
Research and development costs	$ 692	736	681	616	524
Long-term debt	$ 4,669	5,105	4,820	4,294	5,021
Total debt	$ 5,536	6,382	7,909	7,878	7,885
Fixed charge coverage ratio (SEC definition)	9.5	9.7	9.6	8.8	8.5
Debt to capital (*percent*)	15.3	17.5	20.6	19.0	18.2
Shareholders' equity	$29,443	28,851	29,096	32,012	33,626
Shareholders' equity per share*	$ 17.40	18.42	19.91	22.30	24.38
Average number of shares outstanding (*thousands*)*	1,722,798	1,632,338	1,508,186	1,445,317	1,411,950
Number of shareholders at year-end (*thousands*)	889	839	785	740	732
Wages, salaries, and employee benefits	$ 5,849	5,550	5,381	5,553	4,646
Number of employees at year-end (*thousands*)	151	148	144	102	100

*Reflects August 1987 two-for-one stock split.

Consolidated Balance Sheet

EXXON CORPORATION

	Dec. 31, 1986	Dec. 31, 1987
	(millions of dollars)	
Assets		
Current assets		
Cash	$ 2,908	$ 1,911
Marketable securities	908	620
Notes and accounts receivable, less estimated doubtful amounts	6,784	6,278
Inventories		
Crude oil, products and merchandise	3,603	4,200
Materials and supplies	948	972
Prepaid taxes and expenses	1,169	1,410
Total current assets	16,320	**15,391**
Investments and advances	2,778	3,822
Property, plant and equipment, at cost, less accumulated depreciation and depletion	49,289	53,434
Other assets, including intangibles	1,097	1,395
Total assets	$69,484	**$74,042**
Liabilities		
Current liabilities		
Notes and loans payable	$ 3,584	$ 2,864
Accounts payable and accrued liabilities	9,515	10,248
Income taxes payable	2,121	2,184
Total current liabilities	15,220	**15,296**
Long-term debt	4,294	5,021
Annuity reserves and accrued liabilities	5,121	5,902
Deferred income tax credits	10,828	11,863
Deferred income	466	560
Equity of minority shareholders in affiliated companies	1,543	1,774
Total liabilities	37,472	**40,416**
Shareholders' equity		
Capital stock without par value (authorized 2 billion shares, 1,813 million issued*)	2,822	2,822
Earnings reinvested	37,322	39,476
Cumulative foreign exchange translation adjustment	(196)	1,750
Capital stock held in treasury, at cost (378 million shares in 1986, 434 million shares in 1987*)	(7,936)	(10,422)
Total shareholders' equity	32,012	**33,626**
Total liabilities and shareholders' equity	$69,484	**$74,042**

*Reflects August 1987 two-for-one stock split.

Consolidated Statement of Income — EXXON CORPORATION

	1985	1986	1987
		(millions of dollars)	
Revenue			
Sales and other operating revenue, including excise taxes	$91,620	$74,987	**$82,083**
Earnings from equity interests and other revenue	1,249	1,568	**1,252**
	92,869	76,555	**83,335**
Costs and other deductions			
Crude oil and product purchases	44,536	28,876	34,331
Operating expenses	9,702	9,209	9,315
Selling, general and administrative expenses	4,824	5,230	5,621
Depreciation and depletion	4,274	4,415	4,239
Exploration expenses, including dry holes	1,495	1,231	818
Interest expense	627	614	451
Hawkins provision*	948	—	—
Income taxes	4,688	3,196	2,703
Excise taxes	4,947	5,099	5,667
Other taxes and duties	11,719	13,076	15,084
Income applicable to minority interests	239	249	266
	87,999	71,195	**78,495**
Net income	$ 4,870	$ 5,360	**$ 4,840**
Per share**	$3.23	$3.71	**$3.43**

*Results for 1985 include a provision of $948 million, or $545 million net of income taxes, related to the Hawkins field unit litigation.

Consolidated Statement of Shareholders' Equity **EXXON** CORPORATION

	1985		1986		1987	
	Shares	Dollars	Shares	Dollars	Shares	Dollars
				(millions)		
Capital stock**						
Authorized—2 billion shares without par value						
Issued at end of year	1,813	$ 2,822	1,813	$ 2,822	**1,813**	**$ 2,822**
Earnings reinvested						
At beginning of year		32,302		34,565		37,322
Net income for year		4,870		5,360		4,840
Dividends ($1.725 per share in 1985, $1.80 in 1986 and $1.90 in 1987**)		(2,607)		(2,603)		(2,686)
At end of year		34,565		37,322		**39,476**
Cumulative foreign exchange translation adjustment						
At beginning of year		(1,818)		(1,149)		(196)
Change during the year		669		953		1,946
At end of year		(1,149)		(196)		**1,750**
Capital stock held in treasury, at cost**						
At beginning of year	(247)	(4,455)	(352)	(7,142)	(378)	(7,936)
Acquisitions	(108)	(2,748)	(29)	(867)	(58)	(2,566)
Dispositions	3	61	3	73	2	80
At end of year	(352)	(7,142)	(378)	(7,936)	**(434)**	**(10,422)**
Shareholders' equity						
At end of year		$29,096		$32,012		**$33,626**
Shares outstanding at end of year**	1,461		1,435		**1,379**	

**Reflects August 1987 two-for-one stock split.

Consolidated Statement of Funds Provided and Utilized

EXXON CORPORATION

	1985	1986	1987
	(millions of dollars)		
Funds from operations			
Net income			
Accruing to Exxon shareholders	$ 4,870	$ 5,360	$ 4,840
Accruing to minority interests	239	249	266
Costs charged to income not requiring funds			
Depreciation and depletion	4,274	4,415	4,239
Deferred income tax charges/(credits)	1,174	(413)	110
Annuity and accrued liability provisions	190	(41)	353
Dividends received which were in excess of/(less than) equity in current earnings of equity companies	(49)	(522)	18
Funds provided from operations	10,698	9,048	**9,826**
Funds from other sources, excluding financing activities			
Sales of property, plant and equipment	288	356	336
Reversion of surplus pension assets	—	1,600	—
All other decreases/(increases) in long-term items—net	(140)	1,300	(776)
Changes in working capital, excluding cash and debt			
Reduction/(increase)—Notes and accounts receivable	(161)	743	506
—Inventories	(94)	245	(621)
—Prepaid taxes and expenses	(677)	1,389	(241)
Increase/(reduction)—Accounts payable	2,514	(1,775)	733
—Income taxes payable	(502)	(520)	63
Funds from other sources, excluding notes and loans payable, cash and marketable securities	1,228	3,338	—
Funds provided before financing	11,926	12,386	**9,826**
Funds from/(used in) financing activities			
Additions to long-term debt	429	1,036	1,520
Reductions in long-term debt	(714)	(1,562)	(793)
Net additions/(reductions) in notes and loans payable	1,812	495	(720)
Funds from/(used in) financing activities	1,527	(31)	**7**
Total funds provided, excluding cash items	13,453	12,355	**9,833**
Utilization of funds			
Additions to property, plant and equipment	8,844	5,402	5,787
Cash dividends to Exxon shareholders	2,607	2,603	2,686
Cash dividends to minority interests	131	145	159
Acquisition of Exxon shares—net	2,687	794	2,486
Payment of Hawkins judgment	—	2,069	—
Funds utilized	14,269	11,013	**11,118**
Increase/(decrease) in cash and marketable securities	$ (816)	$ 1,342	**$ (1,285)**

Case 15

Chick-fil-A

How many ways can a chicken breast be cooked? Truett Cathy would answer this question in one way and one way only: the *Chick-fil-A* way. Chick-fil-A is a breast-of-chicken sandwich garnished with a pickle and served on a fresh, buttered bun. The chicken is marinated, seasoned, and pressure-fried using Mr. Cathy's own special seasonings and pressure cooking method. Chick-fil-A is also the name of the restaurant chain that Mr. Cathy founded. In 1983, the nationwide sales reached $134 million, a 29% increase over the previous year. Average per store sales of $510,640 were up 21% from 1982. Average operator income was more than $40,000. This record was achieved in an industry reaching maturity and marked by fierce competition.

The Fast Food Industry

The fast food industry is a maturing industry with emphasis being placed more on market orientation: advertising, purchasing economies, menu innovation, and site selection. Many of the most successful chains are owned by large corporations (see Figure 1). The industry is currently dominated by six major competitors: McDonald's, Burger King, Kentucky Fried Chicken, Wendy's, Hardee's, and Arby's. Thirty-six percent of industry sales is distributed among the first three chains on this list. The fast food industry can be divided into the following segments: chicken; burgers, franks, roast beef; pizza; Mexican; seafood; pancakes; steak, full menu; and sandwich, other. Growth within the various segments of the fast food industry during 1983 ranged from 1% in the hamburger segment to 60% in the pizza segment. The industry average was 24% in 1983. The industry is marked by increasing competition and market saturation resulting from many factors. Among these factors are physical market congestion, a weak economy, and a host of new restaurant and menu concepts.

Figure 1 Corporate Owners of Fast Food Winners

Major Company	Subsidiary(s)
Pillsbury	Burger King
General Foods	Burger Chef
Heublein	Kentucky Fried Chicken
PepsiCo	Pizza Hut
	Taco Bell
Ralston Purina	Jack-in-the-Box

Each segment of the fast food industry is marked by keen competition and each has its own leaders. Who does not recognize the Golden Arches and what they stand for in terms of a fast, hot hamburger? McDonald's is the leader in this segment, with Burger King, Wendy's, and Hardee's nipping at each other's heels for second place. This segment is mature and over-saturated. Competition is characterized by such tactics as Wendy's giving away free magnifying glasses at some locations and calling them free meat detectors. Dinner items are being test-marketed by all major competitors. Full market tests

Prepared by Jean M. Hanebury, Franklin Perdue School of Business, Salisbury State University, and Leslie W. Rue, Department of Management, Georgia State University.

of breakfast items are being run by Wendy's, and those competitors that do not already offer a breakfast menu are considering its addition. Late-night service has been added by some chains—Burger King, Wendy's, and Hardee's, to name a few. In some areas, Hardee's offers 24-hour service. All competitors are concerned with shifts in the economy and share a concern with appealing to a broader customer base. These issues are also operating in most other segments of the market.

Other key issues within the fast food industry include an increase in advertising budgets: In 1983, Hardee's increased its advertising budget by 64%, while McDonald's logged a 20% increase. Non-traditional locations are being sought. McDonald's and Burger King have signed contracts with military bases and universities. Burger King has made a deal with Woolworth's to open outlets in the Woolworth stores. New product introductions have grown to be the key to securing and maintaining a chain's market share. New products, such as the loaded baked potato now served at many fast food outlets, help expand and strengthen the customer base and steal market share from competitors. For example, Wendy's posted a 30% sales gain in one year, stemming from the introduction of baked potatoes.

Franchised restaurants of all types continue to dominate the growth within the fast food industry. Figures 2, 3, and 4 provide comparisons of company-owned and franchisee-owned units from 1982 through 1984. Numbering 64,176 in 1982, franchised restaurants were expected to top 74,000 units by the end of 1984. Many small companies have entered the franchising market, accounting for a gain of 18 franchisors in 1982. At the same time, there have been numerous chains that have gone out of the franchising business. For example, 11 franchisors with a total of 143 restaurants (106 owned by franchisees) went out of business in 1983. At the same time, 21 franchisors with a total of 262 restaurants decided to abandon franchising and to stick to company-owned stores.

According to *Restaurant Business* and U.S. Department of Commerce surveys, franchised restaurants will continue to be the most popular sector of franchising activity. Upscaling menus, service, and decor will be seen in all segments of the fast food market.

The chicken segment of the industry is dominated by Kentucky Fried Chicken's 6,000 restaurants. A number of regional and national chains are vying for the number two position, including Grandy's Country Cookin, Mrs. Winner's Chicken & Biscuits, Bojangles' Famous

Figure 2 Franchise Restaurant Sales, by Restaurant Type (in millions of dollars)

Major Sales Activity	1980	1981	1982*	1983*
Chicken	2,734.0	2,833.0	3,308.0	3,958.4
Burgers, franks, roast beef, etc.	14,027.4	14,327.7	15,990.9	18,100.6
Pizza	2,445.5	3,169.6	3,605.8	4,159.6
Mexican	878.5	1,069.7	1,305.3	1,576.1
Seafood	785.8	888.5	1,027.2	1,211.4
Pancakes, waffles	784.5	847.7	913.3	1,009.8
Steak, full menu	5,935.8	6,566.7	7,043.0	7,849.2
Sandwich, other	265.4	339.5	398.4	518.1
Total	27,867.0	30,042.3	33,592.0	38,383.2

*Estimated by respondents.
Source: U.S. Department of Commerce

Figure 3 U.S. Franchised Restaurants, 1982–1984 Summary

Item	1982	1983*	1984*	Percent Change 1982–1983	Percent Change 1983–1984
Company-owned	20,017	21,351	23,087	6.7	8.1
Franchisee-owned	44,159	47,372	51,755	7.3	9.3
Total number of establishments	64,176	68,723	74,842	7.1	8.9
Company-owned	11,985,068	13,536,111	15,360,844	12.9	13.5
Franchisee-owned	22,173,450	25,128,106	28,786,765	13.3	14.6
Total Sales of products and services ($000)	34,158,518	38,664,217	44,147,609	13.2	14.2
Merchandise (non-food) for resale	60,356	65,852	71,956	9.1	9.3
Supplies (such as paper goods, etc.)	197,305	213,031	234,282	8.0	10.0
Food ingredients	701,442	777,326	863,314	10.8	11.1
Other	29,547	32,466	36,318	9.9	11.9
Total sales of products and services by franchisors to franchisees ($000)	988,650	1,088,675	1,205,870	10.1	10.8

*Data estimated by respondents.
Source: *Restaurant Business,* Mar. 20, 1984, p. 168.

Figure 4 Restaurant Franchising Growth in Units, 1978–1983

	Total Units			Company-owned			Franchisee-owned		
Major Activity	1978	1983*	% Change	1978	1983*	% Change	1978	1983*	% Change
Chicken	6,708	8,528	27	1,870	2,856	53	4,838	5,672	17
Hamburgers, franks, roast beef	26,038	28,563	10	4,648	6,430	38	21,390	22,133	3
Pizza	7,542	12,042	60	3,042	4,099	35	4,500	7,943	76
Mexican	2,329	3,374	45	993	1,505	52	1,336	1,869	40
Seafood	2,297	3,060	33	899	1,447	61	1,398	1,613	15
Pancakes, waffles	1,441	1,640	14	363	514	42	1,078	1,126	4
Steak, full menu	7,924	9,429	19	3,479	4,101	18	4,445	5,328	20
Sandwich and other	1,033	2,087	102	216	399	85	817	1,688	107
Total	55,312	68,723	24	15,510	21,351	38	39,802	47,372	19

*Estimated by survey respondents.
Source: U.S. Department of Commerce, and *Restaurant Business,* Mar. 20, 1984, p. 172.

Chicken 'N Biscuits, and Church's Fried Chicken. Franchising is the way that these newer competitors have chosen to take advantage of the nationwide trend toward lighter food. Grandy's, located in the Southwest, is growing at an average of 40% per year, with 31 company-owned and 51 franchised units. By June 1984 it expects to have 108 restaurants in operation. The initial franchise fee is $27,000. Royalties of 3% of gross sales and a marketing fee of 4% are paid by franchisees. Menu items include chicken, country fried steak, homemade gravies and biscuits, cinnamon rolls, and salad bar. Average unit volume was $1.7 million in 1983. Breakfast accounts for 17% of sales.

Another major competitor, Mrs. Winner's, hopes to capture 25% of the chicken market eventually. Located in the Southeast, Mrs. Winner's has 96 company stores and 27 franchised units. During 1984 Mrs. Winner's plans to add 45 to 50 company-owned and 80 to 100 franchised units. A 68-seat unit costs $550,000 to build. Franchisees pay a $10,000 fee per store and can own more than one unit. They pay $5,000 up front for each of the first ten stores, and the additional $5,000 per unit as each opens. A royalty fee of 4% of net sales is paid by each unit. Another 4% of net sales is allocated for national and local advertising. Mrs. Winner's offers a mildly spicy fried chicken, baked beans, corn on the cob, and mashed potatoes. Chicken and biscuits sales account for 40% of revenues. Average unit sales volume is $640,000 per restaurant.

Located in the Southeast and New York, Bojangles opened 96 units in 1983. During 1984 it plans to add 35 to 40 company-owned and 150 to 160 franchised units. Restaurants seat between 85 and 90 and serve chicken, chicken filet on a biscuit, dirty rice, and cajun pintos. One-third of sales is accounted for by breakfast items like eggs and biscuits. An average unit volume is in excess of $1 million. Franchisers must commit themselves to opening from 3 to 20 restaurants in a locale. A fee of $25,000 per unit is charged. A typical unit costs between $500,000 and $650,000 to build and equip. Royalty fees and marketing fees of 4% each are standard.

Sisters Chicken & Biscuits and Popeye's Famous Fried Chicken are also competitors in the chicken segment of the fast food industry, but Kentucky Fried Chicken (KFC) and Church's Fried Chicken are number one and two, respectively. KFC expects to open 120 new company-owned and 120 new franchised units during 1984. It already operates 4,521 company-owned and 998 franchised units. KFC is expecting to concentrate on growth in the Northeast. Church's had a total of 1,200 company-owned units by the end of 1983. It also has 260 franchised units. Unlike other competitors within this segment, Church's owns 80% of its restaurants. One hundred more company-owned units and 50 franchised restaurants are planned for 1984. Walk-up and drive-through windows are being test-marketed by Church's. It also plans to grow by acquiring small, struggling chicken chains.

In addition, two new contenders are just beginning to penetrate the chicken market with a new menu concept: marinated and open-pit, charcoal-broiled chicken with Mexican side dishes. These new chains are El Pollo Loco and El Pollo Flojo, based in Mexico and Phoenix, Arizona, respectively.

The fast food market is marked by a more discriminating and sophisticated customer base and ever-increasing competition. Therefore, the fast food industry will be moving in the direction of more sophisticated business management practices. Trends for the industry include:

1. Moderate industry growth.

2. Consumer-driven, broader, and more diverse menus.

3. New concepts in fast food, like Mexican food and table service.

4. Increased focus on productivity and asset management, including size and configuration of the unit.

5. Increased emphasis on efficient procurement strategies to provide economies of scale. The cash register as a computer will help streamline all phases of operation from menu planning through inventories.

Chick-fil-A is not included in industry statistics because it is not a public company. But the trends within the whole fast food industry and the chicken segment in particular apply to its operations.

Early Years at Chick-fil-A

The Chick-fil-A concept grew out of long experience in the restaurant business. Mr. Cathy opened his first restaurant on Central Avenue in Hapeville, Georgia, on the outskirts of Atlanta, in 1946. The Hapeville location, originally called the Dwarf Grill, is still in operation today as the Dwarf House Restaurant. It is a popular lunch stop for all those living and working in that area. Ask anyone in Hapeville and he will tell you about the good meals served at the Dwarf House. When Mr. Cathy first went into the restaurant business, hamburgers were the big seller on the menu. Those staples sold for 20 cents. Coke and fried apple or peach pie cost only one nickel. A steak platter was the high-priced item, selling for 90 cents. For that exorbitant amount you got a 7-ounce rib eye, homemade French fries, and rolls!

A second location not far away was the original Dwarf House. This restaurant was Mr. Cathy's favorite, and he was quite devastated when it burned to the ground in 1962. A new Dwarf House was built near the burned-out shell, and self-service was introduced. This first attempt at innovation was not completely successful. Customers used to traditional table service often just got up and walked out when no waitress appeared to take their order. Mr. Cathy's pressing financial obligations and the initial failure of the self-service concept led him to lease the location to Atlanta's first Kentucky Fried Chicken franchise.

One of the problems Mr. Cathy faced at the Dwarf House was supplying fully cooked fried chicken to customers on the run. He experimented with boned chicken in various ways before developing his special recipe for pressure-fried chicken-breast sandwiches. The seasonings are still a secret, but the finished product is a tasty chicken breast cooked for 3½ minutes in peanut oil. To promote his new sandwich idea, Mr. Cathy entered it in the sandwich idea contest sponsored by the National Restaurant Association in 1963. It didn't even earn honorable mention. But Mr. Cathy was undaunted. He heard that Lady Bird Johnson would be campaigning for her husband, President Lyndon Johnson, in Georgia and that she would be hosted by the U.S. Senator and Mrs. Herman Talmadge. The menu was to consist of all kinds of Southern delicacies like country ham and fried chicken. It seemed an ideal place to introduce his new concept in chicken sandwiches. After taking some samples of the product to Mrs. Talmadge, Mr. Cathy earned the privilege of serving Chick-fil-A to the First Lady, Mrs. Johnson. He then faced the problem of how to prepare and deliver a flavorful meal to the location near Savannah, which was 200 miles from the Dwarf House. Cathy made an arrangement with a restaurant near Savannah to use its facilities during off-hours to prepare the meal. Chick-fil-A was so good that Mrs. Johnson commended Mr. Cathy in a personal letter.

Truett Cathy continued to manage his original location, which stayed open 24 hours a day, and franchised the chicken sandwich to other restaurants. The cooking instructions and special seasonings were distributed to many different kinds of establishments. It was soon apparent that there was a problem with quality, however. Mr. Cathy could not count on a consistent, high-quality, good-tasting chicken-breast sandwich. Some operators failed to change the oil often enough; some kept the sandwiches in warmers. The Chick-fil-A high standard of quality was beyond Mr. Cathy's control.

These franchise frustrations led to the establishment of Chick-fil-A as a chain operation centered around the Chick-fil-A sandwich. The first of these operations, which opened at Greenbriar Mall in Atlanta in 1967, was just a tiny "hole in the wall." It was 2 years before another location was opened. By the end of 1983 there were 280 Chick-fil-A restaurants in 31 states. Plans call for 35 additional Chick-fil-A outlets from coast to coast by the end of 1984. About 90% of the money it takes to finance each new unit is still generated internally!

An Emphasis on People

Chick-fil-A is a special business entity in many ways. Its consistent record of growth in the highly competitive fast food business stems from various factors which emphasize all of Chick-fil-A's people, perhaps especially its founder.

The Founder

S. Truett Cathy is a remarkable kind of businessman. He is always immaculately groomed and quiet-spoken. But he is a man who commands immediate respect. His background has shaped him to value service as much as he values good business sense. Just how unique an individual he is can be revealed by a story that is still told in Hapeville. When Mr. Cathy was trying not only to establish his first restaurants but also to gain recognition for his special chicken-breast sandwich, he took advantage of a local feud to advertise his specialty. There were two local newspapers in the area and two local newspaper publishers. These individuals were opposed to each other on every subject, from ballgames to political issues. They also, of course, fought for the local share of advertising dollars. Mr. Cathy decided that he might capitalize on their quest for new advertising. He made an appointment with each after the noon rush on the same day, advising both men that he would like to discuss taking out a full-page advertisement. The one thing he failed to tell them was that he had invited them to the Dwarf House at the same time. Both men arrived, and Mr. Cathy invited them to sit down at the same table and enjoy a free chicken sandwich. It was soon evident how painful it was for each opponent to accept. The meal was quite strained, but when they had both finished, Mr. Cathy made them an offer they could hardly resist. "If you two will shake hands and let me take a picture of it, I'll buy a full-page ad in both your papers." How could either man say no? The resulting advertisement was a blow-up of the historic handshake with the following caption: "We disagree on almost everything, but we both agree this is the best chicken sandwich we have ever eaten." That ad did wonders for local business.

Truett Cathy's business acumen is something he seems to have possessed since he was born. When he was 8 years old, he bought six bottles of Coke for a quarter and sold them for a nickel apiece. He soon added the *Ladies Home Journal* and the *Saturday Evening Post* to the items he had for sale. The energetic young Cathy also worked as a paperboy for *The Atlanta Journal.* When asked about his early career, Mr. Cathy responded: "The family was not very well off. This was my way of getting some spending money. My mother had to take in boarders to provide food for our table." Always independent, Mr. Cathy decided to go into business for himself when he left the Armed Services in the 1940s.

There is another part of Mr. Cathy's personality that he believes has greatly contributed to Chick-fil-A's success. That is his deep religious faith. Mr. Cathy is a Christian businessman. Chick-fil-A's corporate purpose statement, as printed in the annual report and reiterated by Dan Cathy, the founder's son, reflects Mr. Cathy's way of life: "To glorify God by being faithful stewards of all that is entrusted to us. To have a positive influence on all who come into contact with Chick-fil-A." Mr. Cathy is quick to tell anyone who questions the Christian orientation of his firm that as a "business run by Christian principles . . . it is not a prerequisite that you be Christian to be a part of us. We hire people of other religious faiths and we don't see a conflict there."

What does it mean to believe in service and in helping others? Mr. Cathy's whole life is an example of this orientation. In addition to his commitment to the quality of his product and to the excellence of his company, Mr. Cathy has spent as much time as possible helping others develop their potential. He teaches a Sunday School class of 13-year-old boys and often invites one or two to his farm for the weekend. He believes in the value of hard work, and before these boys can ride dirt bikes with their benefactor, they must help with the chores around the farm. He is active in many civic organizations and many local papers carry stories about his charitable works.

Other Corporate Personnel

Chick-fil-A is a privately held firm. Except for a few shares held by relatives, the company's stock is held by Truett Cathy. The founder feels that the firm can remain privately held and controlled almost indefinitely. His family has always been intimately involved in running the company, ever since he started with his first restaurant in Hapeville. Wife, Jeannette, daughter, Trudy, and sons, Don and Dan, have all at one time or another been involved in the daily business at Chick-fil-A. Dan Cathy is Senior Vice President for Operations, and Don Cathy is Senior Director, Field Operations, Northeast Region. The following statement by Dan Cathy reflects their philosophy toward Chick-fil-A:

> We grew up sitting around the table and listening to Dad talk about Chick-fil-A and the restaurant business. It is hard to think of an opportunity or occasion to be apart from Chick-fil-A. Dad's ideas and spiritual values were applied to the business. Each of us grew up with a conviction that we were going to be doing something for the business that would last a lifetime.

The Executive Vice-President, James L. S. Collins, has a long history of service with Chick-fil-A. When Mr. Cathy first decided to build the Dwarf House, he used Mr. Collin's expertise as a restaurant designer. He again got Mr. Collins to help when he was ready to open his prototype Chick-fil-A mall store at Greenbriar. He soon asked Mr. Collins to join the Chick-fil-A family, and they have had a solid working relationship ever since. Industry experts said that Truett Cathy had the perfect chicken sandwich and that Jimmy Collins knew how to design the perfect kitchen. This combination is still going strong.

The corporate staff is listed in Figure 5, and the organizational structure is shown in Figure 6. The corporate headquarters was relocated in 1982 to 75 heavily wooded acres containing three streams and a 1½ acre lake. The 110,000-square-foot building, featuring an 80-foot atrium lobby and a five-story spiral staircase, cost $7.5 million. Each floor opens onto the lobby, which is topped by a clear, skylighted roof. Two glass elevators ride up the outside of the elevator shaft. Mr. Cathy wanted the building to blend into its peaceful surroundings, and it seems almost lost among the trees. It is hard to believe that a busy major highway is nearby. In 1983, about 100 administrative employees were based at the new headquarters. It is expected that about 300 employees will eventually be housed there.

Figure 5 Chick-fil-A Corporate Staff

Philip A. Barrett, *Controller*
Stephen G. Mason, *Director, Field Operations, Midwest/Far West Region*
Nolan C. Robinson, *Sr. Director, Administration*
William L. Baran, Ph.D., *Director, Product Research & Development*
Donald M. Cathy, *Sr. Director, Field Operations, Northeast Region*
John W. Russell, Jr., *Director, National Advertising*
J. Michael Pair, *Director, Field Operations, Southwest Region*
Costelle B. Walker, *Sr. Director, Training & Development*
William H. Lowder, *Director, Data Processing*
H. Allen Smith, *Director, Tax Accounting*
Roger E. Blythe, Jr., *Director, Stores Accounting*
Huie H. Woods, Jr., *Sr. Director, Human Resources*
Jack B. Sentell, *Sr. Director, Field Operations, Southeast Region*
Younger D. Newton, II, *Director, Food Purchasing*

Source: Annual message, Chick-fil-A, 1983.

Figure 6 Organizational Chart

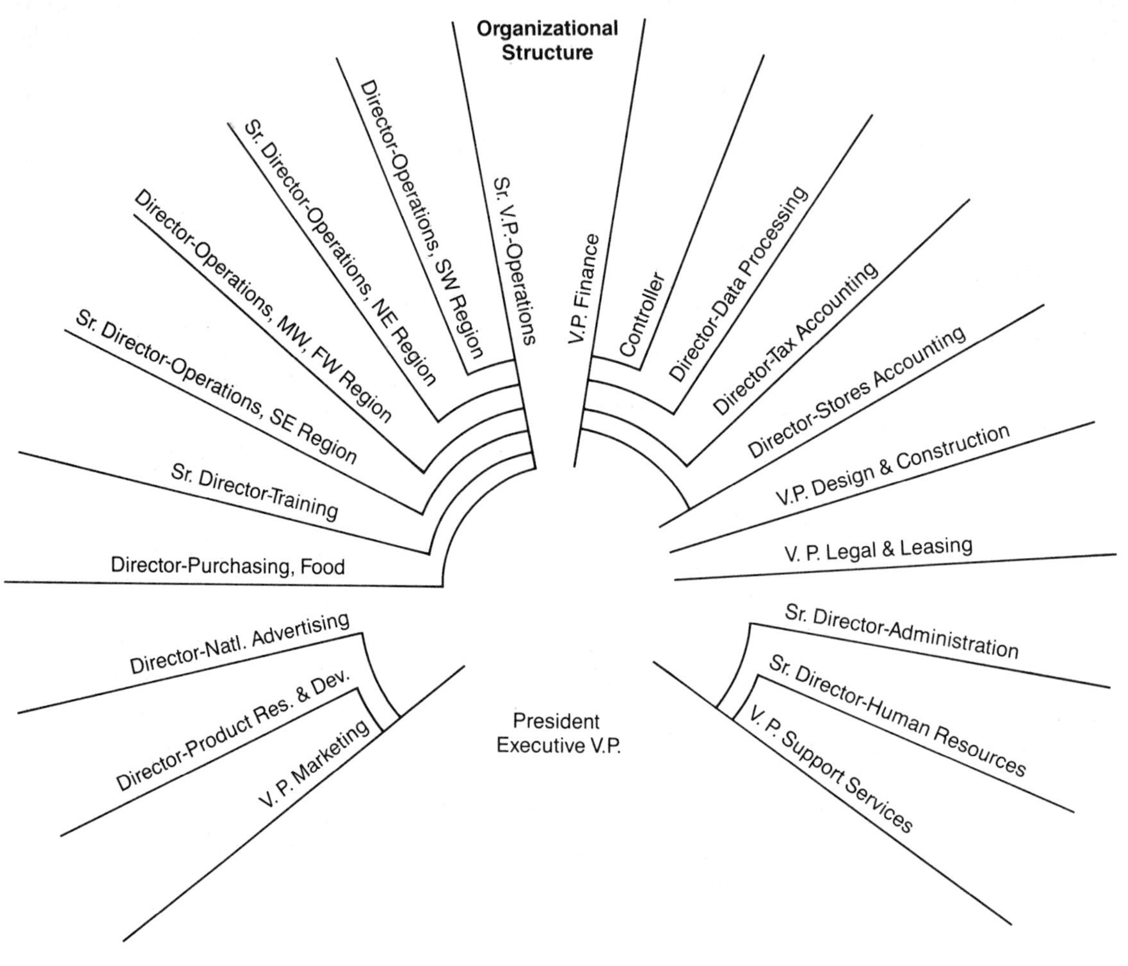

Source: Annual message, Chick-fil-A, 1983.

Owner-Operators

One of Chick-fil-A's most interesting characteristics is its relationship with its owner-operators. Mr. Cathy has structured the owner-operator relationship in a rather unusual manner. Going back to his own philosophy and his experience as a young family man trying to make a living and to have a happy family life, Mr. Cathy incorporated his realizations into the conception of how his restaurants would be organized and staffed. His son, Dan, puts it this way:

> Dad's vision is all based on his prior restaurant experience. You can handle any other pressure if you don't have financial pressure. Consequently the Chick-fil-A system is designed to relieve our owner-operators from financial burdens and requires the owner-operator to invest only $5,000.

For the initial investment of $5,000, an operator is completely trained in the operations end of the business. New operators are guaranteed a minimum income of $20,000 for each of the first 2 years. After this initial period, they are guaranteed $12,000 plus 50% of the net profits. The parent company receives 15% of gross sales each year, and 3¼% of sales is used in the national advertising program. All these monies are spent back in the local markets. There are three or four national advertising campaigns per year. Additionally, hundreds of thousands of pounds of chicken are given away in front of stores per year. A minimum of 100 pounds is distributed at each location per month.

The successful operator must be ready and willing to invest long hours of his time to make his unit a success. The units operate 6 days each week. It is a cardinal rule with Mr. Cathy that no Chick-fil-A will be open on Sunday. The only operator to violate this dictum is no longer with the company. The average operator can reasonably expect to make $40,000 after 5 years. In 1983, 62 owner-operators, or about 26%, made more than $50,000.

One of Truett Cathy's firm convictions is that he will never franchise. He feels that each of his owner-operators can manage just one Chick-fil-A. "Absentee ownership just doesn't work," Mr. Cathy firmly asserts. Mr. Collins sees this philosophy as a key to success. "Each operator must run his own store. Taking on more than one would disturb his [the manager's] effectiveness," emphasizes Mr. Cathy. But unit managers are encouraged to make as much money as possible from their own unit. In fact, they can and do make more money each year than most of the headquarters staff.

Mr. Cathy has a very firm philosophy about the people he attracts to Chick-fil-A and how to get the right people to do the best job. Previous restaurant experience is not a governing criteria. Mr. Cathy often says:

> You can train anyone to cook chicken and make cole slaw. But it is more important to carefully select the person you train because everything else follows from that initial personnel selection. We establish work habits and work attitudes. When you have high expectations, people will do their best. It's like a football team, if you pick the right players and inspire them to work hard, they will be doing their very best for the team.

What kind of person is Chick-fil-A looking for to operate its outlets? Someone with entrepreneurial spirit with a successful track record, a stable family background, and a history of community service is the prime candidate. The selection process is quite protracted. Last year, about 4,000 applicants made initial contacts with Chick-fil-A. Mr. Huie Woods, Senior Director of Human Resources, reiterates the philosophy described earlier. "The boss [Mr. Cathy] insists that human resources are the most important asset that we have. If you are right at the people end of the business, you can't fail."

Most of the emphasis is on the selection end of this human resource process. All selections are made at the Atlanta headquarters. The process is as follows: A prospective owner-operator submits a résumé accompanied by a recent photo and completes an extensive application. A lot of time is spent reviewing these applications, looking for people who hold the same goals and values as those that exemplify the corporate purpose of Chick-fil-A. There were 4,096 applications in 1983 for 12 staff jobs and 26 operator positions. Every inquiry is answered except for blanket résumés obviously sent out at random. Once a good prospect is identified, he or she is invited to the Atlanta headquarters for an initial interview and battery of tests. References are also explored at this point.

Mr. Woods reiterated both Truett and Dan Cathy's words. Chick-fil-A has a Christian orientation. "We don't look for a specific denomination as such, but the people chosen are those with high moral standards, with strong family values, ties in their local community and demonstrated leadership ability." There is another unique Chick-fil-A policy regarding picking the right operator for each location. The company seeks operators in the local community, rather than recruiting and transferring young trainees from another part of the country.

About 10% of those accepted have previous fast food experience. Many have sales experience or have supervised young people in some capacity. It will become increasingly apparent as the operation is developed how much rides on making an informed choice when selecting Chick-fil-A operators. The initial investment of $5,000 is a prerequisite, but Mr. Cathy has often helped candidates finance this initial investment if they show the potential he is always seeking in those around him. It is not unusual for an employee who started out making the cole slaw at a Chick-fil-A location to eventually become an owner-operator himself.

There are field consultants and regional directors of field operations who keep in contact with each location. After the first 2 months in a new location, one of these corporate representatives will visit to offer assistance and to see how the new operator is coping with the infant business. Dan Cathy reports that once the initial training and evaluation is completed successfully, there may be no further on-site visits from field representatives for 2 to 3 years. As long as all indications such as sales growth, employee turnover, and supply costs are in line, the operator and his location are deemed healthy. Operator turnover runs between 4 and 6% per year. In 1983, turnover was 5.8%. The industry average for restaurant managers is between 100 and 200% each year!

Chick-fil-A offers its owner-operators a special benefit package. Ongoing management training is one facet of the package. As noted in the 1983 annual message, "Every February Chick-fil-A invites Operators and their spouses to an expense paid, five-day seminar at a luxury resort. For 1984, we held the seminar at the Southampton Princess Hotel in Bermuda." These yearly retreats provide an opportunity for more than state-of-the-business reports, awards ceremonies, operational workshops, and new marketing plans. "Operators and their spouses enjoy the camaraderie of sharing with old and new friends." Chick-fil-A's incentive package includes the "Symbol of Success" program. "Operators who increase their restaurant's sales by 40 percent or more are awarded the use of a new Lincoln Continental Mark VII for one year." Should the operator continue his 40% sales growth through another year, the car is his to keep. In 1983, 46 operators were presented with the Symbol of Success.

Sharing between corporate staff and operators is encouraged. Two house organs, *Chick-fil-A Operator Newsletter* and *Chicken Chatter,* keep the Chick-fil-A family in touch. Operators share promotional ideas and get reports on new corporate directions. Personal milestones, like new babies, marriages, and other personal or family triumphs, are also shared.

Career Development Program. A 1-year internship is offered to 4-year college graduates between the ages of 22 and 26 who might consider becoming an operator. Salary for the year is $16,000 and 75 to 80% of the time is spent in operating different Chick-fil-A units on an interim basis. The program is geared to introducing young people to all aspects of the owner-operator concept. About 18 to 20 of these positions are offered each year.

There are usually only one or two full-time personnel other than the operator at each location. In many instances the operator's spouse or another family member makes up the core of the crew. Other employees are called "crew members." Eighty percent of the employees are students. They are part-time employees with an average work week of 20 hours. These crew members, too, are another focus of Chick-fil-A's recipe for success.

Crew Members

As indicated previously, Chick-fil-A operators make all other hiring decisions. They staff their location and decide how much to pay each worker. Using tested methods developed over the years by the headquarters staff, each location trains its own crew members. Dan Cathy described the kinds of young people that Chick-fil-A operators attract:

> Lots of these youngsters are class leaders. They are the kind of young people who attract other

> prospective employees. It is also not unusual for brothers and sisters to follow one another into the Chick-fil-A ranks. Often younger children can't wait to follow an older sibling as a Chick-fil-A employee. We have had as many as three members of one family as crew members at the same time.

In fact, this is the kind of relationship that the corporate and local managers strive to develop. It exemplifies the team and family spirit that has made Chick-fil-A a success.

Crew training is quite extensive. New employees start in the back of the location, making the fresh food from scratch each day. They are carefully cross-trained in all aspects of the operation, from cutting cabbage for cole slaw to manning the counter. A friendly atmosphere is important, so the new crew members are gradually introduced to public contact. Pleasing the customer is another key to success and each Chick-fil-A team member must have that in mind. Each new employee receives an individual "Crew Member Training Program." To quote Dan Cathy:

> One of the most fulfilling aspects of operating a Chick-fil-A Unit is observing the development of business skills in crew members. For many, employment at Chick-fil-A is their first business exposure. Having the privilege of taking an active involvement in their development is a great responsibility.

Figure 7 lists the objectives of the Crew Member Training Program. Three training Levels, I, II, and III, are administered according to the individual's progression through the previous levels of training. Industrywide turnover for employees like the youngsters who serve you hamburgers at Wendy's or McDonald's is over 400%. Turnover at Chick-fil-A has remained in the 40 to 50% range.

Benefits for crew members are something special at Chick-fil-A. The annual report states: "Student workers are offered special incentives to stay and grow with Chick-fil-A. Any student who works an average of 20 hours a week for a period of two years or more, while maintaining a 'C' or better grade average, receives a $1,000 scholarship to the college of his or her choice." More than $2 million in scholarships has been awarded since 1973. More than $500,000 was awarded in 1983 alone.

The year 1984 marks a milestone for the Chick-fil-A crew member incentive package and perhaps for the industry. Chick-fil-A and Berry College, a 4-year liberal arts institution located in Rome, Georgia, entered into a scholarship grant program. Berry is situated in northwest Georgia on 28,000 acres of forests, fields, moun-

Figure 7 Crew Member Training Goals

1. Meet on-going training needs by providing continuous training and retraining in order to fully capitalize on employee potential.
2. Systematically provide required training by breaking training into "bite-size" pieces. In other words, the program does not encourage teaching complete jobs, but centers on teaching the tasks which make up complete jobs.
3. Challenge employees to become competent in all areas of operations and reduce, if not eliminate, the need for specialists.
4. To improve profitability in the Unit through more consistent and uniform implementation of cost control procedures in food portioning, waste control and employee productivity.
5. Provide a system of recognition and incentives to motivate crew members to constantly strive for increased levels of performance and productivity.
6. Be manageable in that the Operator need not be required to devote an unreasonable amount of time administering the program.

tains, lakes, and streams. Chick-fil-A's founder, Truett Cathy, and Berry's founder, Martha Berry, shared common goals: to incorporate religion into life; to excel in work and study; and to take pride in a job well done. This philosophy is well illustrated in the letter Martha Berry left to be opened on her death (see Figure 8).

Approximately 1,500 students from all over the United States and several foreign countries make up the student body. In 1984, the joint grant program will allow about 75 young people from Chick-fil-A restaurants nationwide to begin college at Berry. Students sponsored by Chick-fil-A will be housed in the Berry Academy, a former secondary school located on the main campus. To be eligible for the grant, interested students must have worked for Chick-fil-A for 6 months. They must apply and be accepted for admission to Berry before receiving approval from Chick-fil-A to enter the grant program. Additional opportunities for individual growth and leadership development will be made available through recreational, academic, and religious programs sponsored by Chick-fil-A. Mr. Cathy, in his President's Message for 1984, stated:

> The time is coming when a large number of operators and staff will come from this pool of young people who work in Chick-fil-A restaurants. For instance, one new Chick-fil-A operator, age 22, has nine years of experience with the company already. He started out as a crew member at age 13 wiping tables after school.

Careful Selection Pays Off

At this point it is important to note some statistics that relate to Mr. Cathy's emphasis on choosing the right people for each operation. Not one of Chick-fil-A's locations has ever closed. There has been operator turnover as indicated above, but it has remained well below industry standards. Average incomes of owner-operators are higher than those of other managers in the

Figure 8 Miss Berry's Final Letter to Alumni

The Berry Schools
Mount Berry, Georgia
July 1, 1925

To the Graduates of the Berry Schools:

When I am gone, I want you to always think of me as alive—alive beyond your farthest thoughts, and near and loving you, and growing more like God wants me to become. I want you to love the Berry Schools and stand ready to help them in every emergency. Use all of your influence to hold the Schools *to the original plan, simple living, work, prayer, the Bible being taught, Christian teachers; keeping the Schools a separate community, protecting and guarding the property and the good name of the Schools.* I feel that I shall not be separated from the Schools which have been my life and work and which I have always loved so dearly. I shall not be separated from any of the boys and girls who are my logical heirs. I shall just be closer to God, and will understand better the way in which prayer and faith can open the ways through which God can keep and guard our beloved Berry Schools.

I would like to leave an especial message to the graduates of the Berry Schools who are *giving back in service what you have gotten from the Schools.* You who are putting your lives into the work are the real dependence of the Schools and I want to ask you especially to be faithful and guard and protect the Berry Schools. My prayer is that the Schools may stand through the ages, for the honor and glory of God and for the Christian training of poor boys and girls of the mountains and country districts.

I leave with each one of you the motto which I have kept on my desk for years, "Prayer Changes Things."

Faithfully Yours,

Martha Berry

Note—This letter was attached to Miss Berry's will and marked, "To be opened after Miss Berry's death."

mall locations, including large chain stores. On the average, Chick-fil-A units generate more sales per square foot than any other fast food tenant in malls with Chick-fil-A locations. Chick-fil-A has been recognized in many industry publications as having a friendly, positive attitude among its employees. This friendliness and positive attitude also is noted by its customers.

Mr. Cathy says, "Keep your chin up and your knees down and it is impossible to fall." His tenacious spirit and careful supervision of the selection process continues to guide Chick-fil-A to excellence. He still personally interviews each of the final employment candidates for all corporate and owner-operator positions.

Figure 9 Average Unit Sales

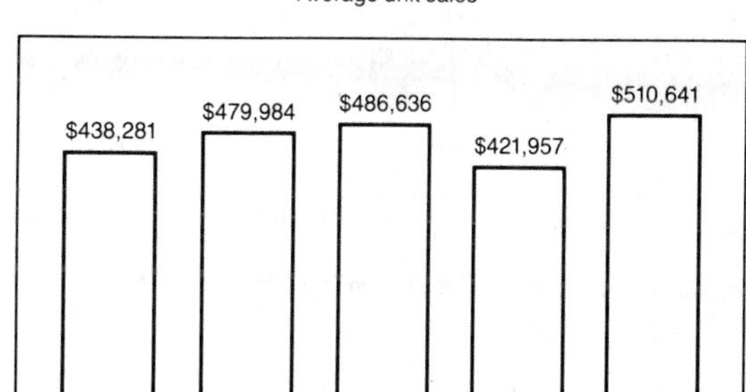

Source: Annual message, Chick-fil-A, 1983.

Operations

As with other aspects of the business, a firm set of guidelines organizes all phases of operation, from the construction of the unit through the menu served at each location. Monthly profit and loss statements from each location are the strongest management tool used by corporate headquarters to monitor and modify the business. Each afternoon, after 5 P.M., owner-operators call into the main computer at headquarters to enter daily sales data. In the next year or two, Dan Cathy hopes to have personal computers located at each unit so that analysis of sales can be done on-site.

Average unit sales for 1979 through 1983 are found in Figure 9. About 6 of the 285 units didn't make a profit in 1983, but they were mostly the new locations. An increase in sales of 29% over 1982 was recorded in 1983. The average sales per square foot is over $340.

Chick-fil-A has units in 32 states. Seventy-five percent are located in Texas, Florida, North Carolina, and Georgia. New units in the Northeast are heavily concentrated in the Philadelphia area and New Jersey. Much new expansion is centered in the Southwest and California. There are also 15 mall locations in the Chicago area that are prime candidates for the Chick-fil-A concept. Over half of all Chick-fil-A units have opened in the last 4 years.

A Typical Chick-fil-A Unit

With three exceptions to date, all Chick-fil-A units are mall locations. The company selects all the sites. Chick-fil-A looks for enclosed malls having the following specifications:

1. 50,000 square feet or more

2. Two or more anchor stores (such as Sears or Penney's)

3. Sixty or more in-line merchants

Regional malls have been the primary targets of Chick-fil-A's development plans. Chick-fil-A's location strategy also is quite different from the industry norm. It is very unusual for mall owners to sign long-term leases with tenants. Chick-fil-A always seeks and receives a 10- or 15-year lease agreement. Once the site is located, a typical unit costs about $250,000 to build and equip. Chick-fil-A corporate headquarters handles all details of leasing, building, and equipping the location. The local owner-operator is sought in conjunction with long-term development plans in each area. Eighty percent or more of the annual construction budget is internally financed. Each unit is custom-designed—not a clone of every other unit, as in many fast food chain competitors like McDonald's or Hardee's.

Malls usually receive a set amount of rent for each unit or 6% of gross sales, whichever is higher. Typically, the 6% figure is received. Because of the returns mentioned previously, Chick-fil-A is a tenant that is vigorously sought by mall developers across the nation.

All locations are built to the specifications initially developed by Mr. Collins. Whenever possible, Chick-fil-A does not locate in a food cluster part of the mall. Experience has indicated that it is more attractive to repeat customers to locate away from other fast food operations. The rationale behind the choice of mall location is to be in a high-traffic area while keeping costs low and size small. Chick-fil-A wants to attract the shopper who wants quick food that is hot and tasty. The typical Chick-fil-A is 1,800 square feet, while the typical McDonald's or Wendy's is 4,000 to 5,000 square feet. Table service is not offered in any Chick-fil-A location.

Renegotiations of the original contracts for additional 12- to 15-year leases are not unusual. In fact, Chick-fil-A has never pulled out of a mall location or failed to complete construction of a unit. As Huie Woods said, echoing the Cathys: "We are going to make it. That's why the mall developers seek us." Once the new location is equipped and staffed, it usually takes about 2 to 3 years to become profitable.

Once the selection has been made, the new operator travels to corporate headquarters in Atlanta to undergo an extensive 4-week training program. Every aspect of the business is explored, although this session only touches on personnel training. Next, the new operator returns to his brand new unit and organizes his operation. All local hires, personnel policies (including things like insurance coverage), pay scales, and local sales promotions—in fact, all aspects of the business, including buying supplies—are up to the individual Chick-fil-A operator. Operators have no control over the following items:

1. Contracts cannot be negotiated individually with poultry suppliers. Five poultry houses supply the special seasoned and sized chicken breasts. Breast trimmings become nuggets.

2. Recipes cannot be altered.

The Menu

Like the many other fast food operations, Chick-fil-A started out with a limited menu centered around the Chick-fil-A sandwich. The company has stuck to this limited menu, perhaps more consistently than some of its competitors. All items on the menu, with the exception of french fries, are made from scratch every day. The core element is the marinated filet breast of chicken that goes into the Chick-fil-A sandwich, which is still served with a pickle on a buttered bun without condiments. The sandwich relies on the taste of the chicken itself, not of some special sauce. Fresh lemonade, homemade cole slaw, and homemade lemon pie complete the original menu. Soft drinks and iced tea are also available. Chicken nuggets have recently been added and are an increasingly popular item. Truett Cathy feels his sandwich is the model for chicken sandwiches copied by other fast food competitors. There has been some pressure on supply and demand for chicken, as it is selling at the highest price in years. There is some feeling also that when fast food competitors like Burger King introduced a lower-quality chicken sandwich, some customers were driven away from all chicken sandwiches. Figure 10 shows the results of a recent taste test conducted by Marketing & Research Counselors, Inc.

Various items have been added to the menu in some locations in the last few years, and others are under development. Added items include soup made from chicken breasts and breakfast menu items such as biscuits. Twenty percent of McDonald's sales is now in breakfast menu items. The test market for breakfast items has been the new freestanding locations in downtown Houston and Atlanta. The breakfast menu will be expanded during 1984.

Figure 10 Chick-fil-A Rates Number One

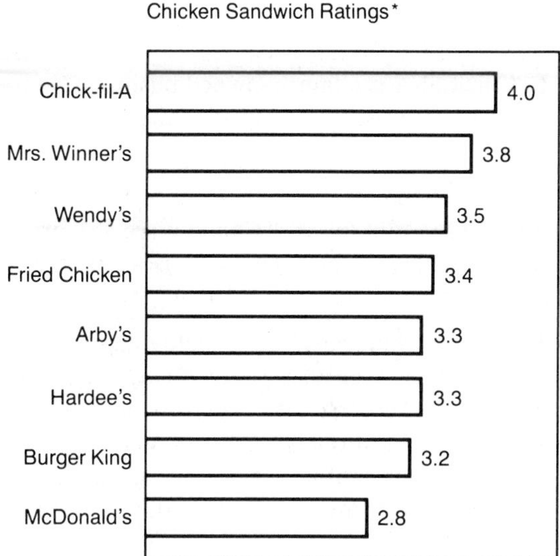

Source: Annual message, Chick-fil-A, 1983.

New Directions

The discussion of new menu items leads to the exploration of new directions for Chick-fil-A. Dan Cathy, head of operations, talked at length about many potential directions for the company. Talk centered around menu expansion, more freestanding Chick-fil-A units, and a possible new restaurant concept.

New Menus

Much marketing research has been done by Chick-fil-A as competition has heated up in the chicken niche of the fast food market. There are many factors which have triggered Chick-fil-A experiments with new menu items. Recent demographic trends have indicated that more families are visiting malls in the evenings, more apartments are being built around malls, and customers are increasingly concerned with the nutritional value of the food they consume.

Dan Cathy emphasized that not only is Chick-fil-A a delicious meal, but it has always been a nutritious one. Several entree dinner items are being tested for possible expansion of the Chick-fil-A menu.

New Freestanding Locations

Although there are still mall locations to be reached in various areas of the United States, corporate staff has begun to plan alternatives for the time in the future when mall operations become a saturated market. The existing units in non-mall locations in downtown Houston and Atlanta are situated in renovated buildings along with other businesses. They are not innovative other than as test markets for breakfast items. So Chick-fil-A has already begun to explore the freestanding Chick-fil-A concept, to design these locations, and to build several pilot locations. Two freestanding Chick-fil-A units are planned for 1984. This will allow Chick-fil-A to fine-tune the Chick-fil-A basic concept. It may need to be modified or adapted in some way to continue to maximize success in a new setting. For example, table service will probably be added in freestanding locations. These new locations will feature menus different from those in mall units.

A Brand New Restaurant

Much of the corporate headquarters is still unoccupied. In one of these areas that has yet to be finished, Chick-fil-A has constructed a restaurant complete with a replica Mark VII at the drive-through window. The prototype represents a new idea that Chick-fil-A has been developing over the last several years. Not only has Chick-fil-A already entered a large portion of the most desirable mall locations but also market studies show that people's behavior and tastes are changing. These factors have been considered, so the prototype of the new freestanding restaurant chain—based on a combination of the menus, facilities, and operations of both the Dwarf House and Chick-fil-A—now sits on the third floor of corporate headquarters. At present, the proposed name for the new chain would be Dwarf House Restaurant. Twenty-four-hour service is envisioned, along with a combination of waitress and self-service.

During discussions with Truett and Dan Cathy, each returned many times to the elder Cathy's philosophy. Both feel strongly the gift and the tremendous responsibility that come along with the more conventional rewards of owning a successful business. They believe in Christian stewardship. They feel a responsibility to operators, crew members, corporate personnel, and the public in general. Truett Cathy and all that he has helped to develop at Chick-fil-A seem to espouse the same ideals of service. Truett Cathy summed it up with these words: "Our strongest commitment is to people. We don't even bring an operator or a member of the staff in unless it is a person we want to be with until one of us retires or dies."

Questions for Discussion

1. Chick-fil-A is a family-owned business. Compare and contrast its operation to that of a public firm.

2. What elements of the culture at Chick-fil-A contribute to its success? Can you see any problems that may stem from the close-knit family culture that pervades the company?

3. The fast food business is highly competitive and mature. Analyze Chick-fil-A's internal strengths and compare its owner-operator system to the more traditional franchise system followed by major competitors. What are Chick-fil-A's strengths as compared with other systems? Where are their weaknesses?

Case 16

Pacific Telesis Group—New Directions and Challenges

On January 1, 1984, Pacific Telesis became totally independent of AT&T. Divestiture had been characterized as similar to taking apart a 747 airliner in flight and reassembling it into a 767, all without spilling any coffee on the passengers. The separation occurred on time and the phones kept ringing through it all. In addition, PacTel felt it obtained the right people, assets, and financial status it needed to continue to do the job. Exhibit 1 shows the financial improvements made. Exhibit 2 shows the position of PacTel in light of other *Fortune* 500 firms.

This case describes the actions taken by the Pacific Telesis Group, formerly the Pacific Telephone and Telegraph Co., during the year immediately preceding divestiture; the organization of the firm after divestiture; and the challenges faced by Sam Ginn, Vice-Chairman and Group President of Diversified Businesses at Pacific Telesis.

Organizing to Meet the Future

After his appointment as strategic planning officer, Sam Ginn set into motion the processes necessary to accomplish the divestiture from AT&T and to develop a strategic plan for the soon-to-be-independent regional company. This included assembling a group to coordinate the divestiture process, establishing a strategic planning group, and organizing to run the businesses after divestiture.

Divestiture Team Set-Up

An experienced team of PT&T managers was quickly assembled to identify, assign, and monitor the myriad of tasks to be accomplished before divestiture on January 1, 1984. These people were selected for their overall knowledge of the firm, their willingness to change, and their commitment to make divestiture work. More than $19 billion in Pacific Telephone assets had to be reviewed and divided between PacTel and AT&T. This included about 3,000 buildings and all the telecommunications equipment they contained. In addition, provisions had to be made to transfer almost 20,000 employees to AT&T. Other key issues that had to be resolved included the financial status of the separated company and use of the Bell symbol. This divestiture team enlisted the support of all the areas of the business. They met regularly in their status room, dubbed the "War Room," to coordinate the divestiture and to track the progress of each task. These tasks were charted on big boards that covered all four walls of the room. The team's efforts were characterized by long, hard hours and a problem-solving, "can-do" attitude.

This case was prepared by Assistant Professor David B. Jemison and Ms. Chris Cairns of Pacific Telesis as a basis for class discussion rather than to illustrate either effective or ineffective handling of an administrative situation.

Support for the development of this case was provided in part by the Strategic Management Program, Graduate School of Business, Stanford University.

Exhibit 1 Financial Highlights and Projections Pacific Telesis Group

Normalized Net Income
(in Millions of Dollars)
Projected improvements in Pac Tel Group cost effectiveness continue the trend of year over year growth.

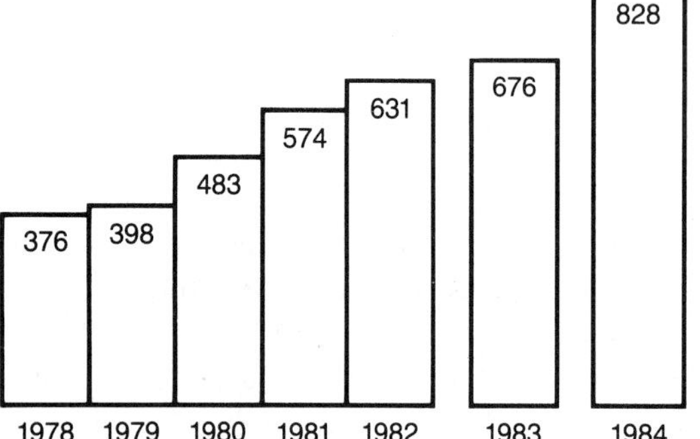

Normalized Pretax Interest Coverage Ratio
With projected 1984 results, Pacific Telesis Group will achieve the highest pretax interest coverage since Pacific Telephone's 1973 performance.

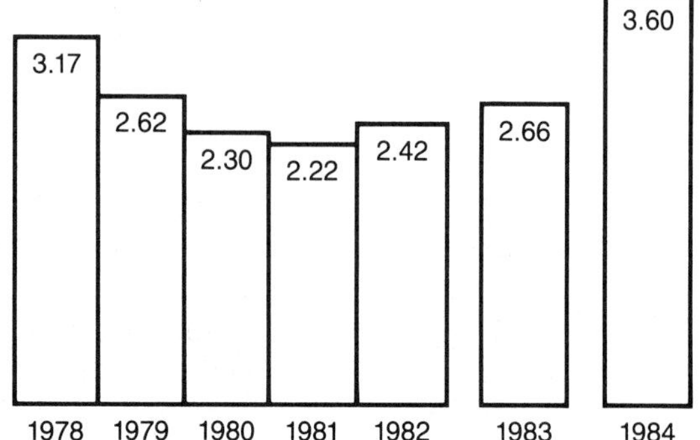

Debt Ratio
(Percentage)
With divestiture, Pacific Telesis will have a debt ratio of 46.5%—a level competitive with other Sunbelt companies.

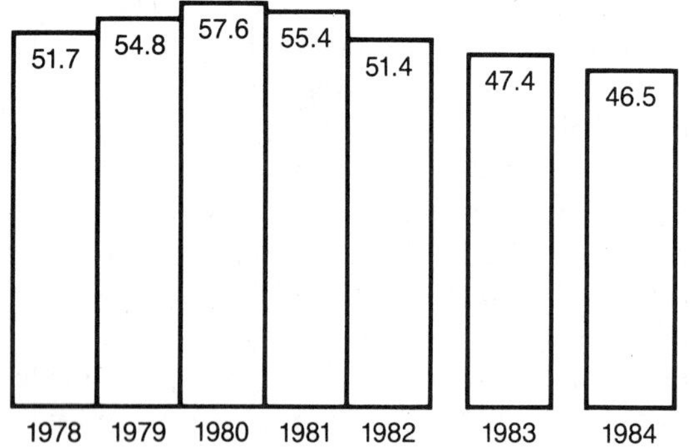

Percentage of Capital Generated Internally
(Percentage)
Pacific Telesis will continue to fund a substantial portion of its construction requirements internally.

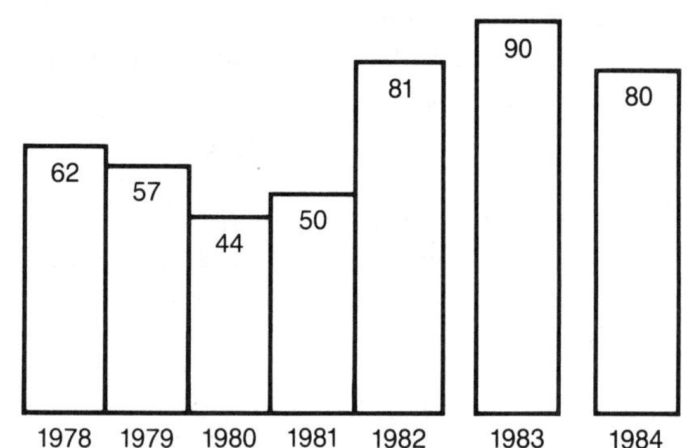

Notes:
*The years 1978 through 1983 reflect financial results for *Pacific Telephone.*
*Normalized results for 1978 through 9 months 1983 net income, pretax interest coverage ratio, and debt ratio have been restated to reflect, in the years to which they are applicable, the impacts of recent congressional legislation (including the effect of the June 1983 closing agreement with the IRS) reducing certain back-tax liabilities and changes to bring the accounting for deferred taxes in line with ratemaking practices.
*The 1984 projections are for Pacific Telesis Group for the calendar year 1984.
Source: Annual Reports and Internal Documents.

Strategic Planning Takes Shape

A strategic planning function was established at PacTel with a staff of planners and analysts and the creation of a Strategic Planning Board. Key officers from each major part of the PT&T organization formed the Board. They met regularly to address the major strategic, legal, and regulatory issues facing the corporation. Sam used this forum to discuss, work through, and gain acceptance for the strategic direction that was

Exhibit 2 *Fortune* 500 Comparisons

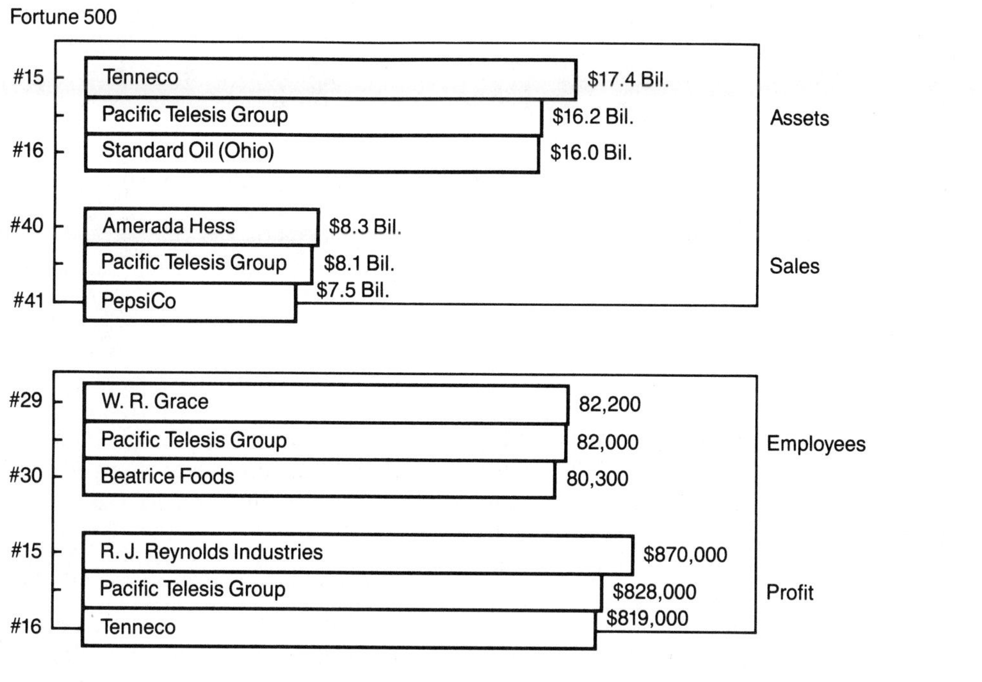

Source: *Value Line.*

emerging for PT&T. He saw the Strategic Planning Board as critical to successful operation of the firm after divestiture, since it represented each major portion of the business. During this time, the board met monthly.

The small staff group of strategic planners and analysts provided procedural guidance and analytical support to the board. In addition to PT&T managers, outside experienced planners were hired to minimize the learning period. The group acted in an analytical capacity, as well as independently, identifying the critical issues facing Pacific Telephone that would insure the best outcome from divestiture. They had wide authority to call upon the resources of the entire PT&T organization to resolve the issues they struggled with in very tight time constraints.

A process was also established to evaluate alternative business plans, allocate resources, and monitor results. The Pacific Management System, as it became known, provided this evaluation, allocation, and monitoring support in the context of a business planning cycle (see Exhibit 3) to insure regular review of the business plans from various parts of the company.

Major Outcomes of the Strategic Planning Process

Diversification Strategy Adopted

Sam Ginn and his planners recognized that Pacific Telephone was at an important crossroads. They saw two distinct options. The company could remain a traditional telephone utility. Alternatively, it could adopt an aggressive diversification strategy. There were advantages and risks to both options.

Exhibit 3 Business Planning Cycle

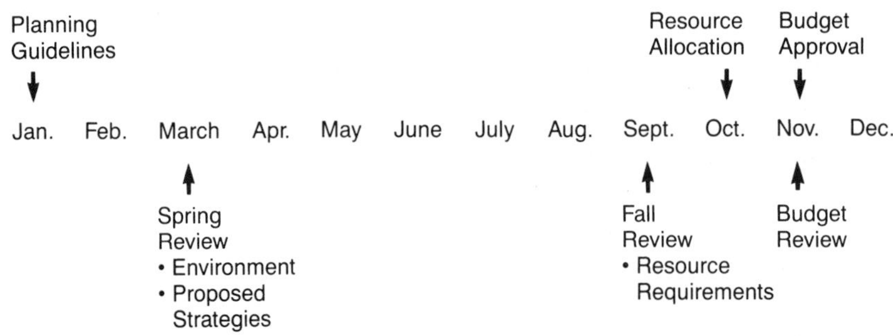

Remaining a traditional telephone utility had appeal because the people in the firm knew this business so well. However, there were substantial risks in standing still as the industry changed dramatically. The traditional revenue stream from regulated services was vulnerable to incursion from competitors who sought to use new technologies to lure selective, profitable customers. This would leave the regulated utility at a continual disadvantage. As competitors skimmed off profitable customers, other customers would be asked to pay more for maintaining service, a scenario that was fraught with regulatory peril.

The company chose to adopt an aggressive diversification strategy, both within and outside the confines of regulation. This would allow Pacific Telephone to explore opportunities for growth in a wide range of enterprises and give it the capability to meet competition in a variety of different arenas. In addition, as it would eliminate the sole dependency on the regulatory process for earnings, it would improve investor perceptions of the firm and, as a consequence, increase financing flexibility.

This diversification was allowed by a provision of Judge Green's Modified Final Judgment on Divestiture. This provision indicated that the regional telephone companies could enter diversified businesses by obtaining waivers from him upon showing that there was no substantial possibility the corporation could use their monopoly power to impede competition in the markets they sought to enter.

New Organization Structure Put in Place

Mr. Donald Guinn, Chairman of the Board, announced a new strategic direction, structure, and name for the firm on August 8, 1983. A holding company, Pacific Telesis, was created with two lines of business: regulated telephone service and diversified businesses (Exhibit 4). The regulated telephone business of Pacific Bell and Nevada Bell were structurally separated from the new diversified businesses. This separation was necessary in light of Judge Greene's order and also allowed the companies to compete freely in their respective markets. In addition, it was hoped that this would enhance Pacific Telesis's growing image as a diversified corporation with multiple sources of revenue and profit.

To insure the continuance of the strategic planning process, the position of vice-president, strategic planning, was established. Mr. John Gaulding, who had been managing partner of a consulting firm that had done a significant amount of work for Pacific Telephone, was hired in this capacity. Mr. Gaulding reported directly to the chairman, rather than in one of the two sections of the Pacific Telesis Group.

A key portion of the diversification strategy

Exhibit 4 Pacific Telesis Group

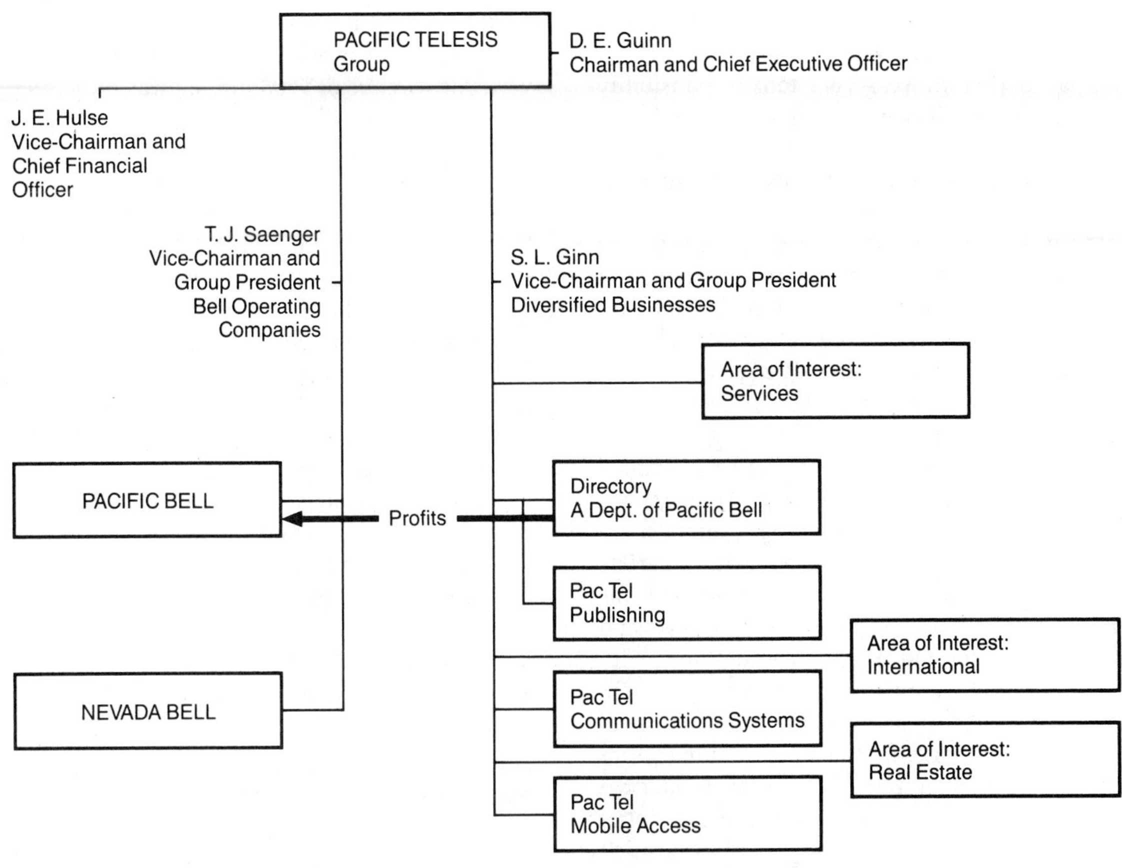

Source: Company records.

called for seeking new opportunities in the traditional regulated side of the business, as well as on the diversified business side. With this in mind, the telephone company's marketing organization was restructured. John Lockton, previously president of Warner Amex Cable Corporation and a senior officer with Dun and Bradstreet Inc., was appointed to the newly created position of executive vice-president, marketing, for the telephone side of the business. In this position, Mr. Lockton was responsible for developing enhanced regulated services, such as specialized terminals for home banking and shopping, and contracting with municipalities for multiuse cable systems.

New Diversified Business

Sam Ginn was appointed vice-chairman and group president—diversified businesses. Several promising opportunities were identified for immediate pursuit, and subsidiary companies were created to develop these businesses. The presidents of each of the diversified subsidiaries reported to Ginn. A brief description of each of the diversified subsidiaries, as well as the major areas of interest for possible future subsidiaries, follows.

PacTel Communications Systems

As part of divestiture, AT&T took responsibility for terminal equipment: maintenance of existing in-place leased telephones and sales of new phones and systems. AT&T also took over all the Phone Center Store outlets and personnel. However, a modification to the final divestiture judgment allowed the local companies to reenter the terminal equipment sales business on January 1, 1984, if they would establish a separate subsidiary for this purpose. PacTel Communications Systems was established by Pacific Telesis to enter this market.

PacTel Communications Systems planned to market a line of technically superior telephone terminal equipment. Beginning operation on January 1, 1984, they contracted with a variety of manufacturers to provide a broad-based line of basic telephones, designer phones, speaker and cordless phones, and telephones combined with other appliances such as clock radios and answering devices. In addition, they targeted small and large businesses for sales of communications systems and data products. Product offerings provided excellent value in terms of warranties and service contracts were designed to position PacTel as the premier service provider in the industry.

The initial revenue projection for PacTel Communications Systems was over $200 million in 1984. The organization began the year with about 250 employees. About 40 percent of these came from Pacific Bell, but a high percentage of the salespeople were hired from other companies, such as IBM, Xerox, and other communications equipment vendors.

Directory

The Directory Department of Pacific Bell (the regulated part of the Pacific Telesis Group) was responsible for producing the *White Pages* and *Yellow Pages* directories. This portion of the telephone business was exempted from regulation in 1978, although the profits were still to be used to support basic telephone service. For 1984, advertising revenue of $508 million was projected. Directory, although a part of Pacific Bell, was managed as a diversified business under Sam Ginn. About 500 management and nonmanagement (sales and production) persons made up the Directory Department, which had been a longstanding department in the telephone company.

The reason that Directory reported to Ginn was that their managers also had responsibilities for managing PacTel Publishing, a completely separate subsidiary. To satisfy terms of the divestiture and regulatory requirements, the head of Directory, the vice-president, directory services, and Directory's chief financial officer became holding company employees so that they could report to Sam Ginn and facilitate their additional responsibilities for PacTel Publishing.

PacTel Publishing

A small group, initially composed of six persons, was selected to begin PacTel Publishing. The purpose of this subsidiary was to develop new publishing ventures in four areas.

- National directory publications, for example, industrial or trade directories.
- Localized publishing products, such as visitor's guides or convention guides.
- Directory services under contract for other publishers or telephone companies.
- Electronic publishing, such as shop-at-home services.

This group, which except for the marketing vice-president came from the Directory organization, was expected in 1984 to sign contracts that would bring in at least $2 million in revenue in 1985. The group was expected to break even in early 1986 and to become a profit contributor later that year.

PacTel Mobile Access

Originally formed as a nationwide subsidiary of AT&T and called Advanced Mobile Phone Service, AMPS was (as a part of the divestiture decree) split up and assigned to the seven regional holding companies. The California/Nevada portion of AMPS, now part of the Pacific Telesis Group, was named PacTel Mobile Access.

PacTel Mobile Access planned an advanced, high-quality state-of-the-art mobile phone system for use by executives and other people who needed telephone service from their automobiles. They planned to market their services in two ways: on the retail level using their own agents and on a wholesale basis to resellers who would market the service under their own name with their own terminal equipment.

Because of the use of radio waves in this business, the FCC granted franchises for certain areas to partnerships of firms that already provided wire-line telephone services to customers in the area. This business was still in the formative stages nationwide with only a small portion of the major market-area franchises determined. The first service in the Pacific region was planned for the Los Angeles area beginning in May 1984, in time for the Summer Olympics. PacTel Mobile Access was the general partner in providing this service with several other limited partners, including GTE.

PacTel Mobile Access was staffed by about 100 persons and planned to double that size in about eight years. Most employees at all levels in the company had a Bell System background. Revenues for 1984 were estimated at $7 million and were expected to climb dramatically as the service became available in more areas. Estimates of PacTel Mobile Access share of the market approached $200 million in five years.

PacTel Mobile Service

A small group was spun off from PacTel Mobile Access in mid-1984. Their mission was to provide mobile telephone service and equipment sales outside the carrier markets served by Mobile Access. This organizational change was driven by the evolving regulatory environment.

Pacific Telesis International

The international market for telecommunications products and services was exploding. Pacific Telesis International was formed as the vehicle for marketing Telesis's expertise overseas. They would meet international customers' needs with creative solutions to large telecommunications and information problems. Offerings would include services (such as consulting), information systems, telecommunications systems, project management, training, and operational and administrative support systems.

Potential customers would include both governments and private firms; competitors in this business included such well-established firms as ITT, Cable and Wireless PLC, Nippon Electric Company, and AT&T International. If a waiver to enter this business were sought and obtained, a small group of 20–25 persons as a separate subsidiary could be set up. As contracts were obtained, labor and resources from Pacific Bell could be utilized as necessary and charged to the project on a fully distributed cost basis.

PacTel Properties

PacTel Properties was formed to service Pacific Bell and other affiliated companies as a real estate broker and developer. With more than 2,000 owned and leased buildings totaling about 50 million square feet of space, Pacific Bell had in the past generated $1–3 million annually in real estate brokerage commissions and had relied on outside developers for major office complex development. The subsidiary captured some of these commissions and managed project development with favorable financing terms as a result of having Pacific Bell as a guaranteed major tenant. In addition, real estate development had the possibility for certain tax advantages the holding company could utilize. Properties would begin to participate in the broader real estate market when it received a waiver from the court.

A group of about ten persons, primarily from Pacific Bell's Building, Engineering, and Real Estate groups, staffed this separate subsidiary. The president of such a subsidiary might be recruited from outside Pacific Bell, given the specialized expertise required.

PacTel Finance
A small company was formed to provide lease financing for customers of the Diversified Businesses. It had already begun to service PacTel Mobile Services and would be more fully developed in 1985.

PacTel Services
A support group called Services was also considered. This group would provide the administrative staff support needed for the Diversified Businesses Group. With about 20 people, it would assist in strategic planning, budgeting and financial management, and personnel administration in support of the other subsidiaries in the Diversified Businesses Group.

Included in this Services organization would be a small group that would identify and study new ventures that could develop into additional diversified subsidiaries. They would scan a wide range of business possibilities and develop preliminary analyses on promising opportunities. If results of the preliminary analyses were favorable, more in-depth analysis would determine whether or not a new business would be formed. Sam met twice a month with this New Ventures Group to review results and direct their activities.

Management of the New Diversified Corporation

With the decision to diversify came the need to rethink the style of management that had pervaded the Bell System and to decide what was appropriate for the new Pacific Telesis Group. In the past, key strategic decisions were made by AT&T, and the local telephone companies implemented these decisions. As much planning as possible was done on a nationwide basis to ensure uniformity. Compensation plans were similar throughout the Bell System. Pay scales were standard with annual general increases for almost everyone and the possibility of modest individual merit awards for some at the end of the year. The benefit plan was considered by employees to be among the best, partly because of gains made over the years in union contract negotiations.

With the advent of Pacific Telesis as a diversified corporation, there was a need, especially in the Diversified Businesses Group, to develop a management style that best suited these new and varied businesses. In the Diversified Businesses Group, a decentralized management approach was established. Each subsidiary president was now made responsible for attaining certain profit goals.

The Diversified Businesses Group developed monitoring, measurement, and incentive systems, as well as benefit plans that were different from those for the regulated telephone business. Sam Ginn set up a systematic plan for monitoring and controlling the subsidiaries. Regular monthly meetings were scheduled with each subsidiary president. These meetings included reviews of key financial items; discussion of operations matters; possible modifications of strategic direction, such as new markets, products, or channels of distribution; and any current legal or regulatory matters. At the end of each meeting they would decide on the agenda items for the following month. The staff of PacTel Services coordinated the presentation of results and followed up on areas identified for further study. If a major deviation in the business plan results remained uncorrected, Sam could send a task force of PacTel service analysts to visit the subsidiary to assist in problem solving.

With the decentralized management approach came a new measurement system. When

Sam had been in charge of Network for Pacific Telephone, he reviewed more than 300 indicators of expense control and quality of service every month. However, with the diversified subsidiaries, he had decided to routinely track three or four key financial measures (e.g., gross revenue, net income, return on sales, return on equity, asset turnover) together with a few selected "strategic milestones" that indicated how well the new businesses were being established and positioned. These indicators were also the factors on which the managers' compensation was based.

An incentive compensation plan was developed that tied managers' salaries directly to the financial success of each subsidiary, with a portion of each manager's salary placed "at risk" for the possible attainment of a greater incentive award if the financial goals of the subsidiary were exceeded. To accompany this, a new slimmed-down benefit plan was designed for the Diversified Businesses. It was a flexible plan that could be tailored to meet individual needs, while reducing expenses to the corporation as a whole.

Sam Ginn's New Challenges

Sam saw his new role as group president—Diversified Businesses as even more challenging than his last assignment as strategic planning officer. He mused that his recent jobs had coincided with the more critical issues facing the corporation. A few years back, the quality of telephone service had deteriorated in California to the point where the CPUC threatened to withhold needed rate relief. Sam had undertaken the challenge of spearheading the service recovery drive. Next, he had coordinated the divestiture from AT&T, with the attendant development of new strategic direction and organization structure. As a somewhat overlapping assignment, he had introduced strategic planning to the corporation. Now, he was being asked to do what no other telephone company executive had ever done—successfully build a series of diversified businesses in tandem with a regulated telephone utility.

In his new position, Sam had to wear many different hats. He would possibly be a member of seven different boards of directors, including Pacific Telesis, Pacific Bell, and each of the present Diversified Businesses. The number of board meetings Sam Ginn would have to include in his schedule would grow as more new businesses were formed. In addition to being on the Mills College Board of Trustees, Sam Ginn was elected president of the Industry Education Council of California and the Alumni Advisory Board of the Stanford Business School Sloan Program. He also often took time to speak at various industry and educational conferences on behalf of Pacific Telesis.

Sam knew there were some important new activities he had to initiate to fulfill PacTel's strategic direction. For example, to be viewed as truly diversified, a corporation must obtain a significant portion of its revenues and profits from diversified sources. An important part of his charter was to grow the diversified businesses to a point where they made material revenue and profit contributions to the entire PacTel Group. It would take quite a bit to do this when the size of the current diversified businesses for which he was responsible was small compared with the $8 billion in annual revenues on the regulated side. One possible solution would be to acquire other established businesses. But PacTel had never made any acquisitions before. Another avenue for growth was the development and nurturing of new start-up ventures within the firm. They would be an outgrowth of the efforts of the New Ventures Group in the Services Staff.

As Sam reviewed all his efforts, he realized their success hinged on a successful legal and regulatory strategy to obtain waivers to enter new businesses not authorized under the Divestiture Decree and to keep his new businesses from falling under regulatory oversight, with profits taken to support the cost of basic telephone service.

Another factor he saw as crucial to the diversification strategy was the initial success of the first few new businesses. Sam felt responsible for these businesses, although a decentralized form of management had been installed, with the president of each business responsible for its own profitability. However, Sam intensely wanted each to succeed, as that could build credibility for the overall strategic direction of Pacific Telesis. The financial markets and his colleagues in the old Bell System were waiting to see if the ambitious diversification could be managed successfully.

As he jogged through the fog at dawn in the streets near his office in the heart of San Francisco, Sam saw these as the key questions he must address:

1. How do I organize my job and my time to accomplish all my goals?

2. How do I develop a management system that will evolve as the organization grows, so I can understand and manage the group?

3. How do I insure the success of the existing new businesses, with additional ones to come in the future?

4. How should I try to meet my growth goals: by acquisition, by internal development, or by both? How should each be managed? If I try to build the business by acquisitions, how do I develop and implement a successful acquisitions strategy? Should I strictly use consultants and investment bankers to analyze targets, or should an internal capability be developed?

5. Then, if we make acquisitions, how should they be incorporated in our Diversified Businesses Group?

6. What have I missed that I should be wary of?

Case 16 Update*

Chairman's Letter to Shareowners

I am pleased to report that Pacific Telesis Group posted 1987 annual net income of $950 million or $2.21 per share on revenues of $9.1 billion. Excluding one-time expenses and the impact of retroactive rate reductions, our 1987 annual net earnings would have increased 8 percent to $1.14 billion or $2.64 per share. We achieved these results despite significant rate reductions ordered by the California Public Utilities Commission (CPUC) and increased expenses resulting from steps we took, in the fourth quarter, to improve cost efficiency and enhance future performance.

I'd like to expand briefly on these fourth quarter special items. First, as most of you know, in September we offered management employees an opportunity to voluntarily retire early—nearly 3,000 people accepted that offer. The early retirement plan increased fourth quarter expenses by $217 million. However, the corporation expects to realize annual savings of approximately 60 to 80 percent of this amount beginning in 1988.

Second, the restructuring of the PacTel Communications Companies, which began in 1987 and will continue into 1988, will allow them to improve their financial performance. It includes the previously announced closure of some of PacTel InfoSystems' stores and a strengthening and restructuring of the Communications Companies' relationship with Northern Telecom in serving medium and large PBX business customers.

A third factor causing the decline in our 1987 earnings was the impact of rate reductions ordered by the CPUC in connection with Pacific Bell's 1986 rate case and its attrition case. For a more comprehensive review of these issues and other financial results, I encourage you to read the Financial Review which follows.

How We've Developed Our Management Team
Sam Ginn, now our president and chief operating officer, had extensive experience in the regulated side of our business before he became the architect of our diversification strategy. He's made a significant contribution in developing our cellular company into an asset with an estimated market value of $2 billion.

John Hulse, our chief financial officer since 1981 and vice chairman since 1983, continues to act as the linchpin helping to assure our financial performance and growth in shareowner value. The financial strategies he has developed and executed have been instrumental in enabling us to achieve the financial gains we've made since divestiture.

Art Latno has served as executive vice president of external affairs since 1975. Art manages our relations with federal and state governments, with federal regulatory agencies, and with the public. He also guides our corporate philanthropy programs.

Bob Blanz joined the corporation as executive vice president of corporate strategy in September 1987, after serving for five years as president of Mountain Bell. An engineer by education, Bob has held managerial positions in network, regulatory, and operations within the Bell System since 1954.

Jim Moberg, elected executive vice president of human resources in late 1987, has held managerial posts in external affairs, marketing, operations, and information systems with Pacific Telesis and Pacific Bell since 1961.

*Source: Excerpts from Pacific Telesis 1987 annual report, pp. 5–7, 34–35, 38–41.

Dick Odgers was elected executive vice president-law in November 1987. Previously a senior partner with the San Francisco law firm of Pillsbury, Madison & Sutro, he represented Pacific Bell and Pacific Telesis for many years and specializes in antitrust and regulatory law.

Lee Cox, president and chief executive officer of PacTel Corporation and group president of Pacific Telesis Group, presides over our diversified PacTel Companies. Previously, Lee served as executive vice president of operations and marketing for Pacific Bell.

Phil Quigley is president and chief executive officer of Pacific Bell and group president of Pacific Telesis Group responsible for Pacific Bell, Nevada Bell, and Pacific Bell Directory. Earlier he was executive vice president of PacTel Corporation and president of PacTel Personal Communications.

Ben Dial, executive vice president of human resources, retired at year end. He helped forge a new business and labor partnership that will help Pacific Bell and Nevada Bell grow with changes brought by Information Age technology.

Ted Saenger, president of Pacific Bell for ten years and vice chairman of Pacific Telesis Group, also retired at year end. His many contributions over the years included significantly raising the level of technical capability, efficiency, and profitability at Pacific Bell and Nevada Bell.

Bob Dalenberg, executive vice president, general counsel, and secretary, retires in March 1988. His counsel and development of a full-service legal department helped us maintain a prudent course in the face of great change and uncertainty resulting from divestiture.

We will miss Ben, Ted, and Bob's wisdom and counsel.

This letter marks my fourth and final report to the shareowners of Pacific Telesis. As most of you know, I announced last July that I would retire in 1988. At that time, we also announced a succession plan to ensure continuity in the management of your investment.

Today, we have a group of managers who work closely as a team, anticipating and planning for change. Eight years ago, we began developing that team by advancing highly capable managers already in the company and by bringing in other top managers from outside—a strategy we still follow. We then put into practice a collegial form of decision-making at the top of the business. That's now paying high dividends as we respond to changes in our fast-paced industry.

On these two pages I've told you about the members of the Telesis Policy Group, the team of senior managers working to enhance the value of your investment. Current members and those retiring are pictured here along with a brief description of their roles in guiding corporate policy.

Financial Comparisons in Brief

A. Revenues.

Total revenues increased 1.7 percent from 1986 due to increased revenues in the PacTel Companies and Pacific Bell Directory. The PacTel Companies as a group, however, are not yet profitable. Higher local and toll service volumes offset significant rate reductions in Pacific Bell. These reductions included $49 million in state revenue decreases relating to 1986 business.

B. Costs and expenses.

Operating expenses increased 8.3 percent from 1986. Expenses, in general, increased due to the cost of an early retirement program offered to management employees of Pacific Telesis and Pacific Bell and a one-time charge for a restructuring of PacTel Communications Companies. Depreciation and amortization expense increased 13.0 percent primarily due to the recognition of shorter depreciation periods for telephone equipment and increases in the amount of telephone assets. Maintenance and repairs expense continued to decrease in 1987.

C. **Interest expense.**
Interest expense decreased by 2.4 percent compared to 1986 due to Pacific Bell's refinancing program in 1986 and 1985 and the reduction of long-term debt and short-term borrowings in 1987. The decrease in interest expense was partially offset by external financing activities at Nevada Bell in June 1986.

D. **Net income.**
Net income for 1987 decreased 12.0 percent from 1986. This reduction resulted from several one-time charges, including costs of an early retirement program, a reduction in Pacific Bell's revenues retroactive to March 1986, and expenses relating to a restructuring of PacTel Communications Companies.

E. **Earnings per share.**
Earnings per share decreased from $2.51 in 1986 to $2.21 in 1987. The special items described above decreased 1987 earnings per share by $0.43.

F. **Dividends per share.**
Quarterly dividends were $0.41 per share, totaling $1.64 per share for the year, an increase of 7.9 percent.

G. **Return on shareowners' equity.**
In 1987, return on equity was 11.9 percent compared with 14.2 percent in 1986. This reduction reflects the one-time charges and resulting decrease in net income.

H. **Shareowners' equity.**
The Pacific Telesis Group Board of Directors declared a two-for-one stock split, effective March 25, 1987, resulting in the issuance of approximately 215,400,300 new shares. The Corporation purchased 6,519,600 of its outstanding common shares with general corporate funds as part of a plan to purchase up to 10,000,000 shares of its stock.

I. **Internally generated funds ratio.**
The percentage of internally generated funds decreased to 93.8 percent in 1987. This decline of 13.7 percentage points from the 107.5 percent achieved in 1986 occurred primarily because of the one-time charges mentioned previously and the effects of the Tax Reform Act of 1986 on income taxes.

J. **Capital expenditures.**
Capital expenditures in 1987 include a $333 million acquisition of cellular operations in the Michigan and Ohio areas which operate under the name Cellular One. Expenditures also include property, plant and equipment purchases, systems improvements, and replacements.

K. **Network access lines in service.**
Network access lines increased by approximately 462,000 lines in 1987 reflecting continuing growth in Pacific Bell's and Nevada Bell's customer bases.

L. **Employees.**
The Corporation's work force declined by 3,060 employees during 1987. This reduction does not include approximately 1,600 management employees who accepted the early retirement offer but worked through December 31, 1987. In total, approximately 3,000 employees elected to take the voluntary early retirement option. The decline in work force reflects the Corporation's continued efforts in controlling costs and increasing operational efficiency.

Selected Financial and Operating Data

(Dollars in millions, except per share amounts)	1987	1986	1985	1984	1983
Results of Operations					
A. Revenues	**$ 9,131**	$ 8,977	$ 8,498	$ 7,824	$ 8,133
B. Costs and expenses	**7,026**	6,488	6,245	5,849	6,405
Operating income	**$ 2,105**	$ 2,489	$ 2,253	$ 1,975	$ 1,728
C. Interest expense	**$ 541**	$ 554	$ 596	$ 568	$ 679
Income taxes	**$ 650**	$ 876	$ 778	$ 618	$ 441
Extraordinary item	—	—	—	—	$ 216
D. Net income	**$ 950**	$ 1,079	$ 929	$ 829	$ 848
Per Share Amounts*					
E. Earnings	**$ 2.21**	$ 2.51	$ 2.27	$ 2.12	—
F. Dividends	**$ 1.64**	$ 1.52	$ 1.43	$ 1.35	—
Market price at December 31	**$ 26.63**	$ 26.63	$ 21.16	$ 17.22	—
Performance Measurements					
G. Return on shareowners' equity (%)	**11.9**	14.2	13.5	13.2	10.0
Return on capital (%)	**10.2**	11.2	10.8	10.7	9.2
Capitalization at December 31					
Total assets	**$21,056**	$20,321	$19,538	$18,433	$19,322
Short-term obligations	**$ 468**	$ 238	$ 220	$ 447	$ 276
Long-term obligations	**$ 5,321**	$ 5,515	$ 5,804	$ 5,499	$ 6,506
Minority interest	**$ 22**	$ 50	$ 218	$ 475	$ 511
H. Shareowners' equity	**$ 7,890**	$ 7,753	$ 7,317	$ 6,482	$ 6,698
Debt ratio (%)	**42.3**	42.4	44.4	46.1	48.5
Internally Generated Funds					
Internally generated funds from operations	**$ 1,866**	$ 2,220	$ 2,039	$ 1,811	$ 1,666
I. Internally generated funds ratio (%)	**93.8**	107.5	92.9	89.7	94.4
J. Capital expenditures	**$ 2,028**	$ 2,103	$ 2,257	$ 2,082	$ 1,829
Operating Data					
Toll messages (millions)	**2,622**	2,389	2,168	1,995	3,698
Carrier access minutes-of-use (millions)	**30,973**	28,287	25,960	23,612	—
K. Network access lines in service at December 31 (thousands)	**12,525**	12,063	11,630	11,307	10,930
L. Employees at December 31	**71,877**	74,937	71,488	76,881	97,647

Financial and operating data for 1983 relate to Pacific Bell and Nevada Bell, telephone subsidiaries of Pacific Telesis Group. The financial and operating data presented for 1984–1987 generally is not comparable to the results in 1983 due to the changes required as a result of the breakup of the Bell System. This also explains why 1983 per share amounts are not meaningful.

*Per share amounts have been restated for 1986, 1985, and 1984 to reflect a two-for-one stock split, effective March 25, 1987.

Consolidated Statements of Income

	For the Year Ended December 31		
(Dollars in millions, except per share amounts)	**1987**	**1986***	**1985***
Revenues			
Local service	**$3,068**	$2,957	$2,820
Network access—interstate	**1,641**	1,733	1,670
Network—intrastate	**898**	962	1,045
Toll service	**2,143**	1,999	1,743
Other revenues	**1,381**	1,326	1,220
Total revenues	**9,131**	8,977	8,498
Costs and expenses			
Maintenance and repairs	**1,458**	1,534	1,676
Depreciation and amortization	**1,707**	1,511	1,238
Marketing and customer services	**705**	720	673
Pensions and other employee benefits	**741**	609	588
Network and operator services	**443**	440	462
Payroll-related, property and other taxes	**372**	360	337
Provision for uncollectibles	**116**	110	108
Other costs and expenses	**1,484**	1,204	1,163
Total costs and expenses	**7,026**	6,488	6,245
Operating income	**2,105**	2,489	2,253
Other income and expenses			
Interest expense	**(541)**	(554)	(596)
Miscellaneous income and deductions	**53**	44	82
Income before provision for income taxes	**1,617**	1,979	1,739
Income taxes	**650**	876	778
Income before minority interest	**967**	1,103	961
Minority interest	**17**	24	32
Net income	**$ 950**	$1,079	$ 929
Earnings per share	**$2.21**	$2.51	$2.27
Dividends per share	**$1.64**	$1.52	$1.43
Average shares outstanding (thousands)	**430,630**	430,126	409,295

*Share data have been restated for a two-for-one stock split effective March 25, 1987.
The accompanying Notes are an integral part of the Consolidated Financial Statements.

Consolidated Balance Sheets

(Dollars in millions, except per share amounts)	December 31 1987	1986
Assets		
Cash and temporary cash investments	**$ 5**	$ 201
Accounts receivable—net of allowances for uncollectibles of $92 and $72	**1,434**	1,391
Inventories and supplies	**161**	116
Prepaid expenses and other current assets	**632**	449
Total current assets	**2,232**	2,157
Property, plant and equipment	**23,142**	22,334
Less: accumulated depreciation	**(5,950)**	(5,089)
Property, plant and equipment—net	**17,192**	17,245
Deferred charges and other non-current assets	**1,632**	919
Total assets	**$21,056**	$20,321
Liabilities and shareowners' equity		
Accounts payable and accrued liabilities	**$ 1,700**	$ 1,760
Dividends payable	**175**	164
Short-term borrowings	**142**	22
Current portion of long-term obligations	**326**	216
Other current liabilities	**442**	243
Total current liabilities	**2,785**	2,405
Deferred income taxes	**3,513**	3,355
Unamortized investment tax credits	**943**	1,005
Other deferred credits	**582**	238
Total deferred credits	**5,038**	4,598
Long-term obligations	**5,321**	5,515
Minority interest	**22**	50
Common stock ($0.10 par value; 432,827,595 and 215,274,878 shares issued; 427,122,153 and 215,274,878 shares outstanding)	**43**	22
Additional paid-in capital	**5,100**	5,068
Reinvested earnings	**2,908**	2,663
Less: treasury stock, at cost (5,705,442 shares)	**(161)**	—
Total shareowners' equity	**7,890**	7,753
Total liabilities and shareowners' equity	**$21,056**	$20,321

The accompanying Notes are an integral part of the Consolidated Financial Statements.

Consolidated Statements of Shareowners' Equity

	For the Year Ended December 31		
(Dollars in millions)	**1987**	**1986**	**1985**
Common stock			
Balance at beginning of year	**$ 22**	$ 11	$ 10
Issuance of shares	—	—	1
Two-for-one stock split	**21**	11	—
Balance at end of year	**43**	22	11
Additional paid-in capital			
Balance at beginning of year	**5,068**	5,064	4,561
Issuance of shares	**53**	15	505
Two-for-one stock split	**(21)**	(11)	—
Other changes	—	—	(2)
Balance at end of year	**5,100**	5,068	5,064
Reinvested earnings			
Balance at beginning of year	**2,663**	2,242	1,911
Net income	**950**	1,079	929
Dividends declared	**(705)**	(654)	(594)
Other changes	—	(4)	(4)
Balance at end of year	**2,908**	2,663	2,242
Treasury stock			
Balance at beginning of year	—	—	—
Purchase of shares	**(184)**	—	—
Issuance of treasury shares	**23**	—	—
Balance at end of year	**(161)**	—	—
Total shareowners' equity	**$7,890**	$7,753	$7,317

The accompanying Notes are an integral part of the Consolidated Financial Statements.

Consolidated Statements of Changes in Financial Position

(Dollars in millions)	For the Year Ended December 31 1987	1986	1985
Funds from operations			
Net income	**$ 950**	$1,079	$ 929
Items not requiring (providing) funds currently:			
Depreciation and amortization	**1,707**	1,511	1,238
Deferred income taxes—net	**15**	398	427
Investment tax credits—net	**(62)**	(75)	100
Interest charged construction	**(39)**	(39)	(61)
Total funds from operations	**2,571**	2,874	2,633
Dividends declared on common shares	**(705)**	(654)	(594)
Internally generated funds from operations	**1,866**	2,220	2,039
Funds from (used for) financing activities			
Issuance of common shares	**53**	15	505
Purchase of common shares	**(184)**	—	—
Issuance of treasury shares	**23**	—	—
Issuance of long-term debt	**138**	1,177	851
Retirement of long-term debt	**(206)**	(1,285)	(400)
Decrease in capital lease obligations	**(26)**	(21)	(38)
Increase (decrease) in short-term borrowings—net	**120**	19	(302)
Decrease in minority interest	**(28)**	(168)	(257)
Funds from (used for) financing activities	**(110)**	(263)	359
Funds used for capital expenditures			
Capital expenditures	**(2,028)**	(2,103)	(2,257)
Interest charged construction	**39**	39	61
Funds used for capital expenditures	**(1,989)**	(2,064)	(2,196)
Other sources (uses) of funds			
Changes in non-cash working capital:*			
Current assets	**(128)**	7	15
Accounts payable and accrued liabilities	**(60)**	360	(173)
Dividends payable and other current liabilities	**210**	44	22
Total funds from (used by) changes in non-cash working capital	**22**	411	(136)
Other changes:			
Deferred charges	**(641)**	(292)	(80)
Other—net	**656**	163	36
Total other sources (uses) of funds	**37**	282	(180)
Increase (decrease) in cash and temporary cash investments	**(196)**	175	22
Cash and temporary cash investments at January 1	**201**	26	4
Cash and temporary cash investments at December 31	**$ 5**	$ 201	$ 26

Excluding cash and temporary cash investments, deferred income tax benefits, short-term borrowings, and current portion of long-term obligations.
The accompanying Notes are an integral part of the Consolidated Financial Statements.

Case 17

GENICOM CORPORATION

GENICOM CORPORATION

Curtis W. Powell, President of GENICOM CORPORATION, faced the morning of June 18, 1985 with uncertainty. His upcoming meeting with the labor union at the firm's Waynesboro, Virginia facility was one which raised some disturbing questions about the company's future, and even its past.

Prior to today's meeting, GENICOM had proposed wage and benefit reductions, which resulted in increasing confrontation with union representatives. Mr. Powell pondered what strategic alternatives the company should pursue if the union did not accept the proposed reductions. And even if the union did make the concessions needed, what strategy should GENICOM follow in the competitive computer printer market over the next 3 to 5 years?

Background

GENICOM was founded in June 1983, as a result of a leveraged buy-out of General Electric's (GE) Data Communication Products Business Department in Waynesboro, a relatively self-contained entity which produced computer printers and relay components. The department operated as one of GE's strategic business units.

GE came to Waynesboro, a small town in Central Virginia, in 1954 as part of a major decentralization effort which also included establishing facilities nearby in Lynchburg and Salem, Virginia. Between 1954 and 1974, the Waynesboro plant produced a wide variety of highly sophisticated electro-mechanical devices such as process controls, numerical controls, and aircraft controls, many of which are now produced by other GE divisions.

Products once manufactured in the Waynesboro facility accounted for several hundred million dollars in annual sales revenues for GE. As a result, the Waynesboro factory had a longstanding reputation for its skill in electro-mechanical design and engineering and for its ability to solve difficult design tasks in its highly vertically integrated facilities.

The first electro-mechanical printer was created by GE in Waynesboro as a result of the firm's own dissatisfaction with the performance of the Teletype 33 printers. The new GE printer was three times faster than the Teletype 33 and gained quick popularity. In 1969, a send-receive printer was introduced with such success that it evolved into one of GE's fastest-growing product lines. Other products were added using the same technology, and by 1977 the business in Waynesboro had attained annual revenues of $100,000,000 while being very profitable.

In 1980, GE changed corporate leadership. The new GE Chairman, John F. Welch, initiated a major review of the corporation's businesses to determine which ones were critical to GE's future strategies. Businesses with products which did not rank number one or number two in their

---

This case was prepared by Per V. Jenster, John M. Gwin, and David B. Croll. McIntire School of Commerce, University of Virginia, Charlottesville, Virginia 22903. This case was used in the fifth McIntire Commerce Invitational (MCI V) held at the University of Virginia on February 13–15, 1986. We gratefully acknowledge the General Electric Foundation for support of the MCI and the writing of this case.

served industries or did not have the technological leadership to become first or second required special review. The Waynesboro products did not rank number one or number two in their served industry, nor were they critical to GE's long-term strategies, and in 1981, the department's Strategic Planning process investigated the possibility of divestiture as an alternative course of action.

During 1981, the then current General Manager resigned and Curtis Powell, the Financial Manager and long-term GE employee, was appointed the new General Manager.[1]

During the same time frame the printer business' line of reporting was dismantled; the General Manager, the Division Manager and his superior, the Group Vice President, left GE and the Executive Vice President and Sector Executive retired. As a result, there were no administrative levels between the Waynesboro facility and a newly appointed Sector Executive. Mr. Powell received the dual task of (1) positioning the business for divestiture and (2) making it viable if no acceptable buyers could be found. To accomplish these two objectives, Mr. Powell implemented programs to improve the competitiveness of the Department's printer products and productivity programs to reduce the cost of operations. To support aggressive new product design efforts, funding of research and development activities were increased by $1.0MM per year. The first product, the new 3000 Series printer, was introduced in the latter part of 1981. By 1982, the 3000 Series product had received an excellent reception in the marketplace. Variable cost had been reduced by 28%, primarily as a result of the relocation of 300 jobs from Waynesboro to the Department's Mexican facility, fixed costs had been reduced by 25% and net assets in the business had been reduced by $14.0MM. Despite the successful introduction of the new printer product and rapidly increasing orders, GE was still interested in divesting the business.

After several months of meetings with potential acquirers, GE had not received an acceptable offer. During the fourth quarter of 1982, Mr. Powell and a group of plant managers offered to purchase the Waynesboro based business from GE.

The Buy-Out Of GENICOM

During early 1983, GE agreed to sell the business as a leveraged buy-out, but required a substantial cash payment. In order to complete the transaction, the Management team was joined by two New York based venture capital firms who provided the financial resources needed to purchase the business.

The price agreed upon for the business was net depreciated value plus $8.0MM (note that the business had been in Waynesboro since 1954 and the net depreciated value was significantly less than the appraised value). The purchase price amounted to less than six months sales revenue.

The assets purchased included every printer ever designed by the Waynesboro facility, all customers and contracts, all patents and cross licenses, tools, and buildings, as well as the Relay business. The purchase agreement was signed October 23, 1983, at which time GE received approximately 75% of the purchase price in cash and subordinated notes for the balance. The purchase amount was financed through sale of shares to the venture capital firms and to local management (approximately 45 of the top managers received stock or stock options). Twelve million dollars were borrowed against fixed assets in the business, and a revolving credit line was secured against equipment leases, receivables, and selected inventory. Given the assessed value of the firm, GENICOM had not exceeded 65% of its borrowing capacity.

[1]In this respect, it is important to understand GE's organizational structure. GE was organized as follows: The chairman, three vice-chairmen, seven industry sectors, numerous groups and divisions, each containing many departments. The Waynesboro factory was a department.

The GENICOM Corporation

By 1983, GENICOM was one of the larger independent computer printer companies which manufactured teleprinters (i.e., keyboard send/receive units), dot-matrix printers, and line printers. These printers were primarily industrial grade, and thus were not widely used for personal computer output. They served a wide variety of data processing and telecommunication needs, with printing speeds ranging from 60 cps (characters per second) in the teleprinter version to 400 lpm (lines per minute) in their line printer series. GENICOM was also the industry leader in crystal relays sold to defense, space, and other industries where there was a need for highly reliable electrical switches.

GENICOM was also a multi-national company with production facilities in Waynesboro (1300 employees) and Mexico (700 employees). Approximately 20% of the 1984 sales revenue of $140.0MM was derived from International customers, primarily Original Equipment Manufacturers (OEM's). GENICOM was in the process of establishing its own sales affiliates in the United Kingdom, France, Germany, and Sweden in order to further serve its foreign customers.

Prior to the change in ownership, GENICOM's management negotiated a comprehensive benefits package which was essentially the same as GE's. Furthermore, a new agreement with the Union was settled, and customers and suppliers were briefed. All but fifteen current employees were offered positions with GENICOM at the same salary and similar benefits as provided by GE and all accepted.

According to Mr. Powell, "Everything considered, the buy-out went extremely well. 1984 was an excellent year, a very successful year for GENICOM. We are still trying to change the culture we inherited from GE, where people feel they have unlimited resources to a small company climate, a climate in which costs must be contained. Some of our people in Waynesboro believe that the success we had in 1984 will continue forever. They don't realize that in our industry product life cycles are short and even if your products are doing well today, you need to prepare for tomorrow. This transition from GE to GENICOM has been difficult."

"When we were a part of GE all employees were paid GE wages and salaries. Other firms in our industry and other firms in Waynesboro paid considerably less than GE rates." As part of the two largest employers in Waynesboro, GENICOM's actions when dealing with its employees became public very soon. "We have a very quality conscious work force in Waynesboro and quality has always been extremely important to us. But in our competitive market quality is not enough, we must be cost competitive also."

Management and Structure

GENICOM's management inherited an organizational structure and an information system which reflected GE's standards and procedures. Consequently, GENICOM was probably the most vertically integrated printer company in the world (largely encouraged by GE's capital budgeting and performance evaluation system), making almost everything in-house from tools to printer ribbons to sales brochures. This high degree of vertical integration enabled GENICOM to respond quickly to specific requests for redesign of products to suit individual customer needs.

The firm's information system was also aligned with GE's reporting system, which led one outside observer to conclude that he "had never seen an organization with such a sophisticated information system which used it so little." As an illustration, Exhibit 1 shows GENICOM's MIS budget *vis-a-vis* industry averages. Exhibit 2 compares GENICOM's data processing department with a similar organization in the industry. According to Coopers and Lybrand, a consulting firm retained by GENICOM, the cost problem, highlighted in these two exhibits, could

Exhibit 1 MIS Budgets: Industry Averages and Genicom, 1983–1984

	Manufacturing (electronics, electrical)			Genicom		
	Thousands of Dollars[a]	Percent of Revenue	Percent of MIS Budget	Thousands of Dollars[a]	Percent of Revenue	Percent of MIS Budget
Total revenue	$75,590	100.00%	n/a	$165,000	100.00%	n/a
MIS operating budget	723	1.01	100	2,567.4[b]	1.56	100.0%
Personnel	308	0.43	42.5	1,271.0	0.77	49.5
Hardware	208	0.29	28.4	400.6[c]	0.24	15.6
System software	21	0.03	3.1	27.5	0.02	1.1
Application software	36	0.05	4.9	76.5	0.05	3.0
Supplies	57	0.08	7.8	110.3	0.07	4.2
Outside services	36	0.05	7.8	559.0	0.34	21.8
Communications	21	0.03	3.3	19.8	0.01	0.8
Other	36	0.05	5.0	102.7[d]	0.06	4.0

[a]Average amounts reported in source survey.
[b]Genicom's IS&S actual expenses, January-May 1985, have been annualized and have been modified to (1) remove office services expenses and (2) add estimated hardware depreciation expense and estimated occupancy expense in order to correlate with survey figures.
[c]This category includes equipment rental, maintenance, and depreciation expense. Depreciation expense is drawn from Genicom's fixed asset register and includes annual depreciation (book) for all assets acquired through December 1984.
[d]This category includes occupancy expense, estimated at 4% of total MIS expense budget.
Sources: Infosystems 25th and 26th Annual Salary Surveys, June 1984 and June 1983. A survey of 642 firms conducted for Datamation and published March 15, 1985, shows that firms averaging $200 million in revenue employ an average of 20.1 people in data processing (equivalent to IS&S at Genicom without office services), for an index of average revenue of $9,950,200 per data-processing employee.

Exhibit 2 MIS Characteristics, Genicom and a Similar Organization, 1985

	Genicom	Other Firm
Hardware	5 H-P 3000s	4 H-P 3000s
Number of data centers	1 current 1 planned	2
Annual revenues	$165,000,000 (1985 budget)	$500,000,000
Type of business	Manufacturing	Manufacturing
Number of employees in MIS	34[a]	44[b]
Salary expense	$1,051,300	$1,075,200[c]
Processing characteristics	In-house plus heavy use of remote computing service	In-house plus heavy use of remote computing service
Company revenues per MIS employee	$4,852,900	$12,500,000

[a]Includes staff at one data center.
[b]Includes staff at two data centers.
[c]1984 budget plus 5%.

also be found in other areas: Finance, Materials, Shop Operations, Manufacturing Engineering, Quality Control, Marketing, Product Engineering, and Relays.

The management team of GENICOM (April 1985) consists of the following members:

Curtis W. Powell, President/Chief Executive Officer: Mr. Powell graduated from Lynchburg College, Lynchburg, Virginia in 1961 with a BA Degree in Business Administration - Economics. Prior to the purchase of the Waynesboro business by GENICOM, Mr. Powell had served 22 years in various General Electric assignments; the last two as Department General Manager of the Waynesboro business.

John V. Harker, Executive Vice President: Mr. Harker was responsible for the Sales and Marketing functions, including Product Planning, Market and New Business Development, Marketing Administration, Customer Service, Domestic Sales and International Operations. He formerly held positions as Senior Vice President for Marketing and Corporate Development at Dataproducts, Vice President of Booz, Allen, and Hamilton, Inc., a Management Consulting firm, and with IBM in various Marketing capacities. Upon joining GENICOM, he initiated the hiring of six new Marketing and Sales Executives from the computer peripherals industry.

Robert C. Bowen, Vice President & Chief Financial Officer: Mr. Bowen has served in various financial capacities with GE since 1964, and with Genicom's predecessor for the past ten years.

W. Douglas Drumheller, Vice President of Manufacturing: Mr. Drumheller joined GE's Manufacturing Management Program in 1970 and was appointed Vice President at GENICOM in 1983.

Dennie J. Shadrick, Vice President of Engineering: Mr. Shadrick recently joined GENICOM after seventeen years with Texas Instruments, where he served in a variety of Engineering and Management positions in the terminal and printer business unit.

Charles A. Ford, Vice President of Relay Operations: Mr. Ford has had a long career with GE and GENICOM serving in the areas of Manufacturing, Engineering, and General Management.

Robert B. Chapman, Treasurer: Mr. Chapman has been with GENICOM since 1984, after holding positions with Centronics Data Computer Corporation, Honeywell, Inc., and the Datapoint Corporation, where he was Assistant Treasurer.

"Part of our GE heritage was a strong Engineering and Manufacturing orientation and this is a valuable asset. However, as a new and independent company, we needed to establish a Marketing presence, we needed a new and aggressive approach to our Marketing and Sales Activities. One of our first action items was to recruit the best Marketing and Sales executives we could locate. GENICOM's strategy for developing marketing strengths has been to bring experienced and capable people from other firms in the computer peripherals industry."

Financial Statements

The 1984 financial statements and footnotes are included in Exhibits 3-7. Due to the time period constraints associated with any financial statements, GENICOM's balance sheet for December 30, 1984 did not include the subsequent private placement of stock that took place on January 3, 1985. GENICOM sold 353,000 shares of its unissued common stock for $5 per share. If these shares had been issued at December 30, 1984, unaudited *pro forma* stockholders' equity would have been $16,993,000.

Exhibit 3 Genicom Corporation and Subsidiaries Consolidated Balance Sheet, 1984 (in thousands of dollars)

	December 30, 1984	January 1, 1984
Assets		
Current assets		
Cash	$ 451	$ 3,023
Accounts receivable, less allowance for doubtful accounts of $958 and $483	21,224	22,459
Inventories	26,917	24,343
Prepaid expenses and other assets	1,368	356
Total current assets	$49,960	$50,181
Property, plant, and equipment	27,821	27,314
Other assets	239	180
Total assets	$78,020	$77,675
Liabilities and Capital		
Current liabilities		
Current portion of long-term debt	$ 1,600	$11,841
Accounts payable and accrued expenses	16,104	15,682
Deferred income	1,519	1,359
Income taxes (note 8)	5,579	
Total current liabilities	$24,802	$28,882
Long-term debt, less current portion	36,400	44,500
Deferred income taxes	1,590	504
Redeemable preferred stock, $1 par value; 32,000 shares issued and outstanding at January 1, 1984; stated at liquidation value of $100 per share	-0-	$ 3,200
Stockholders' equity		
Common stock, $0.01 par value; 20,000,000 shares authorized; shares outstanding: December 30, 1984, 10,995,500; January 1, 1984, 8,575,000	$ 110	$ 86
Additional paid-in capital	9,297	772
Retained earnings (deficit)	5,821	(269)
Total stockholders' equity	$15,228	$ 589
Total liabilities and stockholders' equity	$78,020	$77,675

The accompanying notes are an integral part of the financial statements.

The two period comparisons used in the financials entitled "December 30, 1984" and "January 1, 1984" are not true comparisons since the time periods covered are not equal. The first column for the year ending December 30, 1984 represents a 12-month period, but the second column for the year ending January 1, 1984 represents only a two-month, ten-day period.

The remaining statements and ten footnotes are complete and self-explanatory. The strong fi-

Exhibit 4 Genicom Corporation and Subsidiaries Consolidated Statement of Income, 1984 (in thousands of dollars except per share amounts)

	Year ended December 30, 1984	October 21, 1983, to January 1, 1984
Net sales	$136,661	$26,752
Cost of goods sold	90,647	20,403
Gross profit	$ 46,014	$ 6,349
Expenses		
Selling, general, and administration	$ 22,442	$ 3,965
Engineering, research, and product development	4,795	890
Interest	6,900	1,386
Total expenses	$ 34,137	$ 6,241
Income before income taxes	$ 11,877	$ 108
Income tax expense (note 8)	5,787	377
Net income (loss)	$ 6,090	$ (269)
Net income (loss) per common share and common share equivalent		
Primary	$ 0.61	$ (0.03)
Fully diluted	$ 0.59	$ (0.03)
Weighted average number of common shares and common share equivalents		
Primary	9,967	8,753
Fully diluted	10,292	8,892

The accompanying notes are an integral part of the financial statements.

nancial orientation of the management is evident in the statement presentation.

Cost Accounting

A major cost accounting issue was that GENICOM's product costs were well above those of their competitors. GENICOM's willingness to customize their products to meet their customers' individual needs allowed them to charge a premium price. The costs that seemed disproportionately high were salary and hourly wages. GENICOM's salary and wage structures were established over many years while it was a part of GE. General Electric traditionally provided its employees with both a generous base salary and a generous fringe package. As wages and benefits were negotiated with the union on an overall corporate basis, the printer department had avoided serious conflicts with the union.

Consultants from Coopers and Lybrand were hired by GENICOM to evaluate the firm's cost structure. Although the study was not completed, preliminary research had focused on this labor cost problem. The preliminary findings suggested that most areas of the firm seemed overstaffed and salary and wage levels exceeded both industry norms and local community standards (e.g., see Exhibits 1 & 2).

Exhibit 5 Genicom Corporation and Subsidiaries Consolidated Statement of Changes in Capital Accounts for the Year Ended December 30, 1984 and the Period from October 21, 1983 (commencement of operations) to January 1, 1984

	Redeemable Preferred Stock	Common Stock	Additional Paid-In Capital	Retained Earnings
Issued in connection with acquisition:				
32,000 shares of redeemable preferred stock	$ 3,200			
8,000,000 shares of common stock		$ 80	$ 721	
Issuance of 525,000 shares of common stock		5	47	
Exercise of stock options		1	4	
Net loss				$ (269)
Balance, January 1, 1984	$ 3,200	$ 86	$ 772	$ (269)
Issuance of 1,297,000 shares of common stock		13	5,288	
Redemption of preferred stock	$(3,200)	6	3,194	
Exercise of stock options		5	43	
Net income				6,090
Balance, December 30, 1984	—	$110	$9,297	$5,821

The accompanying notes are an integral part of the financial statements.

An interesting point was that GENICOM's wage and salary differential over other local companies was so great that it proved detrimental to some laid-off employees. Other companies in the region had reported that they were hesitant to hire a laid-off GENICOM employee knowing that, as soon as an opening existed, the employee would be lost back to GENICOM.

Union Negotiations

Negotiations with Local 124 of the United Electrical Radio and Machine Workers (UE) of America started on April 23, 1985. Management's primary goal was to reduce the average costs of an applied direct labor hour by four dollars. Included in the employee benefit package were vacation (five weeks maximum), holidays (ten days), comprehensive medical benefits, life insurance, temporary disability, overtime premium, pension, breaks, night-shift bonus, paid sick days/personal time, and job structures which included seventeen pay grades. Appendices 1–6 provide a picture of the negotiations as the confrontation grew.

Earlier in April, a different local of UE in a nearby Virginia town had been involved in an almost identical situation. A former department of Westinghouse which had been sold to outside interests, confronted with wage and benefit structures originally negotiated at the national level, attempted to win major financial concessions from its workforce in order to become cost competitive in its market. The local refused to accept any cutbacks in its package and, after several months of negotiation, went on strike. Two days later the company announced it would begin hiring permanent replacements for the striking workers on the following Monday and placed help wanted ads in the local newspapers. On Sunday afternoon, in a close vote, the union members voted to end the strike and accept management's proposals.

Exhibit 6 Genicom Corporation and Subsidiaries Consolidated Statement of Changes in Financial Position, 1984 (in thousands of dollars)

	Year Ended December 30, 1984	October 21, 1983, to January 1, 1984
Sources of working capital		
From operations		
Net income (loss)	$ 6,090	$ (269)
Charges to income not affecting working capital		
Depreciation	4,664	630
Amortization	49	
Deferred income taxes	1,086	504
Working capital from operations	$ 11,889	$ 865
Issued or assumed in connection with acquisition		
Redeemable preferred stock		$ 3,200
Common stock		801
Long-term debt		57,841
Proceeds from issuance of common stock	8,501	52
Exercise of options	48	5
Other, net	357	(189)
Total sources	$ 20,795	$62,575
Applications of working capital		
Additions to property, plant, and equipment	$ 5,636	$ 918
Noncurrent assets purchased in acquisition		27,017
Reduction of long-term debt	8,100	13,341
Redemption of preferred stock	3,200	-0-
Total applications	$ 16,936	$41,276
Analysis of working capital components		
Increase (decrease) in current assets		
Cash	$ (2,572)	$ 3,023
Accounts receivable	(1,235)	22,459
Inventories	2,574	24,343
Prepaid expenses and other assets	1,012	356
Total	$ (221)	$50,181
Increase (decrease) in current liabilities		
Current portion of long-term debt	$(10,241)	$11,841
Accounts payable and accrued expenses	422	15,682
Deferred income	160	1,359
Income taxes	5,579	
Total	$ (4,080)	$28,882
Increase in working capital	$ 3,859	$21,299
Working capital, beginning of period	21,299	-0-
Working capital, end of period	$ 25,158	$21,299

The accompanying notes are an integral part of the financial statements.

Exhibit 7 GENICOM Corporation and Subsidiaries Notes to Consolidated Financial Statements

1. *Incorporation and Acquisition:*

GENICOM Corporation (the "Company") was incorporated on June 1, 1983 and had no activity other than organizational matters until October 21, 1983 when it acquired substantially all of the net assets of the Data Communication Products Business Department and all of the outstanding common stock of Datacom de Mexico, S.A. de C.V., both wholly owned by General Electric Company ("GE"), a related party. These entities together functioned as a single business unit and were acquired in a purchase transaction for consideration totaling $62.1 million. The consideration was financed by (a) borrowing $41.0 million under a revolving credit and term loan agreement, (b) issuing $16.8 million in subordinated notes to GE, (c) assuming $340,000 of liabilities and (d) selling $800,000 of common stock and $3.2 million of redeemable preferred stock.

The consideration was allocated to working capital ($35.1 million) and property, plant and equipment and other assets ($27.0 million). The allocation of the purchase price to assets acquired and liabilities assumed is subject to adjustment resulting from refinements in the application of purchase method accounting.

If the acquisition is assumed to have been made as of January 1, 1983, unaudited pro forma consolidated net sales, net loss and net loss per share (computed by adjusting historical operations for acquisition financing and purchase method accounting) would approximate the following for the year ended January 1, 1984 (dollar amounts in millions, except per share amounts): net sales—$113.5; net loss—$3.4; net loss per common share and common share equivalent: primary—$.42 and fully diluted—$.42.

2. *Summary of Significant Accounting Policies:*

The Company, one of the largest independent computer printer companies, is a manufacturer and leading supplier of teleprinters, serial dot matrix printers, and line printers serving a wide variety of data processing and telecommunication markets. Additionally, the Company is a recognized leader in the manufacturer and supply of high quality, crystal/can relays, which are used in the Aerospace and Defense industries.

a. Principles of consolidation: The consolidated financial statements include the accounts of the Company and its wholly owned subsidiaries. All significant intercompany accounts and transactions have been eliminated.

b. Fiscal year: The Company's fiscal year ends on the Sunday nearest December 31. Accordingly, the Company is reporting on the period October 21, 1983 (commencement of operations) to January 1, 1984 and for the 52-week period ended December 30, 1984.

c. Inventories: Inventories are stated at the lower of cost or market. Cost is determined on a first-in, first-out basis.

d. Property, plant and equipment: Property, plant and equipment is stated at cost. Depreciation is computed using the straight-line method for financial reporting purposes based on estimates of useful lives at their acquisition date (generally 15 to 25 years for buildings and 3 to 8 years for machinery and equipment). Significant improvements and the cost of tooling are capitalized, while repairs and maintenance costs are charged to operations.

e. Income taxes: Timing differences exist in the computation of income for financial and tax reporting purposes which give rise to deferred taxes. The principal reason for these differences is the use of alternative methods for computing depreciation. The Company accounts for investment tax credits as a reduction of current taxes in the year realized.

f. Research and development: Research and development costs are charged to operations as incurred. The costs were $3,367,000 for the year ended December 30, 1984 and $475,000 for the period October 21, 1983 to January 1, 1984.

g. Foreign currency translation: Through its subsidiary, Datacom de Mexico, S.A. de C.V., the Company operates in a country considered to have a highly inflationary economy. As such, translation adjustments, which are not material, are included in results of operations. The consolidated financial statements of the Company include foreign assets and liabilities of $2,643,000 and $526,000 at December 30, 1984 and $1,291,000 and $96,000 at January 1, 1984.

h. Employee benefit plans: Substantially all of the Company's employees are eligible to participate under the Company's employee benefit plans described in Note 5. These plans are

Exhibit 7 *(continued)*

contributory and each employee must elect to participate and make contributions to the plans. Employee contributions vest immediately.

l. Net income per common share and common share equivalent: Primary net income (loss) per share was computed by dividing net income (loss) by the weighted average number of common shares and common share equivalents outstanding during the period. Common share equivalents include the weighted average number of shares issuable upon the assumed exercise of outstanding stock options and warrants after assuming the applicable proceeds from such exercise were used to acquire treasury shares at the average market price during the period.

Fully diluted net income (loss) per share was based upon the further assumption that the applicable proceeds from the exercise of the outstanding stock options and warrants were used to acquire treasury shares at the market price at the end of the period if higher than the average market price during the period.

3. *Supplemental Balance Sheet Information:*
Inventories consist of:

(Amounts in thousands)	December 30, 1984	January 1, 1984
Raw materials	$10,110	$ 9,897
Work in process	9,781	9,708
Finished goods	7,026	4,738
	$26,917	$24,343

Property, plant, and equipment consist of:

(Amounts in thousands)	December 30, 1984	January 1, 1984
Land	$ 709	$ 709
Buildings	5,383	5,268
Machinery and equipment	25,628	21,760
Construction in progress	1,291	207
	$33,011	$27,944
Less accumulated depreciation	5,190	630
	$27,821	$27,314

Accounts payable and accrued expenses consist of:

(Amounts in thousands)	December 30, 1984	January 1, 1984
Trade accounts payable	$ 6,297	$ 7,881
Accrued liabilities:		
Compensated absences	2,801	2,532
Payroll and related liabilities	1,589	808
Interest	1,337	1,426
Employee benefits	1,830	332
Other	2,250	2,703
	$16,104	$15,682

4. *Long-Term Debt:*
Long-term debt consists of:

(Amounts in thousands)	December 30, 1984	January 1, 1984
Revolving credit notes	$21,000	$27,500
Term loan	12,000	12,000
Subordinated notes payable to GE	5,000	16,841
	38,000	56,341
Less current portion	1,600	11,841
	$36,400	$44,500

On October 21, 1983, the Company entered into a financing agreement with several banks which provides the Company with $31 million of revolving credit and a $12 million term loan.

The revolving credit and term loan bear interest at the price rate (10¾% at December 30, 1984) plus 1½%, payable quarterly. In addition, a commitment fee of ½ of 1% is payable quarterly on the average daily unused portion of the revolving credit borrowing base. The Company is also required to maintain compensating balances of at least 5% of the total outstanding revolving credit and term loan. Withdrawal of the compensating balances is not legally restricted and any deficiency in maintaining such balances is subject to a fee based upon an average borrowing rate on amounts outstanding under this agreement.

The initial revolving loan base of $31 million decreases by $1.55 million beginning on October

(continued)

Exhibit 7 *(continued)*

1, 1986, and continues to decrease by $1.55 million each quarter thereafter and expires on October 1, 1991.

The term loan is payable in quarterly installments of $600,000 beginning October 1, 1985.

All borrowings by the Company under the agreement are collateralized by liens on all of the Company's assets. The agreement requires the Company to meet certain financial ratios related to indebtedness, net worth and current assets and current liabilities. The agreement also limits additional borrowing, purchase of property and equipment, the sale or disposition of certain assets, and restricts the payment of dividends to 50% of retained earnings. Under the most restrictive covenant $2.9 million of retained earnings was available for payment of dividends at December 30, 1984.

In connection with the acquisition, at October 21, 1983, the Company issued subordinated notes to GE in the amount of $16.8 million. These notes bear interest at the prime rate, payable quarterly. During 1984 in accordance with the terms, the Company paid $11.8 million of the notes. The remaining $5 million is payable as follows: October 21, 1985—$1 million; October 21, 1986—$2 million; and October 21, 1987—$2 million.

Maturities of long-term debt for the five fiscal years subsequent to December 30, 1984 are (in millions): 1985—$1.6; 1986—$4.4; 1987—$4.4; 1988—$6.4; and 1989—$8.6.

5. *Employee Benefit Plans:*

Effective January 1, 1984, the Company established a defined benefit pension plan for hourly employees. Employees must elect to participate and the plan is contributory. Employee contributions are 3% of compensation in excess of $12,000 per year. The Company makes contributions to the plan and records as pension expense an amount that is actuarially determined to be sufficient to provide benefits provided for under the plan, including amortization of unfunded liabilities over a maximum of 30 years. For the year ended December 30, 1984, pension expense was $408,000. Details of accumulated plan benefits and net plan assets as of the initial valuation date (January 1, 1984) are as follows:

Actuarial present value of accumulated plan benefits are:

Vested	$ 74,777
Nonvested	28,067
	$102,844
Market value of assets	$ 49,969
Rate of return assumed	7½%

Certain hourly employees have the additional benefit of receiving Unemployment Supplemental Income if their employment is terminated due to reductions in the Company's workforce.

Substantially all salaried employees are eligible to participate in the Company's deferred compensation and savings plan. The plan provides for contributions to be made by employees through salary reductions. The Company makes certain matching contributions which are allocated to the participants and vest as called for by the plan. For the year ended December 30, 1984, the Company's expense under this plan was $1,002,000.

6. *Warrants and Redeemable Preferred Stock:*

In connection with the acquisition the Company issued to GE stock purchase warrants to acquire 2,500,000 shares of the Company's common stock at a price of $.50 per share. The warrants are currently exercisable and expire October 21, 1988.

On December 20, 1984, the Company redeemed all of the outstanding redeemable preferred stock ($3.2 million) by issuing 640,000 shares of common stock. Holders of the redeemable preferred stock waived payment of the cumulative preferred stock dividends for all periods the stock was outstanding.

7. *Restricted Stock Purchase and Incentive Stock Option Plans:*

Under the Company's restricted stock purchase plan, the Company may offer to sell up to 975,000 shares of common stock to employees of the Company at a price per share equal to 100% of the fair market value as determined by the Board of Directors on the date of offer. Purchased shares vest to the employees as provided for under the agreement and, in certain cases, is dependent upon the attainment of annual financial objectives. Shares issued under the plan which are not vested at an employee's termination are subject to repurchase by the Company at the lower of original issue price or their then fair market value.

At December 30, 1984, 200,000 shares of common stock are reserved for future grants under this plan. The following table summarizes the activity of the plan during the respective fiscal periods (fair market value as determined at date of purchase): *see table A.*

Effective October 21, 1983, the Company adopted an incentive stock option plan whereby 1,300,000 shares of unissued common stock was reserved for future issuance. The plan was amended on October 20, 1984 to reduce the number of shares

Exhibit 7 *(continued)*

available under the plan from 1,300,000 to 1,025,000. Stock option activity for the respective fiscal periods is as follows: *see table B.*

The plan provides for the exercise of the outstanding options at 20% per year beginning five years from date of grant. The Company accelerated the exercising provisions of 475,000 options granted, and these options were exercised prior to December 30, 1984. Of these shares issued, 425,000 shares are restricted and subject to certain vesting provisions related to annual financial objectives. Additionally, under the plan, other options granted also become exercisable at earlier dates if these same financial objectives are attained. During the year ended December 30, 1984, such objectives were attained and 45,000 shares of those restricted above accrued to the benefit of the holders and 63,500 options became exercisable of which 58,500 were exercised and shares of common stock issued. The Company must continue to attain certain financial objectives annually in order to continue to have accelerated exercise dates (with respect to options) and continue to vest (with respect to restricted shares). In the event of employee termination prior to full vesting in these shares, the Company may purchase such shares at the lower of fair market value at date of termination or the original option price.

Table A

	Year ended December 30, 1984		October 21, 1983 to January 1, 1984	
	Number of Shares	Market Value	Number of Shares	Market Value
Unvested shares outstanding, beginning of period	525,000	$ 52,500		
Shares issued	250,000	95,000	525,000	$52,500
Shares vested	(175,000)	(17,500)		
Unvested shares outstanding, end of period	600,000	$130,000	525,000	$52,500

Table B

	Year ended December 30, 1984			October 21, 1983 to January 1, 1984		
		Option Price			Option Price	
	Number of Shares	Per Share	Total	Number of Shares	Per Share	Total
Outstanding, beginning of period	780,000	$.10	$78,000			
Granted	82,500	$.20–$1.00	46,500	830,000	$.10	$83,000
Exercised	483,500	$.10	48,350	50,000	$.10	5,000
Cancelled	65,000	$.10–$.20	7,250			
Outstanding, end of period	314,000		$68,900	780,000		$78,000
Options exercisable, end of period	5,000	$.10	$ 500			
Options available for future grants	177,500					

(continued)

Exhibit 7 *(continued)*

8. *Income Taxes:*
Income tax expense consists of:

(Amounts in thousands)	Year ended December 30, 1984	October 21, 1983 to January 1, 1984
Current:		
Federal	$4,788	
State	936	
Foreign	(72)	
	5,652	–
Deferred:		
Federal	73	$ 302
State	1	75
Foreign	61	
	135	377
	$5,787	$ 377

Total tax expense amounted to an effective rate of 48.7% for the year ended December 30, 1984 and 449% for the period October 21, 1983 to January 1, 1984. Income tax expense was different from that computed at the statutory U.S. Federal income tax rate of 46% for the following reasons:

(Amounts in thousands)	Year ended December 30, 1984	October 21, 1983 to January 1, 1984
Tax expense at statutory rate	$5,463	$ 50
Increases (decreases) related to:		
Investment tax credits	(249)	(56)
State income tax, net of federal income tax benefit	515	40
Purchase method accounting for inventories	103	370
DISC income	(70)	
Other, net	25	(27)
Actual tax expense	$5,787	$ 377

Deferred income tax expense results from timing differences in the recognition of revenue and expense for tax and financial statement purposes. The sources of these differences and the tax effect of each are as follows:

(Amounts in thousands)	Year ended December 30, 1984	October 21, 1983 to January 1, 1984
Depreciation	$ 728	$ 497
Inventory valuation	(668)	
Other, net	75	(120)
	$ 135	$ 377

9. *Leasing Arrangements:*

As Lessee

The Company leases certain manufacturing and warehousing property. Rent expense included in the consolidated statement of income amounted to $740,000 for the year ended December 30, 1984 and $120,000 for the period October 21, 1983 to January 1, 1984.

Annual future minimum lease commitments for operating leases as of December 30, 1984 are immaterial.

As Lessor

The Company has rental plans for the leasing of printers. Operating lease terms vary, generally from one to 60 months. Rental income for the year ended December 30, 1984 and for the period October 21, 1983 to January 1, 1984 was $18,139,000 and $3,807,000, respectively. Minimum future rental revenues on noncancellable operating leases with terms of one year or longer at December 30, 1984 are (in thousands): 1985—$2,900; 1986—$500; 1987—$400; and 1988—$300.

At December 30, 1984 and January 1, 1984, the cost of equipment leased was (in thousands) $4,087 and $4,040, which is included in property, plant and equipment, net of accumulated depreciation of $1,072 and $131, respectively.

10. *Related-Party Transactions:*

The Company presently utilizes GE for various services, such as repair services for customers and data processing, under contracts expiring generally in 1985. The Company also purchases various raw materials from GE. The cost of these materials and services for the year ended December 30, 1984 and the period October 21, 1983 to January 1, 1984, totaled $8.4 million and $1.1 million, respectively.

Exhibit 7 *(continued)*

Sales to GE were $12.4 million for the year ended December 30, 1984 and $3.3 million for the period October 21, 1983 to January 1, 1984. In addition, sales to GE affiliates, who serve as distributors to third party customers in certain markets, and sales of parts for maintenance services to customers amounted to $14.4 million for the year ended December 30, 1984 and $1.7 million for the period October 21, 1983 to January 1, 1984. Accounts receivable from GE were $4.6 million at December 30, 1984 and $5.2 million at January 1, 1984; accounts payable to GE were $.8 million at December 30, 1984 and $.9 million at January 1, 1984.

The Printer Industry

The demand for printer hardware is derived from the demand for computing machinery. As the demand for computing capability shifted from mainframe computers to minicomputers to microcomputers, so did the demand for printing capacity shift from output capability to output quality. Similarly, the attributes of printers which determined their success in the marketplace changed from reliability and performance when dealing with mainframe applications to price and capability when dealing with microcomputer applications. At the same time, as business applications of microcomputers moved into networking situations, where a number of microcomputers are linked to a central database and a single printer, the demands placed on the printer hardware changed from the demands of a stand-alone microcomputer.

In addition to the changes that took place in the printer industry as a result of changes in the computer industry, there was change in the competitive structure of the marketplace. The presence of the Japanese manufacturers had altered the competitive nature of the industry. As had been the strategy in other industries, Japanese manufacturers entered the market at the bottom of the price structure. Because of lower labor rates and efficient production capability, the Japanese products forced extreme price pressure into the market. Once established, the Japanese manufacturers then began to "trade up" through product improvement and brand extension. As a result, the Japanese printer manufacturers became a formidable force in the marketplace, particularly in the microprinter (for personal computer use) segment. This set of competitors was a force all U.S. manufacturers of printers must have accounted for in the formulation of new product introductions and pricing strategies. A number of U.S. manufacturers had licensed "offshore" (Mexican, Korean, Taiwanese, and Japanese) manufacturers to produce price competitive products under the U.S. manufacturer brand names as a means of competing with the Japanese manufacturers.

The Market

The total market for printers of all types was predicted to be $10.44 billion in 1986. The breakdown of sales by printer type is shown in Exhibit 8. The market was segmented by impact (printers which use a printhead that actually strikes the paper) and non-impact (printers which do not strike the paper, but apply ink in some other fashion). Within the impact market, printers were also segmented by dot-matrix (printers which use dots to form the characters printed) and fully formed (printers which print an entire character at once, such as a "daisy wheel" printer). This market was further segmented according to whether a printer was a serial printer (one which prints character by character in a serial fashion) or a line printer (one which prints an entire line at a time—in general, line printers are called "high speed" and print faster than serial printers, but often at a lower quality); finally, the impact market segment was subdivided according to speed of printing. The non-impact segment was divided further according to printer

Exhibit 8 The U.S. Printer Market, 1983 and 1986

	1983				1986			
	Number of Units	Percent Share	Value (millions of dollars)	Percent Share	Number of Units	Percent Share	Value (millions of dollars)	Percent Share
Serial daisy wheel	712,000	25%	1,370	25%	2,000,000	24%	$ 2,400	23%
Serial dot matrix	1,857,000	66	2,280	41	4,600,000	54	4,140	40
Serial non-impact[a]	132,000	5	162	3	1,600,000	19	990	9
Nonimpact page printers[b]	5,200	0	222	4	150,000	2	1,000	10
Fully formed line printers	86,000	3	1,130	21	100,000	1	1,400	13
Dot matrix line printers	31,000	1	318	6	55,000	0	510	5
Total	2,823,000	100%	5,482	100%	8,505,000	100%	10,440	100%

[a]Ink-jet and thermal transfer printers
[b]Laser and similar printers.
[c]Source: Datek Information Services, Inc.

technology (electrostatic, ink jet, laser), and by speed (in characters per second). Certain non-impact printers were also segmented as page printers (those which print a complete page at a time). All non-impact printers were considered to have fully formed characters. A schematic representation of the complete market for printers is shown in Exhibit 9.

Besides print quality, different classes of printers had advantages and disadvantages for end users. Fully-formed character printers, whether daisywheel or band line, offered no graphics capability since they were limited to alphanumeric characters. These printers also were very noisy while printing unless special quietized enclosures were used to surround them. Additionally, daisywheel printers, which were found almost exclusively in offices for word processing applications, were extremely slow.

The primary drawback to dot matrix printers was perceived print quality, although a number of technological developments had improved their performance. These printers, however, supplied excellent adaptability to applications needs—graphics, spreadsheets, data and word processing, for instance—and prices had been dropping very rapidly in this market segment.

Non-impact printers offered much of the best aspects of performance—quiet operation, flexible application, and outstanding print quality—but drawbacks included high prices, inability to print multiple copies simultaneously (i.e., continuous multipart forms printing), higher cost of operation because of their utilization of consumable supplies such as toner, and some perception of the part of users that non-impact printers, like the copiers their technology was derived from, were less reliable.

As advances in technology decreased the cost of non-impact printers, the growth of sales in these segments was expected to increase. The prices of nonimpact printers were still high rel-

Exhibit 9 Electronic Printer Market Breakdown

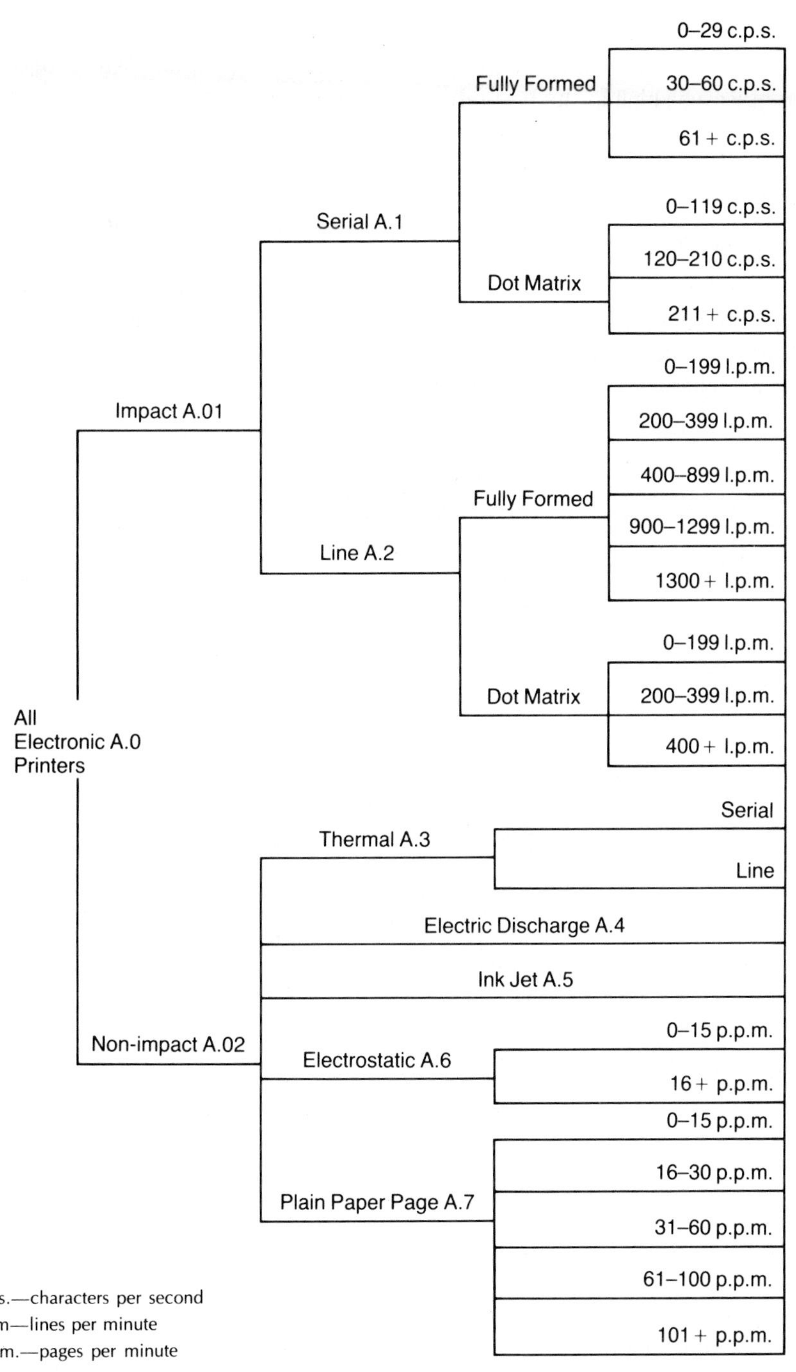

Source: DATAQUEST, Inc.

ative to impact offerings, and the impact printers still enjoyed a speed advantage. However, the non-impact printers were much quieter than their impact counterparts, and the quality of their output was at least as high as the best fully-formed impact output. Exhibit 10 shows the characteristics of printer types, as compared against the "ideal" printer.

GENICOM Product Line

By April of 1985, GENICOM primarily produced dot matrix impact printers, though $6,000,000 in 1984 revenue was derived from a 300 lpm fully formed character line printer. The company produced line and serial printers which could print from 60 cps in an office environment to 600 lpm in a high speed line printer used for volume production. Most of the GENICOM product line also offered letter-quality printing at slower speeds, so the machines were flexible, depending on the user's needs. GENICOM offered branded printers as peripheral devices, and produced OEM printers for a number of major customers. GENICOM's products generally were more expensive than those of their major competitors, but had higher performance capabilities and greater durability. GENICOM sales by product for 1984 are shown in Exhibit 11.

Exhibit 10 Personal Computer Printer Trends: Characteristics by Technology

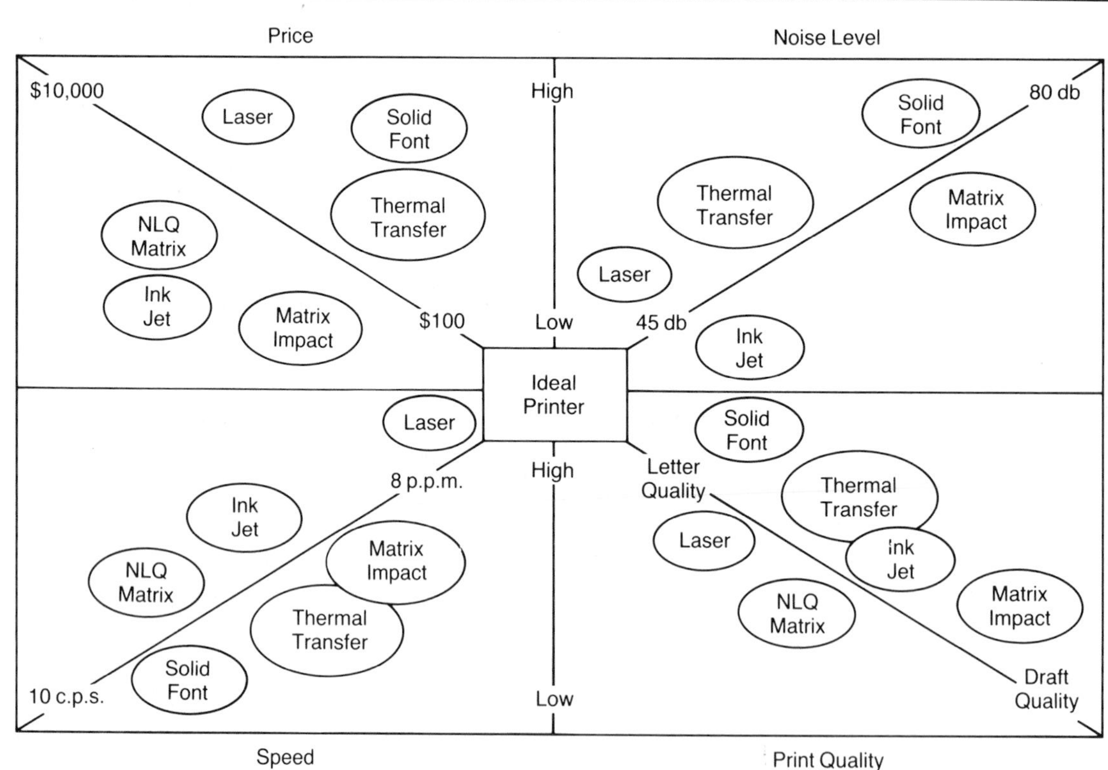

Source: FUTURE COMPUTING INCORPORATED

Exhibit 11 Genicom Sales, 1984

Printers	Thousands of dollars	Number of Units
340/510	$ 5,980	1,749
200	8,564	4,016
2030	6,131	9,623 (2030 and 2120 combined)
2120	5,011	
3000	30,924	20,495
3014/3024	3,879	5,036
4000	—	—
Other	399	—
Total printers	$ 60,888	40,919
Parts	16,962	
Ribbons	7,846	
Lease	18,140	
Service	9,380	
Total printer business	$113,216	
Relays	23,426	
Total company business	$136,642	

GENICOM Competitors

GENICOM had a number of major competitors in each of the market segments it served. Its two major U.S. competitors were Centronics and Dataproducts, both competing essentially "head on" with GENICOM in almost every market segment. There were other, smaller competitors for special applications and certain of GENICOM's market segments. Exhibit 12 offers market share estimates for major competitors in each major segment.

End User

The end user for GENICOM products was faced with a complex decision process in the choice of a printer. The current products operated faster, printed more legibly, and cost less than those of a few years ago. However, there were more machines to choose from, so the choice needed to be carefully made.

GENICOM Marketing Strategy

GENICOM's general marketing strategy had been one of improving current products and expanding product lines rather than developing entirely new products or diversifying into new technologies. The strategy could have been characterized as "evolutionary" rather than "revolutionary." GENICOM's main distinctive competencies in the market had been flexibility in production and the quality of its products. They had traditionally been on the upper end of price points for similar products and had sought to gain market share by stressing the advantages their machines offered relative to the competition. Each of GENICOM's products offered some distinct advantage–speed, print quality, quietness, or flexibility–which was thought to offset price disadvantages.

GENICOM had an important presence in the OEM market, offering those customers a

Exhibit 12 Market Share, U.S. Printer Markets, 1984 (in units)

U.S. Serial Impact Printer Market, 1984 (market share in units)

Country of Manufacture	Manufacturer	% Share	Fully-formed	Dot Matrix
Japan	Epson	20.1		×
	C. Itoh (TEC)	13.9	×	×
	Okidata	11.4		×
	Star	3.2		×
	NEC	2.4	×	×
	Brother	2.0	×	×
	Ricoh	2.0	×	
	Toshiba	1.1		×
	Canon	0.9		×
	Juki	0.9	×	
	Fujitsu	0.6	×	×
	Subtotal	58.5		
United States	Xerox	3.2	×	
	IBM	3.0	×	
	Texas Instruments	2.2		×
	DEC	2.2		×
	Teletype	2.0		×
	Quae	2.0	×	
	Centronics	1.6		×
	Genicom	1.1		×
	Anadex	0.6		×
	Datasouth	0.4		×
	Dataproducts	1.6	×	×
	Subtotal	19.9		
Europe	Mannesmann	0.9		×
	Facit	0.5	×	×
	Philips	0.3		×
	Hermes	0.2		×
	Subtotal	1.9		
Other		19.7		

U.S. Nonimpact Printer Market, 1984 (market share in units)

Country of Manufacture	Manufacturer	% Share	Page	Thermal	Ink jet
Japan	Canon	17.3	×		×
	Okidata	17.0		×	×
	Star	12.8		×	
	Sharp	8.5		×	×
	Brother	4.5		×	
	Subtotal	60.1			
United States	IBM	8.0	×	×	×
	Hewlett-Packard	4.5		×	×
	Xerox	3.6	×	×	×
	Texas Instruments	2.5		×	
	Subtotal	18.6			
Europe	Siemens	3.5	×		×
	Honeywell	1.0	×		
	Subtotal	4.5			
Other		16.8			

Exhibit 12 *(continued)*

U.S. Line Impact Printer Market, 1984 (market share in units)

Country of Manufacture	Manufacturer	% Share	Fully Formed	Dot Matrix
United States	Dataproducts	31.0	×	
	IBM	23.0	×	×
	Teletype	8.0	×	
	Centronics	7.0	×	
	Hewlett-Packard	6.0		×
	Printronix	6.0	×	×
	Genicom	1.5	×	
	Subtotal	82.5		
Japan	NBC	4.1	×	
	Fujitsu	1.6	×	
	Hitachi	0.7	×	×
	Subtotal	6.4		
Europe	Mannesmann	2.1	×	
Other		8.0		

wide variety of choices regarding specifications for products. The GENICOM presence in the branded printer market was not so strong, though efforts were underway to increase the importance of that market.

The product positioning of the GENICOM line had been for the professional user. Both for data processing and for word processing, the strength of GENICOM's product line had been in the commercial rather than the personal segments. The current product line was more durable, had more capability, and was more expensive than the bulk of the personal printer market. The GENICOM products could be compared to IBM office typewriters; they were generally considered "over-engineered" for the home market. GENICOM was giving some consideration to the personal printer market, to compete with Epson, Okidata, Toshiba and others. It recognized that among other factors a new product line, rather than modification of an existing product, would be necessary to compete in this highly price-competitive market.

Distribution

In early 1985, GENICOM products were distributed through a distributor network which focused on industrial users and on wholesale/retail distributors who serviced end user needs. Consideration was given to entering retail distributorship relations with large companies or with independently owned and franchised chains.

The GENICOM distribution system was not vertically integrated at that time. Although GENICOM had been contemplating expanding the distributor network slightly to effect better geographic coverage of markets, other plans suggested that they develop recognition of authorized dealers through the current distributor network. A schematic representation of the GENICOM distribution system is presented in Exhibit 13.

While prices and margins for dot-matrix impact printers had been dropping as market pressures grew, the future could be said to be nothing but certain. Curtis Powell considered the union negotiations a critical turning point in the firm's history.

Exhibit 13 Domestic Multi-Tier Distribution Channels

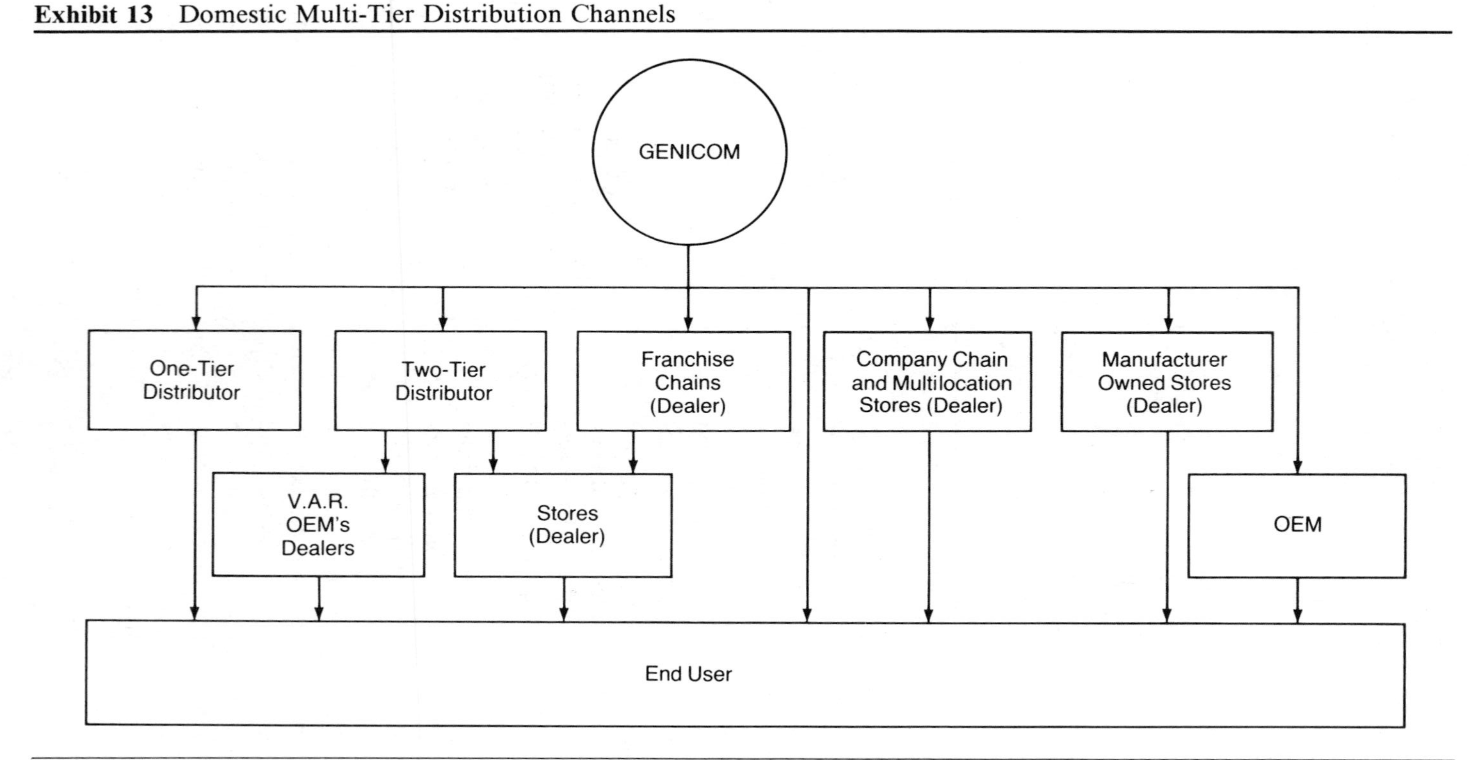

The United Effort

Local 124 Park Station P.O. Box 2245 Waynesboro, Va. 22980

Negotiations Report

On Tuesday afternoon the negotiating committee met with Relations and a lawyer to start contract talks. Right away, without putting any paperwork on the table, this lawyer wanted us to tell him ways management can cut *four dollars an hour* off the cost of labor. According to him, the cost per hour, including wages and benefits, is fourteen dollars an hour and this is, "significantly higher" than other workers are making in Waynesboro and must drop to ten dollars total of wages and benefits. He was even so helpful as to offer selections, like a smorgasbord, if you will, of items from which *we* could decide where to make the cuts.

For our consideration he laid out: rate cuts, night shift differential pay, vacation time cuts and other paid time off, give up bump rights, retraining, premium pay for some overtime, call in pay, medical benefits and the list goes on. All he wants *us* to do is decide where to cut to come up with a four dollar price cut. He pointed out that the wages in the lower job rates are much to high and will have to be cut to make us more comparable with other wage earners in Waynesboro.

Based on the claim that Genicom needs for us to cough up four dollars worth of wages and benefits, we naturally figured the company was going broke so we asked a question about the financial condition of the business. The reply was contrary to what you might suspect based on them wanting cost cuts. It turns out that the company is *making* money but wants to make *more* money and in order to do that they want to get into our pocket.

Just as we figured, when the word got out in the plant, you became furious to think that the company would be so greedy as to come after the wages and benefits you have worked years for and some of you even walked a picket line for a hundred and two days in 1969 to get. There is a growing demand from the union membership to hold work stoppages to protest these unrealistic demands by management and it appears the time will come for that kind of action! The next meeting with management is scheduled for May 6th and Boris "Red" Block will be here for that meeting. We will have a full membership meeting the next day, Tuesday, May 7th, to let you know what is going on and how negotiations are progressing. At that time we will be *led by the membership* about what action you want to take.

After we listened to what management had to say about their thoughts we laid out our proposals and informed them that the list was only a partial list of what we think is needed in a new contract. Some of what we are looking at includes strong job security language, improvement in pensions and downward adjustments in our contributions to the pension plan, a better severance pay clause, insurance coverage to be nothing less than we now have, improvements in S&A benefits, cost of living clause, contract language improvements and a general wage increase. And, as we pointed out, there are other things we are looking at which we will lay on the table later. What happens in negotiations and what we are able to do is directly dependent on you and how much support you are willing to give.

It's your Local and "The Members Run This Union!"

Appendix 2

The United Effort

Local 124 Park Station P.O. Box 2245 Waynesboro, Va. 22980

The Members Decide

At the end of the second session of negotiations management still insists on demanding a $4.00 an hour wage and benefit concession from you. They set the record straight so there would be no mistake in anyones mind we were told "we are taking it." We asked time and time again what they would do with the $4.00 if they can take it and we were told rather matter of factly, "we are going to put in in our pockets." It's not that Genicom didn't make a profit last year its just plain and simple they just want to add an additional $3200.00 an hour to their pockets (300 employees × $4.00 per hr. = $3200.00 an hour) at your expense.

At a full house special membership meeting, 1st and 2nd shift, the committee was instructed to take a secret ballot strike vote. We normally keep the meetings to one hour but due to the number of members who wanted to speak, the meeting lasted well over the normal length of time and then a vote was taken, which was in favor of a strike action. As we have said before, this local doesn't have a history of strike action but the workers at Genicom feel they have no choice but to fight on the issues of wages and working conditions in this plant. Management sometime ago decided to cut the rate of the mold machine operators from R13 to R9 and it seems this only wet their appetite to want to take even more. We filed a grievance and processed it through the required steps of the grievance procedure and we will be taking action on that grievance at the proper time of which you will be notified.

We don't need to tell you how important it is for everyone to support the strike action. The issue is over a rate cut on one job but remember, the bigger issue is now management is saying they are going to cut $4.00 off of everyone in wages and benefits. Whether they can get away with it or not depends on you and everyone in the plant. The stakes are high and it's up to you to decide. Do you just fork over the $4.00 in wages and benefits or do you join your fellow workers and fight?

Shop Steward Election

There will be a meeting at Jim Durcin's desk today, five minutes before the end of lunch break, to nominate and elect a shop steward.

Appendix 3

GENICOM Printer Flash

Date May 31, 1985 No. 85-6

To All Employees:

In response to the excessive amount of publicity in the local press concerning GENICOM's negotiations with the UE Local 124, the following advertisement will appear in tomorrow's Waynesboro News-Virginion and Sunday's Stanton News Leader. We felt you, as GENICOM employees, should be the first to have this information.

What's Really Happening at GENICOM

GENICOM and its negotiations with Local 124 have been the subject of much discussion in our community and among GENICOM employees in recent weeks. All the information to this point has come from the Union. Since so much is at stake for GENICOM, its employees, and our community, we believe management should do its best to assure that the people who may be affected understand what is happening—and why.

GENICOM is a Waynesboro company that is dedicated to remaining a Waynesboro company. That dedication is reflected in GENICOM's proposals to UE Local 124 to establish a wage and benefit program that will allow GENICOM to meet competition while providing GENICOM workers with wages and benefits in line with community standards.

As part of the negotiations process, GENICOM provided wage survey data to Local 124 on both GENICOM's national competition and its Waynesboro neighbors. Reflecting that data, GENICOM's proposal includes job rates from $6.50 to $12 per hour, three weeks paid vacation, eight holidays, medical and dental insurance at a cost of $4 per week to employees, a defined benefit pension plan with limited contributions by employees, as well as company paid life and disability programs.

Starting in 1954, and for nearly 30 years, General Electric Company conducted manufacturing operations at the current GENICOM facility in Waynesboro. Under General Electric, wages were negotiated on a national basis. As a result, Waynesboro wage and salary costs reached levels which are out of line with the electronics industry and with the Waynesboro community. GENICOM Corporation was formed to operate the Business purchased from G.E. GENICOM is now managed by people who are committed to establishing and maintaining a successful and profitable business—because it is our only business. In the 19 months since GENICOM acquired its business, it has been operated on a profitable basis. This was particularly true in 1984, when the market for computers and related equipment was robust. The Business is less profitable now that its market has become much softer and competition for sales of electronic products such as GENICOM's has become very intense. GENICOM management is determined and committed to reducing costs and competing.

These costs reductions can be accomplished either by moving operations to GENICOM's existing lower cost locations or by lowering costs in Waynesboro. GENICOM has decided to stay in Waynesboro. The wage and benefit concessions requested will make Waynesboro a competitive manufacturing location—a manufacturing location with a future. These concessions will not be easy or insignificant for GENICOM workers to accept, but they are not unreasonable. Competitive wages will make operations in Waynesboro much more economically attractive for GENICOM and increase GENICOM's incentive to maintain and expand those operations, thus offering more job security to Waynesboro workers and greater stability to the Waynesboro community.

C.W. Powell
President and Chief Executive Officer
GENICOM Corporation

Appendix 4

The United Effort

Local 124 Park Station P.O. Box 2245 Waynesboro, Va. 22980

Genicom Should Tell It Like It Is, Instead of Wanting to Pocket 6½ Million Dollars of Its Employees and the Community

Thats what Genicom wants in concessions from the hourly workers. Genicom said thats not all. They are going to get a like amount from the lower paid salary workers and supervisors.

Not once have they said they are going to cut top paid Genicom employees such as Mr. Powell.

Genicom says they are dedicated to remaining in Waynesboro. If that is so, why have they moved over 600 jobs to Mexico, and continue to move jobs out of Waynesboro. They say they need concessions from their employees to do this. But they refuse to put in writing to the Union that these concessions will keep jobs in Waynesboro.

Instead the Company tells us they want to "put the money in their pockets." They go on to say they will use some of this money to buy other plants in other states. This will not bring jobs to Waynesboro. The Company is going to run the plants where they buy them. Not once has the Company said they would brings jobs back from Mexico with the $4 per hour concessions that they want.

The Truth Is!

The Company proposal to the Union means 2 less paid holidays per year, it means that most employees would lose 2 weeks paid vacation per year. All employees would take pay cuts. Some Genicom families would take cuts of $12,000 per year. As for the pensions and the insurance, the proposal is to leave it as it is now. The Company proposal would take away all of the night shift bonus, the few sick days workers have now, and would do away with rest breaks.

If the company really means that they will bring more jobs to Waynesboro. They should be willing to put it in writing.

If the Company really means to have greater stability for the Community they should reinvest the extra profits in the Genicom Waynesboro plant. Not take the money and buy plants in other states.

Genicom would like the Community to believe that GE negotiated the last Union contract. *THAT IS NOT SO. GENICOM NEGOTIATED THE LAST CONTRACT.* Mr. Stoner of Genicom Management was part of the last negotiations and he is part of this negotiations. Mr. Stoner plays a big part in negotiations.

The Company admits in their paid ad that they made money with the last Union Contract. They could make money with the new contract that has no cuts.

Its time for Genicom to put in writing to its employees that the Company will keep jobs in Waynesboro. Genicom is making a profit. They should let the employees keep what they have. There should be NO CUTS. Workers should keep their 6 1/2 Million Dollars. This would keep the money in the Community. Not take it to other States and Mexico.

If Genicom takes this money and "puts it in their pockets." Merchants will lose, taxes for other people in the Community will go up and everyone in the Community will lose.

Only top management like Mr. Powell will gain when they line their pockets with our money at Community expense.

Appendix 5

GENICOM

June 13, 1985
This letter was mailed to all hourly employees on 6/14/85. This copy is for your information.

TO: OUR GENICOM EMPLOYEES AND THEIR FAMILIES

I would like to take this opportunity to express my appreciation for the patience being displayed by the majority of our employees during a very difficult time in which we are negotiating a new labor agreement.

GENICOM and its Management team remain dedicated to the resolution of differences with UE Local 124 and the adoption of a new collective bargaining agreement through the negotiation process. Nevertheless, in reflecting on Local 124's recent newsletter concerning strike preparations, we feel compelled to offer our thoughts on some questions and other appropriate subjects that should be addressed by the Union's lawyer at Sunday's meeting.

QUESTION: Is the Company required to pay wages to strikers during an economic strike?

ANSWER: No, the Company is not required to pay wages to economic strikers.

QUESTION: Is the Company required to pay the premiums to continue health insurance, life insurance and other benefits for strikers during an economic strike?

ANSWER: No, the Company is not required to continue payments for benefits to economic strikers.

QUESTION: Are economic strikers eligible for Virginia unemployment benefits during an economic strike?

ANSWER: No, state law disqualifies employees involved in a "labor dispute."

QUESTION: Is it possible for the UE to guarantee that GENICOM will change its proposals because of strike action?

ANSWER: No, negotiations are a give and take process that may remain unchanged in the face of employee strikes or Company lockouts.

QUESTION: If there is no agreement for a new contract by June 23rd, is the Company required to keep the current contract in effect?

ANSWER: No, at that time the Company may unilaterally implement its final proposal.

QUESTION: Can economic strikers be permanently replaced by new workers if the Company decides to continue operations without them?

ANSWER: Yes, federal law allows a company to continue operations with new employees. The law also does not require the Company to discharge these employees to allow returning strikers to resume their jobs. Replaced strikers who indicate they wish to return to work on the Company's terms may fill open positions if any exist or be placed on a hiring list ahead of non-employees.

Once again let me say we, as GENICOM's Management team, remain dedicated to reaching agreement with UE Local 124 *without* any strike action. However, we are also dedicated to continue the growth of a viable business in Waynesboro. In order to accomplish this, we *must* reduce our cost structure to a level that will allow GENICOM to meet our competition.

Currently, the demand for our printers is poor due to a downturn in the computer market and foreign competition. This market situation, and GENICOM's decision to maintain Waynesboro as our primary production location, demand the changes we have proposed to the UE.

We have furnished wage data on Waynesboro and our national competition to the Union negotiating committee establishing that our proposals are competitive with both Waynesboro and national rates.

Under one proposal, wages would run between $6.00 per hour and $11.50 per hour and benefits would remain at current levels or slightly better. In recognition of the economic impact that such concessions may have, we have offered alternative proposals such as eliminating sick days, night shift differential and afternoon breaks. These reductions would increase the wage proposal to between $6.50 and $12.00 per hour. All other benefits would remain the same or slightly better.

We hope that our employees, their families and their collective bargaining representatives will consider all these factors before taking any action that could be injurious to both the Employees and the Company.

Sincerely,
Curtis W. Powell
President/Chief Executive Officer

GENICOM SEEKS WORKERS; UNION CLAIMS 'A THREAT'

By SERGIO BUSTOS
Staff Writer

WAYNESBORO—Genicom's advertisement in area newspapers seeking immediate applications for production and maintenance workers was seen as "a threat" Monday by a union representative as negotiations between both sides continue toward a June 23 contract deadline.

The company advertised in two newspapers, including The Daily News Reader today, seeking immediate applications for production and maintenance employees "to fill regular, full-time positions . . ."

The company is advertising "an excellent compensation package, including competitive pay rates, beginning at $6.50 per hour, up to $12 per hour . . ." It also offers medical and dental benefits as well as up to three weeks paid vacation.

"We figure it's a threat—a form of intimidation," said George Stevens, the union representative for United Electrical Radio and Machine Workers local 124. He said he was "not surprised" by management's action.

"We are still a long way apart in negotiations," added Stevens, who said Monday's negotiations saw a change in management's position.

"It's still the same basic proposal of a $4 cut in wages and benefits," said Stevens.

Genicom management officials would not comment when reached Monday.

William Freeman, union president, however, said management's latest move would "intimidate workers" and result in their not joining further work stoppages. He added it "was a definite threat" and "was not expected."

"I imagine it (management's action) would work," said Freeman, who said Monday's negotiation session between the two was "terrible."

"I'm amazed that each offer (from management) is worse than the one made before," said Freeman.

Management's action is similar to the action taken by the McQuay division of Snyder General in April when its workers went on strike.

Following six days of striking, however, McQuay union workers agreed to a three-year contract after management threatened to hire non-union workers.

Negotiations between Genicom management and the union began late in April and will continue until June 23, according to Stevens.

A LEADING MANUFACTURER OF ELECTRONIC EQUIPMENT IS SEEKING IMMEDIATE APPLICATIONS

For Production & Maintenance Employees To FNI Regular, Full-Time Positions Including: janitors, assemblers, machine operators, inspectors, testors, stock keepers, drivers, material handlers, painters, machinists, machine repairers, electricians, electronic technicians, and tool & die makers.

The company offers an excellent compensation package including competitive pay rates, beginning at $6.50 per hour, up to $12 per hour (depending upon skill); substantial medical & dental benefits; company paid life & disability programs; eight paid holidays; up to three weeks paid vacations; and a defined benefit pension plan.

INTERESTED, QUALIFIED
CANDIDATES SHOULD APPLY
BY CALLING
(703)949-7553 or (703) 949-7652

Case 18

Applied CAD Knowledge, Inc. (A)

> Something is seriously wrong with this planet. Look at us. I'm working a hundred and twenty hours a week or more, and not catching up. I've got these two friends—both recently divorced, like me—who aren't working at all: they're living off their girl friends, and loving it. One of them is basking in Hawaii. But here I am, busting my ass and giving my customers problems anyhow.
>
> Some guys go on television and say, "Send money now," and people *do.* I ask my best customer to send money, and he goes bankrupt instead. What's wrong with this picture?

Jeff Stevens, president and 90% owner of Applied CAD Knowledge, Inc., was reporting on current sales and production levels to the two business school professors who comprised his Board of Directors. It was late August of 1987, and the three men sat in a booth at Bogie's restaurant. The waitress, Patty, was accustomed to these monthly meetings; she offered another round of Lite beer. "Make mine cyanide," said Stevens. "On the rocks, please."

Applied CAD, a small service bureau which designed electronic circuit boards, was experiencing the highest sales levels in its three-year history. June sales had reached $50,000—leaving a backlog of $90,000; July shipments had set a record at $58,000; August would be nearly as high. The problem facing Stevens through the summer of 1987 was a shortage of good designers to work as part-time freelancers. The surge in business saw Stevens sitting at the computer consoles himself, doing design work on second and third shifts, six or seven days a week. After eight weeks of this schedule, the strain was showing. One director asked about the longer-range sales picture, and Stevens summed it up:

> Can I borrow a .45 automatic? I'd like a good game of Russian Roulette.
>
> There's nothing on the books at all for late Fall, and not much likely. Every major customer we have is in "busy phase" right now. When these designs are finished, it will be another four to six months before their next generation of product revisions. In the meantime, everybody is burned out. All I'm hoping for right now is a front porch, a rocking chair, a lobotomy and a drool cup.

The Electronics Industry and Circuit Board Design

The United States electronics industry in 1987 was a sprawling giant, some of whose sectors were growing while others remained in a protracted slump. In 1986, total industry size was estimated by *Electronic Business* magazine (December 10, 1985) as $100.5 billion to $182 billion. The same article projected industry revenues for 1995 to be $295.4 billion to $512 billion. The magazine concluded that its industry represented a major driving force for the American economy. The Value Line investment service reports separately on four segments of the electronics industry (see Exhibit 1).

This case was prepared by John A. Seeger, Bentley College, and Raymond M. Kinnunen, Northeastern University, as a basis for class discussion. Distributed by the North American Case Research Association. The case has accompanying videotapes featuring Jeff Stevens, president and owner of Applied CAD Knowledge, Inc., in a question and answer session with an Executive MBA class that can be purchased from Northeastern University, Boston, MA 02115.

Exhibit 1 Electronics Industry Revenues (in $ Billions)

Industry Sector	Number of Companies	1982	1983	1984	1985	1986	(est.) 1987
Electronics	35	16.4	17.7	21.6	21.2	22.0	24.0
U.S. Semiconductors	14	11.4	13.0	17.2	15.6	16.0	17.8
Computers/Peripherals	34	78.6	88.4	104.4	110.5	115.0	127.5
Electrical Equipment	25	50.9	51.2	54.9	56.5	64.7	72.0

Source: *Value Line,* May 8, 1987

Printed Circuit Boards

A basic part of nearly every electronic product—whichever segment of the industry produced or used it—was the printed circuit board to which a variety of electronic components were attached. These components ranged from old-fashioned resistors, capacitors and vacuum tubes to transistors and the most modern integrated circuit chips. All components needed some sort of platform to sit on, and some way to make connection with the other components of the circuit.

In the 1930s and '40s, circuit boards were made from thin, non-conducting fiberboard with metal pins and sockets attached. Assembly operators wound the wire leads of the circuit's resistors, capacitors, etc. around the proper pins and soldered them in place. By the 1960s, the technology of wiring boards and assembling components had advanced to a highly-automated stage. Numerically controlled machines positioned components and connected pins to one another with wires. During this decade, electronic components became increasingly miniaturized and more reliable, complex and powerful. With these technological developments, the "printed circuit board" (PCB) was developed; its use and technical sophistication accelerated rapidly.

In a printed circuit, the wires leading from one pin to another are replaced by electrically conductive lines "printed" or plated onto (or under) the surface of the board itself. The pins themselves are gone; wire leads from electrical components are inserted through small holes in the board and soldered on the underside. By the 1980s, components could be mounted directly on the board's surface, in contact with the printed "wires."

The increasing complexity of electronic circuits presents a problem for PCB technology. When connections were made with wires, assemblers simply attached one end, routed the wire over the top of everything between the two pins involved, and attached the other end where it belonged. With printed circuits, however, designers are constrained to two dimensions on a flat board; they must route the line between two pins without touching any other lines, and they cannot go "over the top" without leaving the surface of the board. Furthermore, efficient design calls for the components to be tightly packed together, grouped by function. Designers frequently find situations where they cannot lay out a trace from one point to another without interfering with other traces.

"Multilayer" PCBs ease this problem by providing "upstairs" layers on the board, allowing the designer to go over the top. Multilayer boards contain at least three layers of traces, and sometimes more than twenty layers. Skilled designers seek to minimize the number of layers required for a given circuit, in order to reduce manufacturing costs of the board: multilayer PCBs are far more expensive to manufacture. In 1983, multilayer boards had sales of $900 million, or 26% of the PCB market. By 1993, they were forecast to reach sales of $5.6 billion, or 41% market share. Exhibit 2 shows PCB sales and projections by type of board.

Exhibit 2 Sales and Projections for PCBs by Type of Board

	1983			1993	
PCB Type	**Sales in $ Millions**	**Market Share**	**Annual Growth Rate**	**Sales in $ Millions**	**Market Share**
Multilevel	900	26%	20%	$5,600	41%
Double-sided	2,000		13%	6,700	
Flexible	353		10%	916	
Single-sided	307	8.8%	4%	454	3.3%
	$3,560	100%		$13,670	100%

*Source: *Electronic Business,* Feb. 1, 1985, p. 87.

Board design was made more complicated by increasing density of components, by sensitivity of components to heat (some threw off large amounts of heat, while others would go haywire if their operating temperature was disturbed), and by radio-frequency interference (some components generated static, while others might "hear" the noise and try to process it). The layout of components on the board had tremendous impact on how well the finished product worked, as well as on its manufacturing cost.

Printed circuit boards offered many technical advantages over the previous method for fashioning circuits:

1) *Greater Miniaturization:* PCBs can be highly miniaturized, allowing progressively more powerful and complex electronic circuits for smaller, lighter products;

2) *Improved Performance:* Product reliability is much greater than in pin-to-pin circuitry, permitting applications in extreme environmental conditions;

3) *Manufacturing advantages:* For high volume products, manufacturing costs are greatly reduced. PCB applications range from simple consumer products to the most powerful mainframe computers.

4) *Maintenance advantages:* PCBs allowed designers to "package" electronic systems into discrete modules which, if not functioning properly, could be replaced without the immediate need of determining where the problem was within the board.

Frost and Sullivan, Inc., a New York market research firm, estimated (in "The Printed Circuit Board Market in the U.S.," July, 1986, quoted by permission) that total U.S. PCB market reached $3.7 billion in sales in 1985, a decrease of 12 per cent from 1984's production. PCBs were projected to grow to a likely $6.5 billion by 1990 and to $10.8 billion in 1995. Multi-layer PCBs were expected to be the fastest-growing type, averaging 15.7 per cent per year annual growth. A little over half the market was served in 1985 by independent PCB makers, as opposed to captive suppliers, Frost & Sullivan said.

Trends in Circuit Board Design Equipment

Originally (and still, for simple circuits), an engineer or technician worked from a "schematic" drawing of the circuit, which showed how the various components were connected. On a large layout table, the PCB designer manually drew in the components and linked them with black tape (or ink), to produce a "photo master" film which was in turn used to project the design photographically onto the base material of the circuit board. As circuits became more complex, the manual process bogged down.

As boards became more complex, specialized computer hardware and software began to help designers and engineers solve complex design problems. By the mid 1970s, system vendors began to offer CAD systems specifically developed for PCB designing. Racal-Redac, Inc., a British firm, was the first to offer a powerful special-purpose PCB-oriented system. Based on Digital Equipment Corp.'s PDP-11 computer, the Redac product was the first to permit PCB designers to interact with the computer, trying various routings of traces and seeing how they looked on the graphic display. This approach competed well against established systems such as Computervision, whose general-purpose equipment was priced in the $500,000 class and still lacked the interactive design capability.

By 1982, prices for PCB design systems had fallen below $100,000. New CAD equipment makers entered the field, with automated routing or documentation features which carried substantial advantages over the established Redac software. Calay and Cadnetix, as examples, introduced strong entries—neither being compatible with the Redac or Sci-Cards equipment already in the field. Racal-Redac Ltd., however, had perhaps taken the greatest strides to tailor its software to run on a variety of hardware platforms. Said Ian Orrock, chief executive of Redac's electronics CAD division in England, "We're all going to end up being software houses."

Another important feature of the new CAD equipment was ease of use; the older CAD/CAM systems might require months of learning time before a designer became proficient. In the late 70s, with high equipment costs and low availability of trained designers, only the largest electronics firms designed and produced their own PCBs. Service bureaus took advantage of the market opportunity, acting as the primary design resource for smaller clients and as peak load designers for firms with in-house capacity. As electronics firms purchased and began to use the newer systems, however, they wanted service bureaus to be equipped with similar or compatible machines. Service bureaus felt the pressure to acquire the most up-to-date hardware and software available, in order to qualify as bidders on that work.

Service Bureau Operations

When a service bureau invested in CAD equipment, the sheer size of the investment created pressure to use the equipment intensively. Multi-shift operations were common, but the supply of designers to man them was severely limited. Typically, a service bureau did not hire permanent staff for all three shifts: the work load was too unpredictable. Service bureaus generally hired moonlighting designers from established electronics firms to staff their second and third shifts.

Printed circuit board design requires a peculiar combination of skills, primarily in spatial geometry, circuit insight, memory, and persistence. A talented designer—perhaps capable of completing a complex design in three weeks of console time—might be several times more productive than a "journeyman". In the early 1980s, talented designers willing to work odd shifts were earning over $100,000 per year; few of them had college educations.

Most customers requested separate quotations for each board; often, customers asked for bids from several service bureaus. Design clients always ran on tight schedules, Jeff Stevens observed, wanting their work to be delivered "yesterday":

> Circuit board design is usually one of the last steps before a new product goes into production. Our design time is the customer's time-to-market. It's natural for them to be in a hurry.

For the design of a large, complex, 4-layered PCB a client might pay between $10,000 to $15,000. Such a project might require 5–6 man weeks of labor input (two thirds of which might be designer's time); it might involve extensive communication between Applied CAD and a wide variety of the client's technical personnel, and it would often require Applied CAD personnel to work through the night at various project stages to make deadlines. In such a typical project, much of Applied CAD's time would be spent sorting out and coordinating conflicting information and directions from different technical people in the client company. Stevens noted,

> "Even our clients themselves won't always know completely what they want. When we take their directions to their logical conclusions, problems often occur. Then we have to show them what developed. You spend a lot of time on the phone with clients, sometimes at 3 a.m. Often, I wind up making decisions for the client, so the work can go ahead; later, I have to convince the client the decision was right."

Design reliability remained a key attribute of a service bureau's reputation, since whole product lines (or engineers' jobs) might depend on the PCB design's working properly, and on its prompt delivery:

> We had one job, in the old days, where a satellite was literally sitting on the launch pad, waiting for a corrected module design. The engineers had discovered a design flaw. They flew into town with the specs, and then took turns sitting behind the designer at the scope, or sitting beside their hotel room telephone, waiting to answer any questions that might come up. In this business, you have to deliver.

When the design phase of a job was finished, the computer tape or disk would be carried to a second service bureau for creation of the film photoplots needed for manufacturing. The equipment for photoplotting was far more complex and expensive than the computer systems needed for design. Only a few design shops in the New England area had their own photoplotting capability; they performed this work for other service bureaus and in-house design departments as well as for their own design clients.

The actual production of PCBs might be done by the client company itself or by a fabrication shop which specialized in the work. The New England area was home to some 80 to 100 fab shops, many of which offered design as well as manufacturing services. A few large firms (Hadco at $125 million in sales) were equipped to service very large orders—100,000 or more boards of a design—but most fab shops fell in the $1 to $2 million size range, with an average order size of 25 to 30 relatively small boards. One shop estimated its average PCB was priced at $22 each, with a setup charge of $150.

Trends in PCB Design

By the end of 1986, a number of vendors had developed PCB design packages to run on personal computers—primarily the IBM XT or AT machines. These software systems, some including automatic routing, were priced as low as a few hundred dollars or as high as $13,000, and varied widely in their features and capabilities. In-house design capability became practical for most electronics firms, although many lacked the PCB expertise that still marked the better service bureaus. Freelance designers, too, could acquire their own equipment. Exhibit 3 compares the features and prices of 24 such software packages.

Clients were inclined to stay with their existing service bureaus, unless they were severely burned. Good relationships between service staff and engineering personnel helped minimize communication errors, and availability of the data base from the original job allowed for revisions or modifications at much lower cost.

In the 1980s, as the cost of entering the service bureau business dropped, many new firms appeared. Jeff Stevens observed, "When I started at Redac in 1978, there were three service bureaus in New England. By 1983 there were maybe a dozen. Now there might be seventy-five, and it could reach 100 in another year." In 1987, several competing service bureaus in the area were owned by former employees of Recal-Redac, where Jeff himself had learned the business. Exhibit 4 lists the major competitors in the Northeastern United States in 1986.

Exhibit 3 Low Cost PC Board Design Software Available, Spring, 1987

Representative Low-Cost PC-Board Layout Packages

Company	Product	Base Price	Required Hardware	Operating System	Auto-Router	Auto-Router Price
ABACUS SOFTWARE	PC BOARD DESIGNER	$195	ATARI 520ST OR 1040ST	GEM	•	
ACCEL TECHNOLOGIES	TANGO-PCS	$495	IBM PC/XT OR PC/AT	MS-DOS	•	
APTOS SYSTEMS	CRITERION II	$4,000	ARTIST 1 CARD AND IBM PC/XT OR PC/AT	MS-DOS	•	$5,000
AUTOMATED IMAGES	PERSONAL 870	$8,000	IBM PC/XT OR PC/AT	MS-DOS		
B&C MICROSYSTEMS	PCB/DE	$395	IBM PC/XT OR PC/AT	MS-DOS (AND THE AUTOCAD DRAFTING PACKAGE)		
CAD SOFTWARE	PADS-PCB	$975	IBM PC/XT OR PC/AT	MS-DOS	•	$750
CASE TECHNOLOGY	VANGUARD PCB	$4,250	IBM PC/AT, SUN-3, OR DEC MICROVAX	MS-DOS, UNIX, OR VMS	•	$5,500
DAISY SYSTEMS	PERSONAL BOARDMASTER	$8,000	IBM PC/AT OR DAISY PL386	DNIX		
DASOFT DESIGN	PROJECT: PCB	$950	IBM PC/XT OR PC/AT	MS-DOS	•	
DESIGN COMPUTATION	DRAFTSMAN-EE	$1,147	IBM PC/XT OR PC/AT	MS-DOS	•	$2,450
DOUGLAS ELECTRONICS	DOUGLAS CAD/CAM	$395	APPLE MACINTOSH	MACINTOSH		
ELECTRONIC DESIGN TOOLS	PROCAD	$2,495	IBM PC/XT OR PC/AT AND 68000 COPROCESSOR	MS-DOS	•	$2,495

ELECTRONIC INDUSTRIAL EQUIPMENT	EXECUTIVE CAD	$11,000	IBM PC/XT OR PC/AT	MS-DOS	•	
FUTURENET	DASH-PCB	$13,000	IBM PC/AT AND 32032 COPROCESSOR	UNIX	•	
HEWLETT-PACKARD	EGS	$7,000	HP 9000	HP-UX		
KONTRON	KAD-286	$10,400	IBM PC/AT	MS-DOS		
PERSONAL CAD SYSTEMS	PCB-1	$6,000	IBM PC/XT OR PC/AT	MS-DOS	•	$6,000
RACAL-REDAC	REDBOARD	$12,000	IBM PC/XT OR PC/AT	MS-DOS	•	
SEETRAX (IN US, CIRCUITS AND SYSTEMS)	RANGER	$5,000	IBM PC/AT	MS-DOS	•	$2,000
SOFTCIRCUITS	PCLOPLUS	$1,024	COMMODORE AMIGA 1000	AMIGADOS	•	
VAMP	McCAD	$395	APPLE MACINTOSH	MACINTOSH	•	$995
VISIONICS	EE DESIGNER II	$1,875	IBM PC/XT OR PC/AT	MS-DOS	•	$1,475
WINTEK	SMARTWORK	$895	IBM PC/XT OR PC/AT	MS-DOS	•	
ZIEGLER INSTRUMENTS (IN US, CADDY)	CADDY ELECTRONIC SYSTEM	$2,495	IBM PC/XT OR PC/AT	MS-DOS	•	$2,500

(continued)

Exhibit 3 *(continued)*

Representative Low-Cost PC-Board Layout Packages

Auto Replacement	Compatible Net Lists	Maximum Number of Colors	Maximum Number of Traces	Maximum Number of Components	Maximum Number of Layers	Packaging Technologies
		2	1100 LINES	250	2	
	ACCEL, OMATION, ORCAD	16	26,000 LINES	1000	9	SMD
•	APTOS,FUTURENET, P-CAD	16	2000 NETS	1000	50	SMD, ECL, ANALOG
	APPLICON, FUTURENET, ORCAD	16			16	SMD, HYBRID
	B&C	16				
•	FUTURENET	16	4511 NETS	764	30	SMD, FINE-LINE
•	CASE	16	2000 NETS	1000	256	SMD
	DAISY	7	14,000 LINES	14,000	255	SMD
	DASOFT	6			4	SMD
•		16	4000 NETS	300	20	FINE-LINE
		2				SMD, ANALOG
•	ELECTRONIC DESIGN TOOLS	16	10,000 NETS	3000	56	SMD, CONSTANT-IMPEDANCE
•	ELECTRONIC INDUSTRIAL EQUIPMENT	16			4	SMD, ECL
	FUTURENET	4			10	FINE-LINE
	HP	15			255	HYBRID
	KONTRON	64	5300 LINES	3200	255	ECL, SMD, HYBRID
•	P-CAD, FUTURENET	16	1000 NETS	300	50	SMD
•	RACAL-REDAC	16	1900 NETS	511	16	SMD
•	SEETRAX	16	10,000 LINES	1400	16	SMD
		16				
•	VAMP	2	32,000 LINES	32,000	6	SMD, METRIC
•		16		999	26	SMD
	WINTEK	3			6	
	ZIEGLER	16			128	ANALOG

Source: *EDN*, March 18, 1987, pp 140–141. Used by permission.

Exhibit 4 PC Design Service Bureaus in New England

Design Houses by Sales Volume 0–1 Million Dollars/Year

Name	Page
Abington Labs.	1
Berkshire Design	14
Cad Tec	17
Cadtronix, Ltd.	19
Computer Aided Circuits, Inc.	21
Dataline PCB Corp.	24
Design Services	25
Energraphics	27
Graphics Technology Corp.	29
Herbertons, Inc.	30
Het Printed Circuit Design	31
High Tech Cad Service Co.	33
Jette Fabrication	35
LSI Engineering	37
P C Design Company	40
Pac-Lab, Inc.	41
Packaging for Electronics	42
PC Design Services	43
Point Design, Inc.	46
Power Processing, Inc.	47
Product Development Co.	48
Qualitron Corp.	49
Quality Circuit Design, Inc.	51
Research Labs, Inc.	53
Scientific Calculations, Inc.	54
Tracor Electro-Assembly Inc.	60
Winter Design	63

Design Houses by Sales Volume 1–2 Million Dollars/Year

Name	Page
Automated Images, Inc.	13
Automated Design, Inc.	11
CAD Services, Inc.	16
Antal Associates	7
Multiwire of New England	38
Teccon	57
Tech Systems & Design	58
Kenex, Inc.	36
Alternate Circuit Design Technology	5
Photofabrication Technology, Inc.	44

Design Houses by Sales Volume 2–5 Million Dollars/Year

Name	Page
Tek-Art Associates	59
Strato Reprographix	55
Altek Co.	3
Eastern Electronics Mfg. Corp.	26
Datacube, Inc.	23
Owl Electronic Laboratories, Inc.	39

Design Houses by Sales Volume 5–10 Million Dollars/Year

Name	Page
Triad Engineering Co.	62
Photronic Labs, Inc.	45

Design Houses by Sales Volume 10 + Million Dollars/Year

Name	Page
Algorex Corp.	2
ASI Automated Systems, Inc.	9
Augat Interconnection Systems Group	10
Racal-Redac Service Bureau	52
Synermation, Inc.	56

Source: Beacon Technology, "New England Printed Circuit Directory."

For the longer run, some industry analysts speculated that constant advances in miniaturizing electronic circuits might permit semiconductor technology to reduce certain whole PCBs (such as those developed for computer memory) into a single IC chip.

Applied CAD Knowledge, Inc.: History

Jeff Stevens had learned the rudiments of circuit board design in his first job after high school graduation, as a technician in a five-person product development laboratory. Here, in 1975, one of his duties was to prepare enlarged prints of circuits, using black tape on white mylar. In another, concurrent job as a technician in an electronics manufacturing firm, he learned how the circuits themselves worked.

In 1977, Stevens left his two technician jobs for an entry-level design position with Racal-Redac in Littleton, Massachusetts. Redac operated a service bureau to complement its sales of DEC hardware and British software. As a pioneer in the field, Redac at the time boasted a near-monopoly in powerful systems dedicated to PCB design. Jeff Stevens, in a training rotation, joined Redac's service bureau as a data-entry technician.

> We had three computer systems—about 20 people altogether. A system then cost about $200,000 and a lot of companies didn't have enough design work to justify buying one.
>
> In data entry, you prepare code to represent all the terminals and components on the board. I refused to code the first job they gave me, and nearly got fired. Finally I convinced them that the job *shouldn't* be coded: the turkey who engineered it had the diodes in backward, and the circuit wasn't going to work. About a week later, they put me in charge of data entry, supervising the guy who had wanted to fire me.

Stevens became a designer, then a lead designer, then operations manager of the service bureau. Under his leadership, the operation dramatically improved its reputation for quality and on-time delivery, as well as its financial performance:

> When I took over in October of 1981, monthly sales were $50,000 and monthly expenses were $110,000. In six months we turned it around: monthly sales were $110,000 and expenses were $50,000. There had been a tremendous amount of dead wood. We had a big bonfire with it, and went from 26 people to 16. In some ways, it was a brutal campaign, I guess.

In June 1983, Stevens left Recal-Redac to work as a consulting designer, helping electronics firms with their CAD decisions as well as doing freelance design work. He had developed design and management expertise and established a reputation in industry circles which he could now broker directly to clients who were familiar with his previous work.

In December 1983, Jeff established Applied CAD while still working from his home in Pepperell, Massachusetts. By purchasing used computer equipment and installing it himself in his living room, Stevens was able to hold his initial investment to $35 thousand; the largest cost element was $28,000 for the software purchased from his former employer. (Financial data on Applied CAD's latest three years of operation are shown in Exhibit 5.)

> The equipment pretty well filled up the living room, and through the summer I couldn't run it during the daytime: we didn't have enough electricity to cool it down. Winter solved that problem, though; I heated the house with a PDP-11.

In late 1984, Applied CAD leased a 1,000 square foot office suite on the ground floor of a new building near the Merrimack River in Tyngsboro, Mass. Jeff Stevens designed the interior space to hold a central computer room (with special air conditioning), a darkened "console room" for the actual design work, and a large front office. By January of 1985, the computing equipment was installed and operating. The console room was furnished with two Recaro ergonometric chairs (at $1,100 each) for the design-

Exhibit 5 Financial Statements of Applied CAD Knowledge, Inc.

Balance Sheet

	1985	1986	1987
Assets			
Current assets:			
Cash	$128,568	$ 14,148	$ 33,074
Accounts receivable, trade	18,865	15,375	14,250
Prepaid taxes and other current assets	4,853	1,200	5,074
Total current assets	152,286	30,723	52,398
Property and equipment	174,079	190,079	203,079
Less accumulated depreciation	48,697	86,357	124,062
Total Property and Equipment	125,382	103,722	79,017
Total Assets	$277,668	$134,445	$131,415
Liabilities and Stockholder's Equity			
Current liabilities:			
Accounts payable, trade	$127,685	$ 9,025	$ 21,823
Current maturities of long-term debt	13,300		
Income taxes payable	4,008		2,303
Other current liabilities	5,000	5,373	70
Total current liabilities	149,993	14,398	24,196
Long-term debt, less current maturities	41,121	83,247	53,663
Stockholder's equity:			
Common stock, no par value; authorized 15,000 shares, issued and outstanding 1,000 shares	25,000	25,000	25,000
Retained earnings	61,554	11,800	28,556
Total stockholder's equity	86,554	36,800	53,556
Total Liabilities and Stockholder's Equity	$277,668	$134,445	$131,415
Statement of Income and Retained Earnings			
Net Revenues	$328,262	$232,540	$346,627
Cost of revenue:			
Salaries, wages and outside services	134,686	116,835	209,998
Research and development	14,154	7,551	13,731
Software costs	65,131	18,864	
Total cost of revenue	$213,971	$143,250	$223,729
Gross profit	114,291	89,290	122,898
Selling, general and administrative expenses	72,320	143,051	77,732
Operating profit	41,971	(53,761)	45,166
Bad Debt Expense			(28,660)
Interest income (expense), net	2,331	3,176	(10,103)
Income before income taxes	44,302	(50,185)	6,403
Income taxes	4,508	0	0
Net income	39,794	(50,185)	6,403
Retained earnings, beginning of year	21,760	62,385	22,154
Retained earnings, end of year	$ 61,554	$ 11,800	$28,557

ers' use; the front office held a large receptionist's desk and a sparse collection of work tables, file cabinets and spare hardware.

Applied CAD's Organization

Jeff oversaw all operations in his company, did all the high level marketing/sales contact work with clients, and did much of the technical design work as well. Another full-time designer was hired in May of 1985 but had to be terminated in September of 1986 due to persistent personal problems. Steve Jones, Jeff's data manager and former assistant at Redac, became a full time employee in January, 1986. Among other duties, Steve covered the telephone, coordinated technical work done by freelance contractors in Jeff's absence, and performed various administrative duties. Steve had a B.S. in Engineering and, before Redac, had worked for other PCB electronics companies. In April of 1987 Jeff hired John Macnamara, a former subcontract designer, on a full-time salaried basis.

In May of 1987 Jeff also hired a part time person to keep the books, write checks, and handle other office related matters. For her first three months she focused on straightening out the books and tax related items. She was also trying to find time to set up an accounting package on the personal computer. The package had been purchased in August of 1986 (at the request of Board members), for the purpose of generating accurate monthly statements. Since the company's founding, the Board had been asking for accurate end-of-month data on sales, accounts receivable, cash balance, backlog and accounts payable. They also wanted monthly financial statements, although Stevens himself saw little point in them: cash flow projections served his immediate needs. The accounting package was chosen by one of the Board members, based partly on its broad capabilities. For example, it could assist in invoicing and aging receivables.

Jeff had other capable designers "on call"—available for freelance project work when the company needed them. Depending upon the market, there were time periods when Jeff could obtain the services of several contractors to meet peak work loads. In general, design contractors worked on a negotiated fixed-fee basis for completing a specific portion of a design project. In July of 1987, however, (after sales in June reached approximately $50 thousand and the backlog reached $90 thousand) Jeff found it difficult to attract contract designers with free time. The backlog consisted of about 15 boards ranging in price from $800 to $15,000. The electronics industry had turned upward and in busy times everyone was busy. Consequently, free-lance designers were committed to their own customers or employers who were also busy.

Jeff's Board of Directors consisted of Jeff and two college professors at well-known institutions in the Boston area. Since the Fall of 1985 the Board had met monthly for 3 to 4 hours, usually during the first week of the month. At most meetings the Board first discussed the previous month's sales and current levels of cash, accounts receivable, backlog and payables. Other typical agenda items ranged from the purchase of new equipment and/or software, to marketing, to personnel problems.

At most meetings, the Board spent considerable time discussing the current business climate and the future sales outlook. This usually led to a discussion of hiring someone to take over the marketing and sales function. It was generally agreed that such a person could not only contribute to the company's growth in sales but also free up a considerable amount of Jeff's time that could be devoted to design and operational matters. When Applied CAD was busy, however, Jeff had very little time to devote to finding, hiring, and working with such a person. When the firm was not busy, Jeff's concern over the reliability of future cash flows made him hesitant to make the major salary commitment that a marketing professional would require. He was aware of the contrary pressures: "I can't get out of the 'boom-splat' syndrome," he said.

To Jeff, the "splat" came when backlogs and cash balances fell. The winter of 1987, for example, had felt to him like hitting a wall. (Exhibit 6 shows monthly totals of sales, accounts receivable, backlogs and cash balances, as estimated by Jeff at monthly Board meetings.)

Hardware and Software

After moving into his new quarters, Jeff Stevens located another PDP-11/34 computer—this one for sale at $7,000. Adding it to his shop required purchase of another Redac software package, but the added capacity was needed. Other, competing CAD systems were now available, but the decision to stick with Redac seemed straightforward to Jeff:

> Recal-Redac systems had several advantages. They were specifically dedicated to PCB design work and they had software that was brutally efficient. They were familiar to most of the freelance designers in the area. Wide acceptance of Redac's software makes it easier to get overflow work from companies who demanded compatibility with their own equipment. Not to mention that I know this gear backward and forward, and could keep several machines busy at once.

The Redac software was originally developed in 1972, which made it very old by industry standards. Jeff pointed out, however, that because machines were slower in 1972 and had much less memory, their software *had* to be extremely efficient. Having used this software for a long time, he said, "I've been able to make process modifications to improve its efficiency, and I know all its intricacies." Jeff had developed some proprietary software for PCB design work which he believed kept him at the cutting edge of the competition. At times, he wondered about the possibilities of licensing his proprietary software to other PCB design firms. He concluded, however, that the small market for this type of software product would probably not justify the necessary marketing and additional product development costs.

Exhibit 6 Monthly Sales and Month-End Receivables, Backlogs, Cash Levels (All in $000's)

	A/R	Sales	Backlog	Cash
January 1986	18	20	20	$98
February	—	10	—	N/A
March	18	10	12	62
April	18	10	20	28
May	24	20	26	26
June	—	10	—	N/A
July	14	25	—	18
August	70	50	30	15
September	90	40	—	8
October	50	30	—	26
November	19	5	10	17
December	24	10	18	14
January 1987	13	3	—	7
February	40	21	—	8
March	35	28	22	6
April	32	22	37	11
May	25	22	50	5
June	50	50	90	10
July	90	58	30	10

In addition to the original equipment purchased by Jeff in 1983 the company purchased a VAX Model 11/751 and a Calay Version 03 in December of 1985 at a cost of approximately $170,000. (See Exhibit 6 for the cash flow statements prepared for the Bank to obtain a loan). The VAX was intended to be used as a communications and networking device and as a platform for developing new software. The Calay was a dedicated hardware system that included an automatic router which could completely design certain less complex boards without an operator. On more complex boards it could complete a major percentage of the board, leaving a designer to do the remainder. In September of 1986 a software upgrade to Calay Version 04 was purchased at a cost of approximately $28,000. Although bank financing was available, Jeff decided to pay cash for this equipment, to avoid raising his monthly fixed expenses. The new purchases gave Applied CAD enough machine capacity to support some $2 million in annual sales.

When the Calay machine was purchased Jeff and the Board felt that its automatic routing capability might open a new market for the company for less complex boards. Since the Calay was virtually automatic on certain applications the final price of these boards could be much less than if they were done by hand. Because of the lower price to the customer the Calay was also appropriate for designing boards that would be produced in smaller quantities. Finally, Jeff and the Board felt that the manufacturer of the Calay as well as the Calay user group would supply new customer leads. Some of these expectations had been met.

The VAX, however, was not being fully used as originally intended—to allow hands-off automation of the firm's varied pieces of computing equipment, as well as providing batch data processing capacity. In its ultimate form, the VAX might actually operate the older, more cumbersome systems. It would be able to juggle dozens of design tasks between work stations and autorouters, queueing and evaluating each job and calling for human intervention when needed. One director, visualizing robots sitting in Applied CAD's Recaro chairs, called this the "Robo-Router plan." To carry it out would require an additional investment of approximately $15,000 in hardware and another $10 to $20 thousand in programming, along with a significant amount of Jeff's time. The investment would result in very substantial cost reductions and reduced dependence on freelance designers, but it would only pay for itself under high volume conditions.

Current Business Options

In August of 1987 Jeff was contemplating the current business climate, his accomplishments with Applied CAD over the past 3 years, and where the company was headed. His major objective, agreed with the Board, was growth. Jeff had discussed many times with his Board the need for a marketing person and a promotional brochure for the company. On occasion, he had talked with marketing people about Applied CAD's needs, but most of these prospective employees lacked the level of skills and PCB experience Jeff hoped to acquire. He had also talked with commercial artists about design of a brochure. Jeff and his Board felt that a "first class" brochure would cost between $5 and $10 thousand.

Marketing in the PCB business, especially among companies with sales of under $1 million, was characterized as informal. Very few companies had full-time people devoted to the marketing task; in most cases it was the owner-president who handled marketing and sales. Most small companies had their own list of faithful customers and new customers tended to come by word of mouth. In the under $1 million segment it was not uncommon for a company when extremely overloaded with work to farm out a board to a competitor. Also, certain other services, such as photoplotting, were done by shops that also did design work. Consequently, there was considerable communication among the competitors; the players seemed to know who got what jobs.

The marketing job at a company like Applied CAD consisted mainly of coordinating the advertising and a sales brochure, calling on present customers, and attempting to find new customers. Such a person needed a working knowledge of PCB design which required experience in the industry. People with the qualifications necessary normally made a $40–50,000 base salary plus commissions; frequently their total compensation exceeded $100,000 per year. Of major concern to Jeff was Applied CAD's erratic history of sales and cash balances, and the difficulty of predicting sales volume any further than 2 months in advance (see Exhibit 7). He balked at taking on responsibility for an executive-level

Exhibit 7 Applied CAD Knowledge, Inc. Cash Flow Projections as of December 16, 1985

	Dec 1985	Jan 1986	Feb 1986	March 1986	April 1986	May 1986	June 1986	July 1986	Aug 1986	Sept 1986	Oct 1986	Nov 1986	Dec 1986	Total $(000s)
Sales	25	30	30	30	30	30	30	30	30	30	30	30	30	360
Expenses[6]	20	24	29.5	29.5	29.5	29.5	29.5	29.5	29.5	29.5	29.5	29.5	29.5	348.5
Profit	5	6	.5	.5	.5	.5	.5	.5	.5	.5	.5	.5	.5	11.5
Opening Cash	141	148	102	102.5	88	88.5	89	89.5	90	90.5	91	91	91.5	
Receivables	37	17	30	30	30	30	30	30	30	30	30	30	30	
Disbursements[5]	30	24[1]	29.5[3]	29.5	29.5	29.5	29.5	29.5	29.5	29.5	29.5	29.5	29.5	
Taxes[4]		29[2]		15										
Closing Cash	148	102	102.5	88	88.5	89	89.5	90	90.5	91	91	91.5	92	

1. Includes loan payment of 4K/mth
2. 25% of equipment costing 156K
3. Includes new employees at 66K/yr
4. Taxes based on the following assumptions: 1985 Profit of 150K; 50K software expense on new equipment; 20K depreciation on new equipment; 10K misc. expenses; Investment tax credit of 15K
5. Figures do not include depreciation which would only influence total profit
6. Expenses include rent, heat, light, power, salaries, contract work, telephone, etc. This level of expenses will support sales double those projected.

salary, lacking confidence in the future. "This would probably be somebody with kids to feed or send to college," Jeff said. "How could I pay them, in slow times?"

Still, marketing appeared to be the function most critical to achieving the growth rates Jeff Stevens and his Board hoped for. It was key, also, in meeting the major potential threat posed by the recent availability of inexpensive software which could enable personal computers to design printed circuit boards (see Exhibit 3). Jeff had heard that some of that software could perform almost as well as the more expensive equipment that was being used by Applied CAD. He wondered how the advent of PC-based design might be viewed as an opportunity, not a threat.

Four possible responses had occurred to Jeff and his people: Applied CAD could ignore the PC software, adopt it, distribute it, or sell its own software to the PC users. Ignoring the new technology might work in the short run, since the complex boards designed by Applied CAD would not be the first affected; in the long run, however, failure to keep up with technology would leave more and more jobs subject to low-cost competition.

By adopting the new software for his next equipment expansion, Applied CAD could take a proactive stance. Jeff could buy a system or two to see how good they were, and hire people to work on the new systems on a freelance basis. Of course, he would need a flow of jobs to experiment with. A variation of this alternative was to sit back and wait while ready to move quickly if he saw something developing.

A third alternative, acting as a distributor for the PC software, would give Applied CAD a product to sell to prospects who insisted on doing their own design. This could establish relationships with people who might later need overload capacity.

Fourth, Applied CAD could proceed with development of its proprietary software, creating a product to sell to PC users. Jeff estimated that his Automated Design Review System could save both time and grief for other designers. In some tasks, it could cut the required design time in half. In all jobs, the capability to check the finished design against the original input automatically and completely could improve quality. ADRS already existed in rough form; it was one of the elements which would make up the "Robo-Router" system, if that were implemented.

Many of these options seemed to require significant marketing skills—strengths, where the company was presently weak. The technical questions could be answered, if Jeff had the time to work on them. But the marketing questions called for a person with extensive industry experience, broad contacts, a creative imagination, and the ability to make things happen.

Amid all the other problems facing the owner of a small business, Jeff was trying to figure out how to shape his business for the long-range future, and how to attract the kind of person he could work with to assure growth—and survival.

Case 19

Applied CAD Knowledge, Inc. (B)

In September of 1987, as the summer rush slowed, Jeff Stevens began to talk seriously with Jerry King, Regional Sales Manager of Calay Systems, Inc., about the marketing problems of Applied CAD Knowledge, Inc. Stevens wanted someone to become in effect a co-owner and officer of the small firm. King had been a principal in his own service bureau in the very early days of automated PCB design, and retained friendships and contacts with high level personnel in many electronics firms. (Exhibit 1 shows King's resume.)

After a month of conversations and negotiations, including a meeting with the Board of Directors, the two men reached tentative agreement on employment terms which would give King a 3% commission on all company sales, a car allowance, and a base salary of $40,000 per year. Since the marketing person would be influential in pricing many jobs, it was important to preserve his regard for profitability; King was offered a stock interest in Applied CAD, contingent on the bottom line at the end of 1988. With a handshake of agreement, Stevens set out to reduce the terms to an employment contract letter.

The following night, Jerry King called Stevens to express his regret that he would be unable to accept the Marketing VP position, after all: he had just received an offer from AT&T, to set up Australian operations for a new venture. It was simply too good an offer to refuse, King said. A dejected Jeff Stevens reported the development at the next Board meeting; "We're back to square one," he said. "And the next 'splat' is just about to arrive."

Applied CAD's monthly sales dropped to half their mid-1987 level, and the backlog dropped to near zero. On December 8, however, Jerry King called Jeff to say he had just decided against Australia, and would like to apply again for the Marketing Vice President position, if it was still open. Jeff agreed, and the next day Jerry presented to Jeff and the Board a plan for reaching $1 million in sales in 1988, and for growing by $1 million per year in the following two years. (This plan is partially reproduced in Exhibit 2.) Concerned with the timing of cash flows, one of the directors asked how long it would take to generate enough new sales to cover their added marketing expenses. King responded, "If I couldn't provide more than enough sales to cover my pay, I wouldn't take the job."

Although not officially joining Applied CAD until January 4, Jerry spent the rest of December in joint calling, with Jeff, on customers where Calay and Applied CAD shared some interests. In these first weeks, the "chemistry" Jeff Stevens had hoped for became readily apparent. The two men's skills complemented each other well: this would be a highly effective team, Stevens felt.

As 1988 began, King and Stevens continued to work closely together. Since Applied CAD's office layout did not provide the privacy needed

---

This case was prepared by Raymond M. Kinnunen, Northeastern University, and John A. Seeger, Bentley College, as a basis for class discussion. Distributed by the North American Case Research Association. The case has accompanying videotapes featuring Jeff Stevens, president and owner of Applied CAD Knowledge, Inc., in a question and answer session with an Executive MBA class that can be purchased from Northeastern University, Boston, MA 02115.

for telephone prospecting, Jerry worked out of his home, joining Jeff several times per week on joint sales calls. At the January 8 meeting of the Board of Directors, the two men presented detailed sales projections for the first quarter and broader estimates for the entire year (see Exhibit 3). One account alone—California PrinCo—held the promise of some $250,000 in sales over the next four months. An old and steady customer of Applied CAD, PrinCo was nearing a decision on a major expansion in their use of circuit boards.

January sales totalled only $6,000 but many prospects seemed close to signing for large orders. At the February 19 Board meeting, Jeff and Jerry predicted sales of $100,000 per month for February and March; it appeared a 1988 sales goal of $1,000,000 might still be reachable. (Exhibit 4 shows monthly sales and backlogs through January, 1988.)

Exhibit 1 Resume

Jerry King

Married
Four Children
Excellent Health

EDUCATION:

FAIRLEIGH DICKENSON UNIVERSITY, Madison, New Jersey
Major: Business Administration

U.S. NAVY, Electronics "A" School, Pearl Harbor, Hawaii

CONTINUING EDUCATION, including numerous seminars and workshops in Corporate Finance, Power Base Selling, Territory Time Management, The Art of Negotiating, Computer Graphics in Electronics, Sales Management and Marketing Techniques.

EXPERIENCE:

GENERAL BUSINESS MANAGEMENT: Establishing policies and procedures for high volume cost efficient business operations, planning promotions for new business development, hiring, training and supervising personnel, including management level, designing and conducting management, sales, marketing and CAD/CAM training seminars internationally.

TECHNICAL BACKGROUND: Twenty one years of direct Printed Circuit Design, Fabrication and Electronics CAD/CAM marketing experience. Helped to create detailed business plans for three start-up companies including a high volume printed circuit design service bureau and raised five million dollars in venture capital used to purchase state-of-the-art CAD/CAM systems and other related equipment. Managed the development and marketing of a PCB Design Automation turn-key system which was sold exclusively to Calma/GE in 1977 and integrated with their GDS1 TRI-DESIGN system. Very strong market knowledge in Computer Aided Engineering (CAE), Computer Aided Design (CAD), Computer Aided Test (CAT), and Computer Aided Manufacturing (CAM).

ACCOMPLISHMENTS:

Particularly effective in areas of personnel management, motivation and training, thereby increasing sales volume production flow, productivity and employee morale. Significant career accomplishments in customer relations, marketing and sales leadership and management.

EMPLOYMENT HISTORY:

1986–Present Calay Systems Incorporated, Waltham, Massachusetts
SENIOR ACCOUNT MANAGER

Responsible for a direct territory consisting of Northern Massachusetts, Vermont, New Hampshire, Maine and Quebec.

1985–1986 Automated Systems Incorporated, Nashua, N.H.
EASTERN REGIONAL SALES MANAGER.

Exhibit 1 *(continued)*

Responsible for regional design and fabrication service sales with a regional quota in excess of $5 million.

1981–1985 Engineering Automation Systems, Inc., San Jose, California.
WESTERN REGIONAL SALES MANAGER.

Responsible for new Printed Circuit Design CAD/CAM system. Set up regional office, hired and trained sales and support staff of twelve people. Western regional sales were in excess of fifty percent of the company's business.

September 1984 PROMOTED TO NATIONAL SALES MANAGER.

1978–1981 Computervision Corporation, Bedford, Massachusetts
NATIONAL PRODUCT SALES MANAGER.

Responsible for all electronic CAD/CAM system sales and related products. Provided direct sales management and training to the national field sales team, conducted sales training internationally, assisted in developing competitive strategy, technical support and new product development. Reported to the Vice President of North American Division.

March 1980 PROMOTED TO MANAGER, CORPORATE DEMONSTRATION and BENCHMARK CENTER.

Managed team of 38 people who performed all corporate level demonstrations and benchmarks. Supported field offices with technical information and people worldwide. Reported to the Vice President of Marketing Operations. THIS WAS A KEY MANAGEMENT POSITION FOR THE COMPANY.

1966–1978 King Systems, Inc., San Diego, California (A Printed Circuit Design CAD/CAM and NC Drilling Service Bureau.)
FOUNDER, PRESIDENT, CHAIRMAN AND MAJOR STOCKHOLDER.

Served as Chief Executive Officer in charge of all aspects of the operation. Primary activities in sales management, direct field sales and customer relations. Responsible for financial adminstration, production operations and personnel administration. Assesssed future needs and created business planning for increasing market share, facilities capability and penetrating new market opportunity. Developed a new concept in contract services for blanket sales to large government and commercial prime contractors.

Exhibit 2 Excerpts from Jerry King's Dec. 9, 1987, Board Presentation

Introduction

The plan is a detailed road map for taking Applied CAD Knowledge, Incorporated (ACK) from the current sales volume to more than three million annual sales volume over the next three years. It identifies target markets, competitive environment, and sales tactics which will be used for achieving the sales projections during the plan period from January 1st 1988 through December 31st 1990. The projections show a monthly breakdown for 1988 and a yearly number for 1989 and 1990. The monthly projections were created on Lotus and provide for projected, forecasted and actual sales bookings for each month. As each month passes the actual numbers are entered and a goal status report is generated as part of the end of month reporting. At the end of each quarter a new quarter will be added so that there will always be four consecutive quarters of monthly projections.

The aggressive growth which is outlined will require significant expansion of facilities, personnel and equipment in order to maintain consistent QUALITY and ON TIME deliveries and insure REPEAT BUSINESS from established customers. It is required that the management

(continued)

Exhibit 2 *(continued)*

and the Board of Directors of ACK provide the necessary production controls and capital/operating budgets to support expansion commensurate with sales volume increases over the term of the plan.

The PCB design service market can be divided into three major segments. Each of these segments will include companies who design and manufacture electronic equipment for Commercial, Industrial, Aerospace and Military vertical market areas.

Major Accounts & Government Sub-Contractors (MA)
Major Accounts are Fortune 1000 companies. They present a significant opportunity for multiple board contracts and blanket purchase agreements. Any one company could fill ACK's capacity.

Primary Accounts (PA)
Primary accounts are companies who have been doing business for more that three years (not a start-up) and typically do between 5–500 million in annual sales. These companies represent the most consistent level of business. The type of contracts available from this market segment are usually on the level of one to four board designs per month. Typically, each board of project has to be sold separately at the project engineering level.

Venture Start-Up Accounts (VA)
Venture start-up companies usually are operating on stringent budgets. They typically have no internal CAD capability and therefore must rely on outside service. The business potential for this market segment is very significant. This market represents a high risk and therefore is avoided by the major competitors leaving more opportunity for the smaller operation. It is not unusual to obtain sole source product level contracts from companies in this market.

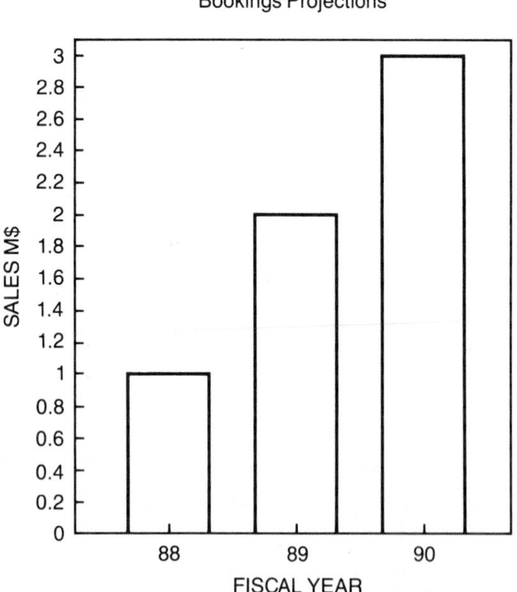

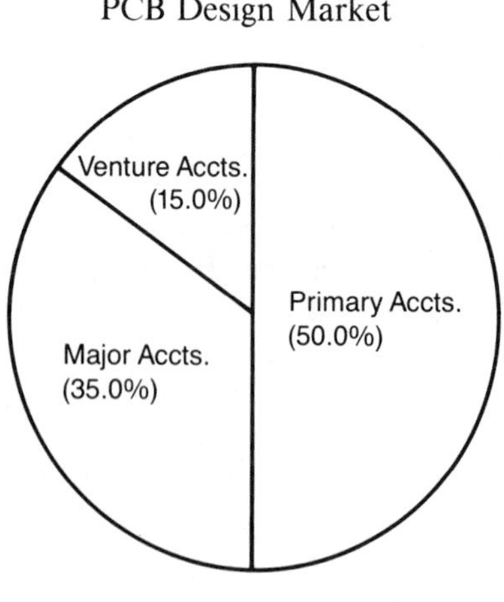

Source: Frost & Sullivan, Oct. 1985.

Exhibit 3 Sales Projections Presented to the Board, January 8, 1988

Forecast Q1 1988: Sales by Customer

Account Name	Jan. 50%	90%	Feb. 50%	90%	Mar. 50%	90%	Total 50%	Total 90%	Grand Total
Customer A	0.0	20.0	0.0	8.0	20.0	0.0	20.0	28.0	48.0
Prospect I	0.0	7.0	0.0	0.0	0.0	0.0	0.0	7.0	7.0
Prospect II	5.0	0.0	2.0	0.0	2.0	0.0	9.0	0.0	9.0
Customer B	0.0	0.0	12.0	0.0	0.0	0.0	12.0	0.0	12.0
Customer C	12.0	0.0	0.0	0.0	0.0	0.0	12.0	0.0	12.0
Customer D	0.0	0.0	12.0	0.0	0.0	0.0	12.0	0.0	12.0
Customer E	0.0	30.0	0.0	0.0	20.0	0.0	20.0	30.0	50.0
Prospect III	0.0	0.0	15.0	0.0	20.0	0.0	35.0	0.0	35.0
Prospect IV	0.0	0.0	15.0	0.0	20.0	0.0	35.0	0.0	35.0
Prospect V	0.0	6.5	0.0	0.8	0.0	3.8	0.0	11.1	11.1
Customer F	0.0	0.0	0.0	7.0	0.0	0.0	0.0	7.0	7.0
Total	17.0	63.5	56.0	15.8	82.0	3.8	155.0	83.1	238.1

Forecast FY 1988: Bookings by Product Type

	Service	Software	Total	Accum Total
January	33	15	48	48
February	48	5	53	101
March	53	15	68	169
Quarter 1	**124**	**35**	**169**	
April	60	5	65	234
May	68	15	83	317
June	75	5	80	397
Quarter 2	**203**	**25**	**228**	
July	80	15	95	492
August	85		85	577
September	88	15	103	680
Quarter 3	**253**	**30**	**283**	
October	90	8	98	778
November	95	15	110	888
December	98	15	113	1001
Quarter 4	**283**	**38**	**321**	

(continued)

Exhibit 3 *(continued)*

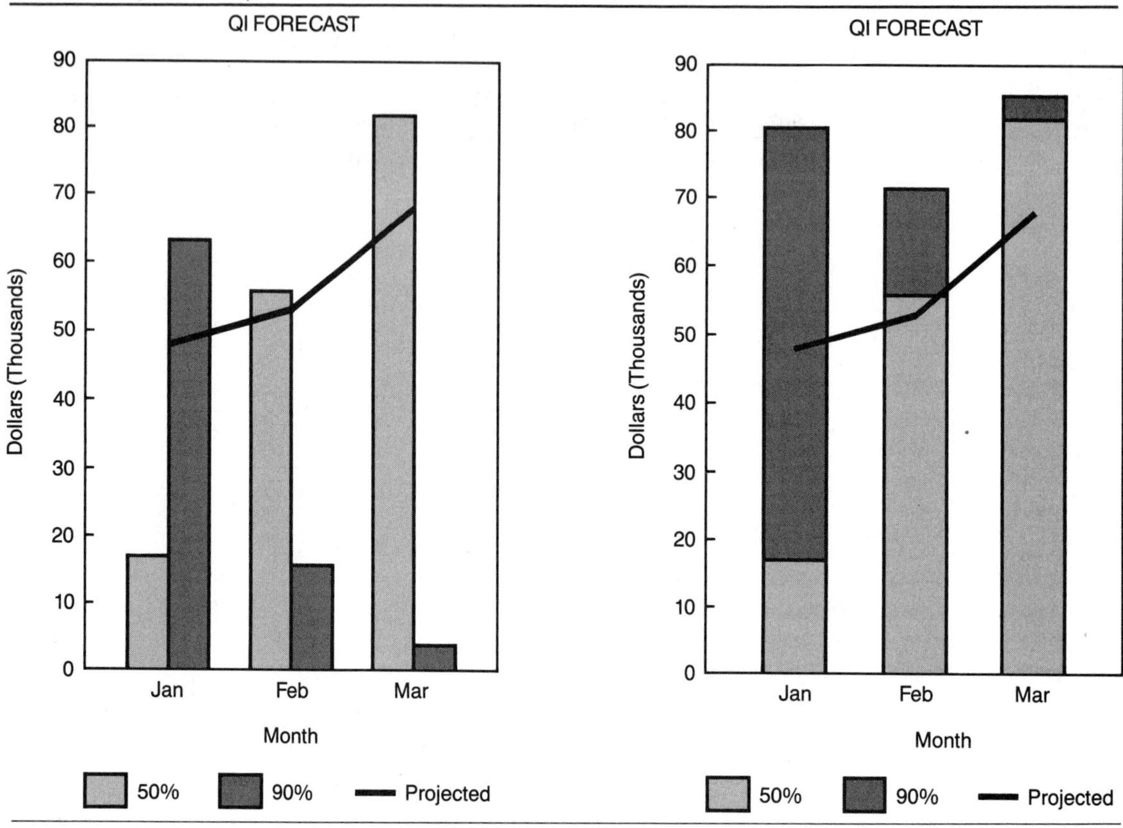

Exhibit 4 Monthly Sales and Month-End Receivables, Backlogs, Cash Levels (All in $000's)

	A/R	Sales	Backlog	Cash		A/R	Sales	Backlog	Cash
January 1986	18	20	20	$98	January 1987	13	3	—	7
February	—	10	—	N/A	February	40	21	—	8
March	18	10	12	62	March	35	28	22	6
April	18	10	20	28	April	32	22	37	11
May	24	20	26	26	May	25	22	50	5
June	—	10	—	N/A	June	50	50	90	10
July	14	25	—	18	July	90	58	30	10
August	70	50	30	15	August	—	25	—	10
September	90	40	—	8	September	34	25	50	21
October	50	30	—	26	October	62	48	9	8
November	19	5	10	17	November	50	24	—	—
December	24	10	18	14	December	14	34	9	33
					January 1988	8	6	—	19

Case 20

The Lincoln Electric Company, 1989

> People are our most valuable asset. They must feel secure, important, challenged, in control of their destiny, confident in their leadership, be responsive to common goals, believe they are being treated fairly, have easy access to authority and open lines of communication in all possible directions. Perhaps the most important task Lincoln employees face today is that of establishing an example for others in the Lincoln organization in other parts of the world. We need to maximize the benefits of cooperation and teamwork, fusing high technology with human talent, so that we here in the USA and all of our subsidiary and joint venture operations will be in a position to realize our full potential.
>
> *George Willis, CEO, The Lincoln Electric Company*

The Lincoln Electric Company is the world's largest manufacturer of arc welding products and a leading producer of industrial electric motors. The firm employs 2400 workers in two U.S. factories near Cleveland and an equal number in eleven factories located in other countries. This does not include the field sales force of more than 200. The company's U.S. market share (for arc-welding products) is estimated at more than 40 percent.

The Lincoln incentive management plan has been well known for many years. Many college management texts make reference to the Lincoln plan as a model for achieving higher worker productivity. Certainly, the firm has been successful according to the usual measures.

James F. Lincoln died in 1965 and there was some concern, even among employees, that the management system would fall into disarray, that profits would decline, and that year-end bonuses might be discontinued. Quite the contrary, twenty-four years after Lincoln's death, the company appears as strong as ever. Each year, except the recession years 1982 and 1983, has seen high profits and bonuses. Employee morale and productivity remain very good. Employee turnover is almost nonexistent except for retirements. Lincoln's market share is stable. The historically high stock dividends continue.

A Historical Sketch

In 1895, after being "frozen out" of the depression-ravaged Elliott-Lincoln Company, a maker of Lincoln-designed electric motors, John C. Lincoln took out his second patent and began to manufacture his improved motor. He opened his new business, unincorporated, with $200 he had earned redesigning a motor for young Herbert Henry Dow, who later founded the Dow Chemical Company.

Started during an economic depression and cursed by a major fire after only one year in business, the company grew, but hardly prospered, through its first quarter century. In 1906, John C. Lincoln incorporated the business and moved from his one-room, fourth-floor factory to a new three-story building he erected in east Cleveland. He expanded his work force to 30 and sales grew to over $50,000 a year. John preferred being an engineer and inventor rather than a manager,

---

This case was prepared by Arthur Sharplin, McNeese State University, Lake Charles, LA 70601. Reprinted with permission.

though, and it was to be left to another Lincoln to manage the company through its years of success.

In 1907, after a bout with typhoid fever forced him from Ohio State University in his senior year, James F. Lincoln, John's younger brother, joined the fledgling company. In 1914 he became active head of the firm, with the titles of General Manager and Vice President. John remained president of the company for some years but became more involved in other business ventures and in his work as an inventor.

One of James Lincoln's early actions was to ask the employees to elect representatives to a committee which would advise him on company operations. This "Advisory Board" has met with the chief executive officer every two weeks since that time. This was only the first of a series of innovative personnel policies which have, over the years, distinguished Lincoln Electric from its contemporaries.

The first year the Advisory Board was in existence, working hours were reduced from 55 per week, then standard, to 50 hours a week. In 1915, the company gave each employee a paid-up life insurance policy. A welding school, which continues today, was begun in 1917. In 1918, an employee bonus plan was attempted. It was not continued, but the idea was to resurface later.

The Lincoln Electric Employees' Association was formed in 1919 to provide health benefits and social activities. This organization continues today and has assumed several additional functions over the years. In 1923, a piecework pay system was in effect, employees got two weeks paid vacation each year, and wages were adjusted for changes in the Consumer Price Index. Approximately thirty percent of the common stock was set aside for key employees in 1914. A stock purchase plan for all employees was begun in 1925.

The Board of Directors voted to start a suggestion system in 1929. The program is still in effect, but cash awards, a part of the early program, were discontinued several years ago. Now, suggestions are rewarded by additional "points," which affect year-end bonuses.

The legendary Lincoln bonus plan was proposed by the Advisory Board and accepted on a trial basis in 1934. The first annual bonus amounted to about 25 percent of wages. There has been a bonus every year since then. The bonus plan has been a cornerstone of the Lincoln management system and recent bonuses have approximated annual wages.

By 1944, Lincoln employees enjoyed a pension plan, a policy of promotion from within, and continuous employment. Base pay rates were determined by formal job evaluation and a merit rating system was in effect.

In the prologue of James F. Lincoln's last book, Charles G. Herbruck writes regarding the foregoing personnel innovations:

> They were not to buy good behavior. They were not efforts to increase profits. They were not antidotes to labor difficulties. They did not constitute a "dogooder" program. They were expression of mutual respect for each person's importance to the job to be done. All of them reflect the leadership of James Lincoln, under whom they were nurtured and propagated.

During World War II, Lincoln prospered as never before. By the start of the war, the company was the world's largest manufacturer of arc-welding products. Sales of about $4,000,000 in 1934 grew to $24,000,000 by 1941. Productivity per employee more than doubled during the same period. The Navy's Price Review Board challenged the high profits. And the Internal Revenue Service questioned the tax deductibility of employee bonuses, arguing they were not "ordinary and necessary" costs of doing business. But the forceful and articulate James Lincoln was able to overcome the objections.

Certainly since 1935 and probably for several years before that, Lincoln productivity has been well above the average for similar companies. The company claims levels of productivity more than twice those for other manufacturers from 1945 onward. Information available from outside sources tends to support these claims.

Company Philosophy

James F. Lincoln was the son of a Congregational minister, and Christian principles were at the center of his business philosophy. The confidence that he had in the efficacy of Christ's teachings is illustrated by the following remark taken from one of his books:

> The Christian ethic should control our acts. If it did control our acts, the savings in cost of distribution would be tremendous. Advertising would be a contact of the expert consultant with the customer, in order to give the customer the best product available when all of the customer's needs are considered. Competition then would be in improving the quality of products and increasing efficiency in producing and distributing them; not in deception, as is now too customary. Pricing would reflect efficiency of production; it would not be a selling dodge that the customer may well be sorry he accepted. It would be proper for all concerned and rewarding for the ability used in producing the product.

There is no indication that Lincoln attempted to evangelize his employees or customers—or the general public for that matter. Neither the chairman of the board and chief executive, George Willis, nor the president, Donald F. Hastings, mention the Christian gospel in their recent speeches and interviews. The company motto, "The actual is limited, the possible is immense," is prominently displayed, but there is no display of religious slogans, and there is no company chapel.

Attitude toward the Customer

James Lincoln saw the customer's needs as the *raison d'etre* for every company. "When any company has achieved success so that it is attractive as an investment," he wrote, "all money usually needed for expansion is supplied by the customer in retained earnings. It is obvious that the customer's interests, not the stockholder's, should come first." In 1947 he said, "Care should be taken . . . not to rivet attention on profit. Between 'How much do I get?' and 'How do I make this better, cheaper, more useful?' the difference is fundamental and decisive." Willis, too, ranks the customer as management's most important constituency. This is reflected in Lincoln's policy to "at all times price on the basis of cost and at all times keep pressure on our cost . . ." Lincoln's goal, often stated, is "to build a better and better product at a lower and lower price." "It is obvious," James Lincoln said, "that the customer's interests should be the first goal of industry."

Attitude toward Stockholders

Stockholders are given last priority at Lincoln. This is a continuation of James Lincoln's philosophy: "The last group to be considered is the stockholders who own stock because they think it will be more profitable than investing money in any other way." Concerning division of the largess produced by incentive management, he wrote, "The absentee stockholder also will get his share, even if undeserved, out of the greatly increased profit that the efficiency produces."

Attitude toward Unionism

There has never been a serious effort to organize Lincoln employees. While James Lincoln criticized the labor movement for "selfishly attempting to better its position at the expense of the people it must serve," he still had kind words for union members. He excused abuses of union power as "the natural reactions of human beings to the abuses to which management has subjected them." Lincoln's idea of the correct relationship between workers and managers is shown by this comment: "Labor and management are properly not warring camps; they are parts of one organization in which they must and should cooperate fully and happily."

Beliefs and Assumptions about Employees

If fulfilling customer needs is the desired goal of business, then employee performance and productivity are the means by which this goal can best be achieved. It is the Lincoln attitude toward employees, reflected in the following comments by James Lincoln, which is credited by many with creating the success the company has experienced:

> The greatest fear of the worker, which is the same as the greatest fear of the industrialist in operating a company, is the lack of income . . . The industrial manager is very conscious of his company's need of uninterrupted income. He is completely oblivious, evidently, of the fact that the worker has the same need.
>
> He is just as eager as any manager is to be part of a team that is properly organized and working for the advancement of our economy . . . He has no desire to make profits for those who do not hold up their end in production, as is true of absentee stockholders and inactive people in the company.
>
> If money is to be used as an incentive, the program must provide that what is paid to the worker is what he has earned. The earnings of each must be in accordance with accomplishment.
>
> Status is of great importance in all human relationships. The greatest incentive that money has, usually, is that it is a symbol of success . . . The resulting status is the real incentive . . . Money alone can be an incentive to the miser only.
>
> There must be complete honesty and understanding between the hourly worker and management if high efficiency is to be obtained.

Lincoln's Business

Arc-welding has been the standard joining method in shipbuilding for decades. It is the predominant way of connecting steel in the construction industry. Most industrial plants have their own welding shops for maintenance and construction. Manufacturers of tractors and all kinds of heavy equipment use arc-welding extensively in the manufacturing process. Many hobbyists have their own welding machines and use them for making metal items such as patio furniture and barbecue pits. The popularity of welded sculpture as an art form is growing.

While advances in welding technology have been frequent, arc-welding products, in the main, have hardly changed. Lincoln's Innershield process is a notable exception. This process, described later, lowers welding cost and improves quality and speed in many applications. The most widely-used Lincoln electrode, the Fleetweld 5P, has been virtually the same since the 1930's. The most popular engine-driven welder in the world, the Lincoln SA-200, has been a gray-colored assembly including a four-cylinder continental "Red Seal" engine and a 200 ampere direct-current generator with two current-control knobs for at least four decades. A 1989 model SA-200 even weighs almost the same as the 1950 model, and it certainly is little changed in appearance.

The company's share of the U.S. arc-welding products market appears to have been about forty percent for many years. The welding products market has grown somewhat faster than the level of industry in general. The market is highly price-competitive, with variations in prices of standard items normally amounting to only a percent or two. Lincoln's products are sold directly by its engineering-oriented sales force and indirectly though its distributor organization. Advertising expenditures amount to less than three-fourths of a percent of sales. Research and development expenditures typically range from $10 million to $12 million, considerably more than competitors.

The other major welding process, flame-welding, has not been competitive with arc-welding since the 1930s. However, plasma-arc-welding, a relatively new process which uses a conducting stream of super heated gas (plasma) to confine the welding current to a small area, has made some inroads, especially in metal tubing manufacturing, in recent years. Major advances in technology which will produce an alternative superior to arc-welding within the next decade or so appear unlikely. Also, it seems likely that changes in the machines and techniques used in arc-welding will be evolutionary rather than revolutionary.

Products

The company is primarily engaged in the manufacture and sale of arc-welding products—electric welding machines and metal electrodes. Lincoln also produces electric motors ranging from one-half horsepower to 200 horsepower. Motors constitute about eight to ten percent of total sales. Several million dollars has recently been invested in automated equipment that will double Lincoln's manufacturing capacity for 1/2 to 20 horsepower electric motors.

The electric welding machines, some consisting of a transformer or motor and generator arrangement powered by commercial electricity and others consisting of an internal combustion engine and generator, are designed to produce 30 to 1,500 amperes of electrical power. This electrical current is used to melt a consumable metal electrode with the molten metal being transferred in super hot spray to the metal joint being welded. Very high temperatures and hot sparks are produced, and operators usually must wear special eye and face protection and leather gloves, often along with leather aprons and sleeves.

Lincoln and its competitors now market a wide range of general purpose and specialty electrodes for welding mild steel, aluminum, cast iron, and stainless and special steels. Most of these electrodes are designed to meet the standards of the American Welding Society, a trade association. They are thus essentially the same as to size and composition from one manufacturer to another. Every electrode manufacturer has a limited number of unique products, but these typically constitute only a small percentage of total sales.

Welding electrodes are of two basic types: (1) Coated "stick" electrodes, usually fourteen inches long and smaller than a pencil in diameter, which are held in a special insulated holder by the operator, who must manipulate the electrode in order to maintain a proper arc-width and pattern of deposition of the metal being transferred. Stick electrodes are packaged in six- to fifty-pound boxes. (2) Coiled wired, ranging in diameter from .035″ to 0.219″, which is designed to be fed continuously to the welding arc through a "gun" held by the operator or positioned by automatic positioning equipment. The wire is packaged in coils, reels, and drums weighing from fourteen to 1,000 pounds and may be solid or flux-cored.

Manufacturing Processes

The main plant is in Euclid, Ohio, a suburb on Cleveland's east side. The layout of this plant is shown in Exhibit 1. There are no warehouses. Materials flow from the half-mile long dock on the north side of the plant through the production lines to a very limited storage and loading area on the south side. Materials used on each work station are stored as close as possible to the work station. The administrative offices, near the center of the factory, are entirely functional. A corridor below the main level provides access to the factory floor from the main entrance near the center of the plan. *Fortune* magazine recently declared the Euclid facility one of America's ten best-managed factories, and compared it with a General Electric plant also on the list:

> Stepping into GE's spanking new dishwasher plant, an awed supplier said, is like stepping "into the Hyatt Regency." By comparison, stepping into Lincoln Electric's 33-year-old, cavernous, dimly lit factory is like stumbling into a dingy big-city YMCA. It's only when one starts looking at how these factories do things that similarities become apparent. They have found ways to merge design with manufacturing, build in quality, make wise choices about automation, get close to customers, and handle their work forces.

Exhibit 1 Main Factory Layout

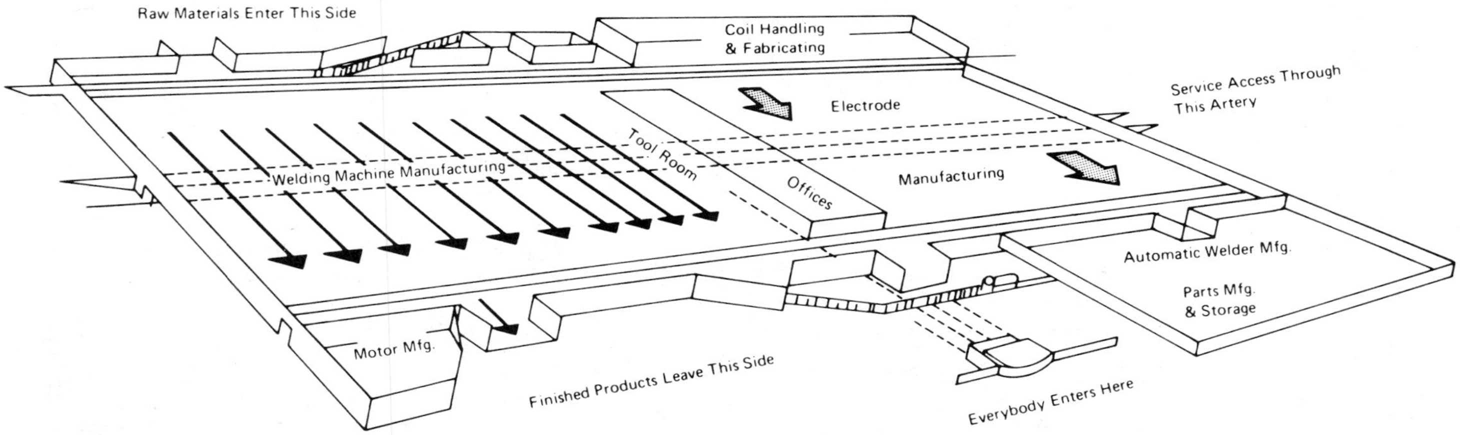

A new Lincoln plant, in Mentor, Ohio, houses some of the electrode production operations, which were moved from the main plant.

Electrode manufacturing is highly capital intensive. Metal rods purchased from steel producers are drawn down to smaller diameters, cut to length and coated with pressed-powder "flux" for stick electrodes or plated with copper (for conductivity) and put into coils or spools for wire. Lincoln's Innershield wire is hollow and filled with a material similar to that used to coat stick electrodes. As mentioned earlier, this represented a major innovation in welding technology when it was introduced. The company is highly secretive about its electrode production processes, and outsiders are not given access to the details of those processes.

Lincoln welding machines and electric motors are made on a series of assembly lines. Gasoline and diesel engines are purchased partially assembled but practically all other components are made from basic industrial products, e.g., steel bars and sheets and bar copper conductor wire.

Individual components, such as gasoline tanks for engine-driven welders and steel shafts for motors and generators, are made by numerous small "factories within a factory." The shaft for a certain generator, for example, is made from raw steel bar by one operator who uses five large machines, all running continuously. A saw cuts the bar to length, a digital lathe machines different sections to varying diameters, a special milling machine cuts a slot for the keyway, and so forth, until a finished shaft is produced. The operator moves the shafts from machine to machine and makes necessary adjustments.

Another operator punches, shapes and paints sheetmetal cowling parts. One assembles steel laminations onto a rotor shaft, then winds, insulates and tests the rotors. Finished components are moved by crane operators to the nearby assembly lines.

Worker Performance and Attitudes

Exceptional worker performance at Lincoln is a matter of record. The typical Lincoln employee earns about twice as much as other factory workers in the Cleveland area. Yet the company's labor cost per sales dollar in 1989, 26 cents, is well below industry averages. Worker turnover is practically nonexistent except for retirements and departures by new employees.

Sales per Lincoln factory employee currently exceed $150,000. An observer at the factory quickly sees why this figure is so high. Each worker is proceeding busily and thoughtfully about the task at hand. There is no idle chatter. Most workers take no coffee breaks. Many operate several machines and make a substantial component unaided. The supervisors are busy with planning and record keeping duties and hardly glance at the people they "supervise." The manufacturing procedures appear efficient—no unnecessary steps, no wasted motions, no wasted materials. Finished components move smoothly to subsequent work stations.

Appendix A includes summaries of interviews with employees.

Organization Structure

Lincoln has never allowed development of a formal organization chart. The objective of this policy is to insure maximum flexibility. An open door policy is practiced throughout the company, and personnel are encouraged to take problems to the persons most capable of resolving them. Once, Harvard Business School researchers prepared an organization chart reflecting the implied relationships at Lincoln. The chart became available within the company, and present management feels that had a disruptive effect. Therefore, no organizational chart appears in this report.

Perhaps because of the quality and enthusiasm of the Lincoln workforce, routine supervision is almost nonexistent. A typical production foreman, for example, supervises as many as 100 workers, a span-of-control which does not allow more than infrequent worker-supervisor interaction.

Position titles and traditional flows of authority do imply something of an organizational structure, however. For example, the Vice-President, Sales, and the Vice-President, Electrode Division, report to the President, as do various staff assistants such as the Personnel Director and the Director of Purchasing. Using such implied relationships, it has been determined that production workers have two or, at most, three levels of supervision between themselves and the President.

Personnel Policies

As mentioned earlier, it is Lincoln's remarkable personnel practices which are credited by many with the company's success.

Recruitment and Selection

Every job opening is advertised internally on company bulletin boards and any employee can apply for any job so advertised. External hiring is permitted only for entry level positions. Selection for these jobs is done on the basis of personal interviews—there is no aptitude or psychological testing. Not even a high school diploma is required—except for engineering and sales positions, which are filled by graduate engineers. A committee consisting of vice presidents and supervisors interviews candidates initially cleared by the Personnel Department. Final selection is made by the supervisor who has a job opening. Out of over 3,500 applicants interviewed by the Personnel Department during a recent period fewer than 300 were hired.

Job Security

In 1958 Lincoln formalized its guaranteed continuous employment policy, which had already been in effect for many years. There have been no layoffs since World War II. Since 1958, every worker with over two year's longevity has been guaranteed at least 30 hours per week, 49 weeks per year.

The policy has never been so severely tested as during the 1981–83 recession. As a manufacturer of capital goods, Lincoln's business is highly cyclical. In previous recessions the company was able to avoid major sales declines. However, sales plummeted 32 percent in 1982 and another 16 percent the next year. Few companies could withstand such a revenue collapse and remain profitable. Yet, Lincoln not only earned profits, but no employee was laid off and year-end incentive bonuses continued. To weather the storm, management cut most of the nonsalaried workers back to 30 hours a week for varying periods of time. Many employees were reassigned and the total workforce was slightly reduced through normal attrition and restricted hiring. Many employees grumbled at their unexpected misfortune, probably to the surprise and dismay of some Lincoln managers. However, sales and profits—and employee bonuses—soon rebounded and all was well again.

Performance Evaluations

Each supervisor formally evaluates subordinates twice a year using the cards shown in Exhibit 2. The employee performance criteria, "quality," "dependability," "ideas and cooperation," and "output," are considered to be independent of each other. Marks on the cards are converted to numerical scores which are forced to average 100 for each evaluating supervisor. Individual merit rating scores normally range from 80 to 110. Any score over 110 requires a special letter to top management. These scores (over 110) are not considered in computing the required 100 point average for each evaluating supervisor. Suggestions for improvements often result in recommendations for exceptionally high performance scores. Supervisors discuss individual performance marks with the employees concerned. Each warranty claim is traced to the individual employee whose work caused the defect. The employee's performance score may be reduced, or the worker may be required to repay the cost of

Exhibit 2 Merit Rating Cards

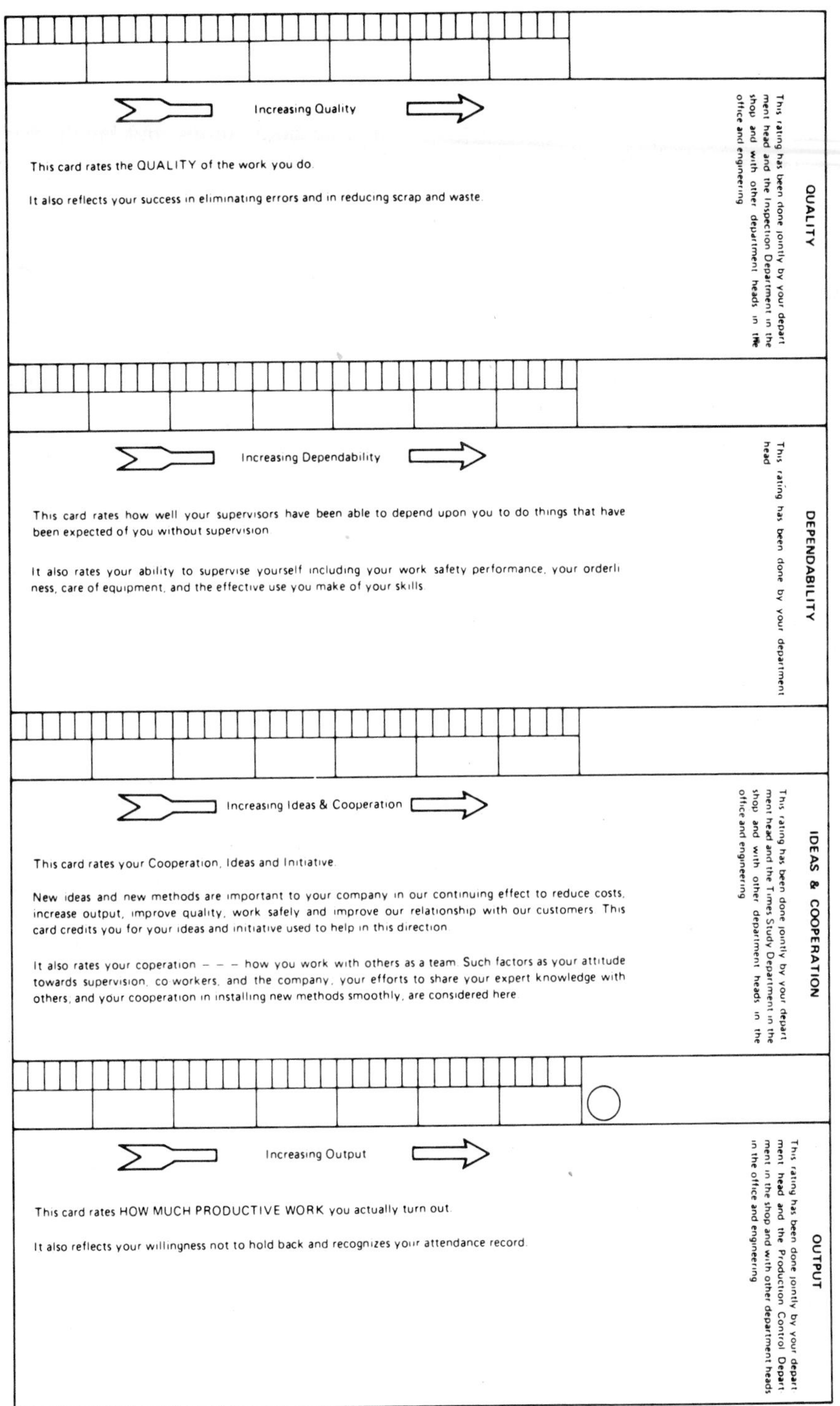

Increasing Quality

This card rates the QUALITY of the work you do.

It also reflects your success in eliminating errors and in reducing scrap and waste.

QUALITY

This rating has been done jointly by your department head and the Inspection Department in the shop and with other department heads in the office and engineering

Increasing Dependability

This card rates how well your supervisors have been able to depend upon you to do things that have been expected of you without supervision.

It also rates your ability to supervise yourself including your work safety performance, your orderliness, care of equipment, and the effective use you make of your skills.

DEPENDABILITY

This rating has been done by your department head

Increasing Ideas & Cooperation

This card rates your Cooperation, Ideas and Initiative.

New ideas and new methods are important to your company in our continuing effect to reduce costs, increase output, improve quality, work safely and improve our relationship with our customers. This card credits you for your ideas and initiative used to help in this direction.

It also rates your coperation – – – how you work with others as a team. Such factors as your attitude towards supervision, co workers, and the company, your efforts to share your expert knowledge with others, and your cooperation in installing new methods smoothly, are considered here.

IDEAS & COOPERATION

This rating has been done jointly by your department head and the Times Study Department in the shop and with other department heads in the office and engineering

Increasing Output

This card rates HOW MUCH PRODUCTIVE WORK you actually turn out.

It also reflects your willingness not to hold back and recognizes your attendance record.

OUTPUT

This rating has been done jointly by your department head and the Production Control Department in the shop and with other department heads in the office and engineering servicing the warranty claim by working without pay.

Compensation

Basic wage levels for jobs at Lincoln are determined by a wage survey of similar jobs in the Cleveland area. These rates are adjusted quarterly in accordance with changes in the Cleveland area wage index. Insofar as possible, base wage rates are translated into piece rates. Practically all production workers and many others—for example, some forklift operators—are paid by piece rate. Once established, piece rates are never changed unless a substantive change in the way a job is done results from a source other than the worker doing the job.

In December of each year, a portion of annual profits is distributed to employees as bonuses. Incentive bonuses since 1934 have averaged about ninety percent of annual wages and somewhat more than after-tax profits. The average bonus for 1988 was $21,258. Even for the recession years 1982 and 1983, bonuses had averaged $13,998 and $8,557, respectively. Individual bonuses are proportional to merit-rating scores. For example, assume the amount set aside for bonuses is 80 percent of total wages paid to eligible employees. A person whose performance score is 95 will receive a bonus of 76 percent (0.80×0.95) of annual wages.

Vacations

The company is shut down for two weeks in August and two weeks during the Christmas season. Vacations are taken during these periods. For employees with over 25 years of service, a fifth week of vacation may be taken at a time acceptable to superiors.

Work Assignment

Management has authority to transfer workers and to switch between overtime and short time as required. Supervisors have undisputed authority to assign specific parts to individual workmen, who may have their own preferences due to variations in piece rates. During the 1982–1983 recession, fifty factory workers volunteered to join sales teams and fanned out across the country to sell a new welder designed for automobile body shops and small machine shops. The result—$10 million in sales and a hot new product.

Employee Participation in Decision Making

Thinking of participative management usually evokes a vision of a relaxed, nonauthoritarian atmosphere. This is not the case at Lincoln. Formal authority is quite strong. "We're very authoritarian around here," says Willis. James F. Lincoln placed a good deal of stress on protecting management's authority. "Management in all successful departments of industry must have complete power," he said, "Management is the coach who must be obeyed. The men, however, are the players who alone can win the game." Despite this attitude, there are several ways in which employees participate in management at Lincoln.

Richard Sabo, Assistant to the Chief Executive Officer, relates job enlargement/enrichment to participation. He said, "The most important participative technique that we use is giving more responsibility to employees. We give a high school graduate more responsibility than other companies give their foremen." Management puts limits on the degree of participation which is allowed, however. In Sabo's words:

> When you use "participation," put quotes around it. Because we believe that each person should participate only in those decisions he is most knowledgeable about. I don't think production employees should control the decisions of the chairman. They don't know as much as he does about the decisions he is involved in.

The Advisory Board, elected by the workers, meets with the Chairman and the President every two weeks to discuss ways of improving operations. As noted earlier, this board has been in existence since 1914 and has contributed to many innovations. The incentive bonuses, for example, were first recommended by this committee. Every employee has access to Advisory Board members, and answers to all Advisory Board suggestions are promised by the following meeting. Both Willis and Hastings are quick to point out, though, that the Advisory Board only recommends actions. "They do not have direct authority," Willis says, "And when they bring up something that management thinks is not to the benefit of the company, it will be rejected."

Under the early suggestion program, employees were awarded one-half of the first year's savings attributable to their suggestions. Now, however, the value of suggestions is reflected in performance evaluation scores, which determine individual incentive bonus amounts.

Training and Education

Production workers are given a short period of on-the-job training and then placed on a piecework pay system. Lincoln does not pay for off-site education, unless very specific company needs are identified. The idea behind this latter policy, according to Sabo, is that everyone cannot take advantage of such a program, and it is unfair to expend company funds for an advantage to which there is unequal access. Recruits for sales jobs, already college graduates, are given on-the-job training in the plant followed by a period of work and training at one of the regional sales offices.

Fringe Benefits and Executive Perquisites

A medical plan and a company-paid retirement program have been in effect for many years. A plant cafeteria, operated on a break-even basis, serves meals at about sixty percent of usual costs. The Employee Association, to which the company does not contribute, provides disability insurance and social and athletic activities. The employee stock ownership program has resulted in employee ownership of about fifty percent of the common stock. Under this program, each employee with more than two years of service may purchase stock in the corporation. The price of these shares is established at book value. Stock purchased through this plan may be held by employees only. Dividends and voting rights are the same as for stock which is owned outside the plan. Approximately 75 percent of the employees own Lincoln stock.

As to executive perquisites, there are none—crowded, austere offices, no executive washrooms or lunchrooms, and no reserved parking spaces. Even the top executives pay for their own meals and eat in the employee cafeteria. On one recent day, Willis arrived at work late due to a breakfast speaking engagement and had to park far away from the factory entrance.

Financial Policies

James F. Lincoln felt strongly that financing for company growth should come from within the company—through initial cash investment by the founders, through retention of earnings, and through stock purchases by those who work in the business. He saw the following advantages of this approach:

1. Ownership of stock by employees strengthens team spirit. "If they are mutually anxious to make it succeed, the future of the company is bright."

2. Ownership of stock provides individual incentive because employees feel that they will benefit from company profitability.

3. "Ownership is educational." Owners-employees "will know how profits are made and lost; how success is won and lost. . . . There are few socialists in the list of stockholders of the nation's industries."

4. "Capital available from within controls expansion." Unwarranted expansion would not occur, Lincoln believed, under his financing plan.

5. "The greatest advantage would be the development of the individual worker. Under the incentive of ownership, he would become a greater man."

6. "Stock ownership is one of the steps that can be taken that will make the worker feel that there is less of a gulf between him and the boss. . . .

Stock ownership will help the worker to recognize his responsibility in the game and the importance of victory."

Until 1980, Lincoln Electric borrowed no money. Even now, the company's liabilities consist mainly of accounts payable and short-term accruals.

The unusual pricing policy at Lincoln is succinctly stated by Willis: "At all times price on the basis of cost and at all times keep pressure on our cost." This policy resulted in the price for the most popular welding electrode then in use going from 16 cents a pound in 1929 to 4.7 cents in 1938. More recently, the SA-200 Welder, Lincoln's largest selling portable machine, decreased in price from 1958 through 1965. According to Dr. C. Jackson Grayson of the American Productivity Center in Houston, Texas, Lincoln's prices increased only one-fifth as fast as the Consumer Price Index from 1934 to about 1970. This resulted in a welding products market in which Lincoln became the undisputed price leader for the products it manufactures. Not even the major Japanese manufacturers, such as Nippon Steel for welding electrodes and Osaka Transformer for welding machines, were able to penetrate this market.

Substantial cash balances are accumulated each year preparatory to paying the year-end bonuses. The bonuses totaled $54 million for 1988. The money is invested in short-term U.S. government securities and certificates of deposit until needed. Financial statements are shown in Exhibit 3. Exhibit 4 shows how company revenue was distributed in the late 1980s.

How Well Does Lincoln Serve Its Stakeholders?

Lincoln Electric differs from most other companies in the importance it assigns to each of the groups it serves. Willis identifies these groups, in the order of priority ascribed to them, as (1) customers, (2) employees, and (3) stockholders.

Certainly the firm's customers have fared well over the years. Lincoln prices for welding machines and welding electrodes are acknowledged to be the lowest in the marketplace. Quality has consistently been high. The cost of field failures for Lincoln products was recently determined to be a remarkable 0.04 percent of revenues. The "Fleetweld" electrodes and SA-200 welders have been the standard in the pipeline and refinery construction industry, where price is hardly a criterion, for decades. A Lincoln distributor in Monroe, Louisiana, says that he has sold several hundred of the popular AC-225 welders, which are warranted for one year, but has never handled a warranty claim.

Perhaps best-served of all management constituencies have been the employees. Not the least of their benefits, of course, are the year-end bonuses, which effectively double an already average compensation level. The foregoing description of the personnel program and the comments in Appendix A further illustrate the desirability of a Lincoln job.

While stockholders were relegated to an inferior status by James F. Lincoln, they have done very well indeed. Recent dividends have exceeded $11 a share and earnings per share have approached $30. In January 1980, the price of restricted stock, committed to employees, was $117 a share. By 1989, the stated value, at which the company will repurchase the stock if tendered, was $201. A check with the New York office of Merrill Lynch, Pierce, Fenner and Smith at that time revealed an estimated price on Lincoln stock of $270 a share, with none being offered for sale. Technically, this price applies only to the unrestricted stock owned by the Lincoln family, a few other major holders, and employees who have purchased it on the open market. Risk associated with Lincoln stock, a major determinant of stock value, is minimal because of the small amount of debt in the capital structure, because of an extremely stable earnings record, and because of Lincoln's practice of purchasing the restricted stock whenever employees offer it for sale.

Exhibit 3 Condensed Comparative Financial Statements ($000,000)*

	Balance Sheets								
	1979	**1980**	**1981**	**1982**	**1983**	**1984**	**1985**	**1986**	**1987**
Assets									
Cash	2	1	4	1	2	4	2	1	7
Bonds & CDs	38	47	63	72	78	57	55	45	41
N/R & A/R	42	42	42	26	31	34	38	36	43
Inventories	38	36	46	38	31	37	34	26	40
Prepayments	1	3	4	5	5	5	7	8	7
Total CA	121	129	157	143	146	138	135	116	137
Other assets**	24	24	26	30	30	29	29	33	40
Land	1	1	1	1	1	1	1	1	1
Net buildings	22	23	25	23	22	21	20	18	17
Net M&E	21	25	27	27	27	28	27	29	33
Total FA	44	49	53	51	50	50	48	48	50
Total assets	189	202	236	224	227	217	213	197	227
Claims									
A/P	17	16	15	12	16	15	13	11	20
Accrued wages	1	2	5	4	3	4	5	5	4
Accrued taxes	10	6	15	5	7	4	6	5	9
Accrued div.	6	6	7	7	7	6	7	6	7
Total CL	33	29	42	28	33	30	31	27	40
LT debt	—	4	5	6	8	10	11	8	8
Total debt	33	33	47	34	41	40	42	35	48
Common stock*	4	3	1	2	0	0	0	0	2
Ret. earnings	152	167	189	188	186	176	171	161	177
Total SH equity	156	170	190	190	186	176	171	161	179
Total claims	189	202	236	224	227	217	213	197	227

	Income Statements								
	1979	**1980**	**1981**	**1982**	**1983**	**1984**	**1985**	**1986**	**1987**
Income	385	401	469	329	277	334	344	326	377
CGS	244	261	293	213	180	223	221	216	239
Selling, G&A***	41	46	51	45	45	47	48	49	51
Incentive bonus	44	43	56	37	22	33	38	33	39
IBT	56	51	69	35	30	31	36	27	48
Income taxes	26	23	31	16	13	14	16	12	21
Net income	30	28	37	19	17	17	20	15	27

*Columns totals may not check and amounts less than $500,000 (0.5) are shown as zero, due to rounding.
**Includes investment in foreign subsidiaries, $29 million in 1987.
***Includes pension expense and payroll taxes on incentive bonus.

Exhibit 4 Revenue Distribution

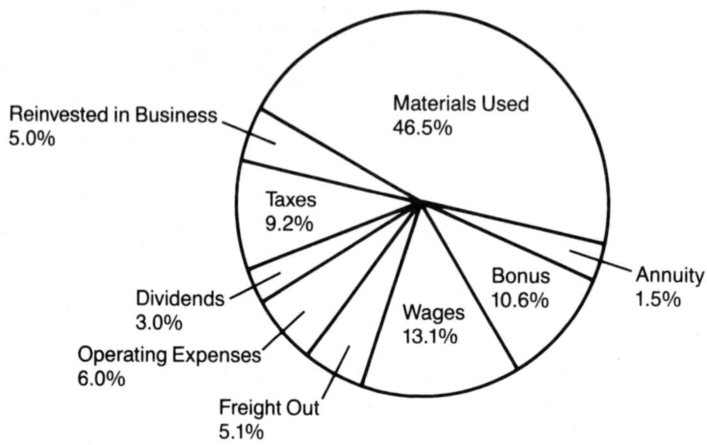

A Concluding Comment

It is easy to believe that the reason for Lincoln's success is the excellent attitude of the employees and their willingness to work harder, faster, and more intelligently than other industrial workers. However, Sabo suggests that appropriate credit be given to Lincoln executives, whom he credits with carrying out the following policies:

1. Management has limited research, development, and manufacturing to a standard product line designed to meet the major needs of the welding industry.

2. New products must be reviewed by manufacturing and all producing costs verified before being approved by management.

3. Purchasing is challenged to not only procure materials at the lowest cost, but also to work closely with engineering and manufacturing to assure that the latest innovations are implemented.

4. Manufacturing supervision and all personnel are held accountable for reduction of scrap, energy conservation, and maintenance of product quality.

5. Production control, material handling, and methods engineering are closely supervised by top management.

6. Management has made cost reduction a way of life at Lincoln, and definite programs are established in many areas, including traffic and shipping, where tremendous savings can result.

7. Management has established a sales department that is technically trained to reduce customer welding costs. This sales approach and other real customer services have eliminated nonessential frills and resulted in long-term benefits to all concerned.

8. Management has encouraged education, technical publishing, and long range programs that have resulted in industry growth, thereby assuring market potential for the Lincoln Electric Company.

Sabo writes, "It is in a very real sense a personal and group experience in faith—a belief that together we can achieve results which alone would not be possible. It is not a perfect system and it is not easy. It requires tremendous dedication and hard work. However, it does work and the results are worth the effort."

Appendix A

Employee Interviews

During the late summer of 1980, the author conducted numerous interviews with Lincoln employees. Typical questions and answers from those interviews are presented below. In order to maintain each employee's personal privacy, the names used for the interviewees are fictitious.

Interview with Betty Stewart, a 52-year-old high school graduate who had been with Lincoln 13 years and who was working as a cost-accounting clerk at the time of the interview.

Q. What jobs have you held here besides the one you have now?
A. I worked in payroll for a while, and then this job came open and I took it.
Q. How much money did you make last year, including your bonus?
A. I would say roughly around $20,000, but I was off for back surgery for a while.
Q. You weren't paid while you were off for back surgery?
A. No.
Q. Did the employee association help out?
A. Yes. The company doesn't furnish that, though. We pay $6 a month into the employee association. I think my check from them was $105.00 a week.
Q. How was your performance rating last year?
A. It was around 100 points, but I lost some points for attendance with my back problem.
Q. How did you get your job at Lincoln?
A. I was bored silly where I was working, and I had heard that Lincoln kept their people busy. So I applied and got the job the next day.
Q. Do you think you make more money than similar workers in Cleveland?
A. I know I do.
Q. What have you done with your money?
A. We have purchased a better home. Also, my son is going to the University of Chicago, which costs $10,000 a year. I buy the Lincoln stock which is offered each year, and I have a little bit of gold.
Q. Have you ever visited with any of the senior executives, like Mr. Willis or Mr. Irrgang?
A. I have known Mr. Willis for a long time.
Q. Does he call you by name?
A. Yes. In fact he was very instrumental in my going to the doctor that I am going to with my back. He knows the director of the clinic.
Q. Do you know Mr. Irrgang?
A. I know him to speak to him, and he always speaks, always. But I have known Mr. Willis for a good many years. When I did Plant Two accounting I did not

understand how the plant operated. Of course you are not allowed in Plant Two, because that's the Electrode Division. I told my boss about the problem one day, and the next thing I knew Mr. Willis came by and said, "Come on, Betty, we're going to Plant Two." He spent an hour and a half showing me the plant.

Q. Do you think Lincoln employees produce more than those in other companies?

A. I think with the incentive program the way that it is, if you want to work and achieve, then you will do it. If you don't want to work and achieve, you will not do it no matter where you are. Just because you are merit rated and have a bonus, if you really don't want to work hard, then you're not going to. You will accept your 90 points or 92 or 85 because, even with that, you make more money than people on the outside.

Q. Do you think Lincoln employees will ever join a union?

A. I don't know why they would.

Q. What is the most important advantage of working for Lincoln Electric?

A. You have an incentive, and you can push and get something for pushing. That's not true in a lot of companies.

Q. So you say that money is a very major advantage?

A. Money is a major advantage, but it's not just the money. It's the fact that, having the incentive, you do wish to work a little harder. I'm sure that there are a lot of men here who, if they worked some other place, would not work as hard as they do here. Not that they are overworked—I don't mean that—but I'm sure they wouldn't push.

Q. Is there anything that you would like to add?

A. I do like working here. I am better off being pushed mentally. In another company if you pushed too hard you would feel a little bit of pressure, and someone might say, "Hey, slow down; don't try so hard." But here you are encouraged, not discouraged.

Interview with Ed Sanderson, 23-year-old high school graduate who had been with Lincoln four years and who was a machine operator in the Electrode Division at the time of the interview.

Q. How did you happen to get this job?

A. My wife was pregnant, and I was making three bucks an hour and one day I came here and applied. That was it. I kept calling to let them know I was still interested.

Q. Roughly what were your earnings last year including your bonus?

A. $37,000.

Q. What have you done with your money since you have been here?

A. Well, we've lived pretty well, and we bought a condominium.

Q. Have you paid for the condominium?

A. No, but I could.

Q. Have you bought your Lincoln stock this year?

A. No, I haven't bought any Lincoln stock yet.

Q. Do you get the feeling that the executives here are pretty well thought of?
A. I think they are. To get where they are today, they had to really work.
Q. Wouldn't that be true anywhere?
A. I think more so here because seniority really doesn't mean anything. If you work with a guy who has 20 years here, and you have two months and you're doing a better job, you will get advanced before he will.
Q. Are you paid on a piece rate basis?
A. My gang is. There are nine of us who make the bare electrode, and the whole group gets paid based on how much electrode we make.
Q. Do you think you work harder than workers in other factories in the Cleveland area?
A. Yes, I would say I probably work harder.
Q. Do you think it hurts anybody?
A. No, a little hard work never hurts anybody.
Q. If you could choose, do you think you would be as happy earning a little less money and being able to slow down a little?
A. No, it doesn't bother me. If it bothered me, I wouldn't do it.
Q. What would you say is the biggest disadvantage of working at Lincoln, as opposed to working somewhere else?
A. Probably having to work shift work.
Q. Why do you think Lincoln employees produce more than workers in other plants?
A. That's the way the company is set up. The more you put out, the more you're going to make.
Q. Do you think it's the piece rate and bonus together?
A. I don't think people would work here if they didn't know that they would be rewarded at the end of the year.
Q. Do you think Lincoln employees will ever join a union?
A. No.
Q. What are the major advantages of working for Lincoln?
A. Money.
Q. Are there any other advantages?
A. Yes, we don't have a union shop. I don't think I could work in a union shop.
Q. Do you think you are a career man with Lincoln at this time?
A. Yes.

Interview with Roger Lewis, 23-year-old Purdue graduate in mechanical engineering who had been in the Lincoln sales program for 15 months and who was working in the Cleveland sales office at the time of the interview.

Q. How did you get your job at Lincoln?
A. I saw that Lincoln was interviewing on campus at Purdue, and I went by. I later came to Cleveland for a plant tour and was offered a job.

Q. Do you know any of the senior executives? Would they know you by name?
A. Yes, I know all of them—Mr. Irrgang, Mr. Willis, Mr. Manross.
Q. Do you think Lincoln salesmen work harder than those in other companies?
A. Yes. I don't think there are many salesmen for other companies who are putting in 50- to 60-hour weeks. Everybody here works harder. You can go out in the plant, or you can go upstairs, and there's nobody sitting around.
Q. Do you see any real disadvantage of working at Lincoln?
A. I don't know if it's a disadvantage but Lincoln is a Spartan company, a very thrifty company. I like that. The sales offices are functional, not fancy.
Q. Why do you think Lincoln employees have such high productivity?
A. Piecework has a lot to do with it. Lincoln is smaller than many plants, too; you can stand in one place and see the materials come in one side and the product go out the other. You feel a part of the company. The chance to get ahead is important, too. They have a strict policy of promoting from within, so you know you have a chance. I think in a lot of other places you may not get as fair a shake as you do here. The sales offices are on a smaller scale, too. I like that. I tell someone that we have two people in the Baltimore office, and they say, "You've got to be kidding." It's smaller and more personal. Pay is the most important thing. I have heard that this is the highest-paying factory in the world.

Interview with Jimmy Roberts, a 47-year-old high school graduate, who had been with Lincoln 17 years and who was working as a multiple drill press operator at the time of the interview.

Q. What jobs have you had at Lincoln?
A. I started out cleaning the men's locker room in 1963. After about a year I got a job in the flux department, where we make the coating for welding rods. I worked there for seven or eight years and then got my present job.
Q. Do you make one particular part?
A. No, there are a variety of parts I make—at least 25.
Q. Each one has a different piece rate attached to it?
A. Yes.
Q. Are some piece rates better than others?
A. Yes.
Q. How do you determine which ones you are going to do?
A. You don't. Your supervisor assigns them.
Q. How much money did you make last year?
A. $47,000.
Q. Have you ever received any kind of award or citation?
A. No.
Q. Was your rating ever over 110?
A. Yes. For the past five years, probably, I made over 110 points.
Q. Is there any attempt to let others know?
A. The kind of points I get? No.

Q. Do you know what they are making?
A. No. There are some who might not be too happy with their points, and they might make it known. The majority, though, do not make it a point of telling other employees.
Q. Would you be just as happy earning a little less money and working a little slower?
A. I don't think I would—not at this point. I have done piecework all these years, and the fast pace doesn't really bother me.
Q. Why do you think Lincoln productivity is so high?
A. The incentive thing—the bonus distribution. I think that would be the main reason. The paycheck you get every two weeks is important too.
Q. Do you think Lincoln employees would ever join a union?
A. I don't think so. I have never heard anyone mention it.
Q. What is the most important advantage of working here?
A. The amount of money you make. I don't think I could make this type of money anywhere else, especially with only a high school education.
Q. As a black person, do you feel that Lincoln discriminates in any way against blacks?
A. No. I don't think any more so than any other job. Naturally, there is a certain amount of discrimination, regardless of where you are.

Interview with Joe Trahan, 58-year-old high school graduate who had been with Lincoln 39 years and who was employed as a working supervisor in the toolroom at the time of the interview.

Q. Roughly what was your pay last year?
A. Over $50,000—salary, bonus, stock dividends.
Q. How much was your bonus?
A. About $23,000.
Q. Have you ever gotten a special award of any kind?
A. Not really.
Q. What have you done with your money?
A. My house is paid for—and my two cars. I also have some bonds and the Lincoln stock.
Q. What do you think of the executives at Lincoln?
A. They're really top notch.
Q. What is the major disadvantage of working at Lincoln Electric?
A. I don't know of any disadvantage at all.
Q. Do you think you produce more than most people in similar jobs with other companies?
A. I do believe that.
Q. Why is that? Why do you believe that?
A. We are on the incentive system. Everything we do, we try to improve to make a better product with a minimum of outlay. We try to improve the bonus.

Q. Would you be just as happy making a little less money and not working quite so hard?
A. I don't think so.
Q. You know that Lincoln productivity is higher than that at most other plants. Why is that?
A. Money.
Q. Do you think Lincoln employees would ever join a union?
A. I don't think they would ever consider it.
Q. What is the most important advantage of working at Lincoln?
A. Compensation.
Q. Tell me something about Mr. James Lincoln, who died in 1965.
Q. You are talking about Jimmy, Sr. He always strolled through the shop in his shirtsleeves. Big fellow. Always looked distinguished. Gray hair. Friendly sort of guy. I was a member of the advisory board one year. He was there each time.
Q. Did he strike you as really caring?
A. I think he always cared for people.
Q. Did you get any sensation of a religious nature from him?
A. No, not really.
Q. And religion is not part of the program now?
A. No.
Q. Do you think Mr. Lincoln was a very intelligent man, or was he just a nice guy?
A. I would say he was pretty well educated. A great talker—always right off the top of his head. He knew what he was talking about all the time.
Q. When were bonuses for beneficial suggestions done away with?
A. About 15 years ago.
Q. Did that hurt very much?
A. I don't think so, because suggestions are still rewarded through the merit rating system.
Q. Is there anything you would like to add?
A. It's a good place to work. The union kind of ties other places down. At other places, electricians only do electrical work, carpenters only do carpenter work. At Lincoln Electric we all pitch in and do whatever needs to be done.
Q. So a major advantage is not having a union?
A. That's right.

Case 21

Wal-Mart Stores, Inc.

In January 1982, amid a distressed economy, Wal-Mart continues to pace the discount-chain industry, leaving K-Mart, Target, and Woolco behind. The chain emerged in 1962 with one store serving a small community in Arkansas and has grown to 491 stores serving 13 different states at the close of 1981. Jack Shewmaker, President of Wal-Mart, says the chain will continue to grow into markets where we can get the right profitability and return on investment.

History and Background

Wal-Mart Stores, Inc., headquartered in Bentonville, Arkansas, had its origin in the variety-store business. Sam Walton opened his first variety store, under the Ben Franklin franchise, in Newport, Arkansas, in 1945. One year later, he was joined by his brother, J. L. "Bud" Walton, now Senior Vice-President, who opened a similar store in Versailles, Missouri. The two brothers went on to assemble a group of 15 Ben Franklin stores, and subsequently developed the concept of larger discount department stores in communities of small size. This concept emerged in 1962 when the first Wal-Mart Discount City store in Rogers, Arkansas opened. Wal-Mart Stores, Inc., became a publicly held corporation in October 1970. After the company was listed on the over-the-counter market, stock began trading on the New York Stock Exchange in mid-1972. The founder, Sam Walton, continues to serve as chairman of the board and chief executive officer.

In 1982, Wal-Mart has 491 discount department stores servicing the general merchandise needs of its customers. The discount stores range in size from 30,000 to 90,000 square feet, with the average store size being about 52,000 square feet. Wal-Mart stores are usually organized with 36 departments and carry merchandise such as wearing apparel for the entire family, household furnishings, appliances, and other hard-line merchandise. These stores are located in 13 states across the south and the southeast.

Unlike many other major discount chains, Wal-Mart has devoted itself almost exclusively to serving small towns and medium-sized cities. In their respective communities, Wal-Mart Discount Cities are the largest nonfood retailers. The largest cities in which the company operates, at this time, are: Little Rock, Arkansas; Shreveport, Louisiana; Springfield, Missouri; Huntsville, Alabama; Nashville, Tennessee.

Management

Wal-Mart has exercised a highly entrepreneurial, participatory, and goal-oriented style of management. Responsibility for Wal-Mart's style has been attributed to Sam Walton, chief executive officer and chairman of the board. Serving below him are some of the most respected top-level management personnel in the discount-store industry. Heading these top-level executives is Jack Shewmaker, President (see Exhibit 1).

One of the chain's historical strengths, though, has been that it has a single-minded phi-

---

Source: This case was prepared by Monya Giggar, Gregg Gunchick, and David Miller, under the supervision of Professor Sexton Adams, University of North Texas, and Professor Adelaide Griffin, Texas Woman's University. Permission to use granted by Sexton Adams. This case is based on library research.

Exhibit 1 Organization Chart

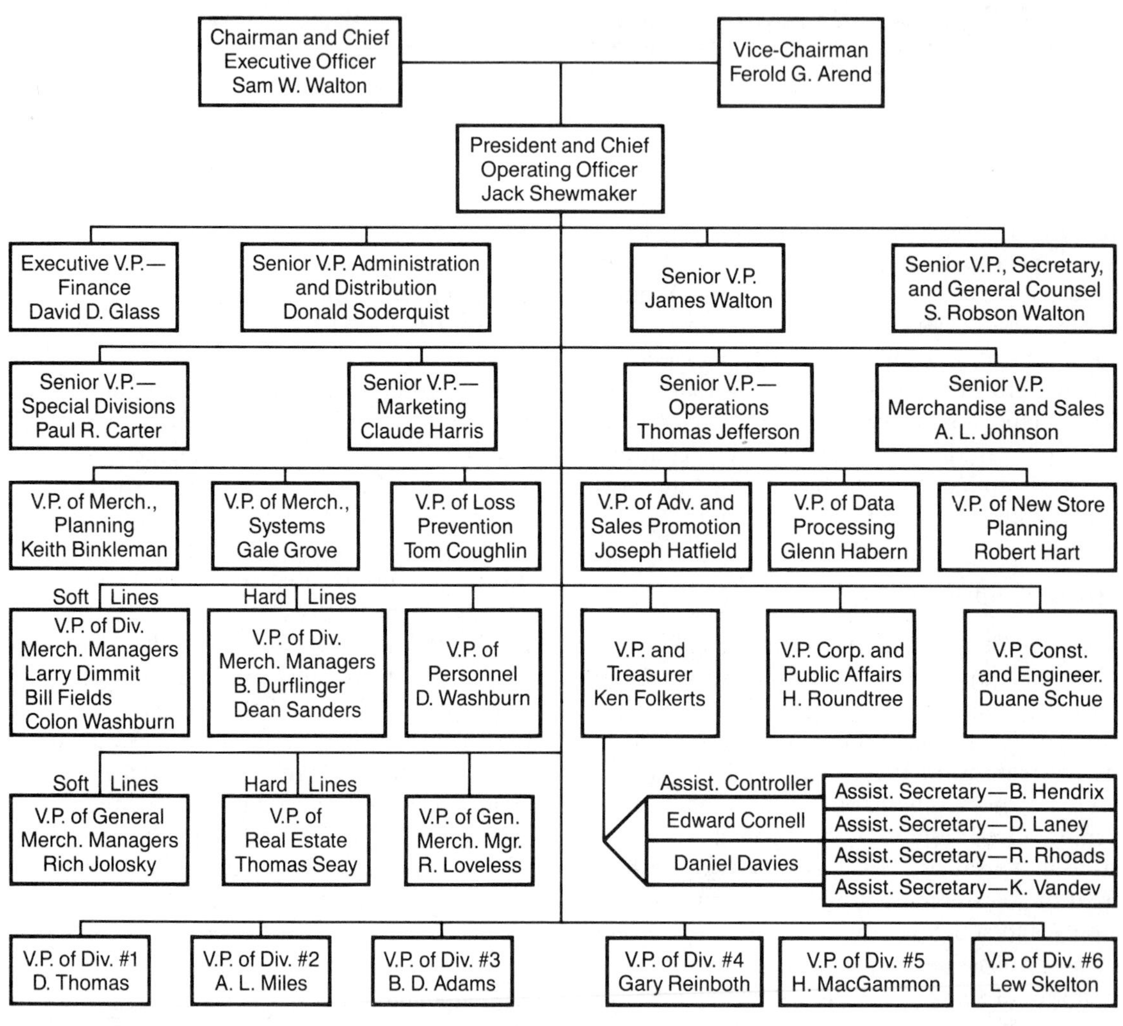

losophy that has kept it on the straight and narrow path established by Sam Walton 36 years ago. Sam's personal attitude has been reflected in the manner which he has established special relationships with many of the employees, whom he calls "associates." In the early years at Wal-Mart, Sam visited all the stores twice a year, exchanging open communication on ideas and problems. Theo Ashcraft, Vice-President of the Lease Department, said that Sam has always listened to people . . . learning (from them) everyday.

In 1982, the geographical expansion of Wal-Mart makes it impossible for Sam Walton to visit and communicate at a personal level with the employees of all 491 stores. Therefore, Jack Shewmaker has inherited many responsibilities, handed-down by the aging Sam Walton. Shewmaker, of the Sam Walton mold, is a strong believer in participatory management. He says,

"Wal-Mart's system is people supportive. This is a major factor in our operational strategy. We design programs so systems and procedures can be overridden by the manager, assistant manager, or the store manager who has first-hand contact with the problem." In addition to his support of Sam Walton's participatory management style, Shewmaker also maintains a personal relationship with Sam Walton, accompanying him on various hunting expeditions.

Grass-Roots Involvement

Wal-Mart practices management objectives called "grass-roots involvement." Jack Shewmaker refers to these objectives as "the involvement of our associates in every aspect of our business and the recognition of their ideas, suggestions, and problems is a key factor to our productivity gains." This policy was designed to provide continuous communication between top management and field operations. Starting at the store level, ideas and thoughts on improving the company's operations are written down by the associates and forwarded to headquarters. The overall corporate plan consolidates these individual goals and objectives to produce Wal-Mart's plan for action.

However, the corporate plans are composed in a centralized fashion at corporate headquarters. Every Saturday Sam Walton meets with the top-level executives and corporate planners to discuss future strategies. Sam continues to have the final word.

Another facet of Wal-Mart's strategy is an extension of the participatory management style to get employees involved. "We believe in sharing vital information on sales, expenses, and profits with every associate throughout the company," says Shewmaker. Among other vital information available, ". . . each month we prepare departmental reports showing percentage to total and comparative performance on sales, markdowns, inventory turnover, and gross margin. Each person is made to feel that he/she can affect the results."

Each of the store managers is evaluated on overall sales from his store, with consideration given to location and size of community. They are also evaluated on appearance, contributions in the form of ideas to corporate headquarters, and their ability to compete in their region.

Wal-Mart's most successful incentive program is its VPI or Volume Producing Item contest. This program allows individual store departments free rein to price and promote certain merchandise of their own choice. Walton claims that many faltering products have been revived as a result. "This is another way to keep people involved and thinking. Each month everyone knows where they rank in the chain and what percentage of a store's business they have," he explains.

The responses of Wal-Mart employees have been overwhelmingly in favor of the people-oriented programs. A clerk said that she "had worked for another chain for three years before coming to Wal-Mart, and I started off earning more here and there's no feeling of strain or pressure." A manager stated, "It's so much more open. You know where you stand all the time. You're not left in the dark."

Merchandising

Consumers' perceptions of Wal-Mart in Russellville, Arkansas, a typical Wal-Mart market, are just fantastic. In a Wal-Mart survey conducted in Russellville, many consumers responded positively to the chain with comments such as they have better quality merchandise, their prices are lower than K-Mart's, and they have a big selection. Wal-Mart's merchandising program has found the right combination of brand names, low prices, promotions and presentations, item merchandising, and fashion sense to attract and keep its customers.

Wal-Mart combines a strong brand-name merchandising philosophy with its domination of categories and subcategories. An example of its brand-name appeal is the Wrangler program. The complete size assortment of Wrangler jeans are displayed in special dark-stained wooden cubicles. Inside the display or adjacent to it in both the men's and women's departments, are accessories (hats, belts, boots, and shirts) positioned to encourage tie-in sales. Brand programs are also extended to the hard lines. The Wal-Mart strategy is that it carries all the usual hard-line brands, but adds fringe items to bolster the price/value perception of its shoppers. In health and beauty aids, a line of old-favorite fragrances like Wind Song, Jontue, and Emeraud is joined by a selection of limited semirestricted lines, like Charlie, Cie, Sophia, and Scoundrel. These limited additions are stocked heavily in multiple facings on open shelves, unlike many other chains that keep limited lines under lock-and-key. The philosophy for having the lines accessible was that one cannot sell the lines where the shoppers cannot get to them.

Another area where perception plays a key role is in Wal-Mart's pricing policies. As one consumer states, Wal-Mart's prices are lower than K-Mart's. The selection is better, too. Wal-Mart, T.G. & Y., and K-Mart are often locked into intense competition in the markets they all share (small-towns and rural areas). In setting pricing policies, each chain must devise an assortment strategy. Of the two competitors, T.G. & Y. tends to be overassorted—similar to the variety stores of the past. K-Mart, on the other hand, tends to narrow its assortments and fill-in the gaps with private label brands, such as K-Mart toilet tissue and facial tissue. Wal-Mart's strategy calls for splitting the difference. First, it out-assorts K-Mart, then it beats the prices offered by T.G. & Y. Additionally, much of Wal-Mart's perceived lower prices is revealed in a comparison of shelf-prices of the three discount retailers that was conducted in Bartlesville, Oklahoma (1981). The results of the shelf-price study are shown in Exhibit 2. There were four random categories chosen and several subcategories within these categories. The total price differential for a 36-item market basket amounted to less than 7½ percent between competitors. These results are indicative of the closeness of the competition.

Much of Wal-Mart's success in developing consumer perceptions is accredited to its promotional programs. The program emphasis provides the impact of name brands and good values that make key departments dominant in the marketplace. "Power alley," a Wal-Mart promotional characteristic, is the high-powered promotional race track in all the stores. The alley promotions are lined down each aisle in the store's race track. In most stores, the power alley will have 100 or more promotional tables or platforms. These tables/platforms contain merchandise with average tickets that are sometimes 100 percent lower than at most chains. This promotional effort is the key to the volume production that has enabled Wal-Mart to maintain its growth. Included among the 100 or more tables and platforms that make up the total program are assorted 2 × 2 ft. cubes, 3 × 3 ft. tables, and 5 ft. square tables and platforms, occasionally joined together. The 2 × 2 cubes are used in health and beauty aids, with 18 to 24 items set in a double row down the center of an interior aisle. Requiring lower inventory investments, the small cubes are also used to pull shoppers into the automotive department located at the right (or left) rear corner of the race track aisle.

Wal-Mart's strategy also entails the use of item merchandising. It is a concept by which an unusual "item" is positioned near or adjacent to a department to build category dominance. To create a bigger share of the bed-sheet market and to build brand image, Cannon sheets at attractive prices are promoted on a table adjacent to the domestics department. The item sets the scene for the particular department and serves as a way to draw shoppers into the department. All Wal-Mart chains practice this concept with their "million-dollar" items. These are basic everyday needs (sheets, socks, mattress covers) that help build a category of major brand-name goods that help build the brand-name image.

The profitable lure of apparel is also becoming increasingly evident in Wal-Mart stores. Over the next five years, Wal-Mart intends to build its stake in soft lines to 35 percent, ac-

Exhibit 2 Shelf-Price Comparison, Bartlesville, Oklahoma, Shelf Prices

Item	Wal-Mart	T.G. & Y.	K-Mart
H & BA			
Bayer 100's	$ 1.57	$ 1.60	$ 1.57
Excedrin X-Strength 100's	2.58	3.37	2.06[a]
Bufferin 100's	2.13	2.13	2.13
Bufferin A.S.	1.67[a]	2.09	2.43
Tylenol X-Strength 100's	3.54	3.27	3.29
Tylenol X-Strength 50's	2.33	2.53	2.33
Anacin 200's	3.68	3.97	3.68
Anacin 100's	1.42[a]	1.99	1.97
Flex 16oz. Shampoo	1.68	1.68	1.74
Suave Baby Shampoo 28oz.	1.06	1.14	1.48
Faberge Organic X-tra Body	1.18	1.18	1.18
No More Tears 16oz. Shampoo	2.62	3.12	1.97[a]
Wella Balsam 8oz. Shampoo	1.78	1.77	1.67
Head & Shoulders 15oz. tube	2.97	2.99	1.58[a]
Head & Shoulders 11oz. bottle	2.46	2.67	2.46
Prell tube 5oz.	1.92	1.72	1.92
Pert 15oz.	1.83[a]	2.44	2.13
Silkience 15oz.	2.56	2.78	2.16
Small Electrics			
Mr. Coffee 10 cup	22.88	22.99	24.97
GE automatic percolator	28.42	28.96	28.87
Regal Poly-Perk hot pot	9.96	9.99	10.62
Automotive			
Rain Dance 16oz.	5.54	5.99	5.07
Turtle Zip Wax 18oz.	1.84	2.17	2.07
Phillips TropArctic oil	0.97	0.95	0.97
Quaker State oil	0.97	0.95	0.97
Penzoil 10W-40	0.97	0.95	0.97
PL nondetergent	0.68	0.77	0.74
Hardware			
Powerlok II 20 ft.	11.57	12.99	12.48
Stanley 16oz.	8.44	5.67[a]	9.97
Steelmaster 16oz.	12.76	14.30	11.88
Black & Decker			
7104 Drill	16.88	17.87	15.77
7004 Drill	12.97	12.99	11.97
7504 Jig saw	12.97	11.77	13.48
7580 VSR drill	42.46	34.57	33.88
7308 Circular saw	29.96	35.97	27.88
7300 Circular saw 5½ in.	24.97	27.77	27.97
TOTAL	$284.19	$290.06	$268.31

Source: Discount Store News Research, December 14, 1981, p. 43.
[a]Sale item.

cording to the chain's executives. This is evident in the newer stores opened. In recent stores, the format is upgraded and total space-to-apparel and major soft-lines is as high as 43 percent. Wal-Mart has placed large, prominently placed departmental signs that tend to resemble J. C. Penney's signs. Brand emphasis is concentrated more and more on the apparel side of the store as is obvious with the Wrangler brand emphasis in boys', men's, and women's wear. Most store units also stock Garan knit sport shirts and display them on an eye-catching "brand displayer." Also, Wal-Mart is now trying to build identity in men's socks by displaying signs that read, "Alder from Burlington." Overall, Wal-Mart steers clear of no-names, especially in categories where image counts.

Advertising

The advertising policy, displayed in all Wal-Mart stores, is to take sale advertisements from any other store and match the price. Under this policy, historically, it has held advertising expenditures to 1.5 percent of sales or less. Recent expansion, however, will raise this level to about 1.7 percent of sales or nearly $2.4 billion a year. According to company sources, one third of that total will be spent on newspaper advertising, and television spots will be increased from $6 million to the $7 or $8-million dollar level. Expansion into urban areas has entered Wal-Mart into markets where television time, newspaper space, and radio time are substantially more costly.

In addition to its added level of expansion, Wal-Mart has begun running more expensive, up-scale advertising. In the small town of Fayetteville, Arkansas, where it was opening an 85,000 square foot store, Wal-Mart ran a 36-page, four-color, all-photo, magazine-size, "catalog" circular. This new style resembled a J. C. Penney's catalog. All 36 pages, 11 or so pages of apparel and the remainder of consumables, seasonal merchandise, and hardlines, were full four-color and the circular used models and/or product photography. In contrast to the bigger-store advertisements, smaller units' circulars are usually 10-page broadsheets with false four-color on the front and back and black and white inside.

Wal-Mart is devising two separate merchandising and advertising strategies: the typical hard-line-oriented 40,000 to 50,000 square foot store and the 85,000 to 90,000 square foot stores that give greater emphasis to the fashion apparel side. This strategy is important to Wal-Mart's future in the ever-changing marketplace.

Distribution Centers

A basic practice of Wal-Mart has been to limit its store operations to about a 450-500-mile radius of distribution to centers, to achieve speed of restocking and savings in delivery costs. As Wal-Mart continues pushing its geographical limits, distribution that is cost-effective becomes more critical.

Located near headquarters in Bentonville, a 525,000 square foot distribution complex handled, in the past, 80 percent of all the goods sold by Wal-Mart. The expansion of the chain has resulted in additional distribution centers being constructed. In Searcy, Arkansas, an equal capacity center was opened to aid in Wal-Mart's expansion into southern Arkansas. Long-range plans called for the construction of a 512,000 square foot center in Palestine, Texas. This center fully came on-line, at the close of 1981. In 1982, a 900,000 square foot distribution center will be built in Cullman, Alabama.

The Palestine distribution center helped Wal-Mart penetrate the Texas border and Gulf Coast markets. Sam Walton is convinced that he can "double, even triple" the size of his company, just with locations in Texas and Louisiana. Shreveport, Louisiana, Houston, Corpus Christi, and Dallas—Fort Worth, Texas have been sited for the expansion of Wal-Mart. Management has already sited the Rio Grande valley and eight more sites in the area for prime expansion moves.

The new Alabama distribution center may be even more critical to the chain's expansion than the Palestine center. Coming on-stream in 1983, the center will provide overnight delivery into the states where the Big K acquisition brought the chain. It will extend into the Carolinas, Georgia, and Florida. These areas could be potential sites for Wal-Mart Country expansion.

Wal-Mart distribution centers (existing, as well as those to be built) are mechanized, utilizing conveyor systems to expedite the flow of merchandise and each serve an approximate proportion of the chain's stores. There are two additional distribution centers in Bentonville that are used for the inspecting and processing of fashion clothing; warehousing for jewelry and sporting goods; operations and accumulation of sale merchandise for shipment to stores as close to the sale as possible. The centers' radius span is to allow Wal-Mart's own trucking fleet to make deliveries in one day.

Wal-Mart trucks are expected to travel about 20-million miles in 1982 at a cost of about $18 million. The distribution centers' total expenses run approximately 2.5 percent of the goods shipped through them (now about 85 percent of the chain's total merchandise assortment). Wal-Mart's move toward establishing distribution centers and trucking fleets in Texas and Alabama is part of its long-range plan to expand its markets outward.

The Acquisition of Big K

Wal-Mart acquired the Kuhn's Big K chain, headquartered in Nashville, Tennessee, in August 1981. The total cost for 92 Big K stores, a large distribution center, headquarters, all of Big K's liabilities, and inventories within each store was about $100 million. Each store is estimated at costing $125,000 each to convert to the Wal-Mart label.

The conversion process (at the close of 1981) was first applied to the five least profitable Big K stores. This served as an acid test of the validity of the acquisition. According to Sam Walton, the average sales gains in these renovated stores have been in excess of 150 percent. In the first quarter as part of the Wal-Mart chain, the renovated stores contributed $70 million in sales volume.

The purchase helped Wal-Mart's future plans become more attainable. With the Big K stores, Wal-Mart gained penetration of Tennessee, Kentucky, and large "clusters" in Alabama and Mississippi. It also brought Wal-Mart into the new areas of Georgia and South Carolina. Thus, by purchasing a bargain expansion and getting good locations that are profitable to the chain, Wal-Mart stands ready to face the future.

Financing

The company has financed its capital expenditures for expansion primarily through internally generated funds. Funds from operations, $74 million in fiscal 1981, are the primary source of liquidity for the company. For additional externally generated funds, Wal-Mart offered one million shares in 1981 that generated almost $33 million for the company. At fiscal year end, 1981, Wal-Mart had access to $176 million of unused short-term credit.

As far as controlling expenses, Wal-Mart has done so using several strategies: (1) negotiating harder with landlords for store sites (its current occupancy cost is 1.75 percent of sales), (2) store payrolls are tight—currently 7.5 percent (store managers work on smaller base salaries but with richer profit-sharing plans), (3) discouraging employee theft by sharing half the savings with employees, (4) tough bargaining stances on key line items from suppliers, and (5) advertising costs are kept at less than 1.2 percent of sales.

Wal-Mart's operating, selling, general, and administrative expenses (1981) rose 138 percent since 1977, and the cost of goods sold at the chain increased even more by 139.7 percent. Sales of the company rose 142.2 percent during that same period. Earnings for Wal-Mart also increased 193.8 percent since 1977.

The financial statements that follow detail Wal-Mart's impressive financial record. Exhibit 3 is the consolidated balance sheet, and Exhibit

Exhibit 3 Consolidated Balance Sheet

	January 31 1981	January 31 1980
	(Dollar Amounts in Thousands)	
Assets		
Current assets:		
Cash	$ 6,927	$ 5,090
Short-term money market investments	11,528	—
Receivables	12,666	7,806
Recoverable costs from sale/leaseback	31,325	15,557
Inventories	280,021	235,315
Prepaid expenses	2,737	2,849
Total Current Assets	345,204	266,617
Property, plant, and equipment, at cost:		
Land	5,903	15,002
Buildings and improvements	51,200	42,287
Fixtures and equipment	80,411	56,072
Transportation equipment	12,969	9,012
	150,483	122,373
Less accumulated depreciation	33,702	23,613
Net property, plant and equipment	116,781	98,760
Property under capital leases	152,882	109,608
Less accumulated amortization	23,721	17,806
Net property under capital leases	129,161	91,802
Other assets and deferred charges	1,199	700
Total Assets	$592,345	$457,879
Liabilities and Stockholders' Equity		
Current liabilities:		
Notes payable	$ 15,000	$ 25,080
Accounts payable	97,445	100,102
Accrued liabilities:		
Salaries	11,229	12,889
Taxes, other than income	9,627	6,619
Other	25,748	15,148
Accrued federal and state income taxes	11,907	5,365
Long-term debt due within one year	3,375	2,314
Obligations under capital leases due within one year	3,270	2,704
Total Current Liabilities	177,601	170,221
Long-term debt	30,184	24,862
Long-term obligations under capital leases	134,896	97,212
Deferred income taxes	1,355	740
Stockholders' equity:		
Preferred stock	—	—
Common stock	3,234	1,512
Capital in excess of par value	67,481	35,064
Retained earnings	177,594	128,268
Total Stockholders' Equity	248,309	164,844
Total Liabilities and Stockholders' Equity	$592,345	$457,879

Source: 1981 Annual Report.

4 is the consolidated statement of income. Exhibit 5 highlights the two-year comparison and the five-year financial review of Wal-Mart's performance. Exhibit 6 provides a review of 10 years of growth for Wal-Mart.

Wal-Mart vs. "The Other Guys"

Wal-Mart's five-year financial record through 1981 has paced the discount-store industry. Exhibit 7 shows five-year averages for Wal-Mart and two of its competitors. While running above the industry median, Wal-Mart has stiff competition to face. As Wal-Mart moves into larger metropolitan areas, its competition expands from Magic Mart, Gibson's, T.G. & Y., and K-Mart to include Dayton Hudson's Target, Woolworth, Murphy, and the Caldwell chain.

Although K-Mart is Wal-Mart's closest competitor, Target stores have been making moves to expand into Arkansas, Wal-Mart's home state. At the close of 1981, Target and Wal-Mart vie only in Nashville, Tennessee. However, the Dayton Hudson discount chain purchased three shuttered Woolco stores in Little Rock, an 80,000 square foot unit and two 10,000 square footers. The stores are to be remodeled in early 1982. Over the next two years, industry observ-

Exhibit 4 Consolidated Statement of Income

	Years Ended January 31 (Dollar Amount in 000) 1981	1980	1979
Number of stores in operation at the end of the year	330	276	229
Revenues:			
Net sales	$1,643,199	$1,248,176	$900,298
Rentals from licensed departments	5,331	4,804	6,344
Other income—net	6,732	5,288	3,271
	1,655,262	1,258,268	909,913
Costs and expenses:			
Cost of sales	1,207,802	919,305	661,062
Operating, selling and general and administrative expenses	331,524	251,616	182,365
Interest costs:	5,808	4,438	3,119
Debt	10,849	8,621	6,595
Capital leases	1,555,983	1,183,980	853,141
Income before income taxes	99,279	74,288	56,772
Provision for federal and state income taxes:			
Current	42,982	31,649	28,047
Deferred	615	1,488	(722)
	43,597	33,137	27,325
Net income	$ 55,682	$ 41,151	$ 29,447
Net income per share:			
Primary and fully diluted	$1.73	$1.34[a]	$.97[a]

Source: 1981 Annual Report.
[a]Adjusted to reflect the 100 percent stock dividend paid on December 16, 1980. See accompanying notes.

Exhibit 5 Wal-Mart's Financial Highlights

Two-Year Comparison
(Dollar amount in thousands)

	1981	1980
Current assets	$345,204	$266,617
Current liabilities...	177,601	170,221
Working capital....	167,603	96,396
Current ratio	1.94	1.57
Stockholders' equity	$248,309	$164,844
Number of shares outstanding	32,342,445	30,242,522[a]

Five-Year Financial Review
(Dollar amounts in thousands except per share data)

	1981	1980	1979	1978	1977
Net sales.........	$1,643,199	$1,248,176	$900,298	$678,456	$478,807
Income before income taxes....	99,279	74,288	56,772	40,847	30,857
Net income	55,682	41,151	29,447	21,191	16,039
Net income per share:					
Primary	$ 1.73	$ 1.34[a]	$ .97[a]	$ .74[a]	$ .58[a]
Fully diluted.....	1.73	1.34[a]	.97[a]	.71[a]	.54[a]
Number of stores in operation at the end of the period	330	276	229	195	153

Source: 1981 Annual Report.
[a]Adjusted to reflect the 100 percent stock dividend paid December 16, 1980 to holders of Wal-Mart common stock.

ers say that Texas appears a likely mark for expansion as Target currently covers the state with roughly half the number of stores as Wal-Mart.

The past performance of Wal-Mart in its smaller towns has been aided by its assimilation of technological advances. Exhibit 8 provides the data to support Wal-Mart's operational power among its competition. Thus, the expansive strength of Wal-Mart will be tested by all its competitors in the years to come.

Industry Trends

Within the discount-store industry, there is a definite trend toward upscaled merchandise presentation. K-Mart is adopting a new merchandising program that, for example, is dropping all synthetic fibers in favor of natural blends. In addition, in view of Wal-Mart's success in rural markets, K-Mart is targeting expansion outside of metropolitan areas. Increasing emphasis on promotionally priced goods has caused reductions in many chains' profit margins. According to Kenneth Mache, president of Dayton Hudson (Target), this additional promotional activity will depress the bottom lines for the major chains by cutting into already reduced margins. To combat these problems, many discounters are turning to more updated apparel lines and cosmetics while at the same time reducing the number of items carried.

Macroeconomic factors have a direct impact on industry strategies. In the recessionary environment of early 1982, for example, discounters

Exhibit 6 Ten Years of Growth for Wal-Mart

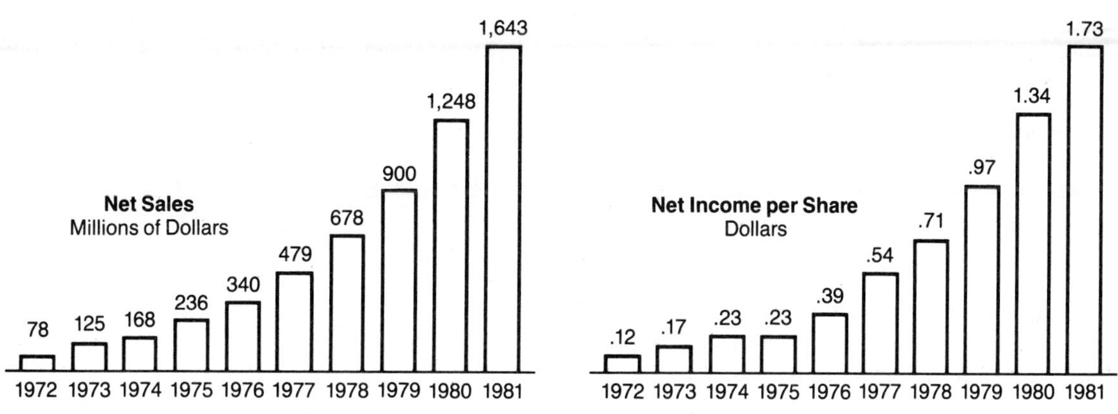

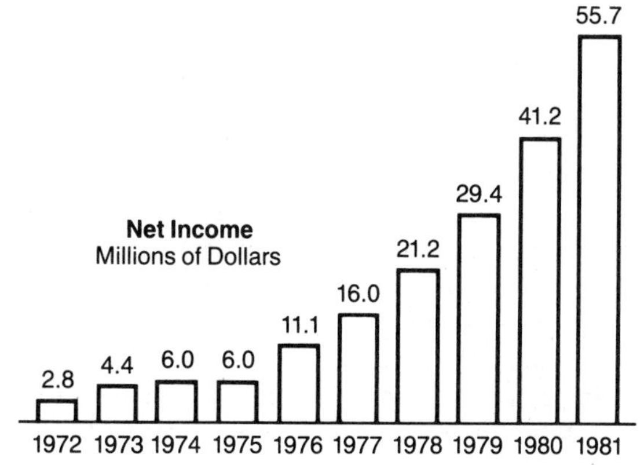

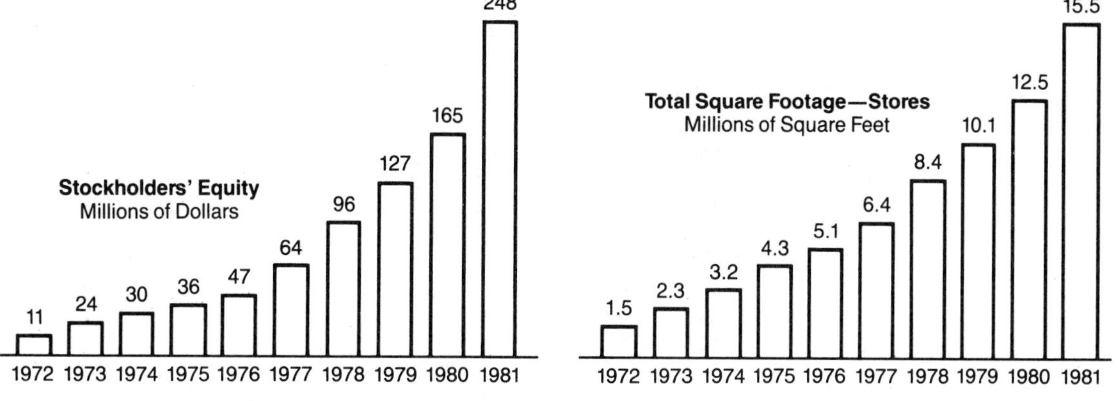

Exhibit 7 Five-Year Averages

Stores	Return on Equity	Sales Growth	Profit Margin
Wal-Mart	30.6%	37.4%	3.3%
K-Mart	16.0	17.1	1.5
Woolworth	11.8	9.6	1.6
Industry Median	12.1	9.7	2.2

Source: "Sam's Song," as published in *Forbes*, January 1982.

are caught in a squeeze between declining real income of consumers because of inflation as well as a very high unemployment rate. As a result, consumers are shopping less frequently, and seeking out sale-priced items when they do shop. Of this, a Merrill Lynch analyst, Jeffrey Feiner, remarks, this pattern may reverse itself following the scheduled 10 percent tax cut in July 1982. But retailers believe that consumers are settling into the habit of sale shopping and will not change quickly.

Industry merchandisers are becoming more selective on the merchandise carried in their stores. Today's successful merchant carefully scrutinizes inventories, making sure that goods do not sit on shelves by stepping up promotions. The test for discounters in the future is to combine a low-cost structure with the most innovative merchandising techniques to move the goods.

There is also a trend toward greater similarity between major competitors in the discount-store industry. Many of the more successful innovations of one chain are quickly adopted by its competitors. Examples of this include racetrack configurations in store layouts, heavy use of promotional tables in merchandising, and upgraded apparel quality and presentation, to name a few.

Company Outlook

The important things have changed very little for Wal-Mart over the years. The company still makes strong presentations of basic merchandise, still benefits from Sam Walton's entrepreneurial spirit, and still concentrates on the small towns and surrounding rural areas where the store can be the primary source for shoppers. It also still uses the best merchandise techniques and develops or attracts the best mechandise talent, always experimenting with new goods and new ways to present these goods.

Wal-Mart has evolved an intense, high-profile management style that brings together field supervisors and store managers into a chainwide

Exhibit 8 How Wal-Mart Outruns the Competition (Sales in billions/Earnings in millions)

	T.G. & Y.		K-Mart		Wal-Mart		Target		
1981	—		+14%	16.5	+28%	2.44	+26%	2.07	Sales
	—		−20%	210.0	+30%	79.5	—		Earnings
1980	+22%	1.4	+14%	14.2	+29%	1.7	+27%	1.5	Sales
	—		−27%	260.5	+26%	55.7	—		Earnings
1979	+19%	1.3	+13%	12.7	+38%	1.2	+20%	1.1	Sales
	—		+4%	358.0	+28%	41.1	—		Earnings
1978	+18%	1.2	+18%	11.7	+28%	0.9	—		Sales
	—		+18%	343.7	+17%	29.4	—		Earnings
1977	+14%	1.0	+18%	9.9	+42%	0.5	—		Sales
	—		+12%	302.9	+31%	21.4	—		Earnings

Source: Discount Store News Research, December 14, 1981, p. 13–14.

merchandising emphasis, providing new ideas for the company. The best ideas are put into the corporate framework and encouraged to be fulfilled. This is but one of several practices that have helped Wal-Mart gain its current status. Others include the perception of every day low prices by the consumers, and commitment to innovative, cost-control systems with the savings passed on to the consumer. The company utilizes technological advances in its operations for maximum efficiency and productivity. One example, is that the main computer in Bentonville talks directly to vendor computers, resulting in lower out-of-stocks.

Wal-Mart's 1981 annual report reflects its view of the future:

> The retailing environment is constantly changing. Competition will continue to improve and become more intense. Life styles will change, and today's solutions will soon be obsolete. But, with a flow of new programs, with the continuing contribution of our dedicated associates and with our commitment to avoid any short-term strategy that does not enhance our long-range goals, we are convinced that improved productivity will be achieved. Our people have truly made the difference, and as they respond to the ever-changing environment, we will serve our customers with the "best value in town."

Case 21 Update*

To Our Shareholders

What's Important Is You! You . . . our customers, associates, vendors and shareholders.

Record sales and earnings marked the year long celebration of our Company's Twenty-Fifth Anniversary. Sales increased 34% to $15.959 billion from $11.909 billion. Net income increased 39% to $627.643 million from $450.086 million. Fully diluted net income per share rose to $1.11, up 41% from $.79 in the prior year.

Sales increases in comparable stores were 11% which follows a 13% same store sales increase in the previous year. These levels of sales increases in our comparable stores indicate we continue to increase our market share. Strong sales advances in a period of very limited inflation and an otherwise slow-growth economic environment are a result of our dedicated associates performing better than ever before. During this past year, they concentrated on the operating philosophies that have sustained our growth in many different economic climates: improving customer service, offering our customers genuine value at the lowest possible everyday prices, effective inventory management, controlling and reducing expenses and listening to one another. We are proud of our associates and their accomplishments. Some of the highlights of these achievements are:

- Sales productivity in comparable Wal-Mart stores reached $213 per gross square foot of store space, up from $194 last year and $145 just five years ago.
- Our total retail space was expanded to 77.804 million square feet, a net increase of 14.531 million square feet, up 23% from last year. Store openings included 134 new Wal-Mart stores, 35 Sam's Wholesale Clubs, six dot Discount Drug stores and two Hypermart★USA stores.

Total Store Square Footage (Millions of Square Feet)

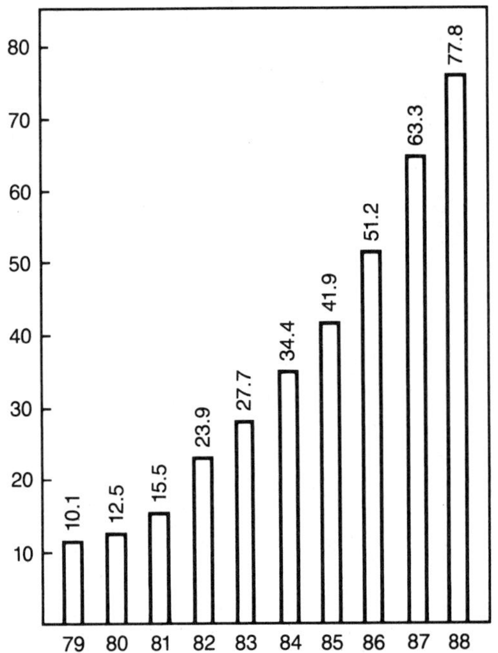

- Our store renovation and update program included 20 relocations of existing stores into larger units, 25 expansions, 23 remodels, 77 stockroom additions and 106 facelifts and in-store refurbishings. These 251 projects on existing stores impacted 39% of Wal-Mart stores three years old or older.
- Completion of the largest private satellite communication system in the United States which links all operating units of the Company and the general office with two-way voice, two-way data and one-way video communication. The inau-

*Excerpts from Wal-Mart Stores, Inc. 1988 annual report, pp. 2–3, 12–15, 18–21.

guration of this system featured a live broadcast from Sam Walton to all Wal-Mart associates.

▪ The addition of 1.477 million square feet to our distribution center system capacity. We expanded three existing facilities and in January 1988, opened our 11th facility in Laurens, South Carolina, a 583 thousand square-foot facility.

▪ "Store-within-a-store", a new tool to involve and equip assistant managers with the necessary skills to develop their retailing careers, by giving them total management responsibilities for several departments within their assigned store, was successfully implemented in our Wal-Mart stores.

▪ Net profit as a percentage of sales increased to 3.9% this year compared with 3.8% last year. Planned reductions in initial markup, as well as the increased percentage of Sam's sales to the total and the pass-through of the lower federal income tax rates, were largely offset by a reduction in total expenses.

▪ Significant improvement in the Company's financial position as a result of strong profit production. Net income, net of dividends, raised shareholders' equity to $2.257 billion from $1.690 billion last year, a 34% increase which follows 32% and 30% increases in fiscal 1987 and 1986, respectively.

Percentage of Return on Common Shareholder's Equity (Millions of Dollars)

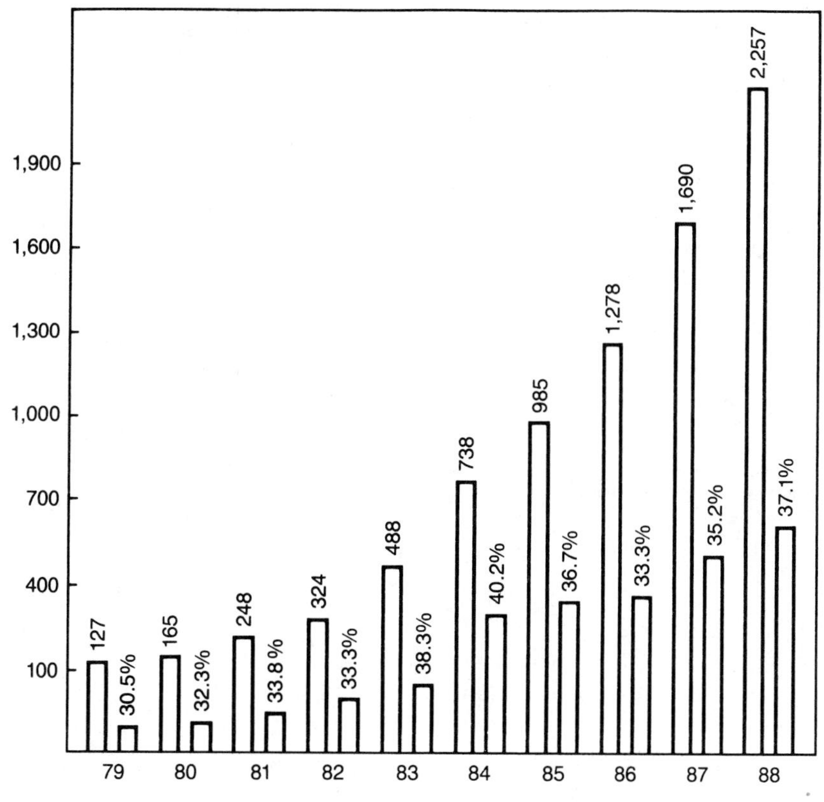

▪ Sam's Wholesale Clubs sales increased 62% to $2.711 billion from $1.678 billion a year ago, representing a 249% increase over sales of $776 million of just two years ago. Sam's opened 35 units this past year, 17 of which were acquired in the June, 1987 acquisition of Super Saver Warehouse Club, Inc. These 17 units are located throughout the Southeast, complementing existing Sam's units and accelerating Sam's market saturation.

▪ Hypermart★USA opened its doors in Garland, Texas, a suburb of Dallas, in December, 1987

Ten-Year Financial Summary

Wal-Mart Stores, Inc. and Subsidiaries

(Dollar amounts in thousands except per share data)	**1988**	1987	1986
EARNINGS			
Net sales	**$15,959,255**	$11,909,076	$8,451,489
Licensed department rentals and other income-net	**104,783**	84,623	55,127
Cost of sales	**12,281,744**	9,053,219	6,361,271
Operating, selling and general and administrative expenses	**2,599,367**	2,007,645	1,485,210
Interest costs:			
Debt	**25,262**	10,442	1,903
Capital leases	**88,995**	76,367	54,640
Taxes on income	**441,027**	395,940	276,119
Net income	**627,643**	450,086	327,473
Per share of common stock:			
Net income	**1.11**	.79*	.58*
Dividends	**.12**	.085*	.07*
Stores in operation at the end of the period			
Wal-Mart Stores	**1,114**	980	859
Sam's Wholesale Clubs	**84**	49	23
FINANCIAL POSITION			
Current assets	**$2,905,145**	$2,353,271	$1,784,275
Net property, plant, equipment and capital leases	**2,144,852**	1,676,282	1,303,450
Total assets	**5,131,809**	4,049,092	3,103,645
Current liabilities	**1,743,763**	1,340,291	992,683
Long-term debt	**185,672**	179,234	180,682
Long-term obligations under capital leases	**866,972**	764,128	595,205
Preferred stock with mandatory redemption provisions	**–**	–	4,902
Common shareholders' equity	**2,257,267**	1,690,493	1,277,659
FINANCIAL RATIOS			
Current ratio	**1.7**	1.8	1.8
Inventories/working capital	**2.3**	2.0	1.8
Return on assets**	**15.5**	14.5	14.8
Return on shareholders' equity**	**37.1**	35.2	33.3

*Adjusted to reflect 100% common stock dividend paid July 10, 1987.

**On beginning of year balances.

and Topeka, Kansas in January, 1988. Hypermart★USA may be described as a blend of the best of a Wal-Mart store, a combination supermarket/general merchandise store and a Sam's Wholesale Club. A true experiment, Hypermart★USA has received strong initial customer acceptance, but our ability to achieve satisfactory profit objectives is still unknown.

We are very pleased with fiscal 1988's profit and sales performance, but even more gratifying has been the opportunity to witness the further

1985	1984	1983	1982	1981	1980	1979
$6,400,861	$4,666,909	$3,376,252	$2,444,997	$1,643,199	$1,248,176	$900,298
52,167	36,031	22,435	17,650	12,063	10,092	9,615
4,722,440	3,418,025	2,458,235	1,787,496	1,207,802	919,305	661,062
1,181,455	892,887	677,029	495,010	331,524	251,616	182,365
5,207	4,935	20,297	16,053	5,808	4,438	3,119
42,506	29,946	18,570	15,351	10,849	8,621	6,595
230,653	160,903	100,416	65,943	43,597	33,137	27,325
270,767	196,244	124,140	82,794	55,682	41,151	29,447
.48*	.35*	.23*	.16*	.11*	.08*	.06*
.0525*	.035*	.0225*	.0163*	.0125*	.0095*	.007*
745	642	551	491	330	276	229
11	3					
$1,303,254	$1,005,567	$ 720,537	$ 589,161	$ 345,204	$ 266,617	$191,860
870,309	628,151	457,509	333,026	245,942	190,562	131,403
2,205,229	1,652,254	1,187,448	937,513	592,345	457,879	324,666
688,968	502,763	347,318	339,961	177,601	170,221	98,868
41,237	40,866	106,465	104,581	30,184	24,862	25,965
449,886	339,930	222,610	154,196	134,896	97,212	72,357
5,874	6,411	6,861	7,438	—	—	—
984,672	737,503	488,109	323,942	248,309	164,844	127,476
1.9	2.0	2.1	1.7	1.9	1.6	1.9
1.8	1.5	1.5	2.0	1.7	2.4	1.9
16.4	16.5	13.2	14.0	12.2	12.7	11.7
36.7	40.2	38.3	33.3	33.8	32.3	30.5

development of our associates. Once again, they have excelled, proving that together we can maintain profitable growth in diverse economic conditions and effectively compete against an ever changing and challenging retailing environment.

We approach this new year, fiscal 1989, confident in our people and the plans they have developed for continued success. We are cognizant of projected economic downturn and the continued sluggishness of the "oil patch", but we believe our strategies and plans will be executed, producing continued gains in market share, expense control and inventory management. We plan to expand our retail square footage to beyond 90 million. Construction will include 125 Wal-Mart stores, 18 Sam's Wholesale Clubs, two dot Discount Drug stores and two Hypermart★USA stores (one joint venture and one wholly owned). Expansions and relocations of 58 existing stores, including the relocation of three Wal-Mart stores into experimental combination supermarket/general merchandise stores to be operated as Wal-Mart SuperCenters, are also planned.

Exciting new concept development, experimentation, increased sales productivity, lower expenses, new store growth, advanced systems development and continued dedication to improved profitability is indeed challenging, but it's

Consolidated Statements Of Income

Wal-Mart Stores, Inc. and Subsidiaries

(Amounts in thousands except per share data)	Fiscal year ended January 31,		
	1988	1987	1986
Revenues:			
Net sales	**$15,959,255**	$11,909,076	$8,451,489
Rentals from licensed departments	**9,215**	10,779	13,011
Other income-net	**95,568**	73,844	42,116
	16,064,038	11,993,699	8,506,616
Costs and expenses:			
Cost of sales	**12,281,744**	9,053,219	6,361,271
Operating, selling and general and administrative expenses	**2,599,367**	2,007,645	1,485,210
Interest costs:			
Debt	**25,262**	10,442	1,903
Capital leases	**88,995**	76,367	54,640
	14,995,368	11,147,673	7,903,024
Income before income taxes	**1,068,670**	846,026	603,592
Provision for federal and state income taxes:			
Current	**432,133**	373,508	258,197
Deferred	**8,894**	22,432	17,922
	441,027	395,940	276,119
Net income	**$ 627,643**	$ 450,086	$ 327,473
Net income per share	**$ 1.11**	$ .79*	$ .58*

*Adjusted to reflect 100% common stock dividend paid on July 10, 1987.

See accompanying notes.

nothing new to Wal-Mart - it is Wal-Mart! Our confidence in our 200,000 dedicated Wal-Mart associates has never been stronger. Our 25 years of success and profitable growth are a direct product of their innovative ideas, commitment, suggestions, "entrepreneurial" spirit and hard work. These involved associates serve as the foundation of a mutually beneficial partnership with our customers, shareholders and suppliers.

This report is dedicated to this partnership and its 25 years of pride and success.

Sam M. Walton
Chairman

David D. Glass
President and
Chief Executive Officer

Net Income (Millions of Dollars)

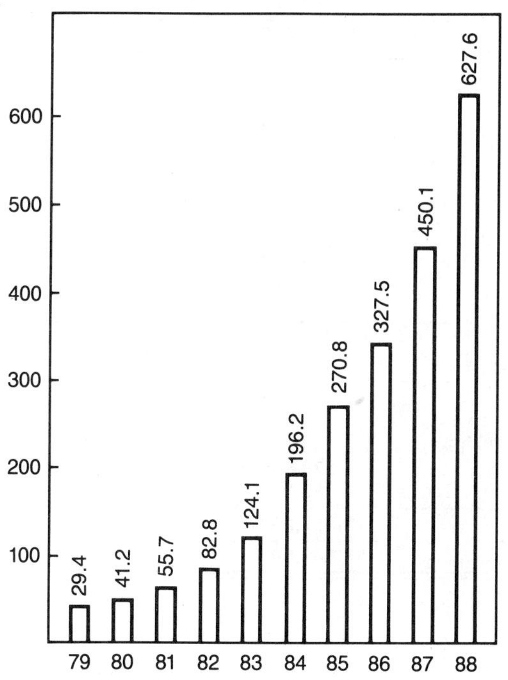

1,114 Wal-Mart Stores in 23 States
(Fiscal year ending January 31, 1988)

Wal-Mart Stores in Each State	
Alabama	62
Arkansas	75
Colorado	17
Florida	75
Georgia	59
Illinois	57
Indiana	16
Iowa	18
Kansas	36
Kentucky	47
Louisiana	64
Minnesota	4
Mississippi	48
Missouri	101
Nebraska	10
New Mexico	15
North Carolina	12
Oklahoma	79
South Carolina	30
Tennessee	73
Texas	204
Virginia	2
Wisconsin	10

Source: Wal-Mart 1988 annual report

Consolidated Balance Sheets

Wal-Mart Stores, Inc. and Subsidiaries

(Amounts in thousands)	January 31, 1988	1987
ASSETS		
Current assets:		
Cash	**$ 11,325**	$ 8,527
Short-term money market investments	**–**	157,018
Receivables	**95,928**	90,380
Recoverable costs from sale/leaseback	**126,917**	47,160
Inventories	**2,651,760**	2,030,972
Prepaid expenses	**19,215**	19,214
TOTAL CURRENT ASSETS	**2,905,145**	2,353,271
Property, plant and equipment, at cost:		
Land	**209,211**	134,351
Buildings and improvements	**621,023**	402,845
Fixtures and equipment	**855,926**	655,253
Transportation equipment	**46,301**	45,346
	1,732,461	1,237,795
Less accumulated depreciation	**374,193**	267,722
Net property, plant and equipment	**1,358,268**	970,073
Property under capital leases	**952,305**	832,337
Less accumulated amortization	**165,721**	126,128
Net property under capital leases	**786,584**	706,209
Goodwill	**47,034**	–
Other assets and deferred charges	**34,778**	19,539
Total assets	**$5,131,809**	$4,049,092
LIABILITIES AND SHAREHOLDERS' EQUITY		
Current liabilities:		
Notes payable	**$ 104,382**	$ —
Accounts payable	**1,099,961**	924,654
Accrued liabilities:		
Salaries	**89,118**	62,774
Taxes, other than income	**81,064**	46,496
Other	**229,921**	159,985
Accrued federal and state income taxes	**120,773**	132,833
Long-term debt due within one year	**2,046**	1,448
Obligations under capital leases due within one year	**16,498**	12,101
TOTAL CURRENT LIABILITIES	**1,743,763**	1,340,291
Long-term debt	**185,672**	179,234
Long-term obligations under capital leases	**866,972**	764,128
Deferred income taxes	**78,135**	74,946
Common shareholders' equity:		
Common stock (shares outstanding, 565,112 in 1988 and 282,182 in 1987)	**56,511**	28,218
Capital in excess of par value	**170,440**	191,857
Retained earnings	**2,030,316**	1,470,418
TOTAL COMMON SHAREHOLDERS' EQUITY	**2,257,267**	1,690,493
Total liabilities and shareholders' equity	**$5,131,809**	$4,049,092

See accompanying notes.

Consolidated Statements Of Common Shareholders' Equity

Wal-Mart Stores, Inc. and Subsidiaries

(Amounts in thousands)	Number of shares	Common stock	Capital in excess of par value	Retained earnings	Total
Balance - January 31, 1985	140,223	$14,022	$189,907	$ 780,743	$ 984,672
Net income				327,473	327,473
Cash dividends:					
Common stock ($.07* per share)				(39,302)	(39,302)
Preferred stock ($2.00 per share)				(396)	(396)
Accretion of preferred stock redemption premium				(70)	(70)
Exercise of stock options	65	7	334		341
Conversion of preferred stock	86	9	977		986
100% common stock dividend	140,374	14,038	(14,038)		
Exercise of stock options	288	28	954		982
Tax benefit from stock options			3,352		3,352
Conversion of preferred stock	9	1	54		55
Other			(434)		(434)
Balance - January 31, 1986	281,045	28,105	181,106	1,068,448	1,277,659
Net income				450,086	450,086
Cash dividends:					
Common stock ($.085* per share)				(47,850)	(47,850)
Preferred stock ($1.50 per share)				(266)	(266)
Exercise of stock options	346	34	812		846
Tax benefit from stock options			5,122		5,122
Conversion of preferred stock	791	79	4,817		4,896
Balance - January 31, 1987	282,182	28,218	191,857	1,470,418	1,690,493
Net income				627,643	627,643
Cash dividends:					
Common stock ($.12* per share)				(67,745)	(67,745)
Exercise of stock options	37	4	452		456
100% common stock dividend	282,219	28,222	(28,222)		
Exercise of stock options	821	82	1,739		1,821
Tax benefit from stock options			9,213		9,213
Other	(147)	(15)	(4,599)		(4,614)
Balance - January 31, 1988	565,112	$56,511	$170,440	$2,030,316	$2,257,267

*Cash dividends on common stock prior to July 10, 1987, have been adjusted to reflect the 100% common stock dividend paid on that date.

See accompanying notes.

Consolidated Statements Of Changes In Financial Position

Wal-Mart Stores, Inc. and Subsidiaries
(Amounts in thousands)

	Fiscal years ended January 31,		
	1988	1987	1986
Source of funds:			
Current operations:			
Net income	**$627,643**	$450,086	$327,473
Items not affecting working capital in current period:			
Depreciation and amortization	**165,962**	123,639	89,749
Deferred income taxes	**3,189**	22,432	17,922
Total from current operations	**796,794**	596,157	435,144
Net proceeds from exercise of options, and conversion of preferred stock	**6,876**	10,864	5,282
Additions to long-term debt	**11,645**	—	141,120
Additions to long-term obligations under capital leases	**131,192**	184,262	156,453
Reduction of other assets	**1,522**	1,300	18,609
Disposal of assets	**37,341**	90,920	9,913
	985,370	883,503	766,521
Application of funds:			
Acquisition of Super Saver Warehouse Club, Inc.			
Property, plant and equipment	**10,422**	—	—
Other assets	**231**	—	—
Goodwill	**50,034**	—	—
Long-term debt	**(20,570)**	—	—
	40,117	—	—
Additions to property, plant and equipment	**527,960**	403,660	350,667
Additions to property under capital leases	**130,491**	182,955	181,487
Reduction in long-term debt, including changes in current maturities	**25,777**	1,448	1,675
Reduction in long-term lease obligations, including changes in current obligations	**28,348**	15,339	11,134
Preferred stock conversions	**—**	4,902	971
Dividends paid	**67,745**	48,116	39,768
Additions to other assets and deferred charges	**16,530**	5,695	3,513
	836,968	662,115	589,215
Increase in working capital	**$148,402**	$221,388	$177,306
Changes in components of working capital:			
Increase (decrease) in current assets:			
Cash	**$ 2,798**	($ 723)	$ 7,398
Short-term money market investments	**(157,018)**	(8,150)	165,168
Receivables	**5,548**	32,718	12,084
Recoverable costs from sale/leaseback	**79,757**	(105,250)	10,021
Inventories	**620,788**	642,804	284,243
Prepaid expenses	**1**	7,597	2,107
	551,874	568,996	481,021
Increase (decrease) in current liabilities:			
Notes payable	**104,382**	—	—
Accounts payable and accrued liabilities	**306,155**	301,910	286,840
Accrued federal and state income taxes	**(12,060)**	43,434	16,040
Long-term debt due within one year	**598**	(157)	(1,377)
Obligations under capital leases due within one year	**4,397**	2,421	2,212
	403,472	347,608	303,715
Increase in working capital	**$148,402**	$221,388	$177,306

Case 22

A Note on the Forest Products Industry

Historical Development

The major products of the forest product industry—paper, lumber, veneer, and plywood—date back to antiquity. The Chinese were first credited with making paper from the pounded bark of the mulberry tree. By 4000 B.C., the Egyptians had 8-foot-long metal saws which they used to cut both stone and wood. In approximately 1500 B.C., the Egyptians were manufacturing veneered furniture, which was later found by archeologists in the tombs of the Pharaohs.

The first sawmills in the United States were believed to have been established at Jamestown, Virginia around 1625 and at Berwick, Maine around 1631. These initial sawmills were likely water powered frame saws which had been employed in Europe since about 1200 A.D. The initial lumber indústry of the early colonies was centered in the white pine forests of the New England states. As the nation grew and expanded, so did its need for more wood. The lumber industry moved to the white pine forests of Michigan, Wisconsin, and Minnesota, and later in the early 1900s to the southern pine forests of the southeastern United States. The great timber stands of the Pacific Northwest were also being opened up, and by the 1920s, they were supplying a large portion of the nation's lumber needs.

The early lumber industry in the United States was blessed with a low-cost plentiful supply of raw material. Markets were relatively strong because the nation needed considerable quantities of lumber and other wood products to support its rapid growth. By 1909, lumber production in the United States reached its all-time peak of 45,000,000,000 board feet.

Although paper had been manufactured dating back to the Chinese mulberry bark paper and the Egyptian papyrus, the early manufacture of paper was not from wood. It was not until approximately 1840 that the manufacture of wooden pulp was accomplished. This early manufacture of wood pulp was accomplished by forcing a log against a rotating stone in a water slurry. The rotating stone ground off small fibers of wood which were carried away in the water slurry. This new process for making pulp was called the ground wood process and was introduced into the United States in the early 1860s.

The first United States paper mill actually had been built much earlier in 1690 to produce paper from the fibers of old rags and not from wood pulp. These early paper mills produced paper sheet by sheet in a slow time consuming process. The first paper machine was installed in the United States in 1827 allowing the continuous production of a long, wide sheet of paper. This new technology was a significant boost to the paper industry.

By the 1880s, chemical methods of pulping wood appeared. In 1880, the sulfite process was available and by 1884, the Kraft or sulfate process was available to produce wood pulp. Both of these methods relied on using chemicals to dissolve the part of the wood that held its fibers

---

This case was written by Steven A. Sinclair, Professor of Forest Products Marketing, Virginia Polytechnic Institute and State University.

together. In 1909, the first Kraft mill using southern pine was built in Roanoke Rapids, North Carolina beginning the growth of the strong southern pulp and paper industry.

Between the two world wars, early leaders in the forest products industry began to utilize their raw material resources more completely. Several large predominantly western lumber companies, such as Weyerhaeuser, led the way by moving into the pulp and paper field. Prior to this point, firms in the industry specialized in either the lumber or paper segments of the industry.

The addition of pulp and paper capacity to a traditional lumber manufacturing firm allowed it to make optimum use of its resources. This was accomplished by taking the waste material from lumber production and the timber unsuitable for lumber production from company lands and using it as raw material for their pulp and paper mills. Increasing timber prices further encouraged better utilization practices, and other western lumber companies followed the lead of Weyerhaeuser by purchasing or building pulp and paper facilities in the 1940s and 1950s.

At the same time, companies that had traditionally been pulp and paper companies, such as St. Regis Paper Company and International Paper Company, began to move into the lumber business. The paper companies moved into the lumber business to enable them to process their high quality timber into more valuable lumber products rather than paper.

Producing both lumber and paper products also helped to diversify company earnings because the sales of paper and lumber tended to be somewhat counter cyclical. In addition, paper prices have historically been more stable than lumber and plywood prices as shown in Exhibit 1. By the late 1950s and early 1960s, the forest products industry was taking on the appearance that it still had in the 1980s. That was an industry increasingly dominated by large fully integrated firms in most product and market segments as shown in Exhibits 2 through 5.

Major Competitors in the Forest Products Industry

The forest products industry typically produced large bulky products that were relatively expensive to transport. As a result, the early stages of development in the U.S. forest products industry centered on local sawmills and paper mills supplying products for local markets. With the advent of rail and steamship transportation, however, strong competition was possible between firms some distance apart. This competition has intensified and continued to this day.

Several major competitors in the two major segments of this industry are profiled here. The segments are those firms predominantly producing paper products and those firms predominantly producing lumber and other wood products. In addition, two new entrants to the industry are profiled in this section.

Paper Products Firms

Boise Cascade

In 1957, 36-year-old Robert Hansberger, the President of Boise Payette Lumber Company, arranged a merger with another lumber producer of similar size, the Cascade Lumber Company. The merger of these two Idaho lumber companies formed the new Boise Cascade Corporation. Boise Cascade Corporation, under Hansberger's leadership, grew at a rapid rate through a long series of acquisitions during the late 1950s and 1960s.

Boise Cascade's initial acquisition strategy was that of integrated utilization. That is, Boise grouped complementary timber conversion operations together in order to achieve the maximum return from each log. In a typical sawmill as much as 50% of the round log became waste materials as square lumber was produced. In the past, many firms simply burnt this waste. However, by utilizing this waste as a raw material to produce other forest products, such as paper or particle board, Boise Cascade began to integrate

Exhibit 1 Relative Price Indexes of Softwood Plywood, Softwood Lumber, and Paper Compared to Indexed Housing Starts from 1967 to 1983

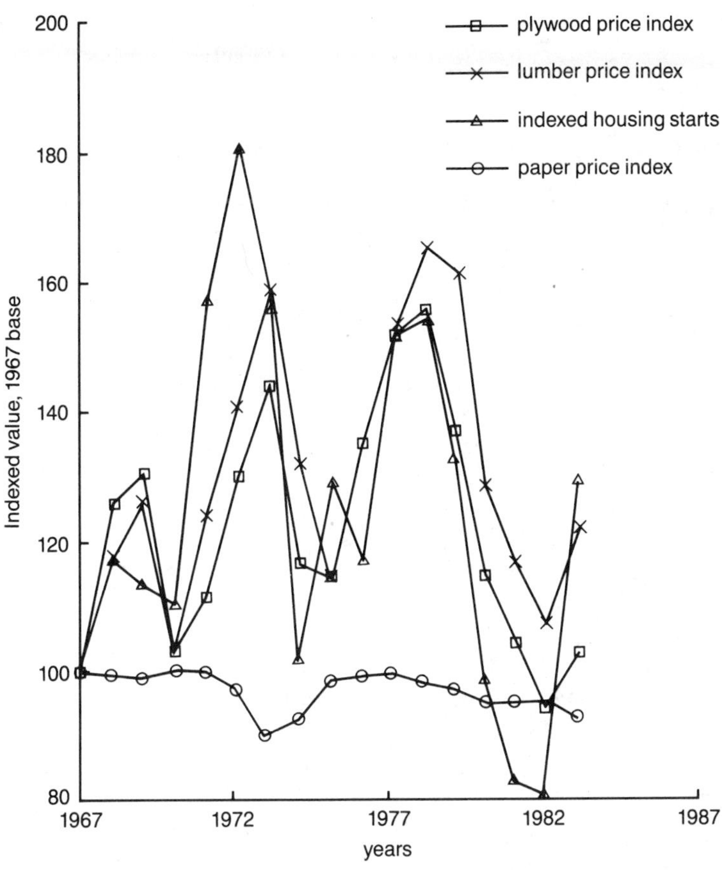

Source: Alice H. Ulrich, *U.S. Timber Production, Trade, Consumption and Price Statistics 1950–83* (Washington D.C.: U.S. Dept. of Agriculture, 1984), pp. 53–72.

its utilization facilities achieving higher returns from its logs.

Through additional mergers in the 1960s, Boise Cascade also became a significant producer of paper and packaging products. It also ventured into home building and land development. Hansberger noted at that time that his company was in the shelter business. Boise Cascade further integrated its operations to include retail level concerns within the building products industry, becoming one of the very few major integrated forest products firms to have a significant building products retail group.

Hansberger was caught up in diversification fever in the late 1960s and proceeded to turn Boise Cascade into a conglomerate. One of the more unusual acquisitions was the Cuban Electric Company, for which Boise had had claims against the Cuban government since 1960. For a while, it seemed this diversification strategy was working and Boise Cascade became one of the glamour conglomerates. In the 1970s, how-

Exhibit 2 1983 Sales Data for Major U.S. Forest-Products Firms

Forbes 1983 sales 500 rank		Total sales ($ mil)	% of sales by business segment		
			Wood products	Paper products	Other
82	Georgia-Pacific	6,469	61	27	12
121	Weyerhaeuser	4,883	53	39	8
144	International Paper	4,357	17	81	2
151	Champion International	4,264	41	59	0
197	Boise Cascade	3,451	35	65	nm
210	Kimberly-Clark	3,274	nm	98	2
245	St. Regis	2,775	15	84	1
248	Crown Zellerbach	2,709	9	90	1
276	Scott Paper	2,465	4	81	5
284	Mead	2,367	nm	95	5
311	James River Corp.	2,104	0	100	nm
365	Union Camp	1,688	9	75	16
380	Hammermill Paper	1,623	9	91	0
400	Great Northern Nekoosa	1,565	6	87	7
401	Westvaco	1,564	nm	89	11
496	Temple-Inland	1,175	25	72	7
*	Louisiana-Pacific	1,265	85	15	0
*	Willamette Industries	1,045	30	70	0

*Unranked.
nm = not a meaningful %.
Sources: "The Nation's Largest Companies Ranked Four Ways," *Forbes,* April 30, 1984, pp. 172–178. Also Corporate annual reports for 1983.

Exhibit 3 1983 U.S. Lumber Market-Share Estimates

Company	Production (MMBf)	Estimated market share
Weyerhaeuser	3,123	8.7%
Georgia-Pacific	1,802	5.0%
Louisiana-Pacific	1,680	4.7%
Champion International	1,272	3.6%
Boise Cascade	844	2.4%
Top 5 Total		24.4%
International Paper	760	2.1%
St. Regis	583	1.6%

Total 1983 consumption = 35,695 MMBf.
Source: "Lumber Firms Enjoyed '83 But '84 Outlook Is Dimmer," *Forest Industries,* July 1984, p. 16.

Exhibit 4 1983 U.S. Plywood Market-Share Estimates

	Production (mm sq f, ⅜″ basis)	Estimated market share
Georgia-Pacific	4,872	23.9%
Champion International	1,822	8.9%
Boise Cascade	1,381	6.8%
Weyerhaeuser	1,319	6.5%
Willamette	1,282	6.3%
Top 5 Total		52.4%

Total 1983 consumption = 20,348 mm sq f (⅜″ basis).
Sources: Corporate annual reports for 1983. Also Robert G. Anderson, *Regional Production and Distribution Patterns of the Structural Panel Industry* (Tacoma, Wash.: American Plywood Association, 1983), p. 11.

Exhibit 5 1981 U.S. Pulp and Paper Capacity, by Category and Top Five Companies

Category	Company	1000 short tons
Newsprint*	Bowater	1,313
	St. Regis	815
	Boise Cascade	610
	Publishers Paper	537
	Kimberly-Clark	526
		3,801
		(57% of total capacity)
Printing and Writing Papers	International Paper	1,525
	Boise Cascade	1,390
	Great Northern Nekoosa	1,238
	Champion International	1,126
	Mead	903
		6,182
		(42% of total capacity)
Tissue	Scott Paper	1,060
	Proctor and Gamble	900
	Kimberly-Clark	532
	Fort Howard Paper	530
	Georgia-Pacific	500
		3,522
		(83% of total capacity)
Unbleached Kraft	St. Regis	861
	Georgia-Pacific	547
	Union Camp	454
	Continental Group	370
	International Paper	260
		2,492
		(64% of total capacity)
Bleached Packaging	International Paper	320
	James River	230
	Hammermill Paper	189
	Crown Zellerbach	140
	Longview Fibre	140
		1,019
		(67% of total capacity)
Paperboard	International Paper	3,205
	Container Corp. (Mobil Oil)	1,941
	Weyerhaeuser	1,900
	Champion International	1,553
	Mead	1,485
		10,084
		(33% of total capacity)
Market Pulp*	Weyerhaeuser	1,213
	Georgia-Pacific	871
	ITT Rayonier	871
	International Paper	500
	Brunswick Pulp & Paper	467
		3,922
		(53% of total capacity)

*Canadian companies have a substantial share of the North American capacity in these categories.
Source: Thomas P. Clephane and J. Carroll, *Timber Survey* (New York: Morgan Stanley and Company, 1982), pp. 52–63.

ever, this strategy almost proved disastrous and Hansberger was forced to resign.

In 1972, the board of directors chose John B. Fery as the new Chairman and Chief Executive Officer of Boise Cascade. Fery sold off much of the earlier diversified operations acquired by Hansberger. The income generated by selling these non-forest products assets was reinvested back into its core forest products businesses. As a result of Fery's actions, many credit him with rescuing Boise Cascade from near disaster.

Fery instituted a sophisticated planning system for Boise Cascade with 5 and 10 year plans along with comprehensive business reviews. These became the basis for strategic decision making at Boise Cascade headquarters and in its operating units. Since the early 1970s, Boise spent nearly $3,000,000,000 to move the corporation into what Fery believed were young markets with high growth potential. Boise moved rapidly into white paper production, the demand for which was being constantly strengthened by the office computer and copy machine. At the same time, Fery lessened Boise's dependence on wood and building materials, which were very vulnerable to the cyclical nature of the housing market.

When Fery took over, Boise Cascade was largely a lumber company with wood products accounting for half of its total sales. Even in 1983, the company was the fifth largest lumber producer and the third largest plywood producer in the U.S. As a result of Fery's actions, however, paper operations for Boise Cascade had grown and accounted for approximately two-thirds of 1983 sales. In addition, Fery pursued a niche strategy in the wood products business by emphasizing distribution to the remodeling market rather than materials for new construction. By 1983, Boise Cascade owned 87 retail building material centers, which served primarily the small remodeling contractors and do-it-yourself consumers. These retail building material centers were supported by 15 wholesale distribution units. All of these facilities were located in high growth areas of the West and southwestern United States.

Boise Cascade also operated a string of 40 office products distribution centers which served all 50 states. These distribution centers gave it a strong position in the office products market and provided a unique marketing outlet for Boise's fast growing white paper production.

In 1983, Boise Cascade had total sales of $3,500,000,000 and 28,708 employees. It owned 3,200,000 acres of timberlands and controlled another 4,500,000 acres through long-term leases and contracts.

International Paper

International Paper was incorporated in 1898. For most of the time since then, it has been the largest paper manufacturer in the world. The acquisition of St. Regis Corporation by Champion International in 1984, however, gave Champion International claim to that title.

International Paper was quick to apply new technology to achieve a dominant position in the paper industry during the early part of this century. However, by the 1960s, the rate of return on net worth for International Paper and its growth in sales were much lower than competing paper companies (Exhibit 6). Rumors on Wall Street that a group of investors were attempting to buy sufficient shares of International Paper stock to control the company shocked the directors out of complacency.

Under the leadership of Edward Hinman and Frederick Kappell (a former chairman of AT&T), International Paper began a drive in the late 1960s to expand and diversify. International Paper moved into the consumer tissues and disposable diapers market, purchased a producer and distributor of specialty health care products, and spent over $1,000,000,000 to increase its paper capacity by 25%. All of this served to leave International Paper strongly in debt after having almost no debt as late as 1965. To better manage this situation, Paul Gorman took over the helm of International Paper in early 1971. Gorman

Exhibit 6 Selected Financial Data for Major U.S. Forest-Products Firms from Value Line's Value/Screen Data Base, January 1985

	Return on net worth	Price/book value	5 year earnings per share growth	Financial strength	Long term debt/total debt
James River Co.	17.1%	1.60	20.5%	C++	43%
Kimberly-Clark	12.7%	1.40	8.0%	A+	25%
Union Camp	11.0%	1.40	3.5%	A	34%
Great Northern Nekoosa	9.3%	1.00	5.5%	A	34%
Georgia-Pacific	8.7%	1.20	−11.9%	B++	39%
Scott Paper	8.3%	1.10	4.0%	B++	27%
Crown Zellerbach	7.7%	0.90	−16.9%	B+	35%
Westvaco Corporation	7.6%	1.20	3.5%	A	28%
Hammermill Paper	7.5%	1.00	6.0%	B+	38%
Temple-Inland	6.8%	1.30	nm	B	22%
Weyerhaeuser	6.3%	1.30	−11.9%	A	29%
International Paper	5.8%	0.80	1.5%	A	20%
Champion International	4.6%	0.70	−18.9%	B++	35%
Willamette Industries	4.5%	1.30	−18.9%	B	37%
Boise Cascade	4.3%	0.80	−10.9%	B++	30%
Louisiana-Pacific	3.8%	0.90	−26.9%	B++	19%
Mead Corporation	3.4%	1.20	−18.9%	B	40%

nm = not a meaningful %.
Source: Value/Screen Data Base (New York: Value Line, Inc., 1985).

was apparently chosen because of his strong financial abilities.

Gorman immediately began to close and/or sell the unprofitable acquisitions and to modernize International Paper's financial systems. With these new controls in place, he began to manage more to turn a profit and not just to attempt to be the largest paper company.

After Gorman's retirement in 1974, the new chairman, J. Stanford Smith, signaled a new strategy indicating that International Paper was no longer just in the paper or even the forest products business, but rather was in the land resource management business. This thinking led International Paper to acquire new companies that had the expertise needed to develop oil deposits that had been discovered on the company's large land holdings. In addition, a new emphasis was placed on solid wood products in the mid to late 1970s when the markets for lumber and other wood products were strong.

In 1979, when Dr. Edwin A. Gee assumed the chairmanship of International Paper, another strategic change was signaled. Gee moved to consolidate International Paper's operations around its original central core of basic forest products. The oil and gas subsidiaries were sold along with other assets which were not directly related to its core business. Cash raised through these sales was plowed back into a five-year capital spending program to upgrade aging paper mills. Between 1979 and 1984, International Paper spent approximately $4,000,000,000 in modernizing its facilities.

International Paper had a stated goal to become a low-cost producer of white paper, packaging, container board and bleached board. To achieve this goal, International Paper began the process of converting and modernizing some of its paper mills to produce uncoated white papers. At the same time, the firm announced its intention to move out of the newsprint business and converted newsprint mills to produce other paper products or sold them.

In 1983, International Paper owned 15 pulp and paper mills, 22 wood products manufacturing facilities, and 57 packaging plants. These operations generated sales of approximately \$4,400,000,000 that year. International Paper had the largest timberland base in the forest products industry, totaling approximately 7,000,000 acres, and employed 33,600 people in 1983.

Wood Products Firms

Weyerhaeuser

By 1900, Frederick Weyerhaeuser had already been active in the lumber and timber industry for 43 years. He led a group of midwestern lumbermen to Tacoma, Washington, in that year to organize a new lumber company. This new company was incorporated as Weyerhaeuser Timber Company. When many people think of the forest products industry, Weyerhaeuser is the name that first comes to mind. Furthermore, six of the nine men who led this giant had the Weyerhaeuser name.

Weyerhaeuser first purchased 900,000 acres of timberland from the Northern Pacific Railroad and later purchased its first sawmill in Everett, Washington in 1902. The company expanded slowly, opening Weyerhaeuser Sales Company in St. Paul, Minnesota, in 1919 and acquiring its first sulfite pulp mill in 1931 in Longview, Washington. Weyerhaeuser was an early leader in the industry in promoting integrated utilization by purchasing pulp mills to use the residues available from its sawmilling operations. Weyerhaeuser was also an early leader in the development of tree farms and the reforestation of cut-over forest land. In addition, Weyerhaeuser was one of the first major forest products firms to institute a research and development program.

Weyerhaeuser remained in the Pacific Northwest until the mid-1950s, at which time it moved into the Southeast and south central United States through a strong acquisition program. Timberlands were first acquired in Mississippi and Alabama in 1956, then in North Carolina and Virginia in 1957. One of the largest southern timberland acquisitions came in 1969 when Weyerhaeuser acquired Dierk's Forests Inc., adding 1,800,000 acres of timberlands in Arkansas and Oklahoma, along with various forest products mills.

Weyerhaeuser tended to be a leader in the forest products industry, instituting such slogans in early advertising as "we're the tree-growing company" and "high-yield forestry." Beginning in mid-1961, George Weyerhaeuser, then the executive vice president of Weyerhaeuser Timber Company, announced a basic shift from commodity selling of lumber to end-user marketing of wood products. This signaled Weyerhaeuser's move into the consumer market with specialty products and a decreasing emphasis on the commodity grades of lumber. The company's huge reserves of prime high-quality timber supported this move and allowed them to produce many high-quality specialty wood products such as prefinished paneling, glue-laminated trusses, preprimed siding, and molded wood products. This same product policy was extended to the pulp and paper division. The emphasis there shifted to a wide variety of printing papers and finished paper products. The marketing-to-end-users theme carried forward into the 1980s when Weyerhaeuser even became the largest U.S. manufacturer of private-labeled disposable diapers.

While emphasizing end-user marketing, Weyerhaeuser also became the tenth largest home builder in the United States in 1983 and one of the country's largest mortgage bankers. Weyerhaeuser developed a system of 64 wholesale customer service centers with the stated goal of becoming a lending force in the wholesale marketing of building products in the 1980s. Weyerhaeuser's current advertising theme "first choice" was keyed upon making each customer service center a separate profit center, giving the manager considerable autonomy to provide a mix of products appropriate for the local building markets.

Beginning in the late 1950s, Weyerhaeuser began to expand its operations into various foreign countries. By 1983, 22% of the net corporate sales were from overseas subsidiaries.

Weyerhaeuser was the only major U.S. forest-products producer that had sufficient timberlands to support 100% of its wood and fiber needs. While this approach had its advantages and disadvantages, it did free the corporation from a heavy dependence on expensive government timber contracts in the Pacific Northwest and from privately owned timber in the Southeast. In all, the company owned approximately 5,900,000 acres of commercial timberland, 54% in the South and 46% in the Pacific Northwest.

In 1983, Weyerhaeuser was the leading U.S. lumber producer with an 8.7% market share. Its total corporate sales in 1983 were $4,880,000,000, second behind Georgia-Pacific, with a net income after taxes of $204,843,000. In the same year, the company employed 42,600 people, principally in its forest-products businesses.

Georgia-Pacific

In 1927, a Virginian named Owen Cheatham borrowed $12,000 and purchased a wholesale lumber yard in Augusta, Georgia. It wasn't long before Cheatham enticed his college friend, Robert Pamplin, to join him in this new business. Together these two men built the company known as Georgia-Pacific.

The early years of Georgia-Pacific were marked by the Great Depression and World War II; however, by 1946 the company owned five lumber mills in Alabama, Arkansas, Mississippi, and South Carolina along with its original lumber yard in Georgia. In addition, sales offices were established in New York City and Portland, Oregon.

Beginning in the late 1940s, Georgia-Pacific entered into an era of tremendous growth. The company moved into the plywood business by purchasing and building several West Coast plywood mills. This was considered quite risky at that time because plywood was a very new product with an unsure market potential. Beginning in the 1950s, Georgia-Pacific moved aggressively into the pulp and paper field and began to acquire some of the last remaining large tracts of old growth West Coast timberlands. The corporation borrowed very heavily to acquire these lands and then, through accelerated harvesting schedules, generated enough cash to repay its short-term creditors and bring its long-term debt down to a manageable level.

The corporate offices were moved from Augusta, Georgia to Portland, Oregon. However, beginning in the 1960s, Georgia-Pacific made a strong move back to its original base in the southern U.S. Large tracts of land were acquired in the Crossett, Arkansas area and in other deep south states. In 1963, Georgia-Pacific built the first southern pine plywood plant. Later that same year four additional plants were running which gave it about a one-year head start over its major competitors. Georgia-Pacific continued its emphasis on plywood and other specialty panels and was the world's largest plywood manufacturer producing approximately 4,900,000,000 square feet of plywood in 1983.

Georgia-Pacific tried to emphasize market positions in fast-growth fields throughout its history. Early on, it chose to emphasize plywood production over that of lumber and also emphasized the rapidly expanding pulp and paper segment. Like Weyerhaeuser, it decided to emphasize the distribution of building products to building material retailers, believing this gave it a strong advantage in the marketplace. By 1983, Georgia-Pacific's 145 wholesale distribution centers made it the world's largest distributor of building products.

Perhaps the largest set back to Georgia-Pacific's growth resulted from a 1972 Federal Trade Commission ruling. It held the company had illegally restricted competition within the softwood plywood industry. The settlement resulted in the company selling 20% of its assets centered in Louisiana. As a result, the Louisiana-Pacific Corporation was created and was immediately the sixth largest domestic producer of lumber. In addition, the Georgia-Pacific Corporation was prohibited from purchasing any additional softwood plywood producers in the United States for 10 years.

In the early 1980s, Georgia-Pacific began construction of a new corporate headquarters in Atlanta, Georgia. It decided to move its corporate headquarters from Portland to Atlanta to be nearer the major part of Georgia-Pacific's assets. By 1983, the corporation owned 4,600,000,000 acres of timberlands in North America, of which 65% was in the southern U.S., 16% in the Pacific Northwest, and 19% in the eastern U.S. and eastern Canada. In that same year, Georgia-Pacific had total sales of $6,500,000,000, ranking it 82nd in sales on the Forbes 500 list and 1st among forest products corporations.

Back in the late 1950s, Georgia-Pacific diversified into the chemical industry to manufacture the resins necessary for its plywood plants. Georgia-Pacific's corporate goals in the 1980s, as articulated by Chief Executive Officer T. Marshall Hahn, were to liquidate all but the most profitable of its chemical operations and to invest the proceeds in modernizing the core forest-products businesses of the corporation.

New Entrants into the Industry

The threat of new entrants building greenfield plants in the forest-products industry continued to be limited. The tremendous cost of a new pulp and paper mill ($500,000,000 to $1,000,000,000) and the necessary timberland base to support such a facility presented an almost insurmountable barrier for a new company. In addition, the new firm would be forced to develop its own marketing channels, manufacturing skills, etc.

While the threat of new entrants was low, the threat of other established firms taking over undervalued forest-products firms was a significant threat. A number of acquisition attempts, takeovers, and spin-offs of forest-products business units occurred. This activity continued to the mid-1980s, and it seems likely to continue in the future. Clearly, it has the potential to alter the traditional structure of the industry.

Louisiana—Pacific

A 1971 complaint to the Federal Trade Commission against Georgia-Pacific ultimately resulted in Louisiana-Pacific Corporation. On January 5, 1973, Georgia-Pacific spun off $327,000,000 of assets to create Louisiana-Pacific. Harry A. Merlo, a former Georgia-Pacific executive, was named president of the new corporation. Merlo wasted no time getting started and in 1973 the company made 17 acquisitions, invested over $21,000,000 in capital improvements, and added 1,800 employees.

On January 5, 1973, 26,320,000 shares of Louisiana-Pacific stock began trading on the New York Stock Exchange. Later in that same year the stock was split 2 for 1. Net sales in that first year of operation were approximately $417,000,000. By 1974, company ownership of timberlands climbed to 625,000 acres, and the company had the capacity to supply 2,500,000 seedlings per year to reforest cut-over timberlands.

While its 1979 annual sales reached $1,300,000,000, they declined to $1,100,000,000 in 1983 due to a weak building-products market. Louisiana-Pacific remained primarily a lumber and plywood producer. In 1973, 92% of its sales were from building products and 8% were from pulp and paper operations. By 1983, the distribution of sales between these two segments had changed slightly. Building products contributed 85% of net sales, and pulp and paper products contributed 15%. Of the major integrated forest-products firms, Louisiana-Pacific had the largest exposure to the highly cyclical building-products market.

Louisiana-Pacific had two principal market areas where it was trying to establish a strong leadership position. The first market area involved the new structural composite panel market. Louisiana-Pacific had a stated goal of 1,000,000,000 square feet of capacity in this market segment by 1985. When the plants under construction in 1985 went into production this goal was met. Louisiana-Pacific produced an oriented waferboard product under the brand name of Waferwood. This particular product had the necessary grade stamps from the American Plywood Association to compete as a substitute product against traditional plywood sheathing and underlayment and also against oriented strand-board products. Its 1,000,000,000 square feet of capacity made Louisiana-Pacific one of the top two producers in this product category along with Georgia-Pacific.

The second area where Louisiana-Pacific had stated goals of market leadership was in the southern pine lumber industry. The company stated, in 1981, that its goal was to have 1,000,000,000 board feet of southern pine lumber capacity by 1985. The company pursued this goal by acquiring southern pine sawmills and by constructing new mills in the southern states.

Louisiana-Pacific largely concentrated on the development of its manufacturing base and somewhat ignored the development of its distribution system for building products. However, in 1979, Louisiana-Pacific did acquire a chain of 15 building-material centers in Southern California from Lone Star Industries. By 1983, Louisiana-Pacific operated 12 building products distribution centers in California, one in Texas, and one in Florida. Louisiana-Pacific employed approximately 13,000 employees and operated 111 manufacturing facilities in 1983.

Temple-Inland

Temple-Inland made the most dramatic entry as an independent company into the forest-products industry of any firm in the 1980s. It began operations on January 1, 1984 following its spin-off from Time's forest-products operations. Temple-Inland was formed from two subsidiaries of Time, Inc., Temple-Eastex and Inland Container, which each had long operating histories.

T.L.L. Temple acquired 7,000 acres of timberland in Texas and established the Southern Pine Lumber Company in 1893. By 1894, the Southern Pine Lumber Company's first sawmill was operating in Diboll, Texas, cutting approximately 50,000 board feet of southern pine per day. During the early years of this company, it was primarily a producer of basic lumber products for the construction and furniture industries. In the late 1950s and early 1960s the company moved into the production of particleboard, gypsum wall board, and other building materials, along with entering the mortgage banking, insurance, and construction businesses.

In 1964, the Southern Pine Lumber Company's name was changed to Temple Industries, Inc., and the company's initial 7,000 acres of timberland had grown to more than 450,000 acres.

In the early 1950s, Time, Inc. entered into a joint venture with the Houston Oil Company and established the East Texas Pulp and Paper Company. In 1956, Time purchased Houston Oil's ownership in the East Texas Pulp and Paper Company. Later in 1973, Time acquired Temple Industries, which was merged with Eastex Pulp and Paper Company to form Temple-Eastex, Inc.

Herman C. Krannert was responsible for the origin of Inland Container Corporation. Krannert started the Inland Box Company in Indianapolis in 1925 and soon acquired a second box plant in Middleton, Ohio. Then, in 1938, the company was re-incorporated as Inland Container Corporation. Up until 1946, Inland was primarily a multi-plant box converter relying solely on outside sources for its paper supply. Through a joint venture with Mead Corporation, that same year, the Georgia Kraft Company was formed and a new liner board mill was constructed in Macon, Georgia. Inland Container Corporation was acquired by Time, Inc. in 1978, to be operated as a subsidiary. In the 1980s, Georgia Kraft, 50% owned by Inland Container, operated three liner board mills with five paper machines, plywood and lumber mills, and owned approximately 1,000,000 acres of timberland in Alabama and Georgia.

The formation of Temple-Inland Corporation from the Time subsidiaries of Temple-Eastex and Inland Container produced an integrated forest-products firm. Its 1983 sales of approximately $1,200,000,000 ranked 16th among major U.S. paper and forest-products companies. Temple-Inland had four main areas of operation: paper, containers, building materials, and financial services. The paper activities of Temple-Inland concentrated on two paper grades, container board and bleached paper board. Both of these served as raw materials for its container-producing operations.

Temple-Inland had a diversified building-products product line, designed to serve the rapidly growing Texas and southeastern U.S. markets. In addition to manufacturing operations, the company also owned six building-materials retail distribution centers in Texas and Louisiana. Its financial services group produced 16% of earnings in 1983. This group was comprised primarily of mortgage banking and insurance operations.

Temple-Inland had a substantial timberland base consisting of 1,100,000 acres of timberland in east Texas and 50% ownership of Georgia Kraft Company, which had approximately 1,000,000 acres of timberland in Georgia and Alabama.

Industry Trends

The commitment to strong captive distribution systems was reiterated by several industry leaders in the early 1980s; they publicly stated that expansion of their distribution systems for building products was a top priority. One of the reasons for developing a strong distribution system was to address the increasingly important repair and remodeling market better. This market's potential was better understood when one looked at the ages of existing housing. In 1980, the total U.S. housing inventory consisted of approximately 90,000,000 units. Of these, approximately 45,000,000 were single-family homes that were at least 20 years old, making them prime candidates for expenditures on upkeep and improvement.[1]

In 1983, 22% of the U.S. softwood lumber consumption and 29% of the U.S. structural panel consumption was utilized in the repair and remodeling market, as shown in Exhibits 7 and 8. Total retail sales in the repair and remodeling market were predicted to reach over $65,000,000,000 in 1984 and $116,000,000,000 by 1990.[2] The fastest growing segment of the repair and remodeling market was the do-it-yourself market. Sales in this market were predicted to expand at a compound rate of 12.5% annually between 1984 and 1990, reaching total sales of $75,400,000,000 in 1990.[3] Furthermore, the total repair and remodeling market was strong enough to be called recession proof. If this market continues to expand as predicted, the major forest-products producers can be expected to continue their strong push into it by expanding their distribution systems.

An earlier trend in the 1960s and early 1970s was a diversification move by many forest-products firms. Georgia-Pacific, International Paper, and Boise Cascade, among others, moved into unrelated businesses they knew little about. These acquisitions included oil and gas, land development, chemicals, and in the case of Boise Cascade, even such exotic adventures as Latin American utilities. The forest products industry was highly dependent upon housing starts and general economic trends; however, the diversification schemes of most companies failed to produce the expected result of protecting against

Exhibit 7 1983 U.S. Softwood Lumber Consumption by End-Use Markets

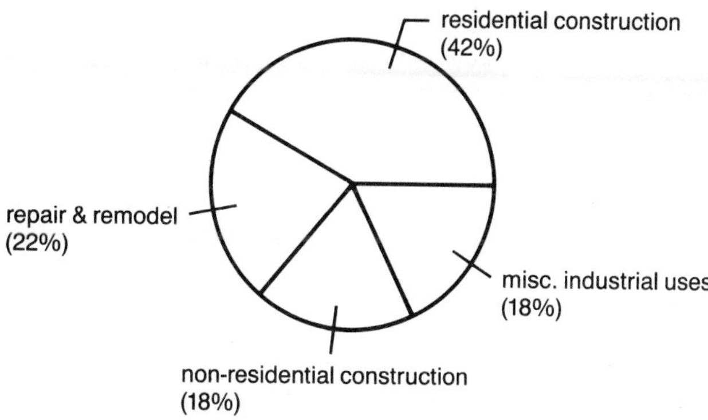

Source: Stuart U. Rich, "Sawmillers Can Profit by Knowing Market Trends," *Forest Industries*, October 1984, p. 21.

Exhibit 8 1983 U.S. Structural Panel Consumption by End-Use Markets

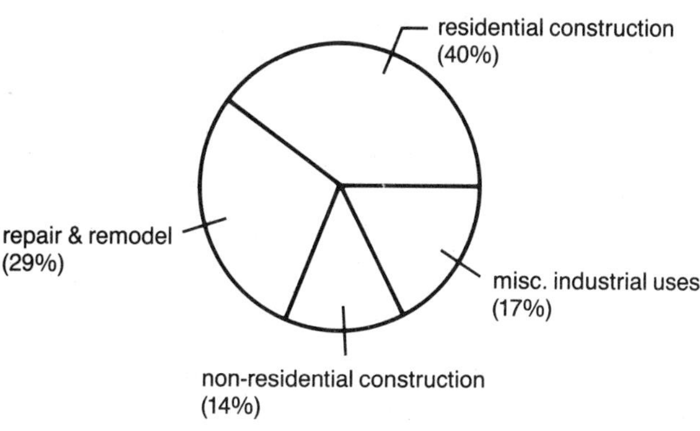

Source: Robert G. Anderson, *Regional Production and Distribution Patterns of the Structural Panel Industry* (Tacoma, Washington: American Plywood Association, 1983), p. 11.

cyclical swings in their forest-products businesses. Beginning in the mid-1970s and continuing until the mid-1980s, many companies started to sell off assets not related to their core forest-products businesses.

A consolidation of firms in the industry occurred. The number of sawmills and planing mills in the United States decreased from 12,189 in 1963 to 7,544 in 1977 and further decreased to 5,881 in 1981.[4] During this period of consolidation, the major forest-products firms increased their market shares. Georgia-Pacific and Weyerhaeuser increased their combined share of the United States lumber market from 6.8% in 1960 to 13.9% in 1981. During the same period, these two companies managed to increase their share of the softwood plywood market from 8.4% in 1960 to 28.8% in 1981.[5]

Another trend was the continued over capacity within the lumber industry, which was capable of producing enough lumber to support housing starts of 2,300,000 units per year in the early 1980s.[6] Although 20% of the western sawmills had gone out of business since 1978, newly built mills and renovations by larger companies kept capacity high. A fair number of old and inefficient plywood plants were in the Pacific Northwest. Many of these were independent operations which were expected to shut down over the next several years. This will reduce the production capacity to bring it more in line with current levels of housing construction, as well as increasing the market share of the major U.S. companies.

An additional trend in the paper segment was to build larger and larger plants to attain economies of scale. The strategy of most major paper producers was to concentrate their production on certain grades of paper to achieve the necessary economies of scale and market clout. Scott Paper Company, for example, continued to emphasize its strength in tissue paper products, including bathroom tissues, paper towels, facial tissues, and napkins. Boise Cascade, a leader in printing and writing papers, continued to strengthen its position in this market segment by bringing two new ultramodern paper machines on line by mid-1980.

Recent Changes in the Forest-Products Industry

The recent federal timber bailout legislation, which was signed into law in late 1984, will likely have a far reaching impact on the forest-products industry. Many Northwest forest-products firms relied heavily on public timber for their supply. During the late 1970s and very early 1980s, the prices bid for this public timber sky rocketed, reaching a peak in 1980 of $429 per thousand board feet for Douglas fir sawtimber. By 1984, that figure had dropped to $139.59 per thousand board feet for the same timber but, unfortunately many Northwest firms were still locked into these earlier contracts at much higher prices. Many of these firms subsequently appealed to the federal government for relief. Industry analysts speculated that many Northwestern forest-products companies would go bankrupt without federal relief. In fact, some firms owed more money on their timber contracts than their company's net worth.

The new legislation provided that the companies can buy out up to 55% of their cutting contracts up to a maximum of 200,000,000 board feet of contracted volume. The other 45% must be harvested under the terms of the original contracts. Timber cutting contracts generally run for a number of years so that some contracts signed in the early 1980s may not need to be cut until 1989.

The part of this legislation which impacted the greatest upon the long-term future of the industry was the restrictions on future timber sales. These restrictions required that annual timber sales in the region not exceed 5,200,000,000 board feet and that timber under contract at the end of any fiscal year not exceed 12,300,000,000 board feet. The annual sales volume for the years 1978 through 1984 was approximately 5,000,000,000 board feet. However, the region in early 1985 had 18,300,000,000 board feet of timber under contract, which greatly exceeded the limitation of 12,300,000,000 board feet at the end of any fiscal year. For the future, this legislation means that in times of strong wood demand the timber offered for sale in the Pacific Northwest from public lands cannot be increased above the current harvest levels.

The production of structural panel products began in the Pacific Northwest in the 1940s with early plywood mills, and this region remained dominant in plywood production until the early 1980s. In the early 1960s, the technology became available to produce plywood from southern pine, and by the early 1980s, the production of southern pine plywood exceeded that of plywood produced in the Pacific Northwest. Recent trends in timber costs and harvesting restrictions in the Pacific Northwest have further enhanced this trend.

Several knowledgeable industry analysts predicted in the early 1980s that the last southern pine plywood mill had been built. They speculated that all new expansion in the structural panel business would come from new, highly engineered composite panels such as waferboard and oriented strand board. These two new products used lower-cost timber and had a more highly automated production process. These two factors significantly lowered production and operating costs for these products versus the traditional plywood panel. Most of the major forest-products companies that had strengths in wood products staked out a position in this new market.

The demand for coated paper stock used for magazine production had been growing at approximately 10% per year. This strong increase in demand was spurred by increased magazine advertising and also rapid increases in the number of special interest magazines dedicated to such subjects as personal computers, physical fitness, self-improvement, and sports in the early 1980s. Demand increased so fast that U.S. coated paper machines operated at 100% of capacity, and yet approximately 425,000,000 tons of coated paper stock were still imported to fill the increasing demand in 1984.

Uncoated white paper used for business purposes and computer printers were also experiencing strong production with operating rates of approximately 95%. The expanding personal computer market was predicted to continue to increase demand for uncoated papers in coming years.

U.S. newsprint production was also up approximately 8% from 1983 levels, reaching approximately 95% of productive capacity in 1984. Canadian imports, however, were very strong in this market, and some U.S. firms appeared ready to pull out of this market altogether.

Threats to the Forest Products Industry

One of the major threats to the forest-products industry, which surfaced several times over the last 20 years, was government timber-cutting policies on federal forest lands. Through the pressure of the environmental movement over the last 15–20 years, a large amount of federal timberlands had been withdrawn from future timber production. This placed increasing pressure on the remaining federal timberlands. In addition, the increasingly stringent environmental regulations on federal timber contracts increased the cost of cutting some timber.

The companies hurt most by these policies were those in the West and Northwest that depended heavily upon federal timberlands for their raw material needs. Many of the companies hardest hit were small- to medium-sized operations with little or no timberland holdings of their own.

Another threat to the forest-products industry was the large role that the federal government played in the housing market. Every time government policies altered interest rates up or down, housing starts typically moved in the opposite direction. The interest cost of a new home represented such a large part of its total cost that any time interest rates were increased, the number of new houses built typically fell. This was especially important to the forest-products industry because in 1983, for instance, 42% of the softwood lumber and 40% of the softwood plywood consumed in this country was used in new residential construction.

Over the years, the federal government supported home ownership. This was evidenced by the interest deduction for home mortgages permitted on individual tax returns. In addition, the government sponsored various programs to make government-backed mortgage money available. If the U.S. Congress were to change the existing laws, this could pose a strong threat to the housing industry and in turn to the forest-products industry. Such proposals as the flat tax legislation that would eliminate the interest deduction for second homes and perhaps limit the interest deduction on first homes could severely damage the new home construction market.

Many segments of the forest-products industry, particularly plywood and most paper segments, were oligopolistic in nature. They were characterized by large firms with fairly large market shares, where price leadership was the norm. A number of times in the past, the Justice Department accused various firms in these oligopolistic segments of the industry of price fixing. These law suits consumed considerable time and effort for forest-products firms and many times resulted in large fines or out-of-court settlements. For instance, in recent plywood price fixing litigation, Georgia-Pacific, Weyerhaeuser, and Willamette reached a settlement of $165,000,000 after an unfavorable jury verdict. They did not admit any guilt, but rather said that the settlement was preferable to the expense and time required for an appeal.

Although the U.S. forest-products industry has been largely free of strong import pressure in most of its product lines, the Canadians had a strong market share in softwood lumber and newsprint. The Canadians had been gaining a larger share of the U.S. softwood lumber market. The National Forest Products Association estimated that Canadian firms supplied approximately 19% of the softwood lumber consumed in the United States in 1975. By 1983, the Canadian share of the U.S. softwood lumber market had risen to almost 34%. In the early 1980s, several major forest-products firms combined forces and filed a countervailing duty petition with the U.S. International Trade Commission. After a major investigation was conducted, the Commission chose to take no action, and Canadian softwood lumber remained free to enter the U.S. without duties.

Suppliers to the Forest Products Industry

Timber supply was the number one ingredient for the forest-products industry. In the production of softwood lumber, for example, the cost of timber comprised approximately 71% of the total cost of lumber production, and for the production of liner board, a paper product, the cost of timber comprised approximately 32% of the total cost of production in the early 1980s.[7] With such high-cost components, it was easy to understand the power that timber supply could have over a forest-products facility. This helped to explain the great concern that forest-products firms had over federal timber-cutting policies and the industry's large privately-owned timber base.

The production of most lumber and panel products was done with relatively little energy consumption; however, the production of pulp and paper products tended to be very energy intensive. The energy crisis of the early and mid-1970s spurred many pulp and paper firms to develop the ability to generate their own energy. As a result, pulp and paper firms and other segments of the forest-products industry helped make the industry one of the most energy self-sufficient industry groups in the U.S.

Buyers of Forest Products

Although several major corporations had strong captive distribution systems at the wholesale level, most of the lumber and plywood still moved through small independently-owned building-materials wholesalers. In the early 1980s, independently owned wholesalers controlled approximately 76% of the sales volume within the lumber, plywood, and millwork markets. With 6,928 wholesalers, mostly small independents, wholesalers exerted relatively little power over the production of forest products by major integrated firms.

The retail side of the wood-products segment was controlled almost entirely by firms without significant manufacturing capabilities. There were 24,940 retail building-material dealers in the early 1980s. The vast majority of these building-material dealers were small, independent firms; however, several large retail building-material chains such as Lowe's, Wickes, and Payless Cashways, all had sales over $1,000,000,000. Wood products sales, however, were only one segment of their total sales. Nonetheless, the size and the growing number of large building-material chains will probably increase their power over the producers of building materials.

The paper segment of the forest-products industry was still highly influenced by the availability and cost of the timber needed to produce paper. However, unlike the wood-products segment, the paper segment sold to buyers in some of its markets that were large enough to influence strongly the price of the product and terms of the sale. One paper market characterized by large buyers was the newsprint market. Most newsprint was sold on the basis of long-term contracts with large established newspapers. Newsprint moved directly from the producing mills to the newspaper firms. In addition, many large newspapers integrated backwards and built or purchased their own newsprint mills, often on a joint venture basis.

The light-weight coated-paper segment of the paper market was also one that dealt with very large buyers. This paper was used in the printing of high quality magazines. Large magazine printers purchased this particular grade of paper in large enough quantities to influence the supplier. Also, buyers in this paper segment had a tendency to integrate backwards into the production of this grade of paper.

For many grades of paper commonly used in everyday life, the major paper producers marketed these products through paper merchants/wholesalers. In 1983, approximately $24,100,000,000 of paper products were sold through the 5,351 paper merchants/wholesalers in the United States. Approximately 80% of these paper merchants were independently owned firms; however, the 20% owned by manufacturers controlled approximately 50% of the sales volume.[8] With so many independent wholesalers and a strong captive wholesaler segment in the paper wholesale market, it was unlikely that any group of buyers could exert undue influence over paper manufacturers.

Substitute Products

Certain segments of the forest-products industry were sensitive to substitute products. One good example was hardwood flooring. Prior to the advent of wall-to-wall carpeting and the introduction of better quality vinyl flooring, hardwood strip flooring enjoyed a large market in the United States. After the advent of these substitute flooring products, however, the hardwood flooring market declined precipitously. From 1969 to 1982, shipments of oak flooring decreased from 387,800,000 board feet to 75,000,000 board feet.

Fortunately most segments of the forest-products industry were not affected to that extent by substitute products. One industry analyst predicted a decrease in the strong relationship between real GNP and paper demand for certain categories of paper products in the late 1980s. This decrease was predicted due to plastic substitutes for certain packaging products and a slight negative influence of electronic transmission of information on newsprint and white-paper demand.

Within the wood-products side of the forest-products industry, the largest market was still for housing. Several substitution trends had the potential to affect the future market for wood building products adversely. Many consumers not able to afford a traditional single-family home were substituting apartments, townhouses, and other multifamily dwellings. A multifamily dwelling consumed approximately half as much lumber and plywood during construction, per housing unit, as the traditional single-family dwelling. Between 1976 and 1980, single-family units represented approximately 71% of total housing starts. By 1981, their market share had dropped to 64%, and Morgan Stanley predicted that in the 1986 to 1990 period, the share of single-family dwellings will drop to approximately 52% of total housing starts.[9]

The Future Outlook

Despite various trends, threats, and substitute products, the outlook for the wood industry as a whole remains strong. In the United States about as much wood, by weight, was used each year as steel, cement, plastics, aluminum, and all other materials combined.[10] With this tremendous usage and a timber supply that is still increasing, the wood-industry future looks bright.

In the wood-products arena, the major forest-products companies need to learn to address better the growing repair and remodelling market. With such firms as K-Mart entering into the retail building material market, many observers predict a competitive shake out in this market place.

Within the paper-products side of the industry, the overall outlook is good. Although electronics and plastic packaging are predicted to impact upon the demand for certain grades of paper, new products on the horizon may boost paper demand even further. One new product is ovenable paper. The increasing use of the microwave in the family kitchen stimulated the need for a tray to hold frozen foods that could be used in a microwave oven. Traditional aluminum packaging for frozen foods like TV dinners was not usable in a microwave. As a result, a new category of paper products was developed. This product allowed frozen foods to be heated in a microwave oven without damage to the microwave circuitry.

Additional interesting paper products on the horizon include asceptic containers made from laminents of paperboard, aluminum foil, and plastic. These containers, used for packaging perishable goods, could keep these goods fresh for long periods of time without refrigeration. Kimberly-Clark recently began test marketing a new treated facial tissue that kills most of the viruses that cause colds and flu. The product is expected to help fight the spread of virus between family members.

A potential cloud on the horizon for many forest-products companies resulted from relatively low stock prices and high initial investments required for new paper capacity. This led to a rash of takeover attempts of paper firms. The largest recent move involved St. Regis, which, after fending off several takeover attempts, finally accepted a friendly offer to merge with Champion International. Continuing mergers and takeovers of this type have the capacity to influence strongly the future shape of the forest products industry.

Notes

1. Stuart U. Rich, "Sawmillers Can Profit By Knowing Market Trends," *Forest Industries*, October 1984, p. 20.
2. "Home Improvement Market Nailing Up New Growth Records," *Building Products Digest*, May 1984, p. 10.
3. "Making Do," *Forbes*, June 1984, p. 8.
4. Rich, p. 21.
5. Thomas P. Clephane and J. Carroll, *Timber Survey* (New York: Morgan Stanley & Co., 1982), p. 133.
6. Standard and Poor's Industry Survey, *Building and Forest Products*, December 1984, p. b65.
7. Clephane, p. 6.
8. *Who's Who in Paper Distribution and Fact Book* (Great Neck, New York: National Paper Trade Association, 1984) p. 14.
9. Clephane, p. 126.
10. James L. Bowyer, "Wood: What Are the Alternatives?" *Northwestern Lumberman*, February 1980, p. 41.

Case 23

James River Corporation of Virginia

On Friday, October 21, 1983, Paul A. Engelmeyer, a staff reporter for *The Wall Street Journal,* reported that Brenton S. Halsey, the chairman and chief executive officer of the James River Corporation, had indicated that the primary goal of the company in the coming years would be consolidation and internal growth. This announcement heralded a change in the corporate strategy of the firm. The revenues of the James River Corporation had grown in a spectacular fashion over the last few years, largely as a result of an aggressive acquisition strategy. Judd Alexander, an executive vice president of the company, observed that if the rate of growth in revenue were to be maintained the firm would have to buy General Motors. And, Mr. Halsey conceded that the current pace of growth would be hard to match in the future, as there are few billion-dollar acquisitions around.

The article in *The Wall Street Journal* went on to discuss other problems associated with the past acquisition strategy of this well-respected paper manufacturing firm. These problems included the substantial debt of the firm and a rise in the price of pulp, which serves as a principal raw material of the firm. Finally, Mr. Alexander was quoted as expressing belief that the environment of the firm had changed because of the present size of the firm, leading him to conclude (as quoted by Mr. Engelmeyer), "You rarely see someone who can start a company and then manage it when it becomes this big."

Source: Prepared by Alan Bauerschmidt, College of Business Administration, University of South Carolina, Columbia, S.C., and Patricia McDougall, Department of Management, Georgia State University.

The shares of the corporation closed that week at 33¾, down 3½ from the previous week, in fairly active trading on the New York Stock Exchange. The Dow-Jones average of the leading industrials traded on the New York Stock Exchange was off 1.16 percent that same week. The shares of James River fell a further 3⅜ during heightened trading the following week, to close at 30⅜. This was paralleled by a further drop in the Dow-Jones average of 2.03 percent. After a smaller drop of ⅝ in the week ending November 4, 1983, shares in the company began a recovery that brought their value back to 37¼ by Friday, December 2, 1983. During the same period the Dow-Jones index rose to its original level. It should be noted that the James River Corporation reported earnings of $1.65 per share for the first half of the fiscal year, during the week of November 15. Earnings for the similar period in the previous year were $1.37.

History of The Corporation

The James River Corporation was founded in 1969 by Mr. Halsey and Robert C. Williams through a leveraged buy-out of a paper mill operated by the Ethyl Corporation. The latter firm was formed as a joint venture of General Motors and Standard Oil of New Jersey to produce a lead additive that would give gasoline a no-knock characteristic. Ethyl later became a public corporation and was acquired by the much smaller Albemarle Paper Company in the early 1960s. The assets of Albemarle became the foundation of the specialty paper operation of the Ethyl Corporation. The merger of these two firms was largely a financial maneuver, rather than an integration of operations.

At the time of the buy-out Mr. Halsey ran a small paper bag factory for the Ethyl Corporation, while Mr. Williams had responsibility for a papermaking R&D department of the corporation. When the managers of Ethyl decided to get rid of the assets of the company in the paper industry, Halsey and Williams borrowed the funds necessary to pay the corporation $1,500,000 for the single-machine mill on the James River in Richmond. The mill was a part of the original assets of the Albemarle Paper Company, and it was involved in the production of unbleached kraft paper that sold for $400 a ton and generated revenues of about $4,500,000. Halsey and Williams, with their backgrounds in engineering and intimate knowledge of the paper industry, converted the mill to produce papers for automotive oil filters that sold for $800 a ton.

The strategy revealed at this early point in the life of the firm has guided its growth over the past 14 years. Halsey and Williams have sought to identify and acquire paper mills and converting plants that require no more than 50 cents of investment per dollar of sales. They then transform the mill from the production of commodity paper products to specialty papers that yield a higher revenue. This requires intimate knowledge of the paper production process and today the company prides itself that the top 50 executives of the firm are so technically knowledgeable that each could operate a paper machine if required.

The spectacular growth of James River began with the acquisition of the Pepperell Paper Company in April of 1971. An 80 percent ownership of the 75-tons-per-day paper mill in East Pepperell, Massachusetts, was purchased from the St. Regis Corporation. This acquisition permitted James River to broaden its involvement in the manufacture of specialty papers. Today the mill produces paper stock that provides the base for masking tape and packaging papers for food products, as well as other grades of converting paper.

In May 1972, James River acquired a mill in Fitchburg, Massachusetts, with a capacity of 52 tons from the Weyerhaeuser Corporation. This mill is operated as a subsidiary, producing a wide variety of special industrial converting papers and other paper products.

A most notable event occurred in 1973, when it was decided to transform the privately held firm into a public corporation. This was accomplished by the sale of 205,000 of the $.10 par value shares of the firm in a public offering accomplished on March 16, at $12.00 per share. The firm retained 515,870 of the 2,000,000 shares authorized on October 29, 1972, as treasury stock, with 2,000 of these earmarked for stock options. The other 1,064,130 shares were distributed to principals associated with the founding of the company.

On October 1, 1974, the firm acquired the Peninsular Paper Company, a small independent producer of text and cover paper in Ypsilanti, Michigan. The acquisition entailed $1,136,006 in notes and 35,018 common shares, plus an additional contingent amount of $200,000. Peninsular is also operated as a subsidiary of the James River Corporation and has a capacity of 50 tons of paper per day.

The capacity of the three acquired mills, plus the mill on the James River, totaled only 199 tons of paper products per day, so the company at this point in time was still relatively small, although it manufactured a variety of specialty papers and was already geographically dispersed in its activities. In 1975, the firm more than doubled this capacity by acquiring five additional paper machines and more than doubling its work force from 598 to 1240 employees.

On September 19 the company paid the Weyerhaeuser Corporation $20,433,000 in cash, notes, and preferred stock for the facilities of Weyerhaeuser-Massachusetts, which contained the five machines. These operations form the hub of the Industrial Products Group of the James River Corporation, and the plant is operated as a subsidiary under the name of James River-Massachusetts. The products of the plant include various types of coated stock such as release backing papers and reprographic papers, with a daily capacity of 238 tons. Two series of preferred stock were developed to consummate the purchase: the first had an 8 percent yield and was convertible into 125,000 shares of common stock; the second series was participating in nature and entitled the holders to 60 percent of the earnings after taxes of the James River-Massachusetts Corporation above $1,000,000.

On January 1, 1977, the firm acquired the privately held Curtis Paper Company. This company operated a mill in Newark, Delaware, and the James River Corporation continues this operation as the Curtis Division, producing 22 tons of bend, text, and cover papers. Later in January—on the 10th of the month—the company acquired the Rochester Paper Company from the Household Finance Company. This acquisition included a mill with a 40-tons-per-day capacity in Adams, Massachusetts, and a mill in Rochester, Michigan, with an 18-ton capacity. Each plant produces a variety of specialty paper products including industrial filters. The James River-Rochester Division is operated as a part of the Filtration Products Group, while the Adams Division is part of the Printing/Packaging Group. During the period in which these two sets of acquisitions were being accomplished the James River Corporation assumed a $15,000,000 note payable quarterly from 1979 to 1991, at 10.25 percent interest. The terms of the note stipulated that the firm must maintain working capital of $15,000,000 and demonstrate certain financial ratios in respect to funded debt. This indebtedness was liquidated during 1982.

During 1977, the company also acquired the Riegal Products Corporation from Southwest Forest Industries. This acquisition included four mills in the western portion of New Jersey which produce a wide variety of specialty papers including inner liners for food packaging. One of these mills with a 15-ton capacity is now idle, while the other three are operated as the Riegal Division of James River; these mills have a capacity of 38, 200, and 75 tons daily, and, therefore, represented the largest acquisition of James River up to that point in time. A portion of the financing of this acquisition included the issue of a third series of participating preferred shares entitled to $4.00 per annum plus dividends on the earnings of the Riegal Products Division above $3,600,000.

On January 30, 1978, the firm acquired the Otis plant of the International Paper Company in Jay, Maine. This plant is now operated as a subsidiary of the James River Corporation, producing coated, conductive, and carbonless specialty papers. The plant has a capacity of 135 tons daily.

During the period of the Otis and Riegal acquisition the firm issued an unsecured senior obligation in the amount of $12,000,000 due during the period 1982–1997 and paying 8.75 percent interest. It also released 40,000 nonparticipating preferred shares in a new series paying $8.75 in dividends.

The firm acquired what has become the James River Graphics Company for approximately $34,800,000 from the Scott Paper Company during December of 1978. This converting operation in South Hadley, Massachusetts, was the firm's first venture into coated film, and the firm uses 12 coating lines of up to 62 inches to produce photographic and reproduction paper, leatherettes, metallic-coated, embossed, decorative, and electrographic papers, along with other products of a coated or moistureproof variety.

The year 1979 provided no new acquisitions by the company and no increase in indebtedness. However, the company increased the number of common shares authorized from 3,000,000 to 10,000,000, and reported that 2,393,898 shares were outstanding (the company has earlier authorized a 3 for 2 split of the common stock). A portion of the new shares—187,000—were issued in conversion of the first series of preferred stock. The second series of preferred stock was repurchased by the company during May.

During June of 1979, the company did reach an agreement to purchase the assets of the Howard Paper Company of Dayton, Ohio, for $7,500,000, but the agreement was never consummated. Howard remains a privately held firm that operates two mills producing coated specialty papers. The mills have a total capacity of 275 tons of paper products per day, and the James River Corporation was prepared to pay $3,700,000 in cash and 165,000 shares of common stock for the firm, while refinancing $2,000,000 of the indebtedness of Howard Paper.

Up to this point in time, James River remained a specialty paper manufacturer which purchased the necessary pulp required as a raw material for its operations. In December of 1980, the firm acquired the Brown Company for $260,000,000 from Gulf & Western; Brown was involved in the production of specialty papers but it also had a pulp mill in New Hampshire. This served to vertically integrate the firm back to the required raw material. The Brown Company also had a towel and tissue operation, a folding carton operation, and a food service operation. Some of these varied activities form the Berlin/Gorham Group of the corporation, headquartered in Berlin, New Hampshire. The pulp mill in Berlin has a daily production of 100 tons of unbleached kraft and 700 tons of bleached kraft; 300 tons of the latter is market pulp. The Gorham plant produces 350 tons of bag and sack paper, creped kraft, and other forms of paper stock. This plant also produces 150 tons of sanitary tissue and interfolded and rolled towels. With this acquisition the *number* of employees of the James River Corporation reached 3,802.

In May of 1981 the firm acquired certain assets of Minerva, Inc., for $3,700,000, and in July 1982 the firm acquired the Dixie/Northern assets of the American Can Company for $480,000,000 in cash and preferred stock for $212,930,000 in working capital and $267,400,000 of other property, gaining a tissue business having a revenue of $600,000,000 and the revenues of the Dixie cup and folding carton operation. The transaction was financed by $372,489,000 of debt, of which $100,000,000 was taken by American Can in the form of a subordinate issue convertible into 5,000,000 shares of James River Corporation common stock. The remainder of the purchase price was obtained from the assumption of $18,841,000 in other long-term debt and liabilities, the sale of $50,000,000 worth of James River common to American Can, and an issue of $39,000,000 in preferred stock to American Can that can be converted to 866,667 shares of common stock.

A major attraction leading to this acquisition was the pulp capacity of the Naheola Mill in Pennington, Alabama, which had a daily output of 1,000 tons of kraft pulp. The Halsey, Oregon, plant produces an additional 350 tons of pulp, of which 125 tons is market pulp. The Ashland and Green Bay, Wisconsin, mills are smaller operations in respect to pulp production, but the former mill produces 51 tons of creped paper based on 50 tons of pulp and the latter produces 410 tons of sanitary tissue, toweling, and converted products while having a capacity of 150 tons of pulp. James River merged the folding carton business obtained through the acquisition of Dixie with the elements obtained from the earlier Brown acquisition to create the Folding Carton Division of the Paperboard Packaging Group. The ranks of the firm grew to 17,700 employees upon completion of this acquisition that added 9,500 individuals.

On October 1, 1983, the James River Corporation concluded the $43,500,000 purchase of the H. P. Smith Paper Company from Phillips Petroleum for cash. The converting plants located in Chicago and Iowa City produce 100 tons of polyethylene-coated paper, board, and oiled papers producing sales of $51,000,000 in the previous year. This acquisition broadened the line of release papers used by industry and food packages and is operated as the KVP Group.

During 1983, James River acquired four mills from the Diamond International Corporation for $75,000,000. The latter firm was acquired by Sir James Goldsmith in 1982, and it was his decision to sell off the pulp and papermaking properties of the firm to the James River Corporation. These acquisitions include a mill in Old Town, Maine, that produces 160 tons per day of tissue and toweling, along with 600 tons of bleached hardwood and softwood kraft pulp. The managers of James River intend to organize a Penobscot division to operate this mill using personnel who performed this activity for the Diamond International Corporation.

The other three acquired mills will be organized as the Groveton Group and include the four-machine paper mill at Groveton, New Hampshire, that produces 300 tons per day of printing paper and 50 tons of facial and toilet tissue. The group will also encompass a mill at Hyde Park, Massachusetts, which produces 200 tons of printing paper daily on two paper machines and a 45-tons-per-day mill at Gouverneur, New York, that produces tissue and napkin paper on a single paper machine.

James River issued 522,057 shares of common stock with a current market value of $19,800,000, and privately placed 760,000 shares of preferred stock with a liquidation value of $76,000,000 to complete the purchase of the mills from Diamond International.

Early in 1984, James River announced that it acquired one quarter of the outstanding shares of A. B. Papers PLC of St. Andrews, Scotland, and will offer to purchase the remaining shares for a total acquisition cost of $7,750,000. The Scottish firm makes printing and specialty papers, and it owns a converting plant in Glasgow that makes heat-seal paper and particle-gum paper used for labels. A. B. Papers reported sales of $27,000,000 for the fiscal year ending on March 31, 1983, and pretax profits of $778,000. This will be the first foreign acquisition by the corporation.

Nature of the Paper Industry

The James River Corporation is a part of the eleventh largest manufacturing industry in the U.S. in volume of sales. The paper and allied products industry accounts for 3.6 percent of the value of all manufacturing in the country, and the value of shipments was $79 billion in 1982, down slightly from the peak shipments of $80.2 billion in 1981. The industry is estimated to have produced 59.8 million short tons of paper and paperboard in 1982, operating at an estimated 85.7 percent of practical maximum capacity. Elements of the industry produced 52.3 million short tons of wood pulp in 1982, of which 5.9 million short tons was marketed as pulp. The industry exported 3.5 million short tons of wood pulp in 1982, and in turn, 3.6 million tons were imported. Exports of paper and paperboard products totaled 4.3 million short tons in 1982, while imports of the same products equaled 7.9 million tons. Imports of newsprint made up 6.6 million tons of the total, while only .3 million tons were exported. The bulk of newsprint imports were from Canada. The major exports from the U.S. were in the form of linerboard and other paperboard products.

The U.S. paper and allied products industry consists of 394 companies producing paper in 655 mills and pulp in 390 mills. In addition there are 4,500 establishments involved in the transformation of the paper and pulp produced in the mills. Some of these converting establishments belong to the 394 companies operating mills, while other establishments belong to companies without mill facilities. Approximately 43.3 percent of the products of the industry are used in packaging, 31.4 percent in printing and publishing, 9.0 percent for stationery and converting, 8.7 percent in building and construction, 5.5 percent as disposable sanitary products, and 2.1 percent as industrial products.

The most distinguishing characteristic of the paper industry is its high level of capital investment. The paper and paperboard mill segment of the industry has approximately one dollar of gross fixed assets for every dollar of shipments. The paper converting segment of the industry is less capital-intensive, with $3.71 in shipments for each dollar of gross fixed assets, while the paperboard converting segment has $2.84 in shipments for each dollar of gross fixed assets. Taken together, the overall industry has shipments of $1.70 per dollar of gross fixed assets.

Papermaking is one of the oldest manufacturing technologies and technological change is relatively infrequent, although firms continue to make innovations in their production processes and the products they offer for sale. In 1980, the industry made capital expenditures of $5.2 billion, representing 17.6 percent of the value-added by paper manufacturing in that year. The overall manufacturing industries had capital expenditures of 9.1 percent in this same year. Another way to appreciate the unusual character of the paper industry in this respect is to observe that the paper and allied products industry made up 3.84 percent of the value-added by manufacturing in 1980, but it accounted for 7.40 percent of the capital expenditures of all manufacturing firms. It is estimated that the amount of capital expenditures made by the paper industry fell by 1.2 percent in 1981, and a further 6.5 percent in 1982.

Modern papermaking dates from the close of the 18th century when the paper machine of today was first developed, replacing the hand molding technique that dated back into antiquity. Paper is formed from pulp on an endless woven-wire cloth that drains and advances the forming paper through a succession of phases depending upon the type and quality of paper to be manufactured. The paper is dried, coated, and calendered as necessary. In this continuous process the web of formed paper is drawn onto a reel, where it is available for shipment or further processing. As mentioned above, various innovations are constantly being developed by equipment and raw material suppliers; however, the basic techniques of the fourdrinier and cylinder-type papermaking machines have been in existence for almost 200 years. This stability of the fundamental technology permits extended years of usefulness of the equipment found in paper and paperboard mills. Some paper machines in America and Europe have been in service for up to a hundred years, although to see such continuous use they have been remodeled again and again to incorporate advancements. The trend of these advancements is in the figures-of-merit associated with greater rates of operating speeds and consistent quality of the web of paper being formed by the machine. The trend in newly installed machines incorporates these figures-of-merit and greater width of paper formation.

The use of wood pulp in the manufacture of paper is of somewhat later origin than the papermaking machine. The wood grinding machine that permitted cheap groundwood papers to be produced was developed in Europe around 1840; however, the acceptance of this new technology took some time, and the availability of rags continued to constrain production of paper on both continents. The first sales of groundwood pulp to papermakers in the U.S. took place in 1867, at a price of eight cents per pound. The price soon dropped to four or 5 cents, and when it eventually fell to a penny a pound it reduced the price of newsprint from 14 cents in 1869, to 2 cents in 1897. This innovation in the raw materials for paper production had a revolutionary impact upon the newspaper industry, where it made the high-speed rotary printing press and the modern newspaper and magazine industries possible.

The use of wood pulp in the manufacture of the various grades and types of papers eventually followed. New uses for paper were developed as the chronic shortage of rags for pulp making disappeared. These new uses required more durable grades of paper than newsprint at a cost intermediate between rag and groundwood. Such paper stocks required the purification of the wood fiber in a chemical process, and the first of these processes that were developed used caustic soda. Today, chemimechanical and semi-chemical processes have improved pulp yields that original chemical methods did not allow. Much of the prepared paperboard now produced in the U.S. is made from the southern pine, which was considered unsuitable for papermaking before adaptation of the kraft sulfate process in the 1930s.

Few firms manufacture pulp to the exclusion of papermaking itself, and few papermaking firms are without pulp making capability in the U.S. It is estimated that 85 percent of the pulp produced in the U.S. is consumed captively at the same location where it is produced. The remaining quantity is shipped as market pulp to other papermaking locations of the same firm, or it is sold domestically and in foreign markets. Imports of pulp to the U.S. exceed exports, and Canada supplies 95 percent of these imports as well as being an active exporter to the rest of the developed nations. In Europe and Japan a great deal of the pulp requirement is met by recycling used paper.

Paper products include unbleached kraft paper which is a brown, somewhat coarse stiff paper used to produce heavy packaging, bags, and sack. Bleached kraft paper is a fine-textured paper manufactured from either softwoods of hardwoods and used to produce fine writing and printing papers and paperboard for packaging; the better papers are produced from softwoods. Newsprint and groundwood printing papers are course-textured papers of low strength and limited durability which tend to yellow with age. Corrugated medium is a course, low-strength paper obtained from the chemical processing of hardwoods and used in corrugated boxes as dividers and stiffeners between the paperboard liners. Linerboard is a stiff, durable, thick paper made primarily from unbleached kraft paper and used to manufacture heavy-duty shipping containers and corrugated boxes. Paperboard is a stiff paper of moderate thickness made from bleached kraft pulp to produce milk cartons, folding boxes, and individual packaging. Coated paper is a printing paper that has been treated with material such as kaolin to improve printability and photo reproduction and then used in the printing of magazines, annual reports, and books. Specialty papers are a diverse group of products ranging from thin filter papers to stiff card stock and used in such products as cigarettes; filter papers, bonded papers (with cotton fibers), index cards, tags, file folders, and postcards. Tissue paper is a thin, soft, absorbent paper manufactured primarily from chemical groundwood pulps and used to manufacture toweling, tissues, and hygienic products. In all, several thousand different kinds of paper and paperboard can be manufactured.

Figure 1 on page 874 lists 30 firms that obtain a substantial portion of their revenues from the sale of such paper products. Various adjustments to the order of the listing could be made to reflect various circumstances, so this listing should not be taken to represent the leading paper manufacturers. Some of the firms such as Crown Zellerbach, Great Northern Nekoosa, Hammermill, Mead, and Scott Paper earn substantial portions of their revenue from the distribution of paper products, rather than from the manufacture of such products. The Hammermill Paper Company, for example, has integrated its downstream activities to the extent that 45 percent of its revenues are attributed to wholesale distribution and only 15 percent of the products being distributed are manufactured by the company. The list could also be modified to reflect the fact that in some cases large portions of the revenues of firms are generated by foreign operations rather than the domestic manufacture and sale of paper and allied products. Figure 2 indicates the proportion of the total revenue of firms that resulted from foreign operations in 1982.

Other measures that might be taken into account in an assessment of the industry could in-

Figure 1 Leading U.S. Paper Firms

Rank in paper business	Company	1982 Revenue from paper business ($ billion)	1982 Total revenue ($ billion)	Paper as percent of total
1	International Paper	3.379	4.015	84
2	Kimberly-Clark	2.870	2.946	97
3	Champion International	2.383	3.737	64
4	St. Regis	2.207	2.556	86
5	Scott Paper	2.117	2.293	92
6	Weyerhaeuser	2.099	4.186	50
7	Boise Cascade	2.068	2.912	71
8	Mead	2.040	2.667	76
9	Mobil	1.951	64.137	3
10	James River	1.875	1.900[a]	99
11	Crown Zellerbach	1.831	2.958	62
12	Georgia-Pacific	1.658	5.402	31
13	Westvaco	1.301	1.450	90
14	Union Camp	1.166	1.526	76
15	Great Northern Nekoosa	1.030	1.430	72
16	Continental Group	.979	4.979[b]	20
17	Time, Inc.	.922	3.564[c]	26
18	Hammermill Paper	.760	1.396	54
19	Owens-Illinois	.679	3.553	19
20	Procter & Gamble	.669	11.994	6
21	Maryland Cup	.656	.656[d]	100
22	Willamette Industries	.641	.929	69
23	Potlatch	.640	.820	78
24	Fort Howard Paper	.537	.537[d]	100
25	Consolidated Papers	.483	.530	91
26	Sonoco Products	.473	.542	87
27	Bemis	.456	.681	67
28	Stone Container	.410	.427[e]	96
29	Dennison Manufacturing	.346	.577	60
30	Longview Fibre	.326	.371	88

[a]Reflects the 1982 acquisition of the American Can properties.
[b]Prior to the 1983 sales of assets that generated $.480 billion of paper and allied products revenue.
[c]Prior to the 1983 divestiture of Temple-Inland.
[d]Prior to Stone Container's 1983 acquisition of assets sold by Continental Group.
[e]These two firms merged in 1983.

clude the relative degree to which firms in the industry have integrated backward to gain ownership or control of forestland that ultimately provides the raw material for the production of paper and paperboard products. Figure 3 provides the best information available on the amount of acreage controlled by the firms previously listed.

A few of the firms report tons of output, and from this a rough gauge can be obtained of the

Figure 2 Proportion of Total Revenues Generated by Foreign Operations in 1982

Company	Percent
International Paper	7
Kimberly-Clark	34
Champion International	13
St. Regis	13
Scott Paper	Nil[a]
Weyerhaeuser	22
Boise Cascade	9
Mead	Nil
Mobil	61[b]
James River	Nil
Crown Zellerbach	16
Georgia-Pacific	Unstated
Westvaco	26
Union Camp	10
Great Northern Nekoosa	Unstated
Continental Group	10
Time, Inc.	25
Hammermill Paper	Nil
Owens-Illinois	20
Procter & Gamble	29
Maryland Cup	Nil
Willamette Industries	Nil
Potlatch	11
Fort Howard Paper	Nil
Consolidated Papers	1
Sonoco Products	24
Bemis	14
Stone Container	7
Dennison Manufacturing	19
Longview Fibre	Nil

[a]Foreign subsidiary operations generate additional revenues of $11.4 billion, but this is considered as an investment return.
[b]Nil in respect to paper and allied products.

Figure 3 Acreage of Forestland Owned or Controlled by Major U.S. Paper Firms

Company	Acreage
International Paper	7,000,000
Kimberly-Clark	2,000,000
Champion International	3,300,000
St. Regis	5,870,000
Scott Paper	3,300,000
Weyerhaeuser	15,000,000
Boise Cascade	7,584,000
Mead	1,702,000
Mobil	1,046,000
James River	1,500,000
Crown Zellerbach	3,311,000
Georgia-Pacific	7,680,000
Westvaco	1,366,000
Union Camp	1,700,000
Great Northern Nekoosa	2,759,000
Continental Group	1,500,000
Time, Inc.	2,000,000
Hammermill Paper	435,000
Owens-Illinois	1,100,000
Procter & Gamble	Unreported
Maryland Cup	Nil
Willamette Industries	558,000
Potlatch	1,400,000
Fort Howard Paper	Nil[a]
Consolidated Papers	667,241
Sonoco Products	265,000[a]
Bemis	Nil
Stone Container	475,000
Dennison Manufacturing	Nil
Longview Fibre	503,000

[a]Both Fort Howard Paper and Sonoco use extensive amounts of recycled wastepaper.

value of the product produced by the various companies. The revenue received per ton of output is shown for these firms in Figure 4.

This illustrates the heterogeneous nature of the paper and allied products industry. Firms operate in various product sectors of the industry and thus add different values to the products produced. A firm such as ITT Rayonier, which is not included in Figure 1, produces and markets pulp to the exclusion of any further process. All the firms in Figure 1 go at least one further step to manufacture paper or form products from the pulp they manufacture or purchase. Some of these papers may be the final product produced—

Figure 4 Revenue per Ton of Product

Company	Tons of pulp paper, and paper products	Dollar revenue per ton
International Paper	5,010,000	674.
Weyerhaeuser	3,695,000	568.
Boise Cascade	1,986,000	1041.
Mead	3,562,000	573.
James River	1,400,000	1339.
Georgia-Pacific	3,000,000	553.
Westvaco	1,993,000	653.
Union Camp	2,196,000	531.
Great Northern Nekoosa	2,243,000	459.
Willamette	1,750,000	366.
Potlatch	587,000	1090.
Consolidated Paper	631,000	765.
Stone Container	785,000	522.
Longview Fibre	599,000	544.

newsprint produced from groundwood pulp would be an example of such a final product. Other papers may be shipped in the rolls for further processing or converted in some fashion in the plant in which the paper was formed from pulp. Firms which purchase paper for further processing into paper products are labeled converters, but the papermaking firms generally are integrated forward into portions of the converting segment of the industry, even if they continue to be considered as papermakers.[1]

The converting of paper is broadly divided into the making of boxes and other containers and the manufacture of other paper products. The latter category of converting is divided into the coating and glazing of paper and the production of envelopes, bags, die-cut paper and board, pressed and molded pulp goods, sanitary paper products, stationery products, and a host of miscellaneous products such as confetti, crepe paper, doilies, gift wrappers, paper tags, and telegraph tape. There is also a segment of the paper industry that is concerned with the conversion of pulp into building paper and board.

The James River Corporation Position in The Industry

The James River Corporation has established positions in both the papermaking and converting portions of the industry. The firm is sufficiently integrated to produce the bulk of the paper and paperboard necessary for its converting operation, while still meeting its desired output of direct paper products. The firm purchases 600,000 tons of pulp to supplement the 700,000 tons of pulp it manufactures. Some 1,200,000 tons of paper and paperboard are manufactured from this pulp, while 100,000 tons of pulp is sold. Over 360,000 tons of the paper and paperboard produced by the firm is in the form of specialty and communications papers. Another 435,000 tons of paper is produced in the form of towel and sanitary tissues. Some 15,000 tons of paper is purchased to meet the additional requirements of the sanitary paper products segment of the business. The remaining 405,000 tons of paperboard produced by the company's mills is supplemented with 190,000 tons of purchased paperboard to produce Dixie cups, for packaging, and to make sales of 150,000 tons of paperboard in the marketplace.

James River considers itself to be the leading firm in the specialty paper products field, with revenues of $485,000,000 generated by this activity in 1982. These products include special paper required by industrial users as well as various forms of communication papers. They include such products as abrasive backings, absorbent papers, antitarnish papers, asphalted papers, battery paper and board, car liner, elec-

[1]The case writers have detected subtle class distinctions among firms in the paper industry in respect to backward and forward integration. Generally, the closer the firm is to the trees the greater the majesty of the firm. This is sometimes rationalized by the notion that the value of paper products devolves from the trees and ultimately any profit generated in papermaking will accrue to the owner of the trees. This conflicts with the other notion that profit has historically been captured by distributors.

trosensitive chart paper, cigarette tipping, duplicator paper, electrical board, electrical cable paper, filter paper, flameproof paper, fluorescent papers, foil backing, gasket stock, gumming paper, impregnated papers, laminating stock, lamp shade paper, latex-treated board and paper, leatherette papers, linen paper, map paper, mimeograph paper, opaque paper, parchment, photomount stock, poly-coated papers, postcard, poster paper, pyroxylin-coated paper, register paper, reproduction base paper, stencil board and paper, synthetic fiber papers, tag board, tag stock, text papers, tracing paper, twising paper, tympan paper, vellum, vulcanizing paper, wrapping papers, and writing papers. These items and others are produced by the six groups which make up the specialty sector of the firm.

The wide nature of the product line of the specialty sector insures a diverse band of competitors. The number of these competitors is almost as numerous as the products produced. Some firms such as the Dexter Corporation and W. R. Grace specialize in a few limited products produced by James River. Other firms such as Kimberly-Clark, Union Camp, Georgia Pacific, and Hammermill have broad lines of products which include many that are manufactured by James River. No firm has a line of products in the specialty category that matches those of the James River Corporation. The Domtar Corporation of Canada has the same broad line of products and many items that are identical in their nature; however, Domtar sells 71 percent of its product domestically and cannot be considered a direct U.S. competitor. There are a number of smaller firms that specialize in products produced by segments of the specialty and communications sectors of the industry; firms such as Hollingsworth and Vose, Howard Paper Mills, the Merrimac Paper Company, Monadnock Paper Mills, and the Mosinee Paper Company. The Mosinee Paper Company manufactures an approximate third of the specialty product line of James River, and it recently acquired the Sorg Paper Company to provide it with a position in two-thirds of the products produced by James River. Before the acquisition of Sorg Paper, Mosinee Paper had revenues of $85,000,000 and an operating income of 12.7 percent.

The specialty and communication papers segment of the industry is generally considered to be mature, with growth largely predicated upon growth in GNP. The James River Corporation believes it is the leading firm in this segment, with a 20 percent share of the market. One sector of the specialty paper market is in a contrasting circumstance to the other segments in respect to growth. Even with the direct threat of substitute plastic products, food industry papers and wraps produced by the KVP group of the James River Corporation have made substantial gains in the last few years, and such gains have defied the most recent recession. Some of the large paper companies such as Georgia-Pacific, Scott, and St. Regis produce the wet-waxed, dry-waxed, wax-laminated products and other release papers used by the food industry, but the risks of substitute products has made this a fertile field for somewhat marginal converters as well as smaller paper companies such as Badger Paper Mills, Bell Fibre Products, and the Mosinee Paper Company.

This same phenomenon of extraordinary growth extends into another line of the James River Corporation business. The paperboard packaging group of the Dixie/Northern sector produces folding boxes for the wet and dry food market. James River estimates that it has 10 percent of the U.S. market, and thus generated revenues of $370,000,000 for the company in 1982. Some 80 percent of sales of folding cartons by the company is to the food industry, while the rest of the folding carton industry has only 32 percent of sales in this category of carton. Competitors to James River's leading position in this market include the Container Corporation of America owned by the Mobil Corporation, and the Folding Carton and Label Division of International Paper. A number of other large paper companies have positions in the sanitary folding box business, but none of these come close to matching the commanding position gained by James River through its acquisitions from the American Can Company.

James River also ranks itself as first in the disposable food and beverage service product business, with 1982 revenues of $460,000,000. The firm estimates that the Dixie Products Group holds 14 percent of the market—a position just ahead of the Maryland Cup operation of the merged Fort Howard Paper Company. Other competing firms are the Solo Cup Company, Lily-Tulip (a spin-off of Owens-Illinois) and the Continental Group.

The final segment of involvement by the James River Corporation in the paper industry is in the market-driven sanitary tissue paper business. The company had revenues of $560,000,000 from this business in 1982, and it believes it ranks third or fourth in respect to bathroom tissue, towels, and napkins. It produces toilet tissues with the "Aurora," "Northern," and "Soft Touch" labels. Scott Paper Company is the leading supplier of toilet tissue, with its "Scott," "Lady Scott," and "Waldorf" brands. Kimberly-Clark follows Scott's 23 percent share of the tissue market with a 17.4 percent share, merchandizing the "Kleenex" and "Delsey" brands. Procter & Gamble holds the third position in the market, with a 14.4 percent share for its "Charmin" and "White Cloud" toilet tissues. James River estimates it holds 12 percent of the combined market, but a 10 percent share of the toilet tissue market may be a realistic estimate.

The over 60 percent of the sanitary paper product market held by these four firms is the most concentrated segment of the entire paper industry. Other firms that compete in this market include Crown Zellerbach, Fort Howard Paper, Marcal Paper Mills, Pope & Talbot, Potlatch, and Statler Tissue Company. The tissue and toweling products that make up the largest part of the segment, along with feminine hygiene products, are noted for their noncommodity nature. These products are heavily advertised to reinforce their differentiated characteristics in the mind of the consumer. The industry uses some of the most sophisticated technology in papermaking to improve such tissue product attributes as absorbency, softness, and strength by using relatively new multilayering and air-lay forming techniques. The value of shipments by the industry is expected to grow by 3 percent in 1983; however, most of the real growth will be in disposable diapers and feminine hygiene products. Growth in sales of toweling, facial tissues, and napkins, along with toilet tissues has been relatively flat in the past few years, and these trends are expected to continue.

Mission, Objectives, and Strategy of the James River Corporation

Bob Williams, who serves as the president and chief operating officer of the corporation, has expressed his belief that the firm will continue its past pattern of growth (see Appendixes A through D for financial performance) and attain annual revenues of $3 billion by 1990. Part of this growth will result from an improved economy that will increase demand for products produced by the company. The firm also intends to increase the capacity of the present plant and introduce certain new products that will result in growth in revenues.

Both Mr. Halsey and Mr. Williams expect a compounded real growth in earnings per share of 15 percent, with a return on equity of 20 percent, and a reduction of debt to 45 percent of total capital. These expectations are predicated on improved operations that will result from capital investments of $800,000,000. This amount will be generated by internal cash flow and the investments will serve to both continue and extend the efficient operations of the company. In addition, the firm intends to enhance the profitable operation of the company by continued improvement in the management of operations. This will be similar to the consolidation of operations that followed the Dixie/Northern acquisition and eliminated 200 staff positions.

The record of acquisitions made by the corporation reveals the commitment of the firm to the paper business. Diversification has been concentrated in its direction toward broadened product lines. It has also led to a degree of vertical integration that is common to the various lines of business in which the firm is involved. In most cases the acquisitions made by the firm have involved to some degree their turnaround into profitable components of the firm. Mr. Halsey and Mr. Williams are depicted as having the ability to size up a candidate for acquisition in respect to potential for turnaround and incorporation into the James River portfolio. Acquired firms which extend the product line are encouraged to make a recovery as a distinct divisional entity of the corporation, with corporate resources and expertise provided as necessary. Acquired firms which have components that are similar to those already in the framework of the corporation are integrated as quickly as possible to achieve potential economics in operation. The two top executives of the corporation were described by *Fortune* magazine as involved in the reformation of some acquisitions even before the sale was final, indicating that each acquisition was the result of extensive planning and not simple opportunism.

The common thread running through the various acquisitions accomplished by the two executives is their focus on products with high value-added. They avoided acquiring plants or firms that were committed to production of commodity-type paper products and depended upon high-volume output. When the firm was limited to the business of industrial and communications papers, Halsey and Williams sought out special market niches. Even after the acquisition of the papermaking assets of American Can they remain focused on noncommodity products, although this acquisition has lead the firm away from lower-volume production and protected niches in the marketplace.

James River attempts to provide products of above-average quality in each of its markets and will never market a product of below-average quality. It will also attempt to produce its above-average-quality products at a cost which is below the industry average, but it will not avoid producing a product at a higher than industry average cost if this is what is required to produce a high-quality product that has active demand and a willingness on the part of customers to pay for such superior quality. It is surprising that the larger firms in the paper industry have not attempted to emulate this philosophical foundation to James River's business strategies.

The executives of the firm believe the company inherited considerable consumer marketing strength in the sanitary paper field when it acquired the operations of American Can. They consider themselves second only to Proctor & Gamble in this regard. The firm also gained an away-from-home sales and marketing organization from Dixie-Marathon that has enhanced institutional sales of both food service and sanitary paper products. James River sees itself as on a par with Scott Paper and only second to Proctor & Gamble in respect to the highly valued performance characteristic of tissue softness at below-average cost of production. Because of the quality of the institutional tissue products sold by James River the executives consider themselves equal to Scott Paper and superior to the lowest-cost producer, Fort Howard. Both the latter and Georgia-Pacific cannot compete in the premium tissue market.

James River considers its strength in the specialty and communications papers fields to revolve about its technical ability, as well as its product development and marketing skill. The firm operates a research center in South Hadley, Massachusetts, and the wide range of products is supported by an extensive and decentralized technical organization. The firm has production flexibility resulting from the large number of diverse types of paper machines in its various mills. Unlike the many small competitors to

James River, the firm has countervailing power to that held by suppliers, and the backward integration of the firm is unusual in this segment of the industry.

Perhaps one of the greatest strengths held by James River in its disposable food and beverage service product business is the Dixie brand name. The firm also has a broad product line that permits production and marketing efficiencies and lower costs. In addition, the firm has a nationwide distribution system, and as already mentioned, they have integrated the institutional sale of towel, tissue, and food service products. The firm manufactures its own bleached paperboard used in the manufacture of the food service products.

This level of integration also extends to the paperboard packaging business of the firm. The firm operates a technical center in Neenah, Wisconsin, to serve its various plants and customers that are widely distributed across the country to best serve the food packaging industry. One of the criteria for success in this line of business is the ability to produce an attractive package, and the firm has graphic capabilities to match demanding customer needs.

Organizational Structure

The corporate level structure of the James River Corporation is depicted in Figure 5. Figure 6 reflects the organization structure of the Dixie/Northern sector of the corporation that integrates activities acquired in the American Can and Brown Company acquisitions. Figure 7 on page 883 presents the structure and interrelationships of the other sectors of the firm. Figures 8 through 13 on pages 884–889 provide details of the structure of the specialty sector of the company.

Conclusion

In an article in the December 1983 issue of *Dun's Business Month,* which announced that periodical's selection of the James River Corporation as one of the five best-managed firms during 1983, Mr. Halsey and Mr. Williams observed that the firm's growth would have to slow somewhat. While they both expect that revenues would pass the $3 billion mark before very long, only 20 percent of that growth would be the result of additional acquisitions. They also indicated their understanding that they could not manage a $2 billion company in the same way that they managed a firm with total revenues of $4 million.

The *Dun's* article evaluated the success of the James River Corporation to be the result of the unusual drive and determination of the two founders. It quoted William's observation that business is a game and at James River there is a driving motivation to win the game. While both the founders were observed to be risk-taking entrepreneurs, they have not sought to dominate the day-to-day management of the firm; they believe they have gone to great lengths to allow employees to participate in the success of the company and provide incentives for such accomplishments.

Figure 5

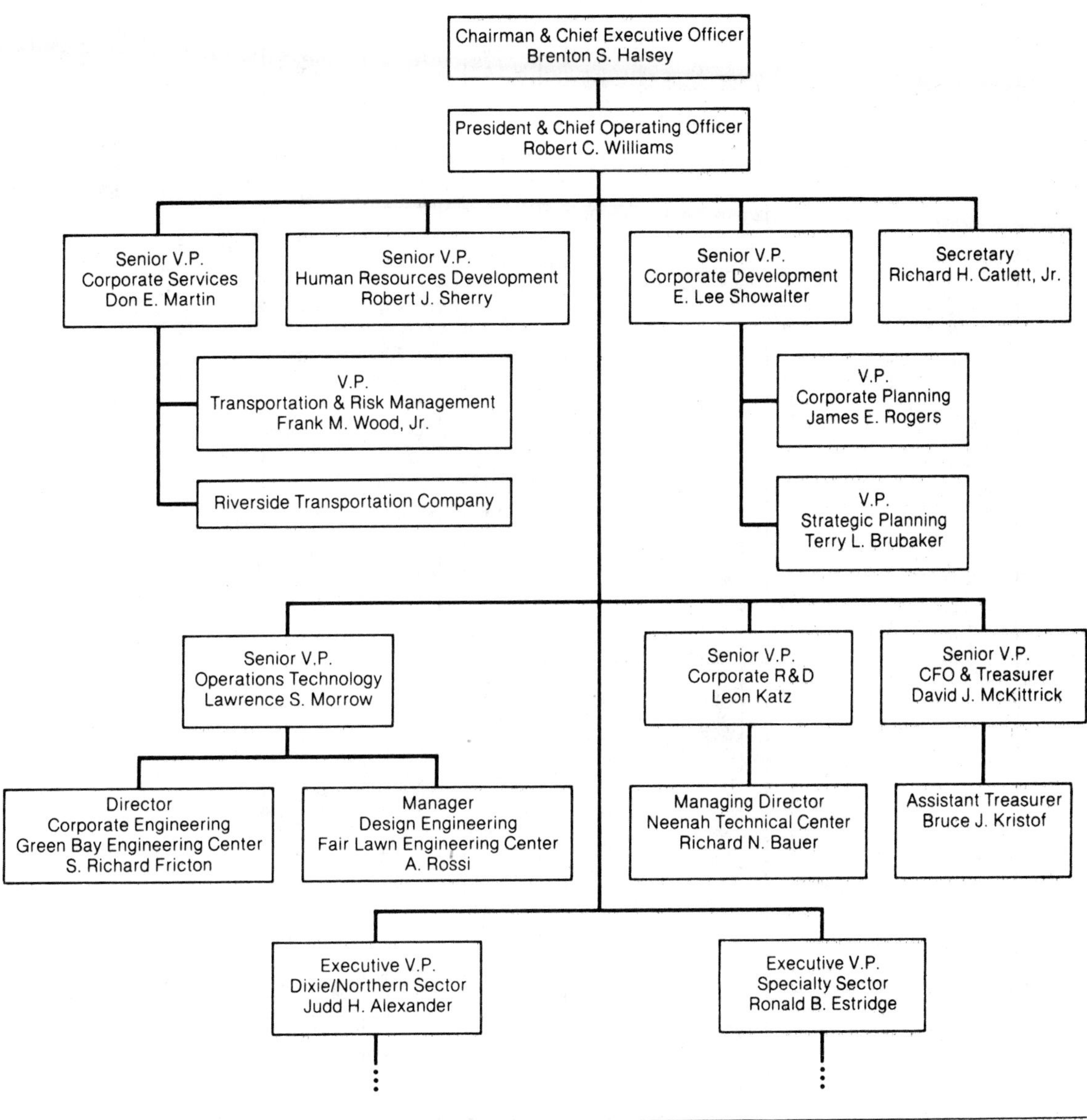
Chairman & Chief Executive Officer
Brenton S. Halsey
President & Chief Operating Officer
Robert C. Williams
Senior V.P.
Corporate Services
Don E. Martin
Senior V.P.
Human Resources Development
Robert J. Sherry
Senior V.P.
Corporate Development
E. Lee Showalter
Secretary
Richard H. Catlett, Jr.
V.P.
Transportation & Risk Management
Frank M. Wood, Jr.
Riverside Transportation Company
V.P.
Corporate Planning
James E. Rogers
V.P.
Strategic Planning
Terry L. Brubaker
Senior V.P.
Operations Technology
Lawrence S. Morrow
Senior V.P.
Corporate R&D
Leon Katz
Senior V.P.
CFO & Treasurer
David J. McKittrick
Director
Corporate Engineering
Green Bay Engineering Center
S. Richard Fricton
Manager
Design Engineering
Fair Lawn Engineering Center
A. Rossi
Managing Director
Neenah Technical Center
Richard N. Bauer
Assistant Treasurer
Bruce J. Kristof
Executive V.P.
Dixie/Northern Sector
Judd H. Alexander
Executive V.P.
Specialty Sector
Ronald B. Estridge

Figure 6

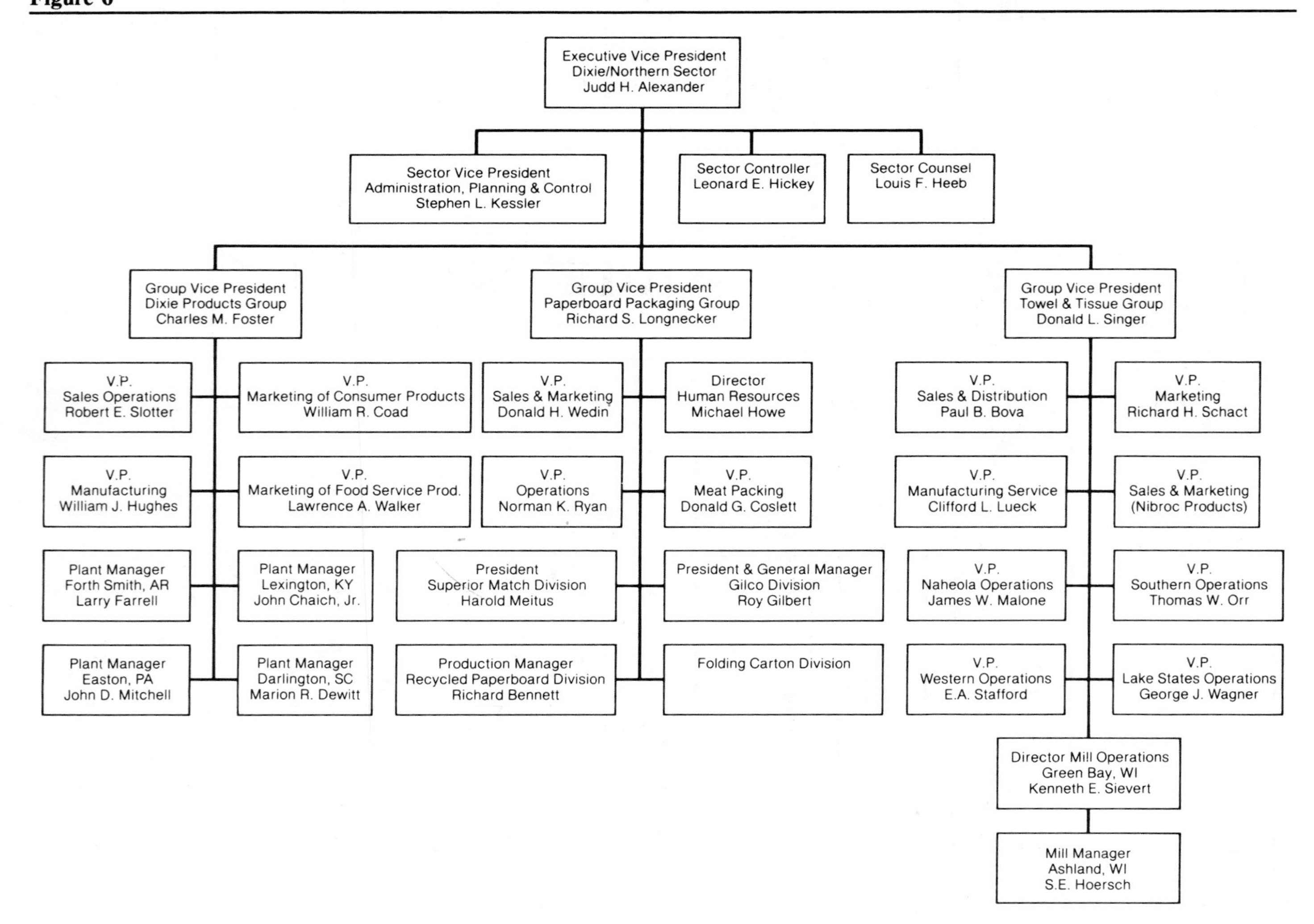
Executive Vice President
Dixie/Northern Sector
Judd H. Alexander
Sector Vice President
Administration, Planning & Control
Stephen L. Kessler
Sector Controller
Leonard E. Hickey
Sector Counsel
Louis F. Heeb
Group Vice President
Dixie Products Group
Charles M. Foster
Group Vice President
Paperboard Packaging Group
Richard S. Longnecker
Group Vice President
Towel & Tissue Group
Donald L. Singer
V.P.
Sales Operations
Robert E. Slotter
V.P.
Marketing of Consumer Products
William R. Coad
V.P.
Manufacturing
William J. Hughes
V.P.
Marketing of Food Service Prod.
Lawrence A. Walker
Plant Manager
Forth Smith, AR
Larry Farrell
Plant Manager
Lexington, KY
John Chaich, Jr.
Plant Manager
Easton, PA
John D. Mitchell
Plant Manager
Darlington, SC
Marion R. Dewitt
V.P.
Sales & Marketing
Donald H. Wedin
Director
Human Resources
Michael Howe
V.P.
Operations
Norman K. Ryan
V.P.
Meat Packing
Donald G. Coslett
President
Superior Match Division
Harold Meitus
President & General Manager
Gilco Division
Roy Gilbert
Production Manager
Recycled Paperboard Division
Richard Bennett
Folding Carton Division
V.P.
Sales & Distribution
Paul B. Bova
V.P.
Marketing
Richard H. Schact
V.P.
Manufacturing Service
Clifford L. Lueck
V.P.
Sales & Marketing
(Nibroc Products)
V.P.
Naheola Operations
James W. Malone
V.P.
Southern Operations
Thomas W. Orr
V.P.
Western Operations
E.A. Stafford
V.P.
Lake States Operations
George J. Wagner
Director Mill Operations
Green Bay, WI
Kenneth E. Sievert
Mill Manager
Ashland, WI
S.E. Hoersch

Figure 7

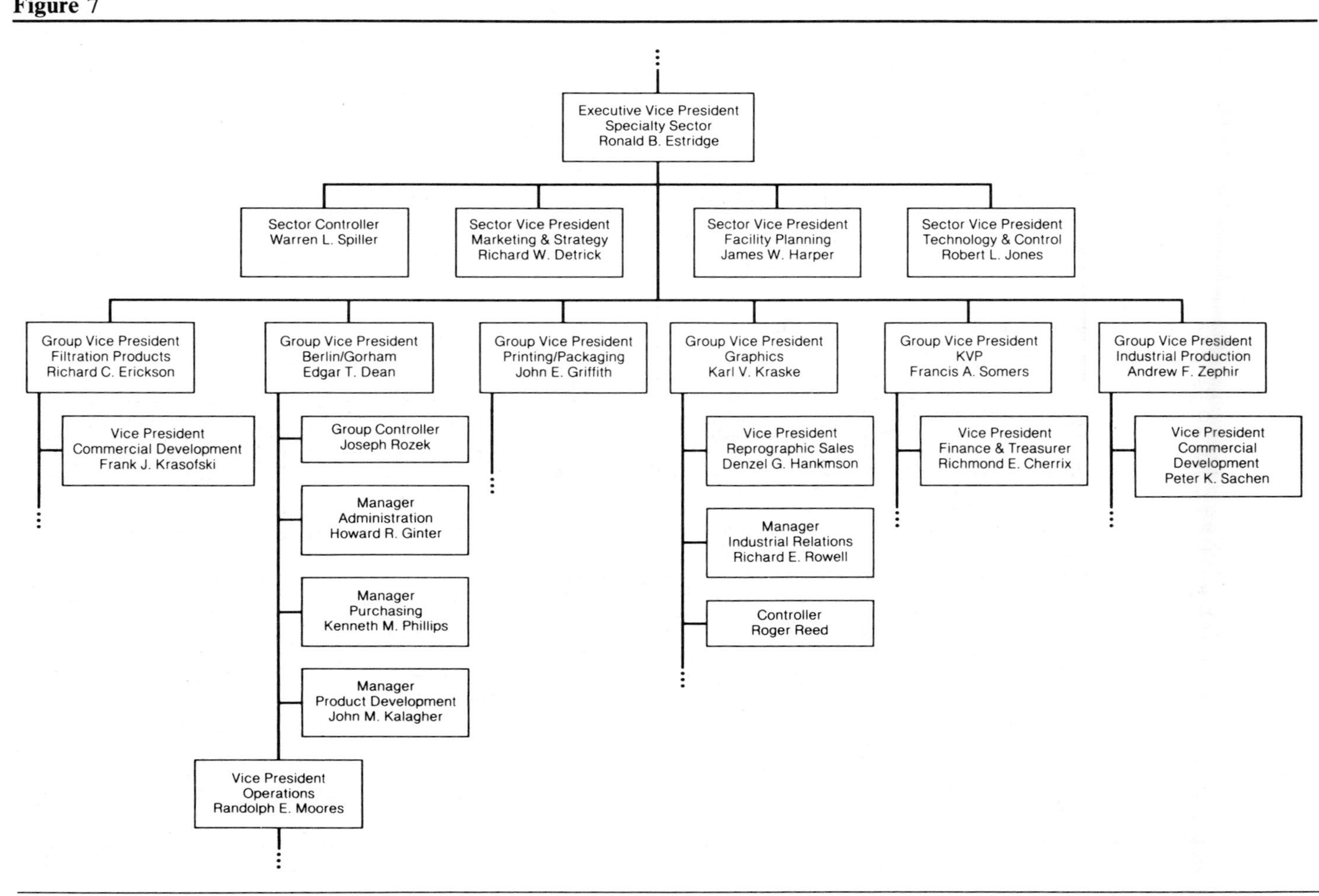
Executive Vice President
Specialty Sector
Ronald B. Estridge
Sector Controller
Warren L. Spiller
Sector Vice President
Marketing & Strategy
Richard W. Detrick
Sector Vice President
Facility Planning
James W. Harper
Sector Vice President
Technology & Control
Robert L. Jones
Group Vice President
Filtration Products
Richard C. Erickson
Vice President
Commercial Development
Frank J. Krasofski
Group Vice President
Berlin/Gorham
Edgar T. Dean
Group Controller
Joseph Rozek
Manager
Administration
Howard R. Ginter
Manager
Purchasing
Kenneth M. Phillips
Manager
Product Development
John M. Kalagher
Vice President
Operations
Randolph E. Moores
Group Vice President
Printing/Packaging
John E. Griffith
Group Vice President
Graphics
Karl V. Kraske
Vice President
Reprographic Sales
Denzel G. Hankmson
Manager
Industrial Relations
Richard E. Rowell
Controller
Roger Reed
Group Vice President
KVP
Francis A. Somers
Vice President
Finance & Treasurer
Richmond E. Cherrix
Group Vice President
Industrial Production
Andrew F. Zephir
Vice President
Commercial
Development
Peter K. Sachen

Figure 8

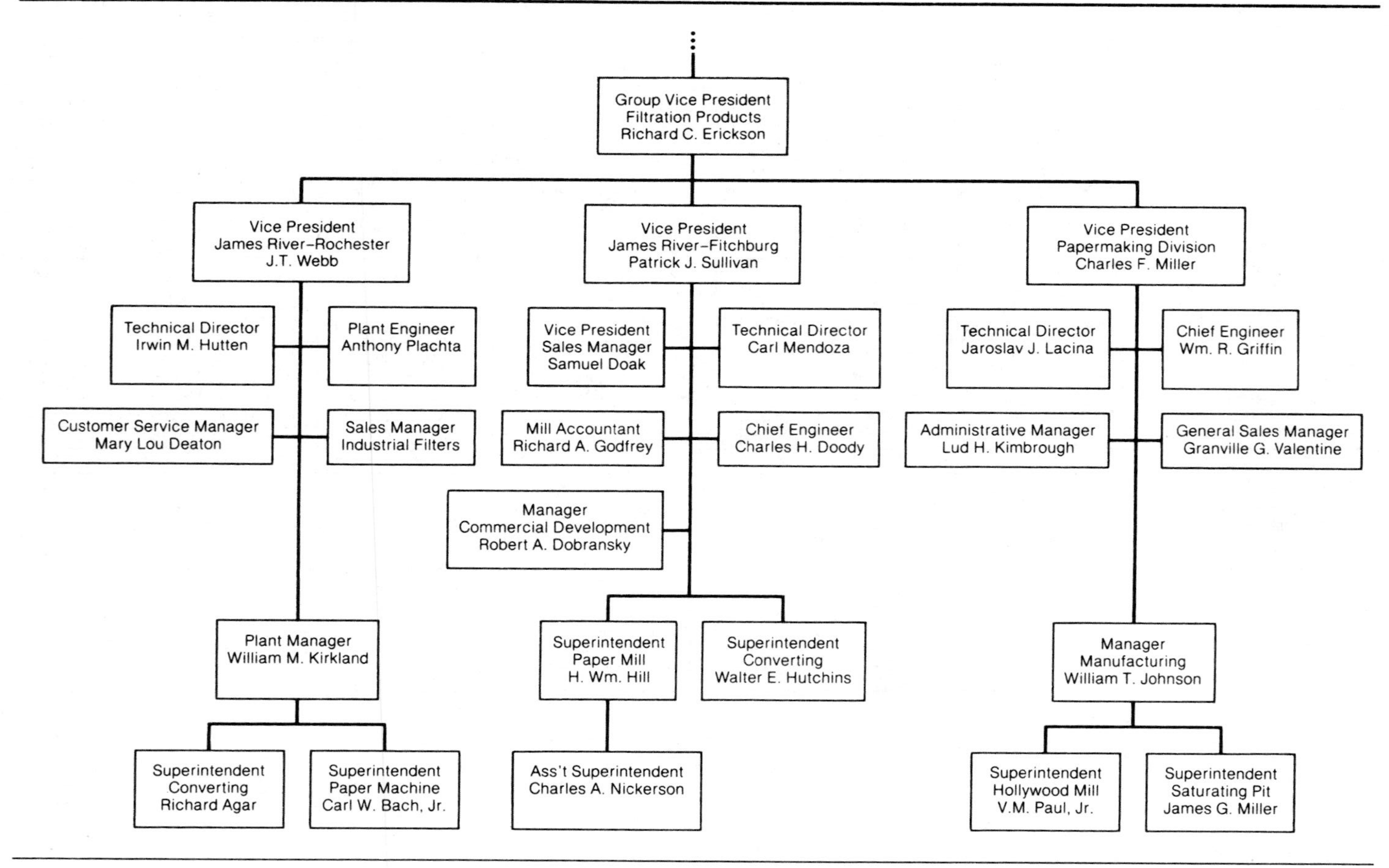
Group Vice President
Filtration Products
Richard C. Erickson
Vice President
James River–Rochester
J.T. Webb
Technical Director
Irwin M. Hutten
Plant Engineer
Anthony Plachta
Customer Service Manager
Mary Lou Deaton
Sales Manager
Industrial Filters
Plant Manager
William M. Kirkland
Superintendent
Converting
Richard Agar
Superintendent
Paper Machine
Carl W. Bach, Jr.
Vice President
James River–Fitchburg
Patrick J. Sullivan
Vice President
Sales Manager
Samuel Doak
Technical Director
Carl Mendoza
Mill Accountant
Richard A. Godfrey
Chief Engineer
Charles H. Doody
Manager
Commercial Development
Robert A. Dobransky
Superintendent
Paper Mill
H. Wm. Hill
Superintendent
Converting
Walter E. Hutchins
Ass't Superintendent
Charles A. Nickerson
Vice President
Papermaking Division
Charles F. Miller
Technical Director
Jaroslav J. Lacina
Chief Engineer
Wm. R. Griffin
Administrative Manager
Lud H. Kimbrough
General Sales Manager
Granville G. Valentine
Manager
Manufacturing
William T. Johnson
Superintendent
Hollywood Mill
V.M. Paul, Jr.
Superintendent
Saturating Pit
James G. Miller

Figure 9

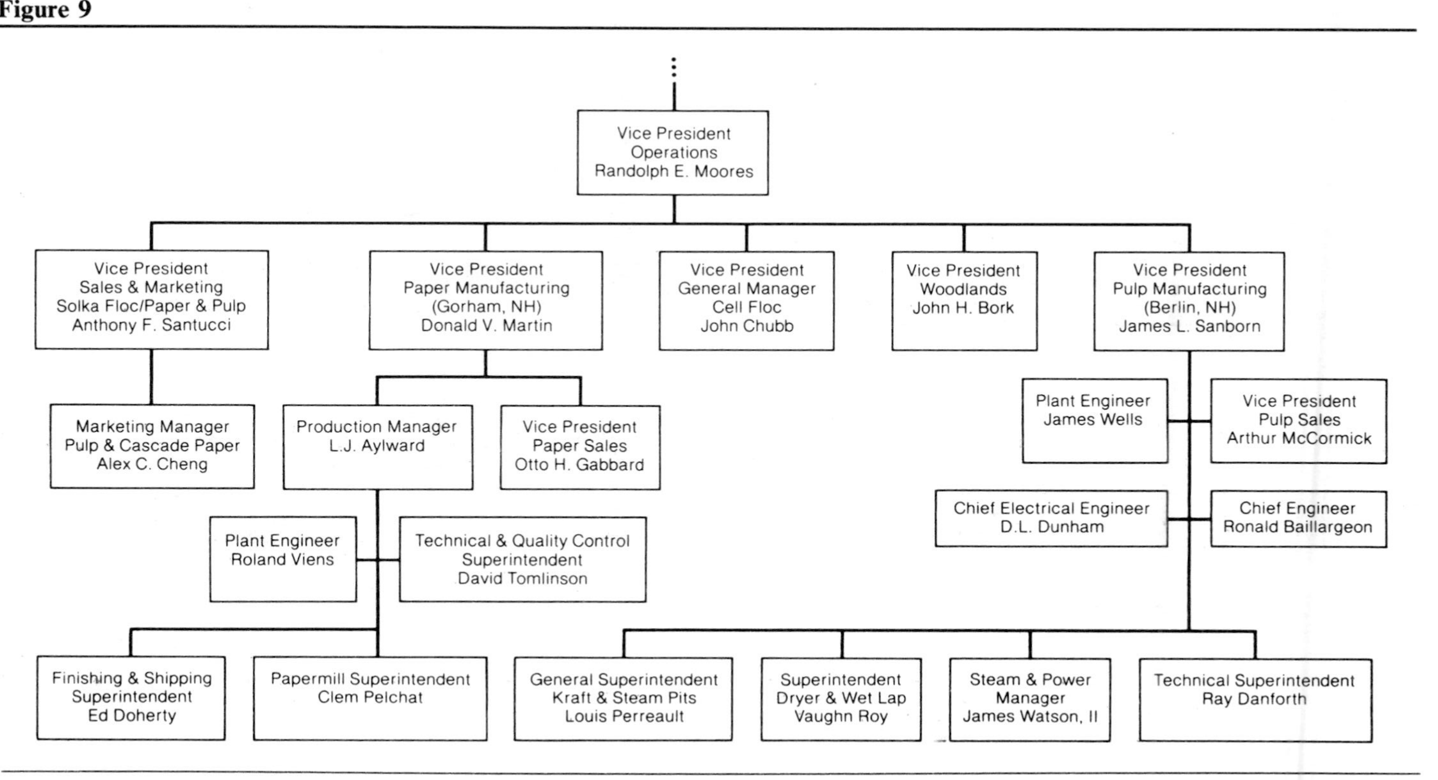

Vice President
Operations
Randolph E. Moores
Vice President
Sales & Marketing
Solka Floc/Paper & Pulp
Anthony F. Santucci
Vice President
Paper Manufacturing
(Gorham, NH)
Donald V. Martin
Vice President
General Manager
Cell Floc
John Chubb
Vice President
Woodlands
John H. Bork
Vice President
Pulp Manufacturing
(Berlin, NH)
James L. Sanborn
Marketing Manager
Pulp & Cascade Paper
Alex C. Cheng
Production Manager
L.J. Aylward
Vice President
Paper Sales
Otto H. Gabbard
Plant Engineer
James Wells
Vice President
Pulp Sales
Arthur McCormick
Chief Electrical Engineer
D.L. Dunham
Chief Engineer
Ronald Baillargeon
Plant Engineer
Roland Viens
Technical & Quality Control
Superintendent
David Tomlinson
Finishing & Shipping
Superintendent
Ed Doherty
Papermill Superintendent
Clem Pelchat
General Superintendent
Kraft & Steam Pits
Louis Perreault
Superintendent
Dryer & Wet Lap
Vaughn Roy
Steam & Power
Manager
James Watson, II
Technical Superintendent
Ray Danforth

Figure 10

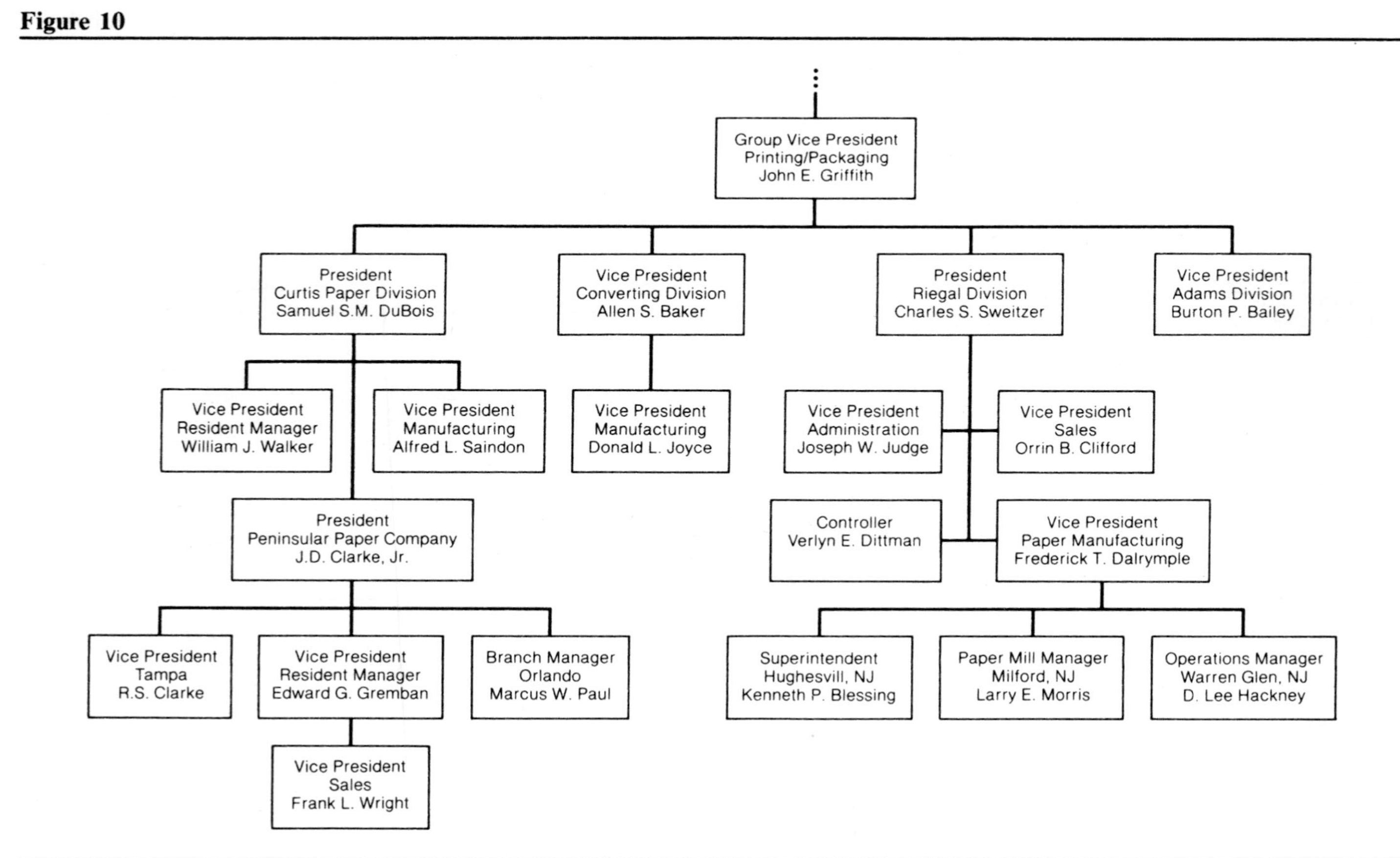
Group Vice President
Printing/Packaging
John E. Griffith
President
Curtis Paper Division
Samuel S.M. DuBois
Vice President
Converting Division
Allen S. Baker
President
Riegal Division
Charles S. Sweitzer
Vice President
Adams Division
Burton P. Bailey
Vice President
Resident Manager
William J. Walker
Vice President
Manufacturing
Alfred L. Saindon
Vice President
Manufacturing
Donald L. Joyce
Vice President
Administration
Joseph W. Judge
Vice President
Sales
Orrin B. Clifford
President
Peninsular Paper Company
J.D. Clarke, Jr.
Controller
Verlyn E. Dittman
Vice President
Paper Manufacturing
Frederick T. Dalrymple
Vice President
Tampa
R.S. Clarke
Vice President
Resident Manager
Edward G. Gremban
Branch Manager
Orlando
Marcus W. Paul
Superintendent
Hughesvill, NJ
Kenneth P. Blessing
Paper Mill Manager
Milford, NJ
Larry E. Morris
Operations Manager
Warren Glen, NJ
D. Lee Hackney
Vice President
Sales
Frank L. Wright

Figure 11

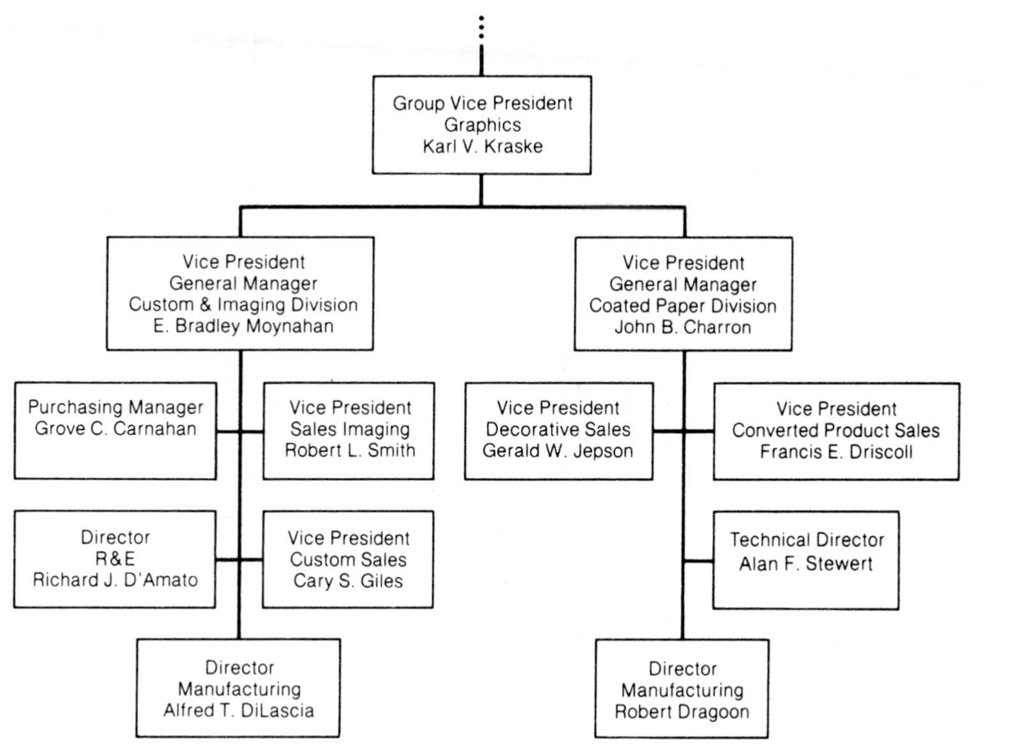
Group Vice President
Graphics
Karl V. Kraske
Vice President
General Manager
Custom & Imaging Division
E. Bradley Moynahan
Vice President
General Manager
Coated Paper Division
John B. Charron
Purchasing Manager
Grove C. Carnahan
Vice President
Sales Imaging
Robert L. Smith
Director
R&E
Richard J. D'Amato
Vice President
Custom Sales
Cary S. Giles
Director
Manufacturing
Alfred T. DiLascia
Vice President
Decorative Sales
Gerald W. Jepson
Vice President
Converted Product Sales
Francis E. Driscoll
Technical Director
Alan F. Stewert
Director
Manufacturing
Robert Dragoon

Figure 12

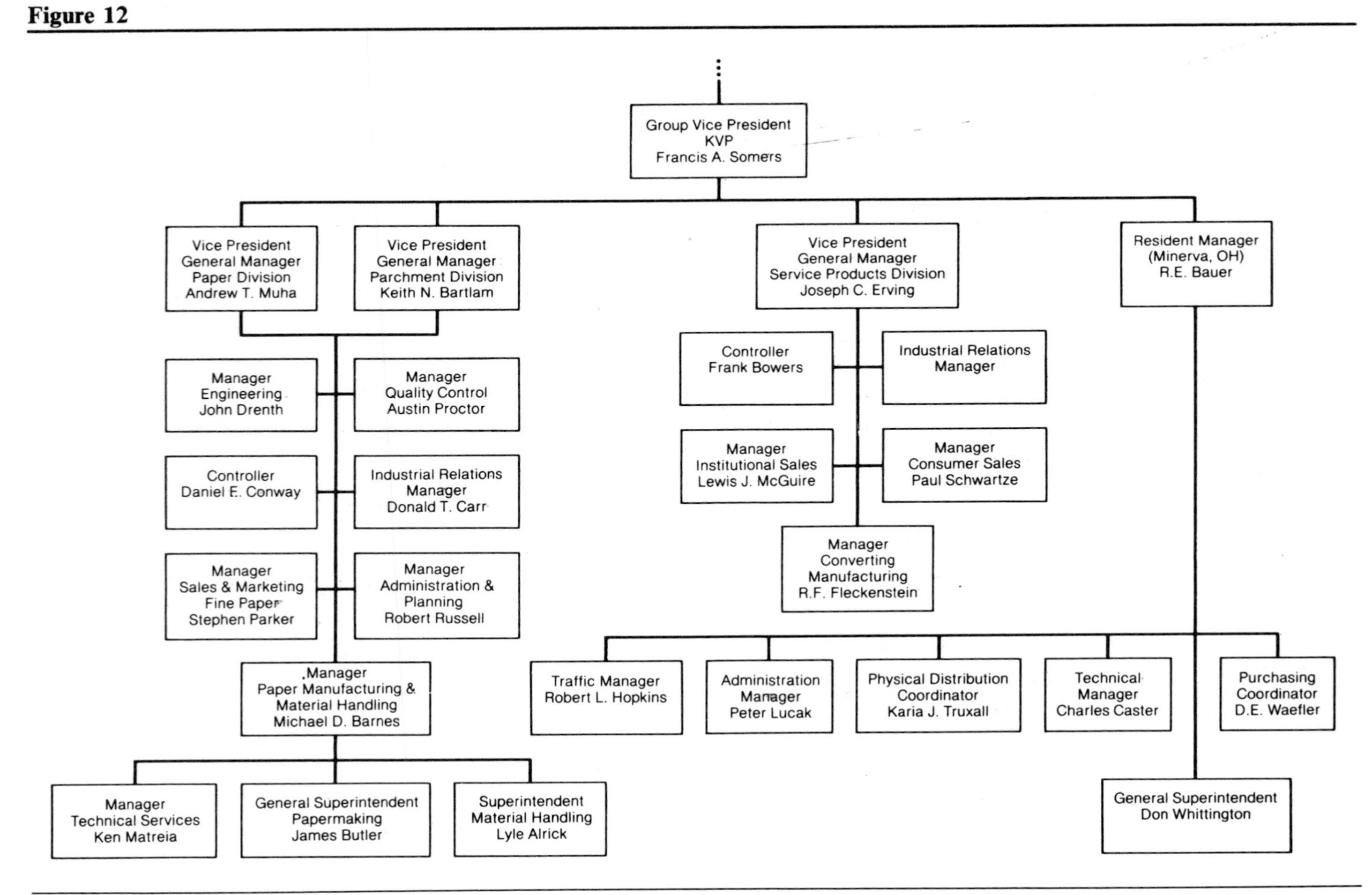
Group Vice President
KVP
Francis A. Somers
Vice President
General Manager
Paper Division
Andrew T. Muha
Vice President
General Manager
Parchment Division
Keith N. Bartlam
Vice President
General Manager
Service Products Division
Joseph C. Erving
Resident Manager
(Minerva, OH)
R.E. Bauer
Manager
Engineering
John Drenth
Manager
Quality Control
Austin Proctor
Controller
Daniel E. Conway
Industrial Relations
Manager
Donald T. Carr
Manager
Sales & Marketing
Fine Paper
Stephen Parker
Manager
Administration &
Planning
Robert Russell
Manager
Paper Manufacturing &
Material Handling
Michael D. Barnes
Manager
Technical Services
Ken Matreia
General Superintendent
Papermaking
James Butler
Superintendent
Material Handling
Lyle Alrick
Controller
Frank Bowers
Industrial Relations
Manager
Manager
Institutional Sales
Lewis J. McGuire
Manager
Consumer Sales
Paul Schwartze
Manager
Converting
Manufacturing
R.F. Fleckenstein
Traffic Manager
Robert L. Hopkins
Administration
Manager
Peter Lucak
Physical Distribution
Coordinator
Karia J. Truxall
Technical
Manager
Charles Caster
Purchasing
Coordinator
D.E. Waefler
General Superintendent
Don Whittington

Figure 13

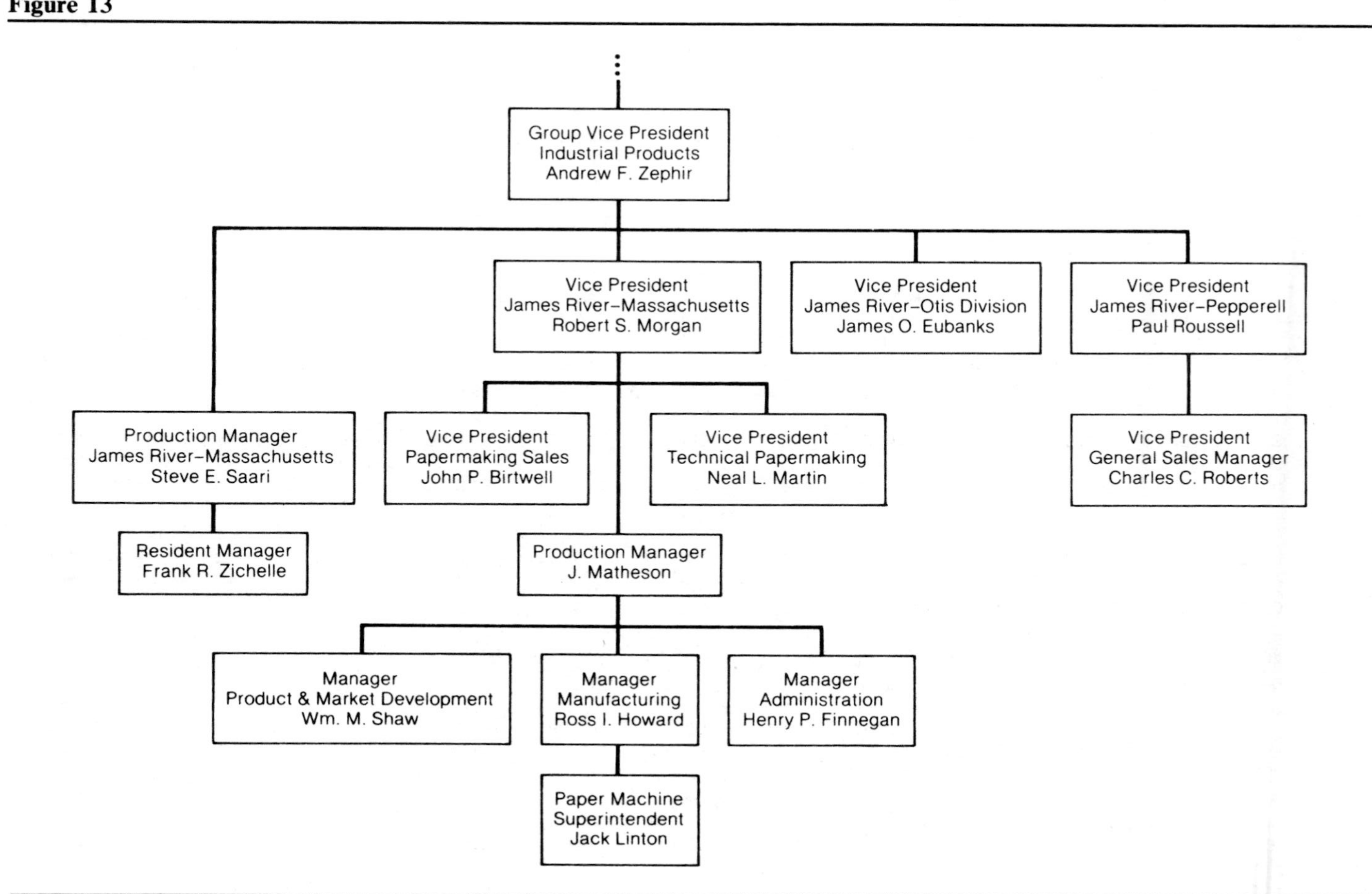
Group Vice President
Industrial Products
Andrew F. Zephir
Vice President
James River–Massachusetts
Robert S. Morgan
Vice President
James River–Otis Division
James O. Eubanks
Vice President
James River–Pepperell
Paul Roussell
Production Manager
James River–Massachusetts
Steve E. Saari
Vice President
Papermaking Sales
John P. Birtwell
Vice President
Technical Papermaking
Neal L. Martin
Vice President
General Sales Manager
Charles C. Roberts
Resident Manager
Frank R. Zichelle
Production Manager
J. Matheson
Manager
Product & Market Development
Wm. M. Shaw
Manager
Manufacturing
Ross I. Howard
Manager
Administration
Henry P. Finnegan
Paper Machine
Superintendent
Jack Linton

Appendix A James River Corporation of Virginia Consolidated Balance Sheet (in thousands of dollars)

	1982	1981	1980	1979	1978	1977	1976	1975	1974	1973	1972
Assets											
Cash & equivalents	25,924	5,703	6,409	18,297	8,286	8,654	3,238	2,682	3,452	2,838	1,156
Accounts receivable	84,222	80,525	39,466	38,706	23,522	12,194	9,400	2,714	3,634	2,648	1,324
Inventories	103,163	107,488	46,010	43,321	27,540	14,594	11,176	4,563	3,085	2,529	1,707
Income tax refund	5,457	—	—	—	—	—	153	291	—	—	—
Prepayments	2,465	3,239	2,732	2,527	1,828	1,327	785	279	172	29	40
Total current assets	221,231	196,955	94,617	102,851	61,178	36,770	24,752	10,482	10,323	8,044	4,227
Constr. funds held by trustee	—	—	—	—	—	—	—	—	2,371	—	—
Net property, etc.	253,352	237,846	71,379	64,778	41,608	25,683	22,468	11,162	5,920	4,750	1,663
Deferred charges & other assets	3,532	3,987	2,594	2,108	1,226	797	346	231	122	35	74
Total assets	478,116	438,788	168,590	169,738	104,013	63,251	47,566	21,875	18,736	12,829	5,964
Liabilities											
Notes payable	—	3,284	1,988	1,585	774	—	4,216	850	200	200	—
Current debt mat	15,558	—	—	—	—	463	1,615	590	811	366	267
Accounts payable & accrs. lia.	86,484	84,053	31,290	34,440	21,791	10,118	7,484	2,312	3,140	2,173	1,116
Income taxes	—	1,312	—	8,024	1,915	734	—	—	655	391	110
Total current liabilities	102,042	88,649	33,277	44,048	24,479	11,316	13,315	3,552	4,806	3,130	1,493
Long-term debt	147,363	137,740	49,939	51,137	36,722	22,247	14,666	8,528	6,826	4,321	2,435
Minority interest	—	—	511	422	304	265	239	184	130	67	82
Deferred income tax	19,944	12,486	7,265	5,146	3,867	2,777	1,555	636	329	138	97
Provision for pension costs	38,790	43,782	730	638	538	404	406	372	67	42	43
Common stock p. $0.10	844	841	430	426	141	140	103	99	95	95	32
Redeem. preferred stock											
A $8 CV. p.f.d. ($10)	—	—	—	—	1,500	150	150	—	—	—	—
B pfd. ($10)	—	—	—	5,000	5,000	500	500	—	—	—	—
C pfd. ($10)	1,724	1,724	1,724	1,970	2,457	—	—	—	—	—	—
D $8.75 pfd. ($10)	4,000	4,000	4,000	4,000	4,000	—	—	—	—	—	—
E $8.75 pfd. ($10)	4,300	4,300	4,300	4,300	—	—	—	—	—	—	—
F $6 CV. pfd. ($10)	—	—	5,000	5,000	—	—	—	—	—	—	—
Sr. G. CV. pfd. stk. ($10)	45,787	45,790	—	—	—	—	—	—	—	—	—
Additional paid-in capital	46,988	46,832	20,544	20,310	9,631	15,414	9,685	3,723	3,324	3,316	892
Retained earnings	66,333	52,643	40,869	27,341	15,372	10,034	6,947	4,781	3,159	1,720	890
Total liabilities	478,116	438,788	168,590	169,738	104,013	63,251	47,566	21,875	18,736	12,829	5,964

Appendix B James River Corporation of Virginia Consolidated Statement of Income (in thousands of dollars except per share data)

	1982	1981	1980	1979	1978	1977	1976	1975	1974	1973	1972
Net sales	772,682	561,318	373,946	297,940	181,922	98,607	70,576	41,848	34,279	24,454	14,884
Other income	2,791	2,118	2,701	1,278	452	601	265	314	256	87	53
Total revenues	775,473	563,436	376,647	299,218	182,374	99,208	70,841	42,162	34,535	24,541	14,937
Cost of goods sold	658,199	477,787	312,961	245,198	155,732	84,524	60,666	35,717	28,906	20,947	12,785
Selling & adm. expenses	66,418	43,784	28,116	21,247	11,742	5,874	4,015	2,711	2,172	1,614	1,121
Interest	16,574	9,842	4,680	4,131	2,831	2,125	1,431	543	401	366	180
	741,191	531,413	357,757	270,576	170,305	92,523	66,112	38,971	31,479	22,927	14,086
Income before income tax exp. & extraordinary charge	34,282	32,023	30,890	28,642	12,069	6,685	4,729	3,191	3,056	1,614	851
Income tax expense	11,929	10,667	14,231	13,933	5,850	3,208	2,341	1,431	1,521	760	393
Income before extraordinary charge	22,353	21,356	16,659	14,709	6,219	3,477	2,388	1,760	1,535	854	458
Extraordinary charge		3,475									
Net income	22,353	17,882	16,659	14,709	6,219	3,477	2,388	1,760	1,535	854	458
Income before extraordinary charge applicable to common shares	17,061	18,006	15,415	12,903	5,718	3,350	2,318	1,760	1,535	854	458
Income before extraordinary charge per common share & com. share equivalent											
Primary	$1.95	$2.29	$2.16	$2.17	$1.15	$ .73	$ .65	$ .51	$ .46	$ .31	$ .20
Fully diluted	$1.92	$2.21	$2.16	$2.09	$1.06	$ .67	$ .61	$ .51	$ .45	$ .31	$ .20
Cash dividends per common share	$ .40	$ .32	$ .30	$ .15	$ .08	$ .05	$ .05	$ .04	$ .03		
Number of common shares & common share equivalents											
Primary	8,751,138	7,971,977	7,263,468	6,004,092	4,953,450	4,613,180	3,582,233	3,433,571	3,352,547	2,730,551	2,307,744
Fully diluted	11,248,599	9,287,168	7,267,676	6,231,210	5,486,606	5,038,538	3,952,673	3,440,469	3,364,028	2,738,337	2,309,057

Appendix C James River Corporation of Virginia Selected Financial Data

	1982	1981	1980	1979	1978	1977	1976	1975	1974	1973	1972
Return on net sales	2.9%	3.8%	4.5%	4.9%	3.4%	3.5%	3.4%	4.2%	4.5%	3.5%	3.1%
Return on average common equity	21.7%	22.6%	28.0%	35.0%	25.5%	21.9%	23.8%	23.2%	26.2%	24.6%	35.2%
Return on average investment	4.9%	5.9%	9.8%	10.7%	7.4%	6.3%	6.9%	8.7%	9.7%	9.5%	10.1%
Current assets to current liabilities	2.17	2.22	2.84	2.34	2.50	3.25	1.86	2.95	2.15	2.57	2.83
Capital expenditures, excluding acquisitions (in thousands)	$42,103	$21,280	$11,113	$9,377	$4,714	$2,627	$1,350	$3,697	$1,581	$1,501	$732
Equity per common share outstanding	$ 13.03	$ 11.43	$ 9.58	$ 7.53	$ 5.27	$ 4.17	$ 3.15	$ 2.57	$ 2.05	$ 1.60	$ 1.12
Common shares outstanding	8,443,408	8,411,760	6,455,276	6,382,619	4,774,691	4,736,357	3,461,370	3,344,426	3,216,707	3,203,291	1,620,000
Price range of common stock	13⅜–23¼	10¾–20½	9⅝–17⅝	6⅝–14⅞	3⅞–6¾	3⅞–7	3⅛–6⅜	2⅜–4	2½–3⅝	3⅛–3⅝	N.A.
Average weekly trading volume, shares	33,850	55,287	59,031	50,157	29,019	28,790	8,826	6,075	8,438	25,988	N.A.

Appendix D James River Corporation of Virginia Consolidated Statement of Changes in Financial Position (in thousands of dollars)

	1982	1981	1980	1979	1978	1977	1976	1975	1974	1973	1972
Sources of working capital											
Operations:											
Income before extraordinary change	22,353	21,356	16,659	14,709	6,219	3,477	2,388	1,760	1,535	889	458
Charges (credits) to income not affecting working capital:											
Depreciation & cost of timber harvested	14,305	9,286	4,289	3,300	1,911	1,343	997	530	409	337	—
Deferred income taxes	7,458	5,221	2,119	1,279	1,090	1,222	937	240	170	41	67
Amortization & other	221	156	175	243	182	118	48	140	164	63	265
Working capital from operations excluding extraordinary change	44,337	36,019	23,242	19,530	9,402	6,160	4,370	2,671	2,279	1,329	790
Extraordinary charge	—	(3,475)	—	—	—	—	—	—	—	(35)	—
Issued or assumed in connection with acquisition:											
Common stock	—	21,437	—	8,812	—	—	—	394	—	—	—
Preferred stock	—	45,790	—	9,265	6,394	—	5,000	—	—	—	—
Long-term debt	—	90,491	—	16,000	14,500	1,500	—	1,136	—	2,042	1,050
Other long-term liabilities	—	43,857	—	—	—	—	—	300	3,050	1,005	—
Working capital from acquisition	—	47,582	—	17,446	10,601	4,049	2,880	772	—	20	—
Increase in long-term debt	25,000	10,800	800	—	—	15,040	267	—	—	—	—
Issuance of common stock on conversion of preferred stock and exercise of options	159	5,262	238	2,187	132	5,767	141	9	9	—	—
Other, net	7,534	3,479	(257)	—	—	—	1,500	—	300	2,522	861
Total sources	77,030	301,243	24,024	73,239	41,029	32,516	14,158	5,281	5,637	6,884	2,701

(continued)

Appendix D *(continued)*

	1982	1981	1980	1979	1978	1977	1976	1975	1974	1973	1972
Applications of working capital											
Additions to property, plant, & equipment	42,103	21,280	11,113	9,377	4,714	2,627	1,350	3,697	1,581	3,424	836
Reduction of long-term debt	15,376	14,915	1,998	1,585	693	9,024	1,436	794	925	1,260	267
Assets acquired from acquisition	—	206,975	—	35,022	23,063	5,987	6,519	1,576	—	—	—
Common stock cash dividends	3,372	2,344	1,887	831	380	263	152	—	—	—	—
Preferred stock cash dividends	5,291	3,763	1,244	1,908	501	127	70	—	—	—	—
Conversion of preferred stock	3	5,000	—	1,500	—	—	—	—	—	—	—
Redemption of preferred stock	—	—	5,246	488	—	—	—	—	—	—	—
Other, net	—	—	—	422	433	470	124	(2,198)	2,527	20	—
Increase in working capital	10,884	46,965	2,537	22,105	11,244	14,017	4,507	1,412	604	2,180	1,597
Total applications	77,030	301,243	24,024	73,239	41,029	32,516	14,158	5,281	5,637	6,884	2,701
Analysis of changes in working capital											
Increase (decrease) in current assets:											
Cash & short-term securities	20,221	(707)	(11,888)	10,011	(368)	5,417	576	(790)	614	1,682	701
Accounts receivable	3,697	41,058	761	15,183	11,328	2,794	6,686	(920)	986	1,324	652
Inventories	(4,325)	61,479	2,688	15,780	12,947	3,418	6,640	1,471	536	822	846
Recoverable income taxes	5,457	—	—	—	—	—	(138)	291	—	—	—
Prepaid expenses	(774)	507	205	698	501	543	506	107	143	(11)	32
Total	24,277	102,337	(8,234)	41,674	24,407	12,172	14,270	158	2,280	3,817	2,232
Increase (decrease) in current liabilities											
Accounts payable & accrued liabilities	2,431	52,763	(3,150)	12,649	11,672	2,634	5,172	(828)	967	1,057	529
Long-term debt, current portion; & collateralized notes payable	12,273	1,297	403	811	311	(5,367)	4,591	229	444	299	155
Income taxes	(1,312)	1,312	(8,024)	6,109	1,180	888	—	(655)	265	280	(50)
Total	13,393	55,372	(10,771)	19,569	13,163	(1,845)	9,763	(1,254)	1,676	1,637	635
Increase in working capital	10,884	46,965	2,537	22,105	11,244	14,017	4,507	1,412	604	2,180	1,597

Case 23 Update*

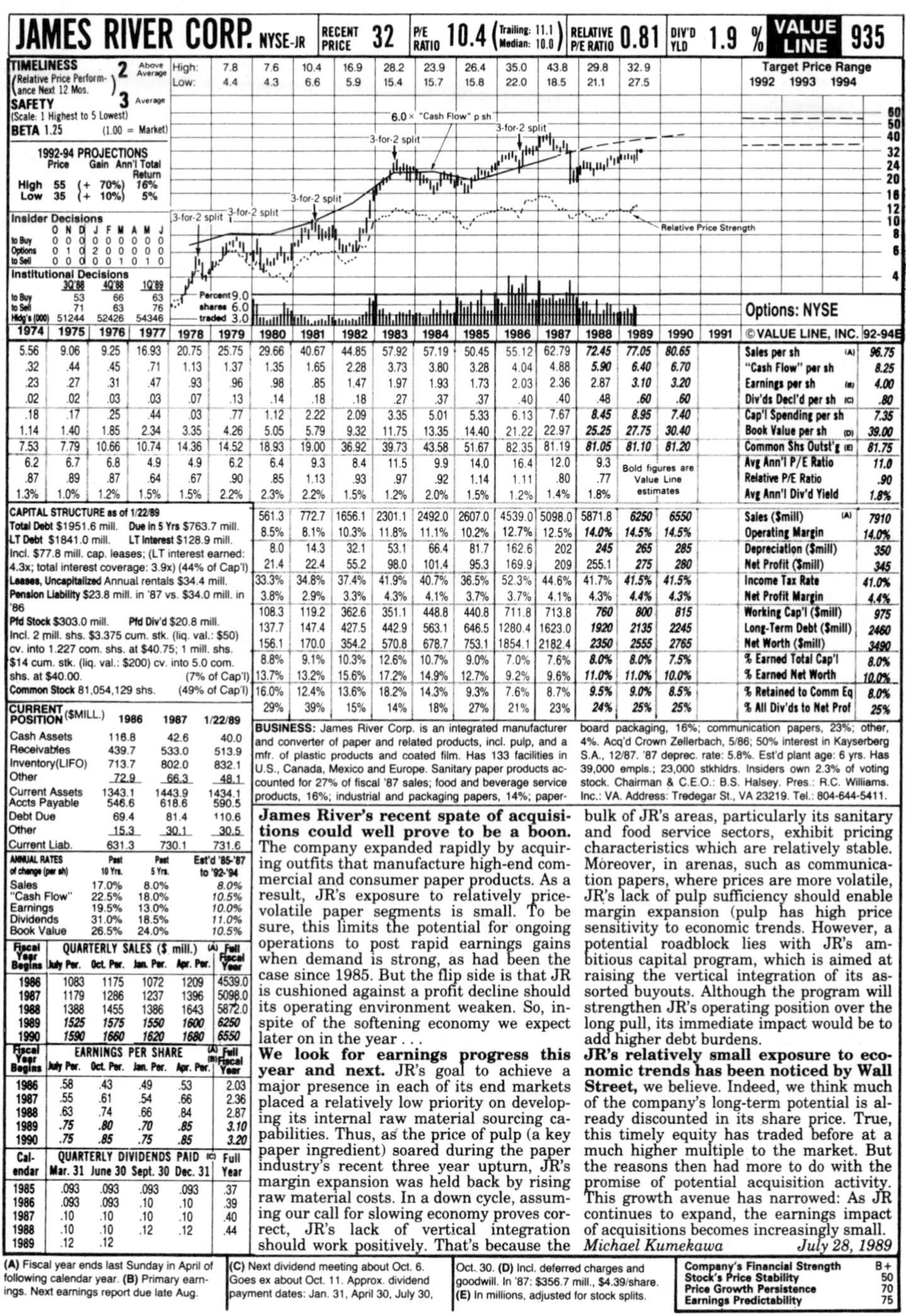

JAMES RIVER CORP. NYSE-JR

RECENT PRICE 32 | P/E RATIO 10.4 (Trailing: 11.1 Median: 10.0) | RELATIVE P/E RATIO 0.81 | DIV'D YLD 1.9 % | VALUE LINE 935

TIMELINESS 2 Above Average (Relative Price Performance Next 12 Mos.)
SAFETY 3 Average (Scale: 1 Highest to 5 Lowest)
BETA 1.25 (1.00 = Market)

	1978	1979	1980	1981	1982	1983	1984	1985	1986	1987	1988	1989
High:	7.8	7.6	10.4	16.9	28.2	23.9	26.4	35.0	43.8	29.8	32.9	
Low:	4.4	4.3	6.6	5.9	15.4	15.7	15.8	22.0	18.5	21.1	27.5	

Target Price Range 1992 1993 1994

1992-94 PROJECTIONS

	Price	Gain	Ann'l Total Return
High	55	(+ 70%)	16%
Low	35	(+ 10%)	5%

Insider Decisions

	O	N	D	J	F	M	A	M	J
to Buy	0	0	0	0	0	0	0	0	0
Options	0	1	0	2	0	0	0	0	0
to Sell	0	0	0	0	0	1	0	1	0

Institutional Decisions

	3Q'88	4Q'88	1Q'89
to Buy	53	66	63
to Sell	71	63	76
Hldg's (000)	51244	52426	54346

1974	1975	1976	1977	1978	1979	1980	1981	1982	1983	1984	1985	1986	1987	1988	1989	1990	1991	© VALUE LINE, INC.	92-94E
5.56	9.06	9.25	16.93	20.75	25.75	29.66	40.67	44.85	57.92	57.19	50.45	55.12	62.79	72.45	77.05	80.65		Sales per sh (A)	96.75
.32	.44	.45	.71	1.13	1.37	1.35	1.65	2.28	3.73	3.80	3.28	4.04	4.88	5.90	6.40	6.70		"Cash Flow" per sh	8.25
.23	.27	.31	.47	.93	.96	.98	.85	1.47	1.97	1.93	1.73	2.03	2.36	2.87	3.10	3.20		Earnings per sh (B)	4.00
.02	.02	.03	.03	.07	.13	.14	.18	.18	.27	.37	.37	.40	.40	.48	.60	.60		Div'ds Decl'd per sh (C)	.80
.18	.17	.25	.44	.03	.77	1.12	2.22	2.09	3.35	5.01	5.33	6.13	7.67	8.45	8.95	7.40		Cap'l Spending per sh	7.35
1.14	1.40	1.85	2.34	3.35	4.26	5.05	5.79	9.32	11.75	13.35	14.40	21.22	22.97	25.25	27.75	30.40		Book Value per sh (D)	39.00
7.53	7.79	10.66	10.74	14.36	14.52	18.93	19.00	36.92	39.73	43.58	51.67	82.35	81.19	81.05	81.10	81.20		Common Shs Outst'g (E)	81.75
6.2	6.7	6.8	4.9	4.9	6.2	6.4	9.3	8.4	11.5	9.9	14.0	16.4	12.0	9.3	Bold figures are Value Line estimates			Avg Ann'l P/E Ratio	11.0
.87	.89	.87	.64	.67	.90	.85	1.13	.93	.97	.92	1.14	1.11	.80	.77				Relative P/E Ratio	.90
1.3%	1.0%	1.2%	1.5%	1.5%	2.2%	2.3%	2.2%	1.5%	1.2%	2.0%	1.5%	1.2%	1.4%	1.8%				Avg Ann'l Div'd Yield	1.8%
						561.3	772.7	1656.1	2301.1	2492.0	2607.0	4539.0	5098.0	5871.8	6250	6550		Sales ($mill) (A)	7910
						8.5%	8.1%	10.3%	11.8%	11.1%	10.2%	12.7%	12.5%	14.0%	14.5%	14.5%		Operating Margin	14.0%
						8.0	14.3	32.1	53.1	66.4	81.7	162.6	202	245	265	285		Depreciation ($mill)	350
						21.4	22.4	55.2	98.0	101.4	95.3	169.9	209	255.1	275	280		Net Profit ($mill)	345
						33.3%	34.8%	37.4%	41.9%	40.7%	36.5%	52.3%	44.6%	41.7%	41.5%	41.5%		Income Tax Rate	41.0%
						3.8%	2.9%	3.3%	4.3%	4.1%	3.7%	3.7%	4.1%	4.3%	4.4%	4.3%		Net Profit Margin	4.4%
						108.3	119.2	362.6	351.1	448.8	440.8	711.8	713.8	760	800	815		Working Cap'l ($mill)	975
						137.7	147.4	427.5	442.9	563.1	646.5	1280.4	1623.0	1920	2135	2245		Long-Term Debt ($mill)	2460
						156.1	170.0	354.2	570.8	678.7	753.1	1854.1	2182.4	2350	2555	2765		Net Worth ($mill)	3490
						8.8%	9.1%	10.3%	12.6%	10.7%	9.0%	7.0%	7.6%	8.0%	8.0%	7.5%		% Earned Total Cap'l	8.0%
						13.7%	13.2%	15.6%	17.2%	14.9%	12.7%	9.2%	9.6%	11.0%	11.0%	10.0%		% Earned Net Worth	10.0%
						16.0%	12.4%	13.6%	18.2%	14.3%	9.3%	7.6%	8.7%	9.5%	9.0%	8.5%		% Retained to Comm Eq	8.0%
						29%	39%	15%	14%	18%	27%	21%	23%	24%	25%	25%		% All Div'ds to Net Prof	25%

CAPITAL STRUCTURE as of 1/22/89
Total Debt $1951.6 mill. **Due in 5 Yrs** $763.7 mill.
LT Debt $1841.0 mill. **LT Interest** $128.9 mill.
Incl. $77.8 mill. cap. leases; (LT interest earned: 4.3x; total interest coverage: 3.9x) (44% of Cap'l)
Leases, Uncapitalized Annual rentals $34.4 mill.
Pension Liability $23.8 mill. in '87 vs. $34.0 mill. in '86
Pfd Stock $303.0 mill. **Pfd Div'd** $20.8 mill.
Incl. 2 mill. shs. $3.375 cum. stk. (liq. val.: $50) cv. into 1.227 com. shs. at $40.75; 1 mill. shs. $14 cum. stk. (liq. val.: $200) cv. into 5.0 com. shs. at $40.00. (7% of Cap'l)
Common Stock 81,054,129 shs. (49% of Cap'l)

CURRENT POSITION ($MILL.)	1986	1987	1/22/89
Cash Assets	116.8	42.6	40.0
Receivables	439.7	533.0	513.9
Inventory(LIFO)	713.7	802.0	832.1
Other	72.9	66.3	48.1
Current Assets	1343.1	1443.9	1434.1
Accts Payable	546.6	618.6	590.5
Debt Due	69.4	81.4	110.6
Other	15.3	30.1	30.5
Current Liab.	631.3	730.1	731.6

ANNUAL RATES of change (per sh)	Past 10 Yrs.	Past 5 Yrs.	Est'd '85-'87 to '92-'94
Sales	17.0%	8.0%	8.0%
"Cash Flow"	22.5%	18.0%	10.5%
Earnings	19.5%	13.0%	10.0%
Dividends	31.0%	18.5%	11.0%
Book Value	26.5%	24.0%	10.5%

Fiscal Year Begins	QUARTERLY SALES ($ mill.) (A) July Per.	Oct. Per.	Jan. Per.	Apr. Per.	Full Fiscal Year
1986	1083	1175	1072	1209	4539.0
1987	1179	1286	1237	1396	5098.0
1988	1388	1455	1386	1643	5872.0
1989	1525	1575	1550	1600	6250
1990	1590	1660	1620	1680	6550

Fiscal Year Begins	EARNINGS PER SHARE (A)(B) July Per.	Oct. Per.	Jan. Per.	Apr. Per.	Full Fiscal Year
1986	.58	.43	.49	.53	2.03
1987	.55	.61	.54	.66	2.36
1988	.63	.74	.66	.84	2.87
1989	.75	.80	.70	.85	3.10
1990	.75	.85	.75	.85	3.20

Cal-endar	QUARTERLY DIVIDENDS PAID (C) Mar. 31	June 30	Sept. 30	Dec. 31	Full Year
1985	.093	.093	.093	.093	.37
1986	.093	.093	.10	.10	.39
1987	.10	.10	.10	.10	.40
1988	.10	.10	.12	.12	.44
1989	.12	.12			

BUSINESS: James River Corp. is an integrated manufacturer and converter of paper and related products, incl. pulp, and a mfr. of plastic products and coated film. Has 133 facilities in U.S., Canada, Mexico and Europe. Sanitary paper products accounted for 27% of fiscal '87 sales; food and beverage service products, 16%; industrial and packaging papers, 14%; paperboard packaging, 16%; communication papers, 23%; other, 4%. Acq'd Crown Zellerbach, 5/86; 50% interest in Kayserberg S.A., 12/87. '87 deprec. rate: 5.8%. Est'd plant age: 6 yrs. Has 39,000 empls.; 23,000 stkhldrs. Insiders own 2.3% of voting stock. Chairman & C.E.O.: B.S. Halsey. Pres.: R.C. Williams. Inc.: VA. Address: Tredegar St., VA 23219. Tel.: 804-644-5411.

James River's recent spate of acquisitions could well prove to be a boon. The company expanded rapidly by acquiring outfits that manufacture high-end commercial and consumer paper products. As a result, JR's exposure to relatively price-volatile paper segments is small. To be sure, this limits the potential for ongoing operations to post rapid earnings gains when demand is strong, as had been the case since 1985. But the flip side is that JR is cushioned against a profit decline should its operating environment weaken. So, inspite of the softening economy we expect later on in the year . . .

We look for earnings progress this year and next. JR's goal to achieve a major presence in each of its end markets placed a relatively low priority on developing its internal raw material sourcing capabilities. Thus, as the price of pulp (a key paper ingredient) soared during the paper industry's recent three year upturn, JR's margin expansion was held back by rising raw material costs. In a down cycle, assuming our call for slowing economy proves correct, JR's lack of vertical integration should work positively. That's because the bulk of JR's areas, particularly its sanitary and food service sectors, exhibit pricing characteristics which are relatively stable. Moreover, in arenas, such as communication papers, where prices are more volatile, JR's lack of pulp sufficiency should enable margin expansion (pulp has high price sensitivity to economic trends. However, a potential roadblock lies with JR's ambitious capital program, which is aimed at raising the vertical integration of its assorted buyouts. Although the program will strengthen JR's operating position over the long pull, its immediate impact would be to add higher debt burdens.

JR's relatively small exposure to economic trends has been noticed by Wall Street, we believe. Indeed, we think much of the company's long-term potential is already discounted in its share price. True, this timely equity has traded before at a much higher multiple to the market. But the reasons then had more to do with the promise of potential acquisition activity. This growth avenue has narrowed: As JR continues to expand, the earnings impact of acquisitions becomes increasingly small.

Michael Kumekawa *July 28, 1989*

(A) Fiscal year ends last Sunday in April of following calendar year. **(B)** Primary earnings. Next earnings report due late Aug. **(C)** Next dividend meeting about Oct. 6. Goes ex about Oct. 11. Approx. dividend payment dates: Jan. 31, April 30, July 30, Oct. 30. **(D)** Incl. deferred charges and goodwill. In '87: $356.7 mill., $4.39/share. **(E)** In millions, adjusted for stock splits.

Company's Financial Strength	B+
Stock's Price Stability	50
Price Growth Persistence	70
Earnings Predictability	75

Case 24

Scott Paper Company: Reassessing the Strategic Plan

Introduction

Scott Paper Company, headquartered in Philadelphia, Pennsylvania, was a multinational forest-products firm that grew, harvested, and sold timber. More importantly, it also manufactured and sold a variety of paper products such as toilet paper, paper towels, napkins, facial tissues, baby wipes, food wraps, and nonwoven materials. In fact, Scott was the world's leading producer of sanitary tissue products for both home and commercial use.

Competition within the paper products industry had grown increasingly intense since the early 1970s. At first, Scott responded rather lethargically; consequently, its market share declined for several key products and its overall profitability suffered. With lower profitability and worsening economic conditions in the late 1970s, Scott Paper became a prime candidate for a takeover. Even though it had millions of acres of valuable timberland, a reputable name, and quality products, its stock price was clearly undervalued. In 1979, Brascan Limited, a Canadian investment firm, began a serious attempt to acquire a majority of Scott Paper Company's stock.

In 1981, Scott Paper Company initiated an aggressive strategic plan that called for the firm to concentrate on its strengths and divest itself of unprofitable operations. In part, this plan was taken to avoid a possible takeover by Brascan Limited or some other firm in the future. The plan appeared to be making some progress after three years, but many analysts still wondered if the effort was too little and too late. Thus, in 1984, Scott Paper Company was considering what additional actions it might take to improve its financial performance and to prevent a takeover from outsiders. Phillip E. Lippincott, Scott Paper's newly promoted President, had actively helped to formulate the plan and was to have prime responsibility for its implementation.

History of Scott Paper Company

In 1867, T. Seymour Scott and E. Irvin Scott left their family farm in Saratoga, New York and moved to Philadelphia, Pennsylvania. There, they opened a store that sold straw paper to local merchants. The brothers incorporated their business in 1879 under the name Scott Paper Company Limited. They bought pulp from other firms and converted it into coarse and straw paper which they sold. They soon added toilet paper (also known as bathroom tissue), which was a new innovation. A major problem in marketing this product was the established business norm of not advertising such personal products. As a result, Scott Paper Company started to ghost manufacture toilet paper under the name of the merchants who sold their product.

This case was written by Fred C. Walters and Larry D. Alexander of Virginia Polytechnic Institute and State University.

Later, in 1910, the Scott brothers decided it was time to produce toilet paper under their own name. They bought their first fully integrated paper mill in nearby Chester, Pennsylvania. This plant was capable of first making the pulp and then producing the paper product itself. Arthur Scott joined his brothers around this time, and he developed Scott Tissue, America's first paper towel. The Scott brothers' philosophy was to produce quality products in high volume, sell them at low prices, and advertise extensively.

The Chester mill grew from one paper-making machine to six machines in 1923. By then, Scott Paper had become the leading toilet paper manufacturer in the world. Four of the five products Scott Paper Company produced at that time had not even been invented when the company first was established. Scott so successfully marketed its products that the name Scott became a household word and even a generic name for some of its products.

Scott Paper Company grew rapidly from 1927 through 1939, even during the heart of the depression. Its plants and machinery were greatly expanded to handle the increased sales during this period. The Chester mill alone increased to nine separate paper machines. A research and engineering department, which had been established, was given the charge to keep the firm at the forefront of the paper industry. To ensure a continuous supply of pulp, Scott joined with Mead Corporation and constructed a chemical pulp mill under the name of the Brunswick Pulp and Paper Company.

In the 1940s, Scott further expanded its operations by purchasing two West Coast pulp mills along with several mills owned by the Marinette Paper Company. By the end of World War II, Scott had acquired seven new plants and introduced three new products, including a line of facial tissues.

In the 1950s, Scott further expanded its operations and began to diversify its product mix. The company introduced Scotkins, a paper napkin of unusually high quality. Scotkins was so popular that customer demand exceeded the available supply for several years. By 1954, when Scott Paper celebrated its 75th year as an incorporated business, it manufactured five basic product lines, which included toilet paper, paper towels, facial tissues, wax paper, and paper napkins.

In the 1960s, Scott further diversified by acquiring the S. D. Warren Company, which produced fine printing, publishing, and specialty papers. While Scott looked to the 1970s and 1980s as an opportunity to participate in new growth markets, these decades, unfortunately, brought adversities to this leading supplier of paper products.

Several factors in the 1970s significantly impacted on Scott's progress. Crippling strikes in 1971 hurt Scott's credibility as a reliable paper supplier. High inflation that racked the decade slowed the growth of the paper industry and many other industries that used paper products. Competition within the sanitary paper products market became more intense as the industry growth rate slowed. For example, Procter & Gamble introduced Bounty paper towels and Charmin toilet paper, which cut deeply into Scott's respective market shares. Scott was also hurt by several generic paper manufacturers which launched an all-out attack on the low price segment of the toilet paper market.

As a result of these competitive challenges, Scott Paper's pretax margins dropped from 16% in the early 1960s to just 7% in 1981. Scott's return on stockholders' equity was 10.6% over the 1976–1981 period. That ranked a disappointing 22nd in profitability out of the 23 leading firms in the forest-products industry.

Scott's Strategic Plan

On February 24th of 1981, Scott Paper Company announced its strategic plan for the 1980s. It was an aggressive five-year strategic plan whose prime objective was to reverse Scott's 20-year downward trend. The plan was designed to improve the profitability of Scott Paper in those core businesses where it had unique competitive strengths. The plan was the result of a thorough two-year analysis of Scott's worldwide operations, its past strategies, and its competitive position within each market segment where it competed.

Scott Paper's new strategy focused on those business segments where it had or could achieve competitive advantages. These included:

1. Value brands and high-quality paper towels and toilet paper for the consumer sanitary-paper market.

2. Paper and nonwoven products for the away-from-home commercial customers.

3. High quality coated commercial printing and publishing papers.

4. Sanitary paper products that were sold internationally.[1]

Within these segments, Scott's strategic plan sought growth in unit volume and market share if, and only if, they could result in improved profitability. To improve its competitive position, the plan called for Scott aggressively to lower its cost position in those manufacturing facilities which produced these core products. One way that costs were to be lowered would be to simplify Scott's product offerings within each product line. If it could concentrate on fewer, more popular brands, it could increase volume for fewer products, which would lower unit costs, and help increase profitability.

Manufacturing/Operations

Scott Paper's extensive worldwide operations, as shown in Exhibit 1, were located in 21 countries. Within the United States alone, it operated 18 manufacturing facilities in 12 states as shown in Exhibit 2. Its largest papermaking mills were located in Chester, Pennsylvania; Everett, Washington; Mobile, Alabama; Muskegon, Michigan; and Westbrook and Winslow, Maine. These and other facilities were grouped into four divisions. They were (1) the Packaged Products Division, (2) the S. D. Warren Division, (3) the Natural Resources Division, and (4) the Nonwovens Division.

The Packaged Products Division, headquartered in Philadelphia, made both consumer sanitary paper products and commercial paper products. J. Richard Leman, age 49, has headed up this division since early 1982. This division was very important to Scott Paper since it accounted for the majority of Scott's total sales. It had been reducing its manufacturing costs since the strategic plan started by improving pulp use, thus completing various cost-reducing capital projects, and by emphasizing its more profitable brands.

The S. D. Warren Division, headquartered in Boston, manufactured commercial printing, publishing, and specialty papers. Robert E. McAvoy, its 55-year-old President, has only held this position since December of 1983. This division operated five pulp and/or paper mills located in Maine, Michigan, and Alabama. A new paper machine was added in 1983 at its Skowhegan, Maine facility at a cost of over $200,000,000. This new machine helped increase the production of lighter weight coated printing paper. In addition, a paper machine at the Muskegon mill was rebuilt during that same year to increase output and lower its unit costs.

This division provided professional advice and technical assistance to more than 800 private landowners through its S. D. Warren tree farm program. Much of the timber harvested from these private woodlots was purchased by Scott Paper Company for use in its mills.

The Natural Resources Division, headquartered in Philadelphia, had responsibility for managing the company's 3,080,000 acres of timberlands and mineral resources. Stephen J. Conway was its vice president for Natural Resources—Timberlands. Scott owned some 2,800,000 acres of timber and had long-term cutting rights (or leased or had purchase rights) for

Exhibit 1 Scott Paper Company's Worldwide Operations

Scott Paper Company

Executive Offices

Scott Plaza
Philadelphia, Pa. 19113
(215) 522-5000

Packaged Products Division

Philadelphia, Pa.

Consumer:

Chester, Pa.; Dover Del.; Everett, Wash.; Ft. Edward, N.Y.; Marinette and Oconto Falls, Wis.; Mobile, Ala.; Winslow, Me.; Lester, Pa. (Excell Paper Sales Company)

Commercial:

Chester, Pa.; Everett, Wash.; Hattiesburg, Miss.; Marinette, Milwaukee and Oconto Falls, Wis.; Mobile, Ala.; Winslow, Me.

S.D. Warren Division

Boston, Mass.
Mobile, Ala.; Muskegon, Mich.; Skowhegan, Westbrook and Winslow, Me.

Managed for Scott Paper International, Inc.:

Belgium (Scott Graphics International, a division of Scott Continental)

Natural Resources Division

Philadelphia, Pa.

Everett, Wash.; Mt Vernon, Ala.; Timberlands in Alabama, Maine, Mississippi and Washington; Timberlands in Georgia, Florida and South Carolina (Scott Timber Company); Alabama (Escuhbia Oil Company); Maine (Greenville Forest Products, 50% owned; Skylark, Inc.); Washington (Three Rivers Timber Company)

Supplier Affiliates:

Brunswick, Pearson and Sterling, Ga.; McCormick, S.C. (Brunswick Pulp & Paper Company, 50% owned); Brunswick, Ga. (Brunswick Pulp Land Company, 50% owned); Tacoma, Wash. (Mountain Tree Farm Company, 50% owned)

From *Scott Paper Company 1983 Annual Report,* p. 48.

Managed for Scott Paper International, Inc.:

New Glasgow, Nova Scotia (Scott Maritimes Limited; Canso Chemicals Limited, 33.3% owned); Parrsboro and Upper Musquodoboit, Nova Scotia, and Timberlands in Nova Scotia (Canadian Timberlands Division; Cape Chignecto Lands Limited); Brazil (Amapá Florestal e Celulose S.A.—AMCEL, 49% owned)

Nonwovens Division

Philadelphia, Pa.

Landisville, N.J.; Rogers, Ark.

Managed for Scott Paper International, Inc.:

Germany (Federal Republic of Germany) (Scott Paper GmbH Nonwovens)

Other Consolidated Operations

Bermuda (Riscott Insurance, Ltd.); Nova Scotia (Owikeno Finance Ltd.)

Scott Paper International, Inc.

Philadelphia, Pa.

Consolidated Operations:

New Glasgow, Nova Scotia (Scott Maritimes Limited); Parrsboro and Upper Musquodoboit, Nova Scotia and Timberlands in Nova Scotia (Canadian Timberlands Division; Cape Chignecto Lands Limited); Nova Scotia (Owikeno Lake Timber Company Limited); Delaware (Discott II, Inc.); Liberia (Scott Finance Liberia, Ltd.); Germany (Federal Republic of Germany) (Scott Paper GmbH Nonwovens)

Supplier Affiliate:

New Glasgow, Nova Scotia (Canso Chemicals Limited, 33.3% owned)

International Affiliates:

Argentina: Celulosa Jujuy, S.A. (33.3% owned)

Australia: The Bowater-Scott Corporation of Australia Limited (50% owned; The Bowater Corporation of Australia Limited owns 50%)

Belgium: Scott Continental and its Scott Graphics International Division

Brazil: Amapá Florestal e Celulose S.A.—AMCEL (49% owned; Indústria e Comércio de Minérios S.A.—ICOMI owns 51%); COPA—Companhia de Papéis (49% owned; Companhia Auxiliar de Emprésas de Mineraçáo—CAEMI owns 51%)

Canada: Scott Paper Limited (50.05% owned)

Colombia: Papeles Scott de Colombia, S.A. (49% owned)

Costa Rica: Scott Paper Company de Costa Rica, S.A. (50% owned)

France: Bouton Brochard Scott, S.A.

Germany: (Federal Republic of Germany): Scott Paper GmbH Nonwovens (a consolidated operation)

Hong Kong: Scott Paper (Hong Kong) Limited (50% owned; Hong Shem & Sons Limited owns 50%)

Italy: Scott S.p.A.

Japan: Sanyo Scott Company Limited (50% owned; Sanyo-Kokusaku Pulp Co., Ltd. owns 50%)

Korea: (Republic of Korea): Ssangyong Paper Co., Ltd. (34% owned)

Malaysia: Scott Paper (Malaysia) Sdn. Bhd. (50% owned; SPP Limited owns 50%)

Mexico: Compañia Industrialde San Cristóbal, S.A. (48.8% owned)

Philippines: Scott Paper Philippines, Inc.

Singapore: Scott Paper (Singapore) Pte. Ltd. (50% owned; SPP Limited owns 50%)

Spain: Gureola-Scott, S.A. (92% owned)

Taiwan (Republic of China): Taiwan Scott Paper Corporation (66.7% owned)

Thailand: Scott Trading Limited (49.8% owned) and Thai-Scott Paper Company Limited (50% owned)

United Kingdom: Bowater-Scott Corporation Limited (50% owned; The Bowater Corporation Limited owns 50%)

(Unless otherwise indicated, Scott or Scott Paper International, Inc. owns 100% of each listed operation.)

Exhibit 2 Scott Paper's Manufacturing Facilities in the United States

Packaged Products Division

Chester, Pennsylvania–consumer and commercial paper products
Dover, Delaware–consumer paper products
Everett, Washington–consumer and commercial paper products and pulp
Ft. Edward, New York–consumer paper products
Hattiesburg, Mississippi–commercial paper products
Marinette, Wisconsin–consumer and commercial paper products
Milwaukee, Wisconsin–commercial paper products
Mobile, Alabama–consumer and commercial paper products and pulp
Oconto Falls, Wisconsin–consumer and commercial paper products
Winslow, Maine–consumer and commercial paper products

S.D. Warren Division

Mobile, Alabama–paper and pulp
Muskegon, Michigan–paper and pulp
Skowhegan, Maine–paper and pulp
Westbrook, Maine–paper and pulp
Winslow, Maine–paper

Natural Resources Division

Mt. Vernon, Alabama–lumber
Parrsboro, Nova Scotia–lumber
New Glasgow, Nova Scotia–pulp

Nonwovens Division

Landisville, New Jersey–nonwoven products
Rogers, Arkansas–nonwoven products

From *Scott Paper Company Form 10-K for 1983,* p. 9.

the remaining 280,000 acres. Scott's timberlands, which were located in the United States and Canada, supplied nearly half of the wood fiber it required for pulp and papermaking. Each year, approximately half of the harvested logs was sold worldwide as logs or converted into lumber to be sold to the commercial market. The other half of the harvested logs was used as raw materials for Scott's pulp manufacturing operations to produce various paper products.

In recent years, Scott's timberlands provided an important fuel source for operating its plants and mills. About 55% of Scott's total energy consumption was supplied from a mix of wood biomass and liquid residues resulting in the conservation of nearly 6,000,000 barrels of crude oil per year. Scott Paper had also placed a heavy emphasis on environmental stewardship wherever it operated. Every mill was in full compliance with both federal and state environmental regulations. The effort to comply with various governmental standards had not come cheaply, since Scott's expenditures totaled over $250,000,000 since the mid-1970s.

The primary objective for Scott's manufacturing operations was to become one of the most cost efficient operations within the paper industry. When Phillip Lippincott was promoted to president and chief operating officer in 1980, Scott had a number of older mills and processing plants. Some of the projects completed already in its five-year capital-spending program included:

1. A new $200,000,000 paper machine at Skowhegan, Maine.
2. A $85,000,000 biomass and coal cogeneration facility at Westbrook, Maine.
3. A $69,000,000 woodyard modernization project at Mobile, Alabama.
4. A $28,000,000 modernization of a papermaking machine at Muskegon, Michigan.
5. A $25,000,000 fiber recycling facility at Winslow, Maine.
6. A $20,000,000 commercial products converting plant at Hattiesburg, Mississippi.
7. A $100,000,000 energy facility at its Chester, Pennsylvania paper mill.

In addition, Scott Paper Company also planned to continue its $300,000,000 project to modernize and upgrade extensively the energy generation facilities at its Mobile, Alabama plant, which was scheduled to be completed in 1985.

Despite these capital improvements, Scott Paper still had other old mills that handicapped its production efficiency.

Marketing/Sales

Scott Paper's products were marketed differently depending on the type of product and market involved.

The Packaged Products Division had sales of $1,570,778,000, which accounted for 63.7% of Scott Paper's total sales in 1983. The various consumer and commercial products offered by this division are shown in Exhibit 3.

The Packaged Products Division's consumer products were targeted at different segments of the market; however, its value segment (sometimes called economy or family pack) was given the most emphasis. Irrespective of the segment, these consumer products were sold primarily through grocery stores, drug stores, general retailers, and discount stores. Scott's four value line products included ScotTissue toilet paper, ScotTowels paper towels, Scotties facial tissues, and Scott Family napkins. These products were all targeted at the medium-priced market segments. In the higher quality segments, Scott brands included Cottonelle and Soft 'n' Pretty toilet paper, Job Squad and Viva paper towels, and Baby Fresh baby wipes. Under Scott's five-year strategic plan, some of the better known brands such as Cottonelle and Soft 'n' Pretty were being milked for whatever cash they could generate; otherwise they might be dropped entirely.

This division's commercial products, by definition, were used in the away-from-home markets, which were growing faster than the home-

Exhibit 3 Scott's Packaged Products Division's Various Products

Packaged Products Division. Trademarked and other products manufactured by the Company's Packaged Products Division, other than pulp, include the following:

Consumer Products

Bathroom Tissues
Cottonelle, Family Scott, ScotTissue, Soft 'n' Pretty, Soft-Weve, Waldorf

Disposable Towels
Job Squad, ScotTowels, Viva

Napkins
Scott Family, *Viva*

Facial Tissues
Scotties

Wax Paper
Cut-Rite

Baby Wipes
Baby Fresh, Wash a-bye Baby

Commercial Products

Washroom Products
Bathroom Tissues—
Escort, ScotTissue, Soft-Weve, Soft Blend, Waldorf
Towels—
Scott, Premiere
Facial Tissues—
Scotties Repete

Food Service Products
Mealmates, Scottex, Scottlin and *Windsor* napkins;
Cut-Rite wax bags;
American placemats, tray covers, table covers, doilies, portion products, fluted containers, specialty cups

Fixtures
Towel, facial tissues, napkin and windshield towel dispensers; bathroom tissue and wiper holders

Wiping Products

Paper—*Assembly Wipes, Micro-Wipes, Sani-Prep, Soft-Cote, Sturdi-Wipes II, Utility Wipes,* Windshield Towels
Scrim Reinforced—*Dura-Weve*

Air Lay—*Heltlon II, Ultralon,* Shop, Service, Autoshop and Roll Wiper Control Towels
Carded Rayon—*Heftlon*
Bonded Cellulose—*Dry-Up, WypAll, WypAll* Blue, Professional Towel

From *Scott Paper Company Form 10-K for 1983,* pp. 2–3.

use market. They included industrial, institutional, commercial, food service, hotel/motel, and government establishments. Whereas the consumer products were generally sold directly to the retail firms themselves, Scott's commercial products were usually sold through distributors, which primarily competed on the basis of price, product quality, and service.

The Packaged Products Division products were noted for high quality, their value for the price, and the Scott name. While the Packaged Products Division had 16 mills, a number of them were older, less efficient production facilities. Scott's natural resources supported this division by providing an unlimited base of raw materials.

The S. D. Warren Division, which manufactured commercial printing, publishing, converting, and specialty papers, posted sales of $686,957,000 in 1983. That represented a 20% increase over 1982. Its principal products were high-quality coated papers used for print advertising, annual reports, and magazines. It also produced uncoated publishing papers of various grades and qualities for a wide range of printed books. The division had made excellent progress in 1983 towards implementing its two-fold strategy. One aspect of it was to expand its market share for lighter weight grades of printing and publishing paper. The other aspect of the strategy was to retain its long standing quality and market position in heavier weight papers.

This division's products were mainly distributed through independent wholesalers throughout the United States. Most of the converting and specialty papers were sold to converters for further processing into a final end-user product. The principal methods of competition in the markets where these products went included price, product quality, and customer service. Many of this division's products had a strong market position and were supported by an effective sales force.

The Natural Resources Division's sales of $86,004,000 for 1983 did not reflect its importance to the other two major divisions. This division had two major objectives. One was to supply wood, pulp, and biomass fuel wood to other Scott operations at the lowest possible cost. The other objective was to become a reliable, long-term supplier of pulp within the pulp-wood market. Half of the logs this division harvested each year were processed into square lumber and the remainder were used by Scott in its pulp manufacturing operations. Scott sold the pulp it made in both the domestic and international markets.

Finance/Accounting

Scott Paper Company's statement of consolidated earnings for 1981–1983 is shown in Exhibit 4. For 1983, its net sales of $2,465,088,000 were an all-time record but so were its costs of goods for that same year. Its 1983 net income after taxes of $123,679,000 was a substantial improvement over the $74,457,000 for 1982, but down somewhat from the previous three years. Scott's consolidated balance sheets for 1982 and 1983 are shown in Exhibit 5. A summary of Scott's business segments for 1981–1983 appears in Exhibit 6. Its income from operations of $140,125,000 for 1983 breaks down as follows: $127,063,000 for the Packaged Products Division, $54,189,000 for the S. D. Warren Division, $25,315,000 for the Forest Products and Materials Division, $9,636,000 from other operations, and $76,078,000 deducted for corporate interest expense. Finally, a ten-year financial summary, from 1974 through 1983, is shown in Exhibit 7.

Scott's financial objective was to increase its stockholders' return on investment, which hovered around 5% in 1981, up to around 12% to 15% by the end of 1986. Several actions were taken in the early 1980s to realize these objectives.

One action was to commit $1,600,000,000 towards a five-year capital spending program as a part of Scott Paper's 1981 strategic plan. The capital spending was needed to upgrade aging plants, buy new machinery, and to expand capacity. This capital spending program was al-

Exhibit 4 Consolidated Earnings for 1981–1983 (in thousands, except on a per share basis)

	1983	1982	1981
Sales	**$2,465,088**	$2,293,436	$2,309,444
Costs and expenses			
Product costs	**1,753,698**	1,592,053	1,580,409
Marketing and distribution	**416,430**	440,977	484,519
Research and development	**29,293**	29,957	31,344
Administration and general	**93,532**	86,401	73,792
Interest expense	**32,010**	21,744	32,642
	2,324,963	2,171,132	2,202,706
Income from operations	**140,125**	122,304	106,738
Other income and (expense)	**18,561**	86,102	58,292
Income before taxes	**158,686**	208,406	165,030
Taxes on income			
Current	**41,223**	19,555	23,297
Deferred	**20,397**	74,610	44,368
	61,620	94,165	67,665
Income before share of earnings of international affiliates	**97,066**	114,241	97,365
Share of earnings (loss) of international affiliates	**26,613**	(39,784)	35,975
Net Income	**123,679**	74,457	133,340
Dividends on preferred shares	**6,262**	5,740	255
Earnings for common shares	**$ 117,417**	$ 68,717	$ 133,085
Earnings for common shares	**$2.58**	$1.61	$3.22
Dividends per common share	**$1.00**	$1.00	$1.00
Average common shares outstanding	**45,534**	42,652	41,375

From *Scott Paper Company 1983 Annual Report*, p. 30.

ready helping Scott Paper to lower its costs and to increase its productivity. Phillip Lippincott noted:

> The capital investment program and the financial strengthening and rationalization measures weren't matters of choice so much as matters of necessity if we were going to maintain, much less improve, our standing in the industry.[2]

Capital expenditures, including equity investments in affiliates, were $350,000,000 for 1981, $402,000,000 for 1982, and $270,000,000 for 1983. An additional $750,000,000 was allocated for 1984 and 1985 combined.

Another action taken towards increasing its stockholders' return on investment focused on how Scott Paper financed its needed capital. Scott used external sources to finance about 50% of its capital spending plan. While not noted for being financially creative, Scott Paper was rather ingenious in how it financed this plan. It sold approximately $50,000,000 worth of tax benefits under the safe harbor provision of the Economic Recovery Tax Act of 1981. It also financed well over $100,000,000 in equipment purchases by using relatively cheap foreign financing, which took advantage of an international tax loophole. Scott also raised $7,000,000 by leasing its equip-

Exhibit 5 Consolidated Balance Sheets for December 25, 1982 and December 31, 1983 (in thousands)

	1983		1982	
Assets:				
Current assets				
Cash		**$ 7,654**		$ 4,769
Marketable securities		**2,352**		3,325
Time deposits		**136,185**		15,646
Receivables		**253,093**		224,021
Inventories		**173,500**		211,666
Prepaid items		**24,287**		14,282
		597,071		473,709
Plant assets, at cost	**$2,665,485**		$2,548,249	
Accumulated depreciation	**(1,116,873)**	**1,548,612**	(1,042,423)	1,505,826
Timber resources, at cost less timber harvested		**95,440**		95,061
Investments in and advances to international affiliates		**280,686**		232,218
Investments in supplier affiliates		**44,696**		40,207
Construction funds held by trustees		**114,521**		1,577
Other assets		**42,130**		33,765
Total		**$2,723,156**		$2,382,363
Liabilities and Shareholders' Equity:				
Current liabilities				
Payable to suppliers and others		**$ 371,438**		$ 344,546
Current maturities of long-term debt		**13,895**		10,645
Accrued taxes on income		**43,910**		18,842
		429,243		374,033
Long-term debt		**566,343**		445,176
Deferred credits, principally deferred income taxes		**246,411**		227,477
		1,241,997		1,046,686
Redeemable preferred shares		**17,608**		45,000
Non-redeemable preferred shares		**7,128**		7,128
Common shareholders' equity				
Common shares	**$ 514,590**		$ 396,254	
Reinvested earnings	**1,010,682**		944,787	
Cumulative translation adjustment	**(58,835)**		(47,212)	
Treasury shares	**(10,014)**	**1,456,423**	(10,280)	1,283,549
Total		**$2,723,156**		$2,382,363

From *Scott Paper Company 1983 Annual Report,* p. 31.

Exhibit 6 A Summary of Scott's Business Segments for 1981-83 (in thousands)

	1983	1982	1981
Sales			
Packaged Products			
Sanitary paper products	**$1,505,741**	$1,473,265	$1,481,631
Market pulp	**65,037**	71,960	69,450
	1,570,778	1,545,225	1,551,081
S.D. Warren			
Printing, publishing, converting, and specialty papers	**666,575**	558,916	564,117
Market pulp	**20,382**	12,899	11,025
	686,957	571,815	575,142
Forest Products and Minerals	**86,004**	64,118	69,309
Other Operations	**121,349**	112,278	113,912
	$2,465,088	$2,293,436	2,309,444
Operating Profits			
Packaged Products			
Sanitary paper products	**$ 143,280**	$ 121,480	$ 69,844
Market pulp	**(16,217)**	(1,925)	14,781
	127,063	119,555	84,625
S.D. Warren			
Printing, publishing, converting and specialty papers	**57,343**	39,203	56,819
Market pulp	**(3,154)**	(3)	2,999
	54,189	39,200	59,818
Forest Products and Minerals	**25,315**	14,526	21,077
Other Operations	**9,636**	7,902	9,069
Corporate	**(76,078)**	(58,879)	(67,851)
Income from operations	**140,125**	122,304	106,738
Other income and (expense)	**18,561**	86,102	58,292
Income before taxes	**$ 156,686**	$ 208,406	$ 165,030

ment to two banks in England as a form of two-country tax shelter. Scott also raised another $91,000,000 by transferring ownership of a new biomass processing boiler to General Electric Corporation under a 25 year contract whereby Scott would buy back the power it uses.

Scott Paper also generated cash internally through the divestiture of several of its affiliates and landholdings. In November of 1983, Scott agreed in principle to sell its Brown Jordan Furniture and Lighting Division to Integrated Resources, Inc. for $83,000,000. Scott was also in the process of selling 220,000 acres of its Northwest timberlands for a sum expected to run in the hundreds of millions of dollars. In addition, these divestitures helped to increase Scott's return on stockholders' investment by spinning off weak performing units, generating needed cash, and emphasizing products in markets where Scott Paper had a competitive advantage.

Exhibit 6 *(continued)*

	1983	1982	1981
Depreciation and Cost of Timber Harvested			
Packaged Products	**$ 69,974**	$ 67,482	$ 61,363
S.D. Warren	**44,729**	30,252	28,288
Forest Products and Minerals	**25,087**	26,390	23,277
Other Operations	**2,578**	2,741	2,243
Corporate	**2,204**	1,519	1,823
	$ 144,572	$ 128,384	$ 116,994
Capital Expenditures			
Packaged Products	**$ 137,055**	$ 145,416	$ 142,494
S.D. Warren	**41,369**	204,621	136,083
Forest Products and Minerals	**29,108**	32,477	30,817
Other Operations	**2,129**	5,688	8,300
Corporate	**11,289**	527	3,405
	$ 220,950	$ 388,729	$ 321,099
Identifiable Assets			
Packaged Products	**$1,145,374**	$1,158,142	$1,143,131
S.D. Warren	**755,036**	678,022	572,556
Forest Products and Minerals	**198,596**	161,682	160,955
Other Operations	—	67,707	64,973
Corporate	**624,150**	316,810	357,068
	$2,723,156	$2,382,363	$2,298,683
Identifiable assets include investments in supplier affiliates of:			
Packaged Products	**$ 39,249**	$ 33,804	$ 39,830
S.D. Warren	**5,100**	6,059	6,324
Forest Products and Minerals	**347**	344	339
	$ 44,696	$ 40,207	$ 46,493

From *Scott Paper Company 1983 Annual Report*, p. 43.

Research and Development

Scott Paper Company's research and development efforts were conducted primarily at facilities located in Philadelphia, Pennsylvania and Westbrook, Maine. Scott spent approximately $30,000,000 per year for various R&D programs. Some of these ongoing programs included research efforts on pulp and papermaking, process control, paper converting, and the development of new and improved paper products.

Ongoing research was also directed at helping Scott achieve its environmental and energy conservation goals. Scott had made significant strides in reducing its use of crude oil through its biomass fuel wood and liquid residue program. For example, Scott was experimenting with a prelogging harvest operation at its Mobile, Alabama papermill. This operation recovered hardwood and small pine stems for fuel, which reduced its use of fuel oil. The project improved

Exhibit 7 A Ten-Year Financial Summary from 1974 through 1983 (in millions)

	1983	1982	1981	1980	1979	1978	1977	1976	1975	1974
Sales	**$2,465.1**	$2,293.4	$2,309.4	$2,083.2	$1,908.1	$1,724.9	$1,520.2	$1,373.8	$1,191.9	$1,109.5
Costs and expenses										
Product costs	**1,753.7**	1,592.0	1,580.4	1,399.9	1,268.7	1,174.3	1,067.9	941.1	827.3	796.9
Marketing and distribution	**416.5**	441.0	484.5	478.2	399.1	344.7	274.9	233.0	195.4	155.3
Research and development	**29.3**	30.0	31.4	31.2	30.0	26.8	25.9	24.4	24.2	23.0
Administration and general	**93.5**	86.4	73.8	65.8	60.4	55.6	46.2	44.8	37.9	34.9
Interest Expense	**32.0**	21.7	32.6	32.4	33.4	34.7	32.6	30.2	28.7	18.1
	2,325.0	2,171.1	2,202.7	2,007.5	1,791.6	1,636.1	1,447.5	1,273.5	1,113.5	1,028.2
Income from operations	**140.1**	122.3	106.7	75.7	116.5	88.8	72.7	100.3	78.4	81.3
Other income and (expense)	**18.6**	86.1	58.3	61.0	21.2	(2.1)	(10.8)	4.7	1.7	—
Income before taxes	**158.7**	208.4	165.0	136.7	137.7	86.7	61.9	105.0	80.1	81.3
Taxes on income	**61.6**	94.2	67.6	47.9	45.1	26.4	19.5	40.7	33.4	31.1
Income before share of earnings of international affiliates	**97.1**	114.2	97.4	88.8	92.6	60.3	42.4	64.3	46.7	50.2
Share of earnings (loss) of international affiliates	**26.6**	(39.7)	35.9	44.2	43.9	32.7	19.2	8.5	17.7	18.9
Income before cumulative effect of accounting change	**123.7**	74.5	133.3	133.0	136.5	93.0	61.6	72.8	64.4	69.1
Cumulative effect of accounting change	**—**	—	—	—	—	—	37.1	—	(.6)	—
Net income	**123.7**	74.5	133.3	133.0	136.5	93.0	98.7	72.8	63.8	69.1
Dividends on preferred shares	**6.3**	5.8	.3	.3	.3	.3	.3	.3	.3	.3
Earnings for common shares	**$ 117.4**	$ 68.7	$ 133.0	$ 132.7	$ 136.2	$ 92.7	$ 98.4	$ 72.5	$ 63.5	$ 68.8

Exhibit 7 *(continued)*

	1983	1982	1981	1980	1979	1978	1977	1976	1975	1974
Dollars per common										
share	**$ 2.58**	$ 1.61	$ 3.22	$ 3.41	$ 3.50	$ 2.40	$ 2.55	$ 2.00	$ 1.84	$ 1.99
Earnings	**$ 2.58**	$ 1.61	$ 3.22	$ 3.41	$ 3.50	$ 2.40	$ 2.55	$ 2.00	$ 1.84	$ 1.99
Dividends	**1.00**	1.00	1.00	1.00	.90	.80	.76	.72	.68	.62
Market price—high	**32¼**	21	28½	23½	20⅞	19	20¾	24⅛	19	18⅛
low	**18⅝**	13⅝	15	13¼	13⅝	12½	13	14¼	12¼	9⅝
Percent of income from operations to sales	**5.7%**	5.3%	4.6%	3.6%	6.1%	5.1%	4.8%	7.3%	6.6%	7.3%
Debt as a percentage of total capitalization	**25.1%**	22.6%	26.4%	28.6%	28.1%	27.9%	37.8%	29.1%	32.4%	29.4%
Return on common shareholders' equity	**8.6%**	5.3%	11.0%	12.4%	14.1%	10.6%	11.8%	10.2%	10.0%	11.7%
Pro forma amounts										
Net income	**$ 123.7**	$ 74.5	$ 133.3	$ 133.0	$ 136.5	$ 93.0	$ 61.6	$ 95.8	$ 70.5	$ 72.3
Earnings per common share	**2.58**	1.61	3.22	3.41	3.50	2.40	1.59	2.64	2.04	2.09
Total assets at year end	**$2,723.2**	$2,382.4	$2,298.7	$2,012.6	$1,827.9	$1,620.3	$1,588.1	$1,464.8	$1,283.5	$1,107.5

(continued)

Exhibit 7 *(continued)*

	1983	1982	1981	1980	1979	1978	1977	1976	1975	1974
Long-term debt at year end	**566.3**	445.2	500.7	474.8	422.3	371.1	430.2	374.1	352.2	270.5
Redeemable preferred shares	**17.6**	45.0	—	—	—	—	—	—	—	—
Capital expenditures for plant and timber	**221.0**	388.7	321.1	252.4	182.2	134.0	149.4	198.6	210.2	147.0
Depreciation and cost of timber harvested	**144.6**	128.4	117.0	109.4	104.3	97.7	88.4	67.7	60.1	54.2
Investments in affiliates	**53.0**	(54.7)	33.4	30.8	46.1	30.0	19.9	12.7	20.1	23.1
(Thousands)										
Common shares										
Average shares outstanding	**45,534**	42,652	41,375	38,896	38,885	38,722	38,619	36,225	34,574	34,573
Number of shareholders	**59.1**	65.0	70.1	74.7	77.7	78.3	75.4	75.9	79.4	82.5
Number of employees	**17.0**	18.6	20.3	20.5	20.8	20.4	21.3	20.6	20.1	20.4

From *Scott Paper Company 1983 Annual Report*, p. 46.

Scott's operations at that facility in several ways. Site preparation costs were substantially lower, and logging costs had been reduced by up to $4.00 per cord. As a result of this program, approximately 55% of the mill's fuel needs were supplied from a mix of biomass fuel wood and liquid residuals.

Scott also emphasized research efforts to improve its forest productivity. Scott's Monroeville, Mississippi, orchard bred genetically superior super trees which were used to replant its harvested timberlands. Scott's foresters believed that the improved seedlings it will plant by the year 2005 will yield at least 40% more volume than ordinary pine trees. Trees which it experimented with in the 1950s were yielding 10% greater volume per acre by the 1980s than ordinary trees. Other projects to increase forest productivity included research to develop trees that can grow in poor soils, shorten the tree growth cycle, and breed disease and insect-resistant pine trees.

Human Resources/Personnel

Since Lippincott took charge in 1981, Scott Paper had been streamlining its work force. Scott had reduced the number of salaried and hourly domestic employees by 15%. In fact, its 17,000 total U.S. employees were down some 1,600 from just the previous year. In 1983, it had 10,800 employees engaged directly in manufacturing operations and 6,200 in administrative, technical, clerical, and sales positions. Scott had also reduced the number of levels in the organization and had increased the average span of management. These actions were taken to reduce overhead costs and to streamline its various business operations to remain competitive.

Scott was placing a greater emphasis on managerial excellence. It tried to create a climate that encouraged its employees to realize their full potential. Scott had adopted new management procedures that gave its employees a greater role in managing Scott's operations. Along with this increased responsibility, Scott had also modified its incentive programs so they would be based more on bottom-line financial measures. The firm believed that tying in personal financial rewards to the overall corporate plan would help improve its return on equity to an acceptable level.

Approximately 9,900 of Scott's hourly-paid work force were represented by labor unions. Since 1981, Scott had taken three costly strikes in an effort to reform work rules to reduce labor costs. A nine-month strike from late 1982 to mid-1983 at Scott's Maritime pulp mill alone was estimated to have cost Scott almost $.10 a share after taxes.[3] However, Scott management believed that it had to take strikes, if necessary, to demonstrate its determination to become a low-cost producer of paper products.

The External Environment: The Art of Papermaking

The modern day steps used to manufacture pulp and paper products operated in a very sophisticated manner. Pulp wood via truck, rail, or water arrived at the mill where it was unloaded and transferred to the barking drum area. The barking drum was a large revolving drum that removed the bark from the tree. The bark was salvaged as fuel for the mill's energy requirements—fuel that cut down on the use of crude oil.

The stripped logs were then taken by conveyor to the chipper, which reduced the logs to tiny chips. The chips were then sorted and packed into large tanks known as digesters. Here, the chips were cooked by steam in an alkaline solution to dissolve the lignin, a glue like substance, which binds the cellulose wood fibers together.

The pulp was then washed in vacuum washers to remove the alkaline chemicals. The pulp could be sold at this point in the pulp wood market or converted into paper products at the papermill.

Within the papermill, the pulp was put through disc refiners to flatten the fibers so they

Exhibit 8 Debt to Capital and Return on Assets Ratios for Leading Forest-Products Firms

Debt/Capital Ratio (%) **Company**	**1979**	**1980**	**1981**	**1982**	**1983**
Paper and Forest Products					
Boise Cascade	31.0	36.8	35.0	34.8	28.0
Champion International	31.7	28.7	31.5	34.1	33.1
Chesapeake Corp. of Virginia	22.6	20.4	26.7	26.6	19.4
Consolidated Papers	8.7	7.3	5.5	4.4	3.4
Crown Zellerbach	31.5	25.9	30.2	34.6	33.5
Domtar Inc.	21.8	22.4	24.4	29.5	28.0
Fort Howard Paper	16.4	15.1	10.2	6.9	16.4
Georgia-Pacific	32.2	32.8	35.7	37.1	33.9
Glatfelter (P.H.)	6.9	4.9	3.3	1.8	0.5
Great Northern Nekoosa	27.4	23.9	22.3	27.5	30.5
Hammermill Paper	35.2	31.7	35.4	38.3	33.1
International Paper	25.4	21.4	17.6	20.7	18.9
Kimberly-Clark	13.4	20.4	15.8	17.4	22.2
Longview Fibre	NA	NA	38.5	41.9	42.2
Louisiana-Pacific	17.5	14.8	12.8	17.2	16.2
MacMillan Bloedel	24.4	32.0	33.8	39.3	34.0
Mead Corp.	32.9	33.9	41.6	48.9	37.8
Pentair Inc.	19.5	32.0	37.4	17.7	20.6
Potlatch Corp.	36.1	36.0	32.6	32.3	28.8
St. Regis Corp.	27.1	32.3	32.5	35.4	29.6
Scott Paper	27.4	27.8	26.0	22.2	27.7
Sonoco Products	8.8	13.6	11.2	12.2	13.4
Southwest Forest Inds.	49.6	47.8	47.4	50.0	54.5
Stone Container	36.4	32.5	39.9	41.9	63.4
Union Camp Corp.	18.6	21.9	20.0	25.3	29.6
Wausau Paper Mills	34.8	50.6	45.6	43.3	41.5
Westvaco Corp.	29.0	27.2	24.8	23.5	25.1
Weyerhaeuser Co.	32.3	31.2	31.4	28.7	26.5
Willamette Inds.	22.1	32.9	39.4	43.8	38.6

NA—Not available. NM—Not meaningful.
Definition: Long-term debt as a % of invested capital.

would knit together on the paper making machines. The papermaking machines, some as long as a football field, had an endlessly moving screen, known as a fourdrinier wire, on which the pulp slurry was spread. It had a consistency of about 99.5% water and 0.5% wood fiber. As the mixture was deposited on the fourdrinier wire, the excess water poured down through the screen. The paper was then transferred to continuously moving felt blankets to remove still more water.

In the final process, the paper passed through colanders, which were heavy revolving steel rollers, that gave the sheet a finished, glazed surface. The paper was then wound onto jumbo rolls about 21 feet long and 8 feet in diameter. The jumbo rolls were cut into smaller rolls which were made to the buyer's specified size.

Exhibit 8 *(continued)*

Return on Assets (%) **Company**	**1979**	**1980**	**1981**	**1982**	**1983**
Paper and Forest Products					
Boise Cascade	8.2	5.5	4.4	0.3	2.2
Champion International	8.2	5.7	3.5	1.1	2.3
Chesapeake Corp. of Virginia	9.6	10.8	10.3	2.8	2.9
Consolidated Papers	16.8	14.4	13.4	9.1	10.4
Crown Zellerbach	6.5	4.3	3.0	NM	3.6
Domtar Inc.	10.7	8.1	4.7	0.7	3.0
Fort Howard Paper	15.3	14.7	15.3	15.1	10.9
Georgia-Pacific	8.9	5.6	3.3	1.0	2.1
Glatfelter (P.H.)	14.1	11.7	8.5	10.0	9.3
Great Northern Nekoosa	8.8	8.6	7.5	5.6	5.1
Hammermill Paper	5.7	5.8	6.0	3.2	3.2
International Paper	7.7	6.2	9.8	2.9	4.6
Kimberly-Clark	16.0	8.3	8.8	7.7	6.8
Longview Fibre	16.8	0.6	3.7	0.9	4.0
Louisiana-Pacific	10.1	5.4	2.3	NM	2.2
MacMillan Bloedel	9.6	5.9	NM	NM	0.1
Mead Corp.	8.8	7.3	5.3	NM	1.3
Pentair Inc.	14.7	12.0	6.2	7.4	6.2
Potlatch Corp.	8.1	4.9	5.2	1.9	3.5
St. Regis Corp.	7.2	6.9	6.4	1.6	1.9
Scott Paper	7.9	6.9	5.9	3.2	4.6
Sonoco Products	11.1	11.4	12.0	8.3	10.0
Southwest Forest Inds.	4.9	4.4	2.0	NM	NM
Stone Container	7.0	8.8	8.1	4.0	NM
Union Camp Corp.	11.3	10.7	9.8	6.5	6.0
Wausau Paper Mills	10.3	8.3	2.5	NM	3.6
Westvaco Corp.	7.8	8.0	8.3	4.8	4.3
Weyerhaeuser Co.	10.8	6.3	4.2	2.4	3.4
Willamette Inds.	11.2	8.2	3.4	0.6	2.4

NA—Not available. NM—Not meaningful.
Definition: Net income divided by average total assets.
From Standard and Poor's Industry Survey, *Building and Forest Products,* September 27, 1984, pp. B85-B86.

The Paper Products Industry

Paper manufacturing was the ninth largest industry in the United States. Paper mills directly employed over 263,000 workers while another 413,000 people were involved in converting and distributing paper products.

The paper industry was characterized by a high degree of vertical integration. Large companies owned or controlled their own timber resource base, saw mills, pulp and paper mills, and converting facilities. In addition, the industry was highly leveraged with average debt to capital ratios between 30% and 40% as shown in Exhibit 8. The exhibit also shows the return on assets ratios for leading firms which varies from 0% up to 10% for 1983. Finally, the industry was very capital intensive. A new papermill cost up to $250,000,000 and took four years to build.

Historically, paper and paperboard production were closely tied to the health of the U.S. economy. Furthermore, sales for many paper and paperboard items were based on a derived demand for some other product that varied with the economy. For example, corrugated box production depended upon the derived demand that various consumer and industrial products had for shipping containers. Similarly, newsprint production depended upon the level of newspaper advertising, which in turn fluctuated with the economy. Because the paper industry was so closely tied to the economy, it experienced an upswing in demand during the second half of 1983 as the economy rebounded. Industry analysts expected the paper industry to continue to prosper well into 1985 and perhaps beyond. This positive outlook was based upon an expectation of record paper production, further price increases for paper products, and a high operating utilization rate.

Because the paper industry incurred huge fixed costs for plant and equipment, operating utilization rates had a critical impact on profitability. The paper industry's overall operating utilization rate was around 97% of capacity in early 1984 and was expected to be even higher by the end of the year. An industry rule of thumb is that below 93% of capacity, gross operating margins for paper firms plummet as in the recession years 1982 and 1975, when rates were 88% and 81%, respectively, because competitors started discounting prices just to keep their machines running.

In the 1980s, industry leaders had become conservative about increasing capacity. They feared that huge federal budget deficits would have an adverse impact on the economy that would particularly hurt their industry. Consequently, most new production capacity and capital spending plans were for smaller projects located in the South. The advantages for locating new production facilities in that region were its longer growing season, proximity to sun belt markets, and its lower labor costs.

The prices and production levels for all grades of paper were up sharply in 1984. Kraft and coated paper production facilities were operating at full capacity. Linerboard production was at full capacity and commanded a price of $320 per ton. Tissue paper products were at 95% capacity, and prices were slightly higher than in 1983. Finally, market pulp, which was used by paper companies to make paper products, was selling for $540 per ton, approximately $100 higher than in 1983.

Industry Threats and Problems

Many of the large vertically integrated paper companies also sold forest products, such as lumber and poles. These products were even more affected by fluctuating interest rates and the general health of the economy. Rising interest rates since the beginning of the 1970s had decreased yearly housing starts, which caused profits to decrease significantly. The early 1980s marked the most severe recession in the forest-products industry since the 1930s. The timber side of the forest-products industry was still facing tough times in 1984, and some firms tried to raise cash by selling off some of their timberlands. The result was a glut of timber on the marketplace, which brought about a substantial decline in the market price of timberland throughout the United States.

The relative strength of the U.S. dollar abroad in 1984, along with the devaluation of some foreign currencies, reeked havoc with the profitability of some multinational paper companies. A continuing strong U.S. dollar would exacerbate the high U.S. trade deficit, thereby generating even greater political pressure for protectionist trade measures. This in turn could threaten future prospects for increased paper product exports. The devaluation of foreign currencies affected operating earnings of foreign affiliates, creating considerable exchange losses.

For instance, Scott Paper Company noted a substantial drop in its Mexican affiliate's earnings due to the devaluation of the peso by approximately 83% in 1982.

The stocks of most forest products firms were selling at low multiples of their earnings. This made many of them vulnerable to possible acquisition. In fact, St. Regis was acquired in 1983 by Champion International, and Fort Howard Paper Company had merged with Maryland Cup Corporation. Other firms like Southwest Forest Industries and Scott Paper Company had faced serious takeover attempts. Acquisitions were popular in this industry because buying additional production capacity was usually cheaper than building it from scratch.

Another threat to the paper firms was their heavy reliance on outside energy sources. Since 1970, the price for crude oil had risen substantially during the 1970s and its availability became less certain. Consequently, many paper firms had made a concerted effort to become more energy self-sufficient. Many firms had started to utilize more fully wood scraps and mill residues to run their mill operations. Some firms had spent hundreds of millions of dollars to convert plant boilers to coal or wood use in an effort to reduce dependency on limited fossil fuel reserves.

Still another threat was the increasing use of plastic as a substitute product for paper bags, sacks, and wraps. Many grocery stores and retailers were switching to plastic because it was stronger and cheaper than paper. Furthermore, plastics were increasingly being used to make disposable cups, bags, and plates.

Three innovations posed a threat to the paper industry. First, the increasing use of computers enabled firms to store tremendous amounts of information on computer files rather than on countless paper reports and documents. Fortunately, at least computers were creating the need for more and more computer paper. Second, the increasing use of microfilm and microfiche, made from plastic, reduced the need for storing bulky paper documents and library materials. Third, the advent of electronic mail, electronic banking, and teleconferencing may well reduce the demand for envelopes, white paper, bank checks, and even newspapers.

Buyers of Paper Products

The paper products industry offered a highly diverse assortment of products including consumer packaged products, specialty papers, pulp- and wood-based chemical derivatives, and timber products. As a result, a variety of distribution methods was used to reach customers in these diverse markets.

Generally, consumer packaged products were sold to supermarkets, grocery stores, and other mass merchandisers either through a direct sales force or wholesale distributors. Commercial packaged products were marketed to industrial and commercial users such as food services, chemical companies, furniture manufacturers, textile operations, and government institutions. These products were generally sold through a direct sales force because most products were specially made to the customer's needs.

Paper products which included specialty and printing papers were usually sold to converters and wholesale distributors. Once again, a direct sales force was used to market these products because orders were specially tailored to the individual customer's needs.

Wood products and pulp were usually sold in the commercial lumber market via a network of wholesalers and distributors. Buyers of these products included contractors, builders, and home-improvement supply centers.

Wood-based chemicals, which were by-products of pulp mill operations, were used mainly in coating, adhesives, printing inks, soaps, detergents, and plastics. Many of these types of products were bought by chemical companies and primary manufacturing operations. In turn, they marketed their products either through a direct sales force or wholesale distributors.

Competitor Profiles

The severe recession in the early 1980s brought about dramatic changes in the strategies used by many paper companies. Before this recession, many paper firms believed that capacity expansion and diversification were the keys to success. Since then, many firms re-evaluated and changed their strategies. Many paper companies were trying to become more cost competitive and starting to emphasize those products in which they had a competitive advantage. Many firms began to divest themselves of poor performing, nonessential business units. Conversely, the proceeds from these divestitures were being plowed back into their high-performance businesses. Capital spending programs were undertaken to lower operating costs and reduce energy dependence rather than increasing capacity. The paper firms hoped that these various actions would help improve bottomline profitability. Scott Paper's key competitors in the paper and pulp industry are overviewed in the following profiles.

International Paper Company

International Paper (I.P.), headquartered in New York City, was the world's largest papermaker. It manufactured and sold products primarily in three business segments: (1) pulp and paper, (2) packaging and packaging materials, and (3) wood products and resources. I.P.'s 1983 sales totaled $4,357,100,000, up some $342,000,000 from the previous year.

Pulp and paper, and packaging were its two dominant business segments. I.P. had invested over $4,000,000,000 since 1979 alone to modernize its plants. Paper and packaging products were sold through its own sales force directly to users or converters for manufacture. International Paper maintained manufacturing plants and sales offices throughout the United States as well as in various locations throughout the world. The firm owned approximately 7,000,000 acres of timberlands in the United States. Of this total, 67% was located in the South, 26% in the Northeast, and 7% in the West. These timberlands collectively supplied most of the raw materials for its mills.

Because of prospects for a continued slump in timber demand, I.P. was in the process of changing its product mix. In coming years, it planned to take the following actions: (1) increase its dependence on the white paper business, (2) eventually phase out its newsprint business, and (3) substantially cut back on timber harvesting.

In stressing its pulp and paper product segments, International Paper's new strategy was to improve the quality of its products. I.P. planned to do this by: (1) coordinating marketing and manufacturing review of product specifications, (2) emphasizing continually effective customer technical service and product development activities, (3) upgrading process control equipment, and (4) providing additional technical resources and training for its production and management employees.[4]

Westvaco Corporation

Westvaco Corporation was one of the major producers of paper and paperboard in the United States. Westvaco was also headquartered in New York City and employed approximately 15,000 people, of which 7,000 were unionized. It operated facilities in both the United States and Brazil.

Westvaco divided its businesses into three major segments: (1) bleached pulp, papers, and paper products, (2) unbleached papers and paper products, and (3) specialty chemicals. In 1983, Westvaco generated sales of $1,500,000,000, which was a 3% increase over 1982's sales. Ninety percent of its 1983 sales were in the pulp and paper products businesses. The principal markets for Westvaco's products were in the United States, and these markets were reached through the firm's own sales force.

Westvaco owned 1,373,650 acres of timberland in the United States and Brazil, which supplied 37% of its wood fiber needs. Another 1,022,000 acres of additional wood fiber were made available through its cooperative forest management program with private landowners.

Like Scott Paper, Westvaco had unveiled a five-year growth program that was designed to emphasize its strongest products and businesses. The overall objective of this program was to produce significant growth in its earning power and competitive position. Particular emphasis would be placed on increasing productivity, cost reduction, environmental protection, and maintaining its high business ethics and business conduct standards. During these five years, which ran from 1984 through 1988, Westvaco anticipated making capital expenditures of $1,600,000,000 to increase its papermaking capacity by 21%. Westvaco planned to expand and emphasize its bleached board and coated paper business. Finally, Westvaco planned a major increase in its R&D efforts for its products and services.

Union Camp Corporation

Union Camp, headquartered in Wayne, New Jersey, produced and sold paper, paperboard, packaging products, building materials, and chemicals. Almost all of Union Camp's sales were made east of the Rocky Mountains. Its 1983 sales totaled $1,688,254,000 with its paper and paperboard business segments contributing the most to its overall net income after taxes of $132,736,000.

Union Camp employed approximately 17,000 people of which 53% were represented by unions. It had exceptional relations with its unions and had not experienced a strike at any major facility since 1974. Union Camp used four mills to produce paper and paperboard. It satisfied approximately two-thirds of its mills' energy requirements by burning wood waste and spent liquor, which was a by-product of the pulping process. Union Camp owned or controlled 1,700,000 acres of timberland scattered throughout the Southeast, which provided 35% of its wood fiber requirements. Its remaining wood fiber needs were purchased from private landowners, other paper companies, and the federal government.

Union Camp's paper and paperboard operations produced paper bags for grocery outlets, merchandise bags for retailers, and multiwall bags for holding cement, feed, fertilizer, pet food, and mineral products. It also produced corrugated containers used to store and ship canned, bottled, and packaged products. Paper and paperboard were sold both by its own sales force and through wholesale distributors. Using Union Camp's own sales force, packaging materials were sold directly to industrial and agricultural users.

Hammermill Paper Company

Hammermill Paper Company, headquartered in Erie, Pennsylvania, was the largest producer of fine writing papers in the United States. Hammermill had five business groups, which were as follows: (1) fine and printing papers, (2) industrial packaging, (3) converted paper products, (4) wholesale distribution, and (5) forest products. Hammermill's 1983 sales were $1,622,695,000 with net profits after taxes of $32,548,000. It employed 13,000 people and owned 35 manufacturing or processing plants, which were all located within the United States. The company also owned or controlled 425,000 acres of timberland.

Hammermill's strategies were aimed at increasing market position and profit growth. They included:

1. Building leading positions in targeted market segments.
2. Achieving cost competitiveness in all of its operations.
3. Balancing five distinct but related businesses.
4. Expanding productive capacity by increments.
5. Maintaining a strong flexible financial position, which assures the availability of long-term capital.[5]

The prospects for Hammermill for 1985 and beyond were a bit cloudy. Several competitors were planning to start up new white paper machines during 1984 and 1985. This and the continued influx of imported white papers could cause a softening in the market.

Chesapeake Corporation of Virginia

Chesapeake Corporation of Virginia, headquartered in West Point, Virginia, was a major manufacturer of pulp and paper products. They included unbleached kraft paperboard and paper, and bleached hardwood market pulp. Its 1983 total sales were $273,800,000; net income after taxes was $12,500,000.

Chesapeake operated one paper mill located in West Point that employed 2,700 people. It owned 376,000 acres of timberland that supplied approximately 20% of its yearly wood requirements.

In 1983, Chesapeake launched the largest expansion program in its history. It allocated $73,000,000 to construct a new linerboard machine at its West Point mill, which was expected to be fully on line by 1985.

Scott Paper's Outlook for the Future

Scott Paper did better in 1983 than it did in 1982; however, its net profits after taxes from 1979 through 1981 had been even higher. Still Scott Paper was optimistic about the future. The general upturn in several key foreign economies along with a strong U.S. economy in 1984 provided hope for increased sales in the future. On the cost side, greater efficiency and higher productivity were beginning to show results from Scott's strategic plan and its five-year capital spending program. In addition, Scott found out that it could raise prices on some of its core products and so widen operating margins.

The product/market opportunities that Scott might pursue were numerous. The U.S. paper market was booming, and analysts expected the paper industry's operating capacity rates to remain high through 1985. Foreign competitors could not match the U.S. wood fiber base. Furthermore, Scott's steady capital spending in the 1980s in its domestic facilities had made many of Scott's mills some of the most efficient in the world.

With the demand for paper and forest products rapidly increasing in developing countries, Scott Paper might decide to pursue further this largely untapped market. As it stood in 1984, Scott Paper already had a number of international affiliates. While foreign markets might be very lucrative, they were subject to even greater economic swings than the U.S. economy. In effect, when the U.S. economy made a downturn, it had an even greater effect on economies in many foreign countries.

Scott's tree farm program for private landowners provided another opportunity to increase its wood fiber supply. Scott provided professional advice and technical assistance to private landowners in Maine and New Hampshire. This program could possibly be expanded to include private landowners within the southeastern and western regions of the United States as well. The opportunity to increase future yields and provide professional assistance might go a long way toward ensuring Scott's fiber needs for the future.

By increasing the use of its prelogging operations, Scott also had the opportunity to reduce further its dependence on fossil fuels. By expanding the use of this effective program to include other mill locations, Scott might be able to save a substantial amount of crude oil.

Unfortunately, Scott was involved with several legal matters. On September 17, 1981, Scott Paper Company, along with virtually all other pulp producers in the United States, Canada, Portugal, and Scandinavia that sold pulp in the Common Market, was charged with price fixing. If infringement was established, the firms could be fined and required to stop such practices. The case was still pending as of late 1984.

Domestically, Scott Paper Company faced another legal threat. It received a request from the Federal Trade Commission for information to determine whether Scott and numerous other U.S. pulp manufacturers had engaged in unfair methods of competition in violation of section 5 of the Federal Trade Commission Act. The investigation into the above allegation was likewise unresolved by 1984's end.

Finally, Scott was very concerned with another legal issue, namely the possibility of being acquired by Brascan Limited in the future. The situation was at a standstill in 1984, with Brascan holding 23.5% of Scott Paper's stock, and prohibited from increasing its stock holding above 25%. Unfortunately, the agreement between the two parties was set to expire on January 1, 1986, and Brascan's executives had expressed serious interests in gaining a majority control of Scott Paper's stock, whose board of directors already included four Brascan executives. Clearly, the future possibility of a takeover posed a serious threat that Scott's top management wanted to prevent at any costs.

Notes

1. Scott Paper Company, *Scott Paper Company Annual Report 1981,* pp. 6, 9.
2. "Down to the Core: Scott Paper Cuts Back to its Basic Business, Records a Rebound in Earnings," *Barron's,* April 16, 1984, p. 9.
3. Ibid., p. 10.
4. International Paper, *International Paper Company 1983 Annual Report,* p. 11.
5. Hammermill Paper Company, *Hammermill Paper Company Annual Report, 1983,* pp. 2-3.

Case 24 Update*

Letter to Shareholders

Fellow Shareholders and Employees:

As the cover of our 1987 Annual Report stated, "Scott's goal is to be better than the best of our competitors in all aspects of our business: realizing the full potential of our people, satisfying the needs of our customers, managing growth, generating superior financial returns and contributing to the quality of life in our communities. We will be satisfied with nothing less than preeminence in everything we do." In reaching this goal, we will be fulfilling Scott's vision of creating substantial wealth and value for our customers, employees, shareholders and other key stakeholders.

One of the key areas in which we must achieve preeminence is generating competitively attractive financial returns for our shareholders. Our objective is to achieve and sustain a return on common shareholders' equity of at least 18%. This will require improving earnings and cash flow in the future by 15% to 20% annually through increased sales and improved profit margins.

I am pleased to say that in 1988 Scott continued its excellent progress toward the attainment of its financial objectives. We achieved all-time records for sales, income from operations, net income, and primary earnings per share. Net income increased 71% to $400.9 million from $233.8 million. Primary earnings per share were $5.23 compared with $3.05 a year ago, a 71% increase. Income from operations rose 65% to $732.3 million from $442.5 million. Sales were $4.7 billion, up 15% from 1987.

Our 1988 earnings reflect nonrecurring items which resulted in a net gain of $1.22 per share in the third quarter. These items include the sale of Brunswick Pulp & Paper Company, which resulted in a gain of $1.53, and special changes amounting to $.31. Excluding these nonrecurring items, primary earnings per share would have been $4.01, more than 31% above 1987, our best previous year. Return on common shareholders' equity, excluding Brunswick and other nonrecurring items, rose to 18.1% in 1988 from 16.1% the prior year.

As a result of our performance, your Board of Directors also approved a two-for-one stock split of your common shares in 1988 and twice during the year increased the quarterly dividend, resulting in a total increase in the dividend rate of 17.6%.

In addition to our excellent performance in 1988, I believe it is important to note that in the last six years, Scott's sales increased 96%, primary earnings per share have risen an average of 31% per year, and return on shareholders' equity has increased from 5.3% to 18.1%. Dividends were increased 51% and our stock price appreciated 288% compared with 103% for the *S&P 400.*

These results continue to reflect the superior performance of both our worldwide personal care and cleaning and U.S. printing and publishing papers businesses. To support these businesses, major capital investment programs were announced, or continued, during 1988. The most substantial commitment was in our printing and publishing papers business. Our S.D. Warren subsidiary announced a $475 million capital program designed to further strengthen our leadership position in the coated papers industry. The expansion program includes the construction of

*Source: Excerpts from Scott Paper Company 1988 annual report.

a third advanced-technology paper machine at our Somerset mill in Skowhegan, Maine and the rebuild of one of our heavyweight coated paper machines in Muskegon, Michigan. In the last two years, Warren also has invested almost $200 million in other capital projects at its facilities in Muskegon and Westbrook, Maine.

Scott Worldwide, our personal care and cleaning business, took important steps forward in 1988 to capitalize on the significant growth opportunities in the worldwide foodservice business. We acquired the units of Texstyrene Corporation which make polystyrene foam cups, food containers and the base materials for these products. In January 1989, we completed the purchase of Cross Paperware in the U.K., a manufacturer of an extensive, high-quality disposable foodservice product line for the catering and retail industries. Cross is another key element of our aggressive business strategy initiated in 1987 by the announcement of a $250 million expansion program designed to enhance Scott's leadership position in the high-growth European personal care and cleaning market.

In 1988, Scott Worldwide also announced several major capital projects in the Pacific and Canada in order to build on our strong position in those regions.

As part of our global fiber strategy, Scott joined with two other firms in 1988 in the purchase of a partially completed pulp mill in Chile and 80,000 acres of forestland, of which 29,000 acres are maturing eucalyptus trees and the remainder are to be planted with eucalyptus seedlings. Expected to be completed by 1991, the Chilean facility is the second eucalyptus pulp mill that Scott has acquired during the past two years, the first having been purchased in northern Spain.

To sustain our momentum and achieve our growth objectives, we must continue to strengthen our good businesses, shed our weak businesses or those which do not fit our long-term strategy, and add strong related new businesses. Consistent with these objectives, Scott and The Mead Corporation sold their joint ownership in Brunswick Pulp & Paper Company and related timberlands to Georgia-Pacific Corporation for $665 million. Our decision to sell Brunswick was based upon the fact that the fiber it manufactured was no longer ideal for our worldwide paper business. We are focusing our strategy on fibers like eucalyptus, northern softwood kraft and recycled fiber—none of which Brunswick produced.

During 1988, we continued our commitment to improve and contribute to the quality of life in the communities in which we operate. This was reflected in the implementation and continuation of a wide range of programs. Examples of a few of these efforts were: the contribution of more than $450,000 to those organizations in which our employees volunteer time and donate money; a major grant to organizations in our plant communities fighting the battle against AIDS; and sponsorship of the Project ORBIS mission to Thailand. Project ORBIS is the world's only flying eye-care hospital and teaching university. We also donated $1.4 million to Ronald McDonald Houses across the U.S. and in several other countries, bringing to almost $4.5 million Scott's total contribution over the past three years. These donations are generated through the sales of Scott consumer products.

Without question, our record-breaking success in 1988 and the improvements made since the early 1980's, would not have been possible had it not been for the dedication and efforts of the people who make up Scott Paper Company. We are committed to creating an environment in which each employee can develop to his or her full potential. In 1988, I believe we made progress toward this end with new programs to expand the active involvement and impact of our employees in helping Scott achieve its vision of preeminence. Consistent with these objectives, we have also broadened significantly the ability of our salaried employees to share in the benefits of our results through their participation in a variable compensation program tied into different levels of financial accomplishment.

As previously announced, Charles D. Dickey, Jr. did not stand for reelection to Scott's Board of Directors at the Company's 1988 Annual Meeting, having reached the mandatory retirement age for directors. He has been a director for twenty-seven years and served as chairman of the board from 1971 until 1983. Charley contributed more than 41 years of distinguished service to Scott and earned the respect and affection of us all.

While Scott's 1988 performance was outstanding from many perspectives, we still have a great deal to accomplish to achieve our vision of preeminence. Looking back at our progress over the last six years, it is clear that our strategies are sound, our businesses are strong, and we are positioning ourselves to take maximum advantage of the growth opportunities in our various markets. We remain firm in our commitment to be the best at everything we do and to consistently provide superior wealth and value to our customers, employees, shareholders and other key stakeholders. We appreciate your continuing contributions and support.

Philip E. Lippincott
Chairman and Chief Executive Officer
February 21, 1989

Scott Paper Company Business Segments—Consolidated Operations, 1986–1988

BUSINESS SEGMENTS — CONSOLIDATED OPERATIONS

Scott Paper Company's operations are now reported in two segments. Prior to 1988, the Company's operations were reported in three segments: Personal Care and Cleaning; Printing and Publishing Papers; and Pulp, Forest Products and Minerals. In 1988, the Company's Pulp, Forest Products and Minerals operations were combined within the other two segments as they are primarily focused on supplying these segments with raw materials for production.

Scott's two business segments are:

Personal Care and Cleaning — Includes a broad range of sanitary paper products, foodservice products, health care products, personal cleansing products and systems and nonwoven materials. Pulp and timberlands operations which are vertically integrated with those businesses are also included.

Printing and Publishing Papers — Includes printing, publishing and specialty papers and those pulp and timberlands operations vertically integrated with those businesses.

The Company's investment in unconsolidated international affiliates of $210.7 million in 1988, $185.0 million in 1987 and $136.4 million in 1986 is included in Corporate assets. Information concerning the operations of international equity affiliates is shown on pages 46 and 47.

The business segments information presented for 1987 and 1986 has been restated for comparative purposes. Also, on a comparative basis, the Personal Care and Cleaning segment's income before taxes was $185.8 million in 1985 and $186.0 million in 1984, and the Printing and Publishing Papers segment's income before taxes was $149.0 million in 1985 and $160.9 million in 1984.

YEAR 1988	*(Millions)*	*Sales*	*Income Before Taxes*	*Identifiable Assets(1)*	*Capital Expenditures*	*Depreciation and Cost of Timber Harvested*
Business Segment	Personal Care and Cleaning	$3,470.3	$335.3	$2,798.6	$308.2	$167.1
	Printing and Publishing Papers	1,256.1	246.2	1,399.7	193.0	99.8
	Total business segments	4,726.4	581.5	4,198.3	501.2	266.9
	Brunswick sale	—	207.3	—	—	—
	Corporate	—	(56.5)	958.0	7.5	4.6
	Interest expense	—	147.5	—	—	—
	Other income and (expense)	—	16.9	—	—	—
	Consolidated total	$4,726.4	$601.7	$5,156.3	$508.7	$271.5
Geographic Area	United States	$3,502.5	$477.0	$3,165.0		
	Europe	1,092.8	97.9	926.0		
	Pacific	131.1	13.9	107.3		
	Latin America(2)	—	(7.3)	—		
	Subtotal	4,726.4	581.5	4,198.3		
	Brunswick sale	—	207.3	—		
	Corporate	—	(56.5)	958.0		
	Interest expense	—	147.5	—		
	Other income and (expense)	—	16.9	—		
	Consolidated total	$4,726.4	$601.7	$5,156.3		

(1) Includes investments in supplier and other affiliates of: Personal Care and Cleaning — $1.6; Corporate — $41.5, which includes $39.6 in affiliates located in Chile.

(2) Expenses represent regional costs for equity affiliates.

(continued)

YEAR 1987	(Millions)	Sales	Income Before Taxes	Identifiable Assets (1)	Capital Expenditures	Depreciation and Cost of Timber Harvested
Business Segment	Personal Care and Cleaning	$3,014.3	$307.0	$2,577.0	$218.0	$151.5
	Printing and Publishing Papers	1,107.7	182.5	1,284.6	154.2	85.5
	Total business segments	4,122.0	489.5	3,861.6	372.2	237.0
	Corporate	—	(47.0)	618.9	7.9	9.8
	Interest expense	—	139.0	—	—	—
	Other income and (expense)	—	8.6	—	—	—
	Consolidated total	$4,122.0	$312.1	$4,480.5	$380.1	$246.8
Geographic Area	United States	$3,077.7	$397.0	$2,957.6		
	Europe	953.7	89.6	806.7		
	Pacific	90.6	8.0	97.3		
	Latin America (2)	—	(5.1)	—		
		4,122.0	489.5	3,861.6		
	Corporate	—	(47.0)	618.9		
	Interest expense	—	139.0	—		
	Other income and (expense)	—	8.6	—		
	Consolidated total	$4,122.0	$312.1	$4,480.5		

(1) Includes investments in supplier affiliates, whose operations were predominantly domestic, of: Personal Care and Cleaning — $38.3; Printing and Publishing Papers — $1.0.

(2) Expenses represent regional costs for equity affiliates.

YEAR 1986	(Millions)	Sales	Income Before Taxes	Identifiable Assets (1)	Capital Expenditures	Depreciation and Cost of Timber Harvested
Business Segment	Personal Care and Cleaning	$2,487.2	$254.2	$2,260.0	$227.7	$120.9
	Printing and Publishing Papers	949.8	146.8	1,240.2	187.3	77.2
	Total business segments	3,437.0	401.0	3,500.2	415.0	198.1
	Corporate	—	(32.6)	439.2	5.7	4.7
	Interest expense	—	122.0	—	—	—
	Other income and (expense)	—	28.7	—	—	—
	Consolidated total	$3,437.0	$275.1	$3,939.4	$420.7	$202.8
Geographic Area	United States	$2,783.3	$337.5	$2,859.5		
	Europe	585.4	59.8	575.5		
	Pacific	68.3	7.3	65.2		
	Latin America (2)	—	(3.6)	—		
		3,437.0	401.0	3,500.2		
	Corporate	—	(32.6)	439.2		
	Interest expense	—	122.0	—		
	Other income and (expense)	—	28.7	—		
	Consolidated total	$3,437.0	$275.1	$3,939.4		

(1) Includes investments in supplier affiliates, whose operations were predominantly domestic, of: Personal Care and Cleaning — $37.5; Printing and Publishing Papers — $1.9.

(2) Expenses represent regional costs for equity affiliates.

Scott Paper Company Ten-Year Financial Summary, 1979–1988

TEN-YEAR FINANCIAL SUMMARY

Scott Paper Company

(Millions)	**1988**	1987(2)	1986(3)	1985	1984	1983	1982	1981(4)	1980	1979
Sales	**$4,726.4**	$4,122.0	$3,437.0	$3,049.5	$2,847.3	$2,707.6	$2,415.9	$2,442.9	$2,217.7	$2,035.9
Costs and expenses										
Product costs	**3,115.3**	2,713.6	2,264.8	2,019.1	1,905.1	1,921.0	1,676.5	1,667.9	1,490.3	1,356.8
Marketing and distribution	**824.1**	744.1	659.7	577.8	510.6	482.5	489.3	529.0	518.9	434.8
Research, administration and general	**248.0**	206.3	157.5	146.1	127.3	117.1	109.2	100.4	95.4	90.1
Other	**(193.3)**	15.5	(13.4)	10.3	(1.9)	(18.0)	4.0	7.0	14.7	(14.5)
	3,994.1	3,679.5	3,068.6	2,753.3	2,541.1	2,502.6	2,279.0	2,304.3	2,119.3	1,867.2
Income from operations	**732.3**	442.5	368.4	296.2	306.2	205.0	136.9	138.6	98.4	168.7
Interest expense	**147.5**	139.0	122.0	81.4	64.2	42.4	28.0	37.2	36.5	36.1
Other income and (expense)	**16.9**	8.6	28.7	14.4	43.2	3.9	91.9	65.3	75.7	6.7
Income before taxes	**601.7**	312.1	275.1	229.2	285.2	166.5	200.8	166.7	137.6	139.3
Taxes on income	**237.8**	117.1	106.3	75.4	104.2	66.4	94.2	67.2	48.2	46.3
Income before share of earnings of international equity affiliates	**363.9**	195.0	168.8	153.8	181.0	100.1	106.6	99.5	89.4	93.0
Share of earnings (loss) of international equity affiliates	**37.0**	38.8	17.7	47.3	6.0	23.6	(32.1)	33.8	43.6	43.5
Net income	**400.9**	233.8	186.5	201.1	187.0	123.7	74.5	133.3	133.0	136.5
Dividends on preferred shares	**.3**	.3	.3	.3	2.6	6.3	5.8	.3	.3	.3
Earnings for common shares	**$ 400.6**	$ 233.5	$ 186.2	$ 200.8	$ 184.4	$ 117.4	$ 68.7	$ 133.0	$ 132.7	$ 136.2
Dollars per common share(1)										
Earnings — primary	**$5.23**	$3.05	$2.48	$2.26	$1.91	$1.29	$.80	$1.61	$1.71	$1.75
— fully diluted	**5.21**	3.05	2.47	2.26	1.91	1.29	.80	1.61	1.71	1.75
Dividends	**.755**	.68	.635	.605	.56	.50	.50	.50	.50	.45
Market price — high-low	**42¾-32⅜**	43½-27½	33⁵⁄₁₆-24	26⅛-16¹¹⁄₁₆	17⁷⁄₁₆-12⅝	16⅛-9⁹⁄₁₆	10½-6¹³⁄₁₆	14¼-7½	11¾-6⅝	10⁷⁄₁₆-6¹³⁄₁₆
Income from operations as a percentage of sales	**15.5%**	10.7%	10.7%	9.7%	10.8%	7.6%	5.7%	5.7%	4.4%	8.3%
Debt as a percentage of total capitalization	**38.2%**	40.6%	45.5%	48.7%	34.5%	26.6%	25.4%	27.5%	29.9%	29.6%
Return on common shareholders' equity	**23.1%**	16.1%	14.7%	14.1%	12.2%	8.6%	5.3%	11.0%	12.4%	14.1%
(Millions)										
Total assets at year-end	**$5,156.3**	$4,480.5	$3,939.4	$3,517.2	$3,313.3	$2,846.3	$2,490.8	$2,356.3	$2,061.8	$1,876.5
Long-term debt at year-end	**1,450.3**	1,381.9	1,412.3	1,379.1	640.4	582.5	467.7	506.4	480.6	428.5
Redeemable preferred shares	**—**	—	—	—	—	17.6	45.0	—	—	—
Capital expenditures for plant and timber resources	**508.7**	380.1	420.7	514.2	285.8	225.3	390.9	325.8	255.6	184.5
Depreciation and cost of timber harvested	**271.5**	246.8	202.8	167.3	158.8	149.6	131.4	120.9	112.4	107.0
Common shares(1)										
Average shares outstanding (Millions) — primary	**76.6**	76.5	75.0	88.8	96.4	91.0	85.4	82.8	77.8	77.8
— fully diluted	**76.9**	76.5	75.4	88.8	96.4	91.0	85.4	82.8	77.8	77.8
Number of shareholders (Thousands)	**44.2**	44.5	47.5	52.4	55.9	59.1	65.0	70.1	74.7	77.7
Number of employees (Thousands)	**27.0**	25.4	24.9	22.2	20.6	20.9	20.5	21.6	21.9	22.2

(1) Common share data have been restated to reflect a two-for-one split of the common shares effective March 1988.

(2) Certain accounting reclassifications (not affecting net income) have been made to present more clearly the results of operations for years prior to 1988.

(3) Reflects the adoption of FAS 87, Employers' Accounting for Pensions, for U.S. plans, which reduced 1986 pension cost and thereby increased net income by $10.6 million and primary earnings per share by $.28.

(4) In 1981 Scott adopted FAS 52, Foreign Currency Translation and, as permitted, financial statements for prior years were not restated.

COMPANY OPERATIONS

SCOTT PAPER COMPANY

Executive Offices
Scott Plaza
Philadelphia, PA 19113
U.S.A.
(215) 522-5000

SCOTT WORLDWIDE — PERSONAL CARE AND CLEANING

Philadelphia, PA

North America

United States
Chester, PA; Dover, DE; Everett, WA; Ft. Edward, NY; Hattiesburg, MS; Landisville, NJ; Marinette, Milwaukee, Oconto Falls and Oshkosh, WI; Mobile, AL; Rogers, AR; San Antonio, TX; Winslow, ME

Escuhbia Oil Company
Alabama

Excell Paper Sales Company
Lester, PA

Scott Container Products Group, Inc.
Alexandria, VA; City of Industry, CA; Des Plaines, IL; El Campo, TX; Higginsville, MO; Mt. Sterling, OH; Phoenix and Tolleson, AZ; Renton, WA; Shreveport, LA; Stone Mountain, GA; Tinton Falls, NJ

Scott Polymers, Inc.
Fort Worth and Saginaw, TX

Three Rivers Timber Company
Washington

WinCup, Inc.
(87.5% owned) Rancho Dominguez, CA

Timberlands in Alabama, Mississippi and Washington

Canada
Cape Chignecto Lands Limited

Scott Maritimes Limited

Scott Paper Limited
(50% owned)

Scott Polymers, Ltd.

Parrsboro, Nova Scotia

Timberlands in Nova Scotia

Europe
Belgium: *Scott Continental; Scott Paper Coordination Center; Scott Paper International Trade Venture (Europe)*

France: *Scott, S.A.*

Germany (Federal Republic of Germany): *Scott Paper GmbH Nonwovens*

Italy: *Scott S.p.A.*

Portugal: *Scott Paper Portugal Lda.*

Spain: *Scott Iberica, S.A.*

United Kingdom: *Scott Limited; Cross Paperware Limited*[1]

Latin America
Argentina: *Celulosa Jujuy, S.A.* (33.3% owned)[2]

Brazil: *COPA — Companhia de Papéis* (49% owned)

Costa Rica: *Scott Paper Company de Costa Rica, S.A.* (40% owned)[3]

Mexico: *Compañia Industrial de San Cristóbal, S.A.* (48.8% owned)[4]

Pacific
Hong Kong: *Sandollar Limited*

Japan: *Sanyo Scott Company Limited* (50% owned)

Korea (Republic of Korea): *Ssangyong Paper Co., Ltd.* (34% owned)

Malaysia: *Scott Paper (Malaysia) Sdn. Bhd.*

Singapore: *Scott Paper (Singapore) Pte. Ltd.*

Taiwan (Republic of China): *Taiwan Scott Paper Corporation* (66.7% owned)

Thailand: *Scott Trading Limited* (49.8% owned); *Thai-Scott Paper Company Limited* (69.2% owned)

S.D. WARREN COMPANY — PRINTING AND PUBLISHING PAPERS

Boston, MA

Mobile, AL; Muskegon, MI; Skowhegan, Westbrook and Winslow, ME

Skylark, Inc., Maine

Timberlands in Maine

Belgium: *Scott Graphics International* (a division of Scott Continental)

UNCONSOLIDATED SUPPLIER AND OTHER AFFILIATES

Mountain Tree Farm Company (50% owned)
Tacoma, WA

Canada: *Canso Chemicals Limited* (33.3% owned)

Chile: *Forestal e Industrial Santa Fe, S.A.* (20% owned); *Forestal Colcura, S.A.* (20% owned); *Forestal y Agricola Monte Aguila Ltda.* (20% owned)

Cabin Bluff Management Company (50% owned)

Cabin Bluff Partners (50% owned)

OTHER

Bermuda: *Riscott Insurance, Ltd.*

Operations are classified to conform to the Company's management reporting responsibilities during 1988. All operations are 100% owned, directly or indirectly, by Scott Paper Company, unless otherwise indicated. All operations which are shown as being more than 50% owned are consolidated for financial reporting purposes. All unconsolidated operations are reported as described in the Financial Review.

(1) This subsidiary was acquired in January 1989.

(2) The Company has entered into a contract to sell its interest in this affiliate.

(3) The Company's ownership of this affiliate was increased to 51% in January 1989.

(4) An additional 3.1% of this affiliate is owned by a 40%-owned Mexican affiliate.

Case 25

Manville Corporation (1988)[1]

> Perhaps no other mineral is so woven into the fabric of American life as is asbestos. Impervious to heat and fibrous—it is the only mineral that can be woven into cloth—asbestos is spun into fireproof clothing and theater curtains, as well as into such household items as noncombustible drapes, rugs, pot holders, and ironing-board covers. Mixed into slurry, asbestos is sprayed onto girders and walls to provide new buildings with fireproof insulation. It is used in floor tiles, roofing felts, and in most plasterboards and wallboards. Asbestos is also an ingredient of plaster and stucco and of many paints and putties. This "mineral of a thousand uses"—an obsolete nickname: the present count stands at around 3,000 uses—is probably present in some form or other in every home, school, office building, and factory in this country. Used in brake linings and clutch facings, in mufflers and gaskets, in sealants and caulking, and extensively used in ships, asbestos is also a component of every modern vehicle, including space ships.

This was written by columnist Bruce Porter in 1973, just as the dangers of breathing asbestos dust were becoming widely recognized by the general public. The insert below describes certain health effects of breathing asbestos dust.

U.S. consumption of asbestos rose from around 200,000 metric tons per year during the 1930s to a plateau of about 700,000 metric tons a year in the 1950s, 1960s, and early 1970s. U.S. asbestos use dropped sharply after 1972, to just over 100,000 metric tons in 1985.[2] World asbestos production continued to expand rapidly until about the mid 1970s, when it abruptly plateaued at about 4.6 million metric tons a year. Through 1976 world production barely dropped, apparently because increased shipments to developing countries offset declining usage elsewhere.[3]

From about the turn of the century, Johns-Manville Corporation (renamed Manville Corporation in 1981) was the world's leading asbestos company, involved in mining and sale of the raw fibers as well as development, manufacture, and marketing of intermediate and finished asbestos products. Manville was the main target of a trickle of asbestos-health (A-H) lawsuits in the 1920s and early thirties which would become a flood by the 1980s.

> **Asbestos Diseases.** Ingested asbestos causes mechanical injury to moving tissue, especially the lungs. The microscopic fibers are impervious to body fluids and oxygen and are almost impossible to filter out of air. The constant motion of the lungs causes tissue to be penetrated and cut by the fibers. This leads to progressive and irreversible scarring, thickening, and calcification of the lungs and their linings, a condition called asbes-

[1]Prepared by Arthur Sharplin, McNeese State University, Lake Charles, Louisiana 70601. The assistance and encouragement of the Center for Business Ethics at Bentley College in Waltham, Massachusetts, of which the author is a fellow, is gratefully acknowledged as is the research assistance provided by Cam Leach and Jeanette Savoie. Reprinted with permission.

[2]Barry I. Castleman, *Asbestos: Medical and Legal Aspects* (Clifton, NJ: Prentice-Hall Law and Business, 1987), 614.

[3]Ibid., 636-7.

tosis. A rare and always-fatal pleural cancer, mesothelioma, is strongly connected with asbestos exposure as are increased incidence and severity of lung cancer and many other respiratory ailments. The first outward symptoms of asbestos disease typically appear ten to thirty years after exposure begins. But early damage is easily detectable by x-rays and some cancers and respiratory deficiencies show up after only a year or two.

On the evening of August 25, 1982, the Manville board of directors was provided a briefing on bankruptcy reorganization. A petition for protection from creditors under Chapter 11 of the U.S. bankruptcy code had already been prepared. It was approved by the board that night and was filed the next day. It would be more than six years before a plan to emerge from court protection would be final. Many of the asbestos victims would die in the meantime. And the tens of thousands who had been held off during those years by the bankruptcy court would find their claims subordinated to those of commercial creditors as well as to other interests.

Company Background

Until the seventies, Manville was a success by the usual standards. Incorporated in 1901, the company saw consistent growth in sales and profits. Dividends were paid every year except for the war years of 1915–1916 and the depths of the Depression in 1933–1934. Manville was one of the "Dow-Jones Industrial Thirty" for many years.

In the decades before 1970, Manville's sales grew somewhat slower than the Gross National Product. But the company benefitted from relatively low fixed costs, due to a largely depleted and depreciated capital base and the total absence of long-term debt in the capital structure. With low operating and financial leverage, the firm was able to adapt to sales downturns in 1957, 1960, 1967, and 1970 and still earn profits in each of those years. By 1970, Manville had about $400 million ($1.1 billion in 1986 dollars) in book value net worth garnered almost entirely from the mining, manufacture, and sale of asbestos products, for which it still held a dominant market position. Appendix A describes selected pre-1970s events concerning asbestos and health.

During the 1960s, a number of the senior officials who had been with Manville since the 1930s died or retired. Compared to just the 1966 board of directors, the 1970 board had a majority of new members. In 1970, departing from a tradition of promoting from within, the board of directors installed an outsider, psychologist Richard Goodwin, as president. Thus began a prolonged effort to diversify Manville away from asbestos and to change its image.

Goodwin arranged to move the corporate headquarters from its old Madison Avenue brick building to the Denver countryside. There, he purchased the 10,000 acre Ken Caryl Ranch and planned a luxurious "world headquarters," the first phase of which was to cost $60 million.

Goodwin also led the company through more than twenty small acquisitions—in lighting systems, golf carts, irrigation sprinklers, and other products. In the process, Manville's long-term debt went from zero to $196 million and fixed costs increased several fold. A short, steep recession in 1975 cut Manville's profits in half, back to 1970 levels. U.S. asbestos consumption had begun a rapid decline, which was to accelerate and total more than fifty percent by 1982.

And Manville was suffering reverses in its fight against the asbestos tort lawsuits. In 1972, Manville and five other asbestos companies had lost the landmark Clarence Borel asbestos tort lawsuit. The appeals court in that case wrote, "The evidence . . . tended to establish that none of the defendants ever tested its product to determine its effect on industrial insulation workers. . . . The unpalatable facts are that in the twenties and thirties the hazards of working with asbestos were recognized.[4]

[4]Clarence Borel v. Fibreboard Paper Products Corporation, et al., 493 F. 2d. 1076–1109 (5th Cir. 1973).

In an April 1976 deposition, Dr. Kenneth Smith, former Manville medical director, told of his knowledge of asbestos dangers during the 1940s. He also revealed his 1950 finding that the lungs of 704 of the 708 Manville asbestos workers he studied showed asbestos damage. He went on to describe his unsuccessful efforts to get caution labels put on Manville asbestos products.[5]

Then, in April 1977, the "Raybestos-Manhattan Correspondence" was discovered by asbestos plaintiff attorneys. Included were many letters and memoranda among Manville officials and other asbestos industry executives. Most were written during the 1930s. After reading the papers, a South Carolina judge wrote, "The Raybestos-Manhattan Correspondence very arguably shows a pattern of denial of disease and attempts at suppression of information which is highly probative [and] reflects a conscious effort by the industry in the 1930s to downplay, or arguably suppress, the dissemination of information to employees and the public . . ."[6]

Confronted with the new and damning evidence, a growing number of juries awarded punitive damages against Manville during 1981 and 1982, as much as a million dollars per claimant. And many suits named current and former Manville executives as defendants.[7] When Manville sought bankruptcy court protection in August of 1982, asbestos-health claims against the company numbered 20,000 and new suits were being filed at the rate of three an hour every business day.[8] The average cost per case, the company said, was "sharply higher" than in prior years, averaging $40,000 per claim.[9]

The managers at Manville were particularly vulnerable to charges of conspiring to hide past sins of the company, if not for committing them. The top five executives had each been with the firm since 1952 or before. All had been senior officials since at least the early seventies.[10]

The outside directors were eminent in their respective fields, but they too could hardly claim noninvolvement. Among them were the Dean of the School of Architecture at Princeton and the Dean of the Graduate School of Business Administration at New York University. The latter had previously been chief executive of American Can Company. Also included were the chief executive of Ideal Basic Industries, Inc., who had earlier been elected three times as Governor of Colorado, the head of Phelps Dodge Corporation, and the top managers of three other companies.[11] All but two of the eleven directors in 1982 had over ten years tenure, averaging seventeen years on the board. Six had joined the board in the sixties and two others, the inside directors, had worked for Manville since about 1950.[12]

Five months after the Smith deposition, the nine outside directors of Manville demanded the resignation of Richard Goodwin. According to Goodwin, the three directors who transmitted the demand refused to explain their action.[13] A

[5]Dr. Kenneth W. Smith, Discovery deposition, Louisville Trust Company, Administrator of the estate of William Virgil Sampson, v. Johns-Manville Corporation, File no. 164–122, (Court of Common Pleas, Jefferson County, Kentucky, April 21, 1987). A Manville attorney later claimed Smith was an alcoholic.

[6]Amended Order (Survival and Wrongful Death Actions), Bennie M. Barnett, Administrator, for Gordon Luther Barnett, deceased, v. Owens-Corning Fiberglass Corp., et al., (Court of Common Pleas, Greenville County, South Carolina, August 23, 1978), 10 and 5.

[7]Ronald L. Motley (leading asbestos plaintiff attorney), telephone conversation with author, October 9, 1987, Charleston, South Carolina. Also see Manville Corporation, *Quarterly Report on U.S. Securities and Exchange Commission Form 10-Q,* for quarter ended June 30, 1982, II-8 (discussion of Louisiana cases).

[8]G. Earl Parker, "The Manville Decision," Paper presented at the symposium "Bankruptcy Proceedings—The Effect on Product Liability," conducted by Andrews Publications, Inc., Miami, March 1983, 3.

[9]Manville Corporation, "Manville Files for Reorganization," media release, August 26, 1982, 2.

[10]Manville Corporation, *1982 Proxy Statement,* March 25, 1982, 12; *Moody's Industrial Manual,* 2 (New York: Moody's Investor Service, 1971), 1424; (1972), 3222; (1973), 2907–8; and (1974), 2040.

[11]Manville Corporation, *1982 Proxy Statement,* March 25, 1982, 4–7.

[12]Ibid., 4–7.

[13]Herbert E. Meyer, "Shootout at the Johns-Manville Corral," *Fortune,* October 1976, 146–54.

later Manville chief executive would claim Goodwin had been a womanizer and an alcoholic.[14]

John A. McKinney, Manville's legal—who had joined the company before 1950—took over as chief executive. McKinney divested many of the Goodwin acquisitions and turned his attention to what he called "aggressive defense" of the asbestos lawsuits and the search for a "substantial acquisition." He also made plans for a $200 million expansion in the company's fiberglass operations. In his 1977 "Presidents Review," McKinney wrote, "we do not expect asbestos fiber to dominate J-M earnings to the extent it has in the past."[15]

Ideal Basic Industries (IBI), a major producer of potash and portland cement, spurned a Manville buyout initiative in early 1978. It may have been important that the chief executive of IBI, John A. Love was on the Manville board of directors. Next, Manville began a takeover battle (with Texas Eastern Corporation) for Olinkraft Corporation, a wood products company concentrated in paperboard and paper. Olinkraft's main assets were about 600,000 acres of prime southern timberland and several paper mills.

Manville won the contest and closed the deal in the last half of 1978. The purchase price was $595 million, 2.24 times book value and over twice recent market value. About half was paid in cash and the rest was represented by a new issue of cumulative preferred stock which was required to be repurchased beginning in 1987.

The directors and officers were guaranteed indemnification by Manville, a contract they had the company reaffirm in 1981.[16] The importance of such protection is illustrated by attacks by asbestos victims against the estate of Vandiver Brown, Manville vice president and secretary during the 1930s, attacks which would continue into the mid-1980s.[17]

But ordinary business problems after 1978 imperiled the managers' indemnity and rendered even their jobs insecure, not to mention the professional embarrassment failure might bring such illustrious directors and executives. That year, the company began what seemed an irreversible downward slide financially. Revenues (in 1986 dollars) fell from $2.74 billion in 1978 to a $2.18 billion annual rate for the first half of 1982. And earnings available to common stock (also in 1986 dollars) simply evaporated, going from $198 million to an $85 million annual-rate *loss*.[18] Earnings available to common stock does not include dividends on the debt-equivalent preferred stock issued in the Olinkraft acquisition. Despite its acquisitions, Manville remained intensely concentrated in construction-dependent businesses, which all suffered from the construction industry recession that began in 1979. Appendix B provides financial summaries for 1978 through the first half of 1982.

Manville's auditor, Coopers and Lybrand, qualified its opinion on the company's 1980 and 1981 annual reports.[19] Of course, Standard and Poor's and Moody's downgraded the company's debt.[20] And Manville's insurers gave the executives little solace; they stopped paying for most

---

[14]W. Thomas Stephens, conversation with author at Seventh National Conference on Business Ethics, Waltham, MA, October 16, 1987.

[15]Manville Corporation, *1977 Annual Report,* 2.

[16]Manville Corporation, *1981 Proxy Statement,* September 11, 1981, Exhibit 2, 5–7.

[17]"Stay Sought for Lawsuits Against Estate of Vandiver Brown," *Stockholders & Creditors News Service Re. Johns-Manville Corp., et al.* (Edgemont, PA: Andrews Publications, November 5, 1984), 3082.

[18]Manville Corporation, *1982 Annual Report and Form 10-K,* 7 and *U.S. Securities and Exchange Commission Form 10-Q,* for quarter ended June 30, 1982, I-2. Also, Johns-Manville Corporation, *1978 Annual Report,* 36. U.S. Consumer Price Index figures were obtained from Ibbotson Associates, *Stocks, Bonds, Bills, and Inflation: 1987 Yearbook* (Chicago: Ibbotson Associates, Inc., 1987), 30.

[19]Manville Corporation, *1980 Annual Report,* 21, and *1981 Annual Report,* 15.

[20]See, for example, "Manville Ratings Cut by Standard and Poor's," *Wall Street Journal,* June 11, 1982, p. 36.

of the asbestos claims by 1981,[21] and generally could not pay punitive damages anyway.

The small amounts actually paid for "asbestos health costs," $13 million in 1981 and $16 million in 1982,[22] could hardly be blamed for the financial collapse. Those costs never amounted to even one percent of sales. But loss of asbestos profits was clearly a major factor. Until at least 1978, the immensely-profitable asbestos trade was the company's mainstay. Sales of the raw fiber alone produced 41 percent of Manville's operating profit as late as 1976, though accounting for only 12 percent of revenues that year.[23] Further, many of the company's manufactured products were asbestos-based, including asbestos felts, papers, textiles, asbestos-cement shingles, asbestos-cement water and sewer pipe, and asbestos paper and millboard.[24]

Public awareness of asbestos-health dangers continued to increase and U.S. purchases of the substance fell after 1976, by 36 percent in 1980 alone.[25] From a 1974 peak of over 750,000 metric tons, U.S. asbestos consumption would fall to under 200,000 metric tons in 1985.[26] Led by lawyer McKinney, the directors voted to reorganize the company in 1981, placing the non-asbestos operations in separate corporations under the parent Manville.

By 1982, Manville's asbestos-fiber revenues were half the 1976 level. An estimated 60 percent of the fiber was sold internationally, mainly in Western Europe.[27] And each dollar of fiber sales produced markedly less operating profit, 18 cents versus 33 cents in 1976.[28]

The stock market reflected Manville's deteriorating financial condition. By mid-August 1982, the company's common stock price had dropped below $8, less than one-fourth its 1977 high.

In Full Readiness for Chapter 11

The company was well-prepared for a Chapter 11 filing. Manville was still able to pay its bills. But the 1978 bankruptcy amendments had removed insolvency as a requirement for filing. The Olinkraft purchase had been structured so half the cost would not come due until 1987 and later. Filing would void that obligation. The 1981 reorganization had segregated the asbestos assets in separate corporations. Each corporation could file its own Chapter 11 petition. They could submit separate or joint reorganization plans. Management could decide which.

Manville had ready access to the best consultants and attorneys. For fifty years, the firm had been close to Morgan Stanley and Company and Davis Polk and Wardwell. Morgan Stanley was the nation's leading investment banker. Davis Polk was a top New York law firm.

And there were no rebels on the management team. Eight of the eleven directors had been with Manville since the fifties and sixties. After Goodwin took over in 1970, no senior manager came in from outside. In fact, the top five executives in 1982 each had at least thirty years tenure.

Best yet, almost none of the company's $1.1 billion debt was secured. McKinney would soon boast of "nearly $2 billion in unencumbered as-

[21]Manville Corporation, *U.S. Securities and Exchange Commission Form 10-Q,* for quarter ended June 30, 1982, II-11-II-14.

[22]Manville Corporation, *1982 Annual Report and Form 10-K,* 7.

[23]Manville Corporation, *1977 Annual Report,* 1.

[24]Johns-Manville Corporation, *1977 Annual Report,* 8, 10, and 13.

[25]Raymond A. Joseph, "Problems Have Long Plagued Asbestos Firms," *The Wall Street Journal,* August 30, 1982, p. 15 (U.S. Interior Department figures in thousands of metric tons for 1976–1981 are given as 659, 610, 619, 561, 359, and 350, respectively).

[26]Barry I. Castlemen, *Asbestos: Medical and Legal Aspects,* 2nd. ed. (Clifton, NJ: Prentice-Hall Law & Business, 1986), 614.

[27]Manville Corporation, *1982 Annual Report and Form 10-K,* 18 and 30, and Johns-Manville Corporation, *1977 Annual Report,* 1.

[28]Ibid.

sets." That would prove to be a real advantage in bankruptcy. Unsecured creditors have no claim on or control over any particular assets. Their claims can be discharged under a reorganization plan.

The Bankruptcy reorganization

On August 26 that year, Manville filed its bankruptcy petition. The common stock fell from \$7.875 the day before the filing to \$4.625 a few days later. All legal actions against the company, including the asbestos tort lawsuits, were automatically stayed under provisions of the bankruptcy law. Appendix C summarizes the Chapter 11 process.

The company's largest division, Manville Forest Products Corporation, emerged from Chapter 11 protection in 1983. Under the court order, it was obligated to pay its commercial debt, but was free of asbestos claims.[29] Various other units, notably the main asbestos fiber subsidiaries and certain asbestos-cement pipe operations, were sold that year, also free of Manville's asbestos liabilities.[30] Appendix D provides financial summaries for several years following Manville's bankruptcy filing.

A reorganization plan for the remaining divisions was filed by Manville management in 1986. The bankruptcy judge in the case issued a confirmation order December 22, 1986. But full implementation of the plan was held up pending the outcome of two appeals from the order.[31]

The plan provided for essentially full payment of \$472 million of unsecured commercial creditor claims which had not been paid earlier. Secured obligations were to be either paid in full or reinstated with payment of accrued interest. Common stockholders were to be practically dispossessed through issuance of additional shares and rights. Preferred stockholders were to receive a mixture of common and "preference" shares worth an estimated 15 percent of the face value of their preferred shares.

A trust (the A-H trust) set up to pay asbestos-health claims was to receive the following assets: (1) \$615 million in expected insurance settlement proceeds, partly deferred and all contingent on the plan surviving all appeals; (2) \$111 million estimated confirmation-date value in cash and receivables; (3) a zero-coupon bond worth an estimated \$249 million[32]—in an October 1987 debate at the National Conference on Business Ethics, Manville chief executive W. Thomas Stephens said the value of the bond was \$350 million; (4) other debt securities valued at about \$45 million; (5) 50 percent of Manville's common stock, which was to be required to be voted for management's choices for directors for at least four years after plan consummation—sale of the stock was to be restricted for at least five years after consummation; (6) contingent claims on 20 percent of corporate earnings beginning the fourth fiscal year after consummation and on a new issue of convertible preferred stock.[33]

After the publicity surrounding the Manville bankruptcy, hundreds of property-damage (PD) claims began to be filed. They were mainly claims for estimated costs of cleaning asbestos out of the thousands of schools and government and commercial buildings where it had been used as insulation or fire proofing. By 1986 the PD claims totaled over \$70 billion. Manville's plan provided that a PD trust would be set up to pay these claims. It would be initially funded with \$100 million from Manville and \$25 million from the A-H trust. The PD trust was also supposed to get certain extra funds the A-H trust might have.

The A-H claimants committee, consisting of

---

[29]Manville Corporation, *1983 Annual Report and Form 10K,* 13.

[30]Ibid., 15.

[31]See, for example, "Appeals Consolidated in 2nd Circuit (sic), Possible Hearing in October," *Stockholders & Creditors News Service* (Edgemont, PA: Andrews Publications, September 21, 1987), 6953.

[32]Arthur Sharplin, "Liquidation versus 'The Plan.' " *The Asbestos Litigation Reporter* (Edgemont, PA: Andrews Publications, November 21, 1986), 13636–40.

[33]Ibid.

19 lawyers and one asbestos victim, endorsed the Manville plan, emphasizing the $2.5 billion nominal value of the A-H trust. However, one expert used discounted cash flow analysis to calculate the value of the proposed trust assets at $572 million.[34]

How the Managers Fared

Compared to the chaos which imperiled the executives' fortunes and jobs in the months before August 1982, the situation which existed thereafter must have seemed sublime. For the executives and directors, Chapter 11 brought a lightened management load, improved pay and benefits, munificent retirement for those who desired it, and bonuses and "golden parachutes" for others. The pre-filing managers and directors even arranged to continue their power over the corporation after its possible emergence from bankruptcy court protection. Finally, some of the pre-filing managers were able to control, or even own, company assets freed of asbestos claims.

Lightened Management Load

When Manville filed its Chapter 11 petition, the management burden was lightened by a surplus of cash and the ability to generate income out of avoided interest. The company's receivables flowed in and $627 million in unsecured liabilities were frozen, most to be paid only after conclusion of the Chapter 11 proceedings.[35] The company was not required to pay this debt, or even accrue interest on it after the filing. Consequently, Manville's cash and marketable securities balance varied from a little over $200 million in December 1982 to over $440 million December 31, 1986—compared to $27 million on June 30, 1982, shortly before the filing.[36] The pre-filing unsecured debt, including accounts payable and other accrued liabilities, was down to $490 million by December 1986.[37] But if the avoided interest on even that amount had been accrued yearly, Manville would have suffered an overall loss for the five years 1982–1986 instead of the reported $92 million total net profit it reported.

Further, the managers were undoubtedly more comfortable in the legal/administrative milieu of the bankruptcy court than in the economic one of competitive business. Chairman/chief executive/president John A. McKinney and four more of the eleven directors in 1982 were attorneys (although one, William D. Tucker, Jr. had just joined the board that year). The company had been involved in asbestos-tort litigation since the 1920s. The litigation and related public affairs matters had been a dominant concern since the early 1970s. The company's success in staving off the asbestos-health claims until the 1980s contrasted with its inability to reverse the economic downslide which began in 1979.

Improved Pay and Benefits

The directors and top executives of Manville, mostly unchanged after the sixties, increased their pay and improved their benefits while in bankruptcy. For example, chief executive John McKinney's reported cash compensation went from $408,750 in early 1982 to $638,005 in 1985, his last full year of employment. Senior vice president Chester Sulewski's increased by 88 percent from 1982 to 1986. The cash compensation of W. Thomas Stephens, who became president in September 1986, was 39 percent higher that year than in 1985, the first year he appeared in the company's Compensation Table.[38]

The cash compensation of the 32 officers and directors of Manville was shown as $3.9 million in the March 25, *1982 Proxy Statement* (p. 10). The *1986 Annual Report and Form 10-K* (p. 63)

[34]Ibid.

[35]Manville Corporation, *1982 Annual Report and Form 10-K*, December 31, 1982, 6 and 11.

[36]Manville Corporation, *1982 Annual Report and Form 10-K*, 6, *1986 Annual Report and Form 10-K*, 39, and *U.S. Securities and Exchange Commission Form 10-Q*, for the quarter ended June 30, 1982, I-3.

[37]Manville Corporation, *1986 Annual Report and Form 10K*, December 31, 1986, 45.

[38]Manville Corporation, *1982 Proxy Statement*, 10, *1985 Annual Report and Form 10-K*, 79, and *1986 Annual Report and Form 10-K*, 63.

reported cash compensation of $5.5 million for just the 25 executive officers during 1986.

Secure Retirement, "Golden Parachutes," and Bonuses

And the most senior pre-filing managers were able to retire in economic security, shielded by the bankruptcy court and indemnified by Manville against the asbestos victims. The Manville reorganization plan provided that the A-H Trust would be responsible for defending and paying any future asbestos claims against the company, its insurers, or the executives and directors. McKinney's severance agreement, effective September 1, 1986, granted him cash payments totalling $1.3 million, two extra years of fringe benefits, and two extra years of longevity for retirement purposes. Two other managers were given severance agreements at the same time providing for payments totalling $1,030,000 and certain other benefits.

By December 1986, four of the five most highly-paid executives shown in the *1982 Proxy Statement* had left the company. J. T. Hulce resigned as president in 1986, allegedly under pressure from the asbestos victims' committee, and was authorized $530,000 in severance pay.[39] G. Earl Parker, Manville's legal chief under McKinney, retired in March 1987. His severance agreement, approved by the bankruptcy court in September, 1987, provided for payments of $430,000 a year through 1989, a total of $1.2 million, counting from March 1987, when he stepped down.[40] But the Board of Directors remained mostly unchanged from the 1982 board, with only one of the nine outside directors having departed.

The executives left behind were also reassured of large termination payments upon choosing or being asked to leave and probable bonuses in the meantime. At a special board meeting in New York held on October 11, 1985, McKinney discussed "Confidential Minute Number 13," which was said to address severance pay of up to two times annual salary for officers and other "key managerial personnel" upon any termination of employment. It was agreed that the special pay would even apply to persons terminated after any assignment of a trustee in the bankruptcy case.[41]

In mid-July 1987 Manville obtained court approval for a new executive bonus plan for that year increasing the possible bonuses for certain managers from 57.5 percent of annual salaries to 97.1 percent. The allowable bonuses for achieving less than 80 percent of goals were reduced.[42]

Post-Consummation Power

The power of the pre-filing directors and replacement senior managers promised to remain firm for at least four years after plan consummation, if and when that was to occur. Two new directors were appointed at the insistence of a group of preferred shareholders in 1984,[43] but no other new outside director appeared on the 1987 board.[44] A third director, Randall Smith, a limited partner in Bear Stearns & Co., had served briefly. Smith was appointed after Bear Stearns accumulated a large holding of Manville com-

[39] Cynthia F. Mitchell, "Manville to Pay Large Severance to 2 Executives," *The Wall Street Journal,* June 24, 1986, pp. 3 and 5. Also see Cynthia F. Mitchell, "Manville President Quits After Dispute with Asbestos Plaintiff over Top Posts," *Wall Street Journal,* April 30, 1986, p. 34.

[40] Arthur Sharplin, "Liquidation versus 'The Plan,'" *The Asbestos Litigation Reporter,* November 21, 1986, 13636-40. Also see Johns-Manville Corporation, et al., "Application for an Order Approving Severance Pay Agreements," *Stockholders & Creditors News Service* (Edgemont, PA: Andrews Publications, September 8, 1986), 5569–5572, and "Judge Approves Severance Pay for G. Earl Parker," *Stockholders & Creditors News Service* (Edgemont, PA: Andrews Publications, October 5, 1987), 6988–6989.

[41] "Key Manville Officers Allowed Severance in Event of Termination by Trustee," *Stockholders and Creditors News Service* (Edgemont, PA: Andrews Publications, April 7, 1986), 4995.

[42] "New Bonus Plan for Executives Approved by Court," *Stockholders and Creditors News Service* (Edgemont, PA: Andrews Publications, August 10, 1987), 6778–9.

[43] "Manville Adds 3 to Board to Increase Shareholder Input," *Wall Street Journal,* August 3, 1984, p. 4.

[44] Manville Corporation, *1986 Annual Report and Form 10-K,* 56–59.

mon stock.[45] Smith resigned his directorship in late 1985. No annual or special meetings of common shareholders, at which new directors might have been elected, were permitted after the bankruptcy filing.[46]

Further, the Manville reorganization plan provided that at least half of all common shares, those held by the A-H Trust, would be voted for management's nominees to the board of directors for four years after the consummation date.[47] While the initial post-consummation board of directors was to include seven new outside members, six of the pre-filing directors were to remain on the board, as was chief executive W. Thomas Stephens.[48]

Control of Assets Free of Asbestos Claims

Some of the executives who left the company were able to remain in control of substantial assets, assets then free and clear of asbestos claims against Manville. For example, the group which bought Manville's Canadian asbestos division on July 1, 1983 was headed by the chief executive officer of Johns-Manville Canada.[49] Manville even continued to get most of the profits from those divisions' asbestos sales. Aside from about $47 million apparently borrowed on the asbestos assets and remitted to Manville, the $117 million to $150 million (Canadian) selling price was payable "out of 85.5% of available future cash flows from asbestos fiber operations."[50] The other divisions sold that year, notably certain asbestos-cement pipe operations, were presumably transferred with management in place.[51]

After leaving Manville in 1986, former president Hulce and another former Manville executive helped form a company, BMZ Materials, Inc., which purchased several Manville plants with annual sales of $17.5 million. The purchase price was $5.5 million in cash and a $1.5 million promissory note.[52]

Several other sales of Manville assets were approved by the bankruptcy court at about the same time.[53] In all these cases, the assets involved were legally placed out of reach of the asbestos victims.

Even some of the managers who stayed with Manville, those in Manville Forest Products Corporation, controlled assets not subject to asbestos claims. That subsidiary accounted for more than a third of Manville's assets in 1986.[54] As previously mentioned, it emerged from bankruptcy court protection in 1983.

Benefits for Attorneys and Consultants

The Manville executives and directors found themselves able to distribute much of the largess produced by decades of asbestos production to a host of consultants and attorneys. For example, Davis Polk and Wardwell, a New York law firm which had represented Manville since 1928, was co-counsel for the Chapter 11 proceedings and charged over $200,000 a month early in the pro-

---

[45]See Dean Rotbart and Jonathan Dahl, "Manville's Common Stockholders May Have Potent Ally as Bear Stearns Bolsters Holdings," *Wall Street Journal,* July 25, 1984, 51.

[46]See, for example, Manville Corporation, *1986 Annual Report and Form 10-K,* 33.

[47]Manville Corporation, *First Amended Disclosure Statement, Second Amended and Restated Plan of Reorganization, and Related Documents,* August 22, 1986, 41.

[48]Manville Corporation, *1986 Annual Report and Form 10-K,* 56–61.

[49]"Hearing on Sale of J-M Canada Scheduled for August 30," *Stockholders and Creditors News Service* (Edgemont, PA: Andrews Publications, August 15, 1983), 1315.

[50]Ibid.

[51]Ibid., 15.

[52]"3 Manville Manufacturing Plants Sold to Former President Hulce," *The Denver Post,* January 5, 1988, p. 2C, and "Manville Sells Three Plants for $7 million," *Stockholders and Creditors News Service* (Edgemont, PA: Andrews Publications, January 11, 1988), 7, 261–2.

[53]See, for example, "Court Approves Sale by Manville of 100 Acres for $22 Million," "Court Approves Sale of 14 Acres to Manville Joint Venture," and "Order Authorizing Sale of Manville, NJ Property," *Stockholders and Creditors News Service* (Edgemont, PA: Andrews Publications, January 11, 1988), 7261, 7262, and 7264, respectively.

[54]Manville Corporation, *1986 Annual Report and Form 10K,* 53.

ceedings.[55] First Boston Corporation was authorized $100,000 a month in late 1984 to serve as financial adviser to certain creditor groups.[56] Through 1986, Manville had dispensed $64 million in Chapter 11 costs.[57] By October 1987, Manville chief Stephens said the number had exceeded $100 million.[58]

Leon Silverman, the "Legal Representative for Future Claimants" appointed by the bankruptcy court, submitted bills for $2.3 million for August 1, 1984 through December 31, 1986.[59] Dr. Frederick W. Kilbourne was paid $73,550 for work as Manville's actuarial expert during November 1983 through April 1984.[60] The executive director of the Association of Trial Lawyers of America, Marianna S. Smith, was hired as Chief Executive Officer of the A-H Trust, at $250,000 a year.

The pattern continued into 1988. For the first six months of 1987, 22 law firms submitted bills in the Manville Chapter 11 proceeding for $5,733,983.[61] The "Provisional" trust budget for January-August 1987 provided $4.6 million to administer the A-H trust, including $194,000 for executive searches, $840,000 to pay Smith and three assistants, and $257,000 for the six trustees who were scheduled to meet only 7 times.[62] The trust rented 32,038 square feet of office space in Washington, D.C. at an annual cost of $849,007.[63] In addition to their $30,000 annual compensation, each trustee was to get $1,000 a day for meetings, intercontinental travel, and other work performed for the trust.

The managing trustee was authorized $1,500 for each day his part-time trust duties were to occupy over half his time. The trust budget for the ten months September 1987 through June 1988 was $9.6 million, including $2.9 million for salaries and benefits. Adequate funding for such expenses was assured by the transfer of $150 million from Manville to the trust and was approved by the bankruptcy judge November 25, 1987.[64]

Benefits for the Asbestos Victims

By 1988, an estimated 41,500 new A-H claims were waiting to be filed against Manville[65] and, of course, many of the 20,000 1982 claimants had died. Total A-H claims filed in the United States by mid 1987 against all companies were estimated at 70,000.[66] No pre-filing A-H claim had been paid by Manville or the trust. In July

[55]"Four Law Firms Submit Bills Totaling $1.8 Million as of December 31, 1982," *Stockholders and Creditors News Service* (Edgemont, PA: Andrews Publications, March 14, 1983), 794.

[56]In re Johns-Manville Corporation, et al., Debtors, Third Supplemental Order Approving Expanded Retention and Reduced Compensation of Investment Banker, 82 B 11656–76 (BRL) (SD NY November 16, 1984) reprinted in *Stockholders and Creditors News Service* (Edgemont, PA: Andrews Publications, December 10, 1984), 3184.

[57]Manville Corporation, *1986 Annual Report and Form 10-K*, 40, and *1983 Annual Report and Form 10-K*, 6.

[58]Debate at the National Conference on Business Ethics Waltham, MA, October 16, 1987.

[59]In re Johns-Manville Corporation, et al., Debtors, Statement of Compensation of the Legal Representative for Future Claimants and His Counsel, 82 B 11656–62 and 82 B 11664–76 (BRL) (SD NY August 14, 1987) reprinted in *Stockholders and Creditors News Service* (Edgemont, PA: Andrews Publications, September 7, 1987), 6945.

[60]"Affidavit of J. Thomas Beckett in Support of the Motion of the Committee of Unsecured Creditors for an Order Authorizing and Directing Final Payment to Actuarial Experts, 82 B 11656–76 (HCB) (SD NY August 3, 1987)," in *Stockholders and Creditors News Service* (Edgemont, PA: Andrews Publications, August 24, 1987), 6819.

[61]"Firms Seek $5.7 Million in Legal Fees for Six Months Ending June 30," *Stockholders and Creditors News Service* (Edgemont, PA: Andrews Publications, September 7, 1987), 6905.

[62]"Manville Personal Injury Settlement Trust Provisional Budget/Expense Estimates (January through August 1987)," *Stockholders and Creditors News Service* (Edgemont, PA: Andrews Publications, August 10, 1987), 6800.

[63]"Terms of Lease for Personal Injury Trust Quarters Approved," *Stockholders & Creditors News Service* (Edgemont, PA: Andrews Publications, December 7, 1987), 7193.

[64]"Manville Trust Forms Being Printed; $9.2 million (sic) Interim Budget," *Stockholders and Creditors News Service* (Edgemont, PA: Andrews Publications, January 25, 1988), 7295.

[65]"Plan Protects Manville, Shortchanges Victims," *Asbestos Watch* 4:1 (Fall 1986), 1.

[66]"JM Trust to Accept Claims in January, Negotiate Even Before Consummation," *Stockholders & Creditors News Service* (Edgemont, PA: Andrews Publications, July 6, 1987), 6681.

1987, the A-H trustees estimated payments from the trust could begin during the spring of 1988,[67] nearly six years after Manville's bankruptcy filing. By January 1988, it seemed clear the bankruptcy judge's confirmation order would be appealed to the U.S. Supreme Court unless overturned by the court of appeals.[68] The estimate of when payments could begin was moved back to "April to November 1988."[69] But in March 1988 the Second Circuit U.S. Court of Appeals was still mulling one of the appeals.[70] So the consummation date seemed likely to slip into 1989, if not beyond.

In addition to the delay, the asbestos victims had six other reasons to despair. First, consummation of the Manville plan might not occur at all, or might be reversed if it did. Second, A-H representatives in the bankruptcy court had been effectively preempted. Third, the victims were to have little control over Manville or the A-H trust for years after consummation, if and when that was to occur. Fourth, the Manville plan provided for effective subordination of A-H claims to commercial debt, even that which was unsecured. Fifth, many of Manville's pre-filing assets had already been irrevocably insulated from potential claims against them by A-H victims. Sixth, the prospective payments to the A-H trust provided for in the plan were to be substantially uncertain.

Consummation Might Not Occur or Might Be Reversed

Some A-H victims were convinced the Manville plan offered their best hope for compensation. But there were at least two reasons to think consummation might not occur at all—or might be reversed if it did. First, there was evidence the A-H trustees were concerned Manville had made inadequate disclosure of incriminating evidence during reorganization. In March 1988, Manville and the A-H trust urgently began setting up a repository to hold 44 million pages of documents produced in two major lawsuits. The repository was to be ready in six weeks and was to be open to "those involved in resolving health claims against the company."[71]

Second, court rulings in late 1987 and early 1988 seemed to suggest criminal indictments of Manville or its officials were possible. Such indictments could void judge Lifland's ability to protect the company and its managers. In two Delaware cases Raymark Corporation (formerly Raybestos-Manhattan Corporation) was found liable for civil conspiracy with Manville to conceal or misrepresent the health hazards of asbestos. And a court in Washington state ruled Manville and Raymark engaged in "concert of action" to each market asbestos-containing products without warning of their potential dangers.[72]

Concerning the Delaware cases, the court later ruled the standard of proof required in civil conspiracy was "preponderance of evidence," not the "clear and convincing" test Raymark wished to impose. The court did not address whether the stronger test had been met, only that it was not required. The judge wrote, "I find no basis for singling out this type of intentional tort, or intentional torts in general, which involve a greater level of culpability than that involved in

---

[67]"JM Trust to Accept Claims in January, Negotiate Even Before Consummation," *Stockholders & Creditors News Service* (Edgemont, PA: Andrews Publications, July 6, 1987), 6680.

[68]Marianna S. Smith, Executive Director, Manville Personal Injury Settlement Trust, "Memorandum to Attorneys with Prepetition Cases," January 27, 1988, in *Asbestos Litigation Reporter* (Edgemont, PA: Andrews Publications, February 5, 1988), 16503.

[69]Ibid.

[70]"2nd Circuit's Delay in Kane Appeal Causes Speculation," *Stockholders and Creditors News Service* (Edgemont, PA: Andrews Publications, March 7, 1988), 7417.

[71]"All Manville Documents to Be Available at Repository in Denver," *Stockholders & Creditors News Service* (Edgemont, PA: Andrews Publications, March 7, 1988), 7415.

[72]"Delaware Jury Awards $75 Million in Punitive Damages Against Raymark," *Stockholders & Creditors News Service* (Edgemont, PA: Andrews Publications, November 23, 1987), 7171-2; "Delaware Jury Awards $22 Million in Punitive Damages Against Raymark," *Asbestos Litigation Reporter* (Edgemont, PA: Andrews Publications, March 18, 1988), 16723; and "Washington Judge Finds Concert of Action by Raymark and J-M," *Asbestos Litigation Reporter* (Edgemont, PA: Andrews Publications, March 18, 1988), 16724.

negligent conduct, for favored treatment in the proof of the wrongdoing."[73]

A-H Representatives Preempted in Bankruptcy Court

After 1984, the asbestos victims were essentially powerless to affect the outcome of the Chapter 11 process, mainly because Manville management was able to neutralize their committee in the bankruptcy court. The committee consisted of nineteen contingent-fee attorneys and one asbestos victim. Until early 1984, the committee had aggressively confronted Manville management. For example, during September 1983 through January 1984, the committee asked the bankruptcy court to dismiss the bankruptcy filing,[74] rejected management's proposed reorganization plan,[75] requested that Manville's top management be replaced with a trustee,[76] and even petitioned the court to cut the managers' salaries.[77] But in January 1984, Manville obtained a hearing date on its motion to void the A-H attorneys' contingent-fee agreements, which generally gave the attorneys one-third of any settlement or judgement proceeds.[78] Manville had called the fee arrangements "completely unconscionable."[79]

In March, 1984, the A-H committee withdrew its motion to decrease management salaries.[80] For the ensuing two years, the *Asbestos Litigation Reporter,* which reported legal news and filings in asbestos cases,[81] revealed no actions by the A-H committee to contest the authority or benefits of Manville management or to remove the company from bankruptcy court protection.[82] And Manville management relaxed its effort to void the contingent-fee arrangements. By July 1984, Manville was predicting quick agreement to its reorganization plan by all parties, including the A-H committee.[83] Leading asbestos attorney, and member of the A-H committee, Ronald Motley later wrote, "[The] intimation that there is some relationship between Manville's withdrawal of its objection to contingency fees in exchange for the AH Committee's not opposing certain management decisions is both false and insulting."[84]

The A-H committee became a strong management ally in seeking approval of the plan. For example, the committee sponsored promotional brochures for inclusion in the 100,000 information packets and ballots on the plan mailed in September 1986 to persons who provided evi-

[73]"DE Judge: Conspiracy Requires Only 'Preponderance of Evidence' Proof," *Asbestos Litigation Reporter* (Edgemont, PA: Andrews Publications, March 4, 1988), 16665.

[74]"Committee of Asbestos Related Litigants Again Asks Bankruptcy Court to Dismiss Johns-Manville Bankruptcy," *Asbestos Litigation Reporter* (Edgemont, PA: Andrews Publications, September 23, 1983), 7148.

[75]"Asbestos Claimants Committee Rejects Plan," *Asbestos Litigation Reporter* (Edgemont, PA: Andrews Publications, November 25, 1983), 7416.

[76]"Asbestos-Related Litigants Move to Have Bankruptcy Court Appoint Trustee," *Asbestos Litigation Reporter* (Edgemont, PA: Andrews Publications, January 6, 1984), 7625.

[77]"Committee of Asbestos-Related Litigants and/or Creditors Withdraws Its Motion to Reduce Salaries of Manville Officers," *Asbestos Litigation Reporter* (Edgemont, PA: Andrews Publications, March 16, 1984), 7999.

[78]"Hearing Set on Replacement for Plaintiff Contingency Fee Arrangements," *Asbestos Litigation Reporter* (Edgemont, PA: Andrews Publications, February 3, 1984), 7785.

[79]"Johns-Manville Asks Court to Void Asbestos-Claimants Attorney Fees," *Asbestos Litigation Reporter* (Edgemont, PA: Andrews Publications, November 25, 1983), 7411.

[80]"Committee of Asbestos-Related Litigants and/or Creditors Withdraws Its Motion to Reduce Salaries of Manville Officers," *Asbestos Litigation Reporter* (Edgemont, PA: Andrews Publications, March 16, 1984), 7999.

[81]Published by Andrews Publications, Edgemont, PA 19028.

[82]"In re Johns-Manville Corp.," *Asbestos Litigation Reporter: Eight-Year Cumulative Index, February 1979-July 1987,* (Edgemont, PA: Andrews Publications, August 1987), 37-8.

[83]"Essentials of Consensual Plan Should Be Soon," *Asbestos Litigation Reporter* (Edgemont, PA: Andrews Publications, July 20, 1984), 8687.

[84]Letter to author, April 1, 1988.

dence they had asbestos-related disease.[85] The brochures stated, "The Asbestos Victims Committee urges you to vote in favor of the Plan. . . . Vote yes on the Manville Reorganization Plan."[86] Despite the promotional activity, including a nationwide multimedia campaign, one of the two national organizations of asbestos victims opposed the plan and the other refused to endorse it.[87] But the A-H attorneys throughout America apparently acted en masse in voting the asbestos victims' proxies for the plan. And tens of thousands of persons were allowed to vote as asbestos victims though they had never submitted an actual claim. In any case, Manville claimed its plan received 96 percent of the 52,440 A-H votes cast.[88]

The bankruptcy judge further weakened any active opposition to the Manville plan by asbestos victims in late 1987, when he approved the transfer of $150 million into the A-H trust. Victims' hopes were undoubtedly raised because the money was not excluded from eventually being used to pay A-H claims. But the court order approving the transfer provided that if the plan failed to survive all appeals, unspent funds would go first to pay property damage claims and then to "charitable purposes."[89] So if opposition to the Manville plan from any quarter were to prove successful, an additional $150 million of Manville's assets, in this case cash, would be unavailable to pay A-H claims. Besides, much of the money would be consumed by trust administrative expenses, then running about $1 million a month.[90]

Little Control over Manville after Consummation

Even after plan consummation, if and when that were to occur, the A-H claimants would have little power over Manville or the A-H trust. As previously mentioned, six of the pre-filing directors were to remain on the post-consummation board, as was chief executive, W. Thomas Stephens. The trust would own 50 percent of Manville's common stock. But sale of the stock was to be restricted for five years and the stock was to be required to be voted for management's choices for directors for at least four years after consummation.[91]

The A-H trustees, including an investment banker, four lawyers, and a business consultant, were to have lifetime tenure. Vacancies were to be filled by the remaining trustees, after consultation with Manville and selected asbestos counsel.[92]

A-H Claims Subordinated to Those of Commercial Creditors

The plan would effectively subordinate the A-H claims to those of commercial creditors, even unsecured ones. For example, an estimated $473 million in cash would be distributed by Manville

---

[85] "100,000 Ballots and Information Packets Being Mailed This Week," *Stockholders and Creditors News Service* (Edgemont, PA: Andrews Publications, September 8, 1986), 5513.

[86] The Committee of Asbestos-Related Litigants and/or Creditors Representing Asbestos-Health Claimants of Manville Corporation, "Questions and Answers on Asbestos-Health Claims and the Manville Reorganization Plan" and "A Very Important Message for People With Asbestos-Related Diseases," n.d., distributed in August-October 1986.

[87] Continuing personal correspondence with the top official of each organization, 1984–1988.

[88] "Manville Says Overwhelming Majority of Voters Accepted Plan," *Asbestos Litigation Reporter* (Edgemont, PA: Andrews Publications, December 5, 1986), 13677.

[89] "Manville Pays First $150 Million to Settlement Trust Mostly for Claims," *Stockholders and Creditors News Service* (Edgemont, PA: Andrews Publications, December 21, 1987), 7231.

[90] "Manville Trust Claims Forms Being Printed; $9.2 Million (sic) Interim Budget," *Stockholders and Creditors News Service* (Edgemont, PA: Andrews Publications, January 25, 1988), 7295. The budget authorized $9.6 million for the ten months September 1987 through June 1988.

[91] Manville Corporation, *First Amended Disclosure Statement, Second Amended and Restated Plan of Reorganization, and Related Documents,* August 22, 1986, M-41.

[92] Ibid., M-65.

if the plan were to go into effect.[93] *But only $55 million of this would go to the victims' trust* (technically, the trust would get $80 million but would have to give $25 million of that to the property damage trust).[94] In contrast, the general unsecured creditors would get $248 million in cash.[95] The rest of the general unsecured creditors' principal, with interest, would be paid within four and one-half years.[96]

And much of Manville's pre-filing commercial debt had already been reinstated or paid as divisions were reorganized or sold free and clear of asbestos claims during the lengthy Chapter 11 process. As a result, the liabilities subject to Chapter 11 proceedings reported on Manville's balance sheet declined by $161 million from 1982–1986.[97]

The plan would prohibit interest on asbestos-health claims.[98] But unsecured creditors would receive 12 percent interest.[99] They would even get $114 million in debentures for interest while Manville was in bankruptcy.[100] Further, the plan provided that Manville's ability to pledge assets to the victims' trust would be limited until the unsecured creditors were paid in full.[101]

Finally, as discussed below, most payments to the A-H trust would be made from future earnings of the company, earnings which were far from certain. In contrast, general unsecured creditors would be paid from the pool of liquid assets available upon plan confirmation and within four and one-half years thereafter.

[93]Ibid., M-402 and M-407.

[94]Ibid., M-72 and M-180.

[95]Ibid., M-47.

[96]Ibid., M-60.

[97]Annual reports, respective years.

[98]Manville Corporation, *First Amended Disclosure Statement, Second Amended and Restated Plan of Reorganization, and Related Documents,* August 22, 1986, M-46.

[99]Ibid., M-46 and M-47.

[100]Ibid., M-48.

[101]Ibid., M-300 and M-343.

Manville Assets Shielded from A-H Claims

The reorganization of Manville Forest Products corporation in 1983 forever insulated that division's $870 million in assets[102] from victims' claims. Another $301 million in prefiling assets were shielded from the asbestos liabilities through the sale of Manville's U.S. pipe operations in 1982 and the asbestos fiber operations in 1983.[103] In each case, commercial creditors of the affected divisions were either paid in full or had their claims reinstated. Manville's Denver headquarters and a number of other assets were sold in 1987 and 1988, all protected from asbestos claims by the bankruptcy court. In fact, Manville retained responsibility for cleaning up asbestos residue on certain of the transferred property, further decreasing the company's potential profitability.[104]

Payments to A-H Trust Uncertain

As indicated earlier, appeals from the Manville reorganization plan appeared headed for the U.S. Supreme Court in 1988. Of course, all payments to asbestos victims contemplated under the plan were contingent upon it surviving the appeals. In addition, payments under the insurance settlement agreements, which were to constitute the preponderance of A-H trust assets during the decade after consummation, were not to be paid until after the plan became final.[105]

But even if the plan were to be put into effect, little reason was given to expect the A-H trust would have the resources needed to compensate asbestos victims. The major promised source of

[102]Ibid., M-431.

[103]Manville Corporation, *1983 Annual Report and Form 10-K,* 17 and 18.

[104]For example, see "Court Approves Sale by Manville of 100 Acres for $22 million," *Stockholders & Creditors News Service* (Edgemont, PA: Andrews Publications, January 11, 1988), 7261.

[105]Manville Corporation, *First Amended Disclosure Statement, Second Amended and Restated Plan of Reorganization, and Related Documents,* August 22, 1986, M-55 and M-149.

long-term funding for the A-H trust would be an unsecured, zero-interest Manville bond. The bond would provide for semi-annual payments of $37.5 million in the fourth through the twenty-fifth fiscal years after consummation.[106]

Aside from Manville's ability to pay the bond installments, reason was present for concern about the purchasing power they would represent. Using Manville's inflation assumption of 5.2 percent,[107] those payments would each be worth $29 million (consummation-year dollars) in the fifth year, $23 million in the tenth year, $17.5 million in the fifteenth year, and $14 million in the twentieth year. If inflation were to average, say, three percent higher than Manville anticipated, the installments in the twentieth year would each only be worth $8 million. Further, the payments could be reduced after the thirteenth fiscal year.[108]

But, Manville's ability to pay its obligations to the A-H trust seemed problematical at best. The company estimated a $473 million payout under its plan upon consummation, most to commercial creditors, and another $546 million during the ensuing five years. A capital spending program would consume another $800 million over those five years.[109] These amounts total $1.8 billion, compared to Manville's estimated liquidation value for all its assets of $2–2.4 billion.[110] So after paying out over 80 percent of its asset value—over twice its reported net worth[111]—in just five years, Manville promised to honor its further obligations under the plan. These further payments would average $108 million a year for years six, seven, and eight, including the two annual payments of $37.5 million to the A-H trust.[112]

[106]Ibid., M-67, M-68 and M-278.

[107]Ibid., M-76.

[108]Ibid., M-67 and M-68.

[109]Ibid., M-519.

[110]Ibid., M-399.

[111]Ibid., M-418.

[112]Ibid., M-519.

In proving feasibility of the plan, Manville and its investment banker, Morgan Stanley and Company, "projected" the company's cash flows forward through 1991.[113] These figures were then "extrapolated" through 2011.[114] The table below shows Manville's actual sales and net earnings for 1978–1986[115] and the projections for 1987–1991. Also listed are the interest expense amounts for each of those years. As the table illustrates, Manville's net earnings declined from $121 million in 1978 to $60 million in 1981.

Manville Actual and Projected Sales, Earnings, and Interest

	Year	Net Sales	Net Earnings	Interest
Actual:	1978	$1,648	$121	$ 22
	1979	2,276	115	62
	1980	2,267	81	65
	1981	1,895	60	72
	1982	1,685	(98)	52
	1983	1,729	67	26
	1984	1,814	77	21
	1985	1,880	(45)	23
	1986	1,920	81	20
Projected:	1987	2,043	108	112
	1988	2,239	86	114
	1989	2,411	108	116
	1990	2,636	118	115
	1991	2,480	47	106

Then, from 1982–1986 net earnings averaged only $16 million a year. Manville would have lost money for the 1982-86 period except for two non-recurring advantages. First, the company avoided at least $50 million a year in average interest charges on liabilities subject to Chapter 11 proceedings.[116] The unsecured portions of

[113]Ibid., M-405.

[114]Ibid., M-86 and M-87.

[115]Annual reports for respective years.

[116]Annual reports for respective years.

these liabilities varied from $627 million in 1982 to $490 million in 1986. Interest expense was projected to average $85 million a year more in 1987–91 than in 1982–86. Second, other income averaged $52 million in 1982–86.[117] It was put at only $14 million a year for 1987–91.[118]

The projections and extrapolations promised an annual average of $93 million in net earnings for the five years after 1986. This despite the payment of $85 million a year more interest than in 1982–86 and the loss of $38 million a year in other income.

Manville and Morgan Stanley claimed income from operations would reach $370 million in 1990. They estimated it would *average* $283.4 million annually for the five years 1987–91.[119] That is almost exactly double the $145 million average for the preceding five years and more than Manville had ever earned in any single year.[120]

Manville issued extensive disclaimers for itself and Morgan Stanley concerning the projections. For example, the company reported, "NO REPRESENTATIONS CAN BE MADE WITH RESPECT TO THE ACCURACY OF THE PROJECTIONS OR THE ABILITY TO ACHIEVE THE PROJECTED RESULTS . . . the above pro forma and projected financial statements are unaudited . . . Morgan Stanley did not independently verify the information considered in its reviews of [the assumptions upon which the projections were based] and for purposes of its reviews relied upon the accuracy and completeness of all such information. . . . [Under certain] PESSIMISTIC ASSUMPTIONS MANVILLE WOULD NOT GENERATE THROUGH ITS OPERATIONS SUFFICIENT CASH TO MEET ALL OF ITS OBLIGATIONS UNDER THE PLAN DURING THE PERIODS ANALYZED."[121] The presentations were accepted by the bankruptcy court as proving plan feasibility.

Conclusion

On October 16, 1987, Manville chief executive W. Thomas Stephens appeared in a debate before the National Conference on Business Ethics. He generally described past company managers as well intentioned but misinformed. He mentioned certain lessons he had learned: (1) Chapter 11 was the right decision. (2) "Today, its 'Let the seller beware' and it's as it should be." (3) The industry did not tell employees and customers enough about the dangers of asbestos.[122]

On the broad question of toxic waste, Stephens said, "I think the companies and the officers of those companies should be held totally accountable for their actions. . . . Some horrible mistakes have been made in the past. . . . But I think the emphasis should be on solving the problem, learning the lessons from the past, and not bashing the guys that screwed up."[123]

Later Stephens said the advantage of the asbestos victims owning stock through the A-H trust was that they would be long-term investors looking for long-term results, not just a boost in one quarter's earnings. He expressed his hope that Manville would experience a rebirth, "like the Phoenix," when it emerged from Chapter 11. He said, knowing Manville's assets and liabilities gave Manville a competitive advantage.

The cover story in the November 1987 magazine *Corporate Finance* was entitled "Miracle at Manville: How Tom Stephens Raised the Bread to Overcome Bankruptcy." The article

[117]Annual reports for respective years.

[118]*First Amended Disclosure Statement,* M-405.

[119]*First Amended Disclosure Statement,* M-405.

[120]Annual reports for respective years.

[121]*First Amended Disclosure Statement.,* M-75 and M-77.

[122]"Ethical Dilemmas of Chapter 11 Reorganization," transcript of session at the Seventh National Conference on Business Ethics, October 16, 1987. Reprinted in *Stockholders and Creditors News Service Re. Johns-Manville Corp., et al.* (Edgemont, PA: Andrews Publications, Inc.), December 7, 1987, 7,196–7,216.

[123]Ibid., 7,215.

said many considered the Manville bankruptcy "the ultimate management cop-out of all time." It continued, "Soon these critics will have to eat their words."[124]

In a January 1988 *Financier* article, Stephens wrote, "We have set a goal: That the new Manville will be the model of ethical corporate behavior. We have demonstrated what we can and will do. I'm proud of our record."[125]

In March 1988, Stephens took questions from a University of Montana business ethics class. He said he thought Manville's bankruptcy choice was "the most courageous and most ethical decision ever made by a Fortune 500 company."[126]

In March 1988, Manville and the A-H trust announced the creation of a depository for asbestos-related documents, mainly those produced from 1983–1987 in Manville's California lawsuit against its insurance carriers and a Washington, D.C. claims court case the company had filed against the government. That lawsuit had led to the insurance settlements which were to provide most early funding to the A-H trust. The depository, located near Manville's Denver headquarters, was opened in April, 1988 and, according to Manville, was to contain over 44 million pages.

A news service reported some attorneys believed Manville and the A-H trust were anxious to avoid later claims that the full extent of the company's knowledge was hidden during the reorganization. And a person familiar with the case said certain A-H trustees became concerned about such concealment after reading a court-ordered summary of evidence in the Washington claims court case mentioned above. Some attorneys had advised the head of the Asbestos Victims of America that the inadequate disclosure which concerned the A-H trustees might necessitate a new vote by stockholders, creditors, and claimants on the Manville reorganization. One of Manville's attorneys wrote judge Lifland that questions had been raised about the "breadth of the restraining provisions" which protected the A-H trustees and others involved in the trust from legal attack. Judge Lifland issued a new order on March 18, 1987 barring any action concerning "administration, enforcement or settlement of accounts" related to the trust in any court except the bankruptcy court.[127]

On March 30, 1988 the Second Circuit U.S. Court of Appeals issued its long-awaited decision on the remaining appeal from the Manville confirmation order. The other appeal had been rejected earlier and a petition for a rehearing was also rejected, setting the stage for a further appeal to the U.S. Supreme Court. Ninety days were allowed to seek review by the Supreme Court. A spokesperson for the A-H trust said if the Supreme Court refused to hear either of the appeals, consummation of the plan could occur sometime in the fall and payments to victims could begin by year end. Otherwise, consummation would slip into 1989, the seventh year after Manville's bankruptcy filing.

Appendix E contains comments on the Manville bankruptcy by executives and other principals in the case.

---

[124]Stephen W. Quickel, "Miracle at Manville: How Tom Stephens Raised the Bread to Overcome Bankruptcy," *Corporate Finance,* November 1987, (No page numbers; reprint of article provided by Manville Corporation).

[125]W. Thomas Stephens, "Manville-Asbestos Ethical Issues Shaping Business Practice," *Financier,* January 1988, 33–36.

[126]Patricia Sullivan, "The High Cost of Ethics: Manville Chief Defends Bankruptcy Decision," *The Missoulan* (Missoula, Montana newspaper), March 10, 1988, 2.

[127]"Judge Lifland Bars Any Actions Relating to Administration of PI Trust," *Asbestos Litigation Reporter* (Edgemont, PA: Andrews Publications, April 8, 1988), 16798.

Appendix A

Pre-1970 Events Concerning Asbestos and Health

1898: Manville founder and inventor of uses for asbestos, Henry Ward Johns, dies of "dust phthisis pneumonitis," assumedly asbestosis.

1929: Manville defending early lawsuits for asbestos deaths. The company claims employees assumed the risks of employment, knew or should have known the dangers, and were contributorily negligent. Legal documents in these cases bear signatures of senior Manville officials who would remain with the company until the 1960s.

1930: Dr. A. J. Lanza, of Metropolitan Life Insurance Company (Manville's insurer), begins a four-year study on the "Effects of Inhalation of Asbestos Dust upon the Lungs of Asbestos Workers."

1933: Based on interim results of his study, Dr. Lanza suggests Manville engage an outside consultant to do dust counts at company plants. A decision is made to train an insider to do this rather than bring in someone from outside the company.

1934: Asbestosis is considered for classification as a disease for workmen's compensation purposes. Manville's chief attorney writes to the company:

> In particular we have urged that asbestosis should not at the present time be included in the list of compensation diseases, for the reason that it is only within a comparatively recent time that asbestosis has been recognized by the medical and scientific professions as a disease—in fact one of our principal defenses in actions against the company on the common law theory of negligence has been that the scientific and medical knowledge has been insufficient until a very recent period to place on the owners of plants or factories the burden or duty of taking special precautions against the possible onset of the disease in their employees.

After reviewing a draft of Dr. Lanza's report (above, 1930), Manville vice president and corporate secretary Vandiver Brown writes Dr. Lanza requesting changes. His letter states, "All we ask is that all of the favorable aspects of the survey be included and that none of the unfavorable be unintentionally pictured in darker terms than the circumstances justify. I feel confident that we can depend upon you and Dr. McConnel to give us this 'break' . . ."

1935: Brown writes another industry executive, Sumner Simpson, "I quite agree that our interests are best served by having asbestosis receive the minimum of publicity." He is commenting on Simpson's response to a letter by Anne Rossiter (editor of the industry journal *Asbestos*) in which she has written, "You may recall that we have written you on several occasions concerning the publishing of information, or discussion of, asbestosis. . . . Always you have requested that for obvious reasons, we publish nothing, and, naturally your wishes have been respected."

1936: Messrs. Brown and Simpson convince nine other asbestos companies to provide a total of $417 per month for the industry's own three-year study of the effects of asbestos dust on guinea pigs and rabbits by Dr. LeRoy U. Gardner. Simpson writes Gardner, "we could determine from time to time after the findings were made, whether we wish any publication or not." In a separate letter, Brown states, "the manuscript of your study will be submitted to us for approval prior to publication." Gardner will tell the companies of "significant changes in guinea pigs' lungs within a period of one year" and "fibrosis" produced by long fibers and "chronic inflammation" caused by short fibers. He will make several requests for additional funding but will die in 1946 without reporting final results.

1940: Lawsuits have increased in number through the 1930s, but Manville continues to successfully defend or settle them, using the same defenses as in the 1920s but adding a statute-of-limitations defense, made possible by the long latency period of asbestos diseases. The companies continue to be able to prevent significant publicity about asbestos and health.

The war will bring spiralling sales and profits, as thousands of tons of asbestos are used in building war machines, mainly ships—resulting in exposure of tens of thousands of shipyard workers and seamen, thousands of whom will die of asbestos diseases decades later. Manville will later sue the U.S. government, claiming government had "superior knowledge" of the asbestos dangers to shipyard workers. The federal judge will rule against Manville in 1987.

1947: A study by the Industrial Hygiene Foundation of America finds that from three to twenty percent of asbestos plant workers already have asbestosis and a Manville plant employing 300 is producing "5 or 6 cases annually that the physician believes show early changes due to asbestos."

1950: Dr. Kenneth W. Smith, Manville chief physician, has given superiors his report that of 708 workers he studied only four were free of asbestos disease. Concerning the more serious cases he has written, "The fibrosis of this disease is irreversible and permanent so that eventually compensation will be paid to each of these men but as long as the man is not disabled it is felt that he should not be told of his condition so that he can live and work in peace and the company can benefit from his many years of experience."

1952: John A. McKinney, Fred L. Pundsack, Chester E. Shepperly, Monroe Harris, and Chester J. Sulewski, who will be Manville's top five officers as it prepares to seek bankruptcy court protection in 1982, have all joined the company in various capacities.

1953: Dr. Smith tries to convince senior Manville managers to authorize caution labelling for asbestos. In a 1976 deposition he will characterize their responses: "We recognize the potential hazard that you mentioned, the suggested use of a caution label. We will discuss it among ourselves and make a decision." Asked why he was overruled, Smith will say, "application of a caution label identifying a product as hazardous would cut out sales."

1956: The Board of Governors of the Asbestos Textile Institute (made up of Manville and other asbestos companies) meet to discuss the increasing publicity about asbestos and cancer and agree that "every effort should be made to disassociate this relationship until such a time that there is sufficient and authoritative information to substantiate such to be a fact."

1957: The Asbestos Textile Institute rejects a proposal by the Industrial Health Foundation that asbestos companies fund a study on asbestos and cancer. Institute minutes report, "There is a feeling among certain members that such an investigation would stir up a hornet's nest and put the whole industry under suspicion."

1959: An increasing number of articles connecting asbestos with various diseases have appeared in scholarly medical journals over the last few years.

1963: Dr. I. J. Selikoff, of Mt. Sinai Medical Center in New York, reads a report of his study of asbestos workers before the American Medical Association meeting. Like the earlier research, the Selikoff study implicates asbestos ingestion as the causal factor in many thousands of deaths and injuries. Selikoff will soon estimate that at least 100,000 more Americans will die of asbestos diseases this century. The study and the articles, news stories, and academic papers which follow will focus public attention on the asbestos and health issue. An estimated 100 articles on asbestos-related diseases will appear in 1964 alone.

1964: For the first time, Manville agrees to place caution labels on asbestos products. The labels say, "Inhalation of asbestos in excessive quantities over long periods of time may be harmful" and suggests that users avoid breathing the dust and wear masks if "adequate ventilation control is not possible." The company's most profitable—and deadly—product, bags of asbestos fiber for distribution to other manufacturers and insulators throughout the world, will not be caution labeled for another five years.

Appendix B

Manville Financial Summaries, before August 26, 1982

Income Statements (dollar amounts in millions)*

	1982 6 mos.	1981	1980	1979	1978
Sales	$ 949	$2,186	$2,267	$2,276	$1,649
Cost of sales	784	1,731	1,771	1,747	1,190
Selling, G & A exp.	143	271	263	239	193
R&D and eng. exp.	16	34	35	31	33
Operating income	6	151	197	259	232
Other income, net	1	35	26	21	28
Interest expense	35	73	65	62	22
Income before inc. taxes	(28)	112	157	218	238
Income taxes	2	53	77	103	116
Net income	(25)	60	81	115	122
Div. on preferred stock	12	25	25	24	0
Net Income for C.S.	$ (37)	$ 35	$ 55	$ 91	$ 122

Business Segment Information (dollar amounts in millions)*

	1981	1980	1979	1978	1977	1976
Revenues						
Fiberglass products	$ 625	$ 610	$ 573	$ 514	$ 407	$ 358
Forest products	555	508	497	0	0	0
Non-fiberglass insulation	258	279	268	231	195	159
Roofing products	209	250	273	254	204	171
Pipe products & systems	199	220	305	303	274	218
Asbestos fiber	138	159	168	157	161	155
Industrial & spec. prod.	320	341	309	291	301	309
Corporate revenues, net	12	9	11	20	12	(22)
Intersegment sales	(95)	(84)	(106)	(94)	(74)	(56)
Total	$2,221	$2,292	$2,297	$1,677	$1,480	$1,291
Income from Operations						
Fiberglass products	$ 90	$ 91	$ 96	$ 107	$ 82	$ 60
Forest products	39	37	50	0	0	0
Non-fiberglass insulation	20	27	27	35	28	18
Roofing products	(17)	9	14	23	14	8
Pipe products & systems	0	(5)	18	26	24	(3)
Asbestos fiber	37	35	56	55	60	60
Industrial & spec. prod.	50	55	43	36	25	19
Corporate expense, net	(23)	(38)	(23)	(23)	(24)	(49)
Eliminations & adjustments	3	11	(2)	1	3	2
Total	$ 198	$ 223	$ 280	$ 260	$ 212	$ 116

*Totals may not check, due to rounding.

Balance Sheets (millions)*

	June 30	December 31			
	1982	1981	1980	1979	1978
Assets					
Cash	$ 10	$ 14	$ 20	$ 19	$ 28
Marketable securities	17	12	12	10	38
Accounts & notes receivable	348	327	350	362	328
Inventories	182	211	217	229	219
Prepaid expenses	19	19	20	31	32
Total current assets	$ 576	$ 583	$ 619	$ 650	$ 645
Property, plant & equipment					
Land & land improvements		119	118	114	99
Buildings		363	357	352	321
Machinery & equipment		1,202	1,204	1,161	1,043
		$1,685	$1,679	$1,627	$1,462
Less: Accum. depr. & depl.		(525)	(484)	(430)	(374)
		$1,160	$1,195	$1,197	$1,088
Timber & timberland, net		406	407	368	372
	$1,523	$1,566	$1,602	$1,565	$1,460
Other assets	148	149	117	110	113
	$2,247	$2,298	$2,338	$2,324	$2,217
Liabilities					
Short-term debt	$	$ 29	$ 22	$ 32	$ 23
Accounts payable	191	120	126	143	114
Employee comp. & benefits		77	80	54	45
Income taxes		30	22	51	84
Other liabilities	149	58	61	50	63
Total current liab.	$ 340	$ 316	$ 310	$ 329	$ 329
Long-term debt	499	508	519	532	543
Other non-current liab.	93	86	75	73	60
Deferred income taxes	186	185	211	195	150
	$1,116	$1,095	$1,116	$1,129	$1,083
Stockholders' Equity					
Preferred	$ 301	$ 301	$ 300	$ 299	$ 299
Common	60	59	58	208	197
Capital in excess of par	178	174	164	0	0
Retained earnings	642	695	705	692	643
Cum. currency transl. adj.	(47)	(22)	0	0	0
Less: cost of treas. stock	(3)	(3)	(4)	(4)	(6)
	$1,131	$1,203	$1,222	$1,196	$1,134
	$2,247	$2,298	$2,338	$2,324	$2,217

*Totals may not check, due to rounding.

Appendix C

How Chapter 11 Works

Chapter 11 of the U.S. Bankruptcy Code was passed by Congress in 1978 with an effective date of October 1, 1979. This law replaced various business reorganization provisions in earlier law. The new act was amended in 1984 and 1986. An apparent premise of Chapter 11 is the pleasing idea that most businesses are worth at least as much as going concerns as in liquidation.[128] If this supposition is true, stockholders and creditors may get more out of a troubled company by allowing it to continue operating than by shutting the company down. A societal benefit is that employees keep their jobs and the community keeps the tax base and economic and social activity related to the debtor firm. Practically any company or individual may seek Chapter 11 protection. Insolvency is not a requirement.

Administration of the Debtor Firm

A U.S. bankruptcy court assumes oversight of any firm which desires to "reorganize" under Chapter 11. Upon filing, the firm becomes the "debtor in possession" (DIP) with the powers and obligations of a trustee in bankruptcy. The prefiling managers continue to operate the company in "the ordinary course of business" while a plan to emerge from court protection is being formulated, approved, and confirmed.

U.S. bankruptcy judges serve fourteen-year terms. Because these judges do not have the lifetime tenures and salary protection of other federal judges, they are limited to ruling on "noncontroversial" matters. Since many of the issues in bankruptcy are highly controversial, each bankruptcy court operates under the supervision of a federal district court. A U.S. trustee helps in the administration of cases under the bankruptcy court's jurisdiction.

A committee of unsecured creditors is appointed by the U.S. trustee. A committee of equity security holders may also be appointed, and usually is. Other committees or advocates may be established if necessary to represent interests which diverge from those of shareholders and unsecured creditors. In the Manville Corporation case, for example, a committee was set up for present asbestos tort claimants and an individual was appointed as an advocate for future claimants. In the A. H. Robins case, a committee was formed to represent women who had used the company's Dalkon Shield intrauterine device. The committees are charged with representing their respective claimant groups and participating in the formulation of a plan of reorganization.

For the first 120 days after filing, only the DIP can submit a reorganization plan. If a plan is not submitted within 120 days and accepted by "impaired" claimant groups within 180 days, any party in interest, even an individual shareholder or creditor, may file a plan. Both time limits may be extended or shortened for cause by the bankruptcy court. For example, Manville Corporation was given more than four years to prepare its plan and seek approval of it. On the other hand, Worlds of Wonder, Inc. filed for Chapter 11 protection in December 1987. The company's banks and unsecured creditors were allowed to submit a plan, which was approved by the bankruptcy court in March 1988.

The bankruptcy judge is authorized to confirm a plan if the following requirements, among

[128]The popularity of "leveraged buyouts" and takeovers, after which acquisitions are dismembered and sold, suggests this may not be an entirely valid assumption.

others, are met. The plan must be proposed in good faith and the proponent must disclose certain specified information. Each holder of a claim or interest who has not accepted the plan must be allowed at least as much value, as of the plan's effective date, as Chapter 7 liquidation would provide. Each class of claims or interests which is "impaired" under the plan must have accepted the plan—unless the judge rules the plan does not discriminate unfairly and is fair and equitable with respect to the class.[129] In general, a plan is considered fair and equitable with respect to nonapproving impaired classes if it treats them equally in comparison to other classes of equal rank and if their allowed claims will be fully satisfied under the plan before more junior classes receive any distribution at all. Approval of a plan under this provision is called a "cramdown." Finally, confirmation of the plan must not be likely to be followed by the need for further financial reorganization or liquidation.

While the plan is being negotiated, approved, and confirmed, all prefiling claims are automatically stayed and executory contracts may be unilaterally cancelled by the debtor. The court has authority to lift the automatic stay with regard to particular claims. Also, the cancellation of executory contracts may create allowable claims against the debtor estate.

Ideally, the plan will provide that the value of the going concern as of the effective date of the plan will be allocated first to the administrative costs of the proceeding and any post-filing obligations of the debtor and then to the claimant groups in order of their "absolute priority in liquidation." Thus, the allowed prefiling claims on the debtor estate may be satisfied in this sequence: (1) secured debt (up to the value of respective collateral as of the effective date of the plan), (2) unsecured debt (including nominally secured debt above the value of respective collateral), and (3) equity claims in order of preference (e.g., preferred, then common). The "value" may be in the form of cash, securities, or other real or personal property and should be at least equivalent to what each party would have gotten if the company had been liquidated. Any claim not provided for in the final reorganization plan is discharged.

[129]A class of claims or interests is unimpaired if reinstated and the holders compensated for damages or if paid in cash. Acceptance of a plan by a creditor class requires approval by over half in number and at least two-thirds in amount of allowed claims in the class. Classes of interests, such as shareholders, must approve by at least two-thirds in amount of such interests.

Managerial Incentives in Chapter 11

After filing for reorganization, management is bombarded with powerful conflicting demands. Employees want their jobs assured at the same or higher pay levels. Stockholders want share price to be propped up and dividends to be reinstated at the earliest possible time. Creditors demand payment or special considerations such as extra collateral or higher interest rates. The typical bankruptcy judge wants decorum and consensus to prevail and rapid progress to be made toward consummation of a workable plan.

Managers are forestalled from their traditional role of representing only shareholder interests. Shareholders have a committee to look out for them and putting management on their side would prejudice the interests of other claimants. Besides, little or no shareholder equity may be left in the debtor firm, so the court may rule there is no shareholder interest to protect. To prevent shareholders from extracting undue consideration from managers or voting in new ones, shareholders may be disenfranchised during the reorganization process. For example, the judge in the five-years-long Manville case turned down several petitions to require management to conduct annual and special stockholder meetings. He even disbanded the shareholders' committee in the bankruptcy court.

A common premise is that filing for Chapter

11 protection stigmatizes management.[130] But unlike most fiduciaries, management of a Chapter 11 debtor has strong financial interests in its truster. As compared to outright liquidation or austere survival without court protection, bankruptcy reorganization can lead to improved pay and benefits, lengthened careers, lowered job demands, and heightened respectability for the managers. So burdened with profound self interest and faced with an ambiguous charter, managers may seek to turn the reorganization process to personal ends.

---

[130]See, for example, Robert I. Sutton and Anita L. Callahan, "The Stigma of Bankruptcy: Spoiled Organizational Image and Its Management," *Academy of Management Journal,* 1987, 3, 405–436.

Appendix D

Manville Financial Summaries, after August 26, 1982

Income Statements (dollar amounts in millions)*

	1987**	1986	1985	1984	1983	1982
Sales	$1,541	$1,920	$1,880	$1,814	$1,729	$1,772
Other income, net	31	39	62	59	61	34
	1,572	1,959	1,942	1,873	1,791	1,806
Cost of sales	1,136	1,452	1,473	1,400	1,370	1,391
Selling, G & A expenses	166	235	246	238	224	222
R & D and eng. exp.	27	39	35	36	35	28
Operating income	243	233	188	200	161	163
Loss on disp. of assets	(21)	47	151	0	(3)	110
Empl. sep. and ret. costs						39
Asbestos health costs	6	11	52	26	20	16
Interest expense	17	20	23	21	26	52
Chapter 11 costs	8	17	9	17	18	2
Income-cont. oper.	233	138	(47)	135	100	(56)
Income taxes	100	57	(2)	58	40	32
Net. inc.-cont. ops.	133	81	(45)	77	60	(88)
Net inc.-discont. oper.	0	0	0	0	7	(10)
Net income	$ 133	$ 81	$ (45)	$ 77	$ 67	$ (98)

Business Segment Information (dollar amounts in millions)*

	1987**	1986	1985	1984	1983	1982
Revenues						
Fiber glass products	$ 652	$ 809	$ 803	$ 781	$ 718	$ 609
Forest products	450	541	459	451	415	436
Specialty products	469	611	674	645	683	829
Corporate revenues-net	26	31	43	38	36	15
Intersegment sales	(25)	(33)	(37)	(42)	(61)	(82)
Total	$1,572	$1,959	$1,942	$1,873	$1,791	$1,806
Income from Operations						
Fiberglass products	$ 113	$ 133	$ 106	$ 115	$ 97	$ 75
Forest products	84	68	43	63	52	48
Specialty products	45	46	33	28	19	51
Corporate expense-net	(4)	(18)	(1)	(6)	(6)	(18)
Eliminations and adjmts.	5	4	7	0	0	7
Total	$ 243	$ 233	$ 188	$ 200	$ 161	$ 164

*Totals may not check, due to rounding.
**Nine months ended September 30. Sales for the year totaled $2.063 billion.
Net income for 1987 was $73 million, after an extraordinary charge due to payment of $150 million to the A-H trust.

Balance Sheets (dollar amounts in millions)*

	December 31				
	1986	1985	1984	1983	1982
Assets					
Cash	$ 8	$ 7	$ 9	$ 19	$ 11
Mkt securities at cost	437	314	276	240	206
Accounts and notes rec	292	314	285	277	310
Inventories	153	153	164	141	152
Prepaid expenses	24	29	17	22	17
Total current assets	914	817	752	700	696
Property, plant and equip					
Land and improvements	99	95	96	97	108
Buildings	312	299	308	303	332
Machinery and equip	1,234	1,160	1,121	1,036	1,090
Less acc dpr & depl	586	538	513	472	547
	1,059	1,017	1,013	984	983
Timber and tbrland-net	376	385	392	395	402
PP&E-net	1,434	1,402	1,405	1,379	1,385
Other assets	165	174	182	174	154
	$2,513	$2,393	$2,339	$2,253	$2,236
Liabilities and Stockholder Equity					
Short-term debt	$ 30	$ 26	$ 20	$ 94	$ 12
Accounts payable	93	84	102	65	86
Accrued employee compensation and benefits	103	94	81	14	63
Income taxes	16	12	18	9	32
Other accrued liab.	62	69	35	26	29
Total current liab.	304	286	256	209	221
Long-term debt	80	92	84	713	736
Liab-Chap. 11 proceedings	575	578	574	5	12
Other non-current liab.	118	115	67	61	60
Deferred income taxes	161	144	162	136	140
	1,239	1,214	1,142	1,122	1,170
Preferred stock	$ 301	$ 301	$ 301	$ 301	$ 301
Common stock	60	60	60	60	60
Capital in excess of par	178	178	178	178	178
Retained earnings	749	667	713	635	568
Cum. curr. transl. adj.	(11)	(26)	(53)	(41)	(39)
Cost of treas. stock	(2)	(2)	(2)	(2)	(2)
	974	878	896	831	765
	$2,513	$2,393	$2,339	$2,253	$2,236

*Totals may not check, due to rounding.

Appendix E

Comments by Manville Executives and Other Principals

John A. McKinney (letter to author): The suggestion that the Chapter 11 filing was for the benefit of Manville Officers is laughable. . . . The filing preserved the position of the victims as equal creditors (virtually all unsecured) in the event of a financial calamity.

W. Thomas Stephens (letters to author): There are really only two questions. First: How do we compensate for the mistakes already made? And, second: How do we prevent another problem like that from ever arising in our society again. . . . Nothing worse could happen to the asbestos health claimants than to initiate a liquidation process. . . . There are a lot of us in this case who didn't cause this problem. As professionals, however, we were brought in to solve it. . . . Personally, I am proud that we have found a solution to a very, very complex legal, social and financial problem.

Leading A-H Attorney Ronald L. Motley (letters to author): After four years of discussions, negotiations and consultations with our committees and investment consultants, the overwhelming majority of the AH Committee, including the representative of the Asbestos Victims of America, voted in favor of the Plan of Reorganization which was largely shaped by Leon Silverman, in consultation with myself, Stan Levy, and our counsel, Elihu Inselbuch . . . the addition of the property damage weight to the scales led many of us to view the settlement as being in the best interest of the personal injury claimants. . . .

[The] intimation that there is some relationship between Manville's withdrawal of its objection to contingency fees in exchange for the AH Committee's not opposing certain management decisions is both false and insulting.

Case 26

F. W. Woolworth and Co., Limited (Woolworth, U.K.) (C)

"We do not know what the flyers are, so we do not know how fast they can fly," noted an executive of Woolworth U.K., referring to Woolworth's merchandise mix, as he reflected upon the resistance he perceived to the use of the information Management Services generated or could generate. He believed this information would be quite useful to Woolworth's management. "But," a member of Management Services added, "we shall generate this information only if someone asks for it." In the summer of 1981, while attempting to implement numerous changes in its approach to retailing, Woolworth was also experiencing some economic difficulties. Several executives were questioning whether its management systems were providing an adequate support to decision making and strategy implementation, and whether these systems were adequately used by management. As one of them explained: "There are masses of data available, but not much is actually used in reaching decisions."

This case describes the management systems used by Woolworth, with particular emphasis given to its management information systems, its budgeting and reporting systems, its five-year plan and its management committees.

This case was prepared by Research Associate Nancy Newcomer under the direction of Professor Xavier Gilbert as a basis for class discussion rather than to illustrate either effective or ineffective handling of an administrative situation.

Management Information

Management Services was in charge, among other responsibilities, of Woolworth's electronic data processing (EDP). In addition to a number of bookkeeping tasks performed for Finance, EDP processed the Central Ordering System data. This system centralized the orders from the various stores and dispatched them either to the Stocking Centers from which the goods were delivered to the stores, or to the suppliers who delivered directly to the stores. According to Management Services, approximately 55% of the total merchandise range was processed through the Central Ordering System. The other 45% was ordered directly by the stores to the suppliers, a short-circuit allowed by management in a number of cases, particularly for goods ordered on a recurrent basis.

Management Services believed that the data collected through the Central Ordering System could also meet some other information needs. At that time, Management Services only issued the so-called monthly "Green Report" indicating total store orders, per region, per merchandise department. This report was distributed to Senior Management, the Regional Managers and the Buyers. Exhibit 1 on pages 964–965 shows a copy of one of the pages of the Green Report.

"Potentially," observed a member of Management Services, "a lot more information could be obtained from this data base. For example, we could identify the fast moving items and their profitability. This information could be brought together with other data, such as space allocation per department, price lists, etc., and serve as a basis for merchandise analysis. The frequency with which various reports could be circulated could also be adapted to the needs of various users. Unfortunately, this potential source of information is not tapped. I think the buyers do not really want to know. They fear losing representation in the stores."

Point-of-Sale Data Collection

Point-of-sale data collection was another management information system being studied by Management Services. Management Services believed that such a system could provide Woolworth with two benefits: an inventory management system for the stores and statistical information on what the stores actually sold. Point-of-sale data collection functioned by using computer-linked tills to record the code of each item sold. The data collected in this manner could then be processed through a variety of statistical analyses. The coding of all the articles sold by Woolworth had already been performed for the Central Ordering System.

Such systems were generally not yet used in the U.K., according to Management Services, and were just being introduced in the U.S. In the U.K., British Home Stores had been the first retail chain to have one. But, as an executive noted:

> British Home Stores has only 120 stores and some 10,000 items which have a relatively high average value—clothing—and are closely affected by fashion. Supermarkets have also been quicker in introducing point-of-sale data collection systems: they deal with low-gross, fast-moving merchandise.
>
> The problem of Woolworth is of a different nature. The proportion of slow-moving items in Woolworth's merchandise range is in fact increasing: in 1970, 52% of the items had sales of less than six units per store, per week. In 1975, 81% of the items sold by Woolworth were in this situation. I estimate that in 1980, the percentage would be 90% of the items. Consequently, timing of data collection is not so crucial for most of our merchandise. In addition, with 1,000 stores and a merchandise range of 30,000 to 40,000 items, a point-of-sale data collection system would be a considerable project.

In July 1981, Management Services was trying to get the Board's approval to install a point-of-sale data collection system in one store on a trial basis. The cost was estimated to be £40,000 to £50,000. This was after four alternatives had been proposed to the Board to introduce a point-of-sale data collection system, none of which had been approved.

1. A complete system in all stores, identifying each item separately. The total capital investment would be in excess of £33 million.

2. The information could be collected per merchandise department, per store, instead of collecting it per item, per store. It would provide data on the movement of goods, their profitability, the inventory level per department. The capital cost for such a system was estimated at £16 million.

3. The system could be introduced in a sample of stores only. With a sample of 200 stores the capital cost would amount to £5.4 million.

4. The system could be introduced only in the 65 stores of the classes 1–3, excluding Woolco. The capital cost would amount to approximately £3.5 million.

According to Management Services, the reasons for the Board's rejection of all four alternatives were both the cost of the system and the fact that Board Members did not believe that it would be very useful. A member of Management Services reported comments such as "When we had department tills in the stores, instead of central cash registers, we never used the information; we had it in the first Woolco store and we never used the information either." In fact, Management Services believed the information used to be used by the store managers themselves who, at that time, had much more autonomy in the merchandising decisions concerning their stores.

According to one Board Member, however, the reason for the Board's refusal was that the way in which the information generated would be used was still unclear. In August 1981, the proposal to install the system in one store on a trial basis was also rejected as a result of the difficulty of committing funds to an immediately subsequent introduction on a 200 store basis, if the experiment turned out to be favorable.*

Budgeting and Reporting System

The preparation of the yearly budgets was coordinated by the Group Financial Controller, in the Finance Department. The final budgets were prepared by the regions, with inputs from the Sales Department, the Buyers, and other functional units such as Personnel, Store Operations, etc. They were subsequently consolidated by the Group Financial Controller's office.

The input from the Sales Department consisted in sales forecasts per region, while those from Buying consisted in gross margin forecasts per merchandise department. According to management, the reconciliation of these forecasts did not pose any particular problem. Firstly, the executives concerned—Sales Director, Buying Controllers and Buying Directors—were all located in the Executive Offices and could meet easily in order to discuss any discrepancy. Secondly, the forecasts were prepared essentially by extrapolating the previous year, with most of the budget already committed. "This," the Director of Corporate Planning observed, "results in quite comparable forecasts from the various persons involved."

The budgeting process started at the end of September, when the Regional Managers were asked to prepare a forecast of the results of the current fiscal year. This forecast updated the current year budget in terms of Sales, Gross Margin, Expenses, etc.

Then, during the month of October, guidelines concerning personnel and other expenses were prepared respectively by the Personnel Department and by the Expense Control Department. At the same time, the Sales Department prepared its sales forecasts per region and the Buying Department prepared its gross margin forecasts per merchandise department. Also at the same time, store inventory turnover forecasts were prepared per region by the Expense Control Department and inventory forecasts for the warehouses were prepared by the Warehouse Department. On the basis of these forecasts, a preliminary budget was prepared by the Finance Department and approved by management at the beginning of November.

During November, the Regional Offices could then prepare their own budgets within the guidelines sent to them by the Finance Department. These budgets were revised during December, approved by management at the beginning of January, and sent to the U.S. parent company. Once the year-end actual results were available, the budgets could be revised in March-April.

Budgets and actual results were compared on a monthly basis through several monthly reports. These reports included the following:

1. *"Gold Report" (issued on yellow paper).* This was a detailed income statement for the month and for the year to date, per region. Since it showed the trading profit and the profit before tax, its publication was restricted to the Board Members (see Exhibit 2, pages 966–969).

2. *"Blue Report" (on blue paper).* This report covered only part of the information contained in the Gold Report. It was limited to the last month only and, for reasons of secrecy, it did not include the corporate overheads, neither the trading profit nor the profit before tax. Being less sensitive, it had a wider distribution than the Gold Report (see Exhibit 3, pages 970–973).

*In 1982, it was agreed that mechanical trials of suitable equipment would take place in test stores and that a complete system would be put into the experimental new form of city center store due to open at Bristol.

3. *"Green Report" (on green paper).* This report showed the store purchases per merchandise department and per region (Exhibit 1). It was prepared on the basis of the information collected through the Central Ordering System.

4. *Reports from the Regional Managers.* On two to three pages, these reports prepared by the Regional Managers showed the same figures as in the Blue Report, but limited to their region. It included a narrative presenting the figures, typically: "Sales have increased by x% compared to last year but are y% under budget for this year." This was followed by an explanation for the situation: "As a result of bad weather, summer items have gone more slowly than anticipated . . ."

5. *Print-outs of the store results, per store.* This was a 10-cm-thick computer print-out of the income statements limited to the items controllable by the store manager for each store.

Top management received all of the above reports. Regional Managers received only the Blue Report, the Green Report and the store print-outs. Buyers received the Green Report. Store Managers received the results from their store.

Five-Year Plan

The Five-year Plan, a document of approximately 80 pages, represented the yearly formalization of the strategic thinking process through which the Board was engaging on a continued basis. As the Director of Corporate Planning explained: "Strategic issues are discussed on an ongoing basis among Board members."

The Five-year Plan was prepared every year during June and July. The 1980–1984 Plan covered the following sections, consisting of qualitative comments accompanied with figure tables if needed:

I. Examination of present position and outline of future corporate development

II. Evaluation of present and past performance

III. Key Management Areas
   Buying and Merchandising
   D.I.Y. Division
   Textile Division
   Catering Division
   The Variety Base
   Inventory
   Marketing
   Sales Management—Advertising—Sales Promotion
   Press and Public Relations
   Woolco
   Furnishing World
   Shoppers World
   Overseas
   Real Estate and Construction
   Business Administration

IV. Financial forecasts 1980—1984 (Pro Forma Financial Statements)

The narratives on the various key areas were generally obtained from the persons in charge of these areas, although the planning executive in charge of the Five-year Plan (reporting to the Corporate Planning Director) could be quite involved in helping some of them put together the necessary quantitative and qualitative information. Once collected from the various sources, this information was consolidated by Corporate Planning so that it would read as if it had been prepared by one single person; for example, the format of the tables had to be made uniform. The financial forecasts, presented according to the format required by the U.S. parent company, were added at the end and this constituted the Five-year Plan. It was distributed only to the members of the Board of Directors and sent to the U.S. parent company.

Corporate Planning was a small unit, consisting essentially of two executives who reported to the Corporate Planning Director. One of them was responsible for collecting from various sources the data that constituted the corporate plan and for assembling it. Corporate Planning also prepared a number of reports and special studies on various issues related to the evolution of the company. It had limited staff resources. For example, the 1980–1984 Plan had to be typed outside the company.

The Corporate Planning Executive in charge of the Five-year Plan commented:

> The most important aspect of planning is not the plan itself, but the process through which it was prepared and that it makes managers think about the long term future of their activities. People are quite willing to cooperate with me when I go to them and ask for information. At the beginning, they were somewhat reluctant to say something about the future, but then they realized that it did not cause any harm. They also saw that thinking about the future could be useful.

Management Meetings

A number of management meetings were scheduled regularly in order to facilitate the coordination among organizational units.

Corporate Policy Committee

The Corporate Policy Committee met monthly or more frequently if needed. It included the Chairman, the Executive Directors,* the Management Services Executive, the Store Operations Executive and one of the Corporate Planning executives who acted as secretary to the Committee. The purpose of these meetings was to discuss issues of a policy nature. For example, the agenda of a typical meeting (July 1981) included the following:

▪ Approval of the minutes of the previous meeting.

(The minutes of the previous meeting recapitulated the essence of the discussion and the opinions expressed by various members of the committee. They indicated in the margin who was responsible for an action that had been decided. For example, the minutes of the June 1981 meeting indicated that the Director of Corporate Planning had agreed to prepare a paper on concessions in stores.)

▪ Results to date; further actions.

▪ Management update of Nielsen Audit Data; Nielsen presentation. (Nielsen is a marketing research firm specialized in retailing.)

▪ Clothing Division update:
Spring/Summer performance
Autumn buy
(At that time, as a result of bad weather, the spring/summer collection of the clothing division was performing poorly.)

▪ Acquisitions: reaffirm commitment to specific areas.
(Refers to the merchandise/distribution areas selected for priority development.)

▪ D.I.Y. policy.

▪ Growth of cost centers.
(At that time, certain expenses were increasing beyond the budgeted amounts.)

▪ Paper on franchises/concessions presented by the Director of Corporate Planning.
(The issue of renting concessions within stores, for example, to opticians, had been discussed in the previous meeting and the Director of Corporate Planning had agreed to prepare a paper to propose a policy.)

▪ Decision on options for major change in marketing strategy. (Some important changes in the marketing strategy were being considered, but decisions had not yet been reached.)

Buyer's Reviews

There were two types of Buyer's Reviews. The first type, where each individual buyer met with his Buying Controller and the Buying Director,

---

*In addition to the Chairman, the other Executive Directors (i.e., members of the Board of Directors) were the two joint Managing Directors, the Sales Director, the two Buying Directors, the Corporate Planning Director, the Finance Director, the Personnel Director and the Director of Construction and Real Estate.

took place approximately every second year. Its purpose was to review each item in the buyer's merchandise department and to decide on its continuation, its replacement, or the introduction of new items. This did not prevent such decisions at other times, but this formal exercise was gone through at least every second year.

The second type of Buyer's Review was considered a very important meeting. It took place twice a year and involved top management in a formal financial and planning review of each buyer's performance. The Year-end Buyer's Review took place in March. Each buyer appeared in front of the Executive Directors, including the Chairman. Regional Merchandise Managers could also be asked to attend when certain departments were being reviewed. The exercise lasted for three to four days. Buyers appeared individually or as a group of related departments to present individually to the Board, for about half an hour, their performance during the previous year, compared with their forecast. They had to explain any difference and what they intended to do about it during the current year. They also had to explain their plans with respect to their merchandise mix and the expected impact on their department's gross profit. Finally, they answered questions from the Board. Before the meeting, they had to submit a short written review, possibly prepared with their Buying Controller.

Explained the Director of Corporate Planning:

> Previously this session was very much like an oral examination. In the previous Chairman's own words, he gave them "a pat on the back if they were above forecast and a kick up the . . . if they were under." It was expected that, as a result of having been shaken up, the buyer would discover the appropriate merchandise mix to increase his gross profit. The philosophy was "put the buyers under pressure and they'll do what is best for the company." Now, the style has changed but the expected result of the Buyer's Reviews has remained the same.
>
> The Mid-year Buyer's Review took place in October. Its purpose was to discuss the plans for the following years. They had had in the past a rather short-term orientation, the buyers being asked questions on what they had done thus far and what they intended to do before the end of the year. Since 1980, however, an attempt had been made to make this meeting become more a marketing review. Buyers were asked to project their view of their department four or five years ahead, with the idea of using their thoughts as an input for the Five-year Plan. At the same time top management would tell them what the framework of the company was likely to be for the years to come. "It should develop into a two-way discussion of the future," explained the Corporate Planning Director. In 1980, the views expressed by the Buyers in the course of these meetings were recorded and synthesized for the Board by the Marketing Department.

Management believed that the buyers could do much to improve the gross profit of their department. As the Director of Corporate Planning explained:

> It is up to them to be creative and find the merchandise mix that yields the highest gross profit, while meeting the sales targets. As an example, a whole new department was created with kitchenware, using a well-balanced mix of well-designed product. This may be less easy to do, however, when dealing with a mixed bag of variety products, such as those that are found in some other departments. What is also difficult to achieve is a possible coordination between kitchenware, for example, and other more or less related departments.

In order to perform this task, the buyers could use several sources of information. One was the Green Report, indicating the store purchases per department. According to one of the Planning Executives:

> They could also talk with the Regional Managers, the Regional Merchandise Managers, the District Managers and the Store Managers, to get their views on those items that were doing well. Al-

> though the buyers do not have a formal information system that tells them what is actually being sold per item or per department, they can develop informally a certain idea. With the big-ticket items, for example, such as "stereos" the stores may keep a hand count of what is being sold. The clothing sales are identified through a specially coded ticket [Kimbie tag] at the cash registers. So there are in fact many informal possibilities to obtain the necessary information.

Operations Committee Meetings

These monthly meetings had a fixed agenda. They covered essentially the Regional Managers' performance. The meetings were chaired by the Chairman and they were attended by the Executive Directors, the Functional Departments' Executives and the Regional Directors.

For these meetings, the Regional Directors prepared a two-to-three page report (as described in the section on reporting). The purpose of these meetings was to look at problems at the regional, or store class, level, although, according to the Director of Corporate Planning, "there were frequent temptations to look at individual stores."

During these meetings the Executive Directors also introduced items for action or comments within their areas of responsibility: Personnel, Industrial Relations, Store Relations, Buying, etc. "The Operations Committee Meetings also serve a policy implementation purpose," an Executive observed.

Other Meetings

Several other committees met regularly to deal with more specialized issues:

Audit Committee: Met quarterly.

Capital Expenditure Committee: Met every two weeks to review all capital expenditure projects. It could approve the projects between £20,000 and £10 million.

Store Planning and Coordination Committee: Met monthly to coordinate the problems of architecture, design and fixtures.

Systems and Research Committee: Met monthly to review the administrative systems, EDP, equipment, organization and methods.

Exhibit 1 Green Report

Office Only

Accumulative Departmental Report—15 Weeks to 10th May 1979/80

Merchandise Departments	Purchases 14 Weeks to 3rd May (xxxxx/xxxxx)					Merchandise Book at 3rd May			
	Last Year £000's	This Year £000's	Gain %	% of Total		Including Inventory		Excluding Inventory	
			All Stores	Last Year	This Year	Last Year	This Year	Last Year	This Year
010 L B M K W									
D/T									
015 L B M K W									
D/T									
020 L B M K W									
D/T									
021 L B M K W									

+
+
+
+

D/T									
022 L B M K W									
D/T									
023 L B M K W									
D/T									
024 L B M K W									
D/T									
025 L B M K W									
D/T									

Casewriter's Note: The complete Green Report consists of eight pages similar to the above one to cover all 60 Merchandise Departments referenced in the left-hand side.

Exhibit 2 Gold Report

Shop Sales Inflation Index Current Period/Last Year	

F.W. Woolworth and Co. Limited **Page 1**

		Company Results Actual £000's %	(at S.P.)	Budget £000's %	(at S.P.)	Last Year £000's %	(Weeks) (at S.P.)	Budget/ Last Year Inc. %	Actual Last Year Inc. %	Number of Stores*
Sales (Excl. T.K.L.) (Dept. 241)	Regions									
	Shoppers World									
	Footlocker									
	Furnishing									
	World									
	Overseas									
Gross Profit (Before Shrinkage)	Regions									
	Shoppers World									
	Footlocker									
	Furnishing									
	World									
	Overseas									
	E.O. adg.									
Shrinkage (At Cost)	Regions		( )	( )	( )					
	Shoppers World		( )	( )	( )					
	Footlocker		( )	( )	( )					
	Furnishing									
	World		( )	( )	( )					
	Overseas		( )	( )	( )					
	E.O. adj.		( )	( )	( )					
			( )	( )	( )					
Gross Profit	Regions									
	Shoppers World									
	Footlocker									
	Furnishing									
	World									
	Overseas									
	E.O. adj.									
	**Other Income									

Total Salaries	Regions	
	Shoppers World	
	Footlocker	
	Furnishing World	
	Overseas	
Managers Controllable Expense	Regions	
	Shoppers World	
	Footlocker	
	Furnishing World	
	Overseas	
Market Rent Differential	Regions	
	Shoppers World	
	Footlocker	
	Furnishing World	
	Overseas	
Other Expense	Regions	
	Shoppers World	
	Footlocker	
	Furnishing World	
	Overseas	
	E.O. adj.	
Net Profit + (Includes Other Income)	+Regions	
	Shoppers World	
	Footlocker	
	Furnishing World	
	Overseas	
	E.O. adj.	

*Number of stores Shoppers World includes —"Two in One" Units
**Other income from Dept. 241—T.K.L.

(continued)

Exhibit 2 *(continued)*

Shop Sales Inflation Index Current Period/Last Year	

F.W. Woolworth and Co. Limited

		Company Results		(Weeks)	Budget/ Last Year Inc. %	Actual Last Year Inc. %
		Actual £000's %	Budget £000's %	Last Year £000's %		
Net Profit + (Includes Other Income)	+Regions					
	Shoppers World					
	Footlocker					
	Furnishing World					
	Overseas					
	E.O. adj.					
Manager	Regions					
	Shoppers World					
	Footlocker					
	Furnishing World					
	Overseas					
	E.O. adj.					

Debits after W
Credits after W
Market Rent Differential
Trading Profit
Depreciation of Fixed Assets
Interest Paid/Received
Rents Received
Profit on Sales of Properties
Profit Before Tax
Foreign Currency Losses
(X denotes loss)
R.I.
Overseas

Note: The budget for R.I. and Overseas has been converted at current exchange rates. The resulting difference at W level from the original conversion for the company budget is shown as a Foreign Currency loss in the budget column.

R.I. and Overseas Stores Exchange Rates cause distortions between actual and last year.

Exhibit 3 Blue Report

Shop Sales Inflation Index Current Period/Last Year	

F.W. Woolworth and Co. Limited **PAGE 1**

		All Stores Region Results					**(Weeks)**	**Budget/ Last Year Inc. %**	**Actual/ Last Year Inc. %**	**Number of Stores**
		Actual £000's %	**(at S.P.)**	**Budget £000's %**	**(at S.P.)**	**Last Year £000's %**	**(at S.P.)**			
Sales (Excl. T.K.L.) (Dept. 241)	Liverpool									
	R.I.									
	Birmingham									
	Metropolitan									
	Kensington									
Gross profit (Before Shrinkage)	Liverpool									
	R.I.									
	Birmingham									
	Metropolitan									
	Kensington									
Shrinkage (At Cost)	Liverpool		( )	( )	( )					
	R.I.		( )	( )	( )					
	Birmingham		( )	( )	( )					
	Metropolitan		( )	( )	( )					
	Kensington		( )	( )	( )					
			( )	( )	( )					
Gross Profit	Liverpool									
	R.I.									
	Birmingham									
	Metropolitan									
	Kensington									
Other Income (Dept. 241–) (T.K.L.)	Liverpool									
	R.I.									
	Birmingham									
	Metropolitan									
	Kensington									

Total Salaries	Liverpool R.I. Birmingham Metropolitan Kensington		
Managers Controllable Expense	Liverpool R.I. Birmingham Metropolitan Kensington		Actual/ Last Year Mrkt. Rent Inc. %
Other Expense	Liverpool R.I. Birmingham Metropolitan Kensington		
Net Profit	Liverpool R.I. Birmingham Metropolitan Kensington		
Manager	Liverpool R.I. Birmingham Metropolitan Kensington		
	Liverpool R.I. Birmingham Metropolitan Kensington		

(continued)

Exhibit 3 *(continued)*

R.I. Results Converted at:
This Year Punts—£1 (U.K.)
Last Year Punts—£1 (U.K.)

Merchandise Stock at:

	S.P. EST Stock This Month			Maximum Stock at Selling Price	Express of Estimated Stock over Maximum		Merchandise Book to Date	
		T/I	L/Y		This Month	Inc. %	This Year	Last Year
Liverpool R.I. Birmingham Metropolitan Kensington								
Total								

F.W. Woolworth and Co. Limited
Super Stores (Classes 1, 2, and 3) Results (Weeks)

		Actual £000's %	% of Regional Totals	Last Year £000's %	% of Regional Totals	Actual/ Last Year Inc. %
Sales (Excl. T.K.L.) (Dept. 241)	Liverpool R.I. Birmingham Metropolitan Kensington					
Gross Profit (Before Shrinkage)	Liverpool R.I. Birmingham Metropolitan Kensington					
Shrinkage (At Cost)	Liverpool		( )	( )	( )	
	R.I.		( )	( )	( )	
	Birmingham		( )	( )	( )	
	Metropolitan		( )	( )	( )	
	Kensington		( )	( )	( )	
			( )	( )	( )	

Gross Profit	Liverpool	
	R.I.	
	Birmingham	
	Metropolitan	
	Kensington	
Other Income (Dept. 241–) (T.K.L.)	Liverpool	
	R.I.	
	Birmingham	
	Metropolitan	
	Kensington	
Total Salaries	Liverpool	
	R.I.	
	Birmingham	
	Metropolitan	
	Kensington	
Managers Controllable Expense	Liverpool	
	R.I.	
	Birmingham	
	Metropolitan	
	Kensington	
Other Expense	Liverpool	
	R.I.	
	Birmingham	
	Metropolitan	
	Kensington	
Net Profit	Liverpool	
	R.I.	
	Birmingham	
	Metropolitan	
	Kensington	
Manager	Liverpool	
	R.I.	
	Birmingham	
	Metropolitan	
	Kensington	
		Unadjusted for Accruals

Appendix A

Woolworth, Ltd (C).

Biographical Sketch of Directors

G. Rodgers (Chairman and Chief Executive)
Joined Woolworth as Management Trainee and subsequently managed a number of stores in the Liverpool Region. From 1961 has held the following Executive positions:

District Manager

Assistant Regional Manager

Executive responsible for Decimalization

Regional Manager

Director and Regional Manager

Joint Managing Director

Deputy Chairman and Chief Executive

Chairman and Chief Executive

H. R. Johnson (Joint Managing Director)
Joined Woolworth as a Management Trainee and progressed through Store Management in the Liverpool Region. Had extensive experience of setting up Overseas Companies and managing stores in the West Indies. Since 1962 has held the following Executive posts:

District Manager

Regional Departmental Manager

Supervisor Overseas Stores

Buyer—various departments

Executive responsible for formation of catalogue division

General Manager—Shoppers World

Seconded to N.C.R. on Management exchange program

Store Operations Executive

Director—responsible for developing departments

Joint Managing Director

R. E. Jones (Joint Managing Director)
Joined Woolworth as Management Trainee, subsequently managing a number of stores in the Metropolitan Region. Has held the following Executive positions since 1969:

District Manager

Seconded to work with P.A. Consultants on special project

Merchandise Co-ordinator

Buyer

Store Planning Executive

Assistant Regional Manager

Regional Manager

Director and Regional Manager

Joint Managing Director

J. H. Bradwell (Joint Director of Buying)
Joined Woolworth as Management Trainee and progressed through Store Management in the Birmingham Region. Since 1959 has held the following Executive posts:

District Manager

Regional Departmental Manager

Buyer—various departments

Buying Supervisor

Executive in charge of Buying

Director of Buying

J. Blair (Director of Real Estate, Construction and Fixtures)
Joined Woolworth as Management Trainee and subsequently managed stores in the Birmingham Region. From 1961 has held the following positions:

District Manager

Executive in charge of Research

Buyer—Woolworth

Buyer—Woolco

Assistant Buying Supervisor—Woolco

Buying Supervisor—Woolco

Director—responsible for developing departments

Director—in charge of Real Estate, Construction and Fixtures

K. J. Willoughby (Director of Corporate Planning)
Joined Woolworth in 1971. Previous experience had been with Nestle and the Co-operative Wholesale Society. Joined Woolworth as Marketing Manager. Subsequently became:

Director of Store Operations

Director of Corporate Planning

M. P. Downs (Director of Personnel)
Joined Woolworth in 1974. Previous experience had been in retailing in South Africa and Rhodesia. Became Personnel Manager for British Home Stores and later Personnel Manager for the Regional Hospital Boards. Joined Woolworth as Personnel Manager and subsequently appointed Personnel Director.

R. J. Kirkman (Director of Corporate Financing)
Background in accountancy in retail industry and immediately prior to joining Woolworth was Chairman and Managing Director of UDS Group Finance Ltd. Joined Woolworth in 1978 as Director of Finance, following two consecutive incumbents hired since 1971 from outside the Company who had occupied the position and left.

D. Collier (Director of Sales and Advertising)
Joined Woolworth as Management Trainee and progressed through Store Management in the Kensington Region. Since 1968 has held the following Executive positions:

District Manager

Regional Sales Manager

Sales Promotion Executive—major stores

Company Sales and Advertising Executive

Director of Sales and Advertising

J. G. Dodds (Joint Director of Buying)
Joined Woolworth as Management Trainee and subsequently managed both Woolworth and Woolco stores. From 1973 has held the following Executive posts:

Assistant General Manager—Woolco

Assistant Regional Manager—Woolworth

Regional Manager

Director and Regional Manager

Joint Buying Director

Appendix B

Woolworth, Ltd (C)

Classification of Stores by Neighborhood

Area Code	Description
1	*City Centers*—Twelve major centers of national importance and influence
2	*Other Major Conurbations*—Major towns of regional importance including suburban retail nuclei in city-center-based conurbations.
3	*Major Conurbations: Secondary Sites*
4	*Metropolitan Regions:* Urbanized regions with well developed communication and employment infrastructure. Regional town centers exerted strong influence over these surrounding urbanized catchments.
5	*Metropolitan Region:* Secondary Center
6	*Rural Regions:* Areas with limited urban development, isolated from metropolitan centers, predominantly served by "self-contained" market centers of long standing.
7	*Rural Region: Secondary Center*

Questions for Discussion

1. Do you think the proposed system will improve strategic control at Woolworth's?

2. What problems would you anticipate might occur as the system is implemented?

3. Prepare an implementation plan for the new system.

Case 27

The NASA Space Shuttle Disaster: A Case Study

In retrospect, Thiokol Inc.'s perfunctory green light unwittingly reads like a death warrant. For a breathless moment the reader is transfixed with the thought that the shuttle accident might have been avoided (Figure 1). But the lethal calculus of limited O-ring tolerances and subnormal Florida temperatures served not only as the immediate mechanical cause of the Challenger tragedy but also as a symptom of long-unresolved organizational issues. For example, besides advertising America's technological (and, derivatively, political) superiority, what, specifically, was the agency's actual scientific purpose? Was it reasonable to assume that a 14-year-old bureaucracy, driven by an exploratory ethos inspired by the futurology of H. G. Wells, could be readily adapted to a commercial schedule without creating serious organizational tensions? (From "Apollo" to "Shuttle"—the choice of project logos captures the essence of this radical reorientation.) Given the institutionwide appropriation of the original astronauts' style (i.e., "Right Stuff"—an unflinching mix of high-tech, high-macho, and high-risk drama) and the virgin technology employed, did NASA and its galaxy of subcontractors operate with an attention to safety? Who and what defined the margin of error? What kind of adverse data interrupted a final countdown? How was it that after 25 elaborate countdowns and with onboard computers that routinely monitored 2,000 vital functions before every launch, the suspect integrity of the critical rocket joints was left un-"sensored"? Or did the collision of pioneering technology and unknown environmental factors make chance error inevitable? Risk could not be eliminated altogether and still allow spacecraft to be launched.

With the full backing of Presidents Kennedy and Johnson, James Webb, NASA's first and last entrepreneur, dreamed of fashioning an enlightened alliance between science and democratic tradition. Indeed, in light of the agency's dramatic accomplishments, it seemed that Webb's technocratic vision had been fulfilled. No order was too large, and, on the surface at least, the agency's partnership with the private sector produced spectacular results. NASA evoked a public image of detached reason; it was a beacon of order, competence, and hope for Americans jaded by generalized institutional decline. NASA appeared to stand outside the malignant politics, inefficiency, and crossed lines of responsibility that sabotaged the efforts of other major agencies both public and private.

Of course, image and reality do not always correspond. Recent revelations surrounding the decision and communication processes affecting the Challenger launch demonstrate that NASA was foremost a human institution with all the

---

Source: Reprinted by permission of the publisher from "The NASA Space Shuttle Disaster: A Case Study" by Robert Marx, Charles Stubbart, Virginia Traub, and Michael Cavanaugh, *Journal of Management Case Studies* 1987, vol no. 3, pp. 300–318.

Address reprint requests to: Robert Marx, School of Management, University of Massachusetts at Amherst, Amherst, MA 01003.

Figure 1 Copy of Telefax Sent to Kennedy and Marshall Centers by Thiokol

MTI Assessment of Temperature Concern on SRM-25 (51L) Launch

- Calculations show that SRM-25 o-rings will be 20° colder than SRM-15 o-rings
- Temperature data not conclusive on predicting primary o-ring blow-by
- Engineering assessment is that:
  - Colder o-rings will have increased effective durometer (harder")
  - "Harder" o-rings will take longer to "seat"
    - More gas may pass primary o-ring before the primary seal seats (relative to SRM-15)
      - Demonstrated sealing threshold is 3 times greater than 0.038° erosion experienced on SRM-15
  - If the primary seal does not seat, the secondary seal will seat
    - O-ring pressure leak check places secondary seal in outboard position which minimizes sealing time
- MTI recommends STS-51L launch proceed on 28 January 1986
  - SRM-25 will not be significantly different from SRM-15

Joe C. Kilminster, Vice President
Space Booster Programs

MORTON THIOKOL, INC.
WASATCH DIVISION

Source: Rogers Commission Report (1986), p. 79

imperfection that this implies. And perhaps because of this rude shock, we harbor an ongoing sense of institutional loss in addition to the human loss of the seven crew members. Ultimately, beyond all its advances to American rocketry, NASA's most enduring legacy may be to organizational and managerial science.

NASA: A Narrative History

The ongoing saga of America's space program and, particularly, the events surrounding the January 1986 loss of the shuttle Challenger can be better understood if divided into four successive periods: 1) a preliminary period of ad hoc and idiosyncratic research dating from Robert Goddard's pioneering experiments and ending abruptly with the Russian launch of Sputnik I; 2) a second period of public-funded and directed "command technology" commencing with the passage of the National Aeronautics and Space Act of 1958 and closing with the 1968 retirement of James Webb, NASA's first and only "big operator" (McDougall, 1985); 3) a subsequent chapter of organizational decline culminating in the January 1986 explosion of the ill-fated Challenger, a patronless period characterized by mounting national indifference to NASA, shrinking Congressional appropriations, and the unresolved organizational conflicts fueled by the agency's attempt to shift from an exploratory mode to a routine operation; and 4) following the Challenger loss, a self-searching period of mandated change and mission definition.

Period 1—Foundations

The interplanetary designs of Jules Verne and H. G. Wells served as principal inspiration for an entire generation of American and European backyard rocketeers. Yet, in every sense of the phrase, American rocketry was slow to get off the ground. Until World War II, the state remained disinterested. Invention and application of knowledge were generally acknowledged as the proper domain of private individuals and institutions. Indeed, dating from Robert Goddard's early experiments with liquid-fuel rockets in 1926 until the surprise attack on Pearl Harbor 15 years later, U.S. rocketry was relegated to an orphaned status. With the singular exception of the National Advisory Committee for Aeronautics (NACA), conceived at the end of World War I by Charles D. Walcott of the Smithsonian Institution to keep America abreast of advances in European aviation, large-scale government involvement in rocket (or most any other form of scientific) research languished.

World War II permanently altered this laissez-faire philosophy. Traditionally opposed to state assistance, America's political and scientific leadership closed ranks in recognizing the essential role of state-directed R&D in the conduct of modern warfare. Public funds, for instance, underwrote jet-assisted takeoffs and the development of antitank rockets (the bazooka). The war left its own special legacy to American rocket science, a fledgling aerospace industry. Ironically, the first private firm devoted to rocketry, Reaction Motors, Inc., founded in 1941, later became a division of Thiokol Chemical. Residual concerns about mixing politics and science swept aside, the war also facilitated public acceptance of a vast research consortium composed of government, industry, and university, thereby closing a long chapter in amateur invention. The efficacy of government-mobilized R&D was epitomized by the Manhattan Project and (exploiting the experience of captured German rocket scientists) a growing investment in the military applications of jet and rocket propulsion systems.

Although the war had served to resurrect and transform American rocketry, postwar rocket research lacked direction. Following demobilization, congressional and presidential interest waned. Constrained by parsimonious budgets, scientists tinkered with advanced versions of Von Braun's V-2 rocket. And satellite development, despite the promptings of the Rand Corporation, received low priority. Further developments awaited a crisis.

Period 2—Technocracy Achieved

In a 1954 report, Werner von Braun asked for $100,000 to build a space satellite because "a man-made satellite, no matter how humble (five pounds) would be a scientific achievement of tremendous impact." He prophesized that "it would be a blow to U.S. prestige if we did not do it first" (McDougall, 1985, p. 119). In a single stroke, the October 4, 1957 launch of Sputnik I overturned American assumptions about a U.S. technological monopoly and ignited a domestic political crisis. The U.S. response was rapid, however, and was waged along several fronts. The Congress promptly passed the National Defense Education Act to facilitate the recruitment of scientific and engineering talent. New and stricter criteria were promulgated for high school science curricula, backed by across-the-board increases in funding for basic science. On October 1, 1958, less than a full year after the first Soviet launch, the National Aeronautics and Space Act was signed into law creating a civilian bureaucracy to serve as the nation's foremost aeronautical contractor. (NASA performed only a small fraction of actual design and construction. Reviving cottage industry on an unprecedented scale, NASA contracted 80–90% of its work to private subcontractors.) Later, in 1961, impressed by the orbital flight of the Soviet cosmonaut, Yuri Gagarin, and in need of political ammunition to offset setbacks in Laos, the

Congo, and the Bay of Pigs debacle, the new Kennedy Administration declared its commitment to place Americans on the moon within the decade: "This is the new ocean, and I believe the United States must sail on it and be in a position second to none" (John Kennedy, *Time,* Feb. 10, 1986). The young President would marshal American technology to extend America's landlocked frontier. Moreover, the Cold War now included outer space. Space science and the state were inextricably linked. Henceforth, space R&D budgets would be subject to the vicissitudes of superpower rivalry.

Under the energetic stewardship of James Webb, NASA underwrote the Mercury, Gemini, and Apollo programs, culminating in the Apollo 11 moon landing in July 1969. But even at the apex of its power—1964–1965—when the agency received money for the asking (1964 funding totaled $5.1 billion, nearly five times its 1961 budget), the program's long-term objectives remained unclear. Even the NASA field centers failed to reach agreement on charting their own post-Apollo course. Moreover, in the face of the Johnson government's escalating commitments to the Great Society and Vietnam, Webb feared to press for new projects (a manned mission to Mars, a permanent moon base, orbiting space stations) that promised high and unpredictable costs. Not unlike the boom-or-bust revenues of the extractive economies within which it operated (the Gulf states), NASA funding began to evaporate in the second half of the decade. More pressing domestic problems and the relaxation of Cold War tensions undermined vital political support. And many had come to believe "that Apollo was the space program. Once the race was over and won, Americans could turn back to their selfish pursuits" (McDougall, 1985, p. 422).

Finally, in September 1969, the White House unveiled a new charter. A Space Task Group chaired by Spiro Agnew presented the President with three alternatives in descending order of cost. Nixon selected the least expensive—a space station with a shuttle. He later shelved the space station pending development of the shuttle. The message was clear. NASA, for all its technical achievements, was an institution without a coherent mission and was therefore expendable. Another Soviet first could have revived NASA. But having lost the race to the moon, Moscow seemed content to maintain a low profile.

Period 3—The Twilight Zone

"Apollo was a matter of going to the moon and building whatever technology would get us there: the Space Shuttle was a matter of building a technology and going wherever it could take us" (McDougall, 1985, p. 423). After Apollo 11, the agency and the aerospace industry languished. The agency's principal patrons had retired or died. Kennedy was dead. Both LBJ and Webb stepped down in 1968. (NASA chief administrators were replaced with every change in the White House). This was the situation until 1972, when the Nixon administration, convinced of the electoral fallout sure to result from an aerospace depression, agreed to fund the Space Shuttle (or Space Transportation System—STS).

The STS, however, represented a pyrrhic gain for the agency. Most of the original design was bargained away trying to accommodate competing military, commercial, and scientific interests. For instance, to meet Pentagon specifications, the orbiter's payload was increased. The vehicle's fully reusable technology was jettisoned. Furthermore, a zealous Office of Management and Budget trimmed original cost estimates by half. But perhaps most significantly, NASA bowed to Congressional pressure to transform the shuttle operation into a government version of Federal Express (Wilford, 1986, p. 102):

> To satisfy Congress, the system had to pay for itself, which meant that NASA, charted as a research and development agency, was put in the unaccustomed position of hustling business and running an orbital freight operation. The conflicting goals and pressures, as well as the complexity

of the machines themselves, virtually assured that America's Space Transportation—as the shuttle is officially known—would not operate with the efficiency its original designers had planned.

The product of these compromises turned out to be an improvisational instrument useful for ferrying heavy (military) payloads into low earth orbit. But its technical limitations and the cost overruns associated with preflight preparations forfeited the high ground to foreign competition (comsats require higher earth orbits) and pushed the agency into chronic budget overruns.

There was another matter. For James Webb, space conquest was only a spinoff. NASA represented nothing less than a "revolution from above" (McDougall, 1985), an extraordinary opportunity to demonstrate the power of the technological revolution including projected advances in quantitative management. Modeled after the grand patterns of the Tennessee Valley Authority and Manhattan projects, NASA would serve as the prototypic administrative instrument for large-scale social and political change. Like McNamara's efforts to rationalize the Pentagon, Webb aimed to pioneer a new era in management science.

Period 4—Crossroads

Intermittent shuttle launchings notwithstanding, NASA has existed in a suspended state of animation since the spectacular voyage of Apollo 11 in 1969. The agency's most vital period was remarkably brief (1962–1968). In an odd turnabout of events, the American space program is viewed in much the same terms as in its formative, pre-World War II years—an exotic novelty, peripheral to mainstream national concerns.

Such is the power of television that recent American generations distinguish themselves by the media events they recollect. For some it was the Kennedy assassination, for others the Iranian hostage crisis. The haunting TV image of the disintegrating Challenger represents another generation's indelible memory. Measured against previous exploits, the "shuttle chapter" tells the story of an organization in decline. Fourteen years of development and 30 billion invested have produced only 25 flights since 1981. Sponsors were promised 30–60 profit-generating flights annually. NASA's romantic technology was inherently ill-suited for routine operations and commercial (cost-conscious) venture. The disappointment expressed by Dr. Alex Roland, a historian of technology at Duke University, seems almost mean-spirited at this stage: "The shuttle was an economic bust before the accident. It's just crazy to think, as some people in NASA do, that we can return to business as usual" (*New York Times,* Mar. 16, 1986). In the interim, with the shuttle program indefinitely grounded, the Pentagon's STS launch-dependent satellite program is stranded while foreign competitors eagerly vie for American commercial launch contracts.

NASA: A Functional Analysis

NASA—The Organization

Officially, NASA is an agency of the Executive branch, under the control of the President, who directs space policy and appoints NASA's head administrator. Congress sets spending limits and can specify projects to be undertaken. The head administrator has several important tasks, including drawing up proposals and making decisions on future programs, resolving high-level personnel problems, and selling NASA to Congress and the U.S. public. Assistant administrators head various support functions and programs. During the Apollo program, and in the early days of the shuttle, astronauts, who had an appreciation of operations and flight safety, were regularly promoted to management. By the 1980s, this had stopped. NASA has nine field centers, each with its own special mission in support of the overall NASA effort. Private contractors work with, and report to, the field centers.

NASA has undergone several reorganizations in order to meet changing goals. A 1961 reorganization was made to develop a stronger headquarters team that could coordinate efforts among the field centers. In 1963, NASA decentralized to better meet the "man-on-the-moon" goal. After a tragic fire took the lives of three astronauts, organizational changes in 1967 created a centralized structure that could integrate decision making and increase emphasis on safety. Another reorganization occurred in 1983 when the shuttle program was reclassified from "developmental" to "operational." Figure 2 shows how NASA was organized as of January 1986.

Constituencies. From the very beginning, many people feared that NASA would become more political and less scientific. Although it still has a highly scientific orientation, the goals and policies of the agency have been dictated by political considerations. Whether NASA must answer primarily to the Executive branch, Congress, or some other constituency is always a matter of debate. According to veteran observers of NASA, "NASA is a child of Congress, rather than that of the executive branch" (Hirsch and Trento, 1973, p. 126). On the other hand, former NASA Administrator James Beggs saw space-program support as a matter of "the mood of the country and a question of priorities" (*Sky and Telescope,* 1982, p. 333).

Without a doubt, each President set the tone for much of NASA's activities. It was during the Kennedy-Johnson administrations that NASA received its greatest support. In the post-Apollo days, NASA, fueled by the overwhelming technological success of its moon landings, pushed for manned space flight to Mars. One observer described NASA as "an organism that was more responsive to its own internal technological momentum than to externally developed objectives" (Logsdon, 1983, p. 86). The Nixon administration favored more practical goals. And politicians, who controlled matters of budget and set policy, pushed for a program with tangible benefits to science, the economy, and national security.

President Reagan's 1982 policy consisted of two priorities: maintaining U.S. leadership in space, and expanding private-sector involvement and investment. A less publicized policy was the increasing involvement of the Department of Defense and use of the space program for national defense. After three years of lobbying on the part of those supporting a space station, Reagan, in his 1984 State of the Union address, set a goal of an orbiting space station within ten years. Administrator Beggs' push to make the shuttle "operational" may have been in part politically motivated; he recognized this was a necessary step in garnering support for the permanent, manned space station. Many people in NASA supported this goal. So did commercial, private enterprise.

Furthermore, the contracting companies who performed 80–90% of NASA's design and development work had active trade associations and lobbying efforts to promote their interests. With the shuttle in an "operational" state and the potential development of the manned space station, NASA was no longer its own customer. It now had to serve the needs of private industry. In short, there was a close-knit network between NASA, Congress, the Department of Defense, and private industry.

Public Relations. With so many different constituencies, NASA had always been acutely aware of the value of public relations and image. In its earliest days, NASA was particularly concerned with maintaining secrecy. The Kennedy administration felt that openness was a better approach to provide a counterattack to Soviet propaganda and secrecy. It was also a way of getting the most mileage out of the image of the U.S. as the underdog, steadily maintaining its effort to "catch up." The press was eager for involvement in the space program. They knew it made good copy—spaceships, astronaut heroes,

Figure 2 NASA Organization

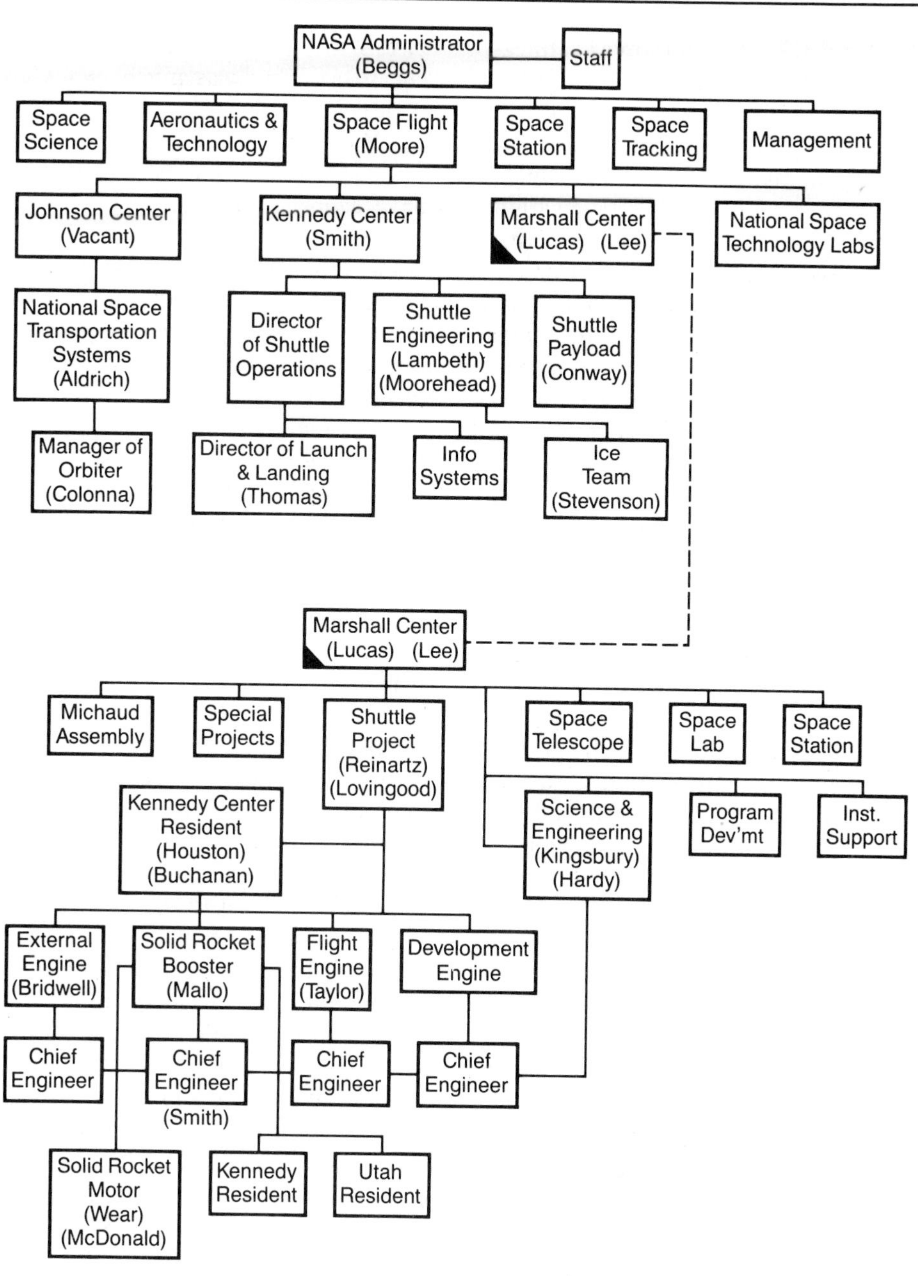

Source: Rogers Commission Report (1986)

patriotism, and American knowhow. Engineers were "scientists" and words like "enhance" and "uprate" replaced the verb "improve." "Integrity" now described machines, and the press became members of an exclusive space-age fraternity.

The merits of manned versus unmanned space flight had been a continuing debate within and outside of NASA. Manned flights were criticized for being expensive, dangerous, and largely unnecessary, particularly in light of improving robotics and computer capabilities. Proponents countered that the intelligence and versatility that on-board humans brought to space missions could not be duplicated by any machine. Even more important was the use of manned missions to win support and bolster enthusiasm of both NASA personnel and the general public.

If anything represented the public's pride in the national space program, it was the original seven Mercury astronauts. They were the nation's "champions" at the same time they were the All-American boys next door. But as the number of astronauts and the size of missions increased, it became harder for the public to keep track of and identify with astronauts. Until the first manned moon flights, a rigid pecking order among the astronauts kept scientist and engineer astronauts on the ground while former fighter and test pilots were selected for moon missions.

Post-Apollo astronauts were selected for their capabilities as scientists. Racial and gender barriers were broken with the selection of female, black, and Asian astronauts. As NASA's programs became increasingly commercialized, it was difficult to retain the astronaut's pioneering and heroic image. Christa McAuliffe, selected as the first teacher in space, represented a new orientation toward the astronaut. The image of the fearless daredevil was no longer appropriate. Instead, outer space belonged to all and now the astronaut was Everyman and Everywoman.

Successes and Failures. Even some of the most disastrous events in the agency's history were viewed as at least partial successes by NASA personnel. Prior to 1961, there were many rocket failures. In 1959, seven out of 17 launches failed. NASA saw these as necessary learning experiences, but there was much public criticism of their cost and delay.

By many accounts, however, the 1967 Apollo tragedy was an accident that should not have happened. In January 1967, during "routine" testing, a flash fire broke out in the command module, killing the three astronauts on board. The NASA review board acknowledged insufficient attention to crew safety. Some aspects of the investigation were suppressed by NASA and later revealed by a Congressional inquiry. Among the Congressional findings were "overconfidence" and "complacency" on the part of NASA and a lack of concern on the part of the prime contractor. A more critical review of the incident characterized Congressional findings as "ambiguous" and asserted that because of its close ties with NASA, Congress was reluctant to do anything that would implicate itself. The critique alleged that "sloppy workmanship and slipshod quality" had been with the program all along.

Despite "official" stringent safety standards, the agency was more concerned with meeting deadlines than with safety issues. NASA used this tragedy to its best advantage. Invoking the memory of the dead, they stressed the importance of getting on with the program because that's what the astronauts would have wanted. In spite of this setback, Kennedy's challenge to land a man on the moon was met.

The lives of three other astronauts were seriously endangered during the Apollo 13 mission. While enroute to the moon, the capsule's main oxygen tank exploded. Anderson, NASA's official biographer, believed that technology saved the day. The system contained sufficient flexibility and depth to permit the astronauts to ride safely back to earth. A review board investigating the incident had another perspective. They attributed the accident to a number of human errors and lack of proper monitoring and testing by NASA personnel and concluded that "the lessons of the Apollo 204 (fire) had not been fully applied" (Hirsch and Trento, 1973, p. 121).

Technical problems and failures with various Skylab and Shuttle missions called forth massive round-the-clock efforts by ground personnel and astronauts. Once again, failures became successes where problems were solved with "human ingenuity and courage" (Anderson, 1981, p. 83).

Finances and Budget. NASA's budget and employment figures are listed in Table 1. In terms of both budget and employment, NASA enjoyed its greatest power in the mid 1960s with the buildup of the man-on-the-moon effort. Funding decreased steadily over the next ten years, as the nation turned its attention and priorities to other matters. Although funding improved with the shuttle, inflation-adjusted figures show little increase, and the watchword has been fiscal restraint.

NASA—Life on the Inside

Decision Making. Decisions had to be made about the agency's overall goals. But NASA could not be a good decision maker because "government policy is based on partisan and interest group politics instead of on business or

Table 1 NASA's Budget and Employment

	Budget (in billions)		Employment	
Fiscal year	**Nominal**	**Real**[a]	**Government**	**Contractor**
1959	0.33	0.37	9,325	31,000
1960	0.51	0.57	10,286	36,500
1961	0.96	1.07	17,077	57,500
1962	1.83	2.02	22,156	115,000
1963	3.67	4.00	27,904	218,400
1964	5.10	5.49	31,984	347,100
1965	5.25	5.56	33,200	376,700
1966	5.18	5.33	33,924	360,000
1967	4.97	4.97	33,726	273,200
1968	4.59	4.40	32,471	235,400
1969	4.00	3.64	31,745	186,600
1970	3.75	3.22	31,223	136,580
1971	3.31	2.73	29,479	121,130
1972	3.36	2.68	27,428	117,540
1973	3.43	2.58	25,955	108,100
1974	3.04	2.06	24,854	100,200
1975	3.23	2.00	24,333	103,400
1976	3.51	2.06	24,039	108,000
1977	3.82	2.10	23,569	100,500
1978	4.06	2.08	23,237	102,800
1979	4.35	2.00	23,237	104,300
1980	5.24	2.12	22,563	101,800
1981	5.52	2.03	21,873	110,000
1982	6.02	2.08	21,652	105,000
1983	6.84	2.29	21,219	107,000

[a]Adjusted for inflation using the 1967 Consumer Price Index.

technological grounds" (Goldman, 1985, pp. 48–49).

Decision making and problem solving around technical issues were accomplished by creating consensus. For example, one of Apollo's early tasks was to plan the mechanics of putting a man on the moon. A number of options were possible. A group of engineers came up with the idea of a lunar orbiter-lander combination. They spent two years refining the idea, arguing their case before various NASA groups, and they even went "out of channels" directly to NASA's general manager. Their idea gradually won adherents and was adopted.

In mid-1968, with the Apollo program seriously behind schedule, the head of the Manned Space Flight Center, George Low, decided that the scope of each mission should be broadened. Specifically, he believed the Apollo 8 mission should orbit the moon rather than the earth, as originally planned. This represented a bold new step in the Apollo program. He presented his idea to Robert Gilruth, the head of the space task group, who responded enthusiastically. Next they polled the senior project managers, who agreed that all current problems appeared to be solvable in time for the launch deadline. Within just a few months, the mission was reconfigured for its newly established goal.

By the mid-1980s, NASA administrators and engineers made a distinction between engineering and program management decisions. This represented a change from years past. An engineer who had been with NASA since 1960 said (Bazell, 1986, p. 12):

> At the beginning, all the decisions were made at the lowest possible level. We worked together toward one goal. It was simply inconceivable that one person could have thought something was wrong—particularly if it was dangerous—and everyone else not know about it.

Another engineer echoed this perspective: "People making the decisions are getting farther and farther away from the people who get their hands dirty" (Bazell, 1986, p. 14).

A Changing Organization. What was clear was that NASA had changed in many ways over the past 25 years; in other ways it remained the same.

NASA at the start faced many challenges on many fronts dealing with rapid expansion and coordination of activities: leapfrogging the Soviets, dealing with the Executive branch and Congress, creating an environment good for scientific and technological creativity. The task was not merely to provide technical resources but also technical management so that a government-industry-university team could be built. The entire organization had to be geared toward flexibility to improve quality and reliability as the problems of space exploration were better understood. The emphasis was on avoiding "quick fixes" so that many small changes did not eventually add up to serious problems. The crash-program atmosphere of intense effort demanded by the program and by Kennedy's end-of-the-decade deadline was not without personal costs (divorces, heart attacks, and suicides) among NASA personnel.

At its 25th anniversary in 1983, NASA was facing a variety of issues, some of them new to the agency: commercialization of space activity; competition with Europe, Japan, and the Soviet Union; working closely with government military and civilian agencies as well as developing private-sector space activities; and meeting customer commitments. While the shuttle program had changed NASA's mandate, its field organizations retained their scientific and engineering orientations. Although this was appropriate for the Apollo era, observers felt this was currently causing problems for the agency.

Even before this time, NASA had shown resistance to certain changes. In 1973, one observer noted that there were difficulties associated with increasing the professional female and nonwhite staff and that the "overwhelming white domination of NASA is making it an increasingly conspicuous and embarrassing anomaly among government agencies" (Holden, 1973). Although NASA had hired a black woman for a top post in the agency's Affirmative Action department, the political realities of the Nixon administration made it a token gesture. She was dismissed for not fitting into the bureaucracy, but some felt her dismissal was precipitated by her refusal to play Nixon-era politics. It is not clear how much had changed by the mid 1980s, for in 1986 Robert Bazell described NASA insiders as a homogeneous group—white males in their fifties, career men with NASA or its contractors.

A 1979 shuttle management review team, headed by USAF General James Abrahmson, called for changes in management structure and philosophy. Some of the team's findings included the following:

> The near-term potential for unanticipated technical problems, schedule slippage and cost growth is high and appropriate reserves should be included in all aspects of program planning.
>
> There has been a lack of adequate long-range planning. . . . Emphasis has been on the current fiscal year, with only secondary attention to succeeding years. . . . Long range planning has not been performed to the extent required for a program as complex as the shuttle.
>
> . . . The successive program changes and associated up and down expenditure rates have resulted in experienced contractor and subcontractor personnel being terminated. Recent and current aerospace industry demand for such personnel is such that experienced people do not remain available, resulting in the employment of inexperienced personnel at a cost to overall efficient performance. This constitutes a major cause for concern, especially for the production phase of the program.
>
> . . . The space transportation system associate administrator (or Level 1 management) has, through an ever increasing personal participation in program activities, became the de facto program director . . . during the course of the fact finding, it became apparent that there was a broad and detailed involvement of Level 1 on technical issues with lesser attention given to cost and schedule.
>
> In the effort to live with funding limitations while still progressing acceptably toward completion, shuttle management has generally set up work schedules that demanded more performance than could be delivered.

Members of the shuttle management review team also mentioned that NASA managers felt the way to keep shuttle costs down was to set up high work performance goals. One NASA manager said (Covault, 1979, pp. 20–21):

> If we hadn't done it this way we could never have converted this thundering herd of Apolloites to more reasonable people. This program would have cost \$10–\$12 billion with the same philosophies we had in Apollo, and then there wouldn't have been any shuttle program.

A concern for costs persisted as the shuttle project progressed. Hans M. Mark, a NASA deputy administrator, reported that, "It is very unlikely that it will be possible to control costs of operations if the developmental attitudes that prevail at Johnson Space Center dominate after the shuttle becomes operational" (Covault, 1981, p. 13).

Despite a changing orientation toward the space program by the administration, many at NASA viewed the shuttle as another Apollo program. Therefore certain considerations, such as technical simplicity, minimizing operational costs, and meeting development schedules were seen by NASA people as less important than the technological development of the shuttle.

Heretofore, NASA had run with a single-flight focus. But because of the pressures of military needs and commercialization of shuttle flights, the program began to include several flights at various stages of readiness. It was becoming difficult to meet the flight schedule and maintain the overall efficiency of the system. By 1986, the schedule allowed for less than one month between flights. Furthermore, certain attitudes persisted from the resource-rich days of Apollo. There was still an inclination toward "can do" spontaneity in responding to crises and technological challenges and a very positive approach to problem solving. This type of enthusiasm was very costly at a time when the shuttle program required nurturing resources. The agency had an established tradition of flexibility, frequently changing shuttle plans as different needs and priorities of its commercial customers arose. These frequent and sometimes last-minute changes were a further drain on resources.

Tight schedules had to be balanced with cost constraints, and NASA contractors had rules governing employee overtime. Some required clearance for overtime in excess of 20 hours per week. Approval was frequently granted. For example, two contractors with employees working at Kennedy Space Center reported the 20-hour limit was exceeded about 5,000 times from October 1985 through January 1986.

During this era of multiple launches, it was necessary for key NASA and contractor personnel-skilled technicians and managers to log 72-hour work weeks and 12-hour days for weeks on end. One team leader worked consecutive work weeks of 60 hours, 96.5 hours, 94 hours, and 81 hours in January 1986. Given this unrelenting pace, it is not surprising that the likelihood for human error increased in early January 1986, when a group of technicians at Kennedy Space Center, working 12-hour shifts, repeatedly misinterpreted fuel-system error messages and made faulty decisions during previous shuttle launch preparations. The mission was scrubbed just 31 seconds before takeoff when an insufficient supply of liquid oxygen in the shuttle's fuel tank triggered alarms. A subsequent investigation attributed the launch abort to human error produced by fatigue. Human safety issues may have taken a back seat to cost considerations, as key personnel were pushed beyond their limits of endurance.

Much of NASA's current staff joined the organization in the Apollo build-up days of the early 1960s. Some were still in mid-career and interested in taking on technological challenges. The changed emphasis to cost and schedule constraints prompted these talented and motivated individuals to leave the organization. However, according to John Pennington, NASA's Director of Human Resources, surveys indicated high motivation and morale and low turnover in the organization (Pennington, 1986).

Nevertheless, the motivation for many of NASA's personnel was still the excitement and challenge of manned missions, large space systems, and interplanetary exploration. Despite the inbred staff of the space program, there was no consensus on what the program's goals should be. For many who remembered the effort and accomplishments of Apollo, there was a growing "return to the moon" movement; others favored focus on a suborbital manned space station. Some people in NASA believed it should become an operational organization, others felt it should remain an R&D agency.

Overall, the lack of a clear mission and the seemingly conflicting roles created difficulties for the agency. There was a tendency at some of the field centers to solve problems in-house rather than pass them up the hierarchy. NASA project managers at some of the centers felt isolated from headquarters and more accountable to their field centers. Conflicting goals, roles, and expectations produced an almost schizoid character. There was difficulty transferring an Apollo-era mood to shuttle realities, in switching from shuttle to routine operations, and in moving from an organization dominated by scientists and engineers to one dominated by bureaucrats and administrators.

Flight Readiness and Safety. Much of NASA's decision making was structured around flight readiness and safety issues. Planning for a shuttle flight began 12–18 months before a shuttle lifted off the pad. Figure 3 shows the steps that each flight had to clear. The Shuttle Flight Readiness Review was a complicated process. Flights required careful coordination among thousands of contractors, subcontractors, and three space centers (Kennedy, Marshall, and Johnson). Besides obvious concerns about the ability of the rocket to fly, officials allocated cargo space, trained the

Figure 3 Flight Readiness Review Process

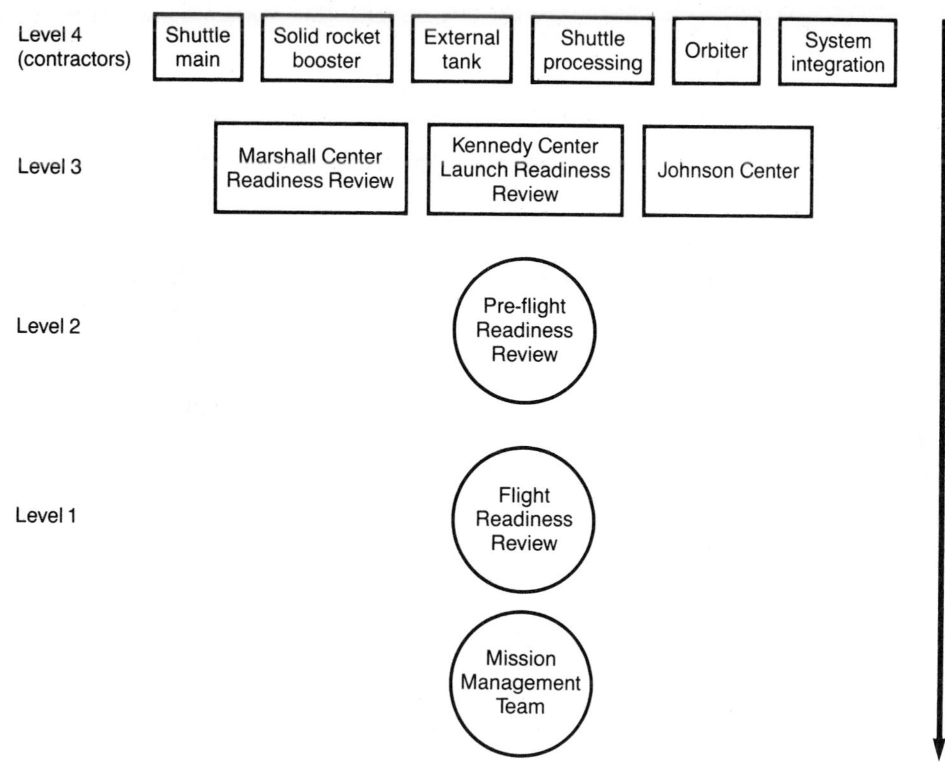

crew, designed a flight plan, scheduled space activities and experiments, and programmed dozens of computers. Literally hundreds of decisions were involved in a shuttle launch. Therefore, NASA had evolved a "Japanese" style of management: disagreements "bubbled up" the hierarchy until somebody resolved them.

The flight design process was the central concern in flight preparation. In this process, NASA officials and scientists set the flight objectives and laid out a detailed schedule of flight activities from launch until landing. Four field centers reported the Space Flight Program: Kennedy (launches), Johnson, Marshall (vehicle design and development), and the National Space Technology Laboratories. The planning went through several steps as outlined below.

Level 4. Level 4 was initiated by a formal directive from the NASA Associate Director of Space Flight. The burden was on contractors at the various space centers (who performed the bulk of the design and development and all of the manufacturing) to certify in writing that their components met the necessary standards.

Level 3. After all certifications were received, the decision making moved down to Level 3. At Level 3, the project managers for the Orbiter, solid rocket, booster, and external tank and main engines at Johnson, Kennedy, and Marshall made official presentations to their respective Center Directors. Each review verified the readiness of launch support elements.

Level 2. Next came the Preflight Readiness Review at Level 2 at Johnson Space Center. In the Level 2 review, each shuttle program element certified that it had satisfactorily completed the manufacture, assembly, tests, and checks on shuttle equipment. The manager of the National Space Transportation Program presided.

Level 1. The reviews culminated with Level 1. Under the direction of the Associate Administrator for Space Flight, the Flight Readiness Review at Level 1 checked previous planning activities, and a Mission Management Team was established.

Mission Management Team. This team takes over management 48 hours before the launch and continues until the shuttle had landed and been secured. This team met 24 hours before the planned launch to take care of unsatisfied requirements, to assess weather forecasts, and to discuss any anomalies. The Mission Management Team encouraged officials at lower levels to report any new problems or difficulties.

The director of the Shuttle Project Office reported to the Director of the Marshall Space Center. But the readiness review process mainly took place outside the normal chain of command. The levels of the Readiness Review paralleled and overlapped the levels of the formal management structure.

NASA's Safety, Reliability, and Quality Assurance Program came under the duties of the Chief Engineer at NASA headquarters. Out of a staff of 20, one person spent 25% of his time, and another spent 10%, on safety. At the various centers, the personnel who developed the shuttle hardware were also responsible for related safety issues. Components were engineered to meet stringent specifications, and they were tested. In 1980, NASA appointed a special committee to study the flight worthiness of the entire shuttle system.

Safety issues often cropped up at various levels of the Readiness Review. Flights had to meet 28 specific criteria before the countdown could begin. Participants mulled over technical specifications, interpretation of test results, and what constituted an adequate margin for safety. Those systems that had no back-up and which might bring about the loss of the vehicle and life were called "critical" and received special attention. In addition, the Flight Readiness Review procedure included official procedures for waiving nonconforming components or systems in the interests of flexibility, expedience, or extenuating circumstances.

Shuttle Flight Procedures: Challenger Flight 51-L

May 1985. Crew training begins.

August 20, 1985. NASA conducts a Preflight Readiness Review. They discuss the crew, storage, engineering status, photo and TV requirements, the Teacher-in-Space program and the launch window.

December 13, 1985. Associate Administrator for Space Flight (Moore) schedules Flight Readiness Review for January 15, 1986.

January 9, 1986. Morton Thiokol (MTI) certifies solid rocket booster flight readiness (Level 4). This is the first stage where equipment problems can delay a launch. The O-rings are a known problem, but MTI and NASA personnel do not believe they are serious enough to stop launch.

January 14, 1986. After weeks of intensive preparation, including a dress rehearsal and a mock firing of the main engines, Kennedy Center Director Richard Smith convenes the Preflight

Readiness Review meeting (Level 2) and sets the schedule for Level 1/Mission Management Team meetings. Over 100 participants from Kennedy, Marshall, Johnson, Lockheed, and various subcontractors discuss what time of day to launch, conditions for viewing Halley's comet, excessive cargo weight, and the schedule of crew activities. No problems with the solid rocket booster were identified. Kennedy Center Director Smith signs launch-readiness certificate.

January 15, 1986. NASA associate administrator Moore chairs Flight Readiness Review Meeting (Level 1). A video teleconference links NASA flight centers to Cape Kennedy. All systems are reviewed in detail, from engineering through flight responsibilities. They decide, "Go."

January 22, 1986. NASA officials are worried about dust storms in Dakar, the main emergency landing site. A shuttle can't go up unless it has a safe place to land if something goes wrong. Countdown is reset for January 26 at 9:36 A.M.

January 25, 1986. 11 A.M. EST. Level 1 team meets again. All unresolved flight readiness review items were reported closed. But rainstorms prompt officials to postpone until the 27th.

January 27, 1986. 12:36 P.M. Mission Management Team scrubs launch because of high winds and overcast at launch site. Rain can damage the shuttle's heat-resistant tiles. Problems with a sticky bolt cause a 90-minute delay in the astronauts' disembarking from the orbiter. Team resets launch for 9:38 A.M., January 28.

2:00 P.M. Mission Management Team meets again. Because weather forecasts predict temperatures in low 20s, someone raises concerns about cold weather effects on launch facility water drains, fire suppression system, and water trays. They decide to activate heaters on the shuttle.

2:30 P.M. in Utah. Morton Thiokol engineers in Wasatch, Utah, hearing about forecast cold temperatures discuss possible effects of cold weather predicted for January 28 on solid rocket booster (see Figure 4 for MTI organization.)

5:45 P.M. First teleconference between NASA Level 3 personnel at Kennedy (Lovingood) and Marshall (Reinartz) and Thiokol personnel in Utah. Morton Thiokol officials express reservations about effects of temperatures on O-rings. They postpone launch until noon or afternoon of 28th. Lovingood proposes going to Level 2 (Aldrich) if MTI stands by no-launch recommendation at second teleconference set for 8:15.

8:45 P.M. Second teleconference between MTI Utah (six members), Kennedy (Reinartz, Mulloy, McDonald—MTI liaison), and Marshall (Hardy, Lovingood, et al.). A technical discussion of O-ring problems and tests. Problems with the O-rings had a long history. One MTI vice president of engineering (Lund) says not to fly 51-L until temperature exceeds 53°F. Another MTI engineer Boisjoly presents charts and tables about problem. Mulloy asks MTI vice president Kilminster for recommendation. Kilminster says he cannot recommend launch. Reinartz, Mulloy, and Hardy challenge MTI conclusions, asking for hard data to support Boisjoly's conjectures. Hardy says he is "appalled" by the recommendation. Mulloy says, "Do you want us to wait until April to launch?" Kilminster asks for time to caucus. Later, Mr. Boisjoly remarks, "This was a meeting where the determination was to launch, and it was up to us to prove beyond a shadow of a doubt that it was not safe to do so . . . usually it is exactly opposite that." Mulloy says, "There was no violation of launch commit criteria . . . [there] were 27 full-scale tests of the O-rings damage tolerances . . . we had experience with this problem" (see Figure 5).

10:30 P.M. to 11:00 P.M. in Utah. MTI personnel discuss O-rings. Two engineers (Boisjoly and Thompson) continue to voice strong objections to launch. Mason asks Lund to "put on his management hat." The MTI top managers decide that objections are not serious enough to justify cancelling 51-L. The MTI officials later

Figure 4 Morton Thiokol Management Structure

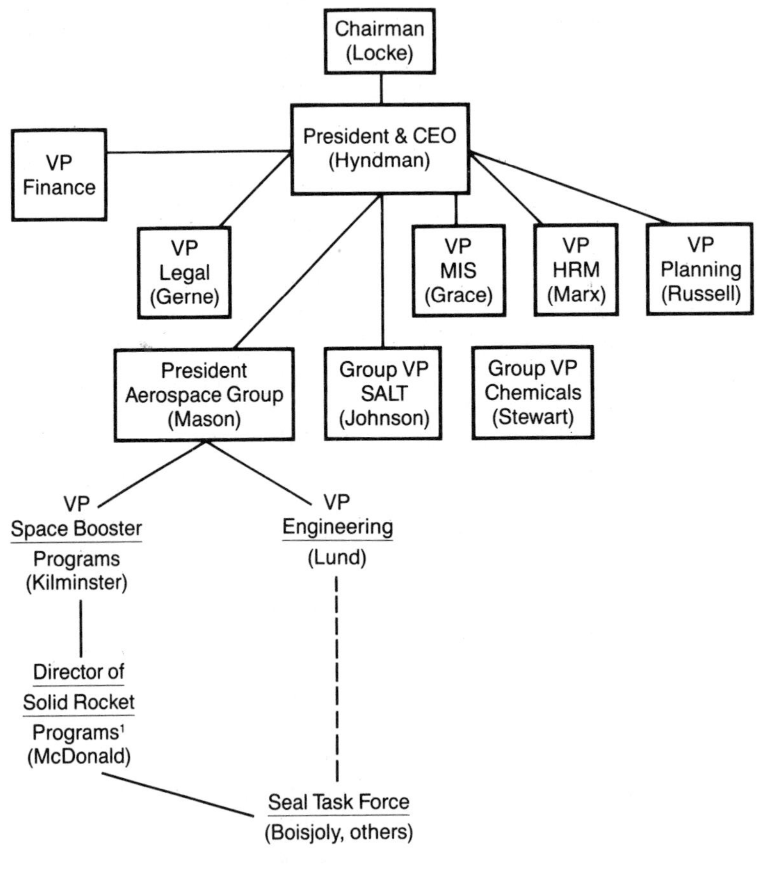

[1]At Kennedy Space Center.

characterize the discussion as "unemotional, rational discussion of the facts as they knew them . . . a judgment call."

10:30 P.M. to 11:00 P.M. at Kennedy. McDonald, Mulloy, Reinartz, Buchanan, and Houston discuss whether to delay. Mulloy says that none of MTI's data change the rationale from previous successful flights.

11:00 P.M. Second teleconference continues. The MTI officials say that O-rings are a concern but data are not conclusive against launch. Kilminster recommends launching. NASA asks MTI to put recommendation in writing.

11:15 P.M. to 11:30 P.M. at Kennedy. McDonald strongly argues for delay, says he would not like to answer to board of inquiry. Mulloy says that the temperature of the fuel in the booster will still meet the Minimum Launch Criteria. Reinartz and Mulloy tell McDonald that it is not his decision, that his concerns are noted and will be passed on. (See Figure 5 for summary of disputants.)

11:30 P.M. to 12:00 A.M. Teleconference at Kennedy. Mulloy, Reinartz, and Aldrich discuss icing in launch area and recovery ships' activities. The O-rings are not mentioned.

Figure 5 Main Players at NASA, Marshall Center, and Morton Thiokol

NASA Top Management	Position	Action (Inaction)
1. Jesse Moore	Associate Administrator for space flight	Made decision to launch 51L did not know of no-go recommendations
2. Arnold Aldrich	Shuttle Manager at Johnson	Knew only Rockwell reservations
Marshall Center		
1. William Lucas	Director	Outside launch chain of command
2. Stanley Reinartz	Mgr., Shuttle Projects	Did not tell superiors about Thiokol reservations
3. Lawrence Mulloy	Chief of Solid Rockets	Did not accept Thiokol engineer's doubts
4. George Hardy	Deputy Director of Space Engineering	Did not accept Thiokol engineer's doubts
Morton Thiokol		
1. Jerald Mason	Senior Vice President	Asked for decision
2. Joseph Kilminster	V.P. for Boosters	Signed "go" memo
3. Robert Lund	V.P. for Engineering	Persuaded to OK launch recommendation
4. Allan MadDonald	Director of Solid Rockets	At Kennedy—opposed launch
5. Rogert Boisjoly	Head of Seals Task Force	Worried about low temp.
6. Arnold Thompson	Engineer	Opposed launch
7. Brian Russell	Engineer	Opposed launch

Source: Rogers Commission Report (1986).

January 28, 1986. 1:30 A.M. to 3:00 A.M. at Kennedy. The Ice crew reports large quantities of ice on pad B. The spacecraft can be damaged by chunks of ice that can be hurled about during the turbulent rocket ignition.

5:00 A.M. at Kennedy. Mulloy tells Lucas of MTI concerns over temperature and resolution and shows the recommendation written by MTI.

7:00 A.M. to 9:00 A.M. at Kennedy. The clear morning sky formed what glider pilots call a "blue bowl." Winds dwindled to 9 mph. During the night temperatures fell to 27°F. The ice crew measures temperatures at 25°F on the right-hand solid rocket booster, 8°F on the left. They are not concerned as there are no Launch Commit Criteria relating to temperatures on rocket surfaces.

8:00 A.M. at Kennedy. Lovingood tells Deputy Director of Marshall (Lee) about previous discussions with MTI.

9:00 A.M. at Kennedy. Mission Management Team meets with Level 1 and 2 managers, project managers, and others. The ice conditions on launch pad are discussed, but not the O-ring issue.

10:30 A.M. at Kennedy. The ice crew reports to the Mission Management Team that ice is still left on booster.

11:18 A.M. A Rockwell engineer in California watching the ice team over closed-circuit television telephones the Cape to advise a delay because of the ice. Kennedy Center Director Smith, advised by the ice team that there is little risk, permits the countdown to continue.

11:28 A.M. Inside Challenger's flight deck (about the size of a 747), Commander Scobee and pilot Smith run through their elaborate checklists. The orbiter's main computer, supported by four backup computers, scans data from 2,000 sensors. If it detects a problem, it will shut down the entire system. In June 1984, the computer aborted four seconds before the rocket ignition. This time, it doesn't.

11:30 A.M. Thousands of motorists pull off highways to face toward the ocean.

11:37 A.M. The launch platform is flooded by powerful streams of water from 7-foot pipes to dampen the lift-off sound levels, which could damage the craft's underside.

11:38 A.M. Flight 51-L is launched. Two rust-colored external fuel tanks, each 154 feet high, carrying 143,351 gallons of liquid oxygen and 385,265 gallons of liquid hydrogen power the rocket. They will burn until the fuel runs out.

11:39 A.M. Everything looked like it was supposed to look. As one MTI engineer watched the rocket lift off the pad into a bright Florida sky he thought, "Gee, it's gonna be all right. It's a piece of cake . . . we made it."

References

Anderson, F. W. (1981) *Orders of Magnitude: A History of NACA and NASA, 1915–1980.* Washington, D.C.: NASA.

Bazell, R. (1986) NASA's Mid Life Crisis. *The New Republic,* Mar. 24, pp. 12–15.

Beatty, J. K. (1982) The "Space Age" (25 Years and Counting). *Sky and Telescope,* 64, pp. 310–313.

Becker, J. (1985) NASA's Projects Reflect a New Attitude as Agency Competes for Launch Services. *EDN,* Aug. 22, pp. 307–311.

Berry, R. (1986) A Busy Year for the Shuttle. *Astronomy,* 14, pp. 8–22.

Brooks, H. (1983) Managing the Enterprise in Space. *Technology Review,* 86, pp. 39–46.

Covault, C. (1979) Changes Expected in Shuttle Management Philosophy. *Aviation Week and Space Technology,* Sept. 24, pp. 20–21.

Covault, C. (1984) NASA Formulates Policy to Spur Private Investment. *Aviation Week and Space Technology,* Nov. 26, pp. 18–19.

Goldman, N. C. (1985) *Space commerce: Free Enterprise on the High Frontier.* Cambridge, MA: Ballinger.

Guterl, F., and Truxal, C. (1983) Militarization: Peace or War? *IEEE Spectrum,* Sept., pp. 35–39.

Hirsch, R., and Trento, J. J. (1973) *The National Aeronautics and Space Administration.* New York: Praeger.

Holden, C. (1973) NASA: Sacking Top Black Woman Stirs Concern for Equal Employment. *Science,* 182, pp. 804–807.

Kennan, E. A., and Harvey, E. H. Jr. (1969) *Mission to the Moon: A Critical Examination of NASA and the Space Program.* New York: William Morrow.

Levine, A. L. (1975) *The Future of the U.S. Space Program.* New York: Praeger.

Levine, A. S. (1982) *Managing NASA in the Apollo Era.* Washington, D.C.: NASA.

Logsdon, J. M. (1983) NASA's Dual Challenge: Serving Yet Striving. *IEEE Spectrum,* Sept., pp. 86–89.

McDougall, W. A. (1985) *The Heavens and the Earth: A Political History of the Space Age.* New York: Basic Books Inc.

Murray, B. (1986) In Search of Presidential Goals. *Issues in Science and Technology,* Spring.

Pennington, J. (NASA Director of Human Resources). (1986) Personal communication, July.

Reichhardt, T. (1985) Twelve Years From the Moon. *Space World,* July, pp. 13–14.

Rogers Commission Report. (1986) Washington D.C.: U.S. Government Printing Office.

Sidey, H. (1986) Pioneers in Love with the Frontier. *Time,* Feb. 10.

Sietzen, F. Jr. (1984) Perspectives on the Apollo Era. *Space World,* July, pp. 4–9.

Sky and Telescope. (1982) An Interview with James Beggs. Oct., pp. 332–333.

Space World. (1983) NASA's First 25 Years. Oct., pp. 25–32.

Space World. (1984) NASA Reorganizations. Jan. pp. 34–35.

Wilford, J. N. (1986) After the Challenger: America's Future in Space. *New York Times,* Mar. 16.

Wolfe, T. (1986) Everyman vs. Astropower. *Newsweek,* Feb. 10, pp. 40–41.

Wolfe, T. (1979) *The Right Stuff.* New York: Farrar, Straus, Giroux.

Case 28

A Note on Starting an Entrepreneurial Business through Venture Capital

Throughout America more and more entrepreneurs are building successful businesses, which range from high technology to food franchising, from manufacturing products to providing services. Venture capital investments are spurring a good deal of the entrepreneurial momentum. In recent years investment bankers and venture capital firms have channeled funds into a variety of companies that demonstrated solid potential for profitable growth.[1]

Owning and managing a small firm is a risky undertaking, however. About 400,000 small businesses fail each year.[2] In fact, by their tenth year of existence, almost 90 percent of all small firms fail (Table 1a). Tables 1b and 1c present the overall new business failure rates and survival rates for one year and four years based on firm size.

The key to starting a successful firm is a good idea. Let us assume for this note that the idea is a new one and that it is patentable. Let us further assume that the entrepreneur has completed the necessary market research and found the potential for this product, process, or service to be outstanding. What he or she lacks is funding.

Table 1a Overall New Business Failure Rates

By the End of:	Percentage that Fail
1st year	40%
2d year	60
10th year	90

Sources: Commerce Department; SBA; Dun & Bradstreet.

Table 1b One-Year Survival Rates by Firm Size

Firm Size (employees)	Survival Percent
0–9	77.8%
10–19	85.5
20–99	95.3
100–249	95.2
250+	100.0

Source: Michael B. Teitz et al., "Small Business and Employment Growth in California," Working Paper No. 348 (Berkeley, Calif.: University of California, March 1981), 42.

Table 1c Four-Year Survival Rates by Firm Size

Firm Size (employees)	D&B Study (1969–1976)	California Study (1976–1980)
0–19	37.4%	49.9%
20–49	53.6	66.9
50–99	55.7	66.9
100–499	67.7	70.0

Sources: David L. Birch, *MIT Studies, 1979–80*; and Michael B. Teitz et al., "Small Business and Employment Growth in California," Working Paper No. 348 (Berkeley, Calif.: University of California, March 1981), p. 22.

[1] *Raising Venture Capital: An Entrepreneur's Guidebook*, Deloitte, Haskins, and Sells, 1985, 72.

[2] Small Business Administration, *The State of Small Business, 1986*.

Table 2 Standard Deviations, *F*-Values: Projected Financial Ratios

	No. Samples Funded	No. Samples Unfunded	Std. Dev. Funded	Std. Dev. Unfunded	*F*-Values
Asset Management					
Sales/fixed assets	15	20	61.83	131.10	4.61**
Sales/current assets	16	21	0.92	1.36	2.18*
Working capital/total assets	17	22	0.51	0.63	1.53
Working capital/sales	16	20	0.32	0.61	3.52**
Profitability					
EBIT/sales	24	37	0.41	0.29	1.99
EBIT/total assets	17	22	0.61	0.54	1.40
EBIT/equity	13	20	0.68	0.56	1.47
Expense Management					
Fixed costs/sales	15	26	0.35	0.46	1.73
Gross margin	20	29	0.53	0.63	1.41
Capital Structure					
LT debt/equity	14	21	0.17	1.93	128.89**

*p · 0.05; **p · 0.01.
Note that due to lack of data in some plans it was impossible to calculate all ratios, so sample sizes vary.
Source: I.C. MacMillan and P.N. Subba Narasimha, "Characteristics Distinguishing Funded from Unfunded Business Plans Evaluated by Venture Capitalists," *Strategic Management Journal* 8 (issue 6, 1987): 583.

What Venture Capitalists Look For

Studies of successful and unsuccessful firms have indicated that firms with properly developed, implemented, and controlled plans are more likely to be successful in obtaining venture capital. A study that considered only the structure of the plan, not the content, distinguished funded from unfunded business plans evaluated by venture capitalists[3] (see Tables 2 and 3). The data revealed that plans that exhibit wide values from the norm go unfunded. It seems clear from the data that financial projections should conform to financial ratios for firms in similar competitive situations. Venture capitalists most often compare forecast figures and typical industry statistics in their early screening. Any differences from the industry should be explained in the plan. Failure to do this usually results in a rejection letter.

Many investment companies publish their investment criteria (Exhibit 1), yet it is still very difficult to obtain venture funding. In fact, only an estimated one in a hundred firms is funded through traditional venture capitalists. Exhibit 2 shows the sources of capital for entrepreneurs starting businesses that were previously nonexistent.

Most venture capitalists look for established industry niches to fund. Because they expect to see sound management practices, it is rare to see a venture funded that has limited management expertise. Mergers and acquisitions expert Robert Ouriel believes that venture capitalists look

[3] I.C. MacMillan and P.N. Subba Narasimha, "Characteristics Distinguishing Funded from Unfunded Business Plans Evaluated by Venture Capitalists," *Strategic Management Journal* 8 (issue 6, 1987), 582–583.

Table 3 Standard Deviations, *F*-Values for Plan Structure

	No. Samples Funded	No. Samples Unfunded	Std. Dev. Funded	Std. Dev. Unfunded	*F*-Value
Marketing percentage of plan	27	55	0.12	0.31	6.67*
Financial percentage of plan	27	55	0.13	0.34	6.81*
Production percentage of plan	27	55	0.12	0.31	6.67*
Management percentage of plan	27	55	0.09	0.18	6.00*
Smallest expense item/largest expense item	16	34	0.12	0.30	6.25*

*$p < 0.01$.
Note that due to lack of data in some plans it was impossible to calculate all ratios, so sample sizes vary.
Source: I.C. MacMillan and P.N. Subba Narsimha, "Characteristics Distinguishing Funded from Unfunded Business Plans Evaluated by Venture Capitalists," *Strategic Management Journal* 8 (issue 6, 1987): 582.

at three things: management, management, and management.

A summary of characteristics of entrepreneurs, as proposed by various authors since the mid-1800s, is given in Table 4. Miner has developed a comprehensive theory of entrepreneurial achievement having at its root McClelland's[4] psychological theory of *n*Ach. Miner's theory specifies five role characteristics and their related motivational patterns.[5] These relationships are summarized as follows:

1. Achievement orientation: A desire to achieve through one's own efforts
2. Personal risk: A desire to take moderate risks
3. Feedback: A desire for some clear index of the level of performance
4. Personal innovation: A desire to introduce novel, creative, or innovative solutions
5. Planning: A desire to think about the future and anticipate future possibilities

A study of technologically innovative entrepreneurs found that these characteristics or motives were relatively strong among more successful entrepreneurs.[6] Entrepreneurs who owned and managed small high-growth electronic firms were found to possess these characteristics as well as sophisticated business plans.[7]

These studies and others lead us to believe that many entrepreneurs are doomed because of a lack of drive and achievement. Barbato and Bracker (1988) studied dislocated (laid off) workers who desired to start their own businesses.[8] Even though they had been in sophisticated positions in large firms, they failed to produce sophisticated business plans for their potential companies after a 12-week training program. Further investigation also found them lacking in many of the motivational areas described by Miner. Therefore, there is a distinct difference between small business people and entrepreneurs. Entrepreneurship reflects a constellation of characteristics and behaviors, and these vary

[4]J.B. Miner, "Limited Domain Theories of Organization Energy," in C.C. Tinder and L.F. Moore, eds., *Middle Range Theory and Study of Organizations* (Boston: Martinus Nijhoff, 1980): 279–280.

[5]Miner, "Limited Domain Theories in Organization Energy," 334–336.

[6]N.R. Smith, J.S. Bracker, and J.B. Miner, "Correlates of Firm and Entrepreneur Success in Technologically Innovative Companies," *Frontiers of Entrepreneurship Research* 7, 337–353.

[7]J.S. Bracker, B. Keats, J.B. Miner, and J.N. Pearson, "Task Motivation, Planning Orientation, and Firm Performance," a paper presented at the National Academy of Management Meeting, Anaheim, California, 1988.

[8]R. Barbato and J.S. Bracker, "Dislocation and Potential Entrepreneurship," *Proceedings*, Santa Barbara Institute Directors Association National Meeting, San Francisco, California, 1988.

Exhibit 1 Investment Criteria of a Typical Investment Company

Industry

- Stable industries not subject to rapid technological change, or wide cyclical swings in volume and profit
- Presence of barriers to market entry

Size

- Revenues of at least $20 million
- Net income after tax of at least $1.5 million in the latest fiscal year or the average of the last three years

Profitability

- Proven record of profitability for a minimum of three years

Balance Sheet

- Relatively low debt/equity ratio

Price

- Purchase price that represents a realistic relationship to demonstrated profit performance

Location

- Anywhere in the United States

Equity Features

- Always required
- Percentage negotiable, never control

Preferred Size of Investment

- $1.0 million to $10.0 million

Purpose of Investments

- Leveraged buyouts
- Divestitures of subsidiaries and divisions
- Leveraged ESOP
- Growing companies

Types of Securities

- Private placements of
  —Subordinated debentures with common stock
  —Subordinated debentures with warrants
  —Preferred stock with common stock
  —Preferred stock with warrants

Types of Financing

- Sole investor/leader
- Lead with participants
- Participant, with another investor leading

Amortization/Redemption Schedules

- 5–10 years

Board of Directors Participation

- Attend board meeting as observer, and/or have the right to sit on the board

Businesses not Favored

- Start-ups
- Turnarounds
- Breaking even or unprofitable operations
- Real estate
- Commodity businesses with little or no control over pricing
- Highly capital intensive businesses that must reinvest most of their cash flow in plant and equipment or working capital in order to remain competitive

Source: Venture Capital Group, Bankers Trust Company, New York, NY.

among all individuals, including small business owners.

Smith identified two types of entrepreneur: opportunist and craftsman.[9] According to his typology, the opportunist reflects an individual who reacts to a broad range of culture; exhibits breadth in education and training; and possesses a high level of social awareness, involvement, flexibility, confidence, and awareness of and orientation toward the future. The craftsman reflects the opposite on each dimension.

[9]N.R. Smith, "The Entrepreneur and his Firm: The Relationship between Type of Man and Type of Company," Michigan State University, East Lansing, Michigan, 1967.

Exhibit 2 Sources of Capital for Entrepreneurs Starting Businesses Previously Nonexistent

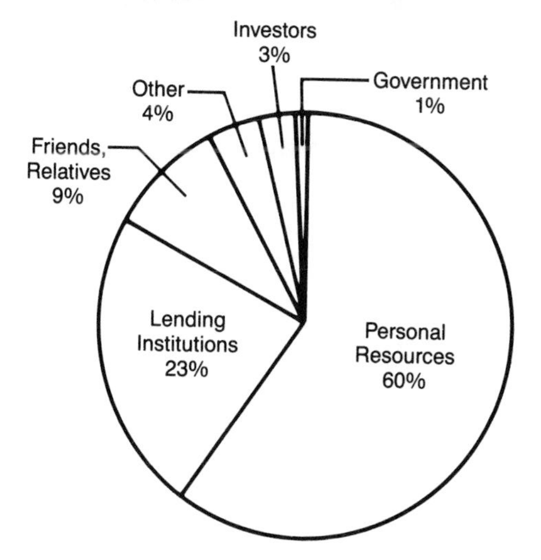

Source: National Federation of Independent Business

Smith's types are consistent with the literature.[10] In general, these typologies suggest that individuals who tend toward the craftsman orientation are motivated to do what they want to do, meet their personal and family needs, and avoid working for others. The opportunistic or managerial types are motivated by a desire to achieve economic gain and build an organization. This motivation is consistent with the goals of venture capital firms with regard to funding and represents the ability to build an organization that will return a significantly higher rate of return than a typical security investment.

Based on our knowledge of venture capital firm funding it seems clear that the business plan developed by the true entrepreneur plays a critical role not only in the success of the firm but in the acquisition of funds to start the firm. Numerous papers and books detail the structure of the plan. It should at a minimum contain: fundamental objectives, description of the company, the products, processes or services, the market, the competition, production and distribution, management, key business advisors, organizational chart, and projected financial information. Central to the plan is a section on how investors will see a return on their investment. The following is taken from a typical business plan:

> The company intends to go public in three to five years. If the company does not go public within that time, investors may realize a return on their investment from either a purchase of the company by a larger health care company, or the exchange of ownership through a pay-out schedule.[11]

The key to investment besides strong management is the construction and presentation of sound financial figures. The accounting firm of Deloitte, Haskins, and Sells has put together an outline of what the figures should look like. They are contained in three important sections: cash-flow forecast, income statement, and pro forma balance sheet (Exhibits 3, 4, and 5).

A Method for Approaching Venture Capitalists

Critical to making the venture capital deal is the method of approaching the venture capitalist. Many firms take a shotgun approach and send business plans to every venture capital firm mentioned in magazines such as *Inc.* or *Venture.* This approach usually brings multiple rejection letters, because the typical large firm might receive nearly a hundred plans a day to evaluate.

[10]See J.W. Carland, Frank Hoy, W.R. Boulton, and J.C. Carland, "Differentiating Entrepreneurs from Small Business Owners: A Conceptualization," *Academy of Management Review* 9 (no. 2, 1984), 356; M.C. Casson, *The Entrepreneur* (Oxford, England: Martin Robertson, 1982); and A.C. Filley and R.J. Aldag, "Characteristics and Measurement of an Organizational Typology," *Academy of Management Journal* 21, 1978, 578–591.

[11]Biosurge, Inc. business plan, 1987.

Table 4 Characteristcs of Entrepreneurs

Date	Author(s)	Characteristics	Normative	Empirical
1848	Mill	Risk bearing	X	
1917	Weber	Source of formal authority	X	
1934	Schumpeter	Innovation; initiative	X	
1954	Sutton	Desire for responsibility	X	
1959	Hartman	Source of formal authority	X	
1961	McClelland	Risk taking; need for achievement		X
1963	Davids	Ambition; desire for independence, responsibility; self-confidence		X
1964	Pickle	Drive/mental; human relations; communication ability; technical knowledge		X
1971	Palmer	Risk measurement		X
1971	Hornaday and Aboud	Need for achievement; autonomy; aggression; power; recognition; innovative/independent		X
1973	Winter	Need for power	X	
1974	Boiland	Internal locus of control		X
1974	Liles	Need for achievement		X
1977	Gasse	Personal value orientation		X
1978	Timmons	Drive/self-confidence; goal oriented; moderate risk taker; locus of control; creativity/innovation	X	X
1980	Sexton	Energetic/ambitious; positive setbacks		X
1981	Welsh and White	Need to control; responsiblity seeker; self-confidence/drive; challenge taker; moderate risk taker		X
1982	Dunkelberg and Cooper	Growth oriented; independence oriented; craftsman oriented		X

Source: James W. Carland, Frank Hoy, William R. Boulton, and Jo Ann C. Carland, "Differentiating Entrepreneurs from Small Business Owners: A Conceptualization," *Academy of Management Review* 9 (No. 2, 1984): 356.

Venture capitalists like to have input into the firm by way of board seats. It would be quite difficult for partners of a California firm to sit on the board of a firm in Maine. Thus logistics of travel and time prompt the new firm to look for funding in its own region.

Most cities have venture capital clubs or associations. Often a contact through the entrepreneur's legal or accounting representation will result in a presentation to these groups. Many times press releases that result in newspaper articles alert venture capitalists to a firm's needs. An example is BioSurge Inc. in Rochester, New York. A short article about its product in *The Wall Street Journal* resulted in eight calls from local and regional venture capital firms.

The key, though, to contacting venture capitalists is personal contacts. Rarely do cold calls or unsolicited letters produce results.

Once the venture capitalist has become interested, the firm must prepare for initial meetings at both its own office and that of the venture firm. Usually the CEO or top financial officer meets initially with the venture capitalist. This meeting is usually a check on figures, a discussion of possible forms of financial participation, and an expressed desire to examine additional information. Often this information is referred to as due diligence. Exhibit 6 is taken from BioSurge's due diligence package. This presents further knowledge of the company and allows the venture capitalist's staff to examine specific technical

Exhibit 3 Cash Flow Forecast

The following format can be used to prepare the cash flow forecast:

BEGINNING CASH BALANCE
CASH RECEIPTS:
- Collection of Receivables
- Interest Income
- Total

CASH DISBURSEMENTS:
- Accounts Payable
- Payments of Other Expenses
- Income Tax Payments
- Total

NET CASH FROM (USED FOR) OPERATIONS
SALE OF STOCK
PURCHASE OF EQUIPMENT
DECREASE (INCREASE) IN FUNDS INVESTED
SHORT-TERM BORROWINGS (REPAYMENTS)
LONG-TERM BORROWINGS (REPAYMENTS)
ENDING CASH BALANCE

This format shows cash receipts and disbursements from operations separate from financing activities and capital acquisitions. It clearly shows the monthly changes in cash flow from operations and will indicate when operations will begin to generate a positive cash flow.

The financing activities are segregated. In using this format, estimate a minimum cash balance to be maintained at the end of every month and project enough borrowings to give you that minimum cash balance. Any excess cash generated during a month is used to repay debt or is invested in money market funds; any shortage of cash is made up by drawdowns of funds previously invested or by additional borrowings.

Source: *Raising Venture Capital: An Entrepreneur's Guidebook*, Deloitte, Haskins, and Sells, 1985.

Exhibit 4 Income Statement

The following format can be used in preparing the income statement:

SALES
COST OF SALES:
- Material
- Labor
- Overhead
- Total

GROSS MARGIN
OPERATING EXPENSES:
- Marketing
- Research and Development
- General and Administrative
- Total

INCOME (LOSS) FROM OPERATIONS
INTEREST INCOME (EXPENSE)
INCOME (LOSS) BEFORE TAXES
TAXES ON INCOME
NET INCOME (LOSS)

To assist the potential investor in evaluating your company, include some operating statistics on the income statement. Calculate your gross margin and each major expense category as a percentage of sales. If any of these statistics are significantly different from industry averages, you should explain why.

Source: *Raising Venture Capital: An Entrepreneur's Guidebook*, Deloitte, Haskins, and Sells, 1985.

details. In the example of BioSurge, these would be its FDA documentation and the strength of its patent applications.

Up to this point the entrepreneur has not revealed any significant technical or marketing information that would have been considered confidential. The presentation of filed patents and, in the case of BioSurge, FDA documentation are crucial business secrets that must be closely controlled. The entrepreneur must make sure that the venture capitalist does not represent a competitor or potential competitor. A signed confidentiality agreement is crucial at this stage. Exhibit 7 provides an example of such an agreement.

What remains now are the negotiations with the venture capital firm. If this is the entrepreneur's first deal, it is important to be accompanied by legal counsel at all times. Most venture capitalists do not like to negotiate initially with attorneys, but having them present is in the best interest of the entrepreneur. However, a con-

Exhibit 5 Pro Forma Balance Sheet

The following format can be used for a pro forma balance sheet:

ASSETS:
Current assets:
  Cash
  Investments
  Accounts Receivable
  Inventory
    Total
Property, Plant, and Equipment—net
  TOTAL ASSETS
LIABILITIES AND STOCKHOLDERS' EQUITY:
Current liabilities:
  Short-Term Debt
  Accounts Payable
  Income Taxes Payable
  Accrued Liabilities
    Total
Long-Term Debt
Stockholders' equity:
  Preferred Stock
  Common Stock
  Retained Earnings (Deficit)
    Total
  TOTAL LIABILITIES AND STOCKHOLDERS' EQUITY

The pro forma balance sheets will help investors to evaluate your understanding of asset management.

Investors use a variety of financial statistics to assist them in evaluating companies. You should calculate these statistics and include them in your forecast. This will make the investors' evaluations easier and show them that you considered these ratios in formulating your plan.

Source: *Raising Venture Capital: An Entrepreneur's Guidebook*, Deloitte, Haskins, and Sells, 1985.

Exhibit 6 Contents Page from a Due Diligence Package

TABLE OF CONTENTS
Introduction to Officers/Directors
Listing of Business Advisors
Organizational Structure
Corporate Resolutions/Agreements
FDA Documentation
Patent Applications

sulting firm can easily assist in lieu of an attorney in the early stages. One such firm is Alimansky Venture Group in New York. Exhibit 8 lists many of the items about which the entrepreneur needs to be knowledgeable when negotiating the deal.

The final decision for the entrepreneur is the percentage of the company to give up. This is a function of economic position, experience, stage of business development, risk involved, and many additional factors. Two of the most common methods today are the sale of preferred stock or private placements. Exhibits 9 and 10 present some of the advantages and disadvantages of each method.

Ultimately the entrepreneur will determine whether the firm is successful. No amount of advisors or money can make a poor idea work. Careful attention to detail and a willingness to work long hard hours and plow revenues back into the firm are musts.

Exhibit 7 Sample Confidentiality Agreement to Business Secrets

CONFIDENTIALITY AGREEMENT

This Agreement is made this __________ day of ______________________, 1988, by and between BioSurge, Inc., a Delaware corporation with a place of business of 919 Westfall Road, Rochester, New York, 14618 (hereinafter referred to as "BioSurge") and ___________, a ____________________ organized and existing under the laws of __________ and having a place of business at ______________________ (hereinafter referred to as "Company").

WHEREAS, the parties hereto desire to discuss areas of mutual interest and benefit, including but not limited to Company investing in BioSurge; and

WHEREAS, in the course of such discussions Company desires to review and evaluate certain Confidential Information (as hereinafter defined) of BioSurge; and

WHEREAS, BioSurge is willing to disclose the Confidential Information to Company only pursuant to the terms of this Agreement;

NOW THEREFORE, in consideration of these premises and mutual covenants herein contained, the parties mutually agree as follows:

1. CONFIDENTIAL INFORMATION. The term "Confidential Information" shall include all information disclosed by BioSurge to Company, or known to Company as a consequence of the relationship between BioSurge and Company, whether in oral, written, graphic or machine-readable form including but not limited to products, plans, procedures, prototypes, clients, trade secrets, patents, copyrights, business information, financial information, ideas and data, including information relating to research, development, manufacturing, purchasing, pricing, selling and marketing. Confidential Information shall not include any information that was known to Company and documented in its files or was in the public domain, publicly known or readily available to the trade or public prior to the date of disclosure by BioSurge, and which is made known by Company to BioSurge with ten (10) days of such disclosure.
2. NON-DISCLOSURE COVENANT. Company agrees that the Confidential Information shall at all times remain property of BioSurge, and that it shall not use the Confidential Information for its own benefit or the benefit of any third party or disclose the Confidential Information to any third party without prior written consent by BioSurge.
3. PROTECTION OF CONFIDENTIAL INFORMATION. Company agrees to use all reasonable means, not less than those employed by Company to preserve and safeguard its own confidential information to maintain the Confidential Information secret and confidential. The Confidential Information shall not be disclosed or revealed to anyone except employees of Company who have a need to know the information and who have entered into a secrecy agreement with Company under which such employees are required to keep confidential the proprietary information of Company, and such employees shall be advised by Company of the confidential nature of the information and that the information shall be treated accordingly. Company shall be responsible for any use or disclosure of the Confidential Information by any of its employees or agents.
4. RETURN OF CONFIDENTIAL INFORMATION. Upon termination of discussions between the parties, or upon request of BioSurge, Company shall immediately return to BioSurge (or at BioSurge's request, destroy) all Confidential Information, including any copies thereof.
5. REPRESENTATION. Company warrants and represents that it is not currently an affiliate of or a substantial investor (with 5% or more equity or voting interest) in an entity whose products are substantially similar to or competitive with BioSurge's proposed products and will immediately inform BioSurge of any such affiliation or interest.
6. EQUITABLE RELIEF. The parties hereto agree that monetary damages shall be insufficient to fully compensate BioSurge for its losses in the event Company violates the provisions of this Agreement. In addition to seeking monetary damages, BioSurge therefore shall be entitled to enjoin Company from violating or continuing to violate the provisions of this Agreement, and Company shall not raise as a defense to any action or proceeding for any injunction the claim that BioSurge would be adequately compensated by monetary damages.
7. TERM. This agreement shall remain in full force and effect both during discussions between the parties and thereafter, whether or not Company actually invests in BioSurge.
8. MISCELLANEOUS.
   8.1 *Severability.* If any part, term or provision of this Agreement shall be held unenforceable, the validity of the remaining portions or provisions shall not be affected thereby.
   8.2 *Modification.* This Agreement shall not be modified or terminated except in writing signed by both parties.
   8.3 *Governing Law.* This Agreement shall be governed by and construed in accordance with the laws of the State of New York.

IN WITNESS WHEREOF, the parties hereto have executed this Agreement as of the day and year first above written.

BIOSURGE, INC.
By: ____________________
Name: ____________________
Title: ____________________
COMPANY
By: ____________________
Name: ____________________
Title: ____________________

Source: BioSurge Inc., Rochester, N.Y.

Exhibit 8 Venture Capital Negotiation Checklist

1. Amount of financing
2. Type of security (e.g., convertible preferred)
3. Price (possibly including performance-based securities)
4. Prefinancing valuation
5. Purchasers
6. Exchange of debt securities
7. Dividend provisions (e.g., preference)
8. Liquidation preference
9. Rights upon merger or consolidation
10. Conversion rights (if applicable)
11. Rights upon a public offering (e.g., automatic conversion, payment of accrued dividends)
12. Antidilution provisions (e.g., stock splits, stock dividends, new stock issued at a purchase price less than the conversion price for this round)
13. Option to require the company to repurchase all or part of the securities issued
14. Voting rights (e.g., on preferred stock)
15. Protective provisions (e.g., consent of 50 percent of holders of new securities required for change in rights)
16. Information rights (e.g., monthly financial statements, annual operating plan, board seat, etc.)
17. Registration rights (e.g., demand registration, "piggyback" registration, S-3 rights, registration expenses, transfer of rights, standoff provisions within 90 days, etc.)
18. Right of first refusal to purchase pro rata any new shares
19. Key man insurance
20. Market standoff agreement (e.g., for 90 days)
21. Employee matters:
    a) Vesting of stock granted to new employees
    b) Proprietary information
    c) Reserved employee shares
    d) Employment contracts
22. Amendments to rights of existing stockholders
23. Conditions to financing (e.g., legal documentation, due diligence, etc.)
24. Investment banking agreement with [our company]
25. Legal fees and expenses to investor's attorney
26. Approval of accounting firm
27. Shareholders agreement
28. Representations and warranties

Source: Alimansky Venture Group Inc., New York, NY, 1988.

Exhibit 9 Obtaining Capital through the Sale of Preferred Stock

Advantages

1. Failure to meet offering terms will not result in bankruptcy.
2. The cost of raising capital is about 30 percent less when preferred is issued instead of secondary common stock.
3. Borrowing reserve and financial insurance are preserved.
4. Preferred carries no maturity unless investors require a sinking fund to guarantee the annual buy-back of a certain number of outstanding shares.
5. If the financial condition of the company is strong, the quality of the common shares is undiminished, nor are debt ratios altered by a preferred offering.

Disadvantages

1. In order to guarantee buy-back of a certain number of shares outstanding every year, the company may have to either establish a sinking fund from available cash, or reissue new shares of preferred to finance the buy-back.
2. If the offering terms are too restrictive in order to satisfy investors, the offering may limit future unsecured borrowing or other long-term debt financing.
3. The quality of common shares may diminish during bad economic times if too much preferred is issued.
4. Management must pay ongoing costs to keep the preferred offering in registration.

Source: Jennifer Lindsay, *The Entrepreneur's Guide to Capital: The Techniques for Capitalizing and Refinancing New and Growing Businesses* (Chicago: Probus Publishing, 1986), 45.

Exhibit 10 Obtaining Capital from Private Investors

Advantages

1. Management can avoid some or all of the time-consuming SEC registration/disclosure requirements of public ownership.
2. Management can raise capital in less time and at slightly less cost by not going public.
3. Friends, employees and associates can acquire private company stock at a more beneficial price with a private offering.
4. More control is retained by company founders/owners/management by remaining private with an exempt offering.

Disadvantages:

1. Regulation D limits the number and qualification of private investors, as well as the amount raised, in some offerings.
2. Resale of private shares is restricted and lack of a public market creates other obvious resale constraints.
3. Private companies do not receive as much media and analyst attention as public entities do.
4. Share price may be lower because of limitations on the number of purchasers and on resale of shares.
5. Private companies cannot apply for NASDAQ or stock exchange listing.

Source: Jennifer Lindsay, *The Entrepreneur's Guide to Capital: The Techniques for Capitalizing and Refinancing New and Growing Businesses* (Chicago: Probus Publishing, 1986), 54–55.

Case 29

Stratton Mountain Ski and Summer Resort (SMSSR)

SMSSR is near the western border of Vermont and New York, in the heart of the snow belt of southern Vermont. Located in the Green Mountains, it is 235 miles from New York City, 135 miles from Boston, 120 from Hartford, and 75 miles from Albany, New York (Exhibit 1).

SMSSR

SMSSR is owned and operated by SMSSR Corporation, which also owns Bromley, an older resort across the valley from SMSSR (Exhibit 2). Each is a complete resort. Bromley, developed in 1937 by Fred Pabst, was one of the first ski centers in the United States. SMSSR was developed in 1961. In 1980, Moore and Munger bought the controlling stock of SMSSR Corporation and made it a subsidiary.

Although SMSSR and Bromley are separate entities, SMSSR administers them as one business. Ski lift tickets are good on both mountains, there is shuttle bus service between the mountains, and a customer arranges for a Stratton-Bromley vacation through the SMSSR Corporation. Lodging arrangements for a "Stratton-Bromley Ski and Summer Vacation" are handled by SMSSR Corporation's lodging service, which represents more than 50 inns and lodges in the area. SMSSR's lodging directory and 1981 price list are shown in Exhibit 3.

The Stratton Resort Area

Stratton is one of the major New England ski resorts with 59 miles of trails and slopes which have a 4,000-foot summit. There are seven distinct skiing areas in the mountains, including the Sun Bowl, which is interconnected with the main face, but which is large enough to form a separate ski area. On the lower mountain, 44 acres are organized into four separate instructional and practice areas for beginners and novices (see Exhibit 4 for statistics about Stratton). SMSSR's trails and base-area facilities are described in Exhibit 5.

The facilities and accommodations include indoor and outdoor tennis courts; two ski shops and rentals located slopeside in the North Face base complex; several restaurants, including a double cafeteria in the base lodge, a quick-lunch counter, several lounges, and quick-lunch counters at the North Face and Sun Bowl summits; a nondenominational chapel near the base lodge; a professional ski patrol and first aid station; and real estate services which handle sales, summer and winter rentals, and services for the chalets, condominiums and cluster homes on the mountain. Additionally, there is the Golf Academy with a 22-acre golf course designed by Geoffery Cornish and considered one of the finest available, and a 20-mile network of trails for cross-country skiers.

Source: "Stratton Mountain Ski and Summer Resort" from *Cases in Marketing Management and Strategy*, pp. 397–423, by Roger D. Blackwell, Wesley J. Johnston and W. Wayne Talarzyk, copyright (c) 1985 by The Dryden Press, a division of Holt, Rinehart and Winston, Inc., reprinted by permission of the publisher.

Exhibit 1 Location of Stratton-Bromley Ski Area

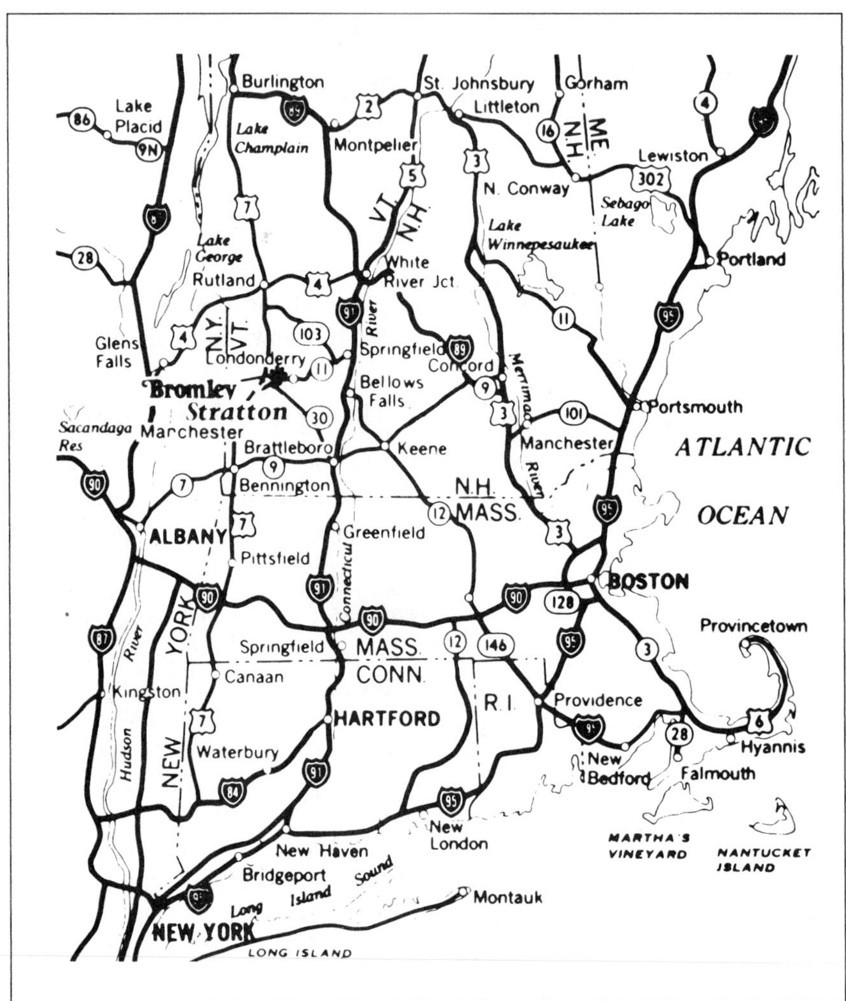

The Bromley Resort Area

Bromley is the only major eastern ski area with a southern exposure, which has earned it the name "the Sun Mountain." For over 40 years, it has been a pioneer in American skiing: special beginners' areas, nurseries for children, and trailside homes were developed and proven at Bromley. Bromley was also the first ski mountain to be groomed, and 83 percent of its trails are covered with artificial snow.

It has over 15 miles of Alpine skiing trails, with a summit of 3,284 feet. From the top, the runs float off in broad, gentle arcs with a few steep trails. On the left is the concave east side, where the runs peel off and drop quickly. Bromley's ski statistics and base area facilities are given in Exhibit 6. Included in the facilities are

Exhibit 2 SMSSR Administers Two Resorts as One

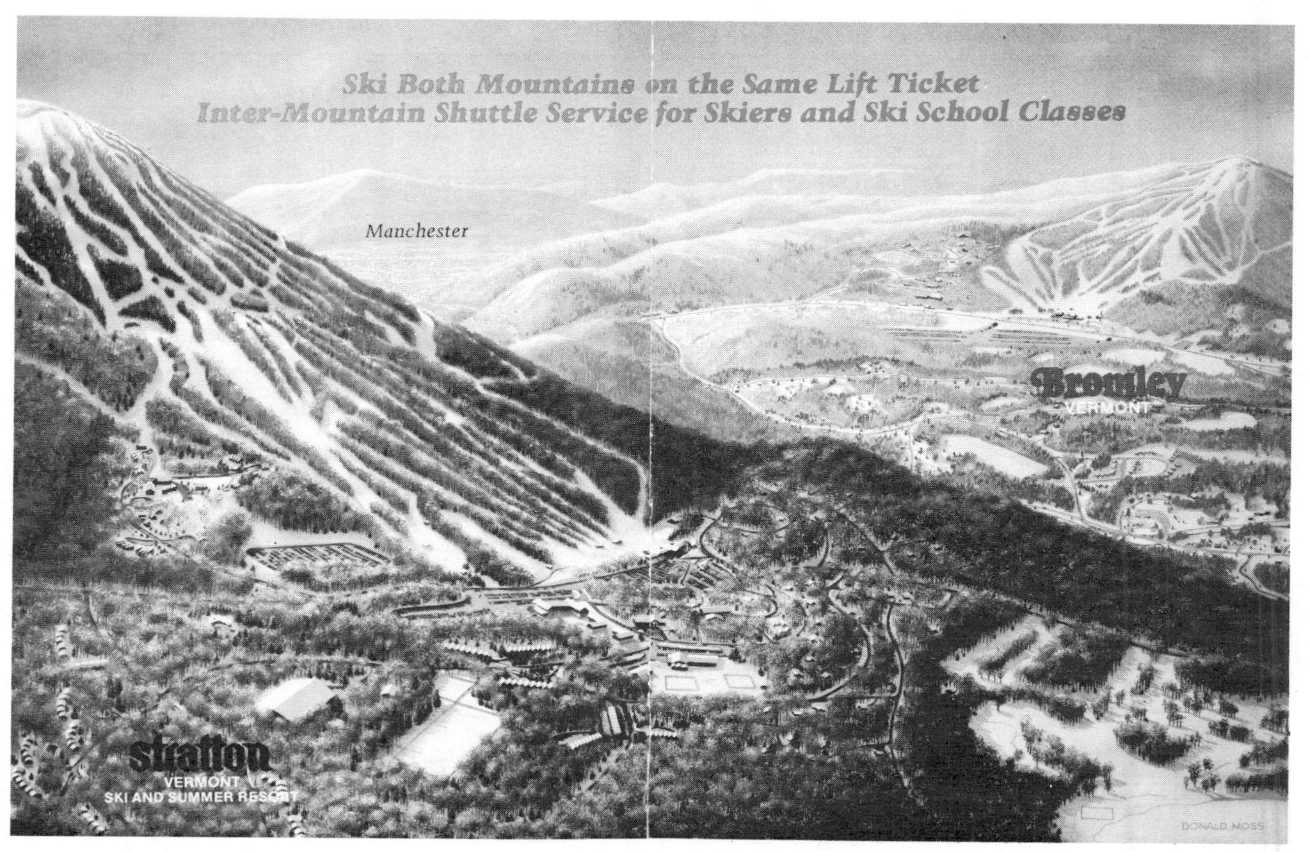

a main lodge with restaurants and cocktail lounges, away from the roadside. In the base area facilities are also a ski shop, the children's nursery, and Bromley Ski School.

Bromley's Alpine Slide

In 1976, the first of Bromley's three Alpine Slides was installed on the mountain. Now, there are three slides, each over 4,100 feet long, with high banked curves, straight slopes and sudden chutes. Customers can control the speed of their descents from the special cart on which they ride down the slides. The slides are open from spring to late fall (Exhibit 7).

Activities at Stratton-Bromley

The programs and activities at Stratton and Bromley encompass the whole year. Although each is primarily a ski resort, the activities include such summer activities as the Stratton Tennis Classic, a vacation at the Golf Academy, sailing, horseback riding, hiking, and a day's fun on the Alpine Slide. Exhibit 8 is a comprehensive list of the 1981 summer activities and their price.

The winter's ski activities and programs at SMSSR include a beginner's ski program, advanced ski programs, a Stratton Ski week, a Woman's Way Ski Seminar, and a ski program for children. SMSSR also hosts a yearly "ski in the Alps tour," and cross-country skiing tours. Exhibit 9 is a comprehensive list of the 1981 winter activities available at Stratton and Bromley, and their price.

Snow Making at SMSSR and Bromley

Fred Pabst pioneered "snow farming" at Bromley: Grooming the trails involves removing stumps and rocks so that it takes less snow to make the trails usable for skiers. Grooming and snow making together are known as snow farming. Although Vermont traditionally has deep snow in the winter, in the late Seventies all the Eastern resorts were plagued by a "snow drought." Fortunately for them, Bromley and SMSSR have two of the finest snow-farming operations in the industry.

Both Stratton and Bromley have two separate systems for making snow. They are the air-water system and the water-only system. The air-water system is a fixed system, in that it is permanently in place and requires the use of huge oil and electric compressors. These compressors send the air and the water through "snow guns" at tremendous pressure. When the water strikes the cold air, it crystalizes into snow before it hits the ground. The colder the temperature, the less air is needed and the more water can be used to make more snow. The warmer it gets, the less efficient the system becomes, because of the increase of air and the decrease of water.

The water-only systems are comprised of portable units, i.e., the compressors are built right onto the snow gun. These Hedco's can be towed to any position on the mountain as long as water can be hooked up. When it is very cold, these guns are extremely efficient.

The two enterprises together have made a huge financial commitment to snow making. The cost of making snow runs into incredible figures. Pat Williams, the head of snow making and lift maintenance, estimates the cost of making snow to be around $250 an hour. This does not include the cost of machinery, the support vehicles or the two six-man crews that work continuous 12-hour shifts. Making snow around the clock, as is done at both Stratton and Bromley, involves staggering costs.

Stratton's system covers 95 acres of skiing terrain from the top to the bottom of its mountains. In cases of dire emergency, this area can be expanded greatly by the use of the portable Hedco's which can be towed to areas not usually covered. It becomes simply a matter of getting the water to the system. As it stands under normal conditions, Stratton covers 10 trails from top to bottom.

Bromley has a total of 140.6 acres of skiable terrain. Of this terrain, 116.87 acres can be covered with synthetic snow, and that figure can be easily raised with the use of the portable Hedco system. According to Bromley's director of operations, Frank Johnson, "There aren't too many places on the mountain that we can't put snow. Even on the trails that we normally don't make snow on, we can patch up areas with the Hedcos. It's just a matter of getting the water to them."

To keep this valuable snow in place and groomed is an enterprise unto itself. The total fleet for the two mountains includes seven grooming machines made by Thiokol, and two Tucker Sno Cats. The cost of these machines is close to $100,000 each: they are used to push snow around for the convenience of the skiing customers. These machines are incredibly efficient, and with the newer equipment such as the snow tiller, they can turn boilerplate into skiable surface. The tiller works much like a garden tiller. Its depth is variable and it cuts the snow, fluffs it up, and packs it to a firm consistency. This innovation has been hailed as the greatest advance since snow making.

Says Johnson, "We have always sold the concept of wide, flat, and smooth. Even in the days before grooming was commonplace, Tut Tuttle would take a bulldozer up the mountain at night to groom the slopes. People thought he was nuts. We do leave a few trails on the East side steep and bumpy for those who like that kind of skiing, but the majority of our skiers like the wide smooth terrain they can cruise and enjoy. We groom every night from the time they leave till they appear again in the morning. We strive to create a smooth trail from treeline to treeline and from top to bottom. Any night during the winter you can look up on the mountain and see the lights as they move up and down the mountain."

As Stratton and Bromley move into the new seasons, the management hopes fervently for the deep natural snow of traditional Vermont winters. If those snows are reluctant to appear, the owners are ready and able to pick up the slack, and their commitment is to provide the finest skiing in the Eastern United States.

SMSSR's Competition

In Vermont alone, there are eighteen major ski resorts. Of these, SMSSR's executives consider Killington, Mount Snow, Stowe, and Sugarbush their major competitors.

Killington is located on five mountains and has 74 trails. Its vertical drop is 3,060 feet. It has seven double chair lifts, four triple chairs and a 3½ mile gondola, the longest in North America. Snow is made to the top of the five mountains, covering 31 miles of trails. Its facilities include six cafeterias, three lounges, a restaurant, three ski shops, three rental shops, a nursery, and a ski school.

Mount Snow is located in 1,000 acres of the Green Mountain area. Its summit is 3,600 feet, and it has three complete mountain faces that are skiable. Its vertical drop is 1,700 feet, and its lifts include ten double chairs, one triple chair, and two gondolas. It has 51 trails and snow-making capability for 22 trails, 6 of which can be covered top-to-bottom from the summit. Its facilities include a ski shop, restaurant, nursery, rental shop, cafeteria, lounge, and ski school.

Stowe is located on two mountains, Mt. Monsfield (Vermont's highest), and Spruce Peak. Its vertical drop is 2,150 feet and it has nine lifts, including four-passenger gondolas. It has 35 trails, and its longest run is 4½ miles. Its snow-making capabilities cover 51 percent of all the terrain to the summit for skiers of all levels of abilities. Its facilities include three ski shops, three rental shops, five restaurants and cafeterias, a lounge, nursery, and ski school.

Sugarbush is located on two of Vermont's 4000-foot mountain peaks. Its vertical drop is 2,600 feet, and its lifts include one gondola, one triple chair, nine double chairs, two pomas, and one T-bar. It has 73 trails and its snow-making capabilities cover 134 acres of trails to the summit. Its facilities include a cafeteria, lounge, rental shop, ski shop, restaurant, nursery, and ski school.

The National Ski Areas Association's (NSAA) First Survey

The NSAA conducted its first national survey of business for the 1979–1980 ski season. The results were published in the fall of 1980, and confirmed a trend dominant in the Seventies: the Rockies were the only major ski region to post a solid 6.5 percent increase in skier-day volume. The other results of the survey are as follows:

- On average, the nation's ski areas reported a 3.8 percent decline in skier volume, based on lift ticket sales, from the 1978–1979 season.
- The sale of season passes dropped by a surprising 10.2 percent.
- More than 60 percent of the responding ski areas reported a decline in both skier volume and season pass sales.
- Although weather was cited as the major reason for both increases and decreases in skier volume and decreases in sales of season passes, the ravages of inflation and recession moved well up on the chart as a secondary cause.
- Especially in the Northeast, which led the league in losses of volume (25.2 percent) and season passes (22.1 percent), smaller areas were hit harder by the bad season than large areas and resorts.

However, the report also contained a few important but less underscored facts:

- The amount of skiing may be smaller than has long been accepted. The 215 (52 percent) of NSAA's 417 members that responded to the survey reported only 34 million skier-days last season, which can be extrapolated to roughly 48 million skier-days for all.

  Since NSAA's membership includes virtually all the large and medium-scale ski areas in the country, and many important small ones as well, this raises some question as to the validity of the widely quoted gospel of 55–60 million skier-days per season. It means that the 300 remaining, nonmember ski areas would have to enjoy 12 million skier-days, which is highly unlikely.
- The Midwest isn't as large a ski market as has been thought, according to the survey. Working with skier-day volume figures for the better of the past two seasons factored by the rate of response (38 percent in the Midwest), the Midwest barely tops 4 million skier-days a season while the Rockies generate 20 million, the Far West 11 million, and the Northeast 10 million. The Southeast, which includes New Jersey and Pennsylvania, has almost the same 4 million as the Midwest.
- Those same figures also suggest that the tourist or destination business may be far better than most observers have suspected, because the population centers (for day or weekend skiers) are located on the coasts and in the Midwest, yet the low-density Rockies dominate in skier-day volume.
- Adding new lifts may not generate an immediate increase in the volume of business because the Rockies had the lowest percentage increase in 1979–1980 in new lifts (1 percent) and vertical transport feet (2.8 percent) while the West, which had the highest (9 percent and 6.8 percent, respectively) declined in skier volume (1.4 percent).

However, for all the sophistication and detail of research, one dominant, long-standing shibboleth of the ski-area business survived intact. Weather is king. Some 42 percent of the areas showing an increase in skier-day volume credited weather as the primary cause, with "promotion effort" (23 percent) and "new facilities" (20 percent) coming next. In contrast, 98 percent showing a decline blamed the weather, with fiscal factors accounting for the other 2 percent.

Still, one of the most disturbing trends identified but not explained in the report was the greater decline suffered by smaller areas in both the Northeast and Southeast. In the Northeast, for instance, areas with one to three lifts lost 45.7 percent of their business in 1978–1979, while the giants—12 lifts or more—declined only 15.8 percent. The decline in the Southeast was even more dramatic. Areas with four to seven lifts increased their business 14 percent, while areas with one to three lifts declined 5.8 percent (Exhibit 10).

Exhibit 3 SMSSR's Directory of Lodges and Price List

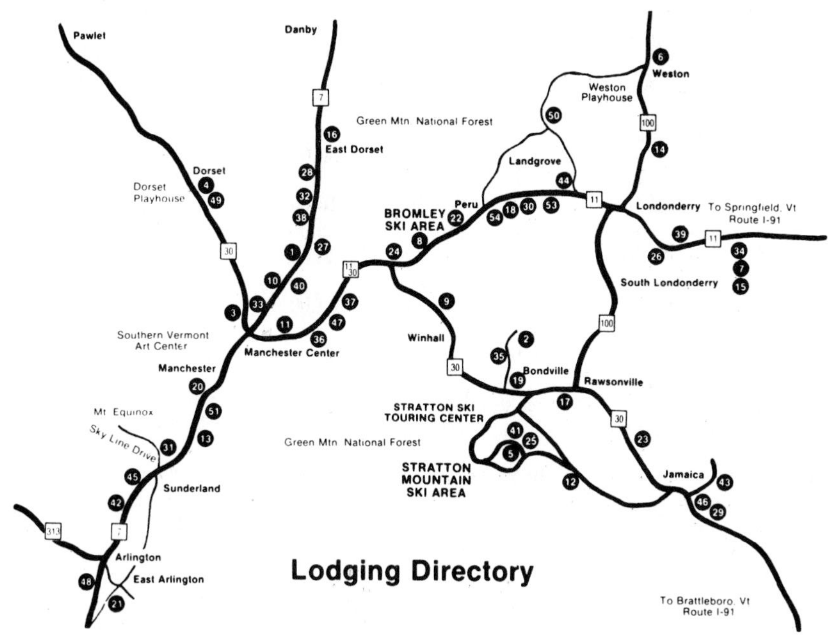

(continued)

Exhibit 3 *(continued)*

Lodges†	Rates per Person Midweek Double Occupancy	Rates per Person Weekend or Holidays Double Occupancy	Rates per Person 5-Day Ski Vacation Nonholiday Double Occupancy	Meal Plan	Semi-Private, Private Baths
The Aspen Motel	$13.50–15.00	$13.50–15.00	$55.00–60.00	EP	P
The Barn Lodge	30.00	30.00	125.00	MAP	P
The Barnstead Motel	15.00–17.00	15.00–17.00	75.00–85.00	EP	P
Barrows House	39.00–48.00	41.00–50.00	194.00–238.00	MAP	S-P
Birkenhaus	55.00	55.00	247.50	MAP	P
Black Shutters	12.50–17.50	14.00–19.50	59.50–83.00	BP	S-P
Blue Gentian Lodge	31.50	37.00	140.00	MAP*	
Bromley Sun Lodge	50.00	50.00	205.00	MAP	P
Bromley View Inn	30.00	35.00	132.00	MAP*	S-P
1878 Carriage House Motel	14.00	16.00	70.00	EP	P
Chalet Motel	16.00	16.00	52.50	EP	P
Chalet Wendland	30.00	30.00	150.00	MAP	S
Cold Spring Motel	11.00	13.00	55.00	EP	P
The Colonial House	16.00–22.00	18.00–24.00	72.00–99.00	BP	S-P
Dostal's Resort Lodge	34.00–39.00	39.00–49.00	155.00–175.00	MAP	P
Erdman's Eyrie	17.00	19.00	68.00	BP	P
The Fundador Lodge	39.50–45.50	39.50–45.50	178.00–200.00	MAP	P
Greenmount Lodge	12.75 –	13.75–14.75	55.00 –	EP**	S-P
Haig's	rates	upon	request	EP	P
The Inn at Manchester	20.00–27.00	20.00–27.00	80.00–115.00	MAP	S/P
Iron Kettle Motel	11.00–12.00	12.00–13.00	50.00–55.00	EP	P
Johnny Seesaw's	27.00–48.00	27.00–48.00	110.00–195.00	MAP	S/P
Jo-Mary's Motel	14.00–17.00	14.00–17.00	63.00–76.50	EP	P
Kandahar Lodge	45.00	45.00	180.00	MAP	S/P
Liftline Lodge/ Berghaus	52.00	52.00	237.00	MAP	P
Liftline Lodge/ Glockenhof	47.00	47.00	214.00	MAP*	P
Magic View Motel	12.00–15.00	14.00–17.00	48.00	BP	P
Manchester View Motel	16.00	17.00	68.00	BP	P
Marbledge Motel	25.50	30.00	120.00	MAP*	P
McKennis' House	17.50	17.50	87.50	BP	S-P
Nordic Inn	37.50–46.50	37.50–46.50 +	155.00–195.00	MAP	S/P
North Shire Motel	17.50	17.50	75.00	BP	P

Exhibit 3 *(continued)*

In-Room Phones	In-Room, Lounge Tele-vision	Enter-tainment	Family Game Room	In-Door Pool, Sauna, Whirpool Baths, Hot Tub	Pets Allowed	Bunks	Con-necting Rooms	Major Credit Cards
	R							MC/V
			•					
	R L		•					MC/V
	L		•	S		•	•	
	L	•	•			•	•	MC/V/AX
	L							MC/V/AX
			•					
•	R L	•	•	P,S	•			MC/V/AX
	L	•				•		MC/V
	R					•		MC/V/AX
•	R L		•	S			•	ALL
						•		
	R				•			MC/V
	R L		•				•	
	R	•	•	P,WB	•	•		MC/V
	R							MC/V/AX
	L		•			•		MC/V/AX
	L		•					
	L	•	•					
	L		•			•	•	
	R		•		•		•	MC/V/AX
	R L		•		•	•	•	MC/V/AX
	R							
	R L	•	•	S	•		•	MC/V/AX
	R L						•	MC/V/AX
	L			HT				MC/V/AX
	R		•		•			MC/V
	R							MC/V/AX
	R L						•	MC/V/AX
	L		•				•	
	L	•						MC/V/AX
	R L							MC/V

(continued)

Exhibit 3 *(continued)*

Lodges†	Rates per Person Midweek Double Occupancy	Rates per Person Weekend or Holidays Double Occupancy	Rates per Person 5-Day Ski Vacation Nonholiday Double Occupancy	Meal Plan	Semi-Private, Private Baths
Olympia Motor Lodge	12.50	17.50–20.00	62.50	EP	P
Palmer House Motel	17.00–21.00	19.00–22.00	85.00	EP	P
The Post Horn Inn	36.00	44.00	165.00	MAP	P
Red Fox Inn	30.00–40.00	30.00–40.00	135.00–180.00	MAP*	S-P
Red Sled Motel	15.00	18.00	65.00	EP	P
Skylight Ski Lodge	21.00	21.00	99.25	MAP	S
Snow Bound Motel	15.00	15.00	60.00	EP	P
Snowdon Motel	14.00	17.00	62.50	BP	P
Stamford Motel	12.00–14.00	13.00–15.00	47.50–60.00	EP	P
Stratton Mountain Inn	52.00	52.00	234.00	MAP	P
Sunderland Motel & Lodge	28.00	29.00	140.00	MAP*	P
Sunny Brook Lodge	15.00	15.00	60.00	BP	S-P
Swiss Inn	32.00–34.00	35.00–38.00	134.00–141.00	MAP	P
Sycamore Inn	24.00	24.00–25.00	110.00	MAP*	S-P
Three Mountain Inn	27.50–35.00	27.50–37.00	140.00–175.00	MAP	S-P
Toll Road Motor Inn	16.00	18.00	80.00	EP	P
Valhalla Motel	12.50	12.50	62.50	EP	
Village Auberge	37.50	40.00	175.00	MAP*	P
The Village Inn	20.00–37.00	20.00–37.00	90.00–165.00	MAP	S-P
Weathervane Motel	10.00–14.00	18.00–22.00	50.00–80.00	EP**	P
West Mountain Inn	12.50–16.00	13.50–17.00	50.00–64.00	EP**	S-P
White Pine Lodge	14.25–18.75	14.25–18.75	56.00–75.00	EP	P
Wiley Foxx Inn	upon request	34.50–37.50	150.00	MAP	S-P

†Add additional 10% during Holidays
*EP Rates also available
**MAP Rates also available

Exhibit 3 *(continued)*

In-Room Phones	In-Room, Lounge Tele-vision	Enter-tainment	Family Game Room	In-Door Pool, Sauna, Whirpool Baths, Hot Tub	Pets Allowed	Bunks	Con-necting Rooms	Major Credit Cards
	R							MC/V/AX
•	R L			S,WB			•	MC/V/AX
	R L		•		•		•	MC/V/AX
	L					•		MC/V/AX
•	R							MC/V
						•		
	R							MC/V/AX
	R						•	
	R				•		•	MC/V/AX
•	R L	•						MC/V/AX
	R L			S	•		•	MC/V
	L							
	R L		•				•	MC/V/AX
	L		•			•	•	MC/V/AX
	L						•	
	R					•		MC/V/AX
	R							MC/V
								MC/V
	L		•	WB,HT			•	MC/V/AX
	R						•	MC/V
			•				•	MC/V/AX
	R		•		•			
	L		•				•	MC/V

Exhibit 4 Ski Statistics: Stratton

- **Elevation:** 3,875 feet
- **Vertical Drop:** Sun Bowl, 2,003 feet; North face, 1,750 feet
- **Lifts:** 7 double chairlifts, 1 triple chairlift
- **Longest Trail:** Wanderer, 14,000 feet; Workroad, Interstate 91, 22,000+ feet
- **Average Snowfall:** 230 inches

Exhibit 5 Stratton: Trails and Facilities

Slopeside Services

Indoor Tennis: Stratton is among the very first of the nation's ski resorts to offer *indoor* tennis. Hourly time on four courts is available.

Ski Shop and Rentals: Both standard and GLM equipment may be rented at First Run Ski and Sports Shop, located slopeside in the North Face base complex. First Run Ski and Sports Shop offers complete ski shop and fashion boutique facilities, plus expert repair services. Storage is also available. Cross country skiing equipment and rentals are available at the Stratton Ski Touring Center.

Restaurants: The Stratton base lodge offers a modern double cafeteria, quick lunch counter, the Bear's Den Lounge, Theodore's Restaurant/Lounge, the Brauhaus, the Wine and Cheese Shop and La Creperie. Quick lunches can also be had at the summit and Sun Bowl warming hut.

Chapel of the Snows: The nondenominational Chapel of the Snows is located on the Mountain Road near the base lodge. Catholic services are conducted on Saturday and Sunday; Protestant services are held on Sunday.

Stratton's Ski Patrol: Our professional Ski Patrol operates from the Summit Patrol Building atop the mountain, with satellite stations at the top of the Standard Chairlift, The Sun Bowl Chairlift and the First Aid Station located on the top floor of the Carlos Otis Stratton Mountain Clinic (next to the base lodge).

Real Estate Services: The Stratton Real Estate Office handles sales, summer and winter rentals and services on the mountain for many fine chalets, condominiums and cluster homes. For more information, phone 802/297-2323, or stop by the Base Lodge office. Open daily.

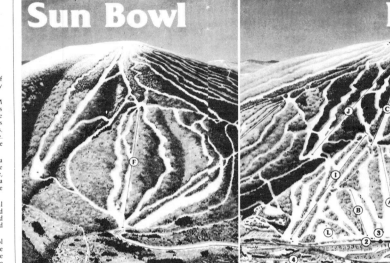

Stratton's 59 Miles of Trails

Sun Bowl

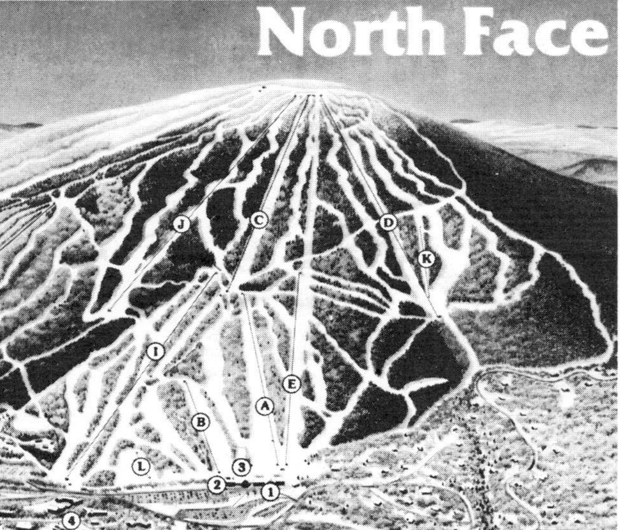

Lifts

I. Tamarack Triple Chairlift: Serves major beginner instructional area. Snowmaking coverage. 3,500'.
L. Little Cub Lift: Children's and beginners instructional area. Snowmaking. 500'.
B. Tyrolienne Double Chairlift: Close to Little Cub, Big Cub and Adult Ski School centers. Teaching carousel. 1,510'.
A. Suntanner Double Chairlift: Site of NASTAR races. Snowmaking coverage. 2,830'.
E. Standard Double Chairlift: Snowmaking coverage. 3,325'.
F. Sun Bowl Chairlift: Restaurant, barbecue area, rest area at base. 4,925'.
J. Grizzly Double Chairlift: 5,000' lift from mid-mountain to summit and Summit House.
C. North American Double Chairlift: 4,000' lift to Summit House Snack Bar, Ski Patrol HQ, rest area. Scenic 4-state view. Snowmaking coverage.
D. Snow Bowl Double Chairlift: 5,000'.
K. Poma Lift: 500'.

Base Area Facilities

1. Stratton Base Complex: Base Lodge, 3 cafeterias, ski shop, Bear's Den Lounge, Theodore's Lounge, Wine & Cheese Shop, Creperies, Medical Center, Ski Patrol HQ, Post Office, Checkroom, Lodging Office, Vacation Sales Center, Real Estate Office, Ticket Sales, rest area, Guest Services and information.
2. First Run Ski Shop: Full service ski equipment rental shop, repair shop, ski & fashion retail sales.
3. Ski School Center: Little Cub and Big Cub ski schools, Day Care Center, Ski School Test Slope and administrative offices, Ski Education Foundation training clubhouse.
4. Stratton Center: John Newcombe Tennis Center (4 indoor courts), Liftline Lodge, Birkenhaus, Stratton Mountain Inn accommodations, Beauty Shop, Boutique, convention facilities, Stratton Mountain School, Chapel of the Snows, Shattarack Cluster Homes.

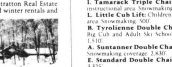

Exhibit 6 Bromley: Trails and Facilities

Slopeside Services

Bromley Vermont

Established in 1937, Bromley was one of the first ski centers in the United States founded by the late Fred Pabst, Jr., Ski Hall of Famer and of the Pabst Blue Ribbon Brewing family. Vice President of Operations: Frank H. Johnson. Ski School Director: Paul Johnston.

Ski Shop and Rentals: The totally refinished First Run Ski and Sports Shop offers complete ski shop and fashion boutique facilities featuring top name clothing and equipment. Standard and GLM equipment may be rented at the First Run, located slopeside in the base area complex, plus expert repair services are handled by a knowledgeable and friendly staff. Open 8 a.m. to 5 p.m. daily.

Restaurants: Bromley base lodge offers two modern cafeterias, The Bromley Room with waitress-served lunch, Pabst Parlor (weekends and holiday weeks) serving buffet lunch and a wine and cheese shop.

Bromley Nursery: The nursery—accredited by Vermont's Department of Human Services—is located at the foot of the mountain. Children from one month to six years are welcome. Facilities include a sleeping room for infants, a playpen/crib room, a large game room and lunchroom with tables and highchairs. The nursery operates daily from 9-4 p.m.

Bromley Ski School: ATM and GLM taught, 1¾-hour class lessons held daily at 9:30 a.m. and 12:45 p.m. Junior Ski School programs for juniors ages 6-14, Snoopy Ski School with classes for all abilities meeting three times daily, Ski and Play Hour for children ages 3-5, All-Day Supervised Skiing for the skiing child and includes lunch, NASTAR daily plus NASTAR Racing Tips, and Beginner's Circle for newcomers or novices who want to learn at their own pace.

Home of the Alpine Slide: The longest slide in North America, with three slides descending 815 feet. Two slides 4060-feet long, one slide over 4100-feet long. Ride chairlift to intermediate get-off and slide down or ride the scenic chairlift down. Open late-May to October.

Elevation: Base: 1,950 ft. Summit: 3,284 ft. Vertical: 1,334 ft.

Snowmaking: Covers 83% of skiable terrain from base to summit (90% novice, 75% intermediate, 95% expert).

Average Snowfall: 150".

Number of Lifts: 5 double chairlifts (3 to summit) 1 J-Bar—Transports 6,300 skiers per hour.

A	Number One Chairlift	E	Proposed Chairlift
B	Plaza Chairlift	F	East Meadow Chairlift
C	Stargazer Chairlift	G	Proposed Chairlift
D	Alpine Chairlift	H	Lord's Prayer J-Bar

Slopes & Trails: 25, totaling over 15 miles of Alpine skiing varying in difficulty—20% Advanced, 60% Intermediate, 20% Beginner. Bromley is the only major ski area facing south (sunnier & warmer).

Longest Run: Run Around/Thruway—2½ miles.

Exhibit 7 Alpine Slide at Bromley

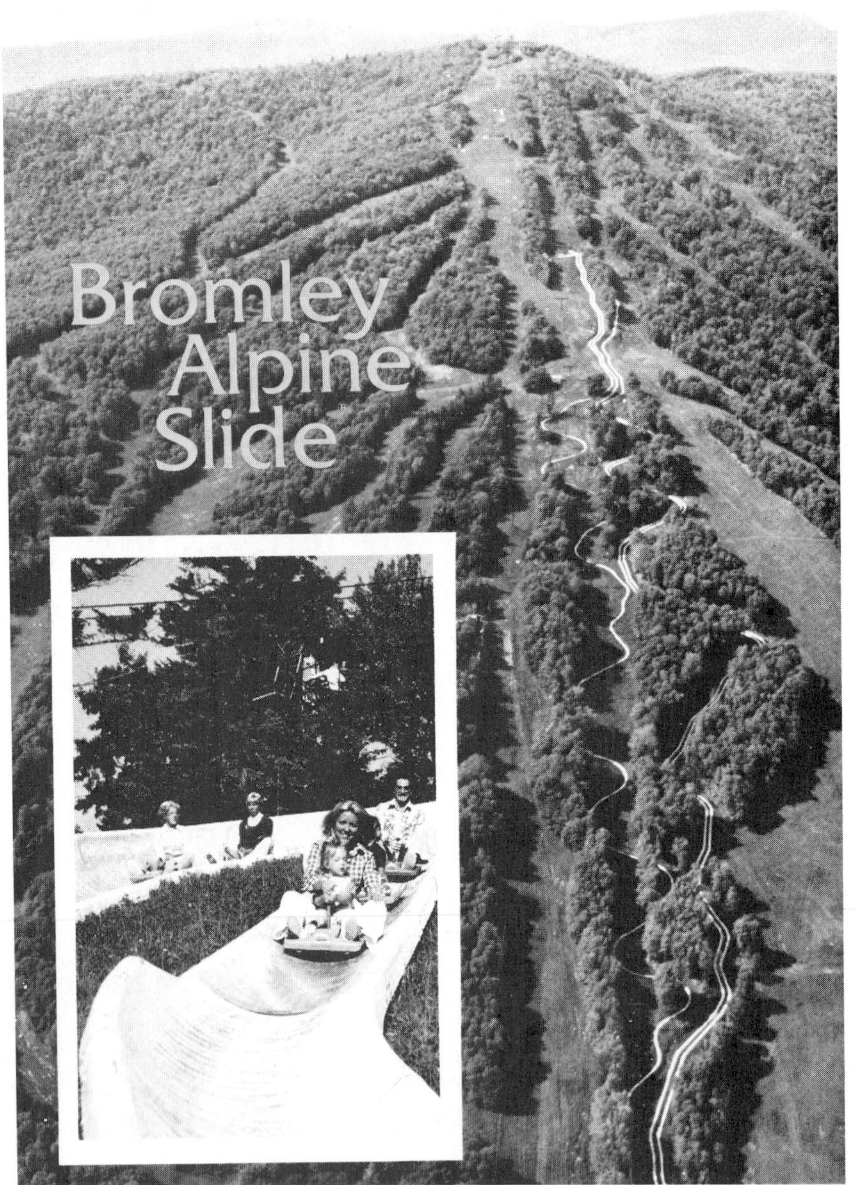

Exhibit 8 "Off-Season" Calendar for Stratton and Bromley

SPECIAL EVENTS

July 2 Manchester
Vermont Symphony Orchestra Pops Concert, Southern Vermont Arts Center, 8:30 pm.

July 3–5 Bromley
Bromleyfest—Three days of music and dancing in the Octoberfest spirit. At the base of the Alpine Slide.

July 2–5 Stratton
NELTA's 45's Tournament, Stratton Mt. Inn.

July 4 Newfane
Annual Family Day, all day, Parade 10 am, fireworks 9 pm.

July 10–11 Newfane
Annual Field Days, Friday 5 til midnight, Saturday 10 am til midnight.

July 10–11 Manchester
Manchester Lions Club Auction, Recreation Center.

July 11 Newfane
Newfane Flower Show, Windham County Court House, 1:30 pm–5:30 pm.

July 11 Dorset
Annual Antique Show, Dorset Village Green, 10–5 pm.

July 15 Stratton
Women's One Day Member Guest, Stratton Country Club.

July 24–26 Stratton
Men's Three Day Member Guest, Stratton Country Club.

July 31–August 2 Stratton
NELTA's 35's Tournament.

July 31–August 1 E. Dorset
Quilt Show, Congregational Church, Friday 1–9 pm, Saturday 10–4 pm.

August 1 Arlington
Bazaar, St. James Church, 10–4 pm.

August 1 Townshend
Grace Cottage Hospital Fair Day, Birthday parade, chicken barbeque, band concert, on the Common, 11–9 pm.

August 5 Manchester
Yankee Male Chorus, Southern Vermont Arts Center, 8:30 pm.

August 5–9 Stratton
Green Mountain Backgammon Tournament. Includes the Vermont State Championhip, The Canadian Open, The 1981 Green Mt. Doubles Championship, Stratton Mountain Inn.

August 6 Dorset
Fair at the Church, 1–4 pm.

August 7–8 Manchester
Sidewalk Sale.

August 8 Stratton
Stratton Country Club Junior Championships, Under 16.

August 9 Stratton
Parent Child Tournament, Stratton Country Club.

August 14–16 Manchester
Southern Vermont Crafts Fair, Magic, Music, Mimes, Recreation area, Friday noon–6 pm, Saturday 10–6 pm, Sunday 10–5 pm, $2.

August 16 Manchester
Manchester Horse Show, Hildene horse ring, River Road, 8 am.

August 20–23 Stratton
Carte Blanche Tennis Legends Championships, John Newcombe Tennis Center. Best players in the world over 35.

August 22–23 Bondville
Bondville Fair, at the Fairgrounds on Rte. 30.

August 23 Stratton
Karen Krantzcke Tennis Tournament. Pro/Am tournament at the Newcombe Tennis Center.

August 29–30 Stratton
Stratton Country Club Mixed Member Guest.

September 4–7 Stratton
Stratton Wurstfest, the best in German food and entertainment, activities for the kids, continuous entertainment, admission charge.

September 4–7 Stratton
NELTA's 50's Tournament.

Sept 12–Oct 12 Stratton
Stratton Arts Festival, Stratton Base Lodge, continuous exhibits of the finest Vermont artists and craftsmen, live concerts and exhibitions.

September 19 Stratton
Tink Smith Trophy Tournament, Stratton Country Club.

September 20 Manchester
Maple Leaf Hall Marathon.

October 2–4 Weston
Weston Antique Show.

October 15 Manchester
Hildene Dinner Auction, Wilburton Inn.

March 1–Nov 30 Bennington
Bennington Museum. American glass, fine art, Grandma Moses School Museum, changing exhibits. Adm.

April 17–August Manchester
Orvis Fly Fishing School. Casting, coaching, lectures. Friday to Sunday and Tuesday to Thursday sessions.

May–September Newfane
Newfane Flea Market. Antiques, junk, guns, tools, knick knacks and everything under the sun. A real experience. Rte 30 between Townshend and Newfane, every Sunday.

Mid–May–October Grafton
Bike Vermont. Weekend and mid-week Vermont Bicycle tours from inn to inn. Limited size groups, all levels of bikers. Fee.

May 23–Oct 25 Manchester
Historic Hildene, home of Robert Todd Lincoln. Special events. Daily 10–4 pm, picnic facilities by appointment, group rates.

(continued)

May 23–October Bellows Falls

Steamtown. World's largest collection of steam locomotives and equipment. Train rides.

May 24–October 12 Weston

Farrar-Mansur House, 1797 tavern, Saturday 1–5 pm, Sunday 2–5 pm, July–Labor Day Wednesday–Saturday 1–5 pm.

May 29–September 27 Stratton

Stratton Golf Academy, golf instruction programs weekend and five day, including lodging, meals, carts, video taping, greens fees, PGA, LPGA teaching pros. Group rates available.

May 29–September 27 Stratton

John Newcombe Tennis Center, complete weekend and five day programs include lodging, meals, video taping, court time, social tennis, activities and indoor courts. Group rates available.

May–October Bromley

Alpine Slide and Scenic Chairlift Rides. Adults $4, Children $3, unlimited sliding $6 Monday through Friday 10–12 pm.

June–Labor Day Stratton

Sailboats. Rent a sunfish and sail the waters of Stratton Lake. Open daily weather permitting.

Newcombe Tennis Center Rates and Information

2-DAY PACKAGES

Tennis includes 4 clinics beginning Friday afternoon at 2:30 p.m. and concluding Sunday at 12 noon. 9 hours of on-court tennis instruction, "Tips on Tennis" lessons each morning, videotape analysis, a meet the pros party, a round robin doubles tournament, special entertainment and free court time.

Accommodations are at your choice of Stratton Mountain Inn, Liftline Lodge or Birkenhaus, which includes lodging and breakfast and dinner for 2 days and nights.

5-DAY PACKAGES

Tennis includes 10 clinics beginning Sunday afternoon at 2:30 p.m. and concluding Friday at 12 noon, 24 hours of on-court tennis instruction, "Tips on Tennis" lessons each morning, videotape analysis, a meet the pros party, pro-guest doubles, a round robin doubles tournament, a pro exhibition, awards party, special entertainment and free court time.

Accommodations are in your choice of Stratton Mountain Inn, Liftline Lodge, or Birkenhaus, which includes lodging and breakfast and dinner for 5 days and nights.

TENNIS ONLY PACKAGES

3-Day Package (Adult)

Includes 4 clinics beginning Friday afternoon at 2:30 p.m. and concluding Sunday at 12 noon, 9 hours of on-court tennis instruction, "Tips on Tennis" lessons each morning, videotape analysis, a meet the pros party, a round robin doubles tournament, special entertainment and free court time.

5-Day Package (Adult)

Includes 10 clinics beginning Sunday afternoon at 2:30 p.m. and concluding Friday at 12 noon, 24 hours of on-court tennis instruction, "Tips on Tennis" lessons each morning, videotape analysis, a meet the pros party, pro-guest doubles, a round robin doubles tournament, a pro exhibition, awards party, special entertainment and free court time.

5-Day Package (Junior)

Includes 20 hours of on-court tennis instruction, "Tips on Tennis" lessons and videotape analysis. Package begins Monday morning at 9:30 a.m. and concludes Friday afternoon at 3:30 p.m. Sessions include drills to develop shot technique and match play to emphasize tactics and strategy.

INDIVIDUAL CLINICS

An individual clinic ticket can be used for any one of the 18 clinics we offer throughout the week. Clinics are 2½ hours in length except for Sundays and Fridays which are 2 hours.

Each clinic begins with a stretching warm up and a courtside demonstration by the pro.

Morning sessions are designed to develop shot technique while afternoons emphasize tactics and strategy.

There are usually 3–4 students per instructor and never more than 5.

Included is videotape analysis and "Tips on Tennis" lessons each morning.

Not included with the ticket is free court time, meet the pros party and afternoon tournaments. These fees are listed below.

Exhibit 8 *(continued)*

Court Rentals

Midweek – $7 per hour. Weekend – $12 per hour.

Afternoon Tournaments

$4 per person

Meet the Pros Party

$5.25 per person

1981 Junior Program

Newk's Training Program is returning to Stratton Mountain in 1981. Our day camp offers weekly and daily packages for juniors, age 15 and under. The available sessions are as follows

June 21–26	August 2–7
June 28–July 3	August 9–14
July 5–10	August 16–21
July 12–17	August 23–28
July 26–31	August 30–September 4

Daily Program—The day's activities include a courtside demonstration by the pro, a concentrated session of drills to develop shot technique, match play to emphasize shot selection, playing percentages and court position, videotape analysis and a session of tactics and strategy. Instruction and groups will be according to ability level.

	Per Person Dbl. Occ.	Per Person Sgl. Occ.	Tennis Only (No meals Lodging)
2 Day	$215	$235	$120
5 Day	$470	$490	$265

Newk's Junior 5 Day Package $110

Package rates do not include 15% gratuities and 5% Vermont meals and room tax.

Daily Clinics	Adult	Junior (15 yrs-under)
Individual Clinic	$ 30	$30 (Day Ticket)
12 Clinic Book	$300	

Private Lessons		Court Rentals
Per Hour—	$30	Mid-Week—$7 per hour
Per Half-Hour—	$15	Weekend—$12 per hour

Stratton Hosts Carte Blanche Legends Tour

Stratton Mountain's John Newcombe Tennis Center will be the site for the seventh stop of the Carte Blanche Tennis Legends Tour, Aug. 20–23. Featuring the world's greatest players, the Tennis Legends Tour brings together the men who have made tennis history for the past 20 years.

Committed to the Stratton tournament are the four greatest players in tennis history. Rod Laver, Ken Rosewall, Roy Emerson, and John Newcombe — all Australians who will comprise four of the eight players competing in the tournament.

The Stratton event will be held on the outdoor courts of the John Newcombe Tennis Center located behind the Stratton Mountain Inn. Box seats and lawn passes will be available for the four day event. Lawn passes will be $6 per day. A box seat will cost $75 for the entire four days (six seats per box).

(continued)

Golf Academy Rates

5 DAY PROGRAM INCLUDES

- greens fees and cart on Sunday afternoon.
- four days of instruction (Monday–Thursday 6 hours/day)—a total of 24 hours including on-course playing lessons.
- golf after instructional hours (Monday–Thursday).
- golf and cart on Friday.
- cocktail party (Monday night).
- graduation banquet (Thursday night).
- Thunderbirds—special trick shot golf show.
- use of golf clubs and golf balls.
- club cleaning and storage.
- color video taping and graph-check analysis.
- private room at one of our luxurious inns for 5 nights, beginning Sunday.
- breakfast and dinner daily from Sunday dinner through Friday breakfast.
- use of swimming pool, tennis courts; evening activities.

WEEKEND PROGRAM INCLUDES

- golf and cart on Friday afternoon and/or use of Training Center with professional supervision.
- instruction Saturday/Sunday (6 hours/day).
- golf after instruction hours Saturday/Sunday.
- cocktail party (Saturday night).
- use of golf clubs and golf balls.
- club cleaning and storage.
- color video taping and graph-check analysis.
- private room at one of our luxurious inns for 2 nights, beginning Friday.
- breakfast and dinner daily from Friday night through Sunday breakfast.
- use of swimming pool, tennis courts; evening activities.

GOLF ACADEMY RATES

All Rates are per person

Weekend Program				5 Day Program			
1/room	2/room	3/room	Non-Golfer	1/room	2/room	3/room	Non-Golfer
$275	$255	$240	$95	$550	$530	$495	$230

Instruction Only without meals and lodging.
Weekend—$160 5 Day—$300

Exhibit 8 *(continued)*

Stratton Resort Special Packages

Riding

On a clear summer day, bring the family to the Stratton Stables for a ride through Vermont's Green Mountain forests. Trail rides are available with guides from July 1 through the end of summer. People of all ages are welcome. The stables are located at the Sun Bowl.

Sailing

Stratton Lake is a beautiful setting for sunning on the beach or sailing a sunfish out to the island. Come take a sailboat and relax in the midst of the mountains on Stratton's clear cool lake. Boats are available for $5 per hour or $16 for the day.

Hiking

The Stratton/Bromley area is a hiker's paradise. Both the Applachian Trail and Vermont's Long Trail wind their way through the valleys and up the mountains of southern Vermont. Pick up the trail at any number of points in the area and find yourself on the top of Stratton, or Bromley, or down by Somerset Reservoir.

Enjoy the beauty and serenity of the Green Mountains the way it was first enjoyed—on foot.

NEW LIFE HEALTH SPA

The New Life Sessions

Any consecutive 7 days 6 nights, arriving at noon for lunch Sunday and departing after lunch the following Saturday.

Double occupancy is $530 per person and single occupancy is $555 per person plus 15% service charge and 5% room and meal tax.

Price includes room with private bath, all meals, yoga and gym classes, daily pool and swim workouts, two massages, participation in all scheduled activities and use of all spa facilities.

Exhibit 9 Stratton and Bromley: Winter Program

Stratton 1980–81 Package Plans

	Lift Tickets		Lifts and Lessons		Lifts, Lessons, and Equipment	
	Non-Holiday	Holiday	Non-Holiday	Holiday	Non-Holiday	Holiday
2-Day Package Plans						
Adult	38	40	–	–	*See 2-Day Learn to Ski Program below*	
Junior	28	30	–	–		
3-Day Package Plans						
Adult	50	60	67	83	91	113
Junior	35	45	52	68	64	83
Big Cub (6–12/all day)	–	–	75	–	87	–
Little Cub (3–6/all day)	–	–	54	–	–	–
5-Day Package Plan						
Adult	75	95	99	129	131	169
Junior	50	70	74	104	90	124
Big Cub (6–12/all day)	–	–	115	–	131	–
Little Cub (3–6/all day)	–	–	88	–	–	–

Holiday periods are December 20 through January 4, and February 7–22, 1981.

Lift Ticket Plans

Our Lift Ticket Plans include unlimited use of all lifts. The lift portions of all Stratton plans are honored at Bromley.

Lifts and Lessons Plans

These plans include daily 1¾ hour lessons, plus video taping with analysis, highlight the 5-day plan. Unlimited use of all lifts is included.

Lifts, Lessons and Equipment Plans

These plans include daily 1¾ hour lessons plus unlimited use of all lifts. Video taping with analysis is included in 5-day plans. First Run Ski Shop provides rental skis, bindings, boots and poles.

Woman's Way Ski Seminars

Again this year, Stratton Mountain will host "Woman's Way Ski Seminars." Founded and conducted by Elissa Slanger (fully certified by the Far West Ski Instructors Association, the Rocky Mountain Ski Instructors Association, and the Professional Ski Instructors of America), Woman's Way Ski Seminars provide the opportunity to replace your skiing fears with confidence to help you ski the way you've always imagined.

The complete 5-day program begins with an orientation party/meeting on Sunday evening. Instruction continues from Monday through Friday, with up to 5 hours of skiing instruction per day in semi-private classes (4–5 students per instructor).

Cost is $240 for instruction. Lift tickets, meals, and lodging not included. A deposit of $100 is required to reserve space in a seminar, and reservations are on a first-come, first-served basis. Enrollment is limited to 35 participants. The remainder of the tuition is due 7 days prior to start of seminar.

Little Cub Ski School

The Little Cub Ski School is designed to teach children, ages 3 to 6, the basics of skiing technique.

Rates are $8 per session or $18 for all day.
Lunch session: $8.

Season Passes Available	Before Nov. 15	After Nov. 15
Lifts, Lessons and Lunch	$260	$275

Big Cub Ski School

The Big Cub Ski School is for children ages 6 to 12. The children learn skiing technique mostly by watching their instructors, and then imitating them.

Session Times and Rates		
All Day	9 a.m.–4 p.m.	$25
¾ hour lessons	9:30–11:15 a.m.; 12:45–2:30 p.m.	10 each
(multiple-lesson books available)		
Lunch Sessions	11:15–12:45 p.m.	8
Snack Session	2:30–4 p.m.	3

Lift ticket required during lessons.

Season Passes	Before Nov. 15	After Nov. 15
Lessons only	$260	$275
Lift & Lessons	484	514

Weekend Programs

Weekend Tripper's Winter Allegro

This program is designed for the advanced skier who wants to work weekends on skills and skiing, in a fun environment, with the same instructor and group.

Cost for entire program is $100, lift tickets required.

(continued)

Exhibit 9 *(continued)*

Beginner's Circle (9:30–2:30 daily)

A continuous teaching program to make skiing fun and rewarding—for beginners and those who have not skied in a long time. You learn at your own pace and may take breaks anytime during the program. Includes special lift ticket, lesson, and skis. (Junior must be five feet tall and weigh at least 100 pounds.) Adult $35, junior $30.

Daily Ski School Rates

All lessons involving the use of lifts require a lift ticket. All Ski School tickets are sold at the Ski School Desk, main level of the Reception Center. Classes are held daily at 9:30 a.m. and 12:45 p.m. Class lessons are 1¾-hours, and assemble at the Ski School Meeting Place located near the Ski School Chalet, slopeside of the Reception Center.

Class Lessons

Single Lesson Ticket	$10
Four Lesson Book	$36
Eight Lesson Book	$66
16 Lesson Book	$120
Special Class Lesson (*8-person limit*)	$74

Private Lessons

1 hour private lesson	$22
Each additional person	$10
1¾ hour private lesson	$33
Each additional person	$14
All day private lesson (9:30–4 p.m.)	$90
Each additional person	$30

Stratton Ski School Racing & Freestyle Programs Rates and Dates, Season 1980–1981

	Liftpass required	Liftpass included
Christmas Camps*: 1. December 20–28 2. December 27–Jan. 4 (9 days each)	$123	$203
Weekends Only Jan. 10–April 5	236	407
Presidents' Birthday weeks* 1. Feb. 7–15 2. Feb. 14–22 (9 days each)	123	203
X-mas camp (9 consec. days) Weekends and Presidents' B'day (9 consec. days)	360	610
X-mas Camp (9 consec. days) and Weekends only	305	518
Presidents' B'day (9 days) & Weekends only	305	518
Christmas Camp (9 days) Presidents' B'day (9 days)	222	365

*Adjusted rates for late start and early departure.

Stratton Instructor Training Course

This special course is open to all who are interested in learning to teach the American Teaching Method (ATM) from beginner to expert skier. The price for the entire course is $105. Individual sessions are available using regular lesson tickets.

Stratton's Handicapped Ski Program

The Stratton Mountain Handicapped Ski Program is open to all interested handicapped persons. No prior skiing or athletic experience is necessary.

Available:

9:30–10:30	$7/hour
10:30–11:30	$7/hour
11:30–12:30	$10/hour–private
1:30– 2:30	$7/hour
2:30– 3:30	$10/hour–private

Ski Touring at Stratton

The Stratton Cross Country School offers certified instruction. Center Director John Eckhardt, who is certified by both the Professional Ski Instructors Association and the Eastern Professional Ski Touring Instructors, leads our staff of professionals.

Single Lesson Ticket: $6

Lessons begin at 10:00 a.m. and 2 p.m. daily. Lessons are 1 hour.

Private Lesson Ticket: $12

Lessons begin at 9 a.m., noon, 1 p.m. or by appointment. Lessons are 1 hour.

Trail Fees: $3

Season Pass: $50/$40 for homeowners/residents

Stratton—Austria Tour

The itinerary is as follows

Fri. May 8 Depart in U.S.A.

Sat. May 9 Arrival in Munich, transfer to Zell am See and Hotel, welcome party in the evening.

12 days Glacier Spring Skiing and/or

- Cablecar ride to the Schmittenhoehe.

Wed. May 13 Evening party, native Austrian specialty dish.

- Discover Zell am See's quaint shops, excellent cafes and restaurants or get a workout on the tennis courts, in the indoor pool or sauna, etc.
- A tour on the gigantic Grossglockner mountain road.
- A trip to Salzburg, the city of music, art and history.
- A trip to Bad Gastein, known all over the world for its Thermal Waters (morning skiing, afternoon swimming in the thermal water).
- A day in Innsbruck, "The Olympic City," visit historic arcades, the massive Olympic ski jumps, etc.
- Skiing Hintertux, Zillertal in Tirol.

Fri. May 22 Shopping, walking, relaxing, evening grill party.

Sat. May 23 Departure to U.S.A.

(continued)

Bromley 1980–81 Package Plans

	Lift Tickets		Lifts and Lessons		Lifts, Lessons and Equipment	
	Non-Holiday	Holiday	Non-Holiday	Holiday	Non-Holiday	Holiday
2-Day Package Plans						
Adult	33	35	–	–	*See 2-Day Learn to Ski Program below.*	
Junior	24	26	–	–		
3-Day Package Plans						
Adult	44	52	61	75	85	105
Junior	30	39	47	62	59	77
5-Day Package Plans						
Adult	65	82	89	116	121	156
Junior	40	60	64	94	80	114

Holiday periods are December 20 through January 4, and February 7–22, 1981.

Lift Ticket Plans

Our Lift Ticket Plans include unlimited use of all lifts.

Lifts and Lessons Plans

These plans include personal attention to your specific weaknesses and strengths on varied terrain, plus video taping with analysis, highlight the 5-day plan. Unlimited use of all lifts is included.

Lifts, Lessons and Equipment Plans

These plans include daily 1¾ hour lessons plus unlimit l use of all lifts. Video taping with analysis is included in 5-day plans. First Run ! κi Shop provides rental skis, bindings, boots and poles.

Beginner's Circle (9:30–2:30 daily)

A continuous teaching program to make skiing fun and rewarding—for beginners and those who have not skied in a long time. You learn at your own pace and may take breaks anytime during the program. Includes special lift ticket, lesson, and skis. (Junior must be five feet tall and weigh at least 100 pounds.) Adult $35, Junior $30.

2-Day Learn to Ski Package

Adult or junior concentrated program for beginners only. Starts in the Beginner's Circle and includes lessons, a special three-lift ticket and rental equipment. Available any two consecutive days, including weekends. Adult $60, Junior $50. Holiday periods: Adult $70, Junior $60.

Junior Specials

Bromley offers a complete range of junior learn-to-ski programs for children up to 14 years old. The Snoopy Ski School meets daily and has classes for all levels of young skiers.

Ski and Play Hour is a special one-hour class which introduces the young child (ages 3–5) to skiing and determines if he or she is ready for the Snoopy Ski School.

All-Day Supervised skiing is designed for the skiing child (7–14) who is a lift-rider. Supervised skiing begins at 9:30 a.m. until 2:30 p.m., and includes lunch. The class is offered weekends and holiday periods.

Exhibit 10 Survey of Ski Resort Business, 1979–1980

1979–80 NSAA End of Season Survey

Volume of Business in Skier Days 1978–79 and 1979–80 by Regions

Region	No. Reporting	Skier Days 1978–79	Skier Days 1979–80	Percent Change
Northeast	76	5,686,559	4,251,111	−25.2
Southeast	21	1,437,572	1,591,000	10.7
Midwest	30	1,885,992	1,665,365	−11.7
Rocky Mtn	45	9,763,158	10,400,847	6.5
West	39	6,263,025	6,174,003	−1.4
U.S. Total	211	25,035,306	24,082,326	−3.8

Proportion of Ski Areas Reporting Increases, No Change or Decreases in Season Pass Sales in 1979–80 by Regions

	Percent Reporting		
Region	Increase	No Change	Decrease
Northeast	11.1	2.8	86.1
Southeast	33.4	5.6	61.0
Midwest	32.0	4.0	64.0
Rocky Mtn	60.5	7.0	32.5
West	37.5	9.4	53.1
U.S. Total	31.6	5.3	63.1

Reasons Selected by Respondents for Decrease in Season Pass Sales in 1979–80

	Rank in Importance			All Selections Summed Without Regard to Rank
Reason	1st	2nd	3rd	
	(Percent Selecting The Reason)			
Prior Conditions	58	9	4	29
Price of Pass	15	15	37	20
Inflation	21	51	18	30
Gas Price		12	32	12
Gas Availability	2	13	9	7
Other	4			2
	100	100	100	100
Number Reporting	119	88	71	278

Case 30

Walsh Petroleum

John Walsh sighed as he looked again at the financial statements his accountant had delivered that morning. When John's father died two years ago, his accountant had advised against selling the business. "It's a good business, John," he said, "and I think you could do a lot to improve it."

While Walsh Petroleum, Inc. had increased profits in 1985, John still considered them unacceptably low. Company sales had declined for the third straight year, and, while John realized that other oil distributors faced the same problems, he had to wonder what type of future he could expect if he stayed with the family business. Now 31 years old and just married, maybe he should consider selling the business and starting another career before he got too old.

Company History

Walsh Petroleum was founded in 1957 by John's mother and father as commission agents in the oil business. By 1976, the senior Walsh converted the company to a conventional oil distributorship. Both the family and the company were well respected in the local community, and the company grew steadily. The 1970's and early 1980's were a period of relative prosperity for Walsh Petroleum. Dollar sales in 1982 were four times higher than sales in 1977 (although most of this increase was a result of increased unit sales prices). Nonetheless, profits were at their highest level in 1982. A year later, sales gallonage started a decline that had continued unabated. In 1984, John's father died, leaving John's mother and John to manage the firm.

Company Operations

Walsh Petroleum distributed oil products throughout a seven-county area of the southeastern United States. Their marketing area was semi-rural, but contained two county seats with populations of 15,000 and 25,000. The area's proximity to a growing, major metropolitan city was expected to result in higher-than-average population growth over the next ten years, but in no way was the area likely to become a suburb of the city. The firm represented a major branded oil company and carried a full line of petroleum products. There were three basic classes of customers for Walsh:

Reseller Accounts

Walsh served as a distributor of oil products to ten reseller locations, most of which were local gas stations. Gaining new reseller customers depended more on financial considerations than marketing techniques, since gasoline and oil products were generally considered commodities, and most distributors offered similar types

---

This case was prepared by George A. Overstreet, Jr., Stewart C. Malone, and Bernard A. Morin. The authors gratefully acknowledge the financial support of the General Electric Foundation and the McIntire School of Commerce at the University of Virginia in the preparation of this case. As well, the cooperation and assistance of the two closely held corporations represented herein is deeply appreciated.

of services. When a new gas station was about to be constructed (an event that had been occurring with decreasing frequency over the past twenty years), the operator would contact several distributors such as Walsh. The distributor would formulate a proposal based on expected sales gallonage. In return for an exclusive, long-term contract to supply the location with gasoline and oil products, the distributor provided the station with fuel storage tanks, pumps, remote consoles and a canopy. Walsh's profit margin per gallon declined as the reseller's volume climbed based on a sliding scale. If up to 50,000 gallons a month were delivered he received 4.5¢ over delivered cost (including freight). If 50,000 to 65,000 gallons a month were delivered he received 4.0¢ per gallon. For 65–75,000 gallons he received 3.65¢, and for over 75,000 gallons he received 3.5¢ per gallon. Over the course of the contract the station operator could switch suppliers if he/she was willing to make a settlement on the equipment provided by the original distributor.

John had recently audited the profitability of his reseller accounts and found that many of the accounts yielded over a 20% after-tax IRR.[1] New reseller contracts also tended to be very lucrative, but there were relatively few high-gallonage locations left in Walsh's trading area, and only two or three new reseller accounts were out for bid each year. The capital requirements for such investments had grown over the years and ranged from $60,000 to $100,000.

In addition to the ten contract locations, Walsh operated a reseller location itself, on which it had constructed a convenience store (C-store). This diversification move was initiated by Mr. Walsh, Sr. in 1983. The C-store facility was located on 3.0 acres with 300 feet of road frontage on a 4-lane U.S. highway. The property had been appraised at $356,000 and included not only the convenience store but also the bulk storage facilities (144,000 gallons). Mrs. Walsh personally owned the site and leased it to Walsh Petroleum at $4,000 per month ($2,500 for the bulk storage plant and $1,500 for the C-store). The property had a $100,000 note payable over five years at 9%.

Home Heating Oil

Active accounts numbered 624, of which 325 were classified as automatic (with refills scheduled by the distributor). While the home heating oil business was relatively profitable, it was also highly seasonal, and, thus, efficient utilization of equipment and personnel was viewed as a problem. Some other distributors had taken on equipment sales and service, as well as related businesses such as air conditioning, in order to balance the seasonality of fuel oil sales. John had concluded that heating oil sales would have to double in order to justify the equipment investment and personnel training for an in-house sales/service department.

Commercial/Agricultural Accounts

Approximately 120 businesses and/or farms maintained their own tanks and pumps for which Walsh supplied oil products. While these accounts had generally shown some degree of loyalty to their petroleum supplier, there was no contractual relationship that would prevent them from changing suppliers.

Within Walsh Petroleum's trading area, there were currently three other gasoline and oil distributors. Competitive pressures were moderate for existing gasoline reseller and home heating oil accounts, but John had recently noticed an increased level of competition for the one or two new reseller locations that were constructed each year. None of the four distributors possessed a large competitive advantage over the others. Each competitor had about the same level of sales, and all possessed a similar amount of financial resources. Since gasoline and oil products have a significant freight cost to value ratio, distributors of these products generally had a

[1]See Appendix B for a discounted cash flow analysis of a recent reseller investment.

trading radius of approximately 75 miles around their terminal or distribution point. While the local competitors did not really worry John, some of the distributors that served the nearby metropolitan area were significantly larger than Walsh, and a move by one of these larger competitors into Walsh's trading area could well upset the competitive equilibrium that had evolved over the years.

Family and Management

Mrs. Walsh assumed the chairmanship of the company following the death of her husband, and she held 52% of the voting stock of the corporation (the remaining 48% being held equally by John and his 2 younger brothers). Having worked with her husband for several years, she was very knowledgeable about the firm's operations. While she held the title of chairman, Mrs. Walsh's duties consisted of supervising the convenience store adjacent to the distributorship and maintaining relationships with the fuel oil customers. A prominent citizen of the local community, Mrs. Walsh also served on the town council.

John Walsh had been employed as a geologist with an energy consulting firm in Denver prior to 1982. When he was visiting home one weekend, he mentioned to his father that he was concerned that his career would be hurt by the recent recession in the oil drilling business. Later that weekend, while having coffee together in the local donut shop, John, Sr. said, "John, our business here is changing rapidly, too. If you have any interest in joining the family business, you better make up your mind soon, because I may just sell the business rather than put up with all the changes that are occurring."

John returned to Denver, but after several months he decided that the opportunity at Walsh Petroleum might offer a better future than his current job. John returned home in late 1982 and began to learn the business from his father. Not only did John assume many of the administrative duties, but he also managed the marketing relationships with the major accounts.

John's two younger brothers were not active in the management of the business at the time, although each held 16% of the corporate stock. Richard was 26 years old and was employed in another city. Daniel was a sophomore in college.

Aside from John and his mother, Walsh Petroleum employed three clerks and four driver/maintenance workers. The three clerks handled much of the administrative paperwork for both the oil distributorship and convenience store. Convenience stores have a multitude of vendors, all of whom expect payment within ten days. Managing the payables took a great deal of time, and Walsh's bookkeeping clerk had complained on more than one occasion that she couldn't keep up with the workload. All of the accounting was done manually, and John planned to install a computer system in the near future.

In addition, there were two full-time and three part-time workers at the convenience store. Salaries and benefits for these workers corresponded to industry averages, and all employees were non-unionized. During the first quarter of 1986, John purchased a new tractor/trailer for $60,000 (9,000 gallon capacity). In addition, Walsh had three older "bobtail" trucks for short deliveries (2,000 gallon capacity), and two used service delivery vans.

The Oil Distribution Industry

Few industries have experienced the volatility and changes connected with the oil business in the past 15 years. In 1973, the Arab oil embargo resulted in a 119% increase in the price of crude oil during a twelve-month period. While demand fell slightly from 1973 to 1981, prices were expected to continue climbing. Spurred by higher prices, oil exploration and refinery construction continued to increase. In 1981, President Reagan decontrolled gasoline and crude oil prices. The acquisition price of crude oil began to drop, and demand also fell as the world economy entered a recession.

Exhibit 1 Average Miles per Gallon 1974–85

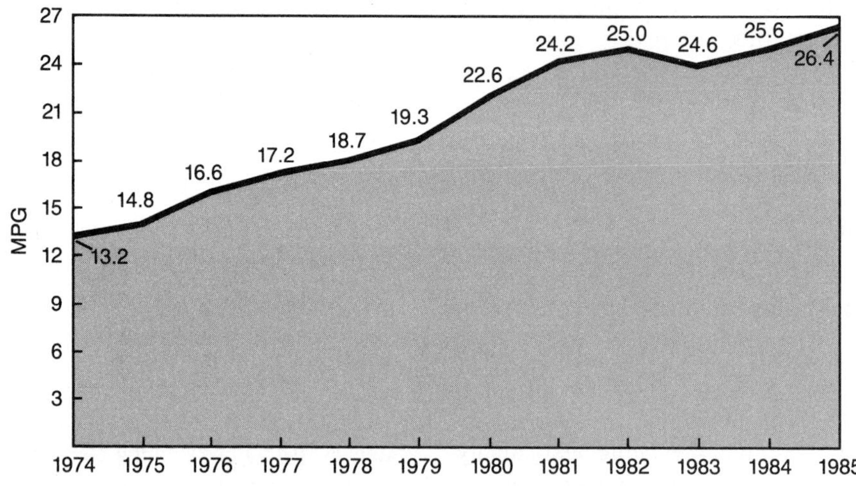

Source: *Forbes,* Citing National Highway Traffic. Safety Administration Data, October 8, 1986, p. 198.

The changes that occurred upstream in the oil production industry had a large impact on the independent petroleum market in the following way:

1. Between 1974 and 1985, American auto manufacturers doubled the miles per gallon of new cars, from 13.2 MPG to 26.4 MPG (see Exhibit 1).

2. During the same period, gasoline consumption of passenger cars declined from approximately 75 billion gallons to 65 billion gallons (see Exhibit 2).

3. The number of service stations (defined as outlets with 50% or more dollar volume from the sale of petroleum products) fell from 226,459 in 1972 to 121,000 in 1985 (see Exhibit 3).

In addition to these changes, oil distributors also faced declining margins, increased real estate costs, and a proliferation of environmental regulations.

News for distributors had not been all bad. The past two years had seen firmer gross profit margins and increased gallonage pumped. Although the market had not recovered to the volume levels of the late 1970's and early 1980's, gasoline gallonage used by motorists increased 1.5% in 1983, 1.5% in 1984, and 3.4% in 1985.[2] A significant portion of the increased demand had to be attributed to the oversupply of world crude and, hence, to lower prices during each of the last three years (−3.3% for 1983, −1.6% for 1984, and −1.6% for 1985).

Independent petroleum marketers are entrepreneurs involved in the sale and distribution of refined petroleum and ancillary products. While the exact number of the companies was unknown, one trade association report estimated their number between 11,000 and 12,000 in 1985.[3] In terms of size, the trade association membership is broken down in Table 1.

Independent petroleum marketers have responded to the pressures in their industry in one

[2] *1986 State of the Convenience Store Industry,* National Association of Convenience Stores, Inc., Alexandria, VA, p. 7.

[3] *1985 Petroleum Marketing Databook,* Petroleum Marketing Education Foundation, Alexandria, VA (1985), p. 12.

Exhibit 2 Gasoline Consumption, 1947–1990 (Passenger Cars)

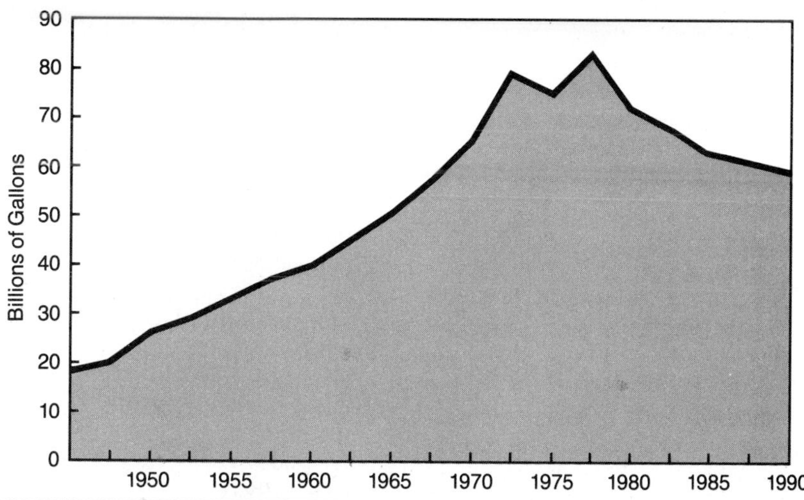

Source: American Petroleum Institute, *Basic Petroleum Data Book,* January 1983, for 1947–1981 figures; 1985 and 1990 projections based on Data Resources, Inc. (DRI), Petroleum Investor's Relations Association (PIRA), and PACE Company Consultants and Engineers (PACE) average projections.

Total U.S. gasoline demand in 1982 was 6.5 million barrels per day. DRI, PIRA, and PACE estimates for 1985 gasoline demand are 6.0, 5.9, and 5.7 million barrels per day, respectively, averaging to 5.87. Their respective 1990 estimates of 5.4, 5.2, and 5.3 million barrels per day average to 5.3. We have applied the 1978–1981 average ratio or total gasoline demand to gasoline consumption for passenger cars to these 1985 and 1990 DRI, PIRA, and PACE averages.

Exhibit 3 The U.S. Gasoline Station Population (1972–1982)

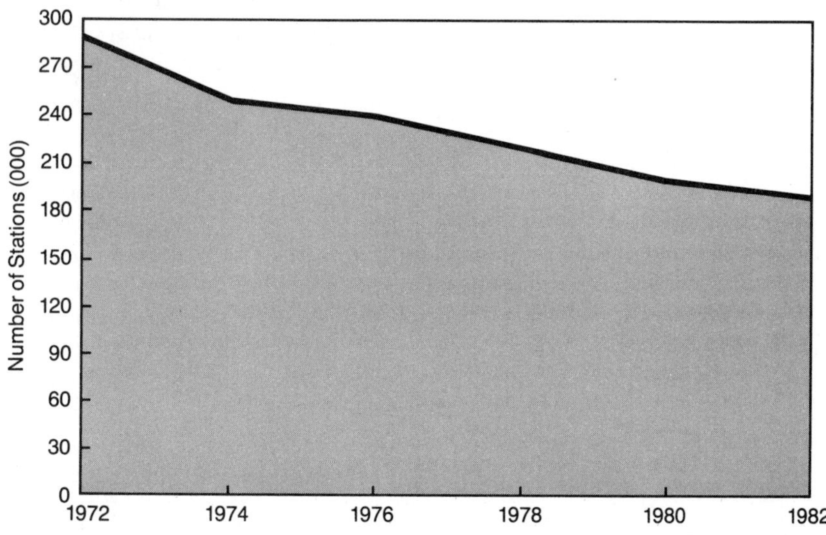

Source: *Lundberg Letter,* October 8, 1982.

Note: Unlike DOE, Lundberg includes gasoline retailers who derive less tan 50% of their revenues from the sale of gasoline.

Table 1 Percentage of Marketers by Size Distribution

Millions of Gallons Sold	1984	1982
Less than 1.0 MM gallons	13.8	18.0
1.0 - 2.49	23.8	26.3
2.5 - 4.99	21.9	20.8
5.0 - 7.49	12.2	9.7
7.5 - 9.99	6.6	6.7
10.0 - 14.99	9.3	7.1
15.0 - 19.99	3.8	2.8
20.0 - 24.99	2.2	1.8
25.0 - 29.99	1.7	1.4
30.0 - 39.99	1.8	1.5
40.0 - 49.99	1.1	1.2
50.0 and above	1.8	2.7
Average Volume	7.80	7.12
Median Volume	3.91	3.18

Source: *1985 Petroleum Marketing Databook* Petroleum Marketing Education Foundation, Alexandria, VA (1985), p. 12

Table 2 1984 Diversified Operations

Operations	Number of Operations
Auto Repair/Maintenance Center	7,081
Auto/Truck/Trailer Rentals	638
Beverage only stores	228
Car washes	2,961
Convenience stores	14,235
Fast food operations	1,002
Heating/Air conditioning service	3,189
Kerosene heater sales	1,275
Lube centers	1,549
Plumbing service	501
Tires/Tires, Battery and Accessory stores	3,507
Truck stops	1,734
Towing service	911
Coal sales	164
Other	1,000

Source: *1985 Petroleum Marketing Databook*, Petroleum Marketing Education Foundation, Alexandria, VA (1985), p. 15.

of two ways: diversification or consolidation (mergers and acquisition). Table 2 shows the number of diversified operations for companies belonging to the major trade association.

Aside from diversifying into other areas, the number of acquisitions had increased in the past few years, spurred by industry decontrol. Independent marketers, particularly larger ones with the capital available to make acquisitions, had acquired other distributors to take advantage of economies of scale in storage, distribution, and other areas such as billing and general administrative services. A 1984 study found that 56 of 135 marketers had purchased one or more marketing companies within the last five years, and 24 of the 56 had purchased more than one.[4] Most of the acquisition activity occurred among marketers with assets greater than $1MM. Of the 90 firms in this category in the sample, 46 had acquired one or more businesses during the period.

As a result of increasing profit pressure, a number of operating changes had occurred on the distribution level.[5] First, the total number of distributor-owned transportation vehicles had declined dramatically from 106,868 in 1982 to 96,972 in 1984. Second, distributors had decreased the amount of their storage facilities from a 2.3 billion-gallon capacity in 1982 to 1.7 billion in 1984. Finally, credit terms to distributors had tightened. In 1982, net 30 day payment terms were reported by 21% of trade association members, while in 1984 this percentage had dropped to 8.2%. These changes and others had led gasoline and oil distributors to redefine the term "good customer." Whereas in the 1960's and 1970's, distributors were willing to inventory product and deliver relatively small amounts of gasoline on small "bobtail" trucks, the new mar-

[4] *1984 Petroleum Marketing Databook*, Petroleum Marketing Education Foundation, Alexandria, VA (1984), p. 19.

[5] *1985 Petroleum Marketing Databook*, Petroleum Marketing Education Foundation, Alexandria, VA (1985), pp. 15–16.

ket realities made these practices less attractive. Instead of inventorying product, successful distributors would now send a large transport truck (9,000-gallon capacity) to the terminal, or distribution point, and transport the gasoline directly to one service station. Since it was inefficient to have the large truck tied up making multiple deliveries, the customer emphasis was on the volume gas station with tank capacity large enough to handle one large delivery. The "mom-and-pop" gasoline retailer was now considered undesirable. John Walsh stated, "In 1980 we considered a good account one that pumped 20,000–25,000 gallons per month, while in 1986 we consider a good account to be in the range of 40,000–50,000 gallons per month."

In addition to the deregulation of gasoline and crude oil prices in 1981, another regulatory development that affected oil distributors was the issuance of EPA regulations regarding leakage of gasoline from underground steel storage tanks. According to one authority, as many as 30% of steel tanks currently in the ground might be leaking.[6] Since both past and present owners of property with underground tanks could be held legally liable for leakage pollution, many companies were completely removing older tanks (more than 10–15 years old) at a cost of approximately $1,000 for a 1,000–3,000 gallon tank. The cost of removing and then reinstalling a similar size tank cost approximately $6,000. If there was a minor leak, clean-up costs would be approximately $5,000 extra. Liability insurance for tank leakage had become exceedingly expensive and difficult to obtain, especially for older, single-wall steel tanks.

The Current Situation

From his study of trade journals and attendance at industry conferences, John Walsh had concluded that basic industry trends portended a bleak future for Walsh Petroleum unless some substantial changes were made in the company's strategy. It seemed apparent to John that his company had to do something different or get out of the business. Being relatively young, John was confident that he could start a career elsewhere, but he enjoyed living in his hometown of Lancaster and liked the idea of being his own boss. Furthermore, his mother was currently receiving an annual salary of $50,000 in addition to rent she received on the C-store. If they sold the company, would the proceeds generate sufficient income to replace his mother's current income?

If they decided not to sell the business, John wondered how the business could be changed? He had received an offer to purchase a competitor, Valley Oil, only weeks before.

The Valley Oil Alternative

In many respects, it seemed as though Valley Oil faced the same problems as Walsh. The two companies sold basically the same product lines, although Valley's percentage of heating fuel sales was higher than Walsh's. This aspect of Valley was attractive to John, since heating fuel commanded higher margins than gasoline (25¢ per gallon versus 8 to 10¢ per gallon), and customers were a little less sensitive to price than gasoline resellers. Overall, though, Valley's unit sales were declining and unit profit margins were being squeezed. Many of Valley's contract resellers were low volume accounts and had experienced declining sales volumes. Furthermore, their underground tanks were old.

The owner of Valley had died recently, and Valley's current 55-year old CEO wanted to get out of the business. Valley's CEO had sent along a copy of the company's recent financial statements which John had given to a consultant to value Valley Oil for him (see Appendix C). Valley's CEO said that, while the company wasn't for sale on the open market yet, he felt that an $800,000 offer would buy the company. John's consultant didn't think Valley was worth that much, but John was skeptical of the consultant's

---

[6] Plenn, Steffen W., *Underground Tankage: The Liability of Leaks,* Petroleum Marketing Education Foundation, Alexandria, VA (1986), pp. 9–12.

conclusions because the consultant did not have experience in the petroleum business.

John thought that acquiring Valley Oil could offer some unique advantages—advantages that many other potential acquirers could not realize. First, many of the selling and administrative expenses that Valley incurred could be performed by Walsh's personnel. A potential buyer from outside the industry would probably have substantially higher operating costs than John would have.

Rather than beginning his analysis with what employees he would be able to eliminate from Valley's payroll, John decided to examine how many people he would have to add to Walsh Petroleum to serve Valley's customers. He figured that initially he would need at least two additional clerks to handle the scheduling and the billing for Valley accounts. Two additional full-time drivers would be needed for deliveries and two seasonal drivers for fuel oil. Salaries for clerks and drivers were estimated at $9,000 and $18,000 a year, respectively, and fringe benefits would probably add about 35%. John thought he could get someone to manage the new business at $30,000 (benefits included). John also felt that if he could get his computerized accounting system up and running within a year for approximately $40,000 he might be able eventually to eliminate one of the clerks. John was also pleased with the thought that the acquisition of Valley would allow him to spread the significant upfront investment in hardware and software over a greater number of accounts, and by adding a delivery scheduling module to the computer system he should be able to schedule his deliveries more efficiently. In addition, John's accountant recommended that he use a conservative tax rate of 30% in his analysis of Valley.

Even with the operating savings John might be able to utilize, Valley would probably be an attractive acquisition to some of the large distributors in the nearby city. Compared to the fierce competition in that city, John's trading area would probably look very attractive to them. While John's knowledge of the local market gave him an advantage, the larger, city-based distributors could achieve many of the operating cost savings that John was contemplating. By purchasing Valley, John felt his gross profit margin would improve due to a reduced level of competition.

The more John thought about the possibility of combining Walsh and Valley, the more likely it seemed that he wouldn't need most of Valley's physical assets to service the accounts he would be acquiring. John had scheduled a lunch with Valley's CEO to discuss the possibility of the acquisition. John's hopes of only acquiring Valley's customers were quickly dashed. Valley's CEO stated that if he was getting out of the business, he was going to sell the whole business as a unit, not hold a "rummage sale". Moreover, he seemed firm about the price of $800,000. The rise in Valley's gross profit margin in 1985 had continued through the first half of 1986 because of the unprecedented drop in oil prices and "sticky" retail prices. However, John knew that Valley's CEO would want to sell the business this year before long-term capital gains rates expired.

A big issue in John's mind was how to finance the acquisition. Neither he nor his mother had enough liquid funds outside the business to acquire Valley. Valley's owners indicated that they might be willing to hold a note, but they would require certain covenants regarding Walsh Petroleum's financial condition in order to protect their position. Also, personal guarantees from John, his mother, and his brother would be required. John decided to try to get Valley's owners to finance 75% of the acquisition price over 10 years. While he would have to pay a premium over the prime rate, in his opinion it might still be a good investment.

The C-Store Alternative

One of the relative bright spots in Walsh Petroleum's operation had been the C-store. C-stores originated as a convenient alternative to the traditional grocery store, and the premise that consumers would pay higher than grocery store prices in exchange for convenience proved correct. Since customers typically bought only a few items, checkout lines were very short. C-stores carried a relatively limited product line of items generally regarded as necessities. Milk, bread, and beer and wine made up a substantial percentage of C-store sales. Although a majority of the products sold in C-stores carried a very similar product mix, opportunities did exist for C-Store operators to differentiate themselves. A number of operators offered video rentals, hot food service (hot dogs, pizza, etc.), and other amenities. Geographic location was also a critical success factor. Customers selected a C-store based on its proximity to their home or their daily route of travel.

Many motor fuel operators had taken the traditional gas station, closed the maintenance bays, and remodeled them into small convenience stores (800–1200 sq. ft.) with gasoline pumps out front. Likewise, convenience store operators, such as Southland (7-Eleven), added self-service gas pumps. According to the National Association of Convenience Stores, gasoline margins averaged 7.3%, while non-gasoline margins averaged 32.2%.[7]

In early 1982, the Walshes had commissioned a marketing consulting group to conduct a feasibility study of a C-store location adjacent to the fuel oil distributorship. The location had approximately 300 feet of frontage on a major highway, and the traffic count looked as though it would make the operation feasible. Mr. Walsh, Sr. had remodeled an existing 2-bay station, and within two years the unit was meeting and then exceeding the marketing consultants' projections.

Walsh Petroleum currently owned an unoccupied two-bay service station on a corner lot with good access from all directions and a stable traffic flow in a growing, nearby community. In the past the Walshes had leased the property to a number of service station operators. None of them had been able to make a success of the operation, and it was John's opinion that the day of the "traditional" two bay station was past its prime. Customers wanted either the pricing and convenience of a self-service station or a super-premium station that provided clearly superior maintenance and service. The turnover of operators was consuming much of Walsh's time, and the station would often sit empty.

John had felt that it might be possible to demolish the station and erect a C-store with self-serve gasoline pumps on the site. To investigate this possibility, John commissioned the same market research firm that had provided the feasibility study for the original C-store to analyze the new location. This firm had developed a forecasting model that would generate fairly accurate sales estimates for both gasoline and in-store sales for a C-store. Among the many variables included in the model was highway traffic flow, store size and layout, distance to the nearest existing C-store, as well as a variety of demographic data on the area. John's corner lot had a traffic count of 14,000 vehicles per day on the main road and 4,000 vehicles a day on the side street. The resulting sales forecast for gasoline was 915,000 gallons with a 24 month maturity and 410,000 gallons in year 1. Kerosene sales were forecast at 7,500 gallons in year 1 and 10,000 gallons per annum thereafter. Inside sales items totalled $213,000 (year 1), $428,000 (year 2), maturing at $530,000 in year 3. Expected margins were 50¢ a gallon for kerosene, 8¢ a gallon for gasoline, and 32% for inside sales.

At the same time, an architectural firm had been retained as a design consultant. Table 3 shows the costs that had been estimated under John's close supervision. Another option John had was to build a C-Store using his major oil supplier's generic C-store design plan. The generic design included a smaller C-store (40 × 50 feet) under a 90 × 40 feet canopy with pumps

[7]"Why the C-store Image Race Could Lead to a Shakeout," *National Petroleum News,* Sept. 1987, p. 40.

Table 3 C-store Estimated Costs

Appraised value of lot	$100,000
Building (≈ $60 for 2400 sq. feet of C-store)	144,400
Market Research	1,000
Equipment Costs:	
Gas equipment	150,000
Food equipment	60,000
Canopy	17,500
Capitalized Site Plan (consultant)	20,000
Inventory:	
Food	40,000
Fuel	14,500
Net Operating Capital	20,000
TOTAL	$567,400
Salvage Value:	
Gas equipment	$13,500
Food equipment	6,000
Canopy	1,750
Capitalized site plan	0
Asset lives:	
Gas equipment	5 years
Food equipment	7 ″
Canopy	10 ″
Site plan & building	31.5 ″
Depreciation Method:	
Gas, Food & Canopy Equip.—Dou. Decl. Bal.	
Site plan & building—Straight Line	

on either side of the store (35 feet from pump to entrance). The advantage to this design was that the major oil company would refund Walsh 2¢ per gallon on all gallons sold (up to 150,000 gallons per month) for 36 months and provide a detailed site plan without charge. John felt he would lose some inside sales with their fatter margins and he wouldn't get to build his own C-store identity and goodwill. The overall cost would be approximately the same for the two options, and John was uncertain which choice was best from a marketing point of view.

Based on those of his other store, John estimated the operating expenses per annum for the new store as follows: salaries and benefits for a 126-hour week at $80,000, utilities at $14,000, property taxes at $2,000 and other miscellaneous expenses at $20,000.

While the research pertaining to the original C-store had been highly accurate, John wondered how reliable the model could be in forecasting future sales for the proposed C-store. Since even the major highways were relatively undeveloped in his rural market, there were certainly some desirable road frontage locations near his site. As a matter of fact, there was a one-acre site directly across the street that could be used for a C-store location. While he had considered buying the property as a defensive move, he felt he really couldn't afford to buy it at $150,000.

John felt that the threat of new C-store competitors was very real. Even though a half-million dollar investment for a C-store was a substantial investment to John, this sum might look like a real bargain to the major C-store chains that had been paying up to a million dollars for prime suburban locations. Surely, John reasoned, a competing C-store within a mile or two of his location would adversely affect the validity of his financial projections. The design consultant had added a drive-in window at a cost of approximately $25,000 to differentiate the store and build customer loyalty. John felt a drive-in window would add 15% annually to projected inside sales.

At a recent petroleum distributors conference, John discussed his C-store plans with several fellow distributors. Most felt that the generic C-store designs offered by the major oil companies were too small to provide the maximum level of in-store sales, particularly in a rural market. They questioned the wisdom of the drive-in window, suggesting a car-wash operation instead.

While John felt the C-store alternative had potential, he also was aware that the move had its risks. Nationally, the number of C-stores had increased rapidly. At the end of 1981, there were 38,000 C-stores, and only 16,416 of these sold gasoline. Just four years later, the C-store population had reached 61,000, with 33,500 selling gasoline.[8]

There was general agreement in the industry that the danger of C-store saturation was greatest in suburban areas, but that substantial opportunities remained in both urban and rural markets. One rural operator, who competed successfully in towns with as few as 1,000 residents, said, "For the rest of the industry, the mark-up on gas is six to eight cents a gallon, while we get eight to ten cents. Often we are the only gas station in town."[9] While gas margins would be higher in rural areas, C-stores often increased margins on other products as well. Fast foods and video rentals were extremely profitable in the absence of strong competitors. Pizza, for example, carried a 70% profit margin. One C-store/pizza vendor said that the pizza concept probably wouldn't work in cities where people could go to a Pizza Hut, "but out in the rural areas, there's no place else to get a good pizza."[10]

Until recently, most of the competitors in the C-store industry were convenience store chains, such as Southland, and locations operated by independent oil distributors. There were increasing indications that the big oil refiners were entering the industry in force. Eight refiner/supplier oil companies, such as Texaco, Mobil, and Exxon, were ranked in the top 50 C-store operators. Many industry observers expected that the entry of the big-oil-owned C-stores would touch off a price war in the industry, particularly in the in-store segment. The rationale behind this expectation was that oil companies would lower in-store merchandise mark-ups in order to increase pump gallonage. However, the major oil companies had tended to concentrate on the urban areas, leaving the rural markets to the distributors.

[8]*Id.*, p. 41.

[9]"Rural vs. Urban: A Site Selection Dilemma," *Convenience Store News*, BAT Publications, New York, NY, July 13-August 2, 1987, p. 54.

[10]*Id.*, p. 54.

The Future of Walsh Oil

During one of the recent executive education programs John had attended, a few sessions had been devoted to evaluating investment opportunities. He knew that he should try to determine an appropriate hurdle rate to use. There were some discussions at these sessions about calculating a cost of capital, but that seemed too academic and complicated. Instead, he went to the library and looked up various interest rates and decided to add a couple of percentage points to them. He figured that a small company like his would have to pay somewhere between 2 and 5 percent over the going rate. The interest rates as of August 1986 are listed in Table 4.

As he reviewed his notes from the training sessions, John found that real estate investments were evaluated differently than other types of investments. Rather than using the total acquisition price as a measure of cash outflow, real estate investments were analyzed on the basis of equity cash outflow to determine the payback. One of John's friends in the real estate business told him that, rather than using the purchase price of the acquisition as a measure of its cost, he should use the down payment, or the immediate cash outflow, as the cost measure and calculate a levered rate of return on investment.

John scheduled an initial meeting with his banker to see what type of financing he might be able to obtain. While the banker expressed interest in the C-store, he didn't feel that the bank would be willing to lend funds for the acquisition of Valley Oil. "John, it's just too risky for us," he said. "Valley's assets just aren't liquid enough

Table 4 Selected Interest Rates–August 1986

Prime rate charged by banks	7.75%
U.S. Treasury bonds–ten years	7.17%
Corporate bonds–Aaa seasoned	8.72%
Home mortgages–FHLBB	10.26%

to qualify as high quality collateral. With those old tanks and trucks, we would never get our money out. Now the C-store is something I could sell to the loan committee. It's my guess that we could finance 80% of the land and building at 11.5% for 15 years.[11] In addition, we could finance 80% of the equipment including the site plan over 7 years at a 9.75% fixed rate."

The banker paused, as if unsure how to proceed. "You know, John, what I'm about to bring up is somewhat sensitive," he said, "so just tell me to stop if I'm out of line. I've watched you work like a dog over the past year to turn your business around, but at some point you have to start thinking about yourself. You can work like hell for thirty years and still only be a minority stockholder. If your mother and two brothers wanted to sell out at some point in the future, all your efforts, not to mention your career, are down the drain."

"Here's an alternative you might just think about," said the banker. "Walsh Petroleum owns the C-store site you are talking about developing. Why don't you buy the land personally and construct the C-store on it? We here at the bank would lend you the money, although we would probably have to have Walsh Petroleum guarantee the loan. You could then lease the C-store back to Walsh Petroleum, and start building up some personal equity for yourself through the real estate investment."

As John Walsh pondered his alternatives, one thing seemed certain to him—he would have to take action very soon. Many of his friends he met at the trade association meetings seemed to be complacent about the pressures on their industry at this time, but as John glanced at the financial statements again, he knew that a few more years like these past two would threaten not only his family's financial security, but his own as well. After all, he was really the only member of the family whose income was directly related to the future of Walsh Petroleum. He remembered the discussion of these issues at a recent dinner with his mother and brothers.

"John, I agree with the idea of expanding the business, and I think it would have pleased your dad," said Mrs. Walsh, "but you have to remember that Walsh Petroleum is really all I have. If we take on too much debt, and get into trouble, I don't know what I'll do in my old age."

"I see your point, Mom," said John, "but the fact is that I'm the only one in the family who is devoting the rest of my life to running the business. You already own C-store #1, and Richard and Daniel either don't want to be in the business or aren't sure yet. I don't want to sound selfish, but my interest in the business is only 16%. I don't want to wake up when I'm fifty and find that I've spent my whole life running this business for the rest of the family and have relatively little to show for it."

Richard puffed on his pipe and said, "John, I'm not sure the C-store alternative is a good idea for the family business. Sure, it's a good deal for you personally, but the rest of us have to guarantee your loan at the bank. I think Walsh Petroleum should give serious consideration to the Valley Oil deal."

"And why do you think that Valley is better than the C-store?" asked John.

"The main reason," Richard replied, "is that Walsh Petroleum is primarily a gasoline distributor. The original C-store was a great idea of Dad's, but the oil business is this family's cash cow. This is an opportunity to take out a competitor. We all agree there aren't a whole lot of new people going into this business, but if a big gasoline distributor in the region buys Valley, then Walsh Petroleum has got some major problems on its hands. The increased competition could certainly lower our gross margin one-to-two cents a gallon, and we all know that there are two large distributors that are interested in Valley."

"But, Richard, can't you see that we're in a declining industry?" said John. "If you looked

---

[11]It should be noted that the bank is refinancing land that Walsh currently owns.

at those financials I sent you, it should be obvious that our gallonage has been declining for several years."

"What do you think, Daniel?" asked Mrs. Walsh. "After all, it's as much your business as it is John's or Richard's."

"I think that John and Richard both have good points," said Daniel." "While John is the only one of us three in the business now, I may want to join the company when I finish school, and I really don't care to be a clerk in a convenience store. And while John certainly has a right to try to accumulate some wealth, I don't know that using the family business's credit rating to guarantee his personal investments is really fair to the rest of us. After all, John is at least getting a decent salary, and Richard and I don't even receive any dividends."

"Wait a second, Dan," said John, somewhat resentfully. "I'm not riding a gravy train here. My thirty thousand dollar salary at Walsh is no higher than what my market worth is, and especially the way things are going, my upside potential is much lower than I could get working for someone else. Even more importantly, the family couldn't find anyone else to do this job for any less than what I'm getting."

The family discussion had ended without resolving anything, but John was certain the business would be worth substantially less if he was unable to turn the operation around. Aside from the purely financial considerations, John knew that the major oil companies were now evaluating their distributors on sales levels and sales growth. A distributor in an attractive market who wasn't showing the appropriate level of sales or sales growth might soon find itself without a supply contract.

Further, while John was anxious to stop the decline in the company's financial performance, he also felt strongly that the business's plan he developed now should lay the foundation for the business growth for the next five-to-ten years. The questions in his mind were, "How do we do it, and is it worth the trouble?"

Appendix A

Walsh Petroleum Statement of Income for the Years Ended 1981–1985

	Year 1981	Year 1982	Year 1983	Year 1984	Year 1985	
Gallons:						
Premium	386,144	687,087	584,076	617,420	593,777	
Unleaded	1,193,536	1,236,757	830,002	898,065	841,184	
Regular	1,930,719	2,656,736	1,660,004	1,290,969	1,039,110	
Lube	24,847	17,793	18,184	16,660	15,725	
Heating Oil	491,583	409,267	327,845	373,609	335,054	
Diesel	375,478	373,704	338,249	348,420	327,098	
Kerosene	79,769	96,215	99,733	138,555	125,182	
Other Products	1,810	414	713	5,301	10,682	
Total	4,483,886	5,477,973	3,858,806	3,688,999	3,287,812	
Sales:						
Premium	322,225	533,091	551,540	517,510	533,998	
Unleaded	1,195,855	1,493,304	1,020,024	1,019,856	881,903	
Regular	2,385,763	2,967,718	1,633,912	1,187,458	854,324	
Lube	84,438	64,681	66,005	60,491	58,988	
Heating Oil	533,368	478,842	368,498	411,344	364,539	
Diesel	397,663	410,090	332,637	345,317	310,858	
Kerosene (Gasahol in '80)	92,252	119,845	117,952	162,359	147,066	
Other Products	53,960	10,757	48,261	140,259	177,768	
Net Sales	5,065,524	6,078,328	4,138,829	3,844,594	3,329,444	
Cost of Sales:						
Beginning Inventory	77,420	84,927	84,804	136,862	131,592	
Purchases Net of Discounts	4,725,693	5,691,682	3,885,577	3,528,264	2,942,582	
Ending Inventory	4,803,113	5,776,609	3,970,381	3,665,126	3,074,174	
	84,927	84,804	136,862	131,592	149,007	
Cost of Sales	4,718,186	5,691,805	3,833,519	3,533,534	2,925,167	
Gross Profit	347,338	386,523	305,310	311,060	404,277	
Selling, General and Admin. Expenses						
Licenses and Non-Income Taxes	22,447	22,462	18,472	22,604	8,917	
Vehicle Expense	23,362	41,510	36,837	43,950	32,583	
Officers' Salaries	68,248	63,370	53,970	52,952	50,780	
Other Salaries and Wages	78,763	92,138	121,160	135,692	140,623	
Other Expense	132,880	135,589	136,903	127,892	150,957	
Depreciation	46,524	68,676	72,842	73,404	69,441	
Interest on Borrowing Needs	6,457	7,410	11,232	11,999	9,299	
Operating Income (Loss)	(31,343)	(44,632)	(146,106)	(157,433)	(58,323)	
Earnings on Marketable Securities	4,456	2,853	3,009	2,943	3,739	
Other Income (Expense)	83,587	112,425	103,109	144,878	85,038	— Hauling income
Earnings before Taxes	56,700	70,646	(39,988)	(9,612)	30,454	
Provision for Federal Income Taxes	6,590	11,870	(15,294)	(2,229)	2,485	
Net Income	50,110	58,776	(24,694)	(7,383)	27,969	

Note: Inventory is recorded on a lifo basis.

Walsh Petroleum Balance Sheet for the Years Ended 1981–1985

	Year 1981	Year 1982	Year 1983	Year 1984	Year 1985	
Assets						
Current Assets						
Cash	36,305	7,704	38,510	55,652	14,003	
Marketable Securities	0	0	0	0	0	
Accounts Rec.	262,047	254,809	190,673	143,802	155,839	
Inventories	84,927	84,804	136,862	131,592	149,007	
Refundable Taxes	3,964	0	27,194	2,665	200	
Prepaid Exp.	5,756	7,121	13,698	8,625	9,609	
Notes Receivable	0	0	0	0	9,368	
Other Current Assets	0	0	0	0	116,607	← Key man life insurance pay off (cash)
Total Current Assets	392,999	354,438	406,937	342,336	454,633	
Property Plant and Equipment						
Land	25,201	28,134	25,489	34,893	30,544	← Market value $100,000
Buildings	0	0	0	0	0	
Equipment	154,029	140,493	163,011	130,797	144,965	← Market value $100,000
Vehicles	51,930	60,678	42,367	37,032	24,604	← Market value $18,000
Furniture and Fixtures	5,544	3,730	3,449	4,102	3,425	
Total	236,704	233,035	234,316	206,824	203,538	
Less Accumulated Depreciation	0	0	0	0	0	
Net Property Plant and Equipment	236,704	233,035	234,316	206,824	203,538	
Other Assets						
Long-Term Investments	677	1,202	1,202	1,202	1,202	
Deposits and Licenses	0	0	0	0	0	
Cash Surrender Value—Officers Life	30,970	35,117	690	3,116	0	
Loan Fees—Net	370	277	195	0	0	
Advances to Affiliated Companies	0	0	0	0	0	
Total Other Assets	32,017	36,596	2,087	4,318	1,202	
Total Assets	661,720	624,069	643,340	553,478	659,373	
Liabilities						
Current Liabilities						
Accounts Payable	264,812	155,012	157,254	80,624	98,505	
Notes Payable	0	0	50,000	30,000	0	
Current Portion of Long-Term Debt	18,163	18,315	18,204	17,900	50,675	
Construction Loan Payable	0	0	0	0	0	
Income Taxes Payable	334	4,506	0	235	2,485	
Advances from Officers	0	0	0	0	0	
Accrued Expenses	42,834	45,944	55,125	44,424	40,724	
Other Current Liabilities	0	0	522	846	0	
Total Current Liability	326,143	223,777	281,105	174,029	192,389	
Long-Term Debt	19,849	10,305	0	0	0	
Other Long-Term	14,572	30,054	26,992	51,592	0	← Equipment demand note payable net of current maturities at Prime +1
Total Liabilities	360,564	264,136	308,097	225,621	192,389	
Owners Equity	301,157	359,933	335,240	327,856	466,984	
Total Liabilities and Owners Equity	661,721	624,069	643,337	553,477	659,373	

Note: Walsh has limited underground tank liability due to placing tanks in resellers name, and having installed double-walled tanks @ the bulk plant over the past 5 years.

Walsh Petroleum Ratio Analysis for the Years Ended 1981–1985

Ratio Analysis	Year 1981	Year 1982	Year 1983	Year 1984	Year 1985
Dupont Analysis:					
Return on Sales	0.99%	0.97%	−0.60%	−0.19%	0.84%
· Asset Turnover	7.66	9.74	6.43	6.95	5.05
= Return on Assets	7.57%	9.42%	−3.84%	−1.33%	4.24%
· Financial Leverage	2.20	1.73	1.92	1.69	1.41
= Return on Equity	16.64%	16.33%	−7.37%	−2.25%	5.99%
Gallonage DuPont:					
Return on Sales	1.12	1.07	−0.64	−0.20	0.85
· Asset Turnover	6.78	8.78	6.00	6.67	4.99
= Return on Assets	7.57%	9.42%	−3.84%	−1.33%	4.24%
· Financial Leverage	2.20	1.73	1.92	1.69	1.41
= Return on Equity	16.64%	16.33%	−7.37%	−2.25%	5.99%
Activity:					
Fixed Asset Turnover	21.40	26.08	17.66	18.59	16.36
Sales Growth (Dollars)	13.48%	19.99%	−31.91%	−7.11%	−13.40%
Sales Growth (Gallons)		22.17%	−29.56%	−4.40%	−10.88%
Profitability:					
Gross Margin	6.86%	6.36%	7.38%	8.09%	12.14%
Salaries Ratio (Offic. Salar. + Sales)	1.35%	1.04%	1.30%	1.38%	1.53%
S,G, & A Ratio (S,G & A + Sales)	6.43%	5.84%	8.88%	9.96%	11.53%
Working Capital Usage:					
Days Payable	19.08	9.31	13.87	7.65	10.80
Collection Period (Days)	18.88	15.30	16.82	13.65	17.08
Days Inventory	6.12	5.09	12.07	12.49	16.34
Cash Cycle ((Collect. + Inv.) − Days Pay)	5.92	11.09	15.02	18.49	22.62
Leverage:					
Total Debt/Assets	54.49%	42.32%	47.89%	40.76%	29.18%
Long-Term Debt/Assets	0.03	0.02	0.00	0.00	0.00
Liquidity:					
Current Ratio	1.20	1.58	1.45	1.97	2.36
Acid Test Ratio	0.94	1.20	0.96	1.21	1.59

Walsh Petroleum Common Size Statement of Income for the Years Ended 1981–1985

	Year 1981	Year 1982	Year 1983	Year 1984	Year 1985
Sales:					
Premium	6.36%	8.77%	13.33%	13.46%	16.04%
Unleaded	23.61%	24.57%	24.65%	26.53%	26.49%
Regular	47.10%	48.82%	39.48%	30.89%	25.66%
Lube	1.67%	1.06%	1.59%	1.57%	1.77%
Heating Oil	10.53%	7.88%	8.90%	10.70%	10.95%
Diesel	7.85%	6.75%	8.04%	8.98%	9.34%
Kerosene	1.82%	1.97%	2.85%	4.22%	4.42%
Other Products	1.07%	0.18%	1.17%	3.65%	5.34%
Net Sales	100.00%	100.00%	100.00%	100.00%	100.00%
Cost of Sales:	0.00%	0.00%	0.00%	0.00%	0.00%
Beginning Inventory	1.53%	1.40%	2.05%	3.56%	3.95%
Purchases Net of Discounts	93.29%	93.64%	93.88%	91.77%	88.38%
	94.82%	95.04%	95.93%	95.33%	92.33%
Ending Inventory	1.68%	1.40%	3.31%	3.42%	4.48%
Cost of Sales	93.14%	93.64%	92.62%	91.91%	87.86%
Gross Profit	6.86%	6.36%	7.38%	8.09%	12.14%
Selling, General and Admin. Expenses					
Licenses and Non-Income Taxes	0.44%	0.37%	0.45%	0.59%	0.27%
Vehicle Expense	0.46%	0.68%	0.89%	1.14%	0.98%
Officers' Salaries	1.35%	1.04%	1.30%	1.38%	1.53%
Other Salaries and Wages	1.55%	1.52%	2.93%	3.53%	4.22%
Other Expense	2.62%	2.23%	3.31%	3.33%	4.53%
Depreciation	0.92%	1.13%	1.76%	1.91%	2.09%
Interest on Borrowing Needs	0.13%	0.12%	0.27%	0.31%	0.28%
Operating Income (Loss)	−0.62%	−0.73%	−3.53%	−4.09%	−1.75%
Earnings on Marketable Securities	0.09%	0.05%	0.07%	0.08%	0.11%
Other Income (Expense)	1.65%	1.85%	2.49%	3.77%	2.55%
Earnings before Taxes	1.12%	1.16%	−0.97%	−0.25%	0.91%
Provision for Federal Income Taxes	0.13%	0.20%	−0.37%	−0.06%	0.07%
Net Income	0.99%	0.97%	−0.60%	−0.19%	0.84%

Walsh Petroleum Common Size (% of Assets) Balance Sheet for the Years Ended 1981–1985

	Year 1981	Year 1982	Year 1983	Year 1984	Year 1985
Assets					
Current Assets					
Cash	5.49%	1.23%	5.99%	10.05%	2.12%
Marketable Securities	0.00%	0.00%	0.00%	0.00%	0.00%
Accounts Rec.	39.60%	40.83%	29.64%	25.98%	23.63%
Inventories	12.83%	13.59%	21.27%	23.78%	22.60%
Refundable Taxes	0.60%	0.00%	4.23%	0.48%	0.03%
Prepaid Exp.	0.87%	1.14%	2.13%	1.56%	1.46%
Notes Receivable	0.00%	0.00%	0.00%	0.00%	1.42%
Other Current Assets	0.00%	0.00%	0.00%	0.00%	17.68%
Total Current Assets	59.39%	56.79%	63.25%	61.85%	68.95%
Property Plant and Equipment					
Land	3.81%	4.51%	3.96%	6.30%	4.63%
Buildings	0.00%	0.00%	0.00%	0.00%	0.00%
Equipment	23.28%	22.51%	25.34%	23.63%	21.99%
Vehicles	7.85%	9.72%	6.59%	6.69%	3.73%
Furniture and Fixtures	0.84%	0.60%	0.54%	0.74%	0.52%
Total	35.77%	37.34%	36.42%	37.37%	30.87%
Less Accumulated Depreciation	0.00%	0.00%	0.00%	0.00%	0.00%
Net Property Plant and Equipment	35.77%	37.34%	36.42%	37.37%	30.87%
Other Assets					
Long-Term Investments	0.10%	0.19%	0.19%	0.22%	0.18%
Deposits and Licenses	0.00%	0.00%	0.00%	0.00%	0.00%
Cash Surrender Value—Officers Life	4.68%	5.63%	0.11%	0.56%	0.00%
Loan Fees—Net	0.06%	0.04%	0.03%	0.00%	0.00%
Advances to Affiliated Companies	0.00%	0.00%	0.00%	0.00%	0.00%
Total Other Assets	4.84%	5.86%	0.32%	0.78%	0.18%
Total Assets	100.00%	100.00%	100.00%	100.00%	100.00%
Liabilities					
Current Liabilities					
Accounts Payable	40.02%	24.84%	24.44%	14.57%	14.94%
Notes Receivable	0.00%	0.00%	7.77%	5.42%	0.00%
Current Portion of Long-Term Debt	2.74%	2.93%	2.83%	3.23%	7.69%
Construction Loan Payable	0.00%	0.00%	0.00%	0.00%	0.00%
Income Taxes Payable	0.05%	0.72%	0.00%	0.04%	0.38%
Advances from Officers	0.00%	0.00%	0.00%	0.00%	0.00%
Accrued Expenses	6.47%	7.36%	8.57%	8.03%	6.18%
Other Current Liabilities	0.00%	0.00%	0.08%	0.15%	0.00%
Other Financing Needed	0.00%	0.00%	0.00%	0.00%	0.00%
Total Current Liability	49.29%	35.86%	43.69%	31.44%	29.18%
Long-Term Debt	3.00%	1.65%	0.00%	0.00%	0.00%
Deferred Taxes	2.20%	4.82%	4.20%	9.32%	0.00%
Total Liabilities	54.49%	42.32%	47.89%	40.76%	29.18%
Owners' Equity	45.51%	57.68%	52.11%	59.24%	70.82%
Total Liabilities and Owners' Equity	100.00%	100.00%	100.00%	100.00%	100.00%

Walsh Petroleum Common Size (% of Sales) Balance Sheet for the Years Ended 1981–1985

	Year 1981	Year 1982	Year 1983	Year 1984	Year 1985
Assets					
Current Assets					
Cash	0.72%	0.13%	0.93%	1.45%	0.42%
Marketable Securities	0.00%	0.00%	0.00%	0.00%	0.00%
Accounts Rec.	5.17%	4.19%	4.61%	3.74%	4.68%
Inventories	1.68%	1.40%	3.31%	3.42%	4.48%
Refundable Taxes	0.08%	0.00%	0.66%	0.07%	0.01%
Prepaid Exp.	0.11%	0.12%	0.33%	0.22%	0.29%
Notes Receivable	0.00%	0.00%	0.00%	0.00%	0.28%
Other Current Assets	0.00%	0.00%	0.00%	0.00%	3.50%
Total Current Assets	7.76%	5.83%	9.83%	8.90%	13.65%
Property Plant and Equipment					
Land	0.50%	0.46%	0.62%	0.91%	0.92%
Buildings	0.00%	0.00%	0.00%	0.00%	0.00%
Equipment	3.04%	2.31%	3.94%	3.40%	4.35%
Vehicles	1.03%	1.00%	1.02%	0.96%	0.74%
Furniture and Fixtures	0.11%	0.06%	0.08%	0.11%	0.10%
Total	4.67%	3.83%	5.66%	5.38%	6.11%
Less Accumulated Depreciation	0.00%	0.00%	0.00%	0.00%	0.00%
Net Property Plant and Equipment	4.67%	3.83%	5.66%	5.38%	6.11%
Other Assets					
Long-Term Investments	0.01%	0.02%	0.03%	0.03%	0.04%
Deposits and Licenses	0.00%	0.00%	0.00%	0.00%	0.00%
Cash Surrender Value—Officers Life	0.61%	0.58%	0.02%	0.08%	0.00%
Loan Fees—Net	0.01%	0.00%	0.00%	0.00%	0.00%
Advances to Affiliated Companies	0.00%	0.00%	0.00%	0.00%	0.00%
Total Other Assets	0.63%	0.60%	0.05%	0.11%	0.04%
Total Assets	13.06%	10.27%	15.54%	14.40%	19.80%
Liabilities					
Current Liabilities					
Accounts Payable	5.23%	2.55%	3.80%	2.10%	2.96%
Notes Payable	0.00%	0.00%	1.21%	0.78%	0.00%
Current Portion of Long-Term Debt	0.36%	0.30%	0.44%	0.47%	1.52%
Construction Loan Payable	0.00%	0.00%	0.00%	0.00%	0.00%
Income Taxes Payable	0.01%	0.07%	0.00%	0.01%	0.07%
Advances from Officers	0.00%	0.00%	0.00%	0.00%	0.00%
Accrued Expenses	0.85%	0.76%	1.33%	1.16%	1.22%
Other Current Liabilities	0.00%	0.00%	0.01%	0.02%	0.00%
Other Financing Needed	0.00%	0.00%	0.00%	0.00%	0.00%
Total Current Liability	6.44%	3.68%	6.79%	4.53%	5.78%
Long-Term Debt	0.39%	0.17%	0.00%	0.00%	0.00%
Deferred Taxes	0.29%	0.49%	0.65%	1.34%	0.00%
Total Liabilities	7.12%	4.35%	7.44%	5.87%	5.78%
Owners' Equity	5.95%	5.92%	8.10%	8.53%	14.03%
Total Liabilities and Owners' Equity	13.06%	10.27%	15.54%	14.40%	19.80%

Walsh Petroleum Statement of Income as a % of Assets for the Years Ended 1981–1985

	Year 1981	Year 1982	Year 1983	Year 1984	Year 1985
Sales:					
Premium	0.4870	0.8542	0.8573	0.9350	0.8099
Unleaded	1.8072	2.3929	1.5855	1.8426	1.3375
Regular	3.6054	4.7554	2.5397	2.1454	1.2957
Lube	0.1276	0.1036	0.1026	0.1093	0.0895
Heating Oil	0.8060	0.7673	0.5728	0.7432	0.5529
Diesel	0.6010	0.6571	0.5170	0.6239	0.4714
Kerosene	0.1394	0.1920	0.1833	0.2933	0.2230
Other Products	0.0815	0.0172	0.0750	0.2534	0.2696
Net Sales	7.6551	9.7398	6.4333	6.9462	5.0494
Cost of Sales:					
Beginning Inventory	0.1170	0.1361	0.1318	0.2473	0.1996
Purchases Net of Discounts	7.1415	9.1203	6.0397	6.3747	4.4627
	7.2585	9.2564	6.1715	6.6220	4.6623
Ending Inventory	0.1283	0.1359	0.2127	0.2378	0.2260
Cost of Sales	7.1302	9.1205	5.9588	6.3842	4.4363
Gross Profit	0.5249	0.6194	0.4746	0.5620	0.6131
Selling, General and Admin. Expenses					
Licenses and Non-Income Taxes	0.0339	0.0360	0.0287	0.0408	0.0135
Vehicle Expense	0.0353	0.0665	0.0573	0.0794	0.0494
Officers' Salaries	0.1031	0.1015	0.0839	0.0957	0.0770
Other Salaries and Wages	0.1190	0.1476	0.1883	0.2452	0.2133
Other Expense	0.2008	0.2173	0.2128	0.2311	0.2289
Depreciation	0.0703	0.1100	0.1132	0.1326	0.1053
Interest on Borrowing Needs	0.0098	0.0119	0.0175	0.0217	0.0141
Operating Income (Loss)	−0.0474	−0.0715	−0.2271	−0.2844	−0.0885
Earnings on Marketable Securities	0.0067	0.0046	0.0047	0.0053	0.0057
Other Income	0.1263	0.1801	0.1603	0.2618	0.1290
Earnings before Taxes	0.0857	0.1132	−0.0622	−0.0174	0.0462
Provision for Federal Income Taxes	0.0100	0.0190	−0.0238	−0.0040	0.0038
Net Income	0.0757	0.0942	−0.0384	−0.0133	0.0424

Walsh Unit Sales Trends (1984–1987)

Unit	Type	Avg. Gal./Month (000's)		
		1984	1985	1986 (EST)
1	4,000 Sq ft rural grocery, owner change in 1984	6.0	10.5	10.8
2	Village 2-bay, financial problems, cash only, pool hall	11.7	16.8	14.3
3	5,000 sq ft rural grocery in low growth area	—	—	8.2
4	C-store in growing rural area	—	6.7	18.1
5	2-bay station with marina service, new C-store competition	20.3	17.9	20.7
6	Rehab 2-bay on front of bulk plant property, owned by mother and leased to corporation, good location on four-lane with crossover access, growth area	28.4	35.3	37.5
7	3-bay station in low-growth rural area, father and son	9.9	9.9	10.1
8	1,500 sq ft rural grocery with new owner, business recovery	14.0	9.1	11.6
9	3,000 sq ft rural C-store with interceptor location, sell on consignment with Walsh controlling price, considering canopy to be leased by Walsh from owner	17.6	18.8	20.0
10	3,000 sq ft rural C-store with interceptor location	21.9	22.4	22.7

Appendix B

Reseller Investment Analysis

Investment	
Underground Costs:	
Storage Tanks & UG Lines	0
Electr. Tank Mon. & Probes	0
Submersible Pumps	0
Installation	0
Fuel Inventory	0
Total	0
Aboveground Costs:	
Dispensors	25,000
Remote Console	3,500
Canopy	8,000
Signage	1,500
Installation	32,000
Total	70,000
Asset Lives:	
Canopy	10 yrs.
All Other	5 yrs.
Financing to Retailer:	
% Equity	100.00%
Principle	25,000
Interest Rate	9.00%
Term	60 Mo.

	1	2	3	4	5	6	7	8	9	10
Operating Costs:										
Property Taxes	500	500	500	500	500	500	500	500	500	500
Maintenance	0	2,000	2,000	2,000	2,000	2,000	2,000	2,000	2,000	2,000
Revenues/Gallon:										
Gasoline	$0.045	$0.045	$0.045	$0.045	$0.045	$0.045	$0.045	$0.045	$0.045	$0.045
Diesel	$0.045	$0.045	$0.045	$0.045	$0.045	$0.045	$0.045	$0.045	$0.045	$0.045
Kerosine	$0.300	$0.300	$0.300	$0.300	$0.300	$0.300	$0.300	$0.300	$0.300	$0.300
Sales Mix:										
Gasoline	90.00%	90.00%	90.00%	90.00%	90.00%	90.00%	90.00%	90.00%	90.00%	90.00%
Diesel	5.00%	5.00%	5.00%	5.00%	5.00%	5.00%	5.00%	5.00%	5.00%	5.00%
Kerosine	5.00%	5.00%	5.00%	5.00%	5.00%	5.00%	5.00%	5.00%	5.00%	5.00%
Total Gallons	450,000	450,000	450,000	450,000	450,000	450,000	450,000	450,000	450,000	450,000
Tax Rate	30.00%	30.00%	30.00%	30.00%	30.00%	30.00%	30.00%	30.00%	30.00%	30.00%
Discount Rate	12.00%									

NOTE: Arrangement here centers around placing the underground tanks in the reseller's name. Walsh loans $25,000 to the reseller for this purpose, as noted above. Terms of the loan and the necessity for such are subject to negotiation.

Financing Schedule

	Month: 1	2	3	4	5	6	7	8	9	10	11	12
Balance	25,000	24,669	24,335	23,998	23,659	23,318	22,974	22,627	22,278	21,926	21,571	21,214
Payment	519	519	519	519	519	519	519	519	519	519	519	519
Principle	331	334	336	339	342	344	347	349	352	355	357	360
Interest	188	185	183	180	177	175	172	170	167	164	162	159

Depreciation Schedule

	Year: 1	2	3	4	5	6	7	8	9	10
Canopy	1,600	1,280	1,024	819	655	524	419	336	268	215
Other	24,800	14,880	8,928	5,357	3,214					

Cash Flow Analysis

	Year: 0	1	2	3	4	5	6	7	8	9	10
Revenues:											
Gas		18,225	18,225	18,225	18,225	18,225	18,225	18,225	18,225	18,225	18,225
Diesel		1,013	1,013	1,013	1,013	1,013	1,013	1,013	1,013	1,013	1,013
Kerosine		6,750	6,750	6,750	6,750	6,750	6,750	6,750	6,750	6,750	6,750
Total		25,988	25,988	25,988	25,988	25,988	25,988	25,988	25,988	25,988	25,988
Operating Costs:											
Taxes		500	500	500	500	500	500	500	500	500	500
Maintenance		0	2,000	2,000	2,000	2,000	2,000	2,000	2,000	2,000	2,000
Depreciation		26,400	16,160	9,952	6,176	3,869	524	419	336	268	215
Total		26,900	18,660	12,452	8,676	6,369	3,024	2,919	2,836	2,768	2,715
Interest Earned		2,082	1,693	1,267	802	293					
Pretax Income		1,169	9,020	14,803	18,114	19,911	22,963	23,068	23,152	23,219	23,273
Less: Taxes		351	2,706	4,441	5,434	5,973	6,889	6,920	6,946	6,966	6,982
Net Income		818	6,314	10,362	12,680	13,938	16,074	16,148	16,206	16,253	16,291
Plus:											
Depreciation		26,400	16,160	9,952	6,176	3,869	524	419	336	268	215
Principle Repayments		4,146	4,535	4,960	5,425	5,934					
Less:											
Initial Principle	(25,000)										
Below Ground Cost	0										
Above Ground Cost	(70,000)										
Cashflow	(95,000)	31,364	27,009	25,274	24,281	23,742	16,599	16,567	16,542	16,522	16,506
Present Value of Annual Cashflows	(95,000)	28,004	21,531	17,990	15,431	13,472	8,409	7,494	6,681	5,958	5,314
Cumulative Present Value Position	(95,000)	(66,996)	(45,465)	(27,475)	(12,044)	1,427	9,837	17,331	24,012	29,970	35,284
IRR	22.02%										
MPV	35,284										

Appendix C

Valuation of Valley Oil Co.

Purpose and Methodology

Fair market value is defined as "the price at which the property would change hands between a willing buyer and a willing seller when the former is not under any compulsion to buy and the latter is not under any compulsion to sell, both parties having reasonable knowledge of relevant facts" (Rev.Rul. 59–60).

Revenue Ruling 59-60 also outlines many techniques appropriate in the determination of fair market value. Among these are the following:

- the economic outlook in general and the condition and outlook of the specific industry in particular;
- the nature of the business and the history of the enterprise from its inception;
- the book value of the stock and the financial condition of the business;
- the earning capacity of the company; and
- whether or not the enterprise has goodwill or other intangible value.[1]

Bearing these points in mind, the analysis will consider the following:

I. Condition of Industry

II. Condition of Company

  A. Position within market and life cycle

  B. Financial trends and earnings capacity

  C. Income-based value

  D. Goodwill potential

III. Adjusted asset value

IV. Conclusion

[1]Burke, Frank M. *Valuation and Valuation Planning for Closely Held Businesses* (Prentice-Hall: Englewood Cliffs, N.J., 1981), pp. 27–7.

I. Condition of Industry

At present, the picture in the petroleum marketing industry is glum; according to a National Petroleum News study, industry observers see a fallout rate of over 17% for the 1985–87 period. Through 1990, the rate is even higher; observers expect little more than two-thirds of the jobbers will still be in business by 1990.[2] Over the past decade, jobber returns have been falling drastically. According to data collected by the Petroleum Marketing Education Foundation, after tax return on equity has fallen from almost 20% in 1979–80 to only 6.9% in 1984–85 (see Table 5). This falling return comes from two main sources. First, as demand remains weak and the age of assets increases, total asset turnover, an asset productivity measure, falls significantly. Second, because of the pressure put on prices by deregulation and by the elimination of benefits from refiners,[3] profit margins have dropped drastically. Although margins improved in 1985, and so far in 1986, these are the result of a market phenomenon, sticky retail prices during periods of unprecedented price decline. In other words, the improvement is a temporary result of the reluctance of marketers to pass price declines on to the consumer. Upon return to normal equilibrium, one finds that the marketer is squeezed from both sides, volume and margin.

Given these factors, it seems logical to place the petroleum marketing industry late in the life cycle. The industry has shown several classic examples of mature (stage three) behavior:

[2]Reid, Marvin. "To Stay In or Sell Out," *National Petroleum News,* August 1985, p. 45.

[3]*Id.* p. 46.

Table 5 Industry DuPont Analysis

Year	Profit Margin ·	Total Asset Turns ·	Financial Leverage Multiplier =	ROE
1976–1977	1.03	4.85	2.33	11.6
1977–1978	0.87	5.40	2.55	12.0
1978–1979	0.92	5.20	2.49	11.9
1979–1980	1.24	6.25	2.57	19.9
1980–1981	0.97	7.21	2.66	18.6
1981–1982	0.58	7.44	2.47	10.7
1982–1983	0.55	7.80	2.51	10.8
1983–1984	0.59	6.87	2.39	9.7
1984–1985	0.47	6.12	2.37	6.9

- Sales, as a percent of assets, have trended down dramatically, showing both old, deteriorating assets and market overcrowding.
- Fallout has reached an all-time high, with a definite buyer's market developing.[4]
- Prices have declined to unprecedented lows.
- The market is composed of fewer, but larger, firms.

This placement in the mature stage of the cycle suggests that, barring revolutionary changes in the industry, nothing but decline can be foreseen.

II. Condition of Company

A. Life Cycle and Market

Valley Oil finds itself in the middle of this declining industry. Its position in the life cycle does not seem to be much better; in fact, Valley appears to have advanced into the early decline stage. Several factors contribute to this assessment:

- Sales/total assets have declined from over 5.8 in 1983 to only 5.31 in 1985. On a gallonage basis, where price fluctuations have less impact, there has still been a close to fifty percent decline since 1979.
- Assets are at an unprecedented old age. An attached chart illustrates the old age of Valley's storage tanks.
- Sales, on both an absolute dollar and a gallonage basis, are declining steadily. Although the actual percentage varies from year to year, the overall trend is distinct.

What does this imply for Valley? First, the firm must cope with trying to maintain market share and profitability in an environment where the potential for both is shrinking. Second, the firm must attempt this in spite of its own inherent limitations; it is burdened with older, shrinking-volume resellers, as well as aged vehicles and tanks.

B. Financial Trends and Earning Capacity

The firm's financial statements do not yield a picture any more bright. First, the downward trend in sales is disturbing. Second, excluding the first half of 1985, the same trend has applied to margin. The combination of these two factors places a vise grip on profitability. In fact, if it were not for the margin windfall in the first half of this year, Valley would have taken a major blow.

C. Income-based Value

In any discounted, income-based valuation, two factors must be determined: the discount rate and the earnings base. Theoretically, the discount rate can be assumed to be the rate of return which an investor could earn on a portfolio of similar risk assets. As a starting point, one can consider that for the week of August 1, the Standard and Poor's 10-bond utility average yielded 9.03%. This range of 9% is consistent with performance over recent months and actually low for the past decade. Working from this starting point, one can logically assume that there would have to be some risk premium; therefore, a minimum capitalization rate would be 10%. As an earnings base, one can use a weighted average of

[4] *Id.* p. 47.

the last five years. This both eliminates any unusual blip in the last year and takes into account the overall trend (See Table 6).

When this average earnings figure is capitalized at 10%, an income-based valuation of $367,280 is determined. Using a more reasonable discount rate of 12% yields a value of $306,067.

D. Goodwill Potential

A study by David Nelson, a consultant to the Petroleum Marketing Education Foundation, shows that, of 37 sales studied in 1983, 19 received "goodwill". This ratio was down from 13 out of 18 in 1981.[5] In addition to the quantitative evidence suggesting that large blue sky premiums are a thing of the past, there are several logical arguments to support this point:

- More and more firms are entering the market on the selling side, suggesting a definite oversupply.[6]
- The firm is completely unleveraged, yet it can barely support its current operating costs. Margins are insufficient to cover fixed costs, leaving hauling fees and finance charges as the only means of profit.

Given that the industry trend is toward little or no blue sky, that Valley would be one of many firms entering the market, and that its margins do not even indicate profitable gallonage, it seems unreasonable to attach any goodwill to the earnings base or to an asset valuation.

III. Adjusted Asset Value

Another step that must be taken in any valuation is an assessment of the asset value of the company. If this market-related asset value is higher that the income-based value, then the business has negative operating value and is worth more liquidated.

[5]*Id.* p. 47.

[6]*Id.* p. 47.

Table 6

Year	Wt. Factor	Income	W · I
1981	1	(1,536)	(1,536)
1982	2	38,032	76,064
1983	3	40,920	122,760
1984	4	42,219	168,876
1985	5	36,951	184,755
	15		550,919

Weighted Average Earnings = $36,728

When this step is taken with Valley, the analysis is fairly simple (see attached chart for complete analysis). All of the current assets can be liquidated at their book value except for accounts receivables. These must be carried across to market less a 10% bad debt adjustment. This brings the value of total current assets to $620,557.

Adjustments for the fixed assets are a bit more complex. First, the land/buildings account must be adjusted to $100,000 market value. Equipment, with the exception of tanks, is valued at about $20,000 (79 pumps @ $250). The vehicles have an appraised market value of $156,500. The market value for furniture and fixtures is $7,050, giving a total market value to long-term assets of $283,550. The next step to be followed is to deduct any liabilities. These are deducted at book value of $203,569.

The final step in the adjusted asset valuation is to consider any hidden assets or liabilities. These can take several forms:

- Undervalued real estate which could actually bring much more than its book value;
- Exclusive distribution contracts or other market-related, hidden assets; and
- Contingent liabilities such as pending lawsuits or potential lawsuits from sources such as leaking underground tanks.

The first of these is ruled out by the fact that Valley owns only one piece of real estate, which was recently appraised and is included in the valuation at its appraised value of $100,000. Neither does the second factor enter into the value—Valley has no unique market-related advantages.

The question of contingent liabilities is important; the possibility that one or more of the approximately 90 tanks could develop or already possess a leak is far from remote. According to Steffen Plenn, author of *Underground Tankage: The Liability of Leaks,* as many as thirty percent of the steel tanks currently in the ground may be leaking. What's worse, that number is expected to rise. The volatile nature of this problem is most clearly seen in its propensity to wind up in court. Plenn explains that these leaks, when discovered, are disasters of a magnitude that will not avoid court.[7] The most serious implication, however, is that the liability has historically extended to all owners of the tanks, both past and present, vis-a-vis the concept of joint and several liability. Thus, in the process of any rationally executed liquidation, the seller would have to remove each of the older tanks. In the case of Valley, this cost would amount to approximately $90,000.[8] Deducting this contingent tank liability (cost of removal) from the previously computed values yields a liquidation value of $610,538.

IV. Conclusion

This now presents us with two different values for consideration:

(1) The income-based value of $367,280 and

(2) The adjusted asset liquidation basis of $610,538.

Realizing that

- the liquidation value exceeds the income-based value;
- there is a trend toward decreasing blue sky premiums;
- goodwill is usually paid for growing or unusually profitable gallons, of which Valley has none;
- there is a significant contingent liability attached to the tanks, all of which cannot be eliminated by tank removal (due to potential for previous leaks); and, finally,
- Valley is a declining firm in a mature industry,

we recommend use of the adjusted asset liquidation value of $610,538 as our best estimate of market value.

Adjusted Asset Valuation Valley Oil Co.

	Book	**Market**
Assets:		
Cash	26,558	26,558
A/R	421,308	421,308
Inventory	153,135	137,821
Refundable Taxes	3,888	3,888
Prepaids	25,883	25,883
Notes Receivable	5,099	5,099
Land/Building	79,942	100,000
Equipment	247,258	20,000
Vehicles*	310,000	156,500
Furn. & Fixt.	37,896	7,050
Less: Acc. Depr.	(475,238)	—
Total Asset Value	835,729	904,107
Liabilities		
A/P	(196,670)	(196,670)
Income Taxes Payable	(6,899)	(6,899)
Total Liabilities Value	(203,569)	(203,569)
Less: Contingent Tank Liability	—	(90,000)
Total Value	632,160	610,538

*One two year old tractor/trailer (9,000-gallon capacity), two older "bobtail" trucks (2,000-gallon capacity) and one older service van.

[7]Plenn, Steffen W., *Underground Tankage: The Liabilities of Leaks,* (Petroleum Marketing Education Foundation: Alexandria, Virginia, 1986), pp. 9–12.

[8]Ascertained in conversation with a local contractor. Confirmed by recent removals of similar tanks.

Valley Oil Co. Income Statement Information for the Years Ended 1984 and 1985

	1984	1985
Other Expenses:		
Advertising	6,254	6,921
Office expense	7,066	10,566
Utilities	5,033	4,806
Insurance	15,360	37,855
Telephone	3,327	4,310
Rent*	27,163	27,940
Professional fees	7,483	10,503
Repairs	34,445	32,026
Directors fees	4,800	4,800
Travel	5,982	10,178
Dues and subscriptions	4,786	4,442
Contributions	1,520	4,403
Sales promotion	5,705	5,736
Miscellaneous	—	673
Pension plan expense	1,072	—
Employee benefits	28,834	33,448
Bad debts	28,091	25,552
Total	186,921	224,159

*Rent on bulk plant and corporate office.

Valley Oil Co. Statement of Income for the Years Ended 1981–1985

	Year 1981	Year 1982	Year 1983	Year 1984	Year 1985	
Gallons:						
Premium	NA	NA	NA	NA	382,869	
Unleaded	NA	NA	NA	NA	1,152,730	
Regular	3,956,353	3,316,151	4,004,842	3,101,595	1,418,560	
Lube	NA	NA	NA	NA	NA	
Heating Oil	978,113	1,004,000	1,057,131	1,137,072	1,267,011	
Diesel	NA	NA	NA	NA	NA	
Kerosene	286,870	286,430	262,802	310,066	315,739	
Other Products	NA	NA	NA	NA	NA	
Total	5,221,336	4,606,581	5,324,775	4,548,733	4,536,909	
Sales:						
Premium	NA	NA	NA	NA	358,038	
Unleaded	NA	NA	NA	NA	1,038,871	
Regular	NA	NA	NA	3,061,113	1,222,758	
Lube	NA	NA	NA	95,781	100,922	
Heating Oil	NA	NA	NA	1,172,390	871,031	
Diesel	NA	NA	NA	NA	355,966	
Kerosene	NA	NA	NA	364,573	359,583	
Other Products	NA	NA	NA	NA	92,493	
Net Sales	4,734,881	4,332,049	4,657,833	4,234,277	4,279,681	
Cost of Sales:						
Beginning Inventory	211,832	210,000	192,449	153,639	160,344	
Purchases Net of Discounts	4,292,934	3,873,798	4,138,784	3,752,969	3,714,003	
	4,504,766	4,083,798	4,331,233	3,906,608	3,874,347	
Ending Inventory	210,000	192,449	153,639	160,344	153,135	
Cost of Sales	4,294,766	3,891,349	4,177,594	3,746,264	3,721,212	
Gross Profit	440,115	440,700	480,239	488,013	558,469	
Selling, General and Admin. Expenses						
Licenses and Non-Income Taxes	23,584	24,450	25,943	25,810	22,252	
Vehicle Expense	100,471	61,397	85,365	74,066	81,748	
Officers' Salaries	45,500	49,414	48,700	51,000	53,100	
Other Salaries and Wages	155,843	142,087	154,104	148,434	162,161	
Other Expense	145,081	168,015	168,076	186,921	224,159	
Depreciation	44,428	38,032	36,920	54,639	61,015	
Interest on Borrowing Needs	10,025	3,496	5,272	7,144	11,203	
Operating Income (Loss)	(84,817)	(46,191)	(44,141)	(60,001)	(57,169)	
Earnings on Marketable Securities	8,746	14,493	5,134	6,426	8,103	
Other Income (Expense)	72,552	74,672	90,703	96,501	95,066	←Hauling income
Earnings before Taxes	(3,519)	42,974	51,696	42,926	46,000	
Provision for Federal Income Taxes	(1,983)	4,942	10,776	707	9,049	
Net Income	(1,536)	38,032	40,920	42,219	36,951	

(From 1981 to 1984, gallonage data is available only as aggregate gasoline sales—these are entered as regular. Likewise, during the entire five year period, heating oil and diesel are combined under heating oil. During the same time period, dollar values are often unavailable.)

Valley Oil Co. Balance Sheet for the Years Ended 1981–1985

	Year 1981	Year 1982	Year 1983	Year 1984	Year 1985
Assets					
Current Assets					
Cash	64,468	31,922	24,076	10,000	26,558
Marketable Securities	0	0	0	0	0
Accounts Rec.	656,187	579,313	471,803	470,120	421,308
Inventories	210,000	192,449	153,639	160,344	153,135
Refundable Taxes	33,054	0	0	9,920	3,888
Prepaid Exp.	2,636	1,535	1,526	1,766	25,883
Notes Receivable	1,804	40,277	14,481	59,342	5,099
Other Current Assets	0	0	0	0	0
Total Current Assets	968,149	845,496	665,525	711,492	635,871
Property Plant and Equipment					
Land	79,942	79,942	79,942	79,942	79,942
Buildings	0	0	0	0	0
Equipment	207,463	216,139	208,116	207,873	227,444
Vehicles	247,339	274,634	253,153	279,634	255,355
Furniture and Fixtures	5,032	21,588	22,393	24,388	30,464
Total	539,776	592,303	563,604	591,837	593,205
Less Accumulated Depreciation	392,800	430,332	427,310	392,465	422,781
Net Property Plant and Equip.	146,976	161,971	136,294	199,372	170,424
Other Assets					
Long-Term Investments	0	0	0	0	0
Deposits and Licenses	0	0	0	0	0
Cash Surrender Value—Officers' Life Insurance	0	0	0	0	0
Loan Fees—Net	0	0	0	0	0
Advances to Affiliated Companies	0	0	0	0	0
Total Other Assets	0	0	0	0	0
Total Assets	1,115,125	1,007,467	801,819	910,864	806,295
Liabilities					
Current Liabilities					
Accounts Payable	670,524	474,892	272,434	295,092	196,670
Notes Payable	0	45,000	0	50,000	0
Current Portion of Long-Term Debt	0	0	0	0	0
Construction Loan Payable	0	0	0	0	0
Income Taxes Payable	0	4,942	5,832	0	6,899
Advances from Officers	0	0	0	0	0
Accrued Expenses	0	0	0	0	0
Other Current Liabilities	0	0	0	0	0
Other Financing Needed	0	0	0	0	0
Total Current Liabilities	670,524	524,834	278,266	345,092	203,569
Long-Term Debt	0	0	0	0	0
Other Long-Term	0	0	0	0	0
Total Liabilities	670,524	524,834	278,266	345,092	203,569
Owners Equity	444,601	482,633	523,553	565,772	602,726
Total Liabilities and Owners' Equity	1,115,125	1,007,467	801,819	910,864	806,295

Valley Oil Co. Selected Ratios

Ratio Analysis	Year 1981	Year 1982	Year 1983	Year 1984	Year 1985
DuPont Analysis:					
Return on Sales	−0.03%	0.88%	0.88%	1.00%	0.86%
· Asset Turnover	4.25	4.30	5.81	4.65	5.31
= Return on Assets	−0.14%	3.78%	5.10%	4.64%	4.58%
· Financial Leverage	2.51	2.09	1.53	1.61	1.34
= Return on Equity	−0.35%	7.88%	7.82%	7.46%	6.13%
Activity:					
Fixed Asset Turnover	32.22	26.75	34.17	21.24	25.11
Sales Growth (Dollars)	−16.28%	−8.51%	7.52%	−9.09%	1.07%
Sales Growth (Gallons)	−30.65%	−11.77%	15.59%	−14.57%	−0.26%
Profitability:					
Gross Margin	9.30%	10.17%	10.31%	11.53%	13.05%
Salaries Ratio (Officers Salaries + Sales)	0.96%	1.14%	1.05%	1.20%	1.24%
S,G,& A Ratio (S,G, & A + Sales)	9.94%	10.28%	10.35%	11.48%	12.70%
Working Capital Usage:					
Days Payable	51.69	40.01	21.35	25.44	16.77
Collection Period (Days)	50.58	48.81	36.97	40.52	35.93
Days Inventory	16.19	16.21	12.04	13.82	13.06
Cash Cycle ((Collect.Pd. + Inven.) − Days Pay.)	15.08	25.01	27.66	28.91	32.22
Leverage:					
Total Debt/Assets	60.13%	52.09%	34.70%	37.89%	25.25%
Long-Term Debt/Assets	0.00	0.00	0.00	0.00	0.00
Times Interest EBIT	−7.46	−12.21	−7.37	−7.40	−4.10
Liquidity:					
Current Ratio	1.44	1.61	2.39	2.06	3.12
Acid Test Ratio	1.13	1.24	1.84	1.60	2.37

Valley Oil Co. Common Size Statement of Income for the Years Ended 1981–1985

	Year 1981	Year 1982	Year 1983	Year 1984	Year 1985
Sales:					
Premium	NA	NA	NA	NA	8.37%
Unleaded	NA	NA	NA	NA	24.27%
Regular	NA	NA	NA	72.29%	28.57%
Lube	NA	NA	NA	2.26%	2.36%
Heating Oil	NA	NA	NA	27.69%	20.35%
Diesel	NA	NA	NA	NA	8.32%
Kerosene	NA	NA	NA	8.61%	8.40%
Other Products	NA	NA	NA	NA	2.16%
Net Sales	100.00%	100.00%	100.00%	100.00%	100.00%
Cost of Sales:	0.00%	0.00%	0.00%	0.00%	0.00%
Beginning Inventory	4.47%	4.85%	4.13%	3.63%	3.75%
Purchases Net of Discounts	90.67%	89.42%	88.86%	88.63%	86.78%
Ending Inventory	95.14%	94.27%	92.99%	92.26%	90.53%
	4.44%	4.44%	3.30%	3.79%	3.58%
Cost of Sales	90.70%	89.83%	89.69%	88.47%	86.95%
Gross Profit	9.30%	10.17%	10.31%	11.53%	13.05%
Selling, General and Admin. Expenses	0.00%	0.00%	0.00%	0.00%	0.00%
Licenses and Non-Income Taxes	0.50%	0.56%	0.56%	0.61%	0.52%
Vehicle Expense	2.12%	1.42%	1.83%	1.75%	1.91%
Officers' Salaries	0.96%	1.14%	1.05%	1.20%	1.24%
Other Salaries and Wages	3.29%	3.28%	3.31%	3.51%	3.79%
Other Expense	3.06%	3.88%	3.61%	4.41%	5.24%
Depreciation	0.94%	0.88%	0.79%	1.29%	1.43%
Interest on Borrowing Needs	0.21%	0.08%	0.11%	0.17%	0.26%
Operating Income (Loss)	−1.79%	−1.07%	−0.95%	−1.42%	−1.34%
Earnings on Marketable Securities	0.18%	0.33%	0.11%	0.15%	0.19%
Other Income (Expense)	1.53%	1.72%	1.95%	2.28%	2.22%
Earnings before Taxes	−0.07%	0.99%	1.11%	1.01%	1.07%
Provision for Federal Income Taxes	−0.04%	0.11%	0.23%	0.02%	0.21%
Net Income	−0.03%	0.88%	0.88%	1.00%	0.86%

Valley Oil Co. Common Size (% of Assets) Balance Sheet for the Years Ended 1981–1985

	Year 1981	Year 1982	Year 1983	Year 1984	Year 1985
Assets					
Current Assets					
Cash	5.78%	3.17%	3.00%	1.10%	3.29%
Marketable Securities	0.00%	0.00%	0.00%	0.00%	0.00%
Accounts Rec.	58.84%	57.50%	58.84%	51.61%	52.25%
Inventories	18.83%	19.10%	19.16%	17.60%	18.99%
Refundable Taxes	2.96%	0.00%	0.00%	1.09%	0.48%
Prepaid Exp.	0.24%	0.15%	0.19%	0.19%	3.21%
Notes Receivable	0.16%	4.00%	1.81%	6.51%	0.63%
Other Current Assets	0.00%	0.00%	0.00%	0.00%	0.00%
Total Current Assets	86.82%	83.92%	83.00%	78.11%	78.86%
Property Plant and Equipment					
Land	7.17%	7.93%	9.97%	8.78%	9.91%
Buildings	0.00%	0.00%	0.00%	0.00%	0.00%
Equipment	18.60%	21.45%	25.96%	22.82%	28.21%
Vehicles	22.18%	27.26%	31.57%	30.70%	31.67%
Furniture and Fixtures	0.45%	2.14%	2.79%	2.68%	3.78%
Total	48.40%	58.79%	70.29%	64.98%	73.57%
Less Accumulated Depreciation	35.22%	42.71%	53.29%	43.09%	52.44%
Net Property Plant and Equip.	13.18%	16.08%	17.00%	21.89%	21.14%
Other Assets					
Long-Term Investments	0.00%	0.00%	0.00%	0.00%	0.00%
Deposits and Licenses	0.00%	0.00%	0.00%	0.00%	0.00%
Cash Surrender Value—Officers' Life Insurance	0.00%	0.00%	0.00%	0.00%	0.00%
Loan Fees—Net	0.00%	0.00%	0.00%	0.00%	0.00%
Advances to Affiliated Companies	0.00%	0.00%	0.00%	0.00%	0.00%
Total Other Assets	0.00%	0.00%	0.00%	0.00%	0.00%
Total Assets	100.00%	100.00%	100.00%	100.00%	100.00%
Liabilities					
Current Liabilities					
Accounts Payable	60.13%	47.14%	33.98%	32.40%	24.39%
Notes Receivable	0.00%	4.47%	0.00%	5.49%	0.00%
Current Portion of Long-Term Debt	0.00%	0.00%	0.00%	0.00%	0.00%
Construction Loan Payable	0.00%	0.00%	0.00%	0.00%	0.00%
Income Taxes Payable	0.00%	0.49%	0.73%	0.00%	0.86%
Advances from Officers	0.00%	0.00%	0.00%	0.00%	0.00%
Accrued Expenses	0.00%	0.00%	0.00%	0.00%	0.00%
Other Current Liabilities	0.00%	0.00%	0.00%	0.00%	0.00%
Other Financing Needed	0.00%	0.00%	0.00%	0.00%	0.00%
Total Current Liabilities	60.13%	52.09%	34.70%	37.89%	25.25%
Long-Term Debt	0.00%	0.00%	0.00%	0.00%	0.00%
Deferred Taxes	0.00%	0.00%	0.00%	0.00%	0.00%
Total Liabilities	60.13%	52.09%	34.70%	37.89%	25.25%
Owners' Equity	39.87%	47.91%	65.30%	62.11%	74.75%
Total Liabilities and Owner's Equity	100.00%	100.00%	100.00%	100.00%	100.00%

Valley Oil Co. Common Size (% of Sales) Balance Sheet for the Years Ended 1981–1985

	Year 1981	Year 1982	Year 1983	Year 1984	Year 1985
Assets					
Current Assets					
Cash	1.36%	0.74%	0.52%	0.24%	0.62%
Marketable Securities	0.00%	0.00%	0.00%	0.00%	0.00%
Accounts Rec.	13.86%	13.37%	10.13%	11.10%	9.84%
Inventories	4.44%	4.44%	3.30%	3.79%	3.58%
Refundable Taxes	0.70%	0.00%	0.00%	0.23%	0.09%
Prepaid Exp.	0.06%	0.04%	0.03%	0.04%	0.60%
Notes Receivable	0.04%	0.93%	0.31%	1.40%	0.12%
Other Current Assets	0.00%	0.00%	0.00%	0.00%	0.00%
Total Current Assets	20.45%	19.52%	14.29%	16.80%	14.86%
Property Plant and Equipment					
Land	1.69%	1.85%	1.72%	1.89%	1.87%
Buildings	0.00%	0.00%	0.00%	0.00%	0.00%
Equipment	4.38%	4.99%	4.47%	4.91%	5.31%
Vehicles	5.22%	6.34%	5.43%	6.60%	5.97%
Furniture and Fixtures	0.11%	0.50%	0.48%	0.58%	0.71%
Total	11.40%	13.67%	12.10%	13.98%	13.86%
Less Accumulated Depreciation	8.30%	9.93%	9.17%	9.27%	9.88%
Net Property Plant and Equip.	3.10%	3.74%	2.93%	4.71%	3.98%
Other Assets					
Long-Term Investment	0.00%	0.00%	0.00%	0.00%	0.00%
Deposits and Licenses	0.00%	0.00%	0.00%	0.00%	0.00%
Cash Surrender Value—Officers' Life Insurance	0.00%	0.00%	0.00%	0.00%	0.00%
Loan Fees—Net	0.00%	0.00%	0.00%	0.00%	0.00%
Advances to Affiliated Companies	0.00%	0.00%	0.00%	0.00%	0.00%
Total Other Assets	0.00%	0.00%	0.00%	0.00%	0.00%
Total Assets	23.55%	23.26%	17.21%	21.51%	18.84%
Liabilities					
Current Liabilities					
Accounts Payable	14.16%	10.96%	5.85%	6.97%	4.60%
Notes Payable	0.00%	1.04%	0.00%	1.18%	0.00%
Current Portion of Long-Term Debt	0.00%	0.00%	0.00%	0.00%	0.00%
Construction Loan Payable	0.00%	0.00%	0.00%	0.00%	0.00%
Income Taxes Payable	0.00%	0.11%	0.13%	0.00%	0.16%
Advances from Officers	0.00%	0.00%	0.00%	0.00%	0.00%
Accrued Expenses	0.00%	0.00%	0.00%	0.00%	0.00%
Other Current Liabilities	0.00%	0.00%	0.00%	0.00%	0.00%
Other Financing Needed	0.00%	0.00%	0.00%	0.00%	0.00%
Total Current Liabilities	14.16%	12.12%	5.97%	8.15%	4.76%
Long-Term Debt	0.00%	0.00%	0.00%	0.00%	0.00%
Deferred Taxes	0.00%	0.00%	0.00%	0.00%	0.00%
Total Liabilities	14.16%	12.12%	5.97%	8.15%	4.76%
Owners' Equity	9.39%	11.14%	11.24%	13.36%	14.08%
Total Liabilities and Owners' Equity	23.55%	23.26%	17.21%	21.51%	18.84%

Valley Oil Co. Statement of Income as a % of Assets for the Years Ended 1981–1985

	Year 1981	Year 1982	Year 1983	Year 1984	Year 1985
Sales:					
Premium	NA	NA	NA	NA	0.4441
Unleaded	NA	NA	NA	NA	1.2885
Regular	NA	NA	NA	3.3607	1.5165
Lube	NA	NA	NA	0.1052	0.1252
Heating Oil	NA	NA	NA	1.2871	1.0803
Diesel	NA	NA	NA	NA	0.4415
Kerosene	NA	NA	NA	0.4002	0.4460
Other Products	NA	NA	NA	NA	0.1147
Net Sales	4.2461	4.2999	5.8091	4.6486	5.3078
Cost of Sales:					
Beginning Inventory	0.1900	0.2084	0.2400	0.1687	0.1989
Purchases Net of Discounts	3.8497	3.8451	5.1617	4.1202	4.6063
Ending Inventory	4.0397	4.0535	5.4018	4.2889	4.8051
	0.1883	0.1910	0.1916	0.1760	0.1899
Cost of Sales	3.8514	3.8625	5.2101	4.1129	4.6152
Gross Profit	0.3947	0.4374	0.5989	0.5358	0.6926
Selling, General and Admin. Expenses	0.0000	0.0000	0.0000	0.0000	0.0000
Licenses and Non-Income Taxes	0.0211	0.0243	0.0324	0.0283	0.0276
Vehicle Expense	0.0901	0.0609	0.1065	0.0813	0.1014
Officers' Salaries	0.0408	0.0490	0.0607	0.0560	0.0659
Other Salaries and Wages	0.1398	0.1410	0.1922	0.1630	0.2011
Other Expense	0.1301	0.1668	0.2096	0.2052	0.2780
Depreciation	0.0398	0.0378	0.0460	0.0600	0.0757
Interest on Borrowing Needs	0.0090	0.0035	0.0066	0.0078	0.0139
Operating Income (Loss)	−0.0761	−0.0458	−0.0551	−0.0659	−0.0709
Earnings on Marketable Securities	0.0078	0.0144	0.0064	0.0071	0.0100
Other Income	0.0651	0.0741	0.1131	0.1059	0.1179
Earnings before Taxes	−0.0032	0.0427	0.0645	0.0471	0.0571
Provision for Federal Income Taxes	−0.0018	0.0049	0.0134	0.0008	0.0112
Net Income	−0.0014	0.0378	0.0510	0.0464	0.0458

Valley Oil Co. Gallonage Based
Total Asset Turnover

Year	Tot. Asset Tur.
1979	9.95
1980	7.51
1981	4.52
1982	4.34
1983	5.89
1984	5.31
1985	5.28

Valley Oil Co. Annual Station Gallons (1985)

Stations:*	
1.	346,279
2.	160,316
3.	128,620
4.	111,702
5.	105,036
6.	116,286
7.	37,894
8.	19,746
9.	121,440
10.**	244,802
11.	304,772
12.	189,422
13.	196,152
14.	148,226
15.	47,118
16.	130,472
17.	100,106
18.	220,440
TOTAL	2,728,829

*Reseller locations with contracts ranging from 2–5 years.
**Wholly owned by Valley Oil with appraised value of $100,000 (good potential, 4-lane interceptor, C-store location).

Valley Oil Co. Capacity and Age of Tanks

Sites*	Capacity	Age	Type	Product
1.	4000	12	steel	gas
	4000	12	″	″
	3000	25	″	″
	4000	25	″	″
	3000	25	″	″
2.	2000	7	″	″
	2000	7	″	″
	1000	2	″	″
3.	1000	8	″	″
	1000	8	″	″
4.	1000	10	″	″
	1000	10	″	″
	1000	10	″	″
5.	2000	20	″	″
	1000	20	″	″
	1000	20	″	″
6.	1000	12	″	″
	1000	10	″	Diesel
	1000	10	″	″
7.	1000	15	″	Gas
	1000	15	″	″
	2000	10	″	″
	1000	1	″	″
	1000	1 month	″	″
8.	1000	25	″	″
	2000	3	″	″
	2000	3	″	″
	2000	3	″	″
9.	2000	10	″	″
	4000	11	″	″
	3000	11	″	″
	3000	11	″	″
	1000	11	″	″
10.	1000	12	″	″
	1000	5	″	″
11.	1000	15	″	Diesel
	1000	15	″	Gas
12.	10000	15	″	″
	4000	15	″	″
	4000	15	″	″
	1000	15	″	Kerosene
13.	1000	12	″	Gas
	1000	12	″	″
	1000	12	″	″
14.	2000	14	″	″
	1000	14	″	″
15.	1000	12	″	″
	1000	12	″	Diesel
	2000	12	″	F.O.
16.	10000	10	″	Gas
	2000	10	″	″
17.	2000	10	″	″
18.	1000	5	″	″
	1000	5	″	″
19.	1000	9	″	″
	1000	9	″	″
	1000	9	″	″
20.	10000	35	″	Diesel
21.	20000	15	″	F.O.
	20000	15	″	″
	20000	15	″	″
	20000	15	″	″
	20000	15	″	Gas
	20000	15	″	″
	20000	15	″	″
	20000	15	″	″
	10000	15	″	″
	6266	35	″	Kerosene
	6266	35	″	″
	5631	35	″	″
	6266	35	″	″
	6266	35	″	″
	6266	35	″	″
	6769	35	″	″
22.	4000	10	″	Gas
	4000	10	″	″
	3000	10	″	″
	3000	25	″	″
	3000	25	″	″
23.	1000	20	″	″
	1000	20	″	″
24.	2000	7	″	″
	1000	7	″	″
	1000	7	″	″
	1000	7	″	Kerosene
25.	2000	11	″	Gas
	2000	11	″	″

*Sites include reseller locations, large individual users, and bulk plant (No. 21).

Appendix D

Motor Fuel Marketers—Indust. Avg. Firms W/Assets $500M–$1MM
Statement of Income for the Year ($000's)

	Year 1980	Year 1981	Year 1982	Year 1983	Year 1984	Year 1985
Gallons:						
Premium	3,936.0	2,920.0	3,189.0	3,532.0	542.4	380.8
Unleaded	0.0	0.0	0.0	0.0	1,286.3	1,193.4
Regular	0.0	0.0	0.0	0.0	1,385.2	2,241.8
Lube	0.0	0.0	0.0	0.0	0.0	0.0
Heating Oil	746.0	245.0	295.0	342.0	287.0	366.3
Diesel	777.0	853.0	920.0	982.0	1,558.4	1,241.1
Kerosene	0.0	0.0	0.0	0.0	59.2	71.3
Other Products	47.0	40.0	65.0	30.0	104.2	62.0
Total	5,506.0	4,058.0	4,469.0	4,886.0	5,222.7	5,556.7
Sales:						
Premium	0	0	0	0	0	0
Unleaded	0	0	0	0	0	0
Regular	0	0	0	0	0	0
Lube	0	0	0	0	0	0
Heating Oil	0	0	0	0	0	0
Diesel	0	0	0	0	0	0
Kerosene (Gasahol in '80)	0	0	0	0	0	0
Other Products	0	0	0	0	0	0
Net Sales	5,775.9	4,930.7	5,427.6	5,241.6	5,646.4	5,086.5
Cost of Sales:						
Beginning Inventory	0.0	158.5	135.4	140.4	143.5	97.7
Purchases Net of Discounts	5,402.0	4,510.2	5,000.1	4,816.5	5,117.3	4,595.7
	5,402.0	4,668.7	5,135.5	4,956.9	5,260.8	4,693.4
Ending Inventory	158.5	135.4	140.4	143.5	97.7	76.4
Cost of Sales	5,243.2	4,533.3	4,995.1	4,813.4	5,163.1	4,617.0
Gross Profit	532.7	397.4	432.5	428.2	483.3	469.5
Selling, General and Admin. Expenses						
Licenses and Non-Income Taxes	25.9	32.4	28.0	19.8	20.4	22.5
Vehicle Expense	69.9	65.2	61.7	58.4	58.5	63.6
Officers' Salaries	49.1	40.6	42.9	40.8	55.4	50.4
Other Salaries and Wages	152.0	104.5	115.2	118.6	96.5	126.2
Other Expense	140.4	81.8	109.7	115.2	144.2	125.9
Depreciation	39.3	37.4	37.9	44.3	53.1	50.6
Interest on Borrowing Needs	19.2	22.4	22.0	16.0	18.5	26.2
Operating Income (Loss)	36.9	13.1	15.1	15.1	36.7	4.1
Earnings on Marketable Securities	0.0	0.0	0.0	0.0	0.0	0.0
Other Income (Expense)	38.0	30.4	26.0	35.3	20.3	32.1
Earnings before Taxes	74.9	43.5	41.1	50.4	57.0	36.2
Provision for Federal Income Taxes	19.4	11.0	8.8	11.8	12.9	11.6
Net Income	55.5	32.5	32.3	38.6	44.1	24.6

Motor Fuel Marketers—Indust. Avg. Firms W/Assets $500M–$1MM
Balance Sheet as of 12/31

	($000's) Year 1980	Year 1981	Year 1982	Year 1983	Year 1984	Year 1985
Assets						
Current Assets						
Cash	79.7	54.2	67.5	87.2	64.7	34.2
Marketable Securities	19.4	14.5	12.8	17.6	6.4	14.8
Accounts Rec.	247.5	224.0	235.2	263.0	264.0	194.4
Inventories	158.5	135.4	140.4	143.5	97.7	76.4
Refundable Taxes	0.0	0.0	0.0	0.0	0.0	0.0
Prepaid Exp.	0.0	0.0	0.0	0.0	0.0	0.0
Notes Receivable	0.0	0.0	0.0	0.0	18.0	23.7
Other Current Assets	20.0	30.1	21.1	16.6	26.6	47.9
Total Current Assets	525.1	458.2	477.0	527.9	477.4	391.4
Property Plant and Equipment						
Land	0	0	0	0	0	0
Buildings	0	0	0	0	0	0
Equipment	0	0	0	0	0	0
Vehicles	0	0	0	0	0	0
Furniture and Fixtures	0	0	0	0	0	0
Total	0	0	0	0	0	0
Less Accumulated Depreciation	0	0	0	0	0	0
Net Property Plant and Equipment	287.1	225.4	215.5	248.8	244.9	218.7
Other Assets						
Long-Term Investments	0.0	0.0	0.0	0.0	10.7	28.9
Deposits and Licenses	0	0	0	0	0	0
Cash Surrender Value—Officers' Life Insurance	0	0	0	0	0	0
Loan Fees—Net	0	0	0	0	0	0
Advances to Affiliated Companies	0	0	0	0	0	0
Total Other Assets	25.4	20.6	25.5	29.1	23.2	43.9
Total Assets	837.6	704.2	718.0	805.8	745.5	654.0
Liabilities						
Current Liabilities						
Accounts Payable	237.7	200.1	190.3	203.2	166.9	121.0
Notes Payable	27.5	29.6	46.1	35.7	68.7	109.8
Current Portion of Long-Term Debt	30.9	15.9	15.4	12.7	0.0	0.0
Construction Loan Payable	0.0	0.0	0.0	0.0	0.0	0.0
Income Taxes Payable	0.0	0.0	0.0	0.0	6.9	1.5
Advances from Officers	0.0	0.0	0.0	0.0	0.0	0.0
Accrued Expenses	0.0	0.0	0.0	0.0	0.0	0.0
Other Current Liabilities	67.3	38.4	39.5	43.3	63.4	66.5
Other Financing Needed	0.0	0.0	0.0	0.0	0.0	0.0
Total Current Liabilities	363.0	284.0	291.3	294.9	305.9	298.8
Long-Term Debt	157.4	130.7	105.1	122.3	98.7	85.9
Other Long-Term	2.7	2.9	8.7	4.3	0.0	0.0
Total Liabilities	523.1	417.6	405.1	421.5	404.6	384.7
Owners' Equity	314.5	286.6	313.0	384.3	340.9	269.4
Total Liabilities and Owners' Equity	837.6	704.2	718.1	805.8	745.5	654.1

Motor Fuel Marketers—Indust. Avg. Firms W/Assets $500M–$1MM Ratio Analysis

Ratio Analysis	Year 1980	Year 1981	Year 1982	Year 1983	Year 1984	Year 1985
DuPont Analysis:						
Return on Sales	0.96%	0.66%	0.60%	0.74%	0.78%	0.48%
· Asset Turnover	6.90	7.00	7.56	6.50	7.57	7.78
= Return on Assets	6.63%	4.62%	4.50%	4.79%	5.92%	3.76%
· Financial Leverage	2.66	2.46	2.29	2.10	2.19	2.43
= Return on Equity	17.65%	11.34%	10.32%	10.04%	12.94%	9.13%
Gallonage DuPont:						
Return on Sales	1.01	0.80	0.72	0.79	0.84	0.44
· Asset Turnover	6.57	5.76	6.22	6.06	7.01	8.50
= Return on Assets	6.63%	4.62%	4.50%	4.79%	5.92%	3.76%
· Financial Leverage	2.66	2.46	2.29	2.10	2.19	2.43
= Return on Equity	17.65%	11.34%	10.32%	10.04%	12.94%	9.13%
Activity:						
Fixed Asset Turnover	20.12	21.88	25.19	21.07	23.06	23.26
Sales Growth (Dollars)	−14.63%	10.08%	−3.43%	7.72%	−9.92%	
Sales Growth (Gallons)	−26.30%	10.13%	9.33%	6.89%	6.40%	
Profitability:						
Gross Margin	9.22%	8.06%	7.97%	8.17%	8.56%	9.23%
Salaries Ratio	0.85%	0.82%	0.79%	0.78%	0.98%	0.99%
S,G, & A Ratio	7.57%	6.58%	6.59%	6.73%	6.64%	7.64%
Working Capital Usage:						
Days Payable	15.00	14.81	12.80	14.15	10.79	8.68
Collection Period (Days)	15.64	16.58	15.82	18.31	17.07	13.95
Days Inventory	10.02	10.02	9.44	9.99	6.32	5.48
Cash Cycle	10.66	11.79	12.46	14.16	12.59	10.75
Leverage:						
Total Debt/Assets	62.45%	59.30%	56.41%	52.31%	54.27%	58.81%
Long Term Debt/Assets	0.19	0.19	0.15	0.15	0.13	0.13
Times Interest EBIT	2.92	1.58	1.69	1.94	2.98	1.16
Liquidity:						
Current Ratio	1.45	1.61	1.64	1.79	1.56	1.31
Acid Test Ratio	1.01	1.14	1.16	1.30	1.24	1.05

Case 31

Memorial Funeral Home

History

The Memorial Funeral Home began as a small family business, founded in 1947 by Donald Kellen. Located in an upper-middle-class suburb of a large city, the business prospered and gained an excellent reputation. After 33 years as director of the business, Donald Kellen retired and was succeeded in 1980 by his son Kenneth.

Memorial is the only funeral home in the suburb. However, funeral homes in neighboring suburbs offer strong competition. Under the guidance of Kenneth Kellen, Memorial began diversifying its services. Currently, Memorial handles 65 funerals a year under its own name. In addition, Memorial supplies removal, embalming, directing, livery service, and rental of funeral vehicles to other funeral homes. While maintaining its primary function as a family-run, neighborhood business concentrating on personal service, Memorial has successfully diversified its operations.

Recognizing the rapidly changing ideas and expectations of society, Kenneth Kellen is adjusting. Economics is beginning to play a major role in funeral decisions. Clients are more sophisticated and informed, necessitating clear-cut definitions of services, costs, and available options.

This case was prepared by Dr. Donald F. Kuratko of the College of Business, Ball State University and is intended to be used as a basis for class discussion. Presented and accepted by the refereed Midwest Case Writers Association Workshop, 1985.

Fundamental Components

A number of fundamental components are associated with the funeral home business:

- *Property.* Land and buildings must be large enough to meet the demands of visitations and funeral services. Owning such property—in a convenient and accessible location where the public can be properly served—constitutes one of the major, ongoing costs of a funeral home operation.
- *Facilities.* A funeral home must be tastefully furnished to provide a homelike atmosphere and must be easily adaptable for visitations and for funeral services. Facilities also must be able to accommodate more than one funeral at a time.
- *Automotive equipment.* Funeral directors must provide the latest in automobiles for transportation between the funeral home and the cemetery. Owning and maintaining this equipment, much of which is specially designed, is costly.
- *Selection room.* Special facilities must be available to house the wide variety of merchandise (caskets, vaults, and clothing) made available by the funeral home for burial purposes. This service requires considerable space and investment in inventory.
- *Professional staff.* Salaries make up the largest part of a funeral home's expense. Personnel must be carefully chosen so that families receive both expert and efficient service. To attract qualified personnel, funeral homes must compete with salaries paid by business, industry, and other professions.

- *Educational requirements.* Funeral directors and embalmers today are required by state law to meet certain college academic standards and pass state board examinations before they may be licensed to practice funeral directing and embalming. This highly specialized training prepares the funeral director to offer expert professional service to bereaved families, and the director must be paid a salary commensurate with his or her knowledge.

- *Documents.* Funeral directors are required by law to complete a number of documents relating to each funeral.

- *Counseling skill.* An intangible factor in funeral cost is that of counseling. An effective funeral director helps families to better accept death, grief, and bereavement. The ability to take a traumatic situation and mold it into a meaningful and impressive service of remembrance for the surviving family is an important part of the funeral director's job and contributes to the survivors' mental and emotional health.

- *Twenty-four-hour service.* The typical funeral home is open continuously for service. This means the telephone must be attended, and personnel must be available to assist those who have experienced a death regardless of the day or the hour.

- *Community service.* The funeral director must be a civic-spirited member of the community. He or she must be actively involved in business, civic, and religious organizations.

Public Perception

According to the National Funeral Directors Association (NFDA), there are approximately 22,000 funeral homes in the United States. A major concern of the industry is the new attitudes of the public regarding the disposition of the dead. The executive secretary of the NFDA has noted that

1. Many people believe that a funeral does meet many needs, including individual, family, religious, and community needs.

2. Some people believe that emotions can be intellectualized and the quickest possible disposition of the deceased is the best course of action.

3. There are those who as yet have formed no definite view. They have had little, if any, experience with death. They are honestly asking what needs arise when a death occurs, and whether the funeral helps to satisfy these needs.

Recent investigations of funeral homes by the Federal Trade Commission, as well as newspaper feature stories in exposé form, have not helped the image of the industry. The public, aroused by the sensational and emotional nature of the issue, is easily persuaded into the belief that some funeral homes are dishonest. A basic lack of understanding about death and the funeral home business lies at the root of the public mistrust.

Death is not the every day experience it once was. Millions of Americans have never been present at the death of someone close to them. Millions of Americans have never been to a funeral, or even seen a funeral procession, except one that was televised. Millions of Americans have never seen a dead body except on television, in a movie, on a battlefield, or on a highway. Even where people have been directly involved in the arrangement of a funeral service, there is often confusion or doubt about the role of the funeral director and the cost of his services.

Often the place of the casket in the funeral service is unclear or undefined. Historically, the funeral director has been a provider of goods and some services. A casket was purchased, and all other services were provided "free." Today, according to the NFDA, on the average the merchandise amounts to only about 20 percent of the total cost of a funeral service.

Financial Structure

People are probably less knowledgeable about funeral costs than about any other aspect of funeral services. The following discussion provides a general description of pricing and payment in Memorial's section of the country.

Methods

The surviving relatives accepting responsibility for payment may be charged under one of three methods or a combination thereof. The method used is chosen by the funeral director. The methods are (1) complete itemized pricing, which itemizes every detail; (2) functional pricing, which gives prices for major categories of costs; and (3) unit pricing, which gives only the complete price.

Complete Itemized Pricing For a typical funeral, the complete itemized pricing is detailed on a form similar to the one in Figure 1. The following is a typical pricing structure:

Professional services	
Funeral director and staff	$400
Funeral home facilities	
Chapel and facilities (one night)	395
Embalming and preparation	215
Preparation room	95
Merchandise	
Casket	504
Cards and register book	135
Transportation	
Removal	95
Hearse	150
Total	$1,989

The range of services available, and therefore the costs, may vary (see Table 1). In the foregoing example of itemized costs, the total of $1,989 minus the casket cost of $504 equals $1,485, which corresponds to Major Services—B in Table 2.

The price of the casket will vary as well, ranging from approximately $65 to $7,685. Available at an extra charge are other services such as the following:

Item	Price Range
Burial vault	$105 to $1,200
Clergyman	$50 to $100
Beautician	$50
Chapel organist	$50
Cemetary charges:	
Grave opening	$295 to $535
Mausoleum	Varies greatly
Death notices (one day, one paper)	$75 (average)
Extra funeral cars:	
Flower car	$110
Limousine	$130
Copies of death certificate	$3 (first), $2 (each additional)
Burial garments	$75
Church soloist	$50

If cremation is desired, costs such as the casket will be eliminated. Additional costs encountered would include the following:

Item	Price Range
Cremation	$ 95–$120
Cremation container (box)	$ 65–$75
Cremation urn	$116–$237

In the complete itemized pricing method, all costs are known. Included in some of the itemized costs are markups by the funeral director.

A comparison can be made between the costs of the Memorial Funeral Home and the average industry costs provided in Table 2, which also lists the industry's range of costs for each item.

Functional Pricing A more compressed presentation of costs is provided under the functional pricing method. In contrast to the eight details

Figure 1 Memorial Funeral Home Pricing Form

Services for: Date:

1. Professional Services:

Professional Care of the Deceased, Staff Service Fee . . . $ ______

Professional Services of Funeral Director and Staff . . . . $ ______

. . . . $ ______

. . . . $ ______

Total Professional Services . . . . $ ______

2. Funeral Home Facilities:

Use of Chapel and Funeral Home for Visitation and Services . . . . $ ______

Preparation/Operating Room . $ ______

. . . . $ ______

. . . . $ ______

Total Facilities . . . . $ ______

3. Merchandise:

Casket . . . . $ ______

Burial Vault . . . . $ ______

Clothing . . . . $ ______

Printing, Clerical, and Sundry Business Expenses . . . . $ ______

. . . . $ ______

Total Merchandise . . . . $ ______

4. Transportation:

Removal . . . . $ ______

Funeral Coach . . . . $ ______

Limousines/Family Cars . . . . . . $ ______

Flower Cars . . . . $ ______

. . . . $ ______

Total Transportation . . . . $ ______

Cash Advances:

As a convenience to the family, we will advance payment for the following:

Clergy Honorarium . . . . $ ______
Beautician . . . . $ ______
Chapel Organist . . . . $ ______
Church Organist . . . . $ ______
Death Notices . . . . $ ______
Certified Copies . . . . $ ______
. . . . $ ______
. . . . $ ______
. . . . $ ______
. . . . $ ______
. . . . $ ______

Total . . . . $ ______

Summary:

Our Charges . . . . $ ______
Sales Tax . . . . $ ______
Cash Advances . . . . $ ______
Less Credits . . . . $ ______

TOTAL BALANCE DUE . . . . $ ______

The foregoing contract has been read by (to) me, and I (we) hereby acknowledge receipt of a copy of same and agree to pay the above funeral account and any such additional services or merchandise as ordered by me (us), on or before ______________________

______________________________ 19____.

The liability hereby assumed is in addition to the liability imposed by law upon the estate and others and shall not constitute a release thereof.

____
Signature Relationship

____
Signature Relationship

____
Signature Relationship

____
Funeral Director

NET DUE ON/BEFORE __________ (30 Days)

This account will become past due and delinquent if payment is not made on or before the above date. An Unanticipated Late Payment Fee of 3/4 of 1% per month (9% annual percentage rate) on the outstanding balance will be charged after that date on all accounts in default.

Table 1 A Range of Funeral Services (Charges Listed by Categories)

Major Services Provided	A	B	C	D	E
Use of chapel and funeral home for visitation and funeral services	2 nights and services next day	1 night and services next day	1 night and no services next day	Visitation on day of service (max. 4 hrs.)	No visitation or service
Removal of deceased from local home or hospital	Included	Included	Included	Included	Included
Professional care of the deceased, preparation room, and staff service fee	Included	Included	Included	Included	Not included
Transportation of deceased to local cemetery or crematory	Hearse included	Hearse included	Service vehicle	Hearse included	Service vehicle
Professional services of funeral director and staff, sundry business expenses	Included	Included	Included	Included	Included
Prayer cards/chapel folders, register book, donation envelopes, and acknowledgment cards	Included	Included	Included	Included	Not included
Total Professional Fee	$1685	$1485	$1260	$925	$425
Deceased transported to our funeral home from out of town	$1175	$ 975	$ 750	$650	Direct to interment $195

Casket, vault, and other items of choice are left to the further discretion of the family and are added to the above service expenditures.

Table 2 The Cost of Funerals

	Average	Range
Funeral Home Costs		
Overhead	$ 440	$ 169 to $ 943
Planning, management, supervision, embalming	237	137 to 422
Staff and salaries	523	276 to 798
Funeral vehicles	196	88 to 655
Casket	584	65 to 7,685
Outer receptacle (grave box or burial vault)	411	101 to 1,475
Burial Costs		
Cemetery burial	582	345 to 1,065
Grave memorial	310	135 to 5,105
Mausoleum entombment	2,520	1,150 to 5,200
Cremation	147	110 to 150
Urn	159	30 to 1,100
Columbarium (place set aside in cemetery for ashes)	336	215 to 580
Funeral director profit	275	Not available
Optional Items		
Death notices	69	31 to 113
Flowers	160	20 to 446
Clothes (for deceased)	72	27 to 104
Donation to church, rabbi, etc.	53	20 to 150
Music, organist, vocalist	38	15 to 220

Source: Funeral Directors Association of Greater Chicago

provided under the complete itemized pricing method, the functional pricing method lists only three major categories:

Professional services	$1,105
Merchandise	639
Transportation	245
Total	$1,989

Functional pricing, like detailed pricing, adds all outside charges to the functional total. This method provides more detail than unit pricing but less than that provided by complete itemized pricing.

Unit Pricing Unit pricing is nothing more than providing the casket and all associated services under one lump sum. The unit total varies with the casket selected and with any increased services that are provided.

Years ago most funeral directors used a cost method known as the four-by-four method. It was based on the casket price with the funeral director's fixed costs and profit built into the calculation. For example, for a casket with a cost of $400, the calculation would be:

Casket	$ 400
	× 4
	$1,600
	+ 400
Total	$2,000

Subsequently, funeral directors used a five-by-six method: $400 × 5 = $2,000 + $600 = $2,600. However, this method is no longer widely employed either. Rather it is common practice to simply determine all costs involved and add a percentage for profit. In the main, unit pricing is declining in popularity because more states are requiring itemized pricing.

Form of Payment

So that there is no misunderstanding about who is to pay the bill, someone has to accept responsibility by signing a legal contract. This, along with the signing of an additional release form, allows removal of the body to take place. Full details are then documented on a comprehensive work sheet.

When services have been selected, certain cash payments must be made. A cash advance is also made to the funeral director to defray out-of-pocket costs. Finally, a direct payment must be made to the cemetery to pay all graveside costs in advance.

The Future

The emphasis today is on low-cost funerals and relatively inexpensive selections. Two kinds of funeral homes predominate in the industry: independent, family-run funeral homes with one location, and large corporate-run funeral homes with many locations, many employees, and many pieces of equipment.

Automobiles are a major capital outlay for the funeral director. In 1987 a new hearse cost from $34,000 to $52,000 (for deluxe models); a new limousine cost approximately $35,000. The initial outlay and future maintenance are major considerations for the independent funeral director.

As an alternative to owning vehicles independently, three or four noncompeting funeral homes sometimes pool their hearses, limousines, and flower cars, thus reducing the large capital expenditure. When necessary, professional services can be rendered by one director if another is busy. These developments are proving important to the survival of independent funeral homes.

The Challenge

Kenneth Kellen realizes that the economy and the environment pose problems for the survival and continued growth of his firm. He knows his expenses will remain high while a questioning public weighs its traditional obligations against current economic conditions. Kenneth's major concern is the direction that his firm must take in the years ahead. In his view, education of the public and adaptability of his business in meeting the changing demands of society are essential to the future of the Memorial Funeral Home.

In an interview with the case writers, Mr. Kellen provided the following information about his services and plans.

- *Grief counseling.* Mr. Kellen has a master's degree and is completing his studies for a Ph.D. in guidance counseling and grief. He believes that his background will help the Memorial Funeral Home in the future because it enables him to provide professional counseling during the grief period.
- *Diversified operations.* Mr. Kellen has begun two service operations for other funeral homes. One provides professional services: embalming, directing, and removal. The other is a livery service that involves the use of his funeral vehicles by other funeral homes.
- *Cooperatives.* Mr. Kellen is not presently engaged in cooperatives with other funeral homes. He does, however, see cooperatives as a viable alternative to vast capital expenditures. Members of cooperatives share facilities, vehicles, and services. The formation of cooperatives allows the small, independent funeral home to compete favorably with the large funeral home that has many locations.

Questions

1. Based on the information and background provided in this case, state whether you believe that the funeral business should be regulated by governmental (federal or state) agencies or whether you believe it should continue its traditional form of self-regulation through its own industry associations (e.g., National Funeral Directors Association). Why?
2. Which pricing method is best for the Memorial Funeral Home? Why?
3. What impact has the change of attitudes and beliefs in today's society had on the small funeral home?
4. What are the alternatives for succeeding in this ever-changing environment? Be complete in your answer.

Case 32

Environcare

The Lawn Care Industry

In 1984, about 14,000 companies will provide about $2.75 billion worth of lawn care services for over four million residences. In 1982 lawn service revenues totaled $1.85 billion. Total revenues have increased by almost 50 percent in just two years.

Thirty-nine chemical lawn care companies had revenues in excess of $1 million in 1983, a 75 percent increase over 1978, when 22 firms had sales above $1 million.

It is estimated that only 16 percent of the potential market—50 million single-family residences—has been penetrated. The market has grown at a rate of 30 percent to 35 percent per year from 1975 to 1983, and it is forecast to continue at the same rate of growth for the next eight years.

Most lawn care firms are privately owned and have annual revenues of less than $200,000. However, the giant of the industry, Chem-Lawn, whose headquarters is in Columbus, Ohio, had $200 million in 1983 sales. It has 167 branches throughout the United States and served 1.3 million homes in 1983. The larger lawn care companies, such as Chem-Lawn, Lawn Doctor, Ever-Green Lawns, Orkin Lawn Care, and Nitro-Green Corporation, either own their own branch operations or have franchise units throughout the United States.

Chemicals are used not only to nurture lawns but also to control pests, both inside and outside of residences and commercial establishments. Firms that provide residential pest control include the Orkin Exterminating Company, the largest in the world, Airex, and numerous other local and regional companies. The control of pests in lawns, trees, and bushes (termed ornamentals) is generally handled by firms other than those that provide interior structural applications. The lawn care firms usually do not compete against exterior pest control firms since the latter spray trees and ornamentals, utilizing spray equipment of a different technology and applying chemicals that are primarily preventive and not restorative—as is the case in lawn care.

Landscaping firms, another segment of outside home care, are concerned with the design of a lawn or garden, the selection of appropriate grasses, trees, flowers, and ornamentals. They utilize their creative talents to create a unique lawn and garden that is tailored to each customer's preferences. They are not at all like the lawn care and pest control specialists that apply similar chemicals to most of the residences that they treat.

Also concerned with residential exterior care are those individuals or companies that trim, cut down, and remove trees. They utilize high-technology tree, limb, and leaf shredders and "cherry-picker" extension vehicles to trim or remove tall tree branches. Trees are removed either to improve the aesthetic appearance of the residence or to eliminate a blighted or diseased condition.

This case was prepared by James W. Clinton, Professor of Management, University of Northern Colorado, Greeley, Colorado, as a basis for class discussion rather than to illustrate either effective or ineffective organizational practices. Presented at Midwest Case Writers Association Workshop, 1984. Reprinted with permission.

Growth and Development of the Industry

The growth and prosperity of professional lawn care companies and those firms that provide related services are due to a combination of the factors discussed below.

Health Concerns

The public is concerned about the possible harmful health effects associated with handling chemicals. The chemical, DDT, was an acceptable pesticide for use around the home and garden for some time after World War II. Rachel Carson's 1962 book, *Silent Spring,* alerted the public that our environment was being adversely affected by the indiscriminate use of chemicals. The public began to carefully scrutinize the use of chemicals in pest control and lawn care after it was learned that "Agent Orange," which was used as a defoliant—destroyer of all growing plants—in the Vietnam War, may also have caused major injury to those who conducted the aerial applications of this herbicide or who were present in the areas contaminated by it.

Today there is increased public concern and awareness of the dangers and toxicity of certain chemicals. Consumers are more wary of manufacturer's claims and also are apprehensive about the potential hazards associated with the use of chemicals on their own lawns, trees, plants, and shrubs. Because of this awareness, and their sensitivity to the dangers of being exposed to or ingesting hazardous chemicals, homeowners are more willing to allow chemical lawn care firms to look after their property.

Leisure Time

Homeowners, until 5 or 10 years ago, tended to spend a great deal of time around their homes on weekends, performing miscellaneous chores and making minor home repairs. Today's homeowners place a greater value on their leisure time and prefer to engage in activities other than yard work. The lawn professionals are willing to perform these services, which many homeowners now disdain and consider to be drudgery, for a fee.

Economics

Families today have larger incomes because there are now more families with two wage earners and they can afford the lawn care fees. In addition, because it buys its chemicals in bulk in wholesale quantities, it is frequently possible for the lawn care service to treat a lawn more cheaply than if the homeowner were to purchase the materials at a retail store and administer the treatment.

Home Appearance

The professional lawn care companies use specialized mechanical sprayers that ensure uniform application of the necessary chemicals. This uniformity produces a consistently even and visually pleasing effect on the lawns. Too many homeowners have experienced the erratic operation of a home lawn spreader that produced a striped effect on their lawns—visual proof to all the neighbors that the homeowner was either too cheap to buy a workable lawn spreader or was incompetent and unable to operate the spreader correctly. In other words, a homeowner can hide the wood-working mistakes around the house, but a botched lawn job is there for all the neighbors to see.

An Investment

The price of the average home in many parts of the United States is over $100,000. The value of a home is not separated from its lawn and garden growth. Consequently, the expenditure of perhaps $150 or more a year is seen as a sound investment in enhancing the property value of a residence. Some lawn care firms go after the upscale homeowner. Clark-Morrell Inc., of Georgia, directs its efforts at the one out of ten homeowners who is interested in "quality care and maintenance," and leaves the other potential customers who are price-conscious to the competition. The company has been very successful.

Rocky Mountain Pest Control Company

The Rocky Mountain Pest Control Company (RMPCC) was established in 1976 in Longmont, Colorado, to provide interior pest control services for residences within 25 miles of Longmont. Included in this radius were the cities of Loveland and Boulder, Colorado.

The founder of RMPCC was David Tokarz, its president. Mildred Tokarz, his wife, is secretary-treasurer. In 1978 David Moon joined the company as its vice president in charge of sales and operations. Its 1978 sales were $39,000. Since 1978 RMPCC has been successful in obtaining several major commercial accounts. Its 1983 revenues were $260,000.

In the early 1980s RMPCC received an increasing number of requests from its customers for pest control services for their trees and ornamentals. Tokarz and Moon, however, did not have the expertise or the manpower to provide such services and typically referred their customers to a lawn care firm or tree spray firm with which they were acquainted.

In the fall of 1982 RMPCC decided that the addition of tree and ornamental spraying to their existing line of business would be a valuable complementary service. They also decided that they would expand their geographic base as quickly as possible because they believed that the tree and ornamental spray business was about to experience significant growth. Through contacts in the industry, they learned that Welco Spray Inc., of Greeley, was available for sale if the price and terms offered were acceptable to the owner. RMPCC's offer of $140,000 for Welco was refused by its owner.

Until the fall of 1983 Tokarz and Moon made no further effort to expand their services or geographic coverage. At that time they again offered to buy Welco Spray Inc. They increased their offer by $40,000 to $180,000. The assets to be purchased consisted of the firm's five trucks, its spray equipment, and its customers' accounts list. They also planned to retain the firm's employees and utilize their expertise. RMPCC proposed terms of no money down and $1,500 a month for ten years, plus interest.

The owner of Welco rejected RMPCC's offer. He made no counter proposal, and gave no reason for his rejection of the offer. RMPCC executives concluded that Welco's owner believed that RMPCC would be unable to service the debt obligation to Welco.

Formation of Environcare

The officers of RMPCC, during their visits to Greeley to bargain with the owner of Welco Spray, became acquainted with Don Smith, Welco's general manager. They were impressed with his technical knowledge of the pest spray business and also believed that he had the ability to manage an operation of similar scale on his own. He had the experience and expertise that they lacked and he was also familiar with the geographic area into which RMPCC wished to expand. Accordingly, after being rebuffed by the owner of Welco, they asked Don Smith if he was interested in being the general manager of a company that would be separate from RMPCC. Smith agreed and Environcare was incorporated in the state of Colorado in February 1984.

Organization

David Tokarz is president of Environcare. David Moon is secretary, and Don Smith was appointed vice president in charge of operations. The firm was incorporated as a separate company because RMPCC's officers believed that state licensing requirements for pest control were too complicated. They believed that it would be very easy for them to violate state licensing requirements unknowingly and either be fined or have their operation suspended for a period of time. The Division of Licenses requires that a firm that is licensed to spray trees and ornamentals have a separate license for applying structural (interior) treatments. Consequently, Environcare is licensed only to spray trees, ornamentals, livestock, and weeds. The employees of Environcare, therefore, are not required to take the additional five licensing tests for structural pest control that are administered by the state of Colorado.

David Moon will handle the marketing and perform limited spraying duties. Part-time help will be hired initially to assist Don Smith spray trees and ornamentals.

Finance

Environcare was capitalized with an initial investment of $25,000, which was borrowed from the Bank of Boulder. The loan consisted of a long-term note for $25,000, due in March 1987, at an interest rate of 1 percent over the prime rate, to be adjusted monthly. The firm authorized the issue of 50,000 shares of common stock, which have not yet been issued.

The company purchased a Ford F-350 pickup truck for $8,000, an FMC high-pressure sprayer for $9,000, and liquid spray and wettable powder supplies for $3,000. It maintained $5,000 for other current expenses, such as advertising, promotion, and salaries.

Environcare plans to sell its services on credit. Bills will be due within 30 days of receipt. The firm will also provide for installment payments over a three-month period. They will offer commercial accounts the option of paying on a quarterly basis or after each spray application. Year-round maintenance accounts, requiring a monthly payment throughout the year, will be offered to both residential and commercial accounts.

Richard Foster, publisher of *Pest Control Technology*, has drawn the following profile of the typical lawn care small business:

High net profit before taxes	30%
Average net profit before taxes	20%
Minimum cash investment	$15,000
Average cash investment	$20,000
Stability of the business	Moderate
Risk factor of the business	Moderate
Growth potential	High

In conjunction with this profile, Foster has also developed the following first-year pro forma income statement as a guide for the small-business lawn care entrepreneur:

Table 1 Pro Forma Income Statement, First Year, Lawn Care Service Business

Expense Item	Millions of Dollars	Percent of Total
Marketing and administration	$ 29.6	23%
Labor	25.8	20
Chemicals/fertilizer	34.8	27
Vehicles/equipment	10.3	8
Advertising/promotion	7.7	6
Rent	3.9	3
Gas/repairs/insurance	12.9	10
Telephone/office expense	3.9	3
	$129.0	100%

Foster estimates that the typical lawn service entrepreneur will break even during his first year and service a total of about 700 customer accounts.

Marketing

Environcare's officers believe that radio advertising is the quickest way for a new firm to reach the public and obtain customer recognition. Also, they chose to emphasize radio because they believe that most potential clients are over 35 years of age and, as homeowners, listen to the radio for community programs and announcements. They plan to use radio spots on two Greeley stations—the times and dates to be arranged but prior to the beginning of the spraying season. The messages will be humorous and will be handled by an advertising agency in Longmont.

Environcare will advertise in the "Work Force" classified ad section in three newspapers so that it can reach potential customers in Boulder, Loveland, Fort Collins, and Boulder (see Figure 1). Its employees will make personal contacts to solicit business. David Moon will also

Figure 1 Northern Front Range, Colorado (Mileages between Greeley and Adjacent Cities)

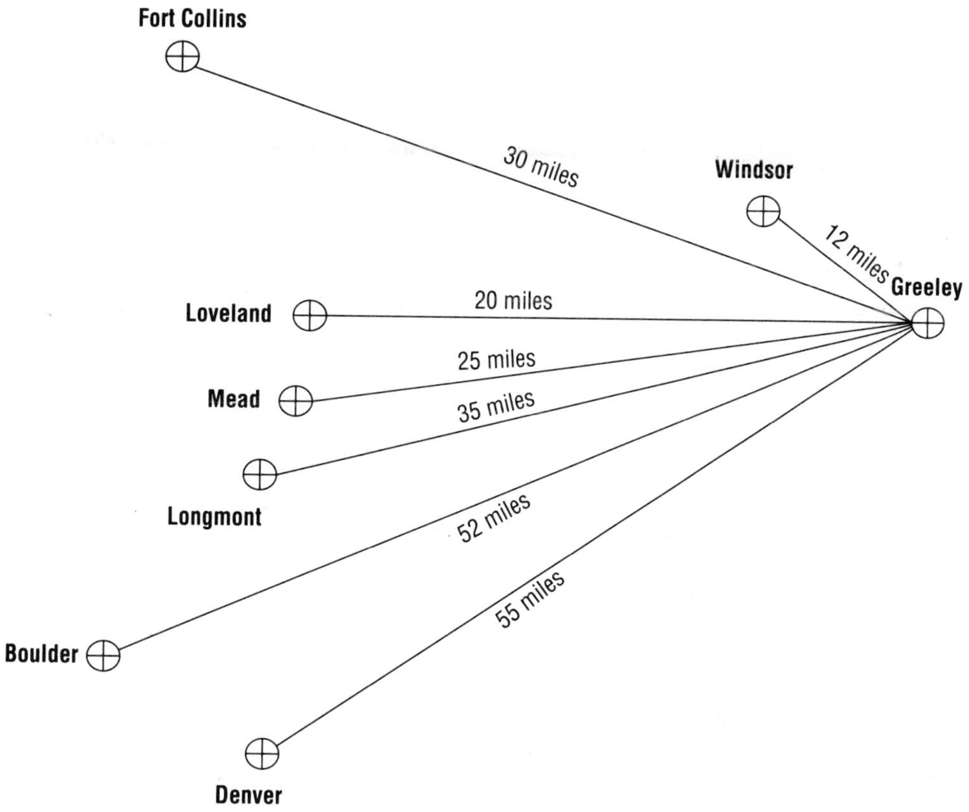

Fort Collins
30 miles
Windsor
12 miles
Greeley
Loveland
20 miles
25 miles
Mead
35 miles
Longmont
52 miles
55 miles
Boulder
Denver

canvass customers, both commercial and residential, by phone. The firm will have an exhibit booth at local home and garden shows held annually in the spring in Greeley, Boulder, and Fort Collins.

Environcare plans to send out three mailings to present customers of RMPCC to solicit business for Environcare. The first mailing will notify customers that they can now receive tree and ornamental spray services from an RMPCC company. The second and third mailings will inform and educate customers about the value of spraying in the high plains and Rocky Mountain foothills (Boulder). Mailers will also be sent to Greeley residents selected by Don Smith, a lifetime Greeley resident, and to commercial firms in the Greeley-Boulder area identified by Don Smith, and Dave Moon. Each mailing of 2,600 pieces will consist of a letter and an enclosed flyer describing Environcare, the services that it provides, its connection with RMPCC, and information about tree and ornamental spraying.

Operations

Environcare will handle both residential and commercial accounts for exterior pest control. Requests for structural pest control treatments will be referred to RMPCC, which, in turn, will provide Environcare with tree and ornamental spray referrals.

Environcare plans to conduct tree spraying in Greeley four days a week and in Boulder/Loveland/Longmont one day a week. Spraying is also done on weekends on an individual basis, as contracted. There will be no extra charge for weekend work.

Customers who call Environcare by phone (there will be separate phone numbers for the Greeley, Fort Collins, Longmont, and Boulder exchanges) will actually be contacting RMPCC's telephone operator/receptionist in Longmont. She will then contact Environcare in Greeley through Don Smith. A receptionist will not be hired for the Greeley office until the additional business warrants it.

Because the public is considered to possess little knowledge about the effects of pest control chemicals, Environcare plans to have its employees explain to its customers the advantages and limitations of such chemicals.

Because of environmental regulations and restrictions, it is difficult to spray more than one home at a time in a neighborhood. Neighbors next door must be notified, as well as those who live across the street. At present this is not a legal requirement, but the owners believe that it may be required in the future.

Neighborhood contact is made in order to avoid lawsuits, harassment by neighbors, or possible adverse publicity. Personal contact with the neighbors is necessary. If possible, the homeowner is asked to assist in notifying his neighbors. Neighbors are inconvenienced because they must close their doors and windows and keep their pets inside their homes while the spray is being applied and for several hours thereafter. A few neighbors are uncooperative and make it difficult for some residences to be sprayed.

The fee for the spray application is determined individually. It depends on the location of the customer, the type of insect, the density of the ornamentals and trees, the area to be covered, and, because of the hazard to fish, the proximity of the plantings to be sprayed to lakes and streams. If such a hazard exists, the trees must be injected with a systemic chemical that converts the tree to a poisoned plant and kills the bugs and insects on contact.

Government Regulations

In accordance with the laws of the state of Colorado, pest control employees must be both licensed and bonded because they apply toxic chemicals in and around inhabited areas. Licensing is not required for the application of fertilizer, also a chemical but not toxic. The bonding requirement ensures that the applicator is capable of absorbing the costs of accidents or harm to people or property due to chemical treatments.

If the chemical to be applied carries a "Danger" label, it is highly toxic and requires that the applicator be certified by the Environmental Protection Agency (EPA). There are approximately 15 categories of chemicals used in tree and ornamental spray that are classified as dangerous. Because of widespread concerns about chemicals, their labeling is much more stringent and restrictive than was the case 5 to 10 years ago.

The state of Colorado's Division of Plant Industry, Department of Agriculture, licenses those who are engaged in pest control and the spraying of trees and ornamentals. There are 15 different categories for licensing, including ornamental pest control for insects and plant diseases; agricultural, industrial, and right-of-way weed control; aquatic pest control, turf pest control, and forest and rangeland pest control.

A licensed individual is expected to know which chemical is appropriate for application in various topographies, the problems encountered in high winds, and how liquids and wettable powders are combined to produce both a curative and a preventive treatment.

Technology

The equipment used for lawn and tree spray has had evolutionary changes during the past three decades. Improvements have increased the efficiency of the pumps used in spraying. The pumps, because they are now smaller, are more mobile and permit easier access to customer lawns. Application times are therefore shorter than before. (In fact, applications are accomplished so quickly that some customers think that they are not getting their money's worth.) Spray nozzles have also been improved so that the application velocity is increased. This allows the sprayers to reach the highest of trees. The City of Denver uses a spraying device that looks like an old civil war cannon but that in reality is a high-powered machine capable of spraying a large number of trees in a very short period of time. Some tree sprayers utilize a device called a roto-mist. It too is capable of rapid coverage of a large area. It is ideal for commercial applications.

There is the possibility that biological insect control will achieve wider acceptance than is the case today. Parasitic wasps are used to eat fly larvae, predatory snails can control slugs, ladybugs can control aphids, and so on. The potential of this type of control is uncertain, and there are few companies that have the expertise to conduct such operations. The Greeley area has many feed lots, and flies are a constant problem. Biological insect control would appear to be an efficient and economical method of controlling such pests. Lace wings, predatory bugs, are used in greenhouses to eat the white flies that attack greenhouse plants. The greenhouses now receive the lace wings direct from an insectary, also called a "bug farm." The best-known insectary in the United States is the Rincon-Vitova, which has three plants in California.

Climate and Insects

Greeley is located on the high desert plains. The humidity is very low and the sun's rays, because of the city's high altitude, are direct and intense. The arid environment, coupled with the heat, makes it more difficult for plants and lawns to survive and thrive. Deeper root systems are needed and proper watering is critical.

Greeley's climate is conducive to the proliferation of a wide variety of insects because the temperatures normally are not cold enough to kill off either the insect's larvae, pupae, or eggs, or even the insects themselves, during the winter months. Different insects thrive in the area's dry climate; others thrive in the dampness that exists around riverbanks, streams, and ponds. This results in a large infestation of insects of one type or another.

There is a wide variety of insects that attack Colorado trees, lawns, and shrubs. The sod webworm feeds on the root systems of grass plants. Grasshoppers are attracted to the leaves of bushes. Elm leaf beetles, elm bark beetles, leaf roller worms, and tent caterpillars, if untreated, will quickly infest trees.

Chemical Applications

The liquid sprays used are primarily systemic. That is, they are absorbed into the plant or tree and spread internally throughout the tree. The pests are destroyed when they touch the tree or plant. This poison is especially effective for use with tall trees when the applicator/technician is not sure that the spray treatment has reached the uppermost branches.

Frequently used liquid chemicals are metasystox-R and Dursban. They are dangerous because they are toxic contact chemicals, i.e., they can cause severe irritation upon contact with the skin. They are safely applied only by licensed technicians, and then only under carefully controlled conditions.

The wettable powders do not dissolve in water. The water serves as an agent to deliver the powder to the tree. The wettable powders have a residual life equal to that of soluble powders. They simply adhere to the tree after the water spray evaporates. The choice of wettable powder or liquid spray depends on the type of insect to be eliminated.

Contact poison chemicals are used against leaf-chewing insects that either absorb the poison on contact with the tree or ornamental or ingest the poison when they chew the poisoned leaves.

Spraying and lawn service contractors must know the watering habits of their customers to ensure that their lawn treatments are effective. Too much or too little water can cause plant and turf problems. Therefore the care and feeding of lawns and gardens is a cooperative venture between the homeowner and the applicator.

The Greeley Market

In 1980, according to U.S. Bureau of the Census figures, there were 20,700 housing units in Greeley. There were estimated to be 21,300 housing units in Greeley in 1984. Slightly more than half of these units are privately owned single-family homes. Somewhat less than half are rental units, either single or multifamily units. The median value of a Greeley single-family home, as of January 1984, was $61,500. Approximately 37 percent of Greeley is zoned either business (10.5 percent) or industrial (26.3 percent). Greeley's physical area covered 21.1 square miles in 1982. This is about one-third larger than its size in 1980, and 148 percent larger than its 1970 area of 8.5 square miles.

Greeley's 1983 population was estimated to be 56,000. Residents under 18 years of age accounted for 28 percent, those between 19 and 64 represented 62 percent, and those over 65, 10 percent. The median family income in Greeley in 1980 was approximately $19,200. Families above the median family income, according to Don Smith, are estimated to use spray treatments twice as frequently as lower-income families. Greeley's water supply and reserves are conservatively expected to be adequate for the city's projected growth for the next 20 years.

Don Smith believes that about one-third of Greeley's residents, i.e., 7,000 homes, have their lawns chemically treated by commercial firms. For about an annual $125 fee, a homeowner receives lawn treatments to fertilize the lawn, kill weeds, and destroy insects harmful to lawns. He also estimates that only about 2,000 residents utilize spray services for trees and ornamentals. On the average, each residence that uses a spray service obtains two treatments per year at $35 per application. (Note: Of the $35 spray application fee, labor is estimated by Don Smith to represent $2.00 of the cost, materials $.80, and truck and spray pump fuel, $.70, for a total of $3.50.)

Greeley schools and city and local governments typically have their own lawn and maintenance employees care for their lawns. Tree spraying, however, is usually let out for bids. Don Smith estimates that this business amounts to $20,000 annually. Shopping centers and local business properties are estimated to represent a present market of $10,000 for tree spraying and $5,000 for lawn care. Property management companies, which administer rentals, apartment complexes, condominiums, and townhouses, represent an estimated present market of $20,000, equally divided between lawn care and tree spraying.

Don Smith estimates that 25 percent of his expected annual revenues will be derived from spraying lawns and that the remainder will come from spraying trees and ornamentals.

Estimated Regional Market Potential

The area in which the Rocky Mountain Pest Control Company and Environcare operate is located along Colorado's Northern Front Range—an area approximately 20 miles wide, running east (from Greeley) to west (Boulder), and about 75 miles long, from north (Fort Collins) to south (Denver). Don Smith estimates that the Fort Collins market potential is about the same as Greeley, that Loveland and Longmont combined represent about one-half of Greeley's potential, and that the Boulder metropolitan market is larger than Greeley's potential by a factor of five. These estimates apply to both lawn care and tree and ornamental spraying.

The Competition

Two companies, Welco Spray Inc. and Greeley

Spray Service, are estimated to have divided the Greeley market pretty much between themselves for the last ten years, with respect to both the spraying of trees and ornamentals and chemical lawn applications. Within the past year, two franchise operations have entered the Greeley market—Ever-Green Lawns and Nitro-Green. These two firms provide only chemical lawn treatments.

There are about 15 firms in Greeley that provide spray service or lawn care, or both. (A discussion of the major competitors will follow.) There are also individuals from outside Greeley who provide lawn care. Some may be conducting their business in violation of a local ordinance, since they may not have a Greeley license to operate. Don Smith anticipates no major change in the nature of the competition. However, he believes it possible that a Denver company or a new franchise operation may enter the Greeley area.

Welco Spray Inc. Welco Spray Inc. was founded in 1966 by J. L. Williams. At first, he sprayed only trees and ornamentals. Pest control services were added in 1975 because a major customer requested this service and assured Williams of a significant return on his investment.

In the fall of 1983 Welco had approximately 3,000 customers. It also had additional inactive accounts—due to customers moving from the area, deaths, switching to another spray company, or just stopping the use of spray services entirely.

Before Environcare was incorporated, Welco had three full-time and four part-time employees. Welco owned five trucks (including five portable spray tanks), a roto-mist machine, two weed sprayers, and a combination tractor-sprayer.

Welco had a good reputation for quality service and, since it was a local firm, a high degree of visibility and acceptance. Welco is only one of three firms that provide both lawn care and tree and ornamental pest control in the Greeley area. It is estimated that lawn care represents 10 percent of its business and trees and ornamentals 90 percent.

Its customer file, which was extensive and comprehensive, was one of Welco's major assets. On the other hand, the firm appeared to lack expertise in money management. It frequently was late in paying its bills. It also had more equipment than appeared to be warranted by its sales volume. One truck generally sat idle in the parking lot.

Welco's sales rose from $15,000 in 1966 to a peak of $175,000 in 1977, and gradually declined to $160,000 in 1983. The firm's expenses were such that during this period it made a profit for only one year (detailed data were not available).

Nitro-Green Nitro-Green has its headquarters in Bismarck, North Dakota. Its 1983 gross revenues, for the treatment of 17,000 lawns, were $1.5 million. It had 20 franchises at the beginning of 1984. One of its strengths is that it is a franchise operation and potential customers have confidence in the name. Its equipment is good, and its trucks, painted in "industry colors" of white and green, are mobile advertisements for their product. Nitro-Green advertises primarily through flyers and inserts that appear in the local newspaper. They also use four-column-wide ads in *The Greeley Tribune,* the city's only daily newspaper.

A local professional sprayer thinks that Nitro-Green employees may not be as knowledgeable about chemicals as they should be in relation to specific pests. That is, they may not use the most effective chemical to treat a particular type of insect. Nitro-Green employs 5 or 6 employees, has three spray trucks and tanks, and has a spray rig set up on a pickup truck. Nitro-Green provides both lawn care (90 percent of its business) and tree spraying (10 percent). One weakness that Don Smith sees is that the firm may not have enough equipment to satisfy customer interest generated from their advertising, which appears to be very effective.

Ever-Green Lawns Ever-Green of Golden bought out Nutra-Lawn of Greeley, a privately owned company, in 1983. It opened a warehouse/office in Windsor, Colorado, 12 miles from Greeley. This is the Golden company's fifth branch. The company reported that its decision to enter the Greeley-Windsor-Fort Collins area was made after it had conducted a market research study of residents in the area.

The Ever-Green Lawns Corporation has gross sales of over $10 million in 1983 for all of its franchise operations. The company was recently purchased by the Hawley Group of London, England, which has additional interests in industrial cleaning and pest control.

The company advertises extensively in the Denver metropolitan area on local television stations, whose signals are received in Greeley with ordinary housetop antennae. It also uses four-color brochures that are inserted in *The Greeley Tribune* and the two major Denver metropolitan dailies that are delivered to Greeley residents. The company also advertises on radio. It continuously solicits business by phone and sends direct mailers to homes, using the mailing lists obtained from the company that it bought out—Nutra-Lawn. There are at least three employees in the Windsor office phoning for new business in the local area.

The company's facility in Windsor is more modern and more complete than any of its competitors'. Its clean white and green vehicles are very visible advertisements on wheels. It appears to have very strong financial resources. When they are first hired, all of its specialized applicators/technicians are required to attend a one-week school run by the parent company in Boulder. They also attend a refresher course every year. A possible weakness is that the firm is not Greeley-based. Each truck is required to do 30 lawns a day, and that may be a high standard for all of its employees to meet. Ever-Green deals exclusively with lawn fertilization. Their employees are not licensed to apply the pest control chemicals associated with tree and ornamental spraying.

Greeley Spray Service The Greeley Spray Service is a subsidiary of Kincaid Tree Service of Fort Collins, Colorado. Its manager is well known and respected by his Greeley customers. However, he comes to Greeley only once or twice a week to perform spray applications. The firm's trucks do not have the distinctive and appealing appearance associated with Nitro-Green and Ever-Green Lawns. Because they come to Greeley infrequently, they do not provide service with the responsiveness and regularity that some Greeley residents prefer.

General Spray and Lawn Service and Colorado Lawn Care Service These two companies lack modern and efficient spray applicator equipment. According to Don Smith, their employees are neither as experienced nor as well trained as those associated with the firms previously discussed. Colorado Lawn Care Service provides both lawn care and pest control spray services.

Competitive Market Share Data Don Smith, vice president of Environcare, estimated that at the approach of the 1984 season the market for the spraying of trees and ornamentals and lawn care was distributed as follows:

Table 2 Estimated Market Shares of the Greeley Area Lawn Care and Trees/Ornamental Spray Business, December 1983

Firm	Trees/ Ornamentals	Lawn Care
Welco Spray	80%	10%
Ever-Green Lawns	0	30
Nitro-Green	2	30
Greeley Spray Service	16	0
General Spray and Lawn Service	1	1
Colorado Lawn Care Service	1	1
Other firms (from Denver, Mead, Loveland, and Fort Collins)	—	28
	100%	100%

Plans for The Future

Don Smith, the general manager of Environcare, hopes some day to own his own business, and that business may be Environcare. He has a target of $500,000 gross sales annually. He also would like to explore the possibilities of biological applications for pest control. At the present time, however, he is devoting all of his time to the start-up of Environcare's tree and ornamental spray business. He comments: "I am not interested in getting into the landscaping business. I think the quality of service I now provide would decline if our services became too broad. I prefer to be friends with the landscapers rather than their competitor. I can provide service to ten landscaping firms. If I am their competitor, I will only get my own referrals for spray service—and none of theirs. Before we can even consider expanding our line of services, we have to learn how to walk before we can run."

Name and Company Index

Subject Index